Microsoft® Excel 2000 Bible, Gold Edition

Microsoft®
Excel 2000 Bible,
Gold Edition

John Walkenbach

IDG Books Worldwide, Inc.
An International Data Group Company

Foster City, CA ✦ Chicago, IL ✦ Indianapolis, IN ✦ New York, NY

Microsoft® Excel 2000 Bible, Gold Edition

Published by
IDG Books Worldwide, Inc.
An International Data Group Company
919 E. Hillsdale Blvd., Suite 400
Foster City, CA 94404
www.idgbooks.com (IDG Books Worldwide Web site)

ISBN: 0-7645-3449-1

Printed in the United States of America

10 9 8 7 6 5 4 3 2 1

XX/RU/QR/QQ/FC

Distributed in the United States by IDG Books Worldwide, Inc.

Distributed by CDG Books Canada Inc. for Canada; by Transworld Publishers Limited in the United Kingdom; by IDG Norge Books for Norway; by IDG Sweden Books for Sweden; by IDG Books Australia Publishing Corporation Pty. Ltd. for Australia and New Zealand; by TransQuest Publishers Pte Ltd. for Singapore, Malaysia, Thailand, Indonesia, and Hong Kong; by Gotop Information Inc. for Taiwan; by ICG Muse, Inc. for Japan; by Intersoft for South Africa; by Eyrolles for France; by International Thomson Publishing for Germany, Austria and Switzerland; by Distribuidora Cuspide for Argentina; by LR International for Brazil; by Galileo Libros for Chile; by Ediciones ZETA S.C.R. Ltda. for Peru; by WS Computer Publishing Corporation, Inc., for the Philippines; by Contemporanea de Ediciones for Venezuela; by Express Computer Distributors for the Caribbean and West Indies; by Micronesia Media Distributor, Inc. for Micronesia; by Chips Computadoras S.A. de C.V. for Mexico; by Editorial Norma de Panama S.A. for Panama; by American Bookshops for Finland.

For general information on IDG Books Worldwide's books in the U.S., please call our Consumer Customer Service department at 800-762-2974. For reseller information, including discounts and premium sales, please call our Reseller Customer Service department at 800-434-3422.

For information on where to purchase IDG Books Worldwide's books outside the U.S., please contact our International Sales department at 317-596-5530 or fax 317-596-5692.

For consumer information on foreign language translations, please contact our Customer Service department at 800-434-3422, fax 317-596-5692, or e-mail rights@idgbooks.com.

For information on licensing foreign or domestic rights, please phone +1-650-655-3109.

For sales inquiries and special prices for bulk quantities, please contact our Sales department at 650-655-3200 or write to the address above.

For information on using IDG Books Worldwide's books in the classroom or for ordering examination copies, please contact our Educational Sales department at 800-434-2086 or fax 317-596-5499.

For press review copies, author interviews, or other publicity information, please contact our Public Relations department at 650-655-3000 or fax 650-655-3299.

For authorization to photocopy items for corporate, personal, or educational use, please contact Copyright Clearance Center, 222 Rosewood Drive, Danvers, MA 01923, or fax 978-750-4470.

Library of Congress Cataloging-in-Publication Data
Walkenbach, John.
    Microsoft Excel 2000 Bible / John Walkenbach.-- Gold ed.
        p.   cm.
    Includes index.
    ISBN 0-7645-3449-1 (alk. paper)
    1. Microsoft Excel for Windows. 2. Electronic spreadsheets. 3. Business--Computer programs. I. Title.
    HF5548.4.M523 W34578 2000
    005.369--dc21   99-056016

is a registered trademark or trademark under exclusive license to IDG Books Worldwide, Inc. from International Data Group, Inc. in the United States and/or other countries.

ABOUT IDG BOOKS WORLDWIDE

Welcome to the world of IDG Books Worldwide.

IDG Books Worldwide, Inc., is a subsidiary of International Data Group, the world's largest publisher of computer-related information and the leading global provider of information services on information technology. IDG was founded more than 30 years ago by Patrick J. McGovern and now employs more than 9,000 people worldwide. IDG publishes more than 290 computer publications in over 75 countries. More than 90 million people read one or more IDG publications each month.

Launched in 1990, IDG Books Worldwide is today the #1 publisher of best-selling computer books in the United States. We are proud to have received eight awards from the Computer Press Association in recognition of editorial excellence and three from Computer Currents' First Annual Readers' Choice Awards. Our best-selling *...For Dummies®* series has more than 50 million copies in print with translations in 31 languages. IDG Books Worldwide, through a joint venture with IDG's Hi-Tech Beijing, became the first U.S. publisher to publish a computer book in the People's Republic of China. In record time, IDG Books Worldwide has become the first choice for millions of readers around the world who want to learn how to better manage their businesses.

Our mission is simple: Every one of our books is designed to bring extra value and skill-building instructions to the reader. Our books are written by experts who understand and care about our readers. The knowledge base of our editorial staff comes from years of experience in publishing, education, and journalism — experience we use to produce books to carry us into the new millennium. In short, we care about books, so we attract the best people. We devote special attention to details such as audience, interior design, use of icons, and illustrations. And because we use an efficient process of authoring, editing, and desktop publishing our books electronically, we can spend more time ensuring superior content and less time on the technicalities of making books.

You can count on our commitment to deliver high-quality books at competitive prices on topics you want to read about. At IDG Books Worldwide, we continue in the IDG tradition of delivering quality for more than 30 years. You'll find no better book on a subject than one from IDG Books Worldwide.

John Kilcullen
Chairman and CEO
IDG Books Worldwide, Inc.

Steven Berkowitz
President and Publisher
IDG Books Worldwide, Inc.

WINNER

*Eighth Annual
Computer Press
Awards ≥1992*

IX

WINNER

*Ninth Annual
Computer Press
Awards ≥1993*

WINNER

*Tenth Annual
Computer Press
Awards ≥1994*

XI

WINNER

*Eleventh Annual
Computer Press
Awards ≥1995*

IDG is the world's leading IT media, research and exposition company. Founded in 1964, IDG had 1997 revenues of $2.05 billion and has more than 9,000 employees worldwide. IDG offers the widest range of media options that reach IT buyers in 75 countries representing 95% of worldwide IT spending. IDG's diverse product and services portfolio spans six key areas including print publishing, online publishing, expositions and conferences, market research, education and training, and global marketing services. More than 90 million people read one or more of IDG's 290 magazines and newspapers, including IDG's leading global brands — Computerworld, PC World, Network World, Macworld and the Channel World family of publications. IDG Books Worldwide is one of the fastest-growing computer book publishers in the world, with more than 700 titles in 36 languages. The "...For Dummies®" series alone has more than 50 million copies in print. IDG offers online users the largest network of technology-specific Web sites around the world through IDG.net (http://www.idg.net), which comprises more than 225 targeted Web sites in 55 countries worldwide. International Data Corporation (IDC) is the world's largest provider of information technology data, analysis and consulting, with research centers in over 41 countries and more than 400 research analysts worldwide. IDG World Expo is a leading producer of more than 168 globally branded conferences and expositions in 35 countries including E3 (Electronic Entertainment Expo), Macworld Expo, ComNet, Windows World Expo, ICE (Internet Commerce Expo), Agenda, DEMO, and Spotlight. IDG's training subsidiary, ExecuTrain, is the world's largest computer training company, with more than 230 locations worldwide and 785 training courses. IDG Marketing Services helps industry-leading IT companies build international brand recognition by developing global integrated marketing programs via IDG's print, online and exposition products worldwide. Further information about the company can be found at www.idg.com.   1/24/99

Credits

Acquisitions Editor
David Mayhew

Development Editor
Laura E. Brown

Technical Editors
Bill Karow
Scott M. Fulton III
Greg Guntle

Copy Editor
Michael D. Welch

Project Coordinator
Linda Marousek

Quality Control Specialists
Chris Weisbart
Laura Taflinger

Graphics and Production Specialists
Mario Amador
Jude Levinson
Michael Lewis
Ramses Ramirez
Victor Pérez-Varela
Dina F Quan

Book Designer
Drew R. Moore

Illustrators
Mary Jo Richards
Clint Lahnen
Karl Brandt

Proofreading and Indexing
York Production Services

Cover Design
Peter Kowaleszyn at Murder By Design

About the Author

John Walkenbach is a leading authority on spreadsheet software, and principal of JWalk and Associates Inc., a Southern California–based consulting firm that specializes in spreadsheet application development. John is the author of about 30 spreadsheet books, and has written more than 300 articles and reviews for a variety of publications, including *PC World*, *InfoWorld*, *PC Magazine*, *Windows*, and *PC/Computing* magazines. He's currently contributing editor for *PC World* and writes the magazine's monthly "Here's How" spreadsheet tips column. He also maintains a popular Internet Web site called "The Spreadsheet Page" at www.j-walk.com/ss, and is the developer of the Power Utility Pak, an award-winning add-in for Microsoft Excel. John graduated from the University of Missouri, and earned a Ph.D. from the University of Montana. John's other interests include guitar, MIDI music, novels, digital photography, and gardening.

Preface

Thanks for purchasing *Microsoft Excel 2000 Bible, Gold Edition*. This book is based on the best-selling books *Microsoft Excel 2000 Bible*, *Microsoft Excel 2000 Power Programming with VBA*, and *Microsoft Excel 2000 Formulas*, all from IDG Books Worldwide.

I've used just about every spreadsheet program available, and Excel 2000 is the best of the bunch. Excel has been around in various incarnations for almost a decade, and each new release pushes the spreadsheet envelope a bit further — in some cases, a *lot* further. My goal in writing this book is to share with you some of what I know about Excel, and in the process make you more efficient on the job.

The book contains everything that you need to know to learn the basics of Excel and then move on to more advanced topics at your own pace. I present many useful examples as well as loads of dynamite tips and slick techniques that I've accumulated over the years.

Is This Book for You?

The "Bible" series from IDG Books Worldwide is designed for beginning, intermediate, and advanced users. This book covers all the essential components of Excel and provides clear and practical examples that you can adapt to your own needs.

Excel can be used at many levels — from the simple to the extremely complex. I've created a good balance here, focusing on the topics that are most useful to most users. The following can help you decide whether this book is for you.

Yes — If you have no spreadsheet experience

If you're new to the world of spreadsheets, welcome to the fold. This book has everything that you need to get started with Excel and then advance to other topics as the need arises.

Yes — If you have used previous versions of Excel

If you've used Excel 97, you're going to feel right at home with Excel 2000. If you're skipping a few upgrades and moving up from Excel 5 or Excel 95, you have lots to learn, because Microsoft has made many improvements in the past few years. In any case, this book can get you up to speed quickly.

Yes — If you have used Excel for the Macintosh

The Macintosh versions of Excel are very similar to the Windows versions. If you're moving over from the Mac platform, you'll find some good background information as well as specific details to make your transition as smooth as possible.

Yes — If you have used DOS versions of 1-2-3 or Quattro Pro

If you're abandoning a text-based spreadsheet such as 1-2-3 or Corel's Quattro Pro in favor of a more modern graphical product, this book can serve you well. You have a head start because you already know what spreadsheets are all about, and you'll discover some great new ways of doing things.

Yes — If you have used Windows versions of 1-2-3 or Quattro Pro

If you've tried the other programs and are convinced that Excel is the way to go, this book quickly teaches you what Excel is all about and why it has such a great reputation. Because you're already familiar with Windows *and* spreadsheets, you can breeze through many introductory topics.

Yes — If you want to learn advanced formula techniques

Formulas, of course, are the key to creating interactive spreadsheet models. This book includes many sophisticated formula examples that, quite frankly, are not available anywhere else.

Yes — If you want to master Excel's VBA macros

I devote 13 chapters to VBA, including in-depth discussions of user interface elements such as dialog boxes, menus, and toolbars.

Software Versions

This book was written for Excel 2000 (also known as Excel 9), but much of the information also applies to Excel 97. If you use a version prior to Excel 97, you'll find that a significant portion of this book does not apply. The earlier versions of Excel are drastically different from the current version.

Conventions This Book Uses

Take a minute to scan this section to learn some of the typographical and organizational conventions that this book uses.

Excel commands

In Excel, as in all Windows programs, you select commands from the pull-down menu system. In this book, such commands appear in normal typeface. An option available under a particular menu is indicated after an ⇨ symbol, as in "Choose File ⇨ Print to print your document."

Filenames, named ranges, and your input

Input that you make from the keyboard appears in **bold**. Named ranges may appear in a code font. Lengthy input usually appears on a separate line. For instance, I may instruct you to enter a formula such as the following:

```
="Part Name: " &VLOOKUP(PartNumber,PartList,2)
```

Key names

Names of the keys on your keyboard appear in normal type. When two keys should be pressed simultaneously, they are connected with a plus sign, like this: "Press Alt+E to select the Edit menu." Here are the key names as I refer to them throughout the book:

Alt	down arrow	Num Lock	right arrow
Backspace	End	Pause	Scroll Lockxi
Caps Lock	Home	PgDn	Shift
Ctrl	Insert	PgUp	Tab
Delete	left arrow	Print Screen	up arrow

Functions

Excel's built-in worksheet functions appear in uppercase, like this: "Enter a SUM formula in cell C20."

Mouse conventions

I assume that you're using a mouse or some other pointing device. You'll come across some of the following mouse-related terms:

✦ **Mouse pointer:** The small graphic figure that moves onscreen when you move your mouse. The mouse pointer is usually an arrow, but it changes shape when you move to certain areas of the screen or when you're performing certain actions.

✦ **Point:** Move the mouse so that the mouse pointer is on a specific item: for example, "Point to the Save button on the toolbar."

✦ **Press:** Press the left mouse button once and keep it pressed. Normally, this is used when dragging.

✦ **Click:** Press the left mouse button once and release it immediately.

✦ **Right-click:** Press the right mouse button once and release it immediately. The right mouse button is used in Excel to pop up shortcut menus that are appropriate for whatever is currently selected.

✦ **Double-click:** Press the left mouse button twice in rapid succession. If your double-clicking doesn't seem to be working, you can adjust the double-click sensitivity using the Windows Control Panel icon.

✦ **Drag:** Press the left mouse button and keep it pressed while you move the mouse. Dragging is often used to select a range of cells or to change the size of an object.

What the Icons Mean

Throughout the book, you'll see special graphic symbols, or *icons*, in the left margin. These call your attention to points that are particularly important or relevant to a specific group of readers. The icons in this book are as follows:

 This symbol denotes features that are new to Excel 2000. If you've upgraded from Excel 97, this icon cues you in on the new features. If you're still using Excel 97, this icon identifies features that aren't available in your version.

 This icon signals the fact that something is important or worth noting. Notes may alert you to a concept that helps you master the task at hand, or they may denote something that is fundamental to understanding subsequent material.

 This icon marks a more efficient way of doing something that may not be obvious.

This icon indicates that the material uses an example file located on this book's companion CD-ROM (see "About the CD-ROM," later in this Introduction).

I use this symbol when a possibility exists that the operation I'm describing could cause problems if you're not careful.

This icon indicates that a related topic is discussed elsewhere in the book.

How This Book Is Organized

Notice that the book is divided into six main parts, followed by three appendixes.

Part I: Getting Started — This part consists of four chapters that provide background about Excel. These chapters are considered required reading for Excel newcomers.

Part II: Working with Excel — The chapters in Part II cover the basic concepts with which all Excel users should be familiar.

Part III: Adding Visual Elements — The chapters in Part III cover topics that make your work look better: formatting, charts, pictures, and maps.

Part IV: Advanced Excel Features — This part consists of nine chapters dealing with topics that are usually considered advanced. Many beginning and intermediate users may find this information useful as well.

Part V: Analyzing Data with Excel — The broad topic of data analysis is the focus of the chapters in Part V. Users of all levels will find some of these chapters of interest.

Part VI: Programming Excel 2000 with VBA — Part VI is for those who want to customize Excel for their own use or who are designing workbooks or add-ins that are to be used by others. It starts with an introduction to programming, and provides in-depth coverage of UserForms, add-ins, toolbars, and menus.

Appendixes — The appendixes consist of supplemental and reference material that may be useful to you.

How to Use This Book

This book is not intended to be read cover-to-cover. Rather, it's a reference book that you can consult when . . .

+ You're stuck while trying to do something.

+ You need to do something that you've never done before.

+ You have some time on your hands, and you're interested in learning something new.

The index is comprehensive, and each chapter typically focuses on a single broad topic. If you're just starting out with Excel, I recommend that you read the first three chapters to gain a basic understanding of the product, and then do some experimenting on your own. After you become familiar with Excel's environment, you can refer to the chapters that interest you most. Some users, however, may prefer to follow the chapters in order. Part II was designed with these users in mind.

Don't be discouraged if some of the material is over your head. Most users get by just fine using only a small subset of Excel's total capabilities. In fact, the 80/20 rule applies here: 80 percent of Excel users use only 20 percent of its features. However, using only 20 percent of Excel's features still gives you *lots* of power at your fingertips.

About the CD-ROM

You find that my writing style emphasizes examples. I know that I learn more from a well-thought-out example than from reading a dozen pages. I've found that this is true for many other people, too. Consequently, I spent a lot of time developing the examples in this book. These example files are available on the companion CD-ROM.

Appendix I describes the material on the CD-ROM.

 When you see this icon, you can open the example file and try out the example for yourself.

Power Utility Pak 2000 Coupon

At the back of the book, you'll find a coupon that you can redeem for a copy of my Power Utility Pak software — a collection of useful Excel utilities and new worksheet functions. This product normally sells for $39.95, but I'm making it available to readers of this book for only $9.95, plus shipping and handling. I developed this package using VBA exclusively, and the complete source files are also available for those who want to learn slick VBA techniques.

Contacting the Author

I'm always happy to hear from readers of my books. The best way to contact me is by e-mail at the following Internet address:

author@j-walk.com

I get lots of e-mail, so I can't promise a personal reply.

Visit The Spreadsheet Page

For even more information on Excel, be sure to check out The Spreadsheet Page on the World Wide Web. Here's the URL:

www.j-walk.com/ss/

Acknowledgments

Thanks to everyone at IDG Books Worldwide who played a part in getting this book into your hands.

Thanks also to all the people throughout the world who have taken the time to let me know that my books have made an impact. My goal is to write books that go well beyond the material found in competing books. Based on the feedback that I've received, I think I'm succeeding.

Many of the ideas for the topics in this book came from postings to the Excel Internet newsgroups and mailing lists. Thanks to all who frequent these services. Your problems and questions were the inspiration for many of the examples I present in this book.

Contents at a Glance

Contents

Part III: Adding Visual Elements 383

Chapter 17: Worksheet Formatting 385

Chapter 18: Chart-Making Basics 413

Part IV: Advanced Excel Features   549

Chapter 23: Creating and Using Worksheet Outlines 551

Chapter 24: Linking and Consolidating Worksheets 563

Chapter 25: Introducing Arrays 579

Part V: Analyzing Data with Excel 697

Part VI: Programming Excel 2000 with VBA   863

Chapter 39: Essentials of Spreadsheet Application Development 865

Chapter 40: Introducing Visual Basic for Applications 885

Getting Started

✦   ✦   ✦   ✦

In This Part

✦   ✦   ✦   ✦

What's New in Excel 2000?

Every new release of Excel is a big event for Excel fans, and Excel 2000 is certainly no exception. Although it doesn't add too many new features (compared to Excel 97), it's by far the best version yet. In this chapter I provide an overview of what's new, what's gone, and what's changed compared to Excel 97.

Installation Improvements

If you've installed previous versions of Excel, you'll notice that Excel 2000 provides a new "intelligent" installation wizard. If you have a previous version installed, you'll get a choice to perform either a similar install or a standard installation. If you choose the former, all of your previous settings will be transferred to Excel 2000.

You also have quite a bit more flexibility in selecting which features to install. Even if you omit a few key features during the initial installation, they will still appear on the menus. If you attempt to access an uninstalled component, you'll get a prompt asking you if you want to install it. Even better, if your installation somehow gets messed up — a critical file gets deleted, for example — the new self-repair feature will detect that fact and re-install the missing file.

New Internet Features

Most of the new features in Excel 2000 deal with the Internet.

✦ **HTML file format:** If you like, you can use HTML as a "native" file format for your Excel work. In other words, you can save a workbook as an HTML file and then re-open it without losing anything. Unless your work needs to be on a corporate intranet, you're much better off sticking with the normal XLS format.

✦ **Save to a server:** Excel 2000 makes it very easy to save a workbook directly to an intranet or an ISP host. In fact, if the server is running Microsoft's FrontPage Server Extensions, it's as easy as saving to a local or network drive. If end users are running Internet Explorer 4.0 or a later version, they can manipulate Excel data (for example, Pivot tables, charts, and worksheets) within the browser.

✦ **Web discussions:** Use the Discussion toolbar to insert and navigate between comments. You can create discussions about the document, or in-line discussions specific to a paragraph. You can reply, edit, or delete from a right-clicked context menu. Comments are indented as in the threaded discussion model common on the Internet , and are threaded with the contributor's name, date, and time stamp.

✦ **Web subscription and notification:** This lets you configure documents and folders to trigger e-mail or Internet Explorer channel updates when a document or related discussion is added, changed, or deleted. You can set notification as daily, weekly, or "within a few minutes." The message provides the date and time, the name of the editor, the document's URL, and a link you can click to cancel further notifications. New comments and replies to remote documents are tracked, but you can't subscribe to e-mail updates on the remote documents and folders themselves.

Cross-Reference   I discuss these features in Chapter 29.

New File Dialog Boxes

The dialog boxes that are displayed when you select File ➪ Save or File ➪ Open have been redesigned so you can see more files at one time and access them more quickly. You can use the icons in the new "Look in" bar along the left side to get to the folders and locations you use the most. Click the History icon to see the last 20–50 documents and folders you have worked with, and then click the Back button to easily return to folders you have recently visited.

PivotTable Enhancements

Excel's PivotTable feature is an extremely useful tool for summarizing data. Excel 2000 adds some new twists:

✦ **Streamlined PivotTable Wizard:** Creating pivot tables is faster than ever. The new PivotTable toolbar displays the filed names, and you can simply drag them to your pivot table.

✦ **PivotChart:** Pivot tables can also now be charted. PivotChart dynamic views are linked to PivotTable.

Automatic Formula Adjustment

Excel 2000 will automatically adjust formulas when you insert a new row directly above the formula. For example, assume you have the following formula in cell A5, which sums the values in A1:A4:

```
=SUM(A1:A4)
```

If you insert a new row directly above row 5 and enter a value into cell A5, the formula adjusts automatically to:

```
=SUM(A1:A5)
```

Caution In most cases, automatic formula adjustment is exactly what you want. In other cases, however, this can cause the formula to display an incorrect result.

See Through Cell Selection

A common complaint among Excel users has been the fact that selecting a cell or range obscures the colors in the cells. Excel 2000 finally addresses that complaint, and now uses a different way of highlighting selected ranges. Now you can still see the colors when you select a range.

Personalized Menus

In an attempt to simplify your life, Excel 2000 is capable of adjusting its menus to your work habits. It does so by displaying only the menu items you use most frequently. You still have access to all commands, of course. At the bottom of the drop-down menu are arrows that can be clicked open to reveal additional menu choices.

Over time, Excel will learn which application features you use most often and then display them higher on the menu list. Less commonly used features are demoted and eventually disappear.

Although some users may see this as a usability enhancement, I think moving the menu commands around is bound to cause confusion. Fortunately, you can turn this feature off. Select View ➪ Toolbars ➪ Customize, and then click the Options tab. Remove the checkmark from the option labeled Menus show recently used commands first.

Easier Toolbar Customization

Excel, of course, is big on toolbars. If you find that you never use some of the buttons on a particular toolbar, it's very easy to remove them. Toolbars now have a small down-pointing arrow button that, when clicked, displays a button labeled Add or Remove Buttons. Click this button to reveal a list of buttons in the toolbar (see Figure 1-1). Simply remove the checkmark to hide a button.

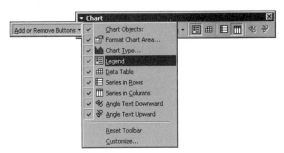

Figure 1-1: Excel 2000 makes it very easy to customize toolbars by showing only the buttons you need.

Documents on the Windows Task Bar

If you use Windows 98, each Excel document appears as a separate task in the Windows task bar.

Enhanced Clipboard

Excel 2000 (along with the other members of Office 2000) uses a special Office clipboard. This enhanced clipboard supports a feature known as "collect and paste"—the ability to store information from several sources and then selectively paste it to a new location.

The Clipboard toolbar (see Figure 1-2) displays icons for each item copied. Unfortunately, this enhanced clipboard only works with the Office applications.

Figure 1-2: Excel 2000 lets you store up to 12 separate items on a special enhanced clipboard.

Euro Currency Symbol

Additional number formats are available with the Euro currency symbol.

New Image Import Options

Excel 2000 lets you import an image directly from a digital camera or scanner. It's no longer necessary to capture the image to a file and then import the file.

A New Help System

Online help in Excel 2000 sports a new look. Microsoft abandoned the traditional Windows help system in favor of a new "HTML Help" system. The system works pretty much like the old one. By default, the help display appears along side of Excel.

 For more information about Excel's online help system, refer to Appendix A.

Office Assistant

The Office Assistant, which debuted in Excel 97, makes an appearance in Excel 2000. I've found that people either love this feature or hate it (I'm in the latter group).

The Office Assistant is a bit less obtrusive in Excel 97 and (finally!) it can be configured in such a way that you never see it again (unless you want to). When you install Excel 2000, an option exists to omit the Office Assistant feature.

Cross-Reference For more information about the Office Assistant, refer to Appendix A.

Multilingual Features

Multilingual users should have it a bit easier with Excel 2000. Excel 2000 can change the language used in its interface (the text in menus, dialog boxes, and so on) on the fly. Doing so is as easy as purchasing the Office language pack. Excel automatically detects the language you're typing in and switches among spelling checker, AutoCorrect, and other proofing tools accordingly.

Modeless UserForms

Finally, macro programmers will welcome a new feature that lets you display custom dialog boxes (UserForms) in a "modeless" manner. In previous versions, everything ground to a halt while a custom dialog box was displayed. In Excel 2000, a macro programmer can keep the dialog box displayed while the user continues working—perfect for displaying status information.

Summary

This chapter provides a brief overview of the new features in Excel 2000.

✦   ✦   ✦

Getting Acquainted with Excel

New users sometimes are overwhelmed when they first fire up Excel. They're greeted with an empty workbook, lots of strange buttons, and unfamiliar commands on the menus. This chapter helps you to feel more at home with Excel, explains its main parts, and gives you a chance to do a few things to get better acquainted with it.

Starting Excel

Before you can use Excel, it must be installed on your system. And before you can install Excel, Microsoft Windows must be installed on your system. Excel 2000 requires a 32-bit operating system, such as Windows 95, Windows 98, or Windows NT. With any luck, Excel is already installed and ready to run. If not, you need to run the Setup program on the Office 2000 CD-ROM.

Excel's Parts

When Excel starts, your screen looks something like Figure 2-1. This figure identifies the major parts of Excel's window, which are explained in the following paragraphs.

Figure 2-1 shows Excel running in VGA mode (800 × 600 pixels). Your screen may look different if you're running Windows in a different video mode that displays more or fewer pixels onscreen.

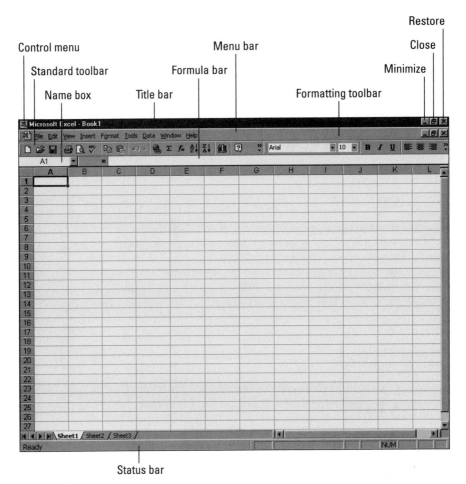

Figure 2-1: Excel runs in a window, which in this case is maximized so that it occupies the full screen.

Title bar

All Windows programs have a title bar, which displays the name of the program and holds some control buttons that you can use to modify the window.

Window control menu button

This button is actually Excel's icon. When you click it, you get a menu that lets you manipulate Excel's window.

Minimize button

Clicking this button minimizes Excel's window and displays it in the Windows taskbar.

Restore button

Clicking this button "unmaximizes" Excel's window so that it no longer fills the entire screen. If Excel isn't maximized, this button is replaced by a Maximize button.

Close button

Clicking this button closes Excel. If you have any unsaved files, you're prompted to save them.

Menu bar

This is Excel's main menu. Clicking a word on the menu drops down a list of menu items, which is one way for you to issue a command to Excel.

The menu bar in Excel 2000 is not fixed in place. In fact, it's actually a toolbar. You can drag it to any side of the window or even make it free-floating if you like.

Toolbars

The toolbars hold buttons that you click to issue commands to Excel. Some of the buttons expand to show additional buttons or commands.

Formula bar

When you enter information or formulas into Excel, they appear in this line.

Name box

This box displays the name of the active cell in the current workbook. When you click the arrow, the list drops down to display all named cells and named ranges (if any) in the active workbook. Select a name to activate the range or cell. You also can use the Name box to name the selected cell or range.

The Name box also displays the name of a selected object, such as a chart or drawing object. However, you cannot use the Name box to select an object or change the name of an object.

Status bar

This bar displays various messages, as well as the status of the Num Lock, Caps Lock, and Scroll Lock keys on your keyboard.

Parts of a Workbook Window

When you work with Excel, your work is stored in workbooks. Each workbook appears in a separate window within Excel's workspace.

Figure 2-2 shows a typical workbook window with its major parts identified. These parts are described in the following paragraphs. Notice that a workbook window has many parts in common with Excel's window.

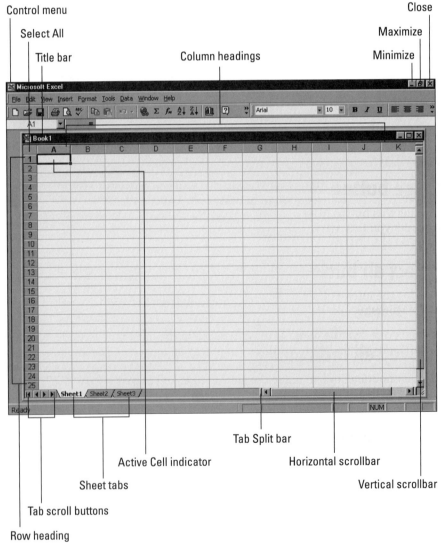

Figure 2-2: An empty Excel workbook, named Book1

Title bar

The title bar shows the name of the workbook and holds some control buttons that you can use to modify the window.

Window control menu button

Clicking this button (actually an icon) displays a menu that lets you manipulate the workbook window.

Minimize button

Clicking this button reduces the workbook window so that only the title bar shows.

Maximize button

Clicking this button increases the workbook window's size to fill Excel's complete workspace. If the window is already maximized, a Restore button appears in its place.

Close button

Clicking this button closes the workbook. If you haven't saved the workbook, Excel prompts you to save it.

Select all button

Clicking the intersection of the row and column headers selects all cells on the active worksheet of the active window.

Active cell indicator

This dark outline indicates the currently active cell (one of the 16,777,216 cells on each worksheet).

Row headings

Numbers ranging from 1 to 65,536 — one for each row in the worksheet. You can click a row heading to select an entire row of cells.

Column headings

Letters ranging from A to IV — one for each of the 256 columns in the worksheet. After column Z comes column AA, which is followed by AB, AC, and so on. After column AZ comes BA, BB, and so on until you get to the last column, labeled IV. You can click a column heading to select an entire column of cells.

Tab scroll buttons

These buttons let you scroll the sheet tabs to display tabs that aren't visible.

Sheet tabs

Each of these notebook-like tabs represents a different sheet in the workbook. A workbook can have any number of sheets, and each sheet has its name displayed in a sheet tab. By default, each new workbook that you create contains three sheets.

Tab split bar

This bar enables you to increase or decrease the area devoted to displaying sheet tabs. When you show more sheet tabs, the horizontal scrollbar's size is reduced.

Horizontal scrollbar

Enables you to scroll the sheet horizontally.

Vertical scrollbar

Let's you scroll the sheet vertically.

If you have a Microsoft IntelliMouse, you can use the mouse wheel to scroll vertically.

A Hands-on Excel Session

The remainder of this chapter consists of an introductory session with Excel. If you've never used Excel, you may want to follow along on your computer to get a feel for how this program works.

This example assumes that you've been asked to prepare a one-page report that shows your company's quarterly sales, broken down by the two sales regions (North and South). This section walks you through the steps required to do the following:

✦ Enter a table of data (the sales figures) into a worksheet

✦ Create and copy a formula (to calculate totals)

✦ Format the data so that it looks good

✦ Create a chart from the data

✦ Save the workbook to a file

✦ Print the data and chart (the one-page report)

When you're finished, you'll have a worksheet that looks like the one shown in Figure 2-3.

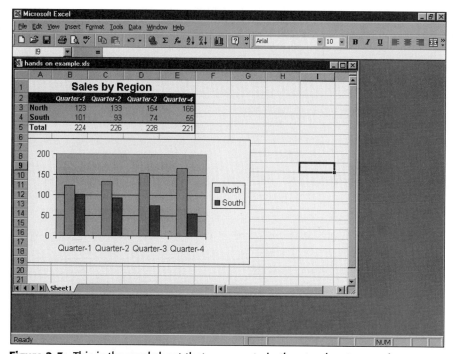

Figure 2-3: This is the worksheet that you create in the step-by-step session.

Note   This section is quite detailed and provides every step that you need to reproduce the worksheet shown in Figure 2-3. If you already have experience with a spreadsheet, you may find this section to be a bit *too* detailed. Don't worry. You'll find that the pace picks up in the remainder of the book.

Getting ready

As a first stage, you start Excel and maximize its window to fill the entire screen. Then you maximize the blank workbook named Book1.

1. If Excel isn't running, start it. You're greeted with a blank window named Book1. If Excel is already running, click its Close button to exit Excel and then restart it so that you see the empty window named Book1.

2. If Excel doesn't fill the entire screen, maximize Excel's window by clicking the Maximize button in Excel's title bar.

3. Maximize the workbook window, so that you can see as much of the workbook as possible. Do this by clicking the Maximize button in Book1's title bar.

Entering the headings

In this stage, you enter the row and column headings into the worksheet named Sheet1 in Book1. After you finish the following steps, the worksheet will look like Figure 2-4.

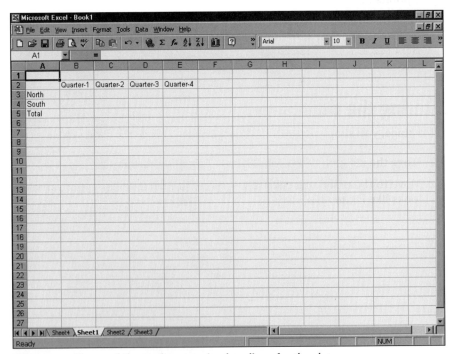

Figure 2-4: The worksheet after entering headings for the data

1. Move the cell pointer to cell A3 by using the direction keys. The Name box displays the cell's address.

2. Enter **North** into cell A3. Just type the text and then press Enter. Depending on your setup, Excel either moves the cell pointer down to cell A4 or the pointer remains in cell A3.

3. Move the cell pointer to cell A4, type **South**, and press Enter.

4. Move the cell pointer to cell A5, type **Total**, and press Enter.

5. Move the cell pointer to cell B2, type **Quarter 1**, and press Enter.

   At this point, you could enter the other three headings manually, but let Excel do the work instead.

6. Move the cell pointer to cell B2 (if it's not already there). Notice the small square at the lower-right corner of the cell pointer. This is called the *fill handle*. When you move the mouse pointer over the fill handle, the mouse pointer changes to a dark cross.

   If the cell doesn't have a fill handle, select the Tools ➪ Options command and then click the Edit tab in the Options dialog box. Place a check mark next to the option labeled Allow cell drag and drop. Then click OK to close the Options dialog box.

7. Move the mouse pointer to the fill handle until the mouse pointer changes to a cross. Then click and drag to the right until you select the three cells to the right (C2, C3, and C4). Release the mouse button and you'll see that Excel filled in the three remaining headings for you. This is an example of AutoFill.

Entering the data

In this stage, you simply enter the values for each quarter in each region.

1. Move the cell pointer to cell B3, type **123**, and press Enter.

2. Move to the remaining cells and enter additional data until your worksheet looks like Figure 2-5.

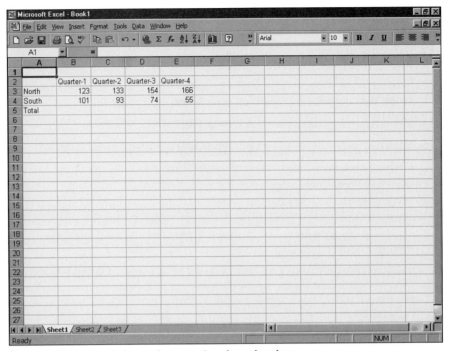

Figure 2-5: The worksheet after entering the sales data

Creating a formula

So far, what you've done has been fairly mundane. In fact, you could accomplish the same effect with any word processor. In this stage, you take advantage of the power feature of a spreadsheet: formulas. You create formulas to calculate the total for each region.

1. Move the cell pointer to cell B5.

2. Locate the AutoSum button on the toolbar below the menu and click it once. The AutoSum button has a Greek sigma on it. The toolbar below the menu is called the Standard toolbar. Notice that Excel inserts the following into the cell:

   `=SUM(B3:B4)`

   This is a formula that calculates the sum of the values in the range B3 through B4.

3. Because this formula is exactly what you want (Excel guessed correctly), press Enter to accept the formula. You see that the sum of the two values is displayed in the cell. You could repeat this step for the remaining three quarters, but it's much easier simply to copy the formula to the three cells to the right.

4. Move the cell pointer to cell B5 (if it's not already there).

5. Move the mouse pointer to the fill handle. When it changes to a cross, click and drag three cells to the right. Release the mouse button and you'll see that Excel copied the formula to the cells that you selected.

At this point, your worksheet should look like Figure 2-6. To demonstrate that these are actual "live" formulas, try changing one or two of the values in rows 3 or 4. You'll see that the cells with the formulas change also. In other words, the formulas are recalculating and displaying new results using the modified data.

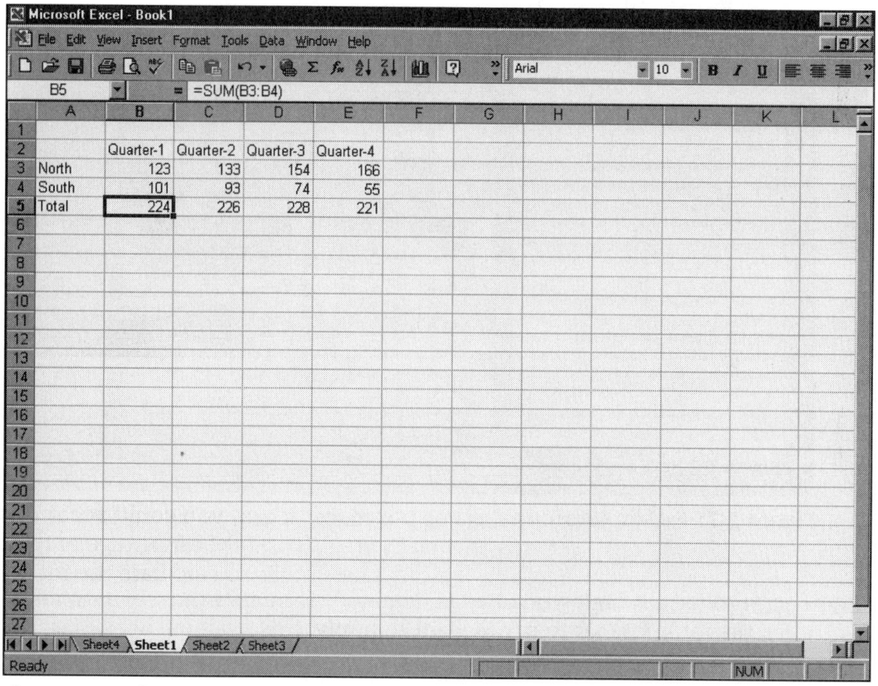

Figure 2-6: The worksheet after inserting a formula and copying it

Formatting the table

The table looks fine, but it could look even better. In this stage, you use Excel's automatic formatting feature to spiff up the table a bit.

1. Move the cell pointer to any cell in the table (it doesn't matter which one because Excel will figure out that table's boundaries).

2. Click the Format menu; it drops down to display its menu items.

3. Select AutoFormat from the list of menu items. Two things happen: Excel determines the table boundaries and highlights the entire table, and it displays the AutoFormat dialog box. Figure 2-7 shows how this looks.

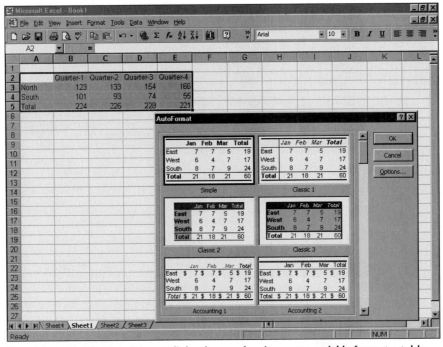

Figure 2-7: Excel's AutoFormat dialog box makes it easy to quickly format a table.

4. The AutoFormat dialog box has 16 "canned" formats from which to choose. Click the table format that you want to apply; this example uses Classic 3.

5. Click the OK button. Excel applies the formats to your table.

Your worksheet should look similar to Figure 2-8.

Note that Excel automatically made the following formatting changes for you:

✦ It changed some of the cell background colors

✦ It changed some of the cell foreground colors

✦ It made the column headings italic

✦ It made the row labels bold

✦ It added borders

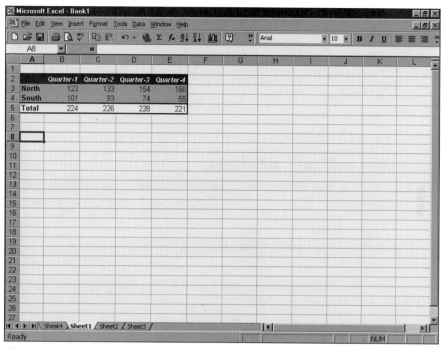

Figure 2-8: Your worksheet after applying automatic formatting.

You could have performed all of these formatting operations yourself, but it probably would have taken several minutes. The AutoFormat feature can save you lots of time.

Adding a title

In this stage, you add a title to the table, make the title bold, and adjust it so that it's centered across the five columns of the table.

1. Move the cell pointer to cell A1.

2. Enter **Sales by Region** and then press Enter.

3. Move the cell pointer back to cell A1 (if it's not there already) and then click the Bold button on the Formatting toolbar (the Bold button has a large *B*). This makes the text bold.

4. Open the Font Size list box (see Figure 2-9) on the Formatting toolbar and select 14 from the list, to make the text larger.

Font Size list box   Merge and Center button

Figure 2-9: The Font Size list box and the Merge and Center button appear on the Formatting toolbar.

5. Click in cell A1 and drag to the right until you select A1, B1, C1, D1, and E1 (that is, the range A1:E1). Don't drag the cell's fill handle. You want to select the cells — not make a copy of cell A1.

6. Click the Merge and Center button on the Formatting toolbar (refer to Figure 2-9). Excel centers the text in cell A1 across the selected cells. In fact, clicking the Merge and Center button merges the five cells into one larger cell.

Your worksheet should look like Figure 2-10.

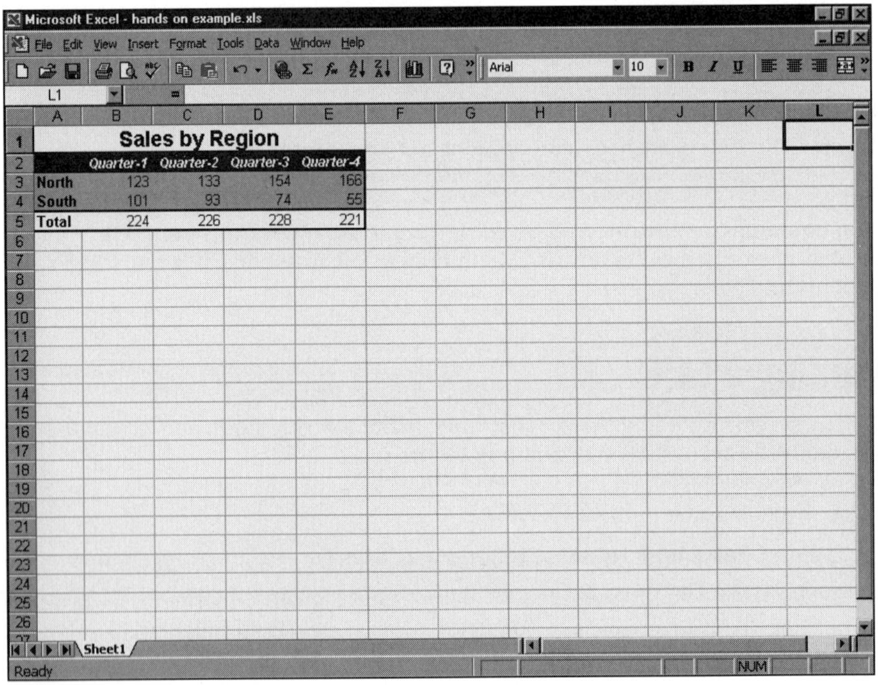

Figure 2-10: Your worksheet after adding a title and formatting it

Creating a chart

In this stage, you create a chart from the data in the table and place it on the worksheet directly below the table.

1. Move the cell pointer to cell A2.

2. Click and drag until you've selected all the cells in the rectangle encompassing A2 at the upper left and E4 at the lower right (15 cells in all). Notice that you're not selecting the cells in the row that displays the totals; you don't want the totals to appear in the chart.

3. With the range A2:E4 selected, click the Chart Wizard button on the Standard toolbar (the Chart Wizard button has an image of a column chart). Excel displays the Office Assistant, which offers you help with charting, and the first in a series of dialog boxes that will help you create the chart that you want (refer to Figure 2-11).

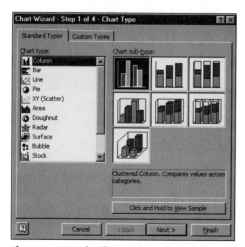

Figure 2-11: The first of four Chart Wizard dialog boxes that help you create a chart

4. First, choose the chart type. The default chart, a Column chart, makes a good choice for the data in the workbook. At this point, you can either click the Next button and specify lots of additional options for the chart or click Finish and accept all of Excel's default choices. Click the Finish button.

Excel creates the chart and displays it on the worksheet. It also displays its Chart toolbar, just in case you want to modify the chart. To get rid of the toolbar, just click the X in its title bar. Your worksheet should look like Figure 2-12.

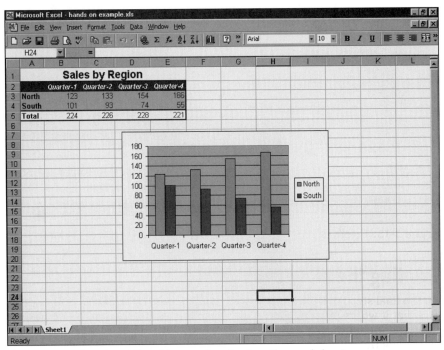

Figure 2-12: The Chart Wizard inserts the chart on the worksheet.

If you want, you can do the following:

✦ Resize the chart by dragging any of the eight handles on its borders (the handles appear only when the chart is selected)

✦ Move the chart by clicking and dragging any of its borders

Saving the workbook

Until now, everything that you've done has occurred in your computer's memory. If the power should fail, all would be lost, so it's time to save your work to a file. Call this workbook **My first workbook**.

1. Click the Save button on the Standard toolbar. The Save button looks like a disk. Excel responds with the Save As dialog box (see Figure 2-13).

2. In the box labeled File name, enter **My first workbook** and then either click Save or press Enter.

Excel saves the workbook as a file. The workbook remains open so that you can work with it some more.

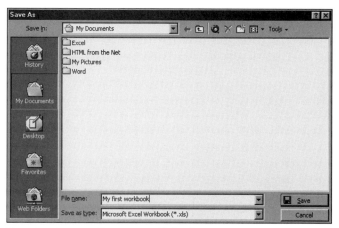

Figure 2-13: Excel's Save As dialog box

Printing the report

As the final step, you print this report, assuming that you have a printer attached and that it works properly. To print the worksheet, just click the Print button on the Standard toolbar (this button has an image of a printer on it). The worksheet (including the chart) is printed using the default settings.

Quitting Excel

Click the Close button in Excel's title bar to exit Excel. Because no changes were made to the workbook since it was last saved, Excel closes without asking whether you want to save the file.

Summary

If this was your first time using Excel, you probably have lots of questions about what you just did in the preceding exercise. Those questions are answered in the following chapters.

If you're the adventurous type, you may have answered some of your own questions by trying out various buttons or menu items. If so, congratulations! Experimenting is the best way to get to know Excel. Just remember, the worst thing that can happen is that you mess up a workbook file. And if you do your experimentation using unimportant files, you have absolutely nothing to lose. And, don't forget about the Office Assistant. You can click the Office Assistant at any time and type a question (using natural language). Your chances are excellent that the Assistant will steer you to a help topic that answers your question.

✦   ✦   ✦

Navigating Through Excel

Because you'll spend lots of time working in Excel, you need to understand the basics of navigating through workbooks and how best to use Excel's user interface. If you're an experienced Windows user, some of this information may already be familiar to you, so this is your chance to learn even more.

If you're new to Excel, some of the information in this chapter may seem confusing. It will become clearer as you progress through the other chapters, however.

Working with Excel's Windows

The files that Excel uses are known as *workbooks*. A workbook can hold any number of sheets, and these sheets can be either worksheets (a sheet consisting of rows and columns) or chart sheets (a sheet that holds a single chart). A *worksheet* is what people usually think of when they think of a spreadsheet.

Figure 3-1 shows Excel with four workbooks open, each in a separate window. One of the windows is minimized and appears near the top-right corner of the screen (when a workbook is minimized, only its title bar is visible).

Worksheet windows can overlap and that the title bar of one window is a different color. That's the window that contains the *active workbook*.

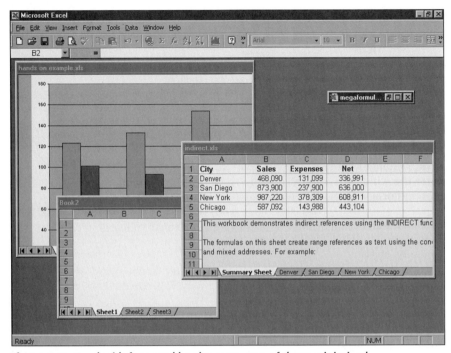

Figure 3-1: Excel with four workbooks open, one of them minimized

The workbook windows that Excel uses work much like the windows in any other Windows program. Excel's windows can be in one of the following states:

✦ **Maximized:** Fills Excel's entire workspace. A maximized window does not have a title bar, and the worksheet's name appears in Excel's title bar. To maximize a window, click its Maximize button.

✦ **Minimized:** Appears as a small window with only a title bar. To minimize a window, click its Minimize button.

✦ **Restored:** A nonmaximized size. To restore a maximized or minimized window, click its Restore button.

If you work with more than one workbook simultaneously (which is quite common), you have to learn how to move, resize, and switch among the workbook windows.

As you're probably aware, Excel itself is contained in a window. Excel's window also can be maximized, minimized, or displayed in a nonmaximized size. When Excel's window is maximized, it fills the entire screen. You can activate other programs by using the Windows taskbar (usually located at the bottom of your screen).

Moving and resizing windows

You *cannot* move or resize a workbook window if it is maximized. You *can* move a minimized window, but doing so has no effect on its position when it is subsequently restored.

To move a window, click and drag its title bar with your mouse. Note that the windows can extend offscreen in any direction, if you want them to.

To resize a window, click and drag any of its borders until it's the size that you want it to be. When you position the mouse pointer on a window's border, the mouse pointer changes shape, which lets you know that you can now click and drag to resize the window. To resize a window horizontally and vertically at the same time, click and drag any of its corners.

If you want all of your workbook windows to be visible (that is, not obscured by another window), you can fiddle around moving and resizing the windows manually, or you can let Excel do it for you. The Window ⇨ Arrange command displays the Arrange Windows dialog box, shown in Figure 3-2. This dialog box has four window-arrangement options. Just select the one that you want and click OK.

Figure 3-2: The Arrange Windows dialog box makes it easy to arrange the windows of all open workbooks.

Switching among windows

As previously mentioned, at any given time, one (and only one) workbook window is the active window. This is the window that accepts your input, and it is the window on which your commands work. The active window's title bar is a different color, and the window appears at the top of the stack of windows.

The following are several ways to make a different window the active workbook:

   ✦ Click another window, if it's visible. The window you click moves to the top and becomes the active window.

✦ Press Ctrl+Tab to cycle through all open windows until the window that you want to work with appears on top as the active window. Shift+Ctrl+Tab cycles through the windows in the opposite direction.

✦ Click the Window menu and select the window that you want from the bottom part of the pull-down menu. The active window has a check mark next to it, as shown in Figure 3-3. This window can display up to nine windows. If you have more than nine workbook windows open, choose More Windows (which appears below the nine window names).

Choose one

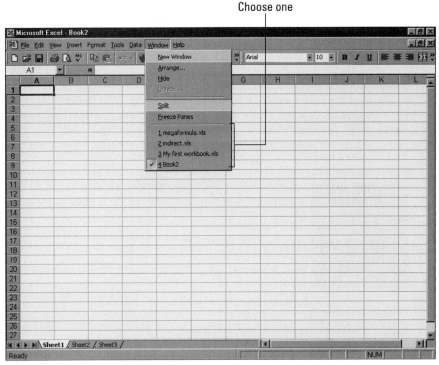

Figure 3-3: You can activate a different window by selecting it from the pull-down Window menu.

Excel 2000 offers another way to make a different window the active workbook: Click the icon in the Windows taskbar that represents the workbook window that you want to view. This feature works only with Windows 98.

Many users (myself included) prefer to do most of their work with maximized workbook windows. This enables you to see more cells and eliminates the distraction of other workbook windows getting in the way. And besides, it's easy to activate another workbook window when you need to use it.

When you maximize one window, all the other windows are maximized, too (but you can't see them). Therefore, if the active window is maximized and you activate a different window, the new active window is also maximized. If the active workbook window is maximized, you can't select another window by clicking it (because other windows aren't visible). You must use either Ctrl+Tab, the Windows taskbar, or the Window menu to activate another window.

When would you *not* want to work exclusively with maximized worksheet windows? Excel also has some handy drag-and-drop features. For example, you can drag a range of cells from one workbook window to another. To do this type of drag and drop, both windows must be visible (that is, not maximized).

Chapter 7 discusses Excel's drag-and-drop features.

You also can display a single workbook in more than one window. For example, if you have a workbook with two worksheets, you may want to display each worksheet in a separate window. All the window-manipulation procedures described previously still apply.

Closing windows

When you close a workbook window, Excel checks whether you have made any changes since the last time you saved the file. If not, the window closes without a prompt from Excel. If you've made any changes, Excel prompts you to save the file, before it closes the window.

You learn more about working with files in Chapter 4.

To close a window, simply click the Close button on the title bar.

Mouseless window manipulation

Although using a mouse to manipulate Excel's windows is usually the most efficient route, you also can perform these actions by using the keyboard. Table 3-1 summarizes the key-combinations that manipulate workbook windows.

Table 3-1
Keystrokes Used to Manipulate Windows

Key Combination	Action
Ctrl+F4	Close a window
Ctrl+F5	Restore a window
Ctrl+F6	Activate the next window
Ctrl+Shift+F6	Activate the previous window
Ctrl+Tab	Activate the next window
Ctrl+Shift+Tab	Activate the previous window
Ctrl+F7	Move a window*
Ctrl+F8	Resize a window*
Ctrl+F9	Minimize a window
Ctrl+F10	Maximize a window
Alt+W[n]	Activate the *n*th window

* Use the direction keys to make the change, and then press Enter.

Moving Around a Worksheet

You'll be spending a lot of time moving around your worksheets, so it pays to learn all the tricks.

Every worksheet consists of rows (numbered 1 through 65,536) and columns (labeled A through IV). After column Z comes column AA; after column AZ comes column BA, and so on. The intersection of a row and a column is a single cell. At any given time, one cell is the *active cell*. You can identify the active cell by its darker border, as shown in Figure 3-4. Its *address* (its column letter and row number) appears in the Name box. Depending on the technique that you use to navigate through a workbook, you may or may not change the active cell when you navigate.

The row and column headings of the active cell are displayed in bold — making it easy to identify the active cell.

The active cell

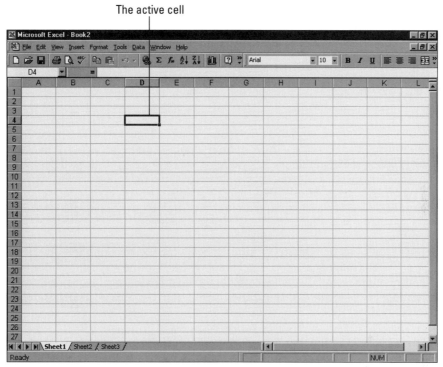

Figure 3-4: The active cell is the cell with the dark border — in this case, cell D4.

How Big Is a Worksheet?

Consider how big a worksheet really is. It has 256 columns and 65,536 rows. Do the arithmetic and you'll find that this works out to 16,777,216 cells. Remember, this is in just one worksheet. A single workbook can hold more than one worksheet — hundreds, if necessary.

If you're using the standard SVGA video mode with the default row heights and column widths, you can see 12 columns and 27 rows (or 324 cells) at a time. This works out to less than 0.001 percent of the entire worksheet. Put another way, more than 100,000 full screens of information are in a single worksheet.

If you started entering a single digit into each cell at a relatively rapid clip of one cell per second, you would take about 194 days, nonstop, to fill a worksheet. Printing the results of your effort would require more than 36,000 sheets of paper.

By the way, don't even think about actually using all the cells in a worksheet. Unless your system is equipped with an unusually large amount of memory, things will slow to a crawl as Windows churns away, swapping information to disk.

Using the keyboard

As you probably already know, you can use the standard navigational keys on your keyboard to move around a worksheet. These keys work just as you would expect: the down arrow moves the active cell down one row, the right arrow moves it one column to the right, and so on. PgUp and PgDn move the active cell up or down one full window (the actual number of rows moved depends on the number of rows displayed in the window).

Tip

When you turn on Scroll Lock, you can scroll through the worksheet without changing the active cell. This can be useful if you need to view another area of your worksheet and then quickly return to your original location. Just press Scroll Lock and then use the direction keys to scroll through the worksheet. When you want to return to the original position (the active cell), press Ctrl+Backspace. Then, press Scroll Lock again to turn it off. When Scroll Lock is turned on, Excel displays SCRL in the status bar at the bottom of the window.

The Num Lock key on your keyboard controls how the keys on the numeric keypad behave. When Num Lock is on, Excel displays NUM in the status bar, and the keys on your numeric keypad generate numbers. Most keyboards have a separate set of navigational keys located to the left of the numeric keypad. These keys are not affected by the state of the Num Lock key.

Table 3-2 summarizes all the worksheet movement keys available in Excel.

Table 3-2	
Excel's Worksheet Movement Keys	
Key	*Action*
Up arrow	Moves the active cell up one row
Down arrow	Moves the active cell down one row
Left arrow	Moves the active cell one column to the left
Right arrow	Moves the active cell one column to the right
PgUp	Moves the active cell up one screen
PgDn	Moves the active cell down one screen
Alt+PgDn	Moves the active cell right one screen
Alt+PgUp	Moves the active cell left one screen
Ctrl+Backspace	Scrolls to display the active cell
Up arrow*	Scrolls the screen up one row (active cell does not change)
Down arrow*	Scrolls the screen down one row (active cell does not change)

Key	Action
Left arrow*	Scrolls the screen left one column (active cell does not change)
Right arrow*	Scrolls the screen right one column (active cell does not change)

* With Scroll Lock on

The actions for some of the keys in the preceding table may be different, depending on the transition options that you've set. Select Tools ⇨ Options and then click the Transition tab in the Options dialog box. If the Transition Navigation Keys option is checked, the navigation keys correspond to those used in older versions of Lotus 1-2-3. Generally, using the standard Excel navigation keys is better than using those for 1-2-3.

Tip

If you know either the cell address or the name of the cell that you want to activate, you can get there quickly by pressing F5 (the shortcut key for Edit ⇨ Go To). This command displays the Go To dialog box.

Just enter the cell address in the Reference box (or choose a named cell from the list), press Enter, and you're there. Using a mouse

Navigating through a worksheet with a mouse also works as you would expect it to work. To change the active cell by using the mouse, click another cell; it becomes the active cell. If the cell that you want to activate is not visible in the workbook window, you can use the scrollbars to scroll the window in any direction. To scroll one cell, click either of the arrows on the scrollbar. To scroll by a complete screen, click either side of the scrollbar's scroll box. You also can drag the scroll box for faster scrolling. Working with the scrollbars is more difficult to describe than to do, so if scrollbars are new to you, I urge you to experiment with them for a few minutes. You'll have it figured out in no time.

When you drag the scrollbar's scroll box, a small yellow box appears that tells you which row or column you will scroll to when you release the mouse button.

If you have a Microsoft IntelliMouse (or a compatible wheel mouse), you can use the mouse wheel to scroll vertically. The wheel scrolls three lines per click at the default rate. Also, if you click the wheel and move the mouse in any direction, the worksheet scrolls automatically in that direction. The more you move the mouse, the faster the scrolling. If you prefer to use the mouse wheel to zoom the worksheet, select Tools ⇨ Options, click the General tab, and then place a check mark next to the option labeled Zoom on roll with IntelliMouse.

Using the scrollbars or scrolling with the IntelliMouse doesn't change the active cell. It simply scrolls the worksheet. To change the active cell, you must click a new cell after scrolling.

Notice that only the active workbook window has scrollbars. When you activate a different window, the scrollbars appear.

Giving Commands to Excel

Excel is designed to take orders from you. You give these orders by issuing commands. You can give commands to Excel by using the following methods:

✦ Menus

✦ Shortcut menus

✦ Toolbar buttons

✦ Shortcut key combinations

In many cases, you can choose how to issue a particular command. For example, if you want to save your workbook to disk, you can use the menu (the File ⇨ Save command), a shortcut menu (right-click the workbook's title bar and click Save), a toolbar button (the Save button on the Standard toolbar), or a shortcut key combination (Ctrl+S). The particular method you use is up to you.

The following sections provide an overview of the four methods of issuing commands to Excel.

Using Excels Menus

Excel, like all other Windows programs, has a menu bar located directly below the title bar (see Figure 3-5). This menu bar is always available and ready for your command. Excel's menus change, depending on what you're doing. For example, if you're working with a chart, Excel's menus change to give you options that are appropriate for a chart. This all happens automatically, so you don't even have to think about it.

Figure 3-5: Excel's menu bar displays different options, depending on the nature of your task.

Note   Technically, Excel 2000's menu bar is just another toolbar. In Excel 2000, toolbars and menu bars are functionally identical. However, I'll continue to discuss menu bars as if they are something different.

Changing Your Mind

When you issue a command to Excel by using any of the available methods, Excel carries out your command. However, just about every command can be reversed by using the Edit ⇨ Undo command. Select this command after issuing a command, and it's as if you never issued the command.

Beginning with Excel 97, the Undo feature became much more useful. Excel 97 and later supports up to 16 levels of Undo. This means that you can reverse the effects of the last 16 commands that you executed! You may not fully appreciate this feature until you someday make a major error (such as deleting a column of formulas) and don't discover it until quite a bit later. You can use Edit ⇨ Undo repeatedly (up to 16 times) until your worksheet reverts to the state that it was in before you made your error.

Rather than use Edit ⇨ Undo, you may prefer to use the Undo button on the Standard toolbar. If you click the arrow on the right side of the button, you can see a description of the commands that are "undoable" (see the accompanying figure). The Redo button performs in the opposite direction of the Undo button: Redo repeats commands that have been undone.

So, as you're working away in Excel, don't forget about Undo. It can be a real lifesaver.

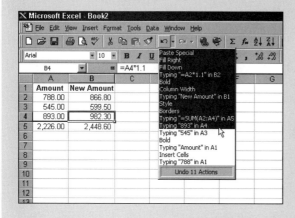

Using a mouse

Opening the menu with a mouse is quite straightforward. Click the menu that you want to open and it drops down to display menu items, also called *commands*, as shown in Figure 3-6. Click the menu item to issue the command.

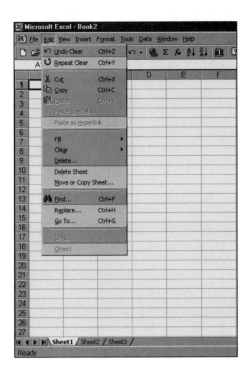

Figure 3-6: Opening Excel's Edit menu displays its menu items.

Some menu items lead to an additional *submenu;* when you click the menu item, the submenu appears to its right. Menu items that have a submenu display a small triangle. For example, the Edit ➪ Clear command has a submenu, shown in Figure 3-7. Excel's designers incorporated submenus primarily to keep the menus from becoming too lengthy and overwhelming to users.

Some menu items also have shortcut keys associated with them. The ones that do usually display the key combination next to the menu item. For example, the Edit ➪ Find command's shortcut key combination is Ctrl+F.

Sometimes, you'll notice that a menu item appears *grayed out.* This simply means that the menu item isn't appropriate for what you're doing. Nothing happens if you select such a menu item.

Menu items that are followed by an ellipsis (three dots) always display a dialog box. Menu commands that don't have an ellipsis are executed immediately. For example, the Insert ➪ Cells command results in a dialog box, because Excel needs more information about the command. The Insert ➪ Rows command doesn't need a dialog box, so Excel performs this command immediately.

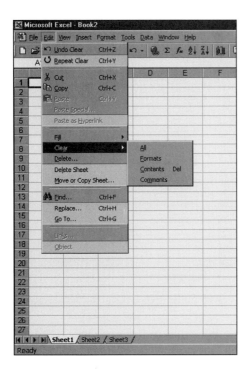

Figure 3-7: The submenu of the
Edit ➩ Clear command

In Excel 2000, your menus may behave differently than they did in previous versions of Excel. When you open a menu, you may see the most recently used commands first. After a few moments, or if you click the arrow at the bottom of the menu, you'll see the rest of the commands for that menu. After you choose a command by clicking the arrow at the bottom of the menu, Excel leaves that command in the list of "recently used" commands; that is, you'll see it immediately among the available commands the next time that you open the menu. To find it again, you won't need to click the arrow at the bottom of the menu or wait until all the commands appear.

Personally, I think this "automatic menu customization" is one of the worst ideas ever—and is practically guaranteed to cause confusion among beginners. I highly recommend that you turn this feature off immediately. Choose Tools ➩ Customize and click the Options tab. Then, remove the check from the check box titled Menus show recently used commands first (see Figure 3-8). Note: Changing this behavior in Excel changes the behavior for *all* Office applications.

Click here

Figure 3-8: Change menu behavior to show all commands by clearing this check box.

Using the keyboard

You can issue menu commands by using the mouse or the keyboard. Although most users tend to prefer a mouse, others find that accessing the menus with the keyboard is more efficient. This is especially true if you're entering data into a worksheet. Using a mouse means that you have to move your hand from the keyboard, locate the mouse, move it, click it, and then move your hand back to the keyboard. Although this takes only a few seconds, those seconds add up.

To issue a menu command from the keyboard, press Alt and then the menu's *hot key*. The hot key is the underlined letter in the menu; for example E is the hot key of the Edit menu. After you open the menu, you can press the appropriate hot key for a command on the menu. For example, to issue the Data ➪ Sort command, press Alt, press D, and then press S.

You also can press Alt alone, or F10. This selects the first menu (the File menu). Next, you use the direction keys to highlight the menu that you want, and then press Enter. In the menu, use the direction keys to choose the appropriate menu item, and press Enter again.

Moving the menu

In Excel 2000, a menu bar is the same as a toolbar. Because the menu bar is a toolbar, you can move the menu to a new location, if you prefer. To move the menu, just click and drag it to its new location. This can be a bit tricky, because you must click the menu in a location that doesn't contain a menu item, such as to the right of the Help menu. You can drag the menu to any of the window borders or leave it free-floating. Figure 3-9 shows the menu after relocating it to the left side of the window.

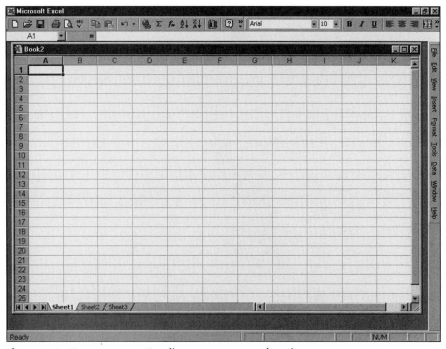

Figure 3-9: You can move Excel's menu to a new location.

Cross-Reference

Learn how to customize Excel's menus (and toolbars) in Chapter 15.

Using Shortcut Menus

Besides the omnipresent menu bar, discussed in the preceding section, Excel features a slew of *shortcut menus*. A shortcut menu is context-sensitive — its contents depend on what you're doing at the time. Shortcut menus don't contain *all* the relevant commands, just those that are most commonly used for whatever is selected. You can display a shortcut menu by right-clicking just about anything in Excel.

As an example, examine Figure 3-10, which shows the shortcut menu (also called a *context menu*) that appears when you right-click a cell. The shortcut menu appears at the mouse-pointer position, which makes selecting a command fast and efficient.

The shortcut menu that appears depends on what is currently selected. For example, if you're working with a chart, the shortcut menu that appears when you right-click a chart part contains commands that are pertinent to what is selected.

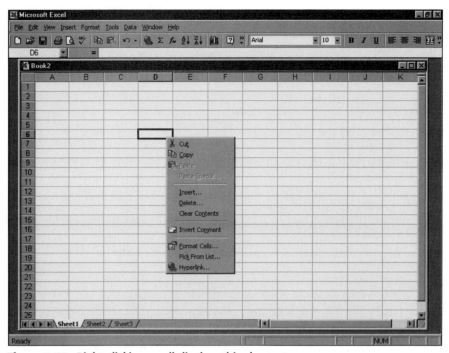

Figure 3-10: Right-clicking a cell displays this shortcut menu.

Tip   Although shortcut menus were invented with mouse users in mind, you also can display a shortcut menu by pressing Shift+F10.

Excel's Toolbars

Excel, like all leading applications, includes convenient graphical toolbars. Clicking a button on a toolbar is just another way of issuing commands to Excel. In many cases, a toolbar button is simply a substitute for a menu command. For example, the Copy button is a substitute for Edit ➪ Copy. Some toolbar buttons, however, don't have any menu equivalent. One example is the AutoSum button, which automatically inserts a formula to calculate the sum of a range of cells. Toolbars can be customized to include menu commands as well as buttons.

By default, Excel displays two toolbars (named *Standard* and *Formatting*). Technically, it displays three toolbars, because the menu bar is actually a toolbar named *Worksheet menu bar*. All told, Excel 2000 has 23 built-in toolbars, plus the menu bar. You have complete control over which toolbars are displayed and where they are located. In addition, you can create custom toolbars, made up of buttons that you find most useful.

Cross-Reference

Learn how to customize toolbars and create new toolbars in Chapter 15.

EXCEL 2000

In Excel 2000, the Standard and Formatting toolbars may appear side by side just below the menu bar. In prior versions, these toolbars appeared separately. Because the toolbars appear side by side, you can't see all the tools on either toolbar; Excel display those tools on each toolbar that you are most likely to use frequently. If you want to use one of the "missing tools," you must click the arrow that appears at the edge of the toolbar to display all the tools available on that toolbar (see Figure 3-11). After you choose a tool from the "missing tools," Excel continues to display that tool, because you recently used it.

If you prefer to see all the tools on a toolbar, you can drag one of the toolbars to a different location. If you want to display one below the other (as previous versions of Excel did), drag one below the other or choose Tools ➪ Customize. Click the Options tab and remove the check from the check box labeled Standard and Formatting toolbars share one row. This check box *is not* available if either toolbar is hidden or both toolbars are floating (you'll learn more about "floating toolbars" later in this chapter). Changing this behavior in Excel affects only Excel.

Instant Help for Commands

Excel's toolbars can be a bit daunting at times, especially for newcomers. One approach — the best approach, in my opinion — is simply to try out things to see what happens (and don't forget about the Edit ➪ Undo command). If you're not that adventurous, an easy way exists to determine the function of a particular menu command or toolbar button.

Drag the mouse pointer over a toolbar button (but don't click it). A small box appears that tells you the name of the button. Often, this provides enough information for you to determine whether the button is what you want.

For context-sensitive help on a menu command or toolbar button, choose the Help ➪ What's This? command (or, press Shift+F1). The mouse pointer turns into an arrow with a question mark beside it. Now, select any menu command or toolbar button, and Excel displays a description of the item. Note that the command itself won't be issued when you click a menu item or toolbar button.

Click here

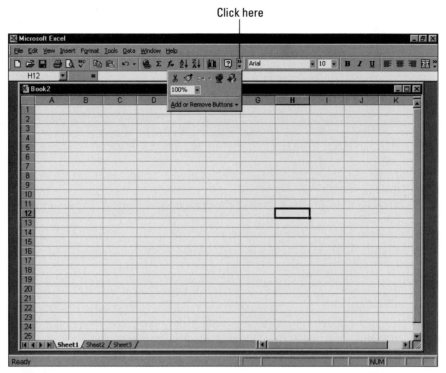

Figure 3-11: Click the arrow to display more tools on the Standard toolbar.

Table 3-3 lists all of Excel's built-in toolbars.

Table 3-3
Excel's Built-in Toolbars

Toolbar	*Use*
Standard	Issue commonly used commands
Formatting	Change how your worksheet or chart looks
Pivot Table	Work with pivot tables
Chart	Manipulate charts
Reviewing	Tools to use workbooks in groups
Clipboard	Tools to copy and paste multiple clipboard selections between Office applications
Forms	Add controls (buttons, spinners, and so on) to a worksheet

Toolbar	Use
Stop Recording	Record macros
External Data	Perform queries on external database files
Auditing	Identify errors in your worksheet
Full Screen	Toggle in and out of full-screen view (one tool only)
Circular Reference	Obtain assistance in identifying circular references in formulas
Visual Basic	Write macros in Visual Basic for Applications
Web	Access the Internet from Excel
Control Toolbox	Add ActiveX controls to a workbook or form
Exit Design Mode	Toggle in and out of design mode (one tool only)
Worksheet Menu Bar	The menu that appears when a worksheet is active
Chart Menu Bar	The menu that appears when a chart is selected
Drawing	Insert or edit drawings on a worksheet
Word Art	Insert or edit a picture composed of words
Picture	Insert or edit graphic images
Shadow Settings	Insert or edit shadows that appear behind objects
3D Settings	Add 3D effects to objects

Sometimes, Excel automatically pops up a toolbar to help you with a particular task. For example, if you're working with a chart, Excel displays its Chart toolbar.

 The Clipboard toolbar (and the way the clipboard functions in Office 2000 applications) is new in Excel 2000.

 See Chapter 7 for more information on the clipboard.

Hiding or showing toolbars

To hide or display a particular toolbar, choose View ➪ Toolbars, or right-click any toolbar. Either of these actions displays a list of common toolbars (but not all toolbars). The toolbars that have a check mark next to them are currently visible. To hide a toolbar, click it to remove the check mark. To display a toolbar, click it to add a check mark.

If the toolbar that you want to hide or show does not appear on the menu list, select View ➪ Toolbars ➪ Customize (or select Customize from the shortcut menu that appears when you right-click a toolbar). Excel displays its Customize dialog box, shown in Figure 3-12. The Toolbars tab of this dialog box shows a list of all toolbars that are available—the built-in toolbars, plus any custom toolbars. The toolbars that have a check mark next to them are currently visible. To hide a toolbar, click it to remove the check mark. To display a toolbar, click it to add a check mark. When you're finished, click the Close button.

Figure 3-12: Choose which toolbars to display in the Customize dialog box.

The Customize dialog box has some other options with which you may want to experiment. Click the Options tab to display these options (see Figure 3-13). The check boxes at the top of the Options tab were discussed earlier in the chapter. The button labeled Reset my usage data, in the middle of Figure 3-13, works in conjunction with the check box titled Menus show recently used commands first. Excel determines the commands to show based on the commands that you use most often. Clicking the Reset my usage data tells Excel to ignore your past usage and reset the menu commands to the defaults that shipped with the product. If you leave the check in the Menus show recently used commands first check box after resetting usage, Excel starts the "monitoring" process over again to determine which commands you're using most often.

Figure 3-13: The Options tab of the Customize dialog box provides some options for toolbars.

If you prefer larger buttons, check the Large icons check box. By default, when you open the Font list box, font names provide a sample of the font (see Figure 3-14). This is useful, but it also slows things down quite a bit. For a faster font list, remove the check from the check box titled List font names in their font. And if you find those pop-up screen tips distracting, uncheck the Show ScreenTips on toolbars check box. You can also specify what type of animation you prefer for the menus.

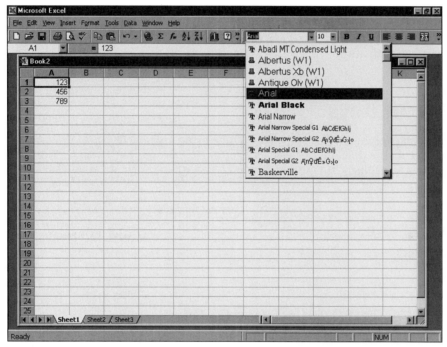

Figure 3-14: By default, font names provide a sample of the font.

Moving toolbars

Toolbars can be moved to any of the four sides of Excel's window, or can be free-floating. A free-floating toolbar can be dragged onscreen anywhere that you want. You also can change a toolbar's size simply by dragging any of its borders. To hide a free-floating toolbar, click its Close button.

Because Excel 2000 menu bars are actually toolbars, this discussion also applies to the menu bars.

When a toolbar isn't free-floating, it's said to be *docked*. A docked toolbar is stuck to the edge of Excel's window and doesn't have a title bar. Therefore, a docked toolbar can't be resized.

To move a toolbar (docked or free-floating), click and drag anywhere on the background of the toolbar (that is, anywhere except on a button). When you drag it toward the window's edge, it automatically docks itself there. When a toolbar is docked, its shape changes to a single row or single column.

Learning more about toolbars

Describing all the toolbar buttons available would take many pages, so I won't even try. You are charged with discovering this handy feature on your own. But, throughout the rest of the book, I point out toolbar buttons that may be useful in particular situations.

Shortcut Keys

This chapter mentioned earlier that some menu commands have equivalent shortcut keys. Usually, the shortcut key combination is displayed next to the menu item — providing a built-in way for you to learn the shortcuts as you select the commands.

Throughout the book, shortcut keys are examined that are relevant to any particular topic.

Appendix E lists all the shortcut keys available in Excel.

Working with Dialog Boxes

As previously stated, menu items that end with an ellipsis (three dots) result in a dialog box. All Windows programs use dialog boxes, so you may already be familiar with the concept.

About dialog boxes

You can think of a dialog box as Excel's way of getting more information from you about the command that you selected. For example, if you choose View ➪ Zoom (which changes the magnification of the worksheet), Excel can't carry out the command until it finds out from you what magnification level you want. Dialog boxes can be simple or much more complicated. Dialog boxes are made up of several items, known as *controls*.

When a dialog box appears in response to your command, you make additional choices in the dialog box by manipulating the controls. When you're finished, click the OK button (or press Enter) to continue. If you change your mind, click the Cancel button (or press Escape) and nothing further happens — it's as if the dialog box never appeared.

If a dialog box obscures an area of your worksheet that you need to see, simply click the dialog box's title bar and drag the box to another location. The title bar in a dialog box has two controls: a Help button (Question-mark icon) and a Close button. When you click the Help button, the mouse pointer displays a question mark. You can click any part of the dialog box to get a description of that part's purpose. Clicking the Close button is the same as clicking the Cancel button or pressing Escape.

Although a dialog box looks like just another window, it works a little differently. When a dialog box appears, you can't do anything in the workbook until the dialog box is closed. In other words, you must dismiss the dialog box before you can do anything.

Dialog box controls

Most people find working with dialog boxes to be quite straightforward and natural. The controls usually work just as you would expect, and they can be manipulated either with your mouse or directly from the keyboard.

The following sections describe the most common dialog box controls and show some examples.

Buttons

A button control is about as simple as it gets. Just click it and it does its thing. Most dialog boxes have at least two buttons. The OK button closes the dialog box and executes the command. The Cancel button closes the dialog box without making any changes. If an ellipsis appears after the text on a button, clicking the button leads to another dialog box.

Pressing the Alt key and the button's underlined letter is equivalent to clicking the button. Pressing Enter is the same as clicking the OK button, and pressing Esc is the same as clicking the Cancel button.

Navigating Dialog Boxes by Using the Keyboard

Although dialog boxes were designed with mouse users in mind, some users prefer to use the keyboard. With a bit of practice, you'll find that navigating a dialog box directly from the keyboard may be more efficient in some cases.

Every dialog box control has text associated with it, and this text always has one underlined letter (a *hot key* or *accelerator key*). You can access the control from the keyboard by pressing the Alt key and then the underlined letter. You also can use Tab to cycle through all the controls on a dialog box. Shift+Tab cycles through the controls in reverse order.

When a control is selected, it appears with a darker outline. You can use the spacebar to activate a selected control.

Option buttons

Option buttons are sometimes known as *radio* buttons, because they work like the preset station buttons on an old-fashioned car radio. Like these car radios, only one option button at a time can be "pressed." Choosing an option button is like choosing a single item on a computerized multiple-choice test. When you click an option button, the previously selected option button is unselected.

Option buttons usually are enclosed in a group box, and a single dialog box can have several sets of option buttons. Figure 3-15 shows an example of a dialog box with option buttons.

Figure 3-15: This dialog box has seven option buttons.

Check boxes

A check box control is used to indicate whether an option is on or off. This is similar to responding to an item on a True/False test. Figure 3-16 shows a dialog box with several check boxes. Unlike option buttons, each check box is independent of the others. Clicking a check box toggles on and off the check mark.

Figure 3-16: An example of check boxes in a dialog box

Range selection boxes

A range selection box enables you to specify a worksheet range by dragging inside the worksheet. A range selection box has a small button that, when clicked, collapses the dialog box, to make it easier for you to select the range by dragging in the worksheet. After you select the range, click the button again to restore the dialog box. Figure 3-17 shows a dialog box with two range selection box controls. The control in the middle is a standard edit box.

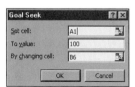

Figure 3-17: A range selection box enables you to specify a worksheet range by dragging in the worksheet.

Spinners

A spinner control makes specifying a number easy. You can click the arrows to increment or decrement the displayed value. A spinner is almost always paired with an edit box. You can either enter the value directly into the edit box or use the spinner to change it to the desired value. Figure 3-18 shows a dialog box with several spinner controls.

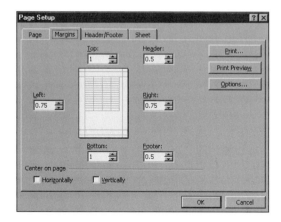

Figure 3-18: This dialog box has several spinner controls.

List boxes

A list box control contains a list of options from which you choose. If the list is longer than will fit in the list box, you can use its vertical scrollbar to scroll through the list. Figure 3-19 shows an example of a dialog box that contains two list box controls.

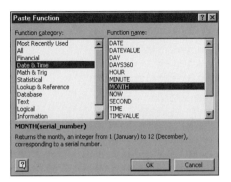

Figure 3-19: Two list box controls in a dialog box

Drop-down boxes

Drop-down boxes are similar to list boxes, but they show only a single option at a time. When you click the arrow on a drop-down box, the list drops down to display additional choices. Figure 3-20 shows an open drop-down box control.

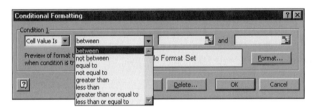

Figure 3-20: A drop-down box control in a dialog box

Tabbed dialog boxes

Many of Excel's dialog boxes are "tabbed" dialog boxes. A tabbed dialog box includes notebook-like tabs, each of which is associated with a different panel. When you click a tab, the dialog box changes to display a new panel containing a new set of controls. The Format Cells dialog box, which appears in response to the Format ➪ Cells command, is a good example. This dialog box is shown in Figure 3-21. Notice that it has six tabs, which makes it functionally equivalent to six different dialog boxes.

Tabbed dialog boxes are quite convenient, because you can make several changes in a single dialog box. After you make all of your setting changes, click OK or press Enter.

Tip   To select a tab by using the keyboard, use Ctrl+PgUp or Ctrl+PgDn, or simply press the first letter of the tab that you want to activate.

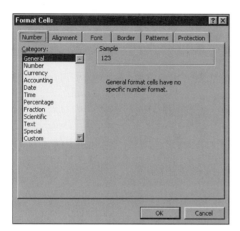

Figure 3-21: The Format Cells dialog box is an example of a tabbed dialog box.

Summary

This chapter covers background information that is essential to using Excel efficiently. It discusses methods to manipulate windows (which hold workbooks), as well as several techniques to move around within a worksheet by using the mouse or the keyboard. It also discusses the various methods used to issue commands to Excel: menus, shortcut menus, toolbar buttons, and shortcut key combinations. This chapter concludes with a general discussion of dialog boxes — an element common to all Windows programs.

✦　　✦　　✦

Working with Files and Workbooks

Computer users won't get too far without understanding the concept of files. Every computer program uses files, and a good understanding of how to manage files stored on your hard drive will make your job easier. This chapter discusses how Excel uses files and what you need to know about files to use Excel.

Some Background on Files

A *file* is an entity that stores information a disk. A hard disk is usually organized into directories (or folders) to facilitate the organization of files. For example, all the files that comprise Excel are stored in a separate folder on your computer. And, your system probably has a directory named Personal (located in your Windows directory) that is used as the default location for storing Excel workbooks.

Files can be manipulated in several ways. They can be copied, renamed, deleted, or moved to another disk or folder. These types of file operations are usually performed by using the tools in Windows (although you also can perform these operations without leaving Excel).

Computer programs are stored in files, and programs also store information that they use in files. Some programs (such as Excel) use files by loading them into memory. Others (such as database programs) access selective parts of a file directly from the disk and don't read the entire file into memory.

Windows makes it easy to access *properties* of files. Properties include information such as file type, size, date created, its read-only status, and so on. Excel enables you access some additional custom properties of files that can help you to locate and categorize your files. For example, you can store information that enables you quickly to locate all workbook files that apply to a particular client.

How Excel Uses Files

When you installed Excel (or the entire Microsoft Office suite) on your system, the Setup program copied many files to your hard disk and created several new folders to hold the files. These files consist of the files that are needed to run Excel, plus some sample files and Help files. The Setup program also made (or modified) some entries in the Windows *Registry*. The Registry is a master database of sorts that keeps track of all configuration information for the operating system and the software installed on your system, and also associates Excel's data files with Excel.

Excel's data files

Excel's primary file type is called a *workbook* file. When you open a workbook in Excel, the entire file is loaded into memory, and any changes that you make occur only in the copy of the file that's in memory. If the workbook is large, your system may not have enough memory to hold the file. In such a case, Windows uses disk-based virtual memory to simulate actual memory (this slows things down considerably). When you save the workbook, Excel saves the copy in memory to your disk, overwriting the previous copy of the file.

Table 4-1 lists the various types of files that Excel supports directly.

<table>
<tr><th colspan="2">Table 4-1
Data Files Used by Excel</th></tr>
<tr><th>File Type</th><th>Description</th></tr>
<tr><td>BAK</td><td>Backup file</td></tr>
<tr><td>XLA</td><td>Excel add-in file (several add-ins are supplied with Excel, and you can create your own add-ins)</td></tr>
<tr><td>XLB</td><td>Excel toolbar configuration file</td></tr>
<tr><td>XLC</td><td>Excel 4 chart file*</td></tr>
<tr><td>XLL</td><td>Excel link library file</td></tr>
<tr><td>XLM</td><td>Excel 4 macro file*</td></tr>
<tr><td>XLS</td><td>Excel workbook file</td></tr>
</table>

File Type	Description
XLT	Excel template file
XLW	Excel workspace file

* These files became obsolete beginning with Excel 5. However, Excel can still read these files for compatibility with previous versions.

Foreign file formats supported

Although Excel's default file format is an XLS workbook file, it also can open files generated by several other applications. In addition, Excel can save workbooks in several different formats. Table 4-2 contains a list of file formats that Excel can read and write.

Cross-Reference Chapter 32 covers file importing and exporting in detail.

Table 4-2	
File Formats Supported by Excel	
File Type	**Description**
WKS	1-2-3 Release 1 spreadsheet format*
WK1	1-2-3 Release 2 spreadsheet format**
WK3	1-2-3 Release 3 spreadsheet format**
WK4	1-2-3 for Windows spreadsheet format
WQ1	Quattro Pro for DOS spreadsheet format
WB1	Quattro Pro for Windows spreadsheet format*
DBF	dBASE database format
SLK	SYLK spreadsheet format
WB1	Quattro Pro for Windows spreadsheet format
HTM, HTML	Hypertext Markup Language files
CSV	Comma-separated value text file format
TXT	Text file format
PRN	Text file format
DIF	Data interchange format

* Excel can open files in this format, but not save them.

** When you open one of these files, Excel searches for the associated formatting file (either FMT or FM3) and attempts to translate the formatting.

Excel 2000 lets you use HTML as a "native" file format. HTML is the file format used by Web browsers. You can save and retrieve files using this format, with no loss of information.

This new HTML feature is discussed in Chapter 29.

Essential Workbook File Operations

This section describes the operations that you perform with workbook files: opening, saving, closing, deleting, and so on. As you read through this section, keep in mind that you can have any number of workbooks open simultaneously, and that at any given time, only one workbook is the active workbook. The workbook's name is displayed in its title bar (or in Excel's title bar if the workbook is maximized).

Creating a new workbook

When you start Excel, it automatically creates a new (empty) workbook called Book1. This workbook exists only in memory and has not been saved to disk. By default, this workbook consists of three worksheets named Sheet1, Sheet2, and Sheet3. If you're starting a new project from scratch, you can use this blank workbook.

You can always create another new workbook in either of three ways:

✦ Use the File ⇨ New command

✦ Click the New Workbook button on the Standard toolbar (this button has an image of a sheet of paper)

✦ Press the Ctrl+N shortcut key combination

If you choose the File ⇨ New command, you're greeted with a dialog box named New (see Figure 4-1). This is a tabbed dialog box that enables you to choose a template for the new workbook. If you don't have any custom templates defined, the General tab displays only one option: Workbook. Clicking this gives you a plain workbook. Templates that are included with Excel are listed in the Spreadsheet Solutions tab. If you choose one of these templates, your new workbook is based on the selected template file.

Templates are discussed later in this chapter.

Pressing Ctrl+N or clicking the New button on the Standard toolbar bypasses the New dialog box and creates a new default workbook immediately. If you want to create a new workbook based on a template, you must use the File ⇨ New command.

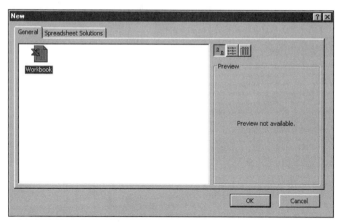

Figure 4-1: The New dialog box enables you to choose a template upon which to base the new workbook.

Tip

If you find that you almost always end up closing the default Book1 workbook that appears when you start Excel, you can set things up so that Excel starts without an empty workbook. To do so, you need to edit the command line that you use to start Excel. For example, if you start Excel by using a shortcut on your Windows desktop, right-click the shortcut icon and choose Properties from the menu. Click the Shortcut tab and add **/e** after the command line listed in the Target field. The following is an example of a command line modified in this manner (the actual drive and path may vary on your system):

```
C:\Program Files\Microsoft Office\Office\excel.exe /e
```

Opening an existing workbook

The following are the ways to open a workbook that has been saved on your disk:

- ✦ Use the File ➪ Open command
- ✦ Click the Open button on the Standard toolbar (the Open button has an image of a file folder opening)
- ✦ Press the Ctrl+O shortcut key combination

All of these methods result in the Open dialog box, shown in Figure 4-2.

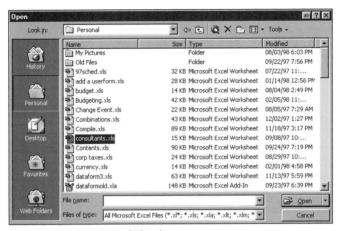

Figure 4-2: The Open dialog box

You also can open an Excel workbook by double-clicking its icon in any folder window. If Excel isn't running, it starts automatically. Or, you can drag a workbook icon into the Excel window to load the workbook.

If you want to open a file that you've used recently, it may be listed at the bottom of the drop-down File menu. This menu shows a list of files that you've worked on recently. Just click the filename and the workbook opens for you (bypassing the Open dialog box).

Tip

You select the number of files to display in the recent file list—from zero up to nine. To change this setting, use Tool ➪ Options. In the Options dialog box, click the General tab and make the change to the Recently used file list setting.

EXCEL 2000

The Open dialog box has a new look in Excel 2000. It provides icons along the left side so that you can quickly activate certain folders. For example, clicking the Desktop icon activates your Windows\Desktop directory—which contains the file and shortcuts displayed on your desktop.

To open a workbook from the Open dialog box, you must provide two pieces of information: the name of the workbook file (specified in the File name field) and its folder (specified in the Look in field).

This dialog box may be a bit overwhelming at first. You can ignore most of it, because many of the controls deal with locating files. If you know what folder the file is in, you simply specify the folder and then select the filename (and don't forget about the new icons on the left side of the Open dialog box). Click Open and the file opens. You also can just double-click the filename to open it.

In Excel 2000, the Open button is actually a drop-down list. Click the arrow and you see the additional options:

✦ **Open:** Opens the file normally.

✦ **Open Read Only:** Opens the selected file in read-only mode. When a file is opened in this mode, changes cannot be saved to the original filename.

✦ **Open as Copy:** Opens a copy of the selected file. If the file is named budget.xls, the workbook that opens is named copy of budget.xls.

✦ **Open in Browser:** Opens the file in your default Web browser.

Tip   You can hold down the Ctrl key and select multiple workbooks. When you click OK, all the selected workbook files will open.

Right-clicking a filename in the Open dialog box displays a shortcut menu with many extra choices. For example, you can copy the file, delete it, modify its properties, and so on.

Specifying a folder

The Look in field is actually a drop-down box. Click the arrow and the box expands to show your system components. You can select a different drive or directory from this list. The Up One Level icon (a file folder with an upward arrow) moves up one level in the folder hierarchy.

As noted previously, you can also click any of the following icons to activate a particular directory:

Icon	Folder
History	c:\windows\recent
Personal	c:\windows\personal
Desktop	c:\windows\desktop
Favorites	c:\windows\favorites
Web Folders	c:\windows\web folders

Filtering by file type

At the bottom of the Open dialog box, the drop-down list is labeled Files of type. When this dialog box is displayed, it shows All Microsoft Excel Files (*.xl*, *.xls, *.xla, *.xlt, *.xlw). This means that the files displayed are filtered, and you see only files that have an extension beginning with the letters XL. In other words, you see only standard Excel files: workbooks, add-ins, templates, and workspace files.

If you want to open a file of a different type, click the arrow in the drop-down list and select the file type that you want to open. This changes the filtering and displays only files of the type that you specify.

File display preferences

The Open dialog box can display your workbook filenames in four different styles:

- ✦ **List:** As a list of filenames only, displayed in multiple columns
- ✦ **Details:** As a list of filenames, with details about each file (its size, file type, and when it was last modified)
- ✦ **Properties:** As a list of filenames, with file properties displayed in a separate panel for the selected file
- ✦ **Preview:** As a list of filenames, with a preview screen displayed in a separate panel for the selected file

You control the style by clicking the View icon and then selecting from the drop-down list. The View icon is located in the upper-right section of the Open dialog box (see Figure 4-3). The style that you choose is entirely up to you.

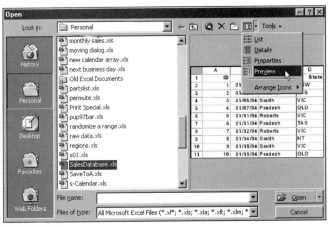

Figure 4-3: The View icon enables you to change the way files are listed in the Open dialog box.

Tip

If you display the files by using the Details style, you can sort the file list by any of the columns displayed (name, size, type, or date). To sort the file list, click the appropriate column heading.

The Tools menu

Clicking the Tools menu, listed last in the upper-right section of the Open dialog box, displays a shortcut menu. The following are the menu items displayed and what they do:

✦ **Find:** Opens a new dialog box that enables you to search for a particular file. See the sidebar, "Finding Lost Workbooks in Excel 2000."

✦ **Delete**: Deletes the selected file(s).

✦ **Rename**: Enables you to rename the selected file.

✦ **Print**: Opens the selected file, prints it, and then closes it.

✦ **Add to Favorites**: Adds to your Favorites directory a shortcut to the selected file.

✦ **Map Network Drive**: Displays a dialog box that enables you to map a network directory to a drive designator.

✦ Properties: Displays the Properties dialog box for the selected file. This enables you to examine or modify the file's properties without actually opening it.

Finding Lost Workbooks in Excel 2000

A common problem among computer users is "losing" a file. You know that you saved a file, but you don't remember the folder that you saved it in. Fortunately, Excel makes it fairly easy to locate such lost files by using the Open dialog box.

The procedure for finding files is much different in Excel 2000 — and also much easier. Select File ⇨ Open, and then click Tools ⇨ Find (or just press Ctrl+F).You'll see the Find dialog box

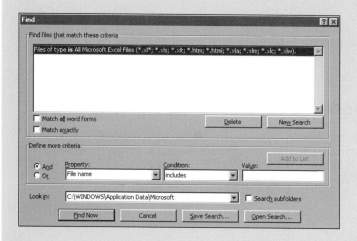

Continued

(continued)

Although this dialog box looks a bit complicated, it's purpose is to collect two pieces of information from you:

✦ Search criteria (what to look for)

✦ Where to look (the search scope)

You can search for files based on virtually any criteria (or combination of criteria) you can think of, including name, size, file type, contents, and so on. And after you define a search, you can save it, so that you can search later by the same criteria. When searching for a file, your search scope can be very broad (a complete hard drive) or very narrow (a specific folder).

If your searches aren't very complex, you may find it faster to use the Windows Find feature. You can search by filename, date, size, and even contents. Click the Windows Start button and then select Find ➪ Files or Folders. Enter your search criteria and click Find Now. A list of matching files will be displayed. To open a file in Excel, just double-click it.

Opening workbooks automatically

Many people find that they work on the same workbooks day after day. If this describes you, you'll be happy to know that you can have Excel open specific workbook files automatically whenever you start Excel.

The XLStart folder is located within the Microsoft Office folder. Any workbook files (excluding template files) that are stored in this folder open automatically when Excel starts. If one or more files open automatically from this folder, Excel won't start up with a blank workbook.

Tip You can specify an alternate startup folder in addition to the XLStart folder. Choose Tools ➪ Options and select the General tab. Enter a new folder name in the field labeled Alternate Startup File Location. After you do that, when you start Excel, it automatically opens all workbook files in both the XLStart folder and the alternate folder that you specified.

Saving workbooks

When you're working on a workbook, it's vulnerable to day-ruining events, such as power failures and system crashes. Therefore, you should save your work to disk often. Saving a file takes only a few seconds, but re-creating four hours of lost work takes about four hours.

Excel provides four ways to save your workbook:

✦ Use the File ⇨ Save command

✦ Click the Save button on the Standard toolbar

✦ Press the Ctrl+S shortcut key combination

✦ Press the Shift+F12 shortcut key combination

If your workbook has already been saved, it's saved again using the same filename. If you want to save the workbook to a new file, use the File ⇨ Save As command (or press F12).

If your workbook has never been saved, its title bar displays a name such as Book1 or Book2. Although Excel enables you to use these generic workbook names for filenames, it's not recommended. Therefore, the first time that you save a new workbook, Excel displays the Save As dialog box (see Figure 4-4) to let you provide a more meaningful name.

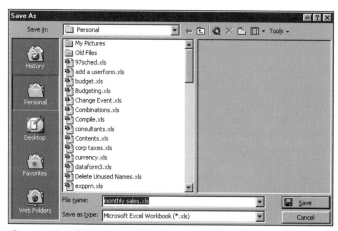

Figure 4-4: The Save As dialog box

The Save As dialog box is somewhat similar to the Open dialog box. Again, you need to specify two pieces of information: the workbook's name and the folder in which to store it. If you want to save the file to a different folder, select the desired folder in the Save in field. If you want to create a new folder, click the Create New Folder icon in the Save As dialog box. The new folder is created within the folder that's displayed in the Save in field.

File Naming Rules

Excel's workbook files are subject to the same rules that apply to other Windows 95 (or later) files. A filename can be up to 255 characters, including spaces. This enables you (finally) to give meaningful names to your files. You can't, however, use any of the following characters in your filenames:

\ (slash)

? (question mark)

: (colon)

* (asterisk)

" (quote)

< (less than)

> (greater than)

| (vertical bar)

You can use uppercase and lowercase letters in your names to improve readability. The filenames aren't case-sensitive, however. If you have a file named My 1999 Budget and try to save another file with the name MY 1999 BUDGET, Excel asks whether you want to overwrite the original file.

If you plan to share your files with others who use Excel 5 or earlier, you should make sure that the filename is no longer than eight characters, with no spaces. Otherwise, the filename will appear rather strange. For example, a file named My 1999 Budget will appear as MY1999~1.XLS, because Windows assigns every file an eight-character filename to be compatible with pre-Windows 95 operating systems.

After you select the folder, enter the filename in the File name field. You don't need to specify a file extension—Excel adds it automatically, based on the file type specified in the Save as type field.

If a file with the same name already exists in the folder that you specify, Excel asks whether you want to overwrite that file with the new file. Be careful with this, because you can't recover the previous file if you overwrite it.

Caution   Remember, saving a file *overwrites* the previous version of the file on disk. If you open a workbook and then completely mess it up, don't save the file! Instead, close the workbook without saving it, and then open the good copy on disk.

The default file location

When you save a workbook file for the first time, the Save As dialog box proposes a folder in which to save it. Normally, this is the Personal folder (located within your \Windows folder). If you want, you can change the default file location. To do so, choose Tools ⇨ Options and click the General tab in the Options dialog box. Then, enter the folder's path into the field labeled Default File Location. After doing so, the Save As dialog box defaults to this folder.

Note, however, that if you override the default folder in the Save As dialog box, the new folder becomes the default folder for the current Excel session. So, if you use the File ⇨ Save As command to save another workbook, Excel proposes the new default folder.

File saving options

The Save As dialog box has a drop-down menu labeled Tools. When you click this menu, one of the options displayed is labeled General Options. Selecting this item displays the Save Options dialog box, shown in Figure 4-5. This dialog box enables you to set the following options:

✦ **Always create backup:** If this option is set, the existing version of the workbook is renamed as a BAK file before the workbook is saved. Doing this enables you to go back to the previously saved version of your workbook. Some users like to use this option because it adds another level of safety. Just be aware that your worksheet files will take up about twice as much disk space, so it's a good idea to delete the backup files occasionally.

✦ **Password to open:** If you enter a password, the password is required before anyone can open the workbook. You're asked to enter the password a second time to confirm it. Passwords can be up to 15-characters long and are case-sensitive. Be careful with this option, because it is impossible to open the workbook (using normal methods) if you forget the password.

✦ **Password to modify:** This option enables you to specify a password that will be required before changes to the workbook can be saved under the same filename. Use this option if you want to make sure that changes aren't made to the original version of the workbook. In other words, the workbook can be saved with a new name, but a password is required to overwrite the original version.

✦ **Read-only recommended:** If this option is checked, the file can't be saved under its original name. This is another way to ensure that a workbook file isn't overwritten.

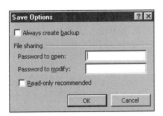

Figure 4-5: The Save Options dialog box

Caution   File security is not one of Excel's strong points. Saving a workbook with a password is not a foolproof method of protecting your work. Several utilities exist that are designed to "crack" passwords in Excel files. Therefore, if you need to keep your work absolutely confidential, Excel is not your best software choice.

Saving Your Work Automatically

If you're the type who gets so wrapped up in your work that you forget to save your file, you may be interested in Excel's AutoSave feature. AutoSave automatically saves your workbooks at a prespecified interval. Using this feature requires that you load an add-in file. This add-in is included with Excel, but normally it's not installed. To load the AutoSave add-in, select Tools ➪ Add-Ins. This displays a dialog box. Click AutoSave in the list of add-ins and then click OK. The add-in will be loaded every time that you run Excel. If you no longer want to use AutoSave, repeat the process and uncheck the AutoSave add-in.

When AutoSave is loaded, the Tools menu has a new menu item: AutoSave. Selecting Tools ➪ AutoSave displays the dialog box shown in the accompanying figure.

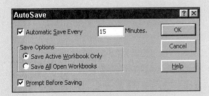

The AutoSave dialog box enables you to specify the time interval for saving. In general, you should specify a time interval equal to the maximum amount of time that you're willing to lose. For example, if you don't mind losing 15 minutes of work, set the interval for 15 minutes.

Option buttons let you choose between saving all open workbooks or just the active workbook. Another option enables you to specify whether you want to be prompted before the save takes place. If you choose to be prompted, you have the opportunity to cancel the save if you're in the middle of something important.

Caution Using AutoSave can be helpful, but it can also be risky. When an Excel workbook is saved, the Undo stack is reset. Therefore, if you make a mistake (such as deleting a range of data) and AutoSave kicks in and saves your file, you won't be able to use Undo to reverse your mistake.

Workbook summary information

When you save a file for the first time by closing the Save As dialog box, Excel may prompt you for summary information by displaying the Properties dialog box, shown in Figure 4-6. This dialog box enables you to specify lots of descriptive information about the workbook, and also displays some details about the file.

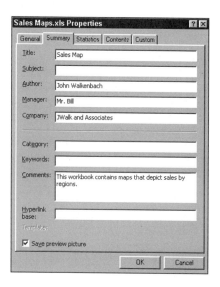

Figure 4-6: You can provide all sorts of information about your workbook in the Properties dialog box.

The Properties dialog box may or may not appear, depending on how Excel is configured. To specify whether to display the Properties dialog box automatically, select Tools ➪ Options, click the General tab, and adjust the setting of the Prompt for File Properties check box.

The Properties dialog box has the following five tabs:

✦ **General:** Displays general information about the file — its name, size, location, date created, and so on. You can't change any of the information in this panel.

✦ **Summary:** Appears by default when you first save the file. It contains nine fields of information that you can enter and modify. You can use the information in this panel to locate workbooks quickly that meet certain criteria. This is discussed later in the chapter.

✦ **Statistics:** Shows additional information about the file, and can't be changed.

✦ **Contents:** Displays the names of the sheets in the workbook, arranged by sheet type.

✦ **Custom:** Can be quite useful if you use it consistently. Basically, it enables you to store in a sort of database a variety of information about the file. For example, if the workbook deals with a client named Smith and Jones Corp., you can keep track of this bit of information and use it to help locate the file later.

You also can access the Properties dialog box for the active workbook at any time by selecting File ➪ Properties from the menu. In addition, you can view the properties of a workbook from the Open dialog box. Right-click the file in which you're interested and choose Properties from the shortcut menu.

Saving files in older formats

If your colleagues also use Excel, you may find yourself exchanging workbook files. If so, it's important that you know which version of Excel they use. Excel 97 and Excel 2000 use the same file format, but previous versions of Excel use different file formats. Generally, newer versions of Excel can open files created in older versions, but older versions of Excel cannot open files created in newer versions.

If you send a workbook to someone who uses a version of Excel prior to Excel 97, you must remember to save the file in a format that the earlier version can read.

Caution   Even though Excel 97 and Excel 2000 use a common file format, this does not ensure complete compatibility. If your workbook makes use of any features new to Excel 2000, these features won't be available if the file is opened in Excel 97.

Excel 5 was the first version to use multisheet workbooks. Prior to Excel 5, worksheets, chart sheets, and macro sheets were stored in separate files. Consequently, if you share a multisheet workbook with someone who still uses one of these older versions, you must save each sheet separately — and in the proper format.

The Save As dialog box has a field labeled Save as type that enables you to choose the format in which to save the file. The Excel file formats are listed in Table 4-3.

Table 4-3
Excel File Formats

Format	What It Does
Microsoft Excel Workbook	Saves the file in the standard Excel 2000 file format (which is identical to the Excel 97 file format)
Microsoft Excel 97–9 and 5.0/95 Workbook	Saves the file in a format that can be read by Excel 5 through Excel 2000
Microsoft Excel 5/95 Workbook	Saves the file in a format that can be read by both Excel 5 and Excel 95

Format	What It Does
Microsoft Excel 4.0 Worksheet*	Saves the file in a format that can be read by Excel 4
Microsoft Excel 3.0 Worksheet*	Saves the file in a format that can be read by Excel 3
Microsoft Excel 2.1 Worksheet*	Saves the file in a format that can be read by Excel 2.1

* These file formats do not support multisheet workbooks.

If you need to send a workbook with three worksheets in it to a colleague who uses Excel 4, you must save it as three separate files and make sure that you select the Microsoft Excel 4.0 Worksheet option from the Save as type drop-down box (see Figure 4-7).

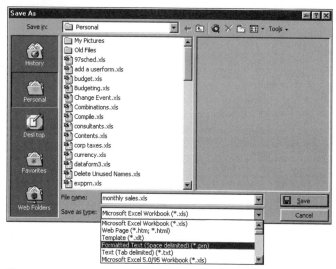

Figure 4-7: You can save an Excel workbook in a format that is readable by previous versions of Excel.

EXCEL 2000

Excel 2000 has an option that enables you to specify the default format for saved workbooks. To change the default setting, select Tools Ì Options, click the Transition tab, and then choose the file type from the drop-down list labeled Save Excel files as.

This is improved over the Excel 97 version of the same feature, which prompts users on every file save if this option is enabled.

Closing workbooks

When you're finished with a workbook, you should close it to free the memory that it uses. You can close a workbook by using any of the following methods:

✦ Use the File ⇨ Close command

✦ Click the Close button in the workbook's title bar

✦ Double-click the Control icon in the workbook's title bar

✦ Press the Ctrl+F4 shortcut key

✦ Press the Ctrl+W shortcut key

If you've made any changes to your workbook since it was last saved, Excel asks whether you want to save the workbook before closing it.

Tip   To close all open workbooks, press the Shift key and choose File ⇨ Close All. This command appears only when you hold down the Shift key while you click the File menu. Excel closes each workbook, prompting you for each unsaved workbook.

Using workspace files

As you know, you can work with any number of workbook files at a time. For example, you may have a project that uses two workbooks, and you like to arrange the windows in a certain way to make it easy to access them both. Fortunately, Excel enables you to save your entire workspace to a file. *Workspace*, as used here, means all the workbooks and their screen positions and window sizes—sort of a snapshot of Excel's current state. Then, you can open the workspace file, and Excel is set up exactly as it was when you saved your workspace.

To save your workspace, use the File ⇨ Save Workspace command. Excel proposes the name resume.xlw for the workspace file. You can use this name or enter a different name in the File name field. Click the Save button, and the workspace will be saved to disk.

Caution   You need to understand that a workspace file doesn't include the workbook files themselves. It includes only the information needed to recreate the workspace. The workbooks in the workspace are saved in standard workbook files. Therefore, if you distribute a workspace file to a coworker, make sure that you also include the workbook files to which the workspace file refers.

Tip   If you save your workspace file in the XLStart folder, Excel opens the workspace file automatically when it starts up. This is handy if you tend to work with the same files every day, because essentially you can pick up where you left off the previous day.

Sharing workbooks with others

If your system is connected to a network, you should be aware of some other issues related to workbook files.

Cross-Reference Chapter 27 is devo.ted entirety to workgroup issues.

Using Template Files

You may be able to save yourself a lot of work by using a template instead of creating a new workbook from scratch. A *template* basically is a worksheet that's all set up with formulas, ready for you to enter data.

The templates distributed with Excel are nicely formatted and relatively easy to customize. When you open a new workbook based on the template, you save the workbook to a new file. In other words, you don't overwrite the template.

Figure 4-8 shows one of the Spreadsheet Solutions templates.

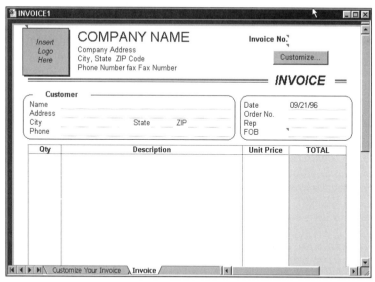

Figure 4-8: Excel includes several templates, designed to perform common tasks. This figure shows the Invoice1 template.

Excel 2000 includes three templates:

✦ **Expense Statement:** Helps you create expense report forms and a log to track them

✦ **Invoice:** Helps you create invoices

✦ **Purchase Order:** Helps you create purchase orders to send to vendors

Another template, named Village, is also available. This isn't really a template. It describes how to purchase additional templates from Village Software.

Tip   You can download additional templates from Microsoft's Web site:

`http://officeupdate.microsoft.com/`

The Spreadsheet Solutions templates are handy, but be aware that they include a lot of overhead — several worksheets, dialog sheets, and a custom toolbar. Consequently, the workbooks that you generate by using these templates may be larger than you would expect. On the positive side, studying how these templates are designed can provide advanced users with some great tips.

Protecting Your Work

The final topic in this chapter offers a few words on backing up your work, to protect yourself from disaster — or at least save yourself the inconvenience of repeating your work. Earlier in the chapter, you learned how to make Excel create a backup copy of your workbook when you save the file. That's a good idea, but it certainly isn't the only backup protection you should use.

If you've been around computers for a while, you probably know that hard disks aren't perfect. I've seen many hard disks fail for no apparent reason and with absolutely no advance warning. In addition, files can get corrupted — which usually makes them unreadable and essentially worthless. If a file is truly important, you need to take extra steps to ensure its safety. The following are several backup options for ensuring the safety of individual files:

✦ **Keep a backup copy of the file on the same drive.** This is essentially what happens when you select the Always create a backup option when you save a workbook file. Although this offers some protection if you create a mess of the worksheet, it won't do you any good if the entire hard drive crashes.

✦ **Keep a backup copy on a different hard drive.** This assumes, of course, that your system has more than one hard drive. This offers more protection than the preceding method, because the likelihood that both hard drives will fail is remote. If the entire system is destroyed or stolen, however, you're out of luck.

✦ **Keep a backup copy on a network server.** This assumes that your system is connected to a server on which you can write files. This method is fairly safe. If the network server is located in the same building, however, you're at risk if the entire building burns down or is otherwise destroyed.

✦ **Keep a backup copy on a removable medium.** This is the safest method. Using a removable medium, such as a floppy disk or tape, enables you physically to take the backup to another location. So, if your system (or the entire building) is damaged, your backup copy remains intact.

Most people with good backup habits acquired them because they've been burned in the past (myself included).

Windows comes with software that you can use to back up your entire system. Consult your Windows manual or online help for details.

Summary

This chapter covers the rather broad topic of files. It starts with an overview of how computers use files and narrows the scope to cover how Excel uses files. The chapter includes a discussion of the essential file operations that you perform from Excel, including creating new workbook files, opening existing files, saving files, and closing files. The chapter concludes with an introduction to the template files that are included with Excel.

✦   ✦   ✦

Working with Excel

Entering and Editing Worksheet Data

People use spreadsheets primarily to store data and perform calculations. This chapter discusses the various types of data that you can enter into Excel.

Types of Worksheet Data

As you know, an Excel workbook can hold any number of worksheets, and each worksheet is made up of cells. A cell can hold any of three types of data:

♦ Values

♦ Text

♦ Formulas

A worksheet also can hold charts, maps, drawings, pictures, buttons, and other objects. These objects actually reside on the worksheet's *draw layer*, which is an invisible layer on top of each worksheet.

Cross-Reference The draw layer is discussed in Chapter 20. This chapter is concerned only with data that you enter into worksheet cells.

Values

Values, also known as numbers, represent a quantity of some type: sales, number of employees, atomic weights, test scores, and so on. Values that you enter into cells can be used in formulas or can be used to provide the data that is used to create a chart. Values also can be dates (such as 6/9/20019) or times (such as 3:24 a.m.), and you'll see that you can manipulate these types of values quite efficiently.

Figure 5-1 shows a worksheet with some values entered in it.

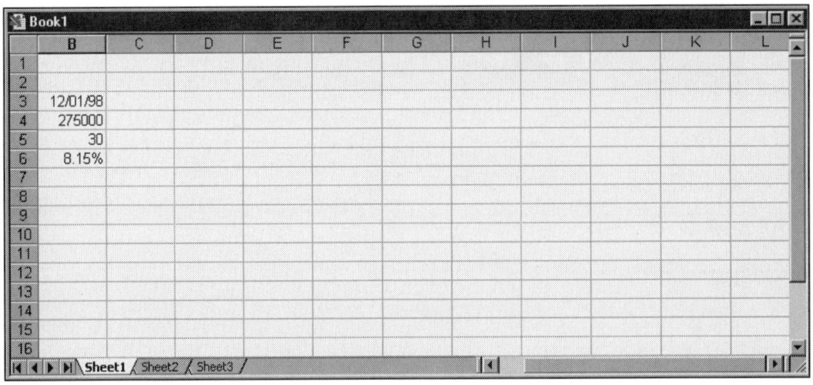

Figure 5-1: Values entered in a worksheet

Text

Most worksheets also include non-numeric text in some of their cells. You can insert text to serve as labels for values, headings for columns, or instructions about the worksheet. Text that begins with a number is still considered text. For example, if you enter an address such as **1425 Main St.** into a cell, Excel considers this to be text rather than a value.

Figure 5-2 shows a worksheet with text in some of the cells. In this case, the text is used to clarify what the values mean.

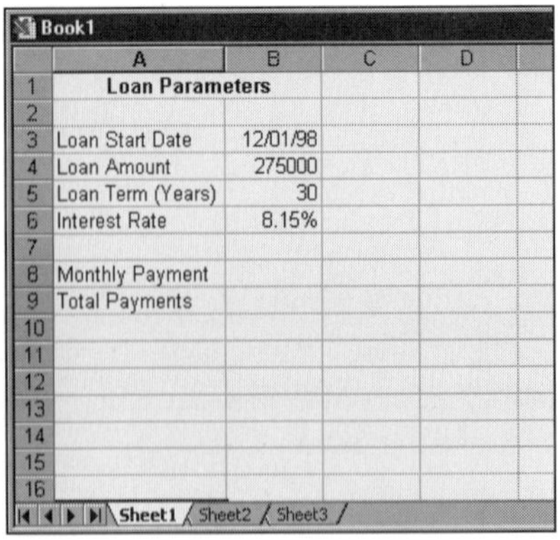

Figure 5-2: This worksheet consists of text and values.

Excel's Numerical Limitations

New users often are curious about the types of values that Excel can handle. In other words, how large can numbers be? And how accurate are large numbers?

Excel's numbers are precise up to 15 digits. For example, if you enter a large value, such as 123,123,123,123,123,123 (18 digits), Excel actually stores it with only 15 digits of precision: 123,123,123,123,123,000. This may seem quite limiting, but in practice, it rarely causes any problems.

Here are some of Excel's other numerical limits:

Largest positive number: 9.9E+307

Smallest negative number: −9.9E+307

Smallest positive number: 1E−307

Largest negative number: −1E-307

These numbers are expressed in scientific notation. For example, the largest positive number is "9.9 times 10 to the 307th power."

Formulas

Formulas are what make a spreadsheet a spreadsheet—otherwise, you'd just have a strange word processor that is good at working with tables. Excel enables you to enter powerful formulas that use the values (or even text) in cells to calculate a result. When you enter a formula into a cell, the formula's result appears in the cell. If you change any of the values used by a formula, the formula recalculates and shows the new result. Figure 5-3 shows a worksheet with values, text, and formulas.

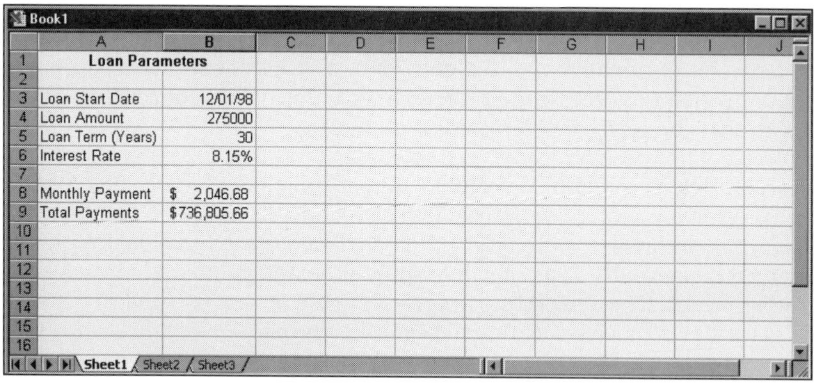

Figure 5-3: Cells B8 and B9 contain formulas that use the other values.

Cross-Reference   Chapter 8 discusses formulas in detail.

Entering Values

Entering values into a cell is quite easy. Just move the cell pointer to the appropriate cell to make it the active cell, enter the value, and then press Enter. The value is displayed in the cell and also appears in Excel's formula bar. You can, of course, include decimal points and dollar signs when entering values and dollar signs, along with plus signs, minus signs, and commas. If you precede a value with a minus sign or enclose it in parentheses, Excel considers it to be a negative number.

Note   Sometimes, the value that you enter won't be displayed exactly as you enter it. More specifically, if you enter a large number, it may be converted to scientific notation. Notice, however, that the formula bar displays the value that you entered originally. Excel simply reformatted the value so that it would fit into the cell. If you make the column wider, the number is displayed as you entered it.

The section "Formatting Values," later in this chapter, discusses the various ways to format values so that they appear differently.

Entering Text

Entering text into a cell is just as easy as entering a value: activate the cell, type the text, and then press Enter. A cell can contain a maximum of about 32,000 characters. To give you an idea of how much text can fit into a single cell, consider the fact that this entire chapter has approximately 37,000 characters.

Caution   Even though a cell can hold a huge number of characters, you'll find that it's not possible to actually display all of these characters.

If you type an exceptionally long text entry into a cell, the characters appear to wrap around when they reach the right edge of the window, and the formula bar expands so that the text wraps around.

What happens when you enter text that's longer than its column's current width? If the cells to the immediate right are blank, Excel displays the text in its entirety, appearing to spill the entry into adjacent cells. If an adjacent cell is not blank, Excel displays as much of the text as possible (the full text is contained in the cell; it's just not displayed). If you need to display a long text string in a cell that's adjacent to a nonblank cell, you can take one of several actions:

✦ Edit your text to make it shorter

✦ Increase the width of the column

✦ Use a smaller font

✦ Wrap the text within the cell so that it occupies more than one line

✦ Use Excel's "shrink to fit" option (see Chapter 17 for details)

Dates and Times

Often, you need to enter dates and times into your worksheet. To Excel, a date or a time is simply treated as a value—but it's formatted to appear as a date or a time.

Working with date values

If you work with dates and times, you need to understand Excel's date and time system. Excel handles dates by using a serial number system. The earliest date that Excel understands is January 1, 1900. This date has a serial number of 1. January 2, 1900, has a serial number of 2, and so on. This system makes it easy to deal with dates in formulas. For example, you can enter a formula to calculate the number of days between two dates.

Most of the time, you don't have to be concerned with Excel's serial number date system. You can simply enter a date in a familiar date format, and Excel takes care of the details behind the scenes. For example, if you need to enter June 1, 1999, you can simply enter the date by typing **June 1, 1999** (or use any of several different date formats). Excel interprets your entry and stores the value 36312—which is the date serial number for that date.

Here is a sampling of the date formats that Excel recognizes. After entering a date, you can format it to appear in a different date format. (Such formatting is covered later in the chapter, in the section "Working with Date Values.")

Entered into a Cell	Excel's Interpretation
6-1-99	June 1, 1999
6-1-1999	June 1, 1999
6/1/99	June 1, 1999
6/1/1999	June 1, 1999
6-1/99	June 1, 1999
June 1, 1999	June 1, 1999
Jun 1	June 1 of the current year
June 1	June 1 of the current year
6/1	June 1 of the current year
6-1	June 1 of the current year

Avoid Year 2000 Surprises

Be careful when entering dates by using two digits for the year. Excel has a rather arbitrary decision point in interpreting your entries. Two-digit years between 00 and 29 are interpreted as 21st century dates. Two-digits years between 30 and 99 are interpreted as 20th century dates. For example, if you enter 12/5/28, Excel interprets your entry as December 5, 2028. But if you enter 12/5/30, Excel sees it as December 5, 1930. To avoid any surprises, it's a good practice to simply enter years using all four digits.

Caution   As you can see, Excel is rather smart when it comes to recognizing dates that you enter into a cell. It's not perfect, however. For example, Excel does *not* recognize any of the following entries as dates: June 1 1999, Jun-1 1999, and Jun-1/1999. Rather, it interprets these entries as text. If you plan to use dates in formulas, make sure that the date you enter is actually recognized as a date; otherwise, your formulas will produce incorrect results.

Tip   After you enter a date, check the formula bar. If the formula bar displays exactly what you entered, Excel didn't interpret the date that you entered as a date. If the formula bar displays your entry in a format like *mm/dd/yyyy*, Excel correctly interpreted your entry as a date.

Working with time values

When you work with times, you simply extend Excel's date serial number system to include decimals. In other words, Excel works with times by using fractional days. For example, the date serial number for June 1, 1999, is 36312. Noon (halfway through the day) is represented internally as 36312.5.

Again, you normally don't have to be concerned with these serial numbers (or fractional serial numbers, for times). Just enter the time into a cell in a recognized format.

Here are some examples of time formats that Excel recognizes:

Entered into a Cell	*Excel's Interpretation*
11:30:00 am	11:30 a.m.
11:30:00 AM	11:30 a.m.
11:30 pm	11:30 p.m.
11:30	11:30 a.m.

The preceding samples don't have a day associated with them. You also can combine dates and times, however, as follows:

Entered into a Cell	Excel's Interpretation
6/1/99 11:30	11:30 a.m. on June 1, 1999

Changing or Erasing Values and Text

Not surprisingly, you can change the contents of a cell after the fact. After you enter a value or text into a cell, you can modify it in several ways:

✦ Erase the cell's contents

✦ Replace the cell's contents with something else

✦ Edit the cell's contents

Erasing the contents of a cell

To erase the value, text, or formula in a cell, just click the cell and press Delete. To erase more than one cell, select all the cells that you want to erase, and then press Delete. Pressing Delete removes the cell's contents, but doesn't remove any formatting (such as bold, italic, or a different number format) that you may have applied to the cell.

For more control over what gets deleted, you can use the Edit ⇨ Clear command. This menu item has a submenu with four additional choices (see Figure 5-4), which are described as follows:

✦ **All:** Clears everything from the cell

✦ **Formats:** Clears only the formatting and leaves the value, text, or formula

✦ **Contents:** Clears only the cell's contents and leaves the formatting

✦ **Comments:** Clears the comment (if one exists) attached to the cell

Replacing the contents of a cell

To replace the contents of a cell with something else, just click the cell and type your new entry, which replaces the previous contents. Any formatting that you applied to the cell remains.

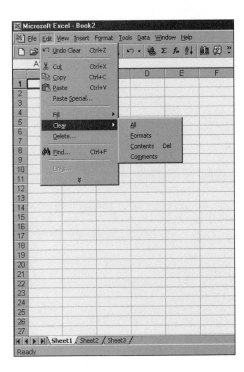

Figure 5-4: Excel provides several options for clearing cells.

Editing the contents of a cell

If the cell contains only a few characters, replacing its contents by typing new data usually is easiest. But if the cell contains lengthy text or a complex formula, and you need to make only a slight modification, you probably want to edit the cell rather than reenter information.

When you want to edit the contents of a cell, you can use one of the following ways to get into cell-edit mode:

✦ **Double-click the cell.** This enables you to edit the cell contents directly in the cell.

✦ **Press F2.** This enables you to edit the cell contents directly in the cell.

✦ **Activate the cell that you want to edit and then click inside the formula bar.** This enables you to edit the cell contents in the formula bar.

You can use whichever method you prefer. Some people find it easier to edit directly in the cell; others prefer to use the formula bar to edit a cell. All of these methods cause the formula bar to display two new icons, as shown in Figure 5-5. The X icon cancels editing, without changing the cell's contents (Esc has the same effect). The Check Mark icon completes the editing and enters the modified contents into the cell (Enter has the same effect).

New icons

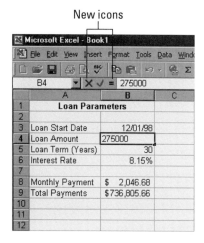

Figure 5-5: The formula bar displays two new icons when you begin editing a cell.

Tip

If the cell contains a formula, you can edit the formula by using any of the techniques listed previously. Or, you can take advantage of the Formula Palette. To activate the Formula Palette, click the = icon in the formula bar.

Cross-Reference

The Formula Palette is explained in detail in Chapter 8.

Editing a cell's contents works pretty much as you might expect. When you begin editing a cell, the insertion point appears as a vertical bar, and you can move the insertion point by using the direction keys. You can add new characters at the location of the insertion point. After you're in edit mode, you can use any of the following keys to move through the cell contents:

✦ **Left/right arrow:** The left- and right-arrow keys move the insertion point left or right one character, respectively, without deleting any characters.

✦ **Ctrl+left/right arrow:** Moves the insertion point one group of characters to the left or right, respectively. A group of characters is defined by a space character.

✦ **Backspace:** Erases the character to the immediate left of the insertion point.

✦ **Delete:** Erases the character to the right of the insertion point, or all selected characters.

✦ **Insert:** When you're editing, pressing the Insert key places Excel in OVR (Overwrite) mode. Rather than add characters to the cell, you *overwrite*, or replace, existing characters with new ones.

✦ **Home:** Moves the insertion point to the beginning of the cell entry.

✦ **End:** Moves the insertion point to the end of the cell entry.

✦ **Enter:** Accepts the edited data.

While editing a cell, you can use the following key combinations to select characters in the cell:

✦ **Shift+left/right arrow:** Selects characters to the left or right, respectively, of the insertion point.

✦ **Shift+Home:** Selects all characters from the insertion point to the beginning of the cell.

✦ **Shift+End:** Selects all characters from the insertion point to the end of the cell.

Tip   You also can use the mouse to select characters while you're editing a cell. Just click and drag the mouse pointer over the characters that you want to select.

Formatting Values

Values that you enter into cells normally are unformatted. In other words, they simply consist of a string of numerals. Typically, you want to format the numbers so that they are easier to read or are more consistent in terms of the number of decimal places shown.

Figure 5-6 shows two columns of values. The first column consists of unformatted values. The cells in the second column have been formatted to make the values easier to read. If you move the cell pointer to a cell that has a formatted value, you find that the formula bar displays the value in its unformatted state. This is because the formatting affects only how the value is displayed in the cell.

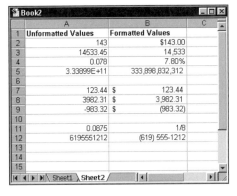

Figure 5-6: Unformatted values (left column) and the same values after formatting

Automatic number formatting

Excel is smart enough to perform some formatting for you automatically. For example, if you enter **12.2%** into a cell, Excel knows that you want to use a percentage format and applies it for you automatically. If you use commas to separate thousands (such as **123,456**), Excel applies comma formatting for you.

And, if you precede your value with a dollar sign, the cell will be formatted for currency.

A new feature in Excel 2000 makes it easier to enter values into cells formatted as a percentage. Select Tools ⇨ Options, and click the Edit tab in the Options dialog box. If the checkbox labeled Enable automatic percent entry is checked, you can simply enter normal value into a cell formatted as a percent (for example, 12.5 for 12.5%). If this checkbox is not checked, you must enter the value as a decimal (for example, .125 for 12.5%).

Formatting numbers using the toolbar

The Formatting toolbar, which is displayed, by default, to the right of the Standard toolbar, contains several buttons that let you quickly apply common number formats. When you click one of these buttons, the active cell takes on the specified number format. You also can select a range of cells (or even an entire row or column) before clicking these buttons. If you select more than one cell, Excel applies the number format to all the selected cells. Table 5-1 summarizes the formats that these Formatting toolbar buttons perform. Remember to click the arrow at the right end of the Formatting toolbar to see all of these buttons.

Table 5-1 **Number-Formatting Buttons on the Formatting Toolbar**	
Button Name	*Formatting Applied*
Currency Style	Adds a dollar sign to the left, separates thousands with a comma, and displays the value with two digits to the right of the decimal point
Percent Style	Displays the value as a percentage, with no decimal places
Comma Style	Separates thousands with a comma and displays the value with two digits to the right of the decimal place
Increase Decimal	Increases the number of digits to the right of the decimal point by one
Decrease Decimal	Decreases the number of digits to the right of the decimal point by one

These five toolbar buttons actually apply predefined "styles" to the selected cells. These styles are similar to those used in word processing programs.

Chapter 17 describes how to modify existing styles and create new styles.

Formatting Numbers by Using Shortcut Keys

Table 5-2 summarizes some shortcut key combinations that you can use to apply common number formatting to the selected cells or range.

Table 5-2 Number-Formatting Keyboard Shortcuts	
Key Combination	**Formatting Applied**
Ctrl+Shift+~	General number format (that is, unformatted values)
Ctrl+Shift+$	Currency format with two decimal places (negative numbers appear in parentheses)
Ctrl+Shift+%	Percentage format, with no decimal places
Ctrl+Shift+^	Scientific notation number format, with two decimal places
Ctrl+Shift+#	Date format with the day, month, and year
Ctrl+Shift+@	Time format with the hour, minute, and a.m. or p.m.
Ctrl+Shift+!	Two decimal places, 1000 separator, and a hyphen for negative values

Other number formats

In some cases, the number formats that are accessible from the Formatting toolbar (or by using the shortcut key combination) are just fine. More often, however, you want more control over how your values appear. Excel offers a great deal of control over number formats.

Figure 5-7 shows Excel's Format Cells dialog box. This is a tabbed dialog box. For formatting numbers, you need to use the tab labeled Number.

Several ways exist to bring up the Format Cells dialog box. Start by selecting the cell or cells that you want to format and then do the following:

✦ Select the Format ➪ Cells command.

✦ Right-click and choose Format Cells from the shortcut menu.

✦ Press the Ctrl+1 shortcut key.

The Number tab of the Format Cells dialog box displays 12 categories of number formats from which to choose. When you select a category from the list box, the right side of the tab changes to display appropriate options. For example, Figure 5-8 shows how the dialog box looks when you click the Number category.

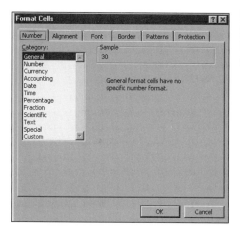

Figure 5-7: The Number tab of the Format Cells dialog box enables you to format numbers in just about any way imaginable.

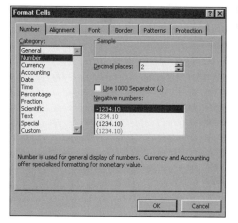

Figure 5-8: Options for the Number category

The Number category has three options that you can control: the number of decimal places displayed, whether to use a comma for the thousand separator, and how you want negative numbers displayed. Notice that the Negative numbers list box has four choices (two of which display negative values in red), and the choices change depending on the number of decimal places and whether you choose to use a comma to separate thousands. Also, notice that the top of the tab displays a sample of how the active cell will appear with the selected number format. After you make your choices, click OK to apply the number format to all the selected cells.

> **Tip** The best way to learn about number formats is to experiment. Enter some values on a worksheet and practice applying number formats.

When Numbers Appear to Add Up Incorrectly

You need to understand that applying a number format to a cell doesn't change the value — formatting changes only how the value looks. For example, if a cell contains .874543, you might format it to appear as 87%. If that cell is used in a formula, the formula uses the full value (.874543), not the displayed value (.87).

In some situations, formatting may cause Excel to display calculation results that appear incorrect, such as when totaling numbers with decimal places (see the accompanying figure). In this example, the values are formatted to display two decimal places. This formatting displays the values after they are rounded. But because Excel uses the full precision of the values in its formula, the sum of these two values appears to be incorrect (10.00 + 10.10 = 20.11). The actual values that are summed are 10.004 and 10.103.

Several solutions to this problem are available. You can format the cells to display more decimal places. Or, you can use the ROUND function on individual numbers and specify the number of decimal places Excel should round to. ROUND and other built-in functions are discussed in Chapter 9.

As another solution, you can instruct Excel to change the worksheet values to match their displayed format. To do this, choose Tools ➪ Options, select the Calculation tab, and then check the Precision as Displayed check box. Excel warns you that the underlying numbers will be permanently changed to match their appearance onscreen. If you want to select this option, backing up the worksheet on disk first is a good idea, in case you change your mind.

The following are the number-format categories, along with some general comments:

✦ **General:** The default format; it displays numbers as integers, decimals, or in scientific notation if the value is too wide to fit in the cell.

✦ **Number:** Enables you to specify the number of decimal places, whether to use a comma to separate thousands, and how to display negative numbers (with a minus sign, in red, in parentheses, or in red and in parentheses).

✦ **Currency:** Enables you to specify the number of decimal places, whether to use a dollar sign, and how to display negative numbers (with a minus sign, in red, in parentheses, or in red and in parentheses). This format always uses a comma to separate thousands.

✦ **Accounting:** Differs from the Currency format in that the dollar signs always line up vertically.

✦ **Date:** Enables you to choose from 15 date formats.

✦ **Time:** Enables you to choose from eight time formats.

✦ **Percentage:** Enables you to choose the number of decimal places and always displays a percent sign.

✦ **Fraction:** Enables you to choose from among nine fraction formats.

✦ **Scientific:** Displays numbers in exponential notation (with an E): 2.00E+05 = 200,000. 2.05E+05 = 205,000. You can choose the number of decimal places to display to the left of E.

✦ **Text:** When applied to a value, causes Excel to treat the value as text (even if it looks like a value). This feature is useful for items such as part numbers.

✦ **Special:** Contains four additional number formats (Zip Code, Zip Code +4, Phone Number, and Social Security Number).

✦ **Custom:** Enables you to define custom number formats that aren't included in any of the other categories. Custom number formats are described in the next section.

Figure 5-9 shows an example from each category.

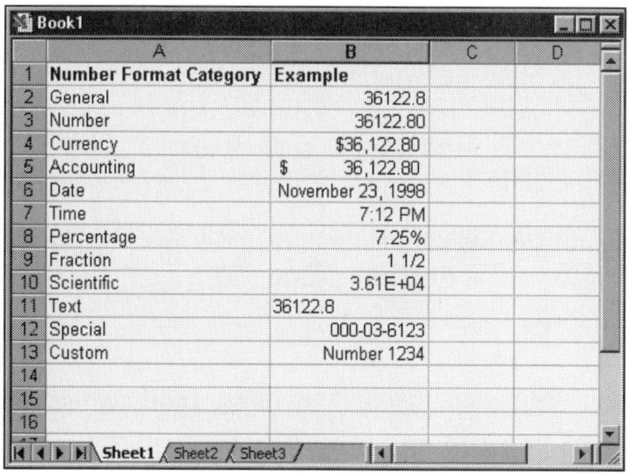

Figure 5-9: Examples of values with various number formats

Preformatting Cells

Usually, you'll apply number formats to cells that already contain values. You also can format cells with a specific number format *before* you make an entry. Then, when you enter information, it takes on the format that you specified. You can preformat specific cells, entire rows or columns, or even the entire worksheet.

Rather than preformat an entire worksheet, however, a better idea is to change the number format for the Normal style (unless you specify otherwise, all cells use the Normal style). You can change the Normal style by selecting Format ⇨ Style. In the Style dialog box, click the Modify button and then choose the new number format for the Normal style.

Note

If the cell displays a series of pound signs (such as #########), it means that the column is not wide enough to display the value by using the number format that you selected. Either make the column wider or change the number format.

You won't see this condition too often, because Excel usually adjusts column widths automatically to accommodate entries as you make them.

Cross-Reference

Refer to Chapter 17 for more information about styles.

Custom number formats

As mentioned in the previous section, the custom number format category enables you to create number formats that aren't included in any of the other categories. Excel gives you much flexibility in creating custom number formats, but doing so can be rather tricky. You construct a number format by specifying a series of codes. You enter this code sequence in the Type field after you select the Custom category on the Number tab of the Format Cells dialog box. Here's an example of a simple number format code:

```
0.000
```

This code consists of placeholders and a decimal point and tells Excel to display the value with three digits to the right of the decimal place. Here's another example:

```
00000
```

This custom number format has five placeholders and displays the value with five digits (no decimal point). This is a good format to use when the cell will hold a ZIP code (in fact, this is the code actually used by the ZIP Code format in the Special category). When you format the cell with this number format and then enter a ZIP code such as 06604 (Bridgeport, CT), the value is displayed with the leading zero. If you enter this number into a cell with the General number format, it displays as 6604 (no leading zero).

If you scroll through the list of number formats in the Custom category in the Format Cells dialog box, you see many more examples. Most of the time, you can use one of these codes as a starting point, and only slight customization will be needed.

Excel also enables you to specify different format codes for positive numbers, negative numbers, zero values, and text. You do so by separating the codes with a semicolon. The codes are arranged in the following structure:

```
Positive format; Negative format; Zero format; Text format
```

The following is an example of a custom number format that specifies a different format for each of these types:

```
[Green]General;[Red]General;[Black]General;[Blue]General
```

This example takes advantage of the fact that colors have special codes. A cell formatted with this custom number format displays its contents in a different color, depending on the value. In this case, positive numbers are green, negative numbers are red, zero is black, and text is blue.

Cross-Reference

If you want to apply cell formatting automatically, such as text or background color, based on the cell's contents, a better solution is to use Excel's Conditional Formatting feature. This feature is discussed in Chapter 17.

The following number format (three semicolons) consists of no format codes for each part of the format structure — essentially hiding the contents of the cell:

```
;;;
```

Table 5-3 lists the formatting codes available for custom formats, along with brief descriptions. These codes are described further in Excel's online help.

Table 5-3
Codes Used to Create Custom Number Formats

Code	Comments
General	Displays the number in General format
#	Digit placeholder
0 (zero)	Digit placeholder
?	Digit placeholder
.	Decimal point

Continued

Table 5-3 *(continued)*

Code	Comments
%	Percentage
,	Thousands separator
E–E+ e–e+	Scientific notation
$ – + / ( ) : space	Displays this character
\	Displays the next character in the format
*	Repeats the next character, to fill the column width
_	Skips the width of the next character
"text"	Displays the text inside the double quotation marks
@	Text placeholder
[color]	Displays the characters in the color specified
[COLOR n]	Displays the corresponding color in the color palette, where *n* is a number from 0 to 56
[condition value]	Enables you to set your own criteria for each section of a number format

Table 5-4 lists the codes that are used to create custom formats for dates and times.

Table 5-4
Codes Used in Creating Custom Formats for Dates and Times

Code	Comments
m	Displays the month as a number without leading zeros (1–12)
mm	Displays the month as a number with leading zeros (01–12)
mmm	Displays the month as an abbreviation (Jan–Dec)
mmmm	Displays the month as a full name (January–December)
d	Displays the day as a number without leading zeros (1–31)
dd	Displays the day as a number with leading zeros (01–31)
ddd	Displays the day as an abbreviation (Sun–Sat)
dddd	Displays the day as a full name (Sunday–Saturday)
yy or yyyy	Displays the year as a two-digit number (00–99), or as a four-digit number (1900–2078)

Code	Comments
h or hh	Displays the hour as a number without leading zeros (0–23), or as a number with leading zeros (00–23)
m or mm	Displays the minute as a number without leading zeros (0–59), or as a number with leading zeros (00–59)
s or ss	Displays the second as a number without leading zeros (0–59), or as a number with leading zeros (00–59)
[ ]	Displays hours greater than 24, or minutes or seconds greater than 60
AM/am/A/a/ PM/pm/P/p	Displays the hour using a 12-hour clock; if no AM/PM indicator is used, the hour uses a 24-hour clock

Note   Custom number formats are stored with the worksheet. To make the custom format available in a different workbook, you must copy a cell that uses the custom format to the other workbook.

Figure 5-10 shows several examples of custom number formats, and the workbook is available at this book's Web site.

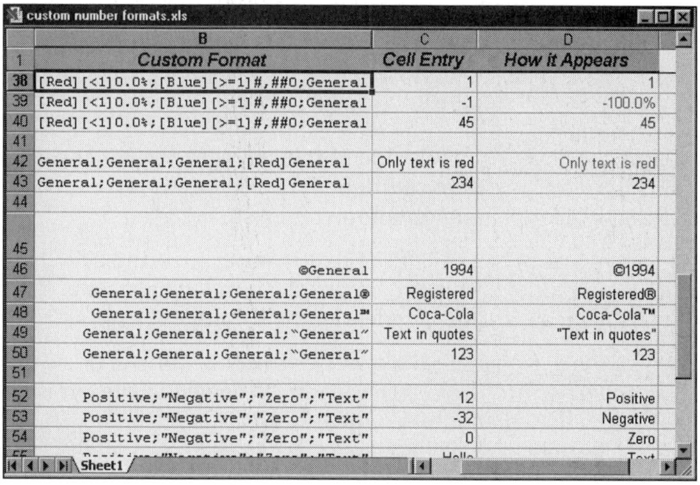

	B	C	D
	Custom Format	Cell Entry	How it Appears
38	[Red][<1]0.0%;[Blue][>=1]#,##0;General	1	1
39	[Red][<1]0.0%;[Blue][>=1]#,##0;General	-1	-100.0%
40	[Red][<1]0.0%;[Blue][>=1]#,##0;General	45	45
41			
42	General;General;General;[Red]General	Only text is red	Only text is red
43	General;General;General;[Red]General	234	234
44			
45			
46	@General	1994	©1994
47	General;General;General;General®	Registered	Registered®
48	General;General;General;General™	Coca-Cola	Coca-Cola™
49	General;General;General;"General"	Text in quotes	"Text in quotes"
50	General;General;General;"General"	123	123
51			
52	Positive;"Negative";"Zero";"Text"	12	Positive
53	Positive;"Negative";"Zero";"Text"	-32	Negative
54	Positive;"Negative";"Zero";"Text"	0	Zero

Figure 5-10: Examples of custom number formats.

Studying these examples will help you understand the concept and may give you some ideas for your own custom number formats.

Basic Cell Formatting

Whereas the preceding section discusses number formatting, this section discusses some of the basic *stylistic* formatting options available to you. These formatting techniques apply to values, text, and formulas. The options discussed in this section are available from the Formatting toolbar. Complete formatting options are available in the Format Cells dialog box, which appears when you choose Format ⇨ Cells (or press Ctrl+1).

Note   If you display the Standard toolbar and the Formatting toolbar side by side, you may not see many of the tools discussed in this section unless you click the arrow at the right edge of the Formatting toolbar.

Remember that the formatting you apply works with the selected cell or cells. Therefore, you need to select the cell (or range of cells) before applying the formatting.

Cross-Reference   The concept of worksheet stylistic formatting is discussed in detail in Chapter 17.

Alignment

When you enter text in a cell, Excel aligns the text with the left edge of the cell. Values, on the other hand, are displayed right-aligned in the cell.

To change the alignment of a cell's contents, select the cell and then click the appropriate button on the Formatting toolbar. The relevant buttons are as follows:

✦ **Align Left:** Aligns the text to the left side of the cell. If the text is wider than the cell, it spills over to the cell to the right. If the cell to the right is not empty, the text is truncated and not completely visible.

✦ **Center:** Centers the text in the cell. If the text is wider than the cell, it spills over to cells on either side, if they are empty. If the adjacent cells aren't empty, the text is truncated and not completely visible.

✦ **Align Right:** Aligns the text to the right side of the cell. If the text is wider than the cell, it spills over to the cell to the left. If the cell to the left is not empty, the text is truncated and not completely visible.

✦ **Merge and Center:** Centers the text in the selected cells and merges the cells into one cell. This feature is described in detail in Chapter 17.

Font and text size

To change the font and the size of the contents of a cell or range, select the cells and then use the Font and Font Size tools on the Formatting toolbar. These tools are drop-down lists. Click the arrow on the tool to display a list of fonts or font sizes (see Figure 5-11). Then, choose the font or size that you want.

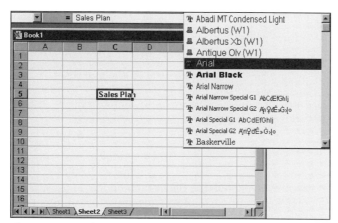

Figure 5-11: Selecting a font from the Font list

 In Excel 2000, fonts in the Font list provide examples of the font they represent, making it easier for you to select the correct font. You can change this default behavior so that the Font list displays all fonts in Arial, as earlier versions of Excel did. Choose Tools ➪ Customer and then click the Options tab. Remove the check from the check box labeled List font names in their font.

Attributes

The Formatting toolbar also has buttons that enable you to make the selected cells bold, italic, or underlined. As you might expect, clicking the appropriate tool makes the change. These buttons actually are toggles, so if the cell is already bold, clicking the Bold button removes the bold.

Borders

Applying a border is another type of formatting. Borders are lines drawn around all or part of selected cells or ranges. When you click the Borders button on the Formatting toolbar, it expands to display 12 border choices in a miniature toolbar. To find the Borders tool, you may need to click the arrow at the right edge of the Formatting toolbar, to display the palette of extra tools (see Figure 5-12). You can drag the toolbar's title bar and move it anywhere you want.

Figure 5-12: The Borders tool on the Formatting toolbar opens to display 12 border choices.

To add a border to the selected cell or cells, just click the icon that corresponds to the type of border you want. The upper-left icon removes all borders from the selected cells.

Note   Normally, Excel displays gridlines to delineate cells in the worksheet. If you add border formatting, you may want to turn off the gridline display. To do so, choose Tools ➪ Options, click the View tab, and then uncheck the Gridlines check box. When you hide gridlines, you can easily see the effects of borders.

Colors

The Fill Color tool lets you quickly change the background color of the cell, and the Font Color tool lets you change the text color. These tools are similar to the Borders tool and also can be moved to a different location.

Data Entry Tips

This chapter wraps up with some useful tips and techniques that can make your data entry more efficient.

Validating data entry

In Excel 2000, you can specify the type of data that a cell or range should hold. For example, you might develop a spreadsheet that will be used by others. Assume that the worksheet has an input cell that is used in a formula. This particular cell might require a value between 1 and 12 to produce valid results in the formula. You can use the data-validation feature to display a message if the user enters a value that does not fall between 1 and 12.

To set up data validation, select the cell or range of cells that you want validated, and then choose Data ➪ Validation. Excel displays the Data Validation dialog box, with its three tabs (see Figure 5-13).

✦ Click the Settings tab and specify the type of data that the cell should contain. The dialog box changes, depending on your choice in the Allow box.

✦ Click the Input Message tab and specify a message that will appear when the cell is selected (optional). The message appears from the Office Assistant (if it's displayed) or in a small pop-up box.

✦ Click the Error Alert tab and specify the message that will appear in a dialog box if invalid data is entered (optional).

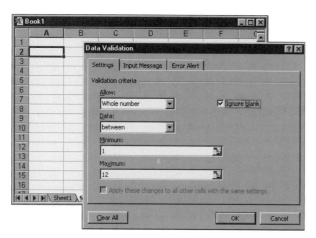

Figure 5-13: The Data Validation dialog box enables you to specify the type of data that will be entered in a cell.

You can set up data validation for as many cells as you want.

Caution   This technique isn't foolproof. The validation does not occur if the user pastes invalid data into a cell that is set up for validation.

Move the cell pointer after entering data?

Depending on how you configure Excel, pressing the Enter key after entering data into a cell may automatically move the cell pointer to another cell. Some users (like myself) find this annoying; others like it. To change this setting, choose Tools ➪ Options and click the Edit tab. The check box that controls this behavior is labeled Move Selection after Enter. You can also specify the direction in which the cell pointer moves (down, left, up, or right).

Use arrows instead of Enter

This chapter mentions several times that you use the Enter key when you're finished making a cell entry. Well, that's only part of the story. You also can use any of the direction keys instead of Enter. And, not surprisingly, these direction keys send you in the direction that you indicate. For example, if you're entering data in a row, press the right-arrow key rather than Enter. The other arrow keys work as expected, and you can even use PgUp and PgDn.

Selecting cells before entering data

Here's a tip that most Excel users don't know about: If you select a range of cells, Excel automatically moves the cell pointer to the next cell in the range when you press Enter. If the selection consists of multiple rows, Excel moves down the column; when it reaches the end of the selection in the column, it moves to the first selected cell in next column. To skip a cell, just press Enter without entering anything. To go backward, use Shift+Enter. If you prefer to enter the data by rows rather than by columns, use Tab rather than Enter.

If you have lots of data to enter, this technique can save you a few keystrokes — and ensure that the data you enter winds up in the proper place.

Use Ctrl+Enter for repeated information

If you need to enter the same data into multiple cells, your first inclination may be to enter it once and then copy it to the remaining cells. Here's a better way: Select all the cells that you want to contain the data, enter the value, text, or formula, and then press Ctrl+Enter. The single entry will be inserted into each cell in the selection.

Automatic decimal points

If you need to enter lots of numbers with a fixed number of decimal places, Excel has a useful tool that works like some adding machines. Select Tools ➭ Options and click the Edit tab. Check the check box labeled Fixed Decimal and make sure that it's set for two decimal places. When the Fixed Decimal option is set, Excel supplies the decimal points for you automatically. For example, if you enter **12345** into a cell, Excel interprets it as 123.45 (it adds the decimal point). To restore things back to normal, just uncheck the Fixed Decimal check box in the Options dialog box.

Note   Changing this setting doesn't affect any values that you have already entered.

Using AutoFill

Excel's AutoFill feature makes it easy to insert a series of values or text items in a range of cells. It uses the AutoFill handle (the small box at the lower left of the active cell). You can drag the AutoFill handle to copy the cell or automatically complete a series.

Cross-Reference   Chapter 8 discusses AutoFill in detail.

Using AutoComplete

With AutoComplete, you type the first few letters of a text entry into a cell, and Excel automatically completes the entry, based on other entries that you've already made in the column. If your data entry task involves repetitious text, this feature is for you.

Here's how it works. Suppose that you're entering product information in a column. One of your products is named *Widgets*. The first time that you enter *Widgets* into a cell, Excel remembers it. Later, when you start typing *Widgets* in that same column, Excel recognizes it by the first few letters and finishes typing it for you. Just press Enter and you're done. It also changes the case of letters for you automatically. If you start entering *widget* (with a lowercase *w*) in the second entry, Excel makes the *w* uppercase, to be consistent with the previous entry in the column.

Besides reducing typing, this feature also ensures that your entries are spelled correctly and are consistent.

Tip   You also can access a mouse-oriented version of this feature by right-clicking the cell and selecting Pick from List from the shortcut menu. With this method, Excel displays a drop-down box that has all the entries in the current column; just click the one that you want.

If you find the AutoComplete feature distracting, you can turn it off on the Edit tab of the Options dialog box. Remove the check mark from the check box labeled Enable AutoComplete for Cell Values.

Entering the current date or time into a cell

Sometimes, you need to date-stamp or time-stamp your worksheet. Excel provides two shortcut keys that do this for you:

   ✦ **Current date:** Ctrl+; (semicolon)
   ✦ **Current time:** Ctrl+Shift+; (semicolon)

Forcing a new line in a cell

If you have lengthy text in a cell, you can force Excel to display it in multiple lines within the cell. Use Alt+Enter to start a new line in a cell. Figure 5-14 shows an example of text in a cell that is displayed in multiple lines. When you add a line break, Excel automatically changes the cell's format to Wrap Text.

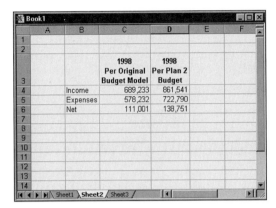

Figure 5-14: Alt+Enter enables you to force a line break in a cell.

 Cross-Reference   Learn more about the Wrap Text formatting feature in Chapter 17.

Entering fractions

If you want Excel to enter a fraction into a cell, leave a space between the whole number and the fraction. For example, to enter the decimal equivalent of $6\frac{7}{8}$, enter **6 7/8** and then press Enter. When you select the cell, 6.875 appears in the formula bar, and the cell entry appears as a fraction. If you have a fraction only (for example, $\frac{1}{8}$), you must enter a zero first, like this: **0 1/8**. When you select the cell and look at the formula bar, you see 0.125. In the cell, you see $\frac{1}{8}$.

Using a data entry form

If you're entering data that is arranged in rows, you may find it easier to use Excel's built-in data form for data entry. Figure 5-15 shows an example of this.

Figure 5-15: Excel's built-in data form can simplify many data entry tasks.

Start by defining headings for the columns in the first row of your data entry range. You can always erase these entries later if you don't need them. Excel needs headings for this command to work, however. Select any cell in the header row and choose Data ➪ Form. Excel asks whether you want to use that row for headers (choose OK). Excel then displays a dialog box similar to the one shown in Figure 5-15. You can use Tab to move between the text boxes and supply information. When you complete the data form, click the New button. Excel dumps the data into a row in the worksheet and clears the dialog box for the next row of data.

Cross-Reference This data form feature has many other useful buttons, which are discussed further in Chapter 33.

Using AutoCorrect for data entry

You can use Excel's AutoCorrect feature to create shortcuts for commonly used words or phrases. For example, if you work for a company named Consolidated Data Processing Corporation, you can create an AutoCorrect entry for an abbreviation, such as cdp. Then, whenever you type *cdp*, Excel automatically changes it to *Consolidated Data Processing Corporation*.

You can customize the AutoCorrect feature by using the Tools ➪ AutoCorrect command. Check the option labeled Replace text as you type, and then enter your custom entries (Figure 5-16 shows an example). You can set up as many custom entries as you like.

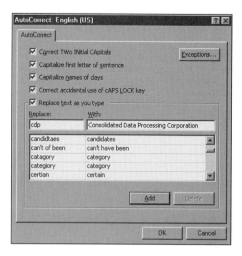

Figure 5-16: You can use Excel's AutoCorrect feature to set up keyboard shortcuts.

Summary

A worksheet cell can contain a value, text, or a formula. This chapter focuses on the task of entering values and formulas. It explains Excel's method of dealing with dates and times and introduces the concept of number formatting—which makes numbers appear differently, but doesn't affect their actual value. This chapter also discusses common editing techniques and basic stylistic formatting, and concludes with a series of general data entry tips.

✦   ✦   ✦

Essential Spreadsheet Operations

This chapter discusses the common spreadsheet
operations that you need to know. A thorough knowledge
of these procedures will help you to work more efficiently.

Working with Worksheets

When you open a new workbook in Excel, the workbook has a
designated number of worksheets in it. You can specify how
many sheets each new workbook will contain. By default, this
number of worksheets is three. Although empty worksheets
really don't use much additional memory or disk storage space,
they just get in the way. And besides, adding a new worksheet
when you need one is easy. I strongly recommend that you
change the default value to one worksheet. To do so, select
Tools ⇨ Options, select the General tab, and then change the
Sheets in new workbook setting to one. After doing this, all new
workbooks will have a single worksheet.

You may find it helpful to think of a workbook as a notebook and
worksheets as pages in the notebook. As with a notebook, you
can activate a particular sheet, add new sheets, remove sheets,
copy sheets, and so on. The remainder of this section discusses
the operations that you can perform with worksheets.

Activating worksheets

At any given time, one workbook is the active workbook,
and one sheet is the active sheet in the active workbook. To
activate a different sheet, just click its sheet tab, located at the

bottom of the workbook window. You also can use the following shortcut keys to activate a different sheet:

✦ **Ctrl+PgUp:** Activates the previous sheet, if one exists

✦ **Ctrl+PgDn:** Activates the next sheet, if one exists

If your workbook has several sheets, all tabs may not be visible. You can use the tab-scrolling buttons (see Figure 6-1) to scroll the sheet tabs.

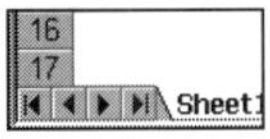

Figure 6-1: The tab-scrolling buttons let you scroll the sheet tabs to display tabs that are not visible.

The sheet tabs share space with the worksheet's horizontal scrollbar. You also can drag the tab split box (see Figure 6-2) to display more or fewer tabs. Dragging the tab split box simultaneously changes the number of tabs and the size of the horizontal scrollbar.

Figure 6-2: Dragging the tab split box enables you to see more (or fewer) sheet tabs.

Tip When you right-click any of the tab-scrolling buttons, Excel displays a list of all sheets in the workbook. You can quickly activate a sheet by selecting it from the list.

Adding a new worksheet

The following are three ways to add a new worksheet to a workbook:

✦ Select the Insert ➪ Worksheet command

✦ Press Shift+F11

✦ Right-click a sheet tab, choose the Insert command from the shortcut menu, and then select Worksheet from the Insert dialog box

Use any of these methods, and Excel inserts a new worksheet before the active worksheet; the new worksheet becomes the active worksheet. The new worksheet, of course, has a sheet tab that displays its name.

Tip To add additional worksheets after inserting a worksheet, press Ctrl+Y (the shortcut for the Edit ⇨ Repeat command) once for each additional sheet that you want to add.

Cross-Reference Chapter 16 discusses how to create and use worksheet templates. This feature enables you to add specially formatted or customized worksheets to an existing workbook.

Deleting a worksheet

If you no longer need a worksheet, or if you want to get rid of an empty worksheet in a workbook, you can delete it in either of two ways:

✦ Select the Edit ⇨ Delete Sheet command

✦ Right-click the sheet tab and choose the Delete command from the shortcut menu

Excel asks you to confirm that you want to delete the sheet.

Tip You can delete multiple sheets with a single command by selecting the sheets that you want to delete. To select multiple sheets, press Ctrl while you click the sheet tabs that you want to delete. Then, use either of the preceding methods to delete the selected sheets.

To select a group of contiguous sheets, click the first sheet tab, press Shift, and then click the last sheet tab.

Caution When you delete a worksheet, it's gone for good. This is one of the few operations in Excel that can't be undone.

Changing the name of a worksheet

Excel uses default names for worksheets: Sheet1, Sheet2, and so on. Providing more meaningful names for your worksheets is usually a good idea. To change a sheet's name, use any of the following methods:

✦ Choose Format ⇨ sheet ⇨ Rename

✦ Double-click the sheet tab

✦ Right-click the sheet tab and choose the Rename command from the shortcut menu

In any of these cases, Excel highlights the name on the sheet tab so that you can edit the name or replace it with a new name.

Sheet names can be up to 31 characters, and spaces are allowed. However, you can't use the following characters in sheet names:

:	colon
/	slash
\	backslash
?	question mark
*	asterisk

Caution Although Excel lets you use square brackets in a worksheet name, you should avoid doing so because it can cause problems with formulas that use external links.

Remember that the name you provide appears on the tab, and that a longer name results in a wider tab. Therefore, if you use lengthy sheet names, you won't be able to see very many sheet tabs without having to scroll.

Moving a worksheet

Sometimes, you may want to rearrange the order of worksheets in a workbook. If you have a separate worksheet for each sales region, for example, arranging the worksheets in alphabetical order or by total sales might be helpful. You also may want to move a worksheet from one workbook to another (to move a worksheet to a different workbook, both workbooks must be open).You can move a worksheet in either of two ways:

✦ Select the Edit ➪ Move or Copy Sheet command. This command is also available when you right-click a sheet tab.

✦ Click the sheet tab and drag it to its desired location (either in the same workbook or in a different workbook). When you drag, the mouse pointer changes to a small sheet and a small arrow guides you.

Dragging is often the easiest method, but if the workbook has many sheets, you may prefer to use the menu command. This command displays the dialog box shown in Figure 6-3, which enables you to select the workbook and the new location.

If you move a worksheet to a workbook that already has a sheet with the same name, Excel changes the name to make it unique. For example, Sheet1 becomes Sheet1 (2).

Tip You also can move multiple sheets at once by selecting them: Press Ctrl while you click the sheet tabs that you want to move.

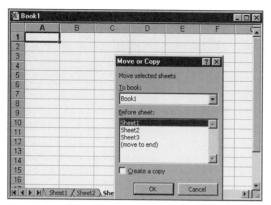

Figure 6-3: The Move or Copy dialog box

Copying a worksheet

You can make an exact copy of a worksheet — either in its original workbook or in a different workbook. The procedures are similar to those for moving a workbook:

✦ Select the Edit ➪ Move or Copy Sheet command. Select the location for the copy and make sure that the check box labeled Create a copy is checked. (The Move or Copy command is also available when you right-click a sheet tab.)

✦ Click the sheet tab, press Ctrl, and then drag it to its desired location (either in the same workbook or in a different workbook). When you drag, the mouse pointer changes to a small sheet with a plus sign on it.

If necessary, Excel changes the name of the copied sheet to make it unique within the workbook.

Note   When you copy a worksheet to a different workbook, the any defined names and custom formats also get copied to the new workbook.

Hiding and unhiding a worksheet

In some cases, you may want to hide a worksheet. Hiding a worksheet is useful if you don't want others to see it or just want to get it out of the way. When a sheet is hidden, its sheet tab is hidden also.

To hide a worksheet, choose Format ➪ Sheet ➪ Hide. The active worksheet (or selected worksheets) will be hidden from view. Every workbook must have at least one visible sheet, so Excel won't allow you to hide all the sheets in a workbook.

To unhide a hidden worksheet, choose Format ➪ Sheet ➪ Unhide. Excel opens a dialog box that lists all hidden sheets. Choose the sheet that you want to redisplay and click OK. You can't select multiple sheets from this dialog box, so you need to repeat the command for each sheet that you want to redisplay.

Zooming worksheets

Excel enables you to scale the size of your worksheets. Normally, everything you see onscreen is displayed at 100 percent. You can change the "zoom percentage" from 10 percent (very tiny) to 400 percent (huge). Using a small zoom percentage can help you to get a bird's-eye view of your worksheet, to see how it's laid out. Zooming in is useful if your eyesight isn't quite what it used to be and you have trouble deciphering those 8-point sales figures. Figure 6-4 shows a window zoomed to 10 percent and a window zoomed to 400 percent.

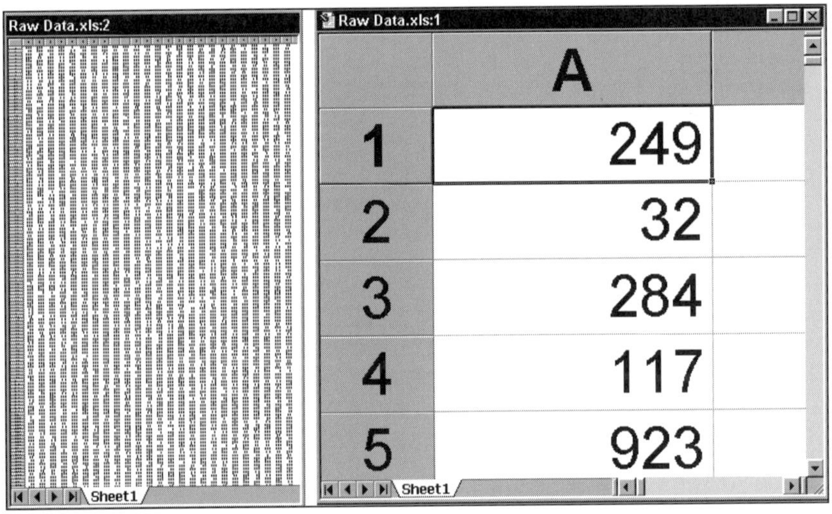

Figure 6-4: A window zoomed to 10 percent and a window zoomed to 400 percent

You can easily change the zoom factor of the active worksheet by using the Zoom tool on the Standard toolbar. Just click the arrow and select the desired zoom factor (see Figure 6-5). Your screen transforms immediately. You can also type a zoom percentage directly into the Zoom tool box. If you choose Selection from the list, Excel zooms the worksheet to display only the selected cells (useful if you want to view only a particular range).

Figure 6-5: The Zoom tool

Zooming affects only the active worksheet, so you can use different zoom factors for different worksheets.

If the Standard toolbar isn't displayed, you can set the zoom percentage by using the View ⇨ Zoom command. This command displays the dialog box shown in Figure 6-6. You can select an option or enter a value between 10 and 400 into the edit box next to the Custom option.

Figure 6-6: The Zoom dialog box

Note   The zoom factor affects only how Excel displays the worksheet onscreen. Zooming has no effect on how the worksheet appears when you print it.

Cross-Reference   Excel contains separate options for changing the size of your printed output (use the File ⇨ Page Setup command). See Chapter 14 for details.

Cross-Reference   If your worksheet uses named ranges (refer to Chapter 7), you'll find that zooming your worksheet to 39 percent or less displays the name of the range overlaid on the cells. This is useful for getting an overview of how a worksheet is laid out.

If you're using a Microsoft IntelliMouse (or a compatible wheel mouse), you can change the zoom factor by pressing Ctrl while you spin the mouse wheel. Each spin changes the zoom factor by 15 percent (but you can't zoom out more than 100 percent). If you find that you do a lot of zooming in, you can change the default behavior for the mouse wheel from scrolling to zooming. To change the default, select Tools ⇨ Options, click the General tab, and then select the Zoom on roll with IntelliMouse check box. After you make this change, you can zoom by spinning the wheel and you won't have to press Ctrl.

Views, Split Sheets, and Frozen Panes

As you add more information to a worksheet, you may find that it gets more difficult to navigate and locate what you want. Excel includes a few options that enable you to view your sheet, and sometimes multiple sheets, more efficiently. This section discusses a few additional worksheet options at your disposal.

Multiple views

Sometimes, you may want to view two different parts of a worksheet simultaneously. Or, you may want to examine more than one sheet in the same workbook simultaneously. You can accomplish either of these actions by opening a new view to the workbook, using one or more additional windows.

To create a new view of the active workbook, choose Window ➪ New Window. Excel displays a new window with the active workbook, similar to Figure 6-7. Notice the text in the windows' title bars: Budget.xls:1 and Budget.xls:2.

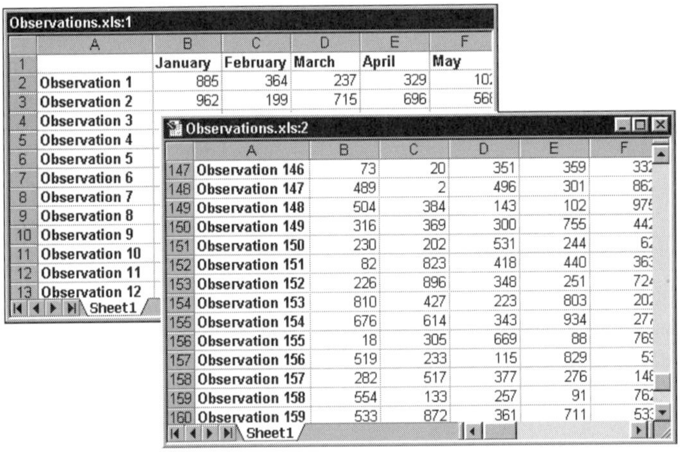

Figure 6-7: Two views of the same workbook

To help you keep track of the windows, Excel appends a colon and a number to each window.

A single workbook can have as many views (that is, separate windows) as you want. Each window is independent of the others. In other words, scrolling to a new location in one window doesn't cause scrolling in the other window(s). This also enables you to display a different worksheet in a separate window. Figure 6-8 shows three views in the same workbook. Each view displays a different worksheet.

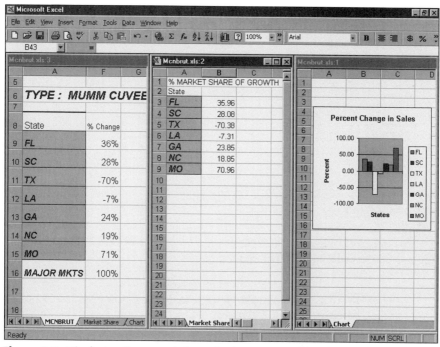

Figure 6-8: Displaying three worksheets in the same workbook

You can close these additional windows by using the standard methods. For example, clicking the Close button title bar closes the active window, but doesn't close the other windows.

As Chapter 7 explains, displaying multiple windows for a workbook also makes it easier to copy information from one worksheet to another. You can use Excel's drag-and-drop procedures to do this.

Splitting panes

If you prefer not to clutter your screen with additional windows, Excel provides another option for viewing multiple parts of the same worksheet. The Window ⇨ Split command splits the active worksheet into two or four separate panes. The split occurs at the location of the cell pointer. You can use the mouse to drag the individual panes to resize them.

Figure 6-9 shows a worksheet split into four panes. Notice that row numbers and column letters aren't continuous. In other words, splitting panes enables you to display in a single window widely separated areas of a worksheet. The two top-to-bottom stacked panes always have the same column headings, and the two side-by-side panes always have the same row headings. To remove the split panes, choose Window ⇨ Remove Split.

	A	B	C	D	K	L	M
1		January	February	March	October	November	December
2	Observation 1	885	364		425	110	689
3	Observation 2	962	199		657	980	400
4	Observation 3	351	148		836	178	472
5	Observation 4	41	396		87	676	499
6	Observation 5	627	383		871	81	775
7	Observation 6	980	826		242	438	968
8	Observation 7	796	714		29	895	85
9	Observation 8	930	654		907	420	621
10	Observation 9	67	790		76	843	197
11	Observation 10	381	436		336	680	202
62	Observation 61	986	155		942	418	56
63	Observation 62	851	879		66	429	963
64	Observation 63	539	763		932	5	374
65	Observation 64	997	762		101	617	561
66	Observation 65	80	167		125	778	768
67	Observation 66	22	825		728	43	374
68	Observation 67	202	651		224	337	500
69	Observation 68	744	381		525	762	403
70	Observation 69	33	384		80	290	292
71	Observation 70	828	861		983	334	238

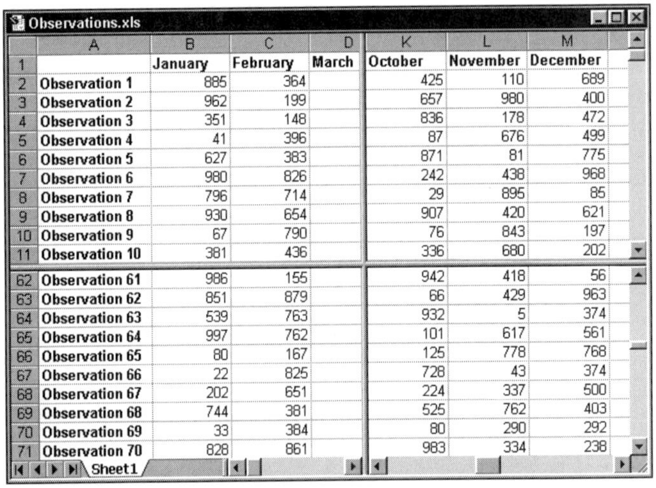

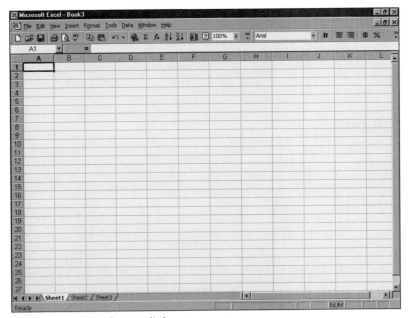

Figure 6-9: This worksheet is split into four panes.

Tip

Another way to split and unsplit panes is to drag either the vertical or horizontal split bar; when you move the mouse pointer over a split bar, the mouse point changes to a pair of parallel lines with arrows pointing outward from each line. Figure 6-10 shows where these split bars are located. To remove split panes by using the mouse, drag the pane separator all the way to the edge of the window, or just double-click it.

Figure 6-10: Drag these split bars to create panes.

Freezing panes

Many worksheets, such as the one shown in Figure 6-11, are set up with row and column headings. When you scroll through such a worksheet, you can easily get lost when the row and column headings scroll out of view, as demonstrated in Figure 6-12. Excel provides a handy solution to this problem: freezing panes.

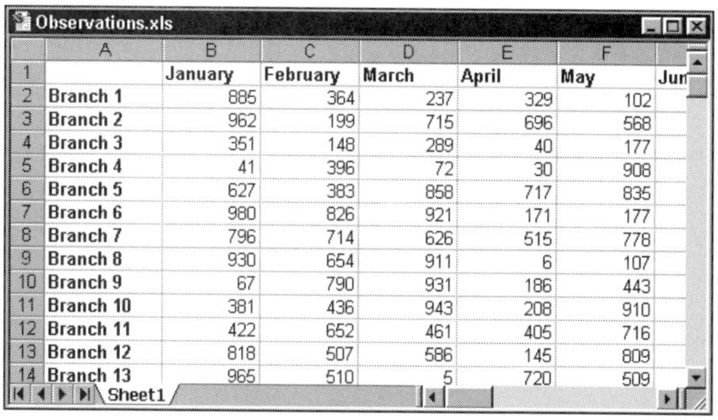

Observations.xls

	A	B	C	D	E	F
1		January	February	March	April	May
2	Branch 1	885	364	237	329	102
3	Branch 2	962	199	715	696	568
4	Branch 3	351	148	289	40	177
5	Branch 4	41	396	72	30	908
6	Branch 5	627	383	858	717	835
7	Branch 6	980	826	921	171	177
8	Branch 7	796	714	626	515	778
9	Branch 8	930	654	911	6	107
10	Branch 9	67	790	931	186	443
11	Branch 10	381	436	943	208	910
12	Branch 11	422	652	461	405	716
13	Branch 12	818	507	586	145	809
14	Branch 13	965	510	5	720	509

Sheet1

Figure 6-11: A worksheet with row and column headings

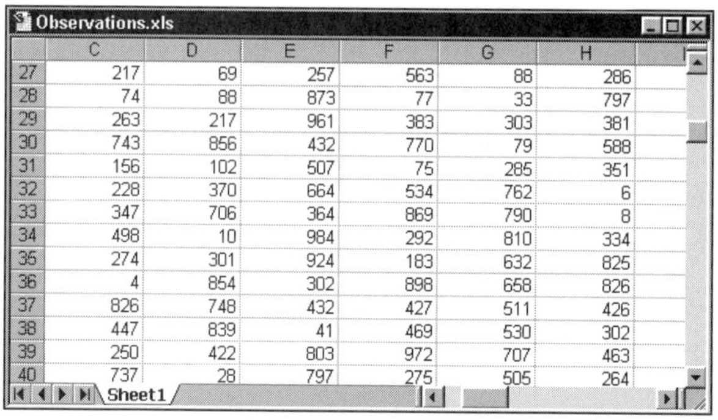

Observations.xls

	C	D	E	F	G	H
27	217	69	257	563	88	286
28	74	88	873	77	33	797
29	263	217	961	383	303	381
30	743	856	432	770	79	588
31	156	102	507	75	285	351
32	228	370	664	534	762	6
33	347	706	364	869	790	8
34	498	10	984	292	810	334
35	274	301	924	183	632	825
36	4	854	302	898	658	826
37	826	748	432	427	511	426
38	447	839	41	469	530	302
39	250	422	803	972	707	463
40	737	28	797	275	505	264

Sheet1

Figure 6-12: You can easily lose your bearings when the row and column headers scroll out of view.

Figure 6-13 shows the worksheet from the previous figure, but with frozen panes. In this case, row 1 and column A are frozen in place. This keeps the headings visible while you are scrolling through the worksheet.

To freeze panes, start by moving the cell pointer to the cell below the row that you want to freeze and to the right of the column that you want to freeze. Then, select Window ⇨ Freeze Panes. Excel inserts dark lines to indicate the frozen rows and columns. You'll find that the frozen row and column remain visible as you scroll throughout the worksheet. To remove the frozen panes, select Window ⇨ Unfreeze Panes.

Observations.xls						
	A	F	G	H	I	J	Oct
1		May	June	July	August	September	
86	Branch 85	351	255	342	939	822	
87	Branch 86	860	230	171	735	13	
88	Branch 87	29	736	458	352	440	
89	Branch 88	582	109	838	916	94	
90	Branch 89	248	167	383	356	858	
91	Branch 90	864	524	109	596	112	
92	Branch 91	480	670	443	953	899	
93	Branch 92	260	365	147	164	892	
94	Branch 93	706	608	12	141	413	
95	Branch 94	514	508	502	113	913	
96	Branch 95	673	994	253	834	142	
97	Branch 96	450	598	260	117	411	
98	Branch 97	827	55	102	379	476	

Figure 6-13: A worksheet with the row and column headings frozen in place

Naming Views

Some users may be interested in a feature called *named views*, which enables you to name various views of your worksheet and to switch quickly among these named views. A view includes settings for window size and position, frozen panes or titles, outlining, zoom factor, the active cell, print area, and many of the settings in the Options dialog box. Optionally, a view can include hidden print settings and hidden rows and columns. If you find that you're constantly fiddling with these settings and then changing them back, using named views can save you lots of effort.

When you select View ➪ Custom Views, you get the dialog box shown in the accompanying figure.

The Custom Views dialog box displays a list of all named views. To select a particular view, just select it from the list and click the Show button. To add a view, click the Add button and provide a name. To delete a named view from the list, click the Delete button.

Working with Rows and Columns

Every worksheet has exactly 65,536 rows and 256 columns. A nice feature would be the capability to specify the number of rows and columns for each worksheet, but these values are fixed and you can't change them. This section discusses some worksheet operations that involve rows and columns.

Inserting rows and columns

Although the number of rows and columns in a worksheet is fixed, you can still insert and delete rows and columns. These operations don't change the number of rows or columns. Rather, inserting a new row moves down the other rows to accommodate the new row. The last row is simply removed from the worksheet, if it is empty. Inserting a new column shifts the columns to the right, and the last column is removed, if it's empty.

Note

If the last row (row 65,536) is not empty, you can't insert a new row. Similarly, if the last column (column IV) contains information, Excel won't let you insert a new column. You can use this to your advantage, however. For example, if you want to ensure that no one adds new rows or columns to your worksheet, simply enter something (anything) into cell IV65536. Attempting to add a row or column displays the dialog box shown in Figure 6-14.

Figure 6-14: Excel's way of telling you that you can't add a new row or column

To insert a new row or rows, you can use any of the following techniques:

✦ Select an entire row or multiple rows by clicking the row numbers in the worksheet border. Select the Insert ➪ Rows command.

✦ Select an entire row or multiple rows by clicking the row numbers in the worksheet border. Right-click and choose Insert from the shortcut menu.

✦ Move the cell pointer to the row that you want to insert and then select Insert ➪ Rows. If you select multiple cells in the column, Excel inserts additional rows that correspond to the number of cells selected in the column.

The procedure for inserting a new column or columns is the same, but you use the Insert ⇨ Column command.

You also can insert cells, rather than just rows or columns. Select the range into which you want to add new cells and then select Insert ⇨ Cells. To insert cells, the other cells must be shifted to the right or shifted down. Therefore, Excel displays the dialog box shown in Figure 6-15 to find out the direction in which you want to shift the cells.

Figure 6-15: When you insert cells, Excel needs to know in which direction to shift the cells to make room.

Caution   Shifting cells around may cause problems in other places in your worksheet, so use caution with the Insert ⇨ Cells command. Better yet, avoid it if you can and insert entire rows or columns. In fact, I've *never* used this command.

Deleting rows and columns

To delete a row or rows, use any of the following methods:

✦ Select an entire row or multiple rows by clicking the row numbers in the worksheet border and then select Edit ⇨ Delete.

✦ Select an entire row or multiple rows by clicking the row numbers in the worksheet border. Right-click and choose Delete from the shortcut menu.

✦ Move the cell pointer to the row that you want to delete and then select Edit ⇨ Delete. In the dialog box that appears, choose the Entire row option. If you select multiple cells in the column, Excel deletes all selected rows.

Deleting columns works the same way. If you discover that you accidentally deleted a row or column, select Edit ⇨ Undo (or Ctrl+Z) to undo the action.

Changing column widths and row heights

Excel provides several different ways to change the widths of columns and the height of rows.

Changing column widths

Column width is measured in terms of the number of characters that will fit into the cell's width. By default, each column's width is 8.43. This is actually a rather meaningless measurement, because in most fonts, the width of individual characters varies — the letter *i* is much narrower than the letter *W*, for example.

Tip If pound signs (#) fill a cell, the column's width isn't wide enough to accommodate the information in the cell. Widen the column to solve the problem. For the most part, Excel automatically adjusts column width as you enter information.

You can change the width of a column or columns in several different ways, which are listed next. Before you change the width, you can select multiple columns, so that the width will be the same for all selected columns. To select multiple columns, either click and drag in the column border or press Ctrl while you select individual columns. To select all columns, click the Select All button in the upper-left corner of the worksheet border (or press Ctrl+Shift+spacebar).

✦ Drag the right-column border with the mouse until the column is the desired width.

✦ Choose Format ➪ column ➪ Width and enter a value in the Column Width dialog box.

✦ Choose Format ➪ column ➪ AutoFit Selection. This adjusts the width of the selected column so that the widest entry in the column fits. If you want, you can just select cells in the column, and the column is adjusted based on the widest entry in your selection.

✦ Double-click the right border of a column to set the column width automatically to the widest entry in the column.

Tip To change the default width of all columns, use the Format ➪ Column ➪ Standard Width command. This displays a dialog box into which you enter the new default column width. All columns that haven't been previously adjusted take on the new column width.

Changing row heights

Row height is measured in points (a standard unit of measurement in the printing trade). The default row height depends on the font defined in the Normal style. Excel adjusts row heights automatically to accommodate the tallest font in the row. So, if you change the font size of a cell to 20 points, for example, Excel makes the column taller so that the entire text is visible.

You can set the row height manually, however, by using any of the following techniques. As with columns, you can select multiple rows.

✦ Drag the lower row border with the mouse until the row is the desired height.

✦ Choose Format ⇨ row ⇨ Height and enter a value (in points) in the Row Height dialog box.

✦ Double-click the bottom border of a row to set the row height automatically to the tallest entry in the row. You also can use the Format ⇨ Row ⇨ AutoFit command for this.

Changing the row height is useful for spacing out rows and is preferable to inserting empty rows between lines of data. Figure 6-16 shows a simple report that uses taller rows to produce a double-spaced effect.

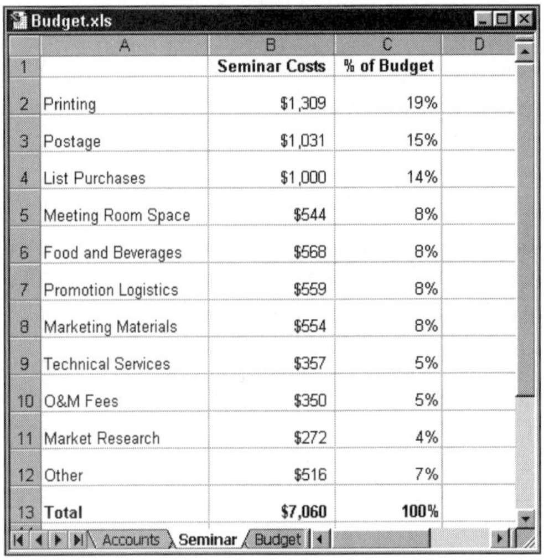

	A	B	C	D
1		Seminar Costs	% of Budget	
2	Printing	$1,309	19%	
3	Postage	$1,031	15%	
4	List Purchases	$1,000	14%	
5	Meeting Room Space	$544	8%	
6	Food and Beverages	$568	8%	
7	Promotion Logistics	$559	8%	
8	Marketing Materials	$554	8%	
9	Technical Services	$357	5%	
10	O&M Fees	$350	5%	
11	Market Research	$272	4%	
12	Other	$516	7%	
13	Total	$7,060	100%	

Budget.xls

◄ ► ►◄ Accounts ∖ Seminar ╱ Budget ◄

Figure 6-16: Changing row heights is the best way to space out the rows in a report.

Hiding rows and columns

Excel lets you hide rows and columns. This may be useful if you don't want users to see particular information.

Tip   You can also hide the rows and columns that aren't used in your worksheet — effectively making your worksheet appear smaller.

Select the row or rows that you want to hide and then choose Format ⇨ RowHide. Or, select the column or columns that you want to hide and then choose Format ⇨ column ⇨ Hide.

You also can drag the row or column's border to hide the row or column. Drag the bottom border of a row upward or the border of a column to the left.

A hidden row is actually a row with its height set to zero. Similarly, a hidden column has a column width of zero. When you use the arrow keys to move the cell pointer, cells in hidden rows or columns are skipped. In other words, you can't use the arrow keys to move to a cell in a hidden row or column.

Unhiding a hidden row or column can be a bit tricky, because selecting a row or column that's hidden is difficult. The solution is to select the columns or rows that are adjacent to the hidden column or row (select at least one column or row on either side). Then, select Format ➪ row ➪ Unhide or Format ➪ column ➪ Unhide. Another method is to select Edit ➪ Go To (or its F5 equivalent) to activate a cell in a hidden row or column. For example, if column A is hidden, you can press F5 and specify cell A1 (or any other cell in column A) to move the cell pointer to the hidden column. Then, you can use the appropriate command to unhide the column.

Summary

This chapter delves into some important operations that all Excel users should know. It covers topics dealing with adding and removing worksheets, renaming worksheets, and moving and copying worksheets. It also discusses topics that help you control the view of your worksheet: freezing panes and splitting panes. This chapter concludes with a discussion of operations that involve entire rows or columns.

✦　　✦　　✦

Working with Cell Ranges

This chapter discusses a variety of techniques that you use to work with cells and ranges.

Cells and Ranges

A cell is a single element in a worksheet that can hold a value, text, or a formula. A cell is identified by its *address*, which consists of its column letter and row number. For example, cell D12 is the cell in the fourth column and the twelfth row.

A group of cells is called a *range*. You designate a range address by specifying its upper-left cell address and its lower-right cell address, separated by a colon.

Here are some examples of range addresses:

A1:B1	Two cells that occupy one row and two columns
C24	A range that consists of a single cell
A1:A100	100 cells in column A
A1:D416	Cells (four rows by four columns)
C1:C65536	An entire column of cells; this range also can be expressed as C:C
A6:IV6	An entire row of cells; this range also can be expressed as 6:6
A1:IV65536	All cells in a worksheet

Alternate Cell Addresses

Typically, you reference cells by their column letter and row number (cell D16 for the cell at the intersection of the fourth column and sixteenth row, for example). You may not know it, but Excel gives you a choice in this matter. You can select Tools ➪ Options (General tab) and then choose the R1C1 reference style option. After selecting this option, the column borders in your worksheets are displayed as numbers rather than letters. Furthermore, all cell references in your formulas use this different notation.

If you find RC notation confusing, you're not alone. RC notation isn't too bad when you're dealing with absolute references. But, when relative references are involved, the brackets can drive you batty.

The numbers in the brackets refer to the relative position of the reference. For example, R[-5]C[-3] specifies the cell that's five rows above and three columns to the left. On the other hand, R[5]C[3] references the cell that's five rows *below* and three columns to the *right*. If the brackets are omitted, it specifies the same row or column: R[5]C refers to the cell five rows below in the same column.

See the following table for examples of how normal formulas translate to RC notation. These formulas are in cell B1 (otherwise known as R1C2).

Formulas Using Column Letters and Row Numbers	Formulas Using RC Notation
=$A$1	=R1C1
=A1+A2+A3	=RC[-1]+R[1]C[-1]+R[2]C[-1]
=(A1+A2)/$A$3	=(RC[-1]+R[1]C[-1])/R3C1

Note   When you're simply navigating through a worksheet or formatting cells, you don't really need to know the range address with which you're working. Understanding cell addresses is most important when you are creating formulas, as you'll see in the next chapter.

Selecting ranges

To perform an operation on a range of cells in a worksheet, you must select the range of cells first. For example, if you want to make the text bold for a range of cells, you must select the range and then click the Bold button on the Formatting toolbar (or, use any of several other methods to make the text bold).

When you select a range, the cells appear highlighted in light blue-gray. The exception is the active cell, which remains its normal color. Figure 7-1 shows an example of a selected range in a worksheet.

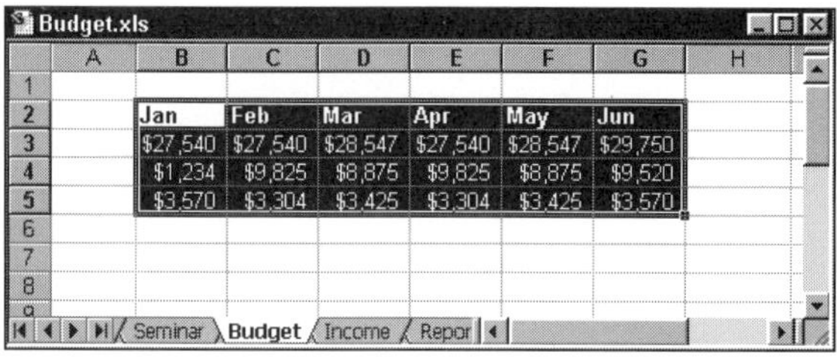

Figure 7-1: When you select a range, it appears highlighted, but the active cell within the range is not highlighted.

EXCEL 2000 Displaying a selected range in light blue-gray is a departure from the behavior of prior versions of Excel, in which the shading of selected cells was black. Microsoft calls this new behavior "See-through View," and it makes it easier to see the actual color formatting of selected cells.

You can select a range in several ways:

✦ Use the mouse to drag, highlighting the range. If you drag to the end of the screen, the worksheet will scroll.

✦ Press the Shift key while you use the direction keys to select a range.

✦ Press F8 and then move the cell pointer with the direction keys to highlight the range. Press F8 again to return the direction keys to normal movement.

✦ Use the Edit ➪ Go To command (or press F5) and enter a range's address manually into the Go To dialog box. When you click OK, Excel selects the cells in the range that you specified.

Tip As you're selecting a range, Excel displays the number of rows and columns in your selection in the Name box (located on the left side of the formula bar).

Selecting complete rows and columns

You can select entire rows and columns in much the same manner as you select ranges, as follows:

✦ Click the row or column border to select a single row or column.

✦ To select multiple adjacent rows or columns, click a row or column border and drag to highlight additional rows or columns.

✦ To select multiple (nonadjacent) rows or columns, press Ctrl while you click the rows or columns that you want.

✦ Press Ctrl+spacebar to select a column. The column of the active cell (or columns of the selected cells) will be highlighted.

✦ Press Shift+spacebar to select a row. The row of the active cell (or rows of the selected cells) will be highlighted.

✦ Click the Select All button (or Ctrl+Shift+spacebar) to select all rows. Selecting all rows is the same as selecting all columns, which is the same as selecting all cells.

Selecting noncontiguous ranges

Most of the time, the ranges that you select will be *contiguous* — a single rectangle of cells. Excel also enables you to work with *noncontiguous ranges*, which consist of two or more ranges (or single cells) that are not necessarily next to each other. This is also known as a *multiple selection*. If you want to apply the same formatting to cells in different areas of your worksheet, one approach is to make a multiple selection. When the appropriate cells or ranges are selected, the formatting that you select is applied to them all. Figure 7-2 shows a noncontiguous range selected in a worksheet.

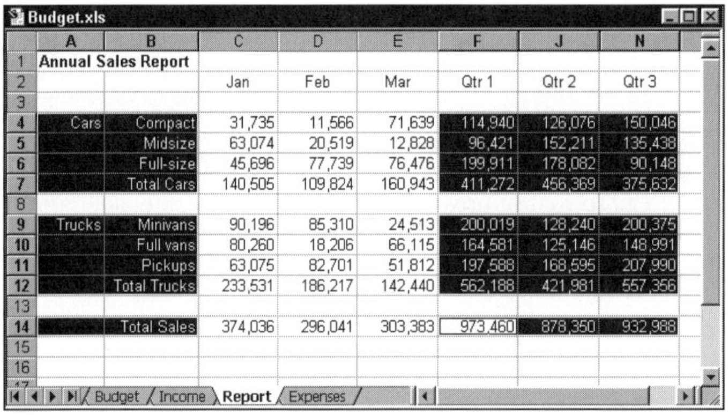

Figure 7-2: Excel enables you to select noncontiguous ranges, as shown here.

You can select a noncontiguous range in several ways:

✦ Hold down Ctrl while you drag the mouse to highlight the individual cells or ranges.

✦ From the keyboard, select a range as described previously (using F8 or the Shift key). Then, press Shift+F8 to select another range without canceling the previous range selections.

✦ Select Edit ➪ Go To and then enter a range's address manually into the Go To dialog box. Separate the different ranges with a comma. When you click OK, Excel selects the cells in the ranges that you specified (see Figure 7-3).

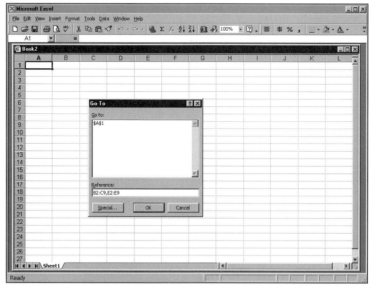

Figure 7-3: Enter a noncontiguous range by separating the ranges with a comma. This example selects a noncontiguous range made up of two ranges: B2:C9 and E2:E9.

Selecting multisheet ranges

So far, this discussion has focused on ranges on a single worksheet. As you know, an Excel workbook can contain more than one worksheet. And, as you might expect, ranges can extend across multiple worksheets. You can think of these as three-dimensional ranges.

Suppose that you have a workbook set up to track expenses by department. A common approach is to use a separate worksheet for each department, making it easy to organize the data. You can click a sheet tab to view the information for a particular department.

Figure 7-4 shows a workbook that has four sheets, named Total, Marketing, Operations, and Manufacturing. The sheets are laid out identically. The only difference is the values. The Total sheet contains formulas that compute the sum of the corresponding items in the three departmental worksheets.

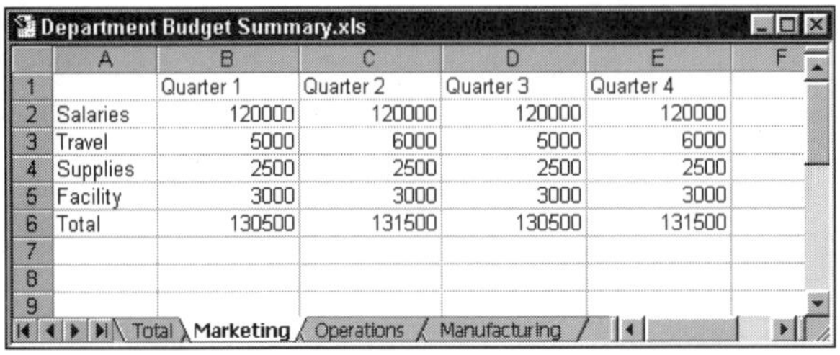

Figure 7-4: A sample workbook that uses multiple worksheets

The worksheets in the Department Budget Summary workbook aren't formatted in any way. If you want to apply number formats, for example, one (not so efficient) approach is simply to format the values in each worksheet separately. A better technique is to select a multisheet range and format the cells in all the sheets simultaneously. The following is a step-by-step example of multisheet formatting, using the workbook shown in Figure 7-4.

1. Activate the Total worksheet.

2. Select the range B2:E6.

3. Press Shift and click the sheet tab labeled Manufacturing. This selects all worksheets between the active worksheet (Totals) and the sheet tab that you click—in essence, a three-dimensional range of cells (see Figure 7-5). Notice that the workbook window's title bar displays [Group]. This is a reminder that you've selected a group of sheets and that you're in Group edit mode.

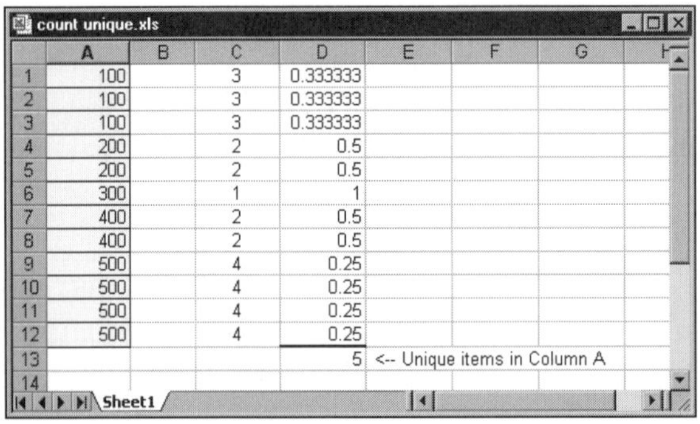

Figure 7-5: Excel in Group mode, with a three-dimensional range of cells selected

4. Click the Comma Style button on the Formatting toolbar. This applies comma formatting to the selected cells.

5. Click one of the other sheet tabs. This selects the sheet and also cancels Group mode; [Group] is no longer displayed in the title bar.

Excel applied comma formatting to all of the values in the selected sheets.

In general, selecting a multisheet range is a simple two-step process: select the range in one sheet and then select the worksheets to include in the range. To select a group of contiguous worksheets, you can press Shift and click the sheet tab of the last worksheet that you want to include in the selection. To select individual worksheets, hold down Ctrl and click the sheet tab of each worksheet that you want to select. If all the worksheets in a workbook aren't laid out the same, you can skip the sheets that you don't want to format. When you make the selection, the sheet tabs of the selected sheets appear in reverse video, and Excel displays [Group] in the title bar.

Tip

To select all sheets in a workbook, right-click any sheet tab and choose Select All Sheets from the shortcut menu.

Special selections

The Edit ⇨ Go To command (or F5) was mentioned earlier as a way to select (or go to) a cell or range. Excel also provides a way to select only "special" cells in the workbook or in a selected range. You do this by choosing Edit ⇨ Go To, which brings up the Go To dialog box. Clicking the Special button displays the Go To Special dialog box, shown in Figure 7-6.

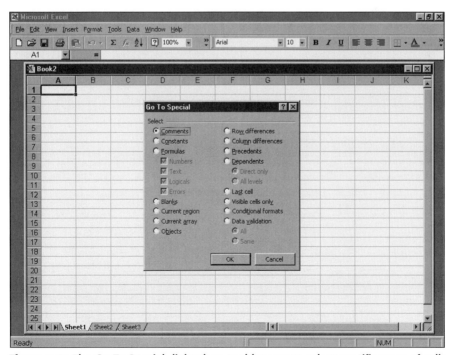

Figure 7-6: The Go To Special dialog box enables you to select specific types of cells.

After you make your choice in the dialog box, Excel selects the qualifying subset of cells in the current selection. Usually, this results in a multiple selection. If no cells qualify, Excel lets you know.

Note   If you bring up the Go To Special dialog box with only one cell selected, Excel bases its selection on the entire active area of the worksheet.

Table 7-1 offers a description of the options available in the Go To Special dialog box. Some of the options can be quite useful.

Table 7-1 Select Special Options	
Option	***What It Does***
Comments	Selects only the cells that contain cell comments (see the next section). Ctrl+Shift+? is the shortcut.
Constants	Selects all nonempty cells that don't contain formulas. This option is useful if you have a model set up and want to clear out all input cells and enter new values. The formulas remain intact.
Formulas	Selects cells that contain formulas. Qualify this by selecting the type of result: numbers, text, logical values (TRUE or FALSE), or errors. These terms are described in the next chapter.
Blanks	Selects all empty cells.
Current Region	Selects a rectangular range of cells around the active cell. This range is determined by surrounding blank rows and columns. Ctrl+* is the shortcut.
Current Array	Selects the entire array. Arrays are covered in Chapters 25 and 26.
Objects	Selects all graphic objects on the worksheet.
Row Differences	Analyzes the selection and selects cells that are different from other cells in each row. Ctrl+\ is the shortcut.
Column Differences	Analyzes the selection and selects the cells that are different from other cells in each column. Ctrl+Shift+| is the shortcut.
Precedents	Selects cells that are referred to in the formulas in the active cell or selection. You can select either direct precedents or precedents at any level.
Dependents	Selects cells with formulas that refer to the active cell or selection. You can select either direct dependents or dependents at any level.

Option	What It Does
Last Cell	Selects the bottom-right cell in the worksheet that contains data or formatting. Ctrl+End is the shortcut.
Visible Cells Only	Selects only visible cells in the selection. This option is useful when dealing with outlines or an autofiltered list.
Conditional Formats	Selects cells that have a conditional format applied (using the Format ➪ Conditional Formatting command).
Data Validation	Selects cells that are set up for data entry validation (using the Data ➪ Validation command). The All option selects all such cells. The Same option selects only the cells that have the same validation rules as the active cell.

Annotating a Cell

Excel's cell-comment feature enables you to attach a comment to a cell. This feature is useful when you need to document a particular value. It's also useful to help you remember what a formula does.

Note   In versions of Excel prior to Excel 97, cell comments were known as *cell notes*.

To add a comment to a cell, select the cell and then choose Insert ➪ Comment (or Shift+F2). Excel inserts a comment that points to the active cell, as shown in Figure 7-7. Initially, the comment consists of your name. Enter the text for the cell comment and then click anywhere in the worksheet to hide the comment.

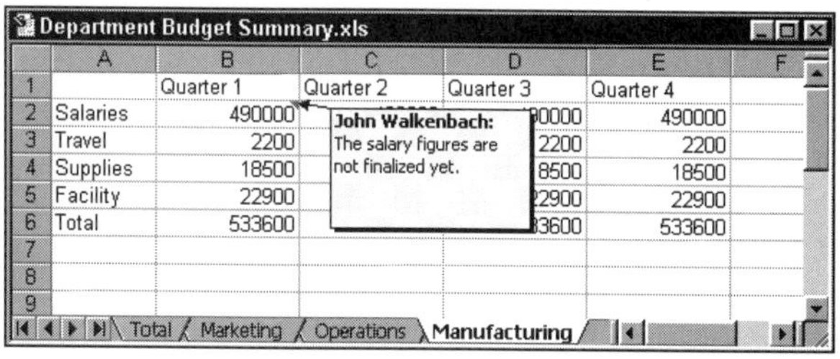

Figure 7-7: Excel enables you to add a descriptive note to a cell.

Cells that have a comment attached display a small red triangle in the upper-right corner. When you move the mouse pointer over a cell that contains a comment, the comment becomes visible.

Note   Select Tools ➪ Options (View tab) to control how cell comment indicators are displayed. You can turn off these indicators if you like.

If you want all cell comments to be visible (regardless of the location of the cell pointer), select View ➪ Comments. This command is a toggle; select it again to hide all cell comments. To edit a comment, activate the cell, right-click, and then choose Edit Comment from the shortcut menu.

To delete a cell comment, activate the cell that contains the comment, right-click, and then choose Delete Comment from the shortcut menu.

Deleting Cell Contents

To erase cells by using only the mouse, select the cell or range to be deleted. Then, click the fill handle—the small square to the lower right of the selection indicator (see Figure 7-8). When you move the mouse pointer over the fill handle, the pointer changes to a cross. As you drag up, Excel grays out the selection. Release the mouse button to erase the contents of the grayed selection.

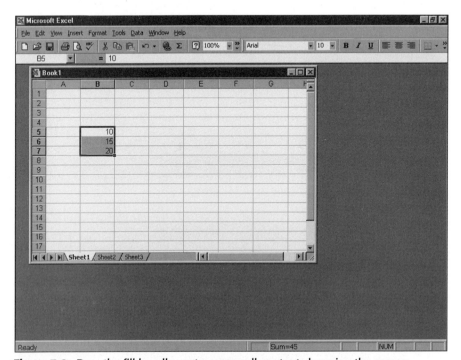

Figure 7-8: Drag the fill handle up to erase cell contents by using the mouse.

Tip   To erase the contents of a cell or range, select the cell or range and press Delete. Or, you can select Edit ➪ Clear, which provides additional options.

Copying a Range

Copying the contents of a cell is a very common operation. You can do any of the following:

✦ Copy a cell to another cell.

✦ Copy a cell to a range of cells. The source cell is copied to every cell in the destination range.

✦ Copy a range to another range. Both ranges must be the same size.

Note   Copying a cell normally copies the cell contents, any formatting that is applied to the original cell (including conditional formatting and data validation), and the cell comment (if it has one). When you copy a cell that contains a formula, the cell references in the copied formulas are changed automatically to be relative to their new destination. More on this in the next chapter.

Copying consists of two steps (although shortcut methods exist, as you'll see later):

1. Select the cell or range to copy (the source range) and copy it to the clipboard.

2. Move the cell pointer to the range that will hold the copy (the destination range) and paste the clipboard contents.

When you paste information, Excel overwrites — without warning — any cells that get in the way. If you find that pasting overwrote some essential cells, choose Edit ➪ Undo (or press Ctrl+Z).

Because copying is used so often, Excel provides many different methods. I discuss each method in the following sections.

Copying by using toolbar buttons

The Standard toolbar has two buttons that are relevant to copying: the Copy button and the Paste button. Clicking the Copy button transfers a copy of the selected cell or range to the Windows clipboard and the Office clipboard. After performing the copy part of this operation, select the cell that will hold the copy and click the Paste button.

The Difference Between the Windows Clipboard and the Office Clipboard

The clipboard is mentioned several times throughout this chapter. Starting with Office 2000, Windows 95 and Windows 98 have two clipboards. The original Windows clipboard remains; whenever you cut or copy information from a Windows program, Windows stores the information on the Windows clipboard, which is an area of memory. Each time that you cut or copy information, Windows replaces the information previously stored on the clipboard with the new information that you cut or copied. The Windows clipboard can store data in a variety of formats. Because information on the clipboard is managed by Windows, it can be pasted to other Windows applications, regardless of where it originated (Chapter 28 discusses the topic of interapplication copying and pasting). Normally, you can't see information stored on the Windows clipboard (nor would you want to).

For Windows programs other than Office programs, you can run the Clipboard Viewer program, which comes with Windows, to view the contents of the Windows clipboard. The Clipboard Viewer may or may not be installed on your system (it is not installed, by default). The accompanying figure shows an example of this program running.

If you open the Clipboard Viewer while working in Excel, by default, you see a row/column reference rather than the actual information you copied. You can use the Clipboard Viewer's Display menu to view the data in different formats, such as the Text format shown in the accompanying figure. You also can save the clipboard contents in a file, which you can then open at a later time.

Chapter 32 contains more information about Clipboard Viewer formats and Excel.

Office 2000 presents a new clipboard, the Office clipboard, which is available only in Office programs. Whenever you cut or copy information in an Office program, such as Excel, the program places the information on both the Windows clipboard and the Office clipboard. However, the program treats information on the Office clipboard differently than it treats information on the Windows clipboard. Instead of replacing information on the Office clipboard, the program appends the information to the Office clipboard. With multiple items stored on the clipboard, you can then paste the items either individually or as a group. You'll learn how the Office clipboard works later in this chapter.

If you're copying a range, you don't need to select an entire range before clicking the Paste button. You need only activate the upper-left cell in the destination range.

Note If you click the Copy button more than once before you click the Paste button, Excel automatically displays the Office Clipboard toolbar.

Copying by using menu commands

If you prefer, you can use the following menu commands for copying and pasting:

✦ **Edit ➪ Copy:** Copies the selected cells to the Windows clipboard and the Office clipboard

✦ **Edit ➪ Paste:** Pastes the Windows clipboard contents to the selected cell or range

Cross-Reference You'll learn more about pasting the contents of the Office clipboard later in this chapter.

Copying by using shortcut menus

You also can use the Copy and Paste commands on the shortcut menu, as shown in Figure 7-9. The Copy command on the shortcut menu places information on both the Windows and Office clipboards. Select the cell or range to copy, right-click, and then choose Copy from the shortcut menu. Then, select the cell in which you want the copy to appear, right-click, and choose Paste from the shortcut menu.

Copying by using shortcut keys

The copy and paste operations also have shortcut keys associated with them:

✦ **Ctrl+C:** Copies the selected cells to both the Windows and Office clipboards

✦ **Ctrl+V:** Pastes the Windows clipboard contents to the selected cell or range

Note These shortcut keys also are used by most other Windows applications.

Copying by using drag and drop

Excel also enables you to copy a cell or range by dragging. Be aware, however, that dragging and dropping *does not* place any information on either the Windows clipboard or the Office clipboard. Select the cell or range that you want to copy and then move the mouse pointer to one of its four borders. When the mouse pointer turns into an arrow pointing up and to the left, press Ctrl; the mouse pointer is augmented with a small plus sign. Then, simply drag the selection to its new location, while you continue to press the Ctrl key. The original selection remains behind, and Excel makes a new copy when you release the mouse button.

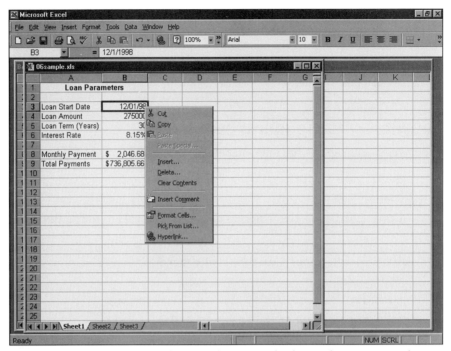

Figure 7-9: Right-clicking anywhere on the screen displays a shortcut menu that contains Copy and Paste commands.

Note

If the mouse pointer doesn't turn into an arrow when you point to the border of a cell or range, you need to make a change to your settings. Select Tools ➪ Options, click the Edit tab, and place a check mark on the option labeled Allow cell drag and drop.

Copying to adjacent cells

Often, you'll find that you need to copy a cell to an adjacent cell or range. This type of copying is quite common when working with formulas. For example, if you're working on a budget, you might create a formula to add the values in column B. You can use the same formula to add the values in the other columns. Rather than reenter the formula, you'll want to copy it to the adjacent cells.

Excel provides some additional options on its Edit menu for copying to adjacent cells. To use these commands, select the cell that you're copying and the cells that you are copying to (see Figure 7-10). Then, issue the appropriate command from the following list for one-step copying:

✦ **Edit ➪ Fill ➪ Down (or Ctrl+D):** Copies the cell to the selected range below

✦ **Edit ➪ Fill ➪ Right (or Ctrl+R):** Copies the cell to the selected range to the right

✦ **Edit ➪ Fill ➪ Up:** Copies the cell to the selected range above

✦ **Edit ➪ Fill ➪ Left:** Copies the cell to the selected range to the left

Note

None of these commands places information on either the Windows clipboard or the Office clipboard.

	A	B	C	D	E	F
1		Quarter 1	Quarter 2	Quarter 3	Quarter 4	
2	Salaries	375000	375000	375000	375000	
3	Travel	3200	3200	3200	3200	
4	Supplies	25000	25000	25000	25000	
5	Facility	13500	13500	13500	13500	
6	Total	416700				
7						
8						
9						
10						

Department Budget Summary.xls

Total / Marketing \ Operations / Manufacturing /

Figure 7-10: To copy to adjacent cells, start by selecting the cell to copy plus the cells in which you want the copy to appear.

You also can use AutoFill to copy to adjacent cells by dragging the selection's fill handle. Excel copies the original selection to the cells that you highlight while dragging. AutoFill doesn't place any information on either the Windows clipboard or the Office clipboard.

Cross-Reference

Chapter 8 discusses more uses for AutoFill.

Copying a Range to Other Sheets

The copy procedures described previously also work to copy a cell or range to another worksheet, even if the worksheet is in a different workbook. You must, of course, activate the other worksheet before you select the location to which you want to copy.

Excel offers a quicker way to copy a cell or range and paste it to other worksheets in the same workbook. Start by selecting the range to copy. Then, press Ctrl and click the sheet tabs for the worksheets to which you want to copy the information (Excel displays [Group] in the workbook's title bar). Select Edit ➪ fill ➪ Across Worksheets, and a dialog box appears that asks what you want to copy (All, Contents, or Formats). Make your choice and then click OK. Excel copies the selected range to the selected worksheets; the new copy will occupy the same cells in the selected worksheets as the original occupies in the initial worksheet.

Caution Be careful with this command, because Excel doesn't warn you if the destination cells contain information. You can quickly overwrite lots of information with this command and not even realize it.

Moving a Cell or Range

Copying a cell or range doesn't modify the cell or range that you copied. If you want to relocate a cell or range to another location, you'll find that Excel is also quite accommodating.

Recall that the Edit ➪ Copy command makes a copy of the selected cell or range and puts the copy on the Windows clipboard and the Office clipboard. The Edit ➪ Cut command also places the selection on both clipboards, but the Edit ➪ Cut command also removes the contents of the selection from its original location. To move a cell or range, therefore, requires two steps:

1. Select the cell or range to cut (the source range) and "cut" it to both of the clipboards.

2. Select the cell that will hold the moved cell or range (the destination range) and paste the contents of one of the clipboards. The destination range can be on the same worksheet or in a different worksheet — or in a different workbook.

You also can move a cell or range by dragging it. Select the cell or range that you want to move and then slide the mouse pointer to any of the selection's four borders. The mouse pointer turns into an arrow pointing up and to the left. Drag the selection to its new location and release the mouse button. This option is similar to copying a cell, except that you don't press Ctrl while dragging; when you drag by moving, you don't place any information on either the Windows clipboard or the Office clipboard.

Other Cell and Range Operations

As you know, the Edit ➪ Copy command and the Edit ➪ Cut command place information on both clipboards. Similarly, the Edit ➪ Paste command transfers the contents of the Windows clipboard to the selected location in your worksheet.

Excel contains two more versatile ways to paste information. You can use the Office clipboard to copy and paste multiple items, or you can use the Paste Special dialog box to paste information in distinctive ways.

Using the Office 2000 clipboard to paste

As mentioned earlier in this chapter, Office 2000 presents a new clipboard, the Office clipboard, which is available only in Office programs. Whenever you cut or copy information in an Office program, such as Excel, the program places the information on both the Windows clipboard and the Office clipboard. However, the program treats information on the Office clipboard differently than it treats information on the Windows clipboard. Instead of *replacing* information on the Office clipboard, the program *appends* the information to the Office clipboard. With multiple items stored on the clipboard, you can then paste the items either individually or as a group.

So far in this chapter, you've seen many ways to copy and cut information to both clipboards. Each of these techniques, however, pastes information from the Windows clipboard, not the Office clipboard. When would you use the Office clipboard? When you want to store multiple items on the Office clipboard and selectively paste them. Or, when you want to store multiple items on the Office clipboard and paste them all simultaneously.

Note   The Office toolbar is available in *all* Office programs. Suppose that you have stored some items from Excel, Access, Outlook, PowerPoint, and Word on the Office clipboard. You can switch to Excel and paste some or all the items from Access. And, you can switch to Word and paste some or all the items from both PowerPoint and Excel.

Suppose that you've created a worksheet like the one shown in Figure 7-11. You have sales, expense, and net information for each individual city stored on the "city" sheets (Denver, San Diego, New York, and Chicago). You want to copy the information from the "city" sheets to the summary sheet, so that you can total the information. In earlier versions of Excel, this task would have been quite tedious. With the Office clipboard, the task is easy.

The process still consists of two basic steps: copy a selection and then paste it. However, when you use the Office clipboard, you copy several times before you paste.

Select the first cell or range that you want to copy to the Office clipboard and copy it by using any of the techniques described earlier in this chapter: Click the Copy tool on the Standard toolbar; choose Edit ➪ Copy; press Ctrl+C; or right-click to choose Copy from the shortcut menu.

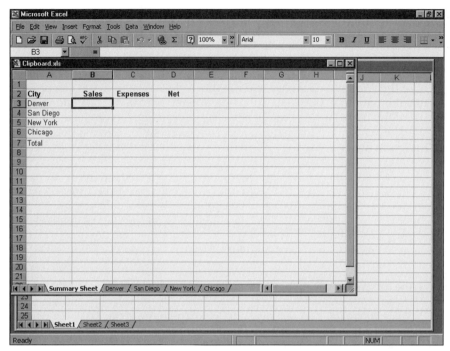

Figure 7-11: Use the Office clipboard to copy information from the "city" sheets to the summary sheet.

Repeat this process, selecting the next cell or range that you want to copy. As soon as you copy the information, the Office clipboard toolbar appears, showing you the number of items that you've copied (see Figure 7-12). The Office clipboard will hold up to 12 items; when you try to add a thirteenth item, you'll see a message asking whether you want to remove the first item that you copied or cancel copying the thirteenth item. Each item stored on the Office Clipboard toolbar contains the symbol for the program from which you copied it; if you point at one of the icons, you'll see a toolbar tip showing you a sample of the information that the item contains.

Note   You can display the Office Clipboard toolbar either by clicking the Copy tool twice, without pasting, or by choosing View ➪ Toolbars ➪ Clipboard.

If necessary, continue copying information. If you want, you can use the Copy tool on the Office Clipboard toolbar; it serves the same purpose and functions in the same way as the Copy tool on the Standard toolbar.

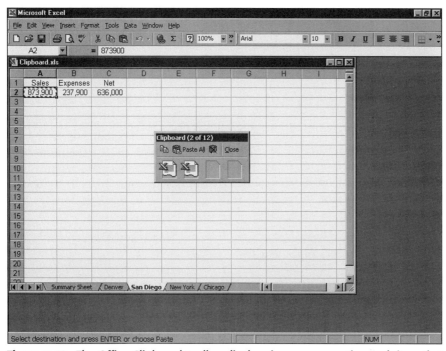

Figure 7-12: The Office Clipboard toolbar displays icons representing each item that you copy.

When you're ready to paste information, select the cell into which you want to copy information. To paste an individual item, click its icon on the Office Clipboard toolbar. To paste all the items that you've copied, click the Paste All button on the Office Clipboard toolbar.

Tip   Although the items appear "across" the Office clipboard, Excel pastes them down a column when you click Paste All — even if you select a range before you click Paste All.

You can clear the contents of the Office clipboard by clicking the Clear Clipboard tool.

Some special notes about the Office clipboard and its functioning:

✦ Excel pastes the contents of the Windows clipboard when you paste either by clicking the Paste tool on the Standard toolbar, by choosing Edit ➪ Paste, by pressing Ctrl+V, or by right-clicking to choose Paste from the shortcut menu.

✦ The last item that you cut or copied appears on both the Office clipboard and the Windows clipboard.

✦ Pasting from the Office clipboard places that item on the Windows clipboard. If you choose Paste All from the Office Clipboard toolbar, you paste all items stored on the Office clipboard onto the Windows clipboard as a single item.

✦ Clearing the Office clipboard also clears the Windows clipboard.

Pasting in special ways

The Edit ➪ Paste Special command is a much more versatile version of the Edit ➪ Paste command. For the Paste Special command to be available, you need to copy a cell or range to the clipboards (using Edit ➪ Cut won't work). Then, select the cell in which you want to paste, and choose Edit ➪ Paste Special. You see the dialog box shown in Figure 7-13. This dialog box has several options, which are explained in the following sections.

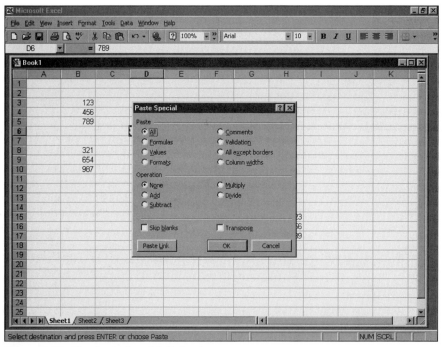

Figure 7-13: The Paste Special dialog box

Pasting all

Selecting the All option in the Paste Special dialog box is equivalent to using the Edit ➪ Paste command. It copies the cell's contents, formats, and data validation from the Windows clipboard.

Pasting formulas as values

Normally, when you copy a range that contains formulas, Excel copies the formulas and automatically adjusts the cell references. The Values option in the Paste Special dialog box enables you to copy the *results* of formulas. The destination for the copy can be a new range or the original range. In the latter case, Excel replaces the original formulas by their current values.

Pasting cell formats only

If you've applied formatting to a cell or range, you can copy only the formatting and paste it to another cell or range. If you've applied lots of formatting to a cell and want to duplicate the formatting elsewhere, use the Formats option in the Paste Special dialog box to save a great deal of time.

Pasting cell comments

If you want to copy only the cell comments from a cell or range, use the Comments option in the Paste Special dialog box. This option doesn't copy cell contents or formatting.

Pasting validation criteria

If you've created validation criteria for a particular cell (by using the Data ⇨ Validation command), you can copy the validation criteria to another cell or range. Use the Validation option in the Paste Special dialog box.

Skipping borders when pasting

Often, you'll want to avoid copying borders around a cell. For example, if you have a table with a border around it, copying a cell from one of the outer cells in the table will also copy the border. To avoid pasting the border, choose the All except borders option in the Paste Special dialog box.

Pasting column widths

You can copy column width information from one column to another. Copy any cell in the column that is set at the width that you want to copy. Select a cell in the column whose width you want to set. In the Paste Special dialog box, choose the Column widths option button.

Performing mathematical operations without formulas

The option buttons in the Operation section of the Paste Special dialog box let you perform an arithmetic operation. For example, you can copy a range to another range and select the Multiply operation. Excel multiplies the corresponding values in the source range and the destination range and replaces the destination range with the new values.

Figure 7-14 shows another example of using a mathematical operation with the Paste Special dialog box. The objective of this example is to increase the values in B4:B10 by ten percent (without using formulas). First, the contents of cell B1 were copied to the clipboard. Then, B4:B10 was selected and the Edit ⇨ Paste Special command was issued. Choosing the Multiply operation causes each cell in B4:B10 to be multiplied by the value on the clipboard, effectively increasing the cell values by ten percent. You also need to select the Value option — otherwise, the cells take on the formatting of the pasted cell.

Figure 7-14: Using the Paste Special command to increase the values in a range by ten percent.

Skipping blanks when pasting

The Skip Blanks option in the Paste Special dialog box prevents Excel from overwriting cell contents in your paste area with blank cells from the copied range. This option is useful if you're copying a range to another area, but don't want the blank cells in the copied range to overwrite existing data.

Transposing a range

The Transpose option in the Paste Special dialog box changes the orientation of the copied range. Rows become columns and columns become rows. Any formulas in the copied range are adjusted so that they work properly when transposed. Note that this check box can be used with the other options in the Paste Special dialog box. Figure 7-15 shows an example of a horizontal range that was transposed to a vertical range.

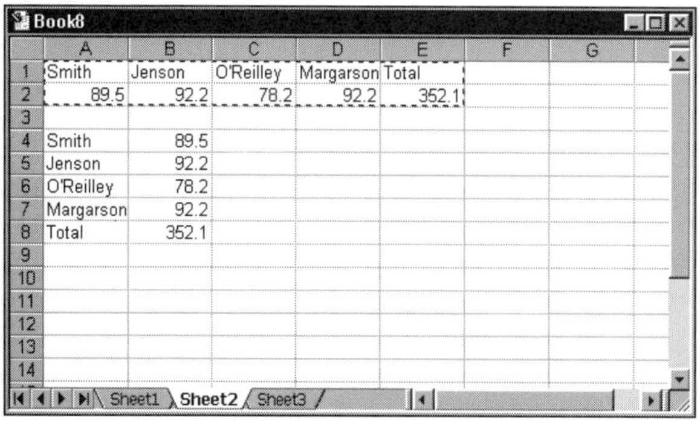

Figure 7-15: The range in A1:E2 was transposed to A4:B8.

Naming Cells and Ranges: The Basics

Dealing with cryptic cell and range addresses can sometimes be confusing (this becomes even more apparent when you deal with formulas, which are covered in the next chapter). Fortunately, Excel enables you to assign descriptive names to cells and ranges. For example, you can give a cell a name such as Interest_Rate, or you can name a range JulySales. Working with these names (rather than cell or range addresses) has several advantages, which are described next.

Advantages of using names

The following are a few advantages of using names:

✦ A meaningful range name (such as Total_Income) is much easier to remember than a cell address (such as AC21).

✦ Entering a name is less error-prone than entering a cell or range address.

✦ You can quickly move to areas of your worksheet either by using the Name box, located at the left side of the formula bar (click the arrow to drop down a list of defined names) or by choosing Edit ➪ Go To (or F5) and specifying the range name.

✦ When you select a named cell or range, the name appears in the Name box.

✦ Creating formulas is easier. You can paste a cell or range name into a formula either by using the Insert ➪ Name ➪ Paste command or by selecting a name from the Name box.

✦ Names make your formulas more understandable and easier to use. A formula such as =Income–Taxes is more intuitive than =D20–D40.

✦ Macros are easier to create and maintain when you use range names rather than cell addresses.

✦ You can give a name to a value or formula — even when the value or formula doesn't exist on the worksheet. For example, you can create the name Interest_Rate for a value of .075. Then, you can use this name in your formulas (more about this in the next chapter).

Valid names

Although Excel is quite flexible about the names that you can define, it does have some rules:

✦ Names can't contain any spaces. You might want to use an underscore or a period character to simulate a space (such as Annual_Total or Annual.Total).

✦ You can use any combination of letters and numbers, but the name must begin with a letter. A name can't begin with a number (such as 3rdQuarter) or look like a cell reference (such as Q3).

✦ Symbols, except for underscores and periods, aren't allowed. Although it's not documented, I've found that Excel also allows a backslash (\ ) and question mark (?).

✦ Names are limited to 255 characters. Trust me — using a name anywhere near this length is not a good idea; in fact, it defeats the purpose of naming ranges.

✦ You can use single letters (except for R or C), but this is generally not recommended because, again, it defeats the purpose of using meaningful names.

Excel also uses a few names internally for its own use. Although you can create names that override Excel's internal names, you should avoid doing so. To be on the safe side, avoid using the following for names: Print_Area, Print_Titles, Consolidate_Area, and Sheet_Title.

Cross-Reference   You can use labels that appear as row and column headings as names; when you do, you don't actually have to define the names. This feature is most useful when you use formulas, so it is discussed in detail in Chapter 8.

Creating names manually

Several ways exist to create names. This section discusses two methods to create names manually.

Using the Define Name dialog box

To create a range name, start by selecting the cell or range that you want to name. Then, select Insert ⇨ name ⇨ Define (or press Ctrl+F3). Excel displays the Define Name dialog box, shown in Figure 7-16.

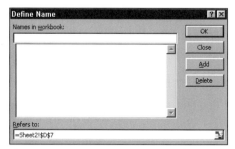

Figure 7-16: Create names for cells or ranges by using the Define Name dialog box.

Type a name in the box labeled Names in workbook (or use the name that Excel proposes, if any). The active or selected cell or range address appears in the Refers to box. Verify that the address listed is correct and then click OK to add the name to your worksheet and close the dialog box. Or, you can click the Add button to continue adding names to your worksheet. If you do this, you must specify the Refers to range either by typing an address (make sure to begin with an equal sign) or by pointing to it in the worksheet. Each name appears in the list box.

Using the Name box

A faster way to create a name is to use the Name box. Select the cell or range to name and then click the Name box and type the name. Press Enter to create the name. If a name already exists, you can't use the Name box to change the range to which that name refers. Attempting to do so simply selects the range.

Note   When you enter a name in the Name box, you *must* press Enter to actually record the name. If you type a name and then click in the worksheet, Excel won't create the name.

The Name box is a drop-down list and shows all names in the workbook (see Figure 7-17). To choose a named cell or range, click the Name box and choose the name. The name appears in the Name box, and Excel selects the named cell or range in the worksheet. Oddly enough, you can't open the Name box by using the keyboard; you must use a mouse. After you click the Name box, however, you can use the direction keys and Enter to choose a name.

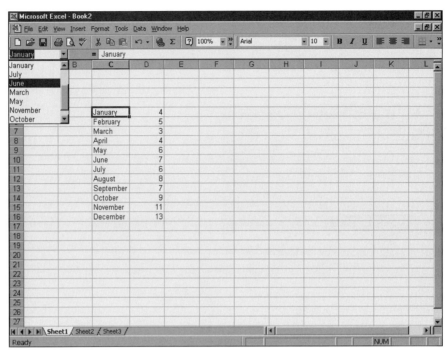

Figure 7-17: The Name box shows all names defined in the workbook.

Creating names automatically

You may have a worksheet that contains text that you want to use for names for adjacent cells or ranges. Figure 7-18 shows an example of such a worksheet. In this case, you might want to use the text in column A to create names for the corresponding values in column B. Excel makes this very easy to do.

Figure 7-18: Excel makes it easy to create names by using text in adjacent cells.

To create names by using adjacent text, start by selecting the name text and the cells that you want to name (these can be individual cells or ranges of cells). The names must be adjacent to the cells that you're naming (a multiple selection is allowed). Then, choose Insert ⇨ Name ⇨ Create (or Ctrl+Shift+F3). Excel displays the Create Names dialog box, shown in Figure 7-19. The check marks in this dialog box are based on Excel's analysis of the selected range. For example, if Excel finds text in the first row of the selection, it proposes that you create names based on the top row. If Excel didn't guess correctly, you can change the check boxes. Click OK and Excel creates the names.

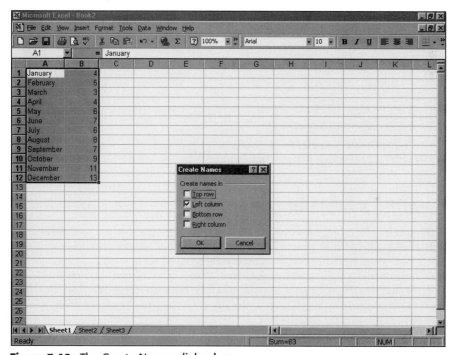

Figure 7-19: The Create Names dialog box

Note   If the text contained in a cell would result in an invalid name, Excel modifies the name to make it valid. For example, if a cell contains the text *Net Income* (which is invalid for a name because it contains a space), Excel converts the space to an underscore character. If Excel encounters a value or a formula where text should be, however, it doesn't convert it to a valid name. It simply doesn't create a name.

Caution   You should double-check the names that Excel creates. Sometimes, the Insert ⇨ name ⇨ Create command works counterintuitively.

Figure 7-20 shows a small table of text and values. If you select the entire table, choose InsertName ➪ Create, and accept Excel's suggestions (Top Row and Left Column options), you'll find that the name Products doesn't refer to A2:A5, as you would expect, but instead refers to B2:C5. If the upper-left cell of the selection contains text and you choose the Top Row and Left Column options, Excel uses that text for the name of the entire data — excluding the top row and left column. So, before you accept the names that Excel creates, take a minute to make sure that they refer to the correct ranges.

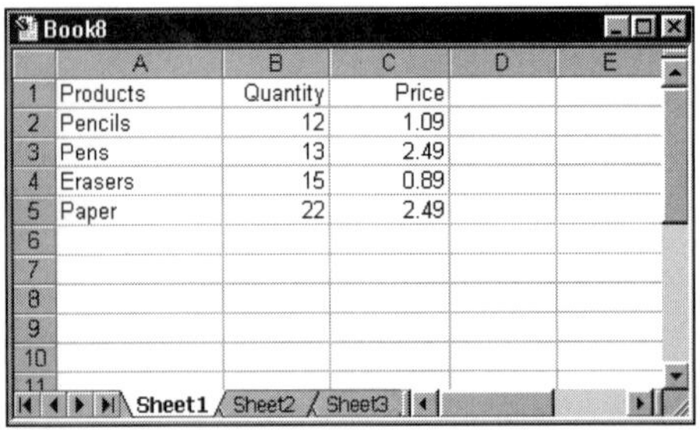

Figure 7-20: Creating names from the data in this table may produce unexpected results.

Creating a table of names

After you create a large number of names, you may need to know the ranges that each name defines, particularly if you're trying to track down errors or document your work. Excel lets you create a list of all names in the workbook and their corresponding addresses. To create a table of names, first move the cell pointer to an empty area of your worksheet — the table is created at the active cell position and will overwrite any information at that location. Use the Insert ➪ name ➪ Paste command (or F3). Excel displays the Paste Name dialog box, shown in Figure 7-21, which lists all the defined names. To paste a list of names, click the Paste List button.

Deleting names

If you no longer need a defined name, you can delete it. Deleting a range name *does not* delete information in the range; it can, however, make formulas in your workbook invalid.

Choose Insert ➪ Name ➪ Define to display the Define Name dialog box. Choose the name that you want to delete from the list and then click the Delete button.

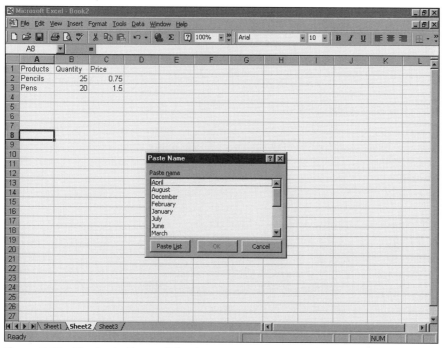

Figure 7-21: The Paste Name dialog box

Caution   Be extra careful when deleting names. If the name is used in a formula, deleting the name causes the formula to become invalid (it will display #NAME?). However, deleting a name can be undone, so if you find that formulas return #NAME? after you delete a name, select Edit ➪ Undo to get the name back.

If you delete the rows or columns that contain named cells or ranges, the names contain an invalid reference. For example, if cell A1 on Sheet1 is named Interest and you delete row 1 or column A, Interest then refers to =Sheet1!#REF! (that is, an erroneous reference). If you use Interest in a formula, the formula displays #REF.

Redefining names

After you define a name, you may want to change the cell or range to which it refers. Select Insert ➪ Name ➪ Define to display the Define Name dialog box. Click the name that you want to change and then edit the cell or range address in the Refers to edit box. If you want to, you can click the edit box and select a new cell or range by pointing in the worksheet.

Note   Excel automatically adjusts the cells to which your names refer. For example, assume that cell A10 is named Summary. If you delete a row above row 10, Summary then refers to cell A9. This is just what you would expect to happen, so you don't need to be concerned about it.

Changing names

Excel doesn't have a simple way to change a name once you create the name. If you create a name and then realize that it's not the name that you want — or, perhaps, that you spelled it incorrectly — you must create the new name and then delete the old name.

Learning more about names

Excel offers some additional features with respect to using names — features unmatched in any of its competitors.

Cross-Reference   These advanced naming features are most useful when working with formulas and therefore are discussed in Chapter 8.

Summary

This chapter discusses the basic worksheet operations that involve cells and ranges. These operations include selecting, copying, moving, deleting, and working with ranges that extend across multiple worksheets in a workbook. This chapter also introduces the topic of names, an important concept that can make your worksheets more readable and easier to maintain.

✦   ✦   ✦

Creating and Using Formulas

Formulas are what make a spreadsheet so useful. Without formulas, a spreadsheet would be little more than a word processor with a very powerful table feature. A worksheet without formulas is essentially dead. Using formulas adds life and lets you calculate results from the data stored in the worksheet. This chapter introduces formulas and helps you get up to speed with this important element.

Introducing Formulas

To add a formula to a worksheet, you enter it into a cell. You can delete, move, and copy formulas just like any other item of data. Formulas use arithmetic operators to work with values, text, worksheet functions, and other formulas to calculate a value in the cell. Values and text can be located in other cells, which makes changing data easy and gives worksheets their dynamic nature. For example, Excel recalculates formulas if the value in a cell used by the formula changes. In essence, you can see multiple scenarios quickly by changing the data in a worksheet and letting formulas do the work.

A formula entered into a cell can consist of any of the following elements:

- ✦ Operators such as + (for addition) and * (for multiplication)
- ✦ Cell references (including named cells and ranges)
- ✦ Values or text
- ✦ Worksheet functions (such as SUM or AVERAGE)

A formula can consist of up to 1,024 characters. After you enter a formula into a cell, the cell displays the result of the formula. The formula itself appears in the formula bar when you select the cell, however.

Here are a few examples of formulas:

=150*.05	Multiplies 150 times 0.05. This formula uses only values and isn't all that useful.
=A1+A2	Adds the values in cells A1 and A2.
=Income–Expenses	Subtracts the cell named Expenses from the cell named Income.
=SUM(A1:A12)	Adds the values in the range A1:A12.
=A1=C12	Compares cell A1 with cell C12. If they are identical, the formula returns TRUE; otherwise, it returns FALSE.

Note   Notice that formulas always begin with an equal sign so that Excel can distinguish formulas from text.

Operators used in formulas

Excel lets you use a variety of operators in your formulas. Table 8-1 lists the operators that Excel recognizes. In addition to these, Excel has many built-in functions that enable you to perform more operations.

Cross-Reference   These functions are discussed in detail in Chapter 9.

Table 8-1 **Operators Used in Formulas**	
Operator	**Name**
+	Addition
-	Subtraction
*	Multiplication
/	Division
^	Exponentiation
&	Concatenation
=	Logical comparison (equal to)

Operator	Name
>	Logical comparison (greater than)
<	Logical comparison (less than)
>=	Logical comparison (greater than or equal to)
<=	Logical comparison (less than or equal to)
<>	Logical comparison (not equal to)

You can, of course, use as many operators as you need (formulas can be quite complex). Figure 8-1 shows a worksheet with a formula in cell B5. The formula is as follows:

```
=(B2-B3)*B4
```

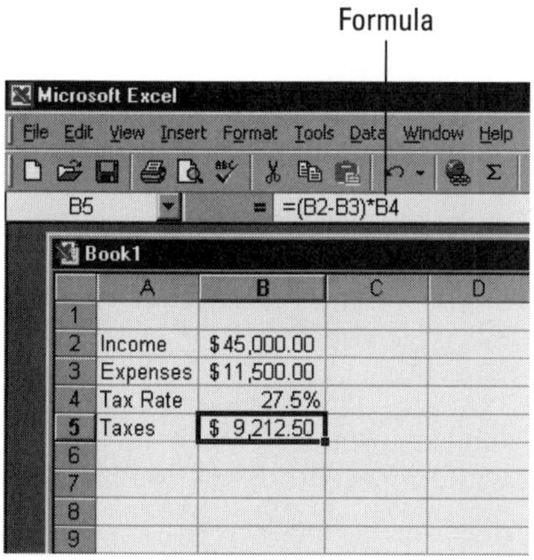

Figure 8-1: A formula that uses two operators

In this example, the formula subtracts the value in B3 from the value in B2 and then multiplies the result by the value in B4. If the worksheet had names defined for these cells, the formula would be a lot more readable. Here's the same formula after naming the cells:

```
=(Income-Expenses)*TaxRate
```

Now, are you beginning to understand the importance of naming ranges? The following are some additional examples of formulas that use various operators.

`="Part-"&"23A"`	Joins *(concatenates)* the two text strings to produce *Part-23A*.
`=A1&A2`	Concatenates the contents of cell A1 with cell A2. Concatenation works with values as well as text. If cell A1 contains 123 and cell A2 contains 456, this formula would return the value 123456.
`=6^3`	Raises 6 to the third power (216).
`=216^(1/3)`	Returns the cube root of 216 (6).
`=A1<A2`	Returns TRUE if the value in cell A1 is less than the value in cell A2. Otherwise, it returns FALSE. Logical comparison operators also work with text. If A1 contained Bill and A2 contained Julia, the formula would return TRUE, because Bill comes before Julia in alphabetical order.
`=A1<=A2`	Returns TRUE if the value in cell A1 is less than or equal to the value in cell A2. Otherwise, it returns FALSE.
`=A1<>A2`	Returns TRUE if the value in cell A1 isn't equal to the value in cell A2. Otherwise, it returns FALSE.

Operator precedence

In an earlier example, parentheses are used in the formula, to control the order in which the calculations occur. The formula without parentheses looks like this:

`=Income-Expenses*TaxRate`

If you enter the formula without the parentheses, Excel computes the wrong answer. To understand why this occurs, you need to understand a concept called *operator precedence*, which basically is the set of rules that Excel uses to perform its calculations. Table 8-2 lists Excel's operator precedence. This table shows that exponentiation has the highest precedence (that is, it's performed first), and logical comparisons have the lowest precedence.

You use parentheses to override Excel's built-in order of precedence. Returning to the previous example, the formula that follows doesn't use parentheses and, therefore, is evaluated using Excel's standard operator precedence. Because multiplication has a higher precedence, the Expense cell is multiplied by the `TaxRate` cell. Then, this result is subtracted from Income. This isn't what was intended.

Table 8-2
Operator Precedence in Excel Formulas

Symbol	Operator	Precedence
^	Exponentiation	1
*	Multiplication	2
/	Division	2
+	Addition	3
-	Subtraction	3
&	Concatenation	4
=	Equal to	5
<	Less than	5
>	Greater than	5

The correct formula, which follows, uses parentheses to control the order of operations. Expressions within parentheses are always evaluated first. In this case, Expenses is subtracted from Income and the result is multiplied by TaxRate.

```
=(Income-Expenses)*TaxRate
```

You can also *nest* parentheses in formulas, which means putting parentheses inside of parentheses. If you do so, Excel evaluates the most deeply nested expressions first and works its way out. Figure 8-2 shows an example of a formula that uses nested parentheses.

```
=((B2*C2)+(B3*C3)+(B4*C4))*B6
```

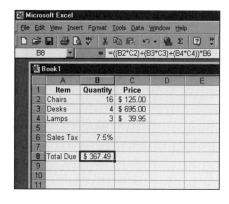

Figure 8-2: A formula with nested parentheses

This formula has four sets of parentheses — three sets are nested inside the fourth set. Excel evaluates each nested set of parentheses and then adds up the three results. This sum is then multiplied by the value in B6.

Using parentheses liberally in your formulas is a good idea. I often use parentheses even when they aren't necessary, to clarify the order of operations and make the formula easier to read. For example, if you want to add 1 to the product of two cells, the following formula will do it:

```
=1+A1*A2
```

I find it much clearer, however, to use the following formula (with superfluous parentheses):

```
=1+(A1*A2)
```

Every left parenthesis, of course, must have a matching right parenthesis. If you have many levels of nested parentheses, it can sometimes be difficult to keep them straight. If the parentheses don't match, Excel displays a message explaining the problem and won't let you enter the formula. Fortunately, Excel lends a hand in helping you match parentheses. When you enter or edit a formula that has parentheses, pay attention to the text. When the insertion point moves over a parenthesis, Excel momentarily bolds it and its matching parenthesis. This lasts for less than a second, so be alert.

In some cases, if your formula contains mismatched parentheses, Excel may propose a correction to your formula. Figure 8-3 shows an example of the Formula AutoCorrect feature. You may be tempted simply to accept the proposed correction, but be careful — in many cases, the proposed formula, although syntactically correct, isn't the formula that you want.

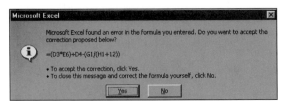

Figure 8-3: Excel's Formula AutoCorrect feature often suggests a correction to an erroneous formula.

Excel's built-in functions

Excel provides a bewildering number of built-in worksheet functions that you can use in your formulas. These include common functions (such as SUM, AVERAGE, and SQRT) as well as functions designed for special purposes, such as statistics or engineering. Functions can greatly enhance the power of your formulas. They can simplify your formulas and make them easier to read; in many cases, functions enable you to perform calculations that would not be possible otherwise. If you can't find a worksheet function that you need, Excel even lets you create your own custom functions.

Cross-Reference Excel's built-in functions are discussed in the Chapter 9, and Chapter 41 covers the basics of creating custom functions by using VBA.

Entering Formulas

As mentioned earlier, a formula must begin with an equal sign to inform Excel that the cell contains a formula rather than text. Basically, two ways exist to enter a formula into a cell: enter it manually or enter it by pointing to cell references. Each of these methods is discussed in the following sections.

Entering formulas manually

Entering a formula manually involves, well, entering a formula manually. You simply type an equal sign (=), followed by the formula. As you type, the characters appear in the cell and in the formula bar. You can, of course, use all the normal editing keys when entering a formula.

Entering formulas by pointing

The other method of entering a formula still involves some manual typing, but you can simply point to the cell references instead of entering them manually. For example, to enter the formula =A1+A2 into cell A3, follow these steps:

1. Move the cell pointer to cell A3.

2. Type an equal sign (=) to begin the formula. Notice that Excel displays Enter in the status bar.

3. Press the up arrow twice. As you press this key, notice that Excel displays a faint moving border around the cell and that the cell reference appears in cell A3 and in the formula bar. Also notice that Excel displays Point in the status bar.

4. Type a plus sign (+). The faint border disappears and Enter reappears in the status bar.

5. Press the up arrow one more time. A2 is added to the formula.

6. Press Enter to end the formula.

Pointing to cell addresses rather than entering them manually is usually more accurate and less tedious.

Tip   When you create a formula that refers to other cells, the cell that contains the formula has the same number format as the first cell it refers to.

Excel includes the Formula Palette feature that you can use when you enter or edit formulas. To display the Formula Palette, click the Edit Formula button in the Formula bar (the Edit Formula button looks like an equal sign). The Formula Palette lets you enter formulas manually or use the pointing techniques described previously. The Formula Palette, shown in Figure 8-4, displays the result of the formula as it's being entered. The Formula Palette usually appears directly below the edit line, but you can drag it to any convenient location (as you can see in the figure).

Edit Formula button

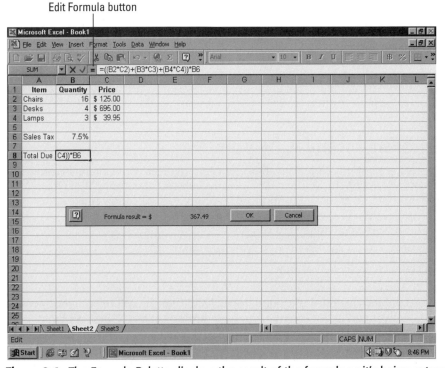

Figure 8-4: The Formula Palette displays the result of the formula as it's being entered.

Pasting names

If your formula uses named cells or ranges, you can either type the name in place of the address or choose the name from a list and have Excel insert the name for you automatically. You have two ways available to insert a name into a formula:

✦ **Select Insert ➪ Name ➪ Paste:** Excel displays its Paste Name dialog box with all the names listed (see Figure 8-5). Select the name and click OK. Or, you can double-click the name, which inserts the name and closes the dialog box.

✦ **Press F3:** This also displays the Paste Name dialog box.

Figure 8-5: The Paste Name dialog box lets you insert a name into a formula.

Referencing Cells Outside the Worksheet

Formulas can refer to cells in other worksheets — and the worksheets don't even have to be in the same workbook. Excel uses a special type of notation to handle these types of references.

Cells in other worksheets

To use a reference to a cell in another worksheet in the same workbook, use the following format:

```
SheetName!CellAddress
```

In other words, precede the cell address with the worksheet name, followed by an exclamation point. Here's an example of a formula that uses a cell on the Sheet2 worksheet:

```
=A1*Sheet2!A1
```

This formula multiplies the value in cell A1 on the current worksheet by the value in cell A1 on Sheet2.

Note   If the worksheet name in the reference includes one or more spaces, you must enclose it in single quotation marks. For example, here's a formula that refers to a cell on a sheet named All Depts:

```
=A1*'All Depts'!A1
```

Cells in other workbooks

To refer to a cell in a different workbook, use this format:

```
=[WorkbookName]SheetName!CellAddress
```

In this case, the workbook name (in square brackets), the worksheet name, and an exclamation point precede the cell address. The following is an example of a formula that uses a cell reference in the Sheet1 worksheet in a workbook named Budget:

```
=[Budget.xls]Sheet1!A1
```

If the workbook name in the reference includes one or more spaces, you must enclose it (and the sheet name) in single quotation marks. For example, here's a formula that refers to a cell on Sheet1 in a workbook named Budget For 1999:

```
=A1*'[Budget For 1999]Sheet1'!A1
```

When a formula refers to cells in a different workbook, the other workbook doesn't need to be open. If the workbook is closed, you must add the complete path to the reference. Here's an example:

```
=A1*'C:\ MSOffice\Excel\[Budget For 1999]Sheet1'!A1
```

Cross-Reference

File linking is covered in detail in Chapter 24.

Entering references to cells outside the worksheet

To create formulas that refer to cells not in the current worksheet, use the pointing technique described earlier (refer to the section "Entering Formulas by Pointing"). Excel takes care of the details regarding the workbook and worksheet references. The workbook that you're using in your formula must be open to use the pointing method.

Note

If you point to a different worksheet or workbook when creating a formula, you'll notice that Excel always inserts absolute cell references. Therefore, if you plan to copy the formula to other cells, make sure that you change the cell references to relative. This concept of absolute versus relative cell references is discussed in the following section.

Absolute Versus Relative References

You need to be able to distinguish between *relative* and *absolute cell references*. By default, Excel creates relative cell references in formulas except when the formula includes cells in different worksheets or workbooks. The distinction becomes apparent when you copy a formula to another cell.

Relative references

Figure 8-6 shows a worksheet with a formula in cell D2. The formula, which uses the default relative references, is as follows:

```
=B2*C2
```

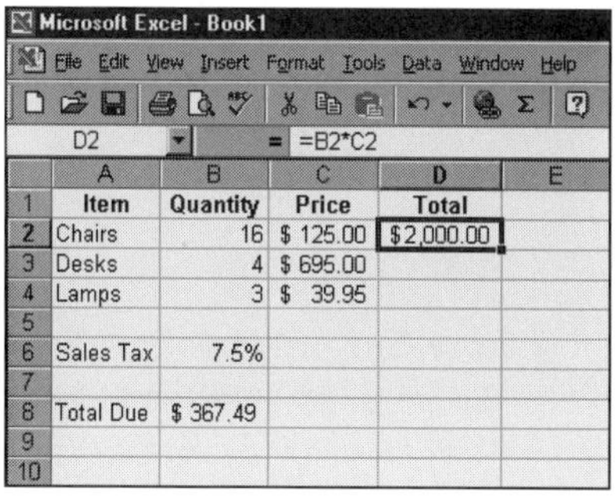

Figure 8-6: The formula in cell D2 will be copied to the cell below.

When you copy this formula to the two cells below it, Excel doesn't produce an exact copy of the formula; rather, it generates these formulas:

✦ **Cell D3:** =B3*C3

✦ **Cell D4:** =B4*C4

Excel adjusts the cell references to refer to the cells that are relative to the new formula. Think of it like this: The original formula contained instructions to multiply the value two cells to the left by the value one cell to the left. When you copy the cell, these *instructions* get copied, not the actual contents of the cell. Usually, this is exactly what you want. You certainly don't want to copy the formula verbatim; if you did, the new formulas would produce the same value as the original formula.

Note   When you cut and paste a formula (move it to another location), the cell references in the formula aren't adjusted. Again, this is what you usually want to happen. When you move a formula, you generally want it to continue to refer to the original cells.

Absolute references

Sometimes, however, you *do* want a cell reference to be copied verbatim. Figure 8-7 shows an example of a formula that contains an absolute reference. In this example, cell B6 contains a sales tax rate. The formula in cell D2 is as follows:

```
=(B2*C2)*$B$6
```

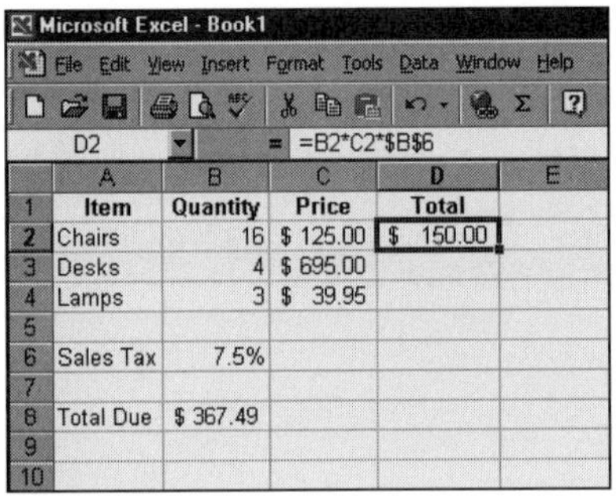

Figure 8-7: A formula that uses an absolute cell reference

Notice that the reference to cell B6 has dollar signs preceding the column letter and the row number. These dollar signs indicate to Excel that you want to use an absolute cell reference. When you copy this formula to the two cells below, Excel generates the following formulas:

✦ **Cell D3:** =(B3*C3)*$B$6

✦ **Cell D4:** =(B4*C4)*$B$6

In this case, the relative cell references were changed, but the reference to cell B6 wasn't changed, because it's an absolute reference.

Mixed references

An absolute reference uses two dollar signs in its address: one for the column letter and one for the row number. Excel also allows mixed references in which only one of the address parts is absolute. Table 8-3 summarizes all the possible types of cell references.

	Table 8-3 **Types of Cell References**
Example	**Type**
A1	Relative reference
$A$1	Absolute reference
$A1	Mixed reference (column letter is absolute)
A$1	Mixed reference (row number is absolute)

When would you use a mixed reference? Figure 8-8 shows an example of a situation in which a mixed reference is appropriate. This worksheet will contain a table of values in which each cell consists of the value in column A multiplied by the value in row 1. The formula in cell B2 is as follows:

```
=B$1*$A2
```

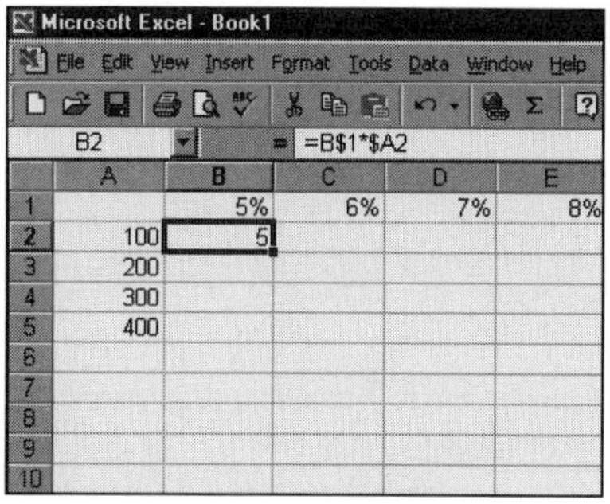

Figure 8-8: This formula uses a mixed reference.

This formula contains two mixed cell references. In the B$1 reference, the row number is absolute, but the column letter is relative. In the $A2 reference, the row number is relative, but the column letter is absolute. You can copy this formula to the range B2:E5 and each cell will contain the correct formula. For example, the formula in cell E5 would be as follows:

```
=E$1*$A5
```

Entering nonrelative references

You can enter nonrelative references (absolute or mixed) manually by inserting dollar signs in the appropriate positions. Or, you can use a handy shortcut: the F4 key. When you're entering a cell reference — either manually or by pointing — you can press F4 repeatedly to have Excel cycle through all four reference types.

For example, if you enter **=A1** to start a formula, pressing F4 converts the cell reference to =$A$1. Pressing F4 again converts it to =A$1. Pressing it again displays =$A1. Pressing it one more time returns to the original =A1. Keep pressing F4 until Excel displays the type of reference that you want.

Note   When you name a cell or range, Excel (by default) uses an absolute reference for the name. For example, if you give the name SalesForecast to A1:A12, the Refers to box in the Define Name dialog box lists the reference as $A$1:$A$12. This is almost always what you want. If you copy a cell that has a named reference in its formula, the copied formula contains a reference to the original name.

When a Formula Returns an Error

Sometimes when you enter a formula, Excel displays a value that begins with a pound sign (#). This is a signal that the formula is returning an error value. You'll have to correct the formula (or correct a cell that the formula references) to get rid of the error display.

As noted previously in this chapter, Excel often suggests a correction for an erroneous formula.

Note   If the entire cell is filled with pound characters, this means that the column isn't wide enough to display the value. You can either widen the column or change the number format of the cell.

Table 8-4 lists the types of error values that may appear in a cell that has a formula. Formulas may return an error value if a cell to which they refer has an error value. This is known as the ripple effect — a single error value can make its way into lots of other cells that contain formulas that depend on the cell.

Editing Formulas

You can edit your formulas just like you can edit any other cell. You might need to edit a formula if you make some changes to your worksheet and need to adjust the formula to accommodate the changes. Or, the formula may return one of the error values described in the previous section, and you need to edit the formula to correct the error.

Table 8-4
Excel Error Values

Error Value	Explanation
#DIV/0!	The formula is trying to divide by zero (an operation that's not allowed on this planet). This also occurs when the formula attempts to divide by a cell that is empty.
#NAME?	The formula uses a name that Excel doesn't recognize. This can happen if you delete a name that's used in the formula or if you have unmatched quotes when using text.
#N/A	The formula is referring (directly or indirectly) to a cell that uses the NA function to signal that data is not available.
#NULL!	The formula uses an intersection of two ranges that don't intersect (this concept is described later in the chapter).
#NUM!	A problem with a value exists; for example, you specified a negative number where a positive number is expected.
#REF!	The formula refers to a cell that isn't valid. This can happen if the cell has been deleted from the worksheet.
#VALUE!	The formula includes an argument or operand of the wrong type. An *operand* is a value or cell reference that a formula uses to calculate a result.

The following are the four ways to get into cell-edit mode:

✦ Double-click the cell, which enables you to edit the cell contents directly in the cell.

✦ Press F2, which enables you to edit the cell contents directly in the cell.

✦ Select the cell that you want to edit, and then click in the formula bar. This enables you to edit the cell contents in the formula bar.

✦ Click the Edit Formula button in the Formula bar to access the Formula Palette.

Cross-Reference

Chapter 5 also discusses these methods.

While you're editing a formula, you can select multiple characters either by dragging the mouse over them or by holding down Shift while you use the direction keys.

You might have a lengthy formula that you can't seem to edit correctly — and Excel won't let you enter it because of the error. In this case, you can convert the formula to text and tackle it again later. To convert a formula to text, just remove the initial equal sign (=). When you're ready to try again, insert the initial equal sign to convert the cell contents back to a formula.

Changing When Formulas Are Calculated

You've probably noticed that Excel calculates the formulas in your worksheet immediately. If you change any cells that the formula uses, Excel displays the formula's new result, with no effort on your part. All this happens when Excel's Calculation mode is set to Automatic. In Automatic Calculation mode (which is the default mode), Excel follows these rules when calculating your worksheet:

✦ When you make a change — enter or edit data or formulas, for example — Excel calculates immediately those formulas that depend on new or edited data.

✦ If Excel is in the middle of a lengthy calculation, it temporarily suspends the calculation when you need to perform other worksheet tasks; it resumes when you're finished.

✦ Formulas are evaluated in a natural sequence. In other words, if a formula in cell D12 depends on the result of a formula in cell D11, Excel calculates cell D11 before calculating D12.

Sometimes, however, you may want to control when Excel calculates formulas. For example, if you create a worksheet with thousands of complex formulas, you'll find that things can slow to a snail's pace while Excel does its thing. In such a case, set Excel's calculation mode to Manual, which you can do in the Calculation tab of the Options dialog box (see Figure 8-9).

To select Manual calculation mode, click the Manual option button. When you switch to Manual calculation mode, Excel automatically places a check in the Recalculate before save check box. You can remove the check if you want to speed up file saving operations.

If your worksheet uses any data tables (described in Chapter 36), you may want to select the Automatic except tables option. Large data tables calculate notoriously slowly.

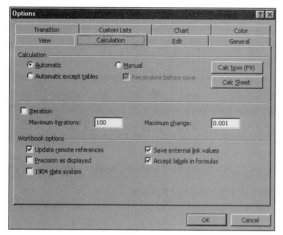

Figure 8-9: The Options dialog box lets you control when Excel calculates formulas.

When you're working in Manual calculation mode, Excel displays Calculate in the status bar when you have any uncalculated formulas. You can use the following shortcut keys to recalculate the formulas:

✦ **F9:** Calculates the formulas in all open workbooks

✦ **Shift+F9:** Calculates only the formulas in the active worksheet. Other worksheets in the same workbook aren't calculated.

✦ **Ctrl+Alt+F9:** This keyboard shortcut combination isn't documented. It forces a complete recalculation. This shortcut became popular when several recalculation bugs in Excel 97 surfaced.

Note   Excel's Calculation mode isn't specific to a particular worksheet. When you change Excel's Calculation mode, it affects all open workbooks, not just the active workbook.

Handling Circular References

When you're entering formulas, you may occasionally see a message from Excel like the one shown in Figure 8-10, indicating that the formula you just entered will result in a *circular reference*. A circular reference occurs when a formula refers to its own value—either directly or indirectly. For example, you create a circular reference if you enter **=A1+A2+A3** into cell A3, because the formula in cell A3 refers to cell A3. Every time the formula in A3 is calculated, it must be calculated again because A3 has changed. The calculation would go on forever—in other words, the answer will never be resolved.

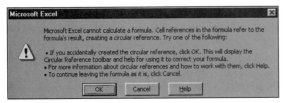

Figure 8-10: Excel's way of telling you that your formula contains a circular reference

When you get the circular reference message after entering a formula, Excel gives you two options:

✦ Click OK to attempt to locate the circular reference

✦ Click Cancel to enter the formula as-is

Usually, you want to correct any circular references, so you should choose OK. When you do so, Excel displays the Help topic on circular references and the Circular Reference toolbar (see Figure 8-11). On the Circular Reference toolbar, click the first cell in the Navigate Circular Reference drop-down list box, and then examine the cell's formula. If you cannot determine whether the cell is the cause of the circular reference, click the next cell in the Navigate Circular Reference box. Continue to review the formulas until the status bar no longer displays Circular.

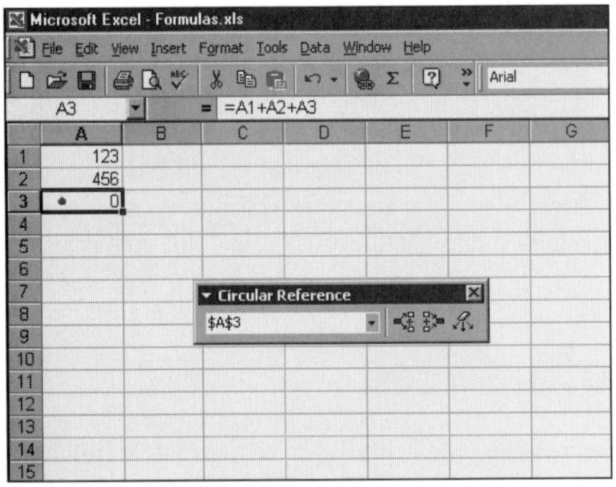

Figure 8-11: The Circular Reference toolbar

If you ignore the circular reference message (by clicking Cancel), Excel lets you enter the formula, and displays a message in the status bar to remind you that a circular reference exists. In this case, the message reads Circular: A3. If you activate a different workbook, the message simply displays Circular (without the cell reference).

Note　Excel won't tell you about a circular reference if the Iteration setting is on. You can check this in the Options dialog box (in the Calculation tab). If Iteration is on, Excel performs the circular calculation the number of times specified in the Maximum iterations field (or until the value changes by less than 0.001 — or whatever value is in the Maximum change field). In a few situations, you may use a circular reference intentionally (explained in a following section). In these cases, the Iteration setting must be on. However, keeping the Iteration setting turned off is best, so that you are warned of circular references. Most of the time, a circular reference indicates an error that you must correct.

Indirect Circular References

Usually, a circular reference is quite obvious and, therefore, easy to identify and correct. Sometimes, however, circular references are indirect. In other words, a formula may refer to a formula that refers to a formula that refers back to the original formula. In some cases, it may require a bit of detective work to get to the problem.

Cross-Reference　You may be able to get some assistance identifying a formula's dependents and precedents by using the tools on the Circular Reference toolbar, which are discussed in Chapter 30.

Intentional Circular References

As mentioned previously, you can use a circular reference to your advantage in some situations. Figure 8-12 shows a simple example.

	A	B	C	D
	Intentional Circular Reference.xls			
1	Gross Income	250,000		
2	Expenses	137,500		
3	Contributions	5,357	=5%*Net_Profit	
4	Net Profit	107,143	=Gross_Income-Expenses-Contributions	
5				
6				
7		Toggle Interation		
8		On/Off		
9				
10				
11				
12				
13				

Figure 8-12: An example of an intentional circular reference

In this example, a company has a policy of contributing five percent of its net profit to charity. The contribution itself, however, is considered an expense and is therefore subtracted from the net profit figure. This produces a circular reference — but this circular reference can be resolved if the Excel's Iteration setting is turned on.

On the CD-ROM   This workbook is available on the companion CD-ROM.

The Contributions cell contains the following formula:

```
=5%*Net_Profit
```

The Net Profit cell contains the following formula:

```
=Gross_Income-Expenses-Contributions
```

These formulas produce a resolvable circular reference. Excel keeps calculating until the formula results don't change anymore. To get a feel for how this works, substitute various values for Gross Income and Expenses. If the Iteration setting is off, Excel displays its Circular Reference message and won't display the correct result. If the Iteration setting is on, Excel keeps calculating until the Contributions value is, indeed, five percent of Net Profit. In other words, the result becomes increasingly more accurate until it converges on the final solution. For your convenience, I include a button on the worksheet that toggles the Iteration setting on and off by using a simple macro.

Note   Depending on your application, you may need to adjust the settings in the Maximum iterations field or the Maximum change field in the Options dialog box. For example, to increase accuracy, you can make the Maximum change field smaller. If the result doesn't converge after 100 iterations, you can increase the Maximum iterations field.

Using AutoFill Rather than Formulas

Chapter 7 discusses AutoFill as a quick way to copy a cell to adjacent cells. AutoFill also has some other uses, which may even substitute for formulas in some cases. I'm surprised to find that many experienced Excel users don't take advantage of the AutoFill feature — which can be a real time-saver.

Besides being a shortcut way to copy cells, AutoFill can quickly create a series of incremental values. For example, if you need a list of values from 1 to 100 to appear in A1:A100, you can do it with formulas. You enter **1** in cell A1, the formula **=A1+1** into cell A2, and then copy the formula to the 98 cells below.

You also can use AutoFill to create the series for you without using a formula. To do so, enter **1** into cell A1 and **2** into cell A2. Select A1:A2 and drag the fill handle down to cell A100. When you use AutoFill in this manner, Excel analyzes the selected cells and uses this information to complete the series. If cell A1 contained 1 and cell A2 contained 3, Excel recognizes this pattern and fills in 5, 7, 9, and so on. This also works with decreasing series (10, 9, 8, and so on) and dates. If no pattern is discernible in the selected cells, Excel performs a linear regression and fills in values on the calculated trend line.

Excel also recognizes common series names, such as days and months. If you enter Monday into a cell and then drag its fill handle, Excel fills in the successive days of the week. You also can create custom AutoFill lists by using the Custom Lists tab of the Options dialog box. Finally, if you drag the fill handle with the right-mouse button, Excel displays a shortcut menu to let you select an AutoFill option.

Advanced Naming Techniques

As promised in the preceding chapter, this section describes some additional techniques that involve names.

Sheet-level names

Usually, you can use a range name that you create anywhere within the workbook. In other words, names, by default, are "workbook level" names rather than "sheet level" names. But what if you have several worksheets in a workbook and you want to use the same name (such as Dept_Total) on each sheet? In this case, you need to create sheet-level names.

To define the name Dept_Total in more than one worksheet, activate the worksheet in which you want to define the name, choose Insert ⇨ name ⇨ Define, and then, in the Names in workbook box, precede the name with the worksheet name and an exclamation point. For example, to define the name Dept_Total on Sheet2, activate Sheet2 and enter the following in the Define Name dialog box:

```
Sheet2!Dept_Total
```

If the worksheet name contains at least one space, enclose the worksheet name in single quotation marks, like this:

```
'Adv Dept'!Dept_Total
```

You also can create a sheet-level name by using the Name box (located at the left side of the formula bar). Select the cell or range, click in the Name box, and enter the name, preceded by the sheet's name and an exclamation point (as shown previously). Press Enter to create the name.

When you write a formula that uses a sheet-level name on the sheet in which it's defined, you don't need to include the worksheet name in the range name (the Name box won't display the worksheet name either). If you use the name in a formula on a different worksheet, however, you must use the entire name (sheet name, exclamation point, and name).

Note Only the sheet-level names on the current sheet appear in the Name box. Similarly, only sheet-level names in the current sheet appear in the list when you open the Paste Name or Define Name dialog boxes.

Using sheet-level names can become complicated if you have an identical book-level name and sheet-level name (yes, Excel does allow this). In such a case, the sheet-level name takes precedence over the book-level name — but only in the worksheet in which you defined the sheet-level name. For example, you might have defined a book-level name of Total for a cell on Sheet1. You also can define a sheet-level name of Total (in, say Sheet2). When Sheet2 is active, Total refers to the sheet-level name. When any other sheet is active, Total refers to the book-level name. You can refer to a sheet-level name in a different worksheet, however, by preceding the name with the worksheet name and an exclamation point (such as Sheet1!Total). To make your life easier, just avoid using the same name at the book level and sheet level.

Using multisheet names

Names even can extend into the third dimension; that is, they can extend across multiple worksheets in a workbook. You can't simply select the multisheet range and enter a name in the Name box, however. Excel makes you do a little additional work to define a multisheet name.

You must use the Define Name dialog box to create a multisheet name, and you must enter the reference in the Refers to box manually. The format for a multisheet reference is as follows:

```
FirstSheet:LastSheet!RangeReference
```

In Figure 8-13, a multisheet name is being defined for A1:C12 that extends across Sheet1, Sheet2, and Sheet3.

After the name is defined, you can use it in formulas. This name won't appear in the Name box, however, or in the Go To dialog box. In other words, Excel lets you define the name, but it doesn't give you a way to select automatically the cells to which the name refers.

Figure 8-13: Creating a multisheet name

Naming constants

Even many advanced Excel users don't realize that you can give a name to an item that doesn't even appear in a cell. For example, if formulas in your worksheet use a sales tax rate, you would probably insert the tax rate value into a cell and use this cell reference in your formulas. To make things easier, you would probably also name this cell something like SalesTax.

Here's another way to do it: Choose Insert ➪ name ➪ Define (or press Ctrl+F3) to bring up the Define Name dialog box. Enter the name (in this case, **SalesTax**) into the Names in workbook field. Then, click the Refers to box, delete its contents, and replace it with a value such as **.075** (see Figure 8-14). Don't precede the constant with an equal sign. Click OK to close the dialog box.

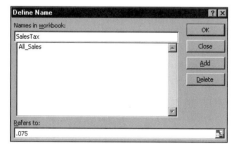

Figure 8-14: Defining a name that refers to a constant

You just created a name that refers to a constant rather than a cell or range. If you type =**SalesTax** into a cell, this simple formula returns 0.075 — the constant that you defined. You also can use this constant in a formula such as =A1*SalesTax.

As with all names, named constants are stored with the workbook. They can be used on any worksheet in the workbook.

In the preceding example, the constant was a value. A constant also can be text, however. For example, you can define a constant for your company's name. If you work for Microsoft, you can define the name MS for Microsoft Corporation.

Note   Named constants don't appear in the Name box or in the Go To dialog box — which makes sense, because these constants don't reside anywhere tangible. They do appear in the Paste Names dialog box, however, which *does* make sense, because you'll use these names in formulas.

As you might expect, you can change the value of the constant by accessing the Define Name dialog box and simply changing the value in the Refers to box. When you close the dialog box, Excel uses the new value to recalculate the formulas that use this name.

Although this technique is useful in many situations, the value is rather difficult to change. Having a constant located in a cell makes it much easier to modify. If the value is truly a "constant," however, you won't need to change it.

Naming formulas

This section takes the preceding section to the next logical level: naming formulas. Figure 8-15 shows an example of this. In this case, the name MonthlyRate refers to the following formula:

```
=Sheet3!$B$1/12
```

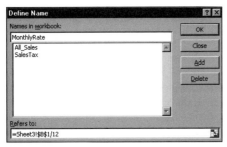

Figure 8-15: Excel lets you give a name to a formula that doesn't exist in the worksheet.

When you use the name MonthlyRate in a formula, it uses the value in B1 divided by 12. Notice that the cell reference is an absolute reference.

Naming formulas gets more interesting when you use relative references rather than absolute references. When you use the pointing technique to create a formula in the Refers to box, Excel always uses absolute cell references, which is unlike its behavior when you create a formula in a cell.

Figure 8-16 shows a name, Power, being created for the following formula:

```
=Sheet1!A1^Sheet1!B1
```

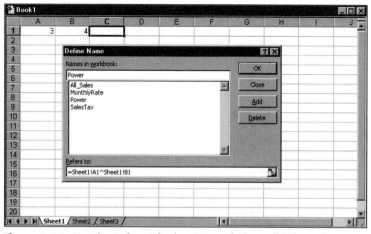

Figure 8-16: Naming a formula that uses relative cell references

Notice that cell C1 is the active cell, which is very important. When you use this named formula in a worksheet, the cell references are always relative to the cell that contains the name. For example, if you enter **=POWER** into cell D12, cell D12 displays the result of B12 raised to the power of the value contained in cell C12.

Range intersections

This section describes an interesting concept that is unique to Excel: *range intersections*. Excel uses an intersection operator — a space — to determine the overlapping references in two ranges. Figure 8-17 shows a simple example. The formula in cell G5 is

```
=B1:B7 A4:E4
```

and returns 180, the value in cell B4 — that is, the value at the intersection of the two ranges.

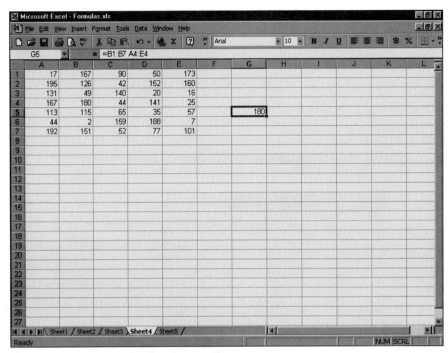

Figure 8-17: An example of an intersecting range

The intersection operator is one of three *reference* operators for ranges. Table 8-5 lists these operators.

Table 8-5
Reference Operators for Ranges

Operator	What It Does
: (colon)	Specifies a range
, (comma)	Specifies the union of two ranges
(space)	Specifies the intersection of two ranges

The real value of knowing about range intersections is apparent when you use names. Examine Figure 8-18, which shows a table of values. I selected the entire table and then used the Insert ⇨ name ⇨ Create command to create names automatically.

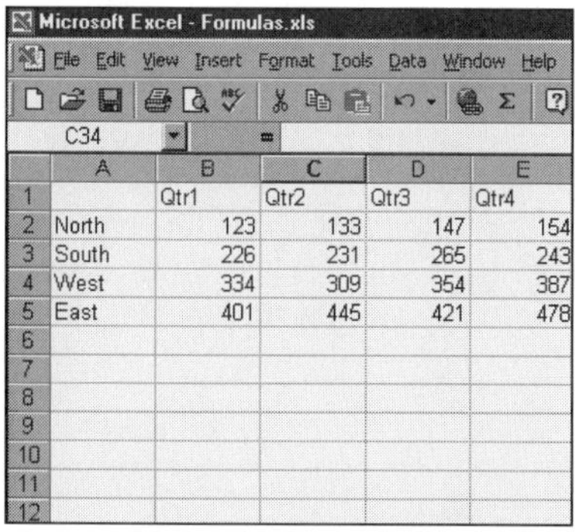

Figure 8-18: This table demonstrates how to use range intersections.

Excel created the following names:

North	=Sheet1!$B$2:$E$2	Qtr1	=Sheet1!$B$2:$B$5
South	=Sheet1!$B$3:$E$3	Qtr2	=Sheet1!$C$2:$C$5
West	=Sheet1!$B$4:$E$4	Qtr3	=Sheet1!$D$2:$D$5
East	=Sheet1!$B$5:$E$5	Qtr4	=Sheet1!$E$2:$E$5

With these names defined, you'll find that you can create formulas that are very easy to read. For example, to calculate the total for Quarter 4, just use this formula:

```
=SUM(Qtr4)
```

But things really get interesting when you use the intersection operator. Move to any blank cell and enter the following formula:

```
=Qtr1 West
```

This formula returns the value for the first quarter for the West region. In other words, it returns the value where the Qtr1 range intersects with the West range. Naming ranges in this manner can help you create very readable formulas.

Applying names to existing references

When you create a new name for a cell or a range, Excel doesn't automatically use the name in place of existing references in your formulas. For example, assume that you have the following formula in cell F10: =A1–A2.

If you define a name Income for A1 and Expenses for A2, Excel won't automatically change your formula to =Income–Expenses. Replacing cell or range references with their corresponding names is fairly easy, however.

Using Row and Column Headings As "Names"

Beginning with Excel 97, you have access to a feature that lets you use "names" without actually defining them. To understand how this feature works, refer to the accompanying figure, which shows a typical table, with row and column headers. Excel lets you use the row and column headers as names in your formulas (and you don't have to define the names). For example, to refer to the cell that holds February sales for the South region, use the following formula:

```
=Feb South
```

In other words, the formula returns the cell that intersects the Feb column and the South row. You can also use this technique with functions. Here's a formula that returns the total sales for March:

```
=SUM(March)
```

Excel handles all the details for you. If you change a row or column heading, all the formulas change automatically to use the new label.

	A	B	C	D	E	F
1		Jan	Feb	Mar	Total	
2	North	11	14	15	40	
3	South	31	34	44	109	
4	West	43	32	56	131	
5	East	109	89	65	263	
6						
7						
8						
9						

This technique has a few limitations. The labels are not "real" names—they don't appear in the Define Name dialog box, nor do they appear in the Name box. For this reason, you can use this method only when the formula refers to cells on the same sheet. The real problem, however, is the inability to document the names. In other words, you can never tell for sure exactly what a name refers to. For that reason, I don't recommend using this feature. Rather, take a few extra seconds and create a "real" range name.

To apply names to cell references in formulas after the fact, start by selecting the range that you want to modify. Then, choose Insert ➪ name ➪ Apply. Excel displays the Apply Names dialog box, shown in Figure 8-19 Select the names that you want to apply by clicking them and then click OK. Excel replaces the range references with the names in the selected cells.

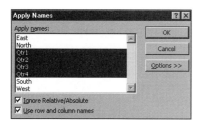

Figure 8-19: The Apply Names dialog box lets you replace cell or range references with names.

The Apply Names dialog box has some options. If you click the Options button, the dialog box expands to display even more options. Most of the time, the defaults work just fine. For more control over the names that you apply, however, you may want to use one or more of its options. These are described in Excel's online Help.

Tips for Working with Formulas

This chapter concludes with a few additional tips and pointers relevant to formulas.

Don't "hard code" values

When you create a formula, think twice before using a value in the formula. For example, if your formula calculates sales tax (which is 6.5 percent), you may be tempted to enter a formula such as the following:

```
+A1*.065
```

A better approach is to insert the sales tax rate in a cell and use the cell reference. Or, you can define it as a named constant by using the technique presented earlier in this chapter. Doing so makes modifying and maintaining your worksheet easier. For example, if the sales tax rate changed to 6.75 percent, you would have to modify every formula that uses the old value. If the tax rate is stored in a cell, you simply change one cell and Excel updates all the formulas.

Using the formula bar as a calculator

If you simply need to perform a calculation, you can use the formula bar as a calculator. For example, enter the following formula—but don't press Enter:

```
=(145*1.05)/12
```

If you press Enter, Excel enters the formula into the cell. But because this formula always returns the same result, you might prefer to store the formula's result rather than the formula. To do so, press F9, and then press Enter. Excel stores the formula's result (12.6875) rather than the formula. This also works if the formula uses cell references.

This is most useful when you use worksheet functions. For example, to enter the square root of 221 into a cell, enter **=SQRT(221)**, press F9, and then press Enter. Excel enters the result: 14.8660687473185. You also can use this technique to evaluate only part of a formula. Consider this formula:

```
=(145*1.05)/A1
```

If you want to convert to a value just the part in the parentheses, select the part of the formula that you want to evaluate (that is, select 145*1.05). Then, press F9, followed by Enter. Excel converts the formula to the following:

```
=152.25/A1
```

Making an exact copy of a formula

As you know, when you copy a formula, Excel adjusts its cell references when you paste the formula to a different location. Sometimes, you may want to make an exact copy of the formula. One way to do this is to convert the cell references to absolute values, but this isn't always desirable. A better approach is to select the formula in edit mode and then copy it to the clipboards as text. You can do this in several ways. Here's a step-by-step example of how to make an exact copy of the formula in A1 and copy it to A2:

1. Double-click A1 to get into edit mode.

2. Drag the mouse to select the entire formula. You can drag from left to right or from right to left.

3. Click the Copy button on the Standard toolbar. This copies the selected text to the clipboards.

4. Press Enter to end edit mode.

5. Select cell A2.

6. Click the Paste button to paste the text into cell A2.

You also can use this technique to copy just *part* of a formula, to use that part in another formula. Just select the part of the formula that you want to copy by dragging the mouse; then, use any of the available techniques to copy the selection to the clipboard. You can then paste the text to another cell.

Formulas (or parts of formulas) copied in this manner won't have their cell references adjusted when they are pasted to a new cell, because the formulas are being copied as text, not as actual formulas.

Converting formulas to values

If you have a range of formulas that will always produce the same result (that is, dead formulas), you may want to convert them to values. As discussed in the previous chapter, you can use the Edit ➪ Paste Special command to do this. Assume that range A1:A20 contains formulas that have calculated results that will never change or that you don't want to change. For example, if you use the @RAND function to create a set of random numbers, and you don't want Excel to recalculate the random numbers each time that you press Enter, convert the formulas to values. To convert these formulas to values:

1. Select A1:A20.

2. Click the Copy button.

3. Select Edit ➪ Paste Special. Excel displays its Paste Special dialog box.

4. Click the Values option button and then click OK.

5. Press Enter or Esc to cancel paste mode.

Array formulas

Excel supports another type of formula called an *array formula*. Array formulas can be extremely powerful, because they let you work with complete ranges of cells rather than individual cells. You'll find that you can perform some amazing feats by using array formulas. This is a rather advanced concept, which is covered in Chapter 26.

Summary

This chapter introduces the concept of formulas. Formulas are entered into cells and use values found in other cells to return a result. This chapter explains how to enter and edit formulas, when to use absolute cell references, how to identify errors in your formulas, and how to handle circular references (either accidental or intentional). It also explains how to set Excel to Manual recalculation mode — and why you would need to do so. The chapter continues by discussing some additional naming techniques that can make your formulas even more powerful. This chapter concludes with a series of tips that can help you get the most out of formulas.

✦   ✦   ✦

Using Worksheet Functions

T he preceding chapter discussed formulas. This chapter continues with coverage of Excel's built-in worksheet functions.

What Is a Function?

Functions, in essence, are built-in tools that you use in formulas. They can make your formulas perform powerful feats and save you a lot of time. Functions can do the following:

✦ Simplify your formulas

✦ Allow formulas to perform calculations that are otherwise impossible

✦ Speed up some editing tasks

✦ Allow "conditional" execution of formulas — giving them rudimentary decision-making capability

Function examples

A built-in function can simplify a formula significantly. To calculate the average of the values in ten cells (A1:A10) without using a function, you need to construct a formula like this:

```
=(A1+A2+A3+A4+A5+A6+A7+A8+A9+A10)/10
```

Not very pretty, is it? Even worse, you would need to edit this formula if you added another cell to the range. You can replace this formula with a much simpler one that uses one of Excel's built-in worksheet functions:

```
=AVERAGE(A1:A10)
```

Next, look at how using a function can enable you to perform calculations that would not be possible otherwise. What if you need to determine the largest value in a range? A formula can't tell you the answer without using a function. Here's a simple formula that returns the largest value in the range A1:D100:

```
=MAX(A1:D100)
```

Functions also can sometimes eliminate manual editing. Assume that you have a worksheet that contains 1,000 names in cells A1:A1000, and all the names appear in all capital letters. Your boss sees the listing and informs you that the names will be mail-merged with a form letter and that all-uppercase is not acceptable: for example, JOHN F. CRANE must appear as John F. Crane. You *could* spend the next several hours reentering the list — or you could use a formula like the following, which uses a function to convert the text in cell A1 to proper case:

```
=PROPER(A1)
```

Enter this formula once in cell B1 and then copy it down to the next 999 rows. Then, select B1:B1000 and use the Edit ➪ Paste Special command (with the Values option) to convert the formulas to values. Delete the original column, and you've just accomplished several hours of work in less than a minute.

One last example should convince you of the power of functions. Suppose that you have a worksheet that calculates sales commissions. If the salesperson sold more than $100,000 of product, the commission rate is 7.5 percent; otherwise, the commission rate is 5.0 percent. Without using a function, you would have to create two different formulas and make sure that you use the correct formula for each sales amount. Here's a formula that uses the IF function to ensure that you calculate the correct commission, regardless of the sales amount:

```
=IF(A1<100000,A1*5%,A1*7.5%)
```

More about functions

All told, Excel includes more than 300 functions. And if that's not enough, you can purchase additional specialized functions from third-party suppliers, and even create your own custom functions (using VBA), if you're so inclined.

You can easily be overwhelmed by the sheer number of functions, but you'll probably find that you use only a dozen or so of the functions on a regular basis. And as you'll see, Excel's Paste Function dialog box (described later in this chapter) makes it easy to locate and insert a function, even if it's not one that you use frequently.

Cross-Reference Appendix C contains a complete listing of Excel's worksheet functions, with a brief description of each.

Function Arguments

In the preceding examples, you may have noticed that all the functions used parentheses. The information inside the parentheses is called an *argument*. Functions vary in how they use arguments. Depending on the function, a function may use:

✦ No arguments

✦ One argument

✦ A fixed number of arguments

✦ An indeterminate number of arguments

✦ Optional arguments

The RAND function, which returns a random number between 0 and 1, doesn't use an argument Even if a function doesn't use an argument, however, you must still provide a set of empty parentheses, like this:

```
=RAND()
```

If a function uses more than one argument, you must separate each argument by a comma. The examples at the beginning of the chapter used cell references for arguments. Excel is quite flexible when it comes to function arguments, however. An argument can consist of a cell reference, literal values, literal text strings, or expressions.

Accommodating Former 1-2-3 Users

If you've ever used any of the 1-2-3 spreadsheets (or any versions of Quattro Pro), you'll recall that these products require you to type an "at" sign (@) before a function name. Excel is smart enough to distinguish functions without you having to flag them with a symbol.

Because old habits die hard, however, Excel accepts @ symbols when you type functions in your formulas — but it removes them as soon as you enter the formula.

These competing products also use two dots (..) as a range operator — for example, A1..A10. Excel also lets you use this notation when you type formulas, but Excel replaces the notation with its own range operator, a colon (:).

This accommodation goes only so far, however. Excel still insists that you use the standard Excel function names, and it doesn't recognize or translate the function names used in other spreadsheets. For example, if you enter the 1-2-3 @AVG function, Excel flags it as an error (Excel's name for this function is AVERAGE).

Using names as arguments

As you've seen, functions can use cell or range references for their arguments. When Excel calculates the formula, it simply uses the current contents of the cell or range to perform its calculations. The SUM function returns the sum of its argument(s). To calculate the sum of the values in A1:D20, you can use:

```
=SUM(A1:A20)
```

And, not surprisingly, if you've defined a name for A1:A20 (such as Sales), you can use the name in place of the reference:

```
=SUM(Sales)
```

In some cases, you may find it useful to use an entire column or row as an argument. For example, the formula that follows sums all values in column B:

```
=SUM(B:B)
```

This technique is particularly useful if the range that you're summing changes (if you're continually adding new sales figures, for instance). If you do use an entire row or column, just make sure that the row or column doesn't contain extraneous information that you don't want included in the sum. You might think that using such a large range (a column consists of 65,536 cells) might slow down calculation time—this isn't true. Excel's recalculation engine is quite efficient.

Literal arguments

A *literal argument* is a value or text string that you enter into a function. For example, the SQRT function takes one argument. In the following example, the formula uses a literal value for the function's argument:

```
=SQRT(225)
```

Using a literal argument with a simple function like this one defeats the purpose of using a formula. This formula always returns the same value, so it could just as easily be replaced with the value 15. Using literal arguments makes more sense with formulas that use more than one argument. For example, the LEFT function (which takes two arguments) returns characters from the beginning of its first argument; the second argument specifies the number of characters. If cell A1 contains the text Budget, the following formula returns the first letter, or *B:*

```
=LEFT(A1,1)
```

Expressions as arguments

Excel also lets you use *expressions* as arguments. Think of an expression as a formula within a formula. When Excel encounters an expression as a function's argument, it evaluates the expression and then uses the result as the argument's value. Here's an example:

```
=SQRT((A1^2)+(A2^2))
```

This formula uses the SQRT function, and its single argument is the following expression:

```
(A1^2)+(A2^2)
```

When Excel evaluates the formula, it starts by evaluating the expression in the argument and then computes the square root of the result.

Other functions as arguments

Because Excel can evaluate expressions as arguments, you shouldn't be surprised that these expressions can include other functions. Writing formulas that have functions within functions is sometimes known as *nesting* functions. Excel starts by evaluating the most deeply nested expression and works its way out. Here's an example of a nested function:

```
=SIN(RADIANS(B9))
```

The RADIANS function converts degrees to radians — which is the unit used by all of Excel's trigonometric functions. If cell B9 contains an angle in degrees, the RADIANS function converts it to radians, and then the SIN function computes the sine of the angle.

With a few exception, you can nest functions as deeply as you need, as long as you don't exceed the 1,024-character limit for a formula.

Ways to Enter a Function

You have two ways available to enter a function into a formula: manually or by using the Paste Function dialog box.

Changeable Range References in Excel 2000

Many functions contain a range reference as an argument. For example, the function that follows uses the range A10:A20:

    =SUM(A10:A20)

If you add a new row between rows 10 and 20, Excel expands the formula's range reference for you automatically. If you add a new row between rows 12 and 13, the formula changes to the following:

    =SUM(A10:A21)

In most cases, this is exactly what you want to happen.

In prior versions of Excel, if you inserted a new row at row 10, however, Excel would *not* include the new row in the range reference; that is, Excel wouldn't automatically expand the argument range reference to include rows that you add at the top or bottom of the range. Because this behavior often confused new users, Microsoft changed Excel's behavior in Excel 2000. In Excel 2000, when you add a row at any place in a referenced range, Excel changes the function that referenced the original range to include the new row automatically.

Entering a function manually

If you're familiar with a particular function — you know how many arguments it takes and the types of arguments — you may choose simply to type the function and its arguments into your formula. Often, this method is the most efficient.

Tip   When you enter a function, Excel always converts the function's name to uppercase. Thus, always using lowercase when you type functions is a good idea: If Excel doesn't convert it to uppercase when you press Enter, then Excel doesn't recognize your entry as a function — which means that you spelled it incorrectly.

If you omit the closing parenthesis, Excel adds it for you automatically. For example, if you type **=SUM(A1:C12** and press Enter, Excel corrects the formula by adding the right parenthesis.

Pasting a function

Formula Palette assists you by providing a way to enter a function and its arguments in a semiautomated manner. Using the Formula Palette ensures that the function is spelled correctly and has the proper number of arguments in the correct order.

To insert a function, start by selecting the function from the Paste Function dialog box, shown in Figure 9-1. You can open this dialog box by using any of the following methods:

✦ Choose the Insert ➪ Function command from the menu

✦ Click the Paste Function button on the Standard toolbar

✦ Press Shift+F3

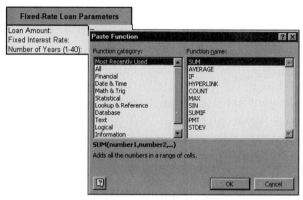

Figure 9-1: The Paste Function dialog box

The Paste Function dialog box shows the Function category list on the left side of the dialog box. When you select a category, the Function name list box displays the functions in the selected category.

The Most Recently Used category lists the functions that you've used most recently. The All category lists all the functions available across all categories. Use this if you know a function's name, but aren't sure of its category.

Tip   To select a function quickly in the Most Recently Used category, click the Edit Formula icon in the formula bar and then select the function from the function list (which occupies the space usually used by the Name box).

When you select a function in the Function name list box, notice that Excel displays the function (and its argument names) in the dialog box, along with a brief description of what the function does.

When you locate the function that you want to use, click OK. Excel's Formula Palette appears, as in Figure 9-2, and the Name box changes to the Formula List box. Use the Formula Palette to specify the arguments for the function. You can easily specify a range argument by clicking the Collapse Dialog button (the icon at the right edge of each box in the Formula Palette). Excel temporarily collapses the Formula Palette to a thin box, so that you can select a range in the worksheet. When you want to redisplay the Formula Palette, click the button again.

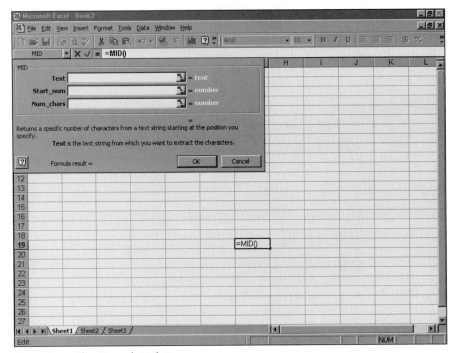

Figure 9-2: The Formula Palette

The Formula Palette usually appears directly below the formula bar, but you can move it to any other location by dragging it.

Inserting a function: An example

This section presents a step-by-step example that explains how to insert a function into a formula. The formula uses the AVERAGE function to compute the average of a range of cells. To insert a function into a formula, proceed as follows:

1. Open a new workbook and enter values into H1:H6 (any values will do).

2. Select cell H7. This cell will contain the formula.

3. Click the Insert Function button on the Standard toolbar. Excel displays its Paste Function dialog box.

4. Because the AVERAGE function is in the Statistical category, click Statistical in the Function category list box. The Function name list box displays the statistical functions.

5. Click AVERAGE in the Function name list box. The dialog box shows the function and its list of arguments. It also displays a brief description of the function.

6. Click the OK button. Excel closes the Paste Function dialog box and displays the Formula Palette (see Figure 9-3) to prompt you for the function's arguments.

Collapse Dialog button

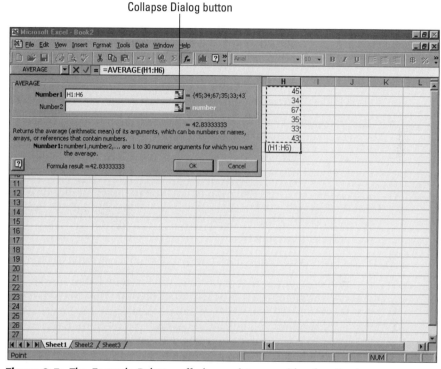

Figure 9-3: The Formula Palette, offering assistance with a function's arguments

Tip

You may not need to complete Steps 7, 8, and 9 if Excel suggests the correct range when the Formula Palette appears.

7. Click the Collapse Dialog button at the right edge of the box labeled Number1 to collapse the Formula Palette temporarily and shift to the worksheet, so that you can select a range.

8. Select the range H1:H6 in the worksheet. This range address appears in the collapsed box, and the formula bar shows the result.

9. Click the Collapse Dialog button again to redisplay the Formula Palette, which shows the formula result.

10. Because you're finding the average of only one range, you don't need to enter any additional arguments. Click the OK button.

Cell H7 now contains the following formula, which returns the average of the values in H1:H6:

```
=AVERAGE(H1:H6)
```

More about entering functions

The following are some additional tips to keep in mind when you use the Formula Palette to enter functions:

✦ Click the Help button (or press F1) at any time to get help about the function that you selected.

✦ If you're starting a new formula, the Formula Palette automatically provides the initial equal sign for you.

✦ If the active cell is not empty when you invoke the Formula Palette, you will be able to edit the formula.

✦ You can use the Paste Function dialog box to insert a function into an existing formula. Just edit the formula and move the insertion point to the location where you want to insert the function. Then, open the Paste Function dialog box and select the function.

✦ If you change your mind about entering a function, click the Cancel button.

✦ The number of boxes that you see in the Formula Palette is determined by the number of arguments used by the function that you selected. If a function uses no arguments, you won't see any boxes. If the function uses a variable number of arguments (such as the AVERAGE function), Excel adds a new box every time that you enter an optional argument.

✦ On the right side of each box, you'll see the current value for each argument.

✦ A few functions, such as INDEX, have more than one form. If you choose such a function, Excel displays another dialog box that lets you choose which form you want to use.

✦ If you only need help remembering a function's arguments, type an equal sign and the function's name, and then press Ctrl+Shift+A. Excel inserts the function with placeholders for the arguments. You need to replace these placeholders with actual arguments.

✦ To locate a function quickly in the Function name list that appears in the Paste Function dialog box, open the list box, type the first letter of the function name, and then scroll to the desired function. For example, if you have selected the All category and want to insert the SIN function, click anywhere on the Function name list box and press S. Excel selects the first function that begins with S — very close to SIN.

✦ If you're using the Formula Palette and want to use a function as the argument for a function (a nested function), click in the box where you want the argument to appear. Then, open the Function List and select the function. Excel will insert the nested function and prompt you for its arguments.

✦ If the active cell contains a formula that uses one or more functions, the Formula Palette lets you edit each function. In the formula bar, click the function that you want to edit. Figure 9-4 shows a formula with multiple functions.

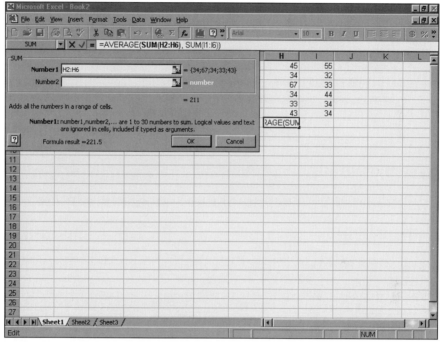

Figure 9-4: If the formula contains multiple functions, click the function in the formula bar to edit it.

Function Examples

This section presents examples of formulas that use functions. It covers all categories listed in the Paste Function dialog box, but not every available function. For more information about a particular function, consult the online Help. For a list of all functions by category, use the Paste Function dialog box.

Cross-Reference

You can also look at Appendix C for more functions by category.

Mathematical and trigonometric functions

Excel provides 50 functions in this category, more than enough to do some serious number crunching. The category includes common functions, such as SUM and INT, as well as plenty of esoteric functions.

INT

The INT function returns the integer (non-decimal) portion of a number by truncating all digits after the decimal point. The example that follows returns 412:

```
=INT(412.98)
```

RAND

The RAND function, which takes no arguments, returns a uniform random number that is greater than or equal to 0 and less than 1. "Uniform" means that all numbers have an equal chance of being generated. This function often is used in worksheets, to simulate events that aren't completely predictable — such as winning lottery numbers — and returns a new result whenever Excel calculates the worksheet.

In the example that follows, the formula returns a random number between 0 and 12 (but 12 will never be generated):

```
=RAND()*12
```

The following formula generates a random integer between two values. The cell named Lower contains the lower bound, and the cell named Upper contains the upper bound:

```
=INT((Upper-Lower+1)*RAND()+Lower)
```

Volatile Functions

Some Excel functions belong to a special class of functions called *volatile*. No, these aren't functions that cause your worksheet to explode. Rather, Excel recalculates a volatile function whenever it recalculates the workbook — even if the formula that contains the function is not involved in the recalculation.

The RAND function is an example of a volatile function, because it generates a new random number every time Excel calculates the worksheet. Other volatile functions are as follows:

AREAS	INDEX	OFFSET
CELL	INDIRECT	ROWS
COLUMNS	NOW	TODAY

A side effect of using these volatile functions is that Excel always prompts you to save the workbook — even if you made no changes. For example, if you open a workbook that contains any of these volatile functions, scroll around a bit (but don't change anything), and then close the file, Excel asks whether you want to save the workbook.

You can circumvent this behavior by using Manual Recalculation mode, with the Recalculate before Save option turned off.

ROMAN

The ROMAN function converts a value to its Roman-numeral equivalent (hey, I never said *all* the functions were useful). Unfortunately for old-movie buffs, no function exists to convert in the opposite direction. The function that follows returns MCMXCVIII:

```
=ROMAN(1998)
```

ROUND

The ROUND function rounds a value to a specified digit to the left or right of the decimal point. This function is often used to control the precision of your calculation. ROUND takes two arguments: the first is the value to be rounded; the second is the digit. If the second argument is negative, the rounding occurs to the left of the decimal point. Table 9-1 demonstrates, with some examples, how this works.

Table 9-1	
Examples of Using the ROUND Function	
Function	*Result*
=ROUND(123.457,2)	123.46
=ROUND(123.457,1)	123.50
=ROUND(123.457,0)	123.00
=ROUND(123.457,-1)	120.00
=ROUND(123.457,-2)	100.00
=ROUND(123.457,-3)	0.00

Caution   Don't confuse rounding a value with number formatting applied to a value. When a formula references a cell that has been rounded with the ROUND function, the formula uses the rounded value. If a number has been formatted to *appear* rounded, formulas that refer to that cell use the actual value stored.

Note   If your work involves rounding, also check out the ROUNDUP and ROUNDDOWN functions. In addition, the FLOOR and CEILING functions let you round to a specific multiple—for example, you can use FLOOR to round a value down to the nearest multiple of 10 (124.5 would be rounded to 130).

PI

The PI function returns the value of π significant to 14 decimal places. It doesn't take any arguments and is simply a shortcut for the value 3.14159265358979. In the example that follows, the formula calculates the area of a circle (the radius is stored in a cell named Radius):

```
=PI()*(Radius^2)
```

SIN

The SIN function returns the sine of an angle. The *sine* is defined as the ratio between the opposite side and the hypotenuse of a triangle. SIN takes one argument — the angle expressed in radians. To convert degrees to radians, use the RADIANS function (a DEGREES function also exists to do the opposite conversion). For example, if cell F21 contains an angle expressed in degrees, the formula that follows returns the sine:

```
=SIN(RADIANS(F21))
```

Excel contains the full complement of trigonometric functions. Consult the online Help for details.

SQRT

The SQRT function returns the square root of its argument. If the argument is negative, this function returns an error. The example that follows returns 32:

```
=SQRT(1024)
```

To compute a cube root, raise the value to the $1/3$ power. The example that follows returns the cube root of 32,768 — which is 32. Other roots can be calculated in a similar manner.

```
=32768^(1/3)
```

SUM

If you analyze a random sample of workbooks, you'll likely discover that SUM is the most widely used function. It's also among the simplest. The SUM function takes from 1 to 30 arguments. To calculate the sum of three ranges (A1:A10, C1:10, and E1:E10), you use three arguments, like this:

```
=SUM(A1:A10,C1:10,E1:E10)
```

The arguments don't have to be all the same type. For example, you can mix and match single cell references, range references, and literals, as follows:

```
=SUM(A1,C1:10,125)
```

Because the SUM function is so popular, the Excel designers made it very accessible — automatic, in fact. To insert a formula that uses the SUM function, just click the AutoSum button on the Standard toolbar. Excel analyzes the context and suggests a range for an argument. If it suggests correctly (which it usually does), press Enter or click the AutoSum button again. If Excel's guess is incorrect, just drag the mouse and make the selection yourself. To insert a series of SUM formulas — to add several columns of numbers, for example — select the entire range and then click AutoSum. In this case, Excel knows exactly what you want, so it doesn't ask you to confirm it.

SUMIF

The SUMIF function is useful for calculating conditional sums. Figure 9-5 displays a worksheet with a table that shows sales by month and by region. The SUMIF function is used in the formulas in column F. For example, the formula in F2 is as follows:

```
=SUMIF(B:B,E2,C:C)
```

	A	B	C	D	E	F	G	H
1	Month	Region	Sales		Regional Summary			
2	Jan	North	16,491		North	54,485		
3	Jan	South	14,557		South	55,089		
4	Jan	West	3,522		West	45,668		
5	Jan	East	22,041		East	61,846		
6	Feb	North	2,061		TOTAL	217,088		
7	Feb	South	21,813					
8	Feb	West	1,169		Monthly Summary			
9	Feb	East	12,486		Jan	56,611		
10	Mar	North	33,956		Feb	37,529		
11	Mar	South	18,318		Mar	79,155		
12	Mar	West	13,500		Apr	43,793		
13	Mar	East	13,381		TOTAL	217,088		
14	Apr	North	1,977					
15	Apr	South	401					
16	Apr	West	27,477					
17	Apr	East	13,938					
18								
19								

Figure 9-5: The SUMIF function returns the sum of values if the values meet specified criteria.

SUMIF takes three arguments. The first argument is the range that you're using in the selection criteria — in this case, the entire column B. The second argument is the selection criteria, a region name in the example. The third argument is the range of values to sum if the criteria are met. In this example, the formula in F2 adds the values in column C only if the corresponding text in column B matches the region in column E.

The figure also shows the data summarized by month. The formula in F9 is the following:

```
=SUMIF(A:A,E9,C:C)
```

You also can use Excel's pivot table feature to perform these operations.

Cross-Reference   Pivot tables are covered in Chapter 35.

Text functions

Although Excel is primarily known for its numerical prowess, it has 23 built-in functions that are designed to manipulate text, a few of which are demonstrated in this section.

CHAR

The CHAR function returns a single character that corresponds to the ANSI code specified in its argument (these codes range from 1 to 255). The CODE function performs the opposite conversion. The formula that follows returns the letter *A*:

```
=CHAR(65)
```

This function is most useful for returning symbols that are difficult or impossible to enter from the keyboard. For example, the formula that follows returns the copyright symbol (©):

```
=CHAR(169)
```

Figure 9-6 shows the characters returned by the CHAR function for arguments from 1 to 255 (using the Arial font).

A	B	C	D	E	F	G	H	I	J	K	L	M	N	O	P	Q	R	S	T	U	V
1	□	26	□	51	3	76	L	101	e	126	~	151	—	176	°	201	É	226	â	251	û
2	□	27	□	52	4	77	M	102	f	127	□	152	˜	177	±	202	Ê	227	ã	252	ü
3	□	28	□	53	5	78	N	103	g	128	□	153	™	178	²	203	Ë	228	ä	253	ý
4	□	29	□	54	6	79	O	104	h	129	□	154	š	179	³	204	Ì	229	å	254	þ
5	□	30	□	55	7	80	P	105	i	130	,	155	›	180	´	205	Í	230	æ	255	ÿ
6	□	31	□	56	8	81	Q	106	j	131	ƒ	156	œ	181	µ	206	Î	231	ç		
7	□	32		57	9	82	R	107	k	132	„	157	□	182	¶	207	Ï	232	è		
8	□	33	!	58	:	83	S	108	l	133	…	158	□	183	·	208	Ð	233	é		
9	□	34	"	59	;	84	T	109	m	134	†	159	Ÿ	184	¸	209	Ñ	234	ê		
10	□	35	#	60	<	85	U	110	n	135	‡	160		185	¹	210	Ò	235	ë		
11	□	36	$	61	=	86	V	111	o	136	ˆ	161	¡	186	º	211	Ó	236	ì		
12	□	37	%	62	>	87	W	112	p	137	‰	162	¢	187	»	212	Ô	237	í		
13	□	38	&	63	?	88	X	113	q	138	Š	163	£	188	¼	213	Õ	238	î		
14	□	39	'	64	@	89	Y	114	r	139	‹	164	¤	189	½	214	Ö	239	ï		
15	□	40	(	65	A	90	Z	115	s	140	Œ	165	¥	190	¾	215	×	240	ð		
16	□	41	)	66	B	91	[	116	t	141	□	166	¦	191	¿	216	Ø	241	ñ		
17	□	42	*	67	C	92	\	117	u	142	□	167	§	192	À	217	Ù	242	ò		
18	□	43	+	68	D	93	]	118	v	143	□	168	¨	193	Á	218	Ú	243	ó		
19	□	44	,	69	E	94	^	119	w	144	□	169	©	194	Â	219	Û	244	ô		
20	□	45	-	70	F	95	_	120	x	145	'	170	ª	195	Ã	220	Ü	245	õ		
21	□	46	.	71	G	96	`	121	y	146	'	171	«	196	Ä	221	Ý	246	ö		
22	□	47	/	72	H	97	a	122	z	147	"	172	¬	197	Å	222	Þ	247	÷		
23	□	48	0	73	I	98	b	123	{	148	"	173		198	Æ	223	ß	248	ø		
24	□	49	1	74	J	99	c	124			149	•	174	®	199	Ç	224	à	249	ù		
25	□	50	2	75	K	100	d	125	}	150	–	175	¯	200	È	225	á	250	ú		

Figure 9-6: Characters returned by the CHAR function

Note Not all codes produce printable characters, and the characters may vary depending on the font used.

LEFT

The LEFT function returns a string of characters of a specified length from another string, beginning at the leftmost position. This function uses two arguments. The first argument is the string and the second argument (optional) is the number of characters. If the second argument is omitted, Excel extracts the first character from the text. In the example that follows, the formula returns the letter *B*:

```
=LEFT("B.B. King")
```

The formula that follows returns the string *Alber*:

```
=LEFT("Albert King",5)
```

Note Excel also has a RIGHT function that extracts characters from the right of a string of characters and a MID function (described after the next section) that extracts characters from any position.

LEN

The LEN function returns the number of characters in a string of text. For example, the following formula returns 12:

```
=LEN("Stratocaster")
```

If you don't want to count leading or trailing spaces, use the LEN function with a nested TRIM function. For example, if you want to know the number of characters in the text in cell A1 without counting spaces, use this formula:

```
=LEN(TRIM(A1))
```

MID

The MID function returns characters from a text string. It takes three arguments. The first argument is the text string. The second argument is the position at which you want to begin extracting. The third argument is the number of characters that you want to extract. If cell A1 contains the text *Joe Louis Walker*, the formula that follows returns *Louis*:

```
=MID(A1,5,5)
```

REPLACE

The REPLACE function replaces characters with other characters. The first argument is the text containing the string that you're replacing. The second argument is the character position at which you want to start replacing. The third argument is the number of characters to replace. The fourth argument is the new text that will replace the existing text. In the example that follows, the formula returns *Albert Collins*:

```
=REPLACE("Albert King",8,4,"Collins")
```

SEARCH

The SEARCH function lets you identify the position in a string of text in which another string occurs. The function takes three arguments. The first argument is the text for which you're searching. The second argument is the string that you want to search. The third argument (optional) is the position at which you want to start searching. If you omit the third argument, Excel starts searching from the beginning of the text.

In the example that follows, assume that cell A1 contains the text *John Lee Hooker*. The formula searches for a space and returns 5, because the first space character was found at the fifth character position.

```
=SEARCH(" ",A1,1)
```

To find the second space in the text, use a nested SEARCH function that uses the result of the first search (incremented by one character) as the third argument:

```
=SEARCH(" ",A1,SEARCH(" ",A1,1)+1)
```

The following formula uses the LEFT function to return the characters to the left of the first space in the text in cell A1. For example, if A1 contains *Jimmy Dawkins*, the formula would return the first name *Jimmy*:

```
=LEFT(A1,SEARCH(" ",A1))
```

The preceding formula has a slight flaw: if the text in cell A1 contains no spaces, the formula results in an error. Here's an improved version that returns the entire string in A1 if it doesn't contains a space:

```
=IF(ISERROR(SEARCH(" ",A1)),A1,LEFT(A1,SEARCH(" ",A1)))
```

UPPER

The UPPER function converts characters to uppercase. If cell A1 contains the text *Lucille*, the formula that follows returns *LUCILLE*:

```
=UPPER(A1)
```

Note

Excel also has a LOWER function (to convert to lowercase) and a PROPER function (to convert to proper case). In proper case, the first letter of each word is capitalized.

Logical functions

The Logical category contains only six functions (although several other functions could, arguably, be placed in this category). This section discusses three of these functions: IF, AND, and OR.

IF

The IF function is one of the most important of all functions. This function can give your formulas decision-making capability.

The IF function takes three arguments. The first argument is a logical test that must return either TRUE or FALSE. The second argument is the result that you want the formula to display if the first argument is TRUE. The third argument is the result that you want the formula to display if the first argument is FALSE.

In the example that follows, the formula returns Positive if the value in cell A1 is greater than zero, and returns Negative otherwise:

```
=IF(A1>0,"Positive","Negative")
```

Notice that the first argument (A1>0) evaluates to logical TRUE or FALSE. This formula has a problem in that it returns the text Negative if the cell is blank or contains 0. The solution is to use a nested IF function to perform another logical test. The revised formula is as follows:

```
=IF(A1>0,"Positive",IF(A1<0,"Negative","Zero"))
```

The formula looks complicated, but when you break it down, you see that it's rather simple. Here's how the logic works. If A1 is greater than 0, the formula displays Positive, and nothing else is evaluated. If A1 is not greater than zero, however, the second argument is evaluated. The second argument is as follows:

```
IF(A1<0,"Negative","Zero")
```

This is simply another IF statement that performs the test on A1 again. If it's less than 0, the formula returns Negative. Otherwise, it returns Zero. You can nest IF statements as deeply as you need to — although it can get very confusing after three or four levels.

Using nested IF functions is quite common, so understanding how this concept works is in your best interest. Mastering IF will definitely help you to create more powerful formulas.

Figure 9-7 shows an example of using the IF function to calculate sales commissions. In this example, the usual commission rate is 5.5 percent of sales. If the total sales of a sales rep exceeds the sales goal, the commission rate is 6.25 percent. The formula in cell C6, shown next, uses the IF function to make a decision regarding which commission rate to use based on the sales amount:

```
=IF(B6>=SalesGoal,B6*BonusRate,B6*CommissionRate)
```

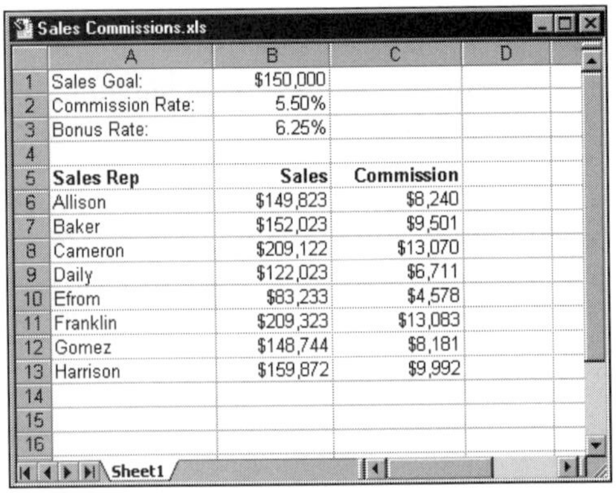

Sales Commissions.xls

	A	B	C	D
1	Sales Goal:	$150,000		
2	Commission Rate:	5.50%		
3	Bonus Rate:	6.25%		
4				
5	**Sales Rep**	**Sales**	**Commission**	
6	Allison	$149,823	$8,240	
7	Baker	$152,023	$9,501	
8	Cameron	$209,122	$13,070	
9	Daily	$122,023	$6,711	
10	Efrom	$83,233	$4,578	
11	Franklin	$209,323	$13,083	
12	Gomez	$148,744	$8,181	
13	Harrison	$159,872	$9,992	
14				
15				
16				

Sheet1

Figure 9-7: Using the IF statement to calculate sales commissions

AND

The AND function returns a logical value (TRUE or FALSE) depending on the logical value of its arguments. If all its arguments return TRUE, the AND function returns TRUE. If at least one of its arguments returns FALSE, AND returns FALSE.

In the example that follows, the formula returns TRUE if the values in cells A1:A3 are all negative:

```
=AND(A1<0,A2<0,A3<0)
```

The formula that follows uses the AND function as the first argument for an IF function. If all three cells in A1:A3 are negative, this formula displays All Negative. If at least one is not negative, the formula returns Not All Negative:

```
=IF(AND(A1<0,A2<0,A3<0),"All Negative","Not All Negative")
```

OR

The OR function is similar to the AND function, but it returns TRUE if at least one of its arguments is TRUE; otherwise, it returns FALSE. In the example that follows, the formula returns TRUE if the value in any of the cells—A1, A2, or A3—is negative:

```
=OR(A1<0,A2<0,A3<0)
```

Information functions

Excel's 15 functions in the Information category return a variety of information about cells. Many of these functions return a logical TRUE or FALSE.

CELL

The CELL function returns information about a particular cell. It takes two arguments. The first argument is a code for the type of information to display. The second argument is the address of the cell in which you're interested.

The example that follows uses the "type" code, which returns information about the type of data in the cell. It returns *b* if the cell is blank, *l* if it contains text (a label), or *v* if the cell contains a value or formula. For example, if cell A1 contains text, the following formula returns *l*:

```
=CELL("type",A1)
```

If the second argument contains a range reference, Excel uses the upper-left cell in the range.

Note   Excel has other functions that let you determine the type of data in a cell. The following functions may be more useful: ISBLANK, ISERR, ISERROR, ISLOGICAL, ISNA, ISNONTEXT, ISNUMBER, ISREF, ISTEXT, and TYPE.

Table 9-2 lists the possible values for the first argument of the CELL function. When using the CELL function, make sure that you enclose the first argument in quotation marks.

Table 9-2	
Codes for the CELL Function Info_Type Argument	

Type	What It Returns
address	The cell's address
col	Column number of the cell
color	1 if the cell is formatted in color for negative values — otherwise, 0
contents	The contents of the cell
filename	Name and path of the file that contains the cell (returns empty text if the workbook has not been saved)
format	Text value corresponding to the number format of the cell
prefix	Text value corresponding to the label prefix of the cell; this is provided for 1-2-3 compatibility

Continued

Table 9-2 *(continued)*

Type	What It Returns
protect	0 if the cell is not locked; 1 if the cell is locked
row	Row number of the cell
type	Text value corresponding to the type of data in the cell
width	Column width of the cell, rounded off to an integer

INFO

The INFO function takes one argument — a code for information about the operating environment. In the example that follows, the formula returns the path of the current folder (that is, the folder that Excel displays when you choose File ➪ Open):

```
=INFO("directory")
```

Table 9-3 lists the valid codes for the INFO function. The codes must be enclosed in quotation marks.

Table 9-3
Codes for the INFO Function

Code	What It Returns
directory	Path of the current folder
memavail	Amount of memory available, in bytes
memused	Amount of memory being used, in bytes
numfile	Number of worksheets in all open workbooks (including hidden workbooks and add-ins)
origin	Returns the cell reference of the top- and leftmost cell visible in the window, based on the current scrolling position
osversion	Current operating system version, as text
recalc	Current recalculation mode — Automatic or Manual
release	Version of Excel
system	Name of the operating environment — mac (for Macintosh) or pcdos (for Windows)
totmem	Total memory available on the system, in bytes

ISERROR

The ISERROR function returns TRUE if its argument returns an error value. Otherwise, it returns FALSE. This function is useful for controlling the display of errors in a worksheet.

Figure 9-8 shows a worksheet that is set up to track monthly sales. Each month, the worksheet is updated with two figures: the number of sales reps on staff and the total sales for the month. Formulas in columns E and F, respectively, calculate the percentage of the sales goal (Actual Sales divided by Sales Goal) and the average sales per sales rep. Notice that the formulas in column F display an error when the data is missing. Cell F2 contains a simple formula:

```
=D2/C2
```

	A	B	C	D	E	F	G	H
1	Month	Sales Goal	Sales Reps	Actual Sales	Pct. Of Goal	Avg. Per Rep		
2	January	500,000	9	510,233	102%	56,693		
3	February	525,000	10	518,733	99%	51,873		
4	March	550,000	10	569,844	104%	56,984		
5	April	575,000	10	560,923	98%	56,092		
6	May	600,000	11	601,923	100%	54,720		
7	June	625,000			0%	#DIV/0!		
8	July	650,000			0%	#DIV/0!		
9	August	675,000			0%	#DIV/0!		
10	September	700,000			0%	#DIV/0!		
11	October	725,000			0%	#DIV/0!		
12	November	750,000			0%	#DIV/0!		
13	December	775,000			0%	#DIV/0!		
14								
15								

Figure 9-8: This worksheet is displaying an error for formulas that refer to missing data.

To avoid displaying an error for missing data, change the formula to the following formula and copy it to the cells that follow. If the division results in an error, the formula displays nothing. Otherwise, it displays the result.

```
=IF(ISERROR(D2/C2),"",D2/C2)
```

Note   Excel offers several other functions that let you trap error values: ERROR.TYPE, ISERR, and ISNA. Also, note that the preceding formula could have used the ISBLANK function to test for missing data.

Date and time functions

If you use dates or times in your worksheets, you owe it to yourself to check out Excel's 14 functions that work with these types of values. This section demonstrates a few of these functions.

To work with dates and times, you should be familiar with Excel's serial number date-and-time system. Refer to Chapter 5.

TODAY

The TODAY function takes no argument. It returns a date that corresponds to the current date — that is, the date set in the system. If you enter the following formula into a cell on June 16, 1998, the formula returns 6/16/98:

```
=TODAY()
```

Note   Excel also has a NOW function that returns the current system date and the current system time.

DATE

The DATE function displays a date based on its three arguments: year, month, and day. This function is useful if you want to create a date based on information in your worksheet. For example, if cell A1 contains 1998, cell B1 contains 12, and cell C1 contains 25, the following formula returns the date for December 25, 1998:

```
=DATE(A1,B1,C1)
```

DAY

The DAY function returns the day of the month for a date. If cell A1 contains the date 12/25/98, the following formula returns 25:

```
=DAY(A1)
```

Note   Excel also includes the YEAR and MONTH functions that extract from a date the year part and month part, respectively.

WEEKDAY

The WEEKDAY function returns the day of the week for a date. It takes two arguments: the date and a code that specifies the type of result (the second argument is optional). The codes are listed in Table 9-4.

Table 9-4	
Codes for the WEEKDAY Function	
Code	**What It Returns**
1 or omitted	Numbers 1–7, corresponding to Sunday through Saturday
2	Numbers 1–7, corresponding to Monday through Sunday
3	Numbers 0–6, corresponding to Monday through Sunday

If cell A1 contains 12/25/98, the formula that follows returns 6—which indicates that this date is a Friday:

```
=WEEKDAY(A1)
```

Tip You also can format cells that contain dates to display the day of the week as part of the format. Use a custom format code of ddd (for abbreviated days of the week) or dddd (for fully spelled days of the week).

TIME

The TIME function displays a time based on its three arguments: hour, minute, and second. This function is useful if you want to create a time based on information in your worksheet. For example, if cell A1 contains 8, cell B1 contains 15, and cell C1 contains 0, the following formula returns 8:15:00 AM:

```
=TIME(A1,B1,C1)
```

HOUR

The HOUR function returns the hour for a time. If cell A1 contains the time 8:15:00 AM, the following formula returns 8:

```
=HOUR(A1)
```

Note Excel also includes the MINUTE and SECOND functions, which extract the minute part and second part, respectively, from a time.

Financial functions

The Financial function category includes 16 functions that are designed to perform calculations that involve money.

Depreciation functions

Excel offers five functions to calculate depreciation of an asset over time. The function that you choose depends on the type of depreciation that you use. Figure 9-9 shows a chart that depicts how an asset is depreciated over time, using each of the five depreciation functions.

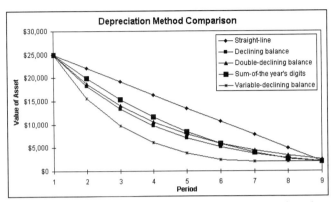

Figure 9-9: A comparison of Excel's five depreciation functions

Table 9-5 summarizes the depreciation functions and the arguments used by each. For complete details, consult the online Help system.

Table 9-5
Excel's Depreciation Functions

Function	Depreciation Method	Arguments*
SLN	Straight-line	Cost, Salvage, Life
DB	Declining balance	Cost, Salvage, Life, Period, [Month]
DDB	Double-declining balance	Cost, Salvage, Life, Period, Month, [Factor]
SYD	Sum-of-the year's digits	Cost, Salvage, Life, Period
VDB	Variable-declining balance	Cost, Salvage, Life, Start Period, End Period, [Factor], [No Switch]

* Arguments in brackets are optional

The arguments for the depreciation functions are described as follows:

✦ **Cost:** Original cost of the asset.

✦ **Salvage:** Salvage cost of the asset after it has been fully depreciated.

✦ **Life:** Number of periods over which the asset will be depreciated.

✦ **Period:** Period in the Life for which the calculation is being made.

✦ **Month:** Number of months in the first year; if omitted, Excel uses 12.

✦ **Factor:** Rate at which the balance declines; if omitted, it is assumed to be 2 (that is, double-declining).

✦ **Rate:** Interest rate per period. If payments are made monthly, for example, you must divide the annual interest rate by 12.

Loan and annuity functions

Table 9-6 lists the functions that can help you perform calculations related to loans and annuities.

	Table 9-6 Loan and Annuity Functions		
Function	**Calculation**	**Arguments***
FV	Future value	Rate, Nper, Pmt, [PV], [Type]
PV	Present value	Rate, Nper, Pmt, [FV], [Type]
PMT	Payment	Rate, Nper, PV, [FV], [Type]
PPMT	Principal payment	Rate, Per, Nper, PV, [FV], [Type]
IPMT	Interest payment	Rate, Per, Nper, PV, [FV], [Type]
ISPMT	Payment interest	Rate, Per, Nper, PV
RATE	Interest rate per period	Nper, Pmt, PV, [FV], [Type], [Guess]
NPER	Number of periods	Rate, Pmt, PV, [FV], [Type]

* Arguments in brackets are optional

Notice that these functions all use pretty much the same arguments — although the exact arguments that are used depend on the function. To use these functions successfully, you must understand how to specify the arguments correctly. The following list explains these arguments:

✦ **Nper:** Total number of payment periods. For a 30-year mortgage loan with monthly payments, Nper is 360.

✦ **Per:** Period in the loan for which the calculation is being made; it must be a number between 1 and Nper.

✦ **Pmt:** Fixed payment made each period for an annuity or a loan. This usually includes principal and interest (but not fees or taxes).

✦ **FV:** Future value (or a cash balance) after the last payment is made. The future value for a loan is 0. If FV is omitted, Excel uses 0.

✦ **Type:** Either 0 or 1, and indicates when payments are due. Use 0 if the payments are due at the end of the period, and 1 if they are due at the beginning of the period.

✦ **Guess:** Used only for the RATE function. It's your best guess of the internal rate of return. The closer your guess, the faster Excel can calculate the exact result.

On the CD-ROM

This book's CD-ROM contains an example workbook that demonstrates the use of the PMT, PPMT, and IPMT functions to calculate a fixed-interest amortization schedule.

Lookup and Reference functions

The 17 functions in the Lookup and Reference category, some of which are demonstrated in this section, are used to perform table lookups and obtain other types of information.

VLOOKUP

The VLOOKUP function can be quite useful when you need to use a value from a table, such as a table of tax rates. This function retrieves text or a value from a table, based on a specific key in the first column of the table. The retrieved result is at a specified horizontal offset from the first row of the table.

Figure 9-10 shows an example of a lookup table (named `PartsList`) in range D2:F9. The worksheet is designed so that a user can enter a part number into cell B2 (which is named `Part`), and formulas in cells B4 and B5 return the appropriate information for the part by using the lookup table. The formulas are as follows:

✦ **Cell B4:** `=VLOOKUP(Part,PartsList,2,FALSE)`

✦ **Cell B5:** `=VLOOKUP(Part,PartsList,3,FALSE)`

	A	B	C	D	E	F
1						
2	Enter Part No. -->	225		Part Number	Name	Unit Cost
3				145	Mesh Rod	$5.95
4	Name:	Toe Bolt		155	Puddle Joint	$12.95
5	Unit Cost:	$0.49		187	Penguin Bold	$1.29
6				205	Finger Nut	$0.98
7				225	Toe Bolt	$0.49
8				319	Piano Nail	$0.99
9				377	Mule Pip	$9.95
10						
11						
12						

Part Lookup.xls — Sheet1

Figure 9-10: A vertical lookup table

The formula in B4 looks up the value in the cell named `Part` in the first column of the table named `PartsList`. It returns the value in the column that corresponds to its third argument (column 2). The fourth argument tells Excel that it must find an exact match. If the fourth argument is TRUE (or omitted), Excel returns the next largest value that is less than the lookup value (the values in the first column must be in ascending order). Using an inexact match is useful for income tax tables, in which a line doesn't exist for every possible income.

If you enter a value that doesn't appear in the table, the formula returns #N/A. You can change the formula to produce a more user-friendly error message by using the ISNA function. The revised formula is as follows:

```
=IF(ISNA(VLOOKUP(Part,PartsList,2,FALSE)),"NotFound",VLOOKUP
(Part,PartsList,2,FALSE))
```

If you enter a part that is not in the list, this formula returns Not Found rather than #N/A.

Note   The HLOOKUP function works exactly like VLOOKUP except that it looks up the value horizontally in the table's first row.

MATCH

The MATCH function searches a range for a value or text and returns the relative row or column in which the item was found. Figure 9-11 shows a simple example. The worksheet contains the month names in A1:A12. Cell D2 contains the following formula:

```
=MATCH(D1,A1:A12,0)
```

The formula returns 7, because cell D1 contains July, and July is the seventh element in the range A1:A12.

	A	B	C	D	E
1	January		Enter a month -->	July	
2	February		Result:	7	
3	March				
4	April				
5	May				
6	June				
7	July				
8	August				
9	September				
10	October				
11	November				
12	December				
13					

Figure 9-11: Using the MATCH function to return a relative position in a range

The third argument for the MATCH function specifies the type of match that you want (0 means an exact match). Use the values of 1 and –1 when you are willing to accept an inexact match.

INDEX

The INDEX function returns a value from a range using a row index (for a vertical range), column index (for a horizontal range), or both (for a two-dimensional range). The formula that follows returns the value in A1:J10 that is in its fifth row and third column:

```
=INDEX(A1:J10,5,3)
```

On the CD-ROM On the CD-ROM, you'll find a workbook that demonstrates the INDEX and MATCH functions. The workbook, shown in Figure 9-12, displays the mileage between selected U.S. cities.

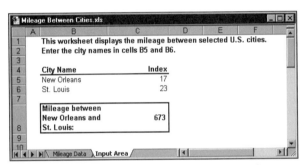

Figure 9-12: This workbook uses the INDEX and MATCH functions to look up the mileage between selected U.S. cities.

The OFFSET function performs a similar function.

INDIRECT

The INDIRECT function returns the value in a cell specified by its text argument. For example, the following formula returns the value (or text) in cell A1:

```
=INDIRECT("A1")
```

This function is most useful when you use a reference as its argument (not a literal, as shown previously). For example, suppose cell C9 contains the text Sales and, in your worksheet, you have defined the name Sales for cell A1; A1 (or Sales) contains the value 46. The following formula returns 46, the value in the cell named Sales:

```
=INDIRECT(C9)
```

This concept can be a bit difficult to grasp, but after you master it, you can put it to good use. Figure 9-13 shows a multisheet workbook with formulas that use the INDIRECT function to summarize the information in the other worksheets in the workbook. Cell B2 contains the following formula, which was copied to the other cells:

```
=INDIRECT("'"&$A2&"'"&"!"&B$1)
```

	A	B	C	D	E	F
1	City	Sales	Expenses	Net		
2	Denver	468,090	131,099	336,991		
3	San Diego	873,900	237,900	636,000		
4	New York	987,220	378,309	608,911		
5	Chicago	587,092	143,988	443,104		
6						
7						
8						
9						
10						

Figure 9-13: These formulas use the INDIRECT function to summarize values contained in the other workbooks.

This formula builds a cell reference by using text in row 1 and column A. Excel evaluates the argument as follows:

```
'Denver'!Sales
```

The Denver sheet has a range named Sales. Therefore, the indirect function returns the value in the cell named Sales on the Denver worksheet.

On the CD-ROM　This file is available on the book's CD-ROM.

Statistical functions

The Statistical category contains a whopping 80 functions that perform various calculations. Many of these are quite specialized, but several are useful for nonstatisticians.

AVERAGE

The AVERAGE function returns the average (arithmetic mean) of a range of values. The *average* is the sum of the range divided by the number of values in the range. The formula that follows returns the average of the values in the range A1:A100:

```
=AVERAGE(A1:A100)
```

If the range argument contains blanks or text, Excel doesn't include these cells in the average calculation. As with the SUM formula, you can supply any number of arguments.

Note   Excel also provides the MEDIAN function (which returns the middle-most value in a range) and the MODE function (which returns the value that appears most frequently in a range).

COUNTIF

The COUNTIF function is useful if you want to count the number of times that a specific value occurs in a range. This function takes two arguments: the range that contains the value to count and a criterion used to determine what to count. Figure 9-14 shows a worksheet set up with student grades. The COUNTIF function is used in the formulas in column E. For example, the formula in E2 is as follows:

```
=COUNTIF(B:B,D2)
```

	A	B	C	D	E	F
1	Student	Grade		Grade	Count	
2	Allen	C		A	6	
3	Baker	C		B	7	
4	Clemens	A		C	8	
5	Daly	C		D	4	
6	Elliot	B		F	1	
7	Franklin	B				
8	Glassheimer	D				
9	Hawkins	A				
10	Ingress	C				
11	Jackson	B				
12	King	B				
13	Lange	F				
14	Martin	D				
15	Nicholson	C				
16	Oswald	C				
17	Peterson	C				
18	Quincy	B				

Figure 9-14: Using the COUNTIF function to create a distribution of grades.

Notice that the first argument consists of a range reference for the entire column B, enabling you to insert new names easily without having to change the formulas.

Cross-Reference   You also can use the Analysis ToolPak add-in to create frequency distributions. See Chapter 38 for details.

COUNT, COUNTA, COUNTBLANK, and COUNTIF

The COUNT function returns the number of values in a range. The COUNTA function returns the number of nonblank cells in a range. For example, the following formula returns the number of nonempty cells in column A:

```
=COUNTA("A:A")
```

COUNTBLANK counts the number of blank cells in a range, and COUNTIF counts the number of cells within a range that meet the criteria that you specify in the argument.

MAX and MIN

Use the MAX function to return the largest value in a range, and the MIN function to return the smallest value in a range. Both MAX and MIN ignore logical values and text. The following formula displays the largest and smallest values in a range named Data; using the concatenation operator causes the result to appear in a single cell:

```
="Smallest: "&MIN(Data)&" Largest: "&MAX(Data)
```

For example, if the values in Data range from 12 to 156, this formula returns Smallest: 12 Largest: 156.

 EXCEL 2000   MAXA and MINA are new to Excel 2000. These functions work like MAX and MIN, respectively, but MAXA and MINA don't ignore logical values and text.

LARGE and SMALL

The LARGE function returns the nth-largest value in a range. For example, to display the second-largest value in a range named Data, use the following formula:

```
=LARGE(Data,2)
```

The SMALL function works just as you would expect; it returns the nth-smallest value in a range.

Database functions

Excel's Database function category consists of a dozen functions that you use when working with database tables (also known as lists) stored in a worksheet. These functions all begin with the letter *D*, and they all have non-database equivalents. For example, the DSUM function is a special version of the SUM function that returns the sum of values in a database that meet a specified criterion. A database table is a rectangular range with field names in the top row. Each subsequent row is considered a record in the database.

To use a database function, you must specify a special criteria range in the worksheet. This type of criteria range is the same one that you use with Excel's Data ⇨ Filter ⇨ Advanced Filter command.

Cross-Reference   This topic is discussed in Chapter 33.

The DSUM function calculates the sum of the values in a specified field, filtered by the criteria table. For example, to calculate the total sales for the North region, enter **North** under the Region field in the criteria range. Then, enter the following formula into any cell (this assumes that the database table is named Data and that the criteria range is named Criteria):

```
=DSUM(Data,"Sales",Criteria)
```

The formula returns the sum of the Sales field, but only for the records that meet the criteria in the range named Criteria. You can change the criteria, and the formula displays the new result. For example, to calculate the sales for January, enter **Jan** under the Month field in the Criteria range (and delete any other entries).

If you want to use several DSUM formulas, you can have each of them refer to a different criteria range (you can use as many criteria ranges as you need).

Excel's other database functions work exactly like the DSUM function.

Analysis ToolPak functions

When you begin to feel familiar with Excel's worksheet functions, you can explore those that are available when you load the Analysis ToolPak. This add-in provides you with dozens of additional worksheet functions.

When you load this add-in, the Paste Function dialog box displays a new category, Engineering. It also adds new functions to the following function categories: Financial, Date & Time, Math & Trig, and Information.

Cross-Reference   The Analysis ToolPak is discussed in Chapter 38. See Appendix C for a summary of the Analysis ToolPak function.

Creating Megaformulas

Often, spreadsheets require intermediate formulas to produce a desired result. After you get the formulas working correctly, you often can eliminate the intermediate formulas and use a single *megaformula* instead (this term is my own — no official name exists for such a formula). The advantages? You use fewer cells (less clutter) and recalculation takes less time. Besides, people in the know will be impressed with your formula-building abilities. The disadvantage? The formula may be impossible to decipher or modify.

Imagine a worksheet with a column of people's names. And suppose that you've been asked to remove all middle names and middle initials from the names — but not all of the names have a middle name or initial. Editing the cells manually would take hours, so you opt for a formula-based solution. Although this task is not a difficult one, it normally involves several intermediate formulas. Also assume that you want to use as few cells as possible in the solution.

Figure 9-15 shows the solution, which requires six intermediate formulas. The names are in column A; the end result is in column H. Columns B through G hold the intermediate formulas. Table 9-7 shows the formulas used in this worksheet, along with a brief description of each.

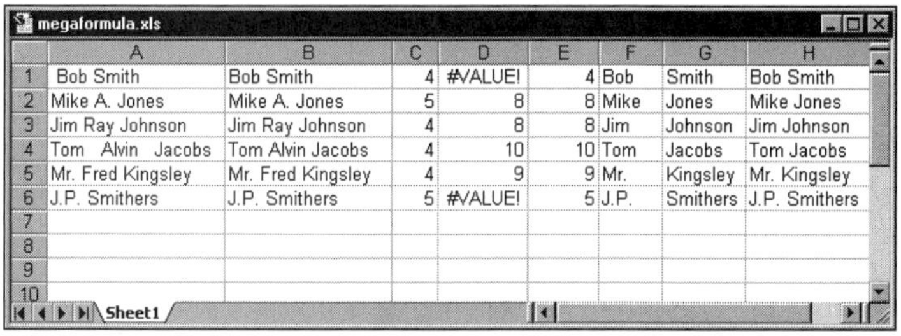
megaformula.xls

	A	B	C	D	E	F	G	H
1	Bob Smith	Bob Smith	4	#VALUE!	4	Bob	Smith	Bob Smith
2	Mike A. Jones	Mike A. Jones	5	8	8	Mike	Jones	Mike Jones
3	Jim Ray Johnson	Jim Ray Johnson	4	8	8	Jim	Johnson	Jim Johnson
4	Tom Alvin Jacobs	Tom Alvin Jacobs	4	10	10	Tom	Jacobs	Tom Jacobs
5	Mr. Fred Kingsley	Mr. Fred Kingsley	4	9	9	Mr.	Kingsley	Mr. Kingsley
6	J.P. Smithers	J.P. Smithers	5	#VALUE!	5	J.P.	Smithers	J.P. Smithers
7								
8								
9								
10								

Sheet1

Figure 9-15: Removing the middle names and initials requires six intermediate formulas.

Table 9-7
Intermediate Formulas

Cell	*Intermediate Formula*	*What It Does*
B1	=TRIM(A1)	Removes excess spaces
C1	=FIND(" ",B1,1)	Locates first space
D1	=FIND(" ",B1,C1+1)	Locates second space (returns an error if no second space exists)
E1	=IF(ISERROR(D1),C1,D1)	Uses the first space if no second space
F1	=LEFT(B1,C1)	Extracts the first name
G1	=RIGHT(B1,LEN(B1)-E1)	Extracts the last name
H1	=F1&G1	Concatenates the two names

You can eliminate all the intermediate formulas by creating a huge formula (what I call a megaformula). You do so by starting with the end result and then replacing each cell reference with a copy of the formula in the cell referred to (but don't copy the equal sign). Fortunately, you can use the clipboard to copy and paste. Keep repeating this process until cell H1 contains nothing but references to cell A1. You end up with the following megaformula in one cell:

```
=LEFT(TRIM(A1),FIND("",TRIM(A1),1))&RIGHT(TRIM(A1),LEN(TRIM(A1)
)-IF(ISERROR(FIND(" ",TRIM(A1),FIND(" ",TRIM(A1),1)+1)),FIND("
",TRIM(A1),1),FIND(" ",TRIM(A1),FIND(" ",TRIM(A1),1)+1)))
```

When you're satisfied that the megaformula is working, you can delete the columns that hold the intermediate formulas, because they are no longer used.

The megaformula performs exactly the same task as all the intermediate formulas — although it's virtually impossible for anyone (even the original author) to figure out. If you decide to use megaformulas, make sure that the intermediate formulas are performing correctly before you start building a megaformula. Even better, keep a copy of the intermediate formulas somewhere, in case you discover an error or need to make a change.

Your only limitation is that Excel's formulas can be no more than 1,024 characters. Because a megaformula is so complex, you may think that using one would slow down recalculation. Actually, the opposite is true. As a test, I created a worksheet that used a megaformula 20,000 times. Then, I created another worksheet that used six intermediate formulas rather than the megaformula. As you can see in Table 9-8, the megaformula recalculated faster and also resulted in a much smaller file.

Table 9-8 Intermediate Formulas Versus Megaformula		
Method	*Recalc Time (seconds)*	*File Size*
Intermediate formulas	9.2	7.1MB
Megaformula	5.1	2.5MB

 This workbook is available on the CD-ROM.

Creating Custom Functions

Although Excel offers more functions than you'll ever need, you may eventually search for a function that you need and not be able to find it. The solution is to create your own.

If you don't have the skills to create your own functions, you may be able to purchase custom Excel functions from a third-party provider that specializes in your industry. Or, you can hire a consultant to develop functions that meet your needs.

To create a custom function, you must be well-versed in Visual Basic for Applications (VBA). When you create a custom function, you can use it in your worksheet, just like the built-in functions.

Cross-Reference   Custom worksheet functions are covered in Chapter 43.

Learning More About Functions

This chapter has just barely skimmed the surface. Excel has hundreds of functions that I haven't mentioned. To learn more about the functions available to you, I suggest that you browse through them by using the Paste Function dialog box and click the Help button when you see something that looks useful. The functions are thoroughly described in Excel's online Help system.

Summary

This chapter discusses the built-in worksheet functions available in Excel. These functions are arranged by category, and you can enter them into your formulas either manually (by typing them) or by using the Paste Function dialog box and the Formula Palette. Many examples of functions across the various categories are also discussed.

✦   ✦   ✦

Manipulating Text

Excel, of course, is best known for its uncanny ability to crunch numbers. However, it also proves its versatility when it comes to handling text. As you know, Excel enables you to enter text for things, such as row and column headings, customer names and addresses, part numbers, and just about anything else. And, as you might expect, you can use formulas to manipulate the text contained in cells.

This chapter contains many examples of formulas that use functions to manipulate text. Some of these formulas perform feats you may not have thought possible.

A Few Words About Text

When you enter data into a cell, Excel immediately goes to work and determines whether you're entering a formula, a number (including a date or time), or anything else. Anything else is considered text.

Note　　You may hear the term *string* used instead of *text*. You can use these terms interchangeably. Sometimes, they even appear together, as in *text string*.

How many characters in a cell?

In Excel 5 and Excel 95, a single cell can hold up to 255 characters. Beginning with Excel 97, however, Microsoft upped the ante significantly. A single cell in Excel 97 can hold up to 32,000 characters. To put things into perspective, this chapter contains about 31,000 characters. I certainly don't recommend using a cell in lieu of a word processor, but if you use Excel 97 or later, you really don't have to lose much sleep worrying about filling up a cell with text.

Caution Although a cell can hold up to 32,000 characters, Excel has a limit on the number of characters that it can actually display. And, as I describe later, some functions may not work properly for text strings greater than 255 characters.

Numbers as text

If you want to "force" a number to be considered as text, you can do one of the following:

✦ Apply the Text number format to the cell. Use Format ➪ Cells, click the Number tab, and select Text from the category list. If you haven't applied other horizontal alignment formatting, the value will appear left-aligned in the cell (like normal text).

✦ Precede the number with an apostrophe. The apostrophe isn't displayed, but the cell entry will be treated as if it were text.

Even though the contents of a cell is formatted as Text (or has an apostrophe preceding it), you can still perform *some* mathematical operations on the cell if the entry *looks* like a number. For example, assume cell A1 contains a value preceded by an apostrophe. The formula that follows will display the value in A1, incremented by 1:

```
=A1+1
```

The formula that follows, however, will treat the contents of cell A1 as 0:

```
=SUM(A1:A10)
```

If switching from Lotus 1-2-3, you'll find this a significant change. Lotus 1-2-3 never treats text as values. In some cases, treating text as a number can be useful. In other cases, it can cause problems. Bottom line? Just be aware of Excel's inconsistency in how it treats a number formatted as text.

Text Functions

Excel has an excellent assortment of worksheet functions that can handle text. For your convenience, Excel's Paste Function dialog box places most of these functions in the Text category. A few other functions that are relevant to Text appear in other function categories. For example, the ISTEXT function is in the Information category in the Paste Function dialog box.

Tip For a listing of Text functions, click the Paste Function toolbar button and scroll through the functions in the Text category.

Most of the text functions are not limited for use with text. In other words, these functions can also operate with cells that contain values. Unlike other spreadsheets (such as 1-2-3), Excel is very accommodating when it comes to treating numbers as text and text as numbers.

The examples discussed in this section demonstrate some common (and useful) things you can do with text. You may need to adapt some of these examples for your own use.

Determining if a cell contains text

In some situations, you may need a formula that determines the type of data contained in a particular cell. For example, you may use an IF function to return a result only if a cell contains text. Excel provides three functions to help you determine if a particular cell contains text:

- ✦ ISTEXT
- ✦ CELL
- ✦ TYPE

As you'll see, however, these functions are not always reliable.

On the CD-ROM The companion CD-ROM includes a workbook that demonstrates these functions (including their problems).

The ISTEXT function

The ISTEXT function takes a single argument, and returns TRUE if the argument contains text, and FALSE if it doesn't contain text. The formula that follows will return TRUE if A1 contains a string:

```
=ISTEXT(A1)
```

Caution The ISTEXT function, although useful, is certainly not perfect. In fact, it will give you an incorrect result in some cases. Although Excel 97 and later can store a huge amount of text in a cell (up to 32,000 characters), the ISTEXT function doesn't seem to realize this fact. The ISTEXT function returns FALSE if its argument refers to a cell that contains more than 255 characters. Excel 2000 corrected this problem, so ISTEXT now works as expected regardless of the amount of text in the cell.

The TYPE function

The TYPE function takes a single argument and returns a value that indicates the type of data in a cell. If cell A1 contains a text string, the formula that follows will return 2 (the code number for text):

```
=TYPE(A1)
```

Caution   The TYPE function falls apart when a cell contains more than 255 characters: It returns 16—the code number for an Error value.

The CELL function

Theoretically, the CELL function should help you determine if a particular cell uses the Text format, or has an apostrophe prefix. The CELL function's first argument can consist of any of 12 keywords, including *format*, *prefix*, or *type*.

None of these options work as advertised when a number is formatted as Text. For example, if you enter a number into cell A1 and then give it a number format of Text, the following formula returns *G*—which means Excel considers it formatted using the General format:

```
=CELL("format",A1)
```

Using *prefix* as the first argument for the CELL function returns an apostrophe if a value is preceded by an apostrophe, but it returns nothing if the cell contains a number and is formatted as Text. Using type as the first argument in the CELL function also yields inconsistent results. For example, if the cell contains more than 255 characters, the function returns *v* (for value).

Working with character codes

Every character that you see on your screen has an associated code number. For Windows systems, Excel uses the standard ANSI character set. The ANSI character set consists of 255 characters, numbered from 1 to 255.

Figure 10-1 shows an Excel worksheet that displays all of the 255 characters. This example uses the Arial font (other fonts may have different characters).

Two functions come into play when dealing with character codes: CODE and CHAR. These functions aren't very useful by themselves. However, they can be quite useful in conjunction with other functions. I discuss these functions in the following sections.

character set.xls

| Font: | Arial | | Size: | 10 | |

#		#		#		#		#		#		#	
1	□	39	'	77	M	115	s	153	™	191	¿	229	å
2	□	40	(	78	N	116	t	154	š	192	À	230	æ
3	□	41	)	79	O	117	u	155	›	193	Á	231	ç
4	□	42	*	80	P	118	v	156	œ	194	Â	232	è
5	□	43	+	81	Q	119	w	157	□	195	Ã	233	é
6	□	44	,	82	R	120	x	158	ž	196	Ä	234	ê
7	□	45	-	83	S	121	y	159	Ÿ	197	Å	235	ë
8	□	46	.	84	T	122	z	160		198	Æ	236	ì
9	□	47	/	85	U	123	{	161	¡	199	Ç	237	í
10	□	48	0	86	V	124	|	162	¢	200	È	238	î
11	□	49	1	87	W	125	}	163	£	201	É	239	ï
12	□	50	2	88	X	126	~	164	¤	202	Ê	240	ð
13	□	51	3	89	Y	127	□	165	¥	203	Ë	241	ñ
14	□	52	4	90	Z	128	€	166	¦	204	Ì	242	ò
15	□	53	5	91	[	129	□	167	§	205	Í	243	ó
16	□	54	6	92	\	130	‚	168	¨	206	Î	244	ô
17	□	55	7	93	]	131	ƒ	169	©	207	Ï	245	õ
18	□	56	8	94	^	132	„	170	ª	208	Ð	246	ö
19	□	57	9	95	_	133	…	171	«	209	Ñ	247	÷
20	□	58	:	96	`	134	†	172	¬	210	Ò	248	ø
21	□	59	;	97	a	135	‡	173	-	211	Ó	249	ù
22	□	60	<	98	b	136	^	174	®	212	Ô	250	ú
23	□	61	=	99	c	137	‰	175	¯	213	Õ	251	û
24	□	62	>	100	d	138	Š	176	°	214	Ö	252	ü
25	□	63	?	101	e	139	‹	177	±	215	×	253	ý
26	□	64	@	102	f	140	Œ	178	²	216	Ø	254	þ
27	□	65	A	103	g	141	□	179	³	217	Ù	255	ÿ
28	□	66	B	104	h	142	Ž	180	´	218	Ú		
29	□	67	C	105	i	143	□	181	µ	219	Û		
30	□	68	D	106	j	144	□	182	¶	220	Ü		
31	□	69	E	107	k	145	'	183	·	221	Ý		
32		70	F	108	l	146	'	184	¸	222	Þ		
33	!	71	G	109	m	147	"	185	¹	223	ß		
34	"	72	H	110	n	148	"	186	º	224	à		
35	#	73	I	111	o	149	•	187	»	225	á		
36	$	74	J	112	p	150	–	188	¼	226	â		
37	%	75	K	113	q	151	—	189	½	227	ã		
38	&	76	L	114	r	152	˜	190	¾	228	ä		

Sheet1

Figure 10-1: The ANSI character set (for the Arial font)

The CODE function

Excel's CODE function returns the character code for its argument. The formula that follows, for example, returns 65—the character code for uppercase *A:*

```
=CODE("A")
```

If the argument for CODE consists of more than one character, the function uses only the first character. Therefore, this formula also returns 65:

```
=CODE("Abbey Road")
```

The CHAR function

The CHAR function is essentially the opposite of the CODE function. Its argument should be a value between 1 and 255, and the function returns the corresponding character. The following formula, for example, returns the letter *A*:

```
=CHAR(65)
```

To demonstrate the opposing nature of the CODE and CHAR functions, try entering this formula:

```
=CHAR(CODE("A"))
```

This formula (illustrative rather than useful) returns the letter *A*. First, it converts the character to its code value (65), and then it converts this code back to the corresponding character.

Assume cell A1 contains the letter *A* (uppercase). The following formula returns the letter *a* (lowercase):

```
=CHAR(CODE(A1)+32)
```

This formula takes advantage of the fact that the alphabetic characters all appear in alphabetical order within the character set, and the lowercase letters follow the uppercase letters (with a few other characters tossed in between). Each lowercase letter lies exactly 32 character positions higher than its corresponding uppercase letter.

How to Find Special Characters

Windows includes a program called Character Map (charmap.exe) that is very useful for locating special characters. For example, you might (for some strange reason) want to include a smiley face character in your spreadsheet. It just so happens that the Wingdings font includes such a character — but you probably have no idea what character code it uses.

Launch the Character Map program and select the Wingdings font (see the accompanying figure). Examine the characters, and you'll find that the smiley face corresponds to the letter J (uppercase). Just type the letter **J** and format the character using the Wingdings font.

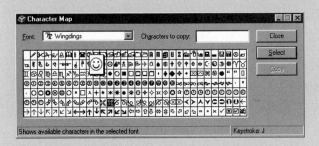

You'll find that some characters cannot be entered using standard keyboard keys. However, Character Map displays an Alt key combination in the lower-right corner. For example, when you select the last character in the Wingdings font (the Windows logo, or character code 255), Character Map displays Alt+0255. You can enter this character by holding down the Alt key and typing 0255 on the numeric keypad of your keyboard. Make sure you use the numeric keypad because the normal number keys will not generate the proper character.

Determining if two strings are identical

You can set up a simple logical formula to determine if two cells contain the same entry. For example, use this formula to determine if cell A1 has the same contents as cell A2:

```
=A1=A2
```

Excel acts a bit lax in its comparisons when involving text. Consider the case in which A1 contains the word *January* (initial capitalization), and A2 contains *JANUARY* (all uppercase). You'll find that the preceding formula returns TRUE, even though the contents of the two cells are not really the same. In other words, the comparison is not case sensitive.

In many cases, you don't need to worry about the case of the text. But if you need to make an exact, case-sensitive comparison, you can use Excel's EXACT function. The formula that follows returns TRUE only if cells A1 and A2 contain *exactly* the same entry:

```
=EXACT(A1,A2)
```

This formula returns FALSE because the first string contains a trailing space:

```
=EXACT("zero ","zero")
```

Joining two or more cells

Excel uses an ampersand as its concatenation operator. *Concatenation* is simply a fancy term that describes what happens when you join the contents of two or more cells. For example, if cell A1 contains the text *San Diego*, and cell A2 contains the text *California*, the formula below will return *San Diego California*.

```
=A1&A2
```

Notice that the two strings are joined together without an intervening space. To add a space between the two entries (to get *San Diego California*), use a formula like this one:

```
=A1&" "&A2
```

Or, even better, use a comma and a space to produce *San Diego, California*:

```
=A1&", "&A2
```

To improve the legibility of the formula, you can eliminate the quote characters and use the CHAR function, with an appropriate argument. Note this example of using the CHAR function to represent a comma (44) and a space (32):

```
=A1&CHAR(44)&CHAR(32)&A2
```

If you'd like to force a "word wrap," concatenate the strings using CHAR (10) and make sure you apply the wrap text format to the cell. The following example joins the text in cell A1 and the text in cell B1, with a line break in between:

```
=A1&CHAR(10)&B1
```

Here's another example of the CHAR function. The formula below returns the string *Stop* by concatenating four characters returned by the CHAR function:

```
=CHAR(83)&CHAR(116)&CHAR(111)&CHAR(112)
```

Below you see a final example of using the & operator. In this case, the formula combines text with the result of an expression that returns the maximum value in Column C.

```
="The largest value in Column C is " &MAX(C:C)
```

Note   Excel also has a CONCATENATE function, which takes up to 30 arguments. This function simply combines the arguments into a single string. You can use this function if you like, but I prefer the & operator's efficiency.

Displaying formatted values as text

Excel's TEXT function enables you to display a value in a specific number format. Although this function may appear to have dubious value, it *does* serve some useful purposes as the examples in this section demonstrate. Figure 10-2 shows a simple worksheet. The formula in cell D1 is:

```
="The net profit is " & B3
```

This formula essentially combines a text string with the contents of cell B3 and displays the result. Note, however, that the contents of B3 are not formatted in any way. You might want to display B3's contents using a currency number format.

Note   Contrary to what you might expect, applying a number format to the cell that contains the formula has no effect because the formula returns a string, not a value.

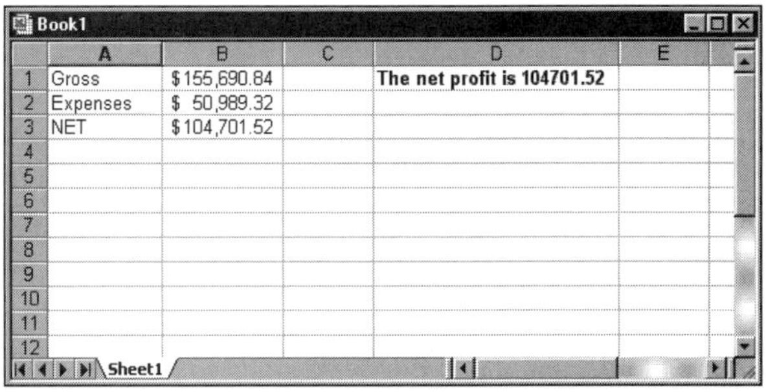

Figure 10-2: The formula in D1 doesn't display the formatted number.

Note this revised formula that uses the TEXT function to apply formatting to the value in B3:

```
="The net profit is " & TEXT(B3,"$#,##0.00")
```

This formula displays the text along with a nicely formatted value: *The net profit is $47,219.79.*

The second argument for the TEXT function consists of a standard Excel number format string. You can enter any valid number format for this argument.

The preceding example uses a simple cell reference (B3). You can, of course, use an expression instead. Here's an example that combines text with a number resulting from a computation:

```
="Average Expenditure: " & TEXT(AVERAGE("A:A","$#,##0.00"))
```

Here's another example that uses the NOW function (which returns the current date and time). The TEXT function displays the date and time, nicely formatted.

```
="Report printed on "&TEXT(NOW(),"mmmm d, yyyy at h:mm AM/PM")
```

The formula might display the following: *Report printed on July 22, 1999 at 3:23 PM.*

Displaying formatted currency values as text

Excel's DOLLAR function converts a number to text using the currency format. It takes two arguments: the number to convert, and the number of decimal places to display. The DOLLAR function always uses the following number format:

```
$#,##0.00_);($#,##0.00).
```

You can sometimes use the DOLLAR function in place of the TEXT function. The TEXT function, however, is much more flexible because it doesn't limit you to a specific number format.

The formula below returns *Total: $1,287.37*. The second argument for the DOLLAR function specifies the number of decimal places.

```
="Total: "&DOLLAR(1287.367, 2)
```

Repeating a character or string

The REPT function repeats a text string (first argument) any number of times you specify (second argument). For example, the formula below returns *HoHoHo*.

```
=REPT("Ho",3)
```

You can also use this function to create crude vertical dividers between cells. This example displays a squiggly line, 20 characters in length:

```
=REPT("~",20)
```

Creating a text histogram

A clever use for the REPT function is to create a crude histogram directly in a worksheet (chart not required). Figure 10-3 shows an example of such a histogram. You'll find this type of graphical display especially useful when you need to visually summarize many values. In such a case, a standard chart may be unwieldy.

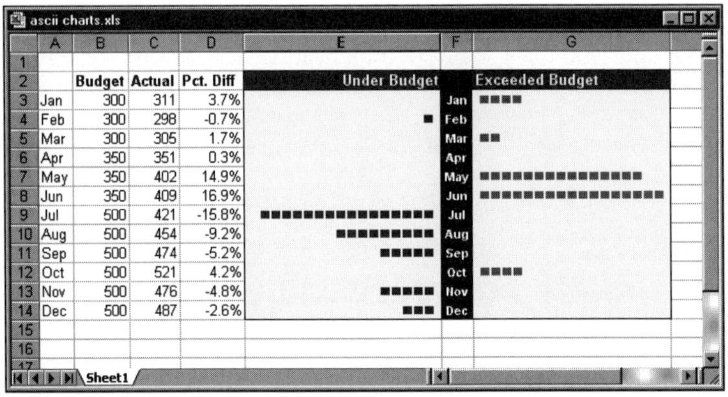

Figure 10-3: Using the REPT function to create a histogram in a worksheet range

The formulas in columns E and G graphically depict monthly budget variances by displaying a series of characters in the Wingdings font. A formula using the REPT function determines the number of characters displayed. Key formulas include:

```
E3:  =IF(D3<0,REPT("n",-ROUND(D3*100,0)),"")
F3:  =A2
G3:  =IF(D3>0,REPT("n",-ROUND(D3*-100,0)),"")
```

Assign the Wingdings font to cells E3 and G3, and then copy the formulas down the columns to accommodate all the data. Right-align the text in column E, and adjust any other formatting. Depending on the numerical range of your data, you may need to change the scaling. Experiment by replacing the 100 value in the formulas. You can substitute any character you like for the n in the formulas to produce a different character in the chart.

Padding a number

You're probably familiar with a common security measure (frequently used on printed checks) in which numbers are padded with asterisks on the right. The following formula displays the value in cell A1, along with enough asterisks to make 24 characters total:

```
=(A1 & REPT("*",24-LEN(A1)))
```

Or, if you'd prefer to pad the number with asterisks on the left, use this formula:

```
=REPT("*",24-LEN(A1))&A1
```

For asterisk padding on both sides of the number, use a formula such as this:

```
=REPT("*",12-LEN(A1))&A1&REPT("*",12-LEN(A1))
```

The preceding formulas are a bit deficient because they don't show any number formatting. Note this revised version that displays the value in A1 (formatted), along with the asterisk padding on the right:

```
=(TEXT(A1,"$#,##0.00")&REPT("*",24-LEN(TEXT(A1,"$#,##0.00"))))
```

Figure 10-4 shows this formula in action.

You can also pad a number by using a custom number format. To repeat the next character in the format to fill the column width, include an asterisk (*) in the custom number format code. For example, use this number format to pad the number with dashes:

```
$#,##0.00*-
```

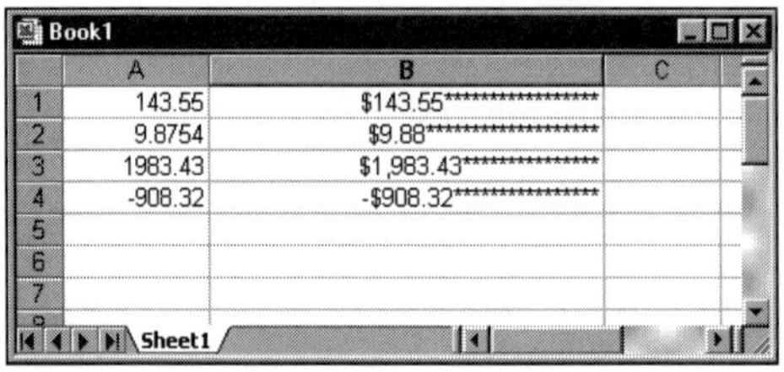

Figure 10-4: Using a formula to pad a number with asterisks

To pad the number with asterisks, use two asterisks like this:

```
$#,##0.00**
```

Removing excess spaces and nonprinting characters

Often, data imported into an Excel worksheet contains excess spaces or strange (often unprintable) characters. Excel provides you with two functions to help whip your data into shape: TRIM and CLEAN.

✦ **TRIM:** Removes all spaces from its text argument except for single spaces between words.

✦ **CLEAN:** Removes all nonprinting characters from a string. These "garbage" characters often appear when you import certain types of data. Of the 255 character codes, 39 of them comprise nonprinting characters. Specifically, the nonprinting character codes include 1-31, 128-129, 141-144, and 157-158.

The example below uses the TRIM function. The formula returns *Fourth Quarter Earnings* (with no excess spaces):

```
=TRIM("   Fourth   Quarter   Earnings   ")
```

Counting characters in a string

Excel's LEN function takes one argument, and returns the number of characters in the cell. For example, if cell A1 contains the string "September Sales," the following formula will return 15:

```
=LEN(A1)
```

Notice that space characters are included in the character count.

The following formula returns the total number of characters in the range A1:A3:

```
{=SUM(LEN(A1),LEN(A2),LEN(A3))}
```

Cross-Reference You will see example formulas that demonstrate how to count the number of specific characters within a string later in this chapter. Also, you may find relevant material in Chapter 12 on counting techniques and Chapter 26 on performing magic with array formulas.

Changing the case of text

Excel provides three handy functions to change the case of text:

- ✦ **UPPER:** converts the text to ALL UPPERCASE
- ✦ **LOWER:** converts the text to all lowercase
- ✦ **PROPER:** Converts the text to "proper" case (The First Letter In Each Word Is Capitalized)

These functions are quite straightforward. The formula that follows, for example, converts the text in cell A1 to proper case. If cell A1 contained the text *MR. JOHN Q. PUBLIC*, the formula would return *Mr. John Q. Public*.

```
=PROPER(A1)
```

These functions operate only on alphabetic characters; they simply ignore all other characters and return them unchanged.

Extracting characters from a string

Excel users often need to extract characters from a string. For example, you may have a list of employee names (first and last names) and need to extract the last name from each cell. Excel provides several useful functions for extracting characters:

- ✦ **LEFT:** Returns a specified number of characters from the beginning of a string
- ✦ **RIGHT:** Returns a specified number of characters from the end of a string
- ✦ **MID:** Returns a specified number of characters beginning at any position within a string

The formula that follows returns the last 10 characters from cell A1. If A1 contains fewer than 10 characters, the formula returns all of the text in the cell.

```
=RIGHT(A1,10)
```

This next formula uses the MID function to return five characters from cell A1, beginning at character position 2. In other words, it returns characters 2-6.

```
=MID(A1,2,5)
```

The following example returns the text in cell A1, with only the first letter in uppercase. It uses the LEFT function to extract the first character and convert it to uppercase. This then concatenates to another string that uses the RIGHT function to extract all but the first character (converted to lowercase).

```
=UPPER(LEFT(A1))&RIGHT(LOWER(A1),LEN(A1)-1)
```

If cell A1 contained the text *FIRST QUARTER*, the formula would return *First quarter*.

Replacing text with other text

In some situations, you may need to replace a part of a text string with some other text. For example, you may import data that contains asterisks, and you need to convert the asterisks to some other character. You could use Excel's Edit ➪ Replace command to make the replacement. If you prefer a formula-based solution, you can take advantage of either of two functions:

✦ **SUBSTITUTE:** Replaces specific text in a string. Use this function when you know the character(s) to be replaced, but not the position.

✦ **REPLACE:** Replaces text that occurs in a specific location within a string. Use this function when you know the position of the text to be replaced, but not the actual text.

The following formula uses the SUBSTITUTE function to replace 1999 with 2000 in the string *1999 Budget*. The formula returns *2000 Budget*.

```
=SUBSTITUTE("1999 Budget","1999","2000")
```

The following formula uses the SUBSTITUTE function to remove all spaces from a string. In other words, it replaces all space characters with an empty string. The formula returns the title of an excellent Liz Phair CD: *Whitechocolatespaceegg*.

```
=SUBSTITUTE("White chocolate space egg"," ","")
```

The formula below uses the REPLACE function to replace one character beginning at position 5 with nothing. In other words, it removes the fifth character (a hyphen) and returns *Part544*.

```
=REPLACE("Part-544",5,1,"")
```

You can, of course, nest these functions to perform multiple replacements in a single formula. The formula that follows demonstrates the power of nested SUBSTITUTE functions. The formula essentially strips out any of the following seven characters in cell A1: space, hyphen, colon, asterisk, underscore, left parenthesis, and right parenthesis.

```
=SUBSTITUTE(SUBSTITUTE(SUBSTITUTE(SUBSTITUTE
(SUBSTITUTE(SUBSTITUTE(SUBSTITUTE(A1," ",""),"-",
""),":",""),"*",""),"_",""),"(",""),")","")
```

Therefore, if cell A1 contains the string *Part-2A-Z(4M1)_A**, the formula returns *Part2AZ4M1A*.

Finding and searching within a string

Excel's FIND and SEARCH functions enable you to locate the starting position of a particular substring within a string.

✦ **FIND:** Finds a substring within another text string and returns the starting position of the substring. You can specify the character position at which to begin searching. Use this function for non-case-sensitive text; you don't need to use wildcard characters.

✦ **SEARCH:** Finds a substring within another text string and returns the starting position of the substring. You can specify the character position at which to begin searching. Use this function for non-case-sensitive text or when you need to use wildcard characters.

The following formula uses the FIND function and returns *7*—the position of the first *m* in the string. Notice that this formula is case sensitive.

```
=FIND("m","Big Mamma Thornton",1)
```

The formula that follows, which uses the SEARCH function, returns *5*—the position of the first *m* (either uppercase or lowercase).

```
=SEARCH("m","Big Mamma Thornton",1)
```

You can use the following wildcard characters within the first argument for the SEARCH function:

✦ **Question mark (?):** Matches any single character

✦ **Asterisk (*):** Matches any sequence of characters

Tip   If you want to find an actual question mark or asterisk character, type a tilde (~) before the question mark or asterisk.

The next formula examines the text in cell A1 and returns the position of the first three-character sequence that has a hyphen in the middle of it. In other words, it looks for any character followed by a hyphen and any other character. If cell A1 contains the text *Part-A90*, the formula returns 4.

```
=SEARCH("?-?",A1,1)
```

Searching and replacing within a string

You can use the REPLACE function in conjunction with the SEARCH function to replace part of a text string with another string. In effect, you use the SEARCH function to find the starting location used by the REPLACE function.

For example, assume cell A1 contains the text "Annual Profit Figures." The following formula searches for the word "Profit," and replaces it with the word "Loss":

```
=REPLACE(A1,SEARCH("Profit",A1),6,"Loss")
```

This next formula uses the SUBSTITUTE function to accomplish the same effect in a more efficient manner:

```
=SUBSTITUTE(A1,"Profit","Loss")
```

Advanced Text Formulas

The examples in this section appear more complex than the examples in the previous section. But, as you'll see, they can perform some very useful text manipulations.

Counting specific characters in a cell

This formula counts the number of Bs (uppercase only) in the string in cell A1:

```
=LEN(A1)-LEN(SUBSTITUTE(A1,"B",""))
```

This formula works by using the SUBSTITUTE function to create a new string (in memory) that has all of the Bs removed. Then, the length of this string is subtracted from the length of the original string. The result reveals the number of Bs in the original string.

The following formula is a bit more versatile. It counts the number of Bs — both upper- and lowercase — in the string in cell A1.

```
=LEN(A1)-LEN(SUBSTITUTE(SUBSTITUTE(A1,"B",""),"b",""))
```

Counting the occurrences of a substring in a cell

The formulas in the preceding section count the number of occurrences of a particular character in a string. The following formula works with more than one character. It returns the number of occurrences of a particular substring (contained in cell B1) within a string (contained in cell A1). The substring can consist of any number of characters.

```
=SUM(LEN(A1)-LEN(SUBSTITUTE(A1,B1,"")))/LEN(B1)
```

For example, if cell A1 contains the text *Blonde On Blonde* and B1 contains the text *Blonde*, the formula returns 2.

The comparison is case sensitive, so if B1 contains the text *blonde*, the formula returns 0. The following formula is a modified version that performs a case-insensitive comparison.

```
=SUM(LEN(A1)-LEN(SUBSTITUTE(UPPER(A1),UPPER(B1),"")))/LEN(B1)
```

Expressing a number as an ordinal

You may need to express a value as an ordinal number. For example, *Today is the 21st day of the month.* In this case, the number 21 converts to an ordinal number by appending the characters *st* to the number.

The characters appended to a number depend on the number. They exhibit no clear pattern, making the construction of a formula more difficult. Most numbers will use the *th* suffix. Exceptions occur for numbers that end with 1, 2, or 3 — except if the preceding number is a 1 (numbers that end with 11, 12, or 13). These may seem like fairly complex rules, but you can translate them into an Excel formula.

The formula that follows converts the number in cell A1 (assumed to be an integer) to an ordinal number:

```
=A1&IF(OR(VALUE(RIGHT(A1,2))={11,12,13}),"th",IF(OR(VALUE(RIGHT
(A1))={1,2,3}),CHOOSE(RIGHT(A1),"st","nd","rd"),"th"))
```

This is a rather complicated formula, so it may help to examine its components. Basically, the formula works as follows:

1. If the last two digits of the number consist of 11, 12, or 13, then use *th*.

2. If Rule #1 does not apply, then check the last digit. If the last digit is 1, use *st*. If the last digit is 2, use *nd*. If the last digit is 3, use *rd*.

3. If neither Rule #1 nor Rule #2 apply, use *rd*.

Cross-Reference   The formula uses two arrays, specified by brackets. Refer to Chapter 25 for more information about using arrays in formulas.

Figure 10-5 shows the formula in use.

	A	B	C	D
1	**Number**	**Adjective**		
2	1	1st		
3	4	4th		
4	7	7th		
5	10	10th		
6	13	13th		
7	16	16th		
8	19	19th		
9	22	22nd		
10	25	25th		
11	28	28th		
12	31	31st		
13	34	34th		
14	37	37th		
15	40	40th		
16	43	43rd		
17	46	46th		
18	49	49th		
19				
20				

Figure 10-5: Using a formula to express a number as an ordinal

Determining a column letter for a column number

This next formula returns a worksheet column letter (ranging from A to IV) for the value contained in cell A1. For example, if A1 contains *29*, the formula returns *AC*.

```
=IF(A1>26,CHAR(CEILING(A1/26,1)+63),"")
&CHAR(IF(MOD(A1,26)=0,26,MOD(A1,26))+64)
```

Note that the formula doesn't check for a valid column number. In other words, if A1 contains a value less than 1 or greater than 256, the formula will still give an answer — albeit a meaningless one. The following modified version includes an IF function to ensure a valid column.

```
=IF(AND(A1>0,A1<257),IF(A1>26,CHAR(CEILING(A1/26,1)+63),"")
&CHAR(IF(MOD(A1,26)=0,26,MOD(A1,26))+64),"")
```

Extracting a file name from a path specification

The following formula returns the file name from a full path specification. For example, if cell A1 contains *c:\windows\desktop\myfile.xls*, the formula returns *myfile.xls*:

```
=MID(A1,FIND("*",SUBSTITUTE(A1,"\","*",LEN(A1)-
LEN(SUBSTITUTE(A1,"\",))))+1,LEN(A1))
```

This formula assumes that the system path separator consists of a backslash (\). It essentially returns all of the text following the last backslash character. If cell A1 doesn't contain a backslash character, the formula returns an error.

Extracting the first word of a string

To extract the first word of a string, a formula must locate the position of the first space character, and then use this information as an argument for the LEFT function. The following formula does just that.

```
=LEFT(A1,FIND(" ",A1)-1)
```

This formula returns all of the text prior to the first space in cell A1. However, the formula has a slight problem: It returns an error if cell A1 consists of a single word. A slightly more complex formula that checks for the error with an IF function solves that problem:

```
=IF(ISERR(LEFT(A1,FIND(" ",A1)-1)),A1,LEFT(A1,FIND(" ",A1)-1))
```

Extracting the last word of a string

Extracting the last word of a string is more complicated, because the FIND function only works from left to right. Therefore, the problem rests with locating the *last* space character. The formula that follows, however, solves this problem. It returns the last word of a string—all of the text following the last space character:

```
=RIGHT(A1,LEN(A1)-FIND("*",SUBSTITUTE(A1," ","*",LEN(A1)-
LEN(SUBSTITUTE(A1," ","")))))
```

This formula, however, has the same problem as the first formula in the preceding section: It fails if the string does not contain at least one space character. The following modified formula uses an IF function to count the number of spaces in cell A1. If it contains no spaces, the entire contents of cell A1 are returned. Otherwise, the preceding formula kicks in.

```
=IF(LEN(A1)-LEN(SUBSTITUTE(A1," ",""))=0,A1,RIGHT(A1,LEN(A1)-
FIND("*",SUBSTITUTE(A1," ","*",LEN(A1)-LEN(SUBSTITUTE(A1,"
","")))))))
```

Extracting all but the first word of a string

The following formula returns the contents of cell A1, except for the first word:

```
=RIGHT(A1,LEN(A1)-FIND(" ",A1,1))
```

Extracting first names, middle names, and last names

Suppose you have a list consisting of people's names in a single column. You have to separate these names into three columns: one for the first name, one for the middle name or initial, and one for the last name. This task is more complicated than you may think, because not every name has a middle initial. However, you can still do it.

Note   The task becomes a *lot* more complicated if the list contains names with titles (such as Mr. or Dr.) or names followed by additional details (such as Jr. or III). In fact, the formulas below will *not* handle these complex cases. However, they still give you a significant head start if you're willing to do a bit of manual editing to handle the special cases.

The formulas that follow all assume that the name appears in cell A1.

You can easily construct a formula to return the first name:

```
=LEFT(A1,FIND(" ",A1)-1)
```

Returning the middle name or initial is much more complicated, because not all names have a middle initial. This formula returns the middle name (if it exists). Otherwise, it returns nothing.

```
=IF(ISERR(MID(A1,FIND(" ",A1)+1,IF(ISERR(FIND(" ",A1,FIND
(" ",A1)+1)),FIND(" ",A1),FIND(" ",A1,FIND(" ",A1)+1))-
FIND(" ",A1)-1)),"",MID(A1,FIND(" ",A1)+1,IF(ISERR(FIND
(" ",A1,FIND(" ",A1)+1)),FIND(" ",A1),FIND(" ",A1,FIND
(" ",A1)+1))-FIND(" ",A1)-1))
```

Finally, this formula returns the last name:

```
=RIGHT(A1,LEN(A1)-FIND("*",SUBSTITUTE(A1," ","*",LEN(A1)-
LEN(SUBSTITUTE(A1," ","")))))
```

As you can see in Figure 10-6, the formulas work fairly well. A few problems exist, however; notably names that contain four "words." But, as I mention above, you can clean these cases up manually.

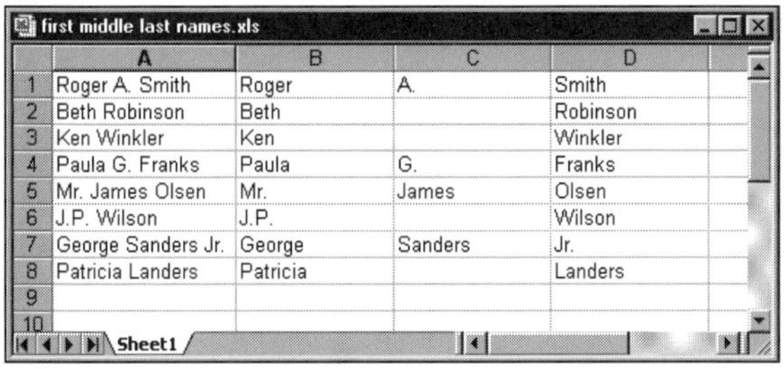

Figure 10-6: This worksheet uses formulas to extract the first name, middle name (or initial), and last name from a list of names in Column A.

Splitting Text Strings Without Formulas

In many cases, you can eliminate the use of formulas and use Excel's Data⇨Text to Columns command to parse strings into their component parts. Selecting this command displays Excel's Convert Text to Columns Wizard—a series of dialog boxes that walk you through the steps to convert a single column of data into multiple columns. Generally, you'll want to select the Delimited option (in Step 1) and use Space as the delimiter (in Step 2).

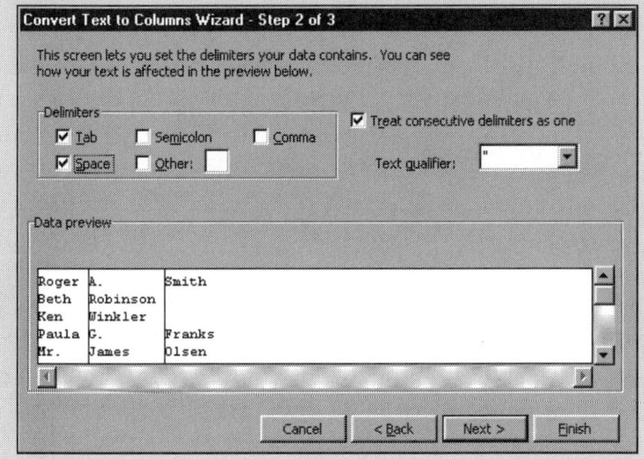

Removing titles from names

You can use the formula that follows to remove three common titles (Mr., Ms., and Mrs.) from a name. For example, if cell A1 contains *Mr. Fred Munster*, the formula would return *Fred Munster*.

```
=IF(OR(LEFT(A1,2)="Mr",LEFT(A1,3)="Mrs",LEFT(A1,2)="Ms"),
RIGHT(A1,LEN(A1) -FIND(" ",A1)),A1)
```

Counting the number of words in a cell

The following formula returns the number of words in cell A1:

```
=LEN(SUBSTITUTE(TRIM(A1),CHAR(32),CHAR(32)&CHAR(32)))-
LEN(TRIM(A1))+1
```

The formula works by creating a new string in memory that consists of the original string without any spaces. Then, you subtract the length of this new string from the original string to determine the number of spaces. A value of one is added to this result to arrive at the number of words. Notice that the TRIM function eliminates any multiple spaces between words.

Custom VBA Text Functions

Excel has many functions that work with text, but it's likely that you'll run into a situation in which the appropriate function just doesn't exist. In such a case, you can often create your own worksheet function using VBA.

✦ **REVERSETEXT:** Returns the text in a cell backwards. For example, using *Evian* as the argument returns *naivE*.

✦ **ACRONYM:** Returns the first letter of each word in its argument. For example, using *Power Utility Pak* as the argument returns *PUP*.

✦ **SPELLDOLLARS:** Returns a number "spelled out" in text — as on a check. For example, using *123.45* as the argument returns *One hundred twenty-three and 45/100 dollars*.

✦ **SCRAMBLE:** Returns the contents of its argument randomized. For example, using *Microsoft* as the argument may return *oficMorts* — or some other random permutation.

✦ **ISLIKE:** Returns TRUE if a string matches a pattern composed of text and wildcard characters.

✦ **CELLHASTEXT:** Returns TRUE if the cell argument contains text, or a value formatted as Text. This function overcomes the problems described at the beginning of this chapter (see "Determining If a Cell Contains Text").

✦ **EXTRACTELEMENT:** Extracts an element from a string based on a specified separator character (such as a hyphen).

Summary

This chapter provided some background on how Excel deals with text entered into cells. It also presented many useful examples that incorporate Excel's text functions.

The next chapter presents formulas that enable you to calculate dates, times, and other time-period values.

✦   ✦   ✦

Working with Dates and Times

Working with dates and times in Excel can be a frustrating experience—until you gain a solid understanding of how this feature works. This chapter provides the information you need to create powerful formulas that manipulate dates and times.

Note   I formatted the dates in this chapter according to the United States English date format: month/day/year. For example, the date 3/1/1952 refers to March 1, 1952, not January 3, 1952.

How Excel Handles Dates and Times

This section presents a quick overview of how Excel deals with dates and times. We'll look at Excel's date and time serial number system and tips for entering and formatting dates and times.

Cross-Reference   Other chapters in this book contain additional date-related information. For example, refer to Chapter 12 for counting examples that use dates.

Understanding date serial numbers

To Excel, a date is simply a number. More precisely, a date is a "serial number" that represents the number of days since January 0, 1900. A serial number of 1 corresponds to January 1, 1900; a serial number of 2 corresponds to January 2, 1900, and so on. This system makes it possible to deal with dates in formulas. For example, you can create a formula to calculate the number of days between two dates.

Choose Your Date System: 1900 or 1904

Excel actually supports two date systems: the 1900 date system and the 1904 date system. Which system you use in a workbook determines what date serves as the basis for dates. The 1900 date system uses January 1, 1900 as the day assigned to date serial number 1. The 1904 date system uses January 1, 1904 as the base date. By default, Excel for Windows uses the 1900 date system, and Excel for Macintosh uses the 1904 date system. Excel for Windows supports the 1904 date system for compatibility with Macintosh files. You can choose the date system from the Options dialog box (select Tools ➪ Options and select the Calculation tab). You cannot change the date system if you use Excel for Macintosh.

Generally, you should use the default 1900-date system. And, you should exercise precaution if you use two different date systems in workbooks that are linked together. For example, assume Book1 uses the 1904 date system and contains the date 1/15/1999 in cell A1. Assume Book2 uses the 1900 date system and contains a link to cell A1 in Book1. Book2 will display the date as 1/14/1995. Both workbooks will use the same date serial number (34713), but they will be interpreted differently.

One advantage in using the 1904 date system is that it enables you to display negative time values. With the 1900 date system, a calculation that results in a negative time (for example 4:00 p.m.–5:30 p.m.) cannot be displayed. When using the 1904 date system, the negative time displays as –1:30 (that is, a difference of one hour and thirty minutes).

You may wonder about January 0, 1900. This "nondate" (which corresponds to date serial number 0) is actually used to represent times that are not associated with a particular day.

To view a date serial number as a date, you must format the cell as a date. Use the Format Cells dialog box (Number tab) to apply a date format.

Note   Excel 97 and later versions support dates from January 1, 1900 through December 31, 9999 (serial number = 2,958,465). Previous versions of Excel support a much smaller range of dates: from January 1, 1900 through December 31, 2078 (serial number = 65,380).

Entering dates

You can enter a date directly as a serial number (if you know it), but more often you'll enter a date using any of several recognized date formats. Excel automatically converts your entry into the corresponding date serial number (which it uses for calculations), and also applies the default date format to the cell so it displays as an actual date rather than a cryptic serial number.

For example, if you need to enter June 1, 2001, you can simply enter the date by typing **June 1, 2001** (or use any of several different date formats). Excel interprets your entry and stores the value 37043 — the date serial number for that date. It also applies the default date format, so the cell contents may not appear exactly as you typed them.

When you activate a cell that contains a date, the formula bar shows the cell contents formatted as a date. It does not display the date's serial number. If you need to find out the serial number for a particular date, format the cell using a nondate number format.

Tip   To change the default date format, you need to change a system-wide setting. Access the Windows Control Panel, and select Regional Settings. In the Regional Settings dialog box, select the Date tab. The selected item for the Short date style determines the default date format used by Excel.

Table 11-1 shows a sampling of the date formats that Excel recognizes.

Table 11-1 **Date Entry Formats Recognized by Excel**	
Entry	**Excel's Interpretation**
6-1-99	June 1, 1999
6-1-1999	June 1, 1999
6/1/99	June 1, 1999
6/1/1999	June 1, 1999
6-1/99	June 1, 1999
June 1, 1999	June 1, 1999
Jun 1	June 1 of the current year
June 1	June 1 of the current year
6/1	June 1 of the current year
6-1	June 1 of the current year

As you can see in Table 11-1, Excel is rather smart when it comes to recognizing dates entered into a cell. It's not perfect, however. For example, Excel does *not* recognize any of the following entries as dates:

✦ June 1 1999

✦ Jun-1 1999

✦ Jun-1/1999

Searching for Dates

If your worksheet uses many dates, you may need to search for a particular date by using Excel's Find dialog box (which you can access with the Edit ➪ Find command, or Ctrl+F). You'll find that Excel is rather picky when it comes to finding dates. You must enter a full four-digit date into the Find what field in the Find dialog box. For example, if your worksheets contain a date displayed as 11/24/99, you must search for that date using 1/24/1999. If you try to locate 11/24/99 with a two-digit year, you won't find it.

Rather, it interprets these entries as text. If you plan to use dates in formulas, make sure that Excel can recognize the date you enter as a date; otherwise, the formulas that refer to these dates will produce incorrect results.

If you attempt to enter a date that lies outside of the supported date range, Excel interprets it as text. If you attempt to format a serial number that lies outside of the supported range as a date, the value displays as a series of pound signs (#########).

Understanding time serial numbers

When you need to work with time values, you simply extend Excel's date serial number system to include decimals. In other words, Excel works with times by using fractional days. For example, the date serial number for June 1, 2001 is 37043. Noon (halfway through the day) is represented internally as 37043.5.

The serial number equivalent of one minute is 0.0006944. The formula that follows calculates this number by multiplying 24 hours by 60 minutes, and dividing the result into 1. The denominator consists of the number of minutes in a day (1,440).

```
=1/(24*60)
```

Similarly, the serial number equivalent of one second is 0.0000115740740740741, obtained by the following formula (1 divided by 24 hours times 60 minutes times 60 seconds). In this case, the denominator represents the number of seconds in a day (86,400).

```
=1/(24*60*60)
```

In Excel, the smallest unit of time is one one-thousandth of a second. The time serial number shown here represents 23:59:59.999, or one one-thousandth of a second before midnight.

```
0.99999999
```

Table 11-2 shows various times of day, along with each associated time serial number.

Table 11-2 Times of Day and Their Corresponding Serial Numbers	
Time of Day	**Time Serial Number**
12:00:00 AM (midnight)	0.00000000
1:30:00 AM	0.06250000
3:00:00 AM	0.12500000
4:30:00 AM	0.18750000
6:00:00 AM	0.25000000
7:30:00 AM	0.31250000
9:00:00 AM	0.37500000
10:30:00 AM	0.43750000
12:00:00 PM (noon)	0.50000000
1:30:00 PM	0.56250000
3:00:00 PM	0.62500000
4:30:00 PM	0.68750000
6:00:00 PM	0.75000000
7:30:00 PM	0.81250000
9:00:00 PM	0.87500000
10:30:00 PM	0.93750000

Entering times

As with entering dates, you normally don't have to worry about the actual time serial numbers. Just enter the time into a cell using a recognized format. Table 11-3 shows some examples of time formats that Excel recognizes.

Table 11-3		
Time Entry Formats Recognized by Excel		
Entry	*Excel's Interpretation*	
11:30:00 am	11:30 a.m.	
11:30:00 AM	11:30 a.m.	
11:30 pm	11:30 p.m.	
11:30	11:30 a.m.	
13:30	1:30 p.m.	

Because the preceding samples don't have a specific day associated with them, Excel (by default) uses a date serial number of 0, which corresponds to the nonday January 0, 1900. Often, you'll want to combine a date and time. Do so by using a recognized date entry format, followed by a space, and then a recognized time-entry format. For example, if you enter the text that follows in a cell, Excel interprets it as 11:30 a.m. on June 1, 2001. Its date/time serial number is 37043.4791666667.

```
6/1/2001 11:30
```

When you enter a time that exceeds 24 hours, the associated date for the time increments accordingly. For example, if you enter the following time into a cell, it is interpreted as 1:00 a.m. on January 1, 1900. The day part of the entry increments because the time exceeds 24 hours.

```
25:00:00
```

Similarly, if you enter a date *and* a time — and the time exceeds 24 hours — the date that you entered is adjusted. The following entry, for example, is interpreted as 9/2/1999 1:00:00 a.m.

```
9/1/1999 25:00:00
```

If you enter a time only (without an associated date), you'll find that the maximum time that you can enter into a cell is 9999:59:59 (just under 10,000 hours). Excel adds the appropriate number of days. In this case, 9999:59:59 is interpreted as 3:59:59 p.m. on 02/19/1901. If you enter a time that exceeds 10,000 hours, the time appears as a text string.

Formatting dates and times

You have a great deal of flexibility in formatting cells that contain dates and times. For example, you can format the cell to display the date part only, the time part only, or both the date and time parts.

You format dates and times by selecting the cells, and then using the Number tab of the Format Cells dialog box, shown in Figure 11-1. The Date category shows built-in date formats, and the Time category shows built-in time formats. Some of the formats include both date and time display. Just select the desired format from the Type list and click OK.

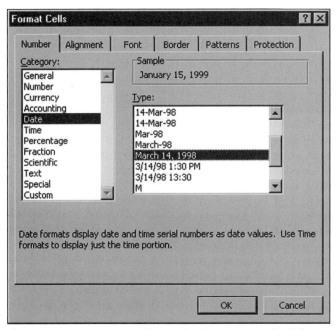

Figure 11-1: Use the Number tab in the Format Cells dialog box to change the appearance of dates and times.

Tip   When you create a formula that refers to a cell containing a date or a time, Excel automatically formats the formula cell as a date or a time. Sometimes, this is very helpful; other times it's completely inappropriate and downright annoying. Unfortunately, you cannot turn off this automatic date formatting. You can, however, use a shortcut key combination to remove all number formatting from the cell. Just select the cell and press Ctrl+Shift+~.

If none of the built-in formats meet your needs, you can create a custom number format. Select the Custom category, and then type the custom format codes into the Type box.

Tip   A particularly useful custom number format for displaying times is:

```
[h]:mm:ss
```

Using square brackets around the hour part of the format string causes Excel to display hours beyond 24 hours. You will find this useful when adding times that exceed 24 hours. For an example, see "Summing Times That Exceed 24 Hours," later in this chapter.

Problems with dates

OK, I admit it: Excel has some problems when it comes to dates. Many of these problems stem from the fact that Excel was designed many years ago, before the acronym Y2K became a household term. And, as I describe, the Excel designers basically emulated Lotus 1-2-3's limited date and time features — which contain a nasty bug duplicated intentionally in Excel. Finally, versions of Excel show inconsistency in how they interpret a cell entry that has a two-digit year.

If Excel were being designed from scratch today, I'm sure it would be much more versatile in dealing with dates. Unfortunately, we're currently stuck with a product that leaves much to be desired in the area of dates.

Excel's leap year bug

A leap year contains an additional day (February 29). Although the year 1900 was not a leap year, Excel treats it as such. In other words, when you type the following into a cell, Excel does not complain. It interprets this as a valid date and assigns a serial number of 60.

```
2/29/1900
```

If you type the following, Excel correctly interprets it as a mistake and *doesn't* convert it to a date. Rather, it simply makes the cell entry text:

```
2/29/1901
```

How can a product used daily by millions of people contain such an obvious bug? The answer is historical. The original version of Lotus 1-2-3 contained a bug that caused it to consider 1900 as a leap year. When Excel was released some time later, the designers knew of this bug, and chose to reproduce it in Excel to maintain compatibility with Lotus worksheet files.

Why does this bug still exist in later versions of Excel? Microsoft asserts that the disadvantages of correcting this bug outweigh the advantages. If the bug were eliminated, it would mess up hundreds of thousands of existing workbooks. In addition, correcting this problem would affect compatibility between Excel and other programs that use dates. As it stands, this bug really causes very few problems because most users do not use dates before March 1, 1900.

Pre-1900 dates

The world, of course, didn't begin on January 1, 1900. People who work with historical information using Excel often need to work with dates before January 1, 1900. Unfortunately, the only way to work with pre-1900 dates is to enter the date into a cell as text. For example, you can enter the following into a cell and Excel won't complain:

```
July 4, 1776
```

You can't, however, perform any manipulation on dates recognized as text. For example, you can't change its numeric formatting, you can't determine which day of the week this date occurred on, and you can't calculate the date that occurs seven days later.

On the CD-ROM

The companion CD-ROM contains an add-in that I developed called Extended Date Functions. When you install this add-in, you'll have access to eight new worksheet functions that enable you to work with any date in the years 0100 through 9999. Figure 11-2 shows a worksheet that uses these functions to calculate the number of days between various pre-1900 dates.

Book4

	A	B	C	D	E
1	**Extended Date Functions Demo**				
2					
3	**Date1**	**Date2**	**Difference (Days)**	**Difference (Years)**	
4	Jan 1, 1776	Jan 1, 1781	1827	5	
5	Jan 1, 1800	Jan 1, 1801	365	1	
6	Apr 12, 1898	Apr 12, 1999	36889	101	
7	Jun 22, 1904	Mar 5, 1881	-8509	-24	
8					
9					
10					
11					

Sheet1

Figure 11-2: The Extended Date Functions add-in enables you to work with pre-1900 dates.

Inconsistent date entries

You need to exercise caution when entering dates by using two digits for the year. When you do so, Excel has some rules that kick in to determine which century to use. And those rules vary depending on the version of Excel that you use.

For Excel 97 and Excel 2000, two-digit years between 00 and 29 are interpreted as 21st century dates, and two-digit years between 30 and 99 are interpreted as 20th century dates. For example, if you enter 12/5/28, Excel interprets your entry as December 5, 2028. But if you enter 12/5/30, Excel sees it as December 5, 1930.

For previous versions of Excel (Excel 3 through Excel 95), two-digit years between 00 and 19 are interpreted as 21st century dates, and two-digit years between 20 and 99 are interpreted as 20th century dates. For example, if you enter 12/5/19, Excel interprets your entry as December 5, 2019. But if you enter 12/5/20, Excel sees it as December 5, 1920.

If for some unknown reason you still use Excel 2, when you enter a two-digit date, it is *always* interpreted as a 20th century date. Table 11-4 summarizes these differences for various versions of Excel.

Table 11-4 How Two-Digit Years Are Interpreted in Various Excel Versions		
Excel Version	*20th Century Years*	*21st Century Years*
2	00–78	N/A
3, 4, 5, 7 (95)	20–99	00–19
8 (97), 9 (2000)	30–99	00–29

To avoid any surprises, you should simply enter *all* years using all four digits for the year.

Date-Related Functions

Excel has quite a few functions that work with dates, and you can use these functions in your formulas. When you use the Paste Function dialog box, these functions appear in the Date & Time function category.

Table 11-5 summarizes the date-related functions available in Excel. Some of Excel's date functions require that you install the Analysis ToolPak.

Function	Description
DATE	Returns the serial number of a particular date
DATEDIF	Calculates the number of days, months, or years between two dates
DATEVALUE	Converts a date in the form of text to a serial number
DAY	Converts a serial number to a day of the month
DAYS360	Calculates the number of days between two dates based on a 360-day year
EDATE*	Returns the serial number of the date that represents the indicated number of months before or after the start date
EOMONTH*	Returns the serial number of the last day of the month before or after a specified number of months
MONTH	Converts a serial number to a month
NETWORKDAYS*	Returns the number of whole workdays between two dates
NOW	Returns the serial number of the current date and time
TODAY	Returns the serial number of today's date
WEEKDAY	Converts a serial number to a day of the week
WEEKNUM*	Returns the week number in the year
WORKDAY*	Returns the serial number of the date before or after a specified number of workdays
YEAR	Converts a serial number to a year
YEARFRAC*	Returns the year fraction representing the number of whole days between start_date and end_date

Table 11-5 title:

**Table 11-5
Date-Related Functions**

* Function is available only when the Analysis ToolPak add-in is installed.

Displaying the current date

The following function displays the current date in a cell:

```
=TODAY()
```

You can also display the date, combined with text. The formula that follows, for example, displays text such as, "Today is Thursday, December 30, 1999."

```
="Today is "&TEXT(TODAY(),"dddd, mmmm d, yyyy")
```

It's important to understand that the TODAY function is updated whenever the worksheet is calculated. For example, if you enter either of the formulas into a worksheet, they will display the current date. But when you open the workbook tomorrow, they will display the current date—not the date when you entered the formula.

Tip To enter a "date stamp" into a cell, press Ctrl+; (semicolon). This enters the date directly into the cell and does not use a formula. Therefore, the date will not change.

Displaying any date

As explained earlier in this chapter, you can easily enter a date into a cell by simply typing it, using any of the date formats that Excel recognizes. You can also create a date by using the DATE function. The following formula, for example, returns a date comprising the year in cell A1, the month in cell B1, and the day in cell C1.

```
=DATE(A1,B1,C1)
```

Note The DATE function accepts invalid arguments and adjusts the result accordingly. For example, this next formula uses 13 as the month argument and returns January 1, 2000. The month argument is automatically translated as month 1 of the following year.

```
=DATE(1999,13,1)
```

Often, you'll use DATE function with other functions as arguments. For example, the formula that follows uses the YEAR and TODAY functions to return the date for Independence Day (July 4th) of the current year:

```
=DATE(YEAR(TODAY()),7,4)
```

The DATEVALUE function converts a text string that looks like a date into a date serial number. The following formula returns 36394, the date serial number for August 22, 1999:

```
=DATEVALUE("8/22/1999")
```

To view the result of this formula as a date, you need to apply a date number format to the cell.

Note Excel's NOW and TODAY functions retrieve their values from the system clock. If your system clock is not set correctly, these functions will not return correct results. Use the Windows Control Panel to adjust your system clock to the correct date and time.

Generating a series of dates

Often, you'll want to insert a series of dates into a worksheet. For example, in tracking weekly sales, you may want to enter a series of dates, each separated by seven days. These dates will serve to identify the sales figures.

The most efficient way to enter a series of dates doesn't require any formulas. Use Excel's AutoFill feature to insert a series of dates. Enter the first date, and drag the cell's fill handle while pressing the right mouse button. Release the mouse button and select an option from the shortcut menu (see Figure 11-3).

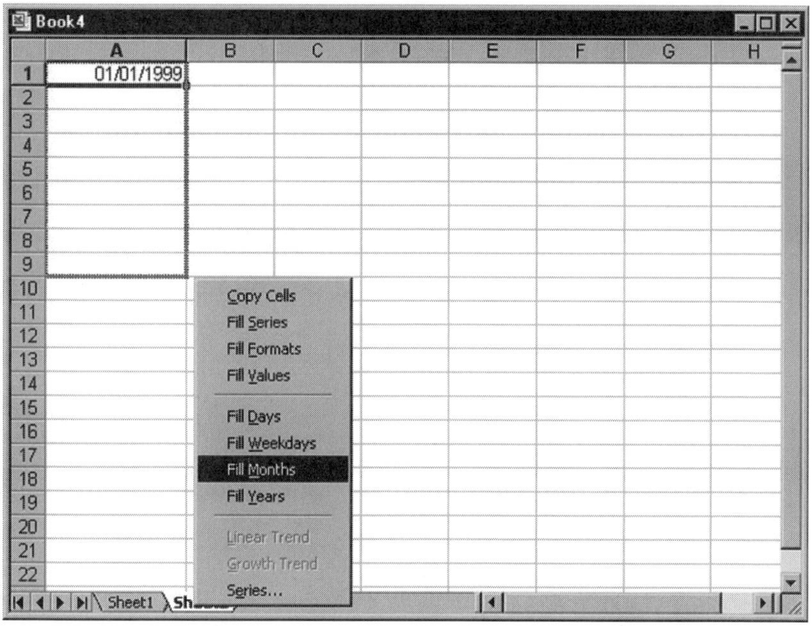

Figure 11-3: Using Excel's AutoFill feature to create a series of dates

The advantage of using formulas to create a series of dates is that you can change the first date and the others will update automatically. You need to enter the starting date into a cell, and then use formulas (copied down the column) to generate the additional dates.

The following examples assume that you entered the first date of the series into cell A1, and the formula into cell A2. You can then copy this formula down the column as many times as needed.

To generate a series of dates separated by seven days, use this formula:

```
=A1+7
```

To generate a series of dates separated by one month, use this formula:

```
=DATE(YEAR(A1),MONTH(A1)+1,DAY(A1))
```

To generate a series of dates separated by one year, use this formula:

```
=DATE(YEAR(A1)+1,MONTH(A1),DAY(A1))
```

To generate a series of weekdays only (no Saturdays or Sundays), use the formula that follows. This formula assumes that the date in cell A1 is not a weekend.

```
=IF(WEEKDAY(A1)=6,A1+3,A1+1)
```

Converting a nondate string to a date

Often, you may import data that contains dates coded as text strings. For example, the following text represents August 21, 1999 (a four-digit year followed by a two-digit month, followed by a two-digit day):

```
19990821
```

To covert this string to an actual date, you can use a formula such as this one that assumes the coded data appears in cell A1:

```
=DATE(LEFT(A1,4),MID(A1,5,2),RIGHT(A1,2))
```

This formula uses text functions (LEFT, MID, and RIGHT) to extract the digits, and then uses these extracted digits as arguments for the DATE function.

Calculating the number of days between two dates

A common type of date calculation determines the number of days between two dates. For example, you may have a financial worksheet that calculates interest earned on a deposit account. The interest earned depends on the number of days the account is open. If your sheet contains the open date and the close date for the account, you can calculate the number of days the account was open.

Because dates store as consecutive serial numbers, you can use simple subtraction to calculate the number of days between two dates. For example, if cells A1 and B1 both contain a date, the following formula returns the number of days between these dates:

```
=A1-B1
```

If cell B1 contains a more recent date than the date in cell A1, the result will be negative.

Note If this formula does not display the correct value, make sure that A1 and B1 both contain actual dates — not text that *looks* like a date.

Sometimes, calculating the difference between two days proves more difficult. To demonstrate, consider the common fence-post analogy. If somebody asks you how many units make up a fence, you can respond with either of two answers: the number of fence posts, or the number of gaps between the fence posts. The number of fence posts always remains one more than the number of gaps between the posts.

To bring this analogy into the realm of dates, suppose you start a sales promotion on February 1 and end the promotion on February 9. How many days was the promotion in effect? Subtracting February 1 from February 9 produces an answer of eight days. Actually, the promotion lasted nine days. In this case, the correct answer involves counting the fence posts, not the gaps. The formula to calculate the length of the promotion (assuming you have appropriately named cells) appears like this:

```
=EndDay-StartDay+1
```

Calculating the number of work days between two dates

Often, you may want to exclude weekends and holidays when calculating the difference between two dates. For example, you may need to know how many business days fall in the month of November. This calculation should exclude Saturdays, Sundays, and holidays. The NETWORKDAYS function can help out. (You can access this function only when you install the Analysis ToolPak.)

Note The NETWORKDAYS function has nothing to do with networks or networking. Rather, it calculates the net workdays between two dates.

The NETWORKDAYS function calculates the difference between two dates, excluding weekend days (Saturdays and Sundays). As an option, you can specify a range of cells that contain the dates of holidays, which are also excluded. Excel has absolutely no way of determining which days are holidays, so you must provide this information in a range.

Figure 11-4 shows a worksheet that calculates the workdays between two dates. The range A2:A9 contains a list of holiday dates. The formulas in column C calculate the workdays between the dates in column A and column B. For example, the formula in cell C13 is:

```
=NETWORKDAYS(A13,B13,A2:A9)
```

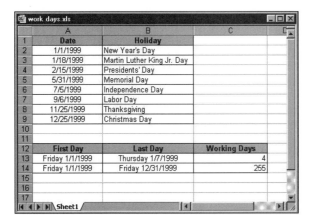

Figure 11-4: Using the NETWORKDAYS function to calculate the number of working days between two dates

This formula returns 4, which means that the seven-day period beginning with January 1 contains four workdays. In other words, the calculation excludes one holiday, one Saturday, and one Sunday.

Offsetting a date using only workdays

The WORKDAY function — available only when you install the Analysis ToolPak — presents the opposite of the NETWORKDAYS function. For example, if you start a project on January 4, and the project requires 10 working days to complete, the WORKDAY function can calculate the date you will finish the project.

The following formula uses the WORKDAY function to determine the date 10 working days from January 4, 1999. A working day consists of a weekday (Monday through Friday).

```
=WORKDAY("1/4/1999",10)
```

The formula returns January 18, 1999 (four weekend dates fall between January 4 and January 18).

The second argument for the WORKDAY function can be negative. And, as with the NETWORKDAYS function, the WORKDAY function accepts an optional third argument — a reference to a range that contains a list of holiday dates.

Calculating the number of years between two dates

The following formula calculates the number of years between two dates. This formula assumes that cells A1 and B1 both contain dates.

```
=YEAR(A1)-YEAR(B1)
```

This formula uses the YEAR function to extract the year from each date, and then subtracts one year from the other. If cell B1 contains a more recent date than the date in cell A1, the result will be negative.

Note that this function doesn't calculate *full* years. For example, if cell A1 contains 12/31/1999 and cell B1 contains 01/01/1998, the formula returns a difference of one year, even though the dates differ by only one day.

Calculating a person's age

A person's age indicates the number of full years that the person has been alive. The formula for calculating the number of years between two dates won't calculate this value correctly. You can use two other formulas, however, to calculate a person's age.

The following formula returns the age of the person whose date of birth you enter into cell A1. This formula uses the YEARFRAC function—available only when you install the Analysis ToolPak add-in.

```
=INT(YEARFRAC(TODAY(),A1,1))
```

The following formula, which doesn't rely on an Analysis ToolPak function, uses the DATEDIF function to calculate an age (see the sidebar, "Where's the DATEDIF Function?"):

```
=DATEDIF(A1,TODAY(),"Y")
```

Where's the DATEDIF Function?

In several places throughout this chapter, I refer to the DATEDIF function. You may notice that this function does not appear in the Paste Function dialog box. Therefore, when you use this function, you must always enter it manually.

The DATEDIF function has its origins in Lotus 1-2-3, and apparently Excel provides it for compatibility purposes. Versions prior to Excel 2000 failed to even mention the DATEDIF function in the online help.

DATEDIF is a handy function that calculates the number of days, months, or years between two dates. The function takes three arguments: start_date, end_date, and a code that represents the time unit of interest. The following table displays valid codes for the third argument (you must enclose the codes in quotation marks).

Continued

(continued)

Unit Code	Returns
"y"	The number of complete years in the period.
"m"	The number of complete months in the period.
"d"	The number of days in the period.
"md"	The difference between the days in start_date and end_date. The months and years of the dates are ignored.
"ym"	The difference between the months in start_date and end_date. The days and years of the dates are ignored.
"yd"	The difference between the days of start_date and end_date. The years of the dates are ignored.

The start_date argument must be earlier than the end_date argument, or the function returns an error.

Determining the day of the year

January 1 is the first day of the year, and December 31 is the last day. But what about all of the days in between? The following formula returns the day of the year for a date stored in cell A1:

```
=A1-DATE(YEAR(A1),1,0)
```

The day of the year is sometimes referred to as a *Julian date.*

The following formula returns the number of days remaining in the year from a particular date (assumed to be in cell A1):

```
=DATE(YEAR(A1),12,31)-A1
```

When you enter either of these formulas, Excel applies date formatting to the cell. You need to apply a nondate number format to view the result as a number.

To convert a particular day of the year (for example, the 90th day of the year) to an actual date in a specified year, use the formula that follows. This formula assumes the year stores in cell A1, and the day of the year stores in cell B1.

```
=DATE(A1,1,B1)
```

PUP 2000 Date Utilities

My Power Utility Pak 2000 (which you can order using the coupon in the back of the book) includes several utilities that work with dates:

✦ **Perpetual Calendar:** Displays a calendar for any month, creates a graphic calendar image, and creates calendars in worksheets.

✦ **Insert-A-Date:** Simplifies date entries. You can insert a date into a cell by clicking a calendar and choosing from a list of common date formats.

✦ **Reminder Alarm:** Displays a reminder (with sound) at a specified time of day, or after a specified period of time has elapsed.

✦ **Time Tracker:** Tracks the amount of time spent working on up to six different projects.

✦ **Date Report:** Creates a useful report that describes all dates in a workbook. This utility is useful for spotting potential Y2K problems.

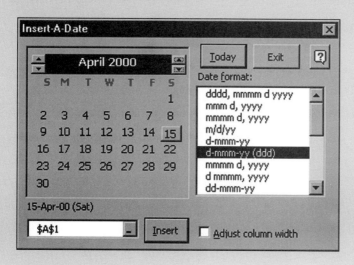

Determining the day of the week

The WEEKDAY function accepts a date argument and returns an integer between 1 and 7 that corresponds to the day of the week. The following formula, for example, returns 7 because the first day of the year 2000 falls on a Saturday:

```
=WEEKDAY(1/1/2000)
```

The WEEKDAY function uses an optional second argument that specifies the day numbering for the result. If you specify 2 as the second argument, the function returns 1 for Monday, 2 for Tuesday, and so on. If you specify 3 as the second argument, the function returns 0 for Monday, 1 for Tuesday, and so on.

Tip   You can also determine the day of the week for a cell that contains a date by applying a custom number format. A cell that uses the following custom number format displays the day of the week, spelled out:

```
dddd
```

Determining the date of the most recent Sunday

You can use the following formula to return the date for the previous Sunday. If the current day is a Sunday, the formula returns the current date:

```
=TODAY()-MOD(TODAY()-1,7)
```

To modify this formula to find the date of a day other than Sunday, change the 1 to a different number between 2 (for Monday) and 7 (for Saturday).

Determining the first day of the week after a date

This next formula returns the specified day of the week that occurs after a particular date. For example, use this formula to determine the date of the first Monday after June 3, 1999. The formula assumes that cell A1 contains a date, and cell A2 contains a number between 1 and 7 (1 for Sunday, 2 for Monday, and so on).

```
=A1+IF(A2<WEEKDAY(A1),7-WEEKDAY(A1)+A2,A2-WEEKDAY(A1))
```

If cell A1 contains June 3, 1999 and cell A2 contains 2 (for Monday), the formula returns June 7, 1999. This is the first Monday after June 3, 1999.

Determining the *n*th occurrence of a day of the week in a month

You may need a formula to determine the date for a particular occurrence of a weekday. For example, suppose your company payday falls on the second Friday of each month, and you need to determine the paydays for each month of the year. The following formula will make this type of calculation:

```
=DATE(A1,A2,1)+IF(A3<WEEKDAY(DATE(A1,A2,1)),7-WEEKDAY
(DATE(A1,A2,1))+A3,A3-WEEKDAY(DATE(A1,A2,1)))+((A4-1)*7)
```

The formula in this section assumes:

✦ Cell A1 contains a year

✦ Cell A2 contains a month

✦ Cell A3 contains a day number (1 for Sunday, 2 for Monday, and so on)

✦ Cell A4 contains the occurrence of interest (for example, 1 to select the first occurrence of the weekday specified in cell A3)

If you use this formula to determine the date of the first Friday in June 2000, it returns June 2, 2000.

Note   If the value in cell A4 exceeds the number of the specified day in the month, the formula returns a date from a subsequent month. For example, if you attempt to determine the date of the sixth Friday in June 2000 (no such date exists), the formula returns the first Friday in July.

Counting the occurrences of a day of the week

You can use the following formula to count the number of occurrences of a particular day of the week for a specified month. It assumes that cell A1 contains a date, and cell B1 contains a day number (1 for Sunday, 2 for Monday, and so on). The formula is an array formula, so you must enter it using Ctrl+Shift+Enter.

```
{=SUM((WEEKDAY(DATE(YEAR(A1),MONTH(A1),ROW(INDIRECT("1:"&
DAY(DATE(YEAR(A1),MONTH(A1)+1,0))))))=B1)*1)}
```

If cell A1 contains the date January 12, 1999, and cell A2 contains the value 2 (for Monday), the formula returns 4 — which reveals that January 1999 contains four Mondays.

The preceding array formula calculates the year and month by using the YEAR and MONTH functions. You can simplify the formula a bit if you store the year and month in separate cells. The following formula (also an array formula) assumes that the year appears in cell A1, the month in cell A2, and the day number in cell B1:

```
{=SUM((WEEKDAY(DATE(A1,A2,ROW(INDIRECT("1:"&
DAY(DATE(A1,A2+1,0))))))=B1)*1)}
```

Figure 11-5 shows this formula used in a worksheet. In this case, the formula uses mixed cell references so you can copy it. For example, the formula in cell C3 is:

```
{=SUM((WEEKDAY(DATE($B$2,$A3,ROW(INDIRECT("1:"&
DAY(DATE($B$2,$A3+1,0))))))=C$1)*1)}
```

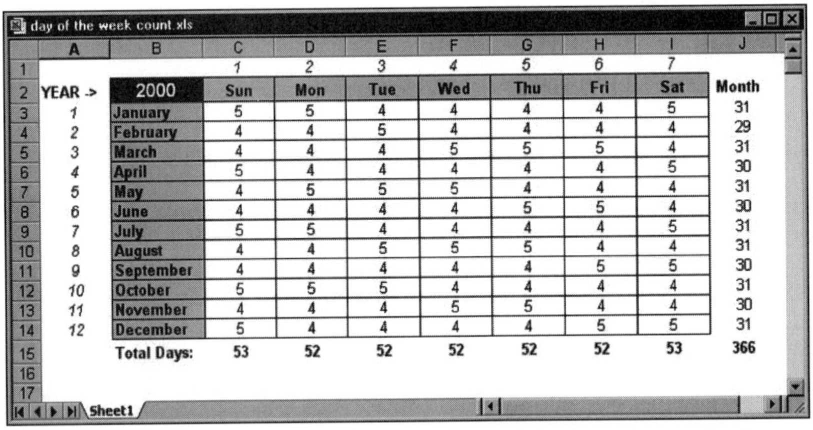

day of the week count.xls

	A	B	C	D	E	F	G	H	I	J
1			1	2	3	4	5	6	7	
2	YEAR ->	2000	Sun	Mon	Tue	Wed	Thu	Fri	Sat	Month
3	1	January	5	5	4	4	4	4	5	31
4	2	February	4	4	5	4	4	4	4	29
5	3	March	4	4	4	5	5	5	4	31
6	4	April	5	4	4	4	4	4	5	30
7	5	May	4	5	5	5	4	4	4	31
8	6	June	4	4	4	4	5	5	4	30
9	7	July	5	5	4	4	4	4	5	31
10	8	August	4	4	5	5	5	4	4	31
11	9	September	4	4	4	4	4	5	5	30
12	10	October	5	5	5	4	4	4	4	31
13	11	November	4	4	4	5	5	4	4	30
14	12	December	5	4	4	4	4	5	5	31
15		Total Days:	53	52	52	52	52	52	53	366
16										
17										

Sheet1

Figure 11-5: Calculating the number of each weekday in each month of a year

Additional formulas use the SUM function to calculate the number of days per month (column J) and the number of each weekday in the year (row 15).

Expressing a date as an ordinal number

You may want to express a date as an ordinal number. For example, you can display 4/6/2000 as April 6th, 2000. The following formula expresses the date in cell A1 as an ordinal date. Note that the result is text, not an actual date.

```
=TEXT(A1,"mmmm ")&DAY(A1)&IF(INT(MOD(DAY(A1),100)/10)=1,
"th",IF(MOD(DAY(A1),10)=1,
"st",IF(MOD(DAY(A1),10)=2,"nd",IF(MOD(DAY(A1),10)=3,
"rd","th"))))&TEXT(A1,", yyyy")
```

The following formula shows a variation that expresses the date in cell A1 in day-month-year format. For example, 4/6/2000 would appear as 4th April, 2000. Again, the result of this formula represents text, not an actual date.

```
=DAY(A1)&IF(INT(MOD(DAY(A1),100)/10)=1, "th",
IF(MOD(DAY(A1),10)=1, "st",IF(MOD(DAY(A1),10)=2,"nd",
IF(MOD(DAY(A1),10)=3, "rd","th"))))& " " &TEXT(A1,"mmmm, yyyy")
```

Calculating dates of holidays

Determining the date for a particular holiday can be tricky. Some, such as New Year's Day and U.S. Independence Day are no-brainers, because they always occur on the same date. For these kinds of holidays, you can simply use the DATE function, which I covered earlier in this chapter. To enter New Year's Day—which always falls on January 1—for a specific year in cell A1, you can enter this function:

```
=DATE(A1,1,1)
```

Other holidays are defined in terms of a particular occurrence of a particular weekday in a particular month. For example, Labor Day falls on the first Monday in September.

Figure 11-6 shows a workbook with formulas to calculate the date for 10 U.S. holidays. The formulas reference the year in cell A1. Notice that because New Year's Day, Independence Day, Veterans Day, and Christmas Day all fall on the same days of the year, the DATE function calculates their dates.

	A	B	C	D
1	2000	<-- Year		
2				
3	**Holiday**	**Description**	**Date**	
4	New Year's Day	1st Day in January	Saturday Jan-01-2000	
5	Martin Luther King Jr. Day	3rd Monday in January	Monday Jan-17-2000	
6	Presidents' Day	3rd Monday in February	Monday Feb-21-2000	
7	Memorial Day	Last Monday in May	Monday May-29-2000	
8	Independence Day	4th Day of July	Tuesday Jul-04-2000	
9	Labor Day	1st Monday in September	Monday Sep-04-2000	
10	Veterans Day	11th Day of November	Saturday Nov-11-2000	
11	Columbus Day	2nd Monday in October	Monday Oct-09-2000	
12	Thanksgiving Day	4thThursday in November	Thursday Nov-23-2000	
13	Christmas Day	25th Day of December	Monday Dec-25-2000	
14				
15				

Figure 11-6: Using formulas to determine the date for various holidays

Martin Luther King Jr. Day

This holiday occurs on the third Monday in January. This formula calculates Martin Luther King Jr. Day for the year in cell A1:

```
=DATE(A1,1,1)+IF(2<WEEKDAY(DATE(A1,1,1)),7-WEEKDAY
(DATE(A1,1,1))+2,2-WEEKDAY(DATE(A1,1,1)))+((3-1)*7)
```

Presidents' Day

Presidents' Day occurs on the third Monday in February. This formula calculates Presidents' Day for the year in cell A1:

```
=DATE(A1,2,1)+IF(2<WEEKDAY(DATE(A1,2,1)),7-WEEKDAY
(DATE(A1,2,1))+2,2-WEEKDAY(DATE(A1,2,1)))+((3-1)*7)
```

Memorial Day

The last Monday in May is Memorial Day. This formula calculates Memorial Day for the year in cell A1:

```
=DATE(A1,6,1)+IF(2<WEEKDAY(DATE(A1,6,1)),7-WEEKDAY
(DATE(A1,6,1))+2,2-WEEKDAY(DATE(A1,6,1)))+((1-1)*7)-7
```

Notice that this formula actually calculates the first Monday in June, and then subtracts 7 from the result to return the last Monday in May.

Labor Day

Labor Day occurs on the first Monday in September. This formula calculates Labor Day for the year in cell A1:

```
=DATE(A1,9,1)+IF(2<WEEKDAY(DATE(A1,9,1)),7-WEEKDAY
(DATE(A1,9,1))+2,2-WEEKDAY(DATE(A1,9,1)))+((1-1)*7)
```

Columbus Day

This holiday occurs on the second Monday in October. The following formula calculates Columbus Day for the year in cell A1:

```
=DATE(A1,10,1)+IF(2<WEEKDAY(DATE(A1,10,1)),7-WEEKDAY
(DATE(A1,10,1))+2,2-WEEKDAY(DATE(A1,10,1)))+((2-1)*7)
```

Thanksgiving Day

Thanksgiving Day is celebrated on the fourth Thursday in November. This formula calculates Thanksgiving Day for the year in cell A1:

```
=DATE(A1,11,1)+IF(5<WEEKDAY(DATE(A1,11,1)),7-WEEKDAY
(DATE(A1,11,1))+5,5-WEEKDAY(DATE(A1,11,1)))+((4-1)*7)
```

Determining the last day of a month

To determine the date that corresponds to the last day of a month, you can use the DATE function. However, you need to increment the month by 1, and use a day value of 0. In other words, the "0th" day of the next month is the last day of the current month.

The following formula assumes that a date is stored in cell A1. The formula returns the date that corresponds to the last day of the month.

```
=DATE(YEAR(A1),MONTH(A1)+1,0)
```

Calculating Easter

You'll notice that I omitted Easter from the previous section. Easter is an unusual holiday because its date is determined based on the phase of the moon and not by the calendar. Because of this, determining when Easter occurs proves a bit of a challenge.

Hans Herber, an Excel master in Germany, once sponsored an Easter formula contest at his Web site. The goal was to create the shortest formula possible that correctly determined the date of Easter for the years 1900 through 2078.

Twenty formulas were submitted, ranging in length from 44 characters up to 154 characters. Some of these formulas, however, work only with European date settings. The following formula, submitted by Thomas Jansen, is the shortest formula that works with any date setting. This formula returns the date for Easter, and assumes the year is stored in cell A1.

```
=DOLLAR(("4/"&A1)/7+MOD(19*MOD(A1,19)-7,30)*14%,)*7-6
```

Please don't ask me to explain this formula. I haven't a clue!

You can use a variation of this formula to determine how many days comprise a specified month. The formula that follows returns an integer that corresponds to the number of days in the month for the date in cell A1.

```
=DAY(DATE(YEAR(A1),MONTH(A1)+1,0))
```

When you enter this formula, Excel applies date formatting to the cell. Apply a nondate number format to view the result as a number.

Determining if a year is a leap year

To determine if a particular year is a leap year, you can write a formula that determines whether the 29th day of February occurs in February or March. You can take advantage of the fact that Excel's DATE function adjusts the result when you supply an invalid argument — for example, a day of 29 when February contains only 28 days.

The following formula returns TRUE if the year of the date in cell A1 is a leap year. Otherwise, it returns FALSE.

```
=IF(MONTH(DATE(YEAR(A1),2,29))=2,TRUE,FALSE)
```

Caution　　This function returns the wrong result (TRUE) if the year is 1900. See "Excel's Leap Year Bug," earlier in this chapter.

Determining a date's quarter

For financial reports, you might find it useful to present information in terms of quarters. The following formula returns an integer between 1 and 4 that corresponds to the calendar quarter for the date in cell A1:

```
=ROUNDUP(MONTH(A1)/3,0)
```

This formula divides the month number by 3, and then rounds up the result.

Converting a year to Roman numerals

Fans of old movies will like this one. The following formula converts the year 1945 to Roman numerals. It returns MCMXLV.

```
=ROMAN(1945)
```

You can access the ROMAN function once you install the Analysis ToolPak. This function returns a text string, so you can't perform any calculations using the result! Unfortunately, Excel doesn't provide a function to convert Roman numerals back to normal numbers.

Creating a calendar in a range

The example calendar you see in Figure 11-7 uses a single formula (an array formula) to display a calendar in a range of cells. The scroll bars are linked to cells that contain the month and year. The month is stored in cell B2 (named *m*) and the year is stored in cell D2 (named *y*). Enter the following array formula into the range B6:H11:

```
{=IF(MONTH(DATE(y,m,1))<>MONTH(DATE(y,m,1)-(WEEKDAY
(DATE(y,m,1))-1)+{0;1;2;3;4;5}*7+{1,2,3,4,5,6,7}-1),
"",DATE(y,m,1)-(WEEKDAY(DATE(y,m,1))-1)+{0;1;2;3;4;5}
*7+{1,2,3,4,5,6,7}-1)}
```

Time-Related Functions

Excel, as you might expect, also includes functions that enable you to work with time values in your formulas. This section contains examples that demonstrate the use of these functions.

Table 11-6 summarizes the time-related functions available in Excel. When you use the Paste Function dialog box, these functions appear in the Date & Time function category.

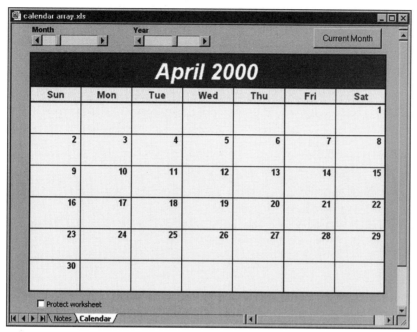

Figure 11-7: You can generate this calendar by using a single array formula, entered into 42 cells.

	Table 11-6
	Time-Related Functions

Function	Description
HOUR	Converts a serial number to an hour
MINUTE	Converts a serial number to a minute
MONTH	Converts a serial number to a month
NOW	Returns the serial number of the current date and time
SECOND	Converts a serial number to a second
TIME	Returns the serial number of a particular time
TIMEVALUE	Converts a time in the form of text to a serial number

Displaying the current time

This formula displays the current time as a time serial number (or, a serial number without an associated date):

```
=NOW()-TODAY()
```

Tip　To enter a time stamp into a cell, press Ctrl+Shift+: (colon).

You need to format the cell with a time format to view the result as a recognizable time. For example, you can apply the following number format:

```
hh:mm AM/PM
```

You can also display the time, combined with text. The formula that follows displays the text "The current time is 6:28 PM."

```
="The current time is "&TEXT(NOW(),"h:mm AM/PM")
```

Note　These formulas are updated only when the worksheet is calculated.

Displaying any time

Earlier in this chapter, I described how to enter a time value into a cell: Just type it into a cell, making sure that you include at least one colon (:). You can also create a time by using the TIME function. For example, the following formula returns a time comprising the hour in cell A1, the minute in cell B1, and the second in cell C1.

```
=TIME(A1,B1,C1)
```

Note　Like the DATE function, the TIME function accepts invalid arguments and adjusts the result accordingly. For example, the following formula uses 80 as the minute argument and returns 10:20:15 AM. The 80 minutes are simply added to the hour, with 20 minutes remaining.

```
=TIME(9,80,15)
```

You can also use the DATE function along with the TIME function in a single cell. The formula that follows generates 36498.7708333333, the serial number that represents 6:30 p.m. on December 4, 1999.

```
=DATE(1999,12,4)+TIME(18,30,0)
```

The TIMEVALUE function converts a text string that looks like a time into a time serial number. The following formula returns 0.2395833333, the time serial number for 5:45 a.m.

```
=TIMEVALUE("5:45 am")
```

To view the result of this formula as a time, you need to apply number formatting to the cell. The TIMEVALUE function doesn't recognize all time formats. For example, the following formula returns an error because Excel doesn't like the periods in "a.m."

```
=TIMEVALUE("5:45 a.m.")
```

Summing times that exceed 24 hours

Many people are dismayed to discover that, when you sum a series of times that exceed 24 hours, Excel doesn't display the correct total. Figure 11-8 shows an example. The range B2:B8 contains times that represent the hours and minutes worked each day. The formula in cell B9 is:

```
=SUM(B2:B8)
```

As you can see, the formula returns an incorrect total (18 hours, 30 minutes). The total should read 42 hours, 30 minutes.

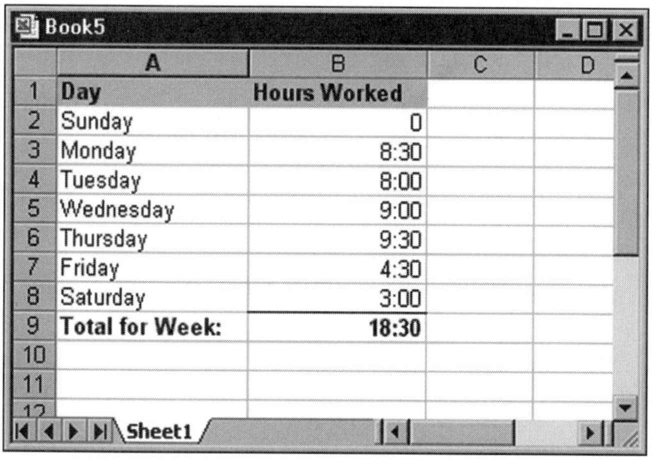

	A	B	C	D
1	Day	Hours Worked		
2	Sunday	0		
3	Monday	8:30		
4	Tuesday	8:00		
5	Wednesday	9:00		
6	Thursday	9:30		
7	Friday	4:30		
8	Saturday	3:00		
9	Total for Week:	18:30		
10				
11				
12				

Figure 11-8: Using the SUM function to add a series of times. The answer is incorrect because cell B9 has the wrong number format.

Unless told otherwise, Excel always displays times as if they comprise part of a day (in other words, limited to 24 hours). To view a time that exceeds 24 hours, you need to change the number format for the cell so square brackets surround the *hour* part of the format string. Applying the number format here to cell B9 displays the sum correctly:

```
[h]:mm
```

Figure 11-9 shows another example of a worksheet that manipulates times. This worksheet keeps track of hours worked during a week (regular hours and overtime hours).

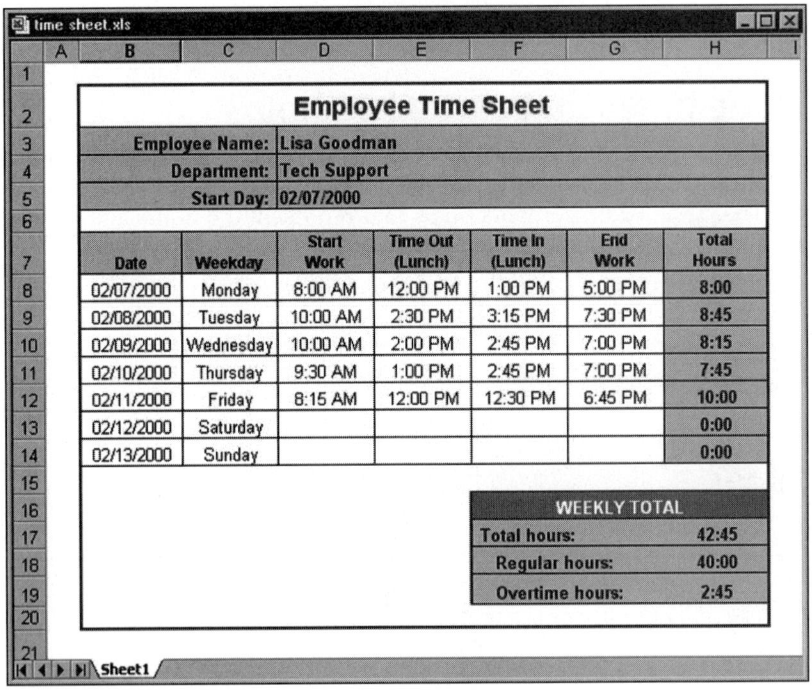
time sheet.xls

Employee Time Sheet

Employee Name:	Lisa Goodman
Department:	Tech Support
Start Day:	02/07/2000

Date	Weekday	Start Work	Time Out (Lunch)	Time In (Lunch)	End Work	Total Hours
02/07/2000	Monday	8:00 AM	12:00 PM	1:00 PM	5:00 PM	8:00
02/08/2000	Tuesday	10:00 AM	2:30 PM	3:15 PM	7:30 PM	8:45
02/09/2000	Wednesday	10:00 AM	2:00 PM	2:45 PM	7:00 PM	8:15
02/10/2000	Thursday	9:30 AM	1:00 PM	2:45 PM	7:00 PM	7:45
02/11/2000	Friday	8:15 AM	12:00 PM	12:30 PM	6:45 PM	10:00
02/12/2000	Saturday					0:00
02/13/2000	Sunday					0:00

WEEKLY TOTAL	
Total hours:	42:45
Regular hours:	40:00
Overtime hours:	2:45

Sheet1

Figure 11-9: An employee timesheet workbook

The week's starting date appears in cell D5, and the formulas in column B fill in the dates for the days of the week. Times appear in the range D8:G14, and formulas in column H calculate the number of hours worked each day. For example, the formula in cell H8 is:

```
=IF(E8<D8,E8+1-D8,E8-D8)+IF(G8<F8,G8+1-G8,G8-F8)
```

The first part of this formula subtracts the time in column D from the time in column E to get the total hours worked before lunch. The second part subtracts the time in column F from the time in column G to get the total hours worked after lunch. I use IF functions to accommodate graveyard shift cases that span midnight — for example, an employee may start work at 10:00 p.m. and begin lunch at 2:00 a.m. Without the IF function, the formula returns a negative result.

The following formula in cell H17 calculates the weekly total by summing the daily totals in column H:

```
=SUM(H8:H14)
```

The formula in cell H18 calculates regular hours (and assumes a 40-hour week). The formula returns the smaller of two values: the total hours, or 40 hours.

```
=MIN(H17,1+TIME(40,0,0))
```

The final formula in cell H19 simply subtracts the regular hours (cell H18) from the total hours (H16) to yield the overtime hours. If your standard workweek consists of something other than 40 hours, make the appropriate change to the formula in H18.

The times in H17:H19 likely will display time values that exceed 24 hours, so these cells use a custom number format:

```
[h]:mm
```

Calculating the difference between two times

Because times are represented as serial numbers, you can subtract the earlier time from the later time to get the difference. For example, if cell A2 contains 5:30:00 and cell B2 contains 14:00:00, the following formula returns 08:30:00 (a difference of eight hours and 30 minutes).

```
=B2-A2
```

If the subtraction results in a negative value, however, it becomes an invalid time; Excel displays a series of pound signs (######) because a time without a date has a date serial number of 0. A negative time results in a negative serial number, which is not permitted. This problem does not occur when you use a date along with the time.

If the direction of the time difference doesn't matter, you can use the ABS function to return the absolute value of the difference:

```
=ABS(B2-A2)
```

This "negative time" problem often occurs when calculating an elapsed time — for example, calculating the number of hours worked given a start time and an end time. This presents no problem if the two times fall in the same day. But if the work shift spans midnight, the result is an invalid negative time. For example, you may start work at 10:00 p.m. and end work at 6:00 a.m. the next day. Figure 11-10 shows a worksheet that calculates the hours worked. As you can see, the shift that spans midnight presents a problem.

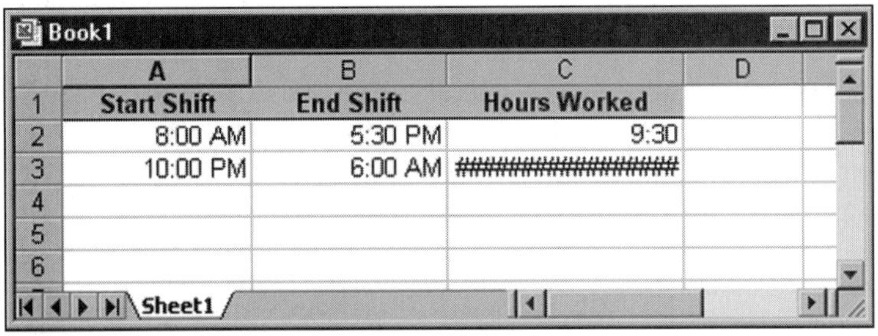

	A	B	C	D
1	**Start Shift**	**End Shift**	**Hours Worked**	
2	8:00 AM	5:30 PM	9:30	
3	10:00 PM	6:00 AM	##################	
4				
5				
6				

Figure 11-10: Calculating the number of hours worked returns an error if the shift spans midnight.

Using the absolute value function (ABS) isn't an option in this case because it returns the wrong result (16 hours). The following formula, however, *does* work.

```
=(B2+(B2<A2)-A2)
```

Another, simpler, formula can do the job:

```
=MOD(B2-A2,1)
```

Tip   Negative times *are* permitted if the workbook uses the 1904 date system. To switch to the 1904 date system, select Tools ➪ Options, and click the Calculation tab. Place a checkmark next to the 1904 date system option. But beware! When changing the workbook's date system, if the workbook uses dates, the dates will be off by four years.

Converting from military time

Military time is expressed as a four-digit number from 0000 to 2459. For example, 1:00 a.m. is expressed as 0100 hours, and 3:30 p.m. is expressed as 1530 hours. The following formula converts such a number (assumed to appear in cell A1) to a standard time:

```
=TIMEVALUE(LEFT(A1,2)&":"&RIGHT(A1,2))
```

The formula returns an incorrect result if the contents of cell A1 do not contain four digits. The following formula corrects the problem and returns a valid time for any military time value from 0 to 2459.

```
=TIMEVALUE(LEFT(TEXT(A1,"0000"),2)&":"&RIGHT(TEXT(A1,"0000"),2)
)
```

Converting decimal hours, minutes, or seconds to a time

To convert decimal hours to a time, divide the decimal hours by 24. For example, if cell A1 contains 9.25 (representing hours), this formula returns 09:15:00 (nine hours, 15 minutes):

```
=A1/24
```

To convert decimal minutes to a time, divide the decimal hours by 1,440 (the number of minutes in a day). For example, if cell A1 contains 500 (representing minutes), the following formula returns 08:20:00 (eight hours, 20 minutes):

```
=A1/1440
```

To convert decimal seconds to a time, divide the decimal hours by 86,400 (the number of seconds in a day). For example, if cell A1 contains 65,000 (representing seconds), the following formula returns 18:03:20 (18 hours, three minutes, and 20 seconds).

```
=A1/86400
```

Adding hours, minutes, or seconds to a time

You can use the TIME function to add any number of hours, minutes, or seconds to a time. For example, assume cell A1 contains a time. The following formula adds two hours and 30 minutes to that time and displays the result:

```
=A1+TIME(2,30,0)
```

You can use the TIME function to fill a range of cells with incremental times. Figure 11-11 shows a worksheet with a series of times in 10-minute increments. Cell A1 contains a time that was entered directly. Cell A2 contains the following formula, which copied down the column:

```
=A1+TIME(0,10,0)
```

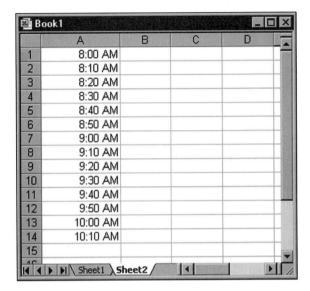

Figure 11-11: Using a formula to create a series of incremental times

Converting between time zones

You may receive a worksheet that contains dates and times in Greenwich Mean Time (GMT, sometimes referred to as Zulu time), and you need to convert these values to local time. To covert dates and times into local times, you need to determine the difference in hours between the two time zones. For example, to convert GMT times to U.S. Central Standard Time, the hour conversion factor is –6.

You can't use the TIME function with a negative argument, so you need to take a different approach. One hour equals 1/24 of a day, so you can divide the time conversion factor by 24, and then add it to the time.

Figure 11-12 shows a worksheet set up to convert dates and times (expressed in GMT) to local times. Cell B1 contains the hour conversion factor (–5 hours for U.S. Eastern Standard Time). The formula in B4, which copies down the column, is:

```
=A4+($B$1/24)
```

This formula effectively adds *x* hours to the date and time in column A. If cell B1 contains a negative hour value, the value subtracts from the date and time in column A. Note that, in some cases, this also affects the date.

	A	B	C	D
	gmt conversion.xls			
1	**Conversion Factor:**	-5 hours		
2				
3	**GMT**	**Local Time**		
4	01/05/1999 01:00 AM	01/04/1999 08:00 PM		
5	01/05/1999 03:30 AM	01/04/1999 10:30 PM		
6	01/05/1999 06:00 AM	01/05/1999 01:00 AM		
7	01/05/1999 08:30 AM	01/05/1999 03:30 AM		
8	01/05/1999 11:00 AM	01/05/1999 06:00 AM		
9	01/05/1999 01:30 PM	01/05/1999 08:30 AM		
10	01/05/1999 04:00 PM	01/05/1999 11:00 AM		
11	01/05/1999 06:30 PM	01/05/1999 01:30 PM		
12	01/05/1999 09:00 PM	01/05/1999 04:00 PM		
13	01/05/1999 11:30 PM	01/05/1999 06:30 PM		
14	01/06/1999 02:00 AM	01/05/1999 09:00 PM		
15	01/06/1999 04:30 AM	01/05/1999 11:30 PM		
16	01/06/1999 07:00 AM	01/06/1999 02:00 AM		
17	01/06/1999 09:30 AM	01/06/1999 04:30 AM		
18	01/06/1999 12:00 PM	01/06/1999 07:00 AM		
19				

Figure 11-12: This worksheet converts dates and times between time zones.

Rounding time values

You may need to create a formula that rounds a time to a particular value. For example, you may need to enter your company's time records rounded to the nearest 15 minutes. This section presents examples of various ways to round a time value.

The following formula rounds the time in cell A1 to the nearest minute:

```
=ROUND(A1*1440,0)/1440
```

The formula works by multiplying the time by 1440 (to get total minutes). This value is passed to the ROUND function; the result is divided by 1440. For example, if cell A1 contains 11:52:34, the formula returns 11:53:00.

The following formula resembles this example, except that it rounds the time in cell A1 to the nearest hour:

```
=ROUND(A1*24,0)/24
```

If cell A1 contains 5:21:31, the formula returns 5:00:00.

The following formula rounds the time in cell A1 to the nearest 15 minutes:

```
=ROUND(A1*24/0.25,0)*(0.25/24)
```

In this formula, 0.25 represents the fractional hour. To round a time to the nearest 30 minutes, change 0.25 to 0.5, as in the following formula:

```
=ROUND(A1*24/0.5,0)*(0.5/24)
```

Working with non-time-of-day values

Sometimes, you may want to work with time values that don't represent an actual time of day. For example, you might want to create a list of the finish times for a race, or record the time you spend jogging each day. Such times don't represent a time of day. Rather, a value represents the time for an event (in hours, minutes, and seconds). The time to complete a test, for instance, might take 35 minutes and 40 seconds. You can enter that value into a cell as:

```
00:35:45
```

Excel interprets such an entry as 12:35:45 AM — which works fine (just make sure that you format the cell so that it appears as you like). When you enter such times that do not have an hour component, you must include at least one zero for the hour. If you omit a leading zero for a missing hour, Excel interprets your entry as 35 hours and 45 minutes.

Figure 11-13 shows an example of a worksheet set up to keep track of someone's jogging activity. Column A contains simple dates. Column B contains the distance, in miles. Column C contains the time it took to run the distance. Column D contains formulas to calculate the speed, in miles per hour. For example, the formula in cell D2 is:

```
=B2/(C2*24)
```

Column E contains formulas to calculate the pace, in minutes per mile. For example, the formula in cell E2 is:

```
=(C2*60*24)/B2
```

Columns F and G contain formulas that calculate the year-to-date distance (using column B), and the cumulative time (using column C). The cells in column G are formatted using the following number format (which permits time displays that exceed 24 hours):

```
[hh]:mm:ss
```

	A	B	C	D	E	F	G	H
				Speed	Pace	YTD	Cumulative	
1	Date	Distance	Time	(mph)	(min/mile)	Distance	Time	
2	01/01/1999	1.50	00:18:45	4.80	12.50	1.50	00:18:45	
3	01/02/1999	1.50	00:17:40	5.09	11.78	3.00	00:36:25	
4	01/03/1999	2.00	00:21:30	5.58	10.75	5.00	00:57:55	
5	01/04/1999	1.50	00:15:20	5.87	10.22	6.50	01:13:15	
6	01/05/1999	2.40	00:25:05	5.74	10.45	8.90	01:38:20	
7	01/06/1999	3.00	00:31:06	5.79	10.37	11.90	02:09:26	
8	01/07/1999	3.80	00:41:06	5.55	10.82	15.70	02:50:32	
9	01/08/1999	5.00	01:09:00	4.35	13.80	20.70	03:59:32	
10	01/09/1999	4.00	00:45:10	5.31	11.29	24.70	04:44:42	
11	01/10/1999	3.00	00:29:06	6.19	9.70	27.70	05:13:48	
12	01/11/1999	5.50	01:08:30	4.82	12.45	33.20	06:22:18	
13								
14								

Figure 11-13: This worksheet uses times not associated with a time of day.

Summary

This chapter explored the date- and time-related features of Excel. I provided an overview of Excel's serial number date and time system, and I described how to enter dates and times into cells. The chapter also listed many examples of formulas that use dates and times.

The next chapter presents various techniques to count data in a spreadsheet.

✦　　✦　　✦

Counting and Summing Formulas

Many of the most frequently asked spreadsheet questions involve counting and summing values and other worksheet elements. It seems that people are always looking for formulas to count or sum various items in a worksheet. If I've done my job, this chapter will answer the vast majority of such questions.

Counting and Summing Worksheet Cells

Generally, a counting formula returns the number of cells in a specified range that meet certain criteria. A summing formula returns the sum of the cells in a range that meet certain criteria. The range you want counted or summed may or may not consist of a worksheet database.

Table 12-1 lists Excel's worksheet functions that come into play when creating counting and summing formulas. If none of the functions in Table 12-1 can solve your problem, it's likely that an array formula can come to the rescue.

Table 12-1
Excel's Counting and Summing Functions

Function	Description
COUNT	Returns the number of cells in a range that contain a numeric value
COUNTA	Returns the number of nonblank cells in a range
COUNTBLANK	Returns the number of blank cells in a range
COUNTIF*	Returns the number of cells in a range that meet a specified criterion
DCOUNT*	Counts the number of records in a worksheet database that meet specified criteria
DCOUNTA	Counts the number of nonblank records in a worksheet database that meet specified criteria
DEVSQ	Returns the sum of squares of deviations of data points from the sample mean; used primarily in statistical formulas
FREQUENCY	Calculates how often values occur within a range of values, and returns a vertical array of numbers; used only in a multicell array formula
SUBTOTAL	When used with a first argument of 2 or 3, returns a count of cells that comprise a subtotal; when used with a first argument of 9, returns the sum of cells that comprise a subtotal
SUM	Returns the sum of its arguments
SUMIF*	Returns the sum of cells in a range that meet a specified criterion
SUMPRODUCT	Multiplies corresponding cells in two or more ranges, and returns the sum of those products
SUMSQ	Returns the sum of the squares of its arguments; used primarily in statistical formulas
SUMX2PY2	Returns the sum of the sum of squares of corresponding values in two ranges; used primarily in statistical formulas
SUMXMY2	Returns the sum of squares of the differences of corresponding values in two ranges; used primarily in statistical formulas
SUMXMY2	Returns the sum of the difference of squares of corresponding values in two ranges; used primarily in statistical formulas.

* Available in Excel 97 or later.

Getting a Quick Count or Sum

In Excel 97, Microsoft introduced a feature known as AutoCalculate. This feature displays — in the status bar — information about the selected range. Normally, the status bar displays the sum of the values in the selected range. You can, however, right-click the AutoCalculate display to bring up a menu with some other options.

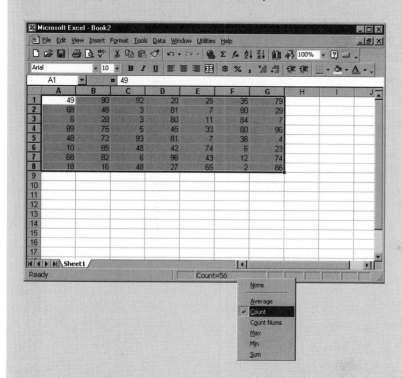

If you select Count, the status bar displays the number of nonempty cells in the selected range. If you select Count Nums, the status bar displays the number of numeric cells in the selected range.

Counting or Summing Records in Databases and Pivot Tables

Special database functions and the use of pivot tables provide additional ways to achieve counting and summing. Excel's DCOUNT and DSUM functions are database functions. They work in conjunction with a worksheet database and require a special criterion range that holds the counting or summing criteria.

Creating a pivot table is a great way to get a count or sum of items without using formulas. Like the database function, using a pivot table is appropriate when your data appears in the form of a database.

Basic Counting Formulas

The basic counting formulas presented here are all straightforward and relatively simple. They demonstrate the ability of Excel's counting functions to count the number of cells in a range that meet specific criteria. Figure 12-1 shows a worksheet that uses formulas (in column E) to summarize the contents of range A1:B10—a 20-cell range named *Data*.

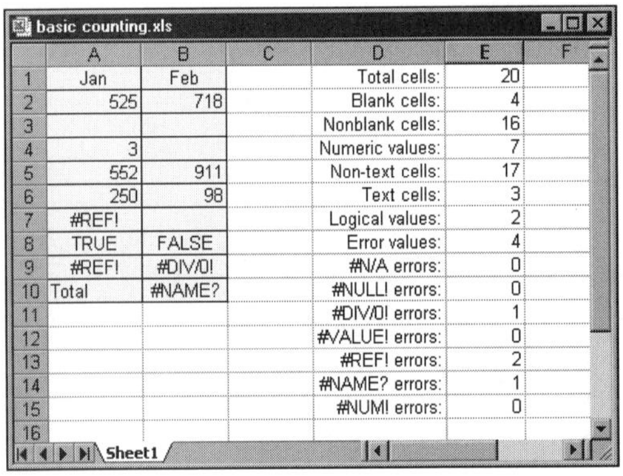

basic counting.xls

	A	B	C	D	E	F
1	Jan	Feb		Total cells:	20	
2	525	718		Blank cells:	4	
3				Nonblank cells:	16	
4	3			Numeric values:	7	
5	552	911		Non-text cells:	17	
6	250	98		Text cells:	3	
7	#REF!			Logical values:	2	
8	TRUE	FALSE		Error values:	4	
9	#REF!	#DIV/0!		#N/A errors:	0	
10	Total	#NAME?		#NULL! errors:	0	
11				#DIV/0! errors:	1	
12				#VALUE! errors:	0	
13				#REF! errors:	2	
14				#NAME? errors:	1	
15				#NUM! errors:	0	
16						

Sheet1

Figure 12-1: Formulas provide various counts of the data in A1:B10.

About This Chapter's Examples

Many of the examples in this chapter consist of array formulas. An array formula, as explained in Chapter 25, is a special type of formula. You can spot an array formula because it is enclosed in brackets. For example:

```
{=Data*2}
```

When you enter an array formula, press Ctrl+Shift+Enter (not just Enter). And don't type the brackets. (Excel inserts the brackets for you.)

Counting the total number of cells

To get a count of the total number of cells in a range, use the following formula. This formula returns the number of cells in a range named *Data*. It simply multiplies the number of rows (returned by the ROWS function) by the number of columns (returned by the COLUMNS function).

```
=ROWS(Data)*COLUMNS(Data)
```

Counting blank cells

The following formula returns the number of blank (empty) cells in a range named *Data*:

```
=COUNTBLANK(Data)
```

The COUNTBLANK function also counts cells containing a formula that returns an empty string. For example, the formula that follows returns an empty string if the value in cell A1 is greater than 5. If the cell meets this condition, then the COUNTBLANK function counts that cell.

```
=IF(A1>5,"",A1)
```

Note　　The COUNTBLANK function does not count cells that contain a zero value, even if you uncheck the Zero values option in the Options dialog box (select Tools ➪ Options, and then click the View tab).

You can use the COUNTBLANK function with an argument that consists of entire rows or columns. For example, this next formula returns the number of blank cells in column A:

```
=COUNTBLANK(A:A)
```

The following formula returns the number of empty cells on the entire worksheet named Sheet1. You must enter this formula on a sheet other than Sheet1, or it will create a circular reference.

```
=COUNTBLANK(Sheet1!1:65536)
```

Counting nonblank cells

The following formula uses the COUNTA function to return the number of nonblank cells in a range named *Data*:

```
=COUNTA(Data)
```

The COUNTA function counts cells that contain values, text, or logical values (TRUE or FALSE).

Counting numeric cells

To count only the numeric cells in a range, use the following formula (which assumes the range is named *Data*):

```
=COUNT(Data)
```

Cells that contain a date or a time are considered to be numeric cells. Cells that contain a logical value (TRUE or FALSE) are not considered to be numeric cells.

Counting nontext cells

The following array formula uses Excel's ISNONTEXT function, which returns TRUE if its argument refers to any nontext cell (including a blank cell). This formula returns the count of the number of cells not containing text (including blank cells):

```
{=SUM(IF(ISNONTEXT(Data),1))}
```

Counting text cells

To count the number of text cells in a range, you need to use an array formula. The array formula that follows returns the number of text cells in a range named *Data*.

```
{=SUM(IF(ISTEXT(Data),1))}
```

Counting logical values

The following array formula returns the number of logical values (TRUE or FALSE) in a range named *Data*.

```
{=SUM(IF(ISLOGICAL(Data),1))}
```

Error values in a range

Excel has three functions that help you determine if a cell contains an error value:

✦ **ISERROR:** Returns TRUE if the cell contains any error value (#N/A, #VALUE!, #REF!, #DIV/0!, #NUM!, #NAME?, or #NULL!)

✦ **ISERR:** Returns TRUE if the cell contains any error value except #N/A

✦ **ISNA:** Returns TRUE if the cell contains the #N/A error value

You can use these functions in an array formula to count the number of error values in a range. The following array formula, for example, returns the total number of error values in a range named *Data*:

```
{=SUM(IF(ISERROR(data),1))}
```

Depending on your needs, you can use the ISERR or ISNA function in place of ISERROR.

If you would like to count specific types of errors, you can use the COUNTIF function. The following formula, for example, returns the number of #DIV/0! error values in the range named *Data*:

```
=COUNTIF(Data,"#DIV/0!")
```

Advanced Counting Formulas

Most of the basic examples I presented previously represent functions or formulas that perform conditional counting. The advanced counting formulas that I present here represent more complex examples for counting worksheet cells, based on various types of criteria.

Counting cells using the COUNTIF function

Excel's COUNTIF function is useful for single-criterion counting formulas. The COUNTIF function takes two arguments:

✦ **Range:** The range that contains the values that determine whether to include a particular cell in the count

✦ **Criteria:** The logical criteria that determine whether to include a particular cell in the count

Table 12-2 lists several examples of formulas that use the COUNTIF function. These formulas all work with a range named *Data*. As you can see, the *criteria* argument is quite flexible. You can use constants, expressions, functions, cell references, and even wildcard characters (* and ?).

Table 12-2
Example Formulas That Use the COUNTIF Function

Formula	What It Returns
=COUNTIF(Data,12)	The number of cells containing the value 12
=COUNTIF(Data,"<0")	The number of cells containing a negative value
=COUNTIF(Data,"<>0")	The number of cells not equal to 0
=COUNTIF(Data,">5")	The number of cells greater than 5
=COUNTIF(Data,A1)	The number of cells equal to the contents of cell A1
=COUNTIF(Data,">"&A1)	The number of cells greater than the value in cell A1
=COUNTIF(Data,"*")	The number of cells containing text
=COUNTIF(Data,"???")	The number of text cells containing exactly three characters
=COUNTIF(Data,"budget")	The number of cells containing the single word budget (not case sensitive)
=COUNTIF(Data,"*budget*")	The number of cells containing the text budget anywhere within the text
=COUNTIF(Data,"A*")	The number of cells containing text that begins with the letter A (not case sensitive)
=COUNTIF(Data,TODAY())	The number of cells containing the current date
=COUNTIF(Data,">"&AVERAGE(Data))	The number of cells with a value greater than the average
=COUNTIF(Data,">"&STDEV(Data)*3)	The number of values exceeding three standard deviations above the mean
=COUNTIF(Data,3)+COUNTIF(Data,-3)	The number of cells containing the value 3 or –3
=COUNTIF(Data,TRUE)	The number of cells containing logical TRUE
=COUNTIF(Data,TRUE)+COUNTIF(Data,FALSE)	The number of cells containing a logical value (TRUE or FALSE)
=COUNTIF(Data,"#N/A")	The number of cells containing the #N/A error value

Counting cells using multiple criteria

In many cases, your counting formula will need to count cells only if two or more criteria are met. These criteria can be based on the cells that are being counted, or based on a range of corresponding cells.

Figure 12-2 shows a simple worksheet that I use for the examples in this section. This sheet shows sales data categorized by Month, SalesRep, and Type. The worksheet contains named ranges that correspond to the labels in row 1.

	A	B	C	D
1	Month	SalesRep	Type	Amount
2	January	Albert	New	85
3	January	Albert	New	675
4	January	Brooks	New	130
5	January	Cook	New	1350
6	January	Cook	Existing	685
7	January	Brooks	New	1350
8	January	Cook	New	475
9	January	Brooks	New	1205
10	February	Brooks	Existing	450
11	February	Albert	New	495
12	February	Cook	New	210
13	February	Cook	Existing	1050
14	February	Albert	New	140
15	February	Brooks	New	900
16	February	Brooks	New	900
17	February	Cook	New	95
18	February	Cook	New	780
19	March	Brooks	New	900
20	March	Albert	Existing	875
21	March	Brooks	New	50
22	March	Brooks	New	875
23	March	Cook	Existing	225
24	March	Cook	New	175
25	March	Brooks	Existing	400
26	March	Albert	New	840
27	March	Cook	New	132

Figure 12-2: This worksheet demonstrates various counting techniques that use multiple criteria.

Using And criteria

An And criterion counts cells if all specified conditions are met. A common example is a formula that counts the number of values that fall within a numerical range. For example, you may want to count cells that contain a value greater than 0 *and* less than or equal to 12. Any cell that has a positive value less than or equal to 12 will be included in the count.

This sort of cell counting requires an array formula. The array formula that follows returns the count of the number of cells in a range named *Data* that are greater than 0 and less than or equal to 12:

```
{=SUM((Data>0)*(Data<=12))}
```

Sometimes, the counting criteria will be based on cells other than the cells being counted. You may, for example, want to count the number of sales that meet the following criteria:

✦ Month is January, *and*

✦ SalesRep is Brooks, *and*

✦ Amount is greater than 1000

The following array formula returns the number of items that meet all three criteria:

```
{=SUM((Month="January")*(SalesRep="Brooks")*(Amount>1000))}
```

Using Or criteria

To count using an Or criterion, you can sometimes simply use multiple COUNTIF functions. The following formula, for example, counts the number of 1s, 3s, and 5s in the range named *Data*:

```
=COUNTIF(Data,1)+COUNTIF(Data,3)+COUNTIF(Data,5)
```

You can also use the COUNTIF function in an array formula. The following array formula, for example, returns the same result as the previous formula:

```
{=SUM(COUNTIF(Data,{1,3,5}))}
```

But if you base your Or criteria on cells other than the cells being counted, the COUNTIF function won't work. Refer back to Figure 12-2. Suppose you want to count the number of sales that meet the following criteria:

✦ Month is January, *or*

✦ SalesRep is Brooks, *or*

✦ Amount is greater than 1000

The following array formula returns the correct count.

```
{=SUM(IF((Month="January")+(SalesRep="Brooks")+(Amount>1000),1))}
```

Combining And and Or criteria

You can combine And and Or criteria when counting. For example, perhaps you want to count sales that meet the following criteria:

✦ Month is January, *and*

✦ SalesRep is Brooks, *or* SalesRep is Cook

This array formula returns the number of sales that meet the criteria.

```
{=SUM((Month="January")*IF((SalesRep="Brooks")+(SalesRep="Cook"),1))}
```

Counting the most frequently occurring entry

Excel's MODE function returns the most frequently occurring value in a range. Figure 12-3 shows a worksheet with values in range A1:A10 (named *Data*). The formula that follows returns 10 because that value appears most frequently in the *Data* range:

```
=MODE(Data)
```

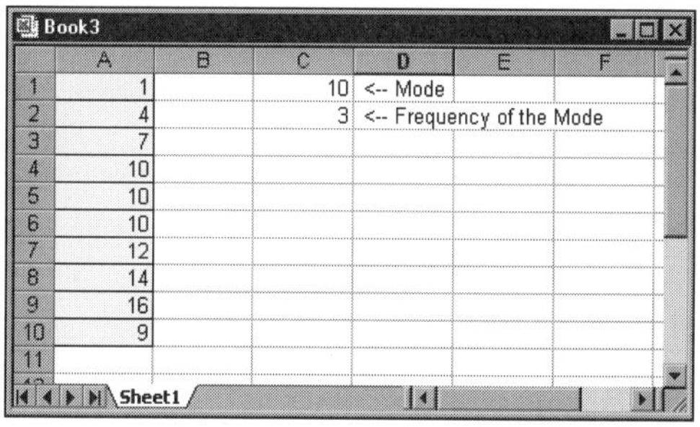

Figure 12-3: The MODE function returns the most frequently occurring value in a range.

To count the number of times the most frequently occurring value appears in the range (in other words, the frequency of the mode), use the following formula:

```
=COUNTIF(Data,MODE(Data))
```

This formula returns 3, because the modal value (10) appears three times in the *Data* range.

The MODE function works only for numeric values. It simply ignores cells that contain text. To find the most frequently occurring text entry in a range, you to need to use an array formula.

To count the number of times the most frequently occurring item (text or values) appears in a range named *Data*, use the following array formula:

```
{=MAX(COUNTIF(Data,Data))}
```

This next array formula operates like the MODE function, except that it works with both text and values.

```
{=INDEX(Data,MATCH(MAX(COUNTIF(Data,Data)),COUNTIF(Data,Data),0))}
```

Counting the occurrences of specific text

The examples in this section demonstrate various ways to count the occurrences of a character or text string in a range of cells. Figure 12-4 shows a worksheet used for these examples. Various text appears in the range A1:A10 (named *Data*); cell B1 is named *Text*.

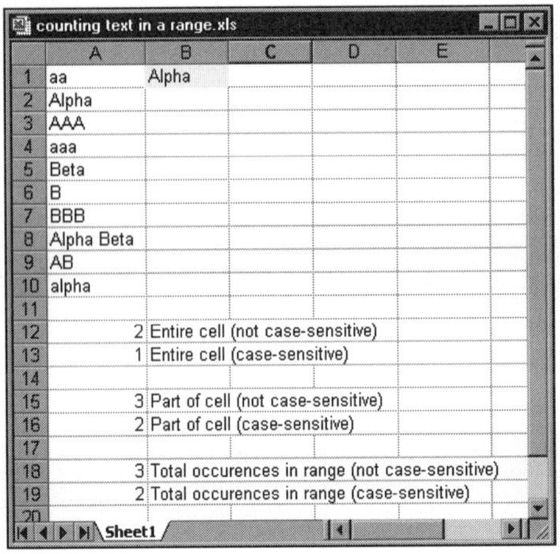

Figure 12-4: This worksheet demonstrates various ways to count characters in a range.

Entire cell contents

To count the number of cells containing the contents of the *Text* cell (and nothing else), you can use the COUNTIF function. The following formula demonstrates:

```
=COUNTIF(Data,Text)
```

For example, if the *Text* cell contains the string "Alpha," the formula returns 2 because two cells in the *Data* range contain this text. This formula is not case-sensitive, so it counts both "Alpha" (cell A2) and "alpha" (cell A10). Note, however, that it does not count the cell that contains "Alpha Beta" (cell A8).

The following array formula is similar to the preceding formula, but this one is case-sensitive:

```
{=SUM(IF(EXACT(Data,Text),1))}
```

Partial cell contents

To count the number of cells that contain a string that includes the contents of the *Text* cell, use this formula:

```
=COUNTIF(data,"*"&Text&"*")
```

For example, if the *Text* cell contains the text "Alpha" the formula returns 3, because three cells in the *Data* range contain the text "alpha" (cells A2, A8, and A10). Note that the comparison is not case sensitive.

If you need a case-sensitive count, you can use the following array formula:

```
{=SUM(IF(LEN(Data)-LEN(SUBSTITUTE(Data,Text,""))>0,1))}
```

If the *Text* cells contain the text "Alpha," the preceding formula returns 2 because the string appears in two cells (A2 and A8).

Total occurrences in a range

To count the total number of occurrences of a string within a range of cells, use the following array formula:

```
{=(SUM(LEN(Data))-SUM(LEN(SUBSTITUTE(Data,Text,""))))/LEN(Text)}
```

If the *Text* cell contains the character "B," the formula returns 7 because the range contains seven instances of the string. This formula is case sensitive.

The following formula is a modified version that is not case sensitive.

```
=(SUM(LEN(Data))-SUM(LEN(SUBSTITUTE(UPPER(Data),UPPER(Text),""))))/LEN(Text)
```

Counting the number of unique values

The following array formula returns the number of unique values in a range named *Data*:

```
{=SUM(1/COUNTIF(Data,Data))}
```

To understand how this formula works, you need a basic understanding of array formulas. (See Chapter 25 for an introduction to this topic.) In Figure 12-5, range A1:A12 is named *Data*. Range C1:C12 contains the following array formula (entered into all 12 cells in the range):

```
{=COUNTIF(Data,Data)}
```

	A	B	C	D	E	F	G	
1	100		3	0.333333				
2	100		3	0.333333				
3	100		3	0.333333				
4	200		2	0.5				
5	200		2	0.5				
6	300		1	1				
7	400		2	0.5				
8	400		2	0.5				
9	500		4	0.25				
10	500		4	0.25				
11	500		4	0.25				
12	500		4	0.25				
13				5	<-- Unique items in Column A			
14								

Figure 12-5: Using an array formula to count the number of unique values in a range

The array in range C1:C12 consists of the count of each value in *Data*. For example, the number 100 appears three times, so each array element that corresponds to a value of 100 in the *Data* range has a value of 3.

Range D1:D12 contains the following array formula:

```
{=1/C1:C12}
```

This array consists of each value in the array in range C1:C12, divided into 1. For example, each cell in the original *Data* range that contains a 200 has a value of 0.5 in the corresponding cell in D1:D12.

Summing the range D1:D12 gives the number of unique items in *Data*. The array formula presented at the beginning of this section essentially creates the array that occupies D1:D12, and sums the values.

This formula has a serious limitation: If the range contains any blank cells, it returns an error. The following array formula solves this problem:

```
{=SUM(IF(COUNTIF(Data,Data)=0,"",1/COUNTIF(Data,Data)))}
```

Cross-Reference To create an array formula that returns a list of unique items in a range, refer to Chapter 26.

Creating a frequency distribution

A frequency distribution basically comprises a summary table that shows the frequency of each value in a range. For example, an instructor may create a frequency distribution of test scores. The table would show the count of As, Bs, Cs, and so on. Excel provides a number of ways to create frequency distributions. You can:

✦ Use the FREQUENCY function

✦ Create your own formulas

✦ Use the Analysis ToolPak add-in

Note   If your data is in the form of a database, you can also use a pivot table to create a frequency distribution.

The FREQUENCY Function

Using Excel's FREQUENCY function presents the easiest way to create a frequency distribution. This function always returns an array, so you must use it in an array formula entered into a multicell range.

Figure 12-6 shows some data in range A1:E20 (named *Data*). These values range from 1 to 500. The range G2:G11 contains the bins used for the frequency distribution. Each cell in this bin range contains the upper limit for the bin. In this case, the bins consist of 1-50, 51-100, 101-150, and so on. See the sidebar, "Creating Bins for a Frequency Distribution," to discover an easy way to create a bin range.

	A	B	C	D	E	F	G	H
1	55	316	223	185	124		**Bins**	
2	124	93	163	213	314		50	
3	211	41	231	241	212		100	
4	118	113	400	205	254		150	
5	262	1	201	172	101		200	
6	167	479	205	337	118		250	
7	489	15	89	362	148		300	
8	179	248	125	197	177		350	
9	456	153	269	49	127		400	
10	289	500	198	317	300		450	
11	126	114	303	314	270		500	
12	151	279	347	314	170			
13	250	175	93	209	61			
14	166	113	356	124	242			
15	152	384	157	233	99			
16	277	195	436	6	240			
17	147	80	173	211	244			
18	386	93	330	400	141			
19	332	173	129	323	188			
20	338	263	444	84	220			
21								

frequency distribution.xls — FREQUENCY Func

Figure 12-6: Creating a frequency distribution for the data in A1:E20

To create the frequency distribution, select a range of cells that correspond to the number of cells in the bin range. Then, enter the following array formula:

```
{=FREQUENCY(Data,G2:G11)}
```

The array formula enters the count of values in the *Data* range that fall into each bin. To create a frequency distribution that consists of percentages, use the following array formula:

```
{=FREQUENCY(Data,G2:G10)/COUNTA(Data)}
```

Figure 12-7 shows two frequency distributions — one in terms of counts, and one in terms of percentages. The figure also shows a chart (histogram) created from the frequency distribution.

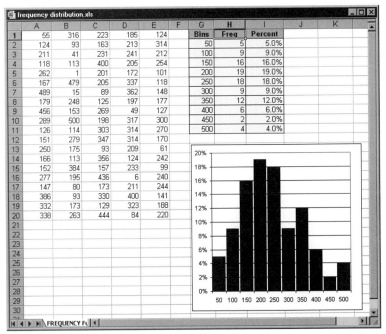

Figure 12-7: Frequency distributions created using the FREQUENCY function

Using formulas to create a frequency distribution

Figure 12-8 shows a worksheet that contains test scores for 50 students in column B (the range is named *Grades*). Formulas in columns G and H calculate a frequency distribution for letter grades. The minimum and maximum values for each letter grade appear in columns D and E. For example, a test score between 80 and 89 (inclusive) qualifies for a B.

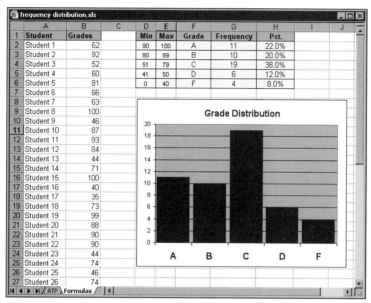

Figure 12-8: Creating a frequency distribution of test scores

Creating Bins for a Frequency Distribution

When creating a frequency distribution, you must first enter the values into the bin range. The number of bins determines the number of categories in the distribution. Most of the time, each of these bins will represent an equal range of values.

To create 10 evenly spaced bins for values in a range named *Data*, enter the following array formula into a range of 10 cells:

```
{=MIN(Data)+(ROW(INDIRECT("1:10"))*
(MAX(Data)-MIN(Data)+1)/10)-1}
```

This formula creates 10 bins, based on the values in the *Data* range. The upper bin will always equal the maximum value in the range.

To create more or fewer bins, use a value other than 10 and enter the array formula into a range that contains the same number of cells. For example, to create five bins, enter the following array formula into a five-cell range:

```
{=MIN(Data)+(ROW(INDIRECT("1:5"))*(MAX(Data)-MIN(Data)+1)/5)-1}
```

The formula in cell G2 that follows is an array formula that counts the number of scores that qualify for an A:

```
{=SUM((Grades>=D2)*(Grades<=E2))}
```

You may recognize this formula from a previous section in this chapter (see "Counting Cells Using Multiple Criteria"). This formula was copied to the four cells below G2.

The formulas in column H calculate the percentage of scores for each letter grade. The formula in H2, which was copied to the four cells below H2, is:

```
=G2/SUM($G$2:$G$6)
```

Using the Analysis ToolPak to create a frequency distribution

Once you install the Analysis ToolPak add-in, you can use the Histogram option to create a frequency distribution. Start by entering your bin values in a range. Then, select Tools ➪ Data Analysis to display the Data Analysis dialog box. Next, select Histogram and click OK. You should see the Histogram dialog box shown in Figure 12-9.

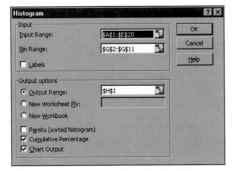

Figure 12-9: The Analysis ToolPak's Histogram dialog box

Specify the ranges for your data (Input Range), bins (Bin Range), and results (Output Range), and then select any options. Figure 12-10 shows a frequency distribution (and chart) created with the Histogram option.

Caution Note that the frequency distribution consists of values, not formulas. Therefore, if you make any changes to your input data, you need to re-run the Histogram procedure to update the results.

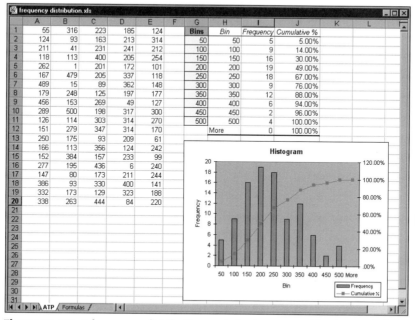

Figure 12-10: A frequency distribution and chart generated by the Analysis ToolPak's Histogram option

Using adjustable bins to create a histogram

Figure 12-11 shows a worksheet with student grades listed in column B (67 students, total). Columns D and E contain formulas that calculate the upper and lower limits for bins, based on the entry in cell E1 (named *BinSize*). For example, if *BinSize* is 10, then each bin contains 10 scores (1–10, 11–20, and so on).

The chart uses two dynamic names in its SERIES formula. You can define the name *Categories* with the following formula:

```
=OFFSET(Sheet1!$E$4,0,0,ROUNDUP(100/BinSize,0))
```

You can define the name *Frequencies* with this formula:

```
=OFFSET(Sheet1!$F$4,0,0,ROUNDUP(100/BinSize,0))
```

The net effect is that the chart adjusts automatically when you change the *BinSize* cell. Figure 12-12, for example, shows the chart with a *BinSize* of 5.

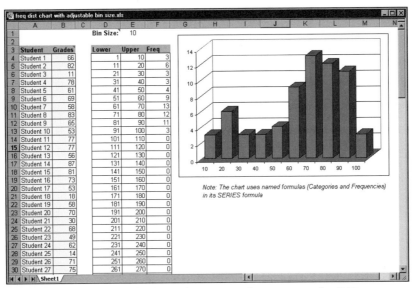

Figure 12-11: The chart displays a histogram; the contents of cell E1 determine the number of categories.

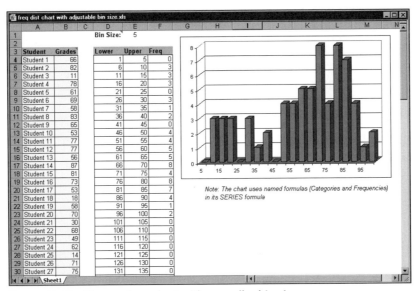

Figure 12-12: The previous chart with a smaller bin size

Summing Formulas

The examples in this section demonstrate how to perform common summing tasks using formulas. The formulas range from very simple to relatively complex array formulas that compute sums using multiple criteria.

Summing all cells in a range

It doesn't get much simpler than this. The following formula returns the sum of all values in a range named *Data*:

```
=SUMData)
```

The SUM function can take up to 32 arguments. The following formula, for example, returns the sum of the values in five noncontiguous ranges:

```
=SUM(A1:A9,C1:C9,E1:E9,G1:G9,I1:I9)
```

You can use complete rows or columns as an argument for the SUM function. The formula that follows, for example, returns the sum of all values in column A. If this formula appears in a cell in column A, it generates a circular reference error.

```
=SUM(A:A)
```

The following formula returns the sum of all values on Sheet1. This formula must appear on a sheet other than Sheet1.

```
=SUM(Sheet1!1:65536)
```

Computing a cumulative sum

Often, you may want to display a cumulative sum of values in a range — sometimes known as a "running total." Figure 12-13 illustrates a cumulative sum. Column B shows the monthly amounts, and column C displays the cumulative (year-to-date) totals.

The formula in cell C2 is:

```
=SUM(B$2:B2)
```

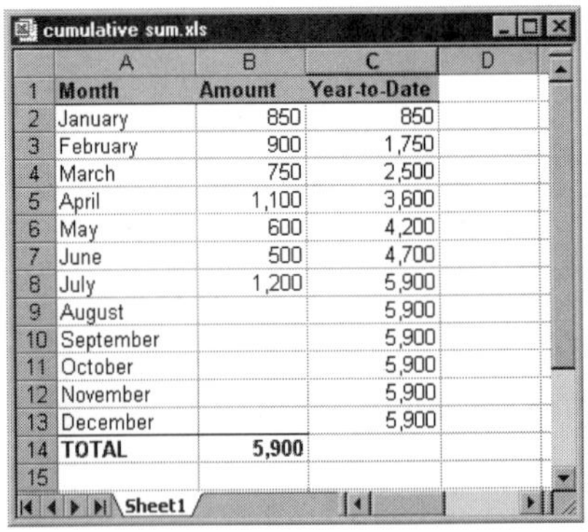

	A	B	C	D
1	Month	Amount	Year-to-Date	
2	January	850	850	
3	February	900	1,750	
4	March	750	2,500	
5	April	1,100	3,600	
6	May	600	4,200	
7	June	500	4,700	
8	July	1,200	5,900	
9	August		5,900	
10	September		5,900	
11	October		5,900	
12	November		5,900	
13	December		5,900	
14	TOTAL	5,900		
15				

Figure 12-13: Simple formulas in column C display a cumulative sum of the values in column B.

Notice that this formula uses a *mixed reference*. The first cell in the range reference always refers to row 2. When this formula is copied down the column, the range argument adjusts such that the sum always starts with row 2 and ends with the current row. For example, after copying this formula down column C, the formula in cell D8 is:

```
=SUM(B$2:B8)
```

You can use an IF function to hide the cumulative sums for rows in which data hasn't been entered. The following formula, entered in cell C2 and copied down the column, is:

```
=IF(B2<>"",SUM(B$2:B2),"")
```

Summing the "top n" values

In some situations, you may need to sum the *n* largest values in a range — for example, the top 10 values. One approach is to sort the range in descending order, and then use the SUM function with an argument consisting of the first *n* values in the sorted range. An array formula such as this one accomplishes the task without sorting:

```
{=SUM(LARGE(Data,{1,2,3,4,5,6,7,8,9,10}))}
```

This formula sums the 10 largest values in a range named *Data*. To sum the 10 smallest values, use the SMALL function instead of the LARGE function:

```
{=SUM(SMALL(Data,{1,2,3,4,5,6,7,8,9,10}))}
```

These formulas use an array constant comprising the arguments for the LARGE or SMALL function. If the value of *n* for your top-*n* calculation is large, you may prefer to use the following variation. This formula returns the sum of the top 30 values in the *Data* range. You can, of course, substitute a different value for 30.

```
{=SUM(LARGE(Data,ROW(INDIRECT("1:30"))))}
```

Conditional Sums Using a Single Criterion

Often, you need to calculate a *conditional sum*. With a conditional sum, values in a range that meet one or more conditions are included in the sum. This section presents examples of conditional summing using a single criterion.

The SUMIF function is very useful for single-criterion sum formulas. The SUMIF function takes three arguments:

- ✦ **Range:** The range containing the values that determine whether to include a particular cell in the sum.

- ✦ **Criteria:** An expression that determines whether to include a particular cell in the sum.

- ✦ **sum_range:** Optional. The range that contains the cells you want to sum. If you omit this argument, the function uses the range specified in the first argument.

The examples that follow demonstrate the use of the SUMIF function. These formulas are based on the worksheet shown in Figure 12-14 — set up to track invoices. Column F contains a formula that subtracts the date in column E from the date in column D. A negative number in column F indicates payment. The worksheet uses named ranges that correspond to the labels in row 1.

	A	B	C	D	E	F	G
1	InvoiceNum	Office	Amount	DateDue	Today	Difference	
2	AG-0145	Oregon	$5,000.00	03-Apr	06-May	-33	
3	AG-0189	California	$450.00	21-Apr	06-May	-15	
4	AG-0220	Washington	$3,211.56	30-Apr	06-May	-6	
5	AG-0310	Oregon	$250.00	02-May	06-May	-4	
6	AG-0355	Washington	$125.50	06-May	06-May	0	
7	AG-0409	Washington	$3,000.00	12-May	06-May	6	
8	AG-0581	Oregon	$2,100.00	25-May	06-May	19	
9	AG-0600	Oregon	$335.39	25-May	06-May	19	
10	AG-0602	Washington	$65.00	30-May	06-May	24	
11	AG-0633	California	$250.00	01-Jun	06-May	26	
12	TOTAL		$14,787.45			36	
13							
14							

Figure 12-14: A negative value in column F indicates a past-due payment.

Let a Wizard Create Your Formula

Beginning with Excel 97, Excel ships with an add-in called Conditional Sum Wizard. Once you install this add-in, you can invoke the Wizard by selecting Tools ⇨ Wizard ⇨ Conditional Sum.

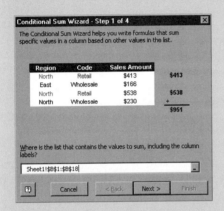

You can specify various conditions for your summing, and the add-in creates the formula for you (always an array formula). The Conditional Sum Wizard add-in, although a handy tool, is not all that versatile. For example, you can combine multiple criteria using an And condition, but not an Or condition.

Summing only negative values

The following formula returns the sum of the negative values in column F. In other words, it returns the total number of past-due days for all invoices. For this worksheet, the formula returns -58.

```
=SUMIF(Difference,"<0")
```

Because you omit the third argument, the second argument (">0") applies to the values in the *Difference* range.

Note　You can also use the following array formula to sum the negative values in the *Difference* range:

```
{=SUM(IF(Difference<0,Difference))}
```

You do not need to hard-code the arguments for the SUMIF function into your formula. For example, you can create a formula such as the following, which gets the criteria argument from the contents of cell G2.

```
=SUMIF(Difference,G2)
```

This formula returns a new result if you change the criteria in cell G2.

Summing values based on a different range

The following formula returns the sum of the past-due invoice amounts (in column C):

```
=SUMIF(Difference,"<0",Amount)
```

This formula uses the values in the *Difference* range to determine if the corresponding values in the *Amount* range contribute to the sum.

Note You can also use the following array formula to return the sum of the values in the *Amount* range, where the corresponding value in the *Difference* range is negative.

```
{=SUM(IF(Difference<0,Amount))}
```

Summing values based on a text comparison

The following formula returns the total invoice amounts for the Oregon office:

```
=SUMIF(Office,"=Oregon",Amount)
```

Using the equal sign is optional. The following formula has the same result:

```
=SUMIF(Office,"Oregon",Amount)
```

To sum the invoice amounts for all offices *except* Oregon, use this formula:

```
=SUMIF(Office,"<>Oregon",Amount)
```

Summing values based on a date comparison

The following formula returns the total invoice amounts that have a due date beyond June 1, 1999.

```
=SUMIF(DateDue,">=6/1/1999",Amount)
```

The formula that follows returns the total invoice amounts that have a future due date (including today).

```
=SUMIF(DateDue,">="&TODAY(),Amount)
```

Notice that the second argument for the SUMIF function is an expression. The expression uses the TODAY function, which returns the current date. Also, the comparison operator, enclosed in quotes, is concatenated (using the & operator) with the result of the TODAY function.

Conditional Sums Using Multiple Criteria

The examples in the preceding section all used a single comparison criterion. The examples in this section involve summing cells based on multiple criteria. Because the SUMIF function does not work with multiple criteria, you need to resort to using an array formula. Figure 12-15 shows the sample worksheet again, for your reference.

	A	B	C	D	E	F	G
1	InvoiceNum	Office	Amount	DateDue	Today	Difference	
2	AG-0145	Oregon	$5,000.00	03-Apr	06-May	-33	
3	AG-0189	California	$450.00	21-Apr	06-May	-15	
4	AG-0220	Washington	$3,211.56	30-Apr	06-May	-6	
5	AG-0310	Oregon	$250.00	02-May	06-May	-4	
6	AG-0355	Washington	$125.50	06-May	06-May	0	
7	AG-0409	Washington	$3,000.00	12-May	06-May	6	
8	AG-0581	Oregon	$2,100.00	25-May	06-May	19	
9	AG-0600	Oregon	$335.39	25-May	06-May	19	
10	AG-0602	Washington	$65.00	30-May	06-May	24	
11	AG-0633	California	$250.00	01-Jun	06-May	26	
12	TOTAL		$14,787.45			36	
13							
14							

Figure 12-15: This worksheet demonstrates summing based on multiple criteria.

Using And criteria

Suppose you want to get a sum of the invoice amounts that are past due, *and* associated with the Oregon office. In other words, the value in the *Amount* range will be summed only if both of the following criteria are met:

✦ The corresponding value in the *Difference* range is negative.

✦ The corresponding text in the *Office* range is "Oregon."

The following array formula does the job:

```
{=SUM((Difference<0)*(Office="Oregon")*Amount)}
```

This formula creates two new arrays (in memory):

✦ A Boolean array that consists of TRUE if the corresponding *Difference* value is less than zero; FALSE otherwise

✦ A Boolean array that consists of TRUE if the corresponding *Office* value equals "Oregon"; otherwise, it consists of FALSE

Multiplying Boolean values results in the following:

```
TRUE * TRUE = 1
TRUE * FALSE = 0
FALSE * FALSE = 0
```

Therefore, the corresponding *Amount* value returns nonzero only if the corresponding values in the memory arrays are both TRUE. The result produces a sum of the *Amount* values that meet the specified criteria.

Note

You may think that you can rewrite the previous array function as follows, using the SUMPRODUCT function to perform the multiplication and addition:

```
{=SUMPRODUCT((Difference<0),(Office="Oregon"),Amount)}
```

For some reason, the SUMPRODUCT function does not handle Boolean values properly, so the formula does not work. This points out another example of inconsistency in Excel's functions.

Using Or criteria

Suppose you want to get a sum of past-due invoice amounts, *or* ones associated with the Oregon office. In other words, the value in the *Amount* range will be summed if either of the following criteria is met:

✦ The corresponding value in the *Difference* range is negative.

✦ The corresponding text in the *Office* range is "Oregon."

The following array formula does the job:

```
{=IF(((Office="Oregon")+(Difference<0),1,0)*Amount}
```

A plus sign (+) joins the conditions; you can include more than two conditions.

Using And and Or criteria

As you might expect, things get a bit tricky when your criteria consists of both And and Or operations. For example, you might want to sum the values in the *Amount* range when the following conditions are met:

✦ The corresponding value in the *Difference* range is negative.

✦ The corresponding text in the *Office* range is "Oregon" or "California."

Notice that the second condition actually consists of two conditions, joined with Or. The following array formula does the trick:

```
{=SUM((Difference<0)*IF((Office="Oregon")+(Office="California"),1)*Amount)}
```

Using VBA Functions to Count and Sum

Some types of counting and summing tasks are simply impossible using Excel's built-in functions, or even array formulas. Fortunately, Excel has a powerful tool that enables you to create custom functions. Excel's Visual Basic for Applications (VBA) language can usually come to the rescue when all else fails.

I devote Part VI of this book to VBA. The following are brief descriptions of several custom functions relevant to counting and summing:

✦ **COUNTBETWEEN:** Returns the number of cells that contain a value between two specified values.

✦ **COUNTVISIBLE:** Returns the number of visible cells in a range.

✦ **DATATYPE:** Returns a string that describes the type of data in a cell. This function enables you to count cells that contain dates (something not normally possible).

✦ **ISBOLD, ISITALIC, FILLCOLOR:** These functions return TRUE if a specified cell has a particular type of formatting (bold, italic, or a specific color). You can use these functions to sum or count cells based on their formatting.

✦ **NUMBERFORMAT:** Returns the number format string for a cell. This function enables you to count or sum cells based on their number format.

✦ **SUMVISIBLE:** Returns the sum of the visible cells in a range.

Summary

This chapter provided many examples of functions and formulas that count or sum cells meeting certain criteria. Many of these formulas are array formulas.

The next chapter covers using formulas to look up specific information in tables or ranges of data.

✦   ✦   ✦

Lookup Formulas

This chapter discusses various techniques that you can use to look up a value in a table. Excel has three functions (LOOKUP, VLOOKUP, and HLOOKUP) designed for this task, but you may find that these functions don't quite cut it. This chapter provides many lookup examples, including alternative techniques that go well beyond Excel's normal lookup capabilities.

What Is a Lookup Formula?

A lookup formula essentially returns a value from a table (in a range) by looking up another value. A common telephone directory provides a good analogy. If you want to find a person's telephone number, you first locate the name (look it up), and then retrieve the corresponding number.

Figure 13-1 shows a simple worksheet that uses several lookup formulas. This worksheet contains a table of employee data (named *EmpData*), beginning in row 9. When you enter a name into cell C2, lookup formulas in D2:G2 retrieve the matching information from the table. The following lookup formulas use the VLOOKUP function:

D2	`=VLOOKUP(C2,EmpData,2,FALSE)`
E2	`=VLOOKUP(C2,EmpData,3,FALSE)`
F2	`=VLOOKUP(C2,EmpData,4,FALSE)`
G2	`=VLOOKUP(C2,EmpData,5,FALSE)`

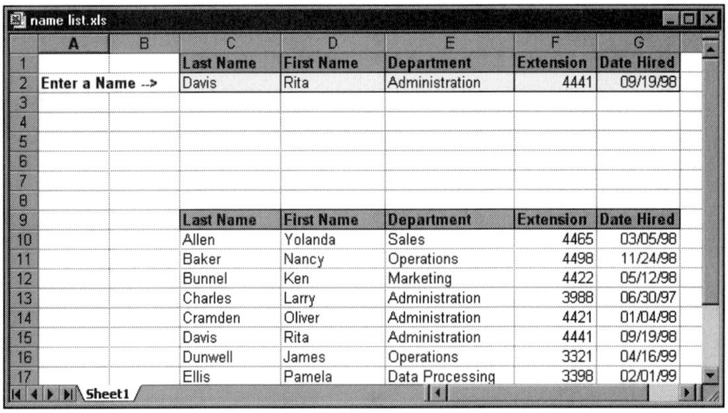

Figure 13-1: Lookup formulas in row 2 look up the information for the employee name in cell C2.

This particular example uses four formulas to return information from the *EmpData* range. In many cases, you'll only want a single value from the table, so use only one formula.

Functions Relevant to Lookups

Several Excel functions are useful when writing formulas to look up information in a table. Table 13-1 lists and describes these functions.

Table 13-1
Functions Used in Lookup Formulas

Function	Description
CHOOSE	Returns a specific value from a list of values (up to 29) supplied as arguments
HLOOKUP	Horizontal lookup. Searches for a value in the top row of a table and returns a value in the same column from a row you specify in the table
INDEX	Returns a value (or the reference to a value) from within a table or range
LOOKUP	Returns a value either from a one-row or one-column range
MATCH	Returns the relative position of an item in a range that matches a specified value
OFFSET	Returns a reference to a range that is a specified number of rows and columns from a cell or range of cells
VLOOKUP	Vertical lookup. Searches for a value in the first column of a table and returns a value in the same row from a column you specify in the table

The examples in this chapter use the functions listed in Table 13-1.

Basic Lookup Formulas

You can use Excel's basic lookup functions to search a column or row for a lookup value to return another value as a result. Excel provides three basic lookup functions: HLOOKUP, VLOOKUP, and LOOKUP. The MATCH and INDEX functions are often used together to return a cell or relative cell reference for a lookup value.

The VLOOKUP function

The VLOOKUP function looks up the value in the first column of the lookup table and returns the corresponding value in a specified table column. The lookup table is arranged vertically. The syntax for the VLOOKUP function is:

```
VLOOKUP(lookup_value,table_array,col_index_num,range_lookup)
```

The VLOOKUP function's arguments are as follows:

✦ **lookup_value:** The value to be looked up in the first column of the lookup table.

✦ **table_array:** The range that contains the lookup table.

✦ **col_index_num:** The column number within the table from which the matching value is returned.

✦ **range_lookup:** Optional. If TRUE or omitted, an approximate match is returned (if an exact match is not found, the next largest value that is — less than *lookup_value* — is returned). If FALSE, VLOOKUP will find search for an exact match. If VLOOKUP cannot find an exact match, the function returns #N/A.

Note

If the *range_lookup* argument is TRUE or omitted, the first column of the lookup table must be in ascending order. If *lookup_value* is smaller than the smallest value in the first column of *table_array*, VLOOKUP returns #N/A. If the *range_lookup* argument is FALSE, the first column of the lookup table need not be in ascending order. If an exact match is not found, the function returns #N/A.

The classic example of a lookup formula involves an income tax rate schedule (see Figure 13-2). The tax rate schedule shows the income tax rates for various income levels.

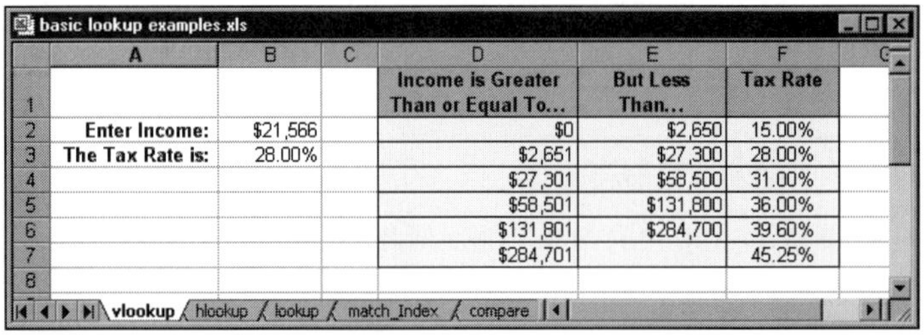

basic lookup examples.xls

	A	B	C	D	E	F
1				Income is Greater Than or Equal To...	But Less Than...	Tax Rate
2	Enter Income:	$21,566		$0	$2,650	15.00%
3	The Tax Rate is:	28.00%		$2,651	$27,300	28.00%
4				$27,301	$58,500	31.00%
5				$58,501	$131,800	36.00%
6				$131,801	$284,700	39.60%
7				$284,701		45.25%
8						

vlookup / hlookup / lookup / match_Index / compare

Figure 13-2: Using VLOOKUP to look up a tax rate

The following formula returns the same result as the LOOKUP formula presented in the previous section:

```
=VLOOKUP(B2,D2:F7,3)
```

The lookup table resides in a range that consists of three columns (D2:F7). Because the last argument for the VLOOKUP function is 3, the formula returns the corresponding value in the third column of the lookup table.

Note that an exact match is not required. If an exact match is not found in the first column of the lookup table, the VLOOKUP function uses the next largest value that is less than the lookup value. In other words, the function uses the row in which the value you want to look up is greater than or equal to the row value, but less than the value in the next row.

The HLOOKUP function

The HLOOKUP function works just like the VLOOKUP function, except that the lookup table is arranged horizontally instead of vertically. The HLOOKUP function looks up the value in the first row of the lookup table and returns the corresponding value in a specified table row.

The syntax for the HLOOKUP function is:

```
HLOOKUP(lookup_value,table_array,col_index_num,range_lookup)
```

The HLOOKUP function's arguments are as follows:

- **lookup_value:** The value to be looked up in the first row of the lookup table.
- **table_array:** The range that contains the lookup table.
- **col_index_num:** The row number within the table from which the matching value is returned.

✦ **range_lookup:** Optional. If TRUE or omitted, an approximate match is returned (if an exact match is not found, the next largest value — less than *lookup_value* — is returned). If FALSE, VLOOKUP will search for an exact match. If VLOOKUP cannot find an exact match, the function returns #N/A.

Figure 13-3 shows the tax rate example with a horizontal lookup table (in the range D1:J3). The formula in cell B3 is:

```
=HLOOKUP(B2,D1:J3,3)
```

	A	B	C	D	E	F	G	H	I	J
1				Income is Greater Than or Equal To...	$0	$2,651	$27,301	$58,501	$131,801	$284,701
2	Enter Income:	$21,566		But Less Than...	$2,650	$27,300	$58,500	$131,800	$284,700	
3	The Tax Rate is:	28.00%		Tax Rate	15.00%	28.00%	31.00%	36.00%	39.60%	45.25%
4										
5										

vlookup \ **hlookup** / lookup / match_Index / compare /

Figure 13-3: Using HLOOKUP to look up a tax rate

The LOOKUP function

The LOOKUP function searches a single-column or single-row table. The syntax for the LOOKUP function is:

```
VLOOKUP(lookup_value,lookup_range,result_range)
```

The LOOKUP function's arguments are as follows:

✦ **lookup_value:** The value to be looked up in the *lookup_range*

✦ **lookup_range:** A single-column or single-row range that contains the values to be looked up

✦ **result_range:** The single-column or single-row range that contains the values to be returned

Note   Values in the *lookup_range* must be in ascending order. If *lookup_value* is smaller than the smallest value in *lookup_range*, LOOKUP returns #N/A.

Figure 13-4 shows the tax table again. This time, the formula in cell B3 uses the LOOKUP function to return the corresponding tax rate. The formula in B3 is:

```
=LOOKUP(B2,D2:D7,F2:F7)
```

basic lookup examples.xls

	A	B	C	D	E	F
1				Income is Greater Than or Equal To...	But Less Than...	Tax Rate
2	Enter Income:	$123,409		$0	$2,650	15.00%
3	The Tax Rate is:	36.00%		$2,651	$27,300	28.00%
4				$27,301	$58,500	31.00%
5				$58,501	$131,800	36.00%
6				$131,801	$284,700	39.60%
7				$284,701		45.25%
8						

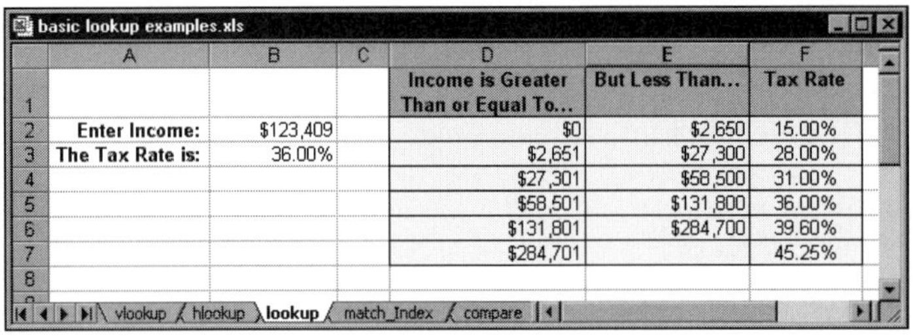

Figure 13-4: Using LOOKUP to look up a tax rate

Caution

If the values in the first column are not arranged in ascending order, the LOOKUP function may return an incorrect value.

Note that LOOKUP (as opposed to VLOOKUP) requires two range references (a range to be looked in, and a range that contains result values). VLOOKUP, on the other hand, uses a single range for the lookup table and the third argument determines which column to use for the result. This argument, of course, can consist of a cell reference.

Combining the MATCH and INDEX functions

The MATCH and INDEX functions are often used together to perform lookups. The MATCH function returns the relative position of a cell in a range that matches a specified value. The syntax for MATCH is:

```
MATCH(lookup_value,lookup_array,match_type)
```

The MATCH function's arguments are as follows:

- ✦ **lookup_value:** The value you want to match in *lookup_array*, which can include wildcard characters * and ?
- ✦ **lookup_array:** The range being searched
- ✦ **match_type:** An integer (-1, 0, or 1) that specifies how the match is determined

Note

If *match_type* is 1, MATCH finds the largest value less than or equal to *lookup_value* (*lookup_array* must be in ascending order). If *match_type* is 0, MATCH finds the first value exactly equal to *lookup_value*. If *match_type* is -1, MATCH finds the smallest value greater than or equal to *lookup_value* (*lookup_array* must be in descending order). If you omit *match_type*, it is assumed to be 1.

The INDEX function returns a cell from a range. The syntax for the INDEX function is:

```
INDEX(array,row_num,column_num)
```

The INDEX function's arguments are as follows:

✦ **array:** A range

✦ **row_num:** A row number within *array*

✦ **col_num:** A column number within *array*

Note   If *array* contains only one row or column, the corresponding *row_num* or *column_num* argument is optional.

Figure 13-5 shows a worksheet with dates, day names, and amounts in columns D, E, and F. When you enter a date in cell B1, the following formula (in cell B2) searches the dates in column D and returns the corresponding amount from column F. The formula in B2 is:

```
=INDEX(F2:F21,MATCH(B1,D2:D21,0))
```

	A	B	C	D	E	F
1	Date:	01/19/2000		**Date**	**Weekday**	**Amount**
2	Amount:	163		01/03/2000	Monday	146
3				01/04/2000	Tuesday	179
4				01/05/2000	Wednesday	149
5				01/06/2000	Thursday	196
6				01/07/2000	Friday	131
7				01/10/2000	Monday	179
8				01/11/2000	Tuesday	134
9				01/12/2000	Wednesday	179
10				01/13/2000	Thursday	193
11				01/14/2000	Friday	191
12				01/17/2000	Monday	176
13				01/18/2000	Tuesday	189
14				01/19/2000	Wednesday	163
15				01/20/2000	Thursday	121
16				01/21/2000	Friday	100
17				01/24/2000	Monday	109
18				01/25/2000	Tuesday	151
19				01/26/2000	Wednesday	138
20				01/27/2000	Thursday	114
21				01/28/2000	Friday	156
22						

Figure 13-5: Using the INDEX and MATCH functions to perform a lookup

To understand how this works, start with the MATCH function. This function searches the range D2:D21 for the date in cell B1. It returns the relative row number where the date is found. This value is then used as the second argument for the INDEX function. The result is the corresponding value in F2:F21.

Tip   In many cases, it's advantageous to use MATCH and INDEX together rather than the LOOKUP or VLOOKUP functions. The MATCH function supports wildcard characters for approximate matches (VLOOKUP and LOOKUP don't support this). An asterisk (*) matches any characters, and a question mark (?) matches any single character. For example, the following formula looks up a string that begins with the letter "B" in *Range1*, and returns the corresponding value in *Range2:*

```
=INDEX(Range2,MATCH("b*",Range1,0))
```

When a Blank Is Not a Zero

Excel's lookup functions treat empty cells as zeros. The worksheet in the accompanying figure contains a two-column lookup table, and this formula looks up the name in cell B1 and returns the corresponding amount:

```
=VLOOKUP(B1,D2:E8,2)
```

Note that the Amount cell for Charlie is blank — but the formula returns a 0.

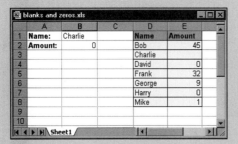

If you need to distinguish zeros from blank cells, you must modify the lookup formula by adding an IF function to check if the length of the returned value is 0. When the looked up value is blank, the length of the return value is 0. In all other cases, the length of the returned value is nonzero. The following formula displays an empty string (a blank) whenever the length of the looked-up value is zero, and the actual value whenever the length is anything but zero:

```
=IF(LEN(VLOOKUP(B1,D2:E8,2))=0,"",(VLOOKUP(B1,D2:E8,2)))
```

Specialized Lookup Formulas

You can use some additional types of lookup formulas to perform more specialized lookups. For instance, you can look up an exact value, search in another column besides the first in a lookup table, perform a case-sensitive lookup, return a value from among multiple lookup tables, and perform other specialized and complex lookups.

Looking up an exact value

As demonstrated in the previous examples, VLOOKUP and HLOOKUP don't necessarily require an exact match between the value to be looked up and the values in the lookup table. In some cases, you may require a perfect match. When the value to be looked up is a text string, you *always* require a perfect match.

To look up an exact value only, use the VLOOKUP (or HLOOKUP) function with the optional fourth argument set to FALSE.

Figure 13-6 shows a worksheet with a lookup table that contains employee numbers (column C) and employee names (column D). The lookup table is named *EmpList*. The formula in cell B2, which follows, looks up the employee number entered in cell B1 and returns the corresponding employee name:

```
=VLOOKUP(B1,EmpList,2,FALSE)
```

	A	B	C	D
	employee list.xls			
1	Employee No:	107035	**Employee Number**	**Employee Name**
2	Employee Name:	#N/A	104566	Yolanda Allen
3			204555	Nancy Baker
4			227402	Ken Franklin
5			331743	Larry Magadan
6			211090	Oliver Nory
7			107031	Rita Rudolph
8			199732	James Storey
9			123487	Pamela Victor
10			201981	Ed Wilson
11				
12				
13				

Figure 13-6: This lookup table requires an exact match.

Because the last argument for the VLOOKUP function is FALSE, the function returns a value only if an exact match is found. If the value is not found, the formula returns #N/A. This, of course, is exactly what you want to happen because returning an approximate match for an employee number makes no sense. Also, notice that the employee numbers in column C are not in ascending order. If the last argument for VLOOKUP is FALSE, the values need not be in ascending order.

 Tip   If you prefer to see something other than #N/A when the employee number is not found, you can use an IF function to test for the #N/A result (using the ISNA function) and substitute a different string. The following formula displays the text "Not Found" rather than #N/A.

```
=IF(ISNA(VLOOKUP(B1,EmpList,2,FALSE)),"Not Found",
VLOOKUP(B1,EmpList,2,FALSE))
```

Looking up a value to the left

The VLOOKUP function always looks up a value in the first column of the lookup range. But what if you want to look up a value in a column other than the first column? It would be helpful if you could supply a negative value for the third argument for VLOOKUP — but you can't.

Figure 13-7 illustrates the problem. Suppose you want to look up the batting average (column B, in a range named *Averages*) of a player in column C (in a range named *Players*). The player you want data for appears in a cell named *LookupValue*. The VLOOKUP function won't work because the data is not arranged correctly. One option is to rearrange your data, but sometimes that's not possible.

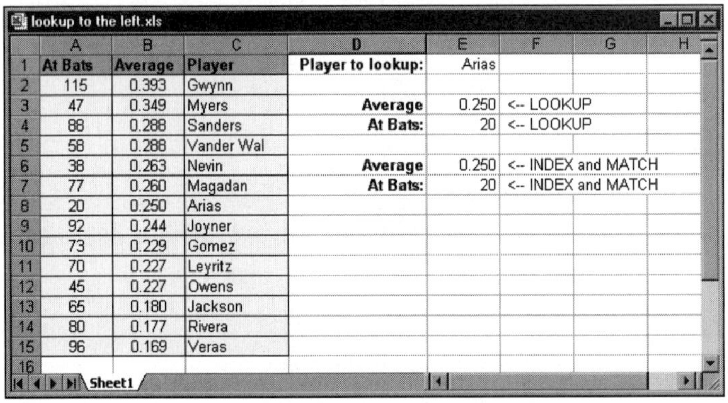

Figure 13-7: The VLOOKUP function can't look up a value in column B, based on a value in column C.

One solution is to use the LOOKUP function, which requires two range arguments. The following formula returns the batting average from column B of the player name contained in the cell named *LookupValue*.

```
=LOOKUP(LookupValue,Players,Averages)
```

This formula suffers from a slight problem: If you enter a nonexistent player (in other words, the *LookupValue* cell contains a value not found in the *Players* range), the formula returns an erroneous result.

A better solution uses the INDEX and MATCH functions. The formula that follows works just like the previous one, except that it returns #N/A if the player is not found.

```
=INDEX(Averages,MATCH(LookupValue,Players,0))
```

Performing a case-sensitive lookup

Excel's lookup functions (LOOKUP, VLOOKUP, and HLOOKUP) are not case sensitive. For example, if you write a lookup formula to look up the text *budget*, the formula considers any of the following a match: *BUDGET, Budget,* or *BuDgEt*.

Figure 13-8 shows a simple example. Range D2:D7 is named *Range1*, and range E2:E7 is named *Range2*. The word to be looked up appears in cell B1 (named *Value*).

case-sensitive lookup.xls

	A	B	C	D	E	F
1	**Word**	DOG		**Range1**	**Range2**	
2	**Result:**	300		APPLE	100	
3				apple	200	
4				DOG	300	
5				dog	400	
6				CANDY	500	
7				candy	600	
8						
9						

Sheet1

Figure 13-8: Using an array formula to perform a case-sensitive lookup

The array formula that follows is in cell B2. This formula does a case-sensitive lookup in *Range1* and returns the corresponding value in *Range2*.

```
{=INDEX(Range2,MATCH(TRUE,EXACT(Value,Range1),0))}
```

The formula looks up the word `DOG` (uppercase) and returns 300. The following standard LOOKUP formula returns 400.

```
=LOOKUP(Value,Range1,Range2)
```

Choosing among multiple lookup tables

You can, of course, have any number of lookup tables in a worksheet. In some cases, your formula may need to decide which lookup table to use. Figure 13-9 shows an example.

multiple lookup tables.xls

	A	B	C	D	E	F	G	H	I	J	K
1	**Sales Rep**	**Years**	**Sales**	**Comm. Rate**	**Commission**		**<3 Years Tenure**			**3+ Years Tenure**	
2	Benson	2	120,000	7.00%	8,400		**Amt Sold**	**Rate**		**Amt Sold**	**Rate**
3	Davidson	1	210,921	7.00%	14,764		0	1.50%		0	2.00%
4	Ellison	1	100,000	7.00%	7,000		5,000	3.25%		50,000	6.25%
5	Gomez	2	87,401	6.00%	5,244		10,000	3.50%		100,000	7.25%
6	Hernandez	6	310,983	9.25%	28,766		20,000	5.00%		200,000	8.25%
7	Kelly	3	43,902	2.00%	878		50,000	6.00%		300,000	9.25%
8	Martin	2	121,021	7.00%	8,471		100,000	7.00%		500,000	10.00%
9	Oswald	3	908	2.00%	18		250,000	8.00%			
10	Reginald	1	0	1.50%	0						
11	Veras	4	359,832	9.25%	33,284						
12	Wilmington	4	502,983	10.00%	50,298						
13											

Sheet1

Figure 13-9: This worksheet demonstrates the use of multiple lookup tables.

This workbook calculates sales commission and contains two lookup tables: G3:H9 (named *Table1*) and J3:K8 (named *Table2*). The commission rate for a particular sales representative depends on two factors: the sales rep's years of service (column B) and the amount sold (column C). Column D contains formulas that look up the commission rate from the appropriate table. For example, the formula in cell D2 is:

```
=VLOOKUP(C2,IF(B2<3,Table1,Table2),2)
```

The second argument for the VLOOKUP function consists of an IF formula that uses the value in column B to determine which lookup table to use.

The formula in column E simply multiplies the sales amount in column C by the commission rate in column D. The formula in cell E2, for example, is:

```
=C2*D2
```

Determining letter grades for test scores

A common use of a lookup table is to assign letter grades for test scores. Figure 13-10 shows a worksheet with student test scores. The range E2:F6 (named *GradeList*) displays a lookup table used to assign a letter grade to a test score.

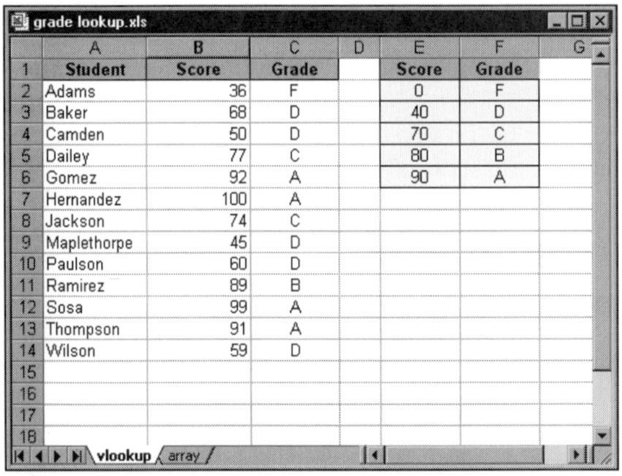

	A	B	C	D	E	F	G
1	Student	Score	Grade		Score	Grade	
2	Adams	36	F		0	F	
3	Baker	68	D		40	D	
4	Camden	50	D		70	C	
5	Dailey	77	C		80	B	
6	Gomez	92	A		90	A	
7	Hernandez	100	A				
8	Jackson	74	C				
9	Maplethorpe	45	D				
10	Paulson	60	D				
11	Ramirez	89	B				
12	Sosa	99	A				
13	Thompson	91	A				
14	Wilson	59	D				
15							
16							
17							
18							

Figure 13-10: Looking up letter grades for test scores

Column C contains formulas that use the VLOOKUP function and the lookup table to assign a grade based on the score in column B. The formula in C2, for example, is:

```
=VLOOKUP(B2,GradeList,2)
```

Tip   When the lookup table is small (as in the example shown in with Figure 13-10), you can use a literal array in place of the lookup table. The formula that follows, for example, returns a letter grade without using a lookup table. Rather, the information in the lookup table is hard-coded into a literal array. See Chapter 25 for more information about literal arrays.

```
=VLOOKUP(B2,{0,"F";40,"D";70,"C";80,"B";90,"A"},2)
```

Calculating a grade point average

A student's grade point average (GPA) is a numerical measure of the average grade received for classes taken. This discussion assumes a letter grade system, in which each letter grade is assigned a numeric value (A=4, B=3, C=2, D=1, and F=0). The GPA comprises an average of the numeric grade values, weighted by the credit hours of the course. A one-hour course, for example, receives less weight than a three-hour course. The GPA ranges from 0 (all Fs) to 4.00 (all As).

Figure 13-11 shows a worksheet with information for a student. This student took five courses, for a total of 13 credit hours. Range B2:B6 is named *CreditHours*. The grades for each course appear in column C (Range C2:C6 is named *Grades*). Column D uses a lookup formula to calculate the grade value for each course. The lookup formula in cell D2, for example, follows. This formula uses the lookup table in G2:H6 (named *GradeTable*).

```
=VLOOKUP(C2,GradeTable,2,FALSE)
```

	A	B	C	D	E	F	G	H
1	Course	Credit Hrs	Grade	Grade Val	Weighted Val		GradeTable	
2	Psych 101	3	A	4	12		A	4
3	PhysEd	2	C	2	4		B	3
4	PoliSci 101	4	B	3	12		C	2
5	IndepStudy	1	A	4	4		D	1
6	IntroMath	3	A	4	12		F	0
7								
8	GPA:	3.38	<-- Requires multiple formulas and lookup table					
9								
10								

Figure 13-11: Using multiple formulas to calculate a GPA

Formulas in column E calculate the weighted values. The formula in E2 is:

```
=D2*B2
```

Cell B8 computes the GPA using the following formula:

```
=SUM(E2:E6)/SUM(B2:B6)
```

The preceding formulas work fine, but you can streamline the GPA calculation quite a bit. In fact, you can use a single array formula to make this calculation and avoid using the lookup table and the formulas in columns D and E. This array formula does the job:

```
{=SUM((MATCH(Grades,{"F","D","C","B","A"},0)-1)*CreditHours)/SUM(CreditHours)}
```

Performing a two-way lookup

Figure 13-12 shows a worksheet with a table that displays product sales by month. The user enters a month in cell B1 and a product name in cell B2.

	A	B	C	D	E	F	G	H
					Widgets	Sprockets	Snapholytes	Combined
1	Month:	July						
2	Product:	Sprockets		January	2,892	1,771	4,718	9,381
3				February	3,380	4,711	2,615	10,706
4	Month Offset:	8		March	3,744	3,223	5,312	12,279
5	Product Offset:	3		April	3,221	2,438	1,108	6,767
6	Sales:	3,337		May	4,839	1,999	1,994	8,832
7				June	3,767	5,140	3,830	12,737
8				July	5,467	3,337	3,232	12,036
9	Single-formula -->	3,337		August	3,154	4,895	1,607	9,656
10				September	1,718	2,040	1,563	5,321
11				October	1,548	1,061	2,590	5,199
12				November	5,083	3,558	3,960	12,601
13				December	5,753	2,839	3,013	11,605
14				Total	44,566	37,012	35,542	117,120

Figure 13-12: This table demonstrates a two-way lookup.

To simplify things, the worksheet uses the following named ranges:

Name	Refers To
Month	B1
Product	B2
Table	D1:H14
MonthList	D1:D14
ProductList	D1:H1

The following formula (in cell B4) uses the MATCH function to return the position of the *Month* within the *MonthList* range. For example, if the month is January, the formula returns 2 because January is the second item in the *MonthList* range (the first item is a blank cell, D1).

```
=MATCH(Month,MonthList,0)
```

The formula in cell B5 works similarly, but uses the *ProductList* range.

```
=MATCH(Product,ProductList,0)
```

The final formula, in cell B6, returns the corresponding sales amount. It uses the INDEX function with the results from cells B4 and B5.

```
=INDEX(Table,B4,B5)
```

You can, of course, combine these formulas into a single formula as shown here:

```
=INDEX(Table,MATCH(Month,MonthList,0),MATCH(Product,ProductList,0))
```

Tip   If use Excel 97 or later, you can use the Lookup Wizard add-in to create this type of formula (see Figure 13-13).

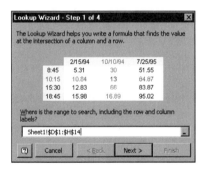

Figure 13-13: The Lookup Wizard add-in can create a formula that performs a two-way lookup.

Tip   Another way to accomplish a two-way lookup is to provide a name for each row and column of the table. A quick way to do this is to select the table and use Insert ➪ Name ➪ Create. After creating the names, you can use a simple formula, such as = Sprockets July. This formula, which uses the range intersection operator (a space), returns July sales for Sprockets.

Performing a two-column lookup

Some situations may require a lookup based on the values in two columns. Figure 13-14 shows an example.

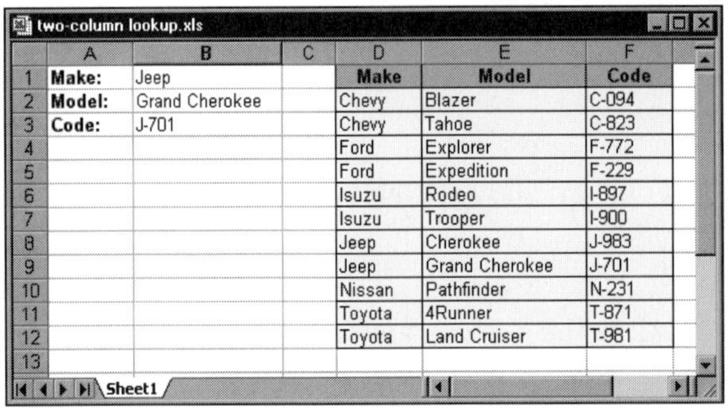

Figure 13-14: This workbook performs a lookup using information in two columns (D and E).

The lookup table contains automobile makes and models, and a corresponding code for each. The worksheet uses named ranges, as shown here:

F2:F12	Czode
B1	*Make*
B2	*Model*
D2:D12	*Range1*
E2:E12	*Range2*

The following array formula displays the corresponding code for an automobile make and model.

```
{=INDEX(Price,MATCH(Make&Model,Range1&Range2,0))}
```

This formula works by concatenating the contents of *Make* and *Model*, and then searching for this text in an array consisting of the concatenated corresponding text in *Range1* and *Range2*.

Determining the address of a value within a range

Most of the time, you want your lookup formula to return a value. You may, however, need to determine the cell address of a particular value within a range. For example, Figure 13-15 shows a worksheet with a range of numbers that occupy a single column (named *Data*). Cell B1, which contains the value to look up, is named *Target*.

Figure 13-15: The formula in cell B2 returns the address in the *Data* range for the value in cell B1.

The formula in cell B2, which follows, returns the address of the cell in the *Data* range that contains the *Target* value.

```
=ADDRESS(ROW(Data)+MATCH(Target,Data,0)-1,COLUMN(Data))
```

If the *Data* range occupies a single row, use this formula to return the address of the *Target* value:

```
=ADDRESS(ROW(Data),COLUMN(Data)+MATCH(Target,Data,0)-1)
```

If the *Data* range contains more than one instance of the *Target* value, the address of the first occurrence is returned. If the *Target* value is not found in the *Data* range, the formula returns #N/A.

Looking up a value using the closest match

The VLOOKUP and HLOOKUP functions are useful in the following situations:

✦ You need to identify an exact match for a target value. Use FALSE as the function's fourth argument.

✦ You need to locate an approximate match. If the function's fourth argument is TRUE or omitted and an exact match is not found, the next largest value less than the lookup value is returned.

But what if you need to look up a value based on the *closest* match? Neither VLOOKUP nor HLOOKUP can do the job.

Figure 13-16 shows a worksheet with student names in column A and values in column B. Range B2:B20 is named *Data*. Cell E2, named *Target*, contains a value to search for in the *Data* range. Cell E3, named *ColOffset*, contains a value that represents the column offset from the *Data* range.

	A	B	C	D	E	F
1	Student	Data				
2	Ann	9,101		Target Value -->	8025	
3	Betsy	8,873		Column Offset -->	-1	
4	Chuck	6,000				
5	David	9,820		Student:	Leslie	
6	George	10,500				
7	Hilda	3,500				
8	James	12,873				
9	John	5,867				
10	Keith	8,989				
11	Leslie	8,000				
12	Michelle	1,124				
13	Nora	9,099				
14	Paul	6,800				
15	Peter	5,509				
16	Rasmusen	5,460				
17	Sally	8,400				
18	Theresa	7,777				
19	Violet	3,600				
20	Wendy	5,400				
21						

Figure 13-16: This workbook demonstrates how to perform a lookup using the closest match.

The array formula that follows identifies the closest match to the *Target* value in the *Data* range, and returns the names of the corresponding student in column A (for example, the column with an offset of -1). The formula returns Leslie (with a matching value of 8,000 — the one closest to the *Target* value of 8,025).

```
{=INDIRECT(ADDRESS(ROW(Data)+MATCH(MIN(ABS(Target-Data)),
ABS(Target-Data),0)-1,COLUMN(Data)+ColOffset))}
```

If two values in the *Data* range are equidistant from the *Target* value, the formula uses the first one in the list.

The value in *ColOffset* can be negative (for a column to the left of *Data*), positive (for a column to the right of *Data*), or 0 (for the actual closest match value in the *Data* range).

Looking up a value using linear interpolation

Interpolation refers to the process of estimating a missing value by using existing values. To illustrate, refer to Figure 13-17. Column D contains a list of values (named *x*), and column E contains corresponding values (named *y*).

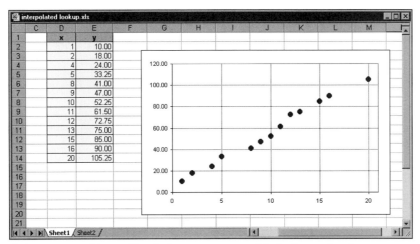

Figure 13-17: This workbook demonstrates a table lookup using linear interpolation.

The worksheet also contains a chart that depicts the relationship between the x range and the y range graphically. As you can see, a linear relationship exists between the corresponding values in the x and y ranges — as x increases, so does y. Notice that the values in the x range are not strictly consecutive. For example, the x range doesn't contain the following values: 3, 6, 7, 14, 17, 18, and 19.

You can create a lookup formula that looks up a value in the x range and returns the corresponding value from the y range. But what if you want to estimate the y value for a missing x value? A normal lookup formula does not return a very good result because it simply returns an existing y value (not an estimated y value). For example, the following formula looks up the value 3, and returns 18.00 (the value that corresponds to 2 in the x range).

```
=LOOKUP(3,x,y)
```

In such a case, you probably want to interpolate. In other words, because the lookup value (3) is halfway between existing x values (2 and 4), you want the formula to return a y value of 21.000 — a value halfway between the corresponding y values 18.00 and 24.00.

Formulas to perform a linear interpolation

Figure 13-18 shows a worksheet with formulas in column B. The value to be looked up is entered into cell B1. The final formula, in cell B16, returns the result. If the value in B3 is found in the x range, the corresponding y value is returned. If the value in B3 is not found, the formula in B16 returns an estimated y value, obtained using linear interpolation.

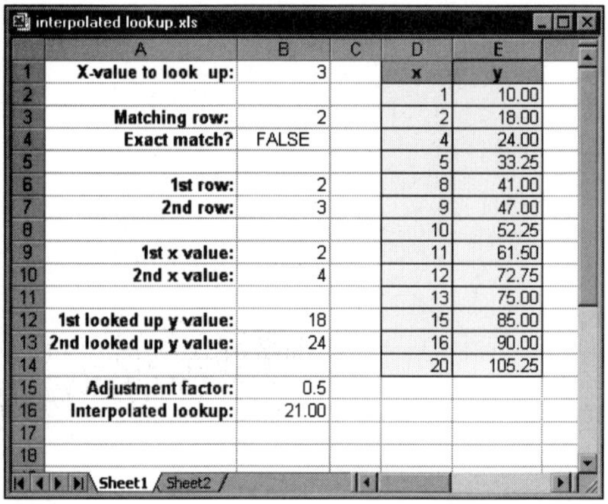

Figure 13-18: Column B contains formulas that perform a lookup using linear interpolation.

It's critical that the values in the *x* range appear in ascending order. If B1 contains a value less than the lowest value in *x* or greater than the largest value in *x*, the formula returns an error value. Table 13-2 lists and describes these formulas.

Table 13-2
Formulas for a Lookup Using Linear Interpolation

Cell	Formula	Description
B3	=LOOKUP(B1,x,x)	Performs a standard lookup, and returns looked-up value in the *x* range.
B4	=B1=B3	Returns TRUE if the looked-up value equals the value to be looked up.
B6	=MATCH(B3,x,0)	Returns the row number of the *x* range that contains the matching value.
B7	=IF(B4,B6,B6+1)	Returns the same row as the formula in B6 if an exact match is found. Otherwise, it adds 1 to the result in B6.
B9	=INDEX(x,B6)	Returns the *x* value that corresponds to the row in B6.
B10	=INDEX(x,B7)	Returns the *x* value that corresponds to the row in B7.
B12	=LOOKUP(B9,x,y)	Returns the *y* value that corresponds to the *x* value in B9.

Cell	Formula	Description
B13	=LOOKUP(B10,x,y)	Returns the y value that corresponds to the x value in B10
B15	=IF(B4,0,(B1-B3)/(B10-B9))	Calculates an adjustment factor based on the difference between the x values.
B16	=B12+((B13-B12)*B15)	Calculates the estimated y value using the adjustment factor in B15.

Combining the LOOKUP and TREND functions

Another slightly different approach, which you may find preferable to performing lookup using linear interpolation, uses the LOOKUP and TREND functions. One advantage is that it requires only one formula (see Figure 13-19).

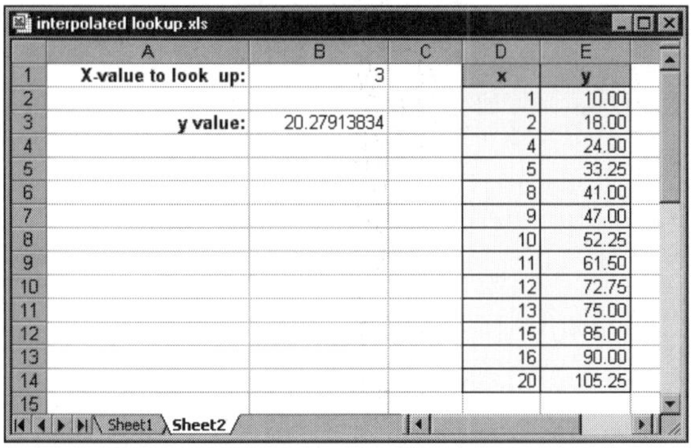

Figure 13-19: This worksheet uses a formula that utilizes the LOOKUP function and the TREND function.

The formula in cell B3 follows. This formula uses an IF function to make a decision. If an exact match is found in the x range, the formula returns the corresponding y value (using the LOOKUP function). If an exact match is not found, the formula uses the TREND function to return the calculated "best-fit" y value (it does not perform a linear interpolation).

```
=IF(B1=LOOKUP(B1,x,x),LOOKUP(INDEX(x,MATCH(LOOKUP(B1,x,x),x,0))
,x,y),TREND(y,x,B1))
```

Summary

This chapter presented an overview of the functions available to perform table lookups. It included many formula examples demonstrating basic lookups, as well as not-so-basic lookups.

The next chapter discusses the various options at your disposal when printing your work.

✦   ✦   ✦

Printing Your Work

Many of the worksheets that you develop with Excel are designed to serve as printed reports. You'll find that printing from Excel is quite easy, and you can generate attractive, well-formatted reports with minimal effort. But, as you'll see, Excel has plenty of options that provide you with a great deal of control over the printed page. These options are explained in this chapter.

One-Step Printing

The Print button on the Standard toolbar is a quick way to print the current worksheet, using the default settings. Just click the button, and Excel sends the worksheet to the printer. If you've changed any of the default print settings, Excel uses the new settings; otherwise, it uses the following default settings:

- ✦ Prints the active worksheet (or all selected worksheets), including any embedded charts or drawing objects

- ✦ Prints one copy

- ✦ Prints the entire worksheet

- ✦ Prints in portrait mode

- ✦ Doesn't scale the printed output

- ✦ Uses 1-inch margins for the top and bottom and .75-inch margins for the left and right

- ✦ Prints with no headers or footers

- ✦ For wide worksheets that span multiple pages, it prints down and then across

As you might suspect, you can change any of these default print settings.

When you print a worksheet, Excel prints only the *active area* of the worksheet. In other words, it won't print all four million cells — just those that have data in them. If the worksheet contains any embedded charts or drawing objects, they also are printed (unless you have modified the Print Object property of the object).

If you create a workbook based on a template, the template may contain different default print settings. Templates are discussed in Chapter 16.

Adjusting Your Print Settings

You adjust Excel's various print settings in two different dialog boxes:

✦ The Print dialog box (accessed either with the File ➪ Print command or Ctrl+P).

✦ The Page Setup dialog box (accessed with the File ➪ Page Setup command). This is a tabbed dialog box with four tabs.

Both of these dialog boxes have a Print Preview button that previews the printed output onscreen.

Settings in the Print Dialog Box

You actually start the printing process from the Print dialog box, unless you use the Print button on the Standard toolbar. After you select your print settings, click OK from the Print dialog box to print your work.

Selecting a printer

Before printing, make sure that you have selected the correct printer (applicable only if you have access to more than one printer) by using the Print dialog box, shown in Figure 14-1. You can select the printer from the Printer drop-down list. This dialog box also lists information about the selected printer, such as its status and where it's connected.

Clicking the Properties button displays a property box for the selected printer. The exact dialog box that you see depends on the printer. The Properties dialog box lets you adjust printer-specific settings. In most cases, you won't have to change any of these settings, but you should be familiar with the settings that you can change.

If you check the Print to file check box, Excel stores the output in a file, prompting you for a filename before printing. The resulting file will *not* be a standard text file. Rather, it will include all the printer codes that are required to print your worksheet.

Printing to a file is useful if you don't have immediate access to a printer. You can save the output to a file and then send this file to your printer at a later time.

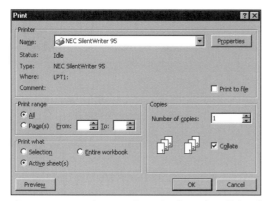

Figure 14-1: Select a printer in the Print dialog box.

 Tip If you want to save your workbook as a text file, use the File ➪ Save As command, and select one of the text file formats from the drop-down list labeled Save as type.

Before printing, you might want to view your worksheets in Page Break Preview mode. To enter this mode, choose the View ➪ Page Break Preview command. The worksheet display changes, and you can see exactly what will be printed and where the page breaks occur. To change the print range, drag any of the dark borders. This feature is discussed in more detail later in this chapter.

After you print a worksheet (or view it in Page Break Preview mode), Excel displays dashed lines to indicate where the page breaks occur. This is a useful feature, because the display adjusts dynamically. For example, if you find that your printed output is too wide to fit on a single page, you can adjust the column widths (keeping an eye on the page-break display) until they are narrow enough to print on one page.

Tip If you don't want to see the page breaks displayed in your worksheet, open the Options dialog box, click the View tab, and remove the check mark from the Automatic Page Breaks check box.

Printing selected pages

If your printed output uses multiple pages, you can select which pages to print, in the Print dialog box. In the Page Range section, indicate the number of the first and last pages to print. You can either use the spinner controls or type the page numbers in the edit boxes.

Specifying what to print

The Print What section of the Print dialog box lets you specify what to print. You have three options:

✦ **Selection:** Prints only the range that you selected before issuing the File ▷ Print command.

✦ **Selected sheet(s):** Prints the active sheet or sheets that you selected. You can select multiple sheets by pressing Ctrl and clicking the sheet tabs. If you select multiple sheets, Excel begins printing each sheet on a new page.

✦ **Entire workbook:** Prints the entire workbook, including chart sheets.

Tip

You can also select File ▷ Print Area ▷ Set Print Area to specify the range or ranges to print. Before you choose this command, select the range or ranges that you want to print. To clear the print area, select File ▷ Print Area ▷ Clear Print Area.

Printing multiple copies

The Print dialog box also enables you to select the number of copies to print. The upper limit is 32,767 copies—not that anyone would ever need that many. You also can specify that you want the copies collated. If you choose this option, Excel prints the pages in order for each set of output. If you're printing only one page, Excel ignores the Collate setting.

Settings in the Page Setup Dialog Box

Using the Page Setup dialog box, you can control page settings and margins, create headers and footers, and adjust sheet settings. Choose File ▷ Page Setup to open the Page Setup dialog box; in Figure 14-2, you see the Page tab of the Page Setup dialog box.

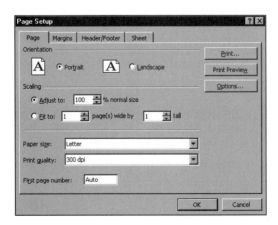

Figure 14-2: You control page settings in the Page tab of the Page Setup dialog box.

Controlling page settings

The Page tab of the Page Setup dialog box enables you to control the following settings:

✦ **Orientation:** Choose either Portrait (tall pages) or Landscape (wide pages). Landscape orientation might be useful if you have a wide range that doesn't fit on a vertically oriented page.

✦ **Scaling:** You can set a scaling factor manually or let Excel scale the output automatically to fit on the number of pages that you specify. Scaling can range from 10 percent to 400 percent of normal size. If you want to return to normal scaling, enter 100 in the box labeled % normal size.

✦ **Paper size:** This setting enables you to select the paper size that you're using. Click the box and see the choices.

✦ **Print quality:** If the installed printer supports it, you can change the printer's resolution — which is expressed in dots per inch (dpi). Higher numbers represent better print quality, but higher resolutions take longer to print.

✦ **First page number:** You can specify a page number for the first page. This is useful if the pages that you're printing will be part of a larger document and you want the page numbering to be consecutive. Use Auto if you want the beginning page number to be 1 — or to correspond to the pages that you selected in the Print dialog box. If you're not printing page numbers in your header or footer, this setting is irrelevant.

Adjusting margins

A margin is the blank space on the side of the page. Wider margins leave less space available for printing. You can control all four page margins from the Margins tab of the Page Setup dialog box, shown in Figure 14-3.

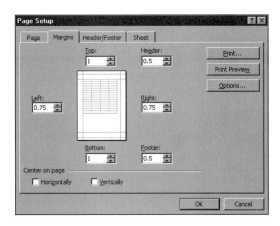

Figure 14-3: The Margins tab of the Page Setup dialog box

To change a margin, click the appropriate spinner (or you can enter a value directly).

Note   The Preview box in the center of the dialog box is a bit deceiving, because it doesn't really show you how your changes look in relation to the page. Rather, it simply displays a darker line to let you know which margin you're adjusting.

In addition to the page margins, you can adjust the distance of the header from the top of the page and the distance of the footer from the bottom of the page. These settings should be less than the corresponding margin; otherwise, the header or footer may overlap with the printed output.

Normally, Excel aligns the printed page at the top and left margins. If you would like the output to be centered vertically or horizontally, check the appropriate check box.

You also can change the margins while you're previewing your output — ideal for last-minute adjustments before printing. Previewing is explained later in the chapter.

Changing the header or footer

A *header* is a line of information that appears at the top of each printed page. A *footer* is a line of information that appears at the bottom of each printed page. You can align information in headers and footers at the left margin, in the center of the header or footer, and at the right margin. For example, you can create a header that prints your name at the left margin, the worksheet name centered in the header, and the page number at the right margin. By default, new workbooks do not have any headers or footers.

The Header/Footer tab of the Page Setup dialog box appears in Figure 14-4. This dialog box displays the current header and footer and gives you other header and footer options in the drop-down lists labeled Header and Footer.

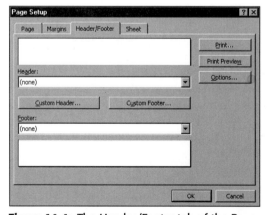

Figure 14-4: The Header/Footer tab of the Page Setup dialog box

When you click the Header (or Footer) drop-down list, Excel displays a list of predefined headers (or footers). If you see one that you like, select it. You then can see how it looks in context — which part is left-justified, centered, or right-justified. If you don't want a header or footer, choose the option labeled (none) for both the Header and Footer drop-down list boxes.

If you don't find a predefined header or footer that is exactly what you want, you can define a custom header or footer. Start by selecting a header or footer that's similar to the one that you want to create (you'll use the selected header or footer as the basis for the customized one). Click the Custom Header or Custom Footer button, and Excel displays a dialog box like the one shown in Figure 14-5.

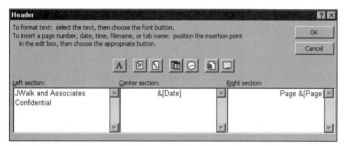

Figure 14-5: If none of the predefined headers or footers is satisfactory, you can define a custom header or custom footer.

This dialog box enables you to enter text or codes in each of the three sections. To enter text, just click in the section and enter the text. To enter variable information, such as the current date or the page number, you can click one of the buttons. Clicking the button inserts a special code. The buttons and their functions are listed in Table 14-1.

Table 14-1
Custom Header/Footer Buttons and Their Functions

Button	Code	Function
Font	Not applicable	Lets you choose a font for the selected text
Page Number	&[Page]	Inserts the page number
Total Pages	&[Pages]	Inserts the total number of pages to be printed
Date	&[Date]	Inserts the current date
Time	&[Time]	Inserts the current time
File	&[File]	Inserts the workbook name
Sheet	&[Tab]	Inserts the sheet's name

You can combine text and codes and insert as many codes as you like into each section. If the text that you enter uses an ampersand (&), you must enter the ampersand twice (because Excel uses an ampersand to signal a code). For example, to enter the text *Research & Development* into a section of a header or footer, enter **Research && Development**.

You also can use different fonts and sizes in your headers and footers. Just select the text that you want to change and then click the Font button. Excel displays its Fonts dialog box so that you can make your choice. If you don't change the font, Excel uses the font defined for the Normal style.

Tip   You can use as many lines as you like. Use Alt+Enter to force a line break for multiline headers or footers.

After you define a custom header or footer, it appears at the bottom of the appropriate drop-down list on the Header/Footer tab of the Page Setup dialog box. You can have only one custom header and one custom footer in a workbook. So, if you edit a custom header, for example, it replaces the existing custom header in the drop-down list.

Unfortunately, you can't print the contents of a specific cell in a header or footer. For example, you might want Excel to use the contents of cell A1 as part of a header. To do so, you need to enter the cell's contents manually — or write a macro to perform this operation.

On the CD-ROM   Excel 2000 still doesn't implement one of the most requested features: The ability to print a workbook's full path and filename in a header or footer. You can print the file name, but you find an option to print the path. The companion CD-ROM contains an add-in that I developed that adds this feature to Excel.

Controlling sheet options

The Sheet tab of the Page Setup dialog box (shown in Figure 14-6) contains several additional options. Each is described in the sections that follow.

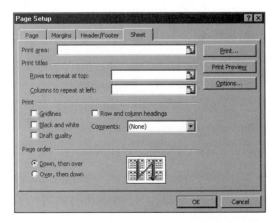

Figure 14-6: The Sheet tab of the Page Setup dialog box

Print area

The Print area box lists the range defined as the print area. If you select a range of cells and choose the Selection option in the Print dialog box, the selected range address appears in this box. Excel also defines this as the reference for the `Print_Area` name.

If the Print area box is blank, Excel prints the entire worksheet. You can activate this box and select a range (Excel will modify its definition of `Print_Area`), or you can enter a previously defined range name into the box.

Print titles

Many worksheets are set up with titles in the first row and descriptive names in the first column. If such a worksheet requires more than one page, reading subsequent pages may be difficult, because the text in the first row and first column won't be printed on subsequent pages. Excel offers a simple solution: *print titles*.

Don't confuse print titles with headers; these are two different concepts. Headers appear at the top of each page and contain information such as the worksheet name, date, or page number. Print titles describe the data being printed, such as field names in a database table or list.

You can specify particular rows to repeat at the top of every printed page, or particular columns to repeat at the left of every printed page. To do so, just activate the appropriate box and select the rows or columns in the worksheet. Or, you can enter these references manually. For example, to specify rows 1 and 2 as repeating rows, enter **1:2**.

In the old days, users often were surprised to discover that print titles appeared twice on the first page of their printouts. This occurred because they defined a print area that included the print titles. Excel now handles this automatically, however, and doesn't print titles twice if they are part of the print area.

You can specify different print titles for each worksheet in the workbook. Excel remembers print titles by creating sheet-level names (Print_Titles).

Print

The section labeled Print contains five check boxes:

> ✦ **Gridlines:** If checked, Excel prints the gridlines to delineate cells. If you turn off the gridline display in the worksheet (in the View tab of the Options dialog box), Excel automatically removes the check from this box for you. In other words, the default setting for this option is determined by the gridline display in your worksheet.

> ✦ **Black and white:** If checked, Excel ignores any colors in the worksheet and prints everything in black and white. By taking advantage of this option, you can format your worksheet for viewing on your monitor and still get readable print output.

✦ **Draft quality:** If checked, Excel prints in draft mode. In draft mode, Excel doesn't print embedded charts or drawing objects, cell gridlines, or borders, which reduces the printing time.

✦ **Row and column headings:** If checked, Excel prints the row and column headings on the printout, enabling you to identify easily specific cells from a printout.

✦ **Comments:** If checked, Excel prints cell notes by using the option that you specify: either At the end of the sheet or As displayed on sheet.

Printer-specific options

The Print dialog box has a button labeled Options (refer to Figure 14-2). Clicking this button displays another dialog box that enables you to adjust properties that are specific to the selected printer. See Figure 14-7 for an example. You can also open this dialog box from the Page Setup dialog box (click the Options button).

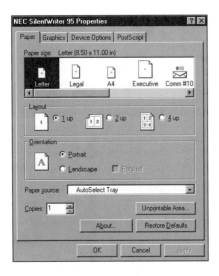

Figure 14-7: The Page Setup dialog box lets you set printer-specific options.

Some of the printer settings can be set directly from Excel. Other settings may not be accessible from Excel, and you can change them in this dialog box. For example, if your printer uses multiple paper trays, you can select which tray to use.

Using Print Preview

Excel's print preview feature displays an image of the printed output on your screen. This is a handy feature that enables you to see the result of the options that you set, before you actually send the job to the printer. It'll save you lots of time—not to mention printing supplies.

Accessing print preview

Several ways exist to preview your document:

✦ Select the File ⇨ Print Preview command.

✦ Click the Print Preview button on the Standard toolbar. Or, you can press Shift and click the Print button on the Standard toolbar (the Print button serves a dual purpose).

✦ Click the Print Preview button in the Print dialog box.

✦ Click the Print Preview button in the Page Setup dialog box.

Any one of these methods changes Excel's window to a preview window, as shown in Figure 14-8.

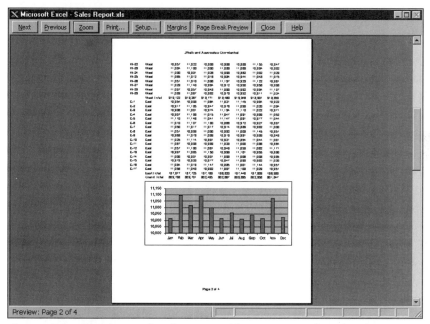

Figure 14-8: The print preview feature enables you to see the printed output before you send it to the printer.

The preview window has several buttons along the top:

✦ **Next:** Displays an image of the next page.

✦ **Previous:** Displays an image of the previous page.

✦ **Zoom:** Zooms the display in or out. This button toggles between the two levels of zooming that are available. You also can simply click the preview image to toggle between zoom modes.

✦ **Print:** Sends the job to the printer.

✦ **Setup:** Displays the Page Setup dialog box, so that you can adjust some settings. When you close the dialog box, you return to the preview screen, so that you can see the effects of your changes.

✦ **Margins:** Displays adjustable columns and margins, described in the next section.

✦ **Page Break Preview:** Displays the worksheet in Page Break Preview mode.

✦ **Close:** Closes the preview window.

✦ **Help:** Displays help for the preview window.

Making changes while previewing

When you click the Margins button in the preview window, Excel adds markers to the preview that indicate column borders and margins (see Figure 14-9). You can drag the column or margin markers to make changes that appear onscreen.

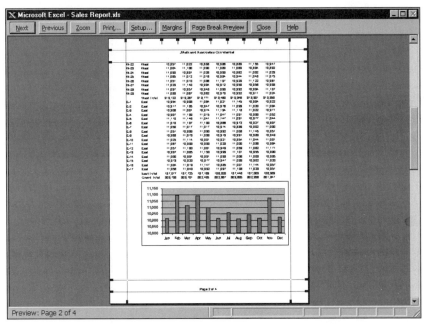

Figure 14-9: You can adjust column widths or margins directly from the print preview window.

For example, if you print a worksheet and discover that Excel is printing the last column on a second page, you can adjust the column widths or margins in the preview window to force all the columns to print on a single page. After you drag one of these markers, Excel updates the display so that you can see what effect it had.

When you make changes to the column widths in the preview window, these changes also are made to your worksheet. Similarly, changing the margins in the preview window changes the settings that appear in the Margins tab of the Page Setup dialog box.

Dealing with Page Breaks

If you print lengthy reports, you know that it's often important to have control over the page breaks. For example, you normally wouldn't want a row to print on a page by itself. Fortunately, Excel gives you superb control over page breaks.

As you may have discovered, Excel handles page breaks automatically. After you print or preview your worksheet, it even displays dashed lines to indicate where page breaks occur. Sometimes, however, you'll want to force a page break — either a vertical or a horizontal one. For example, if your worksheet consists of several distinct areas, you may want to print each area on a separate sheet of paper.

Inserting a page break

To insert a vertical manual page break, move the cell pointer to the cell that will begin the new page, but make sure that you place the pointer in column A; otherwise, you'll insert a vertical page break and a horizontal page break. For example, if you want row 14 to be the first row of a new page, select cell A14. Then, choose Insert ➪ Page Break. Excel displays a dashed line to indicate the page break. The dashed line for manual page breaks is slightly thinner than the lines for natural page breaks.

To insert a horizontal page break, move the cell pointer to the cell that will begin the new page, but in this case, make sure that you place the pointer in row one. Select Insert ➪ Page Break to create the page break.

Removing a page break

To remove a vertical manual page break, move the cell pointer anywhere in the first row beneath the manual page break and then select Insert ➪ Remove Page Break (this command appears only when you place the cell pointer in the first row following a manual page break).

To remove a horizontal manual page break, perform the same procedure, but position the cell pointer anywhere in the first column following a horizontal page break.

Tip To remove all manual page breaks in the worksheet, click the Select All button (or press Ctrl+A); then, choose Insert ➪ Remove Page Break.

Using page break preview

Page Break Preview mode makes dealing with page breaks easy. To use Page Break Preview, choose View ➪ Page Break Preview. The screen changes, as shown in Figure 14-10.

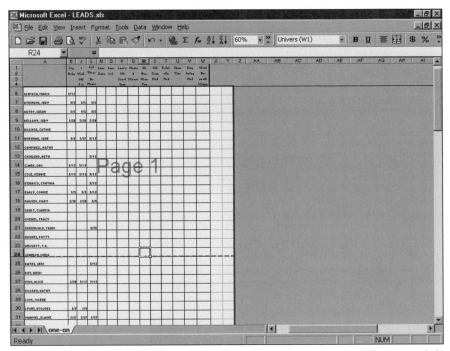

Figure 14-10: Page Break Preview mode gives you a bird's-eye view of your worksheet and shows exactly where the page breaks occur.

When you enter Page Break Preview mode, Excel does the following

✦ Changes the zoom factor so that you can see more of the worksheet

✦ Displays the page numbers overlaid on the pages

✦ Displays the current print range with a white background; nonprinting data appears with a gray background

✦ Displays all page breaks

When you're in Page Break Preview mode, you can drag the borders to change the print range or the page breaks. When you change the page breaks, Excel automatically adjusts the scaling so that the information fits on the pages, per your specifications.

Note   In Page Break Preview mode, you still have access to all of Excel's commands. You can change the zoom factor if you find the text to be too small.

To return to normal viewing, select the View ➪ Normal command.

Using Custom Views

Workbooks commonly are used to store a variety of information, and often, several different reports are printed from such workbooks. If this sounds familiar, you need to know about Excel's custom views feature.

The custom views feature enables you to give names to various views of your worksheet, and you can quickly switch among these named views. A view includes settings for the following:

✦ Print settings, as specified in the Page Setup dialog box (optional)

✦ Hidden rows and columns (optional)

✦ Display settings, as specified in the Options Display dialog box

✦ Selected cells and ranges

✦ The active cell

✦ Window sizes and positions

✦ Frozen panes

For example, you might define a view that hides a few columns of numbers, another view with a print range defined as a summary range only, another view with the page setup set to landscape, and so on.

To create a named custom view, first set up your worksheet with the settings that you want to include in the view. These settings can include any of the settings listed previously. For example, you might create a view that has a specific range of cells defined as the print range. Then, select View ➪ Custom Views, and Excel displays a dialog box that lists all named views. Initially, this list is empty, but you can click the Add button to add a view in the Add View dialog box, shown in Figure 14-11.

Figure 14-11: Use the Add View dialog box to supply a name for a new custom view.

Enter a name for the view and make any adjustments to the check boxes. Click OK, and Excel saves the view. You can add as many views as you want and easily switch among them—just highlight the custom view that you want to display from the Custom Views dialog box and then click the Show button.

More About Printing

A few issues related to printing just don't fit anywhere other than a "miscellaneous" section. This section serves as that "miscellaneous" section and provides some additional information regarding printing.

Problems with fonts (when WYS isn't WYG)

Sometimes, you may find that the printed output doesn't match what you see onscreen. You almost always can trace this problem to the fonts that you use. If your printer doesn't have a font that you use to display your worksheet, Windows attempts to match the font as best as it can. Often, the match just isn't good enough.

Simply using TrueType fonts almost always solves this problem; these scalable fonts are designed for both screen viewing and printing.

Printing noncontiguous ranges on a single page

You may have discovered that Excel lets you specify a print area that consists of noncontiguous ranges (a multiple selection). For example, if you need to print, say, A1:C50, D20:F24, and M11:P16, you can press Ctrl while you select these ranges and then issue the File ➪ Print command and choose the Selection option. Better yet, give this multiple selection a range name so that you can quickly choose the same ranges the next time.

Printing multiple ranges is a handy feature, but you may not like the fact that Excel prints each range on a new sheet of paper—and this behavior can't be changed.

You might consider creating live *snapshots* of the three ranges and pasting these snapshots to an empty area of the worksheet. Then, you can print this new area that consists of the snapshots, and Excel won't skip to a new page for each range.

To create a live snapshot of a range, select the range and copy it to the clipboard. Then, to paste a live link (see the Note that follows), select the cell in which you want to paste the snapshot (an empty worksheet is a good choice), press and hold the Shift key, and choose Edit ➪ Paste Picture Link. Repeat this procedure for the other ranges. After you paste them, you can rearrange the snapshots any way you like. Notice that these are truly live links: change a cell in the original range and the change appears in the linked picture. Figure 14-12 shows an example of snapshots made from several ranges.

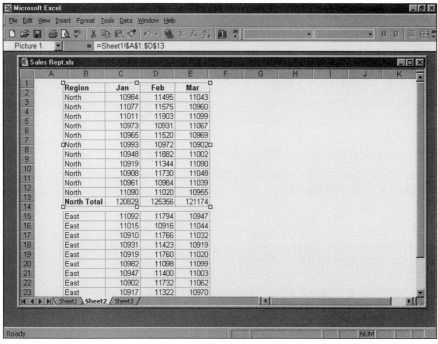

Figure 14-12: These two objects are linked pictures of ranges that exist elsewhere in the workbook, which enables you to print nonadjacent ranges on a single sheet.

Hiding cells before printing

You may have a worksheet that contains confidential information. You may want to print the worksheet, but not the confidential parts. Several techniques prevent certain parts of a worksheet from printing:

✦ When you hide rows or columns, the hidden rows aren't printed.

✦ You can effectively hide cells or ranges by making the text color the same color as the background color.

✦ You can hide cells by using a custom number format that consists of three semicolons (;;;).

✦ You can mask off a confidential area of a worksheet by covering it with a rectangle object. Click the Rectangle tool on the Drawing toolbar and drag the rectangle to the proper size. For best results, you can make the rectangle white with no border.

✦ You can use a text box object, available by using the Text Box tool on the Drawing toolbar, to mask off a range. The advantage to using a text box is that you can add text to it with information about the concealed data (see Figure 14-13).

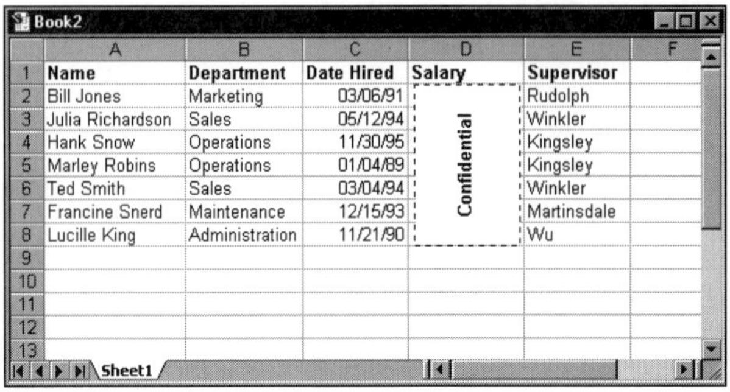

	A	B	C	D	E	F
1	Name	Department	Date Hired	Salary	Supervisor	
2	Bill Jones	Marketing	03/06/91		Rudolph	
3	Julia Richardson	Sales	05/12/94		Winkler	
4	Hank Snow	Operations	11/30/95		Kingsley	
5	Marley Robins	Operations	01/04/89		Kingsley	
6	Ted Smith	Sales	03/04/94	Confidential	Winkler	
7	Francine Snerd	Maintenance	12/15/93		Martinsdale	
8	Lucille King	Administration	11/21/90		Wu	
9						
10						
11						
12						
13						

Sheet1

Figure 14-13: You can use a text box to hide confidential data so that it won't print.

If you find that you must regularly hide data before you print certain reports, consider using the custom views feature to create a named view that doesn't show the confidential information.

Using a template to change printing defaults

If you are never satisfied with Excel's default print settings, you may want to create a template with the print settings that you use most often. After doing so, you can create a new workbook based on the template, and the workbook will have your own print settings for defaults.

Cross-Reference   Chapter 16 discusses template files.

Summary

This chapter presents the basics — and some finer points — of printing in Excel. You learn how to use the Print dialog box and the Page Setup dialog box to control what gets printed and how it is printed. You also learn about the print preview feature that shows how the printed output will look before it hits the paper. The chapter covers features such as manual page breaks, custom views, Page Break Preview mode, tips on printing noncontiguous ranges on a single sheet, and hiding cells that contain confidential information.

✦   ✦   ✦

Customizing Toolbars and Menus

You're probably familiar with many of Excel's built-in
toolbars, and you have most likely thoroughly explored
the menu system. Excel lets you modify both toolbars and
menus. This chapter explains how to customize the built-in
toolbars, create new toolbars, and change the menus that
Excel displays. Although many of these customizations
are most useful when you create macros (discussed in
subsequent chapters), even nonmacro users may find
these techniques helpful.

Menu Bar = Toolbar

Beginning with Excel 97, virtually no distinction exists
between a menu bar and a toolbar. In fact, the menu bar that
you see at the top of Excel's window is actually a toolbar that
is named Worksheet Menu Bar. As with any toolbar, you can
move it to a new location by dragging it (see Figure 15-1).

Many of the menu items display icons in addition to text — a
good sign that Excel's menus are not "real" menus. To further
demonstrate that Excel's menu bars are different from those
used in other programs, note that if you change the colors or
fonts used for menus (using the Windows Control panel),
these changes do not appear in Excel's menus.

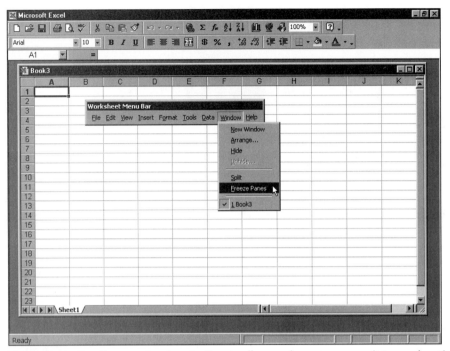

Figure 15-1: Excel's menu bar is actually a toolbar, and you can move it to any location that you want.

Customizing Toolbars

The official term for toolbars, menu bars, and shortcut menus is a *CommandBar*. All told, Excel comes with nearly 100 built-in CommandBars, made up of the following:

✦ Two menu bars (one for worksheets and one for chart sheets)

✦ 40 traditional style toolbars

✦ 51 shortcut menus (the menus that appear when you right-click a selection)

Each CommandBar consists of one or more "commands." A command can take the form of an icon, text, or both. Some additional commands don't appear on any of the prebuilt toolbars.

Many users like to create custom toolbars that contain the commands that they use most often.

How Excel Keeps Track of Toolbars

When you start Excel, it displays the same toolbar configuration that was in effect the last time that you used it. Did you ever wonder how Excel keeps track of this information? When you exit Excel, it updates a file in your Windows folder. This file stores your custom toolbars, as well as information about which toolbars are visible and the onscreen location of each. The file is stored in your Windows directory, and has an XLB extension (the actual filename will vary).

To restore the toolbars to their previous configuration, select File ⇨ Open to open this XLB file. This restores your toolbar configuration to the way that it was when you started Excel. You can also make a copy of the XLB file and give it a different name, which enables you to store multiple toolbar configurations that you can load at any time.

Types of customizations

The following list is a summary of the types of customizations that you can make when working with toolbars (which also include menu bars):

✦ **Move toolbars.** Any toolbar can be moved to another location .

✦ **Remove buttons from built-in toolbars.** You may want to do this to eliminate buttons that you never use.

✦ **Add buttons to built-in toolbars.** You can add as many buttons as you want to any toolbar.

✦ **Create new toolbars.** You can create as many new toolbars as you like, with as many buttons as you like.

✦ **Change the functionality of a button.** You make such a change by attaching your own macro to a built-in toolbar button.

✦ **Change the image that appears on any toolbar button.** A rudimentary but functional toolbar-button editor is included with Excel.

Shortcut menus

The casual user cannot modify Excel's shortcut menus (the menus that appear when you right-click an object). Doing so requires the use of VBA macros.

Moving Toolbars

A toolbar can be either floating or docked. A *docked* toolbar is fixed in place at the top, bottom, left, or right edge of Excel's workspace. *Floating* toolbars appear in an "always-on-top" window, and you can drag them wherever you like.

To move a toolbar, just click its border and drag it to its new position. If you drag it to one of the edges of Excel's window, it attaches itself to the edge and becomes docked. You can create several layers of docked toolbars. For example, the Standard and Formatting toolbars are (normally) both docked along the upper edge.

If a toolbar is floating, you can change its dimensions by dragging a border. For example, you can transform a horizontal toolbar to a vertical toolbar by dragging one of its corners.

Using the Customize Dialog Box

To make any changes to toolbars, you need to be in "customization mode." In customization mode, the Customize dialog box is displayed, and you can manipulate the toolbars in a number of ways. To get into customization mode, perform either of the following actions:

✦ Select View ➪ Toolbars ➪ Customize

✦ Select Customize from the shortcut menu that appears when you right-click a toolbar

Either of these methods displays the Customize dialog box that is shown in Figure 15-2. This dialog box lists all the available toolbars, including custom toolbars that you have created.

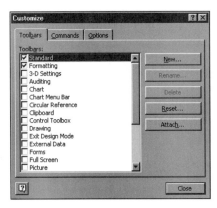

Figure 15-2: The Customize dialog box

The Customize dialog box has three tabs, each of which is described in the following sections.

The Toolbars tab

Figure 15-2 shows the Toolbars tab of the Customize dialog box. The following sections describe how to perform various procedures that involve toolbars.

 Caution   Operations that you perform by using the Customize dialog box cannot be undone.

Hiding or displaying a toolbar

The Toolbars tab displays every toolbar (built-in toolbars and custom toolbars). Add a check mark to display a toolbar; remove the check mark to hide it. The changes take effect immediately.

Creating a new toolbar

Click the New button and then enter a name in the New Toolbar dialog box. Excel creates and displays an empty toolbar. You can then add buttons to the new toolbar. See "Adding or Removing Toolbar Buttons" later in this chapter.

Renaming a custom toolbar

Select a custom toolbar from the list and click the Rename button. Enter a new name in the Rename Toolbar dialog box. You cannot rename a built-in toolbar.

Deleting a custom toolbar

Select a custom toolbar from the list and click the Delete button. You cannot delete a built-in toolbar.

Resetting a built-in toolbar

Select a built-in toolbar from the list and click the Reset button. The toolbar is restored to its default state. If you've added any custom tools to the toolbar, they are removed. If you've removed any of the default tools, they are restored.

The Reset button is not available when a custom toolbar is selected.

Attaching a toolbar to a workbook

If you create a custom toolbar that you want to share with someone else, you can "attach" it to a workbook. To attach a custom toolbar to a workbook, click the Attach button, which presents the Attach Toolbars dialog box. Select the toolbars that you want to attach to a workbook (see Figure 15-3). You can attach any number of toolbars to a workbook.

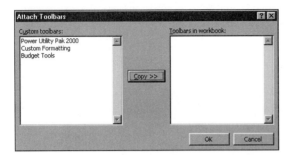

Figure 15-3: You can attach custom toolbars to a workbook in the Attach Toolbars menu.

A toolbar that's attached to a workbook appears automatically when the workbook is opened, unless the workspace already has a toolbar by the same name.

The toolbar that's stored in the workbook is an exact copy of the toolbar at the time that you attach it. If you modify the toolbar after attaching it, the changed version is not stored in the workbook automatically. You must manually remove the old toolbar and then add the edited toolbar.

The Commands tab

The Commands tab of the Customize dialog box contains a list of every tool that's available. Use this tab when you customize a toolbar. This feature is described later in the chapter (see "Adding or Removing Toolbar Buttons").

The Options tab

The Options tab of the Customize dialog box, shown in Figure 15-4, gives you several choices of ways to customize your menus, toolbars, icons, and the like. The following list explains these options.

Figure 15-4: The Options tab of the Customize dialog box

✦ **Personalized Menus and Toolbars:** On the Options tab, the new options of Excel 2000 are Personalized Menus and Toolbars and, in the Other area, List font names in their font. These options provide you with some control over how the menus and toolbars work. Set these options according to your personal preferences.

✦ **Large icons:** To change the size of the icons used in toolbars, select or deselect the Large icons check box. This option only affects the images that are in buttons. Buttons that contain only text (such as buttons in a menu) don't change.

✦ **List font names in their font:** This new feature displays the font names using the actual font. The advantage is that you can preview the font before you select it. The disadvantage is that it's a bit slower.

✦ **Show ScreenTips on toolbar:** ScreenTips are the pop-up messages that display the button names when you pause the mouse pointer over a button. If you find the ScreenTips distracting, remove the check mark from the Show ScreenTips on toolbars check box. The status bar still displays a description of the button when you move the mouse pointer over it.

✦ **Menu animations:** When you select a menu, Excel animates the display of the menu as it is dropping down. You can select the type of animation that you want:

- **Slide:** The menu drops down with a sliding motion

- **Unfold:** The menu unfolds as it drops down

- **Random:** The menu either slides or unfolds randomly

Toolbar Autosensing

Normally, Excel displays a particular toolbar automatically when you change contexts; this is called *autosensing.* For example, when you activate a chart, the Chart toolbar appears. When you activate a sheet that contains a pivot table, the PivotTable toolbar appears.

You can easily defeat autosensing by hiding the toolbar. After you do so, Excel no longer displays that toolbar when you switch to its former context. You can restore this automatic behavior, however, by displaying the appropriate toolbar when you're in the appropriate context. Thereafter, Excel reverts to its normal automatic toolbar display when you switch to that context.

Adding or Removing Toolbar Buttons

As noted earlier in this chapter, you can put Excel into customization mode by displaying the Customize dialog box. When Excel is in customization mode, you have access to all the commands and options in the Customize dialog box. In addition, you can perform the following actions:

✦ Reposition a button on a toolbar

✦ Move a button to a different toolbar

✦ Copy a button from one toolbar to another

✦ Add new buttons to a toolbar by using the Commands tab of the Customize dialog box

New in Excel 2000: An Easier Way to Add or Remove Buttons

Excel 2000 provides a much simpler way to add or remove buttons from a toolbar. Just click the arrow at the end of the toolbar and select Add or Remove Buttons. You'll see a list of all the buttons for the toolbar (see the accompanying figure).

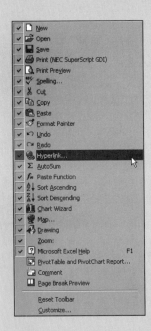

Buttons displayed with a check mark are visible in the toolbar; those without a check mark are not visible in the toolbar. Simply add or remove the check marks according to your preferences. For additional types of customization, you need to use the Customize dialog box.

Moving and copying buttons

When the Customize dialog box is displayed, you can copy and move buttons freely among any visible toolbars. To move a button, drag it to its new location (the new location can be within the current toolbar or on a different toolbar).

To copy a button, press Ctrl while you drag the button to another toolbar. You can also copy a toolbar button within the same toolbar, but no reason really exists to have multiple copies of a button the same toolbar.

Inserting a new button

To add a new button to a toolbar, you use the Commands tab of the Customize dialog box (see Figure 15-5).

Figure 15-5: The Commands tab contains a list of every available button.

The buttons are arranged in 16 categories. When you select a category, the buttons in that category appear to the right in the Commands list box. To determine a button's function, select it and click the Description button.

To add a button to a toolbar, locate it in the Commands tab and then click and drag it to the toolbar.

Other Toolbar Button Operations

When Excel is in customization mode (that is, the Customize dialog box is displayed), you can right-click a toolbar button to get a shortcut menu of additional actions for the tool. Figure 15-6 shows the shortcut menu that appears when you right-click a button in customization mode.

Figure 15-6: In customization mode, right-clicking a button displays this shortcut menu.

These commands are described in the following list (note that some of these commands are not available for certain toolbar tools):

✦ **Reset:** Resets the tool to its original state.

✦ **Delete:** Deletes the tool.

✦ **Name:** Lets you change the name of the tool.

✦ **Copy Button Image:** Makes a copy of the button's image and places it on the clipboard.

✦ **Paste Button Image:** Pastes the image from the clipboard to the button.

✦ **Reset Button Image:** Restores the button's original image.

✦ **Edit Button Image:** Lets you edit the button's image, using Excel's button editor.

✦ **Change Button Image:** Lets you change the image by selecting from a list of 42 button images.

✦ **Default Style:** Displays the tool with its default style (either text only or image and text).

✦ **Text Only (Always):** Always displays text (no image) for the tool.

✦ **Text Only (In Menus):** Displays text (no image) if the tool is in a menu bar.

✦ **Image and Text:** Displays the tool's image and text.

✦ **Begin a Group:** Inserts a divider in the toolbar. In a drop-down menu, a separator bar appears as a horizontal line between commands. In a toolbar, a separator bar appears as a vertical line.

✦ **Assign Hyperlink:** Lets you assign a hyperlink that will activate a Web page.

✦ **Assign Macro:** Lets you assign a macro that is executed when the button is clicked.

EXCEL 2000 Assign Hyperlink is a new feature of Excel 2000.

Creating a Custom Toolbar: An Example

This section walks you through the steps that are used to create a custom toolbar. This toolbar is an enhanced Formatting toolbar that contains many additional formatting tools that aren't found on Excel's built-in Formatting toolbar. You may want to replace the built-in Formatting toolbar with this new custom toolbar.

On the CD-ROM If you don't want to create this toolbar yourself, this workbook is available on this book's CD-ROM.

Adding the first button

The following steps are required to create this new toolbar and add one button (which has five subcommands):

1. Right-click any toolbar and select Customize from the shortcut menu.

   Excel displays its Customize dialog box.

2. Click the Toolbars tab and then click New.

   Excel displays its New Toolbar dialog box.

3. Enter a name for the toolbar: **Custom Formatting**. Click OK.

   Excel creates a new (empty) toolbar.

4. In the Customize dialog box, click the Commands tab.

5. In the Categories list, scroll down and select New Menu.

   The New Menu category has only one command (New Menu), which appears in the Commands list.

6. Drag the New Menu command from the Commands list to the new toolbar.

   This creates a menu button in the new toolbar.

7. Right-click the New Menu button in the new toolbar and change the name to **Font**.

8. In the Customize dialog box, select Format from the Categories list.

9. Scroll down through the Commands list and drag the Bold command to the Font button in your new toolbar.

This step makes the Font button display a submenu (Bold) when the button is clicked.

10. Repeat Step 9, adding the following buttons from the Format category: Italic, Underline, Font Size, and Font.

At this point, you may want to click the Close button in the Customize dialog box to try out your new toolbar. The new toolbar contains only one button, but this button expands to show five font-related commands. Figure 15-7 shows the Custom Formatting toolbar at this stage.

Figure 15-7: A new Custom Formatting toolbar after adding a menu button with five commands. In this example, Underline is selected.

Adding more buttons

If you followed the steps in the previous section, you should understand how toolbar customization works, and you can now add additional buttons by following the procedures that you learned. To finish the toolbar, right-click a toolbar button and select Customize. Then, add additional tools.

Figure 15-8 shows the final version of the Custom Formatting toolbar, and Table 15-1 describes the tools on this toolbar. This customized toolbar includes all the tools that are on the built-in Formatting toolbar — plus quite a few more (38 tools in all). But, because the Custom Formatting toolbar uses five menus (which expand to show more commands), the toolbar takes up a relatively small amount of space.

Figure 15-8: The final version of the Custom Formatting toolbar

You can, of course, customize the toolbar any way that you like. The tools that are listed in the table are my preferences. You may prefer to omit tools that you never use — or add other tools that you use frequently.

Table 15-1
Tools in the Custom Formatting Toolbar

Tool	Subcommands
New Menu (renamed Font)	Bold, Italic, Underline, Font Size, Font
New Menu (renamed Align)	Align Left, Center, Align Right, Decrease Indent, Increase Indent, Merge and Center, Merge Cells, Unmerge Cells, Merge Across
New Menu (renamed Text)	Vertical Text, Rotate Text Up, Rotate Text Down, Angle Text Downward, Angle Text Upward
New Menu (renamed Border)	Clear Border, Apply Outline Borders, Apply Inside Border, Left Border, Right Border, Top Border, Bottom Border, Inside Vertical Border, Inside Horizontal Border, Bottom Double Border
Font Color	(none)
Fill Color	(none)
Pattern	(none)
Clear Formatting	(none)
Format Cells	(none)
New Menu (renamed Number)	Currency Style, Percent Style, Comma Style, Decrease Decimal, Increase Decimal

With two exceptions, all the tools are found in the Formatting category. The Clear Formatting tool is in the Edit category, and the Format Cells tool is in the Built-In Menus category.

Saving the custom toolbar

Excel doesn't have a command to save a toolbar. Rather, the new toolbar is saved when you exit Excel. Refer to the sidebar "How Excel Keeps Track of Toolbars," earlier in this chapter.

Caution   You need to remember that if Excel shuts down by nonnormal means (that is, it crashes!), your custom toolbar will be lost. Therefore, if you invest a lot of time creating a new toolbar, you should close Excel to force the new toolbar to be saved.

Changing a Toolbar Button's Image

To change the image that is displayed on a toolbar button, you have several options:

✦ Choose 1 of the 42 images that are provided by Excel

✦ Modify or create the image by using Excel's Button Editor dialog box

✦ Copy an image from another toolbar button

Each of these methods is discussed in the following sections.

To make any changes to a button image, you must be in toolbar customization mode (the Customize dialog box must be visible). Right-click any toolbar button and select Customize from the shortcut menu.

Using a built-in image

To change the image on a toolbar button, right-click the button and select Change Button Image from the shortcut menu. As you can see in Figure 15-9, this menu expands to show 42 images from which you can choose. Just click the image that you want, and the selected button's image changes.

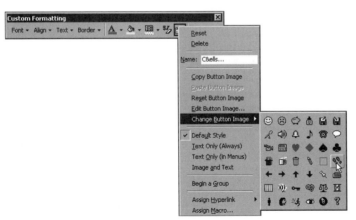

Figure 15-9: The Change Button Image option gives you 42 built-in button images to choose from.

Editing a button image

If not one of the 42 built-in images suits your tastes, you can edit an existing image or create a new image by using Excel's Button Editor.

To begin editing, right-click the button that you want to edit and then choose Edit Button Image from the shortcut menu. The image appears in the Button Editor dialog box (see Figure 15-10), in which you can change individual pixels and shift the entire image up, down, to the left, or to the right. If you've never worked with icons before, you may be surprised at how difficult it is to create attractive images in such a small area.

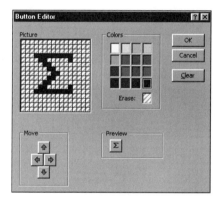

Figure 15-10: The Button Editor dialog box, in which you can design your own button image or edit an existing one

The Edit Button Image dialog box is straightforward. Just click a color and then click a pixel (or drag across pixels). When it looks good, click OK. Or, if you don't like what you've done, click Cancel, and the button keeps its original image.

Copying another button image

Another way to get a button image on a custom toolbar is to copy it from another toolbar button. Right-click a toolbar button, and it displays a shortcut menu that enables you to copy a button image to the clipboard or paste the clipboard contents to the selected button.

Activating a Web Page from a Toolbar Button

You might want to create a button that activates your Web browser and loads a Web page.

EXCEL 2000   This feature is available only in Excel 2000.

To add a new button and attach a hyperlink, make sure that you're in toolbar customization mode. Use the procedure previously described to add a new button and (optionally) specify a button image. Then, right-click the button and select Assign Hyperlink ⇨ Open. You'll see the Assign Hyperlink: Open dialog box, shown in Figure 15-11. Type a URL or select one from the list.

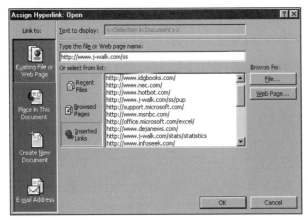

Figure 15-11: The Assign Hyperlink: Open dialog box enables you to assign a hyperlink to a toolbar button.

Summary

This chapter discusses how to modify two components of Excel's user interface: toolbars and menus. Users of all levels can benefit from creating custom toolbars. To create new commands that are executed by toolbar buttons, however, you need to write macros. This chapter also discusses how to change the image that appears on a toolbar button, and then introduces Excel's menu editor, which is most useful for macro writers.

✦   ✦   ✦

Using and Creating Templates

This chapter covers one of the most potentially useful features in Excel — template files. Templates can be used for a variety of purposes, ranging from custom "fill-in-the-blanks" workbooks to a way to change Excel's defaults for new workbooks or new worksheets.

An Overview of Templates

A *template* is essentially a model that serves as the basis for something else. An Excel template is a workbook that's used to create other workbooks. If you understand this concept, you may save yourself a lot of work. For example, you may always use a particular header on your printouts. Conse-quently, every time that you print a worksheet, you need to select File ⇨ Page Setup to add your page header. The solution is to create a new workbook by modifying the template that Excel uses. In this case, you modify the template file by inserting your header into the template. Save the template file, and then every new workbook that you create has your customized page header.

Excel supports three types of templates:

+ **The default workbook template:** Used as the basis for new workbooks.

+ **The default worksheet template:** Used as the basis for new worksheets that are inserted into a workbook.

✦ **Custom workbook templates:** Usually, ready-to-run workbooks that include formulas. Typically, these templates are set up so that a user can simply plug in values and get immediate results. The Spreadsheet Solutions templates (included with Excel) are examples of this type of template.

Each template type is discussed in the following sections.

The default workbook template

Every new workbook that you create starts out with some default settings. For example, the workbook's worksheets have gridlines, text appears in Arial 10-point font, values that are entered display in the General number format, and so on. If you're not happy with any of the default workbook settings, you can change them.

Changing the workbook defaults

Making changes to Excel's default workbook is fairly easy to do, and it can save you lots of time in the long run. Take the following steps to change Excel's workbook defaults:

1. Start with a new workbook.

2. Add or delete sheets to give the workbook the number of worksheets that you want.

3. Make any other changes that you want to make, which can include column widths, named styles, page setup options, and many of the settings that are available in the Options dialog box.

Tip　To change the default formatting for cells, choose Format ➪ Style, and then modify the settings for the Normal style. For example, you can change the default font, size, or number format. Refer to "Using Named Styles" in Chapter 17 for details.

4. When your workbook is set up to your liking, select File ➪ Save As.

5. In the Save As dialog box, select Template (*.xlt) from the Save as type box.

6. Enter **book.xlt** for the filename.

7. Save the file in your \XLStart folder. This folder is probably located within your c:\Program Files\Microsoft Office\Office folder.

   You can also save your book.xlt template file in the folder that is specified as an alternate startup folder. You specify an alternate startup folder in the General tab of the Options dialog box.

8. Close the file.

After you perform the preceding steps, the new default workbook is based on the book.xlt workbook template. You can create a workbook based on your template by using any of the following methods:

✦ Click the New button on the Standard toolbar

✦ Press Ctrl+N

✦ Choose File ➪ New and then select the Workbook icon in the General tab of the New dialog box (see Figure 16-1)

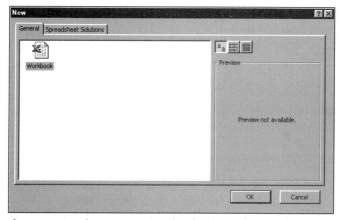

Figure 16-1: After you create a book.xlt template, clicking the Workbook icon creates a new workbook that is based on your template.

Note

Normally, the Xlstart folder does not contain a file named book.xlt. If a file with this name is not present, Excel creates new workbooks using built-in default settings.

Editing the book.xlt template

After you create your book.xlt template, you may discover that you need to change it. You can open the book.xlt template file and edit it just like any other workbook. After you finish with your edits, save the workbook and close it.

Resetting the default workbook

If you create a book.xlt file and then decide that you would rather use the standard default workbook settings, simply delete the book.xlt template file from the Xlstart folder. Excel then resorts to its built-in default settings for new workbooks.

The Default Worksheet Template

When you insert a new worksheet into a workbook, Excel uses its built-in worksheet defaults for the worksheet. This includes items such as column width, row height, and so on.

Note Versions of Excel prior to Excel 97 also use other sheet templates (dialog.xlt and macro.xlt). These templates are not used in Excel 97 or later versions.

If you don't like the default settings for a new worksheet, you can change them by using the following procedure:

1. Start with a new workbook, deleting all the sheets except one.

2. Make any changes that you want to make, which can include column widths, named styles, page setup options, and many of the settings that are available in the Options dialog box.

3. When your workbook is set up to your liking, select File ➪ Save As.

4. In the Save As dialog box, select Template (*.xlt) from the Save as type box.

5. Enter **sheet.xlt** for the filename.

6. Save the file in your \XLStart folder. This folder is probably located within your c:\Program Files\Microsoft Office\Office folder.

   You can also save your book.xlt template file in the folder that is specified as an alternate startup folder. You specify an alternate startup folder in the General tab of the Options dialog box.

7. Close the file.

After performing this procedure, all new sheets that you insert with the Insert ➪ Worksheet command are formatted like your sheet.xlt template.

When you right-click a sheet tab and choose Insert from the shortcut menu, Excel displays its Insert dialog box (which looks just like the New dialog box). If you've created a template named sheet.xlt, you can select it by clicking the icon labeled Worksheet.

Editing the sheet.xlt template

After you create your sheet.xlt template, you may discover that you need to change it. You can open the sheet.xlt template file and edit it just like any other workbook. After you make your changes, save the file and close it.

Resetting the default new worksheet

If you create a sheet.xlt template and then decide that you would rather use the standard default new worksheet settings, simply delete the sheet.xlt template file from the Xlstart folder. Excel then resorts to its built-in default settings for new worksheets.

Custom Workbook Templates

The book.xlt and sheet.xlt templates discussed in the previous section are two special types of templates that determine default settings for new workbooks and new worksheets. This section discusses other types of templates, referred to as *workbook templates,* which are simply workbooks that are set up to be used as the basis for new workbooks.

Why use a workbook template? The simple answer is that it saves you from repeating work. Assume that you create a monthly sales report that consists of your company's sales by region, plus several summary calculations and charts. You can create a template file that consists of everything except the input values. Then, when it's time to create your report, you can open a workbook based on the template, fill in the blanks, and you're finished.

You could, of course, just use the previous month's workbook and save it with a different name. This is prone to errors, however, because you easily can forget to use the Save As command and accidentally overwrite the previous month's file.

How templates work

When you create a workbook that is based on a template, Excel creates a copy of the template in memory so that the original template remains intact. The default workbook name is the template name with a number appended. For example, if you create a new workbook based on a template named Sales Report.xlt, the workbook's default name is Sales Report1.xls. The first time that you save a workbook that is created from a template, Excel displays its Save As dialog box, so that you can give the template a new name if you want to.

Templates that are included with Excel

Excel ships with three workbook templates (called Spreadsheet Solutions templates), which were developed by Village Software. When you select File ➪ New, you can select one of these templates from the New dialog box. Click the tab labeled Spreadsheet Solutions to choose one of the following templates upon which to base your new workbook (see Figure 16-2).

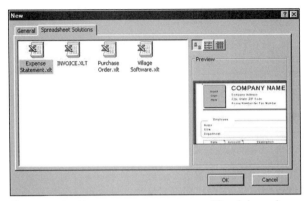

Figure 16-2: You can create a new workbook based on one of the Spreadsheet Solutions templates.

✦ **Expense Statement:** Helps you to create expense report forms and a log to track them

✦ **Invoice:** Helps you to create invoices

✦ **Purchase Order:** Helps you to create purchase orders to send to vendors

EXCEL 2000   The preceding templates are included with Excel 2000.

Note   A fourth template, named Village Software.xlt, describes additional templates that you can obtain from Village Software.

Tip   You can also download some additional templates from Microsoft's Web site: www.microsoft.com/excel.

Creating Custom Templates

This section describes how to create workbook templates, which is really quite simple.

A *custom template* is essentially a normal workbook, and it can use any of Excel's features, such as charts, formulas, and macros. Usually, a template is set up so that the user can enter values and get immediate results. In other words, most templates include everything but the data—which is entered by the user.

If the template is going to be used by novices, you may consider locking all the cells except the input cells (use the Protection panel of the Format Cells dialog box for this). Then, protect the worksheet by choosing Tools ➪ protection ➪ Protect Sheet.

To save the workbook as a template, choose File ⇨ Save As and select Template (*.xlt) from the drop-down list labeled Save as type. Save the template in your Microsoft Office\Templates folder (or a folder within that Templates folder).

Where to Store Your Templates

Template files can be stored anywhere. When you open a template file (by selecting File ⇨ New), you don't actually open the template. Rather, Excel creates a new workbook that's based on the template that you specify. However, your templates are easier to access if you store them in one of the following locations:

✦ **Your \XLStart folder:** This is probably located within c:\Program Files\Microsoft Office\Office. If you create a default workbook template (book.xlt) or a default worksheet template (sheet.xlt), you store these templates in this folder.

✦ **Your \Templates folder:** This is probably located within your c:\Program Files\ Microsoft Office\Office folder. Custom templates that are stored here appear in the New dialog box.

✦ **A folder located in your \Templates folder:** If you create a new folder within this folder, its name appears as a tab in the New dialog box. Clicking the tab displays the templates that are stored in that folder. The accompanying figure shows how the New dialog box looks when a new folder (named John's Templates) is in the Templates folder.

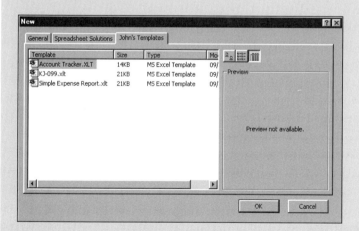

If you've specified an alternate startup folder (using the General panel of the Options dialog box), templates that are stored in that location also appear in the New dialog box.

Before you save the template, you may want to specify that the file be saved with a preview image. Select File ➪ Properties, and check the box that is labeled Save Preview Picture. That way, the New dialog box displays the preview when the template's icon is selected.

If you later discover that you want to modify the template, choose File ➪ Open to open and edit the template (don't use the File ➪ New command, which creates a workbook that is based on the template).

Ideas for Creating Templates

This section provides a few ideas that may spark your imagination for creating templates. A partial list of the settings that you can adjust and use in your custom templates is as follows:

✦ **Multiple formatted worksheets:** You can, for example, create a workbook template that has two worksheets: one formatted to print in landscape mode and one formatted to print in portrait mode.

✦ **Workbook properties:** You can set one or more workbook properties. For example, Excel doesn't store a preview picture of your workbook. Select File ➪ Properties and then change the Save Preview Picture option in the Summary panel.

✦ **Several settings in the View panel of the Options dialog box:** For example, you may not like to see sheet tabs, so you can turn off this setting.

✦ **Color palette:** Use the Color panel of the Options dialog box to create a custom color palette for a workbook.

✦ **Style:** The best approach is to choose Format ➪ Style and modify the attributes of the Normal style. For example, you can change the font or size, the alignment, and so on.

✦ **Custom number formats:** If you create number formats that you use frequently, these can be stored in a template.

✦ **Column widths and row heights:** You may prefer that columns be wider or narrower, or you may want the rows to be taller.

✦ **Print settings:** Change these settings in the Page Setup dialog box. You can adjust the page orientation, paper size, margins, header and footer, and several other attributes.

✦ **Sheet settings:** These are options in the Options dialog box. They include gridlines, automatic page break display, and row and column headers.

Summary

This chapter introduces the concept of templates. Excel supports three template types: a default workbook template, a default worksheet template, and custom workbook templates. This chapter describes how to create such templates and where to store them. It also discusses the Template Wizard, a tool that helps you to create templates that can store data in a central database.

✦　　✦　　✦

Adding Visual Elements

Worksheet Formatting

Chapter 5 discussed number formatting, which enables you to change the way that Excel displays values in their cells. This chapter covers what I refer to as *stylistic* formatting, which is purely cosmetic.

Overview of Stylistic Formatting

The stylistic formatting that you apply to worksheet cells doesn't affect the actual content of the cells. Rather, you should use stylistic formatting with the goal of making your work easier to read or more attractive. In this chapter, you'll learn about the following types of formatting:

✦ Using different type fonts, sizes, and attributes

✦ Changing the way the contents of cells are aligned within cells

✦ Using colors in the background or foreground of cells

✦ Using patterns for cell background

✦ Using borders around cells

✦ Using a graphic background for your worksheet

On the CD-ROM This book's CD-ROM contains a file that demonstrates many of the techniques used in this chapter.

Why bother formatting?

Some users tend to shy away from formatting. After all, it doesn't do anything to make the worksheet more accurate, and formatting just takes valuable time.

I'll be the first to admit that stylistic formatting isn't essential for every workbook that you develop. If no one except you will ever see your workbook, you may not want to bother. If anyone else will use your workbook, however, I strongly suggest that you spend some time applying simple formatting. Figure 17-1 shows how even simple formatting can significantly improve a worksheet's readability.

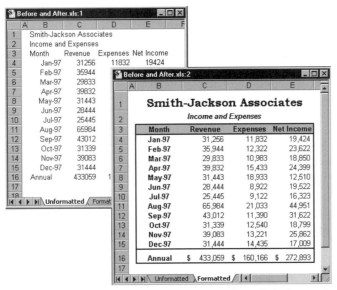

Figure 17-1: Before and after applying simple stylistic formatting

On the other hand, some users go overboard with formatting. I've downloaded many Excel worksheets from the Internet and online services, such as CompuServe. Some of these worksheets are hideous and don't convey a professional image. You disguise your work and make it difficult to read and understand if you use too many different fonts, font sizes, colors, and borders.

Eventually, you'll strike a happy medium with your stylistic formatting: not too much, but enough to clarify what you're trying to accomplish with your worksheet.

When to format

When you're developing a worksheet, you can apply stylistic formatting at any time. Some people prefer to format their work as they go along (I'm in this group). Others wait until the workbook is set up and then apply the formatting as the final step (the icing on the cake). The choice is yours.

The Formatting toolbar

Chapter 5 introduced the Formatting toolbar, shown in Figure 17-2, which you use to apply simple stylistic formatting quickly.

Figure 17-2: The Formatting toolbar contains many tools to apply formats.

In many cases, this toolbar may contain all the formatting tools that you need. But some types of formatting require that you use the Format Cells dialog box. This chapter covers the finer points of stylistic formatting, including options not available on the Formatting toolbar.

The Format Cells dialog box

This chapter refers repeatedly to the Format Cells dialog box. This is a tabbed dialog box from which you can apply nearly any type of stylistic formatting (as well as number formatting). The formats that you choose in the Format Cells dialog box apply to the cells that you have selected at the time.

After selecting the cell or range to format, you can display the Format Cells dialog box by using any of the following methods:

✦ Choose the Format ⇨ Cells command

✦ Press Ctrl+1

✦ Right-click the selected cell or range and choose Format Cells from the shortcut menu

The Format Cells dialog box contains six tabs. When you first open this dialog box, you see the Number tab. You can choose another tab by clicking any of the other tabs. When you open this dialog box again, Excel displays the tab that you used last.

Working with Fonts

Fonts are one of the elements that distinguish a *graphical user interface* (GUI), such as Windows, from a character-based interface (such as plain-old DOS). A GUI can display different fonts in different sizes and with different attributes (bold, italic, underline). A character-based display typically shows one font of the same size and may be capable of handling different font attributes.

Tip   You can use different fonts, sizes, or attributes in your worksheets to make various parts stand out, such as the headers for a table. You also can adjust the font size to make more information appear on a single page.

Reducing the font size so that your report fits on a certain number of pages isn't always necessary.

Cross-Reference   Excel has a handy option that automatically scales your printed output to fit on a specified number of pages, which is discussed in Chapter 14.

About fonts

When you select a font, Excel displays only the fonts that are installed on your system. Windows includes several fonts, and Microsoft Office 2000 includes many additional fonts that you can install on your system. You can acquire fonts from a variety of other sources, too, such as the Internet and online services. For best results, you should use TrueType fonts. You can display and print these fonts in any size, without the "jaggies" (jagged edges) that characterize nonscalable fonts.

Caution   Although you can obtain fonts from many different locations, remember that fonts take up space on your hard drive and use memory. In addition, using too many fonts in a workbook can confuse the reader. You may not ever need any fonts other than those that come with Windows.

If you plan to distribute a workbook to other users, you should stick with the fonts that are included with Windows. If you open a workbook and your system doesn't have the font with which the workbook was created, Windows attempts to use a similar font. Sometimes this works, and sometimes it doesn't. To be on the safe side, use the following fonts only if you plan to share your workbook with others:

- ✦ Arial
- ✦ Courier New
- ✦ Symbol
- ✦ Times New Roman
- ✦ Wingdings

The default font

By default, the information that you enter into an Excel worksheet uses the 10-point Arial font. A font is described by its typeface (Arial, Times New Roman, Courier New, and so on) as well as by its size, measured in points (there are 72 points in one inch). Excel's row height, by default, is 12.75 points. Therefore, 10-point type entered into 12.75-point rows leaves a small amount of blank space between the characters in adjacent rows.

Note   If you have not manually changed a row's height, Excel automatically adjusts the row height based on the tallest text that you enter into the row. You can, of course, override this adjustment and change the row height to any size that you like by using 0.25-point increments. For example, if you enter a row height of 15.35, Excel makes the row 15.5-points high (it always rounds up).

The default font is the font specified by the Normal style for the workbook. All cells use the Normal style unless you specifically apply a different style. If you want to change the font for all cells that use the Normal style, you simply change the font used in the Normal style by using these steps:

1. Choose the Format ⇨ Style command. Excels displays the Style dialog box.

2. Make sure that Normal appears in the *Style name* drop-down box and click the Modify button. Excel displays the Format Cells dialog box.

3. Click the Font tab and choose the font and size that you want as the default.

4. Click OK to return to the Style dialog box.

5. Click OK again to close the Style dialog box.

The font for all cells that use the Normal style changes to the font that you specified. You can change the font for the Normal style at any time. Excel's style feature is discussed later in this chapter.

Cross-Reference   If you want to change the default font permanently, create a template named book.xlt that uses a different font for the Normal style. Templates are covered in Chapter 16.

Changing fonts in Word 2000

Use the Font and Font Size tools on the Formatting toolbar to change the font or size for selected cells. Just select the cells, click the appropriate tool, and then choose the font or size from the drop-down list. In Excel 2000, you can see samples of the fonts when you open the Font list box on the Formatting toolbar (see Figure 17-3). If you prefer the behavior of earlier versions of Excel, in which you don't see font samples when you open this list box, you can change this behavior in the Options dialog box.

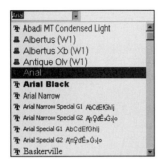

Figure 17-3: The Font list on the Formatting toolbar shows samples as well as choices.

You also can use the Font tab in the Format Cells dialog box, as shown in Figure 17-4. This tab enables you to control several other attributes of the font — from a single dialog box — and preview the font before you select it. Notice that you also can change the font style (bold, italic), underlining, color, and effects (strikethrough, superscript, or subscript). If you click the check box labeled Normal Font, Excel displays the selections for the font defined for the Normal style.

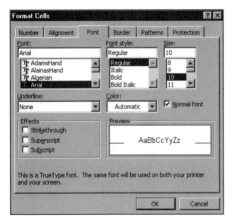

Figure 17-4: The Font tab in the Format Cells dialog box

Figure 17-5 shows examples of font formatting.

Note   Notice in Figure 17-5 that Excel provides four different underlining styles. In the two accounting underline styles, dollar signs and percent signs aren't underlined. In the two nonaccounting underline styles, the entire cell contents are always underlined.

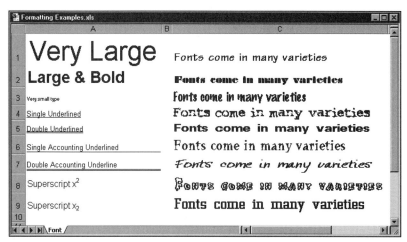

Figure 17-5: Examples of font formatting

Using multiple formatting in one cell

If a cell contains text (not a formula or a value), Excel also enables you to f ormat individual characters in the cell. To do so, switch into edit mode (double-click the cell) and then select the characters that you want to format. You can select characters either by dragging the mouse over them or by holding down the Shift key as you press the left- or right-arrow key. Then, use any of the standard formatting techniques. The changes apply to only the selected characters in the cell. This technique doesn't work with cells that contain values or formulas.

Selecting Fonts and Attributes with Shortcut Keys

If you prefer to keep your hands on the keyboard, you can use the following shortcut keys to format a selected range quickly:

Ctrl+B	Bold
Ctrl+I	Italic
Ctrl+U	Underline
Ctrl+5	Strikethrough

These shortcut keys act as a toggle. For example, you can turn on and off bold by repeatedly pressing Ctrl+B.

Figure 17-6 shows a few examples of using different fonts, sizes, and attributes in a cell.

Figure 17-6: You can use different fonts, sizes, or attributes for selected characters in text.

Changing Cell Alignment

Cell alignment refers to how a cell's contents are situated in the cell. The contents of a cell can be aligned both vertically and horizontally. The effect that you see depends on the cell's height and width. For example, if the row uses standard height, you may not notice any changes in the cell's vertical alignment (but if you increase the row's height, these effects are apparent).

Note   Excel also enables you to display text at a specified orientation — you choose the angle.

Figure 17-7 shows some examples of cells formatted with the various horizontal and vertical alignment options.

Horizontal alignment options

You can apply most of the horizontal alignment options by using the tools on the Formatting toolbar. Or, you can use the Alignment tab in the Format Cells dialog box, as shown in Figure 17-8.

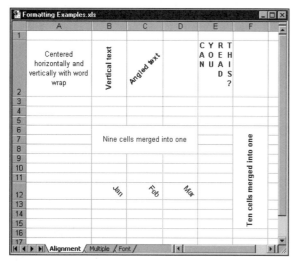

Figure 17-7: Examples of Excel's alignment options

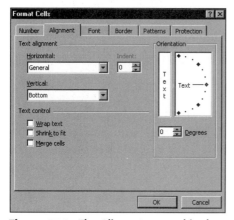

Figure 17-8: The Alignment panel in the Format Cells dialog box

The horizontal alignment options are as follows:

✦ **General:** Aligns numbers to the right, aligns text to the left, and centers logical and error values. This option is the default alignment.

✦ **Left:** Aligns the cell contents to the left side of the cell. If the text is wider than the cell, it spills over to the cell to the right. If the cell to the right is not empty, the text is truncated and not completely visible.

✦ **Center:** Centers the cell contents in the cell. If the text is wider than the cell, it spills over to cells on either side, if they are empty. If the adjacent cells aren't empty, the text is truncated and not completely visible.

✦ **Right:** Aligns the cell contents to the right side of the cell. If the text is wider than the cell, it spills over to the cell to the left. If the cell to the left isn't empty, the text is truncated and not completely visible.

✦ **Fill:** Repeats the contents of the cell until the cell's width is filled. If cells to the right also are formatted with Fill alignment, they also are filled.

✦ **Justify:** Justifies the text to the left and right of the cell. This option is applicable only if the cell is formatted as wrapped text and uses more than one line.

✦ **Center across selection:** Centers the text over the selected columns. This option is useful for precisely centering a heading over a number of columns.

Vertical alignment options

To change the vertical alignment, you must use the Alignment tab of the Format Cells dialog box (these options are not available on the Formatting toolbar). The vertical alignment options are as follows:

✦ **Top:** Aligns the cell contents to the top of the cell

✦ **Center:** Centers the cell contents vertically in the cell

✦ **Bottom:** Aligns the cell contents to the bottom of the cell

✦ **Justify:** Justifies the text vertically in the cell; this option is applicable only if the cell is formatted as wrapped text and uses more than one line

Text control options

The Alignment tab of the Format Cells dialog box offers three additional options, which are discussed in the following sections.

Wrap text

The Wrap text option displays the text on multiple lines in the cell, if necessary. Use this option to display lengthy headings without having to make the columns too wide.

Shrink to fit

Excel includes a Shrink to fit option, which reduces the size of the text so that it fits into the cell without spilling over to the next cell.

If you apply wrap text formatting to a cell, you can't use the shrink-to-fit formatting.

Merging cells

When you merge cells, you don't combine the contents of cells. Rather, you combine a group of cells that occupy the same space into a single cell. Figure 17-9 shows two sets of merged cells. Range C3:G3 has been merged into a single cell that holds the table's title. Range B5:B9 has also been merged to hold a title for the table's rows.

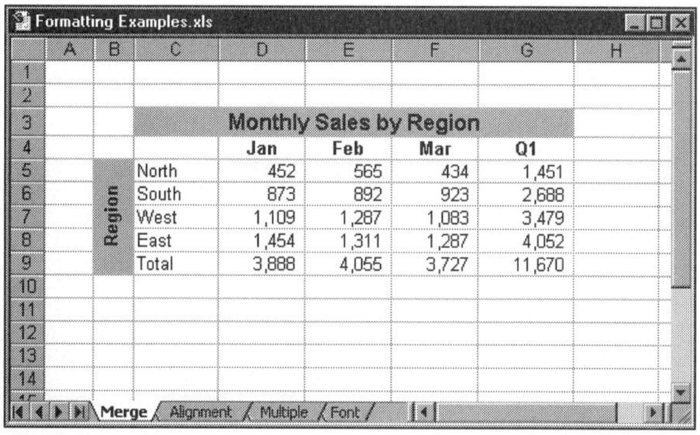

Figure 17-9: The titles for this table appear in merged cells.

You can merge any number of cells, occupying any number of rows and columns. However, the range that you intend to merge should be empty, except for the upper-left cell. If any of the other cells that you intend to merge are not empty, Excel displays a warning.

To merge cells, select the cells that you want to merge and then click the Merge and Center tool on the Formatting toolbar. The only way to "unmerge" cells is to use the Format Cells dialog box. Select the merged cell(s), open the Format Cells dialog box, and, on the Alignment tab, remove the check from the Merge cells box.

Changing a cell's orientation

You can display text horizontally, vertically, or specify an angle. To change the orientation, select the cell or range, open the Format Cells dialog box, and select the Alignment tab. Use the gauge to specify an angle between –90 and +90 degrees.

Figure 17-10 shows an example of text displayed at a 45-degree angle.

Figure 17-10: An example of rotated text

Another Type of Justification

Excel provides another way to justify text, using its Edit ⇨ Fill ⇨ Justify command. This command has nothing to do with the alignment options discussed in this chapter. The Edit ⇨ Fill ⇨ Justify command is useful for rearranging text in cells so that it fits in a specified range. For example, you may import a text file that has very long lines of text.

You easily can justify this text so that it's displayed in narrower lines. The accompanying figure shows a range of text before and after using the Edit ⇨ Fill ⇨ Justify command.

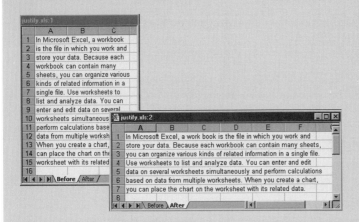

This command works with text in a single column. It essentially redistributes the text in the cells so that it fits into a specified range. You can make the text either wider (so that it uses fewer rows) or narrower (so that it uses more rows).

Select the cells that you want to justify (all in one column) and then extend the selection to the right so that the selection is as wide as you want the end result to be. Choose Edit ⇨ Fill ⇨ Justify, and Excel redistributes the text.

Blank rows serve as paragraph markers. If the range that you select isn't large enough to hold all the text, Excel warns you and lets you continue or abort. Be careful, because justified text overwrites anything that gets in its way.

Colors and Shading

Excel provides the tools to create some very colorful worksheets. I've known people who avoid using color because they are uncertain of how the colors will translate when printed on a black-and-white printer. With Excel, that's not a valid concern. You can instruct Excel to ignore the colors when you print. Choose File ⇨ Page Setup to display the Page Setup dialog box. Click the Sheet tab and place a check in the Black and White check box.

You control the color of the cell's text in the Font tab of the Format Cells dialog box, and you control the cell's background color in the Patterns tab. You can also use tools on the Formatting toolbar (Font Color and Fill Color) to change the color of these items.

A cell's background can be solid (one color) or consist of a pattern that uses two colors. To select a pattern, click the Pattern drop-down list in the Format Cells dialog box. It expands as shown in Figure 17-11. Choose a pattern from the top part of the box and a second color from the bottom part. The first pattern in the list is "None" — use this option if you want a solid background. The Sample box to the right shows how the colors and pattern will look. If you plan to print the worksheet, you need to experiment to see how the color patterns translate to your printer.

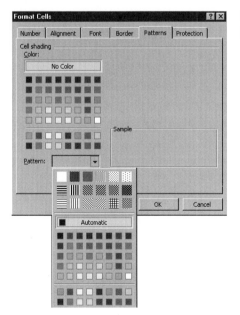

Figure 17-11: Choosing a pattern for a cell background

You might want to use a background color to make a large table of data easier to read. You probably are familiar with computer printer paper that has alternating green-and-white horizontal shading (often referred to as "green bar"). You can use background colors to simulate this effect in Excel. See Figure 17-12 for an example.

Formatting Examples.xls

	A	B	C	D	E	F	G	H
1		Jan	Feb	Mar	Apr	May	Jun	Jul
2	AA-1286	550	3,985	2,176	1,116	3,455	1,017	
3	AA-1287	4,351	2,591	3,324	2,044	1,506	4,512	2,
4	AA-1288	4,908	3,131	3,212	2,340	3,029	710	
5	AA-1289	4,149	1,683	1,504	4,130	1,672	558	4,
6	AA-1290	516	3,130	3,920	4,592	1,441	971	1,
7	AA-1291	1,197	4,289	3,752	2,854	4,039	730	
8	AA-1292	649	884	26	3,055	4,692	3,129	
9	AA-1293	976	1,717	3,746	2,049	4,953	3,208	4,
10	AA-1294	2,792	4,248	3,688	3,452	2,199	1,690	1,
11	AA-1295	2,385	1,080	2,862	1,363	1,227	946	4,
12	AA-1296	3,287	2,182	3,345	1,741	4,041	2,765	2,
13	AA-1297	2,349	648	2,975	4,280	1,556	3,961	
14	AA-1298	4,350	3,586	766	1,474	2,573	4,960	2,
15	AA-1299	547	2,435	564	368	3,449	2,884	
16	AA-1300	1,409	4,335	2,953	1,450	3,676	4,654	3,
17	AA-1301	4,848	1,482	1,074	3,543	2,438	6	
18	AA-1302	137	4,786	531	3,585	1,839	2,930	4,
19	AA-1303	727	923	137	1,022	3,573	1,388	1,
20	AA-1304	1,423	346	2,309	2,838	2,022	4,178	
21	AA-1305	2,733	3,855	3,068	4,470	1,715	1,272	
22	AA-1306	3,987	1,961	2,866	2,527	2,756	1,492	1,
23	AA-1307	2,945	4,748	743	734	4,943	433	2,

⏮ ◀ ▶ ⏭ \ **Shading** ⟋ Orientation ⟋ Merge ⟋ Alignment ⟋ Multiple ◀ ▶ ⏐

Figure 17-12: Shading alternate lines can make a lengthy table easier to read.

Tip

Here's a quick way to apply shading to every other row. This technique assumes that you want to shade every odd-numbered row in the range A1:F100. Start by shading A1:F1 with the color that you want. Then, select A1:F2 (row 1 is shaded and row 2 is not) and copy the range to the clipboard. Next, select A3:F100 and choose Edit ➪ Paste Special (with the Formats option).

To hide quickly the contents of a cell, make the background color the same as the font text color. The cell contents are still visible in the formula bar when you select the cell, however.

Borders and Lines

Borders often are used to group a range of similar cells or simply to delineate rows or columns. Excel offers 13 different styles of borders, as you can see on the Border tab in the Format Cells dialog box (see Figure 17-13). This dialog box works with the selected cell or range and enables you to specify which border style to use for each border of the selection.

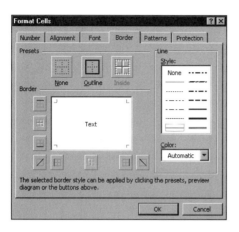

Figure 17-13: The Border tab of the Format Cells dialog box

About the Color Palette

Excel gives you 56 colors from which to choose. These colors are known as the *palette*. You can examine the colors in the palette by clicking the Color or Font Color tool on the Formatting toolbar. You may notice that these colors aren't necessarily unique (some are repeated).

Chances are, you're running Windows in a video mode that supports at least 256 colors. So, why can you use only 56 colors in Excel? Good question. That's just the way Excel was designed.

However, you're not limited to the 56 colors that some unknown techie in Redmond came up with. You can change the colors in the palette to whatever colors you like. To do so, open the Options dialog box and click the Color tab, as shown in the accompanying figure.

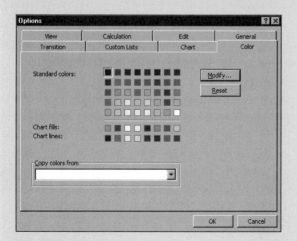

Continued

(continued)

You'll see that the choice of colors for the palette seems to have some rationale. For example, the first 40 colors are designated standard colors. These are followed by 8 chart-fill colors and 8 chart-line colors.

If you want to change a color, select it and click the Modify button. Excel responds with a dialog box named Colors. This dialog box has two tabs: Standard and Custom. Use either tab to select a new color (you have many more choices in the Custom tab). After you select the color, click OK, and the color that you selected replaces the previous color.

If your worksheet uses the replaced color, the new color takes over where that color appeared. If your system is using a video driver that supports only 16 colors, the system creates some of the colors by blending two colors (*dithering*). Dithered colors can be used for cell backgrounds, but text and lines are displayed using the nearest solid color. If you want to revert back to Excel's standard colors, click the Reset button.

Each workbook stores its own copy of the color palette, and you even can copy color palettes from another workbook (which must be open). Use the Options dialog box's drop-down box labeled Copy Colors From.

Before you open this dialog box, select the cell or range to which you want to add borders. First, choose a line style and then choose the border position for the line style by clicking one of the icons.

Notice that the Border tab has three "presets," which can save you some clicking. If you want to remove all borders from the selection, click None. To put an outline around the selection, choose Outline preset. To put borders inside the selection, click Inside preset.

Excel displays the selected border style in the dialog box. You can choose different styles for different border positions and choose a color for the border. Using this dialog box may require some trial and error, but you'll get the hang of it. Figure 17-14 shows examples of borders in a worksheet.

When you apply diagonal lines to a cell or range, the selection looks like it has been crossed out.

 Tip   If you use border formatting in your worksheet, you might want to turn off the grid display, to make the borders more pronounced. Use the View tab of the Options dialog box to do this.

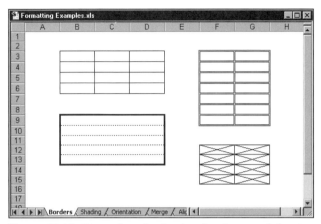

Figure 17-14: Examples of using borders in a worksheet

Producing 3D Effects

You can use a combination of borders and background shading to produce attractive 3D effects on your worksheet. These 3D effects resemble raised or depressed tabs, as shown in the accompanying figure.

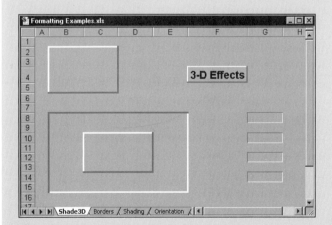

For the best results, use a light-gray background color. To produce a raised effect, apply a white border to the top and left side of the range, and a dark-gray border on the bottom and right side.

Continued

(continued)

To produce a sunken effect, use a dark-gray border on the top and left side, and a white border on the bottom and right side. You can vary the line thickness to produce different effects.

You'll find the 3D Shading utility, which is part of the Power Utility Pak, on this book's CD-ROM.

Adding a Worksheet Background

Excel also enables you to choose a graphics file to serve as a background for a worksheet — similar to the wallpaper that you may display on your Windows desktop. The image that you choose is repeated, so that it tiles the entire worksheet.

Tip　Thousands of background graphics files are available on the World Wide Web. Many Web sites use graphics files for backgrounds, and these files are designed to tile nicely. In addition, these files are usually very small. If you encounter a Web site that uses a good graphic as a background, you can save the file to your hard drive and use it in your Excel workbooks.

To add a background to a worksheet, choose FormatSheet ➪ Background. Excel displays a dialog box that enables you to choose a graphics file. When you locate a file, click OK. Excel tiles your worksheet with the graphic. Some backgrounds make viewing text difficult, so you may want to use a solid background color for cells that contain text (see Figure 17-15). You'll also want to turn off the gridline display, because the gridlines show through the graphic.

Note　The graphic background on a worksheet is for display only — it isn't printed when you print the worksheet.

AutoFormatting

So far, this chapter has described the individual formatting commands and tools at your disposal. Excel also has an *AutoFormatting* feature that can automatically perform many types of formatting for you. Figure 17-16 shows an unformatted table in a worksheet (left side) and the same table formatted using one of Excel's AutoFormats.

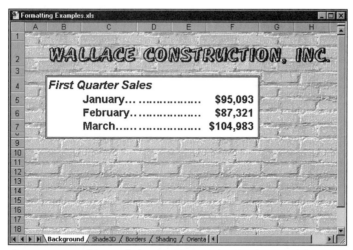

Figure 17-15: This worksheet has a graphic background, but cells that contain text use a white background, which overrides the graphic.

Figure 17-16: A worksheet table before and after using AutoFormat

Cross-Reference   You also can apply AutoFormatting to PivotTables; see Chapter 35.

Copying Formats by Painting

If you want to copy the formats from one cell to another cell or range, you can select Edit ➪ Paste Special and then click the Formats option. Or, use the Format Painter button on the Standard toolbar (the button with the paintbrush image).

Start by selecting the cell or range that has the formatting attributes you want to copy. Then, click the Format Painter button. Notice that the mouse pointer changes to include a paintbrush. Next, select the cells to which you want to apply the formats. Release the mouse button, and Excel completes the painting (and you don't have to clean the brush).

If you double-click the Format Painter button, you can paint multiple areas of the worksheet with the same formats. Excel applies the formats that you copy to each cell or range that you select. To get out of paint mode, click the Format Painter button again (or press Esc).

Using AutoFormats

To apply an AutoFormat, move the cell pointer anywhere within a table that you want to format; Excel determines the table's boundaries automatically. Then, choose Format ➪ AutoFormat. Excel responds with the dialog box shown in Figure 17-17. Choose one of the 17 AutoFormats from the list and click OK. Excel formats the table for you.

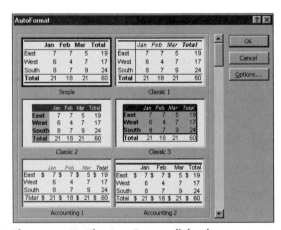

Figure 17-17: The AutoFormat dialog box

Excel applies AutoFormatting rather intelligently. For example, Excel analyzes the data contained in the table and then formats the table to handle items such as subtotals. Figure 17-18 shows an example of a table that contains a subtotal line for each department. When I applied an AutoFormat, Excel took these subtotals into account and produced an attractive table in about one second.

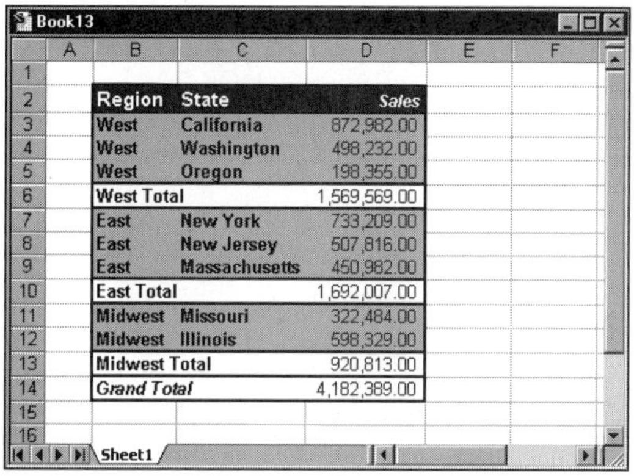

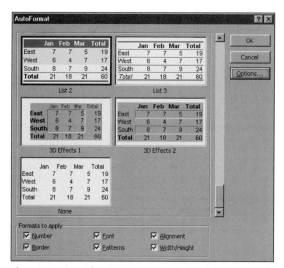

Figure 17-18: AutoFormatting even accommodates subtotals in a table.

Controlling AutoFormats

Although you can't define your own AutoFormats, you can control the type of formatting that is applied. When you click the Options button in the AutoFormat dialog box, the dialog box expands to show six options (see Figure 17-19).

Figure 17-19: The AutoFormat dialog box, expanded to show its options

Initially, the six check boxes are all checked — which means that Excel will apply formatting from all six categories. If you want it to skip one or more categories, just remove the check from the appropriate box before you click OK. For example, when I use AutoFormats, I hardly ever want Excel to change the column widths, so I turn off the Width/Height option. If you've already formatted the numbers, you may want to turn off the Number option.

Using Conditional Formatting

Excel's conditional formatting feature changes cell formats based on the contents of the cell. For example, if the cell contains a negative number, the cell appears bold with a red background. To apply conditional formatting to a cell or range, select the range and then choose Format ➪ Conditional Formatting. You'll see the dialog box shown in Figure 17-20, which enables you to specify up to three conditions for the selected cells.

Figure 17-20: Excel enables you to specify formats based on the cell's value.

The condition can be based on either the cell's value or a formula that you specify (the formula must be a logical formula and return either True or False). Follow these steps to apply conditional formatting:

1. In the first drop-down list, choose either Cell Value Is or Formula Is.

2. If you chose Cell Value Is in Step 1, specify the conditions by using the controls in the dialog box. For example, you can specify between 0 and 100. You can enter values or cell references.

3. If you chose Formula Is in Step 1, specify a reference to the formula. Remember, the formula must return either True or False.

4. Click the Format button and specify the formatting that will be used when the condition is true.

5. If you want to specify another conditional format for the selection, click the Add button. The dialog box expands so that you can repeat Steps 1 through 4 for another condition.

6. When you finish, click OK.

Note Conditional formatting is a great feature, but it's not foolproof. If you copy a value and paste it into a cell that has conditional formatting, the formatting will not be applied. In fact, copying a value to a cell that has conditional formatting wipes out the conditional formatting information. In other words, the feature works only for data that is entered into a cell manually or calculated by a formula.

Using Named Styles

The *named style* feature — borrowed from word processing — is, perhaps, one of the most underutilized features in Excel (named styles may also be the most underutilized feature in word processors).

If you find that you continually are applying the same combination of fonts, lines, and shading in your worksheets, you can save time and effort if you create and use named styles. Named styles apply, in a single step, the formats that you specify, helping you to apply consistent formats across your worksheets.

The real power of styles lies in what happens when you change a component of a style; in this case, all the cells that use that named style automatically incorporate the change. Suppose that you apply a particular style to a dozen cells scattered throughout your worksheet. Later, you realize that these cells should have a font size of 14 points rather than 12 points. Rather than change each cell, simply edit the style. All cells with that particular style change automatically.

A style can consist of settings for six different attributes, although a style doesn't have to use all the attributes. You may recognize these attributes; they correspond to the six tabs in the Format Cells dialog box. The attributes that make up a style are the following:

✦ Number format

✦ Font (type, size, and color)

✦ Alignment (vertical and horizontal)

✦ Borders

✦ Pattern

✦ Protection (locked and hidden)

By default, all cells have the Normal style. In addition, Excel provides five other built-in styles — all of which control only the cell's number format. The styles that are available in every workbook are listed in Table 17-1. If these styles don't meet your needs (and they probably don't), you can easily create new styles.

	Table 17-1 Excel's Built-In Styles	
Style Name	**Description**	**Number Format Example**
Normal	Excel's default style	1234
Comma*	Comma with two decimal places	1,234.00
Comma[0]	Comma with no decimal places	1,234
Currency*	Left-aligned dollar sign with two decimal places	$ 1,234.00
Currency[0]	Left-aligned dollar sign with no decimal places	$ 1,234
Percent*	Percent with no decimal places	12%

* This style can be applied by clicking a button the Standard toolbar.

Applying styles

This section discusses the methods that you can use to apply existing styles to cells or ranges.

Toolbar buttons

As mentioned in the preceding section, you can use three buttons on the Standard toolbar to attach a particular style to a cell or range. You need to understand that when you use these buttons to format a value, you're really changing the cell's style. Consequently, if you later want to change the Normal style, cells formatted with any of these buttons won't be affected by the change.

Using the Style tool

If you plan to work with named styles, you might want to make an addition to one of your toolbars. In fact, I strongly suggest that you do so. Excel has a handy Style tool available. However, this tool (oddly) is not on any of the built-in toolbars — maybe this is why the named style feature is underutilized. To add the Style tool to a toolbar (the Formatting toolbar is a good choice), follow these steps:

1. Right-click any toolbar and choose Customize from the shortcut menu. Excel displays its Customize dialog box.

2. Click the Commands tab.

3. In the Categories list box, click Formatting. The Buttons box displays all available tools in the Formatting category.

4. Click the Style tool (it's a list box labeled *Style*) and drag it to your Formatting toolbar. If you drag the Style tool to the middle of the toolbar, the other tools scoot over to make room for it.

5. Click the Close button in the Customize dialog box.

The new Style tool displays the style of the selected cell and also lets you quickly apply a style — or even create a new style. To apply a style by using the Style tool, select the cell or range, open the Style list box, and then choose the style that you want to apply.

Using the Format ➪ Style command

You also can apply a style by using the Format ➪ Style command, which prompts Excel to display its Style dialog box. Just choose the style that you want to apply from the Style Name drop-down list. However, using the Style tool, as described in the previous section, is a much quicker way to apply a style.

The CD-ROM for this book contains a workbook that defines several styles. You may want to open this workbook and experiment.

Creating new styles

Two ways are available to create a new style: use the Format ➪ Style command or use the Style tool. To create a new style, first select a cell and apply all the formatting that you want to include in the new style. You can use any of the formatting that is available in the Format Cells dialog box.

After you format the cell to your liking, choose Format ➪ Style. Excel displays its Style dialog box, shown in Figure 17-21. Excel displays the name of the current style of the cell (probably Normal) in the Style Name drop-down. This box is highlighted, so that you can simply enter a new style name by typing it. When you do so, Excel displays the words *By Example* to indicate that it's basing the style on the current cell.

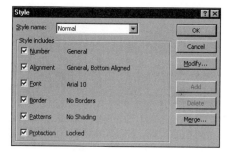

Figure 17-21: You can create a new style by using the Style dialog box.

The check boxes display the current formats for the cell. By default, all check boxes are checked. If you don't want the style to include one or more format categories, remove the check(s) from the appropriate box(es). Click OK to create the style.

You also can create a style from scratch in the Style dialog box. Just enter a style name and then click the Modify button to select the formatting.

Tip   If you added the Style tool to one of your toolbars, you can create a new style without using the Style dialog box. Just format a cell, click inside the Style tool list box, and then type the name. Using this method, you can't specify which formatting categories to omit from the style, but, as you learn next, you can easily modify an existing style.

Overriding a style

After you apply a style to a cell, you can apply additional formatting to it by using any formatting method discussed in this chapter. Formatting modifications that you make to the cell don't affect other cells that use the same style.

Modifying a style

To change an existing file, open the Style dialog box. From the Style name drop-down box, choose the style that you want to modify. You can make changes to the check boxes to include or exclude any of the format categories, or you can click the Modify button to display the familiar Format Cells dialog box. Make the changes that you want and click OK. Click OK again to close the Style dialog box. Excel modifies all the cells formatted with the selected style by applying the new formatting.

Tip   You also can use the Style tool to change a style. Start by modifying the formatting of a cell that uses the style. Then, click inside the Style tool list box, select the style name, and press Enter. Excel asks whether you want to redefine the style based on the selection. Respond in the affirmative to change the style — and all of the cells that use the style.

Deleting a style

If you no longer need a style, you can delete it. To do so, open the Style dialog box, choose the style from the list, and then click Delete. All the cells that had the style revert back to the Normal style.

Suppose that you applied a style to a cell and then applied additional formatting. If you delete the style, the cell retains all of its additional formatting.

Merging styles from other workbooks

You may create one or more styles that you use frequently. Although you could go through the motions and create these styles for every new workbook, a better approach is to merge the styles from a workbook in which you previously created them.

To merge styles from another workbook, open both the workbook that contains the styles that you want to merge *and* the workbook into which you want to merge styles. From the workbook *into which* you want to merge styles, choose Format ➪ Style and click the Merge button. Excel displays a list of all open workbooks, as shown in Figure 17-22. Select the workbook that contains the styles you want to merge and click OK. Excel copies styles from the workbook that you selected into the active workbook.

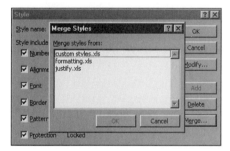

Figure 17-22: Merging styles from another workbook is a good way to make your workbooks look consistent.

When you're merging styles, colors are based on the palette stored with the workbook in which you use the style. Therefore, if the two workbooks involved in the merge use different color palettes, the colors used in the styles may not look the same in each workbook.

Controlling Styles with Templates

When you start Excel, it loads with several default settings, including the settings for stylistic formatting. If you spend a lot of time changing the default elements, you should know about templates.

Here's an example. You may prefer to use 12-point Arial rather than 10-point Arial as the default font. And maybe you prefer Wrap Text to be the default setting for alignment. Templates provide an easy way to change defaults.

The trick is to create a workbook with the Normal style modified to the way that you want it. Then, save the workbook as a template in your XLStart folder. After doing so, you can select File ➪ New to displays a dialog box from which you can choose the template for the new workbook. Template files also can store other named styles, providing you with an excellent way to give your workbooks a consistent look.

Chapter 16 discusses templates in detail.

Summary

This chapter explores all topics related to stylistic formatting: different fonts and sizes, alignment options, applying colors and shading, and using borders and lines. It discusses Excel's AutoFormat feature, which can format a table of data automatically. The chapter concludes with a discussion of named styles, an important concept that can save you time and make your worksheets look more consistent.

✦　　✦　　✦

Chart-Making Basics

Charts — also known as graphs — have been an integral part of spreadsheets since the early days of Lotus 1-2-3. Charting features have improved significantly over the years, and you'll find that Excel provides you with the tools to create a wide variety of highly customizable charts. In fact, Excel has so much capability in this area that *two* chapters are needed to present the information. This chapter presents the basic information that you need to know to create charts and make simple modifications to them. Chapter 19 continues with a discussion of advanced options and a slew of chart-making tricks and techniques.

Overview of Charts

Basically, a *chart* presents a table of numbers visually. Displaying data in a well-conceived chart can make the data more understandable, and you often can make your point more quickly as a result. Because a chart presents a picture, charts are particularly useful for understanding a lengthy series of numbers and their interrelationships. Making a chart helps you to spot trends and patterns that would be nearly impossible to identify when examining a range of numbers.

You create charts from numbers that appear in a worksheet. Before you can create a chart, you must enter some numbers in a worksheet. Normally, the data that is used by a chart resides in a single worksheet, within one file — but that's not a strict requirement. A single chart can use data from any number of worksheets or even from different workbooks.

When you create a chart in Excel, you have two options for where to place the chart:

✦ Insert the chart directly into a worksheet as an object. A chart like the one that appears in Figure 18-1 is known as an *embedded* chart.

✦ Create the chart as a new chart sheet in your workbook (see Figure 18-2). A chart sheet differs from a worksheet in that a chart sheet can hold a single chart and doesn't have cells.

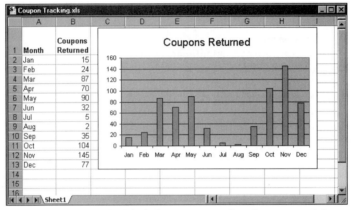

Figure 18-1: An embedded chart appears directly on a worksheet.

Figure 18-2: This chart appears on a separate chart sheet.

Each method has its advantages, as you'll discover later in this chapter. Regardless of the chart-making option that you choose, you have complete control over the chart's appearance. You can change the colors, move the legend, format the numbers on the scales, add gridlines, and so on.

Converting a range of numbers into a chart is quite easy, and many people find this aspect of Excel to be rather fun. You can experiment with different chart types to determine the best way to make your case. If that isn't enough, you can make a variety of adjustments to your charts, such as adding annotations, clip art, and other bells and whistles. The real beauty of Excel's charts, however, lies in their connection to worksheet data — if the numbers in your worksheet change, the charts reflect those changes instantly.

Chart types

You're probably aware of the many types of charts: bar charts, line charts, pie charts, and so on. Excel enables you to create all the basic chart types, and even some esoteric chart types, such as radar charts and doughnut charts. Table 18-1 lists Excel's chart types and the number of subtypes associated with each.

Table 18-1
Excel Chart Types

Chart Type	Subtypes
Area	6
Bar	6
Column	7
Combination	6
Line	7
Pie	6
Doughnut	2
Radar	3
XY (Scatter)	5
Surface	4
Bubble	2
Stock	4
Cylinder	7
Cone	7
Pyramid	7

Cross-Reference   See the "Reference: Excel's Chart Types" section later in this chapter for a complete listing of Excel's chart types.

Which chart type to use?

Beginning chart makers commonly ask how to determine the most appropriate chart type for the data. No good answer exists to this question, and I'm not aware of any hard-and-fast rules for determining which chart type is best for your data. Perhaps the best rule is to use the chart type that gets your message across in the simplest way.

Figures 18-3, 18-4, and 18-5 show the same data plotted using three different chart types. Although all three charts represent the same information, they look quite different.

Figure 18-3: An example of a column chart

Figure 18-4: An example of an area chart

Figure 18-5: An example of a pie chart

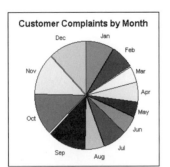

The column chart is probably the best choice for this particular set of data, because it clearly shows the information for each month in discrete units. The area chart may not be appropriate, because it seems to imply that the data (Excel calls each set of data that you chart a *data series*) is continuous — that points exist in between the 12 actual data points (this same argument could be made against using a line chart). The pie chart is simply too confusing. Pie charts are most appropriate for a data series in which you want to emphasize proportions. If you have too many data points, a pie chart can be impossible to interpret.

Fortunately, Excel makes changing a chart's type after you create the chart an easy procedure. Experiment with various chart types until you find the one that represents your data accurately and clearly — and as simply as possible.

The Chart Wizard

You use the Chart Wizard to create a chart. The Chart Wizard consists of a series of dialog boxes that guide you through the process of creating the exact chart that you need. Figure 18-6 shows the first of four Chart Wizard dialog boxes.

Figure 18-6: One of several dialog boxes displayed by the Chart Wizard

Cross-Reference

Chapter 2 presented a step-by-step introductory example that created a simple chart by using the Chart Wizard. If you're new to chart making, you may want to work through that example. The Chart Wizard is explained in detail later in this chapter.

Creating a chart with one keystroke

For a quick demonstration of how easily you can create a chart, follow these instructions. This example bypasses the Chart Wizard and creates a chart on a separate chart sheet.

1. Enter data to be charted into a worksheet. Figure 18-7 shows an
example of data that's appropriate for a chart.

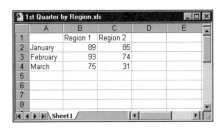

Figure 18-7: This data would make a good chart.

2. Select the range of data that you entered in Step 1, including the row and
column titles. For example, if you entered the data shown in Figure 18-7,
select A1:C4.

3. Press F11. Excel inserts a new chart sheet (named Chart1) and displays
the chart, based on the selected data. Figure 18-8 shows the result.

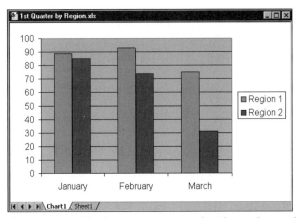

Figure 18-8: This chart was generated with one keystroke.

In this simple example, Excel created its default chart type (which is a two-
dimensional column chart) by using the default settings. For more control
over the chart-making process, you'll want to use the Chart Wizard.

How Excel Handles Charts

A chart is essentially an object that Excel creates. This object consists of one or more data series, displayed graphically; the appearance of the data series depends on the selected chart type. For example, if you create a line chart that uses two data series, the chart contains two lines — each representing one data series. You can distinguish each of the lines by its thickness, color, and data markers. The data series in the chart are linked to cells in the worksheet.

You can include a maximum of 255 data series in most charts; the exception is a standard pie chart, which can display only one data series. If your chart uses more than one data series, you may want to use a legend to help the reader identify each series. Excel also places a limit on the number of categories (or data points) in a data series: 32,000 (4,000 for 3D charts). Most users never run up against this limit.

Charts can use different numbers of axes:

✦ Common charts, such as column, line, and area charts, have a category axis and a value axis. The *category* axis normally is the horizontal axis, and the *value* axis normally is the vertical axis (this is reversed for bar charts, in which the bars extend from the left of the chart rather than from the bottom).

✦ Pie charts and doughnut charts have no axes (but they do have calories). A pie chart can display only one data series. A doughnut chart can display multiple data series.

✦ A radar chart is a special chart that has one axis for each point in the data series. The axes extend from the center of the chart.

✦ True 3D charts have three axes: a category axis, a value axis, and a series axis that extends into the third dimension. Refer to the upcoming sidebar, "3D or Not 3D? That Is the Question," for a discussion about Excel's 3D charts.

A chart is not stagnant. You can always change its type, add custom formatting, add new data series to it, or change an existing data series so that it uses data in a different range.

Before you create a chart, you need to determine whether you want it to be an embedded chart or a chart that resides on a chart sheet.

3D or Not 3D? That Is the Question

Some of Excel's charts are referred to as *3D charts*. This terminology can be a bit confusing, because some of these so-called 3D charts aren't technically 3D charts. Rather, they are 2D charts with a perspective look to them; that is, they appear to have some depth. The accompanying figure shows two "3D" charts.

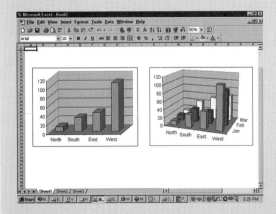

The chart on the left isn't a true 3D chart. It's simply a 2D chart that uses perspective to add depth to the columns. The chart on the right is a true 3D chart, because the data series extend into the third dimension.

A true 3D chart has three axes: a value axis (the height dimension), a category axis (the width dimension), and a series axis (the depth dimension).

Embedded charts

An embedded chart basically floats on top of a worksheet, on the worksheet's draw layer. As with other drawing objects (such as a text box or a rectangle), you can move an embedded chart, resize it, change its proportions, adjust its borders, and perform other operations.

Cross-Reference   Chapter 20 discusses Excel's drawing objects and the draw layer.

To make any changes to the actual chart in an embedded chart object, you must click it to select the chart; Excel's menus, which swap places with the toolbars when you select a chart, include commands that are appropriate for working with charts. In addition, a Chart menu replaces the Data menu. Using embedded charts enables you to print the chart next to the data that it uses.

Figure 18-9 shows an example of a report with a chart embedded.

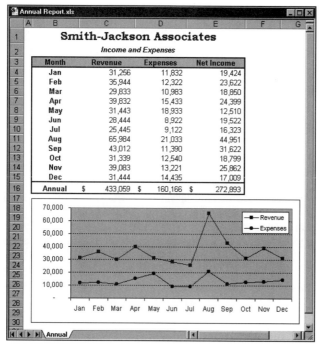

Figure 18-9: This report includes an embedded chart.

Chart sheets

When you create a chart on a chart sheet, the chart occupies the entire sheet. If you plan to print a chart on a page by itself, using a chart sheet is your best choice. If you have many charts to create, you may want to create each one on a separate chart sheet, to avoid cluttering your worksheet. This technique also makes locating a particular chart easier, because you can change the names of the chart sheets' tabs to correspond to the chart that it contains.

Excel's menus change when a chart sheet is active, similar to the way that they change when you select an embedded chart. The Chart menu replaces the Data menu, and other menus include commands that are appropriate for working with charts.

Excel displays a chart in a chart sheet in WYSIWYG mode: the printed chart looks just like the image on the chart sheet. If the chart doesn't fit in the window, you can use the scrollbars to scroll it or adjust the zoom factor.

You also can size the chart in a chart sheet according to the window size by using the View ➪ Sized with Window command. When this setting is enabled, the chart adjusts itself when you resize the workbook window (it always fits perfectly in the window). In this mode, the chart that you're working on may or may not correspond to how it looks when printed.

If you create a chart on a chart sheet, you can easily convert it to an embedded chart. Choose Chart ➪ Location and then select the worksheet that holds the embedded chart from the As object in list box. Excel deletes the chart sheet and moves the chart to the sheet that you specify. This operation also works in the opposite direction: You can relocate an embedded chart to a new chart sheet.

Creating Charts

You can create both embedded charts and charts on chart sheets with or without the assistance of the Chart Wizard.

Note Excel always has a default chart type. Normally, the default is a column chart (but you can change this type, as you'll see later). If you create a chart without using the Chart Wizard, Excel creates the chart by using the default chart type. If you use the Chart Wizard, Excel prompts you for the chart type, so the default chart type becomes irrelevant.

Creating an embedded chart with Chart Wizard

To invoke the Chart Wizard to create an embedded chart:

1. Select the data to be charted (optional).

2. Choose Insert ➪ Chart (or, click the Chart Wizard tool on the Standard toolbar).

3. Make your choices in Steps 1 through 3 of the Chart Wizard.

4. In Step 4 of the Chart Wizard, select the option labeled As object in.

The Chart Wizard is explained in detail later in this chapter.

Creating an embedded chart directly

To create an embedded chart without using the Chart Wizard:

1. Make sure that the Chart toolbar is displayed.

2. Select the data to be charted.

3. Click the Chart Type tool on the Chart toolbar and then select a chart type from the displayed icons.

Excel adds the chart to the worksheet by using the default settings.

Note The Chart Type tool on the Chart toolbar displays an icon for the last selected chart. However, this tool works like a list box; you can expand it to display all 18 chart types (see Figure 18-10). Just click the arrow to display the additional chart types.

Figure 18-10: The Chart Type tool expands so that you can create the type of chart you want.

The Chart Toolbar

The Chart toolbar appears when you click an embedded chart, activate a chart sheet, or choose View ➪ Toolbars ➪ Chart. This toolbar, shown in the accompanying figure, includes nine tools. You can use these tools to make some common chart changes:

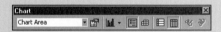

✦ **Chart Objects:** When a chart is activated, you can select a particular chart element by using this drop-down list.

✦ **Format Selected Object:** Displays the Format dialog box for the selected chart element.

✦ **Chart Type:** Expands to display 18 chart types when you click the arrow. After it's expanded, you can drag this tool to a new location — creating, in effect, a miniature floating toolbar.

✦ **Legend:** Toggles the legend display in the selected chart.

✦ **Data Table:** Toggles the display of the data table in a chart.

✦ **By Row:** Plots the data by rows.

✦ **By Column:** Plots the data by columns.

✦ **Angle Text (Downward):** Displays the selected text at a -45-degree angle.

✦ **Angle Text (Upward):** Displays the selected text at a +45-degree angle.

If you press Shift while you click either of the Angle Text tools, Excel no longer angles the selected text.

Excel includes several other chart-related tools that aren't on the Chart toolbar. You can customize the toolbar to include these additional tools, which are located in the Charting category in the Customize dialog box.

In addition, several tools on the other toolbars work with charts, including the Color, Font Color, Bold, Italic, and Font tools.

Creating a chart on a chart sheet with the Chart Wizard

To start the Chart Wizard and create an embedded chart:

1. Select the data that you want to chart (optional).
2. Choose Insert ➪ Chart (or click the Chart Wizard tool on the Standard toolbar).
3. Make your choices in Steps 1 through 3 of the Chart Wizard.
4. In Step 4 of the Chart Wizard, select the option labeled As new sheet.

To create a new chart on a chart sheet by using the default chart type, select the data to be charted and then press the F11 key. This command inserts a new chart sheet. The chart is created from the selected range, without accessing the Chart Wizard.

Creating a Chart with the Chart Wizard

The Chart Wizard consists of four dialog boxes that prompt you for various settings for the chart. By the time that you reach the last dialog box, the chart is usually just what you need.

Selecting the data

Before you start the Chart Wizard, select the data that you want to include in the chart. This step isn't necessary, but it makes creating the chart easier for you. If you don't select the data before invoking the Chart Wizard, you can select it in the second Chart Wizard dialog box.

When you select the data, include items such as labels and series identifiers (row and column headings). Figure 18-11 shows a worksheet with a range of data set up for a chart. This data consists of monthly sales for two regions. You would select the entire range for this worksheet, including the month names and region names.

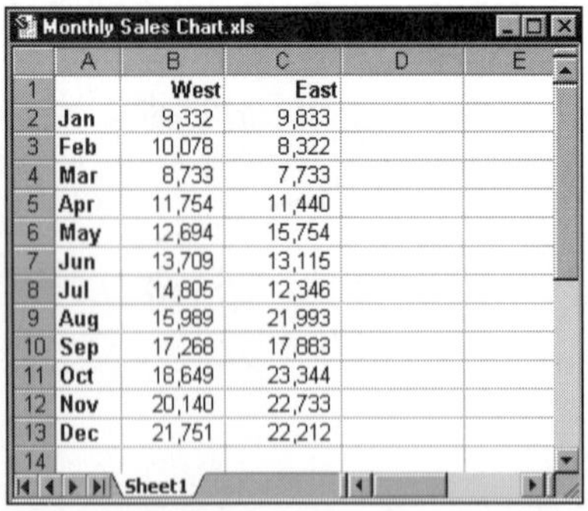
Monthly Sales Chart.xls

	A	B	C	D	E
1		West	East		
2	Jan	9,332	9,833		
3	Feb	10,078	8,322		
4	Mar	8,733	7,733		
5	Apr	11,754	11,440		
6	May	12,694	15,754		
7	Jun	13,709	13,115		
8	Jul	14,805	12,346		
9	Aug	15,989	21,993		
10	Sep	17,268	17,883		
11	Oct	18,649	23,344		
12	Nov	20,140	22,733		
13	Dec	21,751	22,212		
14					

Sheet1

Figure 18-11: Data to be charted

The data that you plot doesn't have to be contiguous. You can press Ctrl and make a multiple selection. Figure 18-12 shows an example of how to select noncontiguous ranges for a chart. In this case, Excel uses only the selected cells for the chart.

Figure 18-12: Selecting noncontiguous ranges to be charted

After you select the data, start the Chart Wizard, either by clicking the Chart Wizard button on the Standard toolbar or by selecting Insert ➪ Chart. Excel displays the first of four Chart Wizard dialog boxes.

At any time while using the Chart Wizard, you can go back to the preceding step by clicking the Back button. Or, you can click Finish to close the Chart Wizard. If you close the Chart Wizard early, Excel creates the chart by using the information that you provided up to that point.

Don't be too concerned about creating the perfect chart. You later can change, at any time, every choice that you make in the Chart Wizard.

Chart Wizard – Step 1 of 4

Figure 18-13 shows the first Chart Wizard dialog box, in which you select the chart type. This dialog box has two tabs: Standard Types and Custom Types. The Standard Types tab displays the 14 basic chart types and the subtypes for each. The Custom Types tab displays some customized charts (including user-defined custom charts).

Tip   When you work in the Custom Types tab, the dialog box shows a preview of your data with the selected chart type. In the Standard Types tab, you get a preview by clicking the button labeled Click and Hold to View Sample. When you click this button, keep the mouse button pressed.

When you decide on a chart type and subtype, click the Next button to move to the next step.

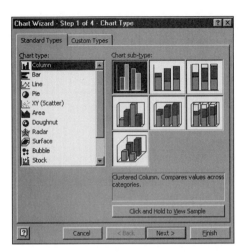

Figure 18-13: The first of four Chart Wizard dialog boxes

Chart Wizard — Step 2 of 4

In the second step of the Chart Wizard (shown in Figure 18-14), you verify the data ranges and specify the orientation of the data (whether it's arranged in rows or columns). The orientation of the data has a drastic effect on the look of your chart. Usually, Excel guesses the orientation correctly — but not always.

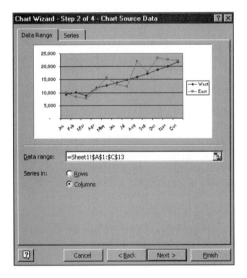

Figure 18-14: In the second Chart Wizard dialog box, you verify the range and specify whether to plot by columns or rows.

If you select the Series tab, you can verify or change the data that is used for each series of the chart. Click the Next button to advance to the next dialog box.

Chart Wizard — Step 3 of 4

In the third Chart Wizard dialog box, shown in Figure 18-15, you specify most of the options for the chart. This dialog box has six tabs:

✦ **Titles:** Add titles to the chart.

✦ **Axes:** Turn on or off axes display and specify the type of axes.

✦ **Gridlines:** Specify gridlines, if any.

✦ **Legend:** Specify whether to include a legend and where to place it.

✦ **Data Labels:** Specify whether to show data labels and what type of labels.

✦ **Data Table:** Specify whether to display a table of the data.

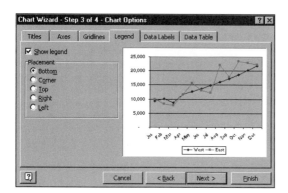

Figure 18-15: You specify the chart options in the third Chart Wizard dialog box.

Note The options available depend on the type of chart that you selected in Step 1 of the Chart Wizard.

After you select the chart options, click Next to move to the final dialog box.

Chart Wizard — Step 4 of 4

Step 4 of the Chart Wizard, shown in Figure 18-16, lets you specify where to place the chart. Make your choice and click Finish.

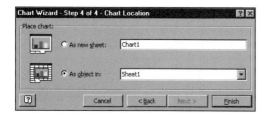

Figure 18-16: Step 4 of the Chart Wizard asks you where to put the chart.

Excel creates and displays the chart. If you place the chart on a worksheet, Excel centers it in the worksheet window and selects it.

Basic Chart Modifications

After you create a chart, you can modify it at any time. The modifications that you can make to a chart are extensive. This section covers some of the more common chart modifications:

✦ Moving and resizing the chart

✦ Changing a chart's location

✦ Changing the chart type

✦ Moving chart elements

✦ Deleting chart elements

 Other types of chart modifications are discussed in Chapter 19.

Activating a chart

Before you can modify a chart, it must be activated. To activate an embedded chart, click it, which also activates the element that you click. To activate a chart on a chart sheet, just click its sheet tab.

Moving and resizing a chart

If your chart is on a chart sheet, you can't move or resize it. You can, however, change the way that it's displayed by selecting View ➪ Sized with Window.

If you embedded the chart, you can freely move and resize it. Click the chart's border to select the chart; eight handles (small black squares) appear on the chart's border. Drag the chart to move it, or drag any of the handles to resize the chart.

Changing a chart's location

Use the Chart ➪ Location command to relocate an embedded chart to a chart sheet, or convert a chart on a chart sheet to an embedded chart. This command displays the Chart Location dialog box.

Tip

If you select an embedded chart and choose an existing chart sheet as its new location, Excel will ask if you'd like to embed the chart on the chart sheet. If you respond Yes, the chart sheet will contain an additional chart. This is a way to overcome the normal limit of one chart per chart sheet. Even better, you can delete the original chart on the chart sheet and then rearrange your embedded charts on a single chart sheet.

Changing the chart type

To change the chart type of the active chart, use either of the following methods:

✦ Click the Chart Type button's drop-down arrow on the Chart toolbar. The button expands to show 18 basic chart types.

✦ Choose the Chart ➪ Chart Type command.

The Chart ➪ Chart Type command displays the dialog box shown in Figure 18-17. You may recognize this dialog box as the first of the Chart Wizard dialog boxes. Click the Standard Types tab to select one of the standard chart types (and a subtype), or click the Custom Types tab to select a customized chart. After you select a chart type, click OK; the selected chart will be changed to the type that you selected.

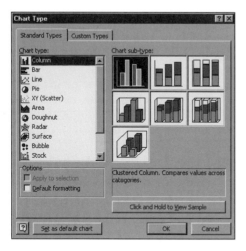

Figure 18-17: The Chart Type dialog box enables you to change the chart's type.

Caution

If you've customized some aspects of your chart, choosing a new chart type from the Custom Types tab may override some or all the changes that you've made. For example, if you've added gridlines to the chart and then select a custom chart type that doesn't use gridlines, your gridlines disappear. Therefore, you should make sure that you're satisfied with the chart before you make too many custom changes to it. However, you can always use Edit ➪ Undo to reverse your actions.

In the Custom Types tab, if you click the User-defined option, the list box displays the name of any user-defined custom formats. If you haven't defined any custom formats, this box shows Default, referring to the default chart type. Changing the default chart type is discussed later in this chapter.

Chapter 19 explains how to create custom formats.

Moving and deleting chart elements

Some of the chart parts can be moved (any of the titles, the legend, or data labels). To move a chart element, simply click it to select it and then drag it to the desired location in the chart. To delete a chart element, select it and then press Delete.

Other modifications

When a chart is activated, you can select various parts of the chart to change. Modifying a chart is similar to everything else you do in Excel. First, you make a selection (in this case, select a chart part). Then, you issue a command to do something with the selection.

You can use the Fill Color tool on the Formatting toolbar to change colors. For example, if you want to change the color of a series, select the series and choose the color that you want from the Fill Color tool. You'll find that many other toolbar tools work with charts. For example, you can select the chart's legend and then click the Bold tool to make the legend text bold.

When you double-click a chart element (or press Ctrl+1 after selecting it), its Formatting dialog box appears, which varies, depending on the item selected. In most cases, the dialog box is of the tabbed variety. Many modifications are self-evident — for example, changing the font used in a title. Others, however, are a bit trickier.

Chapter 19 discusses these chart modifications in detail.

Changing the Default Chart Type

The default chart type is mentioned many times in this chapter. Excel's default chart type is a 2D column chart with a light-gray plot area, a legend on the right, and horizontal gridlines.

If you don't like the looks of this chart or if you typically use a different type of chart, you can easily change the default chart in the following manner:

1. Select the Chart ➪ Chart Type command.

2. Choose the chart type that you want to use as the default chart. This can be a chart from either the Standard Types tab or the Custom Types tab.

3. Click the button labeled Set as default chart type. You are asked to verify your choice.

Tip   If you have many charts of the same type to create, changing the default chart format to the chart type with which you're working is much more efficient than separately formatting each chart. Then, you can create all of your charts without having to select the chart type.

Printing Charts

Printing embedded charts is nothing special; you print them the same way that you print a worksheet (see Chapter 14). As long as you include the embedded chart in the range that you want to print, Excel prints the chart as it appears onscreen.

Tip   If you select an embedded chart and then choose File ⇨ Print (or click the Print button), Excel prints the chart on a page by itself and does *not* print the worksheet.

If you print in Draft mode, Excel doesn't print embedded charts. Also, if you don't want a particular embedded chart to appear on your printout, right-click the chart and choose Format Chart Area from the shortcut menu. Click the Properties tab in the Format Chart Area dialog box and remove the check mark from the Print Object check box.

If you created the chart on a chart sheet, Excel prints the chart on a page by itself. If you open Excel's Page Setup dialog box when the chart sheet is active, the Sheet tab is replaced with a tab named Chart. Figure 18-18 shows the Chart tab of the Page Setup dialog box.

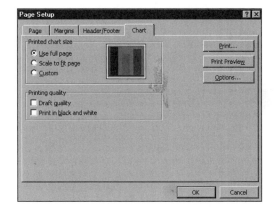

Figure 18-18: The Chart tab of the Page Setup dialog box

This dialog box has several options:

✦ **Use full page:** Excel prints the chart to the full width and height of the page margins. This usually isn't a good choice, because the chart's relative proportions change and you lose the WYSIWYG advantage.

✦ **Scale to fit page:** Expands the chart proportionally in both dimensions until one dimension fills the space between the margins. This option usually results in the best printout.

✦ **Custom:** Prints the chart as it appears on your screen. Select View ➪ Sized with Window to make the chart correspond to the window size and proportions. The chart prints at the current window size and proportions.

The Printing quality options work just like those for worksheet pages. If you choose the Draft quality option for a chart sheet, Excel prints the chart, but its quality may not be high (the actual effect depends on your printer). Choosing the Print in black and white option prints the data series with black-and-white patterns rather than colors.

Tip   Because charts usually take longer to print than text, using the print preview feature before you print a chart is an especially good idea. This feature enables you to see what the printed output will look like, so that you can avoid surprises.

Reference: Excel's Chart Types

For your reference, this chapter concludes with a discussion of Excel's chart types and a listing of the subtypes for each. This section may help you determine which chart type is best for your data.

Column charts

Column charts are one of the most common chart types. This type of chart is useful for displaying discrete data (as opposed to continuous data). You can have any number of data series, and the columns can be stacked on top of each other. Figure 18-19 shows an example of a column chart.

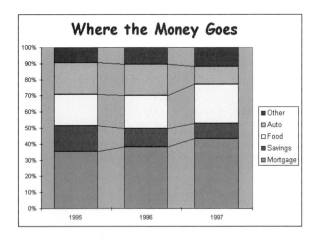

Figure 18-19: This stacked column chart displays each series as a percentage of the total. It may substitute for several pie charts.

Table 18-2 lists Excel's seven column chart subtypes.

Table 18-2 Column Chart Subtypes	
Chart Type	**Description**
Clustered Column	Standard column chart.
Stacked Column	Column chart with data series stacked.
100% Stacked Column	Column chart with data series stacked and expressed as percentages.
3-D Clustered Column	Standard column chart with a perspective look.
3-D Stacked Column	Column chart with a perspective look. Data series are stacked and expressed as percentages.
3-D 100% Stacked Column	Column chart with a perspective look. Excel stacks the data series and expresses them as percentages.
3-D Column	A true 3D column chart with a third axis.

Bar charts

A *bar chart* is essentially a column chart that has been rotated 90 degrees to the left. The advantage in using a bar chart is that the category labels may be easier to read (see Figure 18-20 for an example). You can include any number of data series in a bar chart. In addition, the bars can be stacked from left to right.

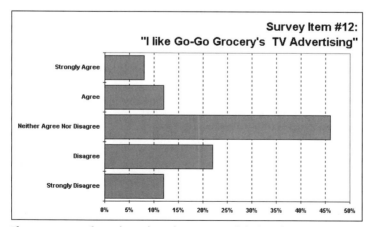

Figure 18-20: If you have lengthy category labels, a bar chart may be a good choice.

Table 18-3 lists Excel's six bar chart subtypes.

Table 18-3 Bar Chart Subtypes	
Chart Type	**Description**
Clustered Bar	Standard bar chart.
Stacked Bar	Bar chart with data series stacked.
100% Stacked Bar	Bar chart with data series stacked and expressed as percentages.
3-D Clustered Bar	Standard bar chart with a perspective look.
3-D Stacked Bar	Bar chart with a perspective look. Excel stacks data series and expresses them as percentages.
3-D 100% Stacked Bar	Bar chart with a perspective look. Excel stacks data series and expresses them as percentages.

Line charts

Line charts are frequently used to plot data that is continuous rather than discrete. For example, plotting daily sales as a line chart may let you spot trends over time. See Figure 18-21 for an example.

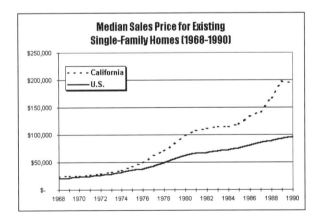

Figure 18-21: A line chart often can help you spot trends in your data.

Table 18-4 lists Excel's seven line chart subtypes.

Table 18-4	
Line Chart Subtypes	
Chart Type	*Description*
Line	Standard line chart.
Stacked Line	Line chart with stacked data series.
100% Stacked Line	Line chart with stacked data series expressed as percentages.
Line with Data Markers	Line chart with data markers.
Stacked Line with Data Markers	Line chart with stacked data series and data markers.
100% Stacked Line with Data Markers	Line chart with stacked data series and line markers, expressed as percentages.
3-D Line	A true 3D line chart with a third axis.

Pie charts

A *pie chart* is useful when you want to show relative proportions or contributions to a whole. Figure 18-22 shows an example of a pie chart. Generally, a pie chart should use no more than five or six data points; otherwise, it's difficult to interpret. A pie chart can use only one data series.

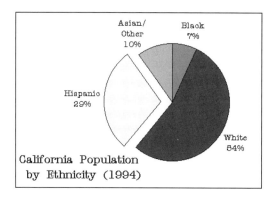

Figure 18-22: A pie chart with one slice exploded

You can explode a slice of a pie chart. Activate the chart and select the slice that you want to explode. Then, drag it away from the center.

Table 18-5 lists Excel's six pie chart subtypes.

Table 18-5
Pie Chart Subtypes

Chart Type	Description
Pie	Standard pie chart.
3-D Pie	Pie chart with perspective look.
Pie of Pie	Pie chart with one slice broken into another pie.
Exploded Pie	Pie chart with one or more slices exploded.
Exploded 3-D Pie	Pie chart with perspective look, with one or more slices exploded.
Bar of Pie	Pie chart with one slice broken into a column.

Cross-Reference   The Pie of Pie and Bar of Pie chart types enable you to display a second chart that clarifies one of the pie slices. You can use the Options tab of the Format Data Series dialog box to specify which data is assigned to the second chart. Refer to Chapter 19 for details.

XY (Scatter) charts

Another common chart type is *XY (Scatter) charts* (also known as *scattergrams*). An XY chart differs from the other chart types in that both axes display values (no category axis exists).

This type of chart often is used to show the relationship between two variables. Figure 18-23 shows an example of an XY chart that plots the relationship between sales calls and sales. The chart shows that these two variables are positively related: months in which more calls were made typically had higher sales volumes.

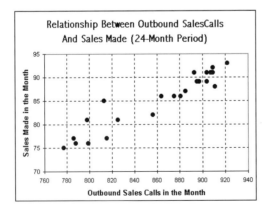

Figure 18-23: An XY (Scatter) chart

Table 18-6 lists Excel's five XY (Scatter) chart subtypes.

Table 18-6 XY (Scatter) Chart Subtypes	
Chart Type	**Description**
Scatter	XY chart with markers and no lines.
Scatter with Smoothed Lines	XY chart with markers and smoothed lines.
Scatter with Smoothed Lines and No Data Markers	XY chart with smoothed lines and no markers.
Scatter with Lines	XY chart with lines and markers.
Scatter with Lines and No Data Markers	XY chart with lines and no markers.

Area charts

Think of an *area chart* as a line chart that has been colored in. Figure 18-24 shows an example of a stacked area chart. Stacking the data series enables you to see clearly the total plus the contribution by each series.

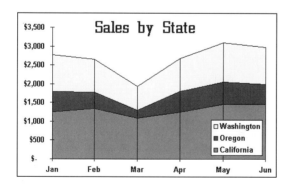

Figure 18-24: An area chart

Table 18-7 lists Excel's six area chart subtypes.

	Table 18-7	
	Area Chart Subtypes	
Chart Type	**Description**	
Area	Standard area chart.	
Stacked Area	Area chart, data series stacked.	
100% Stacked Area	Area chart, expressed as percentages.	
3-D Area	A true 3D area chart with a third axis.	
3-D Stacked Area	Area chart with a perspective look, data series stacked.	
3-D 100% Stacked area	Area chart with a perspective look, expressed as percentages.	

Doughnut charts

A *doughnut chart* is similar to a pie chart, except that it has a hole in the middle. Unlike a pie chart, a doughnut chart can display more than one series of data. Figure 18-25 shows an example of a doughnut chart (the arrow and series descriptions were added manually; these items aren't part of a doughnut chart).

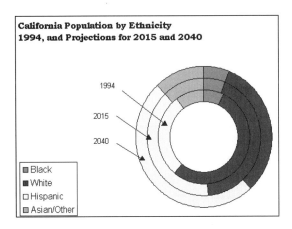

Figure 18-25: A doughnut chart

Notice that Excel displays the data series as concentric rings. As you can see, a doughnut chart with more than one series to chart can be difficult to interpret. Sometimes, a stacked column chart for such comparisons expresses your meaning better than a doughnut chart.

Table 18-8 lists Excel's two doughnut chart subtypes.

Table 18-8	
Doughnut Chart Subtypes	
Chart Type	*Subtype*
Doughnut	Standard doughnut chart.
Exploded Doughnut	Doughnut chart with all slices exploded.

Radar charts

You may not be familiar with radar charts. A *radar chart* has a separate axis for each category, and the axes extend from the center. The value of the data point is plotted on the appropriate axis. If all data points in a series have an identical value, it produces a perfect circle. See Figure 18-26 for an example of a radar chart.

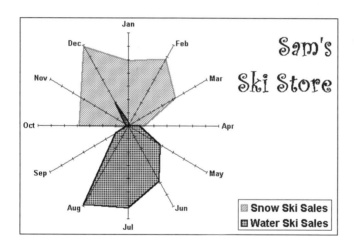

Figure 18-26:
A radar chart

Table 18-9 lists Excel's three radar chart subtypes.

Table 18-9	
Radar Chart Subtypes	
Chart Type	*Subtype*
Radar	Standard radar chart (lines only).
Radar with Data Markers	Radar chart with lines data markers.
Filled Radar	Radar chart with lines colored in.

Surface charts

Surface charts display two or more data series on a surface. As Figure 18-27 shows, these charts can be quite interesting. Unlike other charts, Excel uses color to distinguish values, not to distinguish the data series. You can change these colors only by modifying the workbook's color palette, using the Color tab in the Options dialog box.

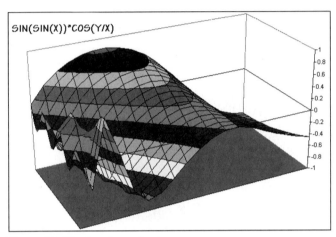

Figure 18-27: A surface chart

Table 18-10 lists Excel's four 3D surface chart subtypes.

Table 18-10 Surface Chart Subtypes	
Chart Type	*Description*
3-D Surface	Standard 3D surface chart.
3-D Surface (wireframe)	3D surface chart with no colors.
Surface (top view)	3D surface chart, as viewed from above.
Surface (top view wireframe)	3D surface chart, as viewed from above, no color.

Bubble charts

Think of a bubble chart as an XY (Scatter) chart that can display additional an data series. That additional data series is represented by the size of the bubbles.

Figure 18-28 shows an example of a bubble chart. In this case, the chart displays the results of a weight-loss program. The x axis represents the original weight, the y axis shows the length of time in the program, and the size of the bubbles represents the amount of weight lost.

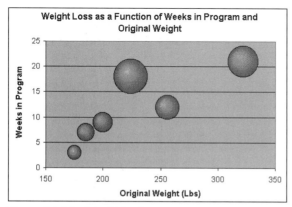

Figure 18-28: A bubble chart

Table 18-11 lists Excel's two bubble chart subtypes.

Table 18-11
Bubble Chart Subtypes

Chart Type	Subtype
Bubble Chart	Standard bubble chart.
Bubble with 3-D effect	Bubble chart with 3D bubbles.

Stock charts

Stock charts are most useful for displaying stock market information. These charts require three to five data series, depending on the subtype.

Figure 18-29 shows an example of a stock chart. This chart uses the High-Low-Close subtype that requires three data series.

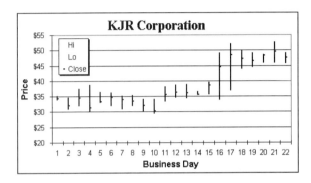

Figure 18-29: A stock chart

Table 18-12 lists Excel's four stock chart subtypes.

Table 18-12 Stock Chart Subtypes	
Chart Type	**Subtype**
High-Low-Close	Displays the stock's high, low, and closing prices.
Open-High-Low-Close	Displays the stock's opening, high, low, and closing prices.
Volume-High-Low-Close	Displays the stock's volume, high, low, and closing prices.
Volume-Open-High-Low-Close	Displays the stock's volume, open, high, low, and closing prices.

Cylinder, Cone, and Pyramid charts

These three chart types are essentially the same — except for the shapes that are used. You usually can use these charts in place of a bar or column chart.

Figure 18-30 shows an example of a pyramid chart.

Figure 18-30: A pyramid chart

Each of these chart types has seven subtypes, which are described in Table 18-13.

Table 18-13 Cylinder, Cone, and Pyramid Chart Subtypes	
Chart Type	**Subtype**
Clustered Column	Standard column chart.
Stacked Column	Column chart with data series stacked.
100% Stacked Column	Column chart with data series stacked and expressed as percentages.
Clustered Bar	Standard bar chart.
Stacked Bar	Bar chart with data series stacked.
100% Stacked Bar	Bar chart with data series stacked and expressed as percentages.
3-D Column	A true 3D column chart with a third axis.

Summary

This chapter introduces Excel's chart-making feature. Charts can be embedded on a worksheet or created in a separate chart sheet. You can either use the Chart Wizard to walk you through the chart-making process or create a default chart in a single step. This chapter also describes how to change the default chart type.

After a chart is created, you can make many types of modifications. A few simple modifications are discussed; Chapter 19 presents additional chart information. Printing charts works much like printing worksheets, although you should be familiar with the page setup options when you're printing chart sheets. The chapter concludes with a complete listing and description of Excel's chart types and subtypes.

✦   ✦   ✦

Advanced Charting

Chapter 18 introduces charting. This chapter takes the topic to the next level. You learn how to customize your charts to the maximum, so that they look exactly as you want. I also share some slick charting tricks that I've picked up over the years.

Chart Customization: An Overview

Often, the basic chart that Excel creates is sufficient for your needs. If you're using a chart to get a quick visual impression of your data, a chart that's based on one of the standard chart types usually does just fine. But, if you want to create the most effective chart possible, you probably want to take advantage of the additional customization techniques available in Excel.

Customizing a chart involves changing its appearance, as well as possibly adding new elements to it. These changes can be purely cosmetic (such as changing colors or modifying line widths) or quite substantial (such as changing the axis scales or rotating a 3D chart). New elements that you might add include features such as a data table, a trendline, or error bars.

Note

Before you can customize a chart, you must activate it on a chart sheet, by clicking its sheet tab. To activate an embedded chart, click the chart's border. To deactivate an embedded chart, just click anywhere in the worksheet.

Tip

In some cases, you may prefer to work with an embedded chart in a separate window. For example, if the embedded chart is larger than the workbook window, working with it in its own window is much easier. To display an embedded chart in a window, right-click the chart's border and select Chart Window from the shortcut menu.

Here's a partial list of the customizations that you can make to a chart:

✦ Change any colors, patterns, line widths, marker styles, and fonts.

✦ Change the data ranges that the chart uses, add a new chart series, or delete an existing series.

✦ Choose which gridlines to display.

✦ Determine the size and placement of the legend (or delete it altogether).

✦ Determine where the axes cross.

✦ Adjust the axis scales by specifying a maximum and minimum, changing the tick marks and labels, and so on. You also can specify that a scale be represented in logarithmic units.

✦ Add titles for the chart and axes, as well as free-floating text anywhere in the chart.

✦ Add error bars and trendlines to a data series.

✦ Display the data points in reverse order.

✦ Rotate a 3D chart to get a better view or to add impact.

✦ Replace line-chart markers with bitmaps.

Note   You can easily become overwhelmed with all the chart customization options. However, the more that you work with charts, the easier it becomes. Even advanced users tend to experiment a great deal with chart customization, and they rely heavily on trial and error — a technique that I strongly recommend.

Elements of a chart

Before chart modifications are discussed, a brief digression is necessary to discuss the various elements of a chart. The number and type of elements in a chart varies with the type of chart — for example, pie charts don't have axes, and only 3D charts have walls and floors.

When a chart is activated, you can select various parts of the chart with which to work. Modifying a chart is similar to everything else that you do in Excel: First you make a selection (in this case, select a chart element) and then you issue a command to do something with the selection. Unlike a worksheet selection, with a chart selection, you can select only one chart element at a time. The exceptions are elements that consist of multiple parts, such as gridlines. Selecting one gridline selects them all.

You select a chart element by clicking it. The name of the selected item appears in the Name box. When a chart is activated, you can't access the Name box; it's simply a convenient place for Excel to display the chart element's name.

The Chart toolbar, which is displayed when you select a chart, contains a tool called Chart Objects (see Figure 19-1). This is a drop-down list of all the named elements in a chart. Rather than selecting a chart element by clicking it, you can use this list to select the chart element that you want to work with.

Figure 19-1: The Chart Objects tool in the Chart toolbar provides another way to select a chart element.

Tip

Yet another way to select a chart element is to use the keyboard. When a chart is activated, press the up arrow or down arrow to cycle through all parts in the chart. When a data series is selected, press the right arrow or left arrow to select individual points in the series.

Table 19-1 lists the various elements of a chart (not all of these parts appear in every chart). You might want to create a chart and practice selecting some of these parts — or use the Chart Objects tool in the Chart toolbar to examine the element names.

Table 19-1	
Chart Elements	
Part	**Description**
Category Axis	The axis that represents the chart's categories.
Category Title	The title for the category axis.
Chart Area	The chart's background.
Chart Title	The chart's title.
Corners	The corners of 3D charts (except 3D pie charts). Select the corners if you want to rotate a 3D chart by using a mouse.
Data Label	A data label for a point in a series. The name is preceded by the series and the point. Example: Series 1 Point 1 Data Label.
Data Labels	Data labels for a series. The name is preceded by the series. Example: Series 1 Data Labels.

Continued

Table 19-1 *(continued)*

Part	Description
Data Table	The chart's data table.
Down-Bars	Down-bars in a stock market chart.
Dropline	A dropline that extends from the data point downward to the axis.
Error Bars	Error bars for a series. The name is preceded by the series. Example: Series 1 Error Bars.
Floor	The floor of a 3D chart.
Gridlines	A chart can have major and minor gridlines for each axis. The element is named using the axis and the type of gridlines. Example: Value Axis Major Gridlines.
High-Low Lines	High-low lines in a stock market chart.
Legend Entry	One of the text entries inside of a legend.
Legend Key	One of the keys inside of a legend.
Legend	The chart's legend.
Plot Area	The chart's Plot Area—the actual chart, without the legend.
Point	A point in a data series. The name is preceded by the series. Example: Series 1 Point 2.
Series Axis	The axis that represents the chart's series (3D charts only).
Series	A line that connects a series.
Trendline	A trendline for a data series.
Up-Bars	Up-bars in a stock market chart.
Value Axis Title	The title for the value axis.
Value Axis	The axis that represents the chart's values. A Secondary Value Axis may also exist.
Walls	The walls of a 3D chart only (except 3D pie charts).

Using the Format dialog box

When a chart element is selected, you can access the element's Format dialog box to format or set options for the element. Each chart element has a unique Format dialog box. You can access this dialog box by using any of the following methods:

✦ Select the Format ⇨ Selected Part Name command (the Format menu displays the actual name of the selected part)

✦ Double-click a chart part

✦ Select the chart element and press Ctrl+1

✦ Right-click the chart element and choose the Format command from the shortcut menu

Any of these methods displays a tabbed Format dialog box that enables you to make many changes to the selected chart element. For example, Figure 19-2 shows the dialog box that appears when the chart's title is selected.

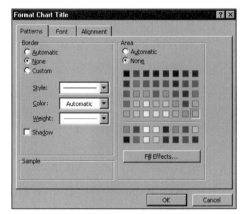

Figure 19-2: The Format dialog box for a chart's title. Each chart element has its own Format dialog box.

In the following sections, the details of the various types of chart modifications are discussed in depth.

Chart Background Elements

As mentioned in the preceding section, a chart consists of many elements. This section discusses two of those elements: the Chart Area and the Plot Area. These chart items provide a background for other elements in the chart.

The Chart Area

The Chart Area is an object that contains all other elements in the chart. You can think of it as a chart's master background. You can't change the size of the Chart Area. For an embedded chart, it's always the same size as the embedded chart object. For a chart sheet, the Chart Area is always the entire sheet.

The following are the three tabs of the Chart Area dialog box and some key points about each:

✦ **Patterns tab:** Enables you to change the Chart Area's color and patterns (including fill effects) and add a border, if you like.

✦ **Font tab:** Enables you to change the properties of *all fonts used in the chart*. Changing the font doesn't affect fonts that you have previously changed, however. For example, if you make the chart's title 20-point Arial and then change the font to 8-point Arial in the Format Chart Area dialog box, the title's font is not affected.

✦ **Properties tab:** Enables you to specify how the chart is moved and sized with respect to the underlying cells. You also can set the Locked property and specify whether the chart will be printed.

Note   If you delete the Chart Area, you delete the entire chart.

Note   Prior to Excel 97, clicking an embedded chart selected the chart object. You could then adjust its properties. To activate the chart, you actually had to double-click it. Beginning with Excel 97, clicking an embedded chart activates the chart contained inside the chart object. You can adjust the chart object's properties by using the Properties tab of the Format dialog box. To select the chart object itself, press Ctrl while you click the chart. You might want to select the chart object to change its name by using the Name box.

The Plot Area

The Chart Area of a chart contains the Plot Area, which is the part of the chart that contains the actual chart. The Plot Area is unlike the Chart Area in that you can resize and reposition the Plot Area. The Format Plot Area dialog box has only one tab: Patterns. This tab enables you to change the color and pattern of the Plot Area and adjust its borders.

Tip   When you select a chart element, you'll find that many of the toolbar buttons that you normally use for worksheet formatting also work with the selected chart element. For example, if you select the chart's Plot Area, you can change its color by using the Fill Color tool on the Formatting toolbar. If you select an element that contains text, you can use the Font Color tool to change the color of the text.

Working with Chart Titles

A chart can have as many as five different titles:

✦ Chart title

✦ Category (X) axis title

✦ Value (Y) axis title

✦ Second category (X) axis title

✦ Second value (Y) axis title

The number of titles that you can use depends on the chart type. For example, a pie chart supports only a chart title, because it has no axes.

To add titles to a chart, activate the chart and use the Chart ⇨ Options command. Excel displays the Chart Options dialog box. Click the Titles tab and enter text for the title or titles (see Figure 19-3).

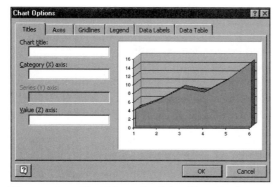

Figure 19-3: The Titles tab of the Chart Options dialog box lets you add titles to a chart.

Tip The titles that Excel adds are placed in the appropriate position, but you can drag them anywhere.

To modify a chart title's properties, access its Format dialog box. This dialog box has tabs for the following:

✦ **Patterns:** Change the background color and borders

✦ **Font:** Change the font, size, color, and attributes

✦ **Alignment:** Adjust the vertical and horizontal alignment and orientation

Tip Text in a chart is not limited to titles. In fact, you can add free-floating text anywhere that you want. To do so, select any part of the chart except a title or data label. Then, type the text in the formula bar and press Enter. Excel adds a Text Box AutoShape that contains the text. You can move the Text Box wherever you want it and format it to your liking.

Working with the Legend

If you create your chart with the Chart Wizard, you have an option (in Step 3) to include a legend. If you change your mind, you can easily delete the legend or add one if it doesn't exist.

To add a legend to your chart, use the Chart ⇨ Options command and then click the Legend tab in the Chart Options dialog box. Place a check mark in the Show legend check box. You also can specify where to place the legend by using the Placement option buttons.

The quickest way to remove a legend is to select the legend and then press Delete. To move a legend, click and drag it to the desired location. Or, you can use the legend's Format dialog box to position the legend (using the Placement tab).

A chart's legend consists of text and keys. A *key* is a small graphic that corresponds to the chart's series. You can select individual text items within a legend and format them separately by using the Format Legend Entry dialog box (which has only a single panel: Font). For example, you may want to make the text bold, to draw attention to a particular data series.

Note You can't use the Chart toolbar's Select Object drop-down list to select a legend entry or legend key. You must either click the item or select the legend itself, and then press the right arrow until the element that you want is selected.

The Legend tool in the Chart toolbar acts as a toggle. Use this button to add a legend, if one doesn't exist, and to remove the legend, if one exists.

Tip After you move a legend from its default position, you may want to change the size of the Plot Area to fill in the gap left by the legend. Just select the Plot Area and drag a border to make it the desired size.

If you didn't include legend text when you originally selected the cells to create the chart, Excel displays *Series 1, Series 2,* and so on in the legend. To add series names, choose Chart ⇨ Source Data and then select the Series tab in the Source Data dialog box (refer to Figure 19-4). Select a series from the Series list box, activate the Name box, and then either specify a cell reference that contains the label or directly enter the series name.

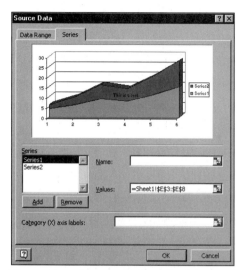

Figure 19-4: Use the Series tab of the Source Data dialog box to change the name of a data series.

Changing Gridlines

Gridlines can help you to determine what the chart series represents numerically. Gridlines simply extend the tick marks on the axes. Some charts look better with gridlines; others appear more cluttered. You can decide whether gridlines can enhance your chart. Sometimes, horizontal gridlines alone are enough, although XY charts often benefit from both horizontal and vertical gridlines.

To add or remove gridlines, choose Chart ⇨ Options and then select the Gridlines tab. This Chart Options dialog box is shown in Figure 19-5.

Each axis has two sets of gridlines: major and minor. *Major* units display a label. *Minor* units are located between the labels. You can choose which to add or remove by checking or unchecking the appropriate check boxes. If you're working with a true 3D chart, the dialog box has options for three sets of gridlines.

To modify the properties of a set of gridlines, select one gridline in the set and access the Format Gridlines dialog box. This dialog has two tabs:

✦ **Patterns:** Changes the line style, width, and color

✦ **Scale:** Adjusts the scale used on the axis

The next section presents an in-depth discussion of scaling.

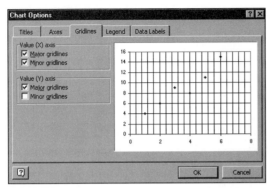

Figure 19-5: The Gridlines tab of the Chart Options dialog box lets you add or remove gridlines from the chart.

Modifying the Axes

Charts vary in the number of axes that they use. Pie and doughnut charts have no axes. All 2D charts have two axes (three, if you use a secondary-value axis; four, if you use a secondary-category axis in an XY chart). True 3D charts have three axes. Excel gives you a lot of control over these axes. To modify any aspect of an axis, access its Format Axis dialog box, which has five tabs:

✦ **Patterns:** Change the axis line width, tick marks, and placement of tick mark labels

✦ **Scale:** Adjust the minimum and maximum axis values, units for major and minor gridlines, and other properties

✦ **Font:** Adjust the font used for the axis labels

✦ **Number:** Adjust the number format for the axis labels

✦ **Alignment:** Specify the orientation for the axis labels

Because the axes' properties can dramatically affect the chart's look, the Patterns and Scale dialog box tabs are discussed separately, in the following sections.

Axes patterns

Figure 19-6 shows the Patterns tab of the Format Axis dialog box.

This tab has four sections:

✦ **Axis:** Controls the line characteristics of the axis (the style, color, and weight of the line).

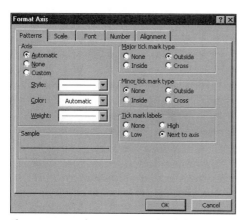

Figure 19-6: The Patterns tab of the Format Axis dialog box

✦ **Major tick mark type:** Controls how the major tick marks appear. You can select None (no tick marks), Inside (inside the axis), Outside (outside the axis), or Cross (on both sides of the axis).

✦ **Minor tick mark type:** Controls how the minor tick marks appear. You can select None (no tick marks), Inside (inside the axis), Outside (outside the axis), or Cross (on both sides of the axis).

✦ **Tick mark labels:** Controls where the axis labels appear. Normally, the labels appear next to the axis. You can, however, specify that the labels appear High (at the top of the chart), Low (at the bottom of the chart), or not at all (None). These options are useful when the axis doesn't appear in its normal position, at the edge of the Plot Area.

Note   Major tick marks are the axis tick marks that normally have labels next to them. Minor tick marks are between the major tick marks.

Axes scales

Adjusting the scale of a value axis can dramatically affect the chart's appearance. Manipulating the scale, in some cases, can present a false picture of the data. Figure 19-7 shows two charts that use the same data; the only difference between the charts is that the Minimum value has been adjusted on the value axis scale. In the first chart, the differences are quite apparent. In the second chart, little difference is apparent between the data points.

The actual scale that you use depends on the situation. No hard-and-fast rules exist about scale, except that you shouldn't misrepresent data by manipulating the chart to prove a point that doesn't exist.

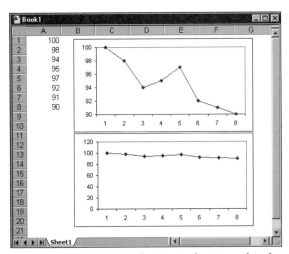

Figure 19-7: These two charts use the same data but different scales.

If you're preparing several charts that use similarly scaled data, keeping the scales the same is a good idea, so that the charts can be compared more easily. The charts in Figure 19-8 show the distribution of responses for a survey. Because the same scale was not used on the value axes, however, comparing the responses across survey items is difficult. All charts in the series should have the same scale.

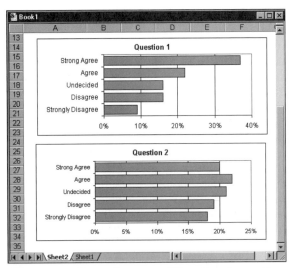

Figure 19-8: These charts use different scales on the value axis, making a comparison between the two difficult.

Excel automatically determines the scale for your charts. You can, however, override Excel's choice in the Scale tab of the Format Axis dialog box (see Figure 19-9).

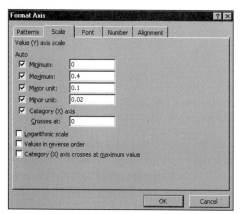

Figure 19-9: The Scale tab of the Format Axis dialog box

Note   The Scale tab varies slightly, depending on which axis is selected.

This dialog box offers the following options:

✦ **Minimum:** Enter a minimum value for the axis. If the check box is checked, Excel determines this value automatically.

✦ **Maximum:** Enter a maximum value for the axis. If the check box is checked, Excel determines this value automatically.

✦ **Major unit:** Enter the number of units between major tick marks. If the check box is checked, Excel determines this value automatically.

✦ **Minor unit:** Enter the number of units between minor tick marks. If the check box is checked, Excel determines this value automatically.

✦ *Axis Type* **axis Crosses at:** Position the axis at a different location. By default, it's at the edge of the Plot Area. The exact wording of this option (*Axis Type*) varies, depending on which axis is selected.

✦ **Logarithmic scale**: Use a logarithmic scale for the axes. A log scale primarily is useful for scientific applications in which the values to plot have an extremely large range. You receive an error message if the scale includes 0 or negative values.

✦ **Values in reverse order:** Make the scale values extend in the opposite direction. For a value axis, for example, selecting this option displays the smallest scale value at the top and the largest at the bottom (the opposite of how it normally appears).

✦ *Axis Type* **crosses at maximum value:** Position the axes at the maximum value of the perpendicular axis (normally, the axis is positioned at the minimum value of the perpendicular axis). The exact wording of this option (*Axis Type*) varies, depending on which axis is selected.

Working with Data Series

Every chart consists of one or more data series. Each series is based on data that is stored in a worksheet. This data translates into chart columns, lines, pie slices, and so on. This section discusses most of the customizations that you can perform with a chart's data series.

To work with a data series, you must first select it. Activate the chart and then click the data series that you want to select. In a column chart, click a column; in a line chart, click a line; and so on. Make sure that you select the entire series and not just a single point. You may find it easier to select the series by using the Chart Object tool in the Chart toolbar.

When you select a data series, Excel displays the series name in the Name box (for example, Series 1, or the actual name of the series), and the SERIES formula in the formula bar. A selected data series has a small square on each element of the series. In addition, the cells used for the selected series are outlined in color.

Many customizations that you perform with a data series use the Format Data Series dialog box, which has as many as seven tabs. The number of tabs varies, depending on the type of chart. For example, a pie chart has four tabs, and a 3D column chart has four tabs. Line and column charts have six tabs, and XY (scatter) charts have seven tabs. The possible tabs in the Format Data Series dialog box are as follows:

✦ **Axis:** Specify which value axis to use for the selected data series. This is applicable only if the chart has two value axes.

✦ **Data Labels:** Display labels next to each data point.

✦ **Options:** Change options specific to the chart type.

✦ **Patterns:** Change the color, pattern, and border style for the data series. For line charts, change the color and style of the data marker in this tab.

✦ **Series Order:** Specify the order in which the data series are plotted.

✦ **Shape:** Specify the shape of the columns (in 3D column charts only).

✦ **X Error Bars:** Add or modify error bars for the X axis. This is available only for XY charts.

✦ **Y Error Bars**: Add or modify error bars for the Y axis.

The sections that follow discuss many of these dialog box options.

Deleting a data series

To delete a data series in a chart, select the data series and press the Delete key. The data series is removed from the chart. The data in the worksheet, of course, remains intact.

Note   You can delete all data series from a chart. If you do so, the chart appears empty. It retains its settings, however. Therefore, you can add a data series to an empty chart, and it again looks like a chart.

Adding a new data series to a chart

A common need is to add another data series to an existing chart. You *could* re-create the chart and include the new data series, but usually, adding the data to the existing chart is easier. Excel provides several ways to add a new data series to a chart:

✦ Activate the chart and select Chart ➪ Source Data. In the Source Data dialog box, click the Series tab (see Figure 19-10). Click the Add button and then specify the data range in the Values box (you can enter the range address or point to it).

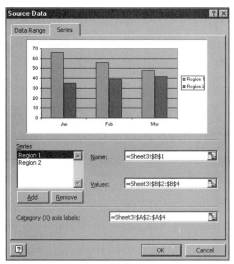

Figure 19-10: Use the Source Data dialog box to add a new data series to a chart.

✦ Select the range to add and copy it to the clipboard. Then, activate the chart and choose Edit ➪ Paste Special. Excel responds with the dialog box shown in Figure 19-11. Complete this dialog box to correspond to the data that you selected (or just use Edit ➪ Paste and let Excel determine how the data fits into the chart).

Figure 19-11: Using the Paste Special dialog box is one way to add new data to a chart.

✦ Select the range to add and drag it into the chart. When you release the mouse button, Excel updates the chart with the data that you dragged in. This technique works only if the chart is embedded on the worksheet.

Changing data used by a series

Often, you create a chart that uses a particular range of data, and then you extend the range by adding new data points in the worksheet. For example, the previous month's sales data arrives in your office, and you enter the numbers into your sales-tracking worksheet. Or, you may delete some of the data points in a range that is plotted; for example, you may not need to plot older information. In either case, you'll find that the chart doesn't update itself automatically. When you add new data to a range, it isn't included in the data series. If you delete data from a range, the chart displays the deleted data as zero values.

Cross-Reference   You can create a chart that updates automatically when you add new data to your worksheet. See "Chart-Making Tricks," later in this chapter.

The following sections describe a few different ways to change the range used by a data series.

Dragging the range outline

The easiest way to change the data range for a data series is to drag the range outline. This technique works only for embedded charts. When you select a series, Excel outlines the data range used by that series. You can drag the small dot in the lower-right corner of the range outline to extend or contract the data series. Figure 19-12 shows an example of how this looks. In this figure, the data series needs to be extended to include the data for July. If the chart uses a range for the category axis, you'll also need to extend that range.

You can drag the outline in either direction, so you can use this technique to expand or contract a range used in a data series.

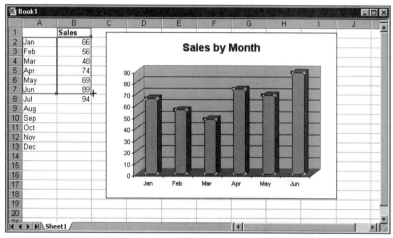

Figure 19-12: To change the range used in a chart's data series, select the data series and drag the small dot at the lower-right corner of the range outline.

Using the Data Source dialog box

To update the chart to reflect a different data range, activate the chart and select Chart ⇨ Source Data. Click the Series tab and then select the series from the Series list box. Adjust the range in the Name box (you can edit the range reference or point to the new range).

Editing the SERIES formula

Every data series in a chart has an associated SERIES formula, which appears in the formula bar when you select a data series in a chart (see Figure 19-13). You can edit the range references in the SERIES formula directly. You can even enter a new SERIES formula manually—which adds a new series to the chart (however, easier ways to do this exist, as described previously).

A SERIES formula consists of a SERIES function with four arguments. The syntax is as follows:

```
=SERIES(Name_ref,Categories,Values,Plot_order)
```

Excel uses absolute cell references in the SERIES function. To change the data that a series uses, edit the cell references (third argument) in the formula bar. The first and second arguments are optional and may not appear in the SERIES formula. If the series doesn't have a name, the Name_ref argument is missing and Excel uses dummy series names in the legend (Series1, Series2, and so on). If no category names exist, the Categories argument is missing, and Excel uses dummy labels (1, 2, 3, and so on).

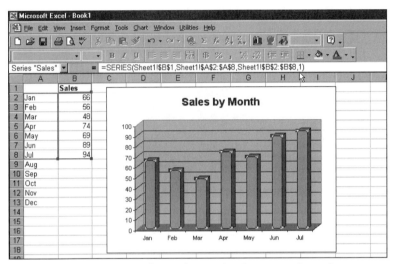

Figure 19-13: When you select a data series, its SERIES formula appears in the formula bar.

 Caution   If the data series uses category labels, make sure that you adjust the reference for the category labels also. This is the second argument in the SERIES formula.

Using names in SERIES formulas

Perhaps the best way to handle data ranges that change over time is to use named ranges. Create names for the data ranges that you use in the chart and then edit the SERIES formula. Replace each range reference with the corresponding range name.

After making this change, the chart uses the named ranges. If you add new data to the range, just change the definition for the name, and the chart is updated.

Displaying data labels in a chart

Sometimes, you may want your chart to display the actual data values for each point. Or, you may want to display the category label for each data point. Figure 19-14 shows an example of both of these options.

You specify data labels in the Data Labels tab of the Chart Options dialog box (see Figure 19-15). This tab has several options. Note that not all options are available for all chart types. If you select the check box labeled Show legend key next to label, each label displays its legend key next to it.

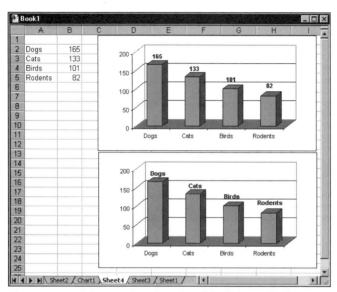

Figure 19-14: The top chart has data labels for each data point; the bottom chart has category labels for each point.

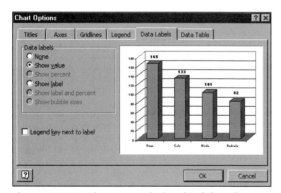

Figure 19-15: The Data Labels tab of the Chart Options dialog box

The data labels are linked to the worksheet, so if your data changes, the labels also change. If you want to override the data label with other text, select the label and enter the new text (or even a cell reference) in the formula bar.

Often, you'll find that the data labels aren't positioned properly—for example, a label may be obscured by another data point. If you select an individual label, you can drag the label to a better location.

Tip   After you add data labels to a series, format the labels by using the Format Data Labels dialog box.

As you work with data labels, you may discover that Excel's Data Labels feature leaves a bit to be desired. For example, it would be nice to be able to specify a range of text to be used for the data labels. This would be particularly useful in XY charts in which you want to identify each data point with a particular text item. Unfortunately, this isn't possible. You can add data labels and then manually edit each label—or, you can use the Chart Data Labeler utility that's included with my Power Utility Pak (use the coupon in the back of the book to get your copy).

Handling missing data

Sometimes, data that you're charting may be missing one or more data points. Excel offers several ways to handle the missing data. You don't control this in the Format Data Series dialog box (as you might expect). Rather, you must select the chart, choose Tools ➪ Options, and then click the Chart tab, which is shown in Figure 19-16. The reason for putting this setting in the Options dialog box is known only to the Excel design team.

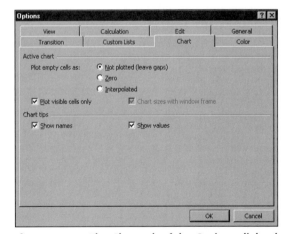

Figure 19-16: The Chart tab of the Options dialog box

Note   A chart must be activated when you select the Tools ➪ Options command, or the options in the Chart panel are grayed.

The options that you set apply to the entire active chart, and you can't set a different option for different series in the same chart.

The following are the *options* in the Chart panel for the active chart:

✦ **Not plotted (leave gaps):** Missing data is simply ignored, and the data series will have a gap.

✦ **Zero:** Missing data is treated as zero.

✦ **Interpolated:** Missing data is calculated by using data on either side of the missing point(s). This option is available only for line charts.

Controlling a data series by hiding data

Usually, Excel doesn't plot data that is in a hidden row or column. You can sometimes use this to your advantage, because it's an easy way to control what data appears in the chart. If you're working with outlines or data filtering (both of which use hidden rows), however, you may not like the idea that hidden data is removed from your chart. To override this, activate the chart and select the Tools ⇨ Options command. In the Options dialog box, click the Chart tab and remove the check mark from the check box labeled Plot visible cells only.

Note
The Plot visible cells only setting applies only to the active chart. A chart must be activated when you open the Options dialog box. Otherwise, the option is grayed. This is another example of a setting that shows up in an unexpected dialog box.

Adding error bars

For certain chart types, you can add error bars to your chart. Error bars often are used to indicate "plus or minus" information that reflects uncertainty in the data. Error bars are appropriate only for area, bar, column, line, and XY charts. Click the Y Error Bars tab in the Format Data Series dialog box to display the options shown in Figure 19-17.

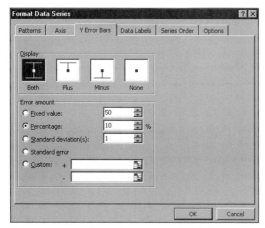

Figure 19-17: The *Y* Error Bars tab of the Format Data Series dialog box

A data series in an *XY* chart can have error bars for both the *X* values and *Y* values. Excel enables you to specify several types of error bars:

✦ **Fixed value:** The error bars are fixed by an amount that you specify.

✦ **Percentage:** The error bars are a percentage of each value.

✦ **Standard deviation(s):** The error bars are in the number of standard-deviation units that you specify (Excel calculates the standard deviation of the data series).

✦ **Standard error:** The error bars are one standard error unit (Excel calculates the standard error of the data series).

✦ **Custom:** The error bar units for the upper or lower error bars are set by you. You can enter either a value or a range reference that holds the error values that you want to plot as error bars.

Figure 19-18 shows a chart with error bars added. After you add error bars, you can access the Format Error Bars dialog box to modify the error bars. For example, you can control the line style and color of the error bars.

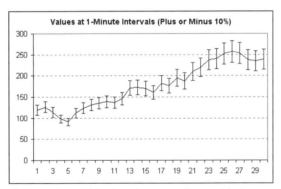

Figure 19-18: This chart has error bars added to the data series.

Adding a trendline

When you're plotting data over time, you may want to plot a trendline that describes the data. A *trendline* points out general trends in your data. In some cases, you can forecast future data with trendlines. A single series can have more than one trendline.

Excel makes adding a trendline to a chart quite simple. Although you might expect this option to be in the Format Data Series dialog box, it's not. The place to go is the Add Trendline dialog box, shown in Figure 19-19, which you access by selecting Chart ➪ Add Trendline. This command is available only when a data series is selected.

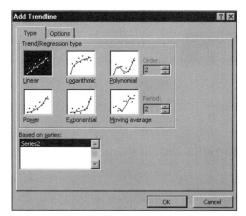

Figure 19-19: The Add Trendline dialog box offers several types of automatic trendlines.

The type of trendline that you choose depends on your data. Linear trends are most common, but some data can be described more effectively with another type. One of the options on the Type tab is Moving average, which is useful for smoothing out "noisy" data. The Moving average option enables you to specify the number of data points to include in each average. For example, if you select 5, Excel averages every five data points.

When you click the Options tab in the Add Trendline dialog box, Excel displays the options shown in Figure 19-20.

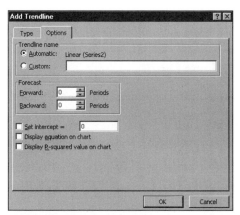

Figure 19-20: The Options tab in the Add Trendline dialog box enables you to smooth or forecast data.

The Options tab enables you to specify a name to appear in the legend and the number of periods that you want to forecast. Additional options let you set the intercept value, specify that the equation used for the trendline should appear on the chart, and choose whether the R-squared value appears on the chart.

Figure 19-21 shows two charts. The chart on the left depicts a data series without a trendline. The chart on the right is the same chart, but a linear trendline has been added that shows the trend in the data.

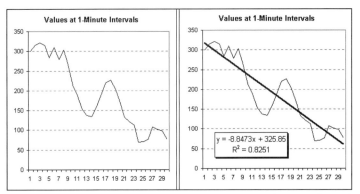

Figure 19-21: Before (chart on the left) and after (chart on the right) adding a linear trendline to a chart

When Excel inserts a trendline, it may look like a new data series, but it's not. It's a new chart element with a name, such as Series 1 Trendline 1. You can double-click a trendline to change its formatting or its options.

Creating Combination Charts

A *combination chart* is a single chart that consists of series that use different chart types. For example, you may have a chart that shows both columns and lines. A combination chart also can use a single type (all columns, for example), but include a second value axis. A combination chart requires at least two data series.

Creating a combination chart simply involves changing one or more of the data series to a different chart type. Select the data series and then choose Chart ⇨ Chart Type. In the Chart Type dialog box, select the chart type that you want to apply to the selected series. Figure 19-22 shows an example of a combination chart.

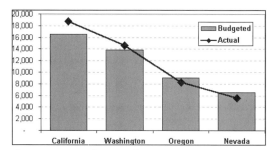

Figure 19-22: This combination chart uses columns and a line.

Note   In some cases, you can't combine chart types. For example, you can't combine a 2D chart type with a 3D chart type. If you choose an incompatible chart type for the series, Excel lets you know.

You can't create combination 3D charts, but if you use a 3D column or 3D bar chart, you can change the shape of the columns or bars. Select a series and access the Format Data Series dialog box. Click the Shape tab and then choose the shape for the selected series.

Using Secondary Axes

If you need to plot data series that have drastically different scales, you probably want to use a *secondary scale*. For example, assume that you want to create a chart that shows monthly sales, along with the average amount sold per customer. These two data series use different scales (the average sales values are much smaller than the total sales). Consequently, the average sales data range is virtually invisible in the chart.

The solution is to use a secondary axis for the second data series. Figure 19-23 shows two charts. The first uses a single value axis, and the second data series (a line) is hardly visible. The second chart uses a secondary axis for the second data series — which makes it easy to see.

To specify a secondary axis, select the data series in the chart and then access the Format Data Series dialog box. Click the Axis tab and choose the Secondary axis option.

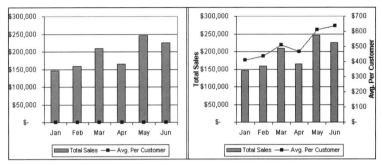

Figure 19-23: These charts show the same data, but the chart on the right uses a secondary axis for the second data series.

Displaying a Data Table

In some cases, you may want to display a *data table*, which displays the chart's data in tabular form, directly in the chart.

To add a data table to a chart, choose Chart ⇨ Chart Options and select the Data Table tab in the Chart Options dialog box. Place a check mark next to the option labeled Show data table. You also can choose to display the legend keys in the data table. Figure 19-24 shows a chart with a data table.

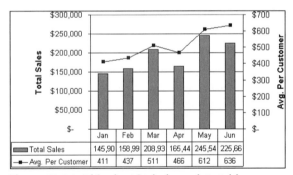

Figure 19-24: This chart includes a data table.

To adjust the formatting or font used in the data table, access the Format Data Table dialog box.

Creating Custom Chart Types

Excel comes with quite a few custom chart types that you can select from the Custom Types tab of the Chart Type dialog box. Each of these custom chart types is simply a standard chart that has been formatted. In fact, you can duplicate any of these custom chart types just by applying the appropriate formatting.

As you might expect, you can create your own custom chart types, called *user-defined* custom chart types.

The first step in designing a custom chart type is to create a chart that's customized the way that you want. For example, you can set any of the colors, fill effects, or line styles; change the scales; modify fonts and type sizes; add gridlines; add a formatted title; and even add free-floating text or graphic images.

When you're satisfied with the chart, choose Chart ➪ Chart Type to display the Chart Type dialog box. Click the Custom Types tab and then select the User-defined option. This displays a list of all user-defined custom chart types.

Click the Add button, which displays the Add Custom Chart Type dialog box, as shown in Figure 19-25. Enter a name for the new chart type and a description. Click OK, and your custom chart type is added to the list.

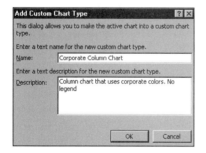

Figure 19-25: The Custom Chart Type dialog box

Working with 3D Charts

One of the most interesting classes of Excel charts is its 3D charts. Certain situations benefit by the use of 3D charts, because you can depict changes over two different dimensions. Even a simple column chart commands more attention if you present it as a 3D chart. Not all charts that are labeled "3D" are true 3D charts, however. A true 3D chart has three axes. Some of Excel's 3D charts are simply 2D charts with a perspective look to them.

How Custom Chart Types Are Stored

The custom chart types that you can select from the Chart Types dialog box are stored in a workbook named Xl8galry.xls, located in the Excel (or Office) folder. If you open Xl8galry, you can see that it contains only chart sheets — one for each custom chart type.

Also notice that the series formulas for these charts don't refer to actual worksheet ranges. Rather, the series formulas use arrays entered directly into the series formulas. This makes the charts completely independent of any specific worksheet range.

If you create a user-defined custom chart type, it's stored in a file called xlusrgal.xls, also in the Excel folder. Each custom chart type that you create is stored as a chart sheet.

If you want your coworkers to have access to your custom chart types, simply put a copy of your xlusrgal.xls file into their Excel (or Office) folders. By copying the file, you enable everyone in your workgroup to produce consistent-looking charts.

Modifying 3D charts

All 3D charts have a few additional parts that you can customize. For example, most 3D charts have a *floor* and *walls,* and the true 3D charts also have an additional axis. You can select these chart elements and format them to your liking. This chapter doesn't go into the details, because the formatting options are quite straightforward. Generally, 3D formatting options work just like the other chart elements.

Rotating 3D charts

When you start flirting with the third dimension, you have a great deal of flexibility regarding the viewpoint for your charts. Figure 19-26 shows a 3D column chart that has been rotated to show four different views.

You can rotate a 3D chart in one of the following two ways:

✦ Activate the 3D chart and choose the Chart ⇨ 3D View command. The dialog box shown in Figure 19-27 appears. You can make your rotations and perspective changes by clicking the appropriate controls. The sample that you see in the dialog box is *not* your actual chart. The displayed sample just gives you an idea of the types of changes that you're making. Make the adjustments and then choose OK to make them permanent (or click Apply to apply them to your chart without closing the dialog box).

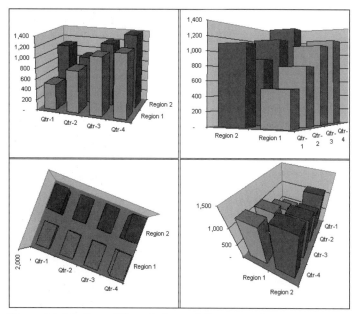

Figure 19-26: Four different views of the same chart

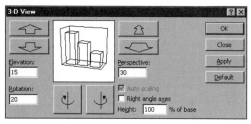

Figure 19-27: The 3D View dialog box enables you to rotate and change the perspective of a 3D chart. You also can drag the chart with the mouse.

✦ Rotate the chart in real time by dragging corners with the mouse. Click one of the corners of the chart. Black handles appear, and the word *Corners* appears in the Name box. You can drag one of these black handles and rotate the chart's 3D box to your satisfaction. This method definitely takes some practice. If your chart gets totally messed up, choose Chart ➪ 3D View and then select the Default button to return to the standard 3D view.

Tip   When you rotate a 3D chart, hold down the Ctrl key while you drag, to see an outline of the entire chart — not just the axes. This technique is helpful, because when
you drag only the chart's axes, you can easily lose your bearings and end up with
a strange-looking chart.

Chart-Making Tricks

In this section, I share chart-making tricks that I've picked up over the years. Some
use little-known features; others are undocumented, as far as I can tell. Several tricks
enable you to make charts that you may have considered impossible to create.

Changing a worksheet value by dragging

Excel provides an interesting chart-making feature that also can be somewhat
dangerous. This feature lets you change the value in a worksheet by dragging the
data markers on two-dimensional line charts, bar charts, column charts, *XY* charts,
and bubble charts.

Here's how it works. Select an individual data point in a chart series (not the entire
series) and then drag the point in the direction in which you want to adjust the value.
As you drag the data marker, the corresponding value in the worksheet changes to
correspond to the data point's new position on the chart. Figure 19-28 shows the
result of dragging the data points around on an *XY* chart with five data series.

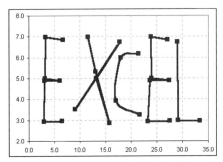

Figure 19-28: This XY chart has five data series.

If the value of a data point that you move is the result of a formula, Excel displays
the Goal Seek dialog box (goal seeking is discussed in Chapter 37). Use this dialog
box to specify the cell that Excel should adjust to make the formula produce the
result that you pointed out on the chart. This technique is useful if you know what

a chart should look like and you want to determine the values that will produce the chart. Obviously, this feature also can be dangerous, because you inadvertently can change values that you shouldn't — so be careful.

Unlinking a chart from its data range

A nice thing about charts is that they are linked to data that is stored in a worksheet. You also can unlink a data series so that it no longer relies on the worksheet data.

To unlink a data series, select the data series and then activate the formula bar. Press F9, and the series formula converts its range references to arrays that hold the values (see the formula bar in Figure 19-29). If you unlink all the series in the chart, you create a dead graph that uses no data in a worksheet. If you want, however, you can edit the individual values in the arrays.

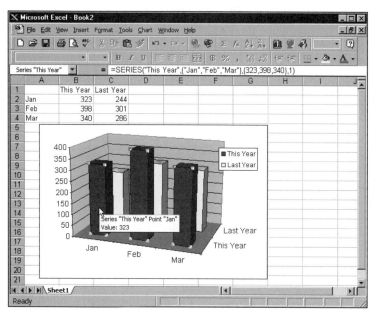

Figure 19-29: This data series no longer uses data in a worksheet.

Creating picture charts

Excel makes it easy to incorporate a pattern, texture, or graphic file for elements in your chart. Figure 19-30 shows an example of a column chart that displays a graphic.

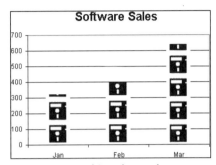

Figure 19-30: This column chart uses a graphic image.

The following sections describe how to create picture charts, using two methods.

Using a graphic file to create a picture chart

To convert a data series to pictures, start with a column or bar chart (either standard or 3D). Then, access the chart's Format Data Series dialog box and select the Patterns tab. Click the Fill Effects button to get the Fill Effects dialog box. Click the Picture tab and then click the Select Picture button to locate the graphics file that you want to use.

Note   Use the Fill Effects dialog box to specify some options for the image.

Using the clipboard to create a picture chart

This section describes another way to create a picture chart—a method with which the image that you want to use doesn't have to exist in a file. This technique works if the image can be copied to the clipboard. It's also the only way to get pictures into the data points for a line or *XY* chart.

The first step is to locate the image that you want to use and copy it to the clipboard. Generally, simpler images work better. You may want to paste it into Excel first, where you can adjust the size, remove the borders, and add a background color, if desired. Or you can create the image by using Excel's drawing tools. In either case, copy the image to the clipboard.

When the image is on the clipboard, activate the chart, select the data series, and then choose Edit ➪ Paste. Your chart is converted. You also can paste the image to a single point in the data series, rather than to the entire data series—simply select the point before you paste.

This technique also works with data markers in line charts, *XY* (scatter) charts, or bubble charts. Figure 19-31 shows an example of a line chart that uses a smiley face instead of the normal data markers. I created this graphic by using Excel's drawing tools (it's one of the AutoShapes in the Basic Shapes category).

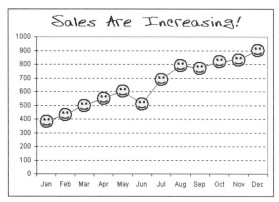

Figure 19-31: A line chart after replacing the data markers with a copied graphic image

Pasting linked pictures to charts

Another useful charting technique involves pasting linked pictures to a chart. Excel doesn't let you do this directly, but this pasting is possible if you know a few tricks. The technique is useful, for example, if you want your chart to include the data that's used by the chart — but the data table feature (discussed earlier in this chapter) isn't flexible enough for you.

Figure 19-32 shows an example of a data range pasted to a chart as a linked picture. If the data changes, the changes are reflected in the chart as well as in the linked picture. Notice that the effect is similar to using a data table, but it provides more formatting options.

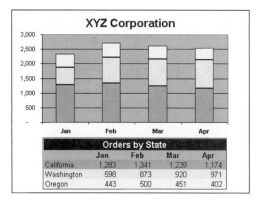

Figure 19-32: This chart uses a linked picture to display the data used in the chart series.

Here are the steps to create the linked picture:

1. Create the chart as usual and format the data range to your liking.

2. Select the data range, press Shift, and select Edit ➪ Copy Picture. Excel displays a dialog box—accept the default options. This copies the range to the clipboard as a picture.

3. Activate the chart and paste the clipboard contents. You'll probably have to resize the Plot Area to accommodate the pasted image.

4. The image that is pasted is a picture, but not a linked picture. To convert the image to a linked picture, select it and then enter the range reference in the formula bar (or simply point it out). For this example, I entered **=Sheet1!A1:E5**.

The picture is now a linked picture. Changing any of the cells that are used in the chart's SERIES formula is reflected immediately in the linked picture.

Simple Gantt charts

Creating a simple Gantt chart isn't difficult when using Excel, but it does require some setup work. *Gantt charts* are used to represent the time required to perform each task in a project. Figure 19-33 shows data that was used to create the Gantt chart in Figure 19-34.

	A	B	C	D	E
	customer survey.xls				
1	Task	Start Date	Duration	End Date	
2	Planning Meeting	12/29/98	1	12/29/98	
3	Develop Questionnaire	12/30/98	11	01/09/99	
4	Print and Mail Questionnaire	01/13/99	9	01/21/99	
5	Receive Responses	01/16/99	15	01/30/99	
6	Data Entry	01/16/99	18	02/02/99	
7	Data Analysis	02/03/99	4	02/06/99	
8	Write Report	02/09/99	12	02/20/99	
9	Distribute Draft Report	02/23/99	1	02/23/99	
10	Solicit Comments	02/24/99	4	02/27/99	
11	Finalize Report	03/02/99	5	03/06/99	
12	Distribute to Board	03/09/99	1	03/09/99	
13	Board Meeting	03/17/99	1	03/17/99	
14					

Figure 19-33: Data used in the Gantt chart

A workbook that demonstrates this technique is available on the companion CD-ROM.

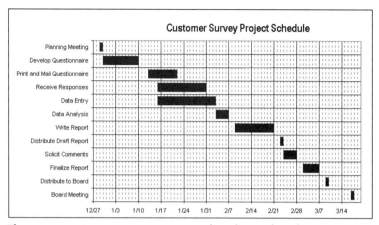

Figure 19-34: You can create a Gantt chart from a bar chart.

Here are the steps to create this chart:

1. Enter the data as shown in Figure 19-33. The formula in cell D2, which was copied to the rows below it, is **=B2+C2-1**.

2. Use the Chart Wizard to create a stacked bar chart from the range **A2:C13**. Use the second subtype, which is labeled Stacked Bar.

3. In Step 2 of the Chart Wizard, select the Columns option. Also, notice that Excel incorrectly uses the first two columns as the Category axis labels.

4. In Step 2 of the Chart Wizard, click the Series tab and add a new data series. Then, set the chart's series to the following:

   Series 1: **B2:B13**

   Series 2: **C2:C13**

   Category (*x*) axis labels: **A2:A13**

5. In Step 3 of the Chart Wizard, remove the legend and then click Finish to create an embedded chart.

6. Adjust the height of the chart so that all the axis labels are visible. You can also accomplish this by using a smaller font size.

7. Access the Format Axis dialog box for the horizontal axis. Adjust the horizontal axis Minimum and Maximum scale values to correspond to the earliest and latest dates in the data (note that you can enter a date into the Minimum or Maximum edit box). You might also want to change the date format for the axis labels.

8. Access the Format Axis dialog box for the vertical axis. In the Scale tab, select the option labeled Categories in reverse order, and also set the option labeled Value (y) axis crosses at maximum category.

9. Select the first data series and access the Format Data Series dialog box. In the Patterns tab, set Border to None and Area to None. This makes the first data series invisible.

10. Apply other formatting, as desired.

Comparative histograms

With a bit of creativity, you can create charts that you may have considered impossible with Excel. For example, Figure 19-35 shows data that was used to create the comparative histogram chart shown in Figure 19-36. Such charts often display population data.

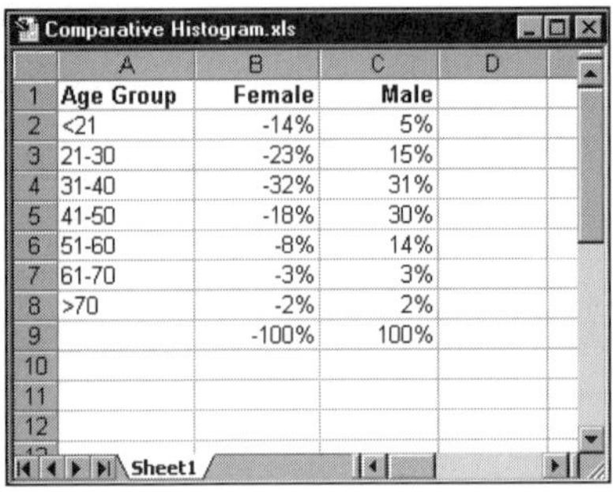

	A	B	C	D
1	Age Group	Female	Male	
2	<21	-14%	5%	
3	21-30	-23%	15%	
4	31-40	-32%	31%	
5	41-50	-18%	30%	
6	51-60	-8%	14%	
7	61-70	-3%	3%	
8	>70	-2%	2%	
9		-100%	100%	

Figure 19-35: Data used in the comparative histogram chart

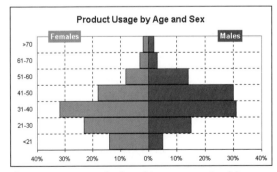

Figure 19-36: Producing this comparative histogram chart requires a few tricks.

A workbook that demonstrates this technique is available on the companion CD-ROM.

Here's how to create the chart:

1. Enter the data as shown in Figure 19-35. Notice that the values for females are entered as negative values.

2. Select A1:C8 and create a 2D bar chart. Use the subtype labeled Clustered Bar.

3. Apply the following custom number format to the horizontal axis: **0%;0%;0%**. This custom format eliminates the negative signs in the percentages.

4. Select the vertical axis and access the Format Axis dialog box. Click the Patterns tab and remove all tick marks. Set the Tick mark labels option to Low. This keeps the axis in the center of the chart but displays the axis labels at the left side.

5. Select either of the data series and then access the Format Data Series dialog box. Click the Options tab and set the Overlap to 100 and the Gap width to 0.

6. Add two text boxes to the chart (**Females** and **Males**), to substitute for the legend.

7. Apply other formatting, as desired.

Charts that update automatically

Earlier in this chapter, I discussed several ways to modify the data range used by a chart series. If you have a chart that displays daily sales, for example, you probably need to change the chart's data range each day when you add new data. Although updating a chart's data range isn't difficult, you might be interested in a trick that forces Excel to update the chart's data range whenever you add new data to your worksheet.

A workbook that demonstrates this technique is available on the companion CD-ROM.

To force Excel to update your chart automatically when you add new data, follow these steps:

1. Create the worksheet shown in Figure 19-37.

2. Select Insert ➪ Name ➪ Define to bring up the Define Name dialog box. In the Names in workbook field, enter **Date**. In the Refers to field, enter this formula:

```
=OFFSET(Sheet1!$A$2,0,0,COUNTA(Sheet1! $A:$A)-1)
```

3. Click Add. Notice that the `OFFSET` function refers to the first data point (cell A2) and uses the `COUNTA` function to get the number of data points in the column. Because column A has a heading in row 1, the formula subtracts 1 from the number.

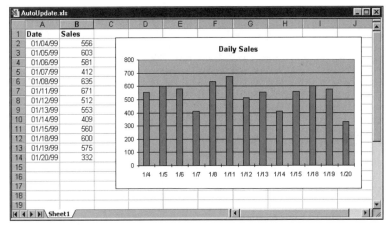

Figure 19-37: This chart is updated automatically whenever you add new data to columns A and B.

4. Type **Sales** in the Names in workbook field, and in the Refers to field enter:

```
=OFFSET(Sheet1!$B$2,0,0,COUNTA(Sheet1!$B:$B)-1)
```

5. Click Add and then OK to close the dialog box.

6. Activate the chart and select the data series. In this example, the formula in the formula bar will read:

```
=SERIES(Sheet1!$B$1,Sheet1!$A$2:$A$10, Sheet1!$B$2:$B$10,1)
```

7. Replace the range references with the names that you defined in Steps 2 and 4. The formula should read:

```
=SERIES(,Sheet1!Date,Sheet1!Sales,1)
```

After you perform these steps, when you add data to columns A and B, the chart will be updated automatically to show the new data.

To use this technique for your own data, make sure that the first argument for the `OFFSET` function refers to the first data point, and that the argument for `COUNTA` refers to the entire column of data. Also, if the columns used for the data contain any other entries, `COUNTA` will return an incorrect value.

Summary

This chapter picks up where Chapter 18 left off by discussing most of the chart customization options in Excel. This chapter demonstrates how to create combination charts and your own custom chart formats — which let you apply a series of customizations with a single command. This chapter also discusses 3D charts, and concludes with several examples that use chart-making tricks.

✦   ✦   ✦

Enhancing Your Work with Pictures and Drawings

In Chapter 18, you learned how to create charts from the numbers in your worksheet. This chapter continues in the same vein by discussing pictures and drawings. Like charts, these objects can be placed on a worksheet's draw layer to add pizzazz to an otherwise boring report. (See the sidebar, "A Word About the Draw Layer," later in this chapter.)

This chapter discusses three major types of images:

✦ Bitmap and line-art graphics imported directly into a workbook or copied from the clipboard

✦ Objects created by using Excel's drawing tools

✦ Objects inserted by using other Microsoft Office tools, such as WordArt and Organization Chart

Cross-Reference   Excel also can create another type of graphic image: maps. But that's the topic of Chapter 21.

Importing Graphics Files

Excel can import a wide variety of graphics files into a worksheet. You have several choices:

✦ Use the Microsoft Clip Gallery to locate and insert an image

✦ Directly import a graphic file

✦ Copy and paste the image by using the Windows clipboard

✦ Import the image from a digital camera or scanner

Using the Clip Gallery

The Clip Gallery is a shared application that is also accessible from other Microsoft Office products.

Note   Besides providing an easy way to locate and insert images, the Clip Gallery enables you to insert sound and video files.

EXCEL 2000   The Clip Gallery is available in both Excel 97 and Excel 2000, but the feature works a bit differently in Excel 2000. In addition, Excel 2000 gives you direct access to Microsoft's Clip Gallery Live on the Web.

You access the Clip Gallery by selecting the Insert ➪ Picture ➪ Clip Art command. This displays the Insert ClipArt dialog box, shown in Figure 20-1. Click the Pictures tab and then click a category, and the images in that category appear. Locate the image that you want and click it. A graphic menu pops up from which you can choose to insert the image, preview the image, add the image to your "favorites," or find similar images. You can also search for clip art by keyword — just enter some text in the Search for clips box, and the matching images are displayed.

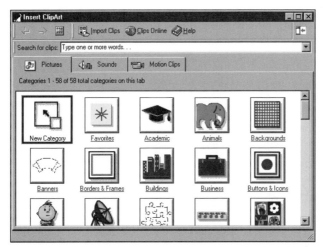

Figure 20-1: The Insert ClipArt dialog box enables you to insert pictures, sounds, or video.

If you select the insert option, the image is embedded in your worksheet. You can then either select additional images from the Clip Gallery or close the Insert ClipArt dialog box.

When an image is selected, Excel displays its Picture toolbar, which contains tools that enable you to adjust the image.

Tip You also can add new files to the Clip Gallery. You might want to do this if you tend to insert a particular graphic file into your worksheets (such as your company logo). Use the Import Clips button to select the file and specify the category for the image.

EXCEL 2000 If you can't find a suitable image, you can go online and browse through the clip art at Microsoft's Web site. In the Insert ClipArt dialog box, click the Clips Online button. Your Web browser will be activated, and you can view the images (or listen to the sounds) and download those that you want. Figure 20-2 shows Microsoft's online Clip Gallery

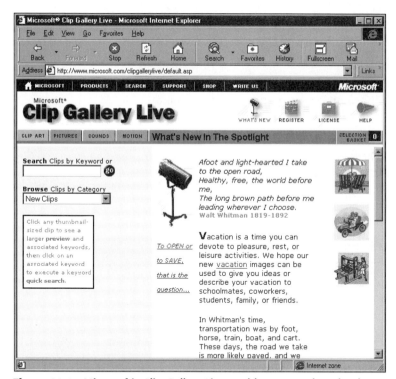

Figure 20-2: Microsoft's Clip Gallery Live enables you to download additional clip art.

Importing graphics files

If the graphic image that you want to insert is available in a file, you can easily import the file into your worksheet by choosing Insert ⇨ Picture ⇨ From File. Excel displays the Insert Picture dialog box, shown in Figure 20-3. This dialog box works just like the Open dialog box. By default, it displays only the graphics files that Excel can import. If you choose the Preview option, Excel displays a preview of the selected file in the right panel of the dialog box.

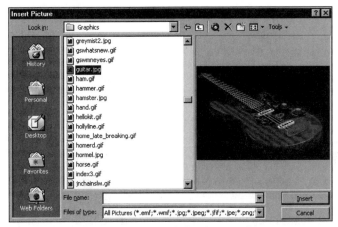

Figure 20-3: The Insert Picture dialog box enables you to embed a picture in a worksheet.

Excel 2000 supports animated GIF files — sort of. If you insert an animated GIF file, the image will be animated only if you save your workbook as a Web page and then view it in a Web browser. Figure 20-4 shows an example of a graphics file in a worksheet.

About Graphics Files

Graphics files come in two main categories: *bitmap* and *vector* (picture). Bitmap images are made up of discrete dots. They usually look pretty good at their original size, but often lose clarity if you increase or decrease the size. Vector-based images, on the other hand, retain their crispness, regardless of their size. Examples of common bitmap file formats include BMP, PCX, DIB, JPG, and GIF. Examples of common vector file formats include CGM, WMF, EPS, and DRW.

Bitmap files vary in the number of colors that they use (even black-and-white images use multiple colors, because these are usually gray-scale images). If you view a high-color bitmap graphic by using a video mode that displays only 256 colors, the image usually doesn't look very good.

You can find thousands of graphics files free for the taking on the Internet and online services such as CompuServe, America Online, and Prodigy.

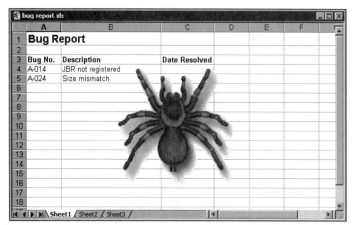

Figure 20-4: An example of a graphics file embedded in a worksheet.

Caution Using bitmap graphics in a worksheet can dramatically increase the size of your workbook, resulting in more memory usage and longer load and save times.

Table 20-1 lists the graphics file types that Excel can import. The most common graphics file formats are GIF, JPG, and BMP.

Table 20-1
Graphics File Formats Supported by Excel

File Type	Description
BMP	Windows bitmap
CDR	CorelDRAW graphics
CGM	Computer Graphics Metafiles
DIB	Windows bitmap
DRW	Micrografx Designer/Draw
DXF	AutoCAD format 2D
EMF	Windows Enhanced Metafile
EPS	Encapsulated PostScript
GIF	Graphic Interchange Format
HGL	HP Graphics Language
JPG	JPEG File Interchange Format

Continued

Table 20-1 *(continued)*

File Type	Description
PCT	Macintosh graphics
PCD	Kodak Photo CD
PCX	Bitmap graphics
PNG	Portable Network Graphics
RLE	Windows bitmap
TGA	Targa graphics format
TIF	Tagged Interchange Format
WMF	Windows metafile
WPG	WordPerfect graphics

Tip

If you want to use a graphic image for a worksheet's background (similar to wall-paper on the Windows desktop), select Format ⇨ Sheet ⇨ Background and then select a graphics file. The selected graphics file is tiled on the worksheet. It won't be printed, however.

Copying graphics by using the clipboard

In some cases, you may want to use a graphic image that is not stored in a separate file or that is in a file that Excel can't import. For example, you may have a drawing program that uses a file format that Excel doesn't support. You may be able to export the file to a supported format, but it may be easier to load the file into the drawing program and copy the image to the clipboard. Then, you can activate Excel and paste the image to the draw layer. (See the sidebar, "A Word About the Draw Layer," later in this chapter.)

This capability also is useful if you don't want to copy an entire image. For example, a drawing may consist of several components, and you may want to use only one element in Excel. In this case, using the clipboard is the only route.

Suppose that you see a graphic displayed onscreen but you can't select it — it may be part of a program's logo, for example. In this case, you can copy the entire screen to the clipboard and then paste it into Excel. Most of the time, you don't want the entire screen — just a portion of it. The solution is to capture the entire screen (or window), copy it to the Windows Paint program, and then copy just the part that you want (or crop out what you don't want) and paste it to your Excel worksheet. Figure 20-5 demonstrates this technique using Paint. In this case, a window was copied and pasted to Paint.

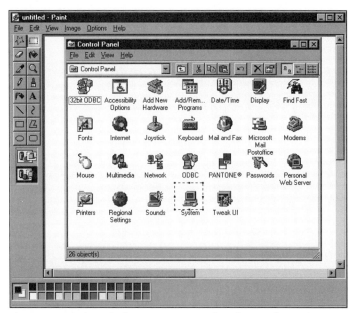

Figure 20-5: The window was captured and pasted to Paint. You can copy the part that you want and paste it to Excel.

Use the following keyboard commands, as needed:

✦ **PrintScreen:** Copies the entire screen to the clipboard

✦ **Alt+PrintScreen:** Copies the active window to the clipboard

Importing from a digital camera or scanner

You can bring in an image directly from a digital camera or a scanner. To use this feature, make sure that your device is connected and set up properly. Then, choose Insert ➪ Picture ➪ From Scanner or Camera. The exact procedure varies, depending on your camera or scanner. In most cases, the image appears in Microsoft Photo Editor. You can adjust the image, if necessary, and then select File ➪ Exit and Return to Excel.

 Importing images from a digital camera or scanner is a new feature in Excel 2000.

Modifying pictures

When you insert a picture on a worksheet, you can modify the picture in various ways by using the Picture toolbar, shown in Figure 20-6. This toolbar appears automatically when you select a picture object. The tools are described in Table 20-2, in left-to-right order on the toolbar.

Figure 20-6: The Picture toolbar enables you to adjust a picture.

Table 20-2	
The Tools on the Picture Toolbar	
Tool Name	*What the Tool Does*
Insert Picture from File	Displays the Insert Picture dialog box.
Image Control	Enables you to change a picture to gray-scale, black and white, or a watermark (semitransparent).
More Contrast	Increases the contrast of the picture.
Less Contrast	Decreases the contrast of the picture.
More Brightness	Increases the brightness of the picture.
Less Brightness	Decreases the brightness of the picture.
Crop	Crops the picture. After clicking this tool, drag any of the picture's handles to make the picture smaller.
Line Style	Selects a border for the picture.
Format Picture	Displays the Format Picture dialog box.
Set Transparent Color	Selects a color that will be transparent. Underlying cell contents appear through the selected transparent color. This option is not available for all types of pictures.
Reset Picture	Returns the picture to its original state.

Using Excel's Drawing Tools

The discussion so far has focused on using graphic images from other sources. If your needs involve simple (or not so simple) graphic shapes, you can use the drawing tools built into Excel to create a variety of graphics.

Beginning with Excel 97, the drawing features have been improved significantly. These tools also are available in the other Microsoft Office applications.

The Drawing toolbar

Excel's drawing tools are available from the Drawing toolbar, shown in Figure 20-7. The drawing objects feature is one of the few features in Excel that's not available from the menus. Notice that the Standard toolbar has a tool named Drawing. Clicking this tool toggles the Drawing toolbar on and off. Normally, the Drawing toolbar appears at the bottom of Excel's window, but (as with all toolbars) you can place it anywhere that you like. As you'll see, this toolbar includes more than meets the eye.

Figure 20-7: Display the Drawing toolbar to create and modify drawings.

Table 20-3 describes the tools in the Drawing toolbar. The tools are listed in the order in which they appear, from left to right.

A Word About the Draw Layer

Every worksheet and chart sheet has as a *draw layer,* an invisible surface that is completely independent of the cells on a worksheet (or the chart on a chart sheet). The draw layer can hold graphic images, drawings, embedded charts, OLE objects, and so on.

Objects placed on the draw layer can be moved, resized, copied, and deleted—with no effect on any other elements in the worksheet. Objects on the draw layer have properties that relate to how they are moved and sized when underlying cells are moved and sized. When you right-click a graphic object and choose Format Object from the shortcut menu, you get a tabbed dialog box (see the accompanying figure). Click the Properties tab to adjust how the object moves or resizes with its underlying cells. Your choices are as follows:

✦ **Move and size with cells:** If this option is selected, the object appears to be attached to the cells beneath it. For example, if you insert rows above the object, the object moves down. If you increase the column width, the object gets wider.

✦ **Move but don't size with cells:** If this option is checked, the object moves if rows or columns are inserted, but it never changes its size if you change row heights or column widths.

✦ **Don't move or size with cells:** This option makes the object completely independent of the underlying cells.

The preceding options control how an object is moved or sized with respect to the underlying cells. Excel also enables you to "attach" an object to a cell. In the Edit panel of the Options dialog box, place a check mark next to the check box labeled Cut, copy, and sort objects with cells. After you do so, graphic objects on the draw layer are attached to the underlying cells.

Because a chart sheet doesn't have cells, objects placed on a chart sheet don't have these options. Such objects do have a property, however, that relates to how the object is sized if the chart size is changed.

Table 20-3
The Tools on the Drawing Toolbar

Tool Name	What the Tool Does
Draw	Displays a menu with choices that enable you to manipulate drawn objects.
Select Objects	Selects one or more graphic objects. If you have several objects and you want to select a group of them, use this tool to drag the outline so that it surrounds all the objects. Click the button again to return to normal selection mode.
Free Rotate	Lets you freely rotate a drawn object.
AutoShapes	Displays a menu of seven categories of shapes. Drag this menu to create an AutoShapes toolbar. You also can display the AutoShapes toolbar with the Insert ➪ Picture ➪ AutoShapes command.
Line	Inserts a line.
Arrow	Inserts an arrow.
Rectangle	Inserts a rectangle or a square.
Oval	Inserts an oval or a circle.
Text Box	Inserts a free-floating box into which you type text.
WordArt	Displays the WordArt Gallery dialog box, which enables you to create attractive titles using text. You also can display this dialog box by selecting Insert ➪ Picture ➪ WordArt.
Insert Clip Art	Displays the Insert ClipArt dialog box . You can also display this dialog box with the Insert ➪ Picture ➪ Clip Art command
Fill Color	Select a fill color or fill effect for an object.
Line Color	Select the line color for an object.
Font Color	Select a font color for text objects.
Line Style	Specify the width of the lines in an object.
Dash Style	Specify the style of the lines in an object.
Arrow Style	Specify the arrow style for arrows.
Shadows	Specify the type of shadow for an object and settings for the shadow.
3-D	Specify the type of perspective effect for an object and settings for the effect.

Insert Clip Art and Line Color are two new tools of Excel 2000.

Drawing AutoShapes

Drawing objects with the AutoShapes tool is quite intuitive. The AutoShapes tool expands to display the following shape categories:

✦ **Lines:** Six styles of lines, including arrows and freehand-drawing capabilities.

✦ **Connectors:** Nine styles of lines designed to indicate connections between other objects. These objects automatically "snap to" other objects.

✦ **Basic Shapes:** Thirty-two basic shapes, including standard shapes, such as boxes and circles, and nonstandard shapes, such as a smiley face and a heart.

✦ **Block Arrows:** Twenty-eight arrow shapes.

✦ **Flowchart:** Twenty-seven shapes suitable for flowchart diagrams.

✦ **Stars and Banners:** Sixteen stars and banners. Stars are handy for drawing attention to a particular cell.

✦ **Callouts:** Twenty callouts, suitable for annotating cells.

✦ **More AutoShapes:** In Excel 2000, you can get even more AutoShapes. Clicking this button brings up a dialog box named More AutoShapes — which contains several additional shapes (actually, these are clip art images).

EXCEL 2000 More AutoShapes is a new feature of Excel 2000.

Click a tool and then drag in the worksheet to create the shape (the mouse pointer changes shape, reminding you that you're in draw mode). When you release the mouse button, the object is selected and its name appears in the Name box (see Figure 20-8).

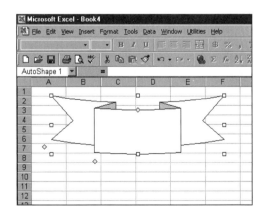

Figure 20-8: This shape was drawn on the worksheet. Its name, AutoShape1, appears in the Name box.

Formatting AutoShape objects

You can format the AutoShape objects at any time. First, you must select the object. If the object is filled with a color or pattern, you can click anywhere on the object to select it. If the object is not filled, you must click the object's border.

You can make some modifications by using the toolbar buttons — for example, change the fill color. Other modifications require that you use the Format AutoShape dialog box. After selecting one or more objects, you can bring up this dialog box by using any of the following techniques:

✦ Choose the Format ➪ AutoShape command

✦ Press Ctrl+1

✦ Double-click the object

✦ Right-click the object and choose Format AutoShape from the shortcut menu

The Format AutoShape dialog box has several tabs, the number of which depends on the type of object and whether it contains text. Each of these tabs is discussed in the following sections.

The Colors and Lines tab

Select the Colors and Lines tab to adjust the colors, lines, and arrow used in the object.

This dialog box contains more than meets the eye, and it can lead to other dialog boxes. For example, click the Color drop-down list and you can select Fill Effects — which brings up another multitabbed dialog box that enables you to specify a wide variety of fill effects.

Beginning with Excel 97, you'll find many new types of fill effects. Spend some time experimenting with these effects, and I'm sure that you'll be impressed.

The Size panel

The Size tab of the Format AutoShape dialog box (shown in Figure 20-9) enables you to adjust the size, rotation, and scale of the object. If the object is a picture, you can use the Reset button to return the object to its original dimensions and rotation.

Note   Contrary to what you might expect, if you rotate an object that contains text, the text *will not* rotate along with the object. You can also change the object's size directly by dragging the object. You can change the rotation directly by clicking the Free Rotate tool on the Drawing toolbar.

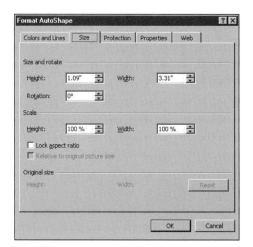

Figure 20-09: The size tab of the Format AutoShape dialog box

The Protection tab

The Protection tab determines whether the object is "locked." Locking has no effect, however, unless the worksheet is protected and the Objects option is in effect. You can protect the worksheet with the Tools ➪ Protection ➪ Protect Sheet command.

Tip

Locking an object prevents the object from being moved or resized. After you format all of your objects to your satisfaction, you should lock all objects and protect the sheet.

The Properties tab

The Properties tab of the Format AutoShape dialog box determines how an object is moved and sized with respect to the underlying cells. (See the sidebar "A Word About the Draw Layer," earlier in this chapter.)

The Font tab

The Font tab appears only if the shape contains text. It should be familiar, because its options are the same as for formatting cells.

The Alignment tab

The Alignment tab appears only if the shape contains text. You can specify the vertical and horizontal alignment of the text, and choose the orientation. Unlike text that is contained in cells, you cannot specify an angle for the orientation (you're limited to 90 degrees).

If you click the Automatic size option, the shape's size adjusts to fit the text that it contains.

The Margins tab

The Margins tab appears only if the shape contains text. Use the controls in this panel to adjust the amount of space along the sides of the text.

The Web tab

If you plan to save your worksheet as a Web page, you can specify some alternative text for the object in this tab. The alternative text appears when the user hovers the mouse pointer over the image in a Web browser.

 EXCEL 2000   The Web tab is a new feature of Excel 2000.

Changing the stack order of objects

As you add drawing objects to the draw layer of a worksheet, you'll find that objects are "stacked" on top of each other in the order in which you add them. New objects are stacked on top of older objects. Figure 20-10 shows an example of drawing objects stacked on top of one another.

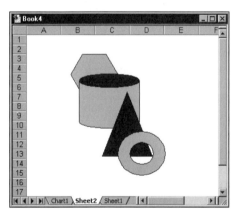

Figure 20-10: These drawing objects are stacked on top of one another.

If you find that an object is obscuring part of another, you can change the order in this stack. Right-click the object and select Order from the shortcut menu. This leads to a submenu with the following choices:

✦ **Bring to Front:** Brings the object to the top of the stack.

✦ **Send to Back:** Sends the object to the bottom of the stack.

✦ **Bring Forward:** Brings the object one step higher toward the top of the stack.

✦ **Send Backward:** Sends the object one step lower toward the bottom of the stack.

Grouping objects

Excel enables you to combine two or more drawing objects into a single object, which is known as *grouping*. For example, if you create a design that uses four separate drawing objects, you can combine them into a group. Then, you can manipulate this group as a single object (move it, resize it, and so on).

To group two or more objects, select all the objects and then right-click. Choose Grouping ➪ Group from the shortcut menu.

Later, if you need to modify one of the objects in the group, you can ungroup them by right-clicking and selecting Grouping ➪ Ungroup from the shortcut menu. This breaks the object into its original components.

Aligning objects

When you have several drawing objects on a worksheet, you may want to align these objects with each other. You can either drag the objects (which isn't very precise) or use the automatic alignment options.

Figure 20-11 shows objects before and after they were aligned to the left.

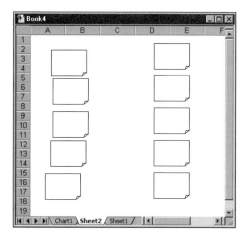

Figure 20-11: The objects on the left are not aligned. Those on the right are aligned to the left.

To align objects, start by selecting them. Then, click the Draw tool on the Drawing toolbar. This tool expands to show a menu. Select the Align or Distribute menu option, followed by any of the six alignment options: Align Left, Align Center, Align Right, Align Top, Align Middle, or Align Bottom.

Note   Unfortunately, you can't specify which object is used as the basis for the align-ment. When you're aligning objects to the left, they are always aligned with the leftmost object. When you're aligning objects to the top, they are always aligned with the topmost object. Alignment in other directions works the same way.

Spacing objects evenly

Excel can also "distribute" three or more objects such that they are equally spaced, horizontally or vertically. Select the objects and then click the Draw tool on the Drawing toolbar. This tool expands to show a menu. Select the Align or Distribute menu option, followed by either Distribute Horizontally or Distribute Vertically.

Changing the AutoShape defaults

You can change the default settings for the AutoShapes that you draw. For example, if you prefer a particular text color or fill color, you can set these as the defaults for all new AutoShapes that you draw.

To change the default settings, create an object and format it as you like. You can change colors, fill effects, line widths and styles, and shadow or 3D effects. Then, select the formatted object, right-click, and select Set AutoShape Defaults from the shortcut menu. You can also access this command from the Draw tool on the Drawing toolbar (this tool expands to show a menu).

Adding shadows and 3D effects

You can apply attractive shadow and 3D effects to AutoShapes (except for those in the Line and Connectors categories). Use the Shadow and 3D tools on the Drawing toolbar to apply these effects.

Shadows and 3D effects are mutually exclusive. In other words, you can apply either a shadow or a 3D effect to an AutoShape—not both.

To apply either of these effects, select an AutoShape that you've drawn on a worksheet and then click either the Shadow or the 3D tool. The tool expands to show a list of options (see Figure 20-12). Select an option, and it's applied to the selected shape.

You can adjust the Shadow or 3D settings by clicking the appropriate tool and then selecting the Shadow Settings or 3D Settings option. Both of these options display a toolbar that enables you to fine-tune the effect. You'll find that *lots* of options are available, and they're all quite straightforward. The best way to become familiar with these effects is to experiment.

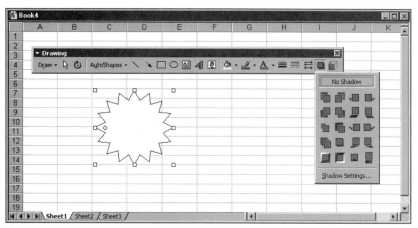

Figure 20-12: Clicking the Shadow tool displays a list of shadow options.

Using WordArt

WordArt is an application that's included with Microsoft Office. You can insert a WordArt image either by using the WordArt tool on the Drawing toolbar or by selecting Insert ➪ Picture ➪ WordArt. Either method displays the WordArt Gallery dialog box (see Figure 20-13). Select a style and then enter your text in the next dialog box. Click OK, and the image is inserted in the worksheet.

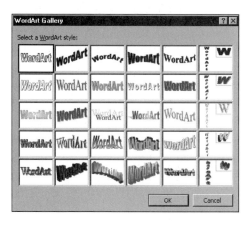

Figure 20-13: The WordArt Gallery dialog box enables you to select a general style for your image.

When you select a WordArt image, Excel displays the WordArt toolbar. Use these tools to modify the WordArt image. You'll find that you have *lots* of flexibility with these tools. In addition, you can use the Shadow and 3D tools to further manipulate the image. Figure 20-14 shows an example of a WordArt image inserted on a worksheet.

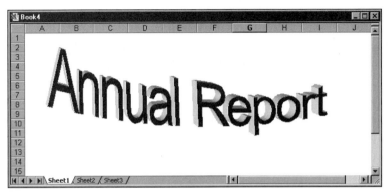

Figure 20-14: An example of WordArt

Drawing Tips

Although drawing objects is quite intuitive, several tips can make this task easier. This section lists some tips and techniques that you should know:

✦ To create an object with the same height and width, press Shift while you draw the object.

✦ To constrain a line or arrow object to angles that are divisible by 15 degrees, press Shift while you draw the object.

✦ To make an object snap to the worksheet row and column gridlines, press the Alt key while you draw the object.

✦ If you press Alt while moving an object, its upper-left corner snaps to the row and column gridlines.

✦ To select multiple objects, press Ctrl while you click them. Or, use the Select Objects tool on the Drawing toolbar to select objects by "lassoing" them.

✦ To select all objects on a worksheet, select Edit ⇨ Go To (or press F5) and then click the Special button in the Go To dialog box. Choose the Objects option button and click OK. All objects are selected. Use this technique if you want to delete all objects (select them all and then press Delete).

✦ You can insert text into most of the AutoShapes (the exceptions are the shapes in the Connectors and Lines categories). To add text to a shape, right-click it and select Add Text from the shortcut menu.

✦ You might find that working with drawing objects is easier if you turn off the worksheet grid line. The snap-to-gridline features work, even if the grid lines aren't visible.

✦ You can control how objects appear onscreen by using the View tab of the Options dialog box. Normally, the Show All option is selected. You can hide all objects by choosing Hide All, or display objects as placeholders by choosing

Show Placeholders (this may speed up things if you have complex objects that take a long time to redraw).

✦ To copy an object with the mouse, single-click it to select it and then press Ctrl while you drag it.

✦ If an object contains text, you can rotate the text 90 degrees by using the Alignment tab on the Format Object dialog box.

✦ By default, drawn objects are printed along with the worksheet. If you don't want the objects to print, access the Sheet panel of the Page Setup dialog box and select the Draft option. Or, right-click the object, select Format from the shortcut menu, and then uncheck the Print Object check box in the Properties panel.

✦ If you want the underlying cell contents to show through a drawn object, access the Colors and Lines tab in the Format dialog box and then set the Fill option to No Fill. You can also select the Semi-transparent option, which enables you to choose a fill color *and* have the cell contents show.

✦ If you save your file as a Web page, each drawn object is stored as a separate GIF file.

A Gallery of Drawing Examples

This section provides you with some examples of using Excel's drawing tools. Perhaps these examples will get your own creative juices flowing.

Calling attention to a cell

The AutoShapes in the Stars and Banners category are useful for calling attention to a particular cell or range to make it stand out from the others. Figure 20-15 shows two examples (one subtle, one more flamboyant) of how you can make one cell's value jump out.

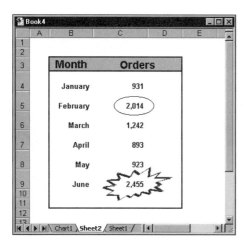

Figure 20-15: Two ways of making a particular cell stand out

Creating shapes with shadow and 3D effects

Figure 20-16 shows a sample of several objects that have various shadow and 3D effects applied. As you can see, the effects can be quite varied.

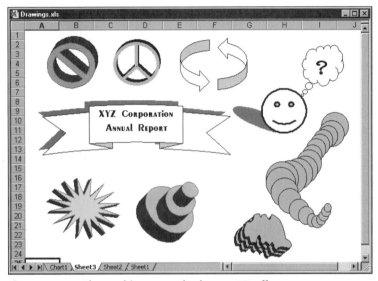

Figure 20-16: These objects use shadow or 3D effects.

Creating organizational charts

Figure 20-17 shows a simple organizational chart that was created with the AutoShape drawing tools. The shapes in the Connectors and Flowchart categories were used and then 3D effects were added. To make the box size consistent, one box was created and then copied several times.

You can also create an organizational chart by selecting Insert ➪ Picture ➪ Organization Chart. This starts the Microsoft Organization Chart application that inserts an OLE object into the worksheet.

Changing the look of cell comments

If a cell contains a cell comment, you can replace the normal comment box with any of the AutoShapes in the Callouts category. Select the cell comment and then click the Draw tool on the Drawing toolbar. This tool expands to show a menu. Select Change AutoShape ➪ Callouts, followed by the desired callout shape. Figure 20-18 shows an example of cell comments that use different AutoShapes.

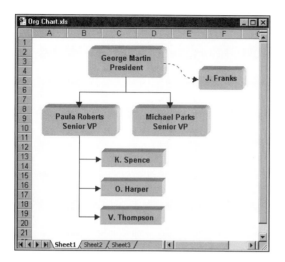

Figure 20-17: This organizational chart was created with Excel's drawing tools.

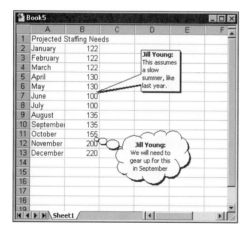

Figure 20-18: These cell comments use different AutoShapes.

Linking text in an object to a cell

As an alternative to typing text directly into an object, consider creating a link to a cell. After doing so, the text displayed in the object reflects the current contents of the linked cell. Figure 20-19 shows an AutoShape that is linked to a cell. The shape is selected; notice that the edit line displays a formula.

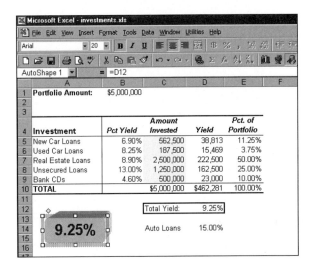

Figure 20-19: The text in the AutoShape is linked to cell D12.

To link an AutoShape to a cell, select the object and then click in the edit line. Enter a simple cell reference, such as =A1, and press Enter. You can format the text in the shape independent of the format of the cell. For best results, access the shape's Format dialog box and change the following settings:

✦ Automatic margins (Margins tab)

✦ Automatic size (Alignment tab)

✦ Center Horizontal alignment and Center Vertical alignment (Alignment tab)

Creating flow diagrams

You also can create flow diagrams by using the drawing tools. The shapes in the Connectors and Flowchart categories are most useful. This capability often is useful to describe how a process or system works. Figure 20-20 shows an example of a flow diagram. After creating the diagram, all the objects were selected and grouped together so that the diagram could be moved as a single unit.

Annotating a chart

One of the most common uses of the drawing tools is to annotate a chart. For example, you can add descriptive text with an arrow, to call attention to a certain data point. This technique works for both embedded charts and charts on chart sheets. Figure 20-21 shows an example of an embedded chart that has been annotated.

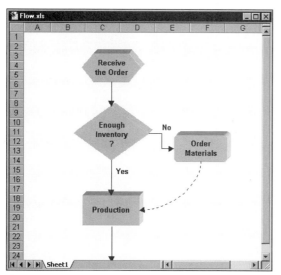

Figure 20-20: This flow diagram was created with Excel's drawing tools.

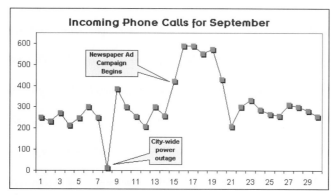

Figure 20-21: Annotating a chart with the drawing tools

Pasting pictures of cells

One of Excel's best-kept secrets is its ability to copy and paste pictures of cells. You can copy a cell or range and then paste a picture of the cell or range on any worksheet. The picture can be static or linked. With a linked picture, the link is to the cells. In other words, if you change the contents of a cell that's in a picture, the picture changes.

To create a picture of a cell or range, select a range and choose Edit ⇨ Copy. Then press Shift and click the Edit menu (pressing Shift is essential). Choose Paste Picture to create a static picture, or choose Paste Picture Link to paste a linked picture of the selection.

If you don't hold down Shift when you select the Edit menu, the Paste Picture and Paste Picture Link commands do not appear.

Figure 20-22 shows an example of a linked picture, with some additional formatting to the picture object (fill color and a shadow). Notice that the picture displays a cell reference in the formula bar.

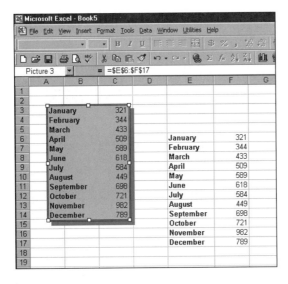

Figure 20-22: This picture is linked to the cells in E6:F17.

Cross-Reference   Using linked pictures is particularly useful for printing noncontiguous ranges. See "Printing Noncontiguous Ranges on a Single Page" in Chapter 14 for more information.

Summary

This chapter covers several types of graphic information that you can add to a worksheet's draw layer: imported graphic images, objects that you draw by using Excel's drawing tools, and other objects, such as WordArt or an OLE object, from Microsoft's Organization Chart application. Several examples demonstrate some ways that you can use these objects in your workbooks.

✦   ✦   ✦

Creating Maps with Microsoft Map

In previous chapters, you saw how you can use a chart to display data in a different — and, usually, more meaningful — way. This chapter explores the topic of mapping and describes how to present geographic information in the form of a map.

The mapping feature is not actually part of Excel. Rather, this feature uses an OLE server application named *Microsoft Map*, which was developed by MapInfo Corporation. You can use this application to insert maps into other Microsoft Office applications. Because the mapping application is not part of Excel, you'll find that the user interface is quite different from that of Excel. When a map is active, Microsoft Map menus and toolbars replace Excel's menus and toolbars.

Mapping an Overview

Mapping, like charting, is a tool that visually presents data. People use maps for a variety of purposes, but the common factor in maps is that they work with data that has a basis in geography. If you classify information by state, province, or country, chances are good that you can represent the data on a map. For example, if your company sells its products throughout the United States, showing the annual sales for each state may be useful.

A mapping example

Figure 21-1 shows sales data for a company, with the data categorized by state. To understand this information, you would have to spend a lot of time examining the data.

	A	B	C	D	E
1	State	Product A	Product B	Combined	
2	AK	262,542	0	262,542	
3	AL	92,629	193,254	285,883	
4	AR	19,690	169,615	189,305	
5	AZ	252,523	183,384	435,907	
6	CA	3,692,909	2,135,068	5,827,977	
7	CO	377,034	149,875	526,909	
8	CT	327,585	425,939	753,524	
9	DC	114,492	63,118	177,610	
10	DE	1,233	108,471	109,704	
11	FL	582,033	851,978	1,434,011	
12	GA	408,371	299,702	708,073	
13	HI	43,428	43,378	86,806	
14	IA	128,260	43,378	171,638	
15	ID	0	122,239	122,239	
16	IL	769,711	837,597	1,607,308	
17	IN	262,542	236,633	499,175	
18	KS	116,416	145,927	262,343	
19	KY	39,430	86,757	126,187	
20	LA	96,676	43,378	140,054	
21	MA	656,947	449,627	1,106,574	
22	MD	402,449	609,373	1,011,822	

Figure 21-1: Raw data that shows sales by state

Figure 21-2 shows the same data displayed in a chart. Although an improvement over the raw-data table, this type of presentation doesn't really work, because it has too many data points. In addition, the chart doesn't reveal any information about sales in a particular region.

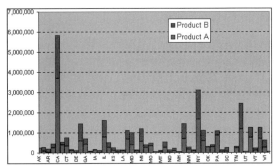

Figure 21-2: The sales data displayed in a chart

Figure 21-3 shows the sales data presented as a map (it looks even better in color). This presentation uses different colors to represent various sales ranges. Looking at the map, you can see clearly that this company performs much better in some regions than in others.

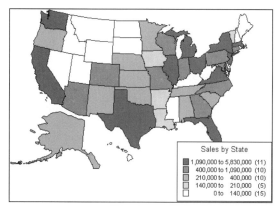

Figure 21-3: The sales data displayed in a map

The map in Figure 21-3 might be even more revealing if the sales were represented relative to the population of each state; that is, in per capita sales. This population data is available as a sample file on the Office CD (Mapstats.xls).

Figure 21-4 shows the contents sheet for this workbook.

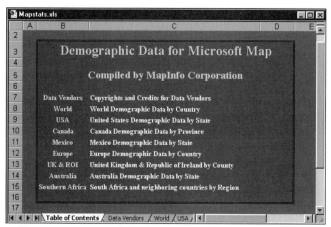

Figure 21-4: The Mapstats workbook contains population statistics that you can use in your maps.

Available maps

The Microsoft Map feature supports a good variety of maps and enables you to create maps in several different formats. A single map can display multiple sets of data, each in a different format. For example, your map can show sales by state and indicate the number of sales offices in each state. In addition, your map can display other accoutrements, such as labels and pin markers.

The maps included with Microsoft Map are listed in Table 21-1. As you'll see later in this chapter, a map can be zoomed to display only a portion of it. Therefore, you can use the Europe map to zoom in on a particular region or country.

Table 21-1
Maps Included with Microsoft Map

Map	Description
Australia	The continent of Australia, by state
Canada	The country of Canada, by province
Europe	The continent of Europe, by country
Mexico	The country of Mexico, by state
North America	The countries of North America (Canada, United States, Mexico)
U.K. Standard Regions	The countries of the United Kingdom, by region
U.S. in North America	United States (excluding Alaska and Hawaii insets), by state
U.S. with AK and HI Insets	United States (with Alaska and Hawaii insets), by state
World Countries	The world, by country

If you would like to order additional maps or data from MapInfo, you can contact the company directly or visit its Web site. For information on how to do so, activate a map and click the Help ➪ About command.

Creating a Map

Creating a basic map with Microsoft Map is simple. In almost all cases, however, you'll want to customize the map. This section discusses the basics of mapmaking.

Setting up your data

The Microsoft Map feature works with data stored in a list format (for an example, refer to Figure 21-1). The first column should contain names of map regions (such as states or countries). The columns to the right should contain data for each area. You can have any number of data columns, because you select the columns to use after the map is created.

Creating the map

To create a map, start by selecting the data. The selection must include one column of area names and at least one column of data. If the columns have descriptive headers, include these in the selection.

Choose Insert ➪ Map (or click the Map button on the Standard toolbar). Click and drag to specify the location and size of the map or just click to create a map of the default size. Unlike charts, maps must be embedded on a worksheet (there are no separate map sheets).

Microsoft Map analyzes the area labels and generates the appropriate map. If two or more maps are possible (or if you've developed any custom map templates), you'll see the Multiple Maps Available dialog box, shown in Figure 21-5. Select the map that you want to use from this list.

Figure 21-5: If multiple maps are available for your data, you can choose from this dialog box which map to use.

You don't have the Insert ➪ Map command? Excel's mapping feature is performed by an OLE server application. The mapping feature is not an integral part of Excel, and it may not be installed on your system. If you don't see a Map command on the Insert menu, you need to install the mapping feature.

To install the mapping feature, you need to rerun Excel's Setup program (or the Microsoft Office Setup program) and specify the mapping feature. Microsoft Map displays the map using the first column of data. It also displays the Microsoft Map Control dialog box, discussed later in the chapter. When the map is created, it is activated. Whenever a map is activated, Microsoft Map's menus and toolbar replace Excel's menus and toolbars. When you click outside the map, Excel's user interface reappears. You can reactivate a map by double-clicking it.

Setting the map format(s)

When a map first appears, the Microsoft Map Control dialog box is visible (see Figure 21-6). Use this dialog box to change the format of the selected map. You can use the Show/Hide Map Control tool to toggle the display of this dialog box.

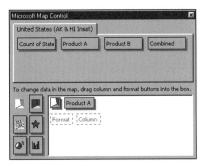

Figure 21-6: The Microsoft Map Control dialog box

By default, you create maps by using the value-shading map format. You can change the format or display two or more formats on a single map. You use the Microsoft Map Control dialog box by dragging the items in it. The top of the dialog box displays all available data fields (which correspond to the columns that you selected when you created the map). The bottom part contains the map format information. Six format icons on the left determine the map format (described in the sections that follow). You combine a map format icon with one or more data fields by dragging the icon. For example, you can replace the default map format icon with another one simply by dragging the new icon over the existing one. Some map formats use more than one data field. In such a case, you can drag additional data fields next to the icon.

To change options for a particular map format, either double-click the format icon or use the Map menu and choose the menu command that is appropriate for the format that you want to change. In either case, you get a dialog box that's appropriate for the map format.

The following sections include descriptions (and samples) of each map format supported by Microsoft Map.

Value shading

With this map format, each map region is shaded based on the value of its data. This format is appropriate for data-quantitative information, such as sales, population, and so on. Figure 21-7 shows an example of a map formatted with value shading (this map is zoomed to show only part of the United States). In this example, the sales are broken down into four ranges, and each sales range is associated with different shading.

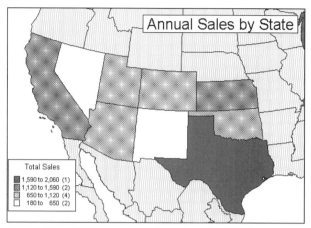

Figure 21-7: This map uses the value-shading format.

You can change the interval ranges in the Format Properties dialog box, shown in Figure 21-8.

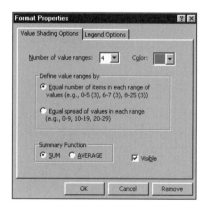

Figure 21-8: The Value Shading Options tab of the Format Properties dialog box

When you're viewing a map that uses value shading, choose Map ➪ Value Shading Options, and Microsoft Map opens the value-shading version of the Format Properties dialog box. You can specify the number of value ranges and the method of defining the ranges — an equal number of areas in each range or an equal spread of values in each range. You also can select a color for the shading. The map displays different variations of the single color that you select. You can choose the summary function to use (SUM or AVERAGE). To hide the format from the map, remove the check mark from the Visible check box.

Category shading

With the category-shading map format, each map region is colored based on a data value. The map legend has one entry (color) for every value of the data range. Therefore, this format is appropriate for data that has a small number of discrete values. For example, you can use the format to identify states that have a sales office, the number of sales reps in a country, and so on. A common use for this format is to identify the states that make up each sales region. Data need not be numeric. For example, the data can consist of text such as Yes and No.

Figure 21-9 shows a map that uses category shading to identify states that met the annual sales goal.

Figure 21-9: This map uses the category-shading format.

To change the colors in the categories, use the Format Properties dialog box. Again, when you're viewing a map that uses category shading, you can open this dialog box by choosing Map ➪ Category Shading Options. Microsoft Map displays the category-shading version of the Format Options dialog box.

Dot density

The dot-density map format displays data as a series of dots. Larger values translate into more dots. The dots are placed randomly within a map region. Figure 21-10 shows an example of a map that uses the dot-density format. This map depicts population in the United Kingdom and Ireland. Each dot represents 100,000 people.

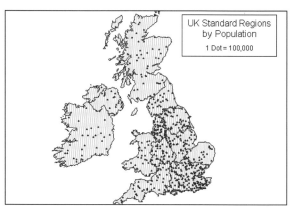

Figure 21-10: A dot-density format map, showing the population of the United Kingdom and Ireland

To change the number of units for each dot or to change the dot size, access the Dot Density Options tab of the Format Properties dialog box, which is shown in Figure 21-11.

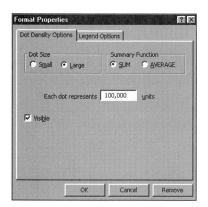

Figure 21-11: The Dot Density Options tab of the Format Properties dialog box

Graduated symbol

The graduated-symbol map format displays a symbol, the size of which is proportional to the area's data value. Figure 21-12 shows an example of this format. I used a Wingdings font character for the symbol. To change the symbol, use the Graduated Symbol Options dialog box. You can select a font, size, and specific character.

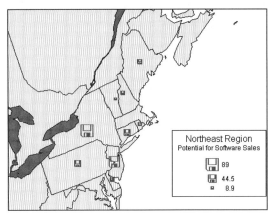

Figure 21-12: A graduated-symbol format map

Pie chart

The pie-chart map format requires at least two columns of data. Maps with this format display a pie chart within each map region. Figure 21-13 shows an example. This map shows a pie chart that depicts the relative sales of three products for each state.

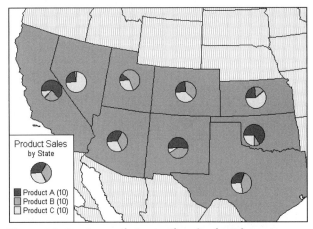

Figure 21-13: A map that uses the pie-chart format

To change the setting for a pie-chart format map, use the Pie Chart Options tab of the Format Properties dialog box, shown in Figure 21-14. This dialog box enables you to select a color for each pie slice. If you choose the Graduated option, the size of each pie is proportional to the sum or average of the data. If you don't use the Graduated option, you also can set the diameter of the pies.

Figure 21-14: The Pie Chart Options tab of the Format Properties dialog box

Column chart

The column-chart map format is similar to the pie-chart format — except that it displays a column chart instead of a pie chart. Figure 21-15 shows an example.

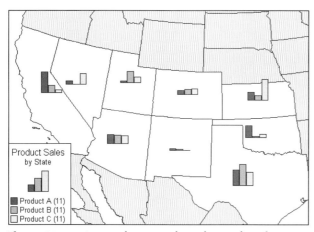

Figure 21-15: A map that uses the column-chart format

Combining map formats

As previously mentioned, a single map can include multiple formats for different data. You do this by stacking groups of icons and data fields in the Microsoft Map Control dialog box. For example, you can display sales as value shading and the number of customers as a dot-density map. Each map format has its own legend.

Overlaying multiple map types has no rules, so some experimentation usually is necessary. Unless the map is very simple, however, you're generally better off using only one or two map types per map; otherwise, the map gets so complicated that the original goal (making the data clear) is lost.

Figure 21-16 shows an example of a map that uses two formats. The value-shading format shows sales broken down into four categories. The graduated-symbol format shows the states that have a sales office.

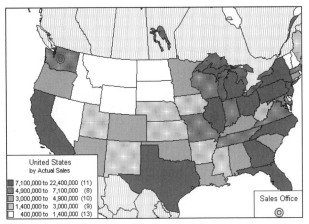

United States
by Actual Sales

7,100,000 to 22,400,000 (11)
4,900,000 to 7,100,000 (8)
3,000,000 to 4,900,000 (10)
1,400,000 to 3,000,000 (9)
400,000 to 1,400,000 (13)

Sales Office

Figure 21-16: An example of a map that uses two map formats: the value-shading format and the graduated-symbol format

Customizing Maps

After you create a map, you have numerous customization options from which to choose, which are described in the following sections.

Zooming in and out

Microsoft Map enables you to zoom your map in and out. Zooming in displays less of the map and zooming out displays more of the map (or makes the entire map smaller). Use the Zoom Percentage of Map control on the toolbar (no menu commands exist).

To zoom in, select a zoom percentage greater than 100 percent. To zoom out, select a zoom percentage less than 100 percent. Before you zoom out, you might want to specify the point that will be the center of the map (use the Center Map toolbar button).

Using the Microsoft Map Toolbar

Whenever a map is activated, the Microsoft Map toolbar appears (see the accompanying figure). Note that this isn't one of Excel's toolbars; rather, this is a special toolbar that appears only when a map is activated. This toolbar is handy for manipulating and customizing the map.

The tools on the Microsoft Map toolbar, from left to right, and their corresponding functions are presented in the following table.

Tool	Purpose
Select Objects	Changes mouse pointer into an arrow, to select objects in the map
Grabber	Reposition the map within the map window
Center Map	Specify the center of the map
Map Labels	Add geography labels or data values in the map
Add Text	Add free-floating text to the map
Custom Pin Map	Add pins to the map, to indicate specific locations
Display Entire	Displays the entire (unzoomed) map
Redraw Map	Redraws the map
Show/Hide Microsoft Map Control	Toggles the display of the floating Microsoft Map Control dialog box
Zoom Percentage of Map	Changes how much of the map that you view
Help	Provides help for a menu item or toolbar button

Repositioning a map

You'll find that, after zooming in or out, the map may not be optimally positioned within the map object rectangle. Use the Grabber tool to move the map image within the map object. Just click and drag the map to reposition it.

Adding labels

Usually, a map doesn't have labels to identify areas. You can't automatically add labels to all areas (for example, all states in the United States), but you can add individual labels, one at a time. You also can insert data values that correspond to a particular map region (such as sales for West Virginia).

Use the Label tool to add labels or data values. When you click the Label tool, the dialog box shown in Figure 21-17 appears. The option button labeled Map feature names refers to labels for the various parts of the map (for example, state names in a U.S. map). When you select the Values from option, you can insert data values from a category in the list box. After closing the dialog box, you can drag the mouse pointer over the map. The label or data value appears when the mouse pointer is over a map region. Just click to place the label or data value and then repeat this procedure for each map label or data value that you want to add. Figure 21-18 shows a map that uses labels and data values.

Figure 21-17: The Map Labels dialog box enables you to add labels or data values to your map.

To move a label, click and drag it to a new location. You can change the font, size, or color of a label by double-clicking it. Stretching the label (by dragging a border) also makes the font larger or smaller.

Figure 21-18: This map has labels and data values.

Adding text

Besides the labels described in the preceding section, you can add free-floating text to your map by using the Text tool. Just click the Text tool, click the area of the map where you want to add text, and enter your text. You can manipulate text the same way that you manipulate labels.

If you don't like the fact that a map title always has a border around it (and the border can't be removed), delete the title and create your own with the Text tool.

Adding pins to a map

In some cases, you may want to add one or more identifier icons to your map. This is similar in concept to inserting pins in a wall map to identify various places.

Clicking the Custom Pin Map tool displays a dialog box that asks you to enter a name for a custom pin map (or choose an existing pin map). Enter a descriptive label; you'll be able to bring these same pins into another map (of the same type) later. For example, if you're identifying sales office locations, you can then add the same pins to another map.

When you close the dialog box, the mouse pointer changes to a pushpin. You can place these pins anywhere in your map. When you click the map to place a pin, you also can enter descriptive text. Double-clicking a pin enables you to change the symbol that is used to something other than a pin. Figure 21-19 shows a map with pins added to it.

Figure 21-19: This map has pins to identify specific locations.

Modifying the legend

You have quite a bit of control over the legend in a map. Note that a map displays a separate legend for each map format that it uses. To modify a legend, double-click it to see the dialog box shown in Figure 21-20.

Figure 21-20: The Legend Options tab of the Format Properties dialog box

You can display a legend in a compact format or in its normal format. A compact format takes up less space, but it doesn't give many details. You also can change the legend's title and subtitle (and enter a different title for a compacted legend). Other buttons enable you to adjust the font (including size and color) and edit the labels that are used in the legend.

To make other changes to the legend — such as changing the number of data ranges that are used — select the appropriate menu item on the Map menu. For example, to change the number of ranges that are used in a value-shading map format, select the Map ⇨ Value Shading Options command.

Adding and removing features

You can add or remove certain features of a map. When you select Map ⇨ Features, you see the Map Features dialog box (see Figure 21-21), which lists all available features for the selected map. To turn on a feature, place a check mark next to it. To turn off a feature, remove the check mark. The features available vary with the map that you're using. If a feature doesn't appear in the list, you can add it by clicking the Add button.

Figure 21-21: The Map Features dialog box

Figure 21-22 shows a North America map with some features added (major cities, major highways, and world oceans) and some features removed (Canada and Mexico).

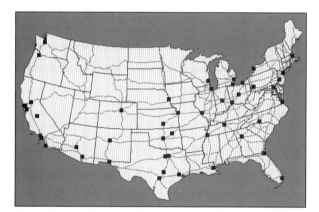

Figure 21-22: This map has features added and removed.

Table 21-2 lists the features available for each map. You can, however, add features from different maps — add world oceans to a North America map, for example.

In some cases, you may want your map to display only specific areas. For example, if your company does business in Missouri, Illinois, Kansas, and Nebraska, you can create a map that shows only these four states. Create a map that includes these states and then remove all features from the map by using the Map ⇨ Features command. The map then shows only those areas that have data. Figure 21-23 shows an example.

Table 21-2 **Available Map Features**	
Map	*Features*
Australia	Airports, Cities, Highways, Major Cities
Canada	Airports, Cities, Forward Sortation Areas, Highways, Lakes, Major Cities
Europe	Airports, Cities, Highways, Major Cities
Mexico	Cities, Highways, Major Cities
U.K.	Two-Digit Post Codes, Airports, Cities, Highways, Major Cities, Standard Regions
U.S. in North America	Five-Digit Zip Code Centers, Highways, Major Cities, Great Lakes
U.S. (AK & HI Inset)	Airports, Cities, Major Cities
World	Capitals, Countries, Graticule, Oceans

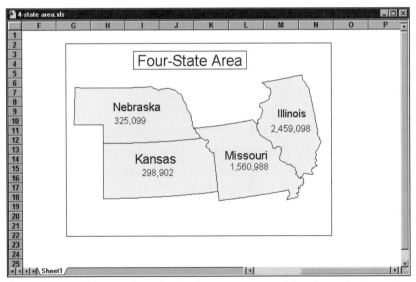

Figure 21-23: This map has all of its features removed, leaving only the states for which data is provided.

Plotting United States ZIP codes

Besides recognizing geographic place names, Microsoft Map recognizes U.S. five-digit ZIP codes. If the data that you select contains more than one type of geographic data (for example, state names and ZIP codes), you need to specify which field to use in the map as the geographic data. Figure 21-24 shows the Specify Geographic Data dialog box, which warns you of the existence of more than one type of data that qualifies as geographic data.

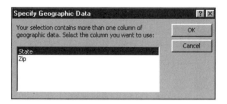

Figure 21-24: The Specify Geographic Data dialog box enables you to select the data to use as geographic data.

If you want to create a map that uses ZIP codes, make sure that your ZIP codes are formatted as values, not as text. Otherwise, Microsoft Map won't recognize them as ZIP codes.

Because ZIP codes are continually being added, Microsoft Map may not recognize all of your ZIP codes. If Microsoft Map encounters an unknown ZIP code, you receive the Resolve Unknown Geographic Data dialog box, shown in Figure 21-25. This dialog box gives you the opportunity to change the ZIP code to another one. Or, you can simply discard that item of data by clicking the Discard button.

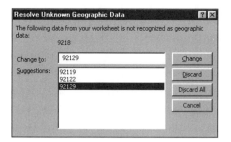

Figure 21-25: Microsoft Map displays the Resolve Unknown Geographic Data dialog box when it doesn't recognize a geographic name.

Figure 21-26 shows a map that depicts customers by their ZIP codes. This is a graduated-symbol map (the default format when ZIP codes are used as data). Note that the symbols appear on the geographic centers of the ZIP codes and don't shade the entire ZIP code areas.

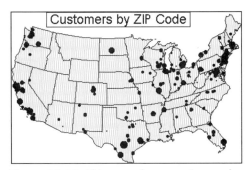

Figure 21-26: This map shows customers by ZIP code centers.

Adding more data to a map

After you create a map, you can add additional data to it. Use the Insert ➪ Data command to add data from a worksheet range, or use the Insert ➪ External Data command to add new data from a database file. Make sure that the data includes geographic labels that match the map to which you're adding data.

Map templates

As you may have figured out by now, getting a map just right can sometimes take a lot of time. Fortunately, you can save a map template, so that you can reuse the settings for another map. To do so, create and customize the map and then choose Map ➪ Save Map Template. You can save a template that includes the following:

✦ The features that you've added or removed

✦ A particular view (zoomed in or out)

✦ Both of the preceding items

Saved templates then appear in the Multiple Maps Available dialog box, which appears when you create a map.

Converting a Map to a Picture

You'll find that working with maps sometimes can be rather sluggish — a great deal of work goes on behind the scenes. When you finish with your map, you can convert it to a static picture that is no longer linked to the data. Click the map once to select it (don't double-click it) and then choose Edit ➪ Copy. Then, select Edit ➪ Paste Special and choose the Picture (Enhanced Metafile) option. This creates an unlinked picture of the map. Then, you can select the original map object and delete it.

If you convert a map to a picture, no way exists to link data back to the picture. If any of your data changes or you want to make modifications to the map, you have to re-create the map.

Learning More

The Microsoft Map feature is relatively complex, and it definitely takes time to master. The best way to master this feature is simply to create some maps and perform customizations. As previously mentioned, the user interface is different from Excel's, so you'll have to try some new techniques. Generally, you can find your way around maps by doing the following:

✦ Double-clicking objects

✦ Right-clicking objects

✦ Exploring the menus (they change somewhat, depending on the type of map)

✦ Using the Microsoft Map toolbar

Summary

This chapter covers Excel's new Microsoft Map feature — which is actually an OLE server application developed by MapInfo Corporation. Some data is more appropriate for a map than for a chart, and this chapter demonstrates the difference. This chapter also describes the basics of creating and customizing maps and provides an example of each map format.

✦   ✦   ✦

Putting It All Together

The preceding chapters present basic information about how Excel works. But you probably already realize that simply knowing the commands and shortcuts won't help you create successful workbooks. This chapter helps you to tie everything together, and provides some pointers and examples to help you develop workbooks that do what you want them to do.

The Audience for Spreadsheets

Before you get too far into this chapter, pause and think about spreadsheets in general. Spreadsheets can be classified in many ways, but the following two broad categories provide a useful place to start:

✦ Spreadsheets that you develop for your own use

✦ Spreadsheets that others will use

As you'll see, the way in which you develop your spreadsheet — and the amount of time and effort that you put into it — often depends on who is the ultimate user (you alone or others).

Developing spreadsheets for yourself

If you're the only person who will use a particular spreadsheet, you should be less concerned with issues such as security, ease of use, and error handling than you would be if you were creating the spreadsheet for others. After all, you develop the spreadsheet and thus know how it is designed. If an error occurs, you can simply track down the source and correct the problem.

Quick-and-dirty spreadsheets

Chances are good that many of the spreadsheets you develop for your own use are "quick-and-dirty"—usually fairly small and developed to solve a problem or answer a question quickly. For example, you're about to buy a new car and want to figure out your monthly payment for various loan amounts. Or, you need to generate a chart that shows your company's monthly sales, so you quickly enter 12 values, whip off a chart, and paste it into your word processing document.

In these examples, you don't really care what the spreadsheet looks like, as long as it gives you the correct answer (or in the case of the second example, produces a nice-looking chart). You can probably input the entire model in a few minutes, and you certainly won't take the time to document your work. In many cases, you won't even bother to save the file.

For-your-eyes-only spreadsheets

As the name implies, this category includes spreadsheets created by you that no one else will ever see or use. For example, a file in which you keep information that is relevant to your income taxes. You open the file whenever a check comes in the mail, you incur an expense that can be justified as business-related, you buy tax-deductible Girl Scout cookies, and so on. Another example is a spreadsheet that you use to keep track of your employees' time records (sick leave, vacation, and such).

Spreadsheets that are for your eyes only differ from the quick-and-dirty ones in that you use them more than once; therefore, you save these spreadsheets to files. Again, though, these are spreadsheets that are not worth spending a great deal of time on—you may apply some simple formatting, but that's about it (after all, you don't really need to impress yourself—or do you?). Like the quick-and-dirty kind, this type of spreadsheet lacks any type of error detection, because you already understand how the formulas are set up and, thus, know enough to avoid inputting data that produces erroneous results. If an error does crop up, you probably immediately know what caused it.

Spreadsheets in this category sometimes increase in sophistication over time. For example, I have an Excel workbook that I use to track my income by source. This workbook was simple when I first set it up, but I tend to add accoutrements to it nearly every time I use it: more summary formulas, better formatting, and even a chart that displays income by month. My latest modification was to add a trend line to the chart to project income based on past trends.

Developing spreadsheets for others

If others will use a spreadsheet that you are developing, you need to pay a lot more attention to minor details. Because of this, such a spreadsheet usually takes longer to create than one that only you will see. The amount of extra effort depends, in large part, on the experience level of the other users. A spreadsheet that will be utilized by an inexperienced computer user is often the most difficult to develop, simply because you need to make sure that it's "bulletproof." In other words, you don't want the user to mess things up (erase a formula, for example). In addition, you have to make perfectly clear how the spreadsheet should be used. This often means adding more formatting and instructions for the user.

As you'll discover in later chapters, you can use Excel as a complete application-development environment and create sophisticated applications that may not even look like a normal spreadsheet. Doing so almost always requires using macros and custom interface elements, such as buttons, custom toolbars, and custom menus.

Characteristics of a Successful Spreadsheet

You create a spreadsheet to accomplish some end result, which could be any of thousands of things. If the spreadsheet is successful, it meets most or all of the following criteria (some of which are appropriate only if the spreadsheet is used by others):

✦ It enables the end-user to perform a task that he or she probably would not be able to do otherwise—or a task that would take *much* longer to do manually.

✦ It's the appropriate solution to the problem.

Using a spreadsheet isn't always the most suitable approach. For example, you can create an organizational chart with Excel, but if you create organizational charts for a living, you're better off with a software product designed specifically for that task.

✦ It accomplishes its goal.

This may seem like an obvious prerequisite, but I've seen many spreadsheets that fail to meet this test.

✦ It produces accurate results.

As you may have discovered by now, creating formulas that produce the wrong results is quite easy. In most cases, returning no answer is better than returning an incorrect one.

✦ It doesn't let the user accidentally (or intentionally) delete or modify important components.

Excel has built-in features to help in this area (see "Applying Appropriate Protection," later in this chapter).

✦ It doesn't let the user enter inappropriate data.

Excel data-validation features make this type of checking easier than ever.

✦ It's laid out clearly so that the user always knows how to proceed.

I've opened far too many spreadsheets and not had a clue as to how to proceed — or even what the purpose of the spreadsheet was.

✦ Its formulas and macros are well documented so that, if necessary, they can be changed.

✦ It is designed so that it can be modified in simple ways without making major changes.

You can create spreadsheets at many different levels, ranging from simple fill-in-the-blank templates to extremely complex applications that utilize custom menus and dialog boxes, and that may not even look like spreadsheets. The remainder of this chapter focuses on relatively simple spreadsheets — those that can be produced by using only the information presented in Parts I and II of this book.

Uses for Spreadsheets

Millions of spreadsheets are in daily use throughout the world. Many fit into the quick-and-dirty or for-your-eyes-only classifications described previously. Of the spreadsheets with lasting value, however, the majority probably fit into one or more of the following broad categories:

✦ Financial or data-analysis models

✦ Reports and presentations

✦ List-management worksheets

✦ Workbooks that enable database access

These types of spreadsheets are discussed in the following sections.

Financial or data-analysis models

Before the days of personal computers, large companies relied on mainframe systems to do their financial analysis. Smaller companies used sheets of accounting paper. But things have changed dramatically over the past decade, and now companies of all sizes can use personal computers to perform sophisticated analyses, in the blink of an eye.

This category of spreadsheets covers a wide variety of applications, including budgeting, investment analysis, modeling, and statistical data analysis. These applications can range from simple tables of numbers to sophisticated mathematical models designed for "what-if" analyses.

One common type of spreadsheet is a *budget spreadsheet,* which typically has months along the top and budget categories along the left. Each intersecting cell contains a projected expense—for example, telephone expenses for June. Budgets use SUM formulas (and maybe SUBTOTAL formulas) to calculate annual totals and totals for each category. Excel's multisheet feature enables you to store on separate sheets the budgets for different departments or divisions.

Budget categories often are arranged hierarchically. For example, you could have a category called Personnel that consists of subcategories such as Salary, Benefits, Bonus, and so on (see Figure 22-1). In such a case, you could create additional formulas to calculate category totals.

					Jan	Feb	Mar	Q1	Apr	May
2	Marketing									
3			Salaries		35,000	35,000	35,000	105,000	35,000	35,000
4			Benefits		7,350	7,350	7,350	22,050	7,350	7,350
5			Bonus		0	0	0	0	0	0
6			**Total Personnel**		**42,350**	**42,350**	**42,350**	**127,050**	**42,350**	**42,350**
7			Office		2,250	2,250	2,250	6,750	2,250	2,250
8			Computer		900	900	900	2,700	900	900
9			**Total Supplies**		**3,150**	**3,150**	**3,150**	**9,450**	**3,150**	**3,150**
10			Transportation		3,000	3,000	3,000	9,000	5,500	3,000
11			Hotel		1,050	1,050	1,050	3,150	3,400	1,050
12			Meals		500	500	500	1,500	1,250	500
13			**Total Travel**		**4,550**	**4,550**	**4,550**	**13,650**	**10,150**	**4,550**
14			Computers		4,500	4,500	4,500	13,500	4,500	4,500
15			Copiers		1,100	1,100	1,100	3,300	1,100	1,100
16			Other		950	950	950	2,850	950	950
17			**Total Equipment**		**6,550**	**6,550**	**6,550**	**19,650**	**6,550**	**6,550**
18			Lease		2,000	2,000	2,000	6,000	2,500	2,500
19			Utilities		450	450	450	1,350	450	450
20			Taxes		540	540	540	1,620	540	540
21			Other		1,200	1,200	1,200	3,600	1,200	1,200
22			Telephone		875	875	875	2,625	875	875
23			Postage		250	250	250	750	250	250
24			**Total Facility**		**5,315**	**5,315**	**5,315**	**15,945**	**5,815**	**5,815**
25		**Total Marketing**			**61,915**	**61,915**	**61,915**	**185,745**	**68,015**	**62,415**
26	Operations									
27			Salaries		210,000	210,000	210,000	630,000	215,000	215,000
28			Benefits		44,100	44,100	44,100	132,300	45,150	45,150

Figure 22-1: This budget worksheet uses formulas to calculate subtotals within each category.

Cross-Reference

Excel's outlining feature is ideal for creating formulas to calculate category totals, which is the topic of Chapter 23.

Another type of financial application is a *what-if model.* A what-if model calculates formulas by using assumptions that are specified in a series of input cells. For example, you can create an amortization spreadsheet that calculates details for a loan, based on the loan amount, the interest rate, and the term of the loan. This model would have three input cells. Excel's Scenario Manager is designed to make this type of model easier to handle.

Chapter 36 discusses various ways to set up what-if models.

Reports and presentations

Some spreadsheets are designed primarily for their end result: printed output. These spreadsheets take advantage of Excel's formatting and chart-making features to produce attractive, boardroom-quality output.

Of course, any spreadsheet can produce good, quality reports, so spreadsheets in this category often fall into another category, as well.

Nowadays, instead of printing your work, you may display it in the form of a Web page, either on the Internet or on your corporate intranet. The new HTML features in Excel 2000 make this task easier than ever.

List management

Another common use for spreadsheets is *list management,* in which a list is essentially a database table stored in a worksheet. A database table consists of field names in the top row and records in the rows below. Beginning with Excel 97, worksheets have 65,536 rows — which means that the potential for list-management applications has improved dramatically.

Excel has some handy tools that enable you to manipulate lists in a variety of ways (see Figure 22-2).

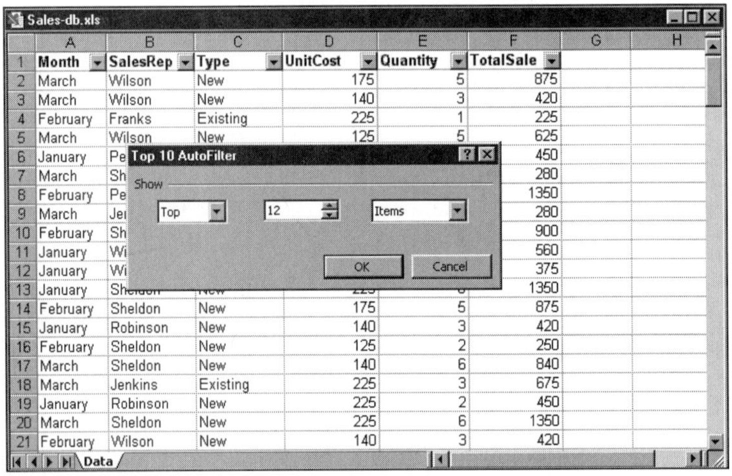

Figure 22-2: Excel makes working with lists of data easy.

List management is the topic of Chapter 33.

Database access

Another category of spreadsheets works with data stored in external databases. You can use Excel to query external databases and bring in a subset of the data that meets criteria that you specify. Then, you can do what you want with this data, independent of the original database.

 Spreadsheets that use external databases are covered in Chapter 34.

Turnkey applications

A *turnkey application* refers to a spreadsheet solution that is programmed to work as a standalone application. Such an application always requires macros, and may involve creating custom menus and custom toolbars.

These applications are large-scale projects that are designed to be used by many people or for a long time. They often interact with other systems (such as a corporate database) and must be very stable. Although this book touches on some elements of developing such applications, they are beyond this book's scope.

Steps in Creating a Spreadsheet

This section discusses the basic steps that you may follow to create a spreadsheet. This discussion assumes that you're creating a workbook that others may use, so you may skip some of these steps if the spreadsheet is for you only. These steps are for relatively simple spreadsheets — those that don't use macros, custom toolbars, or other advanced features. And, of course, these are only basic guidelines. Everyone eventually develops his or her own style, and you may find a method that works better for you. The basic steps are as follows:

1. Think about what you want to accomplish.
2. Consider the audience.
3. Design the workbook layout.
4. Enter data and formulas.
5. Apply appropriate formatting.
6. Test your spreadsheet.
7. Apply protection as necessary.
8. Document your work.

Each of these steps is discussed in the following sections.

Developing a plan

If you're like me, when you set out to create a new spreadsheet, you may have a tendency to jump right in and get to work. Tempting as it may be to create something concrete as quickly as possible, try to restrain yourself. The end product is almost always better if you take some time to determine exactly what you're trying to accomplish and come up with a plan of action. The time that you spend at this stage usually saves you more time later in the project.

Developing a plan for a spreadsheet may involve answering the following questions and collecting the necessary information that is involved:

✦ How is the problem currently being addressed? And what's wrong with the current solution?

✦ Is a spreadsheet really the best solution to the problem?

✦ How long will the spreadsheet be used?

✦ How many people will be using it?

✦ What type of output, if any, will be required?

✦ Does data already exist that can be imported?

✦ Will the requirements for this project change over time?

The point here is to attempt to learn as much as possible about the project that you're developing. With that information, you can determine a plan of action—which may even mean *not* using a spreadsheet for the solution.

Considering the audience

If you'll be the only user of the workbook that you're developing, you can skip this step. But if others will be using your workbook, take some time to find out about these people. Answering the following questions often prevents having to make changes later:

✦ **How experienced are the users?** Can they perform basic operations, such as copying, inserting rows, and so on? Don't assume that everyone knows as much as you do.

✦ **What software will they be using?** For example, if you develop your spreadsheet by using Excel 2000, you need to be aware that it can't be loaded into Excel 95 or earlier versions unless you first save the file in the older format. Users with older versions won't be able to take advantage of the newer features.

✦ **What hardware will they be using?** If your spreadsheet takes 3 minutes to calculate on your Pentium-based system, it may well take 20 minutes on a slower 486 system. Also, be aware of different video modes. If you develop your spreadsheet by using a 1024×768 video mode, users with an 800×600 or 640×480 display will have a much smaller viewing area.

✦ **Do you want to allow changes?** Often, you want to make sure that your formulas don't get modified. If so, you'll need to perform some basic protection (see "Applying Appropriate Protection," later in this chapter).

Designing the workbook layout

An important consideration is how you want to lay out the workbook. Before the days of multisheet workbooks, this was a lot more difficult than it is today. When your file has only a single worksheet, you have to plan it carefully to ensure that making a change doesn't affect something else.

Spreadsheets often consist of distinct blocks of information. In the old days, spreadsheet designers often used a layout like the one shown in Figure 22-3. This example is for a spreadsheet that has three main blocks: an input area, a calculation area, and a report area. This *offset block layout* minimizes the possibility of damage. For example, deleting a column or changing its width affects only one area. If the areas were laid out vertically, this would not be the case.

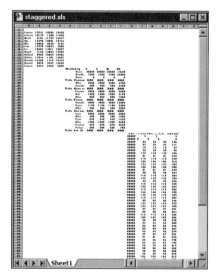

Figure 22-3: This offset block layout is one way to organize a worksheet.

Because Excel uses multiple worksheets in a file, however, this type of layout is rarely necessary. Using a separate worksheet for each block is much easier and more efficient. An added advantage is that you can access the various blocks simply by clicking the tab (which can be named appropriately).

Entering data and formulas

This phase of the spreadsheet development process is often where people begin. But if you've thought through the problem, considered the users, and created an appropriate layout, this phase should go more smoothly than if you jumped right in without the preliminary steps.

The more that you know about Excel, the easier this phase is. Formulas are just one part of a spreadsheet. Sometimes, you may need to incorporate one or more of the following features (all of which are discussed later in the book):

- ✦ Workbook consolidation
- ✦ List management
- ✦ External databases
- ✦ Outlining
- ✦ Data validation
- ✦ Conditional formatting
- ✦ Hyperlinks
- ✦ Statistical analysis
- ✦ Pivot tables
- ✦ Scenario management
- ✦ Solver
- ✦ Mapping
- ✦ Interaction with other applications
- ✦ Custom menus or toolbars (which require macros)

Applying appropriate formatting

Many people prefer to format their work as they go along. If that's not your style, this step must be performed before you unleash your efforts to the end-users. As I mentioned in Chapter 17, almost all worksheets benefit from some stylistic formatting. At the very least, you need to adjust the number formats so that the values appear correctly. If the worksheet will be used by others, make sure that any color combinations you use will be visible for those running on a monochrome system (such as a notebook computer).

Of all the basic steps in creating a spreadsheet, formatting is the one with the most variety. Although beauty may be in the eye of the beholder, you might want to consider a few guidelines:

✦ **Preformat all numeric cells.** Use number formats that are appropriate for the numbers and make sure that the columns are wide enough to handle the maximum values. For example, if a cell is designed to hold an interest rate, format it with a percent sign. And if you create an amortization schedule, make sure that the columns are wide enough to handle large amounts.

✦ **Use only basic fonts.** If others will be using your workbook, stick to the basic TrueType fonts that come with Windows. Otherwise, the fonts may not translate well, and the user may see a string of asterisks rather than a value.

✦ **Don't go overboard with fonts.** As a rule of thumb, never use more than two different typefaces in a single workbook. Usually, one works just fine (Arial is a good choice). If you use different font sizes, do so sparingly.

✦ **Be careful with color.** Colored text or cell backgrounds can make your workbook much easier to use. For example, if you use a lookup table, you can use color to clarify where the table's boundaries are. Or, you may want to color-code the cells that will accept user input. Overuse of colors makes your spreadsheet look gaudy and unprofessional, however. Also, make sure that color combinations will work if the workbook is opened on a monochrome notebook computer.

✦ **Consider identifying the active area.** Many spreadsheets are set up using only a few cells — the active area. Inexperienced users often scroll away from the active area and get lost. One technique is to hide all rows and columns that aren't used. Or, you can apply a color background (such as light gray) to all unused cells. This makes the cells in use very clear.

✦ **Remove extraneous elements.** In some cases, you can simplify things significantly by removing elements that might get in the way or cause the screen to appear more confusing than it is. These elements include automatic page breaks, gridlines, row and column headers, and sheet tabs. These options, which you set in the View panel of the Options dialog box, are saved with the worksheet.

Testing the spreadsheet

Before you actually use your newly created spreadsheet for real work, you should test it thoroughly. This is even more critical if others will be using your spreadsheet. If you've distributed 20 copies of your file and then discover a major error in a formula, you'll have to do a "recall" and send out a corrected copy. Obviously, catching the errors before you send out a spreadsheet is much easier.

Testing basically is the process of ensuring that the formulas produce correct results under all possible circumstances. I don't know of any specific rules for testing a worksheet, so you're pretty much on your own here. I can, however, offer a few guidelines:

✦ **Test with all potential versions.** If some of your end-users are using older versions of Excel, it's critical that you test your work using all the other versions. Saving your file in an older format means that others can open your file with an older version of Excel. It does *not* guarantee that everything will still work correctly!

✦ **Try extreme input values.** If your worksheet is set up to perform calculations using input cells, spend some time and enter very large or very small numbers and observe the effects on the formulas. If the user should enter a percentage, see what happens if you enter a large value. If a positive number is expected, try entering a negative number. This also is a good way to ensure that your columns are wide enough.

✦ **Provide data validation.** Although you can't expect your formulas to yield usable results for invalid entries (garbage in, garbage out), you may want to use Excel's data validation features to ensure that data entered is of the proper type.

✦ **Use dummy data.** If you have a budget application, for example, try entering 1 into each nonformula cell. This is a good way to make sure that all of your SUM formulas refer to the correct ranges. An incorrect formula usually stands out from the others.

✦ **Familiarize yourself with Excel's auditing tools.** Excel has several useful tools that can help you track down erroneous formulas.

Cross-Reference   Excel's auditing tools are discussed in Chapter 30.

Applying appropriate protection

A spreadsheet can be quite fragile. Deleting a single formula often has a ripple effect and causes other formulas to produce an error value or, even worse, incorrect results. I've seen cases in which an inexperienced user deleted a critical formula, panicked, and cemented the mistake by saving the file and reopening it — only to discover, of course, that the original (good) version had been overwritten.

You can circumvent such problems by using the protection features built into Excel. The following are the two general types of protection:

✦ Sheet protection

✦ Workbook protection

Protecting sheets

The Tools ➪ Protection ➪ Protect Sheet command displays the dialog box shown in Figure 22-4.

Figure 22-4: The Protect Sheet dialog box

This dialog box has three check boxes:

✦ **Contents:** Cells that have their Locked property turned on can't be changed.

✦ **Objects:** Drawing objects (including embedded charts) that have their Locked property turned on can't be selected.

✦ **Scenarios:** Defined scenarios that have their Prevent Changes property turned on can't be changed (see Chapter 36 for a discussion of scenario management).

You may provide a password in the Protect Sheet dialog box. If you enter a password, the password must be reentered before the sheet can be unprotected. If you don't supply a password, anyone can unprotect the sheet.

By default, all cells have their Locked property turned on. Before protecting a worksheet, you'll normally want to turn off the Locked property for input cells.

You can change the Locked property of a cell or object by accessing its Format dialog box and clicking the Protection tab. Cells have an additional property: Hidden. This name is a bit misleading, because it doesn't actually hide the cell. Rather, it prevents the cell contents from being displayed in the formula bar. Y ou can use the Hidden property to prevent others from seeing your formulas.

Note You can't change a cell's Locked property while the sheet is protected. You must unprotect the sheet to make any changes, and then protect it again.

Note Protection isn't just for worksheets that others will be using. Many people protect worksheets to prevent themselves from accidentally deleting cells.

Protecting workbooks

The second type of protection is workbook protection. The Tools ➪ Protection ➪ Protect Workbook command displays the dialog box shown in Figure 22-5.

Figure 22-5: The Protect Workbook dialog box

This dialog box has two check boxes:

✦ **Structure:** Protects the workbook window from being moved or resized.

✦ **Windows:** Prevents any of the following changes to a workbook: adding a sheet, deleting a sheet, moving a sheet, renaming a sheet, hiding a sheet, or unhiding a sheet.

Again, you can determine whether to supply a password, depending on the level of protection that you need.

Documenting your work

The final step in the spreadsheet-creation process is documenting your work. Making some notes about your spreadsheet is always a good idea. After all, you may need to modify the spreadsheet later. The elegant formula that you create today may be completely meaningless when you need to change it in six months. The following sections provide some general tips on documenting your spreadsheets.

Use the Properties dialog box

The File ➪ Properties command displays the Properties dialog box (the Summary tab is shown in Figure 22-6). You may want to take a few minutes to fill in the missing information and enter some comments in the Comments box.

Use cell comments

As you know, you can document individual cells by using the Insert ➪ Comment command. The comment appears when you move the mouse pointer over the cell. If you don't like the idea of seeing the cell comments appear, adjust this setting in the View tab of the Options dialog box. Unfortunately, this setting applies to all workbooks, so if you turn off the note indicator for one workbook, you turn it off for all of them.

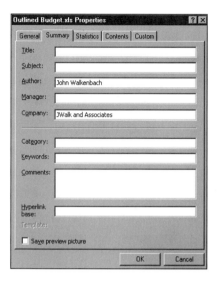

Figure 22-6: The Summary tab of the Properties dialog box

Use a separate worksheet

Perhaps the best way to document a workbook is to insert a new worksheet and store your comments there. Some people also like to keep a running tally of any modifications that they make. You can hide the worksheet so that others can't see it.

A Workbook That's Easy to Maintain

One of the cardinal rules of "spreadsheeting" is that things change. You may have a sales-tracking spreadsheet that you've been using for years, and it works perfectly well. But then you're informed that the company has bought out one of your competitors, and the sales regions will be restructured. Your sales-tracking workbook suddenly no longer applies.

You often can save yourself lots of time by planning for the inevitable changes. You can do a few things to make your worksheets as modifiable as possible:

✦ **Avoid hard-coding values in formulas**. For example, assume that you have formulas that calculate sales commissions by using a commission rate of 12.5 percent. Rather than use the value .125 in the formulas, enter it into a cell and use the cell reference. Or, use the technique described in Chapter 8 (see "Naming Constants") to create a named constant.

✦ **Use names whenever possible.** Cell and range names make your formulas easier to read and more understandable. When the time comes to modify your formulas, you may be able to modify just the range to which a name refers.

✦ **Use simplified formulas.** Beginning users sometimes create formulas that are more complicated than they need to be. Often, this is because they don't know about a particular built-in function. As you gain more experience with Excel, be on the lookout for useful functions that can make your formulas simple and clear. Such formulas are much easier to modify, when needed.

✦ **Use a flexible layout.** Rather than try to cram everything into a single worksheet, use multiple worksheets. You'll find that this makes expanding much easier, should the need arise.

✦ **Use named styles.** Using named styles makes obtaining consistent formatting much easier if you need to add new data to accommodate a change. This feature is discussed in Chapter 17 (see "Using Named Styles").

✦ **Keep it clean.** Keeping your workbooks clean and free of extraneous information is also a good idea. For example, if the workbook has empty worksheets, remove them. If you created names that you no longer use, delete them. If you no longer need a range of cells that you used to perform a quick calculation, delete the range.

When Things Go Wrong

Many types of errors can occur when you work with Excel (or any spreadsheet, for that matter). These errors range from inconvenient errors that can be easily corrected to disastrous, irreparable errors.

For example, a formula may return an error value when a certain cell that it uses contains a zero. Normally, you can isolate the problem and correct the formula, so that the error doesn't appear anymore (this is an example of an easily corrected error). A potentially disastrous error is when you open a worksheet and Excel reports that it can't read the file. Figure 22-7 shows the message that you get. Unless you made a recent backup, you could be in deep trouble. Unfortunately, this type of error (a corrupted file) occurs more often than you might think.

Figure 22-7: When you see an error message like this, you'd better have a recent backup available.

Good testing helps you to avoid problems with your formulas. Making modifications to your work, however, may result in a formula that no longer works. For example, you may add a new column to the worksheet, and the formulas don't pick up the expanded cell reference. This is an example of when using names could eliminate the need to adjust the formulas.

You will encounter cases in which a formula just doesn't work as it should. When this happens, try to isolate the problem as simply as possible. I've found that a good way to deal with such formulas is to create a new workbook with a very simplified example of what I'm trying to accomplish. Sometimes, looking at the problem in a different context can shed new light on it.

The only way to prevent disasters — such as a corrupt file — is to develop good backup habits. If a file is important, you should never have only one copy of it. You should get in the habit of making a daily backup on a different storage medium.

Where to Go from Here

This chapter concludes Part III. If you're following the book in sequential-chapter order, you now have enough knowledge to put Excel to good use.

Excel has many more features that may interest you, however, which are covered in the remaining chapters. Even if you're satisfied with what you already know about Excel, I strongly suggest that you at least browse through the remaining chapters. You may see something that can save you hours.

Summary

This chapter distinguishes two general categories of spreadsheets: those that you create for yourself only and those that others will use. The approach that you take depends on the end-user. This chapter also covers the characteristics of a successful spreadsheet, basic types of spreadsheets, basic steps that you may follow to create a spreadsheet, and features in Excel that let you protect various parts of your work. The chapter concludes with some tips on how to make your spreadsheets easier to maintain and how to handle some common types of errors.

✦　　✦　　✦

Advanced Excel Features

Creating and Using Worksheet Outlines

If you use a word processor, you may be familiar with the concept of an outline. Most word processors have an outline mode that lets you view only the headings and subheadings in your document. You can easily expand a heading to show the detail (that is, the text) below it. To write this book, I used the outline feature in my word processor extensively.

Excel also is capable of using outlines, and understanding this feature can make working with certain types of worksheets much easier for you.

Introducing Worksheet Outlines

You can use outlines to create summary reports in which you don't want to show all the details. You'll find that some worksheets are more suitable for outlines than others. If your worksheet uses hierarchical data with subtotals, it's probably a good candidate for an outline.

An example outline

The best way to understand how worksheet outlining works is to look at an example. Figure 23-1 shows a simple budget model without an outline. Subtotals are used to calculate subtotals by region and by quarter.

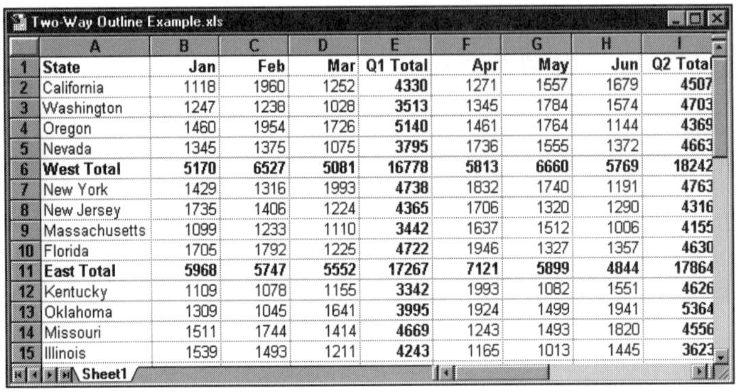

Two-Way Outline Example.xls

	A	B	C	D	E	F	G	H	I
1	**State**	**Jan**	**Feb**	**Mar**	**Q1 Total**	**Apr**	**May**	**Jun**	**Q2 Total**
2	California	1118	1960	1252	**4330**	1271	1557	1679	**4507**
3	Washington	1247	1238	1028	**3513**	1345	1784	1574	**4703**
4	Oregon	1460	1954	1726	**5140**	1461	1764	1144	**4369**
5	Nevada	1345	1375	1075	**3795**	1736	1555	1372	**4663**
6	**West Total**	**5170**	**6527**	**5081**	**16778**	**5813**	**6660**	**5769**	**18242**
7	New York	1429	1316	1993	**4738**	1832	1740	1191	**4763**
8	New Jersey	1735	1406	1224	**4365**	1706	1320	1290	**4316**
9	Massachusetts	1099	1233	1110	**3442**	1637	1512	1006	**4155**
10	Florida	1705	1792	1225	**4722**	1946	1327	1357	**4630**
11	**East Total**	**5968**	**5747**	**5552**	**17267**	**7121**	**5899**	**4844**	**17864**
12	Kentucky	1109	1078	1155	**3342**	1993	1082	1551	**4626**
13	Oklahoma	1309	1045	1641	**3995**	1924	1499	1941	**5364**
14	Missouri	1511	1744	1414	**4669**	1243	1493	1820	**4556**
15	Illinois	1539	1493	1211	**4243**	1165	1013	1445	**3623**

Sheet1

Figure 23-1: A typical budget model with subtotals

Figure 23-2 shows the same worksheet after the outline was created. Notice that Excel adds a new border to the left of the screen. This border contains controls that enable you to determine which level to view. This particular outline has three levels: States, Regions (each region consists of states), and Grand Total (the sum of each region's subtotal). In Figure 23-2, the outline is fully expanded so that you can see all the data.

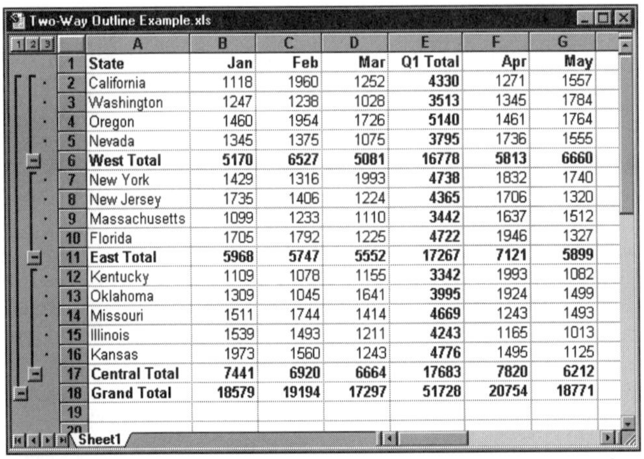

Two-Way Outline Example.xls

	A	B	C	D	E	F	G
1	**State**	**Jan**	**Feb**	**Mar**	**Q1 Total**	**Apr**	**May**
2	California	1118	1960	1252	**4330**	1271	1557
3	Washington	1247	1238	1028	**3513**	1345	1784
4	Oregon	1460	1954	1726	**5140**	1461	1764
5	Nevada	1345	1375	1075	**3795**	1736	1555
6	**West Total**	**5170**	**6527**	**5081**	**16778**	**5813**	**6660**
7	New York	1429	1316	1993	**4738**	1832	1740
8	New Jersey	1735	1406	1224	**4365**	1706	1320
9	Massachusetts	1099	1233	1110	**3442**	1637	1512
10	Florida	1705	1792	1225	**4722**	1946	1327
11	**East Total**	**5968**	**5747**	**5552**	**17267**	**7121**	**5899**
12	Kentucky	1109	1078	1155	**3342**	1993	1082
13	Oklahoma	1309	1045	1641	**3995**	1924	1499
14	Missouri	1511	1744	1414	**4669**	1243	1493
15	Illinois	1539	1493	1211	**4243**	1165	1013
16	Kansas	1973	1560	1243	**4776**	1495	1125
17	**Central Total**	**7441**	**6920**	**6664**	**17683**	**7820**	**6212**
18	**Grand Total**	**18579**	**19194**	**17297**	**51728**	**20754**	**18771**
19							

Sheet1

Figure 23-2: The budget model after creating an outline

Figure 23-3 depicts the outline displayed at the second level. Now, the outline shows only the totals for the regions (the detail rows are hidden). You can partially expand the outline to show the detail for a particular region. Collapsing the outline to level 1 shows only the headers and the Grand Total row.

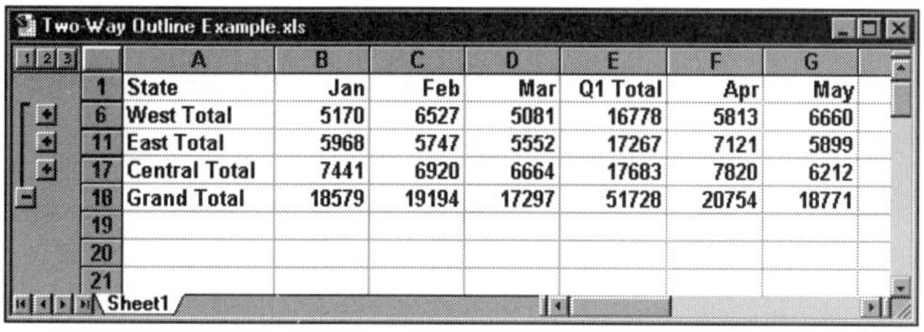

Figure 23-3: The budget model after collapsing the outline to the second level

Excel can create outlines in both directions. In the preceding examples, the outline was a row (vertical) outline. Figure 23-4 shows the same model after a column (horizontal) outline was added. Now, Excel displays another border at the top.

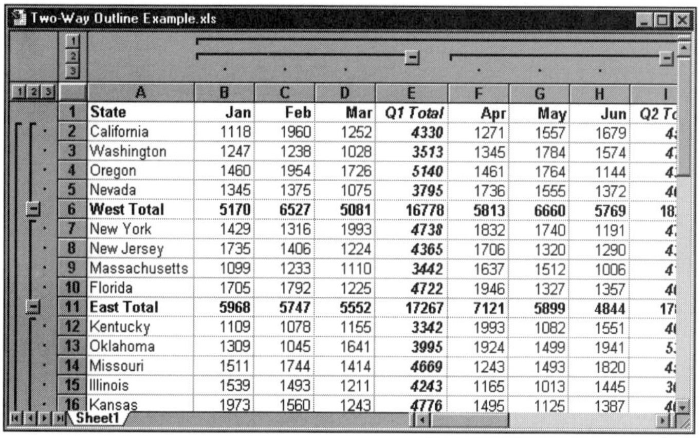

Figure 23-4: The budget model after adding a column outline

If you create both a row and a column outline in a worksheet, you can work with each outline independent of the other. For example, you can show the row outline at the second level and the column outline at the first level. Figure 23-5 shows the model with both outlines collapsed at the second level. The result is a nice summary table that gives regional totals by quarter.

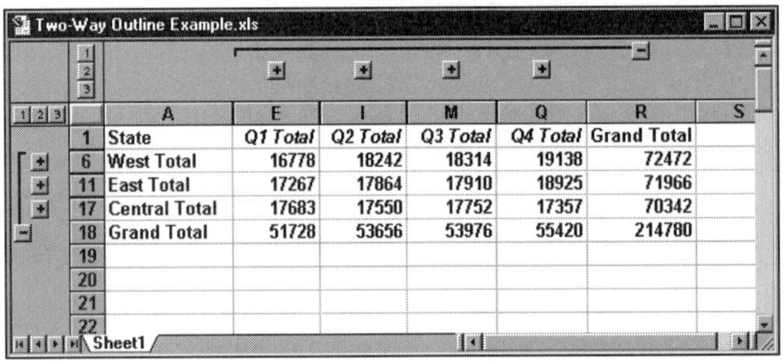

A	E	I	M	Q	R	S
1 State	*Q1 Total*	*Q2 Total*	*Q3 Total*	*Q4 Total*	Grand Total	
6 West Total	16778	18242	18314	19138	72472	
11 East Total	17267	17864	17910	18925	71966	
17 Central Total	17683	17550	17752	17357	70342	
18 Grand Total	51728	53656	53976	55420	214780	

Figure 23-5: The budget model with both outlines collapsed at the second level

On the CD-ROM   You'll find the workbook used in the preceding examples on this book's CD-ROM.

More about outlines

The following are points to keep in mind about worksheet outlines:

✦ A single worksheet can have only one outline (row, column, or both). If you need to create more than one outline, move the data to a new worksheet.

✦ You can either create an outline manually or have Excel do it for you automatically. If you choose the latter option, you may need to do some preparation to get the worksheet in the proper format.

✦ You can create an outline for either all data on a worksheet or just a selected data range.

✦ You can remove an outline with a single command.

✦ You can hide the outline symbols (to free screen space) but retain the outline.

✦ You can have up to eight nested levels in an outline.

Worksheet outlines can be quite useful. But if your main objective is to summarize a large amount of data, you might be better off using a pivot table. A pivot table is much more flexible and doesn't require that you create the subtotal formulas; it does the summarizing for you automatically.

Cross-Reference   Pivot tables are discussed in Chapter 35.

Creating an Outline

In this section, you learn the two ways to create an outline: automatically and manually. But, before getting into the details of those two methods, the all-important first step is examined: getting your data ready for outlining.

Preparing the data

Before you create an outline, you need to ensure the following:

✦ The data is appropriate for an outline

✦ The formulas are set up properly

Determining appropriate data

What type of data is appropriate for an outline? Generally, the data should be arranged in a hierarchy, such as a budget that consists of an arrangement similar to the following:

Company

      Division

            Department

                  Budget Category

                        Budget Item

In this case, each budget item (for example, airfare and hotel expenses) is part of a budget category (for example, travel expenses). Each department has its own budget, and the departments are rolled up into divisions. The divisions make up the company. This type of arrangement is well-suited for a row outline — although most of your outlines probably won't have this many levels.

Once created, you can view the information at any level of detail that you want. When you need to create reports for different levels of management, try using an outline. Upper management may want to see only the Division totals. Division managers may want to see totals by department, and each department manager needs to see the full details for his or her department.

As demonstrated at the beginning of the chapter, you can include time-based information that is rolled up into larger units (such as months and quarters) in a column outline. Column outlines work just like row outlines, however, and the levels need not be time-based.

Setting up the formulas

Before you create an outline, you need to make sure that all the summary formulas are entered correctly and consistently. *Consistently* means that the formulas are in the same relative location. Generally, formulas that compute summary formulas (such as subtotals) are entered below the data to which they refer. In some cases, however, the summary formulas are entered above the referenced cells. Excel can handle either method, but you must be consistent throughout the range that you outline. If the summary formulas aren't consistent, automatic outlining won't produce the results that you want.

Note   If your summary formulas aren't consistent (that is, some are above and some are below the data), you still can create an outline, but you must do it manually.

Creating an outline automatically

Excel can create an outline for you automatically in a few seconds, whereas it might take you ten minutes or more to do the same thing manually.

To have Excel create an outline, move the cell pointer anywhere within the range of data that you're outlining. Then, choose Data ➪ Group and Outline ➪ Auto Outline. Excel analyzes the formulas in the range and creates the outline. Depending on the formulas that you have, Excel creates a row outline, a column outline, or both.

If the worksheet already has an outline, Excel asks whether you want to modify the existing outline. Click Yes to force Excel to remove the old outline and create a new one.

Note   Excel automatically creates an outline when you use the Data ➪ Subtotals command, which inserts subtotal formulas automatically if you set up your data as a list.

Cross-Reference   The Data ➪ Subtotals command is discussed in Chapter 33 (see the section "Creating Subtotals").

Creating an outline manually

Usually, letting Excel create the outline is the best approach. It's much faster and less error-prone. If the outline that Excel creates isn't what you have in mind, however, you can create an outline manually.

When Excel creates a row outline, the summary rows all must be above the data or below the data (they can't be mixed). Similarly, for a column outline, the summary columns all must be to the right of the data or to the left of the data. If your worksheet doesn't meet these requirements, you have two choices:

✦ Rearrange the worksheet so that it does meet the requirements

✦ Create the outline manually

You also need to create an outline manually if the range doesn't contain any formulas. You may have imported a file and want to use an outline to display it better. Because Excel uses the formulas to determine how to create the outline, it is not able to make an outline without formulas.

Creating an outline manually consists of creating groups of rows (for row outlines) or groups of columns (for column outlines). To create a group of rows, click the row numbers for all the rows that you want to include in the group—but do not select the row that has the summary formulas. Then, choose Data ➪ Group and Outline ➪ Group. Excel displays outline symbols for the group. Repeat this for each group that you want to create. When you collapse the outline, Excel hides rows in the group. But the summary row, which is not in the group, remains in view.

Using an Outline for Text

If you need to present lots of textual information in a workbook—as in user instructions, for example—consider arranging the information in the form of an outline. The accompanying figure shows an example that I developed for one of my shareware products. The user manual is contained on a worksheet, and I created an outline to make locating a specific section easier. I also used a simple macro, attached to a check box, to make it easy for users to expand and collapse the outline.

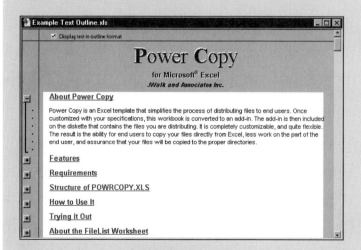

The workbook shown in the figure is available on this book's CD-ROM.

Note   If you select a range of cells (rather than entire rows or columns) before you create a group, Excel displays a dialog box asking what you want to group. It then groups entire rows or columns based on the range that you select.

You also can select groups of groups, to create multilevel outlines. When you create multilevel outlines, always start with the innermost groupings and then work your way out. If you realize that you grouped the wrong rows, you can ungroup the group by selecting Data ➪ Group and Outline ➪ Ungroup.

Excel has toolbar buttons that speed up the process of grouping and ungrouping (see the sidebar "Outlining Tools"). You also can use the following keyboard shortcuts:

✦ **Alt+Shift+right arrow:** Groups selected rows or columns

✦ **Alt+Shift+left arrow:** Ungroups selected rows or columns

Creating outlines manually can be confusing at first, but if you stick with it, you'll become a pro in no time.

Outlining Tools

Excel doesn't have a toolbar devoted exclusively to outlining, but it *does* have one that comes close. The Pivot Table toolbar (see accompanying figure) includes four tools that are handy for working with outlines.

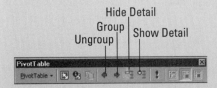

The relevant Pivot Table toolbar buttons are as follows:

Button Name	What It Does
Ungroup	Ungroups selected rows or columns
Group	Groups selected rows or columns
Show Detail	Shows details of selected summary cell
Hide Detail	Hides details of selected summary cell

Using Outlines

This section discusses the basic operations that you can perform with a worksheet outline.

Displaying levels

To display various outline levels, click the appropriate outline symbol. These symbols consist of buttons with numbers on them (1, 2, and so on) and buttons with either a plus sign (+) or a minus sign (–).

Clicking the 1 button collapses the outline so that it displays no detail, just the highest summary level of information. Clicking the 2 button expands the outline to show one level, and so on. The number of numbered buttons depends on the number of outline levels. Choosing a level number displays the detail for that level, plus any lower levels. To display all levels — the most detail — click the highest-level number.

You can expand a particular section by clicking its + button, or you can collapse a particular section by clicking its – button. In short, you have complete control over the details that Excel exposes or hides in an outline.

If you prefer, you can use the Hide Detail and Show Detail commands on the Data ➪ Group and Outline menu, to hide and show details, respectively. Or, you can use one of the buttons on the Pivot Table toolbar to hide or show information.

Tip   If you constantly adjust the outline to show different reports, consider using the Custom Views feature to save a particular view and give it a name. Then, you can quickly switch among the named views. Use the View ➪ Custom Views command for this.

Applying styles to an outline

When you create an outline, you can have Excel automatically apply named styles to the summary rows and columns.

Cross-Reference   Chapter 17 discusses named styles.

Excel uses styles with names in the following formats (where n corresponds to the outline level):

✦ RowLevel_n

✦ ColLevel_n

For example, the named style that is applied to the first row level is RowLevel_1. These styles consist only of formats for the font. Using font variations makes distinguishing various parts of the outline a bit easier. You can, of course, modify the styles in any way that you want. For example, you can use the Format ➪ Style command to change the font size or color for the RowLevel_1 style. After you do so, all the RowLevel_1 cells take on the new formatting. Figure 23-6 shows an outline with the automatic outline styles assigned.

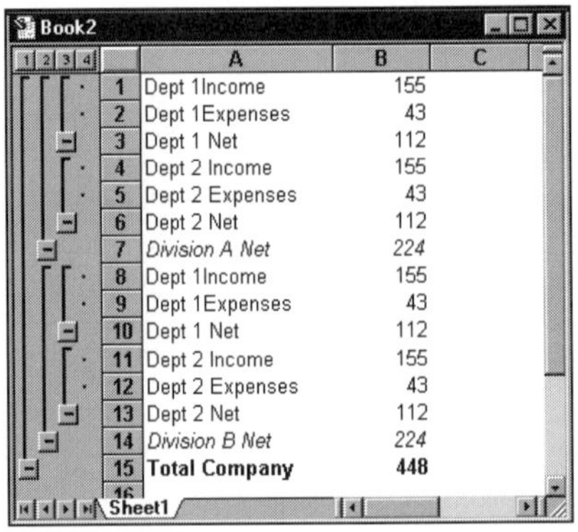

Figure 23-6: This outline has automatic styles

You can have Excel automatically apply the styles when it creates an outline, or you can apply them after the fact. You control this in the Settings dialog box, shown in Figure 23-7. This dialog box appears when you select Data ➪ Group and Outline ➪ Settings.

Figure 23-7: The Settings dialog box

If the *Automatic styles* check box contains a check when you create the outline, Excel automatically applies the styles. To apply styles to an existing outline, select the outline, choose Data ➪ Group and Outline ➪ Settings, and then click the Apply Styles button. Notice that you also can create an outline by using this dialog box.

Tip

You may prefer to use Excel's Format⇨AutoFormat command to format an outline. Several of the AutoFormats use different formatting for summary cells.

Adding data to an outline

You may need to add additional rows or columns to an outline. In some cases, you may be able to insert new rows or columns without disturbing the outline, and the new rows or columns become part of the outline. In other cases, you'll find that the new row or column is not part of the outline. If you create the outline automatically, just select Data⇨Group and Outline⇨Auto Outline again. Excel makes you verify that you want to modify the existing outline. If you create the outline manually, you need to make the adjustments manually, as well.

Removing an outline

If you no longer need an outline, you can remove it by selecting Data⇨Group and Outline⇨Clear Outline. Excel fully expands the outline by displaying all hidden rows and columns, and the outline symbols disappear. The outline styles remain in effect, however.

Caution

You can't "undo" removing an outline, so make sure that you *really* want to remove the outline, before you select this command.

Hiding the outline symbols

The outline symbols Excel displays when an outline is present take up quite a bit of space (the exact amount depends on the number levels). If you want to see as much as possible onscreen, you can temporarily hide these symbols, without removing the outline. The following are the two ways to do this:

✦ Open the Options dialog box, select the View tab, and remove the check from the Outline Symbols check box.

✦ Press Ctrl+8.

Note

When you hide the outline symbols, the outline still is in effect, and the worksheet displays the data at the current outline level. That is, some rows or columns may be hidden.

To redisplay the outline symbols, either place a check mark in the Outline Symbols check box in the Options dialog box or press Ctrl+8.

The Custom Views feature, which saves named views of your outline, also saves the status of the outline symbols as part of the view, enabling you to name some views with the outline symbols and other views without them.

Creating charts from outlines

A worksheet outline also is a handy way to create summary charts. If you have a large table of data, creating a chart usually produces a confusing mess. But, if you create an outline first, then you can collapse the outline and select the summary data for your chart. Figure 23-8 shows an example of a chart created from a collapsed outline. When you expand an outline from which you created a chart, the chart shows the additional data.

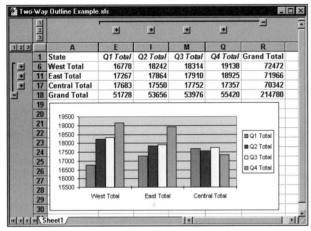

Figure 23-8: This chart was created from the summary cells in an outline.

Note   If your chart shows all the data in the outline, even when it's collapsed, remove the check from the Plot Visible Cells Only check box in the Chart tab in the Options dialog box.

Summary

This chapter discusses the advantages of creating an outline from worksheet data. It teaches you how to create row outlines and column outlines, either automatically or manually. It also discusses how to use an outline after it is created.

✦   ✦   ✦

Linking and Consolidating Worksheets

This chapter discusses two procedures that are common in the world of spreadsheets: linking and consolidation. *Linking* is the process of using references to cells in external workbooks to get data into your worksheet. *Consolidation* combines or summarizes information from two or more worksheets (which can be in multiple workbooks).

Linking Workbooks

When you link worksheets, you connect them together in such a way that one depends on the other. The workbook that contains the link formulas (or external reference formulas) is called the *dependent* workbook. The workbook that contains the information used in the external reference formula is called the *source* workbook. Note, importantly, that you don't need to open the source workbook when you link it to the dependent workbook.

 Cross-Reference You also can create links to data in other applications, such as a database program or a word processor. This is a completely different procedure and is the topic of Chapter 28.

Why link workbooks?

When you consider linking workbooks, you might ask yourself the following question: If Workbook A needs to access data in another workbook (Workbook B), why not just enter the data into Workbook A in the first place? In some cases, you can. But the real value of linking becomes apparent when you continually update the source workbook. Creating a link in Workbook A to Workbook B means that, in Workbook A, you always have access to the most recent information in Workbook B, because Workbook A is updated whenever Workbook B changes.

Linking workbooks also can be helpful if you need to consolidate different files. For example, each regional sales manager might store data in a separate workbook. You can create a summary workbook that first uses link formulas to retrieve specific data from each manager's workbook and then calculates totals across all regions.

Linking also is useful as a way to break up a large model into smaller files. You can create smaller workbook modules that are linked together with a few key external references. Often, this approach makes your model easier to deal with and uses less memory.

Linking has its downside, however. As you'll see later, external reference formulas are somewhat fragile, and accidentally severing the links that you create is relatively easy. You can prevent this from happening if you understand how linking works. Later in the chapter, some of the problems that may arise are discussed, as well as how to avoid them (see "Potential Problems with External Reference Formulas").

Creating external reference formulas

The following are the ways that you can create an external reference formula:

✦ **Type the cell references manually.** These references may be lengthy, because they include workbook and sheet names (and, possibly, even drive and path information). The advantage of manually typing the cell references is that the source workbook doesn't have to be open.

✦ **Point to the cell references.** If the source workbook is open, you can use the standard pointing techniques to create formulas that use external references.

✦ **With the source workbook open, select Edit ➪ Paste Special with the Paste Link button.**

✦ **Use Excel's Data ➪ Consolidate command.** This method is discussed later in the chapter (see "Consolidating Worksheets by Using Data ➪ Consolidate").

Understanding the link formula syntax

This section discusses the concept of external references. The general syntax for an external reference formula is as follows:

```
=[WorkbookName]SheetName!CellAddress
```

Precede the cell address by the workbook name (in brackets), the worksheet name, and an exclamation point. Here's an example of a formula that uses cell A1 in the Sheet1 worksheet of a workbook named Budget:

```
=[Budget.xls]Sheet1!A1
```

If the workbook name or the sheet name in the reference includes one or more spaces, you must enclose the text in single quotation marks. For example, here's a formula that refers to cell A1 on Sheet1 in a workbook named Annual Budget:

```
='[Annual Budget]Sheet1'!A1
```

When a formula refers to cells in a different workbook, that other workbook doesn't need to be open. If the workbook is closed and not in the current folder, you must add the complete path to the reference; for example:

```
='C:\MSOffice\Excel\Budget Files\[Annual Budget]Sheet1'!A1
```

Creating a link formula by pointing

As previously mentioned, you can directly enter external reference formulas, but doing so can cause errors, because you must have every bit of information exactly correct. Instead, have Excel build the formula for you, as follows:

1. Open the source workbook.

2. Select the cell in the dependent workbook that will hold the formula.

3. Enter the formula. When you get to the part that requires the external reference, activate the source workbook and select the cell or range.

4. Finish the formula and press Enter.

You'll see that when you point to the cell or range, Excel automatically takes care of the details and creates a syntactically correct external reference. When you point to a cell reference by using the procedure outlined in the preceding steps, the cell reference is always an absolute reference (such as $A$1). If you plan to copy the formula to create additional link formulas, you can change the absolute reference to a relative reference by removing the dollar signs.

As long as the source workbook remains open, the external reference doesn't include the path to the workbook. If you close the source workbook, however, the external reference formulas change to include the full path. If you use the File ➪ Save As command to save the source workbook with a different name, Excel changes the external references to use the new filename.

Pasting links

The Paste Special command provides another way to create external reference formulas:

1. Open the source workbook.

2. Select the cell or range that you want to link and then copy it to the clipboard.

3. Activate the dependent workbook and select the cell in which you want the link formula to appear. If you're pasting a range, just select the upper-left cell.

4. Choose Edit ➪ Paste Special and then click the Paste Link button.

Working with external reference formulas

You need to understand that a single workbook can contain links that refer to any number of different source workbooks. This section discusses what you need to know about working with links.

Creating links to unsaved workbooks

Excel enables you to create link formulas to unsaved workbooks, and even to nonexistent workbooks. Assume that you have two workbooks open and you haven't saved either of them (they have the names Book1 and Book2). If you create a link formula to Book1 in Book2 and then save Book2, Excel displays the dialog box shown in Figure 24-1. Generally, you should avoid this situation. Simply save the source workbook first.

Figure 24-1: This message indicates that the workbook you're saving contains references to a workbook that you haven't yet saved.

You also can create links to documents that don't exist. You might want to do this if you'll be using a source workbook from a colleague, but the file hasn't arrived. When you enter an external reference formula that refers to a nonexistent workbook, Excel displays its File Not Found dialog box, shown in Figure 24-2. If you click Cancel, the formula retains the workbook name that you entered, but it returns an error. When the source workbook becomes available, the error goes away and the formula displays its proper value.

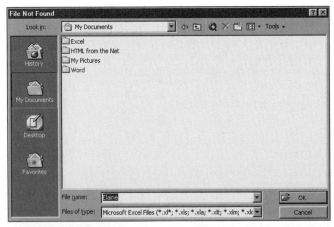

Figure 24-2: When you enter a formula that refers to a nonexistent workbook, Excel displays this dialog box to help you locate the file.

Opening a workbook with external reference formulas

When you open a workbook that contains one or more external reference formulas, Excel retrieves the current values from the source workbooks and calculates the formulas.

If Excel can't locate a source workbook that's referred to in a link formula, it displays its File Not Found dialog box and prompts you to supply a workbook to use for the source workbook.

Examining links

If your workbook uses several workbook links, you might want to see a list of source workbooks. To do so, choose the Edit ➪ Links command. Excel responds with the Links dialog box, shown in Figure 24-3. This dialog box lists all source workbooks, plus other types of links to other documents.

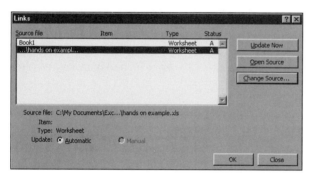

Figure 24-3: The Links dialog box lists all link sources.

 Cross-Reference   These other types of links are explained in Chapter 28.

Updating links

If you want to ensure that your link formulas have the latest values from their source workbooks, you can force an update. This step might be necessary if you just learned that someone made changes to the source workbook and saved the latest version to your network server.

To update linked formulas with their current value, open the Links dialog box (choose Edit ➪ Links), choose the appropriate source workbook, and then click the Update Now button. Excel updates the link formulas with the latest version of the source workbook.

Excel always sets worksheet links to the Automatic update option in the Links dialog box, and you can't change them to Manual. This means that Excel updates the links only when you open the workbook. Excel doesn't automatically update links when the source file changes.

Changing the link source

A time may come when you need to change the source workbook for your external references. For example, you might have a worksheet that has links to a workbook named Preliminary Budget, but you later receive a finalized version named Final Budget.

You *could* change all the cell links manually, or you could simply change the link source. Do this in the Links dialog box. Select the source workbook that you want to change and click the Change Source button. Excel displays a dialog box that enables you to select a new source file. After you select the file, all external reference formulas are updated.

Severing links

If you have external references in a workbook and then decide that you no longer need the links, you can convert the external reference formulas to values, thereby severing the links. To do so, follow these steps:

1. Select the range that contains the external reference formulas and copy it to the clipboard.
2. Choose the Edit ⇨ Paste Special command. Excel displays the Paste Special dialog box.
3. Select the Values option and click OK.
4. Press Esc to cancel cut-copy mode.

All formulas in the selected range are converted to their current values.

Potential problems with external reference formulas

Using external reference formulas can be quite useful, but the links may be unintentionally severed. In almost every case, you'll be able to reestablish lost links. If you open the workbook and Excel can't locate the file, you're presented with a dialog box that enables you to specify the workbook and re-create the links. You also can change the source file by using the Change Source button in the Links dialog box. The following sections discuss some pointers that you must remember when you use external reference formulas.

Renaming or moving a source workbook

If you rename the source document or move it to a different folder, Excel won't be able to update the links. You need to use the Links dialog box and specify the new source document.

Using the File ➪ Save As command

If both the source workbook and the destination workbook are open, Excel doesn't display the full path in the external reference formulas. If you use the File ➪ Save As command to give the source workbook a new name, Excel modifies the external references to use the new workbook name. In some cases, this may be what you want. But in other cases, it may not. Bottom line? Be careful when you use the File ➪ Save As command with a workbook that is linked to another workbook.

Modifying a source workbook

If you open a workbook that is a source workbook for another workbook, be extremely careful if you don't open the destination workbook at the same time. For example, if you add a new row to the source workbook, the cells all move down one row. When you open the destination workbook, it continues to use the old cell references — which are now invalid. You can avoid this problem in the following ways:

✦ **Open the destination workbook when you modify the source workbook.** If you do so, Excel adjusts the external references in the destination workbook when you make changes to the source workbook.

✦ **Use names rather than cell references in your link formula.** This is the safest approach.

Intermediary links

Excel doesn't place many limitations on the complexity of your network of external references. For example, Workbook A can contain external references that refer to Workbook B, which can contain an external reference that refers to Workbook C. In this case, a value in Workbook A can ultimately depend on a value in Workbook C. Workbook B is an *intermediary link*.

I don't recommend these types of links, but if you must use them, be aware that Excel doesn't update external reference formulas if the workbook isn't open. In the preceding example, assume that Workbooks A and C are open. If you change a value in Workbook C, Workbook A won't reflect the change, because you didn't open Workbook B (the intermediary link).

Consolidating Worksheets

The term *consolidation,* in the context of worksheets, refers to several operations that involve multiple worksheets or multiple workbook files. In some cases, consolidation involves creating link formulas. Here are two common examples of consolidation:

✦ The budget for each department in your company is stored in a separate worksheet in a single workbook. You need to consolidate the data and create a company-wide budget.

✦ Each department head submits his or her budget to you in a separate workbook. Your job is to consolidate these files into a company-wide budget.

Using Links to Recover Data from Corrupted Files

Sooner or later (with luck, later), it's bound to happen. You attempt to open an Excel workbook, and you get an error telling you that Excel can't access the file. Most of the time, this indicates that the file (somehow) got corrupted. If you're lucky, you have a recent backup. If you're *very* lucky, you haven't made any changes to the file since you backed it up. But assume that you fell a bit behind on your backup procedures, and the dead file is the only version you have.

Although I don't know of any method to fully recover a corrupt file, I'll share with you a method that sometimes enables you to recover at least some of the data from worksheets in the file (values, not formulas). Your actual success depends on how badly the file is corrupted.

This technique involves creating an external reference formula that refers to the corrupt file. You need to know the names of the worksheets that you want to recover. For example, assume that you have a workbook named Summary Data that you can't open. Further, assume that this workbook is stored on the C drive in a folder named Sheets. This workbook has one sheet, named Sheet1. Here's how to attempt to recover the data from this worksheet:

1. Open a new workbook.

2. In cell A1, enter the following external reference formula:

```
='C:\Sheets\[Summary Data]Sheet1'!A1
```

If you're lucky, this formula returns the value in cell A1 of Sheet1 in the corrupt file.

3. Copy down this formula and to the right to recover as many values as you can.

4. Convert the external reference formulas in the new workbook to values and then save the workbook.

If the corrupt file has additional worksheets, repeat these steps for any other worksheets in the workbook (you need to know the exact sheet names).

These tasks can be very difficult or quite easy; the tasks are easy if the information is laid out exactly the same in each worksheet (as you'll see shortly).

If the worksheets aren't laid out identically, they may be similar enough. In the second example, some budget files submitted to you may be missing categories that aren't used by a particular department. In this case, you can use a handy feature in Excel that matches data by using row and column titles. This feature is discussed later in the chapter (see "Consolidating Worksheets by Using Data ⇨ Consolidate").

If the worksheets bear little or no resemblance to each other, your best bet may be to edit the sheets so that they correspond to one another. In some cases, simply reentering the information in a standard format may be more efficient.

You can use any of the following techniques to consolidate information from multiple workbooks:

✦ Use external reference formulas

✦ Copy the data and use the Paste Special command

✦ Use Excel's Data ⇨ Consolidate command

✦ Use a pivot table (discussed in Chapter 35)

Consolidating worksheets by using formulas

Consolidating with formulas simply involves creating formulas that use references to other worksheets or other workbooks. The primary advantages to using this method of consolidation are the following:

✦ Dynamic updating — if the values in the source worksheets change, the formulas are updated automatically.

✦ The source workbooks don't need to be open when you create the consolidation formulas.

If you are consolidating the worksheets in the same workbook — and if all the worksheets are laid out identically — the consolidation task is quite simple. You can just use standard formulas to create the consolidations. For example, to compute the total for cell A1 in worksheets named Sheet2 through Sheet10, enter the following formula:

```
=SUM(Sheet2:Sheet10!A1)
```

You can enter this formula manually or use the multisheet selection technique discussed in Chapter 7 (see "Selecting Multisheet Ranges"). You can then copy this formula to create summary formulas for other cells. Figure 24-4 shows this technique at work.

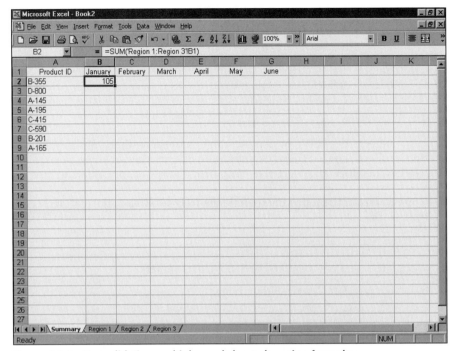

Figure 24-4: Consolidating multiple worksheets by using formulas

If the consolidation involves other workbooks, you can use external reference formulas to perform your consolidation. For example, if you want to add the values in cell A1 from Sheet1 in two workbooks (named Region1 and Region2), you can use the following formula:

```
=[Region1.xls]Sheet1!A1+[Region2.xls]Sheet1!A1
```

You can include any number of external references in this formula, up to the 1,024-character limit for a formula. However, if you use many external references, such a formula can be quite lengthy and confusing, if you need to edit it.

Caution   Remember that Excel expands the references to include the full path — which can increase the length of the formula. Therefore, this expansion may cause the formula to exceed the limit, thus creating an invalid formula.

If the worksheets that you're consolidating aren't laid out the same, you can still use formulas — but you have to ensure that each formula refers to the correct cell.

Consolidating worksheets by using Paste Special

Another method of consolidating information is to use the Edit ➪ Paste Special command. This method is applicable only when all the worksheets that you're consolidating are open. The disadvantage—a major disadvantage—is that the consolidation isn't dynamic. In other words, it doesn't generate a formula. So, if any data that was consolidated changes, the consolidation is no longer accurate.

This technique takes advantage of the fact that the Paste Special command can perform a mathematical operation when it pastes data from the clipboard. Figure 24-5 shows the Paste Special dialog box.

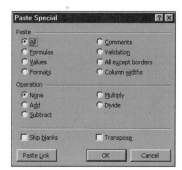

Figure 24-5: The Paste Special dialog box

Here's how to use this method:

1. Copy the data from the first source range.

2. Activate the destination workbook and select the cell in which you want to place the consolidation formula.

3. Select Edit ➪ Paste Special, click the Add option, and then click OK.

Repeat these steps for each source range that you want to consolidate. As you can see, this can be quite error-prone and isn't really a good method of consolidating data.

Consolidating worksheets by Using Data ➪ Consolidate

For the ultimate in data consolidation, use Excel's Data ➪ Consolidate command. This method is quite flexible, and in some cases, it even works if the source worksheets aren't laid out identically. This technique can create consolidations that are static (no link formulas) or dynamic (with link formulas). The Data ⇨ Consolidate command supports the following methods of consolidation:

✦ **By position:** This method is accurate only if the worksheets are laid out identically.

✦ **By category:** Excel uses row and column labels to match data in the source worksheets. Use this option if the data is laid out differently in the source worksheets or if some source worksheets are missing rows or columns.

Figure 24-6 shows the Consolidate dialog box, which appears when you select Data ⇨ Consolidate.

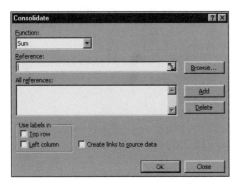

Figure 24-6: The Consolidate dialog box enables you to specify ranges to consolidate.

The following list is a description of the controls in this dialog box:

✦ **Function list box:** Specify the type of consolidation. Usually, you use Sum, but you also can select from ten other options: Count, Avg, Max, Min, Product, Count Nums, StdDev (standard deviation), StdDevp (population standard deviation), Var (variance), or Varp (population variance).

✦ **Reference text box:** Specify a range from a source file that you want to consolidate. You can enter the range reference manually or use any standard pointing technique (if the workbook is open). After you enter the range in this box, click the Add button to add it to the All References list. If you consolidate by position, don't include labels in the range. If you consolidate by category, *do* include labels in the range.

✦ **All references list box:** Contains the list of references that you have added with the Add button.

✦ **Use labels in check boxes:** Use to instruct Excel to perform the consolidation by examining the labels in the top row, the left column, or both positions. Use these options when you consolidate by category.

✦ **Create links to source data check box:** When you select this option, Excel creates an outline that consists of external references to the destination cells in the destination worksheet. Additionally, Excel includes summary formulas in the outline. If you don't select this option, the consolidation doesn't use formulas.

✦ **Browse button:** Displays a dialog box that enables you to select a workbook to open. It inserts the filename in the Reference box, but you have to supply the range reference.

✦ **Add button:** Adds the reference in the Reference box to the All References list.

✦ **Delete button:** Deletes the selected reference from the All References list.

An example consolidation

The simple example in this section demonstrates the power of the Data ⇨ Consolidate command. Figure 24-7 shows three single-sheet workbooks that will be consolidated. These worksheets report product sales for three months. Notice, however, that they don't all report on the same products. In addition, the products aren't even listed in the same order. In other words, these worksheets aren't laid out identically — which makes creating consolidation formulas difficult.

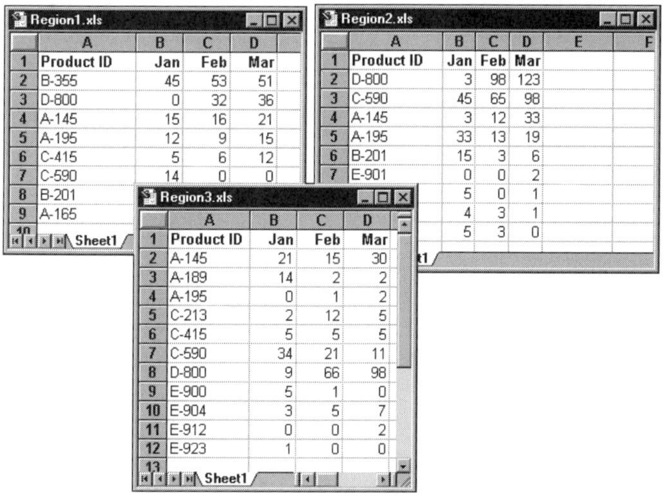

Figure 24-7: Three worksheets to be consolidated

To consolidate this information, start with a new workbook. The source workbooks can be open or not — it doesn't matter. Follow these steps to consolidate the workbooks:

1. Select Data ⇨ Consolidate. Excel displays its Consolidate dialog box.

2. Select the type of consolidation summary that you want to use. Use Sum for this example.
3. Enter the reference for the first worksheet to consolidate. If the workbook is open, you can point to the reference. If it's not open, click the Browse button to locate the file on disk. The reference must include a range. Use **A1:D100**. This range is larger than the actual range to consolidate, but using this range ensures that the consolidation still works if new rows are added to the source file. When the reference in the Reference box is correct, click Add to add it to the All References list.
4. Enter the reference for the second worksheet. You can simply edit the existing reference by changing Region1 to **Region2** and then clicking Add. This reference is added to the All References list.
5. Enter the reference for the third worksheet. Again, you can simply edit the existing reference by changing Region2 to **Region3** and then clicking Add. This final reference is added to the All References list.
6. Because the worksheets aren't laid out the same, select the Left column and Top row check boxes to force Excel to match the data by using the labels.
7. Select the Create links to source data check box to make Excel create an outline with external references.
8. Click OK to begin the consolidation.

In seconds, Excel creates the consolidation, beginning at the active cell. Figure 24-8 shows the result. Notice that Excel created an outline, which is collapsed to show only the subtotals for each product. If you expand the outline, you can see the details. Examine it further, and you'll discover that each detail cell is an external reference formula that uses the appropriate cell in the source file. Therefore, the destination range is updated automatically if any data is changed.

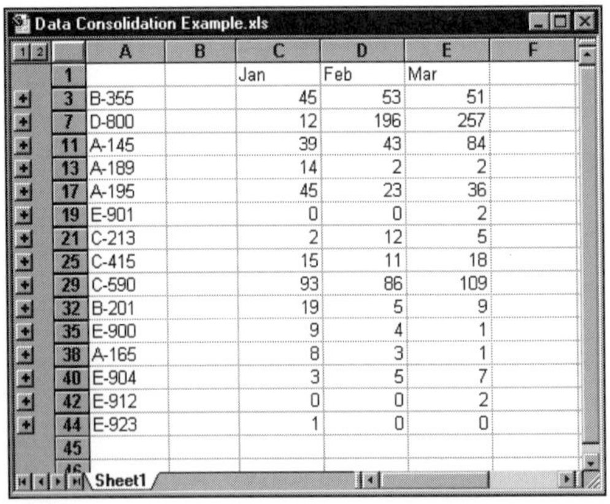

	A	B	C	D	E	F
1			Jan	Feb	Mar	
3	B-355		45	53	51	
7	D-800		12	196	257	
11	A-145		39	43	84	
13	A-189		14	2	2	
17	A-195		45	23	36	
19	E-901		0	0	2	
21	C-213		2	12	5	
25	C-415		15	11	18	
29	C-590		93	86	109	
32	B-201		19	5	9	
35	E-900		9	4	1	
38	A-165		8	3	1	
40	E-904		3	5	7	
42	E-912		0	0	2	
44	E-923		1	0	0	
45						

Figure 24-8: The result of the consolidation

More about consolidation

Excel is very flexible regarding the sources that you can consolidate. You can consolidate data from the following:

- ✦ Workbooks that are open
- ✦ Workbooks that are closed (you have to enter the reference manually — but you can use the Browse button to get the filename part of the reference)
- ✦ The same workbook in which you're creating the consolidation

And, of course, you can mix and match any of the preceding choices in a single consolidation.

Excel remembers the references that you entered in the Consolidate dialog box and saves them with the workbook. Therefore, if you want to refresh a consolidation later, you won't have to reenter the references.

If you perform the consolidation by matching labels, be aware that the matches must be exact. For example, *Jan* does not match *January*. The matching isn't case-sensitive, however, so *April* does match *APRIL*. In addition, the labels can be in any order, and they need not be in the same order in all the source ranges.

If you don't choose the Create links to source data check box, Excel doesn't create formulas, which generates a static consolidation. If the data on any of the source worksheets changes, the consolidation doesn't update automatically. To update the summary information, you need to select the destination range and repeat the Data ⇨ Consolidate command.

 Tip   If you name the destination range **Consolidate_Area**, you don't need to select it before you update the consolidation. Consolidate_Area is a name that has special meaning to Excel.

If you choose the Create links to source data check box, Excel creates an outline. This is a standard worksheet outline, and you can manipulate it by using the techniques described in Chapter 23.

Summary

This chapter discusses two important spreadsheet procedures: linking and consolidation. *Linking* is the process of referring in one worksheet to cells in external workbooks. *Consolidation* is the process of combining or summarizing information from two or more worksheets (which can be in multiple workbooks). This chapter covers various methods of linking and consolidation, and lists potential pitfalls.

✦   ✦   ✦

Introducing Arrays

One of Excel's most interesting (and most powerful) features is its ability to work with arrays in a formula. Although Excel is no longer unique in this area (recent versions of Quattro Pro also support arrays), its implementation is still the most elegant. This chapter introduces the concept of arrays and is required reading for anyone who wants to become a master of Excel formulas. Chapter 36 continues with lots of useful examples.

Array Formulas

If you do any computer programming, you've probably been exposed to the concept of an array. An *array* is simply a collection of items operated on collectively or individually. In Excel, an array can be one-dimensional or two-dimensional. These dimensions correspond to rows and columns. For example, a *one-dimensional array* can be stored in a range that consists of one row (a horizontal array) or one column (a vertical array). A *two-dimensional array* can be stored in a rectangular range of cells. Excel doesn't support three-dimensional arrays.

But, as you'll see, arrays need not be stored in cells. You can also work with arrays that exist only in Excel's memory. You can then use an *array formula* to manipulate this information and return a result. An array formula can occupy multiple cells, or reside in a single cell.

This section presents two examples of array formulas. One is of an array formula that occupies multiple cells, and the other is of another array formula that occupies only one cell.

A multicell array formula

Figure 25-1 shows a simple worksheet set up to calculate product sales. Normally, you would calculate the value in column D (total sales per product) with a formula such as the one that follows, and then copy this formula down the column.

```
=B2*C2
```

After copying the formula, the worksheet contains six formulas in column D.

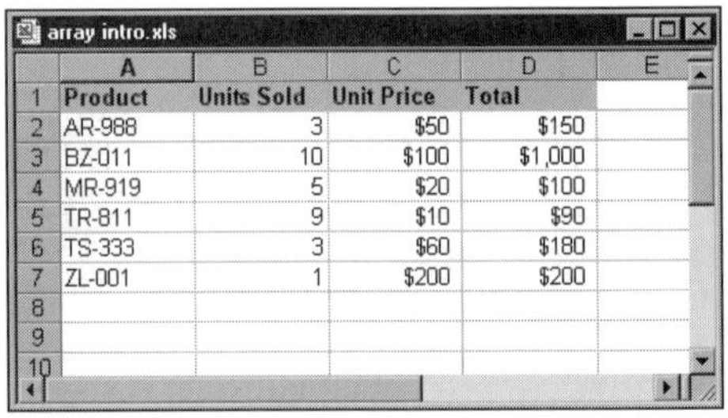
array intro.xls

	A	B	C	D	E
1	Product	Units Sold	Unit Price	Total	
2	AR-988	3	$50	$150	
3	BZ-011	10	$100	$1,000	
4	MR-919	5	$20	$100	
5	TR-811	9	$10	$90	
6	TS-333	3	$60	$180	
7	ZL-001	1	$200	$200	
8					
9					
10					

Figure 25-1: The range D2:D7 contains a single array formula.

Another alternative uses a *single* formula (an array formula) to calculate all six values in D2:D7. This single formula occupies six cells and returns an array of six values.

To create a single array formula to perform the calculations do the following:

1. Select a range to hold the results. In this case, the range is D2:D7.
2. Enter the following formula:
   ```
   =B2:B7*C2:C7
   ```
3. Normally, you press Enter to enter a formula. Because this is an array formula, press Ctrl+Shift+Enter.

The formula is entered into all six of the selected cells. If you examine the formula bar, you'll see the following:

```
{=B2:B7*C2:C7}
```

Excel places brackets around the formula to indicate that it's an array formula.

This formula performs its calculations and returns a six-item array. The array formula actually works with two other arrays, both of which happen to be stored in ranges. The values for the first array are stored in B2:B7, and the values for the second array are stored in C2:C7.

Because it's not possible to display more than one value in a single cell, six cells are required to display the resulting array. That explains why you selected six cells before you entered the array formula.

This array formula, of course, returns exactly the same values as these six normal formulas entered into individual cells in D2:D7:

```
=B2*C2
=B3*C3
=B4*C4
=B5*C5
=B6*C6
=B7*C7
```

Using a single array formula rather than individual formulas does offer a few advantages:

✦ It's a good way of ensuring that all formulas in a range are identical.

✦ Using a multicell array formula makes it less likely you will overwrite a formula accidentally. You cannot change one cell in a multicell array formula.

✦ Using a multicell array formula will almost certainly prevent novices from tampering with your formulas.

A single-cell array formula

Now, it's time to take a look at a single-cell array formula. Refer again to Figure 25-1. The following array formula occupies a single cell:

```
{=SUM(B2:B7*C2:C7)}
```

You can enter this formula into any cell. But when you enter this formula, make sure you use Ctrl+Shift+Enter (and don't type the brackets).

This array formula returns the sum of the total product sales. It's important to understand that this formula does not rely on the information in column D. In fact, you can delete column D and the formula will still work.

This formula works with two arrays, both of which are stored in cells. The first array is stored in B2:B7, and the second array is stored in C2:C7. The formula multiplies the corresponding values in these two arrays and creates a new array (which exists only in memory). The SUM function then operates on this new array and returns the sum of its values.

Creation of an array constant

The examples in the previous section used arrays stored in worksheet ranges. The examples in this section demonstrate an important concept: An array does not have to be stored in a range of cells. This type of array, which is stored in memory, is referred to as an *array constant*.

You create an array constant by listing its items and surrounding them with brackets. Here's an example of a five-item vertical array constant:

```
{1,0,1,0,1}
```

The following formula uses the SUM function, with the preceding array constant as its argument. The formula returns the sum of the values in the array (which is 3).

```
=SUM({1,0,1,0,1})
```

Note   When you specify an array directly (as shown previously), you must provide the brackets around the array elements. When you enter an array formula, on the other hand, you do not supply the brackets.

At this point, you probably don't see any advantage to using an array constant. The formula that follows, for example, returns the same result as the previous formula.

```
=SUM(1,0,1,0,1)
```

Following is a formula that uses two array constants:

```
=SUM({1,2,3,4}*{5,6,7,8})
```

This formula creates a new array (in memory) that consists of the product of the corresponding elements in the two arrays. The new array is:

```
{5,12,21,32}
```

This new array is then used as an argument for the SUM function, which returns the result (70). The formula is equivalent to the following formula, which doesn't use arrays:

```
=SUM(1*5,2*6,3*7,4*8)
```

A formula can work with both an array constant and an array stored in a range. The following formula, for example, returns the sum of the values in A1:D1, each multiplied by the corresponding element in the array constant.

```
=SUM((A1:D1*{1,2,3,4}))
```

This formula is equivalent to:

```
=SUM(A1*1,B1*2,C1*3,D1*4)
```

Array constant elements

An array constant can contain numbers, text, logical values (TRUE or FALSE), and even error values such as #N/A. Numbers can be in integer, decimal, or scientific format. You must enclose text in double quotation marks (for example, "Tuesday"). You can use different types of values in the same array constant, as in this example:

```
{1,2,3,TRUE,FALSE,TRUE,"Moe","Larry","Shemp"}
```

An array constant cannot contain formulas, functions, or other arrays. Numeric values cannot contain dollar signs, commas, parentheses, or percent signs. For example, the following is an invalid array constant:

```
{SQRT(32),$56.32,12.5%}
```

Dimensions of an Array

As stated previously, an array can be either one-dimensional or two-dimensional. A one-dimensional array's orientation can be either vertical or horizontal.

One-dimensional horizontal arrays

The elements in a one-dimensional horizontal array are separated by commas. The following example is a one-dimensional horizontal array constant:

```
{1,2,3,4,5}
```

To display this array in a range requires five cells in a row. To enter this array into a range, select a range of cells that consists of one row and five columns. Then, enter ={1,2,3,4,5} and press Ctrl+Shift+Enter.

If you enter this array into a horizontal range that consists of more than five cells, the extra cells will contain #NA (which denotes unavailable values). If you enter this array into a *vertical* range of cells, only the first item (1) will appear in each cell.

The following example is another horizontal array; it has seven elements and is made up of text strings:

```
{"Sun","Mon","Tue","Wed","Thu","Fri","Sat"}
```

One-dimensional vertical arrays

The elements in a one-dimensional vertical array are separated by semicolons. The following is a six-element vertical array constant:

    {10;20;30;40;50;60}

Displaying this array in a range requires six cells in a column. To enter this array into a range, select a range of cells that consists of six rows and one column. Then, enter ={10;20;30;40;50;60} and press Ctrl+Shift+Enter.

The following is another example of a vertical array; this one has four elements:

    {"Widgets";"Sprockets";"Do-Dads";"Thing-A-Majigs"}

Two-dimensional arrays

A two-dimensional array uses commas to separate its horizontal elements, and semicolons to separate its vertical elements. The following example shows a 3×4 array constant.

    {1,2,3,4;5,6,7,8;9,10,11,12}

To display this array in a range requires 12 cells. To enter this array into a range, select a range of cells that consists of three rows and four columns. Then, type ={1,2,3,4;5,6,7,8;9,10,11,12} and press Ctrl+Shift+Enter. Figure 25-2 shows how this array appears when entered into a range.

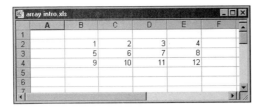

Figure 25-2: A 3×4 array, entered into a range of cells

If you enter an array into a range that has more cells than array elements, Excel displays #NA into the extra cells. Figure 25-3 shows a 3×4 array entered into a 10×5 cell range.

Each row of a two-dimensional array must contain the same number of items. The array that follows, for example, is not valid because the third row contains only two items:

    {1,2,3,4;5,6,7,8;9,10,11}

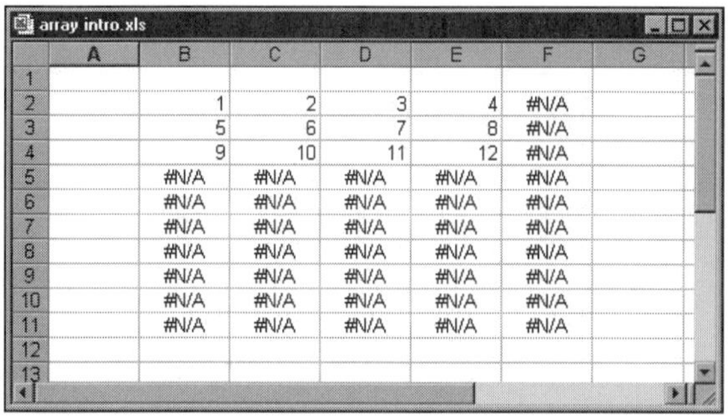

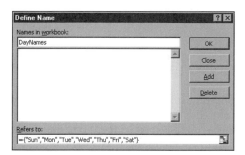

Figure 25-3: A 3×4 array, entered into a 10×5 cell range

Naming Array Constants

You can create an array constant, give it a name, and then use this named array in a formula. Technically, a named array is a named formula.

Figure 25-4 shows a named array being created using the Define Name dialog box. The name of the array is *DayNames*, and it refers to the following array:

```
{"Sun","Mon","Tue","Wed","Thu","Fri","Sat"}
```

Figure 25-4: Creating a named array constant

Notice that, in the Define Name dialog box, the array is defined using a leading equal sign (=). Without this equal sign, the array is interpreted as a text string rather than an array. Also, you must type the brackets when defining a named array constant; Excel does not enter them for you.

After creating this named array, you can use it in a formula. Figure 25-5 shows a worksheet that contains a single array formula entered into the range A1:G1. The formula is:

```
{=DayNames}
```

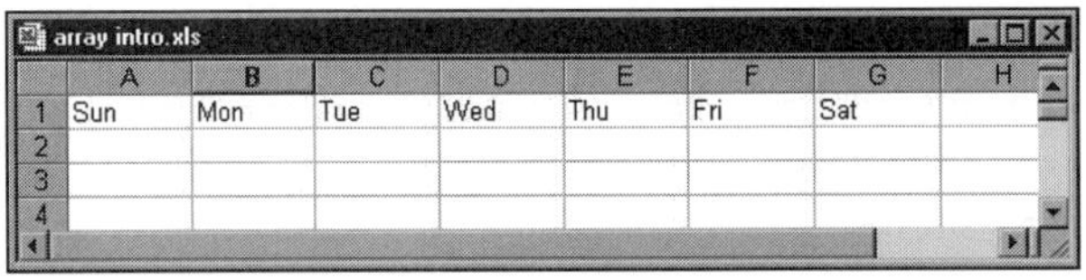

Figure 25-5: Using a named array in an array formula

Because commas separate the array elements, the array has a horizontal orientation. Use semicolons to create a vertical array. Or you can use Excel's TRANSPOSE function to insert a horizontal array into a vertical range of cells (see "Transposing an Array," later in this chapter).

You also can access individual elements from the array by using Excel's INDEX function. The following formula, for example, returns *Wed*, the fourth item in the *DayNames* array:

```
=INDEX(DayNames,4)
```

Working with Array Formulas

This section deals with the mechanics of selecting cells that contain arrays, and entering and editing array formulas. These procedures differ a bit from working with ordinary ranges and formulas.

Entering an array formula

When you enter an array formula into a cell or range, you must follow a special procedure so Excel knows that you want an array formula rather than a normal formula. You enter a normal formula into a cell by pressing Enter. You enter an array formula into one or more cells by pressing Ctrl+Shift+Enter.

You can easily identify an array formula, because the formula is enclosed in brackets in the formula bar. The following formula, for example, is an array formula:

```
{=SUM(LEN(A1:A5))}
```

Don't enter the brackets when you create an array formula; Excel inserts them for you. If the result of an array formula consists of more than one value, you must select all of the cells in the results range *before* you enter the formula. If you fail to do this, only the first element of the result is returned.

Selecting an array formula range

You can select the cells that contain a multicell array formula manually, by using the normal cell selection procedures. Or, you can use either of the following methods:

✦ Activate any cell in the array formula range. Select Edit ➪ Go To (or press F5), click the Special button, and then choose the Current Array option. Click OK to close the dialog box.

✦ Activate any cell in the array formula range and press Ctrl+/ to select the entire array.

Editing an array formula

If an array formula occupies multiple cells, you must edit the entire range as though it is a single cell. The key point to remember is that you can't change just one element of an array formula. If you attempt to do so, Excel displays the messages shown in Figure 25-6.

Figure 25-6: Excel's warning message reminds you that you can't edit just one cell of a multicell array formula.

The following rules apply to multicell array formulas. (If you try to do any of these things, Excel lets you know about it.)

✦ You can't change the contents of any individual cell that makes up an array formula.

✦ You can't move cells that make up part of an array formula (but you can move an entire array formula).

✦ You can't delete cells that form part of an array formula (but you can delete an entire array).

✦ You can't insert new cells into an array range. This rule includes inserting rows or columns that would add new cells to an array range.

To edit an array formula, select all the cells in the array range and activate the formula bar as usual (click it or press F2). Excel removes the brackets from the formula while you edit it. Edit the formula and then press Ctrl+Shift+Enter to enter the changes. All of the cells in the array now reflect your editing changes.

Caution   If you fail to press Ctrl+Shift+Enter after editing an array formula, the formula will no longer be an array formula.

You can't change any individual cell that makes up a multicell array formula. However, you can apply formatting to the entire array or to only parts of it.

Expanding or contracting a multicell array formula

Often, you may need to expand a multicell array formula (to include more cells) or contract it (to include fewer cells). Doing so requires a few steps:

1. Select the entire range that contains the array formula.

2. Press F2 to enter Edit mode.

3. Press Ctrl+Enter. This step enters an identical (nonarray) formula into each selected cell.

4. Change your range selection to include additional or fewer cells.

5. Press F2.

6. Press Ctrl+Shift+Enter.

Array Formulas: The Downside

If you've followed along in this chapter, you probably understand some of the advantages of using array formulas. The main advantage, of course, is that an array formula enables you to perform otherwise impossible calculations. As you gain more experience with arrays, you undoubtedly will discover some disadvantages.

Array formulas are one of the least understood features of Excel. Consequently, if you plan to share a workbook with someone who may need to make modifications, you should probably avoid using array formulas. Encountering an array formula when you don't know what it is can be very confusing.

You may also discover that you can easily forget to enter an array formula by pressing Ctrl+Shift+Enter. If you edit an existing array, you still must use these keys to complete the edits. Except for logical errors, this is probably the most common problem that users have with array formulas. If you press Enter by mistake after editing an array formula, just double-click the cell to get back into Edit mode, and then press Ctrl+Shift+Enter.

Another potential problem with array formulas is that they can slow your worksheet's recalculations, especially if you use very large arrays. On a faster system, this may not be a problem. But, conversely, using an array formula is almost always faster than using a custom VBA function.

Multicell Array Formulas

This section contains examples that demonstrate additional features of array formulas that are entered into a range of cells. These features include creating arrays from values, performing operations, using functions, transposing arrays, and generating consecutive integers.

Creating an array from values in a range

The following array formula creates an array from a range of cells. Figure 25-7 shows a workbook with some data entered into A1:C4. The range D8:F11 contains a single array formula:

```
{=A1:C4}
```

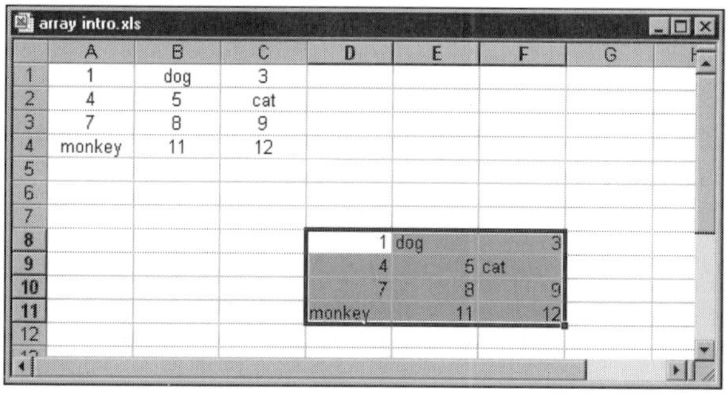

Figure 25-7: Creating an array from a range

The array in D8:F11 is linked to the range A1:C4. Change any value in A1:C4 and the corresponding cell in D8:F11 reflects that change.

Creating an array constant from values in a range

In the previous example, the array formula in D8:F11 essentially created a link to the cells in A1:C4. It's possible to "sever" this link and create an array constant made up of the values in A1:C4.

To do so, select the cells that contain the array formula (the range D8:F11, in this example). Then press F2 to edit the array formula. Press F9 to convert the cell references to values. Press Ctrl+Shift+Enter to reenter the array formula (which now uses an array constant). The array constant is:

```
{1,"dog",3;4,5,"cat";7,8,9;"monkey",11,12}
```

Figure 25-8 shows how this looks in the formula bar.

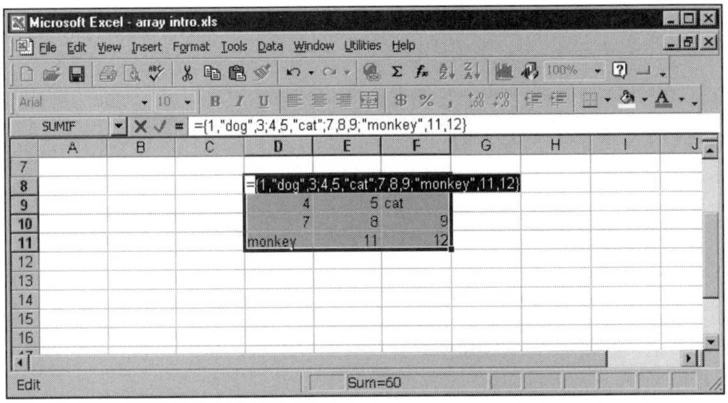

Figure 25-8: After pressing F9, the formula bar displays the array constant.

Performing operations on an array

So far, most of the examples in this chapter simply entered arrays into ranges. The following array formula creates a rectangular array and multiplies each array element by 2:

```
{={1,2,3,4;5,6,7,8;9,10,11,12}*2}
```

Figure 25-9 shows the result when you enter this formula into a range.

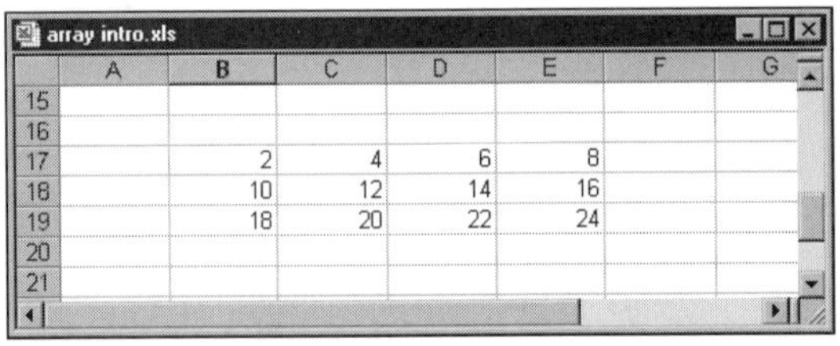

Figure 25-9: Performing a mathematical operation on an array

The following array formula multiplies each array element by itself. Figure 25-10 shows the result when you enter this formula into a range.

```
{={1,2,3,4;5,6,7,8;9,10,11,12}*{1,2,3,4;5,6,7,8;9,10,11,12}}
```

The following array formula is a simpler way of obtaining the same result:

```
{={1,2,3,4;5,6,7,8;9,10,11,12}^2}
```

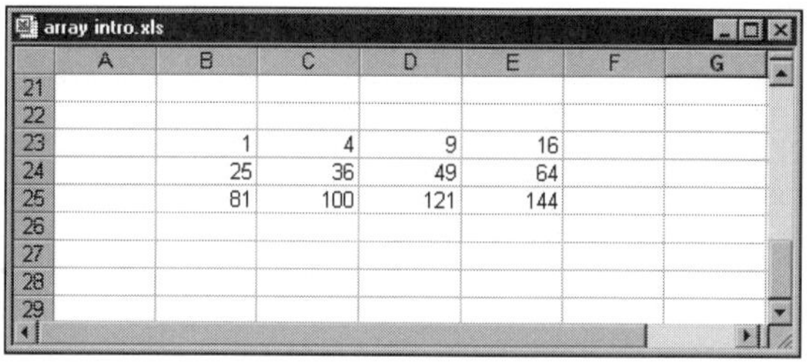

Figure 25-10: Multiplying each array element by itself

If the array is stored in a range (such as A1:C4), the array formula returns the square of each value in the range, as follows:

```
{=A1:C4^2}
```

Using functions with an array

As you might expect, you also can use functions with an array. The following array formula, which you can enter into a 10-cell vertical range, calculates the square root of each array element:

```
{=SQRT({1;2;3;4;5;6;7;8;9;10})}
```

If the array is stored in a range, an array formula such as the one that follows returns the square root of each value in the range:

```
{=SQRT(A1:C4)}{=SQRT(A1:A10)}
```

Transposing an array

When you transpose an array, you essentially convert rows to columns and columns to rows. In other words, you can convert a horizontal array to a vertical array (and vice versa). Use Excel's TRANSPOSE function to transpose an array.

Consider the following one-dimensional horizontal array constant:

```
{1,2,3,4,5}
```

You can enter this array into a vertical range of cells by using the TRANSPOSE function. To do so, select a range of five cells that occupy five rows and one column. Then, enter the following formula and press Ctrl+Shift+Enter:

```
=TRANSPOSE({1,2,3,4,5})
```

The horizontal array is transposed, and the array elements appear in the vertical range.

Transposing a two-dimensional array works in a similar manner. Figure 25-11 shows a two-dimensional array entered into a range normally, and entered into a range using the TRANSPOSE function. The formula in A1:D3 is:

```
{={1,2,3,4;5,6,7,8;9,10,11,12}}
```

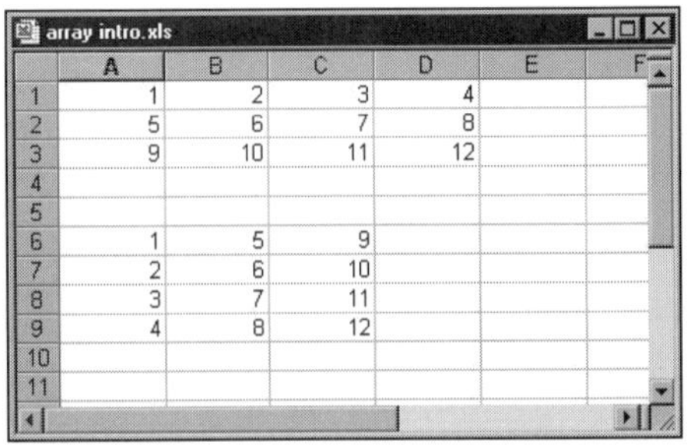

Figure 25-11: Using the TRANSPOSE function to transpose a rectangular array

The formula in A6:C9 is:

```
{=TRANSPOSE({1,2,3,4;5,6,7,8;9,10,11,12})}
```

You can, of course, use the TRANSPOSE function to transpose an array stored in a range. The following formula, for example, uses an array stored in A1:C4 (four rows, three columns). You can enter this array formula into a range that consists of three rows and four columns.

```
{=TRANSPOSE(A1:C4)}
```

Generating an array of consecutive integers

As you will see in Chapter 26, it's often useful to generate an array of consecutive integers for use in an array formula. Excel's ROW function, which returns a row number, is ideal for this. Consider the array formula shown here, entered into a vertical range of 12 cells:

```
{=ROW(1:12)}
```

This formula generates a 12-element array that contains integers from 1 to 12. To demonstrate, select a range that consists of 12 rows and one column, and enter the array formula into the range. You'll find that the range is filled with 12 consecutive integers (see Figure 25-12).

Figure 25-12: Using an array formula to generate consecutive integers

If you want to generate an array of consecutive integers, a formula like the one shown previously is good—but not perfect. To see the problem, insert a new row above the range that contains the array formula. You'll find that Excel adjusts the row references so the array formula now reads:

```
{=ROW(2:13)}
```

The formula that originally generated integers from 1 to 12 now generates integers from 2 to 13.

For a better solution, use this formula:

```
{=ROW(INDIRECT("1:12"))}
```

This formula uses the INDIRECT function, which takes a text string as its argument. Excel does not adjust the references contained in the argument for the INDIRECT function. Therefore, this array formula *always* returns integers from 1-12.

Cross-Reference

Chapter 26 contains several examples that use the technique for generating consecutive integers.

Worksheet Functions That Return an Array

Several of Excel's worksheet functions use arrays; you must enter a formula that uses one of these functions into multiple cells as an array formula. These functions are FORECAST, FREQUENCY, GROWTH, LINEST, LOGEST, MINVERSE, MMULT, and TREND. Consult the online help for more information.

Single-Cell Array Formulas

The examples in the previous section all used a multicell array formula—a single array formula entered into a range of cells. The real power of using arrays becomes apparent when you use single-cell array formulas. This section contains examples of array formulas that occupy a single cell.

Counting characters in a range

Suppose you have a range of cells that contains text entries (see Figure 25-13). If you need to get a count of the total number of characters in that range, the "traditional" method involves creating a formula like the one that follows and copying it down the column:

```
=LEN(A1)
```

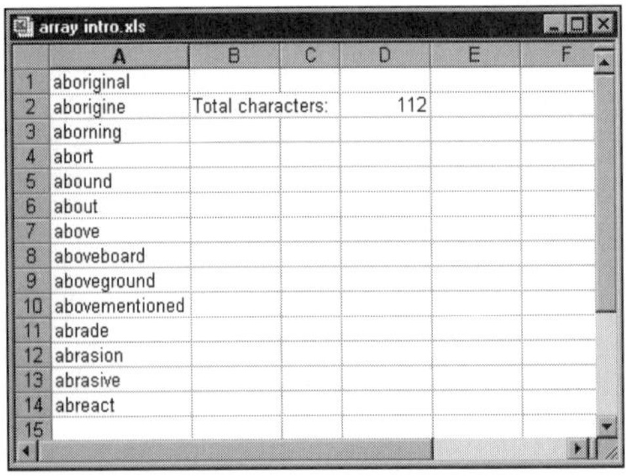

Figure 25-13: A single array formula can count the number of characters in a range of text.

Then, you use a SUM formula to calculate the sum of the values returned by the intermediate formulas.

The following array formula does the job without using any intermediate formulas:

```
{=SUM(LEN(A1:A14))}
```

The array formula uses the LEN function to create a new array (in memory) that consists of the number of characters in each cell of the range. In this case, the new array is:

```
{1,10,9,8,5,6,5,5,10,11,14,6,8,8,7}
```

The array formula is then reduced to:

```
=SUM({1,10,9,8,5,6,5,5,10,11,14,6,8,8,7})
```

Summing the three smallest values in a range

The following formula returns the sum of the three smallest values in a range named *Data*:

```
{=SUM(SMALL(Data,{1,2,3}))}
```

The function uses an array constant as the second argument for the SMALL function. This generates a new array, which consists of the three smallest values in the range. This array is then passed to the SUM function, which returns the sum of the values in the new array.

Figure 25-14 shows an example in which the range A1:A10 is named *Data*. The SMALL function is evaluated three times — each time with a different second argument. The first time, the SMALL function has a second argument of 1, and it returns –5. The second time, the second argument for the SMALL function is 2, and it returns 0 (the second smallest value in the range). The third time, the SMALL function has a second argument of 3, and it returns the third smallest value of 2.

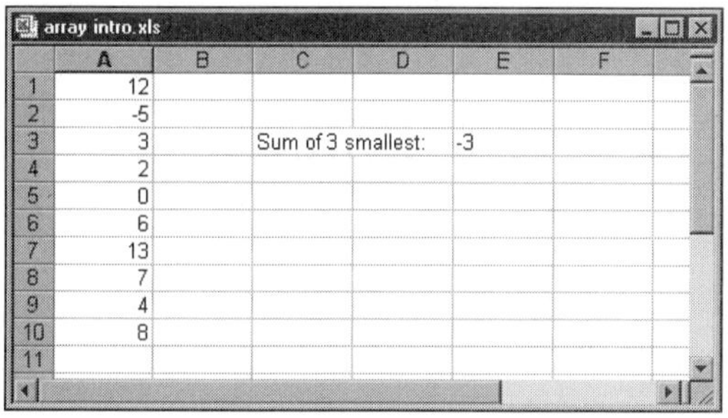

Figure 25-14: An array formula returns the sum of the three smallest values in A1:A10.

Therefore, the array that's passed to the SUM function is:

```
{-5,0,2}
```

The formula returns the sum of the array (-3).

Counting text cells in a range

The following array formula uses the IF function to examine each cell in a range. It then creates a new array (of the same size and dimensions as the original range) that consists of 1s and 0s, depending on whether the cell contains text. This new array is then passed to the SUM function, which returns the sum of the items in the array. The result is a count of the number of text cells in the range.

```
{=SUM(IF(ISTEXT(A1:D5),1,0))}
```

Cross-Reference   This general array formula type (that is, an IF function nested in a SUM function) is very useful for counting. Refer to Chapter 12 for additional examples.

Figure 25-15 shows an example of the preceding formula in cell C8. The array created by the IF Function is:

    {0,1,1,1;1,0,0,0;1,0,0,0;1,0,0,0;1,0,0,0}

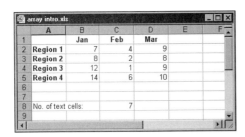

Figure 25-15: An array formula returns the number of text cells in the range.

Notice that this array contains four rows of three elements (the same dimensions as the range).

A variation on this formula follows:

    {=SUM(ISTEXT(A1:D5)*1)}

This formula eliminates the need for the IF function and takes advantage of the fact that:

    TRUE * 1 = 1

and

    FALSE * 1 = 0

Eliminating intermediate formulas

One of the main benefits of using an array formula is that you can eliminate intermediate formulas in your worksheet. This makes your worksheet more compact, and eliminates the need to display irrelevant calculations. Figure 25-16 shows a worksheet that contains pre-test and post-test scores for students. Column D contains formulas that calculate the changes between the pre-test and the post-test scores. Cell D17 contains a formula, shown here, that calculates the average of the values in column D:

    =AVERAGE(D2:D15)

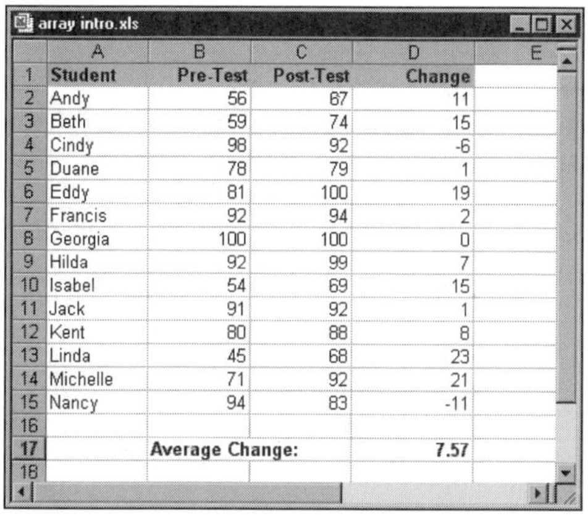

array intro.xls

	A	B	C	D	E
1	Student	Pre-Test	Post-Test	Change	
2	Andy	56	67	11	
3	Beth	59	74	15	
4	Cindy	98	92	-6	
5	Duane	78	79	1	
6	Eddy	81	100	19	
7	Francis	92	94	2	
8	Georgia	100	100	0	
9	Hilda	92	99	7	
10	Isabel	54	69	15	
11	Jack	91	92	1	
12	Kent	80	88	8	
13	Linda	45	68	23	
14	Michelle	71	92	21	
15	Nancy	94	83	-11	
16					
17		Average Change:		7.57	
18					

Figure 25-16: Without an array formula, calculating the average change requires intermediate formulas in column D.

With an array formula, you can eliminate column D. The following array formula calculates the average of the changes, but does not require the formulas in column D:

```
{=AVERAGE(C2:C15-B2:B15)}
```

How does it work? The formula uses two arrays, the values of which are stored in two ranges (B2:B15 and C2:C15). The formula creates a *new* array that consists of the differences between each corresponding element in the other arrays. This new array is stored in Excel's memory, not in a range. The AVERAGE function then uses this new array as its argument and returns the result.

The new array consists of the following elements:

```
{11,15,-6,1,19,2,0,7,15,1,8,23,21,-11}
```

The formula, therefore, is reduced to:

```
=AVERAGE({11,15,-6,1,19,2,0,7,15,1,8,23,21,-11})
```

You can use additional array formulas to calculate other measures for the data in this example. For instance, the following array formula returns the largest change (for example, the greatest improvement). This formula returns 23, which represents Linda's test scores.

```
{=MAX(C2:C15-B2:B15)}
```

The following array formula returns the smallest change (that is, the least improvement). This formula returns –11, which represents Nancy's test scores.

```
{=MIN(C2:C15-B2:B15)}
```

Using an array in lieu of a range reference

If your formula uses a function that requires a range reference, you may be able to replace that range reference with an array constant. This is useful in situations in which the values in the referenced range do not change.

Note   A notable exception to using an array constant in place of a range reference in a function is with the database functions that use a reference to a criteria range (for example, DSUM). Unfortunately, using an array constant instead of a reference to a criteria range does not work.

Figure 25-17 shows a worksheet that uses a lookup table to display a word that corresponds to an integer. For example, looking up a value of 9 returns *Nine* from the lookup table in D1:E10. The formula in cell C1 is:

```
=VLOOKUP(B1,D1:E10,2,FALSE)
```

	A	B	C	D	E	F
1	Number ->	9	Nine	1	One	
2				2	Two	
3				3	Three	
4				4	Four	
5				5	Five	
6				6	Six	
7				7	Seven	
8				8	Eight	
9				9	Nine	
10				10	Ten	
11						

Figure 25-17: You can replace the lookup table in D1:E10 with an array constant.

You can use a two-dimensional array in place of the lookup range. The following formula returns the same result as the previous formula, but it does not require the lookup range in D1:E1:

```
=VLOOKUP(B1,{1,"One";2,"Two";3,"Three";4,"Four";5,"Five";
6,"Six";7,"Seven";8,"Eight";9,"Nine";10,"Ten"},2,FALSE)
```

Summary

This chapter introduced the concept of *arrays*, a collection of items that reside in a range or in Excel's memory. An array formula operates on a range and returns a single value or an array of values.

The next chapter continues this discussion and presents several useful examples that help clarify the concept.

✦   ✦   ✦

Performing Magic with Array Formulas

The previous chapter provided an introduction to arrays and array formulas, and presented some basic examples to whet your appetite. This chapter continues the saga, and provides many useful examples that further demonstrate the power of this feature.

I selected the examples in this chapter to provide a good assortment of the various uses for array formulas. Most can be used as-is. You will, of course, need to adjust the range names or references used. Also, you can modify many of the examples easily to work in a slightly different manner.

More Single-Cell Array Formulas

You enter single-cell array formulas into a single cell. These array formulas work with arrays contained in a range, or that exist in memory.

Summing a range that contains errors

You've probably discovered that Excel's SUM function doesn't work if you attempt to sum a range that contains one or more error values (such as #DIV/0! or #NA). Figure 26-1 shows an example. The SUM formula in cell C9 returns an error value because the range that it sums (C2:C8) contains errors.

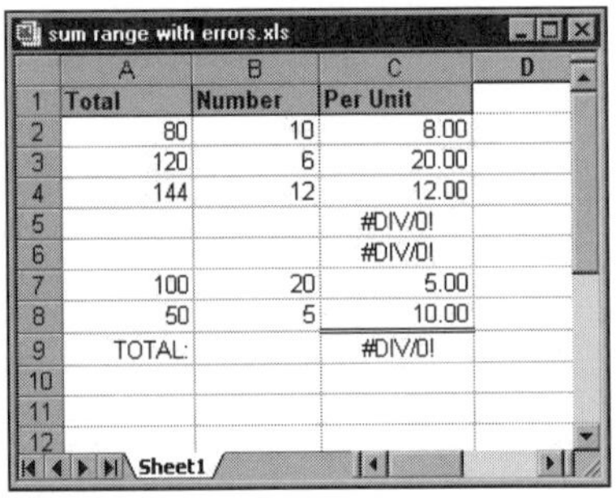

Figure 26-1: An array formula can sum a range of values, even if the range contains errors.

The following array formula returns a sum of the values in a range named *Data*, even if the range contains error values:

```
{=SUM(IF(ISERROR(Data),"",Data))}
```

This formula works by creating a new array that contains the original values, but without the errors. The IF function effectively filters out error values by replacing them with an empty string. The SUM function then works on this "filtered" array. This technique also works with other functions, such as MIN and MAX.

> **Note**   You may want to use a function other than ISERROR. The ISERROR function returns TRUE for any error value: #N/A, #VALUE!, #REF!, #DIV/0!, #NUM!, #NAME?, or #NULL!. The ISERR function returns TRUE for any error except #N/A. The ISNA function returns TRUE only if the cell contains a #N/A.

Counting the number of error values in a range

The following array formula is similar to the previous example, but it returns a count of the number of error values in a range named *Data*.

```
{=SUM(IF(ISERROR(Data),1,0))}
```

This formula creates an array that consists of 1s (if the corresponding cell contains an error) and 0s (if the corresponding cell does not contain an error value).

You can simplify the formula a bit by removing the third argument for the IF function. If this argument is not specified, the IF function returns FALSE if the condition is not satisfied (that is, the cell does not contain an error value). The array formula shown here performs exactly like the previous formula, but doesn't use the third argument for the IF function:

```
{=SUM(IF(ISERROR(Data),1))}
```

Actually, you can simplify the formula even more:

```
{=SUM(ISERROR(Data)*1)}
```

This version of the formula relies on the fact that:

```
TRUE * 1 = 1
```

and

```
FALSE * 1 = 0
```

Summing based on a condition

Often, you need to sum values based on one or more conditions. The array formula that follows, for example, returns the sum of the positive values (it excludes negative values) in a range named *Data*:

```
{=SUM(IF(Data>0,Data))}
```

The IF function creates a new array that consists only of positive values. This array is passed to the SUM function. The *Data* range can consist of any number of rows and columns.

You also can use Excel's SUMIF function for this example. The following function, which is not an array formula, returns the same result:

```
=SUMIF(Data,">0")
```

SUMIF, however, can't be used for multiple conditions. For example, if you want to sum only values that are greater than 0 and less than 5, you need an array formula. This array formula does the job:

```
{=SUM((Data>0)*(Data<=5)*Data)}
```

Caution   Contrary to what you might expect, you cannot use the AND function in an array formula. The following array formula, while quite logical, doesn't return the correct result:

```
{=SUM(IF(AND(Data>0,Data<=5),Data))}
```

You also can combine criteria using an OR condition. For example, to sum the values that are less than 0 or greater than 5, use the following array formula:

```
{=SUM(IF(NOT(NOT((Data<0)+(Data>5))),Data))}
```

Caution

As with the AND function, you cannot use the OR function in an array formula. The following formula, for example, does not return the correct result:

```
{=SUM(IF(OR(Data<0,Data>5),Data))}
```

For an explanation of the workarounds required for using logical functions in an array formula, refer to the following sidebar, "Illogical Behavior from Logical Functions."

Illogical Behavior from Logical Functions

Excel's AND and OR functions are logical functions that return TRUE or FALSE. Unfortunately, these functions do not perform as expected when used in an array formula.

As shown here, columns A and B contain logical values. The AND function returns TRUE if all of its arguments are TRUE. Column C contains nonarray formulas that work as expected. For example, cell C3 contains the following function:

```
=AND(A3,B3)
```

	A	B	C	D	E
			Non-Array	Array with AND	Array formula:
2	Condition 1	Condition 2	Formulas	{=AND(A3:A6,B3:B6)}	{=A3:A6*B3:B6}
3	TRUE	TRUE	TRUE	FALSE	1
4	TRUE	FALSE	FALSE	FALSE	0
5	FALSE	TRUE	FALSE	FALSE	0
6	FALSE	FALSE	FALSE	FALSE	0

The range D3:D6 contains this array formula:

```
{=AND(A3:A6,B3:B6)}
```

You might expect this array formula to return the following array:

```
{TRUE,FALSE,FALSE,FALSE}
```

Rather, it returns only a single item: FALSE. In fact, both the AND function and the OR function always return a single result (never an array). Even when using array constants, the AND function still returns only a single value. For example, this array formula does not return an array:

```
{=AND({TRUE,TRUE,FALSE,FALSE},{TRUE,FALSE,TRUE,FALSE})}
```

I don't know whether or not the formula not returning an array is by design or if it's a bug. In any case, it certainly is inconsistent with how the other functions operate.

Column E contains another array formula, which follows, that returns an array of 0s and 1s. These 0s and 1s correspond to FALSE and TRUE, respectively.

```
{=A3:A6*B3:B6}
```

In array formulas, you must use this syntax in place of the AND function.

The following array formula, which uses the OR function, does not return an array (as you might expect):

```
=OR(A3:A6,B3:B6)
```

Rather, you can use a formula such as the following, which *does* return an array comprising logical OR using the corresponding elements in the ranges:

```
=NOT(NOT(A3:A6+B3:B6))
```

The NOT function works as expected: When used in an array formula, it *does* return an array.

Summing the *n* largest values in a range

The following array formula returns the sum of the 10 largest values in a range named *Data:*

```
{=SUM(LARGE(Data,ROW(INDIRECT("1:10"))))}
```

The LARGE function is executed 10 times, each time with a different second argument (1, 2, 3, and so on up to 10). The results of these calculations are stored in a new array, and that array is used as the argument for the SUM function.

To sum a different number of values, replace the 10 in the argument for the INDIRECT function with another value. To sum the *n smallest* values in a range, use the SMALL function instead of the LARGE function.

Computing an average that excludes zeros

Figure 26-2 shows a simple worksheet that calculates average sales. The formula in cell B11 is:

```
=AVERAGE(B2:B9)
```

This formula, of course, calculates the average of the values in B2:B9. Two of the sales staff had the week off, however, so this average doesn't accurately describe the average sales per representative.

Note   The AVERAGE function ignores blank cells, but does not ignore cells that contain 0.

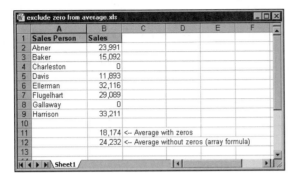

Figure 26-2: The calculated average includes cells that contain a 0.

The following array formula returns the average of the range, but excludes the cells that contain 0.

```
{=AVERAGE(IF(B2:B9<>0,B2:B9))}
```

This formula creates a new array that consists only of the nonzero values in the range. The AVERGAGE function then uses this new array as its argument. You also can get the same result with a regular (nonarray) formula:

```
=SUM(B2:B9)/COUNTIF(B2:B9,"<>0")
```

This formula uses the COUNTIF function to count the number of nonzero values in the range. This value is divided into the sum of the values.

Determining if a particular value appears in a range

To determine whether a particular value appears in a range of cells, you can choose the Edit ➪ Find command and do a search of the worksheet. But, you also can make this determination by using an array formula.

Figure 26-3 shows a worksheet with a list of names in A3:E22 (named *NameList*). An array formula in cell D1 checks the name entered into cell C1 (named *TheName*). If the name exists in the list of names, the formula displays the text *Found*. Otherwise, it displays *Not Found*.

The array formula in cell D1 is:

```
{=IF(OR(TheName=NameList),"Found","Not Found")}
```

This formula compares *TheName* to each cell in the *NameList* range. It builds a new array that consists of logical TRUE or FALSE values. The OR function returns TRUE if any one of the values in the new array is TRUE. The IF function uses this result to determine which message to display.

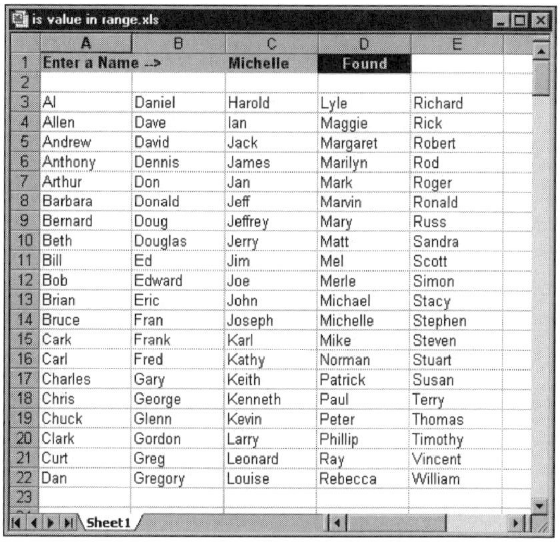

Figure 26-3: Using an array formula to determine if a range contains a particular value

A simpler form of this formula follows. This formula displays TRUE if the name is found; otherwise it displays FALSE.

```
{=OR(TheName=NameList)}
```

Counting the number of differences in two ranges

The following array formula compares the corresponding values in two ranges (named *MyData* and *YourData*) and returns the number of differences in the two ranges. If the contents of the two ranges are identical, the formula returns 0.

```
{=SUM(IF(MyData=YourData,0,1))}
```

The two ranges must be the same size and of the same dimensions.

This formula works by creating a new array of the same size as the ranges being compared. The IF function fills this new array with 0s and 1s (0 if a difference is found, 1 if the corresponding cells are the same). The SUM function then returns the sum of the array.

Returning the location of the maximum value in a range

The following array formula returns the row number of the maximum value in a single-column range named *Data*:

```
{=MIN(IF(Data=MAX(Data),ROW(Data), ""))}
```

The IF function creates a new array that corresponds to the *Data* range. If the corresponding cell contains the maximum value in *Data*, then the array contains the row number; otherwise, it contains an empty string. The MIN function uses this new array as its second argument, and returns the smallest value—the row number of the maximum value in *Data*.

If the *Data* range contains more than one cell that has the maximum value, the row of the first maximum cell is returned.

The following array formula is similar to the previous one, but it returns the actual cell address of the maximum value in the *Data* range. It uses the ADDRESS function, which takes two arguments: a row number and a column number.

```
{=ADDRESS(MIN(IF(Data=MAX(Data),ROW(Data), "")),COLUMN(Data))}
```

Finding the row of a value's *n*th occurrence in a range

The following array formula returns the row number within a single-column range named *Data* that contains the *n*th occurrence of a cell named *Value*:

```
{=SMALL(IF(Data=Value,ROW(Data), ""),n)}
```

The IF function creates a new array that consists of the row number of values from the *Data* range that are equal to *Value*. Values from the Data range that are not equal to *Value* are replaced with an empty string. The SMALL function works on this new array, and returns the *n*th smallest row number.

The formula returns #NUM! if the *Value* is not found or if *n* exceeds the number of the values in the range.

Returning the longest text in a range

The following array formula displays the text string in a range (named *Data*) that has the most characters. If multiple cells contain the longest text string, the first cell is returned.

```
{=INDEX(Data,MATCH(MAX(LEN(Data)),LEN(Data),FALSE),1)}
```

This formula creates four new arrays:

✦ **Array #1:** An array that consists of the length of each cell in the *Data* range (created by the LEN function)

✦ **Array #2:** Another array identical to Array #1

✦ **Array #3:** An array that contains the maximum value in Array #1 (created by the MAX function)

✦ **Array #4:** An array that contains the offset of the cell that contains the maximum length (created by the MATCH function)

The INDEX function works with these arrays and returns the contents of the cell that contains the most characters. This function works only if the *Data* range consists of a single column.

Determining if a range contains valid values

You might have a list of items that you need to check against another list. For example, you might import a list of part numbers into a range named *MyList*, and you want to ensure that all of the part numbers are valid. You can do this by comparing the items in the imported list to the items in a master list of part numbers (named *Master*).

The following array formula returns TRUE if every item in the range named *MyList* is found in the range named *Master*. Both of these ranges must consist of a single column, but they don't need to contain the same number of rows.

```
{=ISNA(MATCH(TRUE,ISNA(MATCH(MyList,Master,0)),0))}
```

The array formula that follows returns the number of invalid items. In other words, it returns the number of items in *MyList* that do not appear in *Master*.

```
{=SUM(1*ISNA(MATCH(MyList,Master,0)))}
```

To return the first invalid item in *MyList*, use the following array formula:

```
{=INDEX(MyList,MATCH(TRUE,ISNA(MATCH(MyList,Master,0)),0))}
```

Summing the digits of an integer

The following array formula calculates the sum of the digits in an integer, which is stored in cell A2. For example, if A2 contains the value 132, the formula returns 6 (the sum of 1, 3, and 2).

```
{=SUM(MID(A2,ROW(INDIRECT("1:"&LEN(A2))),1)*1)}
```

To understand how this formula works, let's start with the ROW function, shown here:

```
=ROW(INDIRECT("1:"&LEN(A2)))
```

This function returns an array of consecutive integers beginning with 1 and ending with the number of digits in the value in cell A2. For example, if cell A2 contains the value 132, then the LEN function returns 3 and the array generated by the ROW functions is:

```
{1,2,3}
```

Cross-Reference   For more information about using the INDIRECT function to return this array, see Chapter 15.

This array is then used as the second argument for the MID function. The MID part of the formula, simplified a bit and expressed as values, is the following:

```
=MID(132,{1,2,3},1)*1
```

This function generates an array with three elements:

```
{4,0,9}{1,3,2}
```

By simplifying again and adding the SUM function, the formula looks like this:

```
=SUM({4,0,9})=SUM({1,3,2})
```

This produces the result of 6.

Note   The values in the array created by the MID function are multiplyied by 1 because the MID function returns a string. Multiplying by 1 forces a numeric value result. Alternatively, you can use the VALUE function to force a numeric string to become a numeric value.

Notice that the formula does not work with a negative value because the negative sign is not a numeric value. The following formula solves this problem by using the ABS function to return the absolute value of the number. Figure 26-4 shows a worksheet that uses this formula in column B.

```
{=SUM(VALUE(MID(ABS(A2),ROW(INDIRECT("1:"&LEN(ABS(A2)))),1))))}
```

	A	B	C
1	Number	Sum of Digits	
2	132	6	
3	9	9	
4	111111	6	
5	980991	36	
6	-980991	36	
7	409	13	
8		0	
9	12	3	
10	123	6	
11			
12			

Figure 26-4: An array formula calculates the sum of the digits in an integer.

Summing rounded values

Figure 26-5 shows a simple worksheet that demonstrates a common spreadsheet problem: rounding errors. As you can see, the grand total in cell E5 appears to display an incorrect amount (that is, it's off by a penny). The values in column E use a number format that displays two decimal places. The actual values, however, consist of additional decimal places that do not display due to rounding (as a result of the number format). The net effect of these rounding errors is a seemingly incorrect total. The total — actually $168.320997 — displays as $168.32.

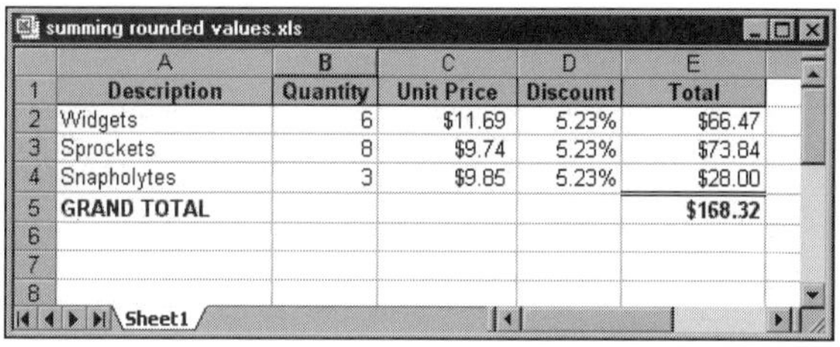

	A	B	C	D	E
1	Description	Quantity	Unit Price	Discount	Total
2	Widgets	6	$11.69	5.23%	$66.47
3	Sprockets	8	$9.74	5.23%	$73.84
4	Snapholytes	3	$9.85	5.23%	$28.00
5	GRAND TOTAL				$168.32
6					
7					
8					

Figure 26-5: Using an array formula to correct rounding errors

The following array formula creates a new array that consists of values in column E, rounded to two decimal places.

```
{=SUM(ROUND(E2:E4,2))}
```

This formula returns $168.31.

You also can eliminate these types of rounding errors by using the ROUND function in the formula that calculates each row total in column E. This technique does not require an array formula.

Summing every *n*th value in a range

Suppose you have a range of values and you want to compute the sum of every third value in the list — the first, the fourth, the seventh, and so on. You can't accomplish this task with a standard formula, but an array formula does the job.

Refer to the data in Figure 26-6. The values are stored in a range named *Data*, and the value of *n* is in cell E6 (named *n*).

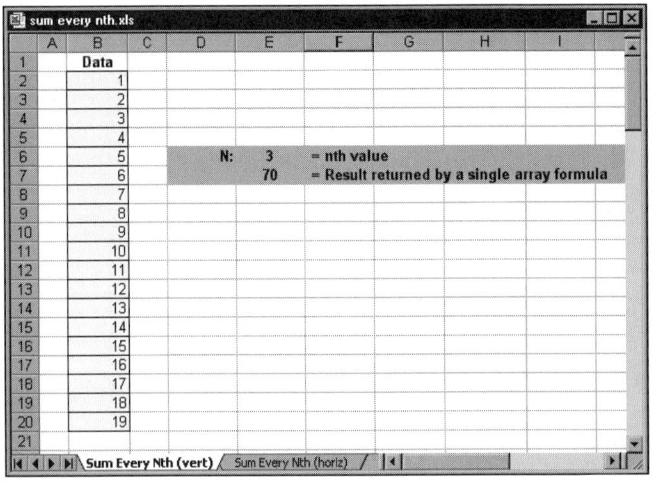

Figure 26-6: An array formula returns the sum of every *n*th value in the range.

The following array formula returns the sum of every *n*th value in the range.

```
{SUM(IF(MOD(ROW(INDIRECT("1:"&COUNT(Data)))-1,n)=0,Data,""))}
```

This formula generates an array of consecutive integers, and the MOD function uses this array as its first argument. The second argument for the MOD function is the value of *n*. The MOD function creates another array, which consists of the remainders (after each row number is divided by *n*). If the array item is 0 (for example, the row is evenly divisible by *n*), the corresponding item in the *Data* range will be included in the sum.

You'll find that this formula fails when *n* is 0 (for example, sums no items). The modified array formula that follows uses an IF function to handle this case:

```
{=IF(n=0,0,SUM(IF(MOD(ROW(INDIRECT("1:"&COUNT(data)))-
1,n)=0,data,""))))}
```

This formula works only when the *Data* range consists of a single column of values. It does not work for a rectangular range, or for a single row of values.

To make the formula work with a horizontal range, you need to transpose the array of integers generated by the ROW function. The modified array formula that follows works only with a horizontal *Data* range:

```
{=IF(n=0,0,SUM(IF(MOD(TRANSPOSE(ROW(INDIRECT("1:"&COUNT(Data)))
)-1,n)=0,Data,""))))}
```

Removing nonnumeric characters from a string

The following array formula extracts a number from a string that contains text. For example, consider the string *ABC145Z*. The formula returns the numeric part, 145.

```
{=MID(A1,MATCH(0,(ISERROR(MID(A1,ROW(INDIRECT("1:"&LEN(A1))),1)
*1)*1),0),LEN(A1)-SUM((ISERROR(MID(A1,ROW
(INDIRECT("1:"&LEN(A1))),1)*1)*1))))}
```

This formula works only with a single embedded number. For example, it fails with a string such as *X45Z99*.

Determining the closest value in a range

The array formula that follows returns the value in a range named *Data* that is closest to a another value (named *Target*):

```
{=INDEX(Data,MATCH(SMALL(ABS(Target-Data),1),ABS(Target-
Data),0))}
```

If two values in the *Data* range are equidistant from the *Target* value, the formula returns the first one in the list. Figure 26-7 shows an example of this formula. In this case, the *Target* value is 45. The array formula in cell D3 returns 48 — the value closest to 45.

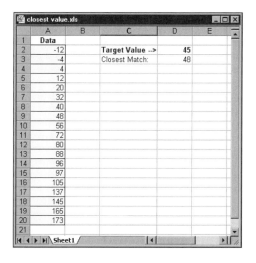

Figure 26-7: An array formula returns the closest match.

Returning the last value in a column

Suppose you have a worksheet that you update frequently by adding new data to columns. You might need a way to reference the last value in column A (the value most recently entered). If column A contains no empty cells, the solution is relatively simple and doesn't require an array formula:

```
=OFFSET(A1,COUNTA(A:A)-1,0)
```

This formula uses the COUNTA function to count the number of nonempty cells in column A. This value (minus 1) is used as the second argument for the OFFSET function. For example, if the last value is in row 100, COUNTA returns 100. The OFFSET function returns the value in the cell 99 rows down from cell A1, in the same column.

If column A has one or more empty cells interspersed — frequently the case — the preceding formula won't work because the COUNTA function doesn't count the empty cells.

The following array formula returns the contents of the last nonempty cell in the first 500 rows of column A:

```
{=INDIRECT(ADDRESS(MAX((ROW(1:500)*(A1:A500<>""))),COLUMN(A:A)))}
```

You can, of course, modify the formula to work with a column other than column A. To use a different column, change the four column references from A to whatever column you need. If the last nonempty cell occurs in a row beyond row 500, you need to change the two instances of "500" to a larger number. The fewer rows referenced in the formula, the faster the calculation speed.

Caution   You cannot use this formula, as written, in the same column with which it's working. Attempting to do so generates a circular reference. You can, however, modify it. For example, to use the function in cell A1, change the references so they begin with row 2.

Returning the last value in a row

The following array formula is similar to the previous formula, but it returns the last nonempty cell in a row (in this case, row 1):

```
=INDIRECT(ADDRESS(1,(MAX((TRANSPOSE(ROW(1:256))*(1:1<>""))))))
```

To use this formula for a different row, change the first argument for the ADDRESS function, and change the 1:1 reference to correspond to the row.

Ranking data with an array formula

Often, computing the rank orders for the values in a range of data is helpful. If you have a worksheet that contains the annual sales figures for 20 salespeople, for example, you may want to know how each person ranks, from highest to lowest.

If you've used Excel's RANK function, you may have noticed that the ranks produced by this function don't handle ties the way that you may like. For example, if two values are tied for third place, the RANK function gives both of them a rank of 3. You may prefer to assign each an average (or midpoint) of the ranks — in other words, a rank of 3.5 for both values tied for third place.

Figure 26-8 shows a worksheet that uses two methods to rank a column of values (named *Sales*). The first method (column C) uses Excel's RANK function. Column D uses array formulas to compute the ranks.

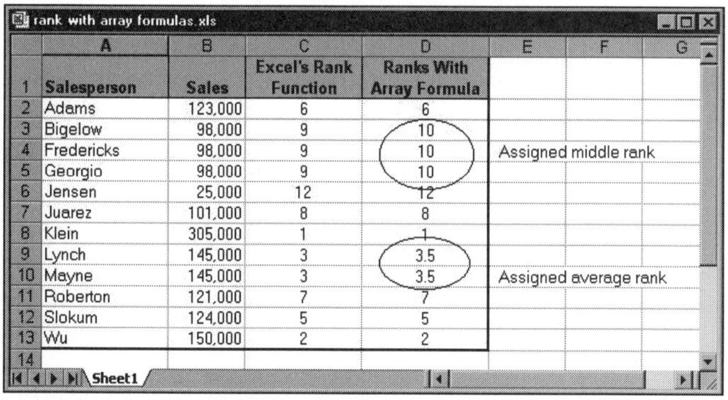

Salesperson	Sales	Excel's Rank Function	Ranks With Array Formula	
Adams	123,000	6	6	
Bigelow	98,000	9	10	
Fredericks	98,000	9	10	Assigned middle rank
Georgio	98,000	9	10	
Jensen	25,000	12	12	
Juarez	101,000	8	8	
Klein	305,000	1	1	
Lynch	145,000	3	3.5	
Mayne	145,000	3	3.5	Assigned average rank
Roberton	121,000	7	7	
Slokum	124,000	5	5	
Wu	150,000	2	2	

Figure 26-8: Ranking data with Excel's RANK function and with array formulas

The following is the array formula in cell D2:

```
{=SUM(1*(B2<=Sales))-(SUM(1*(B2=Sales))-1)/2}
```

This formula copied to the cells below it.

Note

Each ranking is computed with a separate array formula, not with an array formula entered into multiple cells.

Each array function works by computing the number of higher values and subtracting one half of the number of equal values minus 1.

Creating a dynamic crosstab table

A crosstab table tabulates or summarizes data across two dimensions. Take a look at the data in Figure 26-9. This worksheet shows a simple expense account listing. Each item consists of the date, the expense category, and the amount spent. Each column of data is a named range, indicated in the first row.

	A	B	C	D	E	F	G	H	I
1	Date	Category	Amount						
2	04-Jan	Food	23.50			Transp	Food	Lodging	
3	04-Jan	Transp	15.00		04-Jan	160.50	49.57	65.95	
4	04-Jan	Food	9.12		05-Jan	20.00	27.80	89.00	
5	04-Jan	Food	16.95		06-Jan	0.00	101.96	75.30	
6	04-Jan	Transp	145.50		07-Jan	11.50	25.00	112.00	
7	04-Jan	Lodging	65.95						
8	05-Jan	Transp	20.00						
9	05-Jan	Food	7.80						
10	05-Jan	Food	20.00						
11	05-Jan	Lodging	89.00						
12	06-Jan	Food	9.00						
13	06-Jan	Food	3.50						
14	06-Jan	Food	11.02						
15	06-Jan	Food	78.44						
16	06-Jan	Lodging	75.30						
17	07-Jan	Transp	11.50						
18	07-Jan	Food	15.50						
19	07-Jan	Food	9.50						
20	07-Jan	Lodging	112.00						
21									

Figure 26-9: You can use array formulas to summarize data such as this in a dynamic crosstab table.

Array formulas summarize this information into a handy table that shows the total expenses — by category — for each day. Cell F3 contains the following array formula, which copied to the remaining 14 cells in the table:

```
{=SUM(IF($E3&F$2=Date&Category,Amount))}
```

These array formulas display the totals for each day, by category.

The formula sums the values in the *Amount* range, but does so only if the row and column names in the summary table match the corresponding entries in the *Date* and *Category* ranges. It does the comparison by concatenating (using the & operator) the row and column names and comparing the resulting string to the concatenation of the corresponding *Date* and *Category* values. If the two match, the SUM function kicks in and adds the corresponding value in the *Amount* range.

You can customize this technique to hold any number of different categories and any number of dates. You can eliminate the dates, in fact, and substitute people's names, departments, regions, and so on.

Note   You also can use Excel's pivot table feature to summarize data in this way. However, pivot tables do not update automatically when the data changes, so the array formula method I just described has at least one advantage.

More Multicell Array Formulas

The previous chapter introduced array formulas entered into multicell ranges. In this section, I present a few more array multicell formulas. Most of these formulas return some or all of the values in a range, but rearranged in some way.

Returning only positive values from a range

The following array formula works with a single-column vertical range (named *Data*). The array formula is entered into a range that's the same size as *Data*, and returns only the positive values in the *Data* range (0s and negative numbers are ignored).

```
{=INDEX(Data,SMALL(IF(Data>0,ROW(INDIRECT("1:"&ROWS(Data)))),
ROW(INDIRECT("1:"&ROWS(Data)))))}
```

As you can see in Figure 26-10, this formula works but not perfectly. The *Data* range is A2:A21, and the array formula is entered into C2:C21. However, the array formula displays #NUM! error values for cells that don't contain a value.

	A	B	C
1	Data		Positive Vals
2	33		33
3	-33		44
4	44		4
5	4		43
6	-5		99
7	0		5
8	43		6
9	-1		7
10	-2		8
11	-3		9
12	-33		10
13	99		11
14	5		12
15	6		#NUM!
16	7		#NUM!
17	8		#NUM!
18	9		#NUM!
19	10		#NUM!
20	11		#NUM!
21	12		#NUM!
22			
23			

Figure 26-10: Using an array formula to return only the positive values in a range

This more complex array formula avoids the error value display:

```
{=IF(ISERR(SMALL(IF(Data>0,ROW(INDIRECT("1:"&ROWS(Data))))),
ROW(INDIRECT("1:"&ROWS(Data)))),"",INDEX(Data,SMALL(IF
(Data>0,ROW(INDIRECT("1:"&ROWS(Data)))),ROW(INDIRECT
("1:"&ROWS(Data))))))}
```

Returning nonblank cells from a range

The following formula is a variation on the formula in the previous section. This array formula works with a single-column vertical range named *Data*. The array formula is entered into a range of the same size as *Data*, and returns only the nonblank cell in the *Data* range.

```
{=IF(ISERR(SMALL(IF(Data<>"",ROW(INDIRECT("1:"&ROWS(Data))))),
ROW(INDIRECT("1:"&ROWS(Data)))),"",INDEX(Data,SMALL(IF(Data
<>"",ROW(INDIRECT("1:"&ROWS(Data)))),ROW(INDIRECT("1:"&ROWS
(Data))))))}
```

Reversing the order of the cells in a range

The following array formula works with a single-column vertical range (named *Data*). The array formula, which is entered into a range of the same size as *Data*, returns the values in *Data*—but in reverse order.

```
{=IF(INDEX(Data,ROWS(data)-ROW(INDIRECT("1:"&ROWS(Data)))+1)
="","",INDEX(Data,ROWS(Data)-ROW(INDIRECT("1:"&ROWS(Data)))
+1))}
```

Figure 26-11 shows this formula in action. The range A2:A20 is named *Data*, and the array formula is entered into the range C2:C20.

	A	B	C	D	E
1	**Data Entry Range**		**Reversed**		
2	first		10		
3	second		9		
4	third		8		
5	fourth		7th		
6	5th		6th		
7	6th		5th		
8	7th		fourth		
9	8		third		
10	9		second		
11	10		first		
12					
13					
14					
15					
16					
17					
18					
19					
20					
21					

Figure 26-11: A multicell array formula reverses the order of the values in the range.

Sorting a range of values dynamically

Suppose your worksheet contains a single-column vertical range named *Data*. The following array formula — entered into a range with the same number of rows as *Data* — returns the values in *Data*, sorted from highest to lowest. This formula works only with numeric values, not with text.

```
{=LARGE(Data,ROW(INDIRECT("1:"&ROWS(Data))))}
```

To sort the values in *Data* from lowest to highest, use this array formula:

```
{=SMALL(Data,ROW(INDIRECT("1:"&ROWS(Data))))}
```

This formula can be useful if you need to have your data entry sorted immediately. Start by defining the range name *Data* as your data entry range. Then, enter the array formula into another range with the same number of rows as *Data*.

You'll find that the array formula returns #NUM! for cells that don't have a value. This can be annoying if you're entering data. The modified version, which follows, is more complex, but it eliminates the display of the error value.

```
{=IF(ISERR(LARGE(Data,ROW(INDIRECT("1:"&ROWS(Data))))),"",
LARGE(Data,ROW(INDIRECT("1:"&ROWS(Data)))))}
```

Returning a list of unique items in a range

If you have a single-column range named *Data*, the following array formula returns a list of the unique items in the range:

```
{=INDEX(Data,SMALL(IF(MATCH(Data,Data,0)=
ROW(INDIRECT("1:"&ROWS(Data))),MATCH(Data,Data,0),""),
ROW(INDIRECT("1:"&ROWS(Data)))))}
```

This formula does not work if the *Data* range contains any blank cells. The unfilled cells of the array formula display #NUM!. Figure 26-12 shows an example. Range A2:A20 is named *Data*, and the array formula is entered into range C2:C20.

	A	B	C	D
1	**Data**		**Unique Items**	
2	Dog		Dog	
3	Dog		Cat	
4	Dog		Monkey	
5	Dog		Elephant	
6	Cat		Pigeon	
7	Cat		Donkey	
8	Cat		#NUM!	
9	Cat		#NUM!	
10	Monkey		#NUM!	
11	Cat		#NUM!	
12	Elephant		#NUM!	
13	Elephant		#NUM!	
14	Elephant		#NUM!	
15	Pigeon		#NUM!	
16	Pigeon		#NUM!	
17	Pigeon		#NUM!	
18	Donkey		#NUM!	
19	Dog		#NUM!	
20	Monkey		#NUM!	
21				

Figure 26-12: Using an array formula to return unique items from a list

Displaying a calendar in a range

Figure 26-13 shows a calendar displayed in a range of cells. The worksheet has two defined named: *m* (for the month) and *y* (for the year). A single array formula, entered into 42 cells, displays the corresponding calendar. The following array formula is entered into the range B6:H11:

```
{=IF(MONTH(DATE(y,m,1))<>MONTH(DATE(y,m,1)-
(WEEKDAY(DATE(y,m,1))-1)+{0;7;14;21;28;35}+
{0,1,2,3,4,5,6}),"",DATE(y,m,1)-(WEEKDAY(DATE(y,m,1))-
1)+{0;7;14;21;28;35}+{0,1,2,3,4,5,6})}
```

The array formula actually returns date values, but the cells are formatted to display only the day portion of the date. Also, notice that the array formula uses array constants. You can simplify the array formula quite a bit by removing the IF function:

```
{=DATE(y,m,1)-(WEEKDAY(DATE(y,m,1))-1)+{0;7;14;21;28;35}+
{0,1,2,3,4,5,6}}
```

Cross-Reference   See Chapter 25 for more information about array constants.

This version of the formula displays the days from the preceding month and the next month. The IF function checks each date to make sure it's in the current month. If not, the IF function returns an empty string.

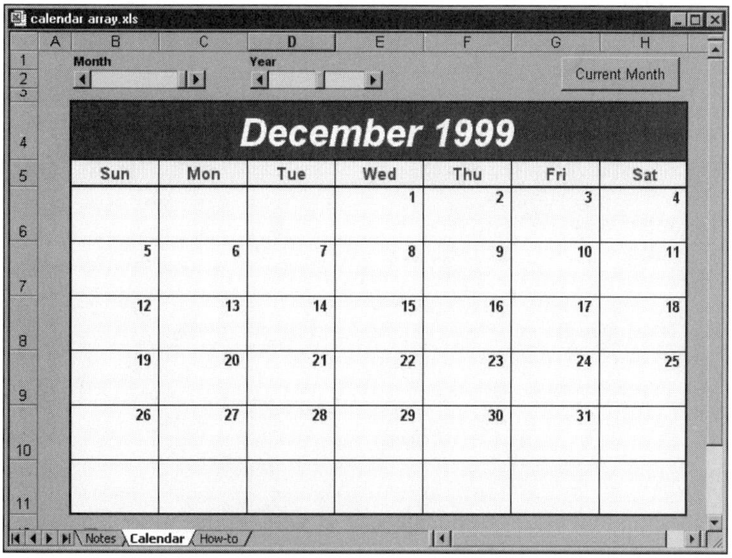

Figure 26-13: Displaying a calendar using a single array formula

Returning an Array from a Custom VBA Function

The chapter's final example demonstrates one course of action you can take if you can't figure out a particular array formula. If Excel doesn't provide the tools you need, you need to create your own.

For example, I struggled for several hours in an attempt to create an array formula that returns a sorted list of text entries. Although you can create an array formula that returns a sorted list of *values* (see "Sorting a Range of Values Dynamically," earlier in this chapter), doing the same for text entries alluded me.

Therefore, I created a custom VBA function called SORTED, which I list here:

```
Function SORTED(rng, Optional ascending) As Variant
    Dim SortedData() As Variant
    Dim CellCount As Long
    Dim Temp As Variant, i As Long, j As Long
    CellCount = rng.Count
    ReDim SortedData(1 To CellCount)

'   Check optional argument
    If IsMissing(ascending) Then ascending = True
```

```
'    Exit with an error if not a single column
     If rng.Columns.Count > 1 Then
         SORTED = CVErr(xlErrValue)
         Exit Function
     End If

'    Transfer data to SortedData
     For i = 1 To CellCount
         SortedData(i) = rng(i)
         If TypeName(SortedData(i)) = "Empty" _
           Then SortedData(i) = ""
     Next i
     On Error Resume Next

'    Sort the SortedData array
     For i = 1 To CellCount
         For j = i + 1 To CellCount
             If SortedData(j) <> "" Then
                 If ascending Then
                     If SortedData(i) > SortedData(j) Then
                         Temp = SortedData(j)
                         SortedData(j) = SortedData(i)
                         SortedData(i) = Temp
                     End If
                 Else
                     If SortedData(i) < SortedData(j) Then
                         Temp = SortedData(j)
                         SortedData(j) = SortedData(i)
                         SortedData(i) = Temp
                     End If
                 End If
             End If
         Next j
     Next i

'    Transpose it
     SORTED = Application.Transpose(SortedData)
End Function
```

The SORTED function takes two arguments: a range reference and an optional second argument that specifies the sort order. The default sort order is ascending order. If you specify FALSE as the second argument, the range is returned sorted in descending order.

Once the SORTED Function procedure is entered into a VBA module, you can use the SORTED function in your formulas. The following array formula, for example, returns the contents of a single-column range named *Data*, but sorted in ascending order. You enter this formula into a range the same size as the *Data* range.

```
{=SORTED(Data)}
```

This array formula returns the contents of the *Data* range, but sorted in descending order:

```
{=SORTED(Data,False)}
```

As you can see, using a custom function results in a much more compact formula. Custom functions, however, are usually much slower than formulas that use Excel's built-in functions.

Figure 26-14 shows an example of this function used in an array formula. Range A2:A17 is named *Data*, and the array formula is entered into range C2:C17.

	A	B	C	D	E
1	**Data Entry**		**Sorted Data**		
2	Ashby		Arias		
3	Leyritz		Ashby		
4	Joiner		Gomez		
5	Veras		Gwynn		
6	Gomez		Hoffman		
7	Arias		Jackson		
8	Sanders		Joiner		
9	Rivera		Leyritz		
10	Gwynn		Meyers		
11	Vander Wall		Rivera		
12	Meyers		Sanders		
13	Jackson		Vander Wall		
14	Hoffman		Veras		
15					
16					
17					
18					
19					

Figure 26-14: Using a custom worksheet function in an array formula

Summary

This chapter provided many examples of useful array formulas. You can use these formulas as is, or adapt them to your needs. It also presented a custom worksheet function that returns an array.

The next chapter presents the use of Excel in a workgroup.

✦   ✦   ✦

Using Excel in a Workgroup

If you use Excel on a standalone computer — a PC that's not connected to a network — you can skip this chapter, because it applies only to users who run Excel on a network.

Using Excel on a Network

A computer network consists of a group of PCs that are linked. A common type of network uses a *client-server model*, in which one or more PCs on the network act as dedicated *servers,* because they store files centrally and supply information, while user PCs are called *clients* (they use data in the centrally stored files on the server). Other networks are *peer-to-peer networks* that don't have a central server. Users on a network can perform the following tasks:

✦ Access files on other systems

✦ Share files with other users

✦ Share resources such as printers and fax modems

✦ Communicate with each other electronically

In many offices, networks now perform functions that formerly required a mainframe system and *dumb* terminals. Networks are usually less expensive, easier to expand, more manageable, and more flexible in terms of software availability than a mainframe system.

This chapter discusses the Excel features that are designed for network users.

File Reservations

Networks provide users with the ability to share information stored on other computer systems. Most networks have one or more file servers attached. A file server stores files that members of a workgroup share. A network's file server may contain, for example, files that store customer lists, price lists, and form letters. Keeping these files on a file server has two major advantages:

✦ It eliminates the need to have multiple copies of the files stored locally on user PCs.

✦ It ensures that the file is always up to date; for example, if everyone makes changes to the same shared copy of a customer list, there's little likelihood that the portions of the list will be correct while other portions will be obsolete.

Some software applications are *multiuser applications*. Most database software applications, for example, enable multiple users to work simultaneously on the same database files. One user may be updating customer records in the database, while another is extracting records. But what if a user is updating a customer record and another user wants to make a change to that same record? Multiuser database software contains record-locking safeguards that ensure only one user at a time can modify a particular record.

Excel is *not* a multiuser application. When you open an Excel file, the entire file is loaded into memory. If the file is accessible to other users, you wouldn't want someone else to open a file that you've opened. If Excel allowed you to open and change a file that someone else on a network has already opened, the following scenario could happen.

Assume that your company keeps its sales information in an Excel file that is stored on a network server. Elaine wants to add this week's data to the file, so she loads it from the server and begins adding new information. A few minutes later, Albert loads the file to correct some errors that he noticed last week. Elaine finishes her work and saves the file. A while later, Albert finishes his corrections and saves the file. Albert's file overwrites the copy that Elaine saved, and her additions are gone.

This scenario *can't happen,* because Excel uses a concept known as *file reservation.* When Elaine opens the sales file, she has the reservation for the file. When Albert tries to open the file, Excel informs him that Elaine is using the file. If he insists on opening it, Excel opens the file as *read-only.* In other words, Albert can open the file, but he can't save it under the same name. Figure 27-1 shows the message that Albert receives if he tries to open a file that is in use by someone else.

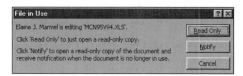

Figure 27-1: The File in Use dialog box appears if you try to open a file that someone else is using.

Albert has these three choices:

✦ **Select Cancel, wait a while, and try again.** He may call Elaine and ask her when she expects to be finished.

✦ **Select Read Only.** This lets him open the file to read it, but doesn't let him save changes to the same filename.

✦ **Select Notify, which opens the file as read-only.** Excel pops up a message when Elaine is finished using the file.

Figure 27-2 shows the message that Albert receives when the file is available.

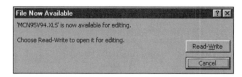

Figure 27-2: The File Now Available dialog box pops up with a new message when the file is available for editing.

Shared Workbooks

Although Excel isn't a multiuser application, it does support a feature known as *shared workbooks,* which enables multiple users to work on the same workbook simultaneously. Excel keeps track of the changes and provides appropriate prompts to handle conflict.

Appropriate workbooks for sharing

Although you can designate any workbook as a shared list, only certain workbooks contain information that is appropriate for sharing. The following are examples of workbooks that work well as shared lists:

✦ **Project tracking:** You may have a workbook that contains status information for projects. If multiple people are involved in the project, they can make changes and updates to the parts that are relevant.

✦ **Customer lists:** With customer lists, changes usually occur infrequently, but records are added and deleted.

✦ **Consolidations:** You may create a budget workbook in which each department manager is responsible for his or her department's budget. Usually, each department's budget appears on a separate sheet, with one sheet serving as the consolidation sheet.

Limitations of shared workbooks

If you plan to designate a workbook as shared, be aware that you cannot perform any of the following actions while sharing the workbook:

✦ Delete worksheets or chart sheets.

✦ Insert or delete a blocks of cells. However, you can insert or delete entire rows and columns.

✦ Merge cells.

✦ Define or apply conditional formats.

✦ Set up or change data-validation restrictions and messages.

✦ Insert or change charts, pictures, drawings, objects, or hyperlinks.

✦ Assign or modify a password to protect individual worksheets or the entire workbook.

✦ Create or modify pivot tables, scenarios, outlines, or data tables.

✦ Insert automatic subtotals.

✦ Make changes to dialog boxes or menus.

✦ Write, change, view, record, or assign macros. However, you can record a macro in a shared workbook that you store in another, unshared workbook.

Designating a workbook as a shared workbook

To designate a workbook as a shared workbook, select Tools ➪ Share Workbook. Excel displays the dialog box that is shown in Figure 27-3. This dialog box has two tabs: Editing and Advanced. In the Editing tab, select the check box to allow changes by multiple users and then click OK. Excel then prompts you to save the workbook.

When you open a shared workbook, the window's title bar displays [Shared]. If you no longer want other users to be able to use the workbook, remove the check mark from the Share Workbook dialog box and save the workbook.

Whenever you're working with a shared workbook, you can find out whether any other users are working on the workbook. Choose Tools ➪ Share Workbook, and the Share Workbook dialog box lists the names of the other users who have the file open, as well as the time that each user opened the workbook.

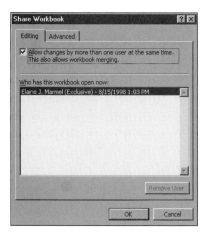

Figure 27-3: The Share Workbook dialog box lets you specify a workbook as a shared workbook.

Advanced settings

Excel enables you to set options for shared workbooks. Select Tools ⇨ Share Workbook and click the Advanced tab to access these options (see Figure 27-4).

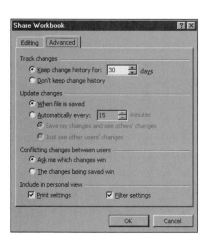

Figure 27-4: The Advanced tab of the Share Workbook dialog box

Tracking changes

Excel can keep track of the workbook's changes — something known as *change history.* When you designate a workbook as a shared workbook, Excel automatically turns on the change history option, enabling you to view information about previous (and perhaps conflicting) changes to the workbook. You can turn off change history by selecting the option labeled Don't keep change history. You can also specify the number of days for which Excel tracks change history.

Updating changes

While you're working on a shared workbook, you can use the standard File ➪ Save command to update the workbook with your changes. The Update changes settings determine what happens when you save a shared workbook:

✦ **When file is saved:** You receive updates from other users when you save your copy of the shared workbook.

✦ **Automatically every:** Lets you specify a time period for receiving updates from other users of the workbook. You can also specify whether Excel should save your changes automatically, too, or just show you the changes made by other users.

Conflicting changes between users

As you may expect, multiple users working on the same file can result in some conflicts. For example, assume that you're working on a shared customer database workbook, and another user also has the workbook open. If you and the other user both make a change to the same cell, a conflict occurs. You can specify the manner in which Excel resolves the conflicts by selecting one of two options in the Advanced tab of the Share Workbook dialog box:

✦ **Ask me which changes win:** If you select this option, Excel displays a dialog box to let you determine how to settle the conflict.

✦ **The changes being saved win:** If you select this option, your changes always take precedence.

Include in personal view

The final section of the Advanced tab of the Share Workbook dialog box enables you to specify settings that are specific to your view of the shared workbook. You can choose to use your own print settings and your own data-filtering settings. If you don't place checks in these check boxes, you can't save your own print and filter settings.

Mailing and Routing Workbooks

Excel provides a few additional workgroup features. To use these features, your system must have one of the following items installed:

✦ Office 2000

✦ Microsoft Exchange

✦ A mail system that is compatible with MAPI (Messaging Application Programming Interface)

✦ Lotus cc:Mail

✦ A mail system that is compatible with VIM (Vendor Independent Messaging)

The procedures vary, depending on the mail system that you have installed; for this reason, discussions in the following sections are general in nature. For specific questions, consult your network administrator.

Mailing a workbook as an e-mail attachment

Electronic mail, or *e-mail*, is commonplace in most offices, and is an extremely efficient means of communication. Unlike a telephone, e-mail doesn't rely on the recipient of the message being available when you want to send the message.

In addition to sending messages by e-mail, you can send complete files — including Excel workbooks. Like a growing number of software applications, Excel is *mail-enabled,* which means that you don't have to leave Excel to send a worksheet to someone by e-mail.

To send a copy of your workbook to someone on your network, select File ⇨ Send To ⇨ Mail Recipient (as Attachment). Excel creates an e-mail message with a copy of the workbook attached, using your default e-mail program; in Figure 27-5, Excel opened Outlook Express to send the workbook. You send this e-mail message the same way that you send any message — from your e-mail program. You also can send the message to multiple recipients, the same way that you send any e-mail message to multiple recipients.

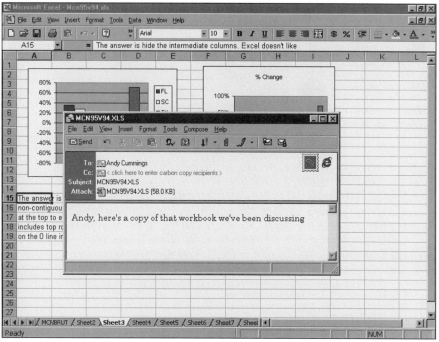

Figure 27-5: Sending a workbook as an attachment to an e-mail message

Note   When you send any file by using an e-mail program, you send a *copy* of the file. If the recipient makes changes to the notebook, the changes do not appear in your copy of the workbook.

Routing a workbook to others

If you choose File ➪ Send To ➪ Routing Recipient, Excel enables you to attach a routing slip to a workbook, similar to the one you see in Figure 27-6. Routing a workbook is most useful when you want the first person in the group to review (and possibly edit) the workbook and then send it to the next person on the list. For example, if you're responsible for your department's budget, you may need input from Alice — and her input may depend on Andy's input. You can set up the workbook and then route it to the others so that they can make their respective additions. When you set up the routing slip, you can tell Excel to return the workbook to you when the routing is finished.

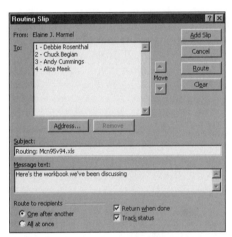

Figure 27-6: Routing a workbook

When you route a workbook, you have the following two options:

✦ **Sequential routing:** Enables you to route the workbook sequentially to workgroup members. When the first recipient is finished, the workbook goes to the second recipient. When the second recipient is finished, the workbook goes to the third, and so on. When all recipients have received the workbook, it can be returned to you. Choose One after another at the bottom of the Routing Slip dialog box for this type of routing.

✦ **Simultaneous routing:** Enables you to route the workbook to all recipients at once. You receive a copy of the workbook from each recipient (not just one copy). This type of routing is useful if you want to solicit comments from a group of coworkers, and you want the responses back quickly (you don't want to wait until a single worksheet makes the circuit). Choose All at once at the bottom of the Routing Slip dialog box for this type of routing.

Click Route to route the workbook immediately. If you don't want to route immediately, click Add Slip. Later, when you're ready to route, choose File ➪ Send To ➪ Next Routing Recipient. Either choice places the workbook in the outgoing mail folder of your e-mail program. To actually route the workbook, open your e-mail program to send the message.

Note

Whether you route or attach a workbook to an e-mail message, Excel uses your e-mail program. Because you can send a workbook to a number of people, either as an e-mail attachment or by using a routing slip, the distinction between the two methods lies in the distinction between sequential and simultaneous routing. If you choose simultaneous routing and you *don't* place a check in the Return when done check box, routing and attaching are identical, because you can't guarantee a reply to e-mail.

Summary

This chapter presents a basic overview of using Excel in a network environment. It explains how the concept of a file reservation prevents two users from modifying a workbook simultaneously. Excel's shared workbook feature, however, lets multiple users work on a single workbook at the same time. The chapter concludes with a discussion of mailing and routing workbooks.

✦   ✦   ✦

Sharing Data with Other Applications

Windows applications are designed to work together. The applications in Microsoft Office are an excellent example. These programs have a common look and feel, and sharing data among these applications is quite easy. This chapter explores some ways that you can make use of other applications while working with Excel, as well as some ways that you can use Excel while working with other applications.

Sharing Data with Other Windows Applications

Besides importing and exporting files, the following are the essential three ways in which you can transfer data to and from other Windows applications:

- ✦ Copy and paste, using either the Windows clipboard or the Office clipboard. Copying and pasting information creates a static copy of the data.

- ✦ Create a link so that changes in the source data are reflected in the destination document.

- ✦ Embed an entire object from one application into another application's document.

The following sections discuss these techniques and present an example for each one.

Using the Windows or Office Clipboards

As you probably know, whenever Windows is running, you have access to the Windows clipboard — an area of your computer's memory that acts as a shared holding area for information that you have cut or copied from an application. The Windows clipboard works behind the scenes, and you usually aren't aware of it. Whenever you select data and then choose either Edit ⇨ Copy or Edit ⇨ Cut, the application places the selected data on the Windows clipboard. Like most other Windows applications, Excel can then access the clipboard data if you choose the Edit ⇨ Paste command (or the Edit ⇨ Paste Special command).

EXCEL 2000

If you copy or cut information while working in an Office application, the application places the copied information on both the Windows clipboard and the Office clipboard.

Note

Once you copy information to the Windows clipboard, it remains on the Windows clipboard even after you paste it, so you can use it multiple times. However, because the Windows clipboard can hold only one item at a time, when you copy or cut something else, the information previously stored on the Windows clipboard is replaced. The Office clipboard, unlike the Windows clipboard, can hold up to 12 separate selections. The Office clipboard operates in all Office applications; for example, you can copy two selections from Word and three from Excel and paste any or all of them in PowerPoint.

Copying information from one Windows application to another is quite easy. The application that contains the information that you're copying is called the *source application*, and the application to which you're copying the information is called the *destination application*.

The general steps that are required to copy from one application to another are as follows. These steps apply to copying from Excel to another application and to copying from another application to Excel.

1. Activate the source document window that contains the information that you want to copy.

2. Select the information by using the mouse or the keyboard. If Excel is the source application, this information can be a cell, range, chart, or drawn object.

3. Select Edit ⇨ Copy. Excel places a copy of the information onto the Windows clipboard and the Office clipboard.

4. Activate the destination application. If the program isn't running, you can start it without affecting the contents of the clipboard.

5. Move to the appropriate position in the destination application (where you want to paste the copied material).

6. Select Edit ➪ Paste from the menu in the destination application. If the clipboard contents are not appropriate for pasting, the Paste command is grayed (not available).

In Step 3 in the preceding steps, you also can select Edit ➪ Cut from the source application menu. This step erases your selection from the source application after placing the selection on the clipboard.

EXCEL 2000

If you repeat Step 3 in any Office application, the Office clipboard toolbar appears automatically. It continues to appear if the destination application that you activate in Step 4 is another Office application.

Note

In Step 6 in the preceding steps, you can sometimes select the Edit ➪ Paste Special command, which displays a dialog box that presents different pasting options.

If you're copying a graphics image, you may have to resize or crop it. If you're copying text, you may have to reformat it by using tools that are available in the destination application. The information that you copy from the source application remains intact, and a copy remains on the clipboard until you copy or cut something else. Figure 28-1 shows an embedded Excel chart. You can easily insert a copy of this chart into a Microsoft Word report. First, select the chart in Excel by clicking it once. Then, copy it to the clipboard by choosing Edit ➪ Copy. Next, activate the Word document into which you want to paste the copy of the chart, and move the insertion point to the place where you want the chart to appear. When you select Edit ➪ Paste from the Word menu bar, the chart is pasted from the clipboard and appears in your document (see Figure 28-2).

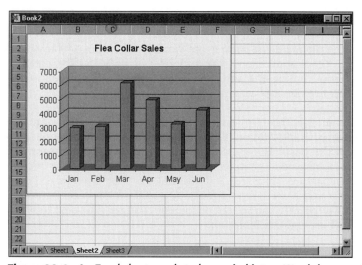

Figure 28-1: An Excel chart, ready to be copied into a Word document

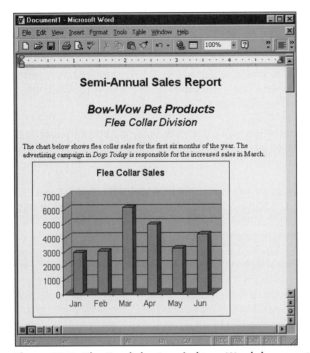

Figure 28-2: The Excel chart copied to a Word document

Note

You need to understand that Windows applications vary in the way that they respond to data that you paste from the clipboard. If the Edit ➪ Paste command is not available (is grayed on the menu) in the destination application, the application can't accept the information from the clipboard. If you copy a range of data from Excel to the clipboard and paste it into Word, Word creates a table when you paste the data. Other applications may respond differently to Excel data. If you plan to do a lot of copying and pasting, I suggest that you experiment until you understand how the two applications handle each other's data.

You should understand that this copy-and-paste technique is static. In other words, no link exists between the information that you copy from the source application and the information that you paste into the destination application. If you're copying from Excel to a word processing document, for example, the word processing document *will not* reflect any subsequent changes that you make in your Excel worksheet or charts. Consequently, you have to repeat the copy-and-paste procedure to update the destination document with the source document changes. The next topic presents a way to get around this limitation.

Linking Data

If you want to share data that may change, the static copy-and-paste procedure described in the preceding section isn't your best choice. Instead, create a dynamic link between the data that you copy from one Windows application to another. In this way, if you change the data in the source document, you don't *also* need to make the changes in the destination document, because the link automatically updates the destination document.

When would you want to use this technique? If you generate proposals by using a word processor, for example, you may need to refer to pricing information that you store in an Excel worksheet. If you set up a link between your word processing document and the Excel worksheet, you can be sure that your proposals always quote the latest prices. Not all Windows applications support dynamic linking, so you must make sure that the application to which you are copying is capable of handling such a link.

Creating links

Setting up a link from one Windows application to another isn't difficult, although the process varies slightly from application to application. The following are the general steps to take:

1. Activate the window in the source application that contains the information that you want to copy.

2. Select the information by using the mouse or the keyboard. If Excel is the source application, you can select a cell, range, or entire chart.

3. Select Edit ⇨ Copy from the source application's menu. The source application copies the information to the Windows clipboard.

4. Activate the destination application. If it isn't open, you can start it without affecting the contents of the clipboard.

5. Move to the appropriate position in the destination application.

6. Select the appropriate command in the destination application to paste a link. The command varies, depending on the application. In Microsoft Office applications, the command is Edit ⇨ Paste Special.

7. A dialog box will probably appear, letting you specify the type of link that you want to create. The following section provides more details.

More about links

Keep in mind the following information when you're using links between two applications:

✦ Not all Windows applications support linking. Furthermore, you can link *from* but not *to* some programs. When in doubt, consult the documentation for the application with which you're dealing.

✦ When you save an Excel file that has a link, you save the most recent values with the document. When you reopen this document, Excel asks whether you want to update the links.

✦ Links can be broken rather easily. If you move the source document to another directory or save it under a different name, for example, the destination document's application won't be able to update the link. You can usually reestablish the link manually, if you understand how the application manages the links. In Excel, you use the Edit ➪ Links command, which displays the Links dialog box, shown in Figure 28-3.

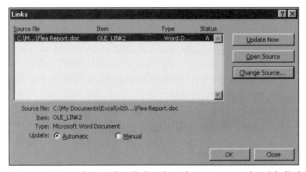

Figure 28-3: The Links dialog box lets you work with links to other applications.

✦ You also can use the Edit ➪ Links command to break a link. After breaking a link, the data remains in the destination document, but is no longer linked to the source document.

✦ In Excel, external links are stored in array formulas. If you know what you're doing, you can modify a link by editing the array formula.

✦ When Excel is running, it responds to link requests from other applications, unless you have disabled remote requests. If you don't want Excel to respond to link-update requests from other applications, choose Tools ➪ Options, select the General tab, and then place a check in the Ignore other applications check box.

Copying Excel Data to Word

One of the most frequently used software combinations is a spreadsheet and a word processor. This section discusses the types of links that you can create by using Microsoft Word.

Note   Most information in this section also applies to other word processors, such as Corel's WordPerfect for Windows and Lotus Word Pro. The exact techniques vary, however. I use Word in the examples because readers who acquired Excel as part of the Microsoft Office have Word installed on their systems. If you don't have a word processor installed on your system, you can use the WordPad application that comes with Windows. The manner in which WordPad handles links is very similar to that for Word.

Figure 28-4 shows the Paste Special dialog box from Microsoft Word after a range of data has been copied from Excel to the clipboard. The result that you get depends on whether you select the Paste or the Paste link option, and on your choice of the type of item to paste. If you select the Paste link option, you can choose to have the information pasted as an icon. If you do so, you can double-click this icon to activate the source worksheet.

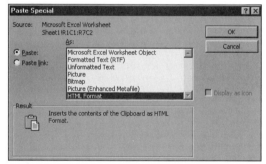

Figure 28-4: The Paste Special dialog box is where you specify the type of link to create.

Pasting without a link

Often, you don't need a link when you copy data. For example, if you're preparing a report in your word processor and you simply want to include a range of data from an Excel worksheet, you probably don't need to create a link.

Table 28-1 describes the effect of choosing the various paste choices when you select the Paste option — the option that *doesn't* create a link to the source data.

Table 28-1
Result of Using the Paste Special Command in Word (Paste Option)

Paste Type	Result
Microsoft Excel Worksheet Object	An object that includes the Excel formatting. This creates an *embedded object*, described in the next section.
Formatted Text (RTF)	A Word table that is formatted as the original Excel range. No link to the source exists. This produces the same result as using Edit ⇨ Paste.
Unformatted Text	Text (not a table) that corresponds to Word's Normal style. Formatting from Excel is not transferred, and no link to the source exists.
Picture	A picture object that retains the formatting from Excel. No link to the source exists. This usually produces better results than the Bitmap option. Double-clicking the object after you paste it enables you to edit the picture.
Bitmap	A bitmap object that retains the formatting from Excel. No link exists to the source. Double-clicking the object after you paste it enables you to edit the bitmap.
HTML Format	A table that is formatted as the original Excel range. No link to the source exists. Use this format when you expect to publish the document as a Web page.

Figure 28-5 shows how a copied range from Excel appears in Word, using each of the paste special formats.

The pasted data *looks* the same regardless of whether the Paste or Paste link option is selected.

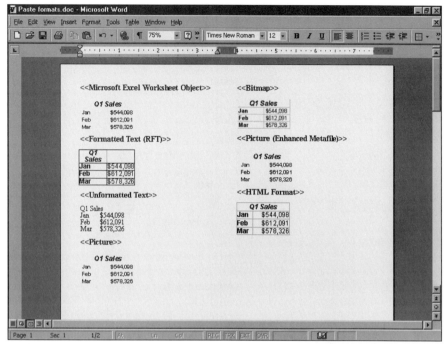

Figure 28-5: Data that is copied from Excel and pasted using various formats

Some Excel formatting does not transfer when pasted to Word as formatted text. For example, Word doesn't support vertical alignment for table cells (but you can use Word's paragraph formatting commands to apply vertical alignment).

Pasting with a link

If you think the data that you're copying will change, you may want to paste a link. If you paste the data by using the Paste link option in the Paste Special dialog box, you can make changes to the source document, and the changes appear in the destination application (a few seconds of delay may occur). You can test these changes by displaying both applications onscreen, making changes to the source document, and watching for them to appear in the destination document.

Table 28-2 describes the effect of choosing the various paste choices in Word's Paste Special dialog box when the Paste link option is selected.

Table 28-2
**Result of Using the Paste Special Command
in Word (Paste Link Option)**

Paste Type	Result
Microsoft Excel Worksheet Object	A linked object that includes the Excel formatting. Double-click the object after pasting it to edit the source data in Excel.
Formatted Text (RTF)	A Word table that is formatted as the original Excel range. Changes in the source are reflected automatically.
Unformatted Text	Text (not a table) that corresponds to Word's Normal style. Formatting from Excel is not transferred. Changes in the source are reflected automatically.
Picture	A picture object that retains the formatting from Excel. Changes in the source are reflected automatically. This usually produces better results than the Bitmap option. Double-click the object after pasting it to edit the source data in Excel.
Bitmap	A bitmap object that retains the formatting from Excel. Changes in the source are reflected automatically. Double-click the object after pasting it to edit the source data in Excel.
HTML Format	A table that is formatted as the original Excel range. Use this format when you expect to publish the document as a Web page.

Embedding Objects

Using *Object Linking and Embedding* (OLE), you can also embed an object to share information between Windows applications. This technique enables you to insert an object from another program and use that program's editing tools to manipulate it. The OLE objects can be items such as those in the following list:

✦ Text documents from other products, such as word processors

✦ Drawings or pictures from other products

✦ Information from special OLE server applications, such as Microsoft Equation

✦ Sound files

✦ Video or animation files

Most of the major Windows applications support OLE. You can embed an object into your document in either of two ways:

✦ Choose Edit ⇨ Paste Special, and select the "object" choice (if it's available). If you do this, select the Paste option rather than the Paste link option.

✦ Select Insert ⇨ Object.

Some applications — such as those in Microsoft Office — can also embed an object by dragging it from one application to another.

The following sections discuss these two methods and provide a few examples using Excel and Word.

Embedding an Excel range in a Word document

This example embeds the Excel range shown in Figure 28-6 in a Word document.

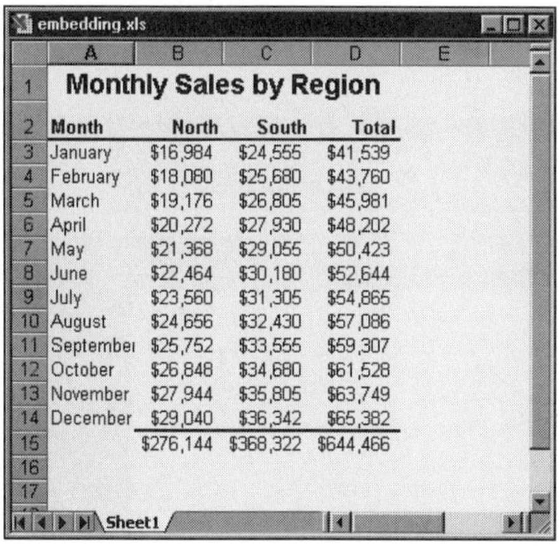

Monthly Sales by Region

Month	North	South	Total
January	$16,984	$24,555	$41,539
February	$18,080	$25,680	$43,760
March	$19,176	$26,805	$45,981
April	$20,272	$27,930	$48,202
May	$21,368	$29,055	$50,423
June	$22,464	$30,180	$52,644
July	$23,560	$31,305	$54,865
August	$24,656	$32,430	$57,086
Septembei	$25,752	$33,555	$59,307
October	$26,848	$34,680	$61,528
November	$27,944	$35,805	$63,749
December	$29,040	$36,342	$65,382
	$276,144	$368,322	$644,466

Figure 28-6: This range will be embedded in a Word document.

To start, select A1:D15 and copy the range to the clipboard. Then, activate (or start) Word, open the document in which you want to embed the range, and then move the insertion point to the location in the document where you want the table to appear. Choose Word's Edit ⇨ Paste Special command. Select the Paste option (not Paste link), and choose the Microsoft Excel Worksheet Object format (see Figure 28-7). Click OK, and the range appears in the Word document.

The pasted object is not a standard Word table. For example, you can't select or format individual cells in the table. Furthermore, it's not linked to the Excel source range. If you change a value in the Excel worksheet, the change does not appear in the embedded object in the Word document.

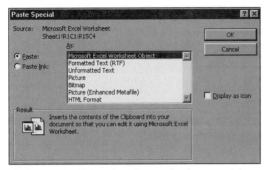

Figure 28-7: This operation embeds an Excel object in a Word document.

If you double-click the object, however, you notice something unusual: Word's menus and toolbars change to those used by Excel. In addition, the embedded object appears with Excel's familiar row and column borders. In other words, you can edit this object *in place* by using Excel's commands. Figure 28-8 shows how this looks. To return to Word, just click anywhere in the Word document.

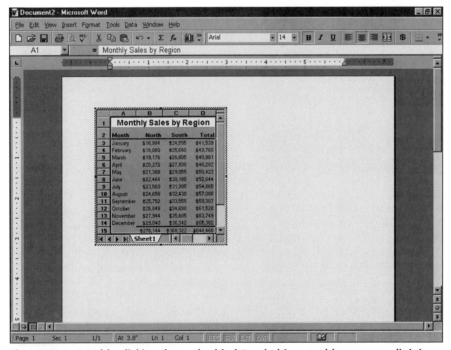

Figure 28-8: Double-clicking the embedded Excel object enables you to edit it in place. Note that Word now displays Excel's menus and toolbars.

Remember that no link is involved here. If you make changes to the embedded object in Word, these changes do not appear in the original Excel worksheet. The embedded object is completely independent from the original source.

Using this technique, you have access to all of Excel's features while you are still in Word. Microsoft's ultimate goal is to enable users to focus on their documents—not on the application that produces the document.

Tip   You can accomplish the embedding previously described by selecting the range in Excel and then dragging it to your Word document. In fact, you can use the Windows desktop as an intermediary storage location. For example, you can drag a range from Excel to the desktop and create a *scrap.* Then, you can drag this scrap into your Word document. The result is an embedded Excel object.

Creating a new Excel object in Word

The preceding example embeds a range from an existing Excel worksheet into a Word document. This section demonstrates how to create a new (empty) Excel object in Word. This may be useful if you're creating a report and need to insert a table of values that doesn't exist in a worksheet. You *could* insert a normal Word table, but you can take advantage of Excel's formulas and functions to make this task much easier.

To create a new Excel object in a Word document, choose Insert ⇨ Object in Word. Word responds with the Object dialog box, shown in Figure 28-9. The Create New tab lists the types of objects that you can create (the contents of the list depends on the applications that you have installed on your system). Choose the Microsoft Excel Worksheet option and click OK.

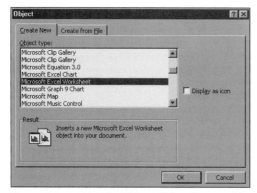

Figure 28-9: Word's Object dialog box enables you to create a new object.

Word inserts an empty Excel worksheet object into the document and activates it for you, as shown in Figure 28-10. You have full access to Excel commands, so you can enter whatever you want into the worksheet object. After you finish, click anywhere in the Word document. You can, of course, double-click this object at any time to make changes or additions.

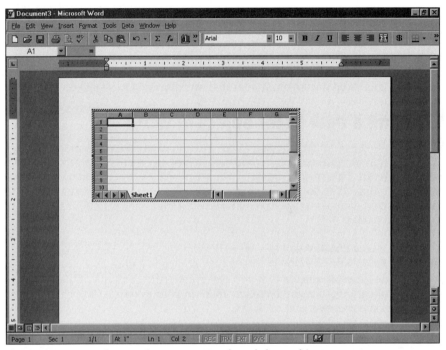

Figure 28-10: Word created an empty Excel worksheet object.

You can change the size of the object while it's activated by dragging any of the sizing handles that appear on the borders of the object. You also can crop the object, so that when it isn't activated, the object displays only cells that contain information. To crop an object in Word, select the object so that you can see sizing handles. Then, display Word's Picture toolbar (right-click any toolbar button and choose Picture). Click the Cropping tool (it looks like a pair of plus signs) and then drag any sizing handle on the object.

Note   Even if you crop an Excel worksheet object in Word, when you double-click the object, you have access to all rows and columns in Excel. Cropping changes only the *displayed* area of the object.

Embedding an existing workbook in Word

Yet another option is to embed an existing workbook into a Word document. Use Word's Insert ➪ Object command. In the Object dialog box, click the tab labeled Create from File (see Figure 28-11). Click the Browse button and locate the Excel workbook that you want to embed.

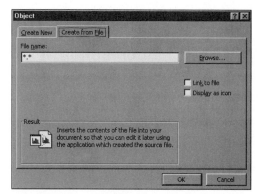

Figure 28-11: This dialog box enables you to locate a file to embed in the active document.

When you use this technique, you embed a *copy* of the selected workbook in the Word document. You can either use it as-is or double-click it to make changes. Note that any changes that you make to this copy of the document are not reflected in the original workbook.

Embedding objects in an Excel worksheet

The preceding examples involve embedding Excel objects in a Word document. The same procedures can be used to embed other objects into an Excel worksheet.

For example, if you have an Excel workbook that requires a great amount of explanatory text, you have several choices:

✦ You can enter the text into cells. This is tedious and doesn't allow much formatting.

✦ You can use a text box. This is a good alternative, but it doesn't offer many formatting features.

✦ You can embed a Word document in your worksheet. This gives you full access to all of Word's formatting features.

To embed an empty Word document into an Excel worksheet, choose Excel's Insert ⇨ Object command. In the Object dialog box, click the Create New tab and select Microsoft Word Document from the Object type list.

The result is a blank Word document, activated and ready for you to enter text. Notice that Word's menus and toolbars replace Excel's menus and toolbars. You can resize the document as you like, and the words wrap accordingly. Figure 28-12 shows an example of a Word document embedded in an Excel worksheet.

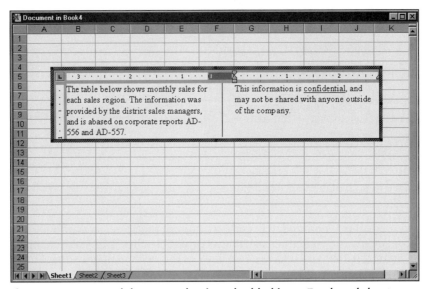

Figure 28-12: A Word document that is embedded in an Excel worksheet

You can embed many other types of objects, including audio clips, video clips, MIDI sequences, and even an entire Microsoft PowerPoint presentation.

When you embed a video clip, Excel doesn't store the actual video clip file in the Excel document. Rather, Excel stores a pointer to the original file. If, for some reason, you want to embed the complete video clip file, you can use the Object Packager application. Be aware, however, that video clip files are typically quite large, and opening and saving the workbook will take a lot of time.

Microsoft Office includes a few additional applications that you may find useful. These all can be embedded in Excel documents:

✦ **Microsoft Equation:** Create equations, such as the one shown in Figure 28-13.

✦ **Microsoft WordArt:** Modify text in some interesting ways, as in Figure 28-14.

✦ **MS Organization Chart:** Create attractive organizational charts, as shown in Figure 28-15.

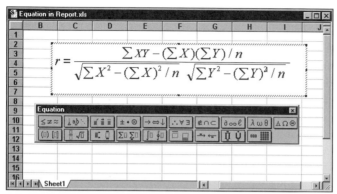

Figure 28-13: This object was created with Microsoft Equation.

Figure 28-14: An example of Microsoft WordArt

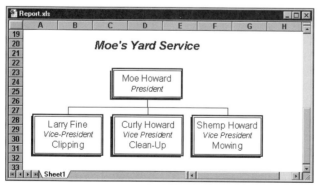

Figure 28-15: An example of an embedded organizational chart

Using Office Binders

If you have Microsoft Office installed, you may take advantage of its binder feature. A *binder* is a container that can hold documents from different applications: Excel, Word, and PowerPoint.

You may find that a binder is useful when you are working on a project that involves documents from different applications. For example, you may be preparing a sales presentation that uses charts and tables from Excel, reports and memos from Word, and slides prepared with PowerPoint. You can store all the information in a single file. And, when you print the entire binder, pages are numbered sequentially.

To use a binder, start the Binder application, and an empty binder appears. You then can add existing documents to the binder or create new documents in the binder. Figure 28-16 shows a binder that contains Word, Excel, and PowerPoint documents. Consult the online Help for complete details on using this application.

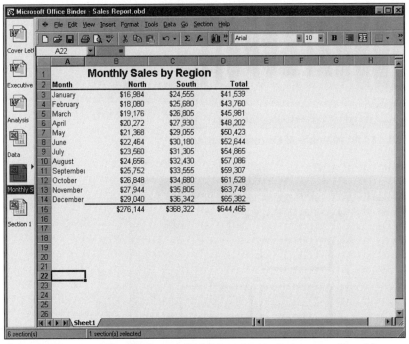

Figure 28-16: An Office binder can hold documents that are produced by different applications.

Note You may need to rerun Office setup if Binder isn't installed on your computer. You'll find it under a category called Office Tools.

Summary

This chapter describes techniques that enable you to use data from other applications. These techniques include standard copy-and-paste options using the Windows and Office clipboards, dynamic linking between applications, and embedding objects. This chapter concludes with a note on Microsoft Office's binder application, which enables you to work with documents that are produced by different applications.

✦   ✦   ✦

Excel and the Internet

Chances are, you're already involved in the Internet in some way. This technology seems to have taken the world by storm. The World Wide Web (WWW or just the Web) is probably the most exciting thing happening these days in the world of computing. In fact, the Web reaches well beyond the computer community and is a pervasive force in our lives. It's now quite common to see Web site addresses listed in TV commercials, in magazine ads, and even on billboards.

The applications in Microsoft Office 2000 — including Excel — have all been revamped to put them on a better footing with the Internet. This chapter provides an introduction to the Internet (for those who have yet to discover this resource) and discusses the Internet features that are available in Excel 2000.

What Is the Internet?

The *Internet,* in a nutshell, is a collection of computers that are located all around the world. These computers are all connected to each other, and they can pass information back and forth. Strange as it may seem, the Internet is essentially a noncommercial system, and no single entity "runs" the Internet.

Most people don't think of the Internet as a collection of computers. Rather, the Internet is a *resource* that contains information — and you use a computer to access that information. The computers that are connected to the Internet simply do the grunt work of passing the information from point A (which could be a computer in Hamburg, Germany) to point B (which could be the computer in your cubicle).

Internet Terminology for Newcomers

If you're just starting to explore the Internet, you'll encounter many new terms (many of which are acronyms). The following is a list of a few common Internet terms and their definitions:

✦ **Browser:** Software that is designed to download HTML documents, interpret them, and display their contents. You can also use a browser to download files from an FTP site. The two leading Web browsers are Microsoft Internet Explorer and Netscape Navigator.

✦ **Download:** To transfer a file from another computer to your computer.

✦ **E-mail:** A method of sending messages to others electronically. You may be able to send and receive e-mail only within your company, or you may be able to send and receive e-mail all over the world by using the Internet.

✦ **FTP:** An acronym for *File Transfer Protocol*. This is one method by which a file is transferred from one computer to another.

✦ **FTP site:** An area of a computer that contains files that can be downloaded. For example, Microsoft maintains several FTP sites that have files that you can download.

✦ **HTML document:** A computer file that contains information that is viewable in a browser. The file includes embedded "tags" that describe how the information is displayed and formatted. Browser software is designed to interpret these tags and display the information. Sometimes known as a *Web document* or a *Web page*.

✦ **HTTP:** An acronym for Hypertext Transfer Protocol. This is the method by which documents are transferred over the Web.

✦ **Hyperlink:** A clickable object (or text) that opens another document. Most Web pages include hyperlinks to enable the user to jump to another topic or Web site.

✦ **Internet:** A network of computers throughout the world that can communicate with each other and pass information back and forth.

✦ **Intranet:** A company-wide network of computers that uses Internet protocols to provide access to information. An intranet can be accessed only by users who have permission.

✦ **URL:** An acronym for *Uniform Resource Locator*. A URL uniquely describes an Internet resource, such as a World Wide Web document or a file. For example, the URL for the opening page of Microsoft's Web site is www.microsoft.com.

✦ **Web site:** A collection of HTML documents and other files located on a particular computer. The files on a Web site are available to anyone in the world. For example, Microsoft maintains a Web site that contains information about its products, technical support, and other resources.

✦ **WWW:** The World Wide Web, which is a part of the Internet that supports the transfer of information between computers throughout the world.

What's available on the Internet?

The amount and variety of information that's available on the Internet is simply mind-boggling. You can think of virtually any topic in the world, and an excellent chance exists that at least some information on that topic can be found on the Internet. Not unexpectedly, computer-related information is especially abundant.

So, where do you get this information? The following are the four primary sources for information on the Internet:

✦ **Web sites:** The Web has rapidly become the most popular part of the Internet. Hundreds of thousands of Web sites are available that you can access with your Web browser software. For example, my own Web site (The Spreadsheet Page) has the following URL: `www.j-walk.com/ss/`.

✦ **FTP sites:** These are computers that have files available for download. You can download these files by using Web browser software or other software that is designed specifically to download files from FTP sites. The following is the URL for Microsoft's FTP site: `ftp://ftp.microsoft.com`.

✦ **Newsgroups:** These are essentially electronic bulletin boards. People post messages or questions, and others respond to the messages or answer their questions. Thousands of newsgroups are available for just about any topic that you can think of. You need special "news reader" software to read or post messages to a newsgroup (although most Web browsers also include this feature). For more information, see the sidebar "Excel Newsgroups."

✦ **Mailing lists:** If you have access to Internet e-mail, you can subscribe to any of several thousand mailing lists that address a broad array of topics. Subscribers send e-mail to the mailing list, and then every other subscriber to the list receives that e-mail. Two popular mailing lists deal with Excel (refer to the "Excel Mailing Lists" sidebar for details).

How do you get on the Internet?

You can access the Internet in a number of ways. Here are some of the most common ways:

✦ **Through your company:** Your company may already be connected to the Internet. If so, just fire up your Web browser and you're there!

✦ **Through an Internet Service Provider (ISP):** Most communities have several companies that can set up an Internet account for you. For a small monthly fee (usually around $20) you can have unlimited (or almost unlimited) access to the Internet. All that's required on your part is a computer, a modem, and a phone line.

✦ **Through an online service:** If you subscribe to any of the following online services, you can access the Internet through that service: America Online, CompuServe, Microsoft Network, or Prodigy.

Excel Newsgroups

Newsgroups are perhaps the best source for help with Excel. Typically, questions posed on a newsgroup are answered within 24 hours—assuming, of course, that the question is asked in a manner that makes others want to reply. The following is a list of newsgroups that deal with Excel:

✦ comp.apps.spreadsheets: Covers all spreadsheets, but about 90 percent of the posts deal with Excel

✦ microsoft.public.excel.programming: Covers Excel programming issues, including VBA and XLM macros.

✦ microsoft.public.excel.123quattro: Covers issues concerning conversion of 1-2-3 or Quattro Pro files to Excel.

✦ microsoft.public.excel.worksheet.functions: Covers worksheet functions.

✦ microsoft.public.excel.charting: Covers topics related to charts.

✦ microsoft.public.excel.printing: Covers topics that deal with printing.

✦ microsoft.public.excel.queryDAO: Discussion area about using the Microsoft Query and Data Access Objects (DAO) in Excel.

✦ microsoft.public.excel.datamap: Covers the Data Map feature in Excel.

✦ microsoft.public.excel.crashesGPFs: Covers General Protection Faults and other system failures.

✦ microsoft.public.excel.misc: A catch-all group for topics that do not fit one of the other categories.

✦ microsoft.public.excel.links: Covers topics related to using links in Excel.

✦ microsoft.public.excel.interopoledde: Discussion area for Object Linking and Embedding (OLE), Dynamic Data Exchange (DDE), and other cross-application issues.

✦ microsoft.public.excel.setup: Covers problems dealing with setup and installation of Excel.

✦ microsoft.public.excel.templates: Discussion area for the Spreadsheet Solutions templates and other XLT files.

Note If your ISP doesn't carry the `microsoft.public.excel.*` groups, you can access them directly from Microsoft's news server. You need to configure your newsreader software or Web browser to access Microsoft's news server, which is `msnews.microsoft.com`.

Excel Mailing Lists

If you like the idea of communicating with other Excel users, you may want to join one of the Excel mailing lists. You can read messages, questions, and answers posted by others and eventually contribute your own messages to the list. If you find that the amount of mail is overwhelming, it's easy to "unsubscribe."

The EXCEL-G mailing list

For Excel users of all levels. To subscribe to the list, send e-mail to LISTSERV@PEACH.EASE. LSOFT.COM. In the body of the message, enter **SUB EXCEL-G YourFirstName YourLastName**. You'll receive complete instructions via e-mail.

The EXCEL-L mailing list

Primarily for Excel developers who discuss more advanced topics. To subscribe to the list, send e-mail to LISTSERV@PEACH.EASE.LSOFT.COM. In the body of the message, enter **SUB EXCEL-L YourFirstName YourLastName**. You'll receive complete instructions via e-mail.

Where to find out more about the Internet

The best place to find out more about the Internet is — you guessed it — the Internet. A good starting place is the IDG Books Web site. To access it, open the following URL in your Web browser: `www.idgbooks.com`.

IDG Books Worldwide publishes numerous Internet books for users of all levels, and you can find these listed and described on the IDG Web site.

Excel's Internet Tools

The remainder of this chapter describes the Internet-related features available in Excel 2000. These features include:

✦ Using HTML as a native file format (instead of the XLS file format).

✦ Saving a worksheet as an interactive Web page.

✦ Using Excel's Web toolbar.

+ Inserting hyperlinks into a worksheet.

+ Creating and using Web queries.

+ Scheduling and conducting online meetings.

+ Creating discussion groups.

Using HTML as a native file format

Excel's standard file format is, of course, an XLS file. Excel 2000, however, has the ability to use HTML as a native file format. This means that you can create a workbook and save it in HTML format. Then, you can reopen the file without losing any information. In other words, your Excel-specific information (such as formulas, charts, pivot tables, and macros) survive the translation to HTML.

If you've used the "save as HTML" feature in Excel 97, you probably know that the HTML file that's created works fine in Web browsers — but if you reopen the file in Excel, all of your formulas (as well as other Excel-specific features) will be gone. With Excel 2000, this problem no longer exists, because the HTML file contains lots of proprietary tags that are ignored by browsers but that enable Excel to re-create the workbook.

To save a workbook in HTML format, select File ➪ Save As. You'll see the familiar Save As dialog box — but with some new options (see Figure 29-1). In the field labeled Save as type, make sure Web Page (*.htm, *.html) is selected. Provide a filename, and click Save. To reopen the file, use the normal File ➪ Open command.

Figure 29-1: Use the Save As dialog box to save a workbook in HTML format.

Caution Unless your workbook is very simple, saving it in HTML format generates additional "supporting" files, because the HTML file format can't handle Excel-specific items, such as macros, charts, and pivot tables. The supporting files are stored in a separate subdirectory within the directory where you save the file. The directory name consists of the file's name, followed by a space and the word "files." Therefore, if you need to transfer the file to another computer, make sure that you also transfer the supporting files in the subdirectory.

If you save your work in HTML format, you should be aware of some additional options. Select Tools ⇨ Options, click the General tab, and then click the Web Options button. You'll see the dialog box shown in Figure 29-2. Most of the time, the default settings work just fine. However, familiarizing yourself with the options available is worthwhile (these are described in the online Help). You can also access the Web Options dialog box from the Tools menu in the Save As dialog box.

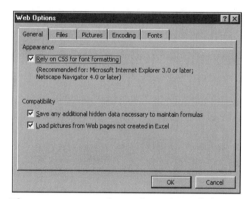

Figure 29-2: Use the Web Options dialog box to set various options for working with HTML files.

When you save a workbook in HTML format, by default, it will not be interactive when it's opened in a browser. The browser displays a good rendition of the worksheet, but it's essentially a "dead" workbook, because the user can't change any cells. The next section describes how to save your Excel workbook in a way that provides interactivity within a Web browser.

Providing interactivity in your Web documents

When you save an Excel workbook in HTML format, you can select an option that makes the file interactive within the browser. This means that the user can perform standard Excel operations directly in the browser. For example, the user can change cells or manipulate data in a pivot table. Saving an Excel file with interactivity is limited to a single sheet.

Note   To take advantage of this interactivity, the user must have Office 2000 installed, or have a licensed copy of the Office Client Pak. The Office Client Pak consists of the ActiveX controls necessary to work with interactive Office documents in a Web browser. Currently, the only browser that supports this technology is Microsoft Internet Explorer.

Figure 29-3 shows an example of an Excel workbook displayed in Internet Explorer. The user can change the values, and the formulas display the calculated results.

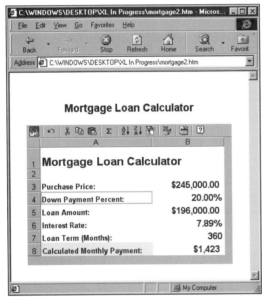

Figure 29-3: An interactive Excel workbook opened in Internet Explorer

You need to understand that the interactivity is limited. For example, you can't execute macros when an interactive Excel file is displayed in a browser.

Using the Web toolbar

Use the Web toolbar (shown in Figure 29-4) to move among files (Excel files and HTML documents); this is similar to using a Web browser. You can jump forward or backward among the workbooks and other files that you've visited, and add the ones that you may use frequently to a "favorites" list.

Figure 29-4: The Web toolbar

Working with hyperlinks

Hyperlinks are shortcuts that provide a quick way to jump to other workbooks and files. You can jump to files on your own computer, your network, and the Internet and Web.

Inserting a hyperlink

You can create hyperlinks from cell text or graphic objects, such as shapes and pictures. To create a text hyperlink, choose the Insert ➪ Hyperlink command (or press Ctrl+K). Excel responds with the dialog box shown in Figure 29-5.

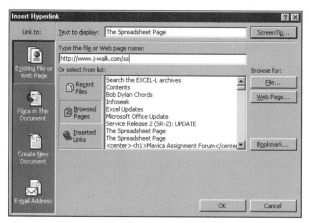

Figure 29-5: The Insert Hyperlink dialog box

Select an icon in the Link to column that represents the type of hyperlink you want to create. Then, specify the location for the file that you want to link to. The dialog box will change, depending on the icon selected. Click OK, and Excel creates the hyperlink in the active cell.

Adding a hyperlink to a graphic object works the same way. Add an object to your worksheet by using the Drawing toolbar. Select the object and then choose the Insert ➪ Hyperlink command. Specify the required information as outlined in the previous paragraph.

Using hyperlinks

When you work with hyperlinks, remember that Excel attempts to mimic a Web browser. For example, when you click a hyperlink, the hyperlinked document replaces the current document — it takes on the same window size and position. The document that contains the hyperlink is hidden. You can use the Back and Forward buttons on the Web toolbar to activate the documents.

Web queries

Excel enables you to pull in data contained in an HTML file by performing a Web query. The data is transferred to a worksheet, where you can manipulate it any way you like. You need to understand that performing a Web query does not actually open the HTML file in Excel.

The best part about a Web query is that Excel remembers where the data came from. Therefore, after you create a Web query, you can "refresh" the query to pull in the most recent data.

Note   The Web query feature is very similar to performing a normal database query (see Chapter 34). The only difference is that the data is coming from a Web page rather than a database file. Figure 29-6 shows a Web page that's a good candidate for a Web query.

To create a Web query, select Data ➪ Get External Data ➪ New Web Query. Excel displays the New Web Query dialog box, shown in Figure 29-7. In part 1, specify the HTML file, using the Browse button if you like. The HTML file can be on the Internet, a corporate intranet, or on a local or network drive. In part 2, select how much of the file you want to use. Most of the time, you'll just want to bring in a particular table. In part 3, specify the type of formatting that you'd like to see. Click the Advanced button for some additional options — these options might be necessary if the data in the HTML file is not in the form of a table. Click OK and you get another dialog box asking where you want to place the data.

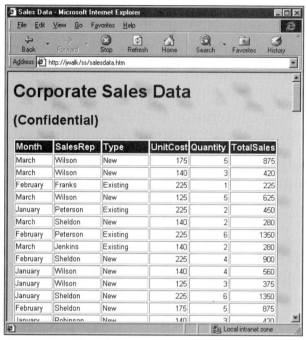

Figure 29-6: The table in this Web page will be brought into a worksheet as a Web query.

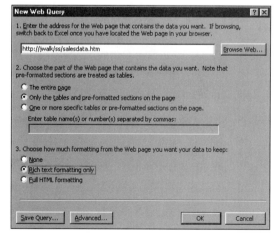

Figure 29-7: Use the New Web Query dialog box to specify the source of the data.

Figure 29-8 shows an Excel workbook, after performing a Web query.

	A	B	C	D	E	F
1	Month	SalesRep	Type	UnitCost	Quantity	TotalSales
2	March	Wilson	New	175	5	875
3	March	Wilson	New	140	3	420
4	February	Franks	Existing	225	1	225
5	March	Wilson	New	125	5	625
6	January	Peterson	Existing	225	2	450
7	March	Sheldon	New	140	2	280
8	February	Peterson	Existing	225	6	1350
9	March	Jenkins	Existing	140	2	280
10	February	Sheldon	New	225	4	900
11	January	Wilson	New	140	4	560
12	January	Wilson	New	125	3	375
13	January	Sheldon	New	225	6	1350
14	February	Sheldon	New	175	5	875
15	January	Robinson	New	140	3	420
16	February	Sheldon	New	125	2	250
17	March	Sheldon	New	140	6	840
18	March	Jenkins	Existing	225	3	675
19	January	Robinson	New	225	2	450
20	March	Sheldon	New	225	6	1350
21	February	Wilson	New	140	3	420
22	February	Robinson	New	140	3	420
23	February	Sheldon	New	140	5	700
24	March	Robinson	New	175	1	175

Figure 29-8: The data in this workbook resulted from a Web query.

After you create your Web query, you have some options. Activate any cell in the data range and select Data ⇨ Get External Data ⇨ Data Range Properties. Or, you can right-click and select the command from the shortcut menu. Either method displays the dialog box shown in Figure 29-9. Adjust the settings to your liking.

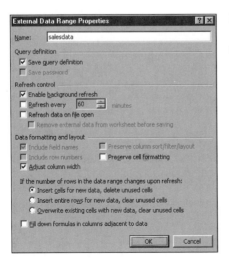

Figure 29-9: The External Data Range Properties dialog box provides you with some options regarding your Web query.

Summary

This chapter provides a brief introduction to the Internet and describes several Internet tools that are available in Excel. It explains how to use HTML as a native file format, use the Web toolbar, work with hyperlinks, and use Web queries.

✦   ✦   ✦

Making Your Worksheets Error-Free

The ultimate goal in developing a spreadsheet solution is to generate accurate results. For simple worksheets, this isn't difficult, and you can usually tell whether the results are correct. But when your worksheets are large or complex, ensuring accuracy becomes more difficult. This chapter provides you with tools and techniques to help you identify and correct errors.

Types of Worksheet Problems

Making a change in a worksheet — even a relatively minor change — may produce a ripple effect that introduces errors in other cells. For example, accidentally entering a value into a cell that formerly held a formula is all too easy to do. This can have a major impact on other formulas, and you may not discover the problem until long after you make the change. Or, you may *never* discover the problem.

An Excel worksheet can have many types of problems. Some problems — such as a formula that returns an error value — are immediately apparent. Other problems are more subtle. For example, if a formula was constructed using faulty logic, it may never return an error value — it simply returns the wrong values. If you're lucky, you can discover the problem and correct it.

Common problems that occur in worksheets are the following:

✦ Incorrect approach to a problem

✦ Faulty logic in a formula

✦ Formulas that return error values

✦ Circular references

✦ Spelling mistakes

✦ A worksheet is new to you, and you can't figure out how it works

Excel provides tools to help you identify and correct some of these problems. In the remaining sections, I discuss these tools along with others that I've developed.

Formula AutoCorrect

When you enter a formula that has a syntax error, Excel attempts to determine the problem and offers a suggested correction.

For example, if you enter the following formula (which has a syntax error), Excel displays the dialog box that is shown in Figure 30-1:

```
=SUM(A1:A12)/3B
```

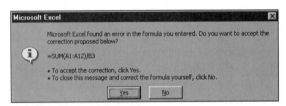

Figure 30-1: Excel can often offer a suggestion to correct a formula.

Caution   Be careful about accepting corrections for your formulas from Excel, because it doesn't always guess correctly. For example, I entered the following formula (which has mismatched parentheses):

```
=AVERAGE(SUM(A1:A12,SUM(B1:B12))
```

Excel proposed the following correction to the formula:

```
=AVERAGE(SUM(A1:A12,SUM(B1:B12)))
```

You may be tempted to accept the suggestion without even thinking. In this case, the proposed formula is syntactically correct — but not what I intended.

Tracing Cell Relationships

Excel has several useful tools that can help you track down errors and logical flaws in your worksheets. This section discusses the following items:

✦ Go To Special dialog box

✦ Excel's built-in auditing tools

These tools are useful for debugging formulas. As you probably realize by now, the formulas in a worksheet can become complicated and refer (directly or indirectly) to hundreds or thousands of other cells. Trying to isolate a problem in a tangled web of formulas can be frustrating.

Before discussing these features, you need to be familiar with the following two concepts:

✦ **Cell precedents:** Applicable only to cells that contain a formula. A formula cell's precedents are all the cells that contribute to the formula's result. A *direct precedent* is a cell that you use directly in the formula. An *indirect precedent* is a cell that isn't used directly in the formula, but is used by a cell to which you refer in the formula.

✦ **Cell dependents:** Formula cells that depend on a particular cell. Again, the formula cell can be a direct dependent or an indirect dependent.

Often, identifying cell precedents for a formula cell sheds light on why the formula isn't working correctly. On the other hand, knowing which formula cells depend on a particular cell is often helpful. For example, if you're about to delete a formula, you may want to check whether it has any dependents.

The Go To Special dialog box

The Go To Special dialog box can be useful, because it enables you to specify the type of cells that you want Excel to select. To display this dialog box, choose Edit ➪ Go To (or press F5). The Go To dialog box appears. Click the Special button, which displays the Go To Special dialog box, as shown in Figure 30-2.

If you select a range before choosing Edit ➪ Go To, the command looks only at the selected cells. If only a single cell is selected, the command operates on the entire worksheet.

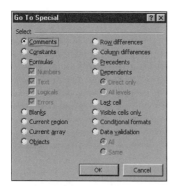

Figure 30-2: The Go To Special dialog box

You can use this dialog box to select cells of a certain type—which can often be helpful in identifying errors. For example, if you choose the Formulas option, Excel selects all the cells that contain a formula. If you zoom the worksheet out to a small size, you can get a good idea of the worksheet's organization (see Figure 30-3). It may also help you spot a common error: a formula that you overwrote with a value. If you find a cell that's not selected amid a group of selected formula cells, chances are good that the cell formerly contained a formula that has been replaced by a value.

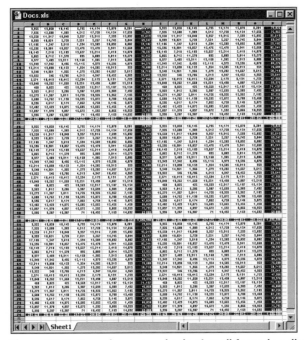

Figure 30-3: Zooming out and selecting all formula cells can give you a good overview of how the worksheet is designed.

You can also use the Go To Special dialog box to identify cell precedents and dependents. In this case, Excel selects all cells that qualify. In either case, you can choose whether to display direct or all levels.

Excel has shortcut keys that you can use to select precedents and dependents. These are listed in Table 30-1.

Table 30-1	
Shortcut Keys to Select Precedents and Dependents	
Key Combination	*What It Selects*
Ctrl+[	Direct precedents
Ctrl+Shift+[	All precedents
Ctrl+]	Direct dependents
Ctrl+Shift+]	All dependents

You also can select a formula cell's direct dependents by double-clicking the cell. This technique, however, works only when you turn off the Edit directly in cell option on the Edit tab of the Options dialog box.

Excel's auditing tools

Excel provides a set of interactive auditing tools that you may find helpful. Access these tools either by selecting Tools ➪ Auditing (which results in a submenu with additional choices) or by using the Auditing toolbar, shown in Figure 30-4.

Figure 30-4: The Auditing toolbar

Pay Attention to the Colors

When you edit a cell that contains a formula, Excel color-codes the cell and range references in the formula. Excel also outlines the cells and ranges used in the formula by using corresponding colors. Therefore, you can see at a glance the cells that are used in the formula.

You can also manipulate the colored outline to change the cell or range reference. To change the references that are used, drag the outline's border or drag the outline's fill handle (at the lower-right corner of the outline).

The tools on the Auditing toolbar, from left to right, are as follows:

✦ **Trace Precedents:** Draws arrows to indicate a formula cell's precedents. Click this multiple times to see additional levels of precedents.

✦ **Remove Precedent Arrows:** Removes the most recently placed set of precedent arrows.

✦ **Trace Dependents:** Draws arrows to indicate a cell's dependents. Click this multiple times to see additional levels of dependents.

✦ **Remove Dependent Arrows:** Removes the most recently placed set of dependent arrows.

✦ **Remove All Arrows:** Removes all precedent and dependent arrows from the worksheet.

✦ **Trace Error:** Draws arrows from a cell that contains an error to the cells that may have caused the error.

✦ **New Comment:** Inserts a comment for the active cell. This really doesn't have much to do with auditing. It lets you attach a comment to a cell.

✦ **Circle Invalid Data:** Draws a circle around all the cells that contain invalid data. This applies only to cells that have validation criteria specified with the Data ➪ Validation command.

✦ **Clear Validation Circles:** Removes the circles that are drawn around cells that contain invalid data.

These tools can identify precedents and dependents by drawing arrows (known as *cell tracers*) on the worksheet, as shown in Figure 30-5. In this case, cell G11 was selected and then the Trace Precedents toolbar button was clicked. Excel drew lines to identify the cells used by the formula in G11 (direct precedents).

Commissions.xls							
	A	B	C	D	E	F	G	H
1	Commission Rate:	5.50%	Normal Commission Rate				
2	Sales Goal:	15%	Improvement From Prior Month				
3	Bonus Rate:	6.50%	Paid if Sales Goal is Attained				
4								
5	Sales Rep	Last Month	This Month	Change	Pct. Change	Met Goal?	Com- mission
6	Murray	101,233	98,744	(2,489)	-2.5%	FALSE	5,431
7	Knuckles	120,933	134,544	13,611	11.3%	FALSE	7,400
8	Lefty	112,344	134,887	22,543	20.1%	TRUE	8,768
9	Lucky	130,933	151,745	20,812	15.9%	TRUE	9,863
10	Scarface	150,932	140,778	(10,154)	-6.7%	FALSE	7,743
11	Totals	616,375	660,698	44,323	7.2%		39,205
12								
13	Average Commission Rate:	5.93%					
14								
15								
16								
17								

Sheet2 / Sheet1

Figure 30-5: Excel draws lines to indicate a cell's precedents.

Figure 30-6 shows what happens when the Trace Precedents button is clicked again. This time, Excel adds more lines to show the indirect precedents. The result is a graphical representation of the cells that are used (directly or indirectly) by the formula in cell G11.

Tip   This type of interactive tracing is often more revealing when the worksheet is zoomed out to display a larger area.

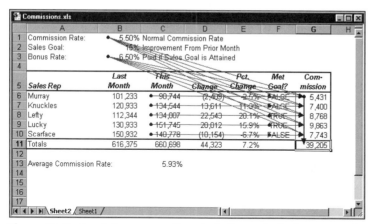

Figure 30-6: Excel draws more lines to indicate the indirect precedents.

The best way to learn about these tools is to use them. Start with a worksheet that has formulas and experiment with the various buttons on the Auditing toolbar.

Tracing error values

The Trace Error button on the Auditing toolbar helps you to identify the cell that is causing an error value to appear. Often, an error in one cell is the result of an error in a precedent cell. Activate a cell that contains an error, and click the Trace Error button. Excel draws arrows to indicate the error source.

Table 30-2 lists the types of error values that may appear in a cell that has a formula. The Trace Error button works with all of these errors.

Table 30-2	
Excel Error Values	
Error Value	**Explanation**
#DIV/0!	The formula is trying to divide by zero (an operation that's not allowed on this planet). This also occurs when the formula attempts to divide by a cell that is empty.
#NAME?	The formula uses a name that Excel doesn't recognize. This can happen if you delete a name that's used in the formula or if you have unmatched quotation marks when using text.
#N/A	The formula refers to an empty cell range.

Continued

Table 30-2 (continued)	
Error Value	**Explanation**
#NULL!	The formula uses an intersection of two ranges that do not intersect (this concept is described later in the chapter).
#NUM!	A problem with a value exists — for example, you specified a negative number where a positive number is expected.
#REF!	The formula refers to a cell that is not valid. This can happen if the cell has been deleted from the worksheet.
#VALUE!	The formula includes an argument or operand of the wrong type.

Circular references

A *circular reference* occurs when a formula refers to its own cell — either directly or indirectly. Usually, this is the result of an error (although some circular references are intentional). When a worksheet has a circular reference, Excel displays the cell reference in the status bar.

Cross-Reference   Refer to the discussion of circular references in Chapter 8.

Other Auditing Tools

The registered version of the Power Utility Pak includes a utility named Auditing Tools. The dialog box for this utility is shown in Figure 30-7.

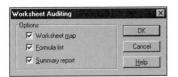

Figure 30-7: The Worksheet Auditing dialog box from the Power Utility Pak

This utility works with the active worksheet and can generate any or all of the following items:

✦ **Worksheet map:** A color-coded graphical map of the worksheet that shows the type of contents for each cell — value, text, formula, logical value, or error. See Figure 30-8.

✦ **Formula list:** A list of all formulas in the worksheet, including their current values.

✦ **Summary report:** An informative report that includes details about the worksheet, the workbook that it's in, and a list of all defined names.

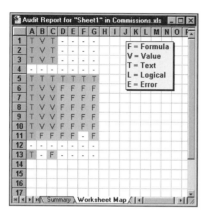

Figure 30-8: This worksheet map was produced by the Auditing Tools utility from the Power Utility Pak.

You can find the shareware version of the Power Utility Pak on this book's CD-ROM. Owners of this book can purchase the Power Utility Pak at a significant discount. Use the coupon in the back of the book to order your copy.

Spelling and Word-Related Options

Excel includes several handy tools to help you with the nonnumeric problems — those related to spelling and words.

Spell checking

If you use a word processing program, you probably run its spelling checker before printing an important document. Spelling mistakes can be just as embarrassing when they appear in a spreadsheet. Fortunately, Microsoft includes a spelling checker with Excel. You can access the spelling checker by using any of these methods:

✦ Select Tools ⇨ Spelling

✦ Click the Spelling button on the Standard toolbar

✦ Press F7

The result of using any one of these methods is the Spelling dialog box that is shown in Figure 30-9.

The extent of the spell checking depends on what you selected before you opened the Spelling dialog box. If you selected a single cell, Excel checks the entire worksheet, including cell contents, notes, text in graphic objects and charts, and page headers and footers. Even the contents of hidden rows and columns are checked. If you select a range of cells, Excel checks only that range. If you select a group of characters in the formula bar, Excel checks only those characters.

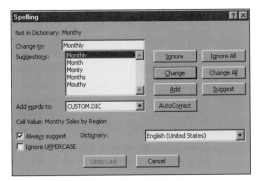

Figure 30-9: The Spelling dialog box

The Spelling dialog box works similarly to other spelling checkers with which you may be familiar. If Excel encounters a word that isn't in the current dictionary or is misspelled, it offers a list of suggestions. You can respond by clicking one of the following buttons:

✦ **Ignore:** Ignores the word and continues the spell check.

✦ **Ignore All:** Ignores the word and all subsequent occurrences of it.

✦ **Change:** Changes the word to the selected word in the Change to edit box.

✦ **Change All:** Changes the word to the selected word in the Change to edit box and changes all subsequent occurrences of it without asking.

✦ **Add:** Adds the word to the dictionary.

✦ **Suggest:** Displays a list of replacement words. This button is grayed if the Always suggest check box is checked.

✦ **AutoCorrect:** Adds the misspelled word and its correct spelling to the list10:
`=SUM(A1:A12)/3B`

Using AutoCorrect

AutoCorrect is a handy feature that automatically corrects common typing mistakes. You also can add words to the list that Excel corrects automatically. The AutoCorrect dialog box appears in Figure 30-10. You access this feature by choosing Tools ➪ AutoCorrect.

This dialog box has several options:

✦ **Correct TWo INitial CApitals:** Automatically corrects words with two initial uppercase letters. For example, *BUdget* is converted to *Budget*. This is a common mistake among fast typists. You can click the Exceptions button to specify a list of exceptions to this rule. For example, my company name is *JWalk and Associates,* so I created an exception for *JWalk*.

✦ **Capitalize first letter of sentence:** Capitalizes the first letter in a sentence.

Figure 30-10: The AutoCorrect dialog box

✦ **Capitalize names of days:** Capitalizes the days of the week. If you enter *monday,* Excel converts it to *Monday.*

✦ **Correct accidental use of cAPS LOCK key:** Corrects errors caused if you accidentally hit the CapsLock key while typing.

✦ **Replace text as you type:** AutoCorrect automatically changes incorrect words as you type them.

Excel includes a long list of AutoCorrect entries for commonly misspelled words. In addition, it has AutoCorrect entries for some symbols. For example, *(c)* is replaced with © and *(r)* is replaced with ®. You can also add your own AutoCorrect entries. For example, if you find that you frequently misspell the word *January* as *Janruary,* you can create an AutoCorrect entry so that it's changed automatically. To create a new AutoCorrect entry, enter the misspelled word in the Replace box and the correctly spelled word in the With box. As I noted previously, you also can do this in the Spelling dialog box.

You also can use the AutoCorrect feature to create shortcuts for commonly used words or phrases. For example, if you work for a company named Consolidated Data Processing Corporation, you can create an AutoCorrect entry for an abbreviation, such as cdp. Then, whenever you type *cdp,* Excel automatically changes it to *Consolidated Data Processing Corporation.*

Using AutoComplete

AutoComplete automatically finishes a word as soon as Excel recognizes it. For Excel to the recognize word, it must appear elsewhere in the same column. This feature is most useful when you're entering a list that contains repeated text in a column. For example, assume that you're entering customer data in a list, and one of the fields is City. Whenever you start typing, Excel searches the other entries in the column. If it finds a match, it completes the entry for you. Press Enter to accept it. If Excel guesses incorrectly, keep typing to ignore the suggestion.

If AutoComplete isn't working, select Tools ➪ Options, click the Edit tab, and check the box labeled Enable AutoComplete for cell values.

You also can display a list of all items in a column by right-clicking and choosing Pick From List from the shortcut menu. Excel then displays a list box of all entries that are in the column (see Figure 30-11). Click the one that you want, and Excel enters it into the cell for you.

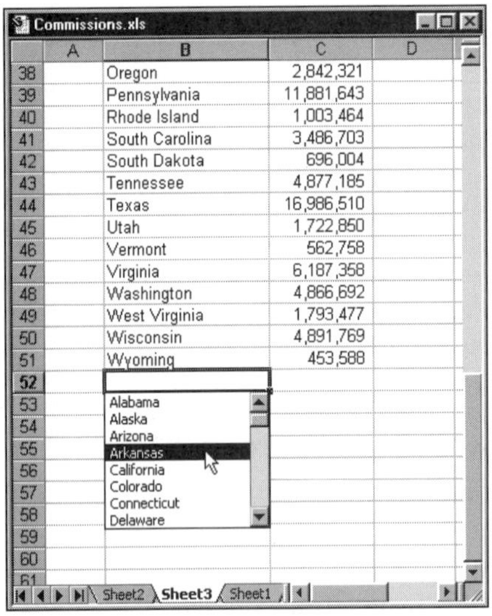

Figure 30-11: Choosing the Pick From List option from the shortcut menu gives you a list of entries from which to choose.

Learning About an Unfamiliar Spreadsheet

When you develop a workbook yourself, you have a thorough understanding of how it's put together. But if you receive an unfamiliar workbook from someone, it may be difficult to understand how it all fits together — especially if it's large.

First, identify the bottom-line cell or cells. Often, a worksheet is designed to produce results in a single cell or in a range of cells. After you identify this cell or range, you should be able to use the cell-tracing techniques described earlier in this chapter to determine the cell relationships.

Although every worksheet is different, a few techniques can help you become familiar with an unfamiliar workbook. I discuss these techniques in the following sections.

Zooming out for the big picture

I find that it's often helpful to use Excel's zoom feature to zoom out to get an overview of the worksheet's layout. You can select View ➪ Full Screen to see even more of the worksheet. When a workbook is zoomed out, you can use all of the normal commands. For example, you can use the Edit ➪ Go To command to select a name range. Or, you can use the options that are available in the Go To Special dialog box (explained previously in this chapter) to select formula cells, constants, or other special cell types.

Viewing formulas

You can become familiar with an unfamiliar workbook by displaying the formulas rather than the results of the formulas. Select Tools ➪ Options, and check the box labeled Formulas on the View tab. You may want to create a new window for the workbook before issuing this command. That way, you can see the formulas in one window and the results in the other.

Figure 30-12 shows an example. The window on the top shows the normal view (formula results). The window on the bottom displays the formulas.

Pasting a list of names

If the worksheet uses named ranges, create a list of the names and their references. Move the cell pointer to an empty area of the worksheet and choose Insert ➪ Name ➪ Paste. Excel responds with its Paste Name dialog box. Click the Paste List button to paste a list of the names and their references into the workbook. Figure 30-13 shows an example.

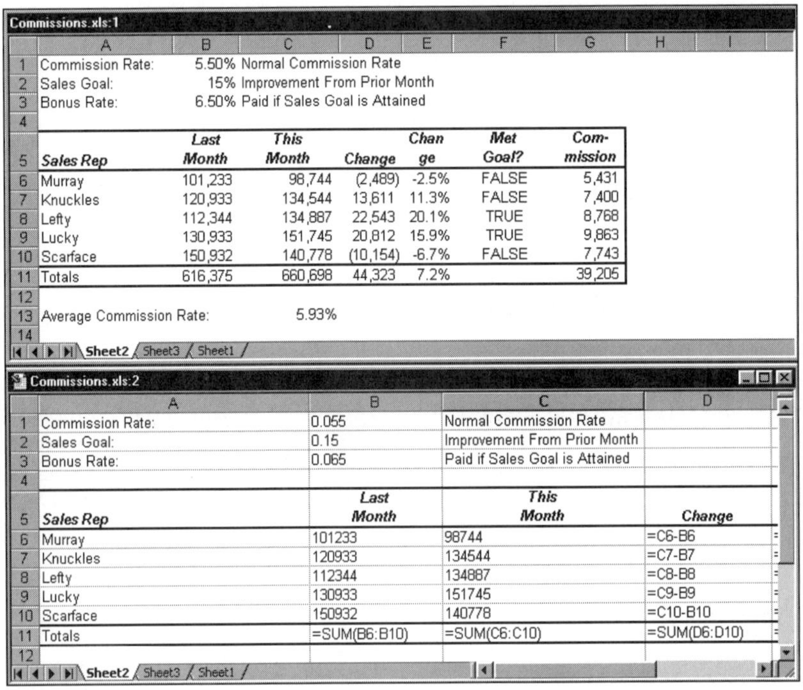

Commissions.xls:1

	A	B	C	D	E	F	G
1	Commission Rate:	5.50%	Normal Commission Rate				
2	Sales Goal:	15%	Improvement From Prior Month				
3	Bonus Rate:	6.50%	Paid if Sales Goal is Attained				
4							
5	*Sales Rep*	*Last Month*	*This Month*	*Change*	*Change*	*Met Goal?*	*Commission*
6	Murray	101,233	98,744	(2,489)	-2.5%	FALSE	5,431
7	Knuckles	120,933	134,544	13,611	11.3%	FALSE	7,400
8	Lefty	112,344	134,887	22,543	20.1%	TRUE	8,768
9	Lucky	130,933	151,745	20,812	15.9%	TRUE	9,863
10	Scarface	150,932	140,778	(10,154)	-6.7%	FALSE	7,743
11	Totals	616,375	660,698	44,323	7.2%		39,205
12							
13	Average Commission Rate:		5.93%				

Commissions.xls:2

	A	B	C	D
1	Commission Rate:	0.055	Normal Commission Rate	
2	Sales Goal:	0.15	Improvement From Prior Month	
3	Bonus Rate:	0.065	Paid if Sales Goal is Attained	
4				
5	*Sales Rep*	*Last Month*	*This Month*	*Change*
6	Murray	101233	98744	=C6-B6
7	Knuckles	120933	134544	=C7-B7
8	Lefty	112344	134887	=C8-B8
9	Lucky	130933	151745	=C9-B9
10	Scarface	150932	140778	=C10-B10
11	Totals	=SUM(B6:B10)	=SUM(C6:C10)	=SUM(D6:D10)

Figure 30-12: The underlying formulas are shown in the bottom window.

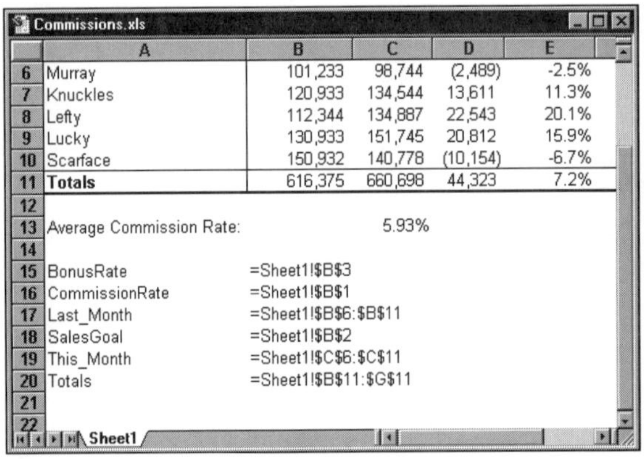

Commissions.xls

	A	B	C	D	E
6	Murray	101,233	98,744	(2,489)	-2.5%
7	Knuckles	120,933	134,544	13,611	11.3%
8	Lefty	112,344	134,887	22,543	20.1%
9	Lucky	130,933	151,745	20,812	15.9%
10	Scarface	150,932	140,778	(10,154)	-6.7%
11	**Totals**	616,375	660,698	44,323	7.2%
12					
13	Average Commission Rate:		5.93%		
14					
15	BonusRate	=Sheet1!$B$3			
16	CommissionRate	=Sheet1!$B$1			
17	Last_Month	=Sheet1!$B$6:$B$11			
18	SalesGoal	=Sheet1!$B$2			
19	This_Month	=Sheet1!$C$6:$C$11			
20	Totals	=Sheet1!$B$11:$G$11			

Figure 30-13: Pasting a list of names (in A15:B20) can sometimes help you understand how a worksheet is constructed.

Summary

In this chapter, I discuss tools that can help you make your worksheets error-free. I identify the types of errors that you're likely to encounter. I also cover three tools that Excel provides, which can help you trace the relationships between cells: the Info window, the Go To Special dialog box, and Excel's interactive auditing tools. I go over text-related features, including spell checking, AutoCorrect, and AutoComplete. I conclude the chapter with general tips that can help you understand how an unfamiliar worksheet is put together.

✦   ✦   ✦

Fun Stuff

Although Excel is used primarily for serious applications, many users discover that this product has a lighter side. This chapter is devoted to the less-serious applications of Excel, including games and interesting diversions.

Games

Excel certainly wasn't designed as a platform for games. Nevertheless, I've developed a few games using Excel and have downloaded several others from various Internet sites. I've found that the key ingredient in developing these games is creativity. In almost every case, I had to invent one or more workarounds to compensate for Excel's lack of game-making features. In this section, I show you a few of my own creations.

The examples in this chapter are either available on the companion CD-ROM or included with the registered version of my Power Utility Pak (see the coupon at the back of the book).

Tick-Tack-Toe

Although Tick-Tack-Toe is not the most mentally stimulating game, everyone knows how to play it. Figure 31-1 shows the Tick-Tack-Toe game that I developed using Excel. In this implementation, the user plays against the computer. I wrote some formulas and VBA macros to determine the computer's moves, and it plays a reasonably good game—about on par with a three-year-old child. I'm embarrassed to admit that the program has even beaten me a few times (okay, so I was distracted!).

This workbook is available on the companion CD-ROM.

You can choose who makes the first move (you or the computer) and which marker you want to use (X or O). The winning games and ties are tallied in cells at the bottom of the window.

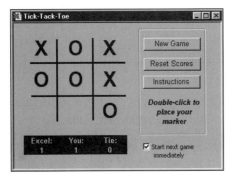

Figure 31-1: My Tick-Tack-Toe game

Moving tile puzzle

At some time in your life, you've probably played one of those moving tile puzzles. They come in several variations, but the goal is always the same: rearrange the tiles so that they are in order.

This workbook is available on the companion CD-ROM.

Figure 31-2 shows a version of this game that I wrote using VBA. This version lets you choose the number of tiles (from a simple 3×3 matrix up to a challenging 6×6 matrix).

Figure 31-2: My Moving Tile puzzle

When you click the tile, it appears to move to the empty position. Actually, no movement is taking place. The program is simply changing the text on the buttons and making the button in the empty position invisible.

Keno

If you've ever spent any time in a casino, you may be familiar with Keno (see Figure 31-3). If you're smart, you probably know to avoid this game like the plague, because it has the lowest return of any casino game. With my Keno for Excel, you don't have to worry about losing any money: all the action takes place on a worksheet, and no money changes hands. And, it's a lot faster than the casino version.

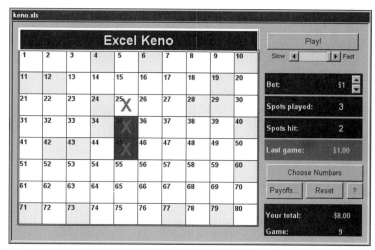

Figure 31-3: Keno for Excel

This workbook is available on the companion CD-ROM. In addition, I've included another workbook that calculates the various odds associated with Keno. Take a look at this workbook and you may never play casino Keno again!

Power Utility Pak Games

The four games listed in this section are included with my Power Utility Pak. Use the coupon in the back of the book to order your copy at a huge discount.

Video Poker

Developing my Video Poker game for Excel (see Figure 31-4) was quite a challenge. I was forced to spend many hours performing research at a local casino to perfect this game so that it captures the excitement of a real poker machine. The only problem is that I haven't figured out a way to dispense the winnings. Oh well, maybe in the next version.

Figure 31-4: My Video Poker game

This version has two games: Joker's Wild (a joker can be used for any card) and Jacks or Better (a pair of jacks or better is required to win). You select which cards to discard by clicking the card face. You can change the game (or the bet) at any time while playing. You can also request a graph that shows your cumulative winnings (or, more typically, your cumulative losses).

Identifying the various poker hands is done using VBA procedures. The game also has a Hide button that temporarily hides the game (pressing Esc has the same effect). You can then resume the game when your boss leaves the room.

This game is included with the registered version of the Power Utility Pak. See the coupon in the back of the book for details on how to get your copy.

Dice Game

The goal of the Dice Game (shown in Figure 31-5) is to obtain a high score by assigning dice rolls to various categories. You get to roll the dice three times on each turn, and you can keep or discard the dice before rolling again. Everything is done using VBA. This game is included with the registered version of the Power Utility Pak. See the coupon in the back of the book for details on how to get your copy.

Bomb Hunt

Windows comes with a game called Minesweeper. I developed a version of this game for Excel and named it Bomb Hunt (see Figure 31-6). The goal is to discover the hidden bombs in the grid. Double-clicking a cell reveals a bomb (you lose) or a number that indicates the number of bombs in the surrounding cells. You use logic to determine where the bombs are located.

This game is included with the registered version of the Power Utility Pak. See the coupon in the back of the book for details on how to get your copy.

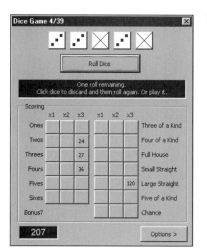

Figure 31-5: My Dice Game

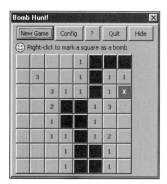

Figure 31-6: My Bomb Hunt game

Hangman

Hangman is another game that almost everyone has played. Figure 31-7 shows a version that I developed for Excel. The objective is to identify a word by guessing letters. Correctly guessed letters appear in their proper position. Every incorrectly guessed letter adds a new body part to the person being hanged (to reduce gratuitous violence, I substituted a skeleton for the hanged gentleman). Ten incorrect guesses and the skeleton is completed—that is, the game is over.

The workbook includes 1,400 words, ranging in length from 6 to 12 letters. You can either choose how many letters you want in the word or have the number of letters determined randomly. The entire game takes place in a dialog box.

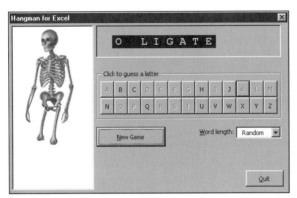

Figure 31-7: My Hangman game

Animated Shapes

With a bit of imagination (and lots of help from VBA), you can create some simple animations in a workbook. I've put together a few examples to demonstrate how it's done. Figure 31-8 shows an example (use your imagination — it really is animated).

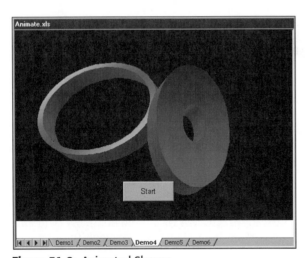

Figure 31-8: Animated Shapes

This workbook is available on the companion CD-ROM.

Symmetrical Pattern Drawing

I must admit, this program is rather addictive—especially for doodlers. It lets you create colorful symmetrical patterns by using the arrow keys on the keyboard. Figure 31-9 shows an example. As you draw, the drawing is reproduced as mirror images in the other three quadrants. When you move the cursor to the edge of the drawing area, it wraps around and appears on the other side. This workbook is great for passing the time on the telephone when you're put on hold.

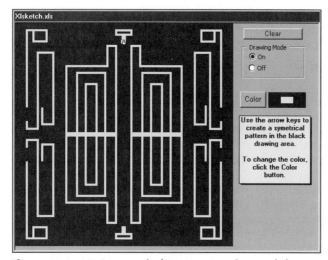

Figure 31-9: My Symmetrical Pattern Drawing worksheet

The drawing is all done with VBA macros. I used the OnKey method to trap the following key presses: left, right, up, and down. Each of these keystrokes executes a macro that shades a cell. The cells in the drawing area are very tiny, so the shading appears as lines.

On the CD-ROM   This workbook is available on the companion CD-ROM

For Guitar Players

If you play guitar, check out this workbook. As you see in Figure 31-10, this workbook has a graphic depiction of a guitar's fret board. It displays the notes (and fret positions) of the selected scale or mode in any key. You can even change the tuning of the guitar, and the formulas automatically recalculate.

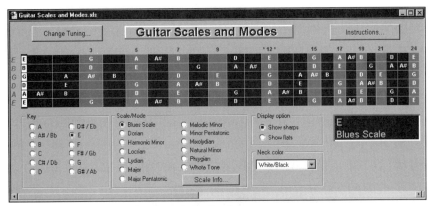

Figure 31-10: My guitar fret board application

This workbook is available on the companion CD-ROM

Other options include the choice to display half-notes as sharps or flats, to pop up information about the selected scale or mode, and to change the color of the guitar neck. This workbook uses formulas to do the calculation, and VBA plays only a minor role. This file was designated a "top pick" on America Online, and I've received positive feedback from fellow pickers all over the world.

An April Fool's Prank

Here's a good April Fool's trick to play on an office mate (with luck, one with a sense of humor). When he or she is out of the office, load this workbook and click the button to reverse the menus. For example, the Insert ➪ Name ➪ Define command becomes the Tresni ➪ Eman ➪ Enifed command. Excel's menus look like they're in a strange language. Figure 31-11 shows how this looks.

This workbook is available on the companion CD-ROM.

The routine performs its mischief by calling a custom function that reverses the text in the captions (except for the ellipses), converts the new text to proper case, and maintains the original hot keys. The net effect is a worksheet menu system that works exactly like the original (and is even keystroke-compatible) but looks very odd.

Clicking the Reset menu button returns the menus to normal.

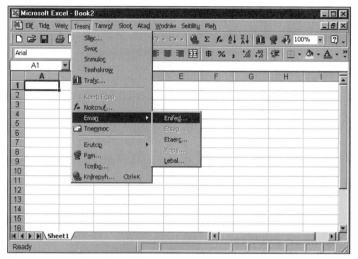

Figure 31-11: Excel with backward menus. The hot keys remain the same.

Creating Word Search Puzzles

Most daily newspapers feature a word search puzzle. These puzzles contain words that are hidden in a grid. The words can be vertical, diagonal, horizontal, forwards, or backwards. If you've ever had the urge to create your own word search puzzle, this workbook can make your job a lot easier by doing it for you. You supply the words; the program places them in the grid and fills in the empty squares with random letters. Figure 31-12 shows the puzzle creation sheet plus a sample puzzle that was created with this application.

This is all done with VBA, and randomness plays a major role. Therefore, you can create multiple puzzles using the same words.

This workbook is available on the companion CD-ROM.

ASCII Art

ASCII art consists of pictures made up of simple ASCII characters. The Internet is filled with thousands of examples of ASCII art. I created a workbook with a few examples that I picked up from the public domain. Figure 31-13 shows an example.

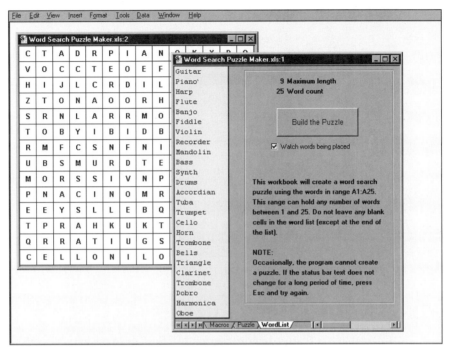

Figure 31-12: My Word Search Puzzle Maker

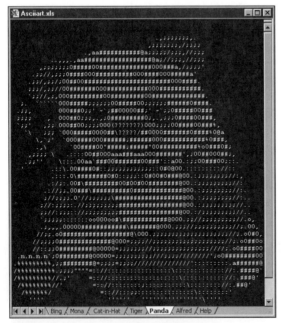

Figure 31-13: An example of ASCII art

This workbfook is available on the companion CD-ROM.

For the image to look correct, you must view ASCII art using a fixed-width font, such as Courier New.

Sound File Player

Excel doesn't have to be quiet. I created a simple macro that lets you play any WAV or MIDI file on your system.

This workbook is available on the companion CD-ROM

Fun with Charts

Excel's charting feature has the potential to be fun. In this section, I provide examples of some nonserious charting applications.

Plotting trigonometric functions

Although I don't know too much about trigonometry, I've always enjoyed plotting various trigonometric functions as XY charts. Sometimes you can come up with attractive images. Figure 31-14 shows an example of a trigonometric plot. Clicking the button changes a random number that makes a new chart.

This workbook is available on the companion CD-ROM.

XY-Sketch

In this workbook, you use the controls to draw an XY chart (see Figure 31-15). Clicking a directional button adds a new X and Y value to the chart's data range, which is then plotted on the chart. You can change the step size, adjust the color, and choose between smooth and normal lines. I include a multilevel Undo button that successively removes data points that you added.

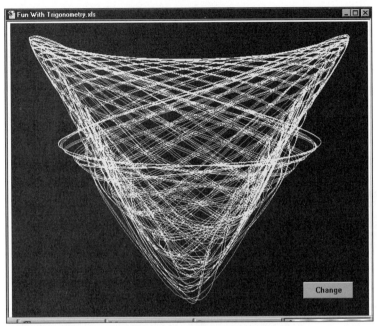

Figure 31-14: This chart plots trigonometric functions.

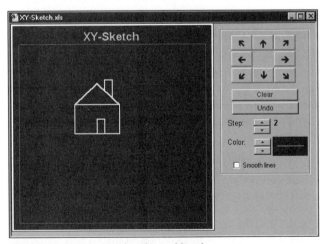

Figure 31-15: My XY-Sketch workbook

 This workbook is available on the companion CD-ROM.

Summary

In this chapter, I present several examples of nonserious applications for Excel. Some of these examples can most likely be adapted and used in more serious applications (well, maybe not).

✦   ✦   ✦

Analyzing Data with Excel

Importing Data from Other Sources

When you get right down to it, Excel can be described as a tool that manipulates data — the numbers and text that you use in a worksheet. But before you can manipulate data, it must be present in a worksheet. This chapter describes a variety of data-importing techniques.

An Overview of Importing

The following are the six basic ways to import data into Excel:

+ Enter the data manually by typing values and text into cells

+ Generate data by using formulas or macros

+ Use Query (or a pivot table) to import data from an external database

+ Import data from an HTML document on the Internet or a Corporate intranet

+ Copy data from another application by using the Windows clipboard

+ Import data from another (non-Excel) file

This chapter deals primarily with the last two methods: clipboard copying and foreign-file importing.

Cross-Reference Chapter 28 is somewhat related to this topic. It deals with linking to and from other applications and embedding objects. Querying external databases is covered in Chapter 34, and pivot tables are covered in Chapter 35. Chapter 29 discusses how Excel works with the Internet.

◆ ◆ ◆ ◆

In This Chapter

An Overview of Importing

A Few Words About Data

File Formats Supported by Excel

Using the Clipboard to Get Data

Importing Text Files

◆ ◆ ◆ ◆

A Few Words About Data

Data is a broad concept that means different things to different people. Data is basically raw information that can come in any number of forms. For example, data can be numbers, text, or a combination. Most of what you do in Excel involves manipulating data in one way or another.

As computers become more commonplace, data is increasingly available in machine-readable formats (otherwise known as *files*). Not too long ago, major data suppliers provided printed reports to their clients. Now, data suppliers commonly offer a choice of formats: paper or disk.

Data that is stored in files can be in a wide variety of formats. Common file formats for distributing data include Lotus 1-2-3 files (WKS and WK1), dBASE files (DBF), and text files (which come in several varieties). Excel's file format is rather complex, and the format tends to change with every new version of Excel. Consequently, the Excel file format is not widely used for the general distribution of data.

Note   The file format for Excel 2000 files is the same as the file format for Excel 97. However, if you use an Excel 2000 file in Excel 97, you will have access only to Excel 97 features.

As an Excel user, you need to understand the types of data that you can access either directly or indirectly.

File Formats Supported by Excel

Rarely does a computer user work with only one application or interact only with people using the same applications he or she uses. Suppose that you're developing a spreadsheet model that uses data from last year's budget, which is stored in your company's mainframe. You can request a printout of the data, of course, and manually enter it into Excel. If the amount of data isn't too large, this route may be the most efficient. But what if you have hundreds of entries to make? Your mainframe probably can't generate an Excel workbook file, but an excellent chance exists that it can send the report to a text file, which you can then import into an Excel worksheet. Potentially, you can save several hours of work and virtually eliminate data-entry errors.

As you know, Excel's native file format is an XLS file. In addition, Microsoft included the capability to read other file formats directly. For example, you can open a file that was created in several other spreadsheet products, such as Lotus 1-2-3 and Quattro Pro. Table 32-1 lists all the file formats that Excel can read (excluding its own file types).

<table>
<tr><td colspan="2" align="center">Table 32-1
File Formats Supported by Excel</td></tr>
</table>

File Type	Description
Text	Space delimited, tab delimited, and comma delimited
Lotus 1-2-3	Spreadsheet files generated by Lotus 1-2-3 for DOS Release 1.x, Release 2.x, Release 3.x, and 1-2-3 for Windows
Quattro Pro/DOS	Files generated by Novell's Quattro Pro for DOS spreadsheet
Microsoft Works 2.0	Files generated by Microsoft Works 2.0
dBASE	Database files in the DBF format
SYLK	Files generated by Microsoft's MultiPlan spreadsheet
Data Interchange Format	Files generated by the VisiCalc spreadsheet
HTML	Files developed for the World Wide Web
Quattro Pro for Windows	Files generated by Corel's Quattro Pro for Windows spreadsheet

To open any of these files, choose File ➪ Open and select the file type from the drop-down list labeled Files of type (see Figure 32-1) to display only the files of the selected type in the file list. If the file is a text file, Excel's Text Import Wizard appears, to help you interpret the file. The Text Import Wizard is discussed later in this chapter.

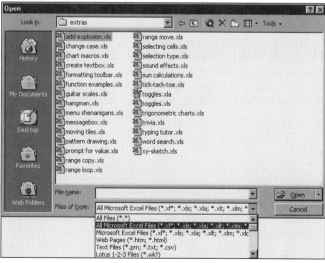

Figure 32-1: Use the Open dialog box to import a foreign file.

You should understand, however, that being able to read a file and translating it perfectly are two different matters. In some cases, you may encounter one or more of the following problems while reading a foreign file into Excel:

✦ Some formulas aren't translated correctly

✦ Unsupported functions aren't translated

✦ Formatting is incorrect

✦ Column widths are incorrect

When you open a file that wasn't produced by Excel, examine it carefully to ensure that Excel retrieved the data correctly.

The following sections discuss the various types of files that Excel can read. Each section discusses a file type and lists that file type's associated file extensions.

If a colleague sends you a file that Excel can't open, don't give up. Simply ask your colleague to save the spreadsheet in a format that Excel *can* read. For example, many applications can save files in 1-2-3 format, and most applications can export to a text file format.

Lotus 1-2-3 spreadsheet files

Lotus spreadsheets come in several flavors:

✦ **WKS files:** Single-sheet files used by 1-2-3 Release 1.*x* for DOS. Excel can read and write these files. If you export a workbook to a WKS file, Excel saves only the active worksheet, because 1-2-3 Release 1.*x* supports only one worksheet per workbook.

✦ **WK1 files:** Single-sheet files used by 1-2-3 Release 2.*x* for DOS. The formatting for these files is stored in ALL files (produced by the Allways add-in) or FM1 files (produced by the WYSIWYG add-in). Excel can read and write all of these file types. When you save a file to the WK1 format, you can choose which (if any) type of formatting file to generate. And, like WKS files, if you export a workbook to a WK1 file, Excel saves only the active worksheet.

✦ **WK3 files:** Multisheet (potentially) files generated by 1-2-3 Release 3.*x* for DOS, 1-2-3 Release 4.*x* for DOS, and 1-2-3 Release 1.*x* for Windows. The formatting for these files is stored in FM3 files (produced by the WYSIWYG add-in). Excel can read and write WK3 files with or without the accompanying FM3 file.

✦ **WK4 files:** Multisheet (potentially) files generated by 1-2-3 Release 4.*x* for Windows and 1-2-3 Release 5.*x* for Windows. Lotus combined formatting and data into one file, eliminating the separate formatting file. Excel can read and write these files.

✦ **123 files:** Multisheet (potentially) files generated by 1-2-3 97 (also known as Release 6) and 1-2-3 Millenium Edition (also known as Release 7). Excel can neither read nor write these files.

If you plan to import or export 1-2-3 files, I urge you to read the online Help for general guidelines and for specific types of information that may not be translated.

Excel evaluates some formulas differently from 1-2-3. To ensure complete compatibility when you work with an imported 1-2-3 file, choose Tools ➪ Options, select the Transition tab, and then check the box labeled Transition Formula Evaluation.

Quattro Pro spreadsheet files

Quattro Pro files exist in several versions:

✦ **WQ1 files:** Single-sheet files generated by Quattro Pro for DOS Versions 1, 2, 3, and 4. Excel can read and write these files. If you export a workbook to a WQ1 file, Excel saves only the active worksheet.

✦ **WQ2 files:** Multisheet (potentially) files generated by Quattro Pro for DOS Version 5. Excel can neither read nor write this file format.

✦ **WB1 files:** Multisheet (potentially) files generated by Quattro Pro for Windows Versions 1 and 5 (Versions 2 through 4 don't exist). Excel can read (but not write) this file format.

✦ **WB2 files:** Multisheet (potentially) files generated by Quattro Pro for Windows Version 6. Excel can neither read nor write this file format.

Database file formats

DBF files are single-table database files generated by dBASE and several other database programs. Excel can read and write DBF files up to and including dBASE 4.

If you have Microsoft Access installed on your system, you can take advantage of feature that converts a worksheet list into an Access database file. To use this feature, you must install the Access Links add-in in Excel (you need your Office 2000 CD-ROM). Use the Data ➪ Convert to MS Access command.

Excel can't read or write any other database file formats directly. If you install the Query add-in, however, you can use Query to access many other database file formats and then copy or link the data into an Excel worksheet.

Cross-Reference See Chapter 34 for details on how to use Query to copy or link data from other database file formats into an Excel worksheet.

Text file formats

Text files simply contain data — no formatting. The following relatively standard text file formats exist, although no standard file extensions exist:

✦ **Tab-delimited files:** Each line consists of fields that are separated by tabs. Excel can read these files, converting each line to a row and each field to a column. Excel also can write these files, using TXT as the default extension.

✦ **Comma-separated files:** Each line consists of fields that are separated by commas. Sometimes, text appears in quotation marks. Excel can read these files, converting each line to a row and each field to a column. Excel can also write these files, using CSV as the default extension.

✦ **Space-delimited files:** Each line consists of fields that are separated by spaces. Excel can read these files, converting each line to a row and each field to a column. Excel also can write these files, using PRN as the default extension.

If you want your exported text file to use a different extension, specify the complete filename and extension in quotation marks. For example, saving a workbook in comma-separated format normally uses the CSV extension. If you want your file to be named output.txt (with a TXT extension), enter **"output.txt"** in the File name box in the Save As dialog box.

When you attempt to load a text file into Excel, the Text Import Wizard kicks in to help you specify how you want Excel to retrieve the file (discussed in detail later in the chapter).

HTML files

Excel can read and save files in HTML (Hypertext Markup Language) format, a file format that is used on the World Wide Web. And, through the use of XML (Extensible Markup Language), HTML files retain all document properties, including fonts and formatting.

Using Excel, you can edit any Excel document from within a Web browser. While you are viewing a page that was created in an Office application, such as Excel, click the Edit button on the browser's toolbar. Office opens the document in the application that was used to create it. You can then edit the Web page and resave it in any of the file formats that the application supports or in HTML.

Other file formats

The following are two other types of file formats that you will rarely encounter; I haven't seen a DIF file in ages, and I've never seen a SYLK file.

✦ **Data Interchange Format (DIF):** Used by VisiCalc. Excel can read and write these files.

✦ **Symbolic Link (SYLK):** Used by MultiPlan. Excel can read and write these files.

Using the Clipboard to Get Data

Using the Windows clipboard is a another method of importing data into your worksheet. The process involves selecting data from another application and copying the data to the clipboard. Then, you reactivate Excel and paste the information to the worksheet. The exact results that you get can vary quite a bit, depending on the type of data that you copied and the clipboard formats that it supports. Obviously, you must have a copy of the other application installed on your system.

Note   If you copy information from another Office application, you use the Office clipboard, not the Windows clipboard. The Office clipboard supports copying and pasting of all formats used in all Office applications.

About the clipboard

As you read in Chapter 7, Office 2000 provides Windows 95 or Windows 98 with two clipboards. The original Windows clipboard remains; whenever you cut or copy information from a Windows program, Windows stores the information on the Windows clipboard, which is an area of memory. Each time that you cut or copy information, Windows replaces the information previously stored on the clipboard with the new information that you cut or copied. The Windows clipboard can store data in a variety of formats. Because Windows manages it, information on the Windows clipboard can be pasted to other Windows applications, regardless of where it originated. Normally, you can't see information stored on the Windows clipboard (nor would you want to).

Note   To view the Windows clipboard contents, you can run the Clipboard Viewer program, which comes with Windows. The Clipboard Viewer may or may not be installed on your system (it is not installed by default). You can use the Clipboard Viewer to view only the last piece of information that you copied to the Office clipboard.

When you copy or cut data to the clipboard, the source application places one or more formats on the clipboard along with the data. Different applications support different clipboard formats. When you paste clipboard data into another application, the destination application determines which format it can handle and typically selects the format that either provides the most information or is appropriate for where you are pasting it. If you view cells copied from Excel in the Clipboard Viewer, by default, you'll see a row/column reference rather than the actual information that you copied (see Figure 32-2). In some cases, you can use the Display command in the Clipboard Viewer application to view the clipboard data in a different format. For example, you can display a range of cells from Excel as a picture, bitmap, text, OEM text, or a DIB bitmap. Figures 32-3, 32-4, 32-5, and 32-6, show examples of the same Excel range as it appears in the Clipboard Viewer when using different Display formats.

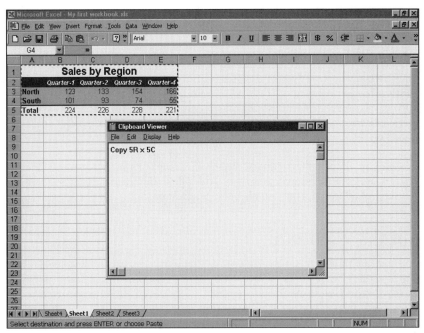

Figure 32-2: The Windows Clipboard Viewer application displaying Excel 2000 data in default format, Display Text

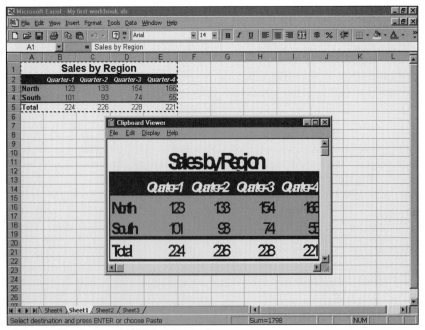

Figure 32-3: The same data in Picture format

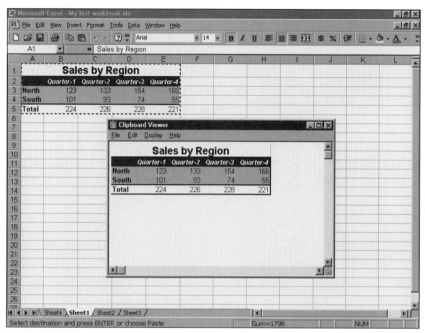

Figure 32-4: Both Bitmap and DIB Bitmap formats closely resemble the formatted appearance of the data in Excel.

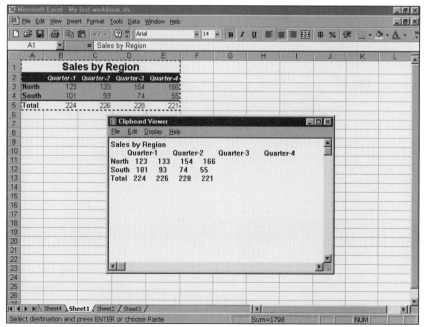

Figure 32-5: The Text format shows the text similar to the way that it appears in the Notepad.

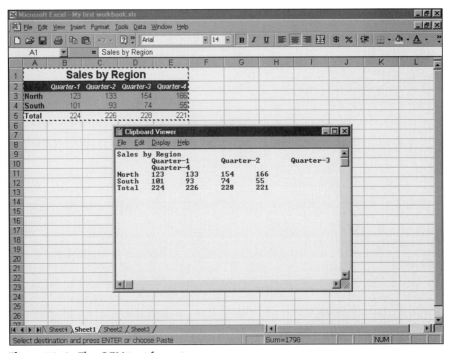

Figure 32-6: The OEM text format

Importantly, the format that you select in the Clipboard Viewer *doesn't* affect how Excel copies the data. In some cases, however, you can use Excel's Edit ➪ Paste Special command to select alternate methods of pasting the data.

Copying data from another Windows application

Copying data from one Windows application to another is quite straightforward. The *source application* contains the data that you're copying, and the *destination application* receives the data that you're copying. Use the following steps to copy data from one application into another:

1. Activate the source document window that contains the information you want to copy.

2. Select the information that you want to copy by using the mouse or the keyboard. If Excel is the source application, this information can be a cell, range, chart, or drawing object.

3. Select Edit ➪ Copy (or any available shortcut). A copy of the information is sent to the Windows clipboard. If you're copying from an Office application, a copy of the information is also sent to the Office clipboard.

4. Activate the destination application. If it isn't open, you can start it without affecting the contents of the clipboard.

5. Move to the position to which you want to paste in the destination application.

6. Select Edit ⇨ Paste from the menu in the destination application. If the clipboard contents aren't appropriate for pasting, the Paste command is grayed (not available).

In Step 3, you also can select Edit ⇨ Cut from the source application menu. This step erases the selection from the source application after it's placed on the clipboard.

Many Windows applications use a common keyboard convention for the clipboard commands. Generally, this technique is a bit faster than using the menus, because these keys are adjacent to each other. The shortcut keys and their equivalents are the following:

Ctrl+C   Edit ⇨ Copy

Ctrl+X   Edit ⇨ Cut

Ctrl+V   Edit ⇨ Paste

You need to understand that Windows applications vary in how they respond to data that you paste from the clipboard. If the Edit ⇨ Paste command isn't available (it is grayed on the menu) in the destination application, the application can't accept the information from the clipboard. If you copy a table from Word for Windows to Excel, the data translates into cells perfectly — complete with formatting. Copying data from other applications may not work as well; for example, you may lose the formatting, or you may end up with all the data in a single column rather than in separate columns. As discussed later in this chapter, you can use the Convert Text to Columns Wizard to convert this data into columns.

If you plan to do a great deal of copying and pasting between two applications, experiment until you understand how the two applications can handle each other's data.

Copying data from a non-Windows application

You also can use the Windows clipboard with non-Windows applications running in a DOS window. As you may know, you can run non-Windows programs from Windows either in a window or in full-screen mode (the application takes over the complete screen).

When you're running a non-Windows application in Windows, you can press Alt+Print Screen to copy the entire screen to the clipboard. The screen contents can then be pasted into a Windows application (including Excel). To copy only part of the screen, you must run the application in a window: press Alt+Enter to toggle between full-screen mode and windowed mode. You can then click the Control menu, choose Edit ⇨ Mark, and select text from the window. This window may or may not have a toolbar displayed. If it does not, follow these steps:

1. Right-click the title bar and select the Toolbar option.

2. Click the Mark tool and select the text to copy.

3. Click the Copy tool to copy the selected text to the clipboard.

4. Activate Excel.

5. Select Edit ➪ Paste to copy the clipboard data into your worksheet.

Figure 32-7 shows Quattro Pro running in a DOS window. Some text is selected.

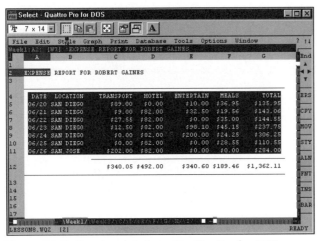

Figure 32-7: Copying data from Quattro Pro for DOS

If you use this technique and copy to Excel, the information is pasted as text in a single column. In other words, even if you copy information from neatly formatted columns, it's all pasted into a single column in Excel. But don't fret — you can use Excel's Convert Text to Columns Wizard to convert this data into columns.

You're limited to copying one screen of information at a time — you can't scroll the DOS application while you're selecting text.

Importing Text Files

Text files (sometimes referred to as ASCII files) are usually considered to be the lowest-common-denominator file type. Such files contain only data, with no formatting. Consequently, most applications can read and write text files. So, if all else fails, you can probably use a text file to transfer data between two applications that don't support a common file format. Because text files are so commonly used, this entire section is devoted to discussing them and explaining how to use Excel's Text Import Wizard.

About text files

You may find it helpful to think of some text files in terms of a database table. Each line in the text file corresponds to a database record, and each record consists of a number of fields. In Excel, each line (or record) is imported to a separate row, and each field goes into a separate column. Text files come in two types: delimited and nondelimited.

Text files consist of plain text and end-of-line markers. *Delimited* text files use a special character to separate the fields on each line — typically a comma, a space, or a tab (but occasionally, you'll see other delimiters used). In addition, text is usually (but not always) enclosed in quotation marks.

Nondelimited files don't contain a special field-separator character. Often, however, each field is a fixed length, enabling you easily to break each line of text into separate columns. When you view a nondelimited file, the data often appears to be in columns.

If you use a proportional font, such as Arial or Times Roman, the fields of text file may appear to not line up, although they actually do. In proportional font sets, each character uses a different amount of horizontal space. For best results, use a nonproportional font, such as Courier New, when working with text files. Excel uses Courier New in its Text Import Wizard dialog box. Figure 32-8 shows the same text displayed in Arial and Courier New fonts.

	A	B	C	D	E	F	G	H
1	DATE LOCATION	TRANSPORT	HOTEL	ENTERTAIN	MEALS	TOTAL		
2	06/20 SAN DIEGO	$89.00	$0.00	$10.00	$36.95	$135.95		
3	06/21 SAN DIEGO	$9.00	$82.00	$32.50	$19.56	$143.06		
4	06/22 SAN DIEGO	$27.55	$82.00	$0.00	$35.00	$144.55		
5	06/23 SAN DIEGO	$12.50	$82.00	$98.10	$45.15	$237.75		
6	06/24 SAN DIEGO	$0.00	$82.00	$200.00	$24.25	$306.25		
7	06/25 SAN DIEGO	$0.00	$82.00	$0.00	$28.55	$110.55		
8	06/26 SAN JOSE	$202.00	$82.00	$0.00	$0.00	$284.00		
9								
10	DATE LOCATION	TRANSPORT	HOTEL	ENTERTAIN	MEALS	TOTAL		
11	06/20 SAN DIEGO	$89.00	$0.00	$10.00	$36.95	$135.95		
12	06/21 SAN DIEGO	$9.00	$82.00	$32.50	$19.56	$143.06		
13	06/22 SAN DIEGO	$27.55	$82.00	$0.00	$35.00	$144.55		
14	06/23 SAN DIEGO	$12.50	$82.00	$98.10	$45.15	$237.75		
15	06/24 SAN DIEGO	$0.00	$82.00	$200.00	$24.25	$306.25		
16	06/25 SAN DIEGO	$0.00	$82.00	$0.00	$28.55	$110.55		
17	06/26 SAN JOSE	$202.00	$82.00	$0.00	$0.00	$284.00		
18								

Figure 32-8: Using a proportional font may obscure columns in a text file.

Excel is quite versatile when importing text files. If each line of the text file is identically laid out, importing is usually problem-free. But if the line contains mixed information, you may need to do some additional work to make the data usable. For example, you create text files in some programs by sending a printed report to a disk file rather than to the printer. These reports often have extra information, such as page headers and footers, titles, summary lines, and so on.

Using the Text Import Wizard

Prior versions of Excel treated importing text files differently from other types of database information. In Excel 2000, if you use the technique described in this section, you'll create a Text File Query, which you can refresh in the same way that you refresh Database and Web queries. This new feature will make the lives easier of those who need to regularly import text files, because they won't need to "set up" the import each time. When you want to update the Excel file that you create by importing a text file, choose Data ➪ Refresh Data. Highlight the text file that you originally imported and click the Import button. Excel automatically updates the Excel version of the file with any new data that may appear in the text file.

Cross-Reference

For more information on Database queries, see Chapter 34. For more information on Web queries, see Chapter 29.

To import a text file into Excel, choose Data ➪ Get External Data ➪ Import Text File. In the Import Text File dialog box, navigate to the folder containing the file that you want to import. The dialog box then displays text files that have an extension of TXT. If the text file that you're importing has a different extension, select the All Files option. Or, you can enter the filename directly into the File name box, if you know the file's name.

Excel displays its Text Import Wizard, a series of interactive dialog boxes in which you specify the information that Excel requires to break the lines of the text file into columns. You can truly appreciate this time-saving feature if, in a previous life, you struggled with the old data-parsing commands that are found in other spreadsheet programs and older versions of Excel.

Text Import Wizard: Step 1 of 3

Figure 32-9 shows the first of three Text Import Wizard dialog boxes. In the Original data type section, verify the type of data file (Excel almost always guesses correctly). You also can indicate the row that Excel should use to start importing. For example, if the file has a title in the first row, you may want to skip the first line.

Notice that you can preview the file at the bottom of the dialog box, using the scrollbars to view more of the file. If the characters in the file don't look right, you may need to change the File Origin; this determines which character set to use (in many cases, it doesn't make any difference). After you finish with this step, click the Next button to move to Step 2.

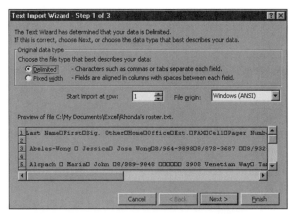

Figure 32-9: Step 1 of the Text Import Wizard

Text Import Wizard: Step 2 of 3

The dialog box that you see for Step 2 of the Text Import Wizard varies, depending on your choice in the Original data type section in Step 1. If you selected Delimited, you see the dialog box shown in Figure 32-10. You can specify the type of delimiter, the text qualifier, and whether to treat consecutive delimiters as a single delimiter; choosing to treat consecutive delimiters as a single delimiter tells Excel to skip empty columns. The Data preview section displays vertical lines to indicate how Excel will break up the fields. The Data preview section changes as you make choices in the dialog box.

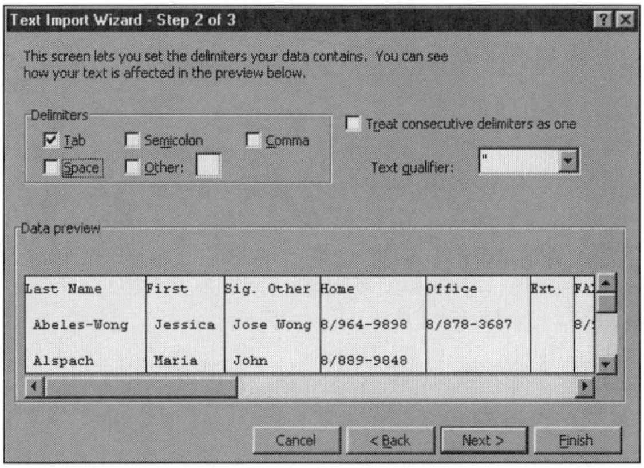

Figure 32-10: Step 2 of the Text Import Wizard (for delimited files)

If you selected Fixed width, you see the dialog box shown in Figure 32-11. At this point, Excel attempts to identify the column breaks and displays vertical break lines to represent how it will break fields apart into columns. If Excel guesses wrong, you can move the lines, insert new ones, or delete lines that Excel proposes. You'll see instructions in the dialog box.

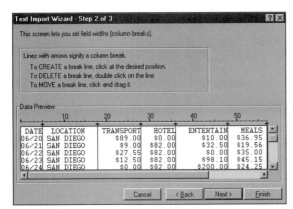

Figure 32-11: Step 2 of the Text Import Wizard (for fixed-width files)

If you're importing a print image file that includes page headers, you can ignore them when you specify the column indicators. Rather, base the columns on the data. When the file is imported, you can then delete the rows that contain the page headers.

When you're satisfied with how the column breaks look, click Next to move to the final step. Or, you can click Back to return to Step 1 and change the file type.

Text Import Wizard: Step 3 of 3

Figure 32-12 shows the last of the three Text Import Wizard dialog boxes. In this dialog box, you can select individual columns and specify the formatting to apply (General, Text, or Data). You also can specify columns to skip—they aren't imported. If you click the Advanced button, you'll see the dialog box shown in Figure 32-13, in which you can specify characters to use as decimal and thousands separators. When you're satisfied with the results, click Finish. Excel prompts you for the starting cell location for the imported data; when you click OK, Excel imports the data and displays the External Data toolbar, which helps you to work with the imported text file (see Figure 32-14). For example, if you click the Data Range Properties tool, you see the External Data Range Properties dialog box, shown in Figure 32-15, which you can use to change how Excel treats the imported file.

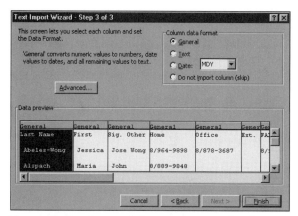

Figure 32-12: Step 3 of the Text Import Wizard

If the results aren't what you expect, close the workbook and try again (text importing often involves trial and error). Don't forget that you can scroll the Data Preview window to make sure that all the data is converted properly. With some files, however, importing all the data properly is impossible. In such cases, you may want to import the file as a single column of text and then break lines into columns selectively. The procedure for doing this is discussed in the next section.

Figure 32-13: The Advanced Text Import Settings dialog box

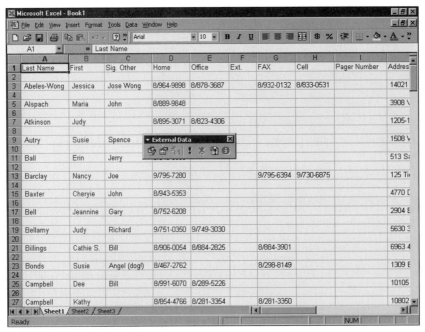

Figure 32-14: Imported text file

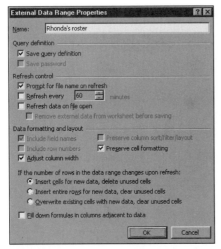

Figure 32-15: Use this dialog box to change the way that Excel treats the imported file.

Using the Text to Columns Wizard

Excel can parse text that is stored in a column. Start by selecting the text (in a single column). Then, choose Data ➪ Text to Columns, and Excel displays the first of three Text to Columns Wizard dialog boxes. These dialog boxes are identical to those used for the Text Import Wizard, except that the title bar text is different.

Unfortunately, you can't use the Data ➪ Text to Columns command on a multiple selection; this would be quite handy for parsing imported files with several different layouts. Even worse, you can't use the Edit ➪ Repeat command to repeat the Text to Columns command.

Summary

This chapter identifies the various sources for getting data into Excel: entering data manually, generating data from formulas or macros, using Query or pivot tables, copying data using the clipboard, and importing foreign files (including text files) into Excel. The chapter focuses on clipboard operations and file importing.

✦   ✦   ✦

Working with Lists

Research conducted by Microsoft indicates that Excel is frequently used to manage lists, or *worksheet databases.* This chapter covers list management and demonstrates useful techniques that involve lists.

What Is a List?

A list is essentially an organized collection of information. More specifically, a list consists of a row of headers (descriptive text), followed by additional rows of data, which can be values or text. You may recognize this as a database table — which is exactly what it is. Beginning with Excel 5, Microsoft uses the term *list* to refer to a database stored in a worksheet and the term *database* to refer to a table of information stored in an external file. To avoid confusion, I adhere to Microsoft's terminology.

Cross-Reference   I cover external database files in Chapter 34.

Figure 33-1 shows an example of a list in a worksheet. This particular list has its headers in row 1 and has 10 rows of data. The list occupies four columns. Notice that the data consists of several different types: text, values, and dates. Column C contains a formula that calculates the monthly salary from the value in column B.

People often refer to the columns in a list as *fields* and to the rows as *records.* Using this terminology, the list shown in the figure has five fields (Name, Annual Salary, Monthly Salary, Location, and Date Hired) and ten records.

The size of the lists that you develop in Excel is limited by the size of a single worksheet. In other words, a list can have no more than 256 fields and can consist of no more than 65,535 records (one row contains the field names). A list of this size would require a great deal of memory and even then may not be possible. At the other extreme, a list can consist of a single cell—not very useful, but it's still considered a list.

	A	B	C	D	E	F
	Name	Annual Salary	Monthly Salary	Location	Date Hired	
1						
2	James Brackman	42,400	3,533	New York	2/1/93	
3	Michael Orenthal	28,900	2,408	Arizona	4/5/94	
4	Francis Jenkins	67,800	5,650	New York	10/12/93	
5	Peter Yolanda	19,850	1,654	Minnesota	1/4/95	
6	Walter Franklin	45,000	3,750	Arizona	2/28/90	
7	Louise Victor	52,000	4,333	New York	5/2/94	
8	Sally Rice	48,500	4,042	New York	11/21/92	
9	Charles K. Barkley	24,500	2,042	Minnesota	6/4/90	
10	Melinda Hintquest	56,400	4,700	Arizona	6/1/87	
11	Linda Harper	75,000	6,250	Minnesota	8/7/91	
12						
13						
14						

Employees.xls — Sheet1

Figure 33-1: An example of a list

Note   In versions of Excel prior to Excel 97, a list was limited to 16,383 records.

What Can You Do with a List?

Excel provides several tools to help you manage and manipulate lists. Consequently, people use lists for a wide variety of purposes. For some users, a list is simply a method to keep track of information (for example, customer lists); others use lists to store data that ultimately will appear in a report. Common list operations include:

✦ Entering data into the list

✦ Filtering the list to display only the rows that meet certain criteria

✦ Sorting the list

✦ Inserting formulas to calculate subtotals

✦ Creating formulas to calculate results on the list filtered by certain criteria

✦ Creating a summary table of the data in the list (this is done using a pivot table; see Chapter 35).

With the exception of the last item, these operations are covered in this chapter.

Designing a List

Although Excel is quite accommodating when it comes to the information that is stored in a list, planning the organization of your list information will pay off. The following are some guidelines to keep in mind when creating lists:

✦ Insert descriptive labels (one for each column) in the first row of the list, called the *header row*. If you use lengthy labels, consider using the Wrap Text format so that you don't have to widen the columns.

See Chapter 17 for information on the Wrap Text format.

✦ Make sure each column contains the same type of information. For example, don't mix dates and text in a single column.

✦ You can use formulas that perform calculations on other fields in the same record. If you use formulas that refer to cells outside the list, make these absolute references; otherwise, you get unexpected results when you sort the list.

✦ Don't leave any empty rows within the list. For list operations, Excel determines the list boundaries automatically, and an empty row signals the end of the list.

✦ For best results, try to keep the list on a worksheet by itself. If you must place other information on the same worksheet as the list, place the information above or below the list. In other words, don't use the cells to the left or the right of a list.

✦ Select Window ⇨ Freeze Panes to make sure that you can see the headings when you scroll the list.

✦ You can preformat entire columns to ensure that the data has the same format. For example, if a column contains dates, format the entire column with the desired date format.

Many people find working in spreadsheets most appealing because changing the layout is relatively easy. Lists behave no differently than any other kind of data in Excel; changing a list's layout is also easy. For example, you may create a list and then decide that it needs another column (field). No problem. Just insert a new column, give it a field name, and Excel expands your list. If you've ever used a database management program, you can appreciate the simplicity of this layout change.

Entering Data into a List

You can enter data into a list in three ways:

✦ Manually, using all standard data entry techniques

✦ By importing it or copying it from another file

✦ By using a dialog box

There's really nothing special about entering data into a list. You just navigate through the worksheet and enter the data into the appropriate cells.

Excel has two features that assist with repetitive data entry:

✦ **AutoComplete:** When you begin to type in a cell, Excel scans up and down the column for entries that match what you're typing. If it finds a match, Excel fills in the rest of the text automatically. Press Enter to make the entry. You can turn this feature on or off in the Edit tab of the Options dialog box.

✦ **Pick Lists:** You can right-click a cell and select Pick from list from the shortcut menu. Excel displays a list box that shows all entries in the column (see Figure 33-2). Click the one that you want to enter into the cell (no typing is required).

	A	B	C	D	E	F	G
1	DATE	REP	REGION	PROD_TYPE	UNIT$	QUANT	AMT$
2	01/03/97	Peterson	North	Entertainment	225	2	450
3	01/04/97	Sheldon	South	Entertainment	202	4	808
4	01/08/97	Robinson	South	Entertainment	25	1	25
5	01/10/97	Jenkins	North	Personal	140	2	280
6	01/12/97	Jenkins	North	Personal	125	6	750
7	01/12/97	Wilson	South	Personal	140	5	700
8	01/13/97	Franks	North	Recreational	175	6	1050
9	01/13/97	Jenkins	North	Entertainment	225	3	675
10	01/13/97	Wilson	South	Recreational	125	3	375
11	01/13/97	Wilson	South	Personal	175	4	700
12	01/14/97	Jenkins	North	Entertainment	175	4	700
13	01/14/97	Jenkins	North	Recreational	140	3	420
14	01/14/97	Peterson	North	Personal	225	2	450
15	01/15/97	Peterson	North	Personal	225	6	1350
16	01/16/97	Franks	North	Recreational	140	4	560
17	01/16/97	Sheldon	South	Personal	125	3	375
18	01/17/97	Franks	North	Entertainment	140	2	280
19	01/18/97	Wilson	South	Recreational	175	3	525
20							
21		Franks					
22		Jenkins					
23		Peterson					
24		Robinson					
25		Sheldon					
26		Wilson					

Figure 33-2: Choosing the Pick from list command on the shortcut menu gives you a list of all items in the current column.

If you prefer to use a dialog box for your data entry, Excel accommodates you. To display a data entry dialog box, move the cell pointer anywhere within the list and choose Data ➪ Form. Excel determines the boundaries of your list and displays a dialog box showing each field in the list. Figure 33-3 depicts an example of such a dialog box. Fields that have a formula don't have an edit box.

Note

If the number of fields exceeds the limit of your display, the dialog box contains two columns of field names. If your list consists of more than 32 fields, however, the Data ➪ Form command doesn't work. You must forgo this method of data entry and enter the information directly into the cells.

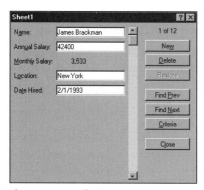

Figure 33-3: The Data ⇨ Form command gives you a handy data entry dialog box.

Entering data with the data form dialog box

When the data form dialog box appears, Excel displays the first record in the list. Notice the indicator in the upper-right corner of the dialog box that tells you the number of the selected record and the total number of records in the list.

To enter a new record, click the New button to clear the fields. Then you can enter the new information into the appropriate fields. Use Tab or Shift+Tab to move among the fields. When you click New (or Close), Excel appends the data that you entered to the bottom of the list. You also can press Enter, which is equivalent to clicking on the New button. If the list contains any formulas, Excel enters them for you automatically into the new record.

Tip

If you named the range of your list **Database**, Excel automatically extends the range definition to include the new row(s) that you add to the list using the data form dialog box. Note that this works only if you name the list **Database**; any other name doesn't work.

Other uses for the data form dialog box

You can use the data form dialog box for more than just data entry. You can edit existing data in the list, view data one record at a time, delete records, and display records that meet certain criteria.

The dialog box contains a number of additional buttons, which are described as follows:

✦ **Delete:** Deletes the displayed record.

✦ **Restore:** Restores any information that you edited. You must click this button before you click the New button.

✦ **Find Prev:** Displays the previous record in the list. If you entered a criterion, this button displays the previous record that matches the criterion.

✦ **Find Next:** Displays the next record in the list. If you entered a criterion, this button displays the next record that matches the criterion.

✦ **Criteria:** Clears the fields and lets you enter a criterion upon which to search for records. For example, to locate records that have a salary greater than $50,000, enter >**50000** into the Salary field. Then you can use the Find Next and Find Prev buttons to display the qualifying records.

✦ **Close:** Closes the dialog box (and enters the data that you were entering, if any).

Using Microsoft Access Forms for data entry

If you have Microsoft Access installed on your system, you can use its form creation tools to develop a data entry form for an Excel worksheet. This feature uses the Access Links add-in, which must be loaded. When the add-in is loaded, you have a new command: Data ⇨ Access Form.

Choosing this command starts Access (if it's not already running) and begins its Form Wizard. Use the Form Wizard to create the data entry form. You can then use this form to add data to your Excel worksheet. Access's Form Wizard places a button on your worksheet that contains the text View Access Form. Click this button to use the form. Figure 33-4 shows an Access form being used to enter data into an Excel worksheet.

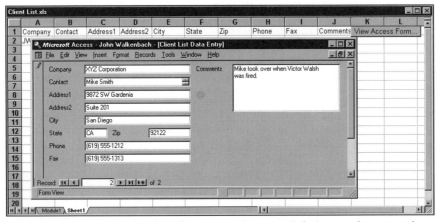

Figure 33-4: This form, developed in Microsoft Access, is being used to enter data into an Excel worksheet.

Filtering a List

Filtering a list is the process of hiding all rows in the list except those that meet some criteria that you specify. For example, if you have a list of customers, you can filter the list to show only those who live in New Jersey. Filtering is a common (and very useful) technique. Excel provides two ways to filter a list:

✦ AutoFilter, for simple filtering criteria

✦ Advance Filter, for more complex filtering

AutoFiltering

To use Excel's AutoFilter feature to filter a list, place the cell pointer anywhere within the list and then choose Data ⇨ Filter ⇨ AutoFilter. Excel analyzes your list and adds drop-down arrows to the field names in the header row, as shown in Figure 33-5.

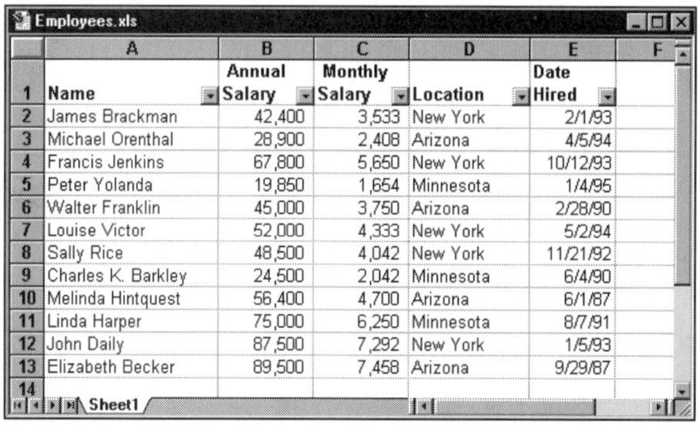

	Name	Annual Salary	Monthly Salary	Location	Date Hired
1	Name	Annual Salary	Monthly Salary	Location	Date Hired
2	James Brackman	42,400	3,533	New York	2/1/93
3	Michael Orenthal	28,900	2,408	Arizona	4/5/94
4	Francis Jenkins	67,800	5,650	New York	10/12/93
5	Peter Yolanda	19,850	1,654	Minnesota	1/4/95
6	Walter Franklin	45,000	3,750	Arizona	2/28/90
7	Louise Victor	52,000	4,333	New York	5/2/94
8	Sally Rice	48,500	4,042	New York	11/21/92
9	Charles K. Barkley	24,500	2,042	Minnesota	6/4/90
10	Melinda Hintquest	56,400	4,700	Arizona	6/1/87
11	Linda Harper	75,000	6,250	Minnesota	8/7/91
12	John Daily	87,500	7,292	New York	1/5/93
13	Elizabeth Becker	89,500	7,458	Arizona	9/29/87

Figure 33-5: When you choose the Data ⇨ Filter ⇨ AutoFilter command, Excel adds drop-down arrows to the field names in the header row.

When you click the arrow in one of these drop-down lists, the list expands to show the unique items in that column. Select an item, and Excel hides all rows except those that include the selected item. In other words, Excel filters the list by the item that you selected.

After you filter the list, the status bar displays a message that tells you how many rows qualified. In addition, the drop-down arrow changes color to remind you that you filtered the list by a value in that column.

AutoFiltering has a limit. Only the first 999 unique items in the column appear in the drop-down list. If your list exceeds this limit, you can use advanced filtering, which is described later.

Besides showing every item in the column, the drop-down list includes five other items:

✦ **All:** Displays all items in the column. Use this to remove filtering for a column.

✦ **Top 10:** Filters to display the "top 10" items in the list; this is discussed later.

✦ **Custom:** Lets you filter the list by multiple items; this is discussed later.

✦ **Blanks:** Filters the list by showing rows that contain blanks in this column.

✦ **NonBlanks:** Filters the list by showing rows that contain nonblanks in this column.

To display the entire list again, click the arrow and choose All — the first item in the drop-down list. Or, you can select Data ➪ Filter ➪ Show All.

To move out of Autofilter mode and remove the drop-down arrows from the field names, choose Data ➪ Filter ➪ AutoFilter again to remove the check mark from the AutoFilter menu item and restore the list to its normal state.

Caution If you have any formulas that refer to data in a filtered list, be aware that the formulas don't adjust to use only the visible cells. For example, if a cell contains a formula that sums values in column C, the formula continues to show the sum for *all* the values in column C — not just those in the visible rows. To solve this problem, use database functions, which I describe later in this chapter.

Multicolumn AutoFiltering

Sometimes you may need to filter a list by values in more than one column. Figure 33-6 shows a list comprised of several fields.

	A	B	C	D	E
1	Month	State	Product	Price	From Ad
2	Jan	CA	Printer	208	Yes
3	Jan	CA	Printer	203	No
4	Jan	IL	Printer	468	No
5	Jan	IL	Printer	226	No
6	Jan	NY	Printer	484	Yes
7	Jan	NY	Printer	373	Yes
8	Jan	CA	Modem	249	Yes
9	Jan	CA	Modem	329	No
10	Jan	IL	Modem	760	Yes
11	Jan	IL	Modem	959	No
12	Jan	NY	Modem	419	No
13	Jan	NY	Modem	555	No
14	Jan	CA	HardDrive	287	Yes
15	Jan	CA	HardDrive	758	No
16	Jan	IL	HardDrive	651	Yes
17	Jan	IL	HardDrive	233	No
18	Jan	NY	HardDrive	332	Yes
19	Jan	NY	HardDrive	852	Yes
20	Jan	CA	Mouse	748	No
21	Jan	CA	Mouse	811	No

Figure 33-6: The list before filtering by multiple columns

Assume that you want to see the records that show modems sold in February. In other words, you want to filter out all records except those in which the Month field is *Feb* and the Product field is *Modem*.

First, get into Autofilter mode. Then click the drop-down arrow in the Month field and select *Feb* to filter the list to show only records with *Feb* in the Month field. Then click the drop-down arrow in the Product field and select *Modem*, filtering the filtered list to show only records that contain *Modem* in the Product column—resulting in a list filtered by values in two columns. Figure 33-7 shows the result.

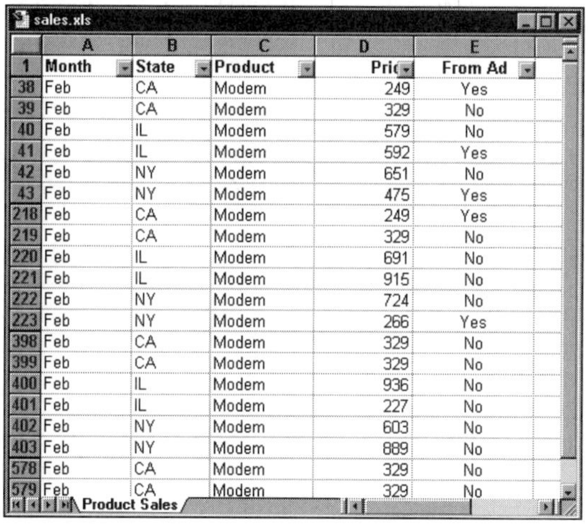

sales.xls

	Month	State	Product	Price	From Ad
38	Feb	CA	Modem	249	Yes
39	Feb	CA	Modem	329	No
40	Feb	IL	Modem	579	No
41	Feb	IL	Modem	592	Yes
42	Feb	NY	Modem	651	No
43	Feb	NY	Modem	475	Yes
218	Feb	CA	Modem	249	Yes
219	Feb	CA	Modem	329	No
220	Feb	IL	Modem	691	No
221	Feb	IL	Modem	915	No
222	Feb	NY	Modem	724	No
223	Feb	NY	Modem	266	Yes
398	Feb	CA	Modem	329	No
399	Feb	CA	Modem	329	No
400	Feb	IL	Modem	936	No
401	Feb	IL	Modem	227	No
402	Feb	NY	Modem	603	No
403	Feb	NY	Modem	889	No
578	Feb	CA	Modem	329	No
579	Feb	CA	Modem	329	No

Product Sales

Figure 33-7: The same list filtered by values in two columns

You can filter a list by any number of columns. Excel applies a different color to the drop-down arrows in the columns that have a filter applied.

Custom AutoFiltering

Usually, AutoFiltering involves selecting a single value for one or more columns. If you choose the Custom option in a drop-down list, you gain a bit more flexibility in filtering the list; Excel displays a dialog box like the one shown in Figure 33-8.

The Custom AutoFilter dialog box lets you filter in several ways:

- **Values above or below a specified value.** For example, sales amounts greater than 10,000.
- **Values within a range.** For example, sales amounts greater than 10,000 AND sales amounts less than 50,000.
- **Two discrete values.** For example, state equal to *New York* OR state equal to *New Jersey*.

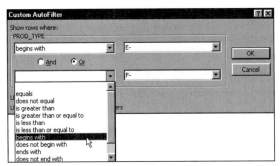

Figure 33-8: The Custom AutoFilter dialog box gives you more filtering options.

✦ **Approximate matches.** You can use the * and ? wildcards to filter in a number of other ways. For example, to display only those customers whose last name begins with *B*, use **B***.

Custom AutoFiltering can be useful, but it definitely has limitations. For example, if you want to filter the list to show only three values in a field (such as New York or New Jersey or Connecticut), you can't do it by AutoFiltering. Such filtering tasks require the advanced filtering feature, which I discuss later in this chapter.

Top 10 AutoFiltering

Sometimes you may want to use a filter on numerical fields to show only the highest or lowest values in the list. For example, if you have a list of employees, you may want to identify the 12 employees with the longest tenure. You could use the custom AutoFilter option, but then you must supply a cutoff date (which you may not know). The solution is to use Top 10 AutoFiltering.

Top 10 AutoFiltering is a generic term; it doesn't limit you to the top *10* items. In fact, it doesn't even limit you to the *top* items. When you choose the Top 10 option from a drop-down list, you see dialog box that is shown in Figure 33-9.

Figure 33-9: The Top 10 AutoFilter gives you more AutoFilter options.

You can choose either Top or Bottom and specify any number. Suppose, for example, that you want to see the 12 employees with the longest tenure. Choose Bottom and 12 to filter the list and show the 12 rows with the smallest values in the Date Hired field. You also can choose Percent or Value in this dialog box. For example, you can filter the list to show the Bottom 5 percent of the records.

Charting filtered list data

You can create some interesting multipurpose charts that use data in a filtered list. The technique is useful because only the visible data appears in the chart. When you change the AutoFilter criteria, the chart updates itself to show only the visible cells.

Note   For this technique to work, select the chart and make sure that the Plot Visible Cells Only option is enabled on the Chart tab of the Options dialog box.

Figure 33-10 shows an example of a chart created with an unfiltered list. It shows sales data for three months for each of four sales regions.

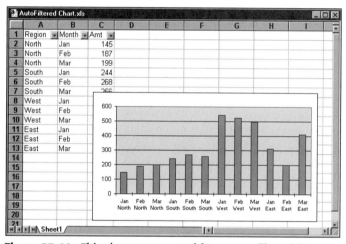

Figure 33-10: This chart was created from an unfiltered list.

Figure 33-11 shows the same chart, but the list was filtered to show only the North sales region. You can apply other filters, and the chart updates automatically. This technique lets a single chart show several different views of the data.

Advanced filtering

In many cases, AutoFiltering does the job. But if you run up against its limitations, you need to use advanced filtering. Advanced filtering is much more flexible than AutoFiltering, but it takes a bit of up-front work to use it. Advanced filtering provides you with the following capabilities:

   ✦ You can specify more complex filtering criteria.

   ✦ You can specify computed filtering criteria.

   ✦ You can extract a copy of the rows that meet the criteria to another location.

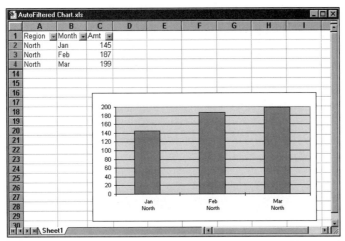

Figure 33-11: The chart from the previous figure, after filtering the list

Setting up a criteria range

Before you can use the advanced filtering feature, you must set up a *criteria range,* a designated range on a worksheet that conforms to certain requirements. The criteria range holds the information that Excel uses to filter the list. It must conform to the following specifications:

✦ It must consist of at least two rows, and the first row must contain some or all field names from the list.

✦ The other rows of the criteria range must consist of your filtering criteria.

Although you can put the criteria range anywhere in the worksheet, it's a good idea not to put it in rows where you placed the list. Because Excel hides some of these rows when filtering the list, you may find that your criteria range is no longer visible after filtering. Therefore, you should generally place the criteria range above or below the list.

Figure 33-12 shows a criteria range, located in A1:D2, above the list that it uses. Only some field names appear in the criteria range. You don't need to include, in the criteria range, field names for fields that you don't use in the selection criteria.

In this example, the criteria range has only one row of criteria. The fields in each row of the criteria range (except for the header row) are joined with an AND operator. Therefore, the filtered list shows rows in which the Month column equals *January* AND the Type column equals *New.* In other words, the list displays only sales to new customers made in January.

	A	B	C	D	E	F	G	
1	**Month**	**SalesRep**	**Type**	**TotalSale**				
2	January		New					
3								
4								
5								
6	**Month**	**SalesRep**	**Type**	**UnitCost**	**Quantity**	**TotalSale**		
7	March	Wilson	New	175	5	875		
8	March	Wilson	New	140	3	420		
9	February	Franks	Existing	225	1	225		
10	March	Wilson	New	125	5	625		
11	January	Peterson	Existing	225	2	450		
12	March	Sheldon	New	140	2	280		
13	February	Peterson	Existing	225	6	1350		
14	March	Jenkins	Existing	140	2	280		
15	February	Sheldon	New	225	4	900		
16	January	Wilson	New	140	4	560		
17	January	Wilson	New	125	3	375		
18	January	Sheldon	New	225	6	1350		
19	February	Sheldon	New	175	5	875		
20	January	Robinson	New	140	3	420		
21	February	Sheldon	New	125	2	250		
22	March	Sheldon	New	140	6	840		
23	March	Jenkins	Existing	225	3	675		
24	January	Robinson	New	225	2	450		
25	March	Sheldon	New	225	6	1350		
26	February	Wilson	New	140	3	420		

Figure 33-12: A criteria range for a list

To perform the filtering, choose Data ➪ Filter ➪ Advanced filter. Excel displays
the dialog box that is shown in Figure 33-13. Specify the list range and the criteria
range, and make sure that you select the option labeled Filter the List in-place.
Click OK, and Excel filters the list by the criteria that you specified.

Figure 33-13: The Advanced
Filter dialog box

Multiple criteria

If you use more than one row in the criteria range, the criteria in each row are
joined with an OR operator. A criteria range can have any number of rows, each
of which is joined to the others with an OR operator. Figure 33-14 shows a criteria
range (A1:D3) with two rows of criteria.

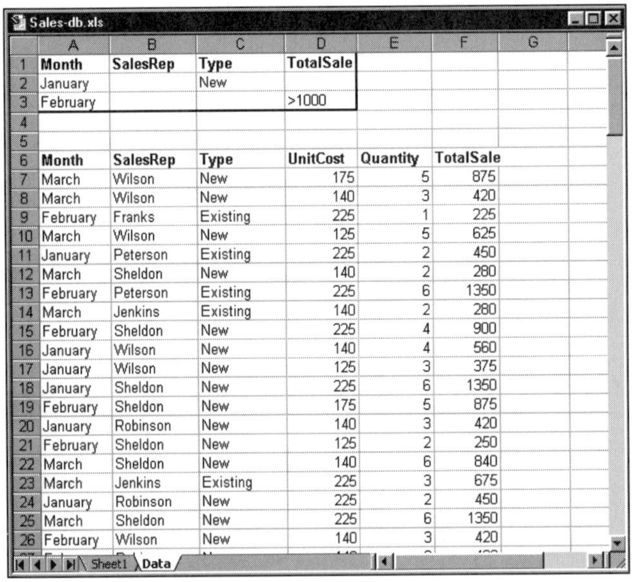

Figure 33-14: This criteria range has two sets of criteria.

In this example, the filtered list shows rows in either of the following:

✦ *The Month field is January AND the Type field is New.*

✦ The Month field is *February* AND the Total Sale field is greater than 1000.

You cannot filter this way with AutoFiltering.

Types of criteria

The entries that you make in the criteria range can be either of the following:

✦ Text or value criteria. The filtering involves comparisons to a value or string, using operators such as equal (=), greater than (>), not equal to (<>), and so on.

✦ **Computed criteria.** The filtering involves a computation of some sort.

Text or value criteria

Table 33-1 lists the comparison operators that you can use with text or value criteria.

Table 33-1
Comparison Operators

Operator	Comparison Type
=	Equal to
>	Greater than
>=	Greater than or equal to
<	Less than
<=	Less than or equal to
<>	Not equal to

Table 33-2 shows examples of criteria that use strings.

Table 33-2
Examples of String Criteria

Criteria	Effect
>K	Text that begins with *L* through *Z*
<>C	All text, except text that begins with C
="January"	Text that matches January
Sm*	Text that begins with Sm
s*s	Text that begins with s and ends with s
s?s	Three-letter text that begins with *s* and ends with *s*

 Note The text comparisons are not case sensitive. For example, si* matches *Simpson* as well as *sick*.

Computed criteria

Using computed criteria can make filtering even more powerful. Computed criteria filter the list based one or more calculations. Figure 33-15 shows a simple list that consists of project numbers, start dates, end dates, and resources. Above the list, in range A1:A2, is the criteria range. Notice, however, that this criteria range does not use a field header from the list — it uses a new field header. A computed criteria essentially computes a new field for the list. Therefore, you must supply new field names in the first row of the criteria range.

	A	B	C	D	E
1	ProjLength				
2	TRUE				
3					
4	Project Number	Start Date	End Date	Resources	
5	AS-109	03/05/97	04/09/97	3,395	
6	AS-110	03/12/97	03/17/97	485	
7	AS-111	04/01/97	04/10/97	873	
8	AS-112	04/01/97	05/03/97	3,104	
9	AS-113	04/12/97	05/01/97	1,843	
10	AS-114	04/21/97	06/05/97	4,365	
11	AS-115	05/03/97	05/15/97	1,164	
12	AS-116	05/21/97	06/09/97	1,843	
13	AS-117	06/02/97	08/01/97	5,820	

Figure 33-15: This list is to be filtered using criteria.

Cell A2 contains the following formula:

```
=C5-B5+1>=30
```

This formula returns a logical value of either *True* or *False*. The result of the formula refers to cells in the first row of data in the list; it does *not* refer to the header row. When you filter the list by this criterion, the list shows only rows in which the project length (End Date–Start Date+1) is greater than or equal to 30 days. In other words, Excel bases the comparison on a computation.

Note You could accomplish the same effect, without using a computed criterion, by adding a new column to the list that contains a formula to calculate the project length. Using a computed criterion, however, eliminates the need to add a new column.

To filter the list to show only the projects that use above-average resources, you could use the following computed criteria formula:

```
=D5>AVERAGE(D:D)
```

This filters the list to show only the rows in which the value of the Resources field is greater than the average of the Resources field.

Keep in mind the following items when using computed criteria:

✦ Don't use a field name in the criteria range that appears in the list. Create a new field name or just leave the cell blank.

✦ You can use any number of computed criteria and mix and match them with noncomputed criteria.

✦ Don't pay attention to the values returned by formulas in the criteria range. These refer to the first row of the list.

✦ If your computed formula refers to a value outside the list, use an absolute reference rather than a relative reference. For example, use $C$1 rather than C1.

✦ Create your computed criteria formulas using the first row of data in the list (not the field names). Make these references relative, not absolute. For example, use C5 rather than $C$5.

Other advanced filtering operations

The Advanced Filter dialog box gives you two other options:

✦ Copy to Another Location

✦ Unique Records Only

Copying qualifying rows

If you choose the Copy to Another Location option in the Advanced Filter dialog box, Excel copies the qualifying rows to another location in the worksheet or a different worksheet. You specify the location for the copied rows in the Copy to edit box. Note that the list itself is not filtered when you use this option.

Displaying only unique rows

Choosing the option labeled Unique records only hides all duplicate rows that meet the criteria that you specify. If you don't specify a criteria range, this option hides all duplicate rows in the list.

Using Database Functions with Lists

It's important to understand that Excel's worksheet functions don't ignore hidden cells. Therefore, if you have a SUM formula that calculates the total of the values in a column of a list, the formula returns the same value when you filter the list.

To create formulas that return results based on filtering criteria, you need to use Excel's database worksheet functions. For example, you can create a formula that calculates the sum of values in a list that meets certain criteria. Set up a criteria range as described previously. Then enter a formula such as the following:

```
=DSUM(ListRange,FieldName,Criteria)
```

In this case, ListRange refers to the list, FieldName refers to the field name cell of the column that you are summing, and Criteria refers to the criteria range.

Excel's database functions are listed in Table 33-3.

	Table 33-3
	Excel's Database Worksheet Functions
Function	**Description**
DAVERAGE	Returns the average of selected database entries
DCOUNT	Counts the cells containing numbers from a specified database and criteria
DCOUNTA	Counts nonblank cells from a specified database and criteria
DGET	Extracts from a database a single record that matches the specified criteria
DMAX	Returns the maximum value from selected database entries
DMIN	Returns the minimum value from selected database entries
DPRODUCT	Multiplies the values in a particular field of records that match the criteria in a database
DSTDEV	Estimates the standard deviation based on a sample of selected database entries
DSTDEVP	Calculates the standard deviation based on the entire population of selected database entries
DSUM	Adds the numbers in the field column of records in the database that match the criteria
DVAR	Estimates variance based on a sample from selected database entries
DVARP	Calculates variance based on the entire population of selected database entries

Cross-Reference   Refer to Chapter 9 for general information about using worksheet functions.

Sorting a List

In some cases, the order of the rows in your list doesn't matter. But in other cases, you want the rows to appear in a specific order. For example, in a price list, you may want the rows to appear in alphabetical order by product name. This makes the products easier to locate in the list. Or, if you have a list of accounts receivable information, you may want to sort the list so that the higher amounts appear at the top of the list (in descending order).

Rearranging the order of the rows in a list is called *sorting*. Excel is quite flexible when it comes to sorting lists, and you can often accomplish this task with the click of a mouse button.

Simple sorting

To quickly sort a list in ascending order, move the cell pointer into the column that you want to sort. Then click the Sort Ascending button the Standard toolbar. The Sort Descending button works the same way, but it sorts the list in descending order. In both cases, Excel determines the extent of your list and sorts all the rows in the list.

When you sort a filtered list, Excel sorts only the visible rows. When you remove the filtering from the list, the list is no longer sorted.

Be careful if you sort a list that contains formulas. If the formulas refer to cells in the list that are in the same row, you don't have any problems. But if the formulas refer to cells in other rows in the list or to cells outside the list, the formulas will not be correct after you sort the list. If formulas in your list refer to cells outside the list, make sure that the formulas use an absolute cell reference.

More complex sorting

Sometimes, you may want to sort by two or more columns. This is relevant to break ties. A tie occurs when rows with duplicate data remain unsorted. Figure 33-16 shows an example of an unsorted list. If you sort this list by Month, Excel places the rows for each month together. But you may also want to show the Sales Reps in ascending order within each month. In this case, you would need to sort by two columns (Month and Sales Rep). Figure 33-17 shows the list after sorting by these two columns.

	A	B	C	D	E	F
7	Month	Sales Rep	Type	Unit Cost	Quantity	Total Sale
8	May	Sheldon	Existing	125	1	125
9	January	Sheldon	Existing	175	1	175
10	January	Sheldon	New	140	6	840
11	January	Jenkins	New	225	1	225
12	February	Robinson	New	225	1	225
13	March	Wilson	Existing	125	4	500
14	April	Robinson	Existing	125	2	250
15	February	Sheldon	Existing	175	1	175
16	March	Robinson	Existing	125	1	125
17	May	Jenkins	New	225	3	675
18	April	Jenkins	New	225	2	450
19	February	Wilson	Existing	125	5	625
20	February	Jenkins	New	225	2	450
21	January	Franks	New	225	4	900
22	May	Wilson	New	225	1	225
23	January	Sheldon	New	225	1	225
24	March	Jenkins	New	225	2	450
25	March	Jenkins	Existing	125	5	625
26	April	Peterson	New	140	2	280
27	February	Franks	Existing	175	2	350
28	May	Robinson	New	140	3	420
29	April	Peterson	Existing	175	6	1050
30	February	Robinson	New	225	3	675

Figure 33-16: This list is unsorted.

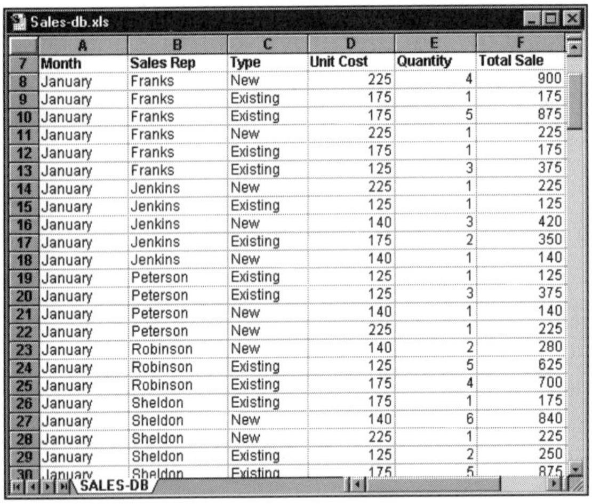
Sales-db.xls

	A	B	C	D	E	F
7	Month	Sales Rep	Type	Unit Cost	Quantity	Total Sale
8	January	Franks	New	225	4	900
9	January	Franks	Existing	175	1	175
10	January	Franks	Existing	175	5	875
11	January	Franks	New	225	1	225
12	January	Franks	Existing	175	1	175
13	January	Franks	Existing	125	3	375
14	January	Jenkins	New	225	1	225
15	January	Jenkins	Existing	125	1	125
16	January	Jenkins	New	140	3	420
17	January	Jenkins	Existing	175	2	350
18	January	Jenkins	New	140	1	140
19	January	Peterson	Existing	125	1	125
20	January	Peterson	Existing	125	3	375
21	January	Peterson	New	140	1	140
22	January	Peterson	New	225	1	225
23	January	Robinson	New	140	2	280
24	January	Robinson	Existing	125	5	625
25	January	Robinson	Existing	175	4	700
26	January	Sheldon	Existing	175	1	175
27	January	Sheldon	New	140	6	840
28	January	Sheldon	New	225	1	225
29	January	Sheldon	Existing	125	2	250
30	January	Sheldon	Existing	175	5	875

SALES-DB

Figure 33-17: The list after sorting on two fields

You can use the Sort Ascending and Sort Descending buttons to do this — but you need to do two sorts. First, sort by the Sales Reps column, and then sort by the Month column. As I explain in the next section, Excel provides a way to accomplish multicolumn sorting with a single command.

Excel's Sorting Rules

Because cells can contain different types of information, you may be curious about how Excel sorts this information. For an ascending sort, the information appears in the following order:

1. **Values:** Excel sorts numbers from smallest negative to largest positive, and treats dates and times as values. In all cases, Excel sorts using the actual values in cells (not their formatted appearance).

2. **Text:** In alphabetical order, as follows: 0 1 2 3 4 5 6 7 8 9 (space) ! " # $ % & ' ( ) * + , − . / : ; < = > ? @ [\ ] ^ _ ` { | } ~ A B C D E F G H I J K L M N O P Q R S T U V W X Y Z.

   By default, sorting is not case sensitive. You can change this behavior, however, in the Sort Options dialog box (described in this chapter).

3. **Logical values:** False comes before True.

4. **Error values:** Error values (such as #VALUE! and #NA) appear in their original order; Excel does not sort them by error type.

5. **Blank cells:** Blanks cells always appear last.

Sorting in descending order reverses this sequence – except that blank cells *still* appear last.

The Sort dialog box

If you want to sort by more than one field, choose Data ➪ Sort. Excel displays the dialog box that is shown in Figure 33-18. Simply select the first sort field from the drop-down list labeled Sort By, and specify Ascending or Descending order. Then, do the same for the second sort field. If you want to sort by a third field, specify the field in the third section. If the Header Row option is set, the first row (field names) is not affected by the sort. Click OK, and the list's rows rearrange in a flash.

Figure 33-18: The Sort dialog box lets you sort by up to three columns.

If the sorting didn't occur as you expected, select Edit ➪ Undo (or press Ctrl+Z) to undo the sorting.

What if you need to sort your list by more than three fields? It can be done, but it takes an additional step. For example, assume that you want to sort your list by five fields: Field1, Field2, Field3, Field4, and Field5. Start by sorting by Field3, Field4, and Field5. Then resort the list by Field1 and Field2. In other words, sort the three "least important" fields first; they remain in sequence when you do the second sort.

Tip

Often, you want to keep the records in their original order but perform a temporary sort just to see how it looks. The solution is to add an additional column to the list with sequential numbers in it (don't use formulas to generate these numbers, but you can use the Fill command). Then, after you sort, you can return to the original order by resorting on the field that contains the sequential numbers. You can also use Excel's undo feature to return the list to its original order. If you use an additional column, you can perform other operations while the list is temporarily sorted (and these operations won't be undone when you undo the sort operation).

Sort options

When you click the Options button in the Sort dialog box, Excel displays the Sort Options dialog box, shown in Figure 33-19.

Figure 33-19: The Sort Options dialog box gives you some additional sorting options.

These options are described as follows:

✦ **First key sort order:** Lets you specify a custom sort order for the sort (see the next section).

✦ **Case sensitive:** Makes the sorting case sensitive so that uppercase letters appear before lowercase letters in an ascending sort. Normally, sorting ignores the case of letters.

✦ **Orientation:** Enables you to sort by columns rather than by rows (the default).

Using a custom sort order

Excel typically sorts either numerically or alphabetically, depending on the data being sorted. In some cases, however, you may want to sort your data in other ways. For example, if your data consists of month names, you usually want it to appear in month order rather than alphabetically. You can use the Sort Options dialog box to perform such a sort. Select the appropriate list from the drop-down list labeled First key sort order. Excel, by default, has four "custom lists," and you can define your own. Excel's custom lists are as follows:

✦ **Abbreviated days:** Sun, Mon, Tue, Wed, Thu, Fri, Sat

✦ **Days:** Sunday, Monday, Tuesday, Wednesday, Thursday, Friday, Saturday

✦ **Abbreviated months:** Jan, Feb, Mar, Apr, May, Jun, Jul, Aug, Sep, Oct, Nov, Dec

✦ **Months:** January, February, March, April, May, June, July, August, September, October, November, December

Note that the abbreviated days and months do not have periods after them. If you use periods for these abbreviations, Excel doesn't recognize them (and doesn't sort them correctly).

You may want to create a custom list. For example, your company may have several stores, and you want the stores to be listed in a particular order (not alphabetically). If you create a custom list, sorting puts the items in the order that you specify in the list. You must use the Data ➪ Sort command to sort by a custom list (click the Options button to specify the custom list).

How Excel Identifies a Header Row

When you use the Data ⇨ Sort command, there's no need to select the list before you choose the command. That's because Excel examines the active cell position and then establishes the list's boundaries for you. In addition, Excel attempts to determine whether the list contains a header row. If the list has a header row, Excel excludes this row is not included from the sort.

How does this happen? I'm not sure exactly, but the following seems to be Excel's "thought" process:

1. Select the current region. (You can do this manually: press F5, click the Special button, select the Current Region option, and click OK.)

2. Examine the first row of the selection.

3. Determine whether the first row contains any blanks. If so, this list has no header row.

4. Determine whether the first row contains text. If so, check the other cells. If they also contain text, this list has no header row.

5. Determine whether the first row contains uppercase text while the list itself contains lowercase or proper case text. If so, this list has a header row.

6. Determine whether the cells in the first row are formatted differently from the other cells in the list. If so, this list has a header row.

Knowing this information can help you eliminate incorrect sorting. For example, if you want to sort a range that doesn't have a header row, you need to make sure that Excel doesn't sort the data as if it had a header row. For best results, use the Sort Ascending and Sort Descending toolbar buttons only when the data that you're sorting has headers. If your data contains no headers, select Data ⇨ Sort and make sure that the No Header Row option is selected.

To create a custom list, use the Custom Lists tab of the Options dialog box, as shown in Figure 33-20. Select the NEW LIST option, and make your entries (in order) in the List Entries box. Or, you can import your custom list from a range of cells by selecting the range and then clicking the Import button.

Custom lists also work with the AutoFill handle in cells. If you enter the first item of a custom list and then drag the cell's AutoFill handle, Excel fills in the remaining list items automatically.

Sorting nonlists

You can, of course, sort any range in a worksheet — it doesn't have to be a list. You need to be aware of a few things, however. The Sort Ascending and Sort Descending toolbar buttons may assume (erroneously) that the top row is a header row and not include these cells in the sort (see the sidebar, "How Excel Identifies a Header Row," earlier in this chapter).

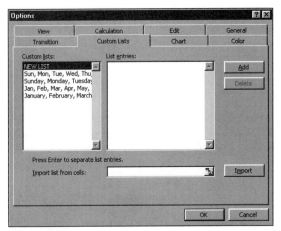

Figure 33-20: Excel lets you create custom sorting lists.

Therefore, to avoid potential errors when sorting nonlists, don't use these toolbar buttons. Rather, select the entire range, and select Data ➪ Sort (making sure that you choose the No Header Row option).

Creating Subtotals

The final topic of this chapter is automatic subtotals—a handy feature that can save you a great deal of time. To use this feature, your list must be sorted, because the subtotals are inserted whenever the value in a specified field changes. Figure 33-21 shows an example of a list, sorted by the Month field, which is appropriate for subtotals.

	A	B	C	D	E	F	G
1	Month	Sales Rep	Type	Unit Cost	Quantity	Total Sale	
2	January	Franks	New	225	4	900	
3	January	Franks	Existing	175	5	875	
4	January	Franks	New	225	1	225	
5	January	Franks	Existing	175	1	175	
6	January	Jenkins	New	225	1	225	
7	January	Jenkins	Existing	125	1	125	
8	February	Franks	New	225	4	900	
9	February	Jenkins	New	225	2	450	
10	February	Jenkins	New	225	3	675	
11	February	Jenkins	New	225	3	675	
12	February	Jenkins	New	225	3	675	
13	February	Jenkins	Existing	175	1	175	
14	February	Peterson	New	225	1	225	
15	February	Peterson	New	225	2	450	
16	March	Peterson	Existing	125	2	250	
17	March	Peterson	New	225	2	450	
18	March	Robinson	Existing	125	1	125	
19	March	Robinson	Existing	125	5	625	
20	March	Robinson	New	225	4	900	
21	April	Franks	New	175	4	700	
22	April	Franks	New	175	3	525	
23	April	Jenkins	New	225	2	450	
24	April	Jenkins	New	140	3	420	

SALES-DB

Figure 33-21: This list is a good candidate for subtotals, which are inserted at each change of the month.

To insert subtotal formulas into a list automatically, move the cell pointer anywhere in the list and choose Data ⇨ Subtotals. You see the dialog box shown in Figure 33-22.

Figure 33-22: The Subtotal dialog box automatically inserts subtotal formulas into a sorted list.

This dialog box offers the following choices:

✦ **At Each Change in:** This drop-down list displays all fields in your list. You must have sorted the list by the field that you choose.

✦ **Use Function: Choose from 11 functions:** You should normally use Sum (the default).

✦ **Add Subtotal to:** This list box shows all the fields in your list. Place a check mark next to the field or fields that you want to subtotal.

✦ **Replace Current Subtotals:** If this box is checked, Excel removes any existing subtotal formulas and replaces them with the new subtotals.

✦ **Page Break Between Groups:** If this box is checked, Excel inserts a manual page break after each subtotal.

✦ **Summary Below Data:** If this box is checked, Excel places the subtotals below the data (the default). Otherwise, the subtotal formulas appear above the totals.

✦ **Remove All:** This button removes all subtotal formulas in the list.

When you click OK, Excel analyzes the list and inserts formulas as specified — and creates an outline for you. The formulas all use the SUBTOTAL worksheet function.

When you add subtotals to a filtered list, the subtotals may no longer be accurate when the filter is removed.

Figure 33-23 shows a worksheet after adding subtotals.

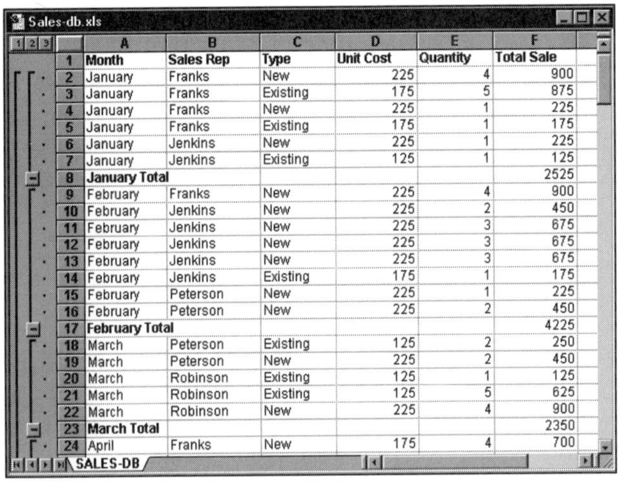

Sales-db.xls

	A	B	C	D	E	F
1	Month	Sales Rep	Type	Unit Cost	Quantity	Total Sale
2	January	Franks	New	225	4	900
3	January	Franks	Existing	175	5	875
4	January	Franks	New	225	1	225
5	January	Franks	Existing	175	1	175
6	January	Jenkins	New	225	1	225
7	January	Jenkins	Existing	125	1	125
8	January Total					2525
9	February	Franks	New	225	4	900
10	February	Jenkins	New	225	2	450
11	February	Jenkins	New	225	3	675
12	February	Jenkins	New	225	3	675
13	February	Jenkins	New	225	3	675
14	February	Jenkins	Existing	175	1	175
15	February	Peterson	New	225	1	225
16	February	Peterson	New	225	2	450
17	February Total					4225
18	March	Peterson	Existing	125	2	250
19	March	Peterson	New	225	2	450
20	March	Robinson	Existing	125	1	125
21	March	Robinson	Existing	125	5	625
22	March	Robinson	New	225	4	900
23	March Total					2350
24	April	Franks	New	175	4	700

SALES-DB

Figure 33-23: Excel added the subtotal formulas automatically—and even created an outline.

Summary

In this chapter, I discuss lists. A list is simply a database table that is stored on a worksheet. The first row of the list (the header row) contains field names, and subsequent rows contain data (records). I offer some pointers on data entry and discuss two ways to filter a list to show only rows that meet certain criteria. AutoFiltering is adequate for many tasks, but if your filtering needs are more complex, you need to use advanced filtering. I end the chapter with a discussion of sorting and Excel's automatic subtotal feature.

✦ ✦ ✦

Using External Database Files

The preceding chapter described how to work with lists that are stored in a worksheet. Many users find that worksheet lists are sufficient for their data tracking. Others, however, choose to take advantage of Excel's capability to access data that is stored in external database files. That's the topic of this chapter.

Why Use External Database Files?

Accessing external database files from Excel is useful when you have the following situations:

✦ You need to work with a very large database.

✦ You share the database with others; that is, other users have access to the database and may need to work with the data at the same time.

✦ You want to work with only a subset of the data — data that meets certain criteria that you specify.

✦ The database is in a format that Excel can't read.

If you need to work with external databases, you may prefer Excel to other database programs. The advantage? After you bring the data into Excel, you can manipulate and format it by using familiar tools.

As you may know, Excel can read some database files directly — specifically, those produced by various versions of dBASE (with a DBF extension). If the database has fewer than 65,535 records and no more than 255 fields, you can load the entire file into a worksheet, memory permitting. Even if you have enough memory to load such a large file, however, Excel's performance would likely be poor.

In many cases, you may not be interested in all the records or fields in the file. Instead, you may want to bring in just the data that meets certain criteria. In other words, you want to *query* the database and load into your worksheet a subset of the external database that meets the criteria. Excel makes this type of operation relatively easy.

Note   To perform queries using external databases, Microsoft Query must be installed on your system. If the Data ➪ Get External Data ➪ Create New Query command is not available, Query is not installed. You must rerun the Excel (or Microsoft Office) setup program and install Query.

In previous versions of Excel, using Microsoft Query required that you load an add-in. That is no longer necessary, starting with Excel 97, although the add-in is still included for compatibility purposes.

To work with an external database file from Excel, use the Query application that is included with Excel. The general procedure is as follows:

1. Activate a worksheet.

2. Choose Data ➪ Get External Data ➪ New Database Query. This starts Query.

3. Specify whether you want to use Query directly or use Query Wizard.

4. Specify the database that you want to use and then create a *query* — a list of criteria that specifies which records you want.

5. Specify how you want the data returned that passes your query — either to a worksheet or as a pivot table.

You can choose to save the query in a file so that you can reuse it later. This means that modifying the query or *refreshing* it (updating it with any changed values) is a simple matter. This is particularly useful when the data resides in a shared database that is continually being updated.

Cross-Reference   The next chapter discusses pivot tables. You can create a pivot table using data in an external file, and use Query to retrieve data.

Using Query: An Example

The best way to become familiar with Query is to walk through an example.

The database file

The file that is used in this example is named Budget.dbf.

On the CD-ROM   If you want to try this example, you can find it on this book's CD-ROM.

This database file is a dBASE IV database with a single table that consists of 15,840 records. This file contains the following fields:

- ✦ **Sort:** A numeric field that holds record sequence numbers.
- ✦ **Division:** A text field that specifies the company division (Asia, Europe, N. America, Pacific Rim, or S. America).
- ✦ **Department:** A text field that specifies the department within the division. Each division is organized into the following departments: Accounting, Advertising, Data Processing, Human Resources, Operations, Public Relations, R&D, Sales, Security, Shipping, and Training.
- ✦ **Category:** A text field that specifies the budget category. The four categories are Compensation, Equipment, Facility, and Supplies & Services.
- ✦ **Item:** A text field that specifies the budget item. Each budget category has different budget items. For example, the Compensation category includes the following items: Benefits, Bonuses, Commissions, Conferences, Entertainment, Payroll Taxes, Salaries, and Training.
- ✦ **Month:** A text field that specifies the month (abbreviated as Jan, Feb, and so on).
- ✦ **Budget:** A numeric field that stores the budgeted amount.
- ✦ **Actual:** A numeric field that stores the actual amount spent.
- ✦ **Variance:** A numeric field that stores the difference between the Budget and Actual fields.

The task

The objective of this exercise is to develop a report that shows the first quarter (January through March) actual compensation expenditures of the training department in the North American division. In other words, the query will extract records for which the following applies:

- ✦ The Division is N. America
- ✦ The Department is Training
- ✦ The Category is Compensation
- ✦ The Month is Jan, Feb, or Mar

Using Query to get the data

You *could* import the entire dBASE file into a worksheet and then choose Data ➪ Filter ➪ AutoFilter to filter the data as required. This approach would work, because the file has fewer than 65,535 records, which isn't always the case. Using Query, however, you import only the data that's required.

Some Database Terminology

People who spend their days working with databases seem to have their own special language. The following terms can help you hold your own among a group of database experts:

- **External database:** A collection of data that is stored in one or more files (not Excel files). Each file of a database holds a single table, and tables are comprised of records and fields.

- **Field:** In a database table, an element of a record that corresponds to a column.

- **ODBC:** An acronym for Open DataBase Connectivity, a standard developed by Microsoft that uses drivers to access database files in different formats. Microsoft Query comes with drivers for Access, dBASE, FoxPro, Paradox, SQL Server, Excel workbooks, and ASCII text files. ODBC drivers for other databases are available from Microsoft and third-party providers.

- **Query:** To search a database for records that meet specific criteria. This term is also used as a noun; you can write a query, for example.

- **Record:** In a database table, a single element that corresponds to a row.

- **Refresh:** To rerun a query to get the latest data. This is applicable when the database contains information that is subject to change, as in a multiuser environment.

- **Relational database:** A database that is stored in more than one table or file. At least one common field (sometimes called the *key field*) connects the tables.

- **Result set:** The data that is returned by a query, usually a subset of the original database. Query returns the result set to your Excel workbook or to a pivot table.

- **SQL:** An acronym for Structured Query Language (usually pronounced *sequel*). Query uses SQL to query data that is stored in ODBC databases.

- **Table:** A record- and field-oriented collection of data. A database consists of one or more tables.

Starting query

Begin with an empty worksheet. Select Data ⇨ Get External Data ⇨ New Database Query; this action launches and activates Microsoft Query, a separate application. Excel continues to run, and you can switch back and forth between Query and Excel, as needed.

Selecting a data source

When Query starts, it displays the Choose Data Source dialog box, shown in Figure 34-1.

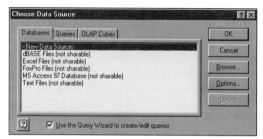

Figure 34-1: The Choose Data Source dialog box

This dialog box contains three tabs:

✦ Databases: Lists the data sources that are known to Query — this tab may be empty, depending on which data sources are defined on your system.

✦ Queries: Contains a list of stored queries. Again, this may or may not be empty.

✦ OLAP Cubes: Lists OLAP databases (see sidebar) that are available for Query.

OLAP Databases

OLAP is an acronym for *online analytical processing*; OLAP presents a new way to organize large databases to suit the way that you analyze and manage information. In an OLAP database, data is organized by level of detail. In a business database, for example, you might want to track sales around the world for the products of a particular company. In an OLAP organization of this information, you would need to consider where and when each product was sold, as well as which product was sold. Each of these aspects of the OLAP database is called a *dimension*, and each dimension is comprised of several fields that can be organized hierarchically, by level of detail. You might call the "where" dimension the Location dimension, and it might contain, for example, fields for country, region, and city. The Time dimension, containing information about when the product was sold, might contain fields for month, date, day, and year.

Dimensions in an OLAP database combine to provide information about the intersecting points; because you can combine several dimensions, OLAP databases are called *cubes.*

You can connect Excel to an OLAP data source created with either the Microsoft DSS (Decision Support Services) Analysis server or other third-party OLAP products that provide data source drivers that are compatible with OLD-DB for OLAP. You connect to an OLAP cube the same way that you connect to other external data sources. Excel can display data that you retrieve from an OLAP cube as either a PivotTable or a PivotChart. You cannot display OLAP data as an external data range of the type discussed in this chapter.

If you've previously worked with a particular database, its name appears in the list of databases. Otherwise, you need to identify the source.

In the Databases tab, select the <New Database Source> option and click OK. This displays the Create New Data Source dialog box, shown in Figure 34-2.

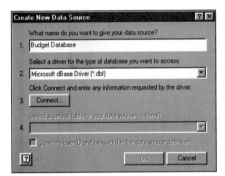

Figure 34-2: The Create New Data Source dialog box

The Create New Data Source dialog box has the following four numbered parts:

1. Enter a descriptive name for the data source. For this example, the name is Budget Database.

2. Select a driver for the data source by selecting from the list of installed drivers. Because the database file in this example is a dBASE file, select the driver named Microsoft dBASE Driver.

3. The Connect button displays the ODBC Setup dialog box that asks for information specific to the driver that you select in Step 2. In this dialog box, you select the directory where the database is located.

4. Select the default data table that you want to use (this step is optional). If the database requires a password, you can also specify that the password be saved with the Data Source definition.

After you supply all the information in the Create New Data Source dialog box, click OK, and Excel redisplays the Choose Data Source dialog box — which now includes the data source that you created.

You have to go through these steps only once for each data source. The next time that you access Query, the Budget Database (and any other database sources that you define) appears in the Choose Data Source dialog box.

Use Query Wizard?

The Choose Data Source dialog box has a check box at the bottom that lets you specify whether to use Query Wizard to create your query. Query Wizard walks you through the steps that are used to create your query, and if you use Query Wizard, you don't have to deal directly with Query. I highly recommend using Query Wizard—and the examples in this chapter use this tool.

In the Choose Data Sources dialog box, make sure that you check the Query Wizard check box at the bottom of the dialog box and then click OK to start Query Wizard.

Query Wizard: Choosing the columns

In the first step of Query Wizard (see Figure 34-3), select the database columns that you want to appear in your query.

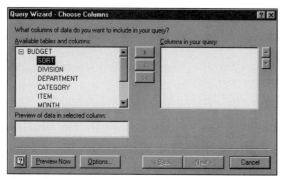

Figure 34-3: In the first step of Query Wizard, you select the columns to use in your query.

The columns that you select determine the fields from the database that Query returns to Excel. Recall that the query for this example involves selecting records based on the following fields: Division, Department, Month, Category, and Actual. You also want to add the Item field. The left tab of the dialog box shows all the available columns. To add a column to the right tab, select the column and click the > button (or, you can double-click the column name).

After you finish adding the columns, the Query Wizard dialog box looks like Figure 34-4.

Using the ODBC Manager

Occasionally, you may need to edit data sources—for example, if you move your database files to a new location. You can do this by using the ODBC Manager utility. This program is available in the Windows Control Panel (it's called *32-bit ODBC*). This utility also lets you add new data sources and remove those that you no longer need.

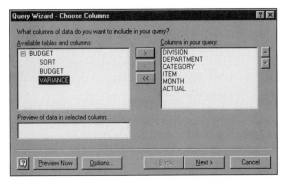

Figure 34-4: Six columns have been added to the query.

If you want to see the data for a particular column, select the column and click the Preview Now button. If you accidentally add a column that you don't need, select it in the right tab and click the < button to remove it. After you select all the columns for the query, click the Next button.

Query Wizard: Filtering data

In the second Query Wizard dialog box, you specify your record selection criteria — how you want to filter the data. This step is optional. If you want to retrieve all the data, just click the Next button to proceed. Figure 34-5 shows the Filter Data dialog box of Query Wizard.

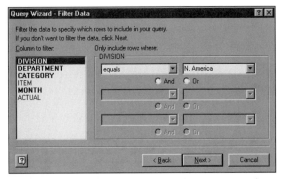

Figure 34-5: In the second step of Query Wizard, you specify how you want to filter the data.

For the example, you don't need all records. Recall that you're interested only in the records in which one of the following applies:

✦ The Division is N. America.

✦ The Department is Training.

✦ The Category is Compensation.

✦ The Month is Jan, Feb, or Mar.

You enter the criteria by column. In this case, you need to specify four criteria (one for each of four columns):

1. In the Column to filter column, select DIVISION. In the right tab, select equals from the first drop-down list, and N. America from the second drop-down list.

2. In the Column to filter column, select DEPARTMENT. In the right tab, select equals from the first drop-down list, and Training from the second drop-down list.

3. In the Column to filter column, select CATEGORY. In the right tab, select equals from the first drop-down list, and Compensation from the second drop-down list.

4. In the Column to filter column, select MONTH. In the right tab, select equals from the first drop-down list, and Jan from the second drop-down list. Because this column is filtered by multiple values, click the Or option and then select equals and Feb from the drop-down lists in the second row. Finally, select equals and Mar from the drop-down lists in the second row.

To review the criteria that you've entered, select the column from the Column to filter list. Query Wizard displays the criteria that you entered for the selected column. After you enter all the criteria, click Next.

Query Operators

The following table lists and describes the operators that are available when you create a query. These operators give you complete control over which rows are returned.

Operator	What It Does
equals	Field is identical to value
does not equal	Field is not equal to value
is greater than	Field is greater than value
is greater than or equal to	Field is greater than or equal to value
is less than	Field is less than value
is less than or equal to	Field is less than or equal to value

Continued

(continued)

Operator	What It Does
is one of	Field is in a list of values, separated by commas
is not one of	Field is not in a list of values, separated by commas
is between	Field is between two values, separated by commas
is not between	Field is not between two values, separated by commas
begins with	Field begins with the value
does not begin with	Field does not begin with value
ends with	Field ends with value
does not end with	Field does not end with value
contains	Field contains value
does not contain	Field does not contain value
like	Field is like value (using * and ? wildcard characters)
not like	Field is not like value (using * and ? wildcard characters)
is Null	Field is empty
is not Null	Field is not empty

Query Wizard: Sort order

The third step of the Query Wizard enables you to specify how you want the records to be sorted (see Figure 34-6). This step is optional, and you can click Next to move to the next step if you don't want the data sorted or prefer to sort it after it's returned to your worksheet.

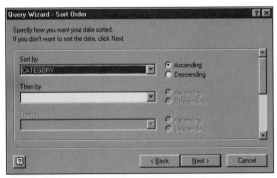

Figure 34-6: In the third step of Query Wizard, you specify the sort order.

For this example, sort by CATEGORY in Ascending order. You can specify as many sort fields as you like. Click Next to move to the next step.

Query Wizard: Finish

The final step of Query Wizard, shown in Figure 34-7, lets you do the following things:

✦ Give the query a name

✦ Save it to a file, so that it can be reused

✦ Specify what to do with the data

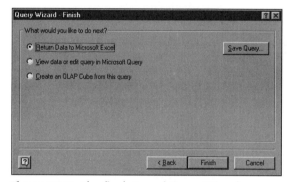

Figure 34-7: The final step of Query Wizard

Normally, you want to return the data to Excel. If you know how to use the Microsoft Query application, you can return the data to Query and examine it, or even modify the selection criteria. Or, you can create an OLAP cube to use in a PivotTable or PivotChart report.

If you plan to reuse this query, you should save it to a file. Click the Save Query button, and you are prompted for a filename. After you make your choices, click Finish.

Specifying a location for the data

Figure 34-8 shows the Returning External Data to Microsoft Excel dialog box, which appears when you click the Finish button in the Query Wizard dialog box.

You can select from the following choices:

✦ **Existing worksheet:** You can specify the upper-left cell.

✦ **New worksheet:** Excel can insert a new worksheet and insert the data beginning in cell A1.

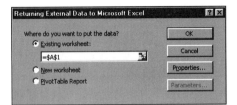

Figure 34-8: Specifying what to do with the data

> ✦ **Pivot Table Report:** Excel can display its Pivot Table Wizard, so that you can specify the layout for a pivot table (see Chapter 35).

Figure 34-9 shows the data that is returned to a worksheet.

	A	B	C	D	E	F
1	DIVISION	DEPARTMENT	CATEGORY	ITEM	MONTH	ACTUAL
2	N. America	Training	Compensation	Payroll Taxes	Feb	3542
3	N. America	Training	Compensation	Benefits	Jan	3283
4	N. America	Training	Compensation	Bonuses	Jan	3331
5	N. America	Training	Compensation	Commissions	Jan	3143
6	N. America	Training	Compensation	Payroll Taxes	Jan	3516
7	N. America	Training	Compensation	Training	Jan	4058
8	N. America	Training	Compensation	Conferences	Jan	4281
9	N. America	Training	Compensation	Entertainment	Jan	3344
10	N. America	Training	Compensation	Salaries	Feb	3972
11	N. America	Training	Compensation	Benefits	Feb	3985
12	N. America	Training	Compensation	Salaries	Jan	4313
13	N. America	Training	Compensation	Commissions	Feb	3288
14	N. America	Training	Compensation	Entertainment	Mar	3205
15	N. America	Training	Compensation	Training	Feb	3757
16	N. America	Training	Compensation	Conferences	Feb	4055
17	N. America	Training	Compensation	Entertainment	Feb	3724
18	N. America	Training	Compensation	Salaries	Mar	3748
19	N. America	Training	Compensation	Benefits	Mar	3808
20	N. America	Training	Compensation	Bonuses	Mar	3809
21	N. America	Training	Compensation	Commissions	Mar	3271
22	N. America	Training	Compensation	Payroll Taxes	Mar	3347
23	N. America	Training	Compensation	Training	Mar	3678
24	N. America	Training	Compensation	Conferences	Mar	4146
25	N. America	Training	Compensation	Bonuses	Feb	2611

Figure 34-9: The results of the query

Working with an External Data Range

Excel stores the data that Query returns in either a worksheet or a pivot table. When Excel stores data in a worksheet, it stores the data in a specially named range, known as an *external data range;* Excel creates the name for this range automatically.

This section describes what you can do with the data that Excel receives from Query and stores in a worksheet.

Adjusting external data range properties

You can adjust various properties of the external data range by using the External
Data Range Properties dialog box (see Figure 34-10).

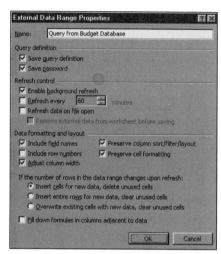

Figure 34-10: The External Data Range
Properties dialog box enables you to
specify various options for an external
data range.

To display this dialog box, the cell pointer must be within the external data range.
You can open this dialog box by using any of three methods:

✦ Right-click and select Data Range Properties from the shortcut menu.

✦ Select Data ➪ Get External Data ➪ Data Range Properties.

✦ Click the Data Range properties tool on the External Data toolbar (this toolbar
appears automatically when you perform a query).

The following list describes the options in the External Data Range Properties
dialog box:

✦ **Name:** The name of the external data range. You can change this name or use
the default name that Excel creates. Excel substitutes, in the range name, the
underscore character for any spaces that you see in the Name box of the
External Data Range Properties box.

✦ **Query definition:** If you check Save query definition, Excel stores the
query definition with the external data range, enabling you to refresh

the data or edit the query, if necessary. If the database requires a password, you can also store the password so that you don't need to enter it when you refresh the query.

✦ **Refresh control:** Determines how and when Excel refreshes the data.

✦ **Data formatting and layout:** Determines the appearance of the external data range.

The External Data Range Properties dialog box has quite a few options. For specific details, click the Help icon in the title bar and then click an option in the dialog box.

You can manipulate data returned from a query just like any other worksheet range. For example, you can sort the data, format it, or create formulas that use the data.

EXCEL 2000 In prior versions of Excel, if you intend to refresh the query, you need to keep the external data range intact. That is, you can't insert new rows or columns in the external data range, because refreshing the query causes the external range to be rewritten. Similarly, you lose any formatting that you applied to the external data range when you refresh the query.

In Excel 2000, refreshing a query *does not* overwrite the external data range. You are free to format the external data range or insert rows and columns. You also can include formulas in those rows and columns that refer to other parts of the external data range. Your work *will not* be destroyed when you refresh the query.

Refreshing a query

After performing a query, you can save the file and then retrieve it later. The file contains the data that you originally retrieved from the external database. The external database may have changed, however, in the interim.

If you checked the Save query definition option in the External Data Range Properties dialog box, then Excel saves the query definition with the workbook. Simply move the cell pointer anywhere within the external data table in the worksheet and then use one of the following methods to refresh the query:

✦ Right-click and select Refresh Data from the shortcut menu

✦ Select Data ➪ Refresh Data

✦ Click the Refresh Data tool on the External Data toolbar

Excel launches Query and uses your original query to bring in the current data from the external database.

Tip If you find that refreshing the query causes undesirable results, use Excel's Undo feature to "unrefresh" the data.

Making multiple queries

A single workbook can hold as many external data ranges as you need. Excel gives each query a unique name, and you can work with each query independently. Excel automatically keeps track of the query that produces each external data range.

Copying or moving a query

After performing a query, you may want to copy or move the external data range, which you can do by using the normal copy, cut, and paste techniques. However, make sure that you copy or cut the entire external data range — otherwise, the underlying query is not copied, and the copied data cannot be refreshed.

Deleting a query

If you decide that you no longer need the data that is returned by a query, you can delete it by selecting the entire external data range and choosing Edit ➪ Delete.

Note If you simply press Delete, the contents of the cells are erased, but the underlying query remains. Excel displays a dialog box asking whether you want to delete the query. If you choose No, you can refresh the query, and the deleted cells appear again, including any formatting that you applied to them.

When you refresh, Query returns only data that is retrieved from the external database. If you delete rows or columns that you inserted into the external data range, Query does not redisplay those rows and columns when you refresh.

Changing your query

If you bring the query results into your worksheet and discover that you don't have what you want, you can modify the query. Move the cell pointer anywhere within the external data table in the worksheet and then use one of the following methods to refresh the query:

✦ Right-click and select Edit Query from the shortcut menu

✦ Select Data ➪ Get External Data ➪ Edit Query

✦ Click the Edit Query tool on the External Data toolbar

Excel then launches (or activates) Query, and you can change the original query. After you finish, choose File ➪ Return Data to Microsoft Excel. Excel reactivates, executes the modified query, and updates the external data range.

Using Microsoft Query Without Query Wizard

Previous sections in this chapter describe how to use Query Wizard to create a database query. Query Wizard is essentially a "front end" for Microsoft Query. In some cases, you may want to use Query itself rather than Query Wizard.

When you select Data ➪ Get External Data ➪ Create New Query, the Choose Data Source dialog box gives you the option of whether to use Query Wizard. If you choose not to use Query Wizard, you work directly with Microsoft Query.

Creating a query

Before you can create a query, you must display the Criteria pane. In Query, open the View menu and confirm that a check appears next to the Criteria command. If you don't see a check, choose View ➪ Criteria to display the Criteria pane in the middle of the window. (See Figure 34-11.)

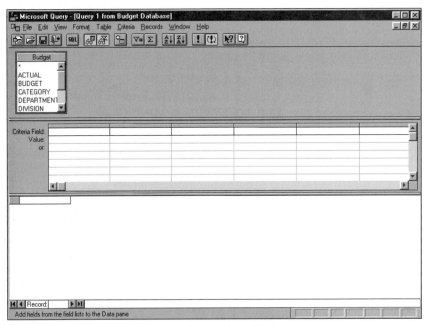

Figure 34-11: Microsoft Query, displaying the Criteria pane

Running Microsoft Query by Itself

Normally, you run Query from Excel. But because Query is a standalone application, you also can run it directly. The executable file is named msqry32.exe and its location can vary (use the Windows Find File feature to locate this program on your system).

If you run Query by itself, you can't return the data to Excel automatically. You can, however, use the clipboard to copy data from the data pane to any application that you want (including Excel).

The Query window has three panes, which are split vertically:

✦ **Tables pane:** The top pane, which holds the data tables for the database. Each data table window has a list of the fields in the table.

✦ **Criteria pane:** The middle pane, which holds the criteria that determine the rows that the query returns.

✦ **Data pane:** The bottom pane, which holds the data that passes the criteria.

Creating a query consists of the following steps:

1. Drag fields from the Tables pane to the Data pane. You can drag as many fields as you want. These fields are the columns that the query will return. You can also double-click a field instead of dragging it.

2. Enter criteria in the Criteria pane. When you activate this pane, the first row (labeled Criteria Field) displays a drop-down list that contains all the field names. Select a field and enter the criteria below it. Query updates the Data pane automatically, treating each row like an OR operator.

3. Choose File ➪ Return Data to Microsoft Excel to execute the query and place the data in a worksheet or pivot table.

Figure 34-12 shows how the query for the example presented earlier in this chapter appears in Query.

Using multiple database tables

The example in this chapter uses only one database table. Some databases, however, use multiple tables. These databases are known as *relational databases*, because a common field links the tables. Query lets you use any number of tables in your queries. To see an example of a relational database, load the sample database (called Northwind Traders) that's provided with Microsoft Query. This particular database has six tables.

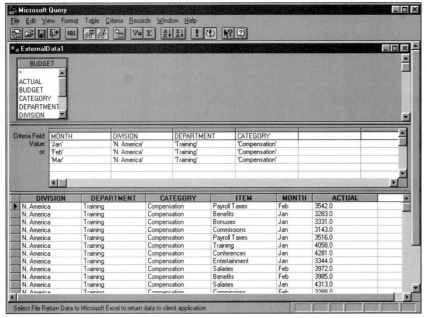

Figure 34-12: The center pane contains a query definition.

Adding and editing records in external database tables

To add, delete, and edit data when you are using Query, make sure that a check appears next to the Records ➪ Allow Editing command. Of course, you can't edit a database file that's set up as read-only. In any case, you need to be careful with this feature, because your changes are saved to disk as soon as you move the cell pointer out of the record that you're editing (you do not need to choose File ➪ Save).

Formatting data

If you don't like the data's appearance in the data pane, you can change the font used, by selecting Format ➪ Font. Be aware that selective formatting isn't allowed (unlike in Excel); changing the font affects all the data in the data pane.

Sorting data

If you need to view the data in the data pane in a different order, choose Records ➪ Sort (or click the Sort Ascending or Sort Descending toolbar icon).

Learning more

This chapter isn't intended to cover every aspect of Microsoft Query. Rather, it discusses the basic features that are used most often. In fact, if you use Query Wizard, you may never need to interact with Query itself. But, if you do need to use Query, you can experiment and consult the online Help to learn more. As with anything related to Excel, the best way to master Query is to use it — preferably with data that's meaningful to you.

Summary

This chapter introduces Microsoft Query — a standalone application that can be executed by Excel. Use Query to retrieve data from external database files. You can specify the criteria, and Query returns the data to your Excel worksheet.

✦   ✦   ✦

Analyzing Data with Pivot Tables

C H A P T E R

35

Excel provides many data analysis tools, but the pivot table feature may be the most useful overall. Pivot tables are valuable for summarizing information that is contained in a database, which can be stored in a worksheet or in an external file.

This chapter demonstrates this innovative feature and suggests how you can use it to view your data in ways that you may not have imagined.

What Is a Pivot Table?

A *pivot table* provides a dynamic summary of data that is contained in a database or list. A pivot table enables you to create frequency distributions and cross-tabulations of several different data dimensions. In addition, you can display subtotals and any level of detail that you want. But, as explained later in this chapter, a pivot table *isn't* appropriate for all databases.

The best way to understand the concept of a pivot table is to see one. Start with Figure 35-1, which shows the data that is being used to create the pivot table in this chapter.

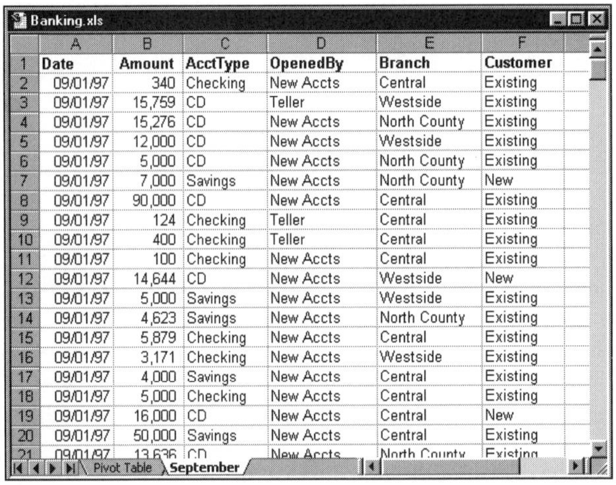
Banking.xls

	A	B	C	D	E	F
1	Date	Amount	AcctType	OpenedBy	Branch	Customer
2	09/01/97	340	Checking	New Accts	Central	Existing
3	09/01/97	15,759	CD	Teller	Westside	Existing
4	09/01/97	15,276	CD	New Accts	North County	Existing
5	09/01/97	12,000	CD	New Accts	Westside	Existing
6	09/01/97	5,000	CD	New Accts	North County	Existing
7	09/01/97	7,000	Savings	New Accts	North County	New
8	09/01/97	90,000	CD	New Accts	Central	Existing
9	09/01/97	124	Checking	Teller	Central	Existing
10	09/01/97	400	Checking	Teller	Central	Existing
11	09/01/97	100	Checking	New Accts	Central	Existing
12	09/01/97	14,644	CD	New Accts	Westside	New
13	09/01/97	5,000	Savings	New Accts	Westside	Existing
14	09/01/97	4,623	Savings	New Accts	North County	Existing
15	09/01/97	5,879	Checking	New Accts	Central	Existing
16	09/01/97	3,171	Checking	New Accts	Westside	Existing
17	09/01/97	4,000	Savings	New Accts	Central	Existing
18	09/01/97	5,000	Checking	New Accts	Central	Existing
19	09/01/97	16,000	CD	New Accts	Central	New
20	09/01/97	50,000	Savings	New Accts	Central	Existing
21	09/01/97	13,636	CD	New Accts	North County	Existing

Pivot Table / September

Figure 35-1: This database is used to create a pivot table.

This database consists of daily new-account information for a three-branch bank. The database contains 350 records and tracks:

- ✦ The date that each account was opened
- ✦ The opening amount
- ✦ The account type (CD, checking, savings, or IRA)
- ✦ Who opened the account (a teller or a new-account representative)
- ✦ The branch at which it was opened
- ✦ Whether a new customer or an existing customer opened the account

On the CD-ROM

You can find this workbook on this book's CD-ROM; it is used in many examples throughout the chapter.

The bank database contains a lot of information, but it's not all that revealing, because, in its present form, the information is difficult to understand. If the data were summarized, it would be more useful. Summarizing a database is essentially the process of answering questions about the data. Here are a few questions that may be of interest to the bank's management:

- ✦ What is the total deposit amount for each branch, broken down by account type?
- ✦ How many accounts were opened at each branch, broken down by account type?

- ✦ What's the dollar distribution of the different account types?
- ✦ What types of accounts do tellers most often open?
- ✦ How is the Central branch doing compared to the other two branches?
- ✦ Which branch opens the most accounts for new customers?

You can use a pivot table to answer questions like these. It takes only a few seconds and doesn't require a single formula.

Figure 35-2 shows a pivot table created from the database that is displayed in Figure 35-1. This pivot table shows the amount of new deposits, broken down by branch and account type. This summary is one of hundreds that you can produce from this data.

Sum of Amount	Branch			
AcctType	Central	North County	Westside	Grand Total
CD	859,438	830,139	344,962	2,034,539
Checking	208,208	92,225	90,597	391,030
IRA	63,380	134,374	10,000	207,754
Savings	332,349	152,607	154,000	638,956
Grand Total	1,463,375	1,209,345	599,559	3,272,279

Figure 35-2: A simple pivot table

Figure 35-3 shows another pivot table that is generated from the bank data. This pivot table uses a page field for the Customer item. In this case, the pivot table displays the data only for new customers. Notice that the orientation of the table is changed. (Branches appear in rows and AcctType appears in columns.)

Customer	New				
Sum of Amount	AcctType				
Branch	CD	Checking	IRA	Savings	Grand Total
Central	123,149	49,228	-	70,600	242,977
North County	152,500	20,070	9,000	39,607	221,177
Westside	71,437	7,419	-	500	79,356
Grand Total	347,086	76,717	9,000	110,707	543,510

Figure 35-3: A pivot table that uses a page field

Data Appropriate for a Pivot Table

Before getting into the details of pivot tables, you need to understand the type of data that's relevant to this feature. The data that you're summarizing must be in the form of a database (although an exception to this does exist, which is discussed later in the chapter). You can store the database in either a worksheet (such a database is sometimes known as a table) or an external database file. Although Excel can convert any database to a pivot table, not all databases benefit.

Generally speaking, fields in a database table can be one of two types:

✦ **Data:** Contains a value. In Figure 35-1, the Amount field is a data field.

✦ **Category:** Describes the data. In Figure 35-1, the Date, AcctType, OpenedBy, Branch, and Customer fields are category fields, because they describe the data in the Amount field.

Pivot Table Terminology

If you're new to Excel, the concept of a pivot table may be a bit baffling. As far as I know, Microsoft invented the name *pivot table*. Understanding the terminology associated with pivot tables is important. Refer to the accompanying figure to get your bearings.

✦ **Column field:** A field that has a column orientation in the pivot table. Each item in the field occupies a column. In the figure, Customer is a column field, and it has two items (Existing and New). Column fields can be nested.

✦ **Data area:** The cells in a pivot table that contain the summary data. Excel offers several ways to summarize the data (sum, average, count, and so on). In the figure, the Data area includes C5:E20.

✦ **Grand totals:** A row or column that displays totals for all cells in a row or column in a pivot table. You can specify that grand totals be calculated for rows, columns, or both (or neither). The pivot table in the figure has grand totals for rows and columns.

✦ **Group:** A collection of items that are treated as a single item. You can group items manually or automatically (group dates into months, for example).

✦ **Item:** An element in a field that appears as a row or column header in a pivot table. In the figure, Existing and New are items for the Customer field. The Branch field has three items: Central, North County, and Westside. AcctType has four items: CD, Checking, IRA, and Savings.

✦ **Page field:** A field that has a page orientation in the pivot table — similar to a slice of a three-dimensional cube. Only one item in a page field can be displayed at one time. In the figure, OpenedBy is a page field that's displaying the NewAccts item; the pivot table shows data only for NewAccts.

✦ **Refresh:** To recalculate the pivot table after changes to the source data have been made.

✦ **Row field:** A field that has a row orientation in the pivot table. Each item in the field occupies a row. Row fields can be nested. In the figure, Branch and AcctType are both row fields.

✦ **Source data:** The data used to create a pivot table. It can reside in a worksheet or an external database.

✦ **Subtotals:** A row or column that displays subtotals for detail cells in a row or column in a pivot table.

	A	B	C	D	E	F	G	H
1	OpenedBy	New Accts ▼						
2								
3	Sum of Amount		Customer ▼					
4	Branch ▼	AcctType ▼	Existing	New	Grand Total			
5	Central	CD	671289	123149	794438			
6		Checking	156884	49228	206112			
7		IRA	27000		27000			
8		Savings	239347	70600	309947			
9	Central Total		1094520	242977	1337497			
10	North County	CD	646184	152500	798684			
11		Checking	55880	20070	75950			
12		IRA	35554	7000	42554			
13		Savings	87136	39607	126743			
14	North County Total		824754	219177	1043931			
15	Westside	CD	143766	71437	215203			
16		Checking	52978	7419	60397			
17		IRA	10000		10000			
18		Savings	153500	500	154000			
19	Westside Total		360244	79356	439600			
20	Grand Total		2279518	541510	2821028			
21								

Banking.xls — Terminology / September / Central / North County

A single database table can have any number of data fields and category fields. When you create a pivot table, you usually want to summarize one or more of the data fields. The values in the category fields, on the other hand, appear in the pivot table as rows, columns, or pages.

Exceptions exist, however, and you may find that Excel's pivot table feature is useful even for databases that don't contain actual numerical data fields. The database in Figure 35-4, for example, doesn't contain numerical data fields, but you can create a useful pivot table that counts fields rather than sums them.

Employee	Month Born	Sex
Miller	September	Female
Santos	February	Female
Alios	June	Male
Chan	December	Female
Henderson	March	Male
Klinger	July	Female
Rosarita	June	Male
Fuller	February	Male
Wilson	January	Female
Quigley	July	Male
Ross-Jacobs	April	Male
Ocarina	August	Female
Yulanderpol	November	Female
Franklin	June	Female

Figure 35-4: This database doesn't have any numerical fields, but you can use it to generate a pivot table.

You can summarize information in pivot tables by using methods other than summing. For example, the pivot table that you see in Figure 35-5 cross-tabulates the Month Born field by the Sex field, and the intersecting cells show the count for each combination of city and sex.

Count of Employee	Sex		
Month Born	Female	Male	Grand Total
January	2	2	4
February	2	2	4
March	0	5	5
April	1	2	3
May	2	0	2
June	3	3	6
July	3	2	5
August	3	2	5
September	4	0	4
October	2	2	4
November	3	1	4
December	2	2	4
Grand Total	27	23	50

Figure 35-5: This pivot table summarizes nonnumeric fields by displaying a count rather than a sum.

Creating a Pivot Table

This section walks you through the steps to create a pivot table by using the PivotTable and PivotChart Wizard. You access the PivotTable and PivotChart Wizard by choosing Data ➪ PivotTable and PivotChart Report.

This section uses the banking account workbook, which is available on this book's CD-ROM.

Identifying where the data is located

When you choose Data ⇨ PivotTable and PivotChart Report, the first of several dialog boxes appears (see Figure 35-6).

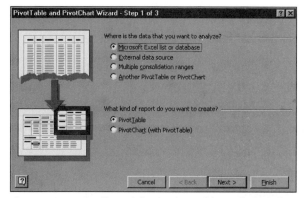

Figure 35-6: The first of three PivotTable and PivotChart Wizard dialog boxes

In this step, you identify the data source. The possible data sources are described in the following sections.

You see different dialog boxes while you work through the Wizard, depending on the location of the data that you want to analyze. The following sections present the Wizard dialog boxes for data located in an Excel list or database, in the context of describing the various possible data sources.

Excel list or database

Usually, the data that you analyze is stored in a worksheet database — which is also known as a *list*. Databases stored in a worksheet are limited to 65,535 records and 356 fields. Working with a database of this size isn't efficient, however (and memory may not even allow it). The first row in the database should be field names. No other rules exist. The data can consist of values, text, or formulas.

External data source

If you use the data in an external database for a pivot table, the data is retrieved by using Query (a separate application). You can use dBASE files, SQL server data, or other data that your system is set up to access. You are prompted for the data source in Step 2 of the PivotTable and PivotChart Wizard.

Chapter 34 discusses external database access, including Query. If you plan to create a pivot table by using data in an external database, you should consult Chapter 34 before proceeding.

Pivot Tables and OLAP Cubes

In Chapter 34, the sidebar, "OLAP Databases" explains that OLAP (*online analytical processing*) presents a new way to organize large databases, to suit the way that you analyze and manage information. In an OLAP database, data is organized by level of detail, and the various aspects of data contained in an OLAP database are called *dimensions.* Because you combine dimensions to obtain information, OLAP databases are called *cubes.*

Generally, creating pivot tables in Excel from OLAP databases is faster than creating pivot tables from other types of external databases, because the OLAP server, not Excel, computes summarized values. Excel, therefore, receives less data from an OLAP cube when you create a pivot table or pivot chart.

Excel contains OLAP Cube Wizard, which helps you to organize data from external relational databases into OLAP cubes. Excel also contains Offline Cube Wizard, which enables you to create cube files that you can query even when you're not connected to your network. Distribute cube files over a network or on the Web to provide access to part, but not all, of a database.

You can create cube files only if you use an OLAP provider that supports creating cube files, such as Microsoft DSS Analysis server.

Multiple consolidation ranges

You also can create a pivot table from multiple tables. This procedure is equivalent to consolidating the information in the tables. When you create a pivot table to consolidate information in tables, you have the added advantage of using all of the pivot table tools while you work with the consolidated data. (An example of this is presented later in the chapter.)

Chapter 24 discusses other consolidation techniques.

Another pivot table

Excel enables you to create a pivot table from an existing pivot table. Actually, this is a bit of a misnomer. The pivot table that you create is based on the *data* that the first pivot table uses (not the pivot table itself). If the active workbook has no pivot tables, this option is grayed, meaning you can't choose it.

Tip   If you need to create more than one pivot table from the same set of data, the procedure is more efficient (in terms of memory usage) if you create the first pivot
table and then use that pivot table as the source for subsequent pivot tables.

Specifying the data

To move on to the next step of the Wizard, click the Next button. Step 2 of the
PivotTable and PivotChart Wizard prompts you for the data. Remember, the dialog
box varies, depending on your choice in the first dialog box; Figure 35-7 shows the
dialog box that appears when you select an Excel list or database in Step 1.

Figure 35-7: In Step 2, you specify the
data range.

Tip   If you place the cell pointer anywhere within the worksheet database when you
select Data ➪ PivotTable Report, Excel identifies the database range automatically
in Step 2 of the PivotTable and PivotChart Wizard.

You can use the Browse button to open a different worksheet and select a range. To
move on to Step 3, click the Next button.

Completing the Pivot Table

The following sections outline how to complete the pivot table. The first step is
to determine the pivot table's location. The dialog box for the final step of the
PivotTable and PivotChart Wizard is shown in Figure 35-8. In this step, you specify
the location for the pivot table.

Figure 35-8: In Step 3, you specify the pivot table's location.

If you select the New worksheet option, Excel inserts a new worksheet for the pivot table. If you select the Existing worksheet option, the pivot table appears on the current worksheet (you can specify the starting cell location).

Pivot table options

You can click the Options button to select some options that determine how the table appears. Refer to the sidebar "Pivot Table Options," later in this chapter. Click OK to redisplay the PivotTable and PivotChart Wizard – Step 3 of 3 dialog box.

Setting up the layout of the pivot table

You can set up the layout of the pivot table in two different ways: either by using the PivotTable and PivotChart Wizard or by using the PivotTable toolbar directly on the worksheet.

Using a dialog box to lay out a pivot table

Click the Layout button of the last Wizard dialog box to see the dialog box shown in Figure 35-9. The fields in the database appear as buttons along the right side of the dialog box. Simply drag the buttons to the appropriate area of the pivot table diagram.

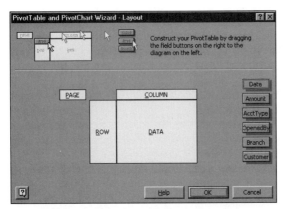

Figure 35-9: Specify the table layout.

The pivot table diagram has four areas

- ✦ **Page:** Values in the field appear as page items in the pivot table.
- ✦ **Row:** Values in the field appear as row items in the pivot table.
- ✦ **Data:** The field is summarized in the pivot table.
- ✦ **Column:** Values in the field appear as column items in the pivot table.

You can drag as many field buttons as you want to any of these locations, and you don't have to use all the fields. Any fields that you don't use simply don't appear in the pivot table.

When you drag a field button to the Data area, the PivotTable and PivotChart Wizard applies the Sum function if the field contains numeric values, and the Count function if the field contains nonnumeric values.

While you're setting up the pivot table, you can double-click a field button to customize it. You can specify, for example, that a particular field be summarized as a Count or other function. You also can specify which items in a field to hide or omit. Be aware, however, that you can customize fields at any time after the pivot table is created; this is demonstrated later in this chapter.

If you drag a field button to an incorrect location, just drag it off the table diagram to get rid of it.

Figure 35-10 shows how the dialog box looks after some field buttons were dragged to the pivot table diagram. This pivot table displays the sum of the Amount field, broken down by AcctType (as rows) and Customer (as columns). In addition, the Branch field appears as a page field. Click OK to redisplay the PivotTable and PivotChart Wizard – Step 3 of 3 dialog box.

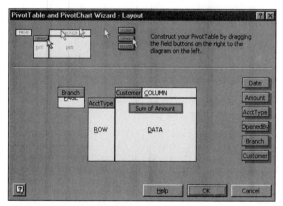

Figure 35-10: The table layout after dragging field buttons to the pivot table diagram

Laying out a pivot table by using the PivotTable toolbar

Starting in Excel 2000, you can lay out a pivot table directly in a worksheet by using the PivotTable toolbar. The technique is very similar to the one just described, because you still drag and drop fields.

The PivotTable toolbar is new to Excel 2000.

Complete the first two steps of the PivotTable and PivotChart Wizard. If you want, set options for the pivot table by using the Options button that appears in the third dialog box of the Wizard. Don't bother with the Layout button, however. Select a location for the pivot table and choose Finish. Excel displays a pivot table template similar to the one you see in Figure 35-11. The template provides you with hints about where to drop various types of fields.

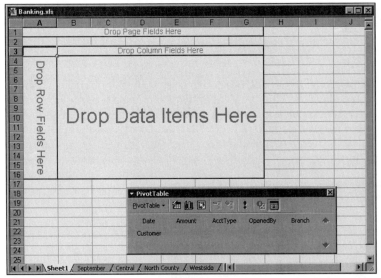

Figure 35-11: Use the PivotTable toolbar to drag and drop fields onto the pivot table template that Excel displays.

Drag and drop fields from the PivotTable toolbar onto the template. As you point at buttons on the toolbar, you'll see tool tips that instruct you to drag the field to the template. Excel continues to update the pivot table as you drag and drop fields; for this reason, you'll find this method easiest to use if you drag and drop data items last.

If you make a mistake, simply drag the field off the template and drop it anyplace on the worksheet — Excel removes it from the pivot table template. All fields remain on the PivotTable toolbar, even if you use them.

The finished product

When you click the Finish button in this last Wizard dialog box, Excel creates the PivotTable. Figure 35-12 shows the result of this example.

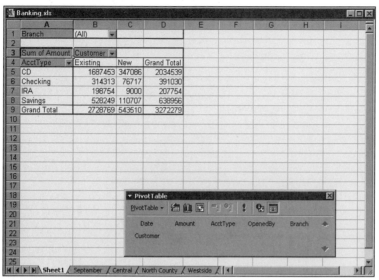

Figure 35-12: The pivot table that is created by the PivotTable and PivotChart Wizard

Notice that the page field is displayed as a drop-down box. You can choose which item in the page field to display by choosing it from the list. You also can choose an item called All, which displays all the data.

Pivot Table Options

Excel provides plenty of options that determine how your pivot table looks and works. To access these options, click the Options button in the final step of the PivotTable and PivotChart Wizard. You can also access this dialog box after you create the pivot table. Right-click any cell in the pivot table and then select Options from the shortcut menu. The accompanying figure shows the PivotTable Options dialog box.

The PivotTable Options dialog box contains the following choices:

✦ **Name:** You can provide a name for the pivot table. Excel provides default names in the form of PivotTable1, PivotTable2, and so on.

✦ **Grand totals for columns:** Check this box if you want Excel to calculate grand totals for items that are displayed in columns.

✦ **Grand totals for rows:** Check this box if you want Excel to calculate grand totals for items that are displayed in rows.

✦ **AutoFormat table:** Check this box if you want Excel to apply one of its AutoFormats to the pivot table. Excel uses the AutoFormat even if you rearrange the table layout.

Continued

(continued)

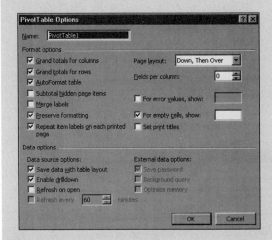

✦ **Subtotal hidden page items:** Check this box if you want Excel to include hidden items in the page fields in the subtotals.

✦ **Merge labels:** Check this box if you want Excel to merge the cells for outer row and column labels. Doing so may make the table more readable.

✦ **Preserve formatting:** Check this box if you want Excel, when it updates the pivot table, to keep any of the formatting that you applied.

✦ **Repeat item labels on each printed page:** Check this box to set row titles that appear on each page when you print a PivotTable report.

✦ **Page layout:** You can specify the order in which you want the page fields to appear.

✦ **Fields per column:** You can specify the number of page fields to show before starting another row of page fields.

✦ **For error values, show:** You can specify a value to show for pivot table cells that display an error.

✦ **For empty cells, show:** You can specify a value to show for pivot table cells that are empty.

✦ **Set print titles:** Check this box to set column titles that appear at the top of each page when you print a PivotTable report.

✦ **Save data with table layout:** If you check this option, Excel stores an additional copy of the data (called a *pivot table cache*), enabling Excel to recalculate the table more quickly when you change the layout. If memory is an issue, you should keep this option unchecked (updating is then a bit slower).

✦ **Enable drilldown:** If checked, you can double-click a cell in the pivot table to view details.

✦ **Refresh on open:** If checked, the pivot table is refreshed whenever you open the workbook.

✦ **Refresh every** *x* **minutes:** If you are connected to an external database, you can specify how often you want the pivot table refreshed while the workbook is open.

✦ **Save password:** If you use an external database that requires a password, you can store the password as part of the query, so that you don't have to reenter it.

✦ **Background query:** If checked, Excel runs the external database query in the background while you continue your work.

✦ **Optimize memory:** This option reduces the amount of memory that is used when you refresh an external database query.

Working with Pivot Tables

After you create a pivot table, it's not a static object. You can continue to modify and tweak it until it looks exactly how you want it to look. This section discusses modifications that you can make to a pivot table.

You'll find the PivotTable toolbar quite useful when you work with pivot tables. This toolbar appears automatically when you activate a worksheet that contains a pivot table.

Changing the Pivot Table structure

Notice that a pivot table, when displayed in a worksheet, includes the field buttons. You can drag any of the field buttons to a new position in the pivot table (known as *pivoting*). For example, you can drag a column field to the row position. Excel immediately redisplays the pivot table to reflect your change. You also can change the order of the row fields or the column fields by dragging the buttons. This action affects how Excel nests the fields and can have a dramatic effect on the appearance of the table.

Figure 35-13 shows the pivot table that was created in the preceding example, after making a modification to the table's structure. The page field button (Branch) has been dragged to the row position. The pivot table now shows details for each item in the AcctType field for each branch.

Describing how to change the layout of a pivot table is more difficult than doing it. I suggest that you create a pivot table and experiment by dragging around field buttons to see what happens.

	A	B	C	D	E	F
	Banking.xls					
1						
2						
3	Sum of Amount		Customer			
4	Branch	AcctType	Existing	New	Grand Total	
5	Central	CD	736,289	123,149	859,438	
6		Checking	158,980	49,228	208,208	
7		IRA	63,380		63,380	
8		Savings	261,749	70,600	332,349	
9	Central Total		1,220,398	242,977	1,463,375	
10	North County	CD	677,639	152,500	830,139	
11		Checking	72,155	20,070	92,225	
12		IRA	125,374	9,000	134,374	
13		Savings	113,000	39,607	152,607	
14	North County Total		988,168	221,177	1,209,345	
15	Westside	CD	273,525	71,437	344,962	
16		Checking	83,178	7,419	90,597	
17		IRA	10,000		10,000	
18		Savings	153,500	500	154,000	
19	Westside Total		520,203	79,356	599,559	
20	Grand Total		2,728,769	543,510	3,272,279	
21						

Sheet1 / September

Figure 35-13: This pivot table has two row fields.

Note   A pivot table is a special type of range, and (with a few exceptions) you can't make any changes to it. For example, you can't insert or delete rows, edit results, or move cells. If you attempt to do so, Excel displays an appropriate error message.

Removing a field

To remove a field from a pivot table, click the field button and drag it away from the pivot table. The mouse pointer changes to include a button with an X across it. Release the mouse button, and Excel updates the table to exclude the field.

Adding a new field

To add a new field to the pivot table, select any field in the pivot table. Then, drag the field that you want to add from the PivotTable toolbar onto the pivot table. Excel updates the pivot table with the new field.

You also can add fields from the PivotTable and PivotChart Wizard; choose Data ➪ PivotTable and PivotChart Report to start the Wizard.

Refreshing a Pivot Table

Notice that pivot tables don't contain formulas. Rather, Excel recalculates the pivot table every time that you make a change to it. If the source database is large, some delay may occur while this recalculation takes place, but for small databases, the update is virtually instantaneous.

In some cases, you may change the source data. When this happens, Excel doesn't update the pivot table automatically. Rather, you must refresh it manually. To refresh a pivot table, you can use any of the following methods:

✦ Choose Data ➭ Refresh Data

✦ Right-click anywhere in the pivot table and select Refresh Data from the shortcut menu

✦ Click the Refresh Data tool on the PivotTable toolbar

Customizing a Pivot Table field

Several options are available for fields within a pivot table. To access these options, simply double-click a field button (or right-click and select Field from the shortcut menu). Excel displays a PivotTable Field dialog box, like the one shown in Figure 35-14.

Figure 35-14: Double-clicking a PivotTable field button displays a dialog box like this one.

You can modify any of the following items:

✦ **Name:** Changes the name that is displayed on the field button. You can also make this change directly by editing the cell that holds the field button.

✦ **Orientation:** Changes how the field's items are displayed. You can also take the more direct approach of dragging the field button to another location, as described previously.

✦ **Subtotals:** Lets you change the type of subtotaling that is displayed. Subtotaling is relevant only if you have more than one field displayed as rows or columns. You can make a multiple selection in the list box, which results in more than one line of subtotals. To eliminate subtotals, click the None option.

✦ **Hide items:** Enables you to hide (not display) one or more items from a field. Click the specific item names that you want to hide.

Excel includes some additional field options that you can specify by clicking the Advanced button in the PivotTable Field dialog box. These options let you specify how the field items are sorted and how many items to show (for example, just the top ten).

Formatting a Pivot Table

When you create a pivot table, Excel, by default, applies an AutoFormat to the table (you can change this by clicking the Options button in Step 3). After Excel creates the pivot table, you can always specify a different AutoFormat. Place the cell pointer in the pivot table and click the Format Report tool on the PivotTable toolbar. Excel displays the AutoFormat dialog box. Select an AutoFormat and click OK.

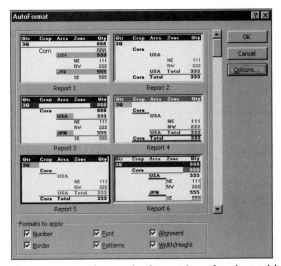

Figure 35-15: Change the formatting of a pivot table.

To change the number format for the pivot table data, use the following procedure:

1. Select any cell in the pivot table's Data area.

2. Right-click and choose PivotTable Field Settings from the shortcut menu. Excel displays its PivotTable Field dialog box.

3. Click the Number button.

4. Select the number format that you want to use.

Tip   If you want Excel to preserve all the formatting that you perform on individual cells, make sure that the Preserve formatting option is turned on. You do this in the PivotTable Options dialog box (right-click a cell and select Table Options from the shortcut menu). If this option is not turned on, Excel returns the formats to the default formats when you refresh the pivot table.

Grouping Pivot Table items

Grouping pivot table items is a handy feature that enables you to group specific items in a field. If one of the fields in your database consists of dates, for example, the pivot table displays a separate row or column for every date. You may find that grouping the dates into months or quarters and then hiding the details is more useful. Fortunately, this is easy to do.

Figure 35-16 shows a pivot table that was created using the bank database. It shows total balances for each AcctType (column field) by the Branch (row field). To create a report that compares the Central branch to the other two branches combined, create a group that consists of the Westside and North County branches.

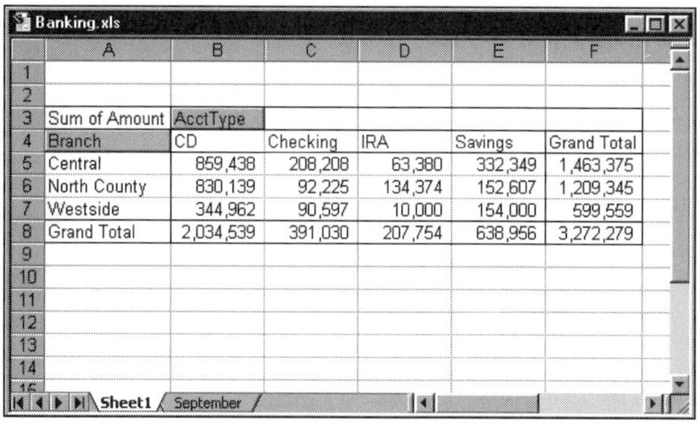

Figure 35-16: This version of the pivot table shows balances for each account type, by branch.

To create the group, select the cells that you want to group — in this case, A6:A7. Then, choose Data ➪ Group and Outline ➪ GroupPivotTable. Excel creates a new field called Branch2, which has two items: Central and Group1 (see Figure 35-17). At this point, you can remove the original Branch field (drag away the field button) and change the names of the field and the items. Figure 35-18 shows the pivot table after making these modifications.

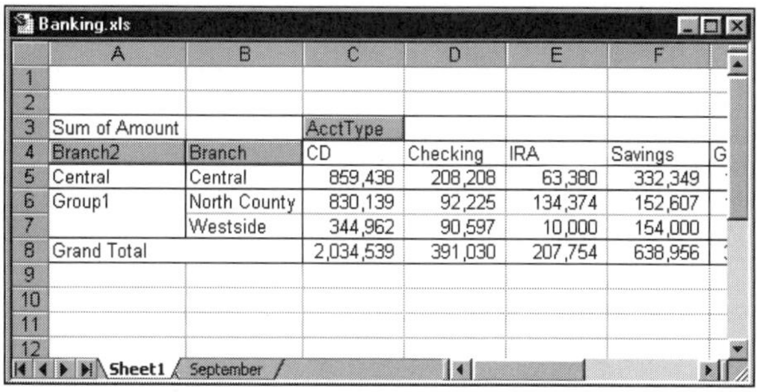

Figure 35-17: The pivot table after grouping the North County and Westside branches

Banking.xls

	A	B	C	D	E	F
1						
2						
3	Sum of Amount	AcctType				
4	Branch2	CD	Checking	IRA	Savings	Grand Total
5	Central	859,438	208,208	63,380	332,349	1,463,375
6	WS & NC	1,175,101	182,822	144,374	306,607	1,808,904
7	Grand Total	2,034,539	391,030	207,754	638,956	3,272,279
8						
9						
10						
11						
12						

Sheet1 / September /

Figure 35-18: The pivot table after removing the original Branch field and renaming the new field and items

Note   The new field name can't be an existing field name. If it is, Excel adds the field to the pivot table. In this example, you can't rename Branch2 to Branch.

Tip   If the items that you want to group are not adjacent to each other, you can make a multiple selection by pressing Ctrl and selecting the items that make up the group.

If the field items that you want to group consist of values, dates, or times, you can let Excel do the grouping for you. Figure 35-19 shows part of another pivot table that was generated from the bank database. This time, Amount is used for the row field and AcctType for the column field. The Data area shows the count for each combination. This report isn't useful, because the Amount field contains so many different items. The report can be salvaged, however, by grouping the items into bins.

Banking.xls

	A	B	C	D	E	F
1						
2						
3	Count of Amount	AcctType				
4	Amount	CD	Checking	IRA	Savings	Grand Total
5	100	0	16	0	0	16
6	124	0	4	0	0	4
7	133	0	4	0	0	4
8	200	0	3	0	3	6
9	240	0	9	0	0	9
10	245	0	1	0	0	1
11	250	0	0	0	3	3
12	275	0	1	0	0	1
13	340	0	1	0	0	1
14	344	0	3	0	0	3
15	400	0	7	0	0	7
16	500	0	2	0	8	10
17	600	0	0	0	5	5
18	1,000	0	7	0	1	8
19	1,325	0	2	0	0	2
20	1,946	0	2	0	0	2
21	2,000	3	0	6	0	9
22	2,749	0	5	0	0	5

Sheet1 / September /

Figure 35-19: This isn't a useful pivot table report, because the Amount field contains too many different items.

To create groups automatically, select any item in the Amount field. Then, choose Data ➪ Group and Outline ➪ Group. Excel displays the Grouping dialog box, shown in Figure 35-20. By default, it shows the smallest and largest values — but you can change these to whatever you want. To create groups of $5,000 increments, enter **0** for the Starting at value, **100000** for the Ending at value, and **5000** for the By value (as shown in Figure 35-20). Click OK, and Excel creates the groups. Figure 35-21 shows the result, which is much more meaningful than the ungrouped data.

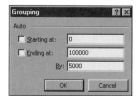

Figure 35-20: The Grouping dialog box instructs Excel to create groups automatically.

Count of Amount	AcctType				
Amount	CD	Checking	IRA	Savings	Grand Total
0-4999	3	127	6	36	172
5000-9999	4	18	13	31	66
10000-14999	56	2	8	1	67
15000-19999	19	0	0	2	21
20000-24999	0	0	0	1	1
25000-29999	1	0	0	1	2
30000-34999	0	0	0	2	2
35000-39999	2	0	0	0	2
40000-44999	0	0	0	1	1
45000-49999	1	0	0	0	1
50000-54999	4	0	0	1	5
65000-69999	0	0	0	2	2
75000-79999	5	0	0	0	5
90000-94999	3	0	0	0	3
Grand Total	98	147	27	78	350

Figure 35-21: The pivot table after grouping the Amount field items

Seeing the details

Each cell in the Data area of a pivot table represents several records in the source database. You may be interested in seeing exactly which fields contribute to a summary value in the pivot table. Using the banking example, you may want to see a list of the records that constitute the total CD accounts in the Central branch. To do so, double-click the appropriate summary cell in the Data area. Excel creates a new worksheet with the records that were used to create the summary. Figure 35-22 shows an example.

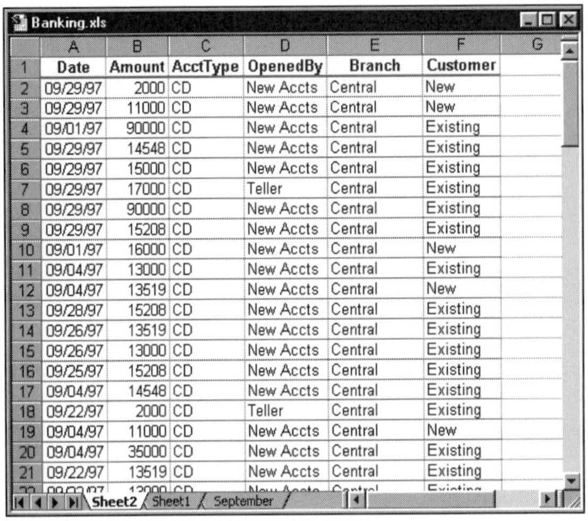

Figure 35-22: Double-clicking a cell in the Data area of a pivot table generates a new worksheet with the underlying data.

Note   If double-clicking a cell doesn't work, make sure that the Enable drilldown option is turned on in the PivotTable Options dialog box (right-click a pivot table cell and select Options from the shortcut menu).

Displaying a Pivot Table on different sheets

If your pivot table displays a field in the Page position, you can see only one sliceof the data at a time, by using the drop-down list box. Excel has an option, however, that puts each item from a page field on a separate sheet, creating a three-dimensional block of data. Click the PivotTable button on the PivotTable toolbar and choose Show Pages from the shortcut menu (or right-click the pivot table and select Show Pages from the shortcut menu). Excel displays the Show Pages dialog box, shown in Figure 35-23, which lists the page fields in your PivotTable. Select the fields that you want, and Excel inserts enough new sheets to accommodate each item in that field.

Figure 35-23: The Show Pages dialog box enables you to display each page field item on a separate worksheet.

Inserting a calculated field into a Pivot Table

As previously noted, a pivot table is a special type of data range, and you can't insert new rows or columns into a pivot table. This means that you can't insert formulas to perform calculations with the data in a pivot table. However, you can create calculated fields for a pivot table. A *calculated field* consists of a calculation that can involve other fields.

Note You cannot create a calculated field in a pivot table that is based on an OLAP database.

In the banking example, for instance, assume that management wants to increase deposits by 15 percent and wants to compare the projected deposits to the current deposits. In this situation, you can use a calculated field. Calculated fields must reside in the Data area of the pivot table (you can't use them in the Page, Row, or Column areas).

Use the following procedure to create a calculated field that consists of the Amount field multiplied by 1.15 (that is, a 15 percent increase):

1. Move the cell pointer anywhere within the pivot table.

2. Right-click and choose Formulas ➪ Calculated Field from the shortcut menu. Excel displays the Insert Calculated Field dialog box, shown in Figure 35-24.

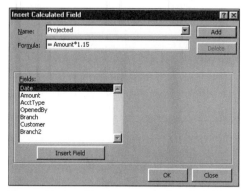

Figure 35-24: The Insert Calculated Field dialog box

3. Enter a descriptive name for the field and specify the formula. The formula can use other fields, but can't use worksheet functions. For this example, the name is Projected, and the formula is the following:

   =Amount*1.15

4. Click Add to add this new field.

5. To create additional calculated fields, repeat Steps 3 and 4. Click OK to close the dialog box.

After you create the field, Excel adds it to the Data area of the pivot table. You can treat it just like any other field, with one exception: you can't move it to the Page, Row, or Column area (it must remain in the Data area). Figure 35-25 shows a pivot table with a calculated field (called Projected).

		OpenedBy		
Branch	(All)			
		OpenedBy		
Customer	Data	New Accts	Teller	Grand Total
Existing	Sum of Amount	2,279,518	449,251	2,728,769
	Sum of Projected	2,621,446	516,639	3,138,084
New	Sum of Amount	541,510	2,000	543,510
	Sum of Projected	622,737	2,300	625,037
Total Sum of Amount		2,821,028	451,251	3,272,279
Total Sum of Projected		3,244,182	518,939	3,763,121

Figure 35-25: This pivot table uses a calculated field.

Tip The formulas that you develop can also use worksheet functions, but the functions cannot refer to cells or named ranges.

Inserting a calculated item into a Pivot Table

The previous section explains how to create a calculated field. Excel also enables you to create *calculated items* for a pivot table field. For example, if you have a field named Months, you can create a calculated item (called Q1, for example) that displays the sum of January, February, and March. You can also do this by grouping the items—but using grouping hides the individual months and shows only the total of the group. Creating a calculated item for quarterly totals shows the total and the individual months. Calculated items must reside in the Page, Row, or Column area of a pivot table (you can't use calculated items in the Data area).

Note You can't create a calculated item in a pivot table based on an OLAP database.

In the banking example, management may want to look at CD accounts combined with savings accounts; you can show this information by creating a calculated item. To create a calculated item, use these steps:

1. Move the cell pointer to a Row, Column, or Page area of the pivot table. The cell pointer cannot be in the Data area.

2. Right-click and choose Formulas ⇨ Calculated Item from the shortcut menu. Excel displays the Insert Calculated Item dialog box, as shown in Figure 35-26.

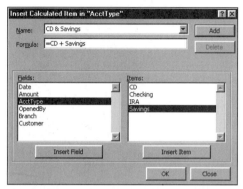

Figure 35-26: The Insert Calculated Item dialog box

3. Enter a name for the new item and specify the formula. The formula can use items in other fields, but can't use worksheet functions. For this example, the new item is named **CD & Savings**, and the formula is as follows:

```
=CD + Savings
```

4. Click Add.

5. Repeat Steps 3 and 4 to create additional items. Click OK to close the dialog box.

After you create the item, it appears in the pivot table. Figure 35-27 shows the pivot table after adding a calculated item.

	A	B	C	D	E	F
1	Branch	(All)				
2						
3	Sum of Amount	Customer				
4	AcctType	Existing	New	Grand Total		
5	CD	1,687,453	347,086	2,034,539		
6	Checking	314,313	76,717	391,030		
7	IRA	198,754	9,000	207,754		
8	Savings	528,249	110,707	638,956		
9	CD & Savings	2,215,702	457,793	2,673,495		
10	Grand Total	4,944,471	1,001,303	5,945,774		

Figure 35-27: This pivot table uses a calculated item.

If you use a calculated item in your pivot table, you may need to turn off the Grand Total display, to avoid double-counting.

Pivot Table Examples

This section describes additional examples of pivot tables, to spark your creativity and help you apply some of these techniques to your own data.

The best way to master pivot tables is to work with them, using your own data—not just read about them.

On the CD-ROM   If you want to work with some prefab pivot tables, I've developed a few for you to use, which you can find on this book's CD-ROM.

Using a Pivot Table to consolidate sheets

Chapter 24 discusses several ways to consolidate data across different worksheets or workbooks. Excel's pivot table feature gives you yet another consolidation option. Figure 35-28 shows three worksheets, each containing monthly sales data for a store (three different stores) in a music store chain. The goal is to consolidate this information into a single pivot table. In this example, all the source data is in a single workbook, but you can consolidate data from different workbooks.

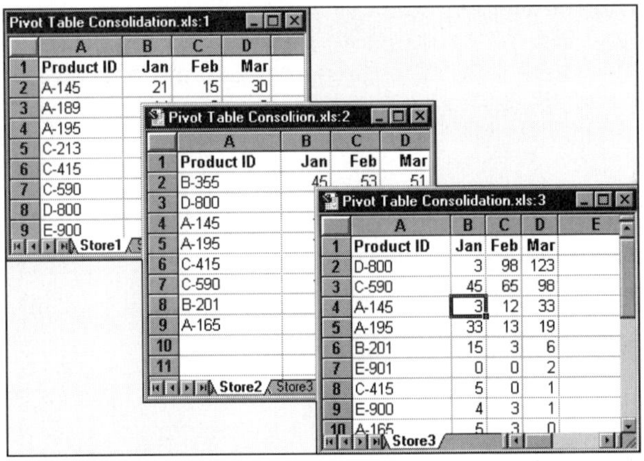

Figure 35-28: You can use a pivot table to consolidate these three worksheets.

On the CD-ROM   You can find this workbook on this book's CD-ROM.

Use the following steps to create this pivot table:

1. Start with a new worksheet named **Summary**.

2. Choose Data ➪ PivotTable and PivotChart Report, to display the PivotTable and PivotChart Wizard.

3. Select the Multiple Consolidation Ranges option and then click Next.
4. In Step 2a of the PivotTable Wizard, select the option labeled Create a single page field for me. Click Next.
5. In Step 2b, specify the ranges to be consolidated. The first range is **Store1!$A$1:$D$12** (you can enter this directly or point to it). Click Add to add this range to the All Ranges list.
6. Repeat this for the other two ranges (see Figure 35-29). Click Next to continue to Step 3.

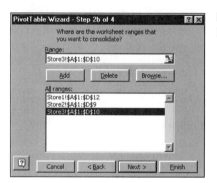

Figure 35-29: Step 2b of the PivotTable Wizard

7. The dialog box in Step 3 of the PivotTable Wizard should look familiar. Click Finish.

Figure 35-30 shows the pivot table. It uses generic names, which you can change to more meaningful names.

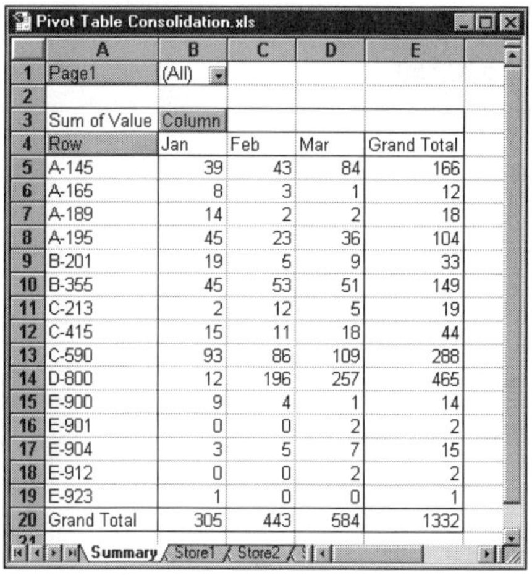
Pivot Table Consolidation.xls

	A	B	C	D	E
1	Page1	(All)			
2					
3	Sum of Value	Column			
4	Row	Jan	Feb	Mar	Grand Total
5	A-145	39	43	84	166
6	A-165	8	3	1	12
7	A-189	14	2	2	18
8	A-195	45	23	36	104
9	B-201	19	5	9	33
10	B-355	45	53	51	149
11	C-213	2	12	5	19
12	C-415	15	11	18	44
13	C-590	93	86	109	288
14	D-800	12	196	257	465
15	E-900	9	4	1	14
16	E-901	0	0	2	2
17	E-904	3	5	7	15
18	E-912	0	0	2	2
19	E-923	1	0	0	1
20	Grand Total	305	443	584	1332

Summary / Store1 / Store2

Figure 35-30: This pivot table uses data from three ranges.

In Step 2a of the PivotTable Wizard, you can choose the option labeled I will create the page fields. Doing so enables you to provide an item name for each item in the page field (rather than the generic Item1, Item2, and Item3).

Creating charts from a Pivot Table

A PivotChart report is a chart that is linked to a pivot table. By using the PivotTable and PivotChart Wizard, you can create simultaneously both a pivot table and a linked chart; you can use the techniques described earlier to drag and drop fields onto the pivot chart or the pivot table. To simultaneously create a pivot table and a pivot chart, choose PivotChart (with PivotTable) in the first dialog box of the PivotTable and PivotChart Wizard. Excel creates a new worksheet and a new chart sheet; both will contain templates for the pivot table and the pivot chart, respectively. Drag fields from the PivotTable toolbar onto either the chart or the table—simply switch between the sheets in the workbook to choose the sheet with which you want to work.

 EXCEL 2000   Pivot chart reports are a new feature of Excel 2000.

Although you can create a pivot chart by using the PivotTable and PivotChart Wizard, you'll find it easier to create the chart from an existing pivot table. While viewing the pivot table, click the Chart Wizard button on the PivotTable toolbar. Excel immediately creates a chart sheet in the workbook based on the pivot table. Figure 35-31 shows the pivot table used as the foundation for the pivot chart shown in Figure 35-32. Excel updates this chart whenever you make changes to the pivot table.

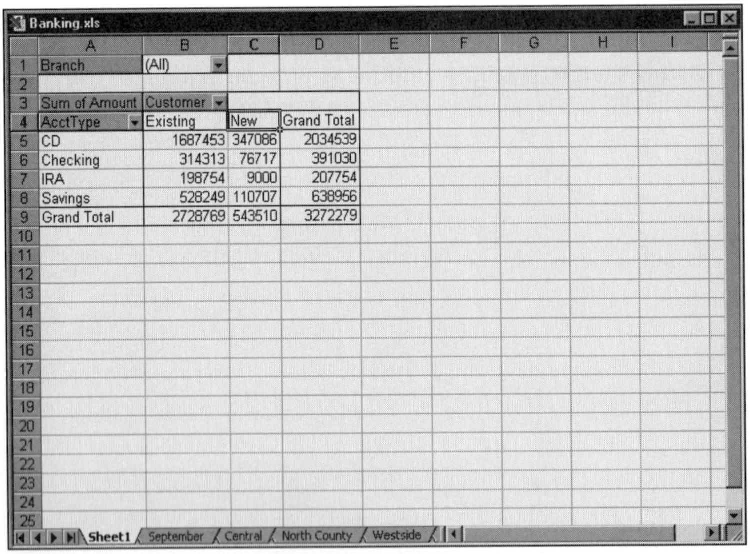

	A	B	C	D
1	Branch	(All)		
2				
3	Sum of Amount	Customer		
4	AcctType	Existing	New	Grand Total
5	CD	1687453	347086	2034539
6	Checking	314313	76717	391030
7	IRA	198754	9000	207754
8	Savings	528249	110707	638956
9	Grand Total	2728769	543510	3272279

Sheet1 / September / Central / North County / Westside

Figure 35-31: The pivot table from which the chart in Figure 35-32 was created

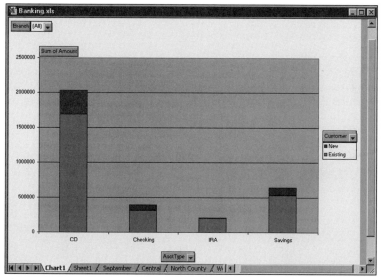

Figure 35-32: The chart changes based on the pivot table.

Tip

A pivot chart is always created on a separate Chart sheet. To convert the chart to an embedded chart on a worksheet, activate the Chart sheet and select Chart ⇨ Location. Select the second option (as object in) and specify a worksheet for the chart.

Analyzing survey data

This example demonstrates how to use a pivot table to analyze survey data that was obtained via a questionnaire. Figure 35-33 shows part of the raw data that is typical of data collected from a survey questionnaire. Each record represents the responses for one respondent.

	A	B	C	D	E	F	G	H	I	J	
1	Name	Sex	Age	State	Item01	Item02	Item03	Item04	Item05	Item06	Iter
2	Subject1	Male	40	Illinois	1	4	4	4	1	1	
3	Subject2	Female	31	Illinois	2	5	1	1	4	2	
4	Subject3	Male	56	New York	1	1	4	2	3	3	
5	Subject4	Male	55	Illinois	2	1	3	5	1	2	
6	Subject5	Female	47	New York	2	2	5	5	4	2	
7	Subject6	Female	51	Illinois	2	4	3	3	1	1	
8	Subject7	Female	48	California	2	4	5	4	5	3	
9	Subject8	Male	39	New York	3	2	1	2	3	4	
10	Subject9	Female	37	California	3	4	4	4	5	1	
11	Subject10	Male	38	New York	2	1	5	5	5	1	
12	Subject11	Male	38	California	4	3	3	2	1	2	
13	Subject12	Female	46	California	2	1	4	5	5	5	
14	Subject13	Female	48	Illinois	4	3	4	3	2	5	
15	Subject14	Female	56	New York	2	3	4	2	1	1	

Figure 35-33: Use a pivot table to tabulate this survey data.

On the CD-ROM   You can find the workbook used in this example on this book's CD-ROM.

Figure 35-34 shows a pivot table that was created to calculate averages for each of the 12 survey items, broken down by sex. Additional page fields enable you to examine the results easily by an age group or a particular state. Or, for a more complex pivot table, you can drag one or both of the page fields to a row or column position.

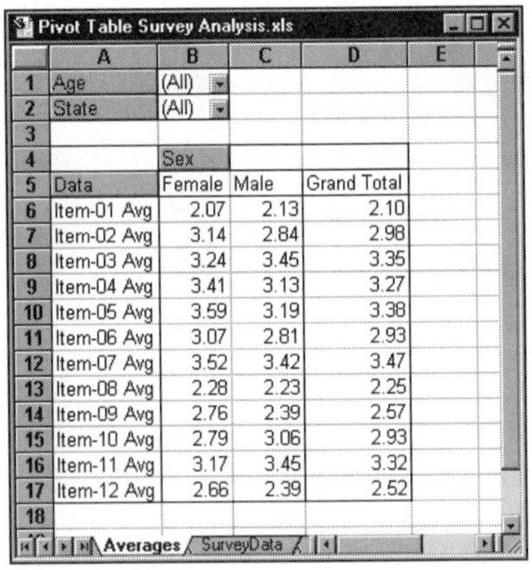

	A	B	C	D	E
	Pivot Table Survey Analysis.xls				
1	Age	(All)			
2	State	(All)			
3					
4		Sex			
5	Data	Female	Male	Grand Total	
6	Item-01 Avg	2.07	2.13	2.10	
7	Item-02 Avg	3.14	2.84	2.98	
8	Item-03 Avg	3.24	3.45	3.35	
9	Item-04 Avg	3.41	3.13	3.27	
10	Item-05 Avg	3.59	3.19	3.38	
11	Item-06 Avg	3.07	2.81	2.93	
12	Item-07 Avg	3.52	3.42	3.47	
13	Item-08 Avg	2.28	2.23	2.25	
14	Item-09 Avg	2.76	2.39	2.57	
15	Item-10 Avg	2.79	3.06	2.93	
16	Item-11 Avg	3.17	3.45	3.32	
17	Item-12 Avg	2.66	2.39	2.52	
18					

Figure 35-34: This pivot table calculates averages for each item.

Figure 35-35 shows another sheet in the workbook. This sheet contains 12 separate pivot tables, one for each survey item. Each pivot table displays the frequency of responses and the percentage of responses. Although you could create each table manually, the workbook includes a macro that creates them all in just a few seconds.

Customer geographic analysis

As a byproduct of creating a pivot table, you end up with a list of unique entries in a field. Figure 35-36 shows part of a database that tracks customers. The field of interest is the State field (which holds the country in the case of non-U.S. orders). The Type field contains a formula that returns either Foreign or Domestic, depending on the length of the entry in the State field. The goal of this example is to create a map that shows sales by state.

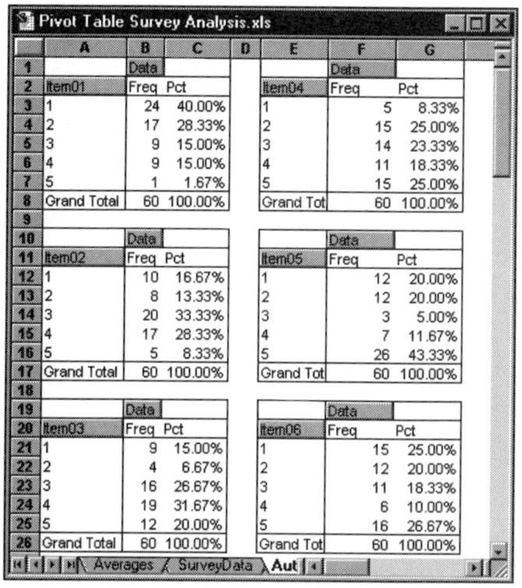
Pivot Table Survey Analysis.xls

	A	B	C	D	E	F	G
1		Data				Data	
2	Item01	Freq	Pct		Item04	Freq	Pct
3	1	24	40.00%		1	5	8.33%
4	2	17	28.33%		2	15	25.00%
5	3	9	15.00%		3	14	23.33%
6	4	9	15.00%		4	11	18.33%
7	5	1	1.67%		5	15	25.00%
8	Grand Total	60	100.00%		Grand Tot	60	100.00%
9							
10		Data				Data	
11	Item02	Freq	Pct		Item05	Freq	Pct
12	1	10	16.67%		1	12	20.00%
13	2	8	13.33%		2	12	20.00%
14	3	20	33.33%		3	3	5.00%
15	4	17	28.33%		4	7	11.67%
16	5	5	8.33%		5	26	43.33%
17	Grand Total	60	100.00%		Grand Tot	60	100.00%
18							
19		Data				Data	
20	Item03	Freq	Pct		Item06	Freq	Pct
21	1	9	15.00%		1	15	25.00%
22	2	4	6.67%		2	12	20.00%
23	3	16	26.67%		3	11	18.33%
24	4	19	31.67%		4	6	10.00%
25	5	12	20.00%		5	16	26.67%
26	Grand Total	60	100.00%		Grand Tot	60	100.00%

Averages / SurveyData / Aut

Figure 35-35: This sheet contains 12 pivot tables, created by a macro.

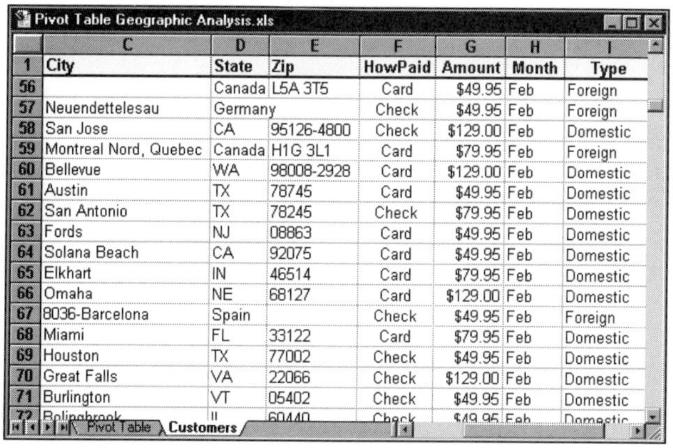
Pivot Table Geographic Analysis.xls

	C	D	E	F	G	H	I
1	City	State	Zip	HowPaid	Amount	Month	Type
56		Canada	L5A 3T5	Card	$49.95	Feb	Foreign
57	Neuendettelesau	Germany		Check	$49.95	Feb	Foreign
58	San Jose	CA	95126-4800	Check	$129.00	Feb	Domestic
59	Montreal Nord, Quebec	Canada	H1G 3L1	Card	$79.95	Feb	Foreign
60	Bellevue	WA	98008-2928	Card	$129.00	Feb	Domestic
61	Austin	TX	78745	Card	$49.95	Feb	Domestic
62	San Antonio	TX	78245	Check	$79.95	Feb	Domestic
63	Fords	NJ	08863	Card	$49.95	Feb	Domestic
64	Solana Beach	CA	92075	Card	$49.95	Feb	Domestic
65	Elkhart	IN	46514	Card	$79.95	Feb	Domestic
66	Omaha	NE	68127	Card	$129.00	Feb	Domestic
67	8036-Barcelona	Spain		Check	$49.95	Feb	Foreign
68	Miami	FL	33122	Card	$79.95	Feb	Domestic
69	Houston	TX	77002	Check	$49.95	Feb	Domestic
70	Great Falls	VA	22066	Check	$129.00	Feb	Domestic
71	Burlington	VT	05402	Check	$49.95	Feb	Domestic
72	Bolingbrook	IL	60440	Check	$49.95	Feb	Domestic

Pivot Table / Customers

Figure 35-36: This customer database would make a good map, but the data is not in the proper format.

On the CD-ROM

You can find this workbook on the CD-ROM.

Figure 35-37 shows a pivot table created from the data displayed in Figure 35-36. It displays the data in terms of total amount, plus a count. Three page fields were used to filter the data.

	A	B	C	D
	Pivot Table Geographic Analysis.xls			
1	HowPaid	(All)		
2	Type	Domestic		
3	Month	(All)		
4				
5		Data		
6	State	Sum of Amount	Count of Amount	
7	AK	$388	4	
8	AL	$50	1	
9	AR	$130	2	
10	AZ	$100	2	
11	CA	$6,556	68	
12	CO	$1,243	12	
13	CT	$1,047	12	
14	DC	$180	3	
15	FL	$1,343	14	
16	GA	$547	5	
17	HI	$129	1	
18	IA	$209	2	
19	IL	$1,553	17	
20	IN	$599	8	
21	KS	$129	1	

Pivot Table / Customers

Figure 35-37: This pivot table contains perfect input for an Excel map.

Figure 35-38 shows the map that was created by using Excel's mapping feature (described fully in Chapter 21).

Figure 35-38: This map was created from the data in the pivot table.

Grouping by month and years

The final pivot table example (see Figure 35-39) demonstrates some techniques that involve grouping by dates. The worksheet contains daily pricing data for two years. I created a macro to change the grouping to days, weeks, months, quarters, or years. The macro also changes the range that is used in the chart.

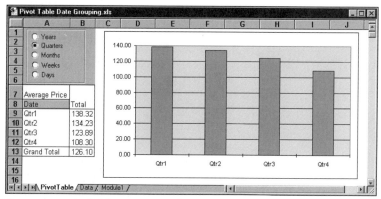

Figure 35-39: Clicking an option button executes a macro that changes the date grouping and updates the chart.

You can find this workbook on the CD-ROM.

Summary

This chapter discusses Excel's pivot table feature, which enables you to summarize data from a database that can be stored in a worksheet or in an external file. The examples in this chapter demonstrate some useful techniques. The best way to master this feature, however, is to use a database with which you're familiar and experiment until you understand how it works.

✦   ✦   ✦

Performing Spreadsheet What-If Analysis

One of the most appealing aspects of a spreadsheet program—including Excel—is that you can use formulas to create dynamic models that instantly recalculate when you change values in cells to which the formulas refer. When you change values in cells in a systematic manner and observe the effects on specific formula cells, you're performing a type of *what-if* analysis. What-if analysis is the process of asking questions such as, "What if the interest rate on the loan changes to 8.5 rather than 9.0 percent?" or "What if we raise the prices of our products by 5 percent?"

If you set up your spreadsheet properly, answering such questions is a matter of plugging in new values and observing the results of the recalculation. Excel provides useful tools to assist you in your what-if endeavors.

A What-If Example

Figure 36-1 shows a spreadsheet that calculates information pertaining to a mortgage loan. The worksheet is divided into two sections: the input cells and the result cells. Column D shows the formulas stored in column C.

With this worksheet, you can easily answer the following what-if questions:

+ What if I can negotiate a lower purchase price on the property?

+ What if the lender requires a 20-percent down payment?

+ What if I can get a 40-year mortgage?

+ What if the interest rate decreases to 7.5 percent?

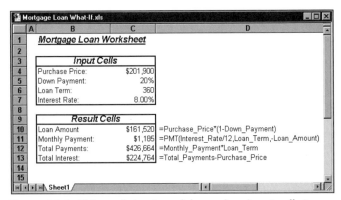

Figure 36-1: This worksheet model uses four input cells to produce the results in the formulas.

You can answer these questions simply by changing the values in the cells in range C4:C7 and observing the effects in the dependent cells (C10:C13). You can, of course, vary any number of input cells simultaneously.

Hard Code Values? No Way!

The mortgage calculation example, simple as it is, demonstrates an important point about spreadsheet design: You should always set up your worksheet so that you have maximum flexibility to make changes. Perhaps the most fundamental rule of spreadsheet design is the following:

Do not hard code (store) values in a formula. Rather, store the values in separate cells, and use cell references in the formula.

The term *hard code* refers to the use of actual values, or *constants,* in a formula. In the mortgage loan example, all the formulas use references to cells, not actual values.

You *could* use the value 360, for example, for the loan term argument of the PMT function in cell C11. Using a cell reference has two advantages. First, you have no doubt about the values that the formula uses (they aren't buried in the formula). Second, you can easily change the value.

Using values in formulas may not seem like much of an issue when only one formula is involved, but just imagine what would happen if this value were hard coded into several hundred formulas that were scattered throughout a worksheet.

Types of What-If Analyses

As you may expect, Excel can handle much more sophisticated models than the preceding example. To perform a what-if analysis using Excel, you have four basic options:

✦ **Manual what-if analysis:** Plug in new values and observe the effects on formula cells.

✦ **Macro-assisted what-if analysis:** Create macros to plug in variables for you.

✦ **Data tables:** Create a table that displays the results of selected formula cells as you systematically change one or two input cells.

✦ **Scenario Manager:** Create named scenarios and generate reports that use outlines or pivot tables.

Manual What-If Analysis

This method doesn't require too much explanation. In fact, the example that opens this chapter is a good one. It's based on the idea that you have one or more input cells that affect one or more key formula cells. You change the value in the input cells and see what happens to the formula cells. You may want to print the results or save each scenario to a new workbook. The term *scenario* refers to a specific set of values in one or more input cells.

This is how most people perform what-if analysis. Manual what-if analysis certainly has nothing wrong with it, but you should be aware of some other techniques.

Macro-Assisted What-If Analysis

A slightly more sophisticated form of manual what-if analysis uses macros. As is discussed in later chapters, a *macro* is a program that performs several operations automatically. Rather than change the input cells manually, you can create a macro to make the changes for you. For example, you may have three macros named BestCase, WorstCase, and MostLikelyCase. Running the BestCase macro enters the appropriate values into the input cells. Executing the WorstCase or MostLikelyCase macros enters other values.

If you understand how to create macros, this technique can be simple to set up. You can attach the macros to buttons, to make running the macros as easy as clicking the button.

Figure 36-2 shows a worksheet designed for what-if analysis. This simple production model contains two input cells: the hourly cost of labor and the unit cost for materials. The company produces three products, and each product requires a different number of hours and a different amount of materials to produce. Excel calculates the combined total profit. Management is trying to predict the total profit but is uncertain what the hourly labor cost and material costs are going to be. They've identified three scenarios, as listed in Table 36-1.

	A	B	C	D	E	F	G	H
1	Resource Cost Variables				Best Case			
2	Hourly Cost	34						
3	Materials Cost	59			Worst Case			
4	Total Profit	$13,008						
5					Most Likely			
6		Model A	Model B	Model C				
7	Hours per unit	12	14	24				
8	Materials per unit	6	9	14				
9	Cost to product	762	1,007	1,642				
10	Sales price	795	1,295	2,195				
11	Unit profit	33	288	553				
12	Units produced	36	18	12				
13	Total profit per model	1,188	5,184	6,636				
14								

Figure 36-2: This worksheet uses macros to display three different combinations of values for the input cells.

Table 36-1
Three Scenarios for the Production Model

Scenario	Hourly Cost	Materials Cost
Best Case	30	57
Worst Case	38	62
Most Likely	34	59

I developed three simple macros and attached one to each of the three buttons on the worksheet. Figure 36-3 shows the VBA macros (also known as subroutines) that Excel executes when you click a worksheet button. These macros simply place values into the named cells on the worksheet. To change the values that any one of the scenarios uses, you must edit the macros.

Note   If you like the idea of instantly displaying a particular scenario, you may be interested in learning about Excel's Scenario Manager, which is described later in this chapter. The Scenario Manager does not require macros.

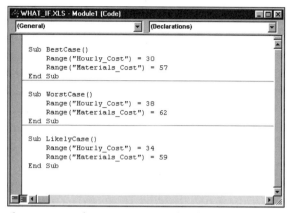

Figure 36-3: These macros simply place different values in the input cells in the worksheet.

Creating Data Tables

When you're working with a what-if model, Excel displays only one scenario at a time. But you can compare the results of various scenarios by using any of the following techniques:

✦ Print multiple copies of the worksheet, each displaying a different scenario.

✦ Copy the model to other worksheets and set it up so that each worksheet displays a different scenario.

✦ Manually create a table that summarizes key formula cells for each scenario.

✦ Use Excel's Data ➪ Table command to create a summary table automatically.

This section discusses the last option — the Data ➪ Table command, which enables you to create a handy data table that summarizes formula cells for various values of either of the following:

✦ A single input cell

✦ Various combinations of two input cells

For example, in the production model example, you may want to create a table that shows the total profit for various combinations of hourly cost and materials cost. Figure 36-4 shows a two-input data table that shows these combinations.

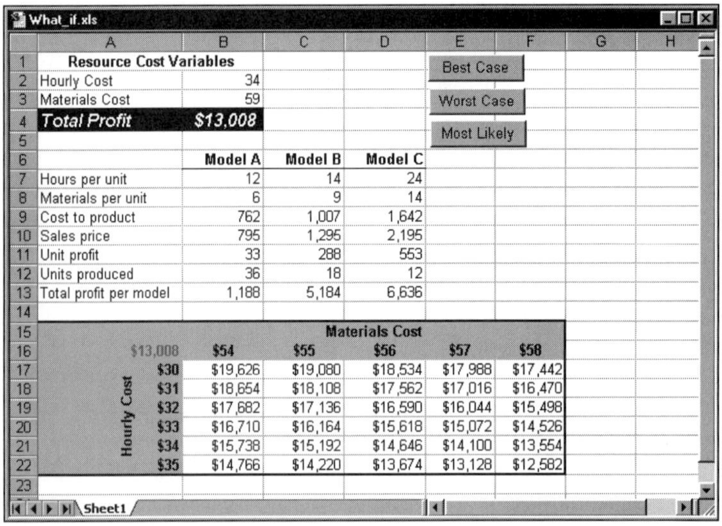
What_if.xls

	A	B	C	D	E	F	G	H
1	Resource Cost Variables				Best Case			
2	Hourly Cost	34						
3	Materials Cost	59			Worst Case			
4	Total Profit	$13,008						
5					Most Likely			
6		Model A	Model B	Model C				
7	Hours per unit	12	14	24				
8	Materials per unit	6	9	14				
9	Cost to product	762	1,007	1,642				
10	Sales price	795	1,295	2,195				
11	Unit profit	33	288	553				
12	Units produced	36	18	12				
13	Total profit per model	1,188	5,184	6,636				
14								
15			Materials Cost					
16	$13,008	$54	$55	$56	$57	$58		
17	Hourly Cost $30	$19,626	$19,080	$18,534	$17,988	$17,442		
18	$31	$18,654	$18,108	$17,562	$17,016	$16,470		
19	$32	$17,682	$17,136	$16,590	$16,044	$15,498		
20	$33	$16,710	$16,164	$15,618	$15,072	$14,526		
21	$34	$15,738	$15,192	$14,646	$14,100	$13,554		
22	$35	$14,766	$14,220	$13,674	$13,128	$12,582		
23								

Sheet1

Figure 36-4: This data table summarizes the total profit for various combinations of the input values.

You can create a data table fairly easily, but data tables have some limitations. In particular, a data table can deal with only one or two input cells at a time. In other words, you can't create a data table that uses a combination of three or more input cells.

The Scenario Manager, discussed later in this chapter, can produce a report that summarizes any number of input cells and result cells.

Creating a one-input data table

A one-input data table displays the results of one or more formulas when you use multiple values in a single input cell. Figure 36-5 shows the general layout for a one-input data table. You can place the table anywhere in the workbook. The left column contains various values for the single input cell. The top row contains formulas or, more often, references to formulas located elsewhere in the worksheet. You can use a single formula reference or any number of formula references. The upper-left cell of the table remains empty. Excel calculates the values that result from each level of the input cell and places them under each formula reference.

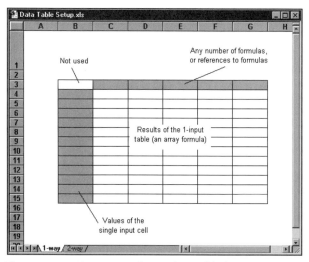

Figure 36-5: How a one-input data table is set up

This example uses the mortgage loan worksheet from earlier in the chapter, which is shown again in Figure 36-6. The goal of this example is to create a table that shows the values of the four formula cells (loan amount, monthly payment, total payments, and total interest) for various interest rates ranging from 7 to 9 percent, in 0.25 percent increments.

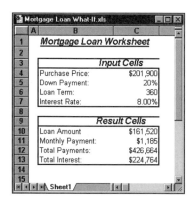

Figure 36-6: This example uses the mortgage loan worksheet to generate a one-input data table.

Figure 36-7 shows the setup for the data table area. Row 2 consists of references to the formulas in the worksheet. For example, cell F3 contains the formula =C10. Column E contains the values of the single input cell (interest rate) that Excel will use in the table. Borders also are added, to indicate where the calculated values go.

Mortgage Loan What-If.xls								
	A	B	C	D E	F	G	H	I
1	*Mortgage Loan Worksheet*				1-Input Data Table			
2				8.00%	$161,520	$1,185	$426,664	$224,764
3		*Input Cells*		7.00%				
4	Purchase Price:		$201,900	7.25%				
5	Down Payment:		20%	7.50%				
6	Loan Term:		360	7.75%				
7	Interest Rate:		8.00%	8.00%				
8				8.25%				
9		*Result Cells*		8.50%				
10	Loan Amount		$161,520	8.75%				
11	Monthly Payment:		$1,185	9.00%				
12	Total Payments:		$426,664					
13	Total Interest:		$224,764					
14								

Figure 36-7: Preparing to create a one-input data table

To create the table, select the range (in this case, E2:I11) and then choose Data ⇨ Table. Excel displays the Table dialog box, shown in Figure 36-8. You must specify the worksheet cell that contains the input value. Because variables for the input cell appear in a column in the data table rather than in a row, you place this cell reference in the text box called Column input cell. Enter **Interest_Rate** (the name for cell C7) or point to the cell in the worksheet. Leave the Row input cell field blank. Click OK, and Excel fills in the table with the appropriate results (see Figure 36-9).

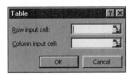

Figure 36-8: The Table dialog box

Mortgage Loan What-If.xls								
	A	B	C	D E	F	G	H	I
1	*Mortgage Loan Worksheet*				1-Input Data Table			
2				8.00%	$161,520	$1,185	$426,664	$224,764
3		*Input Cells*		7.00%	161,520	1,075	386,855	184,955
4	Purchase Price:		$201,900	7.25%	161,520	1,102	396,666	194,766
5	Down Payment:		20%	7.50%	161,520	1,129	406,574	204,674
6	Loan Term:		360	7.75%	161,520	1,157	416,574	214,674
7	Interest Rate:		8.00%	8.00%	161,520	1,185	426,664	224,764
8				8.25%	161,520	1,213	436,840	234,940
9		*Result Cells*		8.50%	161,520	1,242	447,102	245,202
10	Loan Amount		$161,520	8.75%	161,520	1,271	457,444	255,544
11	Monthly Payment:		$1,185	9.00%	161,520	1,300	467,866	265,966
12	Total Payments:		$426,664					
13	Total Interest:		$224,764					
14								

Figure 36-9: The result of the one-input data table

Examine the contents of the cells that Excel entered as a result of this command, and notice that Excel filled in formulas — more specifically, array formulas that use the TABLE function. As discussed in Chapter 25, an array formula is a single formula that produces results in multiple cells. Because the table uses formulas, Excel updates the table that you produce if you change the cell references in the first row or plug in different interest rates in the first column.

Note
You can arrange a one-input table vertically (as in this example) or horizontally. If you place the values of the input cell in a row, you enter the input cell reference in the text box labeled Row input cell in the Table dialog box.

Creating a two-input data table

As the name implies, a two-input data table lets you vary *two* input cells. You can see the setup for this type of table in Figure 36-10. Although it looks similar to a one-input table, the two-input table has one critical difference: it can show the results of only one formula at a time. With a one-input table, you can place any number of formulas, or references to formulas, across the top row of the table. In a two-input table, this top row holds the values for the second input cell. The upper-left cell of the table contains a reference to the single result formula.

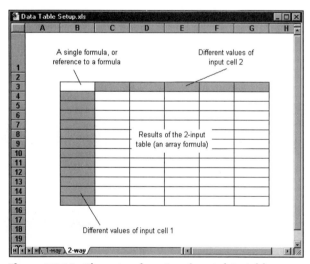

Figure 36-10: The setup for a two-input data table

In the preceding example, you could create a two-input data table that shows the results of a formula (say, monthly payment) for various combinations of two input cells (such as interest rate and down-payment percent). To see the effects on other formulas, you simply create multiple data tables — one for each formula cell that you want to summarize.

The worksheet that is shown in Figure 36-11 demonstrates a two-input data table. In this example, a company wants to conduct a direct-mail promotion to sell its product. The worksheet calculates the net profit from the promotion.

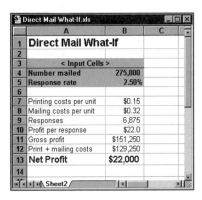

Figure 36-11: This worksheet calculates the net profit from a direct-mail promotion.

This model uses two input cells: the number of promotional pieces mailed and the anticipated response rate. The following items appear in the results area:

✦ **Printing costs per unit:** The cost to print a single mailer. The unit cost varies with the quantity: $0.20 each for quantities less than 200,000; $0.15 each for quantities of 200,001 through 300,000; and $0.10 each for quantities of more than 300,000. The following formula is used:

```
=IF(Number_mailed<200000,0.2,IF(Number_mailed<300000,0.15,0.1))
```

✦ **Mailing costs per unit:** This is a fixed cost, $0.32 per unit mailed.

✦ **Responses:** This is the number of responses, calculated from the response rate and the number mailed. The formula in this cell is the following:

```
=Response_rate*Number_mailed
```

✦ **Profit per response:** This is a fixed value. The company knows that it will realize a profit of $22 per order.

✦ **Gross profit:** This is a simple formula that multiplies the profit per response by the number of responses:

```
=Profit_per_response*Responses
```

✦ **Print + mailing costs:** This formula calculates the total cost of the promotion:

```
=Number_mailed*(Printing_costs_per_unit+Mailing_costs_per_
unit)
```

✦ **Net Profit:** This formula calculates the bottom line — the gross profit minus the printing and mailing costs.

If you plug in values for the two input cells, you see that the net profit varies widely — often going negative to produce a net loss.

Figure 36-12 shows the setup of a two-input data table that summarizes the net profit at various combinations of quantity and response rate; the table appears in the range A15:I25.

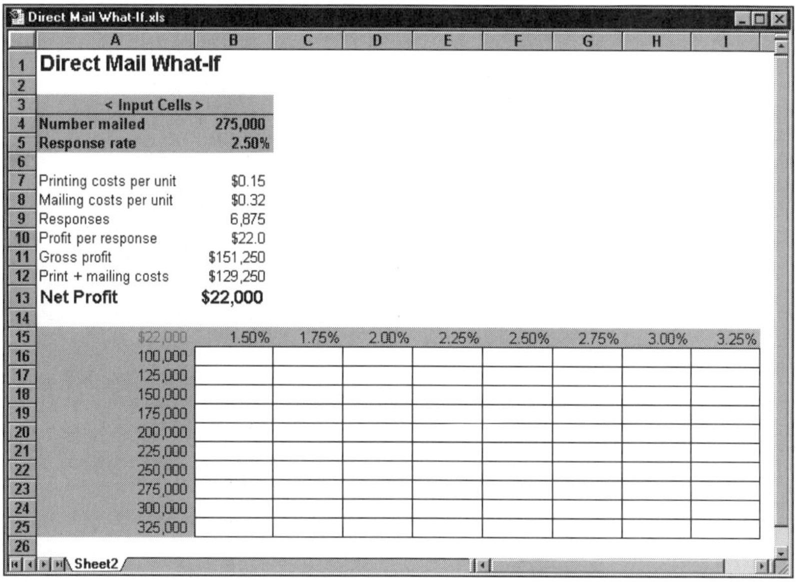

Direct Mail What-If.xls

	A	B	C	D	E	F	G	H	I
1	Direct Mail What-If								
2									
3	< Input Cells >								
4	Number mailed	275,000							
5	Response rate	2.50%							
6									
7	Printing costs per unit	$0.15							
8	Mailing costs per unit	$0.32							
9	Responses	6,875							
10	Profit per response	$22.0							
11	Gross profit	$151,250							
12	Print + mailing costs	$129,250							
13	Net Profit	$22,000							
14									
15	$22,000	1.50%	1.75%	2.00%	2.25%	2.50%	2.75%	3.00%	3.25%
16	100,000								
17	125,000								
18	150,000								
19	175,000								
20	200,000								
21	225,000								
22	250,000								
23	275,000								
24	300,000								
25	325,000								
26									

Sheet2

Figure 36-12: Preparing to create a two-input data table

To create the data table, select the range and choose Data ➪ Table. The Row input cell is Number_Mailed (the name for cell B4), and the Column input cell is Response_Rate (the name for cell B5). Figure 36-13 shows the result of this command.

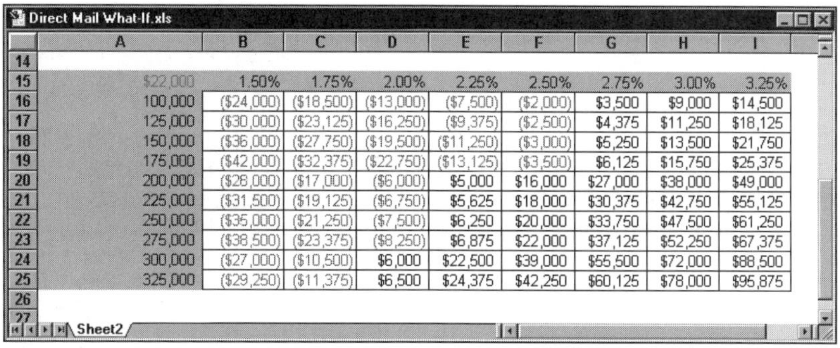

Direct Mail What-If.xls

	A	B	C	D	E	F	G	H	I
14									
15	$22,000	1.50%	1.75%	2.00%	2.25%	2.50%	2.75%	3.00%	3.25%
16	100,000	($24,000)	($18,500)	($13,000)	($7,500)	($2,000)	$3,500	$9,000	$14,500
17	125,000	($30,000)	($23,125)	($16,250)	($9,375)	($2,500)	$4,375	$11,250	$18,125
18	150,000	($36,000)	($27,750)	($19,500)	($11,250)	($3,000)	$5,250	$13,500	$21,750
19	175,000	($42,000)	($32,375)	($22,750)	($13,125)	($3,500)	$6,125	$15,750	$25,375
20	200,000	($28,000)	($17,000)	($6,000)	$5,000	$16,000	$27,000	$38,000	$49,000
21	225,000	($31,500)	($19,125)	($6,750)	$5,625	$18,000	$30,375	$42,750	$55,125
22	250,000	($35,000)	($21,250)	($7,500)	$6,250	$20,000	$33,750	$47,500	$61,250
23	275,000	($38,500)	($23,375)	($8,250)	$6,875	$22,000	$37,125	$52,250	$67,375
24	300,000	($27,000)	($10,500)	$6,000	$22,500	$39,000	$55,500	$72,000	$88,500
25	325,000	($29,250)	($11,375)	$6,500	$24,375	$42,250	$60,125	$78,000	$95,875
26									
27									

Sheet2

Figure 36-13: The result of the two-input data table

Two-input data tables often make good 3D charts. An example of such a chart for the direct-mail example appears in Figure 36-14.

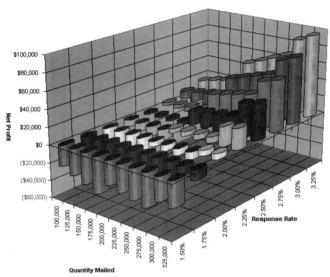

Figure 36-14: Viewing the two-input data table graphically

Using Scenario Manager

Data tables are useful, but they have a few limitations:

- ✦ You can vary only one or two input cells at a time.

- ✦ The process of setting up a data table is not all that intuitive.

- ✦ A two-input table shows the results of only one formula cell (although you can create additional tables for more formulas).

- ✦ More often than not, you're interested in a few select combinations — not an entire table that shows all possible combinations of two input cells.

Excel's Scenario Manager feature makes it easy to automate your what-if models. You can store different sets of input values (called *changing cells* in the terminology of Scenario Manager) for any number of variables and give a name to each set. You can then select a set of values by name, and Excel displays the worksheet by using those values. You can also generate a summary report that shows the effect of various combinations of values on any number of result cells. These summary reports can be an outline or a pivot table.

Your sales forecast for the year, for example, may depend on several factors. Consequently, you can define three scenarios: best case, worst case, and most likely case. You then can switch to any of these scenarios by selecting the named scenario from a list. Excel substitutes the appropriate input values in your worksheet and recalculates the formulas. This process is similar, in some respects, to the macro-assisted what-if technique described earlier. The Scenario Manager is easier to use, however.

Defining scenarios

To introduce you to the Scenario Manager, this section starts with a simple example: the production model used earlier in the chapter.

This example defines three scenarios, as depicted in Table 36-2. The Best Case scenario has the lowest hourly cost and materials cost. The Worst Case scenario has high values for both the hourly cost and the materials cost. The third scenario, Most Likely Case, has intermediate values for both of these input cells (this represents the management's best estimate). The managers need to be prepared for the worst case, however — and they are interested in what would happen under the Best Case scenario.

Table 36-2		
Three Scenarios for the Production Model		
Scenario	*Hourly Cost*	*Materials Cost*
Best Case	30	57
Worst Case	38	62
Most Likely Case	34	59

Access the Scenario Manager by selecting Tools ➪ Scenarios to display the Scenario Manager dialog box, shown in Figure 36-15.

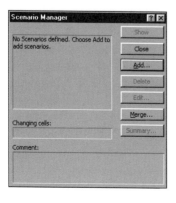

Figure 36-15: The Scenario Manager dialog box lets you assign names to different sets of assumptions.

When you first open this dialog box, it tells you that no scenarios are defined — which is not too surprising, because you're just starting. As you add named scenarios, they appear in this dialog box.

Tip   I strongly suggest that you create names for the changing cells and all the result cells that you want to examine. Excel uses these names in the dialog boxes and in the reports that it generates. If you use names, you'll find that keeping track of what's going on is much easier; names also make your reports more readable.

To add a scenario, click the Add button in the Scenario Manager dialog box. Excel displays its Add Scenario dialog box, shown in Figure 36-16.

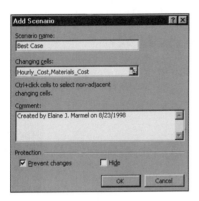

Figure 36-16: The Add Scenario dialog box lets you create a named scenario.

This dialog box consists of four parts:

✦ **Scenario name:** The name for the scenario. You can give it any name that you like — preferably something meaningful.

✦ **Changing cells:** The input cells for the scenario. You can enter the cell addresses directly or point to them. Multiple selections are allowed, so the input cells need not be adjacent. Each named scenario can use the same set of changing cells or different changing cells. The number of changing cells for a scenario is limited to 32.

✦ **Comment:** By default, Excel displays the name of the person who created the scenario and the date that it was created. You can change this text, add new text to it, or delete it.

✦ **Protection:** The two options (preventing changes and hiding a scenario) are in effect only when you protect the worksheet and choose the Scenario option in the Protect Sheet dialog box. Protecting a scenario prevents anyone from modifying it; a hidden scenario doesn't appear in the Scenario Manager dialog box.

In this example, define the three scenarios that are listed in the preceding table. The changing cells are Hourly_Cost (B4) and Materials_Cost (B5).

After you enter the information in the Add Scenario dialog box, click OK. Excel then displays the Scenario Values dialog box, shown in Figure 36-17. This dialog box displays one field for each changing cell that you specified in the previous dialog box. Enter the values for each cell in the scenario. If you click OK, you return to the Scenario Manager dialog box—which then displays your named scenario in its list. If you have more scenarios to create, click the Add button to return to the Add Scenario dialog box.

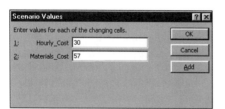

Figure 36-17: You enter the values for the scenario in the Scenario Values dialog box.

Using the Scenarios Tool

Excel has a Scenarios tool, which is a drop-down list that shows all the defined scenarios and enables you to display a scenario or create a new scenario. Oddly, this useful tool doesn't appear on any of the prebuilt toolbars. But, if you use the Scenario Manager, you may want to add the Scenarios tool to one of your toolbars, using the following procedure:

1. Choose Tools ➪ Customize.

2. In the Customize dialog box, click the Commands tab.

3. Select the Tools category.

4. In the Commands tab, locate the Scenarios tool and drag it to any toolbar.

5. Click the Close button.

Refer to Chapter 15 for additional details on customizing toolbars.

Using the Scenarios tool may be more efficient than bringing up the Scenario Manager dialog box to create or view a different scenario.

To create a scenario by using the Scenarios tool, enter the scenario's values, select the changing cells, and then enter the name for the scenario in the Scenario drop-down box. To view a named scenario, just choose it from the list. Scenarios that you define in this manner also appear in the Scenario Manager dialog box. So, if you want to perform any operations on your scenarios (add comments, edit values, or generate reports), you need to select Tools ➪ Scenarios, to display the Scenario Manager dialog box.

Displaying scenarios

After you define all the scenarios and return to the Scenario Manager dialog box, the dialog box displays the names of your defined scenarios. Select one of the scenarios and then click the Show button. Excel inserts the corresponding values into the changing cells and calculates the worksheet to show the results for that scenario.

Modifying scenarios

The Edit button in the Scenario Manager dialog box lets you change one or more of the values for the changing cells of a scenario. Select the scenario that you want to change, click the Edit button, choose OK to access the Scenario Values dialog box, and then make your changes. Notice that Excel automatically updates the Comments box with new text that indicates when the scenario was modified.

Merging scenarios

In workgroup situations, you may have several people working on a spreadsheet model, and several people may have defined various scenarios. The marketing department, for example, may have its opinion of what the input cells should be, the finance department may have another opinion, and your CEO may have yet another opinion.

Excel makes it easy to merge these various scenarios into a single workbook, by using the Merge button in the Scenario Manager dialog box. Clicking this button displays the dialog box shown in Figure 36-18.

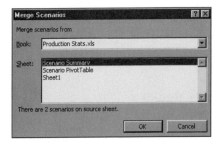

Figure 36-18: The Merge Scenarios dialog box lets you merge scenarios that are defined by others into your workbook.

Before you merge scenarios, make sure that the workbook from which you're merging is open. Then, click the Merge button in the Scenario Manager dialog box. Excel displays its Merge Scenarios dialog box. Choose the workbook from which you're merging in the Book drop-down list. Then, choose the sheet that contains the scenarios you want to merge from the Sheet list box (notice that the dialog box displays the number of scenarios in each sheet as you scroll through the Sheet list box). Click OK, and you return to the previous dialog box, which now displays the scenario names that you merged from the other workbook.

Generating a scenario report

You are ready to take the Scenario Manager through its final feat — generating a summary report. When you click the Summary button in the Scenario Manager dialog box, Excel displays the Scenario Summary dialog box, shown in Figure 36-19.

Figure 36-19: The Scenario Summary dialog box enables you to choose a report type and specify the result cells in which you're interested.

You have a choice of report types:

✦ **Scenario Summary:** The summary report appears in the form of an outline.

✦ **Scenario PivotTable:** The summary report appears in the form of a pivot table (see Chapter 35).

For simple cases of scenario management, a standard Scenario Summary report is usually sufficient. If you have many scenarios defined with multiple result cells, however, you may find that a Scenario Pivot Table provides more flexibility.

The Scenario Summary dialog box also asks you to specify the result cells (the cells that contain the formulas in which you're interested). For this example, select B15:D15 and B17 (a multiple selection) to make the report show the profit for each product, plus the total profit.

Excel creates a new worksheet to store the summary table. Figure 36-20 shows the Scenario Summary form of the report, and Figure 36-21 shows the Scenario Pivot Table form. If you gave names to the changing cells and result cells, the table uses these names. Otherwise, it lists the cell references.

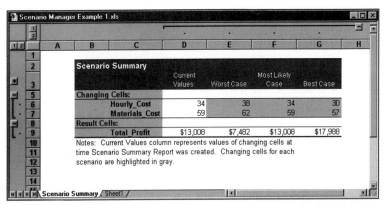

Figure 36-20: A Scenario Summary report produced by the Scenario Manager

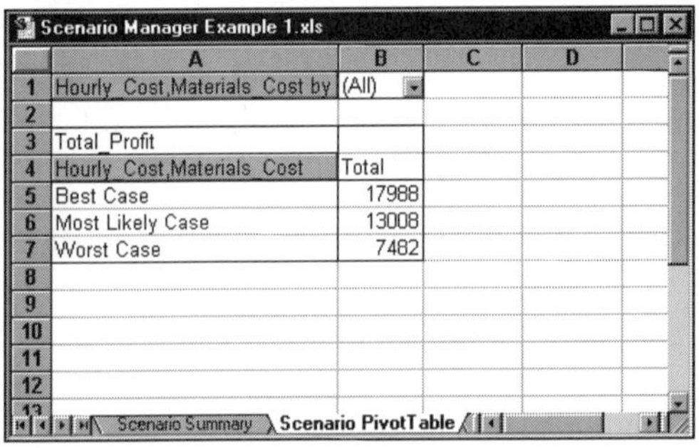

Figure 36-21: A Scenario Pivot Table report produced by the Scenario Manager

Scenario Manager Limitations

As you work with the Scenario Manager, you may discover its main limitation: a scenario can use no more than 32 changing cells. If you attempt to use more, you get the message that is shown in Figure 36-22.

Figure 36-22: The Scenario Manager is limited to 32 changing cells.

You can get around this limitation by splitting your scenarios into parts. For example, assume that you have a worksheet with monthly sales projections for three years (36 changing cells). You may want to define various scenarios for these projections. But, because the number of changing cells exceeds the 32-cell limit, you can break it down into two or three scenarios — each of which uses a different set of changing cells. For example, you can define a scenario for the first 12 months, another for the second 12 months, and yet another for the third 12 months. Then, to display a particular scenario, you must display all three subscenarios. Writing simple macros makes this easy. If you use this technique, be aware that Excel includes superfluous information in summary reports.

Summary

This chapter discusses the concept of spreadsheet what-if analysis. What-if analysis is the process of systematically changing input cells and observing the effects on one or more formula cells. You can perform what-if analysis manually by plugging in different values. You also can use macros to automate this process. Excel's data table feature enables you to summarize the results of various values of a single input cell or various combinations of two input cells. The Scenario Manager feature makes it easy to create scenarios and generate summary reports.

✦   ✦   ✦

Analyzing Data Using Goal Seeking and Solver

The preceding chapter discusses *what-if analysis* — the process of changing input cells to observe the results on other dependent cells. This chapter looks at that process from the opposite perspective: finding the value of one or more input cells that produces a desired result in a formula cell.

What-If Analysis — In Reverse

Consider the following what-if question: "What is the total profit if sales increase by 20 percent?" If you set up your worksheet properly, you can change the value in one cell to see what happens to the profit cell. Goal seeking takes the opposite approach. If you know what a formula result *should* be, Excel can tell you the values that you need to enter in one or more input cells to produce that result. In other words, you can ask a question such as, "How much do sales need to increase to produce a profit of $1.2 million?" Excel provides two tools that are relevant:

+ **Goal seeking:** Determines the value that you need to enter in a single input cell to produce a result that you want in a dependent (formula) cell.

+ **Solver:** Determines the values that you need to enter in multiple input cells to produce a result that you want. Moreover, because you can specify certain constraints to the problem, you gain significant problem-solving ability.

Single-Cell Goal Seeking

Single-cell goal seeking (also known as *backsolving*) is a rather simple concept. Excel determines what value in an input cell produces a desired result in a formula cell. Walk through the following example to understand how single-cell goal seeking works.

A goal-seeking example

Figure 37-1 shows the mortgage loan worksheet that was used in the preceding chapter. This worksheet has four input cells and four formula cells. Originally, this worksheet was used for a what-if analysis example. In this section, the opposite approach is taken — rather than supply different input cell values to look at the calculated formulas, this example lets Excel determine one of the input values.

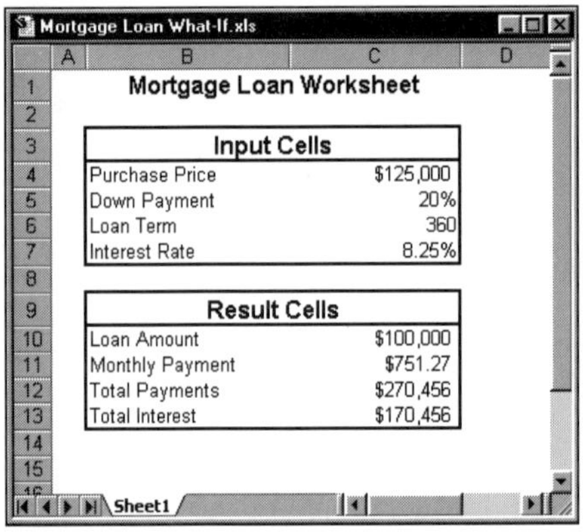

Figure 37-1: This worksheet is a good demonstration of goal seeking.

Assume that you're in the market for a new home and you know that you can afford $1,200 per month in mortgage payments. You also know that a lender can issue a fixed-rate mortgage loan for 8.25 percent, based on an 80 percent loan-to-value (that is, a 20-percent down payment). The question is, "What is the maximum purchase price I can handle?" In other words, what value in cell C4 causes the formula in cell C11 to result in $1,200? You could plug values into cell C4 until C11 displays $1,200; however, Excel can determine the answer much more efficiently.

To answer the question posed in the preceding paragraph, select Tools ➪ Goal Seek. Excel displays the dialog box shown in Figure 37-2. Completing this dialog box is similar to forming a sentence. You want to set cell C11 to 1200 by changing cell C4.

Enter this information in the dialog box either by typing the cell references or by pointing with the mouse. Click OK to begin the goal-seeking process.

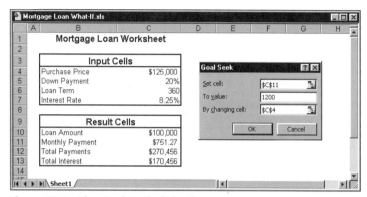

Figure 37-2: The Goal Seek dialog box

In about a second, Excel announces that it has found the solution and displays the Goal Seek Status box, which shows the target value and the value that Excel calculated. In this case, Excel found an exact value. The worksheet now displays the found value in cell C4 ($199,663). As a result of this value, the monthly payment amount is $1,200. At this point, you have two options:

✦ Click OK to replace the original value with the found value.

✦ Click Cancel to restore your worksheet to the form that it had before you chose Tools ➪ Goal Seek.

More about goal seeking

Excel can't always find a value that produces the result for which you're looking—sometimes, a solution simply doesn't exist. In such a case, the Goal Seek Status box informs you of that fact (see Figure 37-3).

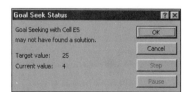

Figure 37-3: When Excel can't find a solution to your goal-seeking problem, it tells you so.

Other times, however, Excel may report that it can't find a solution, but you're pretty sure that one exists. If that's the case, you can try the following options:

✦ Change the current value of the By changing cell box in the Goal Seek dialog box to a value that is closer to the solution, and then reissue the command.

✦ Adjust the Maximum iterations setting in the Calculation tab of the Options dialog box. Increasing the number of iterations makes Excel try more possible solutions.

✦ Double-check your logic and make sure that the formula cell does, indeed, depend on the specified changing cell.

Note   Like all computer programs, Excel has limited precision. To demonstrate this limitation, enter **=A1^2** into cell A2. Then, select Tools ⇨ Goal Seek to find the value in cell A1 (which is empty) that makes the formula return 16. Excel comes up with a value of 4.00002269 (you may need to widen the column to see the complete value), which is close to the square root of 16, but certainly not exact. You can adjust the precision in the Calculation tab of the Options dialog box (make the Maximum change value smaller).

Note   In some cases, multiple values of the input cell produce the same desired result. For example, the formula =A1^2 returns 16 if cell A1 contains either –4 or +4. If you use goal seeking when two solutions are possible, Excel gives you the solution that has the same sign as the current value in the cell.

Perhaps the main limitation of the Tools ⇨ Goal Seek command is its inability to find the value for more than one input cell. For example, it can't tell you what purchase price *and* what down-payment percent will result in a particular monthly payment. If you want to change more than one variable at a time, use Solver (discussed later in this chapter).

Graphical goal seeking

Excel provides another way to perform goal seeking — by manipulating a graph. Figure 37-4 shows a worksheet that projects sales for a startup company. The CFO knows from experience that companies in this industry can grow exponentially according to a formula such as this one:

```
y*(bx)
```

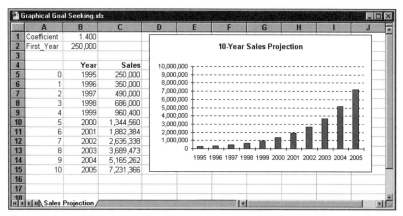

Figure 37-4: This sales projection predicts exponential growth, based on the growth coefficient in cell B1.

Table 37-1 lists and describes the variables.

Table 37-1		
Variables Used in the Sales Growth Formula		
Variable	**Description**	
y	A constant equal to the first year's sales	
b	A growth coefficient	
x	A variable relating to time	

The company managers know that sales during the first year are going to be $250,000, and they want to increase the company's sales to $10 million by the year 2005. The financial modelers want to know the exact growth coefficient that meets this goal. The worksheet that is shown in Figure 37-4 uses formulas to forecast the annual sales, based on the growth coefficient in cell B1. The worksheet has an embedded chart that plots the annual sales.

The initial guess for the growth coefficient is 1.40. As you can see, this number is too low—it results in sales of only $7.231 million for the year 2005. Although you can select Tools ➪ Goal Seek to arrive at the exact coefficient, you have another way to do it.

Click the chart so that you can edit it and then select the chart series. Now, click the last data column to select only that column in the series. Point to the top of the column, and the mouse pointer changes shape. Drag the column upward and watch the value change in the small box displayed next to the mouse pointer. When the value is exactly $10 million, release the mouse button.

Excel responds with the Goal Seek dialog box, with two fields completed, as shown in Figure 37-5. Excel just needs to know which cell to use for the input cell. Specify cell B1 or enter **Coefficient** in the By changing cell edit box. Excel calculates the value of Coefficient that is necessary to produce the result that you pointed out on the chart. If you want to keep that number (which, by the way, is 1.44612554959182), click OK. Excel replaces the current value of Coefficient with the new value, and the chart is updated automatically. You can probably appreciate the fact that it would take quite a while to arrive at this number by plugging in successive approximations.

Figure 37-5: The Goal Seek dialog box appears when you directly manipulate a point on a chart that contains a formula.

You don't want to use this graphical method all the time, however, because the normal Tools ➪ Goal Seek command is more efficient. But, it does demonstrate another way to approach problems that is helpful for those who are more visually oriented.

As you may expect, goal seeking can get much more impressive when it's used with complex worksheets that have many dependent cells. In any event, it sure beats trial and error.

Introducing Solver

Excel's goal-seeking feature is a useful tool, but it clearly has limitations. It can solve for only one adjustable cell, for example, and it returns only a single solution. Excel's powerful Solver tool extends this concept by enabling you to do the following:

✦ Specify multiple adjustable cells.

✦ Specify constraints on the values that the adjustable cells can have.

✦ Generate a solution that maximizes or minimizes a particular worksheet cell.

✦ Generate multiple solutions to a problem.

Although goal seeking is a relatively simple operation, using Solver can be much more complicated. In fact, Solver is probably one of the most difficult (and potentially frustrating) features in Excel. I'm the first to admit that Solver isn't for everyone. In fact, most Excel users have no use for this feature. However, many users find that having this much power is worth spending the extra time to learn about it.

Appropriate problems for Solver

Problems that are appropriate for Solver fall into a relatively narrow range. They typically involve situations that meet the following criteria:

✦ A target cell depends on other cells and formulas. Typically, you want to maximize or minimize this target cell or set it equal to some value.

✦ The target cell depends on a group of cells (called *changing cells*) that Solver can adjust to affect the target cell.

✦ The solution must adhere to certain limitations, or *constraints*.

After you set up your worksheet appropriately, you can use Solver to adjust the changing cells and produce the result that you want in your target cell — and, simultaneously meet all the constraints that you have defined.

On the CD-ROM   You can find all the Solver examples in this chapter on this book's CD-ROM.

A simple Solver example

I start with a simple example to introduce Solver and then present some increasingly complex examples to demonstrate what it can do.

Figure 37-6 shows a worksheet that is set up to calculate the profit for three products. Column B shows the number of units of each product, column C shows the profit per unit for each product, and column C contains formulas that calculate the profit for each product by multiplying the units by the profit per unit.

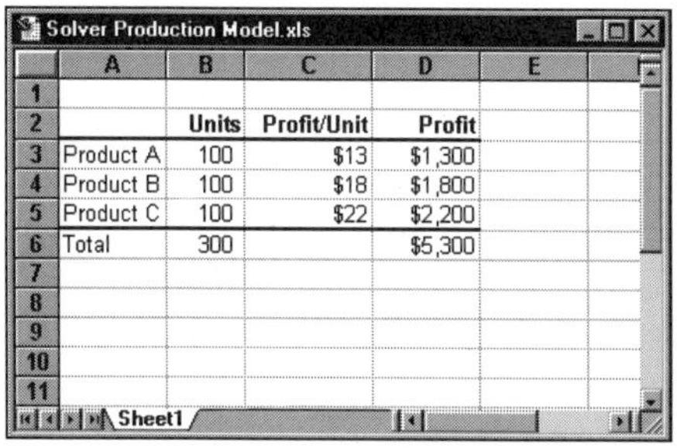

	Units	Profit/Unit	Profit
Product A	100	$13	$1,300
Product B	100	$18	$1,800
Product C	100	$22	$2,200
Total	300		$5,300

Figure 37-6: Use Solver to determine the number of units to maximize the total profit.

It doesn't take an MBA degree to realize that the greatest profit per unit comes from Product C. Therefore, the logical solution is to produce only Product C. If things were really this simple, you wouldn't need tools such as Solver. As in most situations, this company has some constraints to which it must adhere:

✦ The combined production capacity is 300 total units per day.

✦ The company needs 50 units of Product A to fill an existing order.

✦ The company needs 40 units of Product B to fill an anticipated order.

✦ Because the market for Product C is relatively limited, the company doesn't want to produce more than 40 units of this product.

These four constraints make the problem more realistic and challenging. In fact, it's a perfect problem for Solver.

The basic procedure for using Solver is as follows:

1. Set up the worksheet with values and formulas. Make sure that you format cells logically; for example, if you cannot produce portions of your products, format those cells to contain numbers with no decimal values.

2. Bring up the Solver dialog box.

3. Specify the target cell.

4. Specify the changing cells.

5. Specify the constraints.

6. Change the Solver options, if necessary.

7. Let Solver solve the problem.

To start Solver, select Tools ⇨ Solver. Excel displays its Solver Parameters dialog box, shown in Figure 37-7.

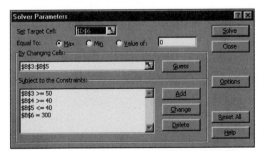

Figure 37-7: The Solver Parameters dialog box

No Tools ⇨ Solver Command?

Solver is an add-in, so it's available only when the add-in is installed. If the Tools menu doesn't show a Solver command, you need to install the add-in before you can use it.

Select Tools ⇨ Add-Ins. Excel displays its Add-Ins dialog box. Scroll down the list of add-ins and place a check mark next to the item named Solver Add-In. Click OK, and Excel installs the add-in and makes the Tools ⇨ Solver command available. If Solver isn't available on your computer, you'll be asked if you want to install it.

In this example, the target cell is D6 — the cell that calculates the total profit for three products. Enter (or point to) cell D6 in the Set Target Cell field of the Solver Parameters dialog box. Because the objective is to maximize this cell, click the Max option. Next, specify the changing cells, which are in the range B3:B5, in the By Changing Cells box.

The next step is to specify the constraints on the problem. The constraints are added one at a time and appear in the box labeled Subject to the Constraints. To add a constraint, click the Add button. Excel displays the Add Constraint dialog box, shown in Figure 37-8. This dialog box has three parts: a cell reference, an operator, and a value. To set the first constraint — that the total production capacity is 300 units — enter B6 as the Cell Reference, choose equal (=) from the drop-down list of operators, and enter 300 as the Constraint value. Click Add to add the remaining constraints. Table 37-2 summarizes the constraints for this problem.

Figure 37-8: The Add Constraint dialog box

Table 37-2
Constraints Summary

Constraint	Expressed As
Capacity is 300 units	B6=300
At least 50 units of Product A	B3>=50
At least 40 units of Product B	B4>=40
No more than 40 units of Product C	B5<=40

After you enter the last constraint, click OK to return to the Solver Parameters dialog box—which now lists the four constraints.

At this point, Solver knows everything about the problem. Click the Solver button to start the solution process. You can watch the progress onscreen, and Excel soon announces that it has found a solution. The Solver Results dialog box is shown in Figure 37-9.

Figure 37-9: Solver displays this dialog box when it finds a solution to the problem.

At this point, you have the following options:

 ✦ Replace the original changing cell values with the values that Solver found

 ✦ Restore the original changing cell values

 ✦ Create any or all three reports that describe what Solver did (press Shift to select multiple reports from this list)

 ✦ Click the Save Scenario button to save the solution as a scenario, so that the Scenario Manager can use it (see Chapter 36)

If you specify any report options, Excel creates each report on a new worksheet, with an appropriate name. Figure 37-10 shows an Answer Report. In the Constraints section of the report, all the constraints except one are *binding,* which means that the constraint was satisfied at its limit, with no more room to change.

This simple example illustrates how Solver works. The fact is, you could probably solve this particular problem manually just as quickly. That, of course, isn't always the case.

More about Solver

Before presenting complex examples, this section discusses the Solver Options dialog box—one of the more feature-packed dialog boxes in Excel. From this dialog box, you control many aspects of the solution process, as well as load and save model specifications in a worksheet range.

Solver Production Model.xls										
A	**B**	**C**	**D**	**E**	**F**	**G**	**H**	**I**	**J**	**K**

1 Microsoft Excel 9.0 Answer Report
2 Worksheet: [Solver Production Model.xls]Sheet1
3 Report Created: 9/4/1998 11:52:06 AM
4
5
6 Target Cell (Max)

	Cell	Name	Original Value	Final Value
7	Cell	Name	Original Value	Final Value
8	$D$6	Profit	$ 5,300	$ 5,310

9
10
11 Adjustable Cells

	Cell	Name	Original Value	Final Value
12	Cell	Name	Original Value	Final Value
13	$B$3	Product A Units	100	50
14	$B$4	Product B Units	100	210
15	$B$5	Product C Units	100	40

16
17
18 Constraints

	Cell	Name	Cell Value	Formula	Status	Slack
19	Cell	Name	Cell Value	Formula	Status	Slack
20	$B$6	Units	300	$B$6=300	Binding	0
21	$B$5	Product C Units	40	$B$5<=40	Binding	0
22	$B$3	Product A Units	50	$B$3>=50	Binding	0
23	$B$4	Product B Units	210	$B$4>=40	Not Binding	170

24

Answer Report 1 / Sheet1

Figure 37-10: One of three reports that Solver can produce

Having Solver report to you that it can't find a solution isn't unusual—even when you know that one should exist. Often, you can change one or more of the Solver options and try again. When you choose the Options button in the Solver Parameters dialog box, Excel displays the Solver Options dialog box shown in Figure 37-11.

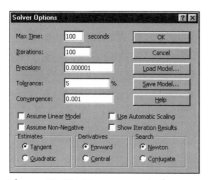

Figure 37-11: You can control many aspects of how Solver solves a problem.

This list describes Solver's options:

✦ **Max Time:** Specify the maximum amount of time (in seconds) that you want Solver to spend on a problem. If Solver reports that it exceeded the time limit, you can increase the amount of time that it spends searching for a solution.

✦ **Iterations:** Enter the maximum number of trial solutions that you want Solver to perform.

✦ **Precision:** Specify how close the Cell Reference and Constraint formulas must be to satisfy a constraint. Excel may solve the problem more quickly if you specify less precision.

✦ **Tolerance:** Designate the maximum percentage of error allowed for integer solutions (relevant only if an integer constraint is used).

✦ **Assume Linear Model:** Choose this option to speed the solution process, but you can use it only if all the relationships in the model are linear. You can't use this option if the adjustable cells are multiplied or divided, or if the problem uses exponents

✦ **Use Automatic Scaling:** Use when the problem involves large differences in magnitude — when you attempt to maximize a percentage, for example, by varying cells that are very large.

✦ **Show Iteration Results:** Instruct Solver to pause and display the results after each iteration, by checking this box.

✦ **Estimates, Derivatives, and Search group boxes:** Use these options to control some technical aspects of the solution. In most cases, you don't need to change these settings.

✦ **Load Model:** Click this button to make Excel display the Load Model dialog box, in which you specify a range containing the model that you want to load.

✦ **Save Model:** Click this button to make Excel display the Save Model dialog box, in which you specify a range where Excel should save the model parameters.

Usually, you want to save a model only when you're using more than one set of Solver parameters with your worksheet, because Excel saves the first Solver model automatically with your worksheet (using hidden names). If you save additional models, Excel stores the information in the form of the formulas that correspond to the specification that you make (the last cell in the saved range is an array formula that holds the options settings).

Solver Examples

The remainder of this chapter consists of examples of using Solver for various types of problems.

Minimizing shipping costs

This example involves finding alternative options for shipping materials while keeping total shipping costs at a minimum (see Figure 37-12). A company has warehouses in Los Angeles, St. Louis, and Boston. Retail outlets throughout the United States place orders, which the company then ships from one of the warehouses. Ideally, the company wants to meet the product needs of all six retail outlets from available inventory in the warehouses — and keep total shipping charges as low as possible.

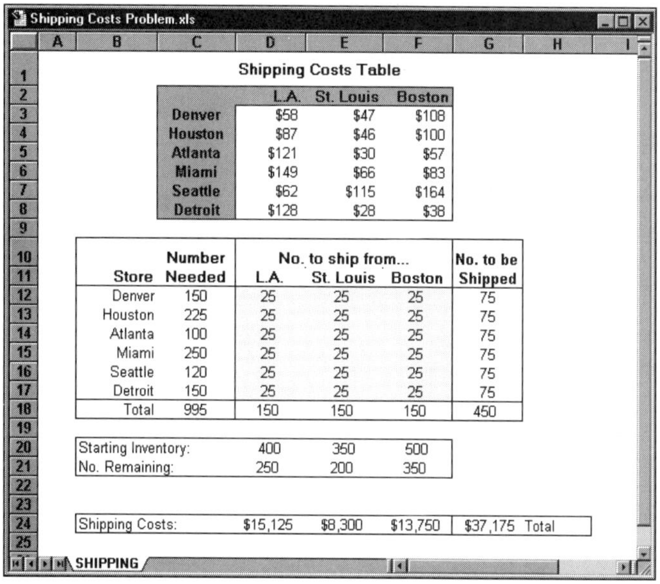

Figure 37-12: This worksheet determines the least expensive way to ship products from warehouses to retail outlets.

This workbook is rather complicated, so each part is explained individually:

✦ **Shipping Costs Table:** This table, at the top of the worksheet, contains per-unit shipping costs from each warehouse to each retail outlet. The cost to ship a unit from Los Angeles to Denver, for example, is $58.

✦ **Product needs of each retail store:** This information appears in C12:C17. For example, Denver needs 150 units, Houston needs 225, and so on. C18 holds the total needed.

✦ **Number to ship:** The shaded range (D12:F17) holds the adjustable cells that Solver varies (they are all initialized with a value of 25, to give Solver a starting value.) Column G contains formulas that total the number of units the company needs to ship to each retail outlet.

✦ **Warehouse inventory:** Row 20 contains the amount of inventory at each warehouse, and row 21 contains formulas that subtract the amount shipped (row 18) from the inventory. For example, cell D21 contains the following formula: =D20–D18.

✦ **Calculated shipping costs:** Row 24 contains formulas that calculate the shipping costs. Cell D24 contains the following formula, which is copied to the two cells to the right of Cell D24:

```
=SUMPRODUCT(D3:D8,D12:D17)
```

This formula calculates the total shipping cost from each warehouse. Cell G24 is the bottom line, the total shipping costs for all orders.

Solver fills in values in the range D12:F17 in such a way that minimizes shipping costs while still supplying each retail outlet with the desired number of units. In other words, the solution minimizes the value in cell C24 by adjusting the cells in D12:F17, subject to the following constraints:

✦ The number of units needed by each retail outlet must equal the number shipped (in other words, all the orders are filled). These constraints are represented by the following specifications:

```
C12=G12    C14=G14    C16=G16
C13=G13    C15=G15    C17=G17
```

✦ The adjustable cells can't be negative, because shipping a negative number of units makes no sense. These constraints are represented by the following specifications:

```
D12>=0    E12>=0    F12>=0
D13>=0    E13>=0    F13>=0
D14>=0    E14>=0    F14>=0
D15>=0    E15>=0    F15>=0
D16>=0    E16>=0    F16>=0
D17>=0    E17>=0    F17>=0
```

✦ The number of units remaining in each warehouse's inventory must not be negative (that is, they can't ship more than what is available). This is represented by the following constraint specifications:

```
D21>=0    E21>=0    F21>=0
```

Note   Before you solve this problem with Solver, you may try your hand at minimizing the shipping cost manually by entering values in D12:F17. Don't forget to make sure that all the constraints are met. This is often a difficult task — and you can better appreciate the power behind Solver.

Setting up the problem is the difficult part. For example, you must enter 37 constraints. When you have specified all the necessary information, click the Solve button to put Solver to work. This process takes a while (Solver's speed depends on the speed of your computer and the amount of memory installed on your computer), but eventually Solver displays the solution that is shown in Figure 37-13.

Store	Number Needed	No. to ship from... L.A.	St. Louis	Boston	No. to be Shipped
Denver	150	150	0	0	150
Houston	225	0	225	0	225
Atlanta	100	0	100	0	100
Miami	250	0	25	225	250
Seattle	120	120	0	0	120
Detroit	150	0	0	150	150
Total	995	270	350	375	995

Starting Inventory:	400	350	500	
No. Remaining:	130	0	125	
Shipping Costs:	$16,140	$15,000	$24,375	$55,515 Total

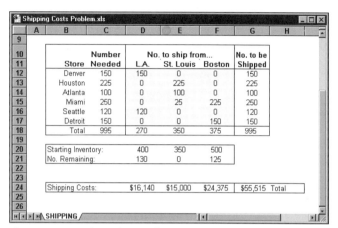

Figure 37-13: The solution that was created by Solver

The total shipping cost is $55,515, and all the constraints are met. Notice that shipments to Miami come from both St. Louis and Boston.

Scheduling staff

This example deals with staff scheduling. Such problems usually involve determining the minimum number of people that satisfy staffing needs on certain days or times of the day. The constraints typically involve such details as the number of consecutive days or hours that a person can work.

Figure 37-14 shows a worksheet that is set up to analyze a simple staffing problem. The question is, "What is the minimum number of employees required to meet daily staffing needs?" At this company, each person works five consecutive days. As a result, employees begin their five-day workweek on different days of the week.

Day	Staff Needed	Staff Scheduled	No. Who Start Work On this Day	Excess Staff
Sun	60	125	25.00	65
Mon	142	125	25.00	-17
Tue	145	125	25.00	-20
Wed	160	125	25.00	-35
Thu	180	125	25.00	-55
Fri	190	125	25.00	-65
Sat	65	125	25.00	60
Total staff needed:			175	

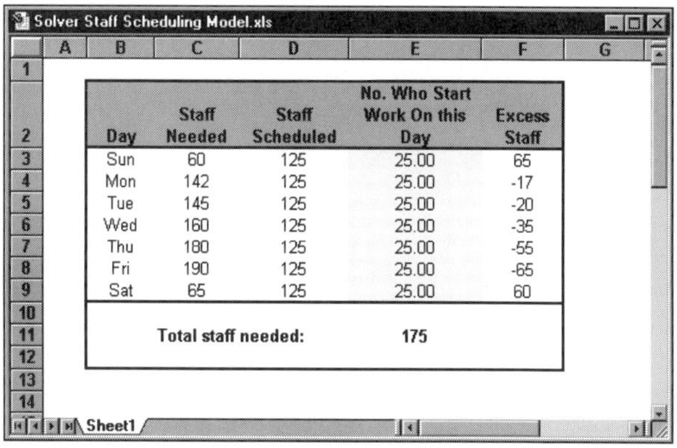

Figure 37-14: This staffing model determines the minimum number of staff members required to meet daily staffing needs.

The key to this problem, as with most Solver problems, is figuring out how to set up the worksheet. This example makes it clear that setting up your worksheet properly is critical to Solver. This worksheet is laid out as follows:

✦ **Day:** Column B consists of plain text for the days of the week.

✦ **Staff Needed:** The values in column C represent the number of employees needed on each day of the week. As you see, staffing needs vary quite a bit by the day of the week.

✦ **Staff Scheduled:** Column D holds formulas that use the values in column E. Each formula adds the number of people who start on that day to the number of people who started on the preceding four days. Because the week wraps around, you can't use a single formula and copy it. Consequently, each formula in column D is different:

```
D3:   =E3+E9+E8+E7+E6
D4:   =E4+E3+E9+E8+E7
D5:   =E5+E4+E10+E9+E8
D6:   =E6+E5+E4+E10+E9
D7:   =E7+E6+E5+E4+E10
D8:   =E8+E7+E6+E5+E4
D9:   =E9+E8+E7+E6+E5
```

✦ **Adjustable cells:** Column E holds the adjustable cells — the numbers to be determined by Solver. These cells are initialized with a value of 25, to give Solver a starting value. Generally, you should initialize the changing cells to values that are as close as possible to the anticipated answer.

✦ **Excess Staff:** Column F contains formulas that subtract the number of staff members needed from the number of staff members scheduled, to determine excess staff. Cell F3 contains =D3 – C3, which was copied to the six cells below it.

✦ **Total staff needed:** Cell E11 contains a formula that sums the number of people who start on each day. The formula is =SUM(E3:E9). This is the value that Solver minimizes.

This problem, of course, has constraints. The number of people scheduled each day must be greater than or equal to the number of people required. If each value in column F is greater than or equal to 0, the constraints are satisfied.

After the worksheet is set up, select Tools ➪ Solver and specify that you want to minimize cell E11 by changing cells E3:E9. Next, click the Add button to begin adding the following constraints:

```
F3>=0
F4>=0
F5>=0
F6>=0
F7>=0
F8>=0
F9>=0
```

Click Solve to start the process. The solution that Solver finds, shown in Figure 37-15, indicates that a staff of 188 meets the staffing needs and that no excess staffing exists on any day.

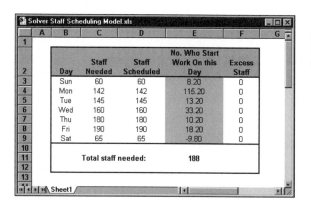

Figure 37-15: This solution offered by Solver isn't quite right – you have to add more constraints.

But wait! If you examine the results carefully, you notice that a few things are wrong here:

✦ Solver's solution involves partial people – who are difficult to find. For example, 8.2 people begin their workweek on Sunday.

✦ Even more critical is the suggestion that a negative number of people should begin their workweek on Saturday.

You can correct both of these problems easily by adding more constraints. Fortunately, Solver enables you to limit the solution to integers, by using the integer option in the Add Constraint dialog box. This means that you must add another constraint for each cell in E3:E9. Figure 37-16 shows how you can specify an integer constraint. Avoiding the negative people problem requires seven more constraints of the form **E3>=0**, one for each cell in E3:E9.

Figure 37-16: With many problems, you have to limit the solution to integers. You can do this by selecting the integer option in the Constraint box of the Add Constraint dialog box.

These two problems (integer solutions and negative numbers) are quite common when using Solver. They also demonstrate that checking the results is important, rather than relying only on Solver's solution.

Tip If you find that adding these constraints is tedious, save the model to a worksheet range. Then, you can add new constraints to the range in the worksheet (and make sure that you don't overwrite the last cell in this range). Next, run Solver again and load the modified model from the range that you edited. The example workbook (available on this book's CD-ROM) has three Solver ranges stored in it.

After adding these constraints, run Solver again. This time it arrives at the solution shown in Figure 37-17. Notice that this solution requires 192 people and results in excess staffing on three days of the week. This solution is the best one possible that uses the fewest number of people — and almost certainly is better than what you would arrive at manually.

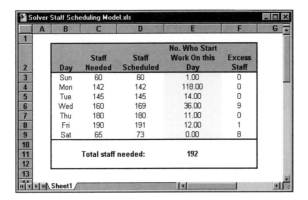

Figure 37-17: Rerunning Solver after adding more constraints produces a better solution to the staffing model problem.

Allocating resources

The example in this section is a common type of problem that's ideal for Solver. Essentially, problems of this sort involve optimizing the volumes of individual production units that use varying amounts of fixed resources. Figure 37-18 shows an example for a toy company.

Figure 37-18: Using Solver to maximize profit when resources are limited

This company makes five different toys, which use six different materials in varying amounts. For example, Toy A requires 3 units of blue paint, 2 units of white paint, 1 unit of plastic, 3 units of wood, and 1 unit of glue. Column G shows the current inventory of each type of material. Row 10 shows the unit profit for each toy. The number of toys to make is shown in the range B11:F11 — these are the values that Solver determines. The goal of this example is to determine how to allocate the resources to maximize the total profit (B13). In other words, Solver determines how many units of each toy to make. The constraints in this example are relatively simple:

✦ Ensure that production doesn't use more resources than are available. This can be accomplished by specifying that each cell in column F is greater than or equal to zero.

✦ Ensure that the quantities produced aren't negative. This can be accomplished by specifying that each cell in row 11 be greater than or equal to zero.

Figure 37-19 shows the results that are produced by Solver. It shows the product mix that generates $12,365 in profit and uses all resources in their entirety, except for glue.

	A	B	C	D	E	F	G	H	I
	Solver Resource Allocation Model.xls								
1				XYZ Toys Inc.					
2				Materials Needed					
3	Material	Toy A	Toy B	Toy C	Toy D	Toy E	Amt. Avail.	Amt. Used	Amt. Left
4	Red Paint	0	1	0	1	3	625	625	0
5	Blue Paint	3	1	0	1	0	640	640	0
6	White Paint	2	1	2	0	2	1,100	1,100	0
7	Plastic	1	5	2	2	1	875	875	0
8	Wood	3	0	3	5	5	2,200	2,200	0
9	Glue	1	2	3	2	3	1,500	1,353	147
10	Unit Profit	$15	$30	$20	$25	$25			
11	No. to Make	194	19	158	40	189			
12	Profit	$2,903	$573	$3,168	$1,008	$4,713			
13	Total Profit	$12,365							
14									
15									

Figure 37-19: Solver determined how to use the resources to maximize the total profit.

Optimizing an investment portfolio

This example demonstrates how to use Solver to help maximize the return on an investment portfolio. Portfolios consist of several investments, each of which has different yields. In addition, you may have some constraints that involve reducing risk and diversification goals. Without such constraints, a portfolio problem becomes a no-brainer: put all of your money in the investment with the highest yield.

This example involves a credit union, a financial institution that takes members' deposits and invests them in loans to other members, bank CDs, and other types of investments. The credit union distributes part of the return on these investments to the members in the form of *dividends*, or interest on their deposits. This hypothetical credit union must adhere to some regulations regarding its investments, and the board of directors has imposed some other restrictions. These regulations and restrictions comprise the problem's constraints. Figure 37-20 shows a workbook set up for this problem.

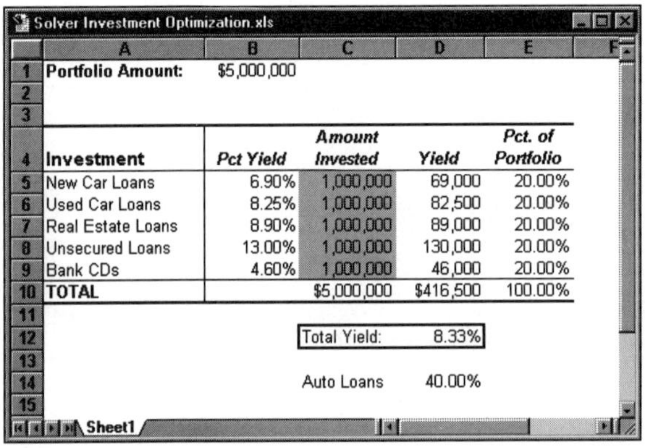

	A	B	C	D	E
1	Portfolio Amount:	$5,000,000			
2					
3					
4	Investment	Pct Yield	Amount Invested	Yield	Pct. of Portfolio
5	New Car Loans	6.90%	1,000,000	69,000	20.00%
6	Used Car Loans	8.25%	1,000,000	82,500	20.00%
7	Real Estate Loans	8.90%	1,000,000	89,000	20.00%
8	Unsecured Loans	13.00%	1,000,000	130,000	20.00%
9	Bank CDs	4.60%	1,000,000	46,000	20.00%
10	TOTAL		$5,000,000	$416,500	100.00%
11					
12			Total Yield:	8.33%	
13					
14			Auto Loans	40.00%	
15					

Figure 37-20: This worksheet is set up to maximize a credit union's investments, given some constraints.

The following constraints are the ones to which you must adhere in allocating the $5 million portfolio:

✦ The amount that the credit union invests in new-car loans must be at least three times the amount that the credit union invests in used-car loans (used-car loans are riskier investments). This constraint is represented as C5>=C6*3.

✦ Car loans should make up at least 15 percent of the portfolio. This constraint is represented as D14>=.15.

✦ Unsecured loans should make up no more than 25 percent of the portfolio. This constraint is represented as E8<=.25.

✦ At least 10 percent of the portfolio should be in bank CDs. This constraint is represented as E9>=.10.

✦ All investments should be positive or zero. In other words, the problem requires five additional constraints to ensure that none of the changing cells go below zero.

The changing cells are C5:C9, and the goal is to maximize the total yield in cell D12. Starting values of 1,000,000 have been entered in the changing cells. When you run

Solver with these parameters, it produces the solution that is shown in Figure 37-21, which has a total yield of 9.25 percent.

Solver Investment Optimization.xls

Portfolio Amount:	$5,000,000			
Investment	***Pct Yield***	***Amount Invested***	***Yield***	***Pct. of Portfolio***
New Car Loans	6.90%	562,500	38,813	11.25%
Used Car Loans	8.25%	187,500	15,469	3.75%
Real Estate Loans	8.90%	2,500,000	222,500	50.00%
Unsecured Loans	13.00%	1,250,000	162,500	25.00%
Bank CDs	4.60%	500,000	23,000	10.00%
TOTAL		$5,000,000	$462,281	100.00%
		Total Yield:	9.25%	
		Auto Loans	15.00%	

Figure 37-21: The results of the portfolio optimization

In this example, the starting values of the changing cells are very important. For example, if you use smaller numbers as the starting values (such as 10) and rerun Solver, you find that it doesn't do as well. In fact, it produces a total yield of only 8.35 percent. This demonstrates that you can't always trust Solver to arrive at the optimal solution with one try—even when the Solver Results dialog box tells you that *All constraints and optimality conditions are satisfied.* Usually, the best approach is to use starting values that are as close as possible to the final solution.

The best advice? Make sure that you understand Solver well before you entrust it with helping you make major decisions. Try different starting values, and adjust the options to see whether Solver can do better.

Summary

This chapter discusses two Excel commands: Tools ➪ Goal Seek and Tools ➪ Solver. The latter command is available only if the Solver add-in is installed. Goal seeking is used to determine the value in a single input cell that produces a result that you want in a formula cell. Solver determines values in multiple input cells that produce a result that you want, given certain constraints. Using Solver can be challenging, because it has many options and the result that it produces isn't always the best one.

✦ ✦ ✦

Analyzing Data with Analysis ToolPak

Although spreadsheets such as Excel are designed primarily with business users in mind, these products can be found in other disciplines, including education, research, statistics, and engineering. One way that Excel addresses these nonbusiness users is with its Analysis ToolPak add-in. Many of the features and functions in the Analysis ToolPak are valuable for business applications as well.

The Analysis ToolPak: An Overview

The Analysis ToolPak is an add-in that provides analytical capability that normally is not available. The Analysis ToolPak consists of two parts:

✦ Analytical procedures

✦ Additional worksheet functions

These analysis tools offer many features that may be useful to those in the scientific, engineering, and educational communities — not to mention business users whose needs extend beyond the normal spreadsheet fare.

This section provides a quick overview of the types of analyses that you can perform with the Analysis ToolPak. Each of the following tools are discussed in detail in the course of this chapter:

✦ Analysis of variance (three types)

✦ Correlation

✦ Covariance

✦ Descriptive statistics

✦ Exponential smoothing

✦ F-test

✦ Fourier analysis

✦ Histogram

✦ Moving average

✦ Random number generation

✦ Rank and percentile

✦ Regression

✦ Sampling

✦ t-test (three types)

✦ z-test

As you can see, the Analysis ToolPak add-in brings a great deal of new functionality to Excel. These procedures have limitations, however, and in some cases, you may prefer to create your own formulas to do some calculations.

Besides the procedures just listed, the Analysis ToolPak provides many additional worksheet functions. These functions cover mathematics, engineering, unit conversions, financial analysis, and dates. These functions are listed at the end of the chapter.

Using the Analysis ToolPak

This section discusses the two components of the Analysis ToolPak: its tools and its functions.

Using the analysis tools

The procedures in the Analysis ToolPak add-in are relatively straightforward. To use any of these tools, you select Tools ➪ Data Analysis, which displays the dialog box shown in Figure 38-1. Scroll through the list until you find the analysis tool that you want to use and then click OK. Excel displays a new dialog box that's specific to the procedure that you select.

Figure 38-1: The Data Analysis dialog box enables you to select the tool in which you're interested.

Usually, you need to specify one or more input ranges, plus an output range (one cell is sufficient). Alternatively, you can choose to place the results on a new worksheet or in a new workbook. The procedures vary in the amount of additional information that is required. In many dialog boxes, you may be able to indicate whether your data range includes labels. If so, you can specify the entire range, including the labels, and indicate to Excel that the first column (or row) contains labels. Excel then uses these labels in the tables that it produces. Most tools also provide different output options that you can select, based on your needs.

Caution   In some cases, the procedures produce their results by using formulas. Consequently, you can change your data, and the results update automatically. In other procedures, Excel stores the results as values, so if you change your data, the results don't reflect your changes. Make sure that you understand what Excel is doing.

Using the Analysis ToolPak functions

After you install the Analysis ToolPak, you have access to all the additional functions (which are described fully in the online Help system). You access these functions just like any other functions, and they appear in the Function Wizard dialog box, intermixed with Excel's standard functions.

Note   If you plan to share worksheets that use these functions, make sure that the other user has access to the add-in functions. If the other user doesn't install Analysis ToolPak add-in, formulas that use any of the Analysis ToolPak functions will return #VALUE.

The Analysis ToolPak Tools

This section describes each tool and provides an example. Space limitations prevent a discussion of every available option in these procedures. However, if you need to use some of these advanced analysis tools, then you probably already know how to use most of the options not covered here.

The analysis of variance tool

Analysis of variance is a statistical test that determines whether two or more samples were drawn from the same population. Using tools in the Analysis ToolPak, you can perform three types of analysis of variance:

✦ **Single-factor:** A one-way analysis of variance, with only one sample for each group of data.

✦ **Two-factor with replication:** A two-way analysis of variance, with multiple samples (or replications) for each group of data.

✦ **Two-factor without replication:** A two-way analysis of variance, with a single sample (or replication) for each group of data.

Figure 38-2 shows the dialog box for a single-factor analysis of variance. Alpha represents the statistical confidence level for the test.

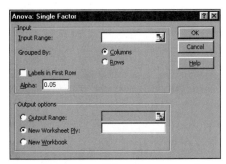

Figure 38-2: Specifying parameters for a single-factor analysis of variance

Figure 38-3 shows the results of an analysis of variance. The output for this test consists of the means and variances for each of the four samples, the value of F, the critical value of F, and the significance of F (P-value). Because the probability is greater than the Alpha value, the conclusion is that the samples were drawn from the same population.

Analysis ToolPak Examples.xls

	F	G	H	I	J	K	L
1	Anova: Single Factor						
2							
3	SUMMARY						
4	Groups	Count	Sum	Average	Variance		
5	Low	8	538	67.25	6680.214		
6	Medium	8	578	72.25	7700.214		
7	High	8	636	79.5	9397.714		
8	Control	8	544	68	6845.714		
9							
10							
11	ANOVA						
12	Source of Variation	SS	df	MS	F	P-value	F crit
13	Between Groups	757	3	252.3333	0.032959	0.991785	2.946685
14	Within Groups	214367	28	7655.964			
15							

Read_Me \ **Anova** / Correlation / Covariance / Descriptive

Figure 38-3: The results of the analysis of variance

The correlation tool

Correlation is a widely used statistic that measures the degree to which two sets of data vary together. For example, if higher values in one data set are typically associated with higher values in the second data set, the two data sets have a positive correlation. The degree of correlation is expressed as a coefficient that ranges from –1.0 (a perfect negative correlation) to +1.0 (a perfect positive correlation). A correlation coefficient of 0 indicates that the two variables are not correlated.

Figure 38-4 shows the Correlation dialog box. Specify the input range, which can include any number of variables, arranged in rows or columns.

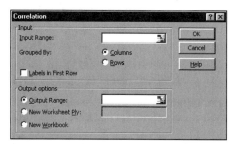

Figure 38-4: The Correlation dialog box

Figure 38-5 shows the results of a correlation analysis for eight variables. The output consists of a correlation matrix that shows the correlation coefficient for each variable paired with every other variable.

	Height	Weight	Sex	Test1	Test2	Test3	Test4	Test5
Height	1							
Weight	0.84031	1						
Sex	0.67077	0.51894	1					
Test1	0.09959	0.16347	0.00353	1				
Test2	-0.2805	-0.2244	-0.1533	0.83651	1			
Test3	-0.4374	-0.3845	-0.0136	-0.445	-0.0203	1		
Test4	0.22718	0.00356	-0.2127	0.07838	0.06727	-0.1515	1	
Test5	-0.1016	-0.1777	0.04521	0.28937	0.20994	-0.3746	0.01266	1

Figure 38-5: The results of a correlation analysis

Note   Notice that the resulting correlation matrix doesn't use formulas to calculate the results. Therefore, if any data changes, the correlation matrix isn't valid. You can use Excel's CORREL function to create a correlation matrix that changes automatically when you change data.

The covariance tool

The Covariance tool produces a matrix that is similar to the one generated by the Correlation tool. *Covariance*, like correlation, measures the degree to which two variables vary together. Specifically, covariance is the average of the product of the deviations of each data point pair from their respective means.

Figure 38-6 shows a covariance matrix. Notice that the values along the diagonal (where the variables are the same) are the variances for the variable.

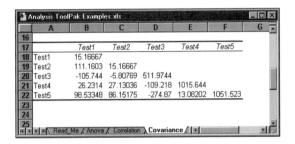

Figure 38-6: The results of a covariance analysis

You can use the COVAR function to create a covariance matrix that uses formulas. The values that are generated by the Analysis ToolPak are *not* the same values that you would get if you used the COVAR function.

The descriptive statistics tool

This tool produces a table that describes your data with some standard statistics. It uses the dialog box that is shown in Figure 38-7. The Kth Largest option and Kth Smallest option each displays the data value that corresponds to a rank that you specify. For example, if you check Kth Largest and specify a value of 2, the output shows the second-largest value in the input range (the standard output already includes the minimum and maximum values).

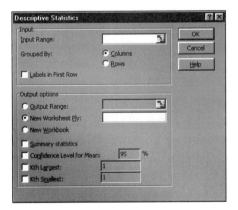

Figure 38-7: The Descriptive Statistics dialog box

Sample output for the Descriptive Statistics tool appears in Figure 38-8. This example has three groups. Because the output for this procedure consists of values (not formulas), you should use this procedure only when you're certain that your data isn't going to change; otherwise, you will need to re-execute the procedure. You can generate all of these statistics by using formulas.

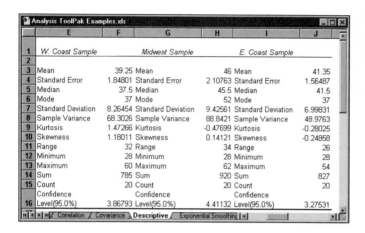

Figure 38-8: Output from the Descriptive Statistics tool

The exponential smoothing tool

Exponential smoothing is a technique for predicting data that is based on the previous data point and the previously predicted data point. You can specify the *damping factor* (also known as a *smoothing constant*), which can range from 0 to 1. This determines the relative weighting of the previous data point and the previously predicted data point. You also can request standard errors and a chart.

The exponential smoothing procedure generates formulas that use the damping factor that you specify. Therefore, if the data changes, Excel updates the formulas. Figure 38-9 shows sample output from the Exponential Smoothing tool.

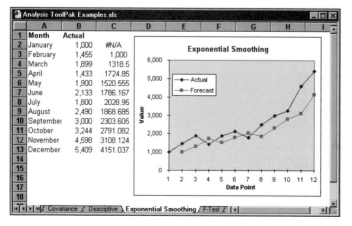

Figure 38-9: Output from the Exponential Smoothing tool

The F-test (two-sample test for variance) tool

The *F-test* is a commonly used statistical test that enables you to compare two population variances. Figure 38-10 shows the dialog box for this tool.

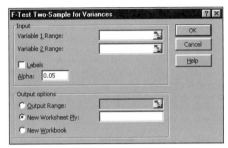

Figure 38-10: The F-Test dialog box

The output for this test consists of the means and variances for each of the two samples, the value of F, the critical value of F, and the significance of F. Sample output appears in Figure 38-11.

Analysis ToolPak Examples.xls							
	A	B	C	D	E	F	G
1	Group 1	Group 2		F-Test Two-Sample for Variances			
2	96	39					
3	78	53			Group 1	Group 2	
4	72	51		Mean	75.44444	46.66667	
5	78	48		Variance	109.5278	25	
6	65	51		Observations	9	9	
7	66	42		df	8	8	
8	69	44		F	4.381111		
9	87	42		P(F<=f) one-tail	0.025855		
10	68	50		F Critical one-tail	3.438103		
11							
12							

Covariance ╱ Descriptive ╱ Exponential Smoothing

Figure 38-11: Sample output for the F-test

The Fourier analysis tool

This tool performs a "fast Fourier" transformation of a range of data. Using the Fourier Analysis tool, you can transform a range limited to the following sizes: 1, 2, 4, 8, 16, 32, 64, 128, 256, 512, or 1,024 data points. This procedure accepts and generates complex numbers, which are represented as labels (not values).

The histogram tool

This procedure is useful for producing data distributions and histogram charts. It accepts an input range and a bin range. A *bin* range is a range of values that specifies the limits for each column of the histogram. If you omit the bin range, Excel creates ten equal-interval bins for you. The size of each bin is determined by a formula of the following form:

```
=(MAX(input_range)-MIN(input_range))/10
```

The Histogram dialog box appears in Figure 38-12. As an option, you can specify that the resulting histogram be sorted by frequency of occurrence in each bin.

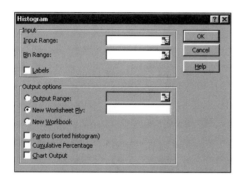

Figure 38-12: The Histogram tool enables you to generate distributions and graphical output.

If you specify the Pareto (sorted histogram) option, the bin range must contain values and can't contain formulas. If formulas appear in the bin range, Excel doesn't sort properly, and your worksheet displays error values.

Figure 38-13 shows a chart generated from this procedure. The Histogram tool doesn't use formulas, so if you change any of the input data, you need to repeat the histogram procedure to update the results.

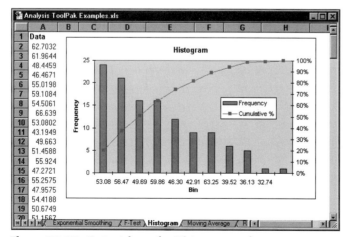

Figure 38-13: Output from the Histogram tool

The moving average tool

The Moving Average tool helps you to smooth out a data series that has a lot of variability. This is best done in conjunction with a chart. Excel does the smoothing by computing a moving average of a specified number of values. In many cases, a moving average enables you to spot trends that otherwise would be obscured by noise in the data.

Figure 38-14 shows the Moving Average dialog box. You can, of course, specify the number of values that you want Excel to use for each average. If you place a check in the Standard Errors check box, Excel calculates standard errors and places formulas for these calculations next to the moving average formulas. The standard error values indicate the degree of variability between the actual values and the calculated moving averages. When you close this dialog box, Excel creates formulas that reference the input range that you specify.

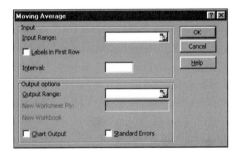

Figure 38-14: The Moving Average dialog box

Figure 38-15 shows the results of using this tool. The first few cells in the output are #N/A because not enough data points exist to calculate the average for these initial values.

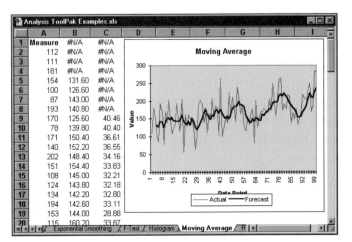

Figure 38-15: Output from the Moving Average tool

The random number generation tool

Although Excel contains a built-in function to calculate random numbers, the Random Number Generation tool is much more flexible, because you can specify what type of distribution you want the random numbers to have. Figure 38-16 shows the Random Number Generation dialog box. The Parameters box varies, depending on the type of distribution that you select.

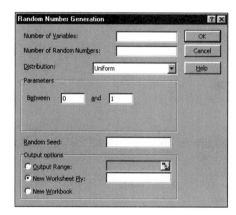

Figure 38-16: This dialog box enables you to generate a wide variety of random numbers.

The Number of Variables refers to the number of columns that you want, and the Number of Random Numbers refers to the number of rows that you want. For example, if you want 200 random numbers arranged in 10 columns of 20 rows, you specify 10 and 20, respectively, in these text boxes.

The Random Seed box enables you to specify a starting value that Excel uses in its random number-generating algorithm. Usually, you leave this blank. If you want to generate the same random number sequence, however, you can specify a seed between 1 and 32,767 (integer values only). You can create the following types of distributions:

✦ **Uniform:** Every random number has an equal chance of being selected. You specify the upper and lower limits.

✦ **Normal:** The random numbers correspond to a normal distribution. You specify the mean and standard deviation of the distribution.

✦ **Bernoulli:** The random numbers are either 0 or 1, determined by the probability of success that you specify.

✦ **Binomial:** This returns random numbers based on a Bernoulli distribution over a specific number of trials, given a probability of success that you specify.

✦ **Poisson:** This option generates values in a Poisson distribution. This is characterized by discrete events that occur in an interval, where the probability of a single occurrence is proportional to the size of the interval. The *lambda* parameter is the expected number of occurrences in an interval. In a Poisson distribution, lambda is equal to the mean, which also is equal to the variance.

✦ **Patterned:** This option doesn't generate random numbers. Rather, it repeats a series of numbers in steps that you specify.

✦ **Discrete:** This option enables you to specify the probability that specific values are chosen. It requires a two-column input range; the first column holds the values, and the second column holds the probability of each value being chosen. The sum of the probabilities in the second column must equal 100 percent.

The rank and percentile tool

This tool creates a table that shows the ordinal and percentile ranking for each value in a range. Figure 38-17 shows the results of this procedure. You can also generate ranks and percentiles by using formulas.

	A	B	C	D	E	F	G	H
1	SalesRep	Sales		Point	Sales	Rank	Percent	
2	Allen	137,676		4	197,107	1	100.00%	
3	Brandon	155,449		3	180,414	2	94.40%	
4	Campaigne	180,414		17	170,538	3	88.80%	
5	Dufenberg	197,107		14	161,750	4	83.30%	
6	Fox	130,814		2	155,449	5	77.70%	
7	Giles	133,283		11	151,466	6	72.20%	
8	Haflich	116,943		19	149,627	7	66.60%	
9	Hosaka	107,684		12	145,088	8	61.10%	
10	Jenson	128,060		1	137,676	9	55.50%	
11	Larson	121,336		18	134,395	10	50.00%	
12	Leitch	151,466		6	133,283	11	44.40%	
13	Miller	145,088		5	130,814	12	38.80%	
14	Peterson	127,995		9	128,060	13	33.30%	
15	Richards	161,750		13	127,995	14	27.70%	
16	Richardson	117,203		10	121,336	15	22.20%	
17	Ryan	102,571		15	117,203	16	16.60%	
18	Serrano	170,538		7	116,943	17	11.10%	
19	Struyk	134,395		8	107,684	18	5.50%	
20	Winfrey	149,627		16	102,571	19	.00%	

Figure 38-17: Output from the rank and percentile procedure

The regression tool

The Regression tool calculates a regression analysis from worksheet data. Use regression to analyze trends, forecast the future, build predictive models, and, often, to make sense out of a series of seemingly unrelated numbers.

Regression analysis enables you to determine the extent to which one range of data (the dependent variable) varies as a function of the values of one or more other ranges of data (the independent variables). This relationship is expressed mathematically, using values that Excel calculates. You can use these calculations to create a mathematical model of the data and predict the dependent variable by using different values of one or more independent variables. This tool can perform simple and multiple linear regressions and calculate and standardize residuals automatically.

Figure 38-18 shows the Regression dialog box.

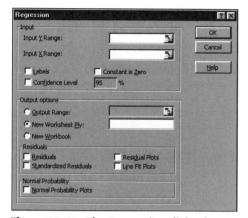

Figure 38-18: The Regression dialog box

As you can see, the Regression dialog box offers many options:

- ✦ **Input Y Range:** The range that contains the dependent variable.

- ✦ **Input X Range:** One or more ranges that contain independent variables.

- ✦ **Confidence Level:** The confidence level for the regression.

- ✦ **Constant is Zero:** If checked, this forces the regression to have a constant of zero (which means that the regression line passes through the origin; when the X values are 0, the predicted Y value is 0).

- ✦ **Residuals:** These options specify whether to include residuals in the output. *Residuals* are the differences between observed and predicted values.

- ✦ **Normal Probability:** This generates a chart for normal probability plots.

The results of a regression analysis appear in Figure 38-19. If you understand regression analysis, the output from this procedure is familiar.

	F	G	H	I	J	K	L
2	SUMMARY OUTPUT						
3							
4	*Regression Statistics*						
5	Multiple R	0.765099405					
6	R Square	0.585377099					
7	Adjusted R Square	0.530094046					
8	Standard Error	370049.2704					
9	Observations	18					
10							
11	ANOVA						
12		*df*	*SS*	*MS*	*F*	*ignificance F*	
13	Regression	2	2.89997E+12	1.45E+12	10.589	0.001356	
14	Residual	15	2.05405E+12	1.3694E+11			
15	Total	17	4.95401E+12				
16							
17		*Coefficients*	*Standard Error*	*t Stat*	*P-value*	*Lower 95%*	*Upper 95%*
18	Intercept	716434.6615	238757.3324	3.0006813	0.009	207535.1	1225334.2
19	Adv	107.6800943	36.20709499	2.97400535	0.0095	30.50645	184.85374
20	bp Diff	25010.94866	6185.924172	4.04320324	0.0011	11825.96	38195.942
21							

Figure 38-19: Sample output from the Regression tool

The sampling tool

The Sampling tool generates a random sample from a range of input values. The Sampling tool can help you to work with a large database by creating a subset of it. The Sampling dialog box appears in Figure 38-20. This procedure has two options: periodic and random. If you choose a periodic sample, Excel selects every *n*th value from the input range, where *n* equals the period that you specify. With a random sample, you simply specify the size of the sample you want Excel to select, and every value has an equal probability of being chosen.

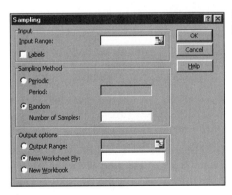

Figure 38-20: The Sampling dialog box is useful for selecting random samples.

The t-test tool

Use the *t-test* to determine whether a statistically significant difference exists between two small samples. The Analysis ToolPak can perform three types of t-tests:

✦ **Paired two-sample for means:** For paired samples in which you have two observations on each subject (such as a pretest and a posttest). The samples must be the same size.

✦ **Two-sample assuming equal variances:** For independent, rather than paired, samples. Excel assumes equal variances for the two samples.

✦ **Two-sample assuming unequal variances:** For independent, rather than paired, samples. Excel assumes unequal variances for the two samples.

Figure 38-21 shows the dialog box for the Paired Two Sample for Means t-test. You specify the significance level (alpha) and the hypothesized difference between the two means (that is, the *null hypothesis*).

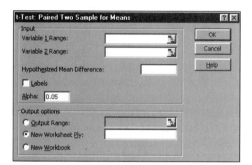

Figure 38-21: The paired t-Test dialog box

Figure 38-22 shows sample output for the paired two sample for means t-test. Excel calculates *t* for both a one-tailed and two-tailed test.

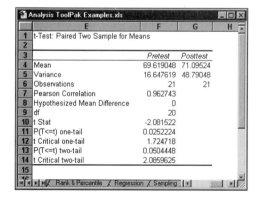

Figure 38-22: Results of a paired two sample for means t-test

The z-test (two-sample test for means) tool

The t-test is used for small samples; the z-test is used for larger samples or populations. You must know the variances for both input ranges.

Analysis ToolPak Worksheet Functions

This section lists the worksheet functions that are available in the Analysis ToolPak. For specific information about the arguments required, click the Help button in the Paste Function dialog box.

Remember, the Analysis ToolPak add-in must be installed to use these functions in your worksheet. If you use any of these functions in a workbook that you distribute to a colleague, make clear to your colleague that the workbook requires the Analysis ToolPak.

These functions appear in the Paste Function dialog box in the following categories:

✦ Date & Time

✦ Engineering (a new category that appears when you install the Analysis ToolPak)

✦ Financial

✦ Information

✦ Math & Trig

Date & Time category

Table 38-1 lists the Analysis ToolPak worksheet functions that you'll find in the Date & Time category.

Table 38-1 Date & Time Category Functions	
Function	**Purpose**
EDATE	Returns the serial number of the date that is the indicated number of months before or after the start date
EOMONTH	Returns the serial number of the last day of the month before or after a specified number of months
NETWORKDAYS	Returns the number of whole workdays between two dates
WEEKNUM	Returns the week number in the year
WORKDAY	Returns the serial number of the date before or after a specified number of workdays
YEARFRAC	Returns the year fraction representing the number of whole days between start_date and end_date

Engineering category

Table 38-2 lists the Analysis ToolPak worksheet functions that you'll find in the Engineering category. Some of these functions are quite useful for nonengineers as well. For example, the CONVERT function converts a wide variety of measurement units.

Table 38-2 Engineering Category Functions	
Function	**Purpose**
BESSELI	Returns the modified Bessel function In(x)
BESSELJ	Returns the Bessel function Jn(x)
BESSELK	Returns the modified Bessel function Kn(x)
BESSELY	Returns the Bessel function Yn(x)
BIN2DEC	Converts a binary number to decimal
BIN2HEX	Converts a binary number to hexadecimal
BIN2OCT	Converts a binary number to octal
COMPLEX	Converts real and imaginary coefficients into a complex number
CONVERT	Converts a number from one measurement system to another
DEC2BIN	Converts a decimal number to binary
DEC2HEX	Converts a decimal number to hexadecimal
DEC2OCT	Converts a decimal number to octal
DELTA	Tests whether two numbers are equal
ERF	Returns the error function
ERFC	Returns the complementary error function
FACTDOUBLE	Returns the double factorial of a number
GESTEP	Tests whether a number is greater than a threshold value
HEX2BIN	Converts a hexadecimal number to binary
HEX2DEC	Converts a hexadecimal number to decimal
HEX2OCT	Converts a hexadecimal number to octal
IMABS	Returns the absolute value (modulus) of a complex number
IMAGINARY	Returns the imaginary coefficient of a complex number
IMARGUMENT	Returns the argument q, an angle expressed in radians

Continued

	Table 38-2 *(continued)*
Function	*Purpose*
IMCONJUGATE	Returns the complex conjugate of a complex number
IMCOS	Returns the cosine of a complex number
IMDIV	Returns the quotient of two complex numbers
IMEXP	Returns the exponential of a complex number
IMLN	Returns the natural logarithm of a complex number
IMLOG10	Returns the base-10 logarithm of a complex number
IMLOG2	Returns the base-2 logarithm of a complex number
IMPOWER	Returns a complex number raised to an integer power
IMPRODUCT	Returns the product of two complex numbers
IMREAL	Returns the real coefficient of a complex number
IMSIN	Returns the sine of a complex number
IMSQRT	Returns the square root of a complex number
IMSUB	Returns the difference of two complex numbers
IMSUM	Returns the sum of complex numbers
OCT2BIN	Converts an octal number to binary
OCT2DEC	Converts an octal number to decimal
OCT2HEX	Converts an octal number to hexadecimal

Financial category

Table 38-3 lists the Analysis ToolPak worksheet functions that you'll find in the Financial category.

	Table 38-3 **Financial Category Functions**
Function	*Purpose*
ACCRINT	Returns the accrued interest for a security that pays periodic interest
ACCRINTM	Returns the accrued interest for a security that pays interest at maturity

Function	Purpose
AMORDEGRC	Returns the prorated linear depreciation of an asset for each accounting period. Similar to the AMORLINC function, except that this function uses a depreciation coefficient that depends on the life of the assets
AMORLINC	Returns the prorated linear depreciation of an asset for each accounting period
COUPDAYBS	Returns the number of days from the beginning of the coupon period to the settlement date
COUPDAYS	Returns the number of days in the coupon period that contain the settlement date
COUPDAYSNC	Returns the number of days from the settlement date to the next coupon date
COUPNCD	Returns the next coupon date after the settlement date
COUPNUM	Returns the number of coupons payable between the settlement date and maturity date
COUPPCD	Returns the previous coupon date before the settlement date
CUMIPMT	Returns the cumulative interest paid between two periods
CUMPRINC	Returns the cumulative principal paid on a loan between two periods
DISC	Returns the discount rate for a security
DOLLARDE	Converts a dollar price, expressed as a fraction, into a dollar price, expressed as a decimal number
DOLLARFR	Converts a dollar price, expressed as a decimal number, into a dollar price, expressed as a fraction
DURATION	Returns the annual duration of a security with periodic interest payments
EFFECT	Returns the effective annual interest rate
FVSCHEDULE	Returns the future value of an initial principal after applying a series of compound interest rates
INTRATE	Returns the interest rate for a fully invested security
MDURATION	Returns the Macauley modified duration for a security with an assumed par value of $100
NOMINAL	Returns the annual nominal interest rate
ODDFPRICE	Returns the price per $100 face value of a security with an odd first period
ODDFYIELD	Returns the yield of a security with an odd first period

Continued

Table 38-3 *(continued)*	
Function	*Purpose*
ODDLPRICE	Returns the price per $100 face value of a security with an odd last period
ODDLYIELD	Returns the yield of a security with an odd last period
PRICE	Returns the price per $100 face value of a security that pays periodic interest
PRICEDISC	Returns the price per $100 face value of a discounted security
PRICEMAT	Returns the price per $100 face value of a security that pays interest at maturity
RECEIVED	Returns the amount received at maturity for a fully invested security
TBILLEQ	Returns the bond-equivalent yield for a Treasury bill
TBILLPRICE	Returns the price per $100 face value for a Treasury bill
TBILLYIELD	Returns the yield for a Treasury bill
XIRR	Returns the internal rate of return for a schedule of cash flows
XNPV	Returns the net present value for a schedule of cash flows
YIELD	Returns the yield on a security that pays periodic interest
YIELDDISC	Returns the annual yield for a discounted security (for example, a Treasury bill)
YIELDMAT	Returns the annual yield of a security that pays interest at maturity

Information category

Table 38-4 lists the two Analysis ToolPak worksheet functions that you'll find in the Information category.

Table 38-4 **Information Category Functions**	
Function	*Purpose*
ISEVEN	Returns TRUE if the number is even
ISODD	Returns TRUE if the number is odd

Math & Trig category

Table 38-5 lists the Analysis ToolPak worksheet functions that you'll find in the Math & Trig category.

Table 38-5 Math & Trig Category Functions	
Function	**Purpose**
GCD	Returns the greatest common divisor
LCM	Returns the least common multiple
MROUND	Returns a number rounded to the desired multiple
MULTINOMIAL	Returns the multinomial of a set of numbers
QUOTIENT	Returns the integer portion of a division
RANDBETWEEN	Returns a random number between the numbers that you specify
SERIESSUM	Returns the sum of a power series based on the formula
SQRTPI	Returns the square root of pi

Summary

This chapter discusses the Analysis ToolPak, an add-in that extends the analytical powers of Excel. It includes 19 analytical procedures and 93 functions. Many of the tools are useful for general business applications, but many are for more specialized uses, such as statistical tests.

✦   ✦   ✦

Programming Excel 2000 with VBA

Essentials of Spreadsheet Application Development

My goal in this chapter is to provide you with some *general* guidelines that you may find useful. No simple, sure-fire recipe exists for developing an effective spreadsheet application. Everyone has his or her own style for creating such applications, and in my experience, I haven't discovered one "best way" that works for everyone. In addition, every project that you undertake will be different and will therefore require its own approach. Finally, the demands and general attitudes of the people you'll be working with (or for) also play a role in how the development process will proceed.

Spreadsheet developers typically perform the following activities:

- ✦ Determine the needs of the user
- ✦ Plan an application that meets these needs
- ✦ Determine the most appropriate user interface
- ✦ Create the spreadsheet, formulas, macros, and user interface
- ✦ Test and debug the application
- ✦ Attempt to make the application bulletproof
- ✦ Make the application aesthetically appealing and intuitive
- ✦ Document the development effort

✦ Develop user documentation and online help

✦ Distribute the application to the user

✦ Update the application when it's necessary

Not all of these steps are required for each application, and the order in which these activities are performed may vary from project to project. Each of these activities is described in the pages that follow; and in most cases, the technical details are covered in subsequent chapters.

Determining User Needs

When you undertake a spreadsheet application development project, one of your first steps is to identify exactly what the end users require. Failure to thoroughly assess the end users' needs early on often results in additional work later when you have to adjust the application so that it does what it was supposed to do in the first place.

In some cases, you'll be intimately familiar with the end users and may even be an end user yourself. In other cases (for example, a consultant developing a project for a new client), you may know little or nothing about the users or their situation.

Following are some guidelines that may help to make this phase easier:

✦ Don't presume that you know what the user needs. Second-guessing at this stage almost always causes problems later on.

✦ If possible, talk directly to the end users of the application, not just their supervisor or manager.

✦ Learn what, if anything, is currently being done to meet the user's needs. You may be able to save some work by simply adapting an existing application. At the very least, looking at current solutions will familiarize you with the operation.

✦ Identify the resources available at the user's site. For example, try to determine whether any hardware or software limitations exist that you must work around.

✦ If possible, determine the specific hardware systems that will be used. If your application will be used on slower systems, you need to take that into account.

✦ Understand the skill levels of the end users. This information will help you design the application appropriately.

✦ Determine how long the application will be used. Knowing this may influence the amount of effort you put into the project.

How do you determine the needs of the user? If you've been asked to develop a spreadsheet application, it's a good idea to meet with the end user and ask very specific questions. Better yet, get everything in writing, create flow diagrams, pay attention to minor details, and do anything else to ensure that the product you deliver is the product that is needed.

One final note: Don't be surprised if the project specifications change before you complete the application. This is quite common, and you'll be in a better position if you *expect* changes rather than if you are surprised by them. Just make sure that your contract (if you have one) addresses the issue of changing specifications.

Planning an Application That Meets User Needs

Once you've determined the end users' needs, it's very tempting to jump right in and start fiddling around in Excel — take it from one who suffers from this problem. But try to restrain yourself. Builders don't construct a house without a set of blueprints, and you shouldn't develop a spreadsheet application without some type of plan. The formality of your plan depends on the scope of the project and your general style of working, but you should at least spend *some* time thinking about what you're going to do and coming up with a plan of action.

Before rolling up your sleeves and settling down at your keyboard, you'll benefit by taking some time to consider the various ways that you can approach the problem. Here is where a thorough knowledge of Excel pays off. Avoiding blind alleys before you stumble into them is always a good idea.

If you ask a dozen Excel gurus to design an application based on very precise specifications, chances are you'll get a dozen different implementations of the project that all meet those specifications. And of those solutions, some will definitely be better than others because Excel often provides several different ways to accomplish a task. If you know Excel inside out, you'll have a pretty good idea of the potential methods at your disposal, and you can choose the one most appropriate for the project at hand. Often, a bit of creative thinking yields an unusual approach that's vastly superior to other methods.

So at the beginning of this planning period, you'll be considering some general options, such as those that follow:

✦ **File structure.** Think about whether you want to use one workbook with multiple sheets, several single-sheet workbooks, or a template file.

✦ **Data structure.** You should always consider how your data will be structured. This includes the use of external database files versus storing everything in worksheets.

✦ **Formulas versus VBA.** Should you use formulas or write VBA procedures to perform calculations? Both have advantages and disadvantages.

✦ **Add-in or XLS file.** In most cases, you probably want your final product to be an XLA add-in, but in some cases, an XLS file is preferable.

✦ **Version of Excel.** Do you want your Excel application to work with Excel 2000 only? With Excel 2000 or Excel 97? What about Excel 95 and Excel 5? Will it also be run on a Macintosh? These are very important considerations because each new version of Excel adds features that aren't available in previous versions.

✦ **How to handle errors.** Error handling is a major issue with applications. You need to determine how your application will detect and deal with errors. For example, if your application applies formatting to the active worksheet, you need to be able to handle a case in which a chart sheet is active.

✦ **Use of special features.** If your application needs to summarize a lot of data, you may want to consider using Excel's pivot table feature. Or, you might want to use Excel's data validation feature as a check for valid data entry.

✦ **Performance issues.** The time to start thinking about increasing the speed and efficiency of your application is at the development stage, not when the application is completed and users are complaining.

✦ **Level of security.** As you may know, Excel provides several protection options to restrict access to particular elements of a workbook. For example, you can lock cells so that formulas cannot be changed, and you can assign a password to prevent unauthorized users from viewing or accessing specific files. Determining up front exactly what you need to protect—and what level of protection is necessary—will make your job easier.

You'll probably have to deal with many other project-specific considerations in this phase. The important thing is that you consider all options and don't settle on the first solution that comes to mind.

Another design consideration is remembering to plan for change. You'll do yourself a favor if you make your application as generic as possible. For example, don't write a procedure that works with only a specific range of cells. Rather, write a procedure that accepts any range as an argument. When the inevitable changes are requested, such a design makes it easier for you to carry out the revisions. Also, you may find that the work you do for one project is similar to the work you do for another. Keeping reusability in mind when you are planning a project is always a good idea.

One thing that I've learned from experience is to avoid letting the end user completely guide your approach to a problem. For example, suppose that you meet with a manager who tells you the department needs an application that writes text files, which will be imported into another application. Don't confuse the user's need with the solution. The user's real need is to share data. Using an intermediate text

Learning While You Develop

Now a few words about reality: Excel is a moving target. Excel's upgrade cycle is approximately 18 months, which means that you have one and one-half years to get up to speed with its current innovations before you have even more innovations to contend with.

Excel 5, which introduced VBA, represented a major paradigm shift for Excel developers. Thousands of people up until that point earned their living developing Excel applications that were largely based on the XLM macro language in Excel 2, 3, and 4. Beginning with Excel 5, dozens of new tools became available and developers — for the most part — eagerly embraced them.

When Excel 97 became available, developers faced yet another shift. This new version introduced a new file format, the Visual Basic editor, and UserForms as a replacement for dialog sheets.

VBA is not difficult to learn, but it definitely takes time to become comfortable with it and even more time to master it. The VBA language is still evolving. Consequently, it's not uncommon to be in the process of learning VBA while you're developing applications with it. In fact, I think it's impossible to learn VBA without developing applications. If you're like me, you'll find it much easier to learn VBA if you have a project that requires it. Learning VBA just for the sake of learning VBA usually doesn't work.

file to do it is one possible solution to the need. There may be other ways to approach the problem — such as direct transfer of information by using DDE or OLE. In other words, don't let the users define their problem by stating it in terms of a solution approach. Determining the best approach is *your* job.

Determining the Most Appropriate User Interface

When you develop spreadsheets that others will use, you need to pay special attention to the user interface. By *user interface,* I mean the method by which the user interacts with the application — clicking buttons, using menus, pressing keys, accessing toolbars, and so on.

Again, it's important that you keep the end user in mind. It's likely that you have much more computer experience than the end users, and an interface that's intuitive to you may not be as intuitive to everyone else.

One way to approach the user interface issue is to rely on Excel's built-in features: its menus, toolbars, scroll bars, and so on. In other words, you can simply set up the workbook and then let the user work with it however he or she wants. This may be the perfect solution if the application will be used only by those who know Excel well. More often, however, you'll find that the audience for your application consists of relatively inexperienced (and often disinterested) users. This makes your job more difficult, and you'll need to pay particular attention to the user interface that drives your application.

Excel provides several features that are relevant to user-interface design:

✦ Custom dialog boxes (UserForms)

✦ ActiveX controls (such as a ListBox or a CommandButton) placed directly on a worksheet

✦ Custom menus

✦ Custom toolbars

✦ Custom shortcut keys

I discuss these features briefly in the following sections and cover them more thoroughly in later chapters.

Creating custom dialog boxes

Anyone who has used Excel for any length of time is undoubtedly familiar with dialog boxes. Consequently, custom dialog boxes play a major role in the user interfaces you design for your applications.

Note   Excel 97 introduced a completely new way to create custom dialog boxes by using UserForms. However, Excel 97 still supports Excel 5/95 dialog sheets. This book focuses exclusively on UserForms.

Figure 39-1 shows a custom dialog box that I developed for an application.

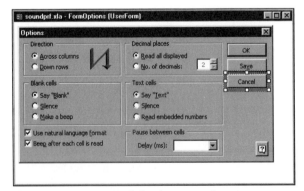

Figure 39-1: Custom dialog boxes are important to an application's user interface.

You can use a custom dialog box to solicit user input, get a user's options or preferences, and direct the flow of your entire application. Custom dialog boxes are stored in UserForms (one dialog box per UserForm). You create and edit custom dialog boxes in the Visual Basic Editor (VBE), which you access by pressing Alt+F11. The elements that make up a dialog box — buttons, drop-down lists, check boxes, and so on — are called controls — more specifically, ActiveX controls. Excel provides a standard assortment of ActiveX controls, and you can also incorporate third-party controls.

After adding a control to a dialog box, you can link it to a worksheet cell so that it doesn't require any macros (except a simple macro to display the dialog box). Linking a control to a cell is easy, but it's not always the best way to get user input from a dialog box. Most of the time, you'll want to develop VBA macros that work with your custom dialog boxes.

Cross-Reference I cover UserForms in detail in Chapters 44 and 45.

Using ActiveX controls on a worksheet

Excel also lets you add the UserForm ActiveX controls to a worksheet's draw layer. Figure 39-2 shows a simple worksheet model with a UserForm inserted directly on the worksheet.

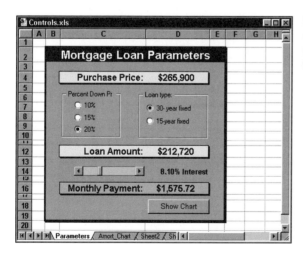

Figure 39-2: Directly adding dialog-box controls may make a worksheet easier to use.

Perhaps the most common control is a CommandButton. By themselves, buttons don't do anything, so you have to attach a macro to each button.

Using dialog-box controls directly in a worksheet often eliminates the need for custom dialog boxes. You can often greatly simplify the operation of a spreadsheet by adding a few ActiveX controls to a worksheet. This lets the user make choices by operating familiar controls rather than making entries into cells.

Note   The ActiveX controls are found on the Control Toolbox toolbar. You can also use Excel 5/95 compatible controls on a worksheet. These controls, which are not ActiveX controls, are available on the Forms toolbar. (These controls are not discussed in this book.)

Customizing menus

Another way to control the user interface in spreadsheet applications is to modify Excel's menus or to create your own menu system. Instead of creating buttons that execute macros, you can add one or more new menus or menu items to execute macros that you've already created. An advantage to custom menus is that the menu bar is always visible, whereas a button placed on a worksheet can easily scroll out of view.

Note   Beginning with Excel 97, Microsoft has implemented an entirely different way of dealing with menus. As you'll see in Chapter 50, a menu bar is actually a toolbar in disguise. Figure 39-3 shows an example of a new menu — something that might be used in a specialized custom application. Each menu item triggers a macro.

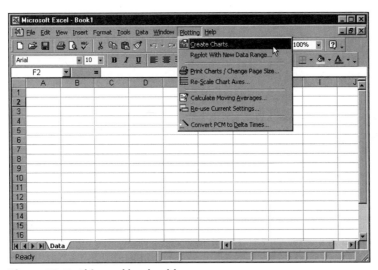

Figure 39-3: This workbook adds a new menu.

You have two ways to customize Excel's menus. You may use VBA code to make the menu modifications, or you can edit the menu directly, using the View ➪ Toolbars ➪ Customize command.

As I explain in Chapter 50, the best approach is usually to use VBA commands to modify the menus. You have complete control over the menus, and can even perform such operations as disabling the menu item or adding a checkmark to the item.

Menu modifications that you make using the View ⇨ Toolbars ⇨ Customize command (see Figure 39-4) are "permanent." In other words, if you make a menu change (such as the removal of a menu item), that change will remain in effect even if you restart Excel.

Figure 39-4: The Customize dialog box is where you make changes to Excel's menu system.

Note The Menu Editor (which debuted in Excel 5) was removed, beginning with Excel 97. Menus that were created using the Menu Editor will continue to function when the workbook is loaded into Excel 97 or Excel 2000.

You'll find that you can customize every menu that Excel displays — even the shortcut menus that appear when you right-click an object. Figure 39-5 shows a customized shortcut menu that appears when you right-click a cell or range. Notice that this shortcut menu has several new commands that aren't normally available.

Figure 39-5: An example of a customized shortcut menu

Cross-Reference I cover custom menus in detail in Chapter 50.

Customizing toolbars

Toolbars are very common in Windows applications, and Excel offers a huge assortment of built-in toolbars. Generally, toolbar buttons serve as shortcuts for commonly used menu commands to give users a quicker way to issue commands. Because a mouse is required to click a toolbar button, a toolbar button generally isn't the *only* way to execute a particular operation. Excel's toolbars, for example, make it possible to do most of the common spreadsheet operations without even using the menus.

You can create a custom toolbar that contains only the tools you want users to be able to access. In fact, if you attach macros to these tools, a custom toolbar becomes the equivalent of a group of buttons placed on a worksheet. The advantage to using the toolbar in this way is that it is always visible and can be repositioned anywhere on the screen. Buttons inserted on a worksheet are fixed in place and can be scrolled off the screen.

Note Beginning with Excel 97, you can also add menus to a toolbar.

You can set up your application so that the toolbar appears whenever your application is loaded. You do this by *attaching* a toolbar to a workbook using the Attach button in the Toolbars tab of the Customize dialog box (see Figure 39-6). This lets you store individual toolbars with a workbook application so that you can distribute them to users of your application.

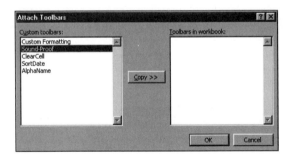

Figure 39-6: You can attach a custom toolbar to a worksheet with the Attach Toolbars dialog box.

Cross-Reference I discuss the topic of toolbars in detail in Chapter 49.

Creating shortcut keys

The final user-interface option at your disposal is custom shortcut keys. Excel lets you assign a Ctrl key (or Shift+Ctrl key) combination to a macro. When the user presses the key combination, the macro executes. Obviously, you have to make it clear to the user which keys are active and what they do. However, if speed is essential, pressing a key combination is usually faster than issuing menu commands, using a toolbar, or working with a dialog box.

You need to be careful, however, not to assign a key combination that's already in use for something else. For example, Ctrl+S is a built-in shortcut key used to save the current workbook. If you assign this key combination to a macro, you lose the ability to save the file with Ctrl+S. In other words, a key combination you assign to a macro takes precedence over the built-in shortcut keys. Shortcut keys are case-sensitive, so you can use a combination such as Ctrl+Shift+S.

Executing the development effort

After you've identified user needs, determined the approach you'll take to meet those needs, and decided on the components you'll use for the user interface, it's time to get down to the nitty-gritty and start creating the application. This step, of course, comprises a great deal of the total time you spend on a particular project.

How you go about developing the application depends on your own personal style and the nature of the application. Except for simple fill-in-the-blanks template workbooks, your application will probably use macros. Developing the macros is the tough part. It's easy to create macros in Excel, but it's difficult to create *good* macros.

Concerning Yourself with the End User

In this segment, I discuss the important development issues that surface as your application becomes more and more workable, and the time to package and distribute your work grows nearer.

Testing it out

How many times have you used a commercial software application, only to have it bomb out on you at a crucial moment? Most likely, the problem was caused by insufficient testing that didn't catch all the bugs. All nontrivial software has bugs; but in the best software, the bugs are simply more obscure. As you'll see, you sometimes have to work around the bugs in Excel to get your application to perform properly.

After you create your application, you need to test it. This is one of the most crucial steps; it's not uncommon to spend as much time testing and debugging an application as you did creating the application in the first place. Actually, you should be doing a great deal of testing during the development phase. After all, while you're writing a VBA routine or creating formulas in a worksheet, you'll want to make sure that the application is working the way it's supposed to work.

Like standard compiled applications, spreadsheet applications that you develop are prone to bugs. A *bug* is usually defined as 1) something that does happen but shouldn't while a program (or application) is running, or 2) something that doesn't happen when it should happen. Both species of bugs are equally nasty, and you should plan on devoting a good portion of your development time to testing the application under all reasonable conditions and fixing any problems you find. In some cases, unfortunately, the problems aren't entirely your fault. Excel, too, has its problems (see the "Bugs? In Excel?" sidebar).

I probably don't need to tell you to thoroughly test any spreadsheet development you develop for others. And depending on its eventual audience, you might want to make your application *bulletproof.* In other words, try to anticipate all the errors and screw-ups that could possibly occur, and make efforts to avoid them — or at least handle them gracefully. This not only helps the end user, but also makes it easier on you and your reputation.

Bugs? In Excel?

You might think that a product like Excel — which is used by millions of people throughout the world — would be relatively free of bugs. Think again, pal. Excel is such a complex piece of software that it is only natural to expect some problems with it. And Excel *does* have some problems.

Getting a product like Excel out the door is not easy, even for a company like Microsoft with seemingly unlimited resources. Releasing a software product involves compromises and trade-offs. It's commonly known that most major software vendors release their products with full knowledge that they contain bugs. Most of the bugs are considered insignificant enough to ignore. Software companies could postpone their releases by a few months and fix most of them, but software, like everything else, is ruled by economics. The benefits of delaying a product often do not exceed the costs involved. Although Excel definitely has its share of bugs, my guess is that the majority of Excel users never encounter one.

In this book, I point out the problems with Excel that I know about. You'll surely discover some more on your own. Some problems occur only under a specific configuration involving hardware and/or software. These are the worst of all bugs because they aren't easily reproducible.

So what's a developer to do? It's called a *workaround.* If something that you try to do doesn't work — and all indications say that it *should* work — it's time to move on to Plan B. Frustrating? Sure. A waste of your time? Absolutely. It's all part of being a developer.

What about Beta Testing?

Software manufacturers typically have a rigorous testing cycle for new products. After extensive internal testing, the prerelease product is usually sent to a group of interested users for *beta testing*. This phase often uncovers additional problems that are usually corrected before the product's final release.

If you're developing an Excel application that more than a few people will use, you may want to consider a beta test. This enables your application to be used in its intended setting on different hardware (usually) and by the intended users.

The beta period should begin after you've completed all of your own testing, and you feel the application is ready to distribute. You'll need to identify a group of users to help you. The process works best if you distribute everything that will ultimately be included in your application — user documentation, installation program, online help, and so on. You can evaluate the beta test in a number of ways, including face-to-face discussions, questionnaires, and phone calls.

You will almost always become aware of problems you need to correct or improvements you need to make before you undertake a widespread distribution of the application. Of course, a beta testing phase takes additional time, and not all projects can afford that luxury.

Although you cannot conceivably test for all possibilities, your macros should be able to handle common types of errors. For example, what if the user enters a text string instead of a value? What if the user tries to run your macro when a workbook isn't open? What if he or she cancels a dialog box without making any selections? What happens if the user presses Ctrl+F6 and jumps to the next window? As you gain experience, issues like this become very familiar, and you'll account for them without even thinking.

Making the application bulletproof

If you think about it, it's fairly easy to destroy a spreadsheet. Erasing one critical formula or value often causes errors throughout the entire worksheet — and perhaps other dependent worksheets. Even worse, if the damaged workbook is saved, it replaces the good copy on disk. Unless a backup procedure is in place, the user of your application could be in trouble — and *you'll* probably be blamed for it.

Obviously, it's easy to see why you need to add some protection when users — especially novices — will be using your worksheets. Excel provides several techniques for protecting worksheets and parts of worksheets:

✦ You can lock specific cells (using the Protection tab in the Format Cells dialog box) so that they cannot be changed. This takes effect only when the document is protected with the Tools ➪ Protection ➪ Protect Sheet command.

✦ You can protect an entire workbook — the structure of the workbook, the window position and size, or both. Use the Tools ⇨ Protection ⇨ Protect Workbook command for this purpose.

✦ You can hide the formulas in specific cells (using the Protection tab in the Format Cells dialog box) so that others can't see them. Again, this takes effect only when the document is protected with Tools ⇨ Protection ⇨ Protect Sheet command.

✦ You can lock objects on the worksheet (using the Protection tab in the Format Object dialog box). This takes effect only when the document is protected with the Tools ⇨ Protection ⇨ Protect Sheet command.

✦ You can hide rows (Format ⇨ Row ⇨ Hide), columns (Format ⇨ Column ⇨ Hide), sheets (Format ⇨ Sheet ⇨ Hide), and documents (Window ⇨ Hide). This helps prevent the worksheet from looking cluttered and also provides some protection against prying eyes.

✦ You can designate Excel workbooks as read-only to ensure that they cannot be overwritten with any changes. You do this by choosing the Options button in the Save As dialog box.

✦ You can assign a password to prevent unauthorized users from opening your file (using the Options button in the Save As dialog box).

✦ You can use a password-protected add-in, which doesn't allow the user to change *anything* on its worksheets.

The way a computer program looks can make all the difference in the world to users, and the same is true with the applications you develop with Excel. Beauty, however, is in the eye of the beholder. If your skills lean more in the analytical direction, consider enlisting the assistance of someone with a more aesthetic sensibility to provide help with design.

Making the application aesthetically appealing and intuitive

If you've used many different software packages, you've undoubtedly seen examples of poorly designed user interfaces, difficult-to-use programs, and just plain ugly screens. If you're developing spreadsheets for other people, you should pay particular attention to how the application looks.

How Secure Are Excel's Passwords?

As far as I know, Microsoft has never advertised Excel as a secure program. And for a good reason: It's actually quite easy to thwart Excel's password system. Several commercial programs are available that can break passwords. Bottom line? Don't think of password protection as foolproof. Sure, it will be effective for the casual user. But if someone *really* wants to break your password, she can.

The users of your applications will appreciate a good-looking user interface, and your applications will have a much more polished and professional look if you devote some additional time to design and aesthetic considerations. An application that looks good demonstrates that its developer cared enough about the product to invest some extra time and effort. Take the following suggestions into account:

✦ Strive for consistency: When designing dialog boxes, for example, try to emulate Excel's dialog box look and feel whenever possible. Be consistent with formatting, fonts, text size, and colors.

✦ A common mistake that developers make is trying to cram too much information into a single screen or dialog box. A good rule of thumb is to present only one or two chunks of information at a time.

✦ If you use an input screen to solicit information from the user, consider breaking it up into several, less crowded screens. If you use a complex dialog box, you might want to break it up by using a MultiPage control (which lets you create a familiar "tabbed" dialog box).

✦ Use color sparingly, because it's very easy to overdo it and make the screen look gaudy. If your application will be used on laptops, make sure that you use color combinations that also look good (and are legible) in monochrome.

✦ Pay attention to numeric formats, type faces and sizes, and borders.

✦ Do whatever you can to make individual parts of the worksheet appear to stay together.

Evaluating aesthetic qualities is very subjective. When in doubt, strive for simplicity and clarity.

Documenting the development effort

Putting a spreadsheet application together is one thing. Making it understandable for other people is another. As with traditional programming, it's important that you thoroughly document your work. Such documentation helps you if you need to go back to it (and you will), and it helps anyone else you may pass it on to.

You may want to consider a couple of things when you document your project. For example, if you were hired to develop an Excel application, you may not want to share all your hard-earned secrets by thoroughly documenting everything. If this is the case, you should maintain two versions: one thoroughly documented and the other partially documented.

How do you document a workbook application? You can either store the information in a worksheet or use another file. You can even use a paper document if you prefer. Perhaps the easiest way is to use a separate worksheet to store your comments and key information for the project. For VBA code, use comments liberally (text preceded with an apostrophe is ignored). An elegant piece of VBA code may seem perfectly obvious to you today—but come back to it in a few months, and your reasoning may be completely obscured.

With regard to user documentation, you basically have two choices: paper-based documentation or electronic (online) documentation. Online help is standard fare in Windows applications. Fortunately, your Excel applications can also provide online help—even context-sensitive help. Developing online help takes quite a bit of additional effort, but for a large project, it may be worth it.

 Cross-Reference   In Chapter 51, I discuss several alternatives for providing online help for your applications.

Distributing the application to the user

You've completed your project, and you're ready to release it to the end users. How do you go about doing this? You can choose from many ways to distribute your application, and the method you choose depends on many factors.

You could just hand over a disk, scribble a few instructions, and be on your way. Or, you may want to install the application yourself—but this is not always feasible. Another option is to develop an official setup program that performs the task automatically. You can write such a program in a traditional programming language, purchase a generic setup program, or write your own in VBA.

 Note   The Developers Edition of Office 2000 includes a Setup Wizard that helps you prepare your applications for distribution.

 EXCEL 2000   Excel 2E000 uses Microsoft Authenticode technology to enable developers to digitally "sign" their applications. This process is designed to help end users identify the author of an application, ensure that the project has not been altered, and help prevent the spread of macro viruses or other potentially destructive code. To digitally sign a project, you must first apply for a digital certificate from a formal certificate authority (or you can self-sign your project by creating your own digital certificate). Refer to the online help or Microsoft's Web site for additional information.

Another point to consider is support for your application. In other words, who gets the phone call if the user encounters a problem? If you aren't prepared to handle routine questions, you'll need to identify someone who is. In some cases you'll want to arrange it so that only highly technical or bug-related issues escalate to the developer.

Why Is There No Run-Time Version of Excel?

When you distribute your application, you need to be sure that each end user has a licensed copy of the appropriate version of Excel. It's illegal to distribute a copy of Excel along with your application. Why, you might ask, doesn't Microsoft provide a run-time version of Excel? A run-time version is an executable program that can load files but not create them. With a run-time version, the end user wouldn't need a copy of Excel to run your application (this is common with database programs).

I've never seen a clear or convincing reason why Microsoft does not have a run-time version of Excel, and no other spreadsheet manufacturer offers a run-time version of its product either. The most likely reason is that spreadsheet vendors fear that doing so would reduce sales of the software. Or, it could be that developing a run-time version would require a tremendous amount of programming that would just never pay off.

Actually, a spreadsheet product *does* exist that can generate executable files. Visual Baler, from TechTools Software (`www.techtools.com/`), is a unique product that enables you to create spreadsheet applications and distribute them, royalty-free, to any number of users. The end users need no additional software to run it. Unfortunately, Baler seems to have been designed more for users of 1-2-3 and Quattro Pro (it bears little resemblance to Excel).

On a related note . . . Microsoft does offer an Excel file *viewer.* This product lets you view Excel files if you don't own a copy of Excel. Even better, it's free. You can get a copy from Microsoft's Web site (`http://officeupdate.microsoft.com`).

Updating the application when necessary

After you distribute your application, you're finished with it, right? You can sit back, enjoy yourself, and try to forget about the problems you encountered (and solved) during the course of developing your application. In rare cases, yes, you may be finished. More often, however, the users of your application will not be completely satisfied. Sure, your application adheres to all of the *original* specifications, but things change. Seeing an application working frequently causes the user to think of other things that the application could be doing. We're talking *updates.*

When you need to update or revise your application, you'll appreciate that you designed it well in the first place and you fully documented your efforts. If not, well . . . we learn from our experiences.

Other Development Issues

You need to keep several other issues in mind when developing an application—especially if you don't know exactly who will be using the application. If you're developing an application that will have widespread use (a shareware application, for example), you have no way of knowing how the application will be used, what type of system it will run on, or what other software will be running concurrently.

The user's installed version of Excel

With every new release of Excel, the issue of compatibility rears its head. As I write this, Excel 2000 is just about ready to be released, yet many large corporations seem to be stuck in a time warp and still use Excel 5 and Windows 3.x.

Unfortunately, you have no guarantee that an application developed for Excel 5 will work perfectly with later versions of Excel. If you need your application to work with Excel 5, Excel 95, Excel 97, and Excel 2000, you're going to have to work with the lowest common denominator (Excel 5)—and then test it thoroughly with all other versions.

Things get even more complicated when you consider Excel's "sub-versions." Microsoft distributes service releases (SRs) to correct problems. For example, users might have the original Excel 97, Excel 97 with SR-1, or Excel 97 with SR-2. And some might even have Excel 97 with the *original* SR-1—which was released and then withdrawn by Microsoft because it caused more problems than it fixed!

Language issues

Consider yourself very fortunate if all of your end users have the English language version of Excel. Non-English versions of Excel aren't always 100 percent compatible, so that would mean additional testing on you part.

System speed

You're probably a fairly advanced computer user and tend to keep your hardware reasonably up-to-date. In other words, you have a fairly powerful system—better than the average user. In some cases, you'll know exactly what hardware the end users of your applications are using. If so, it's vitally important that you test your application on that system. A procedure that executes almost instantaneously on your system may take several seconds on another system. In the world of computers, several seconds may be unacceptable.

Tip   As you gain more experience with VBA, you'll discover that you have ways to get the job done, and ways to get the job done *fast*. It's a good idea to get into the habit of coding for speed. Other chapters in this book will certainly help you out in this area.

Video modes

As you may know, most Windows users use one of three standard video modes: 640 × 480 (that is, standard VGA mode), 800 × 600, and 1024 × 768. If you develop an application in anything but VGA mode, the application may look terrible when it runs on a VGA system.

Note I certainly don't recommend developing your apps in VGA mode! You should, however, test them in that mode if there's a likelihood that they will be used in that mode.

This can be a big problem if your application relies on specific information being displayed on a single screen. For example, if you develop an input screen using 800 × 600 mode, users with a standard VGA display may not be able to see all of the input screen without scrolling. Also, it's important to realize that a restored (that is, not maximized or minimized) workbook is displayed at its previous window size and position. In the extreme case, it's possible that a window saved using a high resolution display may be completely off the screen when opened on a system running in VGA mode.

Although advanced users tend to use higher resolutions in Windows, using VGA is unavoidable in some cases. Some laptop systems, for example, support only VGA for their built-in display. There's no way to automatically scale things so that they look the same regardless of the display resolution. Unless you're certain of the video resolution that the users of your application will be using, it's important that you test your application using the lowest common denominator—VGA mode.

It's possible to determine the user's video resolution by using Windows API calls from VBA. In some cases, you may want to programmatically adjust things depending on the user's video resolution.

Folder structure

Another issue you need to think about is the structure of the user's hard drive—how the folders are arranged and named. For example, you can't assume that Excel is installed in a folder named C:\Program Files\Microsoft Office\Office. And you can't even assume that it's installed on drive C. Similarly, you can't assume that Windows is installed in a directory named Windows. Although these are the default installation locations, many systems won't adhere to these conventions. Fortunately, it's possible to use VBA to determine file storage locations.

Summary

In this chapter, I outlined the basic process for developing a spreadsheet application. Much of the information in this chapter is discussed in more detail later on in the book.

✦   ✦   ✦

Introducing Visual Basic for Applications

Programming Excel essentially boils down to manipulating objects — which you do by writing instructions in a language that Excel can understand. This chapter introduces you to that language and to the objects that make up Excel.

Some BASIC Background

Many hard-core programmers scoff at the idea of programming in BASIC. The name itself (an acronym for Beginner's All-purpose Symbolic Instruction Code) suggests that it's not a professional language. In fact, BASIC was first developed in the early 1960s as a way to teach programming techniques to college students. BASIC caught on quickly and is available in hundreds of dialects for many types of computers.

BASIC has evolved and improved over the years. For example, BASIC was originally an *interpreted* language. Each line was interpreted before it was executed, causing slow performance. Most modern dialects of BASIC allow the code to be compiled, resulting in much faster execution and improved program portability.

BASIC gained quite a bit of respectability in 1991 when Microsoft released Visual Basic for Windows (which is currently in version 6.0). This product made it easy for the masses to develop stand-alone applications for Windows. Visual Basic has very little in common with early versions of BASIC, but BASIC is the foundation on which VBA was built.

About VBA

Excel 5 was the first application on the market to feature Visual Basic for Applications. VBA is best thought of as Microsoft's common application scripting language, and it's now included with all Office 2000 applications—and even applications from other vendors. Therefore, if you master VBA using Excel, you'll be able to jump right in and write macros for other Microsoft (and non-Microsoft) products. Even better, you'll be able to create complete solutions that use features across various applications.

Object models

The secret to using VBA with other applications lies in understanding the *object model* for each application. VBA, after all, simply manipulates objects, and each product (Excel, Word, Access, PowerPoint, and so forth) has its own unique object model. You can program an application using the objects that the application *exposes*.

Excel's object model, for example, exposes several very powerful data analysis objects, such as worksheets, charts, pivot tables, scenarios, and numerous mathematical, financial, engineering, and general business functions. With VBA, you can work with these objects and develop automated procedures. As you work with VBA in Excel, you'll gradually build an understanding of the object model. Warning: it will be very confusing at first. Eventually, however, the pieces will come together and all of a sudden you'll realize that you've mastered it!

VBA versus XLM

Before version 5, Excel used a powerful macro language called XLM. Excel 2000 still executes XLM macros, but the ability to record macros in XLM was removed beginning with Excel 97. As a developer, you should be aware of XLM (in case you ever encounter macros written in that system), but you should use VBA for your development work.

Figures 40-1 and 40-2 show a simple procedure coded in both XLM and VBA. This macro works on the selected cells. It changes the cell background color and the text color, and it makes the text bold. You probably agree that the VBA code is much easier to read. More important, however, the VBA code is also easier to modify when the need arises.

Figure 40-1: A simple macro coded in Excel's XLM language

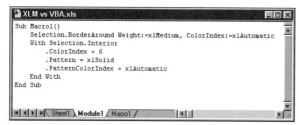

Figure 40-2: A simple macro coded in Excel's VBA language

VBA versus Lotus macros

Lotus 1-2-3 (the DOS version) was the first spreadsheet to incorporate macro capability. Although this feature was great in its day, it's quite crude by today's standards. The original 1-2-3 for DOS macros were based on simple keystroke recording, and then playing back those keystrokes to execute the macro. For example, a 1-2-3 for DOS macro that names a range might look like this:

```
/RNC~
```

This represents the following 1-2-3 command sequence:

```
/Range Name Create (Enter)
```

The keystroke-oriented macro language in 1-2-3 was eventually replaced by a command-oriented language. The most recent versions of 1-2-3 include a scripting language similar to VBA (see the next section).

VBA versus LotusScript

1-2-3 97 and later editions feature LotusScript, a procedural language that has much in common with VBA. My experience with LotusScript is limited, but from what I've seen, VBA offers many advantages.

In light of the fact that VBA has become a "standard" and users have a huge code base to draw on, one wonders why Lotus developed a new (incompatible) language rather than simply licensing VBA from Microsoft.

The Basics of VBA

Before I get into the meat of things, I suggest that you read through the material in this section to get a broad overview of where I'm heading. These are the topics that I cover in the remainder of this chapter.

VBA in a nutshell

Following is a quick-and-dirty summary of what VBA is all about:

✦ You perform actions in VBA by executing VBA code.

✦ You write (or record) VBA code, which is stored in a VBA module.

VBA modules are stored in an Excel workbook, but you view or edit a module using the Visual Basic Editor (VBE).

✦ A VBA module consists of procedures.

A procedure is basically computer code that performs some action on or with objects. Here's an example of a simple a procedure called Test:

```
Sub Test()
    Sum = 1 + 1
    MsgBox "The answer is " & Sum
End Sub
```

✦ A VBA module can also have function procedures.

A function procedure returns a single value. A function can be called from another VBA procedure or used in a worksheet formula. Here's an example of a function named AddTwo:

```
Function AddTwo(arg1, arg2)
    AddTwo = arg1 + arg2
End Function
```

✦ VBA manipulates objects contained in its host application (in this case, Excel 2000).

Excel provides you with more than 100 classes of objects to manipulate. Examples of objects include a workbook, a worksheet, a range on a worksheet, a chart, and a drawn rectangle. Many, many more objects are at your disposal, and you can manipulate them using VBA code.

✦ Object classes are arranged in a hierarchy.

Objects can act as containers for other objects. For example, Excel is an object called `Application`, and it contains other objects, such as `Workbook` and `CommandBar` objects. The `Workbook` object can contain other objects, such as `Worksheet` objects and `Chart` objects. A `Worksheet` object can contain objects such as `Range` objects, `PivotTable` objects, and so on. The arrangement of these objects is referred to as Excel's *object model*.

✦ Like objects form a *collection*.

For example, the `Worksheets` collection consists of all the worksheets in a particular workbook. The `CommandBars` collection consists of all `CommandBar` objects. Collections are objects in themselves

✦ When you refer to a contained or member object, you specify its position in the object hierarchy using a period as a separator between the container and the member.

For example, you can refer to a workbook named Book1.xls as

```
Application.Workbooks("Book1.xls")
```

This refers to the Book1.xls workbook in the `Workbooks` collection. The `Workbooks` collection is contained in the Excel `Application` object. Extending this to another level, you can refer to Sheet1 in Book1 as

```
Application.Workbooks("Book1.xls").Worksheets("Sheet1")
```

You can take it to still another level and refer to a specific cell as follows:

```
Application.Workbooks("Book1.xls").Worksheets("Sheet1").Range
("A1")
```

✦ If you omit a specific reference to an object, Excel uses the *active* objects.

If Book1 is the active workbook, the preceding reference can be simplified as

```
Worksheets("Sheet1").Range("A1")
```

If you know that Sheet1 is the active sheet, you can simplify the reference even more:

```
Range("A1")
```

✦ Objects have *properties*.

A property can be thought of as a *setting* for an object. For example, a `range` object has properties such as `Value` and `Name`. A `chart` object has properties such as `HasTitle` and `Type`. You can use VBA to determine object properties and also to change them.

✦ You refer to properties by combining the object with the property, separated by a period.

For example, you can refer to the value in cell A1 on Sheet1 as

```
Worksheets("Sheet1").Range("A1").Value
```

✦ You can assign values to VBA variables.

To assign the value in cell A1 on Sheet1 to a variable called *Interest*, use the following VBA statement.

```
Interest = Worksheets("Sheet1").Range("A1").Value
```

✦ Objects have *methods*.

A method is an action that is performed with the object. For example, one of the methods for a `Range` object is `ClearContents`. This method clears the contents of the range.

✦ You specify methods by combining the object with the method, separated by a period.

For example, to clear the contents of cell A1 on the active worksheet, use

```
Range("A1").ClearContents
```

✦ VBA also includes all the constructs of modern programming languages, including arrays, looping, and so on.

Believe it or not, the preceding section pretty much describes VBA. Now it's just a matter of learning the details, which is what I cover in the rest of this chapter.

An Analogy

If you like analogies, here's one for you. It may help you understand the relationships between objects, properties, and methods in VBA. In this analogy, I compare Excel with a fast-food restaurant chain.

The basic unit of Excel is a `Workbook` object. In a fast-food chain, the basic unit is an individual restaurant. With Excel, you can add workbooks and close workbooks, and all the open workbooks are known as `Workbooks` (a collection of `Workbook` objects). Similarly, the management of a fast-food chain can add restaurants and close restaurants — and all the restaurants in the chain can be viewed as a collection of `Restaurant` objects.

An Excel workbook is an object, but it also contains other objects such as worksheets, charts, VBA modules, and so on. Furthermore, each object in a workbook can contain its own objects. For example, a `Worksheet` object can contain `Range` objects, `PivotTable` objects, `Shape` objects, and so on.

Continuing with the analogy, a fast-food restaurant (like a workbook) contains objects such as the Kitchen, DiningArea, and ParkingLot. Furthermore, management can add or remove objects from the Restaurant object. For example, management may add a DriveupWindow object. Each of these objects can contain other objects. For example, the Kitchen object has a Stove object, VentilationFan object, a Chef object, Sink object, and so on.

So far, so good—this analogy seems to work. Let's see if I can take it further.

Excel's objects have properties. For example, a Range object has properties such as Value and Name, and a Shape object has properties such as Width, Height, and so on. Not surprisingly, objects in a fast-food restaurant also have properties. The Stove object, for example, has properties such as Temperature and NumberofBurners. The VentilationFan has its own set of properties (TurnedOn, RPM, and so forth).

Besides properties, Excel's objects also have methods, which perform an operation on an object. For example, the ClearContents method erases the contents of a Range object. An object in a fast-food restaurant also has methods. You can easily envision a ChangeThermostat method for a Stove object or a SwitchOn method for a VentilationFan object.

With Excel, methods sometimes change an object's properties. The ClearContents method for a Range object changes the Range's Value property. Similarly, the ChangeThermostat method on a Stove object affects its Temperature property.

With VBA, you can write procedures to manipulate Excel's objects. In a fast-food restaurant, the management can give orders to manipulate the objects in the restaurants ("Turn the stove on and switch the ventilation fan to high."). Now is it clear?

Introducing the Visual Basic Editor

In Excel 5 and Excel 95, a VBA module appeared as a separate sheet in a workbook. Beginning with Excel 97, VBA modules no longer show up as sheets in a workbook. Rather, you use the Visual Basic Editor (VBE) to view and work with VBA modules.

 Note VBA modules are still stored with workbook files; they just aren't visible unless you activate the VBE.

The VBE is a separate application that works seamlessly with Excel. By *seamlessly*, I mean that Excel takes care of the details of opening the VBE when you need it. You can't run VBE separately; Excel 2000 must be running in order for the VBE to run.

Activating the VBE

When you're working in Excel 2000, you can use any of the following techniques to switch to the VBE:

✦ Press Alt+F11.

✦ Select Tools ➪ Macro ➪ Visual Basic Editor.

✦ Click the Visual Basic Editor button, which is located on the Visual Basic toolbar.

Note Don't confuse the Visual Basic Editor with the Microsoft Script Editor. These are two entirely different animals. The Script Editor is used to edit HTML scripts written in VBScript or JavaScript. The Script Editor is not covered in this book.

Figure 40-3 shows the VBE. Chances are, your VBE window won't look exactly like the window shown in the figure. This window is highly customizable — you can hide windows, change their sizes, "dock" them, rearrange them, and so on.

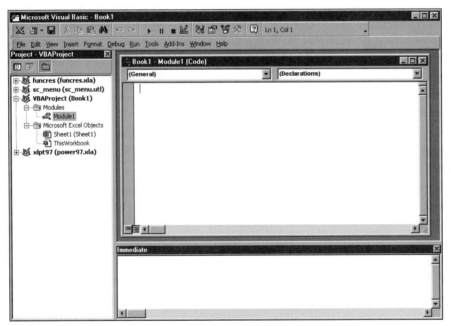

Figure 40-3: The Visual Basic Editor window

The VBE windows

The VBE consists of a number of parts. I briefly describe some of the key components in the sections that follow.

Menu bar

The VBE menu bar, of course, works like every other menu bar you've encountered. It contains commands that you use to work with the various components in the VBE. Many of the menu commands have shortcut keys associated with them. For example, the View ⇨ Immediate Window command has a shortcut key of Ctrl+G.

Tip The VBE also features shortcut menus. As you'll discover, right-clicking virtually anything in a VBE window displays a shortcut menu of common commands.

Toolbars

The Standard toolbar, which is directly under the menu bar by default, is one of six VBE toolbars available. VBE toolbars work just like those in Excel: You can customize toolbars, move them around, display other toolbars, and so forth. Use the View ⇨ Toolbars ⇨ Customize command to work with VBE toolbars.

Project Explorer window

The Project Explorer window displays a tree diagram that consists of every workbook that is currently open in Excel (including add-ins and hidden workbooks). Each workbook is known as a *project*. I discuss the Project Explorer window in more detail in the next section ("Working with the Project Explorer").

If the Project Explorer window is not visible, press Ctrl+R. To hide the Project Explorer window, click the Close button in its title bar (or right-click anywhere in the Project Explorer window, and select Hide from the shortcut menu).

Code window

A code window (sometimes known as a module window) contains VBA code. Every item in a project has an associated code window. To view a code window for an object, double-click the object in the Project Explorer window. For example, to view the code window for the Sheet1 object, double-click Sheet1 in the Project Explorer window. Unless you've added some VBA code, the code window will be empty.

I discuss code windows later on in this chapter (see "Working with Code Windows").

Immediate window

The Immediate window is most useful for executing VBA statements directly, testing statements, and debugging your code. This window may or may not be visible. If the Immediate window isn't visible, press Ctrl+G. To close the Immediate window, click the Close button in its title bar (or, right-click anywhere in the Immediate window and select Hide from the shortcut menu).

Working with the Project Explorer

When you're working in the VBE, each Excel workbook and add-in that's currently open is considered a project. You can think of a project as a collection of objects arranged as an outline. You can "expand" a project by clicking the plus sign (+) at the left of the project's name in the Project Explorer window. You "contract" a project by clicking the minus sign (–) to the left of a project's name. Figure 40-4 shows a Project Explorer window with three projects listed (one add-in and two workbooks).

Figure 40-4: A Project Explorer window with three projects listed

If you try to expand a project that's protected with a password, you'll be prompted to enter the password.

If you have many workbooks and add-ins loaded, the Project Explorer window may be a bit overwhelming. Unfortunately, it's not possible to hide projects in the Project Explorer window. However, you'll probably want to keep the project outlines contracted if you're not working with them.

Every project expands to show at least one "node" called Microsoft Excel Objects. This node expands to show an item for each worksheet and chart sheet in the workbook (each sheet is considered an object) and another object called ThisWorkbook (which represents the ActiveWorkbook object). If the project has any VBA modules, the project listing also shows a Modules node, and the modules are listed there. A project may also contain a node called Forms, which contains UserForm objects (also known as custom dialog boxes).

Adding a new VBA module

To add a new VBA module to a project, select the project's name in the Project Explorer window, and choose Insert ➪ Module. Or you can right-click the project's name, and choose Insert ➪ Module from the shortcut menu.

Tip   When you record a macro, Excel automatically inserts a VBA module to hold the recorded code.

Removing a VBA module

If you need to remove a VBA module from a project, select the module's name in the Project Explorer window and choose File ➪ Remove *xxx*, (where *xxx* is the name of the module). Or you can right-click the module's name, and choose Remove *xxx* from the shortcut menu. You'll be asked whether you want to export the module before removing it. See the next section for details.

Exporting and importing objects

Every object in a project can be saved to a separate file. Saving an individual object in a project is known as *exporting*. And it stands to reason that you can also *import* objects into a project. Exporting and importing objects might be useful if you want to use a particular object (such as a VBA module or a UserForm) in a different project.

To export an object, select it in the Project Explorer window, and choose File ➪ Export File (or press Ctrl+E). You'll get a dialog box that asks for a filename. Note that the object remains in the project (only a copy of it is exported). If you export a UserForm object, any code associated with the UserForm is also exported.

To import a file into a project, select the project's name in the Explorer window, and choose File ➪ Import File. You'll get a dialog box that asks for a file. You can import only a file that has been exported using the File ➪ Export File command.

Tip   If you would like to copy a module or UserForm object to another project, it's not really necessary to export and then import the object. Make sure both projects are open. Then simply activate the Project Explorer, press Ctrl, and drag the object from one project to the other.

Working with Code Windows

As you become proficient with VBA, you'll be spending *lots* of time working in code windows. Each object in a project has an associated code window. To summarize, these objects can be

✦ The workbook itself (`ThisWorkbook` in the Project window)

✦ A worksheet or chart sheet in a workbook (for example, `Sheet1` or `Chart1` in the Project window)

✦ A VBA module

✦ A class module (a special type of module that lets you create new object classes)

✦ A UserForm

Minimizing and maximizing windows

At any given time, VBE may have lots of code windows. Figure 40-5 shows an example of what I mean.

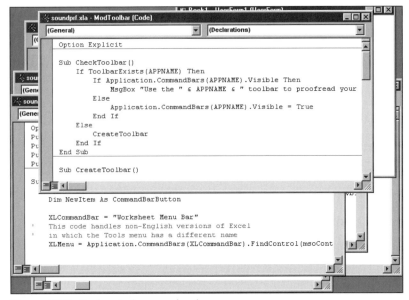

Figure 40-5: Code window overload

Code windows are much like worksheet windows in Excel. You can minimize them, maximize them, hide them, rearrange them, and so forth. Most people find it much easier to maximize the code window that they're working on. Doing so enables you to see more code and keeps you from getting distracted. To maximize a code window, click the maximize button in the window's title bar, or just double-click the title bar. To restore a code window, making it nonmaximized, click the restore button in the window's title bar.

Sometimes, you may want to have two or more code windows visible. For example, you might want to compare the code in two modules or copy code from one module to another.

Minimizing a code window gets it out of the way. You can also click the Close button in a code window's title bar to close the window completely. To open it again, just double-click the appropriate object in the Project Explorer window.

The VBE doesn't let you close a workbook. You must reactivate Excel and close it from there. You can, however, use the Immediate window to close a workbook or add-in. Just activate the Immediate window, type a VBA statement like the following, and press Enter.

```
Workbooks("myaddin.xla").Close
```

As you'll see, this statement executes the Close method of the Workbook object, which closes a workbook.

Storing VBA code

In general, a code window can hold four types of code:

✦ **Sub procedures.** A *procedure* is a set of instructions that performs some action.

✦ **Function procedures.** A *function* is a set of instructions that returns a single value or an array (similar in concept to a worksheet function such as SUM).

✦ **Property procedures.** These are special procedures used in class modules.

✦ **Declarations.** A *declaration* is information about a variable that you provide to VBA. For example, you can declare the data type for variables you plan to use.

A single VBA module can store any number of Sub procedures, function procedures, and declarations. How you organize a VBA module is completely up to you. Some people prefer to keep all their VBA code for an application in a single VBA module; others like to split up the code into several different modules.

Note   Although you have lots of flexibility regarding where to store your VBA code, some restrictions exist. Event-handler procedures must be located in the code window for the object that responds to the event. For example, if you write a procedure that executes when the workbook is opened, that procedure must be located in the code window for the `ThisWorkbook` object, and the procedure must have a special name. This concept will become clearer when I discuss events (Chapter 46) and UserForms (Chapters 44 and 45).

Entering VBA code

Before you can do anything meaningful, you must have some VBA code in a code window. For now, I'll focus on one type of code window: a VBA module.

You can add code to a VBA module in three ways:

✦ Enter the code the old fashioned way — type it from your keyboard.

✦ Use Excel's macro-recorder feature to record your actions and convert them into VBA code.

✦ Copy the code from another module and paste it into the module you are working in.

Entering code manually

Sometimes, the most direct route is the best. Entering code directly involves . . . well, entering the code directly. In other words, you type the code using your keyboard. You can use the Tab key to indent the lines that logically belong together — for example, the conditional statements between an `If` and an `End If` statement. This isn't really necessary, but it makes the code easier to read, so it's a good habit to acquire.

Entering and editing text in a VBA module works just as you would expect. You can select text, copy it or cut it, and then paste it to another location.

Pause for a Terminology Break

Throughout this book, I use the terms *routine*, *procedure*, and *macro*. Programming people typically use the word *procedure* to describe an automated task. Technically, a procedure can be a Sub procedure or a function procedure, both of which are sometimes called *routines*. I use all these terms pretty much interchangeably. An important difference exists, however, between Sub procedures and function procedures. This distinction will become apparent in Chapter 42.

A single instruction in VBA can be as long as you need it to be. For readability's sake, however, you might want to break a lengthy instruction into two or more lines. To do so, end the line with a space followed by an underscore character; then, press Enter, and continue the instruction on the following line. The following code, for example, is a single statement split over four lines:

```
MsgBox "Can't find " & UCase(SHORTCUTMENUFILE) _
    & vbCrLf & vbCrLf & "The file should be located in  _
    " & ThisWorkbook.Path & vbCrLf & vbCrLf & _
    "You may need to reinstall BudgetMan", vbCritical, APPNAME
```

Notice that I indented the last three lines of this statement. Doing so is optional, but it helps clarify the fact that these four lines are, in fact, a single statement.

Tip　Like Excel, the VBE has multiple levels of Undo and Redo. Therefore, if you find that you deleted an instruction that you shouldn't have, you can click the Undo button (or press Ctrl+Z) repeatedly until the instruction comes back. After undoing, you can press F4 to redo changes that were previously undone. This feature can be a lifesaver, so I recommend that you play around with it until you understand how it works.

Try this: Insert a VBA module into a project, and then enter the following statements into the code window of the module:

```
Sub SayHello()
    Msg = "Is your name " & Application.UserName & "?"
    Ans = MsgBox(Msg, vbYesNo)
    If Ans = vbNo Then
        MsgBox "Oh, never mind."
    Else
        MsgBox "I must be clairvoyant!"
    End If
End Sub
```

Figure 40-6 shows how this looks in a VBA module.

Note　As you enter the code, you might notice that the VBE makes some adjustments to the text you enter. For example, if you omit the space before or after an equal sign (=), VBE inserts the space for you. In addition, the color of some of the text is changed. This is all perfectly normal, and you'll appreciate it later.

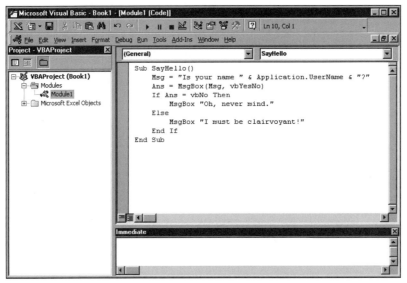

Figure 40-6: Your first VBA procedure

To execute the SayHello procedure, make sure that the cursor is located anywhere within the text you typed. Then, do any of the following:

✦ Press F5.

✦ Select Run ➪ Run Sub/UserForm.

✦ Click the Run Sub/UserForm button on the Standard toolbar.

If you entered the code correctly, the procedure will execute, and you can respond to a simple dialog box (see Figure 40-7). Notice that Excel is activated when the macro executes. At this point, it's not important that you understand how the code works; that becomes clear later in this chapter and in subsequent chapters.

Figure 40-7: The result of running the procedure in Figure 40-6

Note   Most of the time, you'll be executing your macros from Excel. Often, however, it's more efficient to test your macro by running it directly from the VBE.

What you did was write a VBA procedure (also known as a *macro*). When you issued the command to execute the macro, the VBE quickly compiled the code and executed it. In other words, each instruction was evaluated, and Excel simply did what it was told to do. You can execute this macro any number of times, although it tends to lose its appeal after a while.

For the record, this simple procedure uses the following concepts (all of which are covered later):

- ✦ Declaring a procedure (the first line)
- ✦ Assigning a value to variables (Msg and Ans)
- ✦ Concatenating strings (using the & operator)
- ✦ Using a built-in VBA function (MsgBox)
- ✦ Using built-in VBA constants (vbYesNo and vbNo)
- ✦ Using an If-Then-Else construct
- ✦ Ending a procedure (the last line)

Not bad for a first effort, eh?

Using the macro recorder

Another way to get code into a VBA module is to record your actions using Excel's macro recorder.

No matter how hard you try, you have absolutely no way to record the SayHello procedure shown previously. As you'll see, recording macros is very useful, but it has its limitations. In fact, when you record a macro you almost always need to make some adjustments or enter some code manually.

The next example shows how to record a macro that simply changes the page setup to Landscape orientation. If you want to try this, start with a blank workbook, and follow these steps:

1. Activate a worksheet in the workbook (any worksheet will do).
2. Select the Tools ➪ Macro ➪ Record New Macro command.

   Excel displays its Record Macro dialog box.
3. Click OK to accept the defaults.

   Excel automatically inserts a new VBA module into the project. From this point on, Excel converts your actions into VBA code. While recording, Excel displays the word *Recording* in the status bar and also displays a miniature floating toolbar that contains two toolbar buttons (Stop Recording and Relative Reference).

4. Select the File ➪ Page Setup command.

Excel displays its Page Setup dialog box.

5. Select the Landscape option, and click OK to close the dialog box.

6. Click the Stop Recording button on the miniature toolbar (or select Tools ➪ Macro ➪ Stop Recording).

Excel stops recording your actions.

To take a look at the macro, activate the VBE (Alt+F11 is the easiest way), and locate the project in the Project Explorer window. Click the Modules node to expand it. Then click the Module1 item to display the code window (if the project already had a Module1, the new macro will be in Module2). The code generated by this single command is shown in Listing 40-1.

Listing 40-1: Macro for changing page setup to landscape orientation

```
Sub Macro1()
    With ActiveSheet.PageSetup
        .PrintTitleRows = ""
        .PrintTitleColumns = ""
    End With
    ActiveSheet.PageSetup.PrintArea = ""
    With ActiveSheet.PageSetup
        .LeftHeader = ""
        .CenterHeader = "&A"
        .RightHeader = ""
        .LeftFooter = ""
        .CenterFooter = "Page &P"
        .RightFooter = ""
        .LeftMargin = Application.InchesToPoints(0.75)
        .RightMargin = Application.InchesToPoints(0.75)
        .TopMargin = Application.InchesToPoints(1)
        .BottomMargin = Application.InchesToPoints(1)
        .HeaderMargin = Application.InchesToPoints(0.5)
        .FooterMargin = Application.InchesToPoints(0.5)
        .PrintHeadings = False
        .PrintGridlines = True
        .PrintNotes = False
        .CenterHorizontally = False
        .CenterVertically = False
        .Orientation = xlLandscape
        .Draft = False
        .PaperSize = xlPaperLetter
        .FirstPageNumber = xlAutomatic
        .Order = xlDownThenOver
```

```
        .BlackAndWhite = False
        .Zoom = 100
    End With
End Sub
```

You may be surprised by the amount of code generated by this single command (I know I was the first time I tried something like this). Although you changed only one simple setting in the Page Setup dialog box, Excel generated code that reproduced *all* the settings in the dialog box.

This brings up an important concept. Often, the code produced when you record a macro is overkill. If you want your macro only to switch to landscape mode, you can simplify this macro considerably by deleting the extraneous code. This makes the macro easier to read, and the macro also runs faster because it doesn't do things that are not necessary. In fact, this macro can be simplified to

```
Sub Macro1()
    With ActiveSheet.PageSetup
        .Orientation = xlLandscape
    End With
End Sub
```

I deleted all the code except for the line that sets the Orientation property. Actually, this macro can be simplified even more because the With-End With construct isn't needed to change only one property:

```
Sub Macro1()
    ActiveSheet.PageSetup.Orientation = xlLandscape
End Sub
```

In this example, the macro changes the Orientation property of the PageSetup object on the active sheet. By the way, xlLandscape is a built-in constant that's provided to make things easier for you. Variable xlLandscape has a value of 2, and xlPortrait has a value of 1. Most would agree that it's easier to remember the name of the constant than the arbitrary numbers. You can use the online help to learn the relevant constants for a particular command.

You could have entered this procedure directly into a VBA module. To do so, you would have to know which objects, properties, and methods to use. Obviously, it's much faster to record the macro, and this example has a built-in bonus: You also learned that the PageSetup object has an Orientation property.

Note   A point I make clear throughout this book is that recording your actions is perhaps the *best* way to learn VBA. When in doubt, try recording. Although the result may not be exactly what you want, chances are that it will steer you in the right direction. You can use the online help to check out the objects, properties, and methods that appear in the recorded code.

Cross-Reference

I discuss the macro recorder in more detail later in this chapter.

Copying VBA code

So far, I've covered entering code directly and recording your actions to generate VBA code. The final way to get code into a VBA module is to copy it from another module. For example, you may have written a procedure for one project that would also be useful in your current project. Rather than reenter the code, you can simply open the workbook, activate the module, and use the normal clipboard copy-and-paste procedures to copy it into your current VBA module. After you've finished pasting, you can modify the code as necessary.

Tip

As I noted previously in this chapter, you can also import an entire module that has been exported to a file.

Customizing the VBE Environment

If you're serious about becoming an Excel programmer, you'll be spending a lot of time with the VBE window on your screen. To help you make things as comfortable as possible, the VBE provides quite a few customization options.

When VBE is active, choose Tools ⇨ Options. You'll see a dialog box with four tabs: Editor, Editor Format, General, and Docking. I discuss some of the most useful options on these tabs in the sections that follow.

Using the Editor tab

Figure 40-8 shows the options you access by clicking the Editor tab of the Options dialog box.

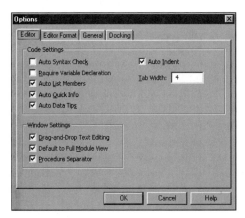

Figure 40-8: The Editor tab of the Options dialog box

Auto Syntax Check option

The Auto Syntax Check setting determines whether the VBE pops up a dialog box if it discovers a syntax error while you're entering your VBA code. The dialog box tells you roughly what the problem is. If you don't choose this setting, VBE flags syntax errors by displaying them in a different color from the rest of the code, and you don't have to deal with any dialog boxes popping up on your screen.

I usually keep this setting turned off because I find the dialog boxes annoying and I can usually figure out what's wrong with an instruction. But if you're new to VBA, you might find this assistance helpful.

Require Variable Declaration option

If the Require Variable Declaration option is set, VBE inserts the following statement at the beginning of each new VBA module you insert:

```
Option Explicit
```

If this statement appears in your module, you must explicitly define each variable that you use. This is an excellent habit to get into. If you don't declare your variables, they will all be of the variant data type, which is flexibe but not efficient in terms of storage or speed. I'll discuss this in more depth later.

Note   Changing the Require Variable Declaration option affects only new modules, not existing modules.

Auto List Members option

If the Auto List Members option is set, VBE provides some help when you're entering your VBA code by displaying a list of member items for an object. These items include methods and properties for the object you typed.

This option is very helpful, and I always keep it turned on. Figure 40-9 shows an example of Auto List Members (which will make a lot more sense when you actually start writing VBA code).

Auto Quick Info option

If the Auto Quick Info option is set, the VBE displays information about functions and their arguments as you type. This can be very helpful, and I always leave this setting on. Figure 40-10 shows this feature in action.

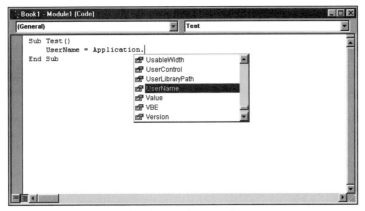

Figure 40-9: An example of Auto List Members

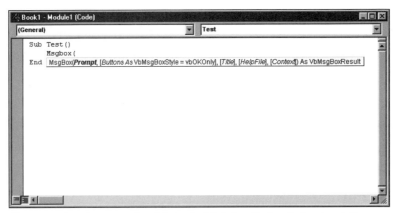

Figure 40-10: An example of Auto Quick Info offering help about the MsgBox function

Auto Data Tips option

If the Auto Data Tips option is set, VBE displays the value of the variable over which your cursor is placed when you're debugging code. When you enter the wonderful world of debugging, you'll definitely appreciate this option.

Auto Indent option

The Auto Indent setting determines whether VBE automatically indents each new line of code by the same amount as the previous line. I'm a big fan of using indentations in my code, so I keep this option on.

Tip   Use the Tab key, not the space bar, to indent your code. You can also use Shift+Tab to "unindent" a line of code.

Tip   VBE's Edit toolbar (which is hidden by default) contains two useful buttons: Indent and Outdent. These buttons let you quickly indent or "unindent" a block of code. Select the code, and then click one of these buttons to change the indenting of the block. These buttons are very useful, so you may want to copy them to your Standard toolbar.

Drag-and-Drop Text Editing option

When enabled, the Drag-and-Drop Text Editing option lets you copy and move text by dragging and dropping. I keep this option turned on, but I almost always use keyboard shortcuts for copying and pasting.

Default to Full Module View option

The Default to Full Module View option sets the default state for new modules (it doesn't affect existing modules). If set, procedures in the code window appear as a single scrollable window. When this option is turned off, you can see only one procedure at a time. I keep this setting turned on.

Procedure Separator option

When the Procedure Separator option is turned on, it displays separator bars at the end of each procedure in a code window. I like the visual cues of knowing where my procedures end, so I keep this option turned on.

Using the Editor Format tab

Figure 40-11 shows the Editor Format tab of the Options dialog box.

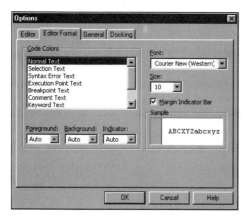

Figure 40-11: The Editor Format tab of the Options dialog box

Code Colors option

The Code Colors option lets you set the text color (foreground and background) and indicator color displayed for various elements of VBA code. This is largely a matter of individual preference. Personally, I find the default colors to be just fine. But for a change of scenery, I occasionally play around with these settings.

Font option

The Font option lets you select the font that's used in your VBA modules. For best results, stick with a fixed-width font such as Courier New. In a fixed-width font, all characters are exactly the same width. This makes your code much more readable because the characters are nicely aligned vertically and you can easily distinguish multiple spaces.

Size setting

The Size setting specifies the size of the font in the VBA modules. This setting is a matter of personal preference determined by your video display resolution and your eyesight. The default size of 10 points works for me.

Margin Indicator Bar option

This option controls the display of the vertical margin indicator bar in your modules. You should keep this turned on; otherwise, you won't be able to see the helpful graphical indicators when you're debugging your code.

Using the General tab

Figure 40-12 shows the options available under the General tab in the Options dialog box. In almost every case, the default settings are just fine.

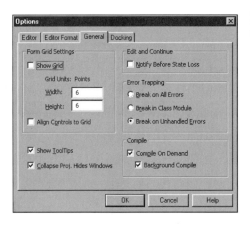

Figure 40-12: The General tab of the Options dialog box

The Error Trapping setting determines what happens when an error is encountered. If you write any error-handling code, make sure that the Break on Unhandled Errors option is set. If the Break on All Errors option is set, error-handling code is ignored (which is hardly ever what you want). I discuss error-handling techniques in Chapter 41.

Using the Docking tab

Figure 40-13 shows the Docking tab of the Options dialog box. These options determine how the various windows in the VBE behave. When a window is docked, it is fixed in place along one of the edges of the VBE window. This makes it much easier to identify and locate a particular window. If you turn off all docking, you'll have a big mess of windows that is very confusing. Generally, you'll find that the default settings work fine.

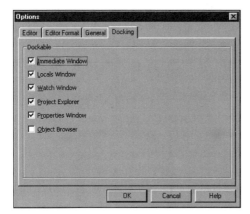

Figure 40-13: The Docking tab of the Options dialog box

The Macro Recorder

Earlier in this chapter, I discussed the macro recorder, a tool that converts your Excel actions into VBA code. This section covers the macro recorder in more detail.

Excel's Visual Basic toolbar has several useful buttons for you. On this toolbar, you'll find the Run Macro, Record Macro, Stop Macro, and Visual Basic Editor buttons useful.

The macro recorder is an *extremely* useful tool, but it's important to remember the following points:

✦ The macro recorder is appropriate only for simple macros or for recording a small part of a more complex macro.

✦ The macro recorder cannot generate code that performs looping (that is, repeating statements), assigns variables, executes statements conditionally, displays dialog boxes, and so on.

✦ The code that is generated depends on certain settings that you specify.

✦ You'll often want to clean up the recorded code to remove extraneous commands.

What is recorded

As you know, Excel's macro recorder translates your mouse and keyboard actions into VBA code. I could probably write several pages describing how this is done, but the best way to show you is by example. Follow these steps:

1. Start with a blank workbook.

2. Make sure Excel's window is not maximized.

3. Press Alt+F11 to activate the VBE window, and make sure *this* window is not maximized.

4. Arrange Excel's window and the VBE window so both are visible. (For best results, minimize any other applications that are running.)

5. Activate Excel, Choose Tools ➪ Macro ➪ Record New Macro, and click OK to start the macro recorder.

   Excel inserts a new module (named Module1) and starts recording on that sheet.

6. Activate the VBE window.

7. In the Project Explorer window, double-click Module1 to display that module in the code window.

Your screen should look like the example in Figure 40-14.

Now, move around in the worksheet, and select various Excel commands. Watch as the code is generated in the window that displays the VBA module. Select cells, enter data, format cells, use the menus and toolbars, create a chart, manipulate graphic objects, and so on. I guarantee that you'll be enlightened as you watch the code being spit out before your very eyes.

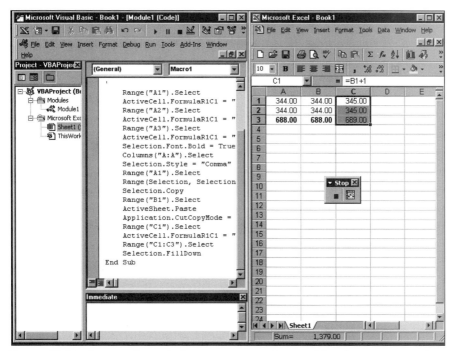

Figure 40-14: A convenient window arrangement for watching the macro recorder do its thing

Relative or absolute?

When recording your actions, Excel normally records absolute references to cells. For example, perform these steps, and examine the code:

1. Activate a worksheet, and start the macro recorder.

2. Activate cell B1.

3. Enter **Jan** into cell B1.

4. Move to cell C1, and enter **Feb**.

5. Continue this process until you've entered the first six months of the year in B1:G1.

6. Click cell B1 to activate it again.

7. Stop the macro recorder.

Excel generates the following code:

```
Sub Macro1()
    Range("B1").Select
    ActiveCell.FormulaR1C1 = "Jan"
    Range("C1").Select
    ActiveCell.FormulaR1C1 = "Feb"
    Range("D1").Select
    ActiveCell.FormulaR1C1 = "Mar"
    Range("E1").Select
    ActiveCell.FormulaR1C1 = "Apr"
    Range("F1").Select
    ActiveCell.FormulaR1C1 = "May"
    Range("G1").Select
    ActiveCell.FormulaR1C1 = "Jun"
    Range("B1").Select
End Sub
```

To execute this macro, choose the Tools ➪ Macro ➪ Macros command (or press Alt+F8), select Macro1 (or whatever the macro is named), and click the Run button.

When executed, the macro re-creates the actions you performed when you recorded it. These same actions occur regardless of which cell is active when you execute the macro. Recording a macro using absolute references always produces the exact same results.

In some cases, however, you'll want your recorded macro to work with cell locations in a *relative* manner. For example, you'd probably want such a macro to start entering the month names in the active cell. In such a case, you'll want to use relative recording to record the macro.

The Stop Recording toolbar, which consists of only two buttons, is displayed when you are recording a macro. You can change the manner in which Excel records your actions by clicking the Relative Reference button on the Stop Recording toolbar. This button is a toggle. When the button appears in a pressed state, the recording mode is relative. When the button appears normally, you are recording in absolute mode. You can change the recording method at any time, even in the middle of recording.

To see how this works, erase the cells in B1:D1, and then perform the following steps:

1. Activate cell B1.

2. Choose Tools ➪ Macro ➪ Record New Macro.

3. Name this macro Relative

4. Click OK to begin recording.

5. Click the Relative Reference button (on the Stop Recording toolbar) to change the recording mode to relative.

When you click this button, it appears pressed.

6. Enter the first six month names in B1:G1, as in the previous example.

7. Select cell B1.

8. Stop the macro recorder.

With the recording mode set to relative, the code that Excel generates is quite different:

```
Sub Macro2()
    ActiveCell.FormulaR1C1 = "Jan"
    ActiveCell.Offset(0, 1).Range("A1").Select
    ActiveCell.FormulaR1C1 = "Feb"
    ActiveCell.Offset(0, 1).Range("A1").Select
    ActiveCell.FormulaR1C1 = "Mar"
    ActiveCell.Offset(0, 1).Range("A1").Select
    ActiveCell.FormulaR1C1 = "Apr"
    ActiveCell.Offset(0, 1).Range("A1").Select
    ActiveCell.FormulaR1C1 = "May"
    ActiveCell.Offset(0, 1).Range("A1").Select
    ActiveCell.FormulaR1C1 = "Jun"
    ActiveCell.Offset(0, -5).Range("A1").Select
End Sub
```

You can execute this macro by activating a worksheet and then choosing the Tools ➪ Macro command. Select the macro's name, and click the Run button.

You'll also notice that I varied the procedure slightly in this example: I activated the beginning cell *before* I started recording. This is an important step when you record macros that use the active cell as a base.

Although it may look strange, this macro is actually quite simple. The first statement simply enters *Jan* into the active cell. (It uses the active cell because it's not preceded by a statement that selects a cell.) The next statement uses the Offset method to move the selection one cell to the right. The next statement inserts more text, and so on. Finally, the original cell is selected by calculating a relative offset rather than an absolute cell. Unlike the preceding macro, this one always starts entering text in the active cell.

Note   You'll notice that this macro generates code that references cell A1 — which may seem strange because cell A1 was not even involved in the macro. This is simply a by-product of the way the macro recorder works. (I discuss the Offset method later in this chapter.) At this point, all you need to know is that the macro works as it should.

By the way, the code generated by Excel is much more complex than it need be, and it's not the most efficient way to code the operation. The macro that follows, which I entered manually, is a simpler and faster way to perform the same operation. This example demonstrates that VBA doesn't have to select a cell before it puts information into it — an important concept that can also speed things up considerably.

```
Sub Macro3()
    ActiveCell.Offset(0, 0) = "Jan"
    ActiveCell.Offset(0, 1) = "Feb"
    ActiveCell.Offset(0, 2) = "Mar"
    ActiveCell.Offset(0, 3) = "Apr"
    ActiveCell.Offset(0, 4) = "May"
    ActiveCell.Offset(0, 5) = "Jun"
End Sub
```

In fact, this macro can be made even more efficient by using the `With-End With` construct:

```
Sub Macro4()
    With ActiveCell
        .Offset(0, 0) = "Jan"
        .Offset(0, 1) = "Feb"
        .Offset(0, 2) = "Mar"
        .Offset(0, 3) = "Apr"
        .Offset(0, 4) = "May"
        .Offset(0, 5) = "Jun"
    End With
End Sub
```

The point here is that the recorder has two distinct modes, and you need to be aware of which mode you're recording in. Otherwise, the result will not be what you expected.

Recording options

When you record your actions to create VBA code, you have several options. Recall that the Tools ➪ Macro ➪ Record New Macro command displays the Record Macro dialog box before recording begins. This dialog box gives you quite a bit of control over your macro. The following paragraphs describe your options.

Macro name

You can enter a name for the procedure that you are recording. By default, Excel uses the names Macro1, Macro2, and so on for each macro you record. I usually just accept the default name and change the name of the procedure later. You, however, may prefer to name the macro up front — the choice is yours.

Shortcut key

The Shortcut key option lets you execute the macro by pressing a shortcut key combination. For example, if you enter **w** (lowercase), you can execute the macro by pressing Ctrl+W. If you enter **W** (uppercase), the macro comes alive when you press Ctrl+Shift+W.

You can add or change a shortcut key at any time, so you don't need to set this option while recording a macro.

Store macro in

The Store macro in option tells Excel where to store the macro that it records. By default, Excel puts the recorded macro in a module in the active workbook. If you prefer, you can record it in a new workbook (Excel opens a blank workbook) or in your Personal Macro Workbook.

Description

By default, Excel inserts five lines of comments (three of them blank) that list the macro name, the user's name, and the date. You can put anything you like here, or nothing at all. As far as I'm concerned, typing anything in is a waste of time because I always end up deleting this in the module.

In versions of Excel prior to Excel 97, the Record Macro dialog box provided an option that let you assign the macro to a new menu item on the Tools menu. For some reason, this option was removed from Excel 97 and later versions. If you want to be able to execute a macro from a menu, you need to set this up yourself. See Chapter 51 for more information.

Cleaning up recorded macros

Earlier in this section, you saw how recording your actions while you issued a single command (the File ⇨ Page Setup command) can produce an enormous amount of VBA code. In many cases, the recorded code includes extraneous commands that you can delete.

The Personal Macro Workbook

If you create some VBA macros that you find particularly useful, you may want to store these routines on your Personal Macro Workbook. This is a workbook (Personal.xls) that is stored in your Xlstart directory. Whenever you start Excel, this workbook is loaded. It's a hidden workbook, so it's out of your way. When you record a macro, one of your options is to record it to your Personal Macro Workbook. The Personal.xls file doesn't exist until you record a macro to it.

It's also important to understand that the macro recorder doesn't always generate the most efficient code. If you examine the generated code, you'll see that Excel generally records what is selected (that is, an object) and then uses the `Selection` object in subsequent statements. For example, here's what is recorded if you select a range of cells and then use the buttons on the Formatting toolbar to change the numeric formatting and apply bold and italic:

```
Range("A1:C5").Select
Selection.NumberFormat = "#,##0.00"
Selection.Font.Bold = True
Selection.Font.Italic = True
```

Tip If you use the Formatting dialog box to record this macro, you'll find that Excel records quite a bit of extraneous code. Recording toolbar button clicks often produces more efficient code.

The preceding example is just *one* way to perform these actions. You can also use the more efficient `With-End With` construct, as follows:

```
Range("A1:C5").Select
With Selection
    .NumberFormat = "#,##0.00"
    .Font.Bold = True
    .Font.Italic = True
End With
```

Or you can avoid the `Select` method altogether and write the code even more efficiently, like this:

```
With Range("A1:C5")
    .NumberFormat = "#,##0.00"
    .Font.Bold = True
    .Font.Italic = True
End With
```

If speed is essential in your application, you'll always want to examine any recorded VBA code closely to make sure that it's as efficient as possible.

You will, of course, need to understand VBA thoroughly before you start cleaning up your recorded macros. But for now, just be aware that recorded VBA code isn't always the best, most efficient code.

About the Code Examples

Throughout this book, I present many small snippets of VBA code to make a point or to provide an example. Often, this code may consist of just a single statement. In some cases, the example consists of only an *expression,* which isn't a valid instruction by itself.

For example, the following is an expression:

```
Range("A1").Value
```

To test an expression, you must evaluate it. The MsgBox function is a handy tool for this:

```
MsgBox Range("A1").Value
```

To try out these examples, you need to put the statement within a procedure in a VBA module, like this:

```
Sub Test()
' statement goes here
End Sub
```

Then put the cursor anywhere within the procedure, and press F5 to execute it. Make sure that the code is being executed within the proper context. For example, if a statement refers to Sheet1, make sure that the active workbook actually has a sheet named Sheet1.

If the code is just a single statement, you can use VBE's Immediate window. The Immediate window is very useful for executing a statement "immediately" — without having to create a procedure. If the Immediate window is not displayed, press Ctrl+G in the VBE.

Just type the VBA statement, and press Enter. To evaluate an expression in the Immediate window, precede the expression with a question mark (?). The question mark is a shortcut for Print. For example, you can type the following into the Immediate window:

```
? Range("A1").Value
```

The result of this expression is displayed in the next line of the Immediate window.

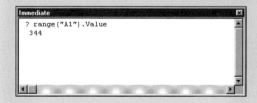

About Objects and Collections

If you've worked through the first part of this chapter, you have an overview of VBA, and you know the basics of working with VBA modules in the VBE. You've also seen some VBA code and were exposed to concepts such as objects and properties. This section gives you some additional details about objects and collections of objects.

As you work with VBA, you must understand the concept of objects and Excel's object model. It helps to think of objects in terms of a *hierarchy*. At the top of this model is the Application object — in this case, Excel itself. But if you're programming in VBA using Microsoft Word, the Application object is Word.

The object hierarchy

The Application object contains other objects. For example, Excel 2000 (the Application object we're interested in) contains 47 objects (many of which are collections). Here are a few examples of objects contained in the Application object:

> Workbooks (a collection of all Workbook objects)
>
> Windows (a collection of all Window objects)
>
> AddIns (a collection of all AddIn objects)
>
> AutoCorrect

Each of these objects can contain other objects. For example, the Workbooks collection consists of all open Workbook objects, and a Workbook object contains other objects, a few of which are as follows:

> Worksheets (a collection of Worksheet objects)
>
> Charts (a collection of Chart objects)
>
> Names (a collection of Name objects)

Each of these objects, in turn, can contain other objects. The Worksheets collection consists of all Worksheet objects in a Workbook. A Worksheet object contains many other objects, which include the following:

> ChartObjects (a collection of ChartObject objects)
>
> Range
>
> PageSetup
>
> PivotTables (a collection of PivotTable objects)

If this seems confusing, trust me, it *will* make sense, and you'll eventually realize that this whole object hierarchy thing is quite logical and well structured. By the way, the complete Excel object model is diagrammed in the online help system.

About collections

Another key concept in VBA programming is *collections*. A collection is a group of objects of the same class (and a collection is itself an object). As I noted previously, Workbooks is a collection of all Workbook objects currently open. Worksheets is a collection of all Worksheet objects contained in a particular Workbook object. You can work with an entire collection of objects or with an individual object in a collection. To reference a single object from a collection, you put the object's name or index number in paren-theses after the name of the collection, like this:

```
Worksheets("Sheet1")
```

If Sheet1 is the first worksheet in the collection, you may also use the following reference:

```
Worksheets(1)
```

You refer to the second worksheet in a Workbook as Worksheets(2), and so on.

A collection also exists called Sheets, which is made up of all sheets in a workbook, whether they're worksheets or chart sheets. If Sheet1 is the first sheet in the workbook, you can reference it as follows:

```
Sheets(1)
```

Object referral

When you refer to an object using VBA, you often must qualify the object by connecting object names with a period (also known as a "dot operator"). What if you had two workbooks open and they both had a worksheet named Sheet1? The solution is to qualify the reference by adding the object's *container,* like this:

```
Workbooks("Book1").Worksheets("Sheet1")
```

To refer to a specific range (such as cell A1) on a worksheet named Sheet1 in a workbook named Book1, you can use the following expression:

```
Workbooks("Book1").Worksheets("Sheet1").Range("A1")
```

The fully qualified reference for the preceding example also includes the Application object, as follows:

```
Application.Workbooks("Book1").Worksheets("Sheet1"). _
  Range("A1")
```

Most of the time, however, you can omit the `Application` object in your references (it is assumed). If the Book1 object is the active workbook, you can even omit that object reference and use this:

```
Worksheets("Sheet1").Range("A1")
```

And — I think you know where I'm going with this — if Sheet1 is the active worksheet, you can use an even simpler expression:

```
Range("A1")
```

Note   Contrary to what you might expect, Excel does not have an object that refers to an individual cell that is called "Cell." A single cell is simply a `Range` object that happens to consist of just one element.

Simply referring to objects (as in these examples) doesn't do anything. To perform anything meaningful, you must read or modify an object's properties or specify a method to be used with an object.

Properties and Methods

It's easy to be overwhelmed with properties and methods; literally thousands are available. In this section I describe how to access properties and methods of objects.

Object properties

Every object has properties. For example, a `Range` object has a property called `Value`. You can write VBA code to display the `Value` property or write VBA code to set the `Value` property to a specific value. Here's a procedure that uses VBA's `MsgBox` function to pop up a box that displays the value in cell A1 on Sheet1 of the active workbook:

```
Sub ShowValue()
    Answer = Worksheets("Sheet1").Range("A1").Value
    MsgBox Answer
End Sub
```

Note   `MsgBox` is a useful keyword that you'll often use to display results while your VBA code is executing. I use it extensively throughout this book.

The code in the preceding example displays the current setting of the Value property of a specific cell: cell A1 on a worksheet named Sheet1 in the active workbook. Note that if the active workbook does not have a sheet named Sheet1, the macro will generate an error.

Now, what if you want to change the Value property? The following procedure changes the value displayed in cell A1 by changing the cell's Value property:

```
Sub ChangeValue()
    Worksheets("Sheet1").Range("A1").Value = 123
End Sub
```

After executing this routine, cell A1 on Sheet1 has the value 123. You might want to enter these procedures into a module and experiment with them.

Note Every object has a default property. For a Range object, the default property is the Value property. Therefore, you can omit the .Value part from the preceding code, and it will have the same effect. It's usually considered good programming practice, however, to include the property, even if it's the default property.

Object methods

In addition to properties, objects also have methods. A *method* is an action that you perform with an object. Here's a simple example that uses the Clear method on a range object. After you execute this procedure, A1:C3 on Sheet1 will be empty.

```
Sub ZapRange()
    Worksheets("Sheet1").Range("A1:C3").Clear
End Sub
```

Most methods also take arguments to define the action further. Arguments for a method are placed in parentheses. Here's an example that copies cell A1 to cell B1 by using the Copy method of the Range object. In this example, the Copy method has one argument (the destination of the copy). Notice that I used the linecontinuation character sequence (a space followed by an underscore) in this example. You can omit the line continuation sequence and type the statement on a single line.

```
Sub CopyOne()
    Worksheets("Sheet1").Range("A1").Copy _
        Worksheets("Sheet1").Range("B1")
End Sub
```

Specifying Arguments for Methods and Properties

An issue that often leads to confusion among VBA programmers concerns arguments for methods and properties. Some methods use arguments to further clarify the action to be taken, and some properties use arguments to further specify the property value. In some cases, one or more of the arguments are optional.

If a method uses arguments, place the arguments after the name of the method, separated by commas. If the method uses optional arguments, you can insert blank *placeholders* for the optional arguments. Consider the Protect method for a workbook object. Check the online help, and you'll find that the Protect method takes three arguments: password, structure, windows. These arguments correspond to the options in the Protect Workbook dialog box.

If you want to protect a workbook named MyBook.xls, for example, you might use a statement like this:

```
Workbooks("MyBook.xls").Protect "xyzzy", True, True
```

If you don't want to assign a password, you can use a statement like this:

```
Workbooks("MyBook.xls").Protect , True, True
```

Notice that the first argument is omitted and that I specified the placeholder with a comma.

Another approach, which makes your code more readable, is to use named arguments. Here's an example of how you use named arguments for the preceding example:

```
Workbooks("MyBook.xls").Protect Structure:=True, Windows:=True
```

Using named arguments is a good idea, especially for methods that have lots of optional arguments and also when you need to use only a few of them.

For properties that use arguments, you must place the arguments in parentheses. For example, the Address property of a Range object takes five arguments, all of which are optional. The following statement is not valid because the parentheses are omitted:

```
MsgBox Range("A1").Address False    ' invalid
```

The proper syntax for such a statement requires parentheses, as follows:

```
MsgBox Range("A1").Address(False)
```

The statement could also be written using a named argument:

```
MsgBox Range("A1").Address(rowAbsolute:=False)
```

These nuances will become clearer as you gain more experience with VBA.

The Comment Object: A Case Study

To help you better understand the properties and methods available for an object, I focus on a particular object: the Comment object. You create a Comment object when you use Excel's Insert ⇨ Comment command to enter a cell comment. In the sections that follow, you'll get a feel for working with objects. If you're a bit overwhelmed by the material in this section, don't fret. These concepts will become much clearer over time.

Online help for the Comment object

One way to learn about a particular object is to look it up in the online help system. Figure 40-15 shows the main help screen for the Comment object.

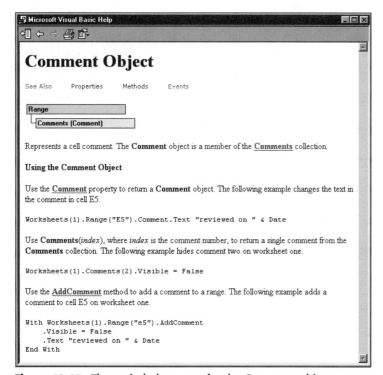

Figure 40-15: The main help screen for the Comment object

Notice that the underlined words are "jumps" that display additional information. For example, you can click Properties to get a list of all properties for the Comment object. Or, click Method to get a list of the object's methods.

Using the Online Help System

The easiest way to get specific help about a particular object, property, or method is to type the word in a code window and press F1. If the word you typed is at all ambiguous, you'll get a dialog box like the one shown in the accompanying figure.

Unfortunately, the items listed in the dialog box are not always clear, so it may require some trial and error to locate the correct help topic. The dialog box in the figure appears when you type **Comment** and then press F1. In this case, although Comment is an object, it may behave like a property. Clicking the first item displays the help topic for the Comment object; clicking the second item displays the help topic for the "Comment property."

Properties of a Comment object

The Comment object has six properties. Table 40-1 contains a list of these properties, along with a brief description of each. If a property is *read-only*, your VBA code can read the property but cannot change it.

Table 40-1 Properties of a Comment Object		
Property	**Read-Only**	**Description**
Application	Yes	Returns the name of the application that created the comment (that is, Excel).
Author	Yes	Returns the name of the person who created the comment.
Creator	Yes	Returns a number that specifies the application that created the object. Not used in Excel for Windows (relevant only for Excel for Macintosh).

Property	Read-Only	Description
Parent	Yes	Returns the parent object for the comment (it is always a Range object).
Shape	Yes	Returns a Shape object that represents the shape attached to the comment.
Visible	No	Is True if the comment is visible.

Methods of a Comment object

Table 40-2 shows the methods that you can use with a Comment object. Again, these methods perform common operations that you may have performed manually with a comment at some point — but you probably never thought of these operations as methods.

Table 40-2	
Methods of a Comment Object	
Method	Description
--------	-------------
Delete	Deletes a comment.
Next	Returns a Comment object that represents the next comment.
Previous	Returns a Comment object that represents the previous comment.
Text	Sets the text in a comment (takes three arguments).

Note You may be surprised to see that Text is a method rather than a property. This leads to an important point: The distinction between properties and methods isn't always clear-cut, and the object model isn't perfectly consistent. In fact, it's not really important that you distinguish between properties and methods. As long as you get the syntax correct, it doesn't matter if a word in your code is a property or a method.

The Comments collection

Recall that a collection is a group of like objects. Every worksheet has a Comments collection, which consists of all Comment objects on the worksheet. If the worksheet has no comments, this collection is empty.

For example, the following code refers to the first comment on Sheet1 of the active workbook:

```
Worksheets("Sheet1").Comments(1)
```

The following statement displays the text contained in the first comment on Sheet1:

```
MsgBox Worksheets("Sheet1").Comments(1).Text
```

Unlike most objects, a `Comment` object does not have a `Name` property. Therefore, to refer to a specific comment, you must use an index number or use the `Comment` property of a `Range` object to return a specific comment (keep reading, and this will make sense).

The `Comments` collection is also an object and has its own set of properties and methods. For example, the following example shows the total number of comments:

```
MsgBox ActiveSheet.Comments.Count
```

The `Comments` collection here has a `Count` property that stores the number of objects in the active worksheet. The next example shows which cell has the first comment:

```
MsgBox ActiveSheet.Comments(1).Parent.Address
```

Here, `Comments(1)` returns the first `Comment` object in the `Comments` collection. The `Parent` property of the `Comment` object returns its container, which is a `Range` object. The message box displays the `Address` property of the `Range`. The net effect is that the statement displays the address of the cell that contains the first comment.

You can also loop through all the comments on a sheet by using the `For Each-Next` construct (this is explained in Chapter 41). Here's an example that displays a separate message box for each comment on the active worksheet:

```
For Each cmt in ActiveSheet.Comments
    MsgBox cmt.Text
Next cmt
```

About the Comment property

In this section I've been discussing the `Comment` object. If you dig through the online help, you'll find that a `Range` object has a property named `Comment`. This property returns an object: a `Comment` object. For example, the following statement refers to the `Comment` object in cell A1:

```
Range("A1").Comment
```

If this were the first comment on the sheet, you could refer to the same `Comment` object as follows:

```
Comments(1)
```

To display the comment in cell A1 in a message box, use a statement like this:

```
MsgBox Range("A1").Comment.Text
```

Note   The fact that a property can return an object is a very important concept — a difficult one to grasp, perhaps, but critical to mastering VBA.

Objects within a Comment object

Working with properties is confusing at first because some properties actually return objects. Suppose that you want to determine the background color of a particular comment on Sheet1. If you look through the list of properties for a `Comment` object, you won't find anything that relates to color. Rather, you must do this:

1. Use the `Comment` object's `Shape` property to return the `Shape` object that's contained in the comment.

2. Use the `Shape` object's `Fill` property to return a `FillFormat` object.

3. Use the `FillFormat` object's `ForeColor` property to return a `ColorFormat` object.

4. Use the `ColorFormat` object's `RGB` property to set the color.

Put another way, getting at the interior color for a `Comment` object involves accessing other objects contained in the `Comment` object. Here's a look at the object hierarchy that's involved.

```
Application (Excel)
   Workbook object
      Worksheet object
         Comment object
            Shape object
               FillFormat object
                  ColorFormat object
```

I'll be the first to admit it: This can get very confusing! But, as an example of the "elegance" of VBA, code to change the color of a comment can be written with a single statement:

```
Worksheets("Sheet1").Comments(1).Shape.Fill.ForeColor.RGB _
    = RGB(0, 255, 0)
```

This type of referencing is certainly not intuitive and can be difficult to get used to. Fortunately, recording your actions in Excel almost always yields some insights regarding the hierarchy of the objects involved. And, if you work with this long enough, it all makes perfect sense. Trust me.

Adding a new Comment object

You may have noticed that the list of methods for the Comment object doesn't include a method to add a new comment. The reason for this is that the AddComment method belongs to the Range object. The following statement adds a comment (an empty comment) to cell A1 on the active worksheet:

```
Range("A1").AddComment
```

If you consult the online help, you'll discover that the AddComment method takes an argument that represents the text for the comment. Therefore, you can add a comment and then add text to the comment with a single statement, like this:

```
Range("A1").AddComment "Formula developed by JW."
```

Note The AddComment method generates an error if the cell already contains a comment.

On the CD-ROM If you'd like to see these Comment object properties and methods in action, check out the example workbook on the companion CD-ROM. This workbook contains several examples that manipulate Comment objects with VBA code. You probably won't understand all the code, but you will get a feel for how you can use VBA to manipulate an object.

Some useful Application properties

As you know, when you're working with Excel, only one workbook at a time can be active. And if the sheet is a worksheet, one cell is the active cell (even if a multicell range is selected).

VBA knows this and lets you refer to these active objects in a simplified manner. This is often useful because you won't always know the exact workbook, worksheet, or range that you want to operate on. VBA handles this by providing properties of the Application object. For example, the Application object has an ActiveCell property that returns a reference to the active cell. The following instruction assigns the value 1 to the active cell:

```
ActiveCell.Value = 1
```

Notice that I omitted the reference to the Application object in the preceding example because it is assumed. It's important to understand that this instruction will fail if the active sheet is not a worksheet. For example, if VBA executes this statement when a chart sheet is active, the procedure halts and you'll receive an error message.

If a range is selected in a worksheet, the active cell will be one of the corner cells of the range (which corner is determined by how the range was selected). In other words, the active cell is always a single cell.

The Application object also has a Selection property that returns a reference to whatever is selected, which could be a single cell (the active cell), a range of cells, or an object such as ChartObject, TextBox, or Shape.

Table 40-3 lists the other Application properties that are useful when working with cells and ranges.

Table 40-3
Some Useful Properties of the Application Object

Property	Object Returned
ActiveCell	The active cell
ActiveSheet	The active sheet (worksheet or chart)
ActiveWindow	The active window
ActiveWorkbook	The active workbook
RangeSelection	The selected cells on the worksheet in the specified window, even when a graphic object is selected
Selection	The object selected (it could be a Range, Shape, ChartObject, and so on)
ThisWorkbook	The workbook that contains the procedure being executed

The advantage of using these properties to return an object is that you don't need to know which cell, worksheet, or workbook is active or to provide a specific reference to it. For example, the following instruction clears the contents of the active cell, even though the address of the active cell is not known:

```
ActiveCell.ClearContents
```

The example that follows displays a message that tells you the name of the active sheet:

```
MsgBox ActiveSheet.Name
```

If you want to know the name of the active workbook, use a statement like this:

```
MsgBox ActiveWorkbook.Name
```

If a range on a worksheet is selected, you can fill the entire range with a value by executing a single statement. In the following example, the Selection property of the Application object returns a Range object that corresponds to the selected cells. The instruction simply modifies the Value property of this Range object, and the result is a range filled with a single value:

```
Selection.Value = 12
```

Note that if something other than a range is selected (such as a ChartObject or a Shape), the preceding statement will generate an error because ChartObjects and Shape objects do not have a Value property.

The following statement, however, enters a value of 12 into the Range object that was selected before a non-Range object was selected. If you look up the RangeSelection property in the online help, you'll find that this property applies to a Window object only.

```
ActiveWindow.RangeSelection.Value = 12
```

Working with Range Objects

Much of the work you will do in VBA involves cells and ranges in worksheets. After all, that's what spreadsheets are designed to do. The earlier discussion on relative versus absolute macro recording exposed you to working with cells in VBA, but you need to know a lot more.

A Range object is contained in a Worksheet object and consists of a single cell or range of cells on a single worksheet. In the sections that follow, I discuss three ways of referring to Range objects in your VBA code:

✦ The `Range` property of a `Worksheet` or `Range` class object

✦ The `Cells` property of a `Worksheet` object

✦ The `Offset` property of a `Range` object

The Range property

The `Range` property returns a `Range` object. If you consult the online help for the `Range` property, you'll learn that this property has two syntaxes:

```
object.Range(cell1)
object.Range(cell1, cell2)
```

The `Range` property applies to two types of objects: a `Worksheet` object or a `Range` object. Here, `cell1` and `cell2` refer to placeholders for terms that Excel will recognize as identifying the range (in the first instance) and *delineating* the range (in the second instance). Following are a few examples of using the `Range` method.

You've already seen examples like the following one earlier in the chapter. The instruction that follows simply enters a value into the specified cell. In this case, it puts a 1 into cell A1 on Sheet1 of the active workbook.

```
Worksheets("Sheet1").Range("A1").Value = 1
```

The `Range` property also recognizes defined names in workbooks. Therefore, if a cell is named "Input," you can use the following statement to enter a value into that named cell:

```
Worksheets("Sheet1").Range("Input").Value = 1
```

The example that follows enters the same value into a range of 20 cells on the active sheet. If the active sheet is not a worksheet, this causes an error message.

```
ActiveSheet.Range("A1:B10").Value = 2
```

The next example produces exactly the same result as the preceding example.

```
Range("A1", "B10") = 2
```

The sheet reference is omitted, however, so the active sheet is assumed. The value property is also omitted, so the default property (which is `Value`, for a `Range` object) is assumed. This example also uses the second syntax of the `Range` property. With this syntax, the first argument is the cell at the top left of the range and the second argument is the cell at the lower right of the range.

The following example uses Excel's range intersection operator (a space) to return the intersection of two ranges. In this case, the intersection is a single cell, C6. Therefore, this statement enters 3 into cell C6:

```
Range("C1:C10 A6:E6") = 3
```

And finally, the next example enters the value 4 into five cells, that is, a noncontiguous range. The comma serves as the union operator.

```
Range("A1,A3,A5,A7,A9") = 4
```

So far, all the examples have used the Range property on a Worksheet object. As I mentioned, you can also use the Range property on a Range object. This can be rather confusing, but bear with me.

Following is an example of using the Range property on a Range object (in this case, the Range object is the active cell). This example treats the Range object as if it were the upper-left cell in the worksheet and then enters a value of 5 into the cell that *would be* B2. In other words, the reference returned is relative to the upper-left corner of the Range object. Therefore, the statement that follows enters a value of 5 into the cell directly to the right and one row below the active cell:

```
ActiveCell.Range("B2") = 5
```

I *said* this is confusing. Fortunately, you have a much clearer way to access a cell relative to a range, called the Offset property. I'll discuss this property after the next section.

The Cells property

Another way to reference a range is to use the Cells property. Like the Range property, you can use the Cells property on Worksheet objects and Range objects. Check the online help, and you'll see that the Cells property has three syntaxes:

```
object.Cells(rowIndex, columnIndex)
object.Cells(rowIndex)
object.Cells
```

I'll give you some examples that demonstrate how to use the Cells property. The first example enters the value 9 into cell 1 on Sheet1. In this case, I'm using the first syntax, which accepts the index number of the row (from 1 to 65536) and the index number of the column (from 1 to 256):

```
Worksheets("Sheet1").Cells(1, 1) = 9
```

Here's an example that enters the value 7 into cell D3 (that is, row 3, column 4) in the active worksheet:

```
ActiveSheet.Cells(3, 4) = 7
```

You can also use the `Cells` property on a `Range` object. When you do so, the `Range` object returned by the `Cells` property is relative to the upper-left cell of the referenced `Range`. Confusing? Probably. An example might help clear this up. The following instruction enters the value 5 into the active cell. Remember, in this case, the active cell is treated as if it were cell A1 in the worksheet:

```
ActiveCell.Cells(1, 1) = 5
```

Note   The real advantage of this type of cell referencing will be apparent when I discuss variables and looping (see Chapter 41). In most cases, you will not use actual values for the arguments. Rather, you'll use variables.

To enter a value of 5 into the cell directly below the active cell, you can use the following instruction:

```
ActiveCell.Cells(2, 1) = 5
```

Think of the preceding example as though it said this: "Start with the active cell and consider this cell to be cell A1. Return the cell in the second row and the first column."

The second syntax of the `Cells` method uses a single argument that can range from 1 to 16,777,216. This number is equal to the number of cells in a worksheet (65,536 rows × 256 columns). The cells are numbered starting from A1 and continuing right and then down to the next row. The 256th cell is IV1; the 257th is A2.

The next example enters the value 2 into cell H3 (which is the 520th cell in the worksheet) of the active worksheet:

```
ActiveSheet.Cells(520) = 2
```

To display the value in the last cell in a worksheet (IV65536), use this statement:

```
MsgBox ActiveSheet.Cells(16777216)
```

This syntax can also be used with a `Range` object. In this case, the cell returned is relative to the `Range` object referenced. For example, if the `Range` object is A1:D10 (40 cells), the `Cells` property can have an argument from 1 to 40 and return one of the cells in the `Range` object. In the following example, a value of 2000 is entered into cell A2 because A2 is the fifth cell (counting from the top and to the right, and then down) in the referenced range:

```
Range("A1:D10").Cells(5) = 2000
```

In the preceding example, the argument for the `Cells` property is not limited to values between 1 and 40. If the argument exceeds the number of cells in the range, the counting continues as if the range were larger than it actually is. Therefore, the preceding statement could change the value in a cell that's outside of the range A1:D10.

The third syntax for the `Cells` property simply returns all cells on the referenced worksheet. Unlike the other two syntaxes, in this one, the return data is not a single cell. This example uses the `ClearContents` method on the range returned by using the `Cells` property on the active worksheet. The result is that the contents of every cell on the worksheet are cleared:

```
ActiveSheet.Cells.ClearContents
```

The Offset property

The `Offset` property (like the `Range` and `Cells` properties) also returns a `Range` object. But unlike the other two methods I discussed, the `Offset` property applies only to a `Range` object and no other class. Its syntax is as follows:

```
object.Offset(rowOffset, columnOffset)
```

The `Offset` property takes two arguments that correspond to the relative position from the upper-left cell of the specified `Range` object. The arguments can be positive (down or right), negative (up or left), or zero. The example that follows enters a value of 12 into the cell directly below the active cell:

```
ActiveCell.Offset(1,0).Value = 12
```

The next example enters a value of 15 into the cell directly above the active cell:

```
ActiveCell.Offset(-1,0).Value = 15
```

By the way, if the active cell is in row 1, the `Offset` property in the preceding example generates an error because it cannot return a `Range` object that doesn't exist.

The `Offset` property is quite useful, especially when you use variables within looping procedures. I discuss these topics in the next chapter.

When you record a macro using the relative reference mode, Excel uses the `Offset` property to reference cells relative to the starting position (that is, the active cell when macro recording begins). For example, I used the macro recorder to generate the following code. I started with the cell pointer in cell B1, entered values into B1:B3, and then returned to B1.

```
Sub Macro1()
    ActiveCell.FormulaR1C1 = "1"
    ActiveCell.Offset(1, 0).Range("A1").Select
    ActiveCell.FormulaR1C1 = "2"
    ActiveCell.Offset(1, 0).Range("A1").Select
    ActiveCell.FormulaR1C1 = "3"
    ActiveCell.Offset(-2, 0).Range("A1").Select
End Sub
```

You'll notice that the generated code references cell A1, which may seem a bit odd, because that cell was not even involved in the macro. This is a quirk in the macro recording procedure that makes the code more complex than necessary. You can delete all references to Range("A1"), and the macro still works perfectly:

```
Sub Modified Macro1()
    ActiveCell.FormulaR1C1 = "1"
    ActiveCell.Offset(1, 0).Select
    ActiveCell.FormulaR1C1 = "2"
    ActiveCell.Offset(1, 0).Select
    ActiveCell.FormulaR1C1 = "3"
    ActiveCell.Offset(-2, 0).Select
End Sub
```

In fact, here's a much more efficient version of the macro (which I wrote myself) that doesn't do any selecting:

```
Sub Macro1()
    ActiveCell = 1
    ActiveCell.Offset(1, 0) = 2
    ActiveCell.Offset(2, 0) = 3
End Sub
```

Things to Know About Objects

The preceding sections introduced you to objects (including collections), properties, and methods. But I've barely scratched the surface.

Esoteric but essential concepts to remember

In this section, I'll add some more concepts that are essential for would-be VBA gurus. These concepts become clearer as you work with VBA and read subsequent chapters:

✦ Objects have unique properties and methods.

Each object has its own set of properties and methods. Some objects, however, share some properties (for example, `Name`) and some methods (such as `Delete`).

✦ You can manipulate objects without selecting them.

This may be contrary to how you normally think about manipulating objects in Excel, especially if you've programmed XLM macros. Fact is, it's usually more efficient to perform actions on objects without selecting them first. When you record a macro, Excel generally selects the object first. This is not necessary and may actually make your macro run slower.

✦ It's important that you understand the concept of collections.

Most of the time, you'll refer to an object indirectly by referring to the collection that it's in. For example, to access a `Workbook` object named Myfile, reference the `Workbooks` collection as follows:

```
Workbooks("Myfile.xls")
```

This reference returns an object, which is the workbook with which you are concerned.

✦ Properties can return a reference to another object. For example, in the following statement, the `Font` property returns a `Font` object contained in a `Range` object:

```
Range("A1").Font.Bold = True
```

✦ There can be many different ways to refer to the same object.

Assume that you have a workbook named `Sales` and that it's the only workbook open. Then assume that this workbook has one worksheet, named Summary. You can refer to the sheet in any of the following ways:

```
Workbooks("Sales.xls").Worksheets("Summary")
Workbooks(1).Worksheets(1)
Workbooks(1).Sheets(1)
Application.ActiveWorkbook.ActiveSheet
ActiveWorkbook.ActiveSheet
ActiveSheet
```

The way you choose is usually determined by how much you know about the workspace. For example, if more than one workbook is open, the second or third way is not reliable. If you want to work with the active sheet (whatever it may be), any of the last three ways would work. To be absolutely sure that you're referring to a specific sheet on a specific workbook, the first way is your best choice.

Learn more about objects and properties

If this is your first exposure to VBA, you're probably a bit overwhelmed by objects, properties, and methods. I don't blame you. If you try to access a property that an object doesn't have, you'll get a run-time error, and your VBA code will grind to a screeching halt until you correct the problem.

Fortunately, you have several good ways to learn about objects, properties, and methods.

Read the rest of the book

Don't forget, the name of this chapter is "Introducing Visual Basic for Applications." The remainder of this book covers lots of additional details and provides many useful and informative examples.

Record your actions

Without question, the absolute best way to become familiar with VBA is simply to turn on the macro recorder and record some actions you make in Excel. This is a quick way to learn the relevant objects, properties, and methods for a task. It's even better if the VBA module in which the code is being recorded is visible while you're recording.

Use the online help system

The main source of detailed information about Excel's objects, methods, and procedures is in the online help system.

Figure 40-16 shows the help topic for the `Value` property. This particular property applies to a number of different objects, and the help topic contains hyperlinks labeled See Also, Example, and Applies To. If you click See Also, you get a list of related topics. If you click Example, another window opens with one or more examples (you can copy the example text and paste it into a VBA module to try it out). Clicking Applies To displays a window that lists all objects that use this property.

Use the Object Browser

The Object Browser is a handy tool that lists every property and method for every object available. When the VBE is active, you can bring up the Object Browser in any of the following three ways:

- ✦ Press F2.
- ✦ Choose the View ➪ Object Browser command from the menu.
- ✦ Click the Object Browser tool on the Standard toolbar.

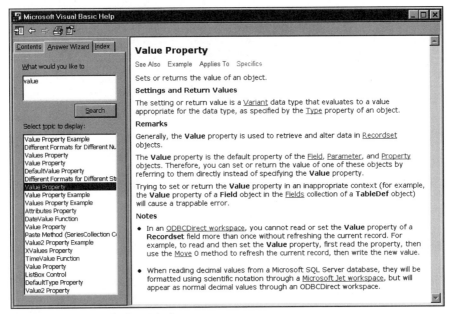

Figure 40-16: A typical VBA help screen

The Object Browser is shown in Figure 40-17.

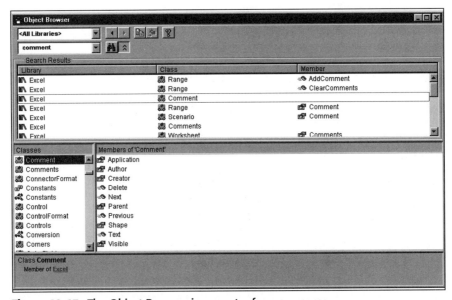

Figure 40-17: The Object Browser is a great reference source

The drop-down list in the upper-left corner of the Object Browser includes a list of all object libraries that you have access to:

✦ Excel itself

✦ MSForms (used to create custom dialog boxes)

✦ Office (objects common to all Microsoft Office applications)

✦ Stdole (OLE automation objects)

✦ VBA

✦ Each open workbook (each workbook is considered an object library because it contains objects)

Your selection in this upper-left drop-down list determines what is displayed in the Classes window, and your selection in the Classes window determines what is visible in the Members of window.

Once you select a library, you can search for a particular text string to get a list of properties and methods that contain the text. You do so by entering the text in the second drop-down list and then clicking the binoculars icon. For example, assume that you're working on a project that manipulates cell comments:

1. Select the library of interest (you probably want to select <All Libraries>).

2. Enter **Comment** in the drop-down list below the library list.

3. Click the binoculars icon to begin the text search.

The Search Results window displays the matching text. Select an object to display its classes in the Classes window. Select a class to display its members (properties, methods, and constants). You can press F1 to go directly to the appropriate help topic.

The Object Browser may seem complex at first, but its usefulness will increase over time.

Experiment with the Immediate window

As I describe in the sidebar earlier in this chapter (see "About the Code Examples"), the Immediate window of the VBE is very useful for testing statements and trying out various VBA expressions. I generally keep the Immediate window visible at all times, and I use it frequently to test various expressions and to help in debugging code.

Summary

In this chapter, I introduced VBA and discussed how VBA compares to other languages. I explained that a VBA module contains procedures and that VBA is based on objects, properties, and methods. I also explained how to use the macro recorder to translate your actions into VBA code.

Chapter 41 discusses programming concepts that are necessary to get the most out of VBA.

✦　　✦　　✦

VBA Programming Fundamentals

◆ ◆ ◆ ◆

In This Chapter

Understanding
VBA's Language
Elements, Including
Variables, Data
Types, Constants,
and Arrays

Using VBA's Built-In
Functions

Manipulating Objects
and Collections

Controlling the
Execution of your
Procedures

◆ ◆ ◆ ◆

In the preceding chapter, I introduced you to VBA; now it's time to get better acquainted. This chapter discusses some of the key language elements and programming concepts in VBA. If you've used other programming languages, much of this information may sound familiar. VBA has a few unique wrinkles, however, so even experienced programmers may find some new information.

VBA Language Elements: An Overview

In Chapter 40, I presented an overview of objects, properties, and methods. But I didn't tell you much about how to manipulate objects so that they do meaningful things. This chapter gently nudges you in that direction by exploring VBA's *language elements*, the keywords and control structures that you use to write VBA routines.

To get the ball rolling, I'll start by presenting a simple procedure. The following procedure is stored in a VBA module and calculates the sum of the first 100 integers. When done, the procedure displays a message with the result.

```
Sub VBA_Demo()
'   This is a simple VBA Example
    Total = 0
    For i = 1 To 100
        Total = Total + i
    Next i
    MsgBox Total
End Sub
```

This procedure uses some common language elements, including a comment (the line preceded by the apostrophe), a variable (Total), two assignment statements (Total = 0 and Total = Total + i), a looping structure (For-Next), and a VBA statement (MsgBox). All these are discussed in subsequent sections of this chapter.

Note VBA procedures need not manipulate any objects. The preceding procedure, for example, doesn't do anything with objects.

Entering VBA Code

VBA code, which resides in a VBA module, consists of instructions. The accepted practice is to use one instruction per line. This standard is not a requirement, however; you can use a colon to separate multiple instructions on a single line. The following example combines four instructions on one line:

```
Sub OneLine()
    x= 1: y= 2: z= 3: MsgBox x + y + z
End Sub
```

Most programmers agree that code is easier to read if you use one instruction per line:

```
Sub OneLine()
    x = 1
    y = 2
    z = 3
    MsgBox x + y + z
End Sub
```

Each line can be as long as you like; the VBA module window scrolls to the left when you reach the right side. For lengthy lines, you may want to use VBA's line continuation sequence: an underscore (_) preceded by a space. For example,

```
Sub LongLine()
    SummedValue = _
        Worksheets("Sheet1").Range("A1").Value + _
        Worksheets("Sheet2").Range("A1").Value
End Sub
```

When you record macros, Excel often uses underscores to break long statements into multiple lines.

After you enter an instruction, VBA performs the following actions to improve readability:

✦ It inserts spaces between operators. If you enter Ans=1+2 (without any spaces), for example, VBA converts it to

```
Ans = 1 + 2
```

✦ VBA adjusts the case of the letters for keywords, properties, and methods. If you enter the following text

```
Result=activesheet.range("a1").value=12
```

VBA converts it to

```
Result = ActiveSheet.Range("a1").Value = 12
```

Notice that text within quotation marks (in this case, `"a1"`) is not changed.

✦ Because VBA variable names are not case sensitive, the interpreter by default adjusts the names of all variables with the same letters so that their case matches the case of letters that you most recently typed. For example, if you first specify a variable as `myvalue` (all lowercase) and then enter the variable as `MyValue` (mixed case), VBA changes all other occurrences of the variable to `MyValue`. An exception occurs if you declare the variable with `Dim` or a similar statement; in this case, the variable name always appears as it was declared.

✦ VBA scans the instruction for syntax errors. If VBA finds an error, it changes the color of the line and may display a message describing the problem. Use the VBE's Tools ➪ Options command to display the Options dialog box, where you control the error color (use the Editor Format tab) and whether the error message is displayed (use the Auto Syntax Check option in the Editor tab).

Comments

A *comment* is descriptive text embedded within your code. The text of a comment is completely ignored by VBA. It's a good idea to use comments liberally to describe what you're doing (an instruction's purpose is not always obvious).

You can use a complete line for your comment, or you can insert a comment *after* an instruction on the same line. A comment is indicated by an apostrophe. VBA ignores any text that follows an apostrophe — except when the apostrophe is contained within quotation marks — up until the end of the line. For example, the following statement does not contain a comment, even though it has an apostrophe:

```
Msg = "Can't continue"
```

The following example shows a VBA procedure with three comments:

```
Sub Comments()
'    This procedure does nothing of value
    x = 0    'x represents nothingness
'    Display the result
    MsgBox x
End Sub
```

Although the apostrophe is the preferred comment indicator, you can also use the Rem keyword to mark a line as a comment. For example,

```
Rem -- The next statement prompts the user for a filename
```

The Rem keyword is essentially a holdover from old versions of BASIC; it is included in VBA for the sake of compatibility. Unlike the apostrophe, Rem can be written only at the beginning of a line, not on the same line as another instruction.

Using comments is definitely a good idea, but not all comments are equally bene-ficial. To be useful, comments should convey information that's not imme-diately obvious from reading the code. Otherwise, you're just chewing up valuable bytes. The following procedure, for example, contains many comments, none of which really adds anything of value:

```
Sub BadComments()
'    Declare variables
     Dim x As Integer
     Dim y As Integer
     Dim z As Integer
'    Start the routine
     x = 100 ' Assign 100 to x
     y = 200 ' Assign 200 to y
'    Add x and y and store in z
     z = x + y
'    Show the result
     MsgBox z
End Sub
```

Following are a few general tips on making the best use of comments:

✦ Use comments to describe briefly the purpose of each procedure you write.

✦ Use comments to describe changes you make to a procedure.

✦ Use comments to indicate that you're using functions or constructs in an unusual or nonstandard manner.

✦ Use comments to describe the purpose of variables so that you and other people can decipher otherwise cryptic names.

✦ Use comments to describe workarounds that you develop to overcome Excel bugs.

✦ Write comments *as* you code rather than after.

Tip

You may want to test a procedure without including a particular instruction or group of instructions. Instead of deleting the instruction, simply turn it into a comment by inserting an apostrophe at the beginning. VBA then ignores the instruction(s) when the routine is executed. To convert the comment back to an instruction, delete the apostrophe.

VBE's Edit toolbar contains two very useful buttons. Select a group of instructions and then use the Comment Block button to convert the instructions to comments. The Uncomment Block button converts a group of comments back to instructions. These buttons are very useful, so you may want to copy them to your Standard toolbar.

Variables, Data Types, and Constants

VBA's main purpose in life is to manipulate data. Some data resides in objects, such as worksheet ranges. Other data is stored in variables that you create.

A *variable* is simply a named storage location in your computer's memory. Variables can accommodate a wide variety of *data types* — from simple Boolean values (True or False) to large, double-precision values (see the following section). You assign a value to a variable by using the equal sign operator (more about this later).

You'll make your life easier if you get into the habit of making your variable names as descriptive as possible. VBA does, however, have a few rules regarding variable names:

✦ You can use alphabetic characters, numbers, and some punctuation characters, but the first character must be alphabetic.

✦ VBA does not distinguish between case. To make variable names more readable, programmers often use mixed case (for example, `InterestRate` rather than `interestrate`).

✦ You cannot use spaces or periods. To make variable names more readable, programmers often use the underscore character (`Interest_Rate`).

✦ Special type declaration characters (#, $, %, &, or !) cannot be embedded in a variable name.

✦ Variable names may comprise as many as 254 characters — but no one in his right mind would create a variable name that long!

The following list contains some examples of assignment expressions that use various types of variables. The variable names are to the left of the equal sign. Each statement assigns the value to the right of the equal sign to the variable on the left.

```
x = 1
InterestRate = 0.075
LoanPayoffAmount = 243089
DataEntered = False
x = x + 1
MyNum = YourNum * 1.25
UserName = "Bob Johnson"
DateStarted = #3/14/94#
```

VBA has many *reserved words*, which are words that you cannot use for variable or procedure names. If you attempt to use one of these words, you get an error message. For example, although the reserved word Next might make a very descriptive variable name, the following instruction generates a syntax error:

```
Next = 132
```

Unfortunately, syntax error messages aren't always very descriptive. The preceding instruction generates this error message: Compile Error: Expected: variable. It would be nice if the error message were something like Reserved word used as a variable. So if an instruction produces a strange error message, check the online help to make sure your variable name doesn't have a special use in VBA.

Defining data types

VBA makes life easy for programmers because it can automatically handle all the details involved in dealing with data. Not all programming languages make it so easy. For example, some languages are *strictly typed,* which means that the programmer must explicitly define the data type for every variable used.

Data type refers to how data is stored in memory—as integers, real numbers, strings, and so on. Although VBA can take care of data typing automatically, it does so at a cost: slower execution and less efficient use of memory. (There's no such thing as a free lunch.) As a result, letting VBA handle data typing may present problems when you're running large or complex applications. If you need to conserve every last byte of memory, you need to be on familiar terms with data types.

Table 41-1 lists VBA's assortment of built-in data types (note that you can also define custom data types, which I describe later in this chapter).

Table 41-1		
VBA's Built-in Data Types		
Data Type	*Bytes Used*	*Range of Values*
Byte	1 byte	0 to 255
Boolean	2 bytes	True or False
Integer	2 bytes	–32,768 to 32,767
Long	4 bytes	–2,147,483,648 to 2,147,483,647

Data Type	Bytes Used	Range of Values
Single	4 bytes	−3.402823E38 to −1.401298E−45 (for negative values); 1.401298E−45 to 3.402823E38 (for positive values)
Double	8 bytes	−1.79769313486232E308 to −4.94065645841247E−324 (negative values); 4.94065645841247E−324 to 1.79769313486232E308 (positive values)
Currency	8 bytes	−922,337,203,685,477.5808 to 922,337,203,685,477.5807
Decimal	14 bytes	+/−79,228,162,514,264,337, 593,543,950,335 with no decimal point; +/−7.92281625 14264337593543950335 with 28 places to the right of the decimal
Date	8 bytes	January 1, 0100 to December 31, 9999
Object	4 bytes	Any object reference
String (variable-length)	10 bytes + string length	0 to approximately 2 billion
String (fixed-length)	Length of string	1 to approximately 65,400
Variant (with numbers)	16 bytes	Any numeric value up to the range of a double data type
Variant (with characters)	22 bytes + string length	0 to approximately 2 billion
User-defined	Varies	Varies by element

EXCEL 2000 The decimal data type is new to Excel 2000. This is a rather unusual data type because you cannot actually declare it. In fact, it is a "subtype" of a variant. You need to use VBA's `CDec` function to convert a variant to the decimal data type.

Generally, it's best to use the data type that uses the smallest number of bytes yet still can handle all the data assigned to it. When VBA works with data, execution speed is a function of the number of bytes VBA has at its disposal. In other words, the fewer bytes used by data, the faster VBA can access and manipulate the data.

Benchmarking Variant Data Types

To test whether data-typing is important, I developed the following routine, which performs some meaningless calculations in a loop and then displays the procedure's total execution time:

```
Sub TimeTest()
    Dim x As Integer, y As Integer
    Dim A As Integer, B As Integer, C As Integer
    Dim i As Integer, j As Integer
    Dim StartTime as Date, EndTime As Date
'   Store the starting time
    StartTime = Timer
'   Perform some calculations
    x = 0
    y = 0
    For i = 1 To 5000
        For j = 1 To 1000
            A = x + y + i
            B = y - x - i
            C = x - y - i
        Next j
    Next i
'   Get ending time
    EndTime = Timer
'   Display total time in seconds
    MsgBox Format(EndTime - StartTime, "0.0")
End Sub
```

On my system, this routine took 7.4 seconds to run (the time will vary, depending on your system's processor speed). I then *commented out* the Dim statements, which declare the data types. That is, I turned the Dim statements into comments by adding an apostrophe at the beginning of the lines. As a result, VBA used the default data type, variant. I ran the procedure again. It took 15.1 seconds, more than twice as long as before.

The moral is simple: If you want your VBA applications to run as fast as possible, declare your variables!

Declaring variables

If you don't declare the data type for a variable that you use in a VBA routine, VBA uses the default data type, variant. Data stored as a variant acts like a chameleon: It changes type, depending on what you do with it. The following procedure demonstrates how a variable can assume different data types.

```
Sub VariantDemo()
    MyVar = "123"
    MyVar = MyVar / 2
    MyVar = "Answer: " & MyVar
    MsgBox MyVar
End Sub
```

In the `VariantDemo` procedure, `MyVar` starts out as a three-character string. Then this "string" is divided by two and becomes a numeric data type. Next, `MyVar` is appended to a string, converting `MyVar` back to a string. The `MsgBox` statement displays the final string: *Answer: 61.5.*

Determining a data type

You can use VBA's `TypeName` function to determine the data type of a variable. Here's a modified version of the previous procedure. This version displays the data type of `MyVar` at each step. You'll see that it starts out as a string, then is converted to a double, and finally ends up as a string again.

```
Sub VariantDemo2()
    MyVar = "123"
    MsgBox TypeName(MyVar)
    MyVar = MyVar / 2
    MsgBox TypeName(MyVar)
    MyVar = "Answer: " & MyVar
    MsgBox TypeName(MyVar)
    MsgBox MyVar
End Sub
```

Thanks to VBA, the data type conversion of undeclared variables is automatic. This process may seem like an easy way out, but remember that you sacrifice speed and memory.

Before you use a variable in a procedure, you may want to *declare* it — that is, tell VBA its name and data type. Declaring variables provides two main benefits:

✦ **Your programs run faster and use memory more efficiently.** The default data type, variant, causes VBA to repeatedly perform time-consuming checks and reserve more memory than necessary. If VBA knows the data type, it doesn't have to investigate, and it can reserve just enough memory to store the data.

✦ **You avoid problems involving misspelled variable names.** Say that you use an undeclared variable named `CurrentRate`. At some point in your routine, however, you insert the statement `CurentRate = .075`. This misspelled variable name, which is very difficult to spot, will likely cause your routine to give incorrect results.

Forcing yourself to declare all variables

To force yourself to declare all the variables that you use, include the following as the first instruction in your VBA module:

```
Option Explicit
```

This statement causes your program to stop whenever VBA encounters a variable name that has not been declared. VBA issues an error message, and you must declare the variable before you can proceed.

Tip   To ensure that the `Option Explicit` statement is automatically inserted whenever you insert a new VBA module, enable the Require Variable Declaration option in the Editor tab of the VBE's Options dialog box. I highly recommend doing so.

Scoping variables

A variable's *scope* determines which modules and procedures the variable can be used in. A variable's scope can be any of the following:

Scope	How a Variable with This Scope Is Declared
Single procedure	Include a `Dim`, `Static`, or `Private` statement within the procedure.
Modulewide	Include a `Dim` statement before the first procedure in a module.
All modules	Include a Public statement before the first procedure in a module.

I discuss each scope further in the following sections.

A Note About the Examples in This Chapter

This chapter contains many examples of VBA code, usually presented in the form of simple procedures. These examples demonstrate various concepts as simply as possible. Most of these examples do not perform any particularly useful task; in fact, the task can often be performed in a different way. In other words, don't use these examples in your own work. Subsequent chapters provide many more code examples that *are* useful.

Local variables

A *local variable* is a variable declared within a procedure. Local variables can be used only in the procedure in which they are declared. When the procedure ends, the variable no longer exists, and Excel frees up its memory.

Note   If you need the variable to retain its value, declare it as a `Static` variable (see "Static Variables" later in this section).

The most common way to declare a local variable is to place a `Dim` statement between a `Sub` statement and an `End Sub` statement (in fact, `Dim` statements usually are placed right after the `Sub` statement, before the procedure's code).

If you're curious about this word, `Dim` is a shortened form of *Dimension*. In old versions of BASIC, this statement was used exclusively to declare the dimensions for an array. In VBA, the `Dim` keyword is used to declare any variable, not just arrays.

The following procedure uses six local variables declared using `Dim` statements:

```
Sub MySub()
    Dim x As Integer
    Dim First As Long
    Dim InterestRate As Single
    Dim TodaysDate As Date
    Dim UserName As String * 20
    Dim MyValue
'    - [The procedure's code goes here] -
End Sub
```

Notice that the last `Dim` statement in the preceding example doesn't declare a data type; it simply names the variable. As a result, that variable becomes a variant.

By the way, you also can declare several variables with a single `Dim` statement. For example,

```
Dim x As Integer, y As Integer, z As Integer
Dim First As Long, Last As Double
```

Caution   Unlike some languages, VBA does not let you declare a group of variables to be a particular data type by separating the variables with commas. For example, the following statement, although valid, does *not* declare all the variables as integers:

```
Dim i, j, k As Integer
```

In VBA, only `k` is declared to be an integer; the other variables are declared variants. To declare `i`, `j`, and `k` as integers, use this statement:

```
Dim i As Integer, j As Integer, k As Integer
```

Another Way of Data-Typing Variables

Like most other dialects of BASIC, VBA lets you append a character to a variable's name to indicate the data type. For example, you can declare the MyVar variable as an integer by tacking % onto the name:

```
Dim MyVar%
```

Type-declaration characters exist for most of VBA's data types (data types not listed don't have type-declaration characters).

Data Type	Type-Declaration Character
Integer	%
Long	&
Single	!
Double	#
Currency	@
String	$

This method of data typing is essentially a holdover from BASIC; it's better to declare your variables using the procedures described in this chapter.

If a variable is declared with a local scope, other procedures in the same module can use the same variable name, but each instance of the variable is unique to its own procedure.

In general, local variables are the most efficient because VBA frees up the memory they use when the procedure ends.

Modulewide variables

Sometimes, you'll want a variable to be available to all procedures in a module. If so, just declare the variable *before* the module's first procedure — outside of any procedures or functions.

In the following example, the Dim statement is the first instruction in the module. Both MySub and YourSub have access to the CurrentValue variable.

```
Dim CurrentValue as Integer

Sub MySub()
```

```
'    - [Code goes here] -
End Sub

Sub YourSub()
'    - [Code goes here] -
End Sub
```

The value of a modulewide variable does not change when a procedure ends.

Public variables

To make a variable available to all the procedures in all the VBA modules in a project, declare the variable at the module level by using the `Public` keyword rather than `Dim`. Here's an example:

```
Public CurrentRate as Long
```

The `Public` keyword makes the `CurrentRate` variable available to any procedure in the project (that is, a single workbook), even those in other modules. You must insert this statement before the first procedure in a module. This type of declaration must also appear in a standard VBA module — not in a code module for a sheet or a UserForm.

Static variables

Static variables are a special case. They are declared at the procedure level, and they retain their value when the procedure ends.

You declare static variables using the `Static` keyword:

```
Sub MySub()
    Static Counter as Integer
    - [Code goes here] -
End Sub
```

Variable Naming Conventions

Some programmers name variables so that their data types can be identified just by looking at their names. Personally, I usually don't use this technique because I think it makes the code more difficult to read. But you might find it helpful.

The naming convention involves using a standard lowercase prefix for the variable's name. For example, if you have a Boolean variable that tracks whether a workbook has been saved, you might name the variable `bWasSaved`. That way, it is clear that the variable is a Boolean variable. The following table lists some standard prefixes for data types:

Continued

(continued)

Data Type	Prefix
Boolean	b
Integer	i
Long	l
Single	s
Double	d
Currency	c
Date/Time	dt
String	str
Object	obj
Variant	v
User-defined	u

Working with constants

A variable's value may, and often does, change while a procedure is executing (that's why it's called a variable). Sometimes, you need to refer to a named value or string that never changes: a *constant*.

Declaring constants

You declare constants using the `Const` statement. Here are some examples:

```
Const NumQuarters as Integer = 4
Const Rate = .0725, Period = 12
Const ModName as String = "Budget Macros"
Public Const AppName as String = "Budget Application"
```

The second example doesn't declare a data type. Consequently, the two constants are variants. Because a constant never changes its value, you'll normally want to declare your constants as a specific data type.

Like variables, constants also have a scope. If you want a constant to be available within a single procedure only, declare it after the `Sub` or `Function` statement to make it a local constant. To make a constant available to all procedures in a module, declare it before the first procedure in the module. To make a constant available to all modules in the workbook, use the `Public` keyword, and declare the constant before the first procedure in a module.

Note If you attempt to change the value of a constant in a VBA procedure, you get an error — which is what you would expect. A constant is a constant, not a variable.

Using constants throughout your code in place of hard-coded values or strings is an excellent programming practice. For example, if your procedure needs to refer to a specific value, such as an interest rate, several times, it's better to declare the value as a constant and use the constant's name rather than its value in your expressions. This technique not only makes your code more readable, it also makes it easier to change should the need arise — you have to change only one instruction rather than several.

Using predefined constants

Excel and VBA contain many predefined constants, which you can use without declaring; in fact, you don't even need to know the value of these constants to use them. The macro recorder generally uses constants rather than actual values. The following procedure uses a built-in constant (xlManual) to change the Calculation property of the Application object (that is, to change Excel's recalculation mode to manual):

```
Sub CalcManual()
    Application.Calculation = xlManual
End Sub
```

I discovered the xlManual constant by recording a macro that changed the calculation mode. I also could have looked in the online help under Calculation Property; all the relevant constants for this property are listed there. And if you have the AutoList Members option turned on, VBA lists all the constants that can be assigned to a property. Usually, the names of the constants are self-explanatory.

The actual value of xlManual is –4135. The constant that changes Excel's mode to automatic calculation is xlAutomatic, and its value is –4105. Obviously, it's easier to use the constant's name than to look up the value.

Note The Object Browser, which I discussed in Chapter 40, contains a list of all Excel and VBA constants. In the VBE, press F2 to bring up the Object Browser.

Working with strings

Like Excel, VBA can manipulate both numbers and text (strings). Two types of strings exist in VBA:

✦ **Fixed-length strings** are declared with a specified number of characters. The maximum length is 65,535 characters.

✦ **Variable-length strings** theoretically can hold up to 2 billion characters.

Each character in a string takes 1 byte of storage, and a small additional amount of storage is used for the header of each string. When you declare a string variable with a Dim statement, you can specify the maximum length if you know it (that is, a fixed-length string), or you can let VBA handle it dynamically (a variable-length string). Working with fixed-length strings is slightly more efficient in terms of memory usage.

In the following example, the MyString variable is declared to be a string with a maximum length of 50 characters. YourString is also declared as a string, but its length is unfixed.

```
Dim MyString As String * 50
Dim YourString As String
```

Working with dates

You can use a string variable to store dates, of course, but you can't perform date calculations on one. Using the date data type is a better way to work with dates.

A variable defined as a date uses 8 bytes of storage and can hold dates ranging from January 1, A.D. 100, to December 31, 9999. That's a span of nearly 10,000 years — more than enough for even the most aggressive financial forecast! The date data type is also useful for storing time-related data. In VBA, you specify dates and times by enclosing them between two pound signs (#), as shown next.

Note The range of dates that VBA can handle is much larger than Excel's own date range — which begins with January 1, 1900. Therefore, be careful that you don't attempt to use a date in a worksheet that is outside of Excel's acceptable date range.

Here are some examples of declaring variables and constants as date data types:

```
Dim Today As Date
Dim StartTime As Date
Const FirstDay As Date = #1/1/2001#
Const Noon = #12:00:00#
```

Note Date variables display dates according to your system's short date format, and times appear according to your system's time format (either 12- or 24-hour). You can modify these system settings by using the Regional Settings option in the Windows Control Panel.

Assignment Expressions

An *assignment expression* is a VBA instruction that makes a mathematical evaluation and assigns the result to a variable or an object. Excel's online help defines *expression* as "a combination of keywords, operators, variables, and constants that yields a string, number, or object. An expression can perform a calculation, manipulate characters, or test data." I couldn't have said it better myself. Much of the work done in VBA involves developing (and debugging) expressions.

If you know how to create formulas in Excel, you'll have no trouble creating expressions in VBA. With a worksheet formula, Excel displays the result in a cell. A VBA expression, on the other hand, can be assigned to a variable or used as a property value.

VBA uses the equal sign (=) as its assignment operator. The following are examples of assignment statements (the expressions are to the right of the equal sign):

```
x = 1
x = x + 1
x = (y * 2) / (z  * 2)
FileOpen = True
FileOpen = Not FileOpen
Range("TheYear").Value = 1995
```

> **Tip**
>
> Expressions can be very complex. You may want to use the continuation sequence (space followed by an underscore) to make lengthy expressions easier to read.

Often, expressions use functions — VBA's built-in functions, Excel's worksheet functions, or custom functions that you develop in VBA. I discuss intrinsic functions later in this chapter.

Operators play a major role in VBA. Familiar operators describe mathematical operations, including addition (+), multiplication (*), division (/), subtraction (-), exponentiation (^), and string concatenation (&). Less-familiar operators are the backslash (\), used in integer division, and the Mod operator, used in modulo arithmetic. The Mod operator returns the remainder of one number divided by another. For example, the following expression returns 2:

```
17 Mod 3
```

VBA also supports the same comparative operators used in Excel formulas: equal to (=), greater than (>), less than (<), greater than or equal to (>=), less than or equal to (<=), and not equal to (<>).

In addition, VBA provides a full set of logical operators, shown in Table 41-2.

	Table 41-2	
	VBA's Logical Operators	
Operator	**What It Does**	
Not	Performs a logical negation on an expression	
And	Performs a logical conjunction on two expressions	
Or	Performs a logical disjunction on two expressions	
XoR	Performs a logical exclusion on two expressions	
Eqv	Performs a logical equivalence on two expressions	
Imp	Performs a logical implication on two expressions	

The order of precedence for operators in VBA is exactly the same as in Excel. Of course, you can add parentheses to change the natural order of precedence.

The following instruction uses the Not operator to toggle the grid-line display in the active window. The DisplayGridlines property takes a value of either True or False. Therefore, using the Not operator changes False to True and True to False.

```
ActiveWindow.DisplayGridlines = _
    Not ActiveWindow.DisplayGridlines
```

The following expression performs a logical And. The MsgBox statement displays True only when Sheet1 is the active sheet *and* the active cell is in row 1.

```
MsgBox ActiveSheet.Name = "Sheet1" And ActiveCell.Row = 1
```

The following expression performs a logical Or. The MsgBox statement displays True when either Sheet1 *or* Sheet2 is the active sheet.

```
MsgBox ActiveSheet.Name = _
    "Sheet1" Or ActiveSheet.Name = "Sheet1"
```

Arrays

An *array* is a group of elements of the same type that have a common name; you refer to a specific element in the array using the array name and an index number. For example, you may define an array of 12 string variables so that each variable corresponds to the name of a different month. If you name the array MonthNames, you can refer to the first element of the array as MonthNames(0), the second element as MonthNames(1), and so on, up to MonthNames(11).

Declaring arrays

You declare an array with a `Dim` or `Public` statement, just as you declare a regular variable. You can also specify the number of elements in the array. You do so by specifying the first index number, the keyword `To`, and the last index number — all inside parentheses. For example, here's how to declare an array comprising exactly 100 integers:

```
Dim MyArray(1 To 100) As Integer
```

 Tip

When you declare an array, you need specify only the upper index, in which case VBA assumes that 0 is the lower index. Therefore, the two statements that follow have the same effect:

```
Dim MyArray(0 to 100) As Integer
Dim MyArray(100) As Integer
```

In both these cases, the array consists of 101 elements.

If you would like VBA to assume that 1 is the lower index for all arrays that declare only the upper index, include the following statement before any procedures in your module:

```
Option Base 1
```

Declaring multidimensional arrays

The arrays examples in the preceding section were one-dimensional arrays. VBA arrays can have up to 60 dimensions, although it's rare to need more than 3 dimensions (a 3D array). The following statement declares a 100-integer array with two dimensions (2D):

```
Dim MyArray(1 To 10, 1 To 10) As Integer
```

You can think of the preceding array as occupying a 10×10 matrix. To refer to a specific element in a 2D array, you need to specify two index numbers. For example, here's how you can assign a value to an element in the preceding array:

```
MyArray(3, 4) = 125
```

You can think of a 3D array as a cube, but I can't tell you how to visualize the data layout of an array of more than three dimensions.

A *dynamic array* doesn't have a preset number of elements. You declare a dynamic array with a blank set of parentheses:

```
Dim MyArray() As Integer
```

Before you can use a dynamic array in your code, however, you must use the ReDim statement to tell VBA how many elements are in the array (or ReDim Preserve if you want to keep the existing values in the array). You can use the ReDim statement any number of times, changing the array's size as often as you need to.

Arrays crop up later in this chapter when I discuss looping.

Object Variables

An *object variable* is a variable that represents an entire object, such as a range or a worksheet. Object variables are important for two reasons:

✦ They can simplify your code significantly.

✦ They can make your code execute more quickly.

Object variables, like normal variables, are declared with the Dim or Public statement. For example, the following statement declares InputArea as a Range object.

```
Public InputArea As Range
```

To see how object variables simplify your code, examine the following procedure, which was written without using object variables:

```
Sub NoObjVar()
    Worksheets("Sheet1").Range("A1").Value = 124
    Worksheets("Sheet1").Range("A1").Font.Bold = True
    Worksheets("Sheet1").Range("A1").Font.Italic = True
End Sub
```

This routine enters a value into cell A1 of Sheet1 on the active workbook and then boldfaces and italicizes the cell's contents. That's a lot of typing. To reduce wear and tear on your fingers, you can condense the routine with an object variable:

```
Sub ObjVar()
    Dim MyCell As Range
    Set MyCell = Worksheets("Sheet1").Range("A1")
    MyCell.Value = 124
    MyCell.Font.Bold = True
    MyCell.Font.Italic = True
End Sub
```

After the variable MyCell is declared as a Range object, the Set statement assigns an object to it. Subsequent statements can then use the simpler MyCell reference in place of the lengthy Worksheets("Sheet1").Range("A1") reference.

Tip

After an object is assigned to a variable, VBA can access it more quickly than it can a normal lengthy reference that has to be resolved. So when speed is critical, use object variables. One way to think about this is in terms of "dot processing." Every time VBA encounters a dot, as in `Sheets(1).Range("A1")`, it takes time to resolve the reference. Using an object variable reduces the number of dots to be processed. The fewer the dots, the faster the processing time. Another way to improve the speed of your code is by using the `With-End With` construct, which also reduces the number of dots to be processed. I discuss this construct later in this chapter.

The true value of object variables will become apparent when I discuss looping later in this chapter.

User-Defined Data Types

VBA lets you create custom, or *user-defined*, data types (a concept much like Pascal records or C structures). A user-defined data type can ease your work with some types of data. For example, if your application deals with customer information, you may want to create a user-defined data type named `CustomerInfo`, as follows:

```
Type CustomerInfo
    Company As String * 25
    Contact As String * 15
    RegionCode As Integer
    Sales As Long
End Type
```

Note

You define custom data types outside of procedures at the top of your module.

After you create a user-defined data type, you use a `Dim` statement to declare a variable as that type. Usually, you define an array. For example,

```
Dim Customers(1 To 100) As CustomerInfo
```

Each of the 100 elements in this array consists of four components (as specified by the user-defined data type, `CustomerInfo`). You can refer to a particular component of the record as follows:

```
Customers(1).Company = "Acme Tools"
Customers(1).Contact = "Tim Robertson"
Customers(1).RegionCode = 3
Customers(1).Sales = 150677
```

You can also work with an element in the array as a whole. For example, to copy the information from `Customers(1)` to `Customers(2)`, use this instruction:

```
Customers(2) = Customers(1)
```

The preceding example is equivalent to the following instruction block:

```
Customers(2).Company = Customers(1).Company
Customers(2).Contact = Customers(1).Contact
Customers(2).RegionCode = Customers(1).RegionCode
Customers(2).Sales = Customers(1).Sales
```

Built-in Functions

Like most programming languages, VBA has a variety of built-in functions that simplify calculations and operations. Often, the functions enable you to perform operations that are otherwise difficult, or even impossible. Many of VBA's functions are similar (or identical) to Excel's worksheet functions. For example, the VBA function `UCase`, which converts a string argument to uppercase, is equivalent to the Excel worksheet function `UPPER`.

Appendix F contains a complete list of VBA's functions, with a brief description of each. All are thoroughly described in the online help system.

To get a list of VBA functions while you're writing your code, type **VBA** followed by a period (.). The VBE displays a list of all functions (see Figure 41-1). If this doesn't work for you, make sure that the Auto List Members option is selected. Choose Tools ⇨ Options, and click the Editor tab.

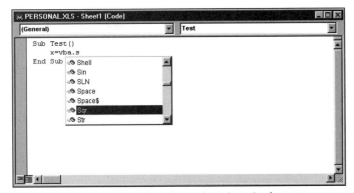

Figure 41-1: Displaying a list of VBA functions in the VBE

You use functions in VBA expressions in much the same way that you use functions in worksheet formulas. For instance, you can nest VBA functions.

Here's a simple procedure that calculates the square root of a variable using VBA's Sqr function, stores the result in another variable, and then displays the result:

```
Sub ShowRoot()
    MyValue = 25
    SquareRoot = Sqr(MyValue)
    MsgBox SquareRoot
End Sub
```

You can use many (but not all) of Excel's worksheet functions in your VBA code. The WorksheetFunction object, which is contained in the Application object, holds all the worksheet functions that you can call from your VBA procedures.

To use a worksheet function in a VBA statement, just precede the function name with

```
Application.WorksheetFunction
```

The following example demonstrates how to use an Excel worksheet function in a VBA procedure. Excel's infrequently used ROMAN function converts a decimal number into a Roman numeral.

```
Sub ShowRoman()
    DecValue = 1999
    RomanValue = Application.WorksheetFunction.Roman(DecValue)
    MsgBox RomanValue
End Sub
```

When you execute this procedure, the MsgBox function displays the string MCMXCIX. Fans of old movies are often dismayed when they learn that Excel doesn't have a function to convert a Roman numeral to its decimal equivalent.

It's important to understand that you cannot use worksheet functions that have an equivalent VBA function. For example, VBA cannot access Excel's SQRT worksheet function because VBA has its own version of that function: Sqr. Therefore, the following statement generates an error:

```
MsgBox Application.WorksheetFunction.Sqrt(123)    'error
```

You can use VBA to create custom worksheet functions that work just like Excel's built-in worksheet functions.

The MsgBox Function

The `MsgBox` function is one of the most useful VBA functions. Many of the examples in this chapter use this function to display the value of a variable.

This function often is a good substitute for a simple custom dialog box. It's also an excellent debugging tool because you can insert `MsgBox` functions at any time to pause your code and display the result of a calculation or assignment.

Most functions return a single value, which you assign to a variable. The `MsgBox` function not only returns a value, but also displays a dialog box that the user can respond to. The value returned by the `MsgBox` function represents the user's response to the dialog. You can use the `MsgBox` function even when you have no interest in the user's response but want to take advantage of the message display.

The official syntax of the `MsgBox` function has five arguments (those in square brackets are optional):

```
MsgBox(prompt[, buttons][, title][, helpfile, context])
```

    prompt   (Required) The message displayed in the pop-up display.

    buttons   (Optional) A value that specifies which buttons and which icon, if any, appear in the message box. Use built-in constants—for example, `vbYesNo`.

    title   (Optional) The text that appears in the message box's title bar. The default is `Microsoft Excel`.

    helpfile   (Optional) The name of the help file associated with the message box.

    context   (Optional) The context ID of the help topic. This represents a specific help topic to display.

You can assign the value returned to a variable, or you can use the function by itself without an assignment statement. The next example assigns the result to the variable `Ans`.

```
Ans = MsgBox("Continue?", vbYesNo + vbQuestion, "Tell me")
If Ans = vbNo Then Exit Sub
```

Notice that I used the sum of two built-in constants (`vbYesNo + vbQuestion`) for the buttons argument. Using `vbYesNo` displays two buttons in the message box: one labeled Yes and one labeled No. Adding `vbQuestion` to the argument also displays a question mark icon (see the accompanying figure). When the first statement is executed, `Ans` contains one of two values, represented by the constants `vbYes` or `vbNo`. In this example, if the user clicks the No button, the procedure ends.

For more information, refer to the online help, which lists all the constants you can use.

Manipulating Objects and Collections

As an Excel programmer, you'll spend a lot of time working with objects and collections. Therefore, you'll want to know the most efficient ways to write your code to manipulate these objects and collections. VBA offers two important constructs that can simplify working with objects and collections:

✦ With-End With constructs

✦ For Each-Next constructs

With-End With constructs

The With-End With instruction construct enables you to perform multiple operations on a single object. To start understanding how the With-End With construct works, examine the following procedure, which modifies five properties of a selection's formatting (the selection is assumed to be a Range object):

```
Sub ChangeFont1()
    Selection.Font.Name = "Times New Roman"
    Selection.Font.FontStyle = "Bold Italic"
    Selection.Font.Size = 12
    Selection.Font.Underline = xlSingle
    Selection.Font.ColorIndex = 5
End Sub
```

This procedure can be rewritten using the With-End With construct. The following procedure performs exactly like the preceding one:

```
Sub ChangeFont2()
    With Selection.Font
        .Name = "Times New Roman"
        .FontStyle = "Bold Italic"
        .Size = 12
        .Underline = xlSingle
        .ColorIndex = 5
    End With
End Sub
```

Some people think that the second incarnation of the procedure is actually more difficult to read. Remember, though, that the objective is increased speed. Although the first version may be more straightforward and easier to understand, a procedure that uses the With-End With construct when changing several properties of an object can be significantly faster than the equivalent procedure that explicitly references the object in each statement.

Note

When you record a VBA macro, Excel uses the With-End With construct every chance it gets. To see a good example of this construct, try recording your actions while you change the page setup by choosing the File ➪ Page Setup command.

For Each-Next constructs

Recall from the preceding chapter that a *collection* is a group of related objects. For example, the Workbooks collection is a collection of all open Workbook objects. You can work with many other collections, and you don't have to know how many elements are in a collection to use the For Each-Next construct.

Suppose that you want to perform some action on all objects in a collection. Or suppose that you want to evaluate all objects in a collection and take action under certain conditions. These are perfect occasions for the For Each-Next construct.

The syntax of the For Each-Next construct is

```
For Each element In group
    [instructions]
    [Exit For]
    [instructions]
Next [element]
```

The following procedure uses the For Each-Next construct to refer to each of the six single-precision members of a fixed-length array one at a time.

```
Sub Macro1()
    Dim MyArray(5)
    For i = 0 To 5
        MyArray(i) = Rnd
    Next i
    For Each n In MyArray
        Debug.Print n
    Next n
End Sub
```

The next procedure uses the For Each-Next construct with the Sheets collection in the active workbook. When you execute the procedure, the MsgBox function displays each sheet's Name property. (If five sheets exist in the active workbook, the MsgBox function is called five times.)

```
Sub CountSheets()
    Dim Item as WorkSheet
    For Each Item In ActiveWorkbook.Sheets
        MsgBox Item.Name
    Next Item
End Sub
```

Note　In the preceding example, Item is an object variable (more specifically, a Worksheet object). There's nothing special about the name *Item;* you can use any valid variable name in its place.

The next example uses For Each-Next to cycle through all objects in the Windows collection.

```
Sub HiddenWindows()
    AllVisible = True
    For Each Item In Windows
        If Item.Visible = False Then
            AllVisible = False
            Exit For
        End If
    Next Item
    MsgBox AllVisible
End Sub
```

If a window is hidden, the value of AllVisible is changed to False, and the For Each-Next loop is exited. The message box displays True if all windows are visible and False if at least one window is hidden. The Exit For statement is optional. It provides a way to exit the For Each-Next loop early. This is generally used in conjunction with an If-Then statement (described later in this chapter).

Here's an example that closes all workbooks except the active workbook. This procedure uses the If-Then construct to evaluate each workbook in the Workbooks collection.

```
Sub CloseInActive()
    For Each Book In Workbooks
        If Book.Name <> ActiveWorkbook.Name Then Book.Close
    Next Book
End Sub
```

My final example of For Each-Next is designed to be executed after the user selects a range of cells. Here, the Selection object acts as a collection that consists of Range objects because each cell in the selection is a Range object. The procedure evaluates each cell and uses VBA's UCase function to convert its contents to uppercase (numeric cells are not affected).

```
Sub MakeUpperCase()
    For Each Cell In Selection
        Cell.Value = UCase(Cell.Value)
    Next Cell
End Sub
```

Controlling Execution

Some VBA procedures start at the top and progress line by line to the bottom. Macros that you record, for example, always work in this fashion. Often, however, you need to control the flow of your routines by skipping over some statements, executing some statements multiple times, and testing conditions to determine what the routine does next.

The preceding section described the For Each-Next construct, which is a type of loop. This section discusses the additional ways of controlling the execution of your VBA procedures:

✦ GoTo statements

✦ If-Then constructs

✦ Select Case constructs

✦ For-Next loops

✦ Do While loops

✦ Do Until loops

GoTo statements

The most straightforward way to change the flow of a program is to use a GoTo statement. This statement simply transfers program execution to a new instruction, which must be preceded by a label (a text string followed by a colon). VBA procedures can contain any number of labels, and a GoTo statement cannot branch outside of a procedure.

The following procedure uses VBA's InputBox function to get the user's name. If the name is not Howard, the procedure branches to the WrongName label and ends. Otherwise, the procedure executes some additional code. The Exit Sub statement causes the procedure to end.

```
Sub GoToDemo()
    UserName = InputBox("Enter Your Name:")
    If UserName <> "Howard" Then GoTo WrongName
    MsgBox ("Welcome Howard...")
'   -[More code here] -
    Exit Sub
WrongName:
    MsgBox "Sorry. Only Howard can run this."
End Sub
```

This simple procedure works, but in general you should use the GoTo statement only when you have no other way to perform an action. In fact, the only time you *really* need to use a GoTo statement in VBA is for error trapping (refer to Chapter 42).

If-Then constructs

Perhaps the most commonly used instruction grouping in VBA is the If-Then construct. This common instruction is one way to endow your applications with decision-making capability. Good decision making is the key to writing successful programs. A successful Excel application essentially boils down to making decisions and acting on them.

The basic syntax of the If-Then construct is

```
If condition Then true_instructions [Else false_instructions]
```

The If-Then construct is used to execute one or more statements conditionally. The Else clause is optional. If included, it lets you execute one or more instructions when the condition you're testing is not true.

The following procedure demonstrates an If-Then structure without an Else clause. The example deals with time. VBA uses the same date-and-time serial number system as Excel. The time of day is expressed as a fractional value—for example, noon is represented as .5. VBA's Time function returns a value that represents the time of day, as reported by the system clock. In the following example, a message is displayed if the time is before noon. If the current system time is greater than or equal to .5, the procedure ends and nothing happens.

```
Sub GreetMe()
    If Time < 0.5 Then MsgBox "Good Morning"
End Sub
```

If you want to display a different greeting when the time of day is after noon, add another If-Then statement, like so:

```
Sub GreetMe()
    If Time < 0.5 Then MsgBox "Good Morning"
    If Time >= 0.5 Then MsgBox "Good Afternoon"
End Sub
```

Notice that I used >= (greater than or equal to) for the second If-Then statement. This covers the extremely remote chance that the time is precisely 12:00 noon.

Another approach is to use the Else clause of the If-Then construct. For example,

```
Sub GreetMe()
    If Time < 0.5 Then MsgBox "Good Morning" Else _
        MsgBox "Good Afternoon"
End Sub
```

Notice that I used the line continuation sequence; `If-Then-Else` is actually a single statement.

If you need to expand a routine to handle three conditions (for example, morning, afternoon, and evening), you can use either three `If-Then` statements or a nested `If-Then-Else` structure. The first approach is the simpler:

```
Sub GreetMe()
    If Time < 0.5 Then MsgBox "Good Morning"
    If Time >= 0.5 And Time < 0.75 Then MsgBox "Good Afternoon"
    If Time >= 0.75 Then MsgBox "Good Evening"
End Sub
```

The value 0.75 represents 6:00 p.m. — three-quarters of the way through the day and a good point at which to call it evening.

The following procedure performs the same action as the previous one but uses the `If-Then-Else` structure:

```
Sub GreetMe()
    If Time < 0.5 Then MsgBox "Good Morning" Else
        If Time >= 0.5 And Time < 0.75 Then MsgBox _
        "Good Afternoon" Else
            If Time >= 0.75 Then MsgBox "Good Evening"
End Sub
```

In both examples, every instruction in the procedure gets executed, even in the morning. A more efficient procedure would include a structure that ends the routine when a condition is found to be true. For example, it might display the Good Morning message in the morning and then exit without evaluating the other, superfluous conditions. True, the difference in speed is inconsequential when you design a procedure as small as this routine. But for more complex applications, you need another syntax:

```
If condition Then
    [true_instructions]
[ElseIf condition-n Then
    [alternate_instructions]]
[Else
    [default_instructions]]
End If
```

Here's how you can use this syntax to rewrite the GreetMe procedure:

```
Sub GreetMe()
    If Time < 0.5 Then
        MsgBox "Good Morning"
    ElseIf Time >= 0.5 And Time < 0.75 Then
        MsgBox "Good Afternoon"
```

```
        ElseIf Time >= 0.75 Then
            MsgBox "Good Evening"
        End If
    End Sub
```

With this syntax, when a condition is true, the conditional statements are executed and the If-Then construct ends. In other words, the extraneous conditions are not evaluated. Although this syntax makes for greater efficiency, some may find the code to be more difficult to understand. There's always a trade-off.

The following is another example that uses the simple form of the If-Then construct. This procedure prompts the user for a value for Quantity and then displays the appropriate discount based on that value. If the InputBox is cancelled, Quantity contains an empty string, and the procedure ends.

```
    Sub Discount1()
        Quantity = InputBox("Enter Quantity: ")
        If Quantity = "" Then Exit Sub
        If Quantity >= 0 Then Discount = 0.1
        If Quantity >= 25 Then Discount = 0.15
        If Quantity >= 50 Then Discount = 0.2
        If Quantity >= 75 Then Discount = 0.25
        MsgBox "Discount: " & Discount
    End Sub
```

Notice that each If-Then statement in this procedure is always executed, and the value for Discount can change. The final value, however, is the desired value.

The following procedure is the previous one rewritten to use the alternate syntax. In this case, the procedure ends after executing the True instruction block.

```
    Sub Discount2()
        Quantity = InputBox("Enter Quantity: ")
        If Quantity = "" Then Exit Sub
        If Quantity >= 0 And Quantity < 25 Then
            Discount = 0.1
        ElseIf Quantity >= 25 And Quantity < 50 Then
            Discount = 0.15
        ElseIf Quantity >= 50 And Quantity < 75 Then
            Discount = 0.2
        ElseIf Quantity >= 75 Then
            Discount = 0.25
        End If
        MsgBox "Discount: " & Discount
    End Sub
```

I find nested If-Then structures rather cumbersome. As a result, I usually use the If-Then structure only for simple binary decisions. When you need to choose among three or more alternatives, the Select Case structure is often a better construct to use.

VBA's IIf Function

VBA offers an alternative to the `If-Then` construct: the `IIf` function. This function takes three arguments and works much like Excel's `IF` worksheet function. The syntax is

```
IIf(expr, truepart, falsepart)
```

expr	(Required) Expression to evaluate
truepart	(Required) Value or expression returned if *expr* is True
falsepart	(Required) Value or expression returned if *expr* is False

The following instruction demonstrates the use of the `IIf` function. The message box displays *Zero* if cell A1 contains a zero or is empty. It displays *Nonzero* if cell A1 contains anything else.

```
MsgBox IIf(Range("A1") = 0, "Zero", "Nonzero")
```

Select Case constructs

The `Select Case` construct is useful for choosing among three or more options. This construct also works with two options and is a good alternative to `If-Then-Else`. The syntax for `Select Case` is as follows:

```
Select Case testexpression
    [Case expressionlist-n
        [instructions-n]]
    [Case Else
        [default_instructions]]
End Select
```

The following example of a `Select Case` construct shows another way to code the `GreetMe` examples presented in the preceding section:

```
Sub GreetMe()
    Select Case Time
        Case Is < 0.5
            Msg = "Good Morning"
        Case 0.5 To 0.75
            Msg = "Good Afternoon"
        Case Else
            Msg = "Good Evening"
    End Select
    MsgBox Msg
End Sub
```

And here's a rewritten version of the `Discount` example, using a `Select Case` construct:

```
Sub Discount3()
    Quantity = InputBox("Enter Quantity: ")
    Select Case Quantity
        Case ""
            Exit Sub
        Case 0 To 24
            Discount = 0.1
        Case 25 To 49
            Discount = 0.15
        Case 50 To 74
            Discount = 0.2
        Case Is >= 75
            Discount = 0.25
    End Select
    MsgBox "Discount: " & Discount
End Sub
```

Any number of instructions can be written below each `Case` statement, and they all are executed if that case evaluates to True. If you use only one instruction per case, as in the preceding example, you may want to put the instruction on the same line as the `Case` keyword (but don't forget VBA's statement-separator character, the colon). This technique makes the code more compact. For example,

```
Sub Discount3()
    Quantity = InputBox("Enter Quantity: ")
    Select Case Quantity
        Case "": Exit Sub
        Case  0 To 24: Discount = 0.1
        Case 25 To 49: Discount = 0.15
        Case 50 To 74: Discount = 0.2
        Case Is >= 75: Discount = 0.25
    End Select
    MsgBox "Discount: " & Discount
End Sub
```

Tip   VBA exits a `Select Case` construct as soon as a True case is found. Therefore, for maximum efficiency, you might want to check the most likely case first.

`Select Case` structures can also be nested. The following procedure, for example, tests for Excel's window state (maximized, minimized, or normal) and then displays a message describing the window state. If Excel's window state is normal, the procedure tests for the window state of the active window and then displays another message.

```
Sub AppWindow()
    Select Case Application.WindowState
```

```
        Case xlMaximized: MsgBox "App Maximized"
        Case xlMinimized: MsgBox "App Minimized"
        Case xlNormal: MsgBox "App Normal"
            Select Case ActiveWindow.WindowState
                Case xlMaximized: MsgBox "Book Maximized"
                Case xlMinimized: MsgBox "Book Minimized"
                Case xlNormal: MsgBox "Book Normal"
            End Select
    End Select
End Sub
```

You can nest `Select Case` constructs as deeply as you need, but make sure that each `Select Case` statement has a corresponding `End Select` statement.

This procedure demonstrates the value of using indentation in your code to clarify the structure. For example, take a look at the same procedure without the indentations:

```
Sub AppWindow()
Select Case Application.WindowState
Case xlMaximized: MsgBox "App Maximized"
Case xlMinimized: MsgBox "App Minimized"
Case xlNormal: MsgBox "App Normal"
Select Case ActiveWindow.WindowState
Case xlMaximized: MsgBox "Book Maximized"
Case xlMinimized: MsgBox "Book Minimized"
Case xlNormal: MsgBox "Book Normal"
End Select
End Select
End Sub
```

Fairly incomprehensible, eh?

Looping blocks of instructions

Looping is the process of repeating a block of instructions. You may know the number of times to loop, or it may be determined by the values of variables in your program.

The following code, which enters consecutive numbers into a range, demonstrates what I call a *bad loop*. The procedure starts by prompting the user for two values: a starting value and the total number of cells to fill in (`InputBox` returns a string, so I used the `Val` function to convert the strings to values). This loop uses the `GoTo` statement to control the flow. If the `CellCount` variable, which keeps track of how many cells are filled, is less than the number requested by the user, program control loops back to `DoAnother`.

```
Sub BadLoop()
    StartVal = Val(InputBox("Enter the starting value: "))
    NumToFill = Val(InputBox("How many cells? "))
    ActiveCell.Value = StartVal
    CellCount = 1
DoAnother:
    ActiveCell.Offset(CellCount, 0).Value = StartVal _
     + CellCount
    CellCount = CellCount + 1
    If CellCount < NumToFill Then GoTo DoAnother Else Exit Sub
End Sub
```

This procedure works as intended, so why is it an example of bad looping? Programmers generally frown on using a GoTo statement when not absolutely necessary. Using GoTo statements to loop is contrary to the concept of structured coding (see the "What is Structured Programming?" sidebar). In fact, a GoTo statement makes the code much more difficult to read because it's almost impossible to represent a loop using line indentations. In addition, this type of unstructured loop makes the procedure more susceptible to error. Furthermore, using lots of labels results in *spaghetti code* — code that appears to have little or no structure and flows haphazardly.

Because VBA has several structured looping commands, you almost never have to rely on GoTo statements for your decision making.

For-Next loops

The simplest type of *good loop* is a For-Next loop, which I've already used in a few previous examples. Its syntax is

```
For counter = start To end [Step stepval]
    [instructions]
    [Exit For]
    [instructions]
Next [counter]
```

What Is Structured Programming?

Hang around with programmers, and sooner or later you'll hear the term *structured programming*. You'll also discover that structured programs are considered superior to unstructured programs.

So what is structured programming? And can you do it with VBA?

Continued

(continued)

The basic premise is that a routine or code segment should have only one entry point and one exit point. In other words, a body of code should be a stand-alone unit, and program control should not jump into or exit from the middle of this unit. As a result, structured programming rules out the GoTo statement. When you write structured code, your program progresses in an orderly manner and is easy to follow — as opposed to spaghetti code, where a program jumps around.

A structured program is easier to read and understand than an unstructured one. More important, it's also easier to modify.

VBA is a structured language. It offers standard structured constructs, such as If-Then-Else and Select Case, and the For-Next, Do Until, and Do While loops. Furthermore, VBA fully supports modular code construction.

If you're new to programming, it's a good idea to form good structured programming habits early.

Following is an example of a For-Next loop that doesn't use the optional Step value or the optional Exit For statement. This routine executes the Sum = Sum + Sqr(Count) statement 100 times and displays the result — that is, the sum of the square roots of the first 100 integers.

```
Sub SumSquareRoots()
    Sum = 0
    For Count = 1 To 100
        Sum = Sum + Sqr(Count)
    Next Count
    MsgBox Sum
End Sub
```

In this example, Count (the loop counter variable) started out as 1 and increased by 1 each time the loop repeated. The Sum variable simply accumulates the square roots of each value of Count.

Caution   When you use For-Next loops, it's important to understand that the loop counter is a normal variable — nothing special. As a result, it's possible to change the value of the loop counter within the block of code executed between the For and Next statements. This is, however, a *ba-a-ad* practice and can cause unpredictable results. In fact, you should take special precautions to ensure that your code does not change the loop counter.

You can also use a Step value to skip some values in the loop. Here's the same procedure rewritten to sum the square roots of the odd numbers between 1 and 100:

```
Sub SumOddSquareRoots()
    Sum = 0
    For Count = 1 To 100 Step 2
        Sum = Sum + Sqr(Count)
    Next Count
    MsgBox Sum
End Sub
```

In this procedure, Count starts out as 1 and then takes on values of 3, 5, 7, and so on. The final value of Count is 99.

The following procedure performs the same task as the BadLoop example found at the beginning of the "Looping Blocks of Instructions" section. I eliminated the GoTo statement, however, converting a bad loop into a good loop that uses the For-Next structure.

```
Sub GoodLoop()
    StartVal = Val(InputBox("Enter the starting value: "))
    NumToFill = Val(InputBox("How many cells? "))
    ActiveCell.Value = StartVal
    For CellCount = 0 To NumToFill - 1
      ActiveCell.Offset(CellCount, 0).Value = StartVal + _
      CellCount
    Next CellCount
End Sub
```

For-Next loops can also include one or more Exit For statements within the loop. When this statement is encountered, the loop terminates immediately, as the following example demonstrates. This procedure determines which cell has the largest value in column A of the active worksheet.

```
Sub ExitForDemo()
    MaxVal = Application.WorksheetFunction.Max(Range("A:A"))
    For Row = 1 To 65536
        Set TheCell = Range("A1").Offset(Row - 1, 0)
        If TheCell.Value = MaxVal Then
            MsgBox "Max value is in Row " & Row
            TheCell.Activate
            Exit For
        End If
    Next Row
End Sub
```

The maximum value in the column is calculated by using Excel's MAX function. This value is then assigned to the MaxVal variable. The For-Next loop checks each cell in the column. If the cell being checked is equal to MaxVal, the Exit For statement ends the procedure. Before terminating the loop, though, the procedure informs the user of the row location and then activates the cell.

The previous examples use relatively simple loops. But you can have any number of statements in the loop, and you can even nest For-Next loops inside other For-Next loops. Here's an example that uses nested For-Next loops to initialize a 10 × 10 × 10 array with the value -1. When the procedure is finished, each of the 1,000 elements in MyArray will contain -1.

```
Sub NestedLoops()
    Dim MyArray(1 to 10, 1 to 10, 1 to 10)
    For i = 1 To 10
        For j = 1 To 10
            For k = 1 To 10
                MyArray(i, j, k) = -1
            Next k
        Next j
    Next i
End Sub
```

Do While loops

A Do While loop is another type of looping structure available in VBA. Unlike a For-Next loop, a Do While loop executes while a specified condition is met. A Do While loop can have either of two syntaxes:

```
Do [While condition]
    [instructions]
    [Exit Do]
    [instructions]
Loop
```

or

```
Do
    [instructions]
    [Exit Do]
    [instructions]
Loop [While condition]
```

As you can see, VBA lets you put the While condition at the beginning or the end of the loop. The difference between these two syntaxes involves the point in time when the condition is evaluated. In the first syntax, the contents of the loop may never be executed. In the second syntax, the contents of the loop are always executed at least one time.

The following example uses a Do While loop with the first syntax.

```
Sub DoWhileDemo()
    Do While Not IsEmpty(ActiveCell)
        ActiveCell.Value = 0
        ActiveCell.Offset(1, 0).Select
    Loop
End Sub
```

This procedure uses the active cell as a starting point and then travels down the column, inserting a zero into the active cell. Each time the loop repeats, the next cell in the column becomes the active cell. The loop continues until VBA's IsEmpty function determines that the active cell is not empty.

The following procedure uses the second Do While loop syntax. The loop will always be executed at least one time, even if the initial active cell is not empty.

```
Sub DoWhileDemo2()
    Do
        ActiveCell.Value = 0
        ActiveCell.Offset(1, 0).Select
    Loop While Not IsEmpty(ActiveCell)
End Sub
```

The following is another Do While loop example. This procedure opens a text file, reads each line, converts the text to upper case, and then stores it in the active sheet, beginning with cell A1 and continuing down the column. The procedure uses VBA's EOF function, which returns True when the end of the file has been reached. The final statement closes the text file.

```
Sub DoWhileDemo1()
    Open "c:\data\textfile.txt" For Input As #1
    LineCt = 0
    Do While Not EOF(1)
        Input #1, LineOfText
        Range("A1").Offset(LineCt, 0) = UCase(LineOfText)
        LineCt = LineCt + 1
    Loop
    Close #1
End Sub
```

Do While loops can also contain one or more Exit Do statements. When an Exit Do statement is encountered, the loop ends immediately.

Do Until loops

The Do Until loop structure is very similar to the Do While structure. The difference is evident only when the condition is tested. In a Do While loop, the loop executes *while* the condition is true. In a Do Until loop, the loop executes *until* the condition is true.

Do Until also has two syntaxes:

```
Do [Until condition]
    [instructions]
    [Exit Do]
    [instructions]
Loop
```

or

```
Do
    [instructions]
    [Exit Do]
    [instructions]
Loop [Until condition]
```

The following example was originally presented for the Do While loop but has been rewritten to use a Do Until loop. The only difference is the line with the Do statement. This example makes the code a bit clearer because it avoids the negative required in the Do While example.

```
Sub DoUntilDemo1()
    Open "c:\data\textfile.txt" For Input As #1
    LineCt = 0
    Do Until EOF(1)
        Input #1, LineOfText
        Range("A1").Offset(LineCt, 0) = UCase(LineOfText)
        LineCt = LineCt + 1
    Loop
    Close #1
End Sub
```

Summary

In this chapter, I discussed the fundamentals of programming in VBA, including variables, constants, data types, arrays, and VBA's built-in functions. I also discussed techniques for manipulating objects and controlling the execution of your procedures.

Chapter 42 focuses on one of the two types of procedures you can write in VBA.

✦ ✦ ✦

Working with VBA Sub Procedures

A *procedure* holds a group of VBA statements that accomplishes a desired task. Most VBA code is contained in procedures. This chapter focuses on *Sub procedures*, which perform tasks but do not return discrete values. VBA also supports Function procedures, which I discuss in Chapter 43.

 Cross-Reference Chapter 43 has many additional examples of procedures that you can incorporate into your work.

About Procedures

A *procedure* is a series of VBA statements that resides in a VBA module, which you access in the VBE. A module can hold any number of procedures.

You have a number of ways to *call*, or execute, procedures. A procedure is executed from beginning to end (but it can also be ended prematurely).

 Tip A procedure can be any length, but it's usually considered good programming practice to avoid creating extremely long procedures that perform many different operations. You may find it easier to write several smaller procedure, each with a single purpose. Then design a main procedure that calls those other procedures. This approach can make your code easier to maintain.

Some procedures are written to receive arguments. An *argument* is simply information that is used by the procedure that is "passed" to the procedure when it is executed. Procedure arguments work much like the arguments you use in Excel worksheet functions. Instructions within the procedure generally perform logical operations on these arguments, and the results of the procedure are usually based on those arguments.

Declaring a Sub procedure

A procedure declared with the Sub keyword must adhere to the following syntax:

```
[Private | Public][Static] Sub name [(arglist)]
    [instructions]
    [Exit Sub]
    [instructions]
End Sub
```

Private	(Optional) Indicates that the procedure is accessible only to other procedures in the same module.
Public	(Optional) Indicates that the procedure is accessible to all other procedures in all other modules in the workbook. If used in a module that contains an Option Private statement, the procedure is not available outside the project.
Static	(Optional) Indicates that the procedure's variables are preserved when the procedure ends.
Sub	(Required) The keyword that indicates the beginning of a procedure.
name	(Required) Any valid procedure name.
arglist	(Optional) Represents a list of variables, enclosed in parentheses, that receive arguments passed to the procedure. Use a comma to separate arguments.
instructions	(Optional) Represents valid VBA instructions.
Exit Sub	(Optional) A statement that forces an immediate exit from the procedure prior to its formal completion.
End Sub	(Required) Indicates the end of the procedure.

Note   With a few exceptions, all VBA instructions in a module must be contained in procedures. Exceptions include module-level variable declarations, user-defined data type definitions, and a few other instructions that specify module-level options (for example, Option Explicit).

Naming Procedures

Every procedure must have a name. The rules governing procedure names are generally the same as for variable names. The exception is that a procedure name cannot be like a cell address. For example, you can't name a procedure J34, because J34 is a cell address.

Ideally, a procedure's name should describe what its contained processes do. A good rule of thumb is to use a name that includes a verb and a noun (for example, `ProcessDate`, `PrintReport`, `Sort_Array`, or `CheckFilename`). Avoid meaningless names such as `DoIt`, `Update`, and `Fix`.

Some programmers use sentence-like names that describe the procedure (for example, `WriteReportToTextFile` and `Get_Print_Options_ and_Print_Report`). Although long names are very descriptive and unambiguous, they are also more difficult to type.

Scoping a procedure

In the preceding chapter, I noted that a variable's scope determines the modules and procedures in which the variable can be used. Similarly, a procedure's scope determines which other procedures can call it.

Public procedures

By default, procedures are *public* — that is, they can be called by other procedures in any module in the workbook. It's not necessary to use the `Public` keyword, but programmers often include it for clarity. The following two procedures are both public:

```
Sub First()
'    ... [code goes here] ...
End Sub

Public Sub Second()
'    ... [code goes here] ...
End Sub
```

Private procedures

Private procedures can be called by other procedures in the same module, but not by procedures in other modules.

Note

When you choose Excel's Tools ➪ Macro ➪ Macros command, the Macro dialog box displays only the public procedures. Therefore, if you have procedures that are designed to be called only by other procedures in the same module, you should make sure that the procedure is declared as `Private`. This prevents the user from running the procedure from the Macro dialog box.

The following example declares a private procedure, named `MySub`:

```
Private Sub MySub()
'    ... [code goes here] ...
End Sub
```

Tip

You can force all procedures in a module to be private — even those declared with the `Public` keyword — by including the following statement before your first `Sub` statement:

```
Option Private Module
```

If you write this statement in a module, you can omit the `Private` keyword from your `Sub` declarations.

Excel's macro recorder normally creates new Sub procedures called `Macro1`, `Macro2`, and so on. These procedures are all public procedures, and they will never use any arguments.

Executing Procedures

In this section I describe the many ways to *execute*, or call, a VBA Sub procedure:

✦ With the Run ➪ Run Sub/UserForm command (in the VBE). Or you can press the F5 shortcut key. Excel executes the procedure at the cursor position. This method doesn't work if the procedure requires one or more arguments.

✦ From Excel's Macro dialog box (which you open by choosing Tools ➪ Macro ➪ Macros). Or you can press the Alt+F8 shortcut key.

✦ Using the Ctrl key shortcut assigned to the procedure (assuming you assigned one).

✦ By clicking a button or a shape on a worksheet. The button or shape must have the procedure assigned to it.

✦ From another procedure you write.

✦ From a Toolbar button.

✦ From a custom menu that you develop.

✦ When an event occurs. These events include opening the workbook, saving the workbook, closing the workbook, making a change to a cell, activating a sheet, and many other things.

✦ From the Immediate window in the VBE. Just type the name of the procedure, write any arguments that may apply, and press Enter.

Note Excel 5 and Excel 95 made it very easy to assign a macro to a new menu item on the Tools menu. For some reason, this feature was removed beginning with Excel 97.

I discuss these methods of executing procedures in the following sections.

Note In many cases, a procedure will not function properly unless it is in the appropriate context. For example, if a procedure is designed to work with the active worksheet, it will fail if a chart sheet is active. A good procedure incorporates code that checks for the appropriate context and exits gracefully if it can't proceed.

Executing a procedure with the Run ⇨ Run Sub/UserForm command

The Run Sub/UserForm menu command is used primarily to test a procedure while you are developing it. You would never expect a user to have to activate the VBE to execute a procedure. Use the Run ⇨ Run Sub/UserForm command (or F5) in the VBE to execute the current procedure (in other words, the procedure that contains the cursor).

If the cursor is not located within a procedure when you issue the Run ⇨ Run Sub/UserForm command, VBE displays its Macro dialog box so that you can select a procedure to execute.

Executing a procedure from the Macro dialog box

Choosing Excel's Tools ⇨ Macro ⇨ Macros command displays the Macro dialog box, shown in Figure 42-1 (you can also press Alt+F8 to access this dialog box). The Macro dialog box lists all available procedures. Use the Macros in drop-down to limit the scope of the macros displayed (for example, show only the macros in the active workbook). The Macro dialog box does not display procedures declared with the `Private` keyword, procedures that require one or more arguments, or procedures contained in add-ins.

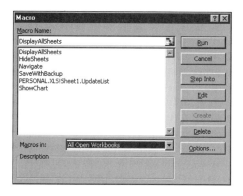

Figure 42-1: The Macro dialog box lists all available procedures.

Executing a procedure using a Ctrl+shortcut key combination

You can assign a Ctrl+shortcut key combination to any procedure that doesn't use any arguments. If you assign the Ctrl+U key combo to a procedure named Update, for example, pressing Ctrl+U executes the Update procedure.

When you begin recording a macro, the Record Macro dialog box gives you the opportunity to assign a shortcut key. However, you can assign a shortcut key at any time. To assign a Ctrl shortcut key to a procedure (or change a procedure's shortcut key), follow these steps:

1. Activate Excel and choose the Tools ➪ Macro ➪ Macros command.

2. Select the appropriate procedure from the list box in the Macro dialog box.

3. Click the Options button to display the Macro Options dialog box (see Figure 42-2).

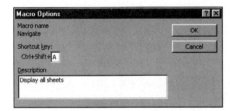

Figure 42-2: The Macro Options dialog box lets you assign a Ctrl key shortcut and an optional description to a procedure.

4. Enter a character into the text box labeled Ctrl+.

   The character that you enter into the text box labeled Ctrl+ is case-sensitive. If you enter a lowercase *s*, the shortcut key combo is Ctrl+S. If you enter an uppercase *S*, the shortcut key combo is Ctrl+Shift+S.

5. Enter a description (optional). If you enter a description for a macro, it is displayed in the Macro dialog box.

6. Click OK to close the Macro Options dialog box, and click Close to close the Macro dialog box.

Caution

If you assign one of Excel's predefined shortcut key combinations to a procedure, your key assignment takes precedence over the predefined key assignment. For example, Ctrl+S is Excel's predefined shortcut key for saving the active workbook. But if you assign Ctrl+S to a procedure, pressing Ctrl+S no longer saves the active workbook.

Tip The following Ctrl+key combinations are *not* used by Excel: E, J, L, M, Q, and T. Excel doesn't use too many Ctrl+Shift+key combinations. In fact, you can safely use any of them *except* F, O, and P.

Executing a procedure from a custom menu

As I describe in Chapter 50, Excel provides two ways for you to customize its menus: using the View ➪ Toolbars ➪ Customize command or writing VBA code. The latter method is preferable, but you can use either technique to assign a macro to a new menu item.

Note Excel 5 and Excel 95 include a menu editor—which was removed beginning with Excel 97.

Following are the steps required to display a new menu item on a menu and to assign a macro to the menu item. It assumes that the new menu item is on the **Data** menu, that the menu item text is **Open Customer File**, and that the procedure is named `OpenCustomerFile`.

1. Choose the View ➪ Toolbars ➪ Customize command. Excel displays the Customize dialog box.

   When the Customize dialog box is displayed, Excel is in a special "customization" mode. The menus and toolbars are not active, but they can be customized.

2. Click the Commands tab in the Customize dialog box.

3. Scroll down and click Macros in the Categories list.

4. In the Commands list, drag the first item (labeled Custom Menu Item) to the bottom of the Data menu (after the Refresh Data item). The Data menu drops down when you click it.

5. Right-click the new menu item (which is labeled Custom Menu Item) to display a shortcut menu.

6. Enter a new name for the menu item: **&Open Customer File** in the text box labeled Name (See Figure 42-3).

7. Click Assign Macro on the shortcut menu.

8. In the Assign Macro dialog box, select the `OpenCustomerFile` procedure from the list of macros.

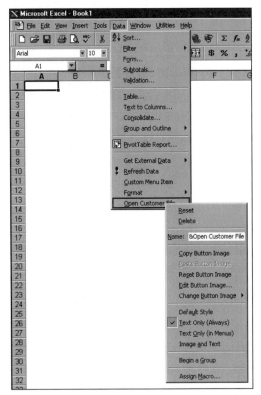

Figure 42-3: Changing the text for a menu item

9. Click OK to close the Assign Macro dialog box, and click Close to close the Customize dialog box.

Caution

After you follow the process mentioned previously, the new menu item always appears on the menu — even when the workbook that contains the macro is not open. In other words, changes you make using the View ➪ Toolbars ➪ Customize command are "permanent." Selecting the new menu item opens the workbook if it's not already open.

Cross-Reference

Refer to Chapter 50 to learn how to use VBA to create menu items that are displayed only when a particular workbook is open.

Executing a procedure from another procedure

One of the most common ways to execute a procedure is from another procedure. You have three ways to do this:

✦ Enter the procedure's name followed by its arguments (if any) separated by commas.

✦ Use the `Call` keyword followed by the procedure's name and then its arguments (if any) enclosed in parentheses and separated by commas.

✦ Use the `Run` method of the `Application` object. You can use this method to execute other VBA procedures or XLM macros. The `Run` method is also useful when you need to run a procedure and the procedure's name is assigned to a variable. You can then pass the variable as an argument to the `Run` method.

The following example demonstrates the first method. In this case, the `MySub` procedure processes some statements (not shown), executes the `UpdateSheet` procedure, and then executes the rest of the statements.

```
Sub MySub()
'    ... [code goes here] ...
     UpdateSheet
'    ... [code goes here] ...
End Sub

Sub UpdateSheet()
'    ... [code goes here] ...
End Sub
```

The following example demonstrates the second method. The `Call` keyword executes the `Update` procedure, which requires one argument; the calling procedure passes the argument to the called procedure. I discuss procedure arguments later in this chapter.

```
Sub MySub()
    MonthNum = InputBox("Enter the month number: ")
    Call UpdateSheet(MonthNum)
'    ... [code goes here] ...
End Sub

Sub UpdateSheet(MonthSeq)
'    ... [code goes here] ...
End Sub
```

Tip   Even though it's optional, some programmers always use the `Call` keyword just to make it perfectly clear that another procedure is being called.

The next example uses the `Run` method to execute the `UpdateSheet` procedure, and passes `MonthNum` as the argument.

```
Sub MySub()
    MonthNum = InputBox("Enter the month number: ")
    Result = Application.Run("UpdateSheet", MonthNum)
```

```
'   ... [code goes here] ...
End Sub

Sub UpdateSheet(MonthSeq)
'   ... [code goes here] ...
End Sub
```

The Run method is also useful when the procedure name is assigned to a variable. In fact, it's the only way to execute a procedure in such a way. The following example demonstrates this. The Main procedure determines the day of the week (an integer between 0 and 6, beginning with Sunday). The SubToCall variable is assigned a string that represents a procedure name. The Run method then calls the appropriate procedure (either WeekEnd or Daily).

```
Sub Main()
    Select Case WeekDay(Now)
        Case 0: SubToCall = "WeekEnd"
        Case 6: SubToCall = "WeekEnd"
        Case Else: SubToCall = "Daily"
    End Select
        Application.Run SubToCall
End Sub

Sub WeekEnd()
    MsgBox "Today is a weekend"
'   Code to execute on the weekend
'   goes here
End Sub

Sub Daily()
    MsgBox "Today is not a weekend"
'   Code to execute on the weekdays
'   goes here
End Sub
```

Note   You can also use the Run method to execute a procedure located in a different workbook. See "Calling a Procedure in a Different Workbook" later in this chapter.

Calling a procedure in a different module

If VBA can't locate a called procedure in the current module, it looks for public procedures in other modules in the same project.

If you need to call a private procedure from another procedure, both procedures must reside in the same module.

You can't have two procedures with the same name in the same module, but you can have identically named procedures in different modules. You can persuade VBA to execute an *ambiguously named* procedure — that is, another procedure in a different module that has the same name. To do so, precede the procedure name with the module name and a dot. For example, say that you define procedures named MySub in Module1 and Module2. If you want a procedure in Module2 to call the MySub in Module1, you can use either of the following statements:

```
Module1.MySub
Call Module1.MySub
```

If you do not differentiate between procedures that have the same name, you get an Ambiguous name detected error message.

Calling a procedure in a different workbook

In some cases, you may need your procedure to execute another procedure defined in a different workbook. To do so, you have two options: Establish a reference to the other workbook, or use the Run method and specify the workbook name explicitly.

To add a reference to another workbook, select the VBE's Tools ➪ References command. Excel displays the References dialog box (see Figure 42-4), which lists all available references, including all open workbooks. Simply check the box that corresponds to the workbook that you want to add as a reference and click OK. After you establish a reference, you can call procedures in the workbook as if they were in the same workbook as the calling procedure.

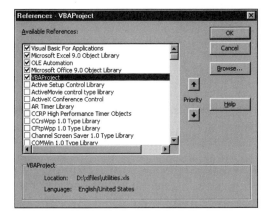

Figure 42-4: The Reference dialog box lets you establish a reference to another workbook.

A referenced workbook does not have to be open; it is treated like a separate object library. Use the Browse button in the References dialog box to establish a reference to a workbook that isn't open. The workbook names that appear in the list of references are listed by their VBE project names. By default, every project is initially named *VBAProject*. Therefore, the list may contain several identically named items. To distinguish a project, change its name in Properties window of the VBE. The list of references displayed in the References dialog box also includes object libraries and ActiveX controls that are registered on your system. Your Excel 2000 workbooks always include references to the following object libraries (and you can't unreference them, because they are essential):

✦ Visual Basic for Applications

✦ Microsoft Excel 9.0 Object Library

✦ OLE Automation

✦ Microsoft Office 9.0 Object Library

If you've established a reference to a workbook that contains the procedure YourSub, for example, you can use either of the following statements to call YourSub:

```
YourSub
Call YourSub
```

To precisely identify a procedure in a different workbook, specify the project name, module name, and procedure name using the following syntax:

```
MyProject.MyModule.MySub
```

Alternatively, you can use the Call keyword:

```
Call MyProject.MyModule.MySub
```

Another way to call a procedure in a different workbook is to use the Run method of the Application object. This technique does not require that you establish a reference. The following statement executes the Consolidate procedure located in a workbook named budget macros.xls:

```
Application.Run "'budget macros.xls'!Consolidate"
```

Why Call Other Procedures?

If you're new to programming, you may wonder why anyone would ever want to call a procedure from another procedure. You may ask, "Why not just put the code from the called procedure into the calling procedure and keep things simple?"

One reason is to clarify your code. The simpler your code, the easier it is to modify. Smaller routines are easier to decipher and then debug. Examine the accompanying procedure, which does nothing but call other procedures. This procedure is so easy to read, it acts like an outline.

```
Sub Main()
    Call GetUserOptions
    Call ProcessData
    Call CleanUp
    Call CloseItDown
End Sub
```

Calling other procedures also eliminates redundancy. Suppose that you need to perform an operation at ten different places in your routine. Rather than enter the code ten times, you can write a procedure to perform the operation and then simply call the procedure ten times.

Also, you may have a series of general purpose procedures that you use frequently. If you store these in a separate module, you can import the module to your current project and then call these procedures as needed — which is much easier than copying and pasting the code into your new procedures.

Remember, creating several small procedures rather than a single large one is simply good programming practice. A modular approach not only makes your job easier, but also makes life easier for the people who wind up working with your code.

Executing a procedure from a toolbar button

You can customize Excel's toolbars to include buttons that execute procedures when clicked. The procedure for assigning a macro to a toolbar button is virtually identical to the procedure for assigning a macro to a menu item.

Assume that you want to assign a procedure to a toolbar button on a toolbar. Here are the steps required to do so:

1. Choose the View ➪ Toolbars ➪ Customize command. Excel displays the Customize dialog box.

   When the Customize dialog box is displayed, Excel is in a special "customization" mode. The menus and toolbars are not active, but they can be customized.

2. Click the Commands tab in the Customize dialog box.

3. Scroll down and click Macros in the Categories list.

4. In the Commands list, drag the second item (labeled Custom Button) to the desired toolbar

5. Right-click the new button to display a shortcut menu.

6. Enter a new name for the button in the text box labeled Name. This is the "tooltip" text that appears when the mouse pointer moves over the button. This step is optional; if you omit it, the tooltip displays *Custom.*

7. Right-click the new button, and select Assign Macro from the shortcut menu.

   Excel displays its Assign Macro dialog box.

8. Select the procedure from the list of macros.

9. Click OK to close the Assign Macro dialog box.

10. Click Close to close the Customize dialog box.

Caution

After you follow the preceding process, the new toolbar button always appears on the assigned toolbar — even when the workbook that contains the macro is not open. In other words, changes you make using the View ⇨ Toolbars ⇨ Customize command are "permanent." Clicking the new toolbar button item opens the workbook if it's not already open.

Cross-Reference

I cover custom toolbars in Chapter 49.

Executing a procedure by clicking an object

Excel has a variety of objects that you can place on a worksheet or chart sheet, and you can attach a macro to any of these objects. These objects are available from three toolbars:

✦ The Drawing toolbar

✦ The Forms toolbar

✦ The Control Toolbox toolbar

Note

The Control Toolbox toolbar contains ActiveX controls — the same controls that you use in a custom dialog box. The Forms toolbar, included for compatibility purposes, contains similar controls (which are not ActiveX controls). The controls on the Forms toolbar were designed for Excel 5 and Excel 95. However, they can still be used in later versions (and may be preferable in some cases). The discussion that follows applies to the Button control on the Forms toolbar. Refer to Chapter 44 for information about using ActiveX controls on worksheets.

To assign a procedure to a Button object (which is on the Forms toolbar), follow these steps:

1. Make sure the Forms toolbar is displayed.

2. Click the Button tool on the Forms toolbar.

3. Drag in the worksheet to create the button.

Excel jumps right in and displays the Assign Macro dialog box. Select the macro you want to assign to the button, and click OK.

To assign a macro to a shape, create a shape using the Drawing toolbar. Right-click the shape and choose Assign Macro from the shortcut menu.

Executing a procedure when an event occurs

You might want a procedure to be executed when a particular event occurs. Examples of events include opening a workbook, entering data into a worksheet, saving a workbook, and many others. A procedure that is executed when an event occurs is known as an *event-handler* procedure. Event-handler procedures are characterized by the following:

✦ They have special names that are made up of an object, an underscore, and the event name. For example, the procedure that is executed when a workbook is opened is called Workbook_Open.

✦ They are stored in the code window for the particular object.

Cross-Reference   Chapter 46 is devoted to event-handler procedures.

Executing a procedure from the Immediate window

You also can execute a procedure by entering its name in the Immediate window of the VBE. If the Immediate window is not visible, press Ctrl+G. The Immediate window executes VBA statements as you enter them. To execute a procedure, simply enter the name of the procedure in the Immediate window and press Enter.

This method can be quite useful when you're developing a procedure because you can insert commands to display results in the Immediate window. The following procedure demonstrates this technique:

```
Sub ChangeCase()
    MyString = "This is a test"
    MyString = UCase(MyString)
    Debug.Print MyString
End Sub
```

Figure 42-5 shows what happens when you enter **ChangeCase** in the Immediate window: The `Debug.Print` statement displays the result immediately.

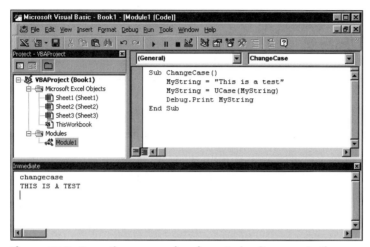

Figure 42-5: Executing a procedure by entering its name in the Immediate window

Passing Arguments to Procedures

A procedure's *arguments* provide it with data that it uses in its instructions. The data that's *passed* by an argument can be any of the following:

- ✦ A variable
- ✦ A constant
- ✦ A literal
- ✦ An array
- ✦ An object

With regard to arguments, procedures are very similar to worksheet functions in the following respects:

- ✦ A procedure may not require any arguments.
- ✦ A procedure may require a fixed number of arguments.
- ✦ A procedure may accept an indefinite number of arguments.
- ✦ A procedure may require some arguments, leaving others optional.
- ✦ A procedure may have all optional arguments.

For example, a few of Excel's worksheet functions such as RAND use no arguments. Others, such as COUNTIF, require two arguments. Others still, such as SUM can use an indefinite number of arguments — up to 30. Still other worksheet functions have optional arguments. The PMT function, for example, can have five arguments (three are required, two are optional).

Most of the procedures that you've seen so far in this book have been declared without any arguments. They were declared with just the Sub keyword, the procedure's name, and a set of empty parentheses. Empty parentheses indicate that the procedure does not accept arguments.

The following example shows two procedures. The Main procedure calls the ProcessFile procedure three times (the Call statement is in a For-Next loop). Before calling ProcessFile, however, a three-element array is created. Inside the loop, each element of the array becomes the argument for the procedure call. The ProcessFile procedure takes one argument (named TheFile) — notice that the argument goes inside parentheses in the Sub statement. When ProcessFile finishes, program control continues with the statement after the Call statement.

```
Sub Main()
    File(1) = "dept1.xls"
    File(2) = "dept2.xls"
    File(3) = "dept3.xls"
    For i = 1 To 3
        Call ProcessFile(File(i))
    Next i
End Sub

Sub ProcessFile(TheFile)
    Workbooks.Open FileName:=TheFile
'    ...[more code here]...
End Sub
```

You can also, of course, pass literals (that is, not variables) to a procedure. For example,

```
Sub Main()
    Call ProcessFile("budget.xls")
End Sub
```

You can pass an argument to a procedure in two ways: by reference and by value. Passing an argument by reference (the default method) simply passes the memory address of the variable. Passing an argument by value, on the other hand, passes a *copy* of the original variable. Consequently, changes to the argument within the procedure are not reflected in the original variable.

The following example demonstrates this concept. The argument for the Process procedure is passed by reference (the default method). After the Main procedure assigns a value of 10 to MyValue, it calls the Process procedure and passes MyValue as the argument. The Process procedure multiplies the value of its argument (named YourValue) by 10. When Process ends and program control passes back to Main, the MsgBox function displays MyValue: 100.

```
Sub Main()
    MyValue = 10
    Call Process(MyValue)
    MsgBox MyValue
End Sub

Sub Process(YourValue)
    YourValue = YourValue * 10
End Sub
```

If you don't want the called procedure to modify any variables passed as arguments, you can modify the called procedure's argument list so that arguments are passed to it *by value* rather than *by reference*. To do so, precede the argument with the ByVal keyword. This technique causes the called routine to work with a copy of the passed variable's data, not the data itself. In the following procedure, for example, the changes made to YourValue in the Process procedure do not affect the MyValue variable in Main. As a result, the MsgBox function displays 10, not 100.

```
Sub Process(ByVal YourValue)
    YourValue = YourValue * 10
End Sub
```

In most cases, you'll be content to use the default reference method of passing arguments. However, if your procedure needs to use data passed to it in an argument — and you absolutely must keep the original data intact — you'll want to pass the data by value.

A procedure's arguments can mix and match by value and by reference. Arguments preceded with ByVal are passed by value; all others are passed by reference.

Note   If you pass a variable defined as a user-defined data type to a procedure, it must be passed by reference. Attempting to pass it by value generates an error.

Because I didn't declare a data type for any of the arguments in the preceding examples, all the arguments have been of the variant data type. But a procedure that uses arguments can define the data types directly in the argument list. The following is a Sub statement for a procedure with two arguments of different data types. The first is declared as an integer, and the second is declared as a string.

```
Sub Process(Iterations As Integer, TheFile As String)
```

When you pass arguments to a procedure, it's important that the data that is passed as the argument matches the argument's data type. For example, if you call `Process` in the preceding example and pass a string variable for the first argument, you get a *type mismatch* error.

Note

Arguments are relevant to both Sub procedures and Function procedures. In Chapter 43, where I focus on Function procedures, I provide more examples of using arguments with your routines, including how to handle optional arguments.

Public Variables versus Passing Arguments to a Procedure

In Chapter 41, I pointed out how a variable declared as `Public` is available to all procedures in the module. In some cases, you may want to access a `Public` variable rather than pass the variable as an argument when calling another procedure.

For example, the procedure that follows passes the value of `MonthVal` to the `ProcessMonth` procedure:

```
Sub MySub()
    Dim MonthVal as Integer
'   ... [code goes here]
    MonthVal = 4
    Call ProcessMonth(MonthVal)
'   ... [code goes here]
End Sub
```

An alternative approach is

```
Public MonthVal as Integer

Sub MySub()
'   ... [code goes here]
    MonthVal = 4
    Call ProcessMonth
'   ... [code goes here]
End Sub
```

In the revised code, because `MonthVal` is a public variable, the `ProcessMonth` procedure can access it, eliminating the need for an argument for the `ProcessMonth` procedure.

Error-Handling Techniques

When a VBA procedure is running, errors can occur — as you undoubtedly know. These include either syntax errors (which you must correct before you can execute a procedure) or run-time errors (which occur while the procedure is running). This section deals with run-time errors.

Caution

For error-handling procedures to work, the Break on All Errors setting *must* be turned off. In the VBE, select Tools ➪ Options and click the General tab in the Options dialog box. If Break on All Errors is selected, VBA ignores your error-handling code. You'll usually want to use the Break on Unhandled Errors option.

Normally, a run-time error causes VBA to stop, and the user sees a dialog box that displays the error number and a description of the error. A good application doesn't make the user deal with these messages. Rather, it incorporates error-handling code to trap errors and take appropriate actions. At the very least, your error-handling code can display a more meaningful error message than the one popped up by VBA.

Cross-Reference

Appendix G lists all the VBA error codes and descriptions.

Trapping errors

You can use the On Error statement to specify what happens when an error occurs. Basically, you have two choices:

+ Ignore the error, and let VBA continue. You can later poll the Err object to determine what the error was, and take action if necessary.

+ Jump to a special error-handling section of your code to take action. This section is placed at the end of the procedure, and marked by a label.

To cause the VBA program to continue when an error occurs, insert the following statement in your code:

```
On Error Resume Next
```

Some errors are inconsequential, and can simply be ignored. But you may want to determine what the error was. When an error occurs, you can use the Err object to determine the error number. VBA's Error function can be used to display the text for Err.Value, which defaults to just Err. For example, the following statement displays the same information as the normal Visual Basic error dialog box (the error number and the error description):

```
MsgBox "Error" & Err & ": " & Error(Err)
```

Figure 42-6 shows a VBA error message, and Figure 42-7 shows the same error displayed in a message box. You can, of course, make the error message a bit more meaningful to your end users by using more descriptive text.

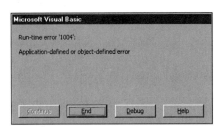

Figure 42-6: VBA's error messages aren't always user friendly.

Figure 42-7: You can create a message box to display the error code and description.

You also use the `On Error` statement to specify a location in your procedure to jump to when an error occurs. You use a label to mark the location. For example,

```
On Error GoTo ErrorHandler
```

Error-handling examples

The first example demonstrates an error that can safely be ignored. The `SpecialCells` method selects cells that meet a certain criteria. (This method is equivalent to selecting the Edit ⇨ Go To command and clicking the Special button to select, for example, cells that contain formulas.)

In the example that follows, the `SpecialCells` method selects all the cells in the current range selection that contain a formula that returns a number. Normally, if no cells in the selection qualify, VBA generates an error message. Using the `On Error Resume Next` statement simply prevents the error message from appearing.

```
Sub SelectFormulas()
    On Error Resume Next
    Selection.SpecialCells(xlFormulas, xlNumbers).Select
End Sub
```

The following procedure uses an additional statement to determine if an error did occur.

```
Sub SelectFormulas2()
    On Error Resume Next
    Selection.SpecialCells(xlFormulas, xlNumbers).Select
    If Err <> 0 Then MsgBox "No formula cells were found."
End Sub
```

If the value of Err is not equal to 0, an error occurred, and a message box displays a notice to the user.

The next example demonstrates error handling by jumping to a label.

```
Sub ErrorDemo()
    On Error GoTo Handler
    Selection.Value = 123
    Exit Sub
Handler:
    MsgBox "Cannot assign a value to the selection."
End Sub
```

The procedure attempts to assign a value to the current selection. If a range is not selected or the sheet is protected, the assignment statement results in an error. The On Error statement specifies a jump to the Handler label if an error occurs. Notice the use of the Exit Sub statement before the label. This prevents the error-handling code from being executed if no error occurs.

Sometimes, you can take advantage of an error to get information. The example that follows simply checks to see whether a particular workbook is open.

```
Sub CheckForFile1()
    FileName = "BUDGET.XLS"
    FileExists = False

    '   Cycle through all workbooks
    For Each book In Workbooks
        If UCase(book.Name) = FileName Then
            FileExists = True
        End If
    Next book

    '   Display appropriate message
    If FileExists Then _
        MsgBox FileName & " is open." Else _
            MsgBox FileName & " is not open."
End Sub
```

Here, a For Each-Next loop cycles through all objects in the Workbooks collection. If the workbook is open, the FileExists variable is set to True. Finally, a message is displayed that tells the user whether the workbook is open.

The preceding routine can be rewritten to use error handling to determine whether the file is open. In the example that follows, the On Error Resume Next statement causes VBA to ignore any errors. The next instruction attempts to reference the workbook and assign its name to a variable. If the workbook is not open, an error occurs. The If-Then-Else structure checks the value property of Err and displays the appropriate message.

```
Sub CheckForFile()
    FileName = "BUDGET.XLS"
    On Error Resume Next
    x = UCase(Workbooks(FileName).Name)
    If Err = 0 Then
        MsgBox FileName & " is open."
    Else
        MsgBox FileName & " is not open."
    End If
End Sub
```

A Realistic Example

In this chapter, I have provided you with a foundation for creating procedures. Most of the previous examples, I will admit, have been rather wimpy. The remainder of this chapter is a real-life exercise that demonstrates many of the concepts covered in this and the preceding two chapters.

This section describes the development of a useful utility that qualifies as an application. More important, I demonstrate the *process* of analyzing a problem and then solving it with VBA. A word of warning to the more experienced users in the audience: I wrote this section with VBA newcomers in mind. As a result, I don't simply present the code, but I show how to find out what you need to know to develop the code.

On the CD-ROM The completed application can be found on the companion CD-ROM.

The goal

The goal of this exercise is to develop a utility that rearranges a workbook by alphabetizing its sheets. If you tend to create workbooks that consist of many sheets, you know that it can be difficult to locate a particular sheet. If the sheets are ordered alphabetically, though, it's much easier to find a desired sheet.

Project requirements

Where to begin? One way to get started is to list the requirements for your application. As you develop your application, you can check your list to ensure that you're covering all the bases.

Here's the list of requirements that I compiled for this example application:

1. It should sort the sheets in the active workbook in ascending order.

2. It should be easy to execute.

3. It should always be available. In other words, the user shouldn't have to open a workbook to use this utility.

4. It should work properly for any open workbook.

5. It should not display any VBA error messages.

What you know

Often, the most difficult part of a project is figuring out where to start. In this case, I started by listing things that I know about Excel that may be relevant to the project requirements:

✦ Excel doesn't have a command that sorts sheets.

✦ I can move a sheet easily by dragging its sheet tab.

Mental note: Turn on the macro recorder and drag a sheet to a new location to find out what kind of code this action generates.

✦ I'll need to know how many sheets are in the active workbook. I can get this information with VBA.

✦ I'll need to know the names of all the sheets. Again, I can get this information with VBA.

✦ Excel has a command that sorts data in worksheet cells.

Mental note: Maybe I can transfer the sheet names to a range and use this feature. Or, maybe VBA has a sorting method that I can take advantage of.

✦ Thanks to the Macro Options dialog box, it's easy to assign a shortcut key to a macro.

✦ If a macro is stored in the Personal Macro Workbook, it will always be available.

✦ I need a way to test the application as I develop it. For certain, I don't want to be testing it using the same workbook in which I'm developing the code.

Mental note: Create a dummy workbook for testing purposes.

✦ If I develop the code properly, VBA won't display any errors.

Mental note: Wishful thinking . . .

The approach

Although I still didn't know exactly how to proceed, I could devise a preliminary, skeleton plan that describes the general tasks required:

1. Identify the active workbook.

2. Get a list of all the sheet names in the workbook.

3. Count the sheets.

4. Sort them (somehow).

5. Rearrange the sheets in the sorted order.

What you need to know

I saw a few holes in the plan. I knew that I had to determine the following:

✦ How to identify the active workbook

✦ How to count the sheets in the active workbook

✦ How to get a list of the sheet names

✦ How to sort the list

✦ How to rearrange the sheets according to the sorted list

Tip

When you lack critical information about specific methods or properties, you can consult this book or the online help. You may eventually discover what you need to know. Your best bet, however, is to turn on the macro recorder and see what it spits out when you perform some relevant actions.

Some preliminary recording

Here's an example of using the macro recorder to learn about VBA. I started with a workbook that contained three worksheets. Then I turned on the macro recorder and specified my Personal Macro Workbook as the destination for the macro. With the macro recorder running, I dragged the third worksheet to the first sheet position. Here's what the macro recorder spat out:

```
Sub Macro1()
    Sheets("Sheet3").Select
    Sheets("Sheet3").Move Before:=Sheets(1)
End Sub
```

I searched the online help for *Move,* and discovered that it's a method that moves a sheet to a new location in the workbook. It also takes an argument that specifies the location for the sheet. Very relevant to the task at hand.

Next I needed to find out how many sheets were in the active workbook. I searched for the word *Count* and found out that it's a property of a collection. I activated the Immediate window in the VBE and typed the following statement:

```
? ActiveWorkbook.Sheets.Count
```

Figure 42-8 shows the result. More useful information.

Figure 42-8: Using VBE's Immediate window to test a statement

What about the sheet names? Time for another test. I entered the following statement in the Immediate window:

```
? ActiveWorkbook.Sheets(1).Name
```

This told me that the name of the first sheet is Sheet3, which is correct. More good information to keep in mind.

Then I remembered something about the For Each-Next construct: It is useful for cycling through each member of a collection. After checking out the online help, I created a short procedure to test it out:

```
Sub Test()
    For Each Item In ActiveWorkbook.Sheets
        MsgBox Item.Name
    Next Item
End Sub
```

Another success. This macro displayed three message boxes, each displaying a different sheet name.

Finally, it was time to think about sorting options. From the online help, I learned that the Sort method applies to a range or a pivot table. So one option was to transfer the sheet names to a range and then sort the range, but that seemed like overkill for this application. I thought a better option was to dump the sheet names into an array of strings and then sort the array by using VBA code.

Initial set-up

Now I knew enough to get started writing some serious code. Before doing so, however, I need to do some initial set-up work. To recreate my steps, follow these instructions:

1. Create an empty workbook with five worksheets, named **Sheet1**, **Sheet2**, **Sheet3**, **Sheet4**, and **Sheet5**.

2. Move the sheets around randomly so that they aren't in any particular order.

3. Save the workbook as **Test.xls**.

4. Activate the VBE and select the **Personal.xls** project in the Project Window.

   If Personal.xls doesn't appear in the Project window in the VBE, you haven't used the Personal Macro Workbook. To have Excel create this workbook for you, simply record a macro (any macro) and specify the Personal Macro Workbook as the destination for the macro.

5. Insert a new VBA module (use the Insert ⇨ Module command).

6. Create an empty procedure called `SortSheets` (see Figure 42-9).

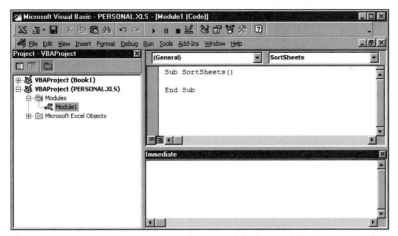

Figure 42-9: An empty procedure in a module located in the Personal Macro Workbook

Actually, you can store this macro in any module in the Personal Macro Workbook. However, it's a good idea to keep each macro in a separate module. That way, you can easily export the module and import it into a different project later on.

7. Activate Excel. Use the Tools ➪ Macro ➪ Macros command (Options button) to assign a shortcut key to this macro. The Ctrl+Shift+S key combination is a good choice.

Code writing

Now it's time to write some code. I knew that I needed to put the sheet names into an array of strings. Because I won't know yet how many sheets are in the active workbook, I used a `Dim` statement with empty parentheses to declare the array. I knew that I could use `ReDim` afterward to redimension the array for the proper number of elements.

I entered the following code, which inserts the sheet names into the `SheetNames` array. I also added a `MsgBox` function within the loop just to assure me that the sheets' names were indeed being entered into the array.

```
Sub SortSheets()
    Dim SheetNames()
    SheetCount = ActiveWorkbook.Sheets.Count
    ReDim SheetNames(1 To SheetCount)
    For i = 1 To SheetCount
        SheetNames(i) = ActiveWorkbook.Sheets(i).Name
        MsgBox SheetNames(i)
    Next i
End Sub
```

To test the preceding code, I activated the Text.xls workbook and pressed Ctrl+Shift+S. Five message boxes appeared, each displaying the name of a corresponding sheet.

I'm a major proponent of testing your work as you go. When you're convinced that your code is working correctly, remove the `MsgBox` statement (these message boxes become annoying after a while).

Tip   Rather than use the `MsgBox` function to test your work, you can use the `Print` method of the `Debug` object to display information in the Immediate window. For this example, use the following statement in place of the `MsgBox` statement:

```
Debug.Print SheetNames(i)
```

You may find this technique less intrusive than using `MsgBox` statements.

At this point, the `SortSheets` procedure simply creates an array of sheet names in the active workbook. Two steps remain: Sort the values in the `SheetNames` array, and then rearrange the sheets to correspond to the sorted array.

Sort procedure writing

It was time to sort the SheetNames array. I could have stuck the sorting code in the SortSheets procedure, but I thought a better approach was to write a general-purpose sorting procedure that I could reuse with other projects (sorting arrays is a common operation).

You may be a bit daunted by the thought of writing a sorting procedure. The good news is that it's relatively easy to find commonly used routines that you can use or adapt. The Internet, of course, is a great source for such information.

You can sort an array in many ways. I chose the *bubble sort* method; although it's not a particularly fast technique, it's easy to code. The bubble sort method uses a nested For-Next loop to evaluate each array element. If the array element is greater than the next element, the two elements swap positions. This evaluation is repeated for every pair of items (that is, n–1 times).

Here's the sorting procedure I developed:

```
Sub BubbleSort(List())
'    Sorts the List array in ascending order
     Dim First As Integer, Last As Integer
     Dim i As Integer, j As Integer
     Dim Temp
     First = LBound(List)
     Last = UBound(List)
     For i = First To Last - 1
         For j = i + 1 To Last
             If List(i) > List(j) Then
                 Temp = List(j)
                 List(j) = List(i)
                 List(i) = Temp
             End If
         Next j
     Next i
End Sub
```

This procedure accepts one argument: a one-dimensional array named List. An array passed to a procedure can be of any length. I use the LBound and UBound functions to define the lower bound and upper bound of the array to the variables First and Last, respectively.

After I was satisfied that this procedure worked reliably, I modified SortSheets by adding a call to the BubbleSort procedure, passing the SheetNames array as an argument. At this point, my module looked like this:

```
Sub SortSheets()
    Dim SheetNames()
```

```
        SheetCount = ActiveWorkbook.Sheets.Count
        ReDim SheetNames(1 To SheetCount)
        For i = 1 To SheetCount
            SheetNames(i) = ActiveWorkbook.Sheets(i).Name
        Next i
        Call BubbleSort(SheetNames)
    End Sub

    Sub BubbleSort(List() As String)
    '    Sorts the List array in ascending order
        Dim First As Integer, Last As Integer
        Dim i As Integer, j As Integer
        Dim Temp

        First = LBound(List)
        Last = UBound(List)
        For i = First To Last - 1
            For j = i + 1 To Last
                If List(i) > List(j) Then
                    Temp = List(j)
                    List(j) = List(i)
                    List(i) = Temp
                End If
            Next j
        Next i
    End Sub
```

At this point, when the SheetSort procedure ends, it contains an array that consists of the sorted sheet names in the active workbook. So far, so good. Now I merely had to write some code to rearrange the sheets to correspond to the sorted items in the SheetNames array.

The code that I recorded earlier, again proved useful. Remember the instruction that was recorded when I moved a sheet to the first position in the workbook?

```
    Sheets("Sheet1").Move Sheets(1)
```

After a little thought, I was able to write a For-Next loop that would go through each sheet and move it to its corresponding sheet location, specified in the SheetNames array.

```
    For i = 1 To SheetCount
        Sheets(SheetNames(i)).Move Sheets(i)
    Next i
```

For example, the first time through the loop, the loop counter (i) is 1. The first element in the SheetNames array is (in this example) Sheet1. Therefore, the expression for the Move method within the loop evaluates to

```
Sheets("Sheet1").Move Sheets(1)
```

The second time through the loop, the expression evaluates to

```
Sheets("Sheet2").Move Sheets(2)
```

I then added the new code to the SortSheets procedure:

```
Sub SortSheets()
    SheetCount = ActiveWorkbook.Sheets.Count
    ReDim SheetNames(1 To SheetCount)
    For i = 1 To SheetCount
        SheetNames(i) = ActiveWorkbook.Sheets(i).Name
    Next i
    Call BubbleSort(SheetNames)
    For i = 1 To SheetCount
        ActiveWorkbook.Sheets(SheetNames(i)).Move _
            ActiveWorkbook.Sheets(i)
    Next i
End Sub
```

I did some testing and it seemed to work just fine for the Test.xls workbook.

Time to clean things up. I declared all the variables used and then added a few comments and blank lines to make the code easier to read. The SortSheets procedure now looked like the following:

```
Sub SortSheets()
'   This routine sorts the sheets of the
'   active workbook in ascending order.

    Dim SheetNames() As String
    Dim SheetCount As Integer
    Dim i As Integer

    SheetCount = ActiveWorkbook.Sheets.Count
    ReDim SheetNames(1 To SheetCount)

'   Fill array with sheet names
    For i = 1 To SheetCount
        SheetNames(i) = ActiveWorkbook.Sheets(i).Name
    Next i

'   Sort the array in ascending order
    Call BubbleSort(SheetNames)

'   Move the sheets
    For i = 1 To SheetCount
        ActiveWorkbook.Sheets(SheetNames(i)).Move _
```

```
              ActiveWorkbook.Sheets(i)
      Next i
  End Sub
```

Everything seemed to be working. To test the code further, I added a few more sheets to Test.xls and changed some of the sheet names. It works like a charm!

More testing

I was tempted to call it a day. However, the fact that the procedure worked with the Test.xls workbook didn't mean that it would work with all workbooks. To test it further, I loaded a few other workbooks and retried the routine. I soon discovered that the application was not perfect. In fact, it was far from perfect. I identified the following problems:

✦ Workbooks with many sheets took a long time to sort because the screen was continually updated during the move operations.

✦ The sorting didn't always work. For example, in one of my tests, a sheet named SUMMARY (all uppercase) appeared before a sheet named Sheet1. This problem was caused by the BubbleSort procedure (an uppercase U is "greater than" a lower case H).

✦ If there were no visible workbook windows, pressing the Ctrl+Shift+S shortcut key combo caused the macro to fail.

✦ If the workbook's structure was protected, the Move method failed.

✦ After sorting, the last sheet in the workbook became the active sheet. Changing the active sheet is not a good practice; it's better to keep the original sheet active.

✦ If I interrupted the macro by pressing Ctrl+Break, VBA displayed an error message.

Screen updating problems

Fixing the screen-updating problem was a breeze. I inserted the following instruction at the beginning of SortSheets to turn screen updating off:

```
Application.ScreenUpdating = False
```

It was also easy to fix the problem with the BubbleSort procedure: I used VBA's UCase function to convert the sheet names to uppercase. That way, all the comparisons were made using uppercase versions of the sheet names. The corrected line read as follows:

```
If UCase(List(i)) > UCase(List(j)) Then
```

Tip

Another way to solve the "case" problem is to add the following statement to the top of your module:

```
Option Text Compare
```

This statement causes VBA to perform string comparisons based on a case-insensitive text sort order. In other words, *A* is considered the same as *a*.

To prevent the error message that appears when no workbooks are visible, I added some error checking. If no active workbook exists, an error occurred. I used On Error Resume Next to ignore the error, and then checked the value of Err. If Err is not equal to 0, it means that an error occurred. Therefore, the procedure ends. The error-checking code is

```
On Error Resume Next
SheetCount = ActiveWorkbook.Sheets.Count
If Err <> 0 Then Exit Sub ' No active workbook
```

There's usually a good reason that a workbook's structure is protected. I decided that the best approach was to display a message box to that effect (with a stop sign icon generated by the vbCritical constant) and then exit the procedure. (If desired, a user can unprotect the workbook and redo the sheet sorting.) Testing for a protected workbook structure was easy — the ProtectStructure property of a Workbook object returns True if a workbook is protected. I added the following block of code:

```
'   Check for protected workbook structure
    If ActiveWorkbook.ProtectStructure Then
        MsgBox ActiveWorkbook.Name & " is protected.", _
            vbCritical, "Cannot Sort Sheets."
        Exit Sub
    End If
```

To reactivate the original active sheet after the sorting is performed, I wrote code that assigned the original sheet to an object variable (OldActive), and then activated that sheet when the routine was finished.

Pressing Ctrl+Break normally halts a macro, and VBA usually displays an error message. But because one of my goals was to avoid VBA error messages, I needed to insert a command to prevent this situation. From the online help, I discovered that the Application object has an EnableCancelKey property that can disable Ctrl+Break. So I added the following statement at the top of the routine:

```
Application.EnableCancelKey = xlDisabled
```

Caution

Be very careful when you disable the cancel key. If your code gets caught in an infinite loop, you can't break out of it. For best results, insert this statement only after you're sure everything is working properly.

After I made all these corrections, the SortSheets procedure looked like Listing 42-1.

Listing 42-1: The final build for the SortSheets procedure

```
Sub SortSheets()
'    This routine sorts the sheets of the
'    active workbook in ascending order.

     Dim SheetNames() As String
     Dim i As Integer
     Dim SheetCount As Integer
     Dim VisibleWins As Integer
     Dim Item As Object
     Dim OldActive As Object

     On Error Resume Next
     SheetCount = ActiveWorkbook.Sheets.Count
     If Err <> 0 Then Exit Sub ' No active workbook

'    Check for protected workbook structure
     If ActiveWorkbook.ProtectStructure Then
         MsgBox ActiveWorkbook.Name & " is protected.", _
             vbCritical, "Cannot Sort Sheets."
         Exit Sub
     End If

'    Disable Ctrl+Break
     Application.EnableCancelKey = xlDisabled

'    Get the number of sheets
     SheetCount = ActiveWorkbook.Sheets.Count

'    Redimension the array
     ReDim SheetNames(1 To SheetCount)

'    Store a reference to the active sheet
     Set OldActive = ActiveSheet

'    Fill array with sheet names and hidden status
     For i = 1 To SheetCount
         SheetNames(i) = ActiveWorkbook.Sheets(i).Name
     Next i

'    Sort the array in ascending order
     Call BubbleSort(SheetNames)

'    Turn off screen updating
     Application.ScreenUpdating = False
```

```
'   Move the sheets
    For i = 1 To SheetCount
        ActiveWorkbook.Sheets(SheetNames(i)).Move _
            ActiveWorkbook.Sheets(i)
    Next i

'   Reactivate the original active sheet
    OldActive.Activate
End Sub
```

Utility availability

Because the `SortSheets` macro is stored in the Personal Macro Workbook, it is available whenever Excel is running. At this point, the macro can be executed by selecting the macro's name from the Macro dialog box (Alt+F8 displays this dialog box), or by pressing Ctrl+Shift+F8.

If you like, you can also assign this macro to a new toolbar button or to a new menu item. Procedures for doing this are described earlier in this chapter.

Evaluating the project

So there you have it. The utility meets all the original project requirements: It sorts all sheets in the active workbook, it can be executed easily, it's always available, it seems to work for any workbook, and I have yet to see it display a VBA error message.

Note The procedure still has one slight problem: The sorting is strict and may not always be "logical." For example, after sorting, Sheet11 is placed before Sheet2. Most would want Sheet2 to be listed before Sheet11.

On the CD-ROM The companion CD-ROM contains another version of the sheet sorting utility that overcomes the problem just described — in most cases. This version of the utility parses the sheet names into two components: the left-most text and the right-most numbers (if any). The parsed data is stored on a worksheet, and the procedure uses Excel's built-in sorting to perform the sort using two sort keys. It's still not perfect because it won't properly sort a sheet with a name like Sheet2Part1.

In this exercise, I tried to demonstrate the process of developing VBA procedures — a valuable lesson even if you're not yet a VBA veteran. I communicated the following points:

✦ Developing a successful procedure is not necessarily a linear process.

✦ It's often useful to use short procedures or the Immediate window to test ideas or approaches before incorporating them into your work.

✦ Even though a procedure appears to work correctly, appearances can be deceiving. Therefore, it's important to test your work in a realistic situation.

✦ You can learn a lot by recording your actions and studying the code that is recorded. Although I didn't actually use any of the recorded code, I learned several things by examining the code.

✦ A project's original requirements aren't always complete. In this example, I didn't think to require that the original active sheet remain the active sheet after the sorting.

Summary

In this chapter, I presented a comprehensive list of ways to execute Sub procedures, and I described how to use arguments. I also gave an example of developing and debugging procedures.

✦   ✦   ✦

Creating Custom Worksheet Functions

As mentioned previously, you can create two types of VBA procedures: subroutines and functions. This chapter focuses on function procedures.

Overview of VBA Functions

Function procedures that you write in VBA are quite versatile. You can use these functions in two situations:

+ As part of an expression in a different VBA procedure

+ On formulas that you create in a worksheet

In fact, you can use a function procedure anywhere that you can use an Excel worksheet function or a VBA built-in function. Custom functions also appear in the Paste Function dialog box, so they appear to be part of Excel.

Excel contains hundreds of predefined worksheet functions. With so many from which to choose, you may be curious as to why anyone would need to develop additional functions. The main reason is that creating a custom function can greatly simplify your formulas by making them shorter — and shorter formulas are more readable and easier to work with. For example, you can often replace a complex formula with a single function. Another reason is that you can write functions to perform operations that would otherwise be impossible.

Note   This chapter assumes that you are familiar with entering and editing VBA code in the Visual Basic Editor (VBE). Refer to Chapter 40 for an overview of the VBE.

An Introductory Example

The process of creating custom functions is relatively easy, once you understand VBA. Without further ado, here's an example of a VBA function procedure. This function is stored in a VBA module, which is accessible from the VBE.

A custom function

This example function, named NumSign, uses one argument. The function returns a text string of Positive if its argument is greater than zero, Negative if the argument is less than zero, and Zero if the argument is equal to zero. The function is shown in Figure 43-1.

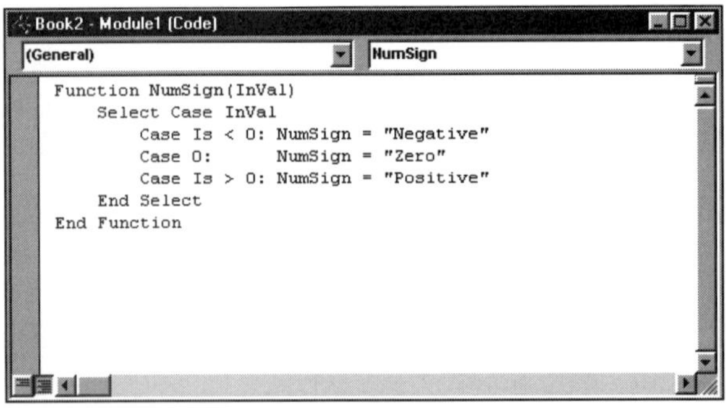

Figure 43-1: A custom function

You could, of course, accomplish the same effect with the following worksheet formula, which uses a nested IF function:

```
=IF(A1=0,"Zero",IF(A1>0,"Positive","Negative"))
```

Many would agree that the custom function solution is easier to understand and to edit than the worksheet formula.

Using the function in a worksheet

When you enter a formula that uses the NumSign function, Excel executes the function to get the result (see Figure 43-2). This custom function works just like any built-in worksheet function. You can insert it in a formula by using the Insert ➪ Function command, which displays the Paste Function dialog box (custom functions are located in the User Defined category). You also can nest custom functions and combine them with other elements in your formulas.

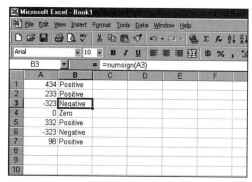

Figure 43-2: Using a custom function in a worksheet formula

Using the function in a VBA subroutine

The following VBA subroutine procedure, which is defined in the same module as the custom NumSign function, uses the built-in MsgBox function to display the result of the NumSign function:

```
Sub ShowSign()
  CellValue = ActiveCell.Value
  MsgBox NumSign(CellValue)
End Sub
```

In this example, the variable CellValue contains the value in the active cell (this variable could contain any value, not necessarily obtained from a cell). CellValue is then passed to the function as its argument. Figure 43-3 shows the result of executing the NumSign subroutine.

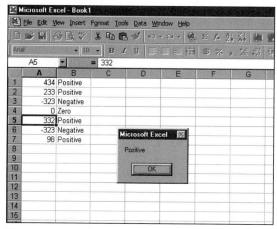

Figure 43-3: Using a custom function in a VBA subroutine

Analyzing the custom function

This section describes the NumSign function. Here again is the code:

```
Function NumSign(InVal)
  Select Case InVal
    Case Is < 0: NumSign = "Negative"
    Case 0:   NumSign = "Zero"
    Case Is > 0: NumSign = "Positive"
  End Select
End Function
```

Notice that the procedure starts with the keyword Function rather than Sub, followed by the name of the function (NumSign). This custom function uses one argument (InVal); the argument's name is enclosed in parentheses. InVal is the cell or variable that is to be processed. When the function is used in a worksheet, the argument can be a cell reference (such as A1) or a literal value (such as –123). When the function is used in another procedure, the argument can be a numeric variable, a literal number, or a value that is obtained from a cell.

The NumSign function uses the Select Case construct to take a different action, depending on the value of InVal. If InVal is less than zero, NumSign is assigned the text Negative. If InVal is equal to zero, NumSign is Zero. If InVal is greater than zero, NumSign is Positive. The value returned by a function is always assigned to the function's name.

The procedure ends with an End Function statement.

About Function Procedures

A custom function procedure has a lot in common with a subroutine procedure. Function procedures have some important differences, however, which are discussed in this section.

Declaring a function

The syntax for declaring a function is as follows:

```
[Public | Private][Static] Function name [(arglist)][As type]
  [statements]
  [name = expression]
  [Exit Function]
  [statements]
  [name = expression]
End Function
```

These elements are defined as follows:

✦ `Public`: Indicates that the function is accessible to all other procedures in all other modules in the workbook. (Optional)

✦ `Private`: Indicates that the function is accessible only to other procedures in the same module. `Private` functions can't be used in worksheet formulas and do not appear in the Paste Function dialog box. (Optional)

✦ `Static`: Indicates that the values of variables declared in the function are preserved between calls, rather than being reset. (Optional)

✦ `Function`: A keyword that indicates the beginning of a function procedure. (Required)

✦ `name`: Any valid variable name. When the function finishes, the single-value result is assigned to the function's name. (Required)

✦ `arglist`: A list (one or more) of variables that represent arguments passed to the function. The arguments are enclosed in parentheses. Use a comma to separate arguments. (Optional)

✦ `type`: The data type that is returned by the function. (Optional)

✦ `statements`: Valid VBA statements. (Optional)

✦ `Exit Function`: A statement that causes an immediate exit from the function. (Optional)

✦ `End Function`: A keyword that indicates the end of the function. (Required)

Keep in mind that a value is assigned to the function's name when a function is finished executing.

To create a custom function, follow these steps:

1. Activate the Visual Basic Editor (or press Alt+F11).

2. Select the workbook in the Project window.

3. Choose Insert ⇨ Module to insert a VBA module (or you can use an existing module).

4. Enter the keyword `Function` followed by the function's name and a list of the arguments (if any) in parentheses.

5. Insert the VBA code that performs the work—and make sure that the variable corresponding to the function's name has the appropriate value (this is the value that the function returns).

6. End the function with an `End Function` statement.

Function names must adhere to the same rules as variable names, and you can't use a name that looks like a worksheet cell (for example, a function named J21 isn't accepted).

What a Function Can't Do

Almost everyone who starts creating custom worksheet functions using VBA makes a fatal mistake: They try to get the function to do more than is possible.

A worksheet function returns a value, and it must be completely "passive." In other words, the function cannot change anything on the worksheet. For example, it's impossible to develop a worksheet function that changes the formatting of a cell (every VBA programmer has tried this, and not one of them has been successful!). If your function attempts to perform an action that is not allowed, the function simply returns an error.

VBA functions that are not used in worksheet formulas can do anything that a regular subroutine can do—including changing cell formatting.

Executing function procedures

Although many ways exist to execute a *subroutine* procedure, you can execute a *function* procedure in just two ways:

✦ Call it from another procedure

✦ Use it in a worksheet formula

Calling custom functions from a procedure

You can call custom functions from a procedure just as you call built-in VBA functions. For example, after you define a function called CalcTax, you can enter a statement such as the following:

```
Tax = CalcTax(Amount, Rate)
```

This statement executes the CalcTax custom function with Amount and Rate as its arguments. The function's result is assigned to the Tax variable.

Using custom functions in a worksheet formula

Using a custom function in a worksheet formula is like using built-in functions. You must ensure that Excel can locate the function procedure, however. If the function procedure is in the same workbook, you don't have to do anything special. If the function is defined in a different workbook, you may have to tell Excel where to find the function. The following are the three ways in which you can do this:

✦ **Precede the function's name with a file reference.** For example, if you want to use a function called CountNames that's defined in a workbook named MyFunctions, you can use a reference such as the following:

```
=MyFunctions.xls!CountNames(A1:A1000)
```

If you insert the function with the Paste Function dialog box, the workbook reference is inserted automatically.

✦ **Set up a reference to the workbook.** If the custom function is defined in a reference workbook, you don't need to precede the function name with the workbook name. You establish a reference to another workbook with the Tools ➪ References command (in the Visual Basic Editor). You are presented with a list of references that includes all open workbooks. Place a check mark in the item that refers to the workbook that contains the custom function (use the Browse button if the workbook isn't open).

✦ **Create an add-in.** When you create an add-in from a workbook that has function procedures, you don't need to use the file reference when you use one of the functions in a formula; the add-in must be installed, however. Chapter 48 discusses add-ins.

Note

If you plan on developing custom worksheet functions, make sure that you heed the warning in the sidebar, "What a Function Can't Do."

Your function procedures don't appear in the Macros dialog box when you select Tools ➪ Macro, because you can't execute a function directly. As a result, you need to do extra, up-front work to test your functions as you're developing them. One approach is to set up a simple subroutine that calls the function. If the function is designed to be used in worksheet formulas, you can enter a simple formula to test it as you're developing the function.

Function Procedure Arguments

Keep in mind the following about function procedure arguments:

✦ Arguments can be variables (including arrays), constants, literals, or expressions.

✦ Some functions do not have arguments.

✦ Some functions have a fixed number of required arguments (from 1 to 60).

✦ Some functions have a combination of required and optional arguments.

The following section presents a series of examples that demonstrate how to use arguments effectively with functions. Coverage of optional arguments is beyond the scope of this book.

Example: A function with no argument

Like subroutines, functions don't necessarily have to use arguments. Excel, for example, has a few built-in worksheet functions that don't use arguments. These include RAND, TODAY, and NOW.

The following is a simple example of a function that has no arguments. This function returns the `UserName` property of the Application object, which is the name that appears in the Options dialog box (General tab). This example is simple, but it can be useful, because no other way is available to get the user's name to appear in a worksheet formula.

```
Function User()
' Returns the name of the current user
    User = Application.UserName
End Function
```

When you enter the following formula into a worksheet cell, the cell displays the name of the current user:

```
=User()
```

As with Excel's built-in functions, when you use a function with no arguments, you must include a set of empty parentheses.

The following example is a simple subroutine that uses the `User` custom function as an argument for the `MsgBox` function. The concatenation operator (&) joins the literal string with the result of the `User` function.

```
Sub ShowUser()
    MsgBox ("The user is " & User())
End Sub
```

Example: A function with one argument

This section contains a more complex function that is designed for a sales manager who needs to calculate the commissions that are earned by the sales force. The commission rate is based on the amount sold — those who sell more earn a higher commission rate. The function returns the commission amount, based on the sales made (which is the function's only argument — a required argument). The calculations in this example are based on the following table:

Monthly Sales	Commission Rate
0–$9,999	8.0%
$10,000–$19,999	10.5%
$20,000–$39,999	12.0%
$40,000+	14.0%

Several ways exist to calculate commissions for various sales amounts that are entered into a worksheet. You could write a formula such as the following:

```
=IF(AND(A1>=0,A1<=9999.99),A1*0.08,IF(AND(A1>=10000,A1<=19999.9
9), A1*0.105
,IF(AND(A1>=20000,A1<=39999.99),A1*0.12,IF(A1>=40000,A1*0.14,0)
)))
```

This is not the best approach, for a couple of reasons. First, the formula is overly complex and difficult to understand. Second, the values are hard coded into the formula, making the formula difficult to modify if the commission structure changes.

A better approach is to use a lookup table function to compute the commissions; for example:

```
=VLOOKUP(A1,Table,2)*A1
```

Using the VLOOKUP function requires that you have a table of commission rates set up in your worksheet.

An even better approach is to create a custom function, such as the following:

```
Function Commission(Sales)
' Calculates sales commissions
  Tier1 = 0.08
  Tier2 = 0.105
  Tier3 = 0.12
  Tier4 = 0.14
  Select Case Sales
      Case 0 To 9999.99: Commission = Sales * Tier1
      Case 1000 To 19999.99: Commission = Sales * Tier2
      Case 20000 To 39999.99: Commission = Sales * Tier3
      Case Is >= 40000: Commission = Sales * Tier4
  End Select
End Function
```

After you define the Commission function in a VBA module, you can use it in a worksheet formula or call it from other VBA procedures.

Entering the following formula into a cell produces a result of 3,000 (the amount, 25,000, qualifies for a commission rate of 12 percent):

```
=Commission(25000)
```

Even if you don't need custom functions in a worksheet, creating function procedures can make your VBA coding much simpler. If your VBA procedure calculates sales commissions, for example, you can use the Commission function and call it from a VBA subroutine. The following is a tiny subroutine that asks the user for a sales amount and then uses the `Commission` function to calculate the commission due and to display it:

```
Sub CalcComm()
    Sales = InputBox("Enter Sales:")
    MsgBox "The commission is " & Commission(Sales)
End Sub
```

The subroutine starts by displaying an input box that asks for the sales amount. Then, the procedure displays a message box with the calculated sales commission for that amount. The `Commission` function must be available in the active workbook; otherwise, Excel displays a message saying that the function is not defined.

Example: A function with two arguments

This example builds on the previous one. Imagine that the sales manager implements a new policy: The total commission paid is increased by one percent for every year that the salesperson has been with the company. For this example, the custom `Commission` function (defined in the preceding section) has been modified so that it takes two arguments — both of which are required arguments. Call this new function `Commission2`:

```
Function Commission2(Sales, Years)
'   Calculates sales commissions based on years in service
    Tier1 = 0.08
    Tier2 = 0.105
    Tier3 = 0.12
    Tier4 = 0.14
    Select Case Sales
        Case 0 To 9999.99: Commission2 = Sales * Tier1
        Case 1000 To 19999.99: Commission2 = Sales * Tier2
        Case 20000 To 39999.99: Commission2 = Sales * Tier3
        Case Is >= 40000: Commission2 = Sales * Tier4
    End Select
    Commission2 = Commission2 + (Commission2 * Years / 100)
End Function
```

The modification was quite simple. The second argument (`Years`) was added to the `Function` statement and an additional computation was included that adjusts the commission, before exiting the function.

The following is an example of how you write a formula by using this function (it assumes that the sales amount is in cell A1, and the number of years that the salesperson has worked is in cell B1):

```
=Commission2(A1,B1)
```

Example: A function with a range argument

The example in this section demonstrates how to use a worksheet range as an argument. Actually, it's not at all tricky; Excel takes care of the details behind the scenes.

Assume that you want to calculate the average of the five largest values in a range named Data. Excel doesn't have a function that can do this, so you can write the following formula:

```
=(LARGE(Data,1)+LARGE(Data,2)+LARGE(Data,3)+LARGE(Data,4)+LARGE
(Data,5))/5
```

This formula uses Excel's LARGE function, which returns the nth largest value in a range. The preceding formula adds the five largest values in the range named Data and then divides the result by 5. The formula works fine, but it's rather unwieldy. And, what if you need to compute the average of the top *six* values? You would need to rewrite the formula — and make sure that all copies of the formula also get updated.

Wouldn't it be easier if Excel had a function named TopAvg? For example, you could use the following (nonexistent) function to compute the average:

```
=TopAvg(Data,5)
```

This is an example of when a custom function can make things much easier for you. The following is a custom VBA function, named TopAvg, which returns the average of the top n values in a range:

```
Function TopAvg(InRange, Num)
' Returns the average of the highest Num values in InRange
  Sum = 0
  For i = 1 To Num
    Sum = Sum + WorksheetFunction.Large(InRange, i)
  Next i
  TopAvg = Sum / Num
End Function
```

This function takes two arguments: InRange (which is a worksheet range) and Num (the number of values to average). The code starts by initializing the Sum variable to 0. It then uses a For-Next loop to calculate the sum of the nth largest values in the range. Note that Excel's LARGE function is used within the loop. You can use an Excel worksheet function in VBA if you precede the function with WorksheetFunction and a period. Finally, TopAvg is assigned the value of Sum divided by Num.

You can use all of Excel's worksheet functions in your VBA procedures, *except* those that have equivalents in VBA. For example, VBA has a Rnd function that returns a random number. Therefore, you can't use Excel's RAND function in a VBA procedure.

Debugging Custom Functions

Debugging a function procedure can be a bit more challenging than debugging a subroutine procedure. If you develop a function to use in worksheet formulas, an error in the function procedure simply results in an error display in the formula cell (usually #VALUE!). In other words, you don't receive the normal run-time error message that helps you to locate the offending statement.

When you are debugging a worksheet formula, using only one instance of the function in your worksheet is the best technique. The following are three methods that you may want to use in your debugging:

✦ **Place MsgBox functions at strategic locations to monitor the value of specific variables.** Fortunately, message boxes in function procedures pop up when the procedure is executed. But, make sure that you have only one formula in the worksheet that uses your function; otherwise, the message boxes appear for each formula that's evaluated.

✦ **Test the procedure by calling it from a subroutine procedure.** Run-time errors display normally, and you can either fix the problem (if you know what it is) or jump right into the debugger.

✦ **Set a breakpoint in the function and then use Excel's debugger to step through the function.** You then can access all the normal debugging tools.

Pasting Custom Functions

Excel's Paste Function dialog box is a handy tool that enables you to choose a worksheet function; you even can choose one of your custom worksheet functions. The Formula Palette prompts you for the function's arguments.

Function procedures that are defined with the Private keyword do not appear in the Paste Function dialog box.

You also can display a description of your custom function in the Paste Function dialog box. To do so, follow these steps:

1. Create the function in a module by using the VBE.
2. Activate Excel.

3. Choose the Tools ⇨ Macro ⇨ Macros command.

Excel displays its Macro dialog box (see Figure 43-4).

Figure 43-4: Excel's Macro dialog box doesn't list functions, so you must enter the function name yourself.

4. In the Macro dialog box, type the name of the function in the box labeled Macro Name. Notice that functions do not normally appear in this dialog box, so you must enter the function name yourself.

5. Click the Options button.

Excel displays its Macro Options dialog box. (See Figure 43-5.)

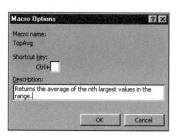

Figure 43-5: Entering a description for a custom function. This description appears in the Paste Function dialog box.

6. Enter a description of the function and then click OK. The Shortcut key field is irrelevant for functions.

The description that you enter appears in the Paste Function dialog box.

Custom functions are listed under the User Defined category, and no straightforward way exists to create a new function category for your custom functions.

Figure 43-6 shows the Paste Function dialog box, listing the custom functions that are in the User Defined category. In the second Function Wizard dialog box, the user is prompted to enter arguments for a custom function — just as in using a built-in worksheet function.

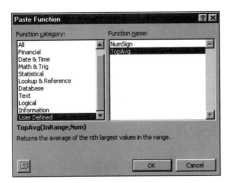

Figure 43-6: Using the Paste Function dialog box to insert a custom function

When you access a *built-in* function from the Paste Function dialog box, the Formula Palette displays a description of each argument. Unfortunately, you can't provide such descriptions for custom functions.

Learning More

The information in this chapter only scratches the surface when it comes to creating custom functions. It should be enough to get you started, however, if you're interested in this topic. You may be able to use the examples in this chapter directly or adapt them for your needs.

Summary

In this chapter, you read about how to create and use custom VBA functions. These functions can be used in worksheet formulas and in other VBA procedures. Several examples are provided.

✦　　✦　　✦

Introducing UserForms

Dialog boxes are, perhaps, the most important user inter-face element in Windows programs. Virtually every Windows program uses them. And most users understand how they work. Excel makes it relatively easy to create custom dialog boxes for your applications. In fact, you can duplicate the look and feel of all Excel's dialog boxes.

Tip   A spreadsheet application that you develop using Excel can consist of any number of elements, or user interface controls. If your application depends on user input, you'll probably want to design custom dialog boxes.

Beginning with Excel 97, things changed substantially with regard to custom dialog boxes. UserForms replaced the clunky old dialog sheets, and gave you much more control over your custom dialog boxes. However, for compatibility purposes, Excel 97 and Excel 2000 still support Excel 5/95 dialog sheets. The good news is that it's much easier to work with User-Forms, and they offer lots of new capabilities.

How Excel Handles Custom Dialog Boxes

A custom dialog box is created on a UserForm, and you access UserForms in the Visual Basic Editor.

Following is the typical sequence of steps you perform when you create a custom dialog box:

1. Insert a new UserForm into your workbook.

2. Write a procedure that displays the UserForm. This procedure is located in a VBA module — not in the code module for the UserForm.

3. Add controls to the UserForm.

4. Adjust some of the properties of the controls you added.

5. Write event-handler procedures for the controls. These procedures, which are located in the code window for the UserForm, are executed when various events (such as a button click) occur.

Inserting a New UserForm

To insert a new UserForm, activate the VBE (Alt+F11), select your workbook's project from the Project window, and select Insert ⇨ UserForm. UserForms have names like UserForm1, UserForm2, and so on.

 Tip   You can change the name of a UserForm to make it easier to identify. Select the form and use the Properties window to change the Name property (press F4 if the Properties window is not displayed). Figure 44-1 shows the Properties window when an empty UserForm is selected.

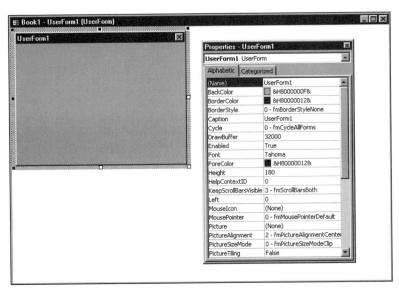

Figure 44-1: The Properties window for an empty UserForm

A workbook can have any number of UserForms, and each UserForm holds a single custom dialog box.

Displaying a UserForm

To display a UserForm, use the `Show` method of the UserForm object. The following procedure, which is contained in a normal VBA module, displays `UserForm1`.

```
Sub ShowForm
    UserForm1.Show
End Sub
```

When the UserForm is displayed, it remains visible onscreen until it is dismissed. Usually, you'll add a CommandButton to the UserForm that executes a procedure that dismisses the UserForm. The procedure can either unload the UserForm (with the `Unload` statement) or hide the UserForm (with the `Hide` method of the User-Form object). This concept becomes clearer later in the chapter.

Adding Controls to a UserForm

To add controls to a custom dialog box, use the Toolbox (the VBE does not have menu commands that add controls). If the Toolbox is not displayed, select View ➪ Toolbox. Figure 44-2 shows the Toolbox.

Figure 44-2: Use the Toolbox to add controls to a UserForm.

Just click the Toolbox button that corresponds to the control you want to add, and then click inside the dialog box. Or, you can click the control and then drag the mouse pointer in the dialog box to specify the dimensions for the control.

When you add a new control, it is assigned a name that combines the control type with the numeric sequence for that type of control. For example, if you add a CommandButton control to an empty dialog box, it is named `CommandButton1`. If you then add a second CommandButton it is named `CommandButton2`.

Tip

> It's a good idea to rename all the controls that you will be manipulating with your VBA code. Doing so enables you to refer to meaningful names (such as `ProductListBox`), rather than generic names such as `ListBox1`. To change the name of a control, use the Properties window in the VBA. Just select the object and enter a new name.

Controls Available to You

In the sections that follow, I briefly describe the controls available to you in the Toolbox.

 Your UserForms can also use other ActiveX controls. See "Customizing the Toolbox" later in this chapter.

CheckBox

A CheckBox control is useful for giving the user a binary choice: yes or no, true or false, on or off, and so on. When a CheckBox is checked, it has a value of True; when it's not checked, the CheckBox's value is False.

ComboBox

A ComboBox control is similar to a ListBox control. A ComboBox, however, is a drop-down box, and it displays only one item at a time. Another difference is that the user may be able to enter a value that does not appear in the given list of items.

CommandButton

Every dialog box that you create will probably have at least one CommandButton. Usually, you'll want to have one CommandButton labeled OK and another labeled Cancel.

Frame

A Frame control is used to enclose other controls. You do this either for aesthetic purposes or to logically group a set of controls. A frame is particularly useful when the dialog box contains more than one set of OptionButton controls.

Image

An Image control is used to display a graphic image, which can come from a file or can be pasted from the clipboard. You might want to use an Image control to display your company's logo in a dialog box. The graphics image is stored in the workbook. That way, if you distribute your workbook to someone else, it is not necessary to include a copy of the graphics file.

Caution   Some graphics files are very large, and using such images can make your work-book increase dramatically in size. For best results, use a file that's as small as possible.

Label

A Label control simply displays text in your dialog box.

ListBox

A ListBox control presents a list of items from which the user can select an item (or multiple items). ListBox controls are very flexible. For example, you can specify a worksheet range that holds the ListBox items, and this range can consist of multiple columns. Or you can fill the ListBox with items using VBA.

MultiPage

A MultiPage control enables you to create tabbed dialog boxes, such as the one that appears when you choose the Tools ➭ Options command. By default, a MultiPage control has two pages. To add additional pages, right-click a tab and select New Page from the shortcut menu.

OptionButton

OptionButtons are useful when the user needs to select from a small number of items. OptionButtons are always used in groups of at least two. When one OptionButton is selected, the other OptionButtons in its group are unselected.

If your dialog box contains more than one set of OptionButtons, each set of OptionButtons must have the same `GroupName` property value. Otherwise, all OptionButtons become part of the same set. Alternately, you can enclose the OptionButtons in a Frame control, which automatically groups the OptionButtons contained in the frame.

RefEdit

A RefEdit control is used when you need to enable the user to select a range in a worksheet.

ScrollBar

A ScrollBar control is similar to a SpinButton control. The difference is that the user can drag the ScrollBar's button to change the control's value in larger increments. The ScrollBar control is most useful for selecting a value that extends across a wide range of possible values.

SpinButton

A SpinButton control enables the user to select a value by clicking one of two arrows; one arrow increases the value and the other arrow decreases the value. A SpinButton is often used in conjunction with a TextBox control or a Label control, both of which display the current value of the SpinButton.

TabStrip

A TabStrip control is similar to a MultiPage control, but it's not as easy to use. In fact, I'm not sure why this control is even included, as the MultiPage control is much more versatile.

TextBox

A TextBox control enables the user to input text.

ToggleButton

A ToggleButton control has two states: on and off. Clicking the button toggles between these two states, and the button changes its appearance. Its value is either True (pressed) or False (not pressed). This is not exactly a "standard" control, and using two OptionButtons is often a better choice.

Using Controls on a Worksheet

Many of the UserForm controls can be embedded directly into a worksheet. These controls are accessible from the Control Toolbox toolbar in Excel (not VBE). Adding such controls to a worksheet requires much less effort than creating a dialog box. In addition, you may not have to create any macros, because you can link a control to a worksheet cell. For example, if you insert a CheckBox control on a worksheet, you can link it to a particular cell by setting its LinkedCell property. When the CheckBox is checked, the linked cell displays TRUE. When the CheckBox is unchecked, the linked cell displays FALSE.

The accompanying figure shows a worksheet that contains some embedded controls.

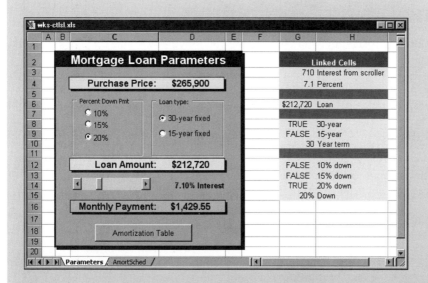

Adding controls to a worksheet can be a bit confusing because controls can come from either of two toolbars:

✦ **Forms toolbar.** These controls are insertable objects (and are compatible with Excel 5 and Excel 95).

✦ **Control Toolbox toolbar.** These are ActiveX controls. These controls are a subset of those that are available for use on UserForms. These controls work only with Excel 97 and Excel 2000, and are not compatible with Excel 5 and Excel 95.

You can use the controls from either of these toolbars, but it's important that you understand the distinctions between them. The controls from the Forms toolbar work much differently than the ActiveX controls.

When you add a control to a worksheet, Excel goes into *design mode.* In this mode, you can adjust the properties of any controls on your worksheet, add or edit event-handler procedures for the control, or change its size or position. To display the Properties window for an ActiveX control, right-click the control and select Properties from the shortcut menu.

For simple buttons, I often use the Button control on the Forms toolbar because it enables me to attach any macro to it. If I use a CommandButton control from the Control Toolbox, clicking it executes its event-handler procedure (for example, `CommandButton1_Click`) in the code module for the `Sheet` object — you can't attach just any macro to it.

When Excel is in design mode, you can't try out the controls. To test the controls, you must exit design mode by clicking the Exit Design Mode button on the Control Toolbox toolbar.

This workbook, plus another that demonstrates all worksheet controls, is available on the companion CD-ROM.

Adjusting Dialog Box Controls

After a control is placed in a dialog box, you can move and resize it using standard mouse techniques.

Tip   You can select multiple controls by Shift-clicking, or by clicking and dragging the pointer to "lasso" a group of controls.

A UserForm may contain vertical and horizontal grid lines which help you align the controls you add. When you add or move a control, it *snaps* to the grid to help you line up the controls. If you don't like to see these grid lines, you can turn them off by choosing Tools ➪ Options in the VBE. In the Options dialog box, select the General tab and set your desired options in the Form Grid Settings section.

The Format menu in the VBE window provides several commands to help you precisely align and space the controls in a dialog box. Before you use these commands, select the controls you want to work with. These commands work just as you would expect, so I don't explain them here. Figure 44-3 shows a dialog box with several OptionButton controls about to be aligned.

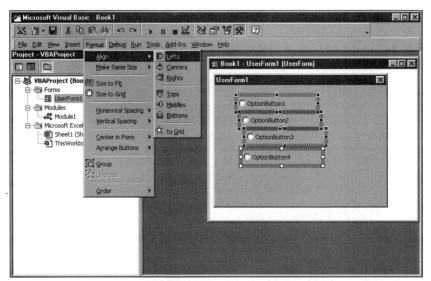

Figure 44-3: Using the Format ➪ Align command to change the alignment of controls

Tip   When you select multiple controls, the last control you select appears with white handles rather than the normal black handles. The control with the white handles is used as the model against which the other black-handle controls are compared for size or position.

Adjusting a Control's Properties

You can change a control's properties at *design time* with the Properties window while you're developing the dialog box or during *run time* when the dialog box is being displayed for the user. You use VBA instructions to change a control's properties at run time.

Using the Properties window

In the VBE, the Properties window adjusts to display the properties of the selected item, which can be a control or the UserForm itself. In addition, you can select a control using the drop-down list at the top of the Properties window (see Figure 44-4).

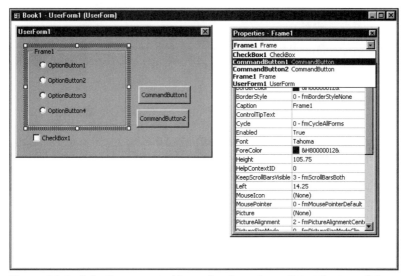

Figure 44-4: Selecting a control from the drop-down list at the top of the Properties window

The Properties window has two tabs. The Alphabetic tab displays the properties for the selected object in alphabetical order. The Categorized tab displays them grouped into logical categories. Both tabs contain the same properties, but in a different order.

To change a property, just click it and specify the new property. Some properties can take on a finite number of values, selectable from a list. If so, the Properties window displays a button with a downward-pointing arrow. Click the button and you'll be able to select the property's value from the list. For example, the TextAlign property can have any of the following values: 1 - fmTextAlignLeft, 2 - fmTextAlignCenter, or 3 - fmTextAlignRight.

A few properties (for example, Font and Picture) display a small button with an ellipsis when selected. Click the button to display a dialog box associated with the property.

The Image control's Picture property is worth mentioning because you can either select a graphic file that contains the image or paste an image from the clipboard. When pasting an image, first copy it to the clipboard, and then select the Picture property for the Image control and press Ctrl+V to paste the clipboard contents.

> **Note** If you select two or more controls at once, the Properties window displays only the properties that are common to the selected controls.

Common properties

Although each control has its own unique set of properties, many of those properties have the same name, and often share a common purpose. For example, every control has a Name property and properties that determine its size and position (Height, Width, Left, and Right).

If you're going to manipulate a control using VBA, you may prefer to provide a meaningful name for the control. For example, the first OptionButton that you add to a UserForm has a default name of OptionButton1. You refer to this object in your code using a statement such as

```
OptionButton1.Value = True
```

But if you give the OptionButton a more meaningful name (such as obLandscape), you can use a statement such as

```
obLandscape.Value = True
```

> **Tip** Many people find it helpful to use a name that also identifies the type of object. In the preceding example, I use *ob* as the prefix to identify the fact that this control is an OptionButton.

Learning more about properties

The best way to learn about the various properties for a control is to use the online help. Simply click a property in the Properties window and press F1. Figure 44-5 shows an example of the type of help provided for a property.

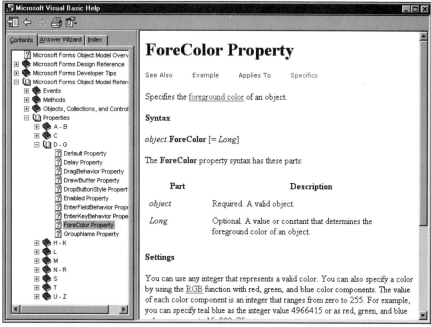

Figure 44-5: The online help provides information about each property for every control.

Accommodating keyboard users

Many users prefer to navigate through a dialog box using the keyboard. The Tab and Shift+Tab keystrokes cycle through the controls, and pressing a hot key operates the control. To make sure that your dialog box works properly for keyboard users, you must be mindful of two issues: tab order and accelerator keys.

Changing the tab order

The tab order determines the sequence in which the controls are activated when the user presses Tab or Shift+Tab. It also determines which control has the initial *focus*. If a user enters text into a TextBox control, for example, the TextBox has the focus. If the user clicks an OptionButton, the OptionButton has the focus. The control that's first in the tab order has the focus when a dialog box is first displayed.

To set the tab order of your controls, choose View ➪ Tab Order. You can also right-click the dialog box and choose Tab Order from the shortcut menu. In either case, Excel displays the Tab Order dialog box shown in Figure 44-6. The Tab Order dialog box lists all the controls, the sequence of which corresponds to the order in which controls pass the focus between each other in the UserForm. To move a control, select it and click the arrow keys up or down. You can choose more than one control (click while pressing Shift or Ctrl) and move them all at once.

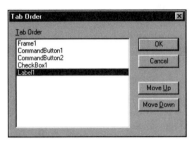

Figure 44-6: Use the Tab Order dialog box to specify the tab order of the controls.

Alternately, you can set an individual control's position in the tab order using the Properties window. The first control in the tab order has a TabIndex property of 0. Changing the TabIndex property for a control may also affect the TabIndex property of other controls. These adjustments are made automatically to ensure that no control has a TabIndex setting that is greater than the total number of controls in the UserForm. If you want to remove a control from the tab order, set its TabStop property to False.

Note Some controls, such as Frame and MultiPage, act as containers for other controls. The controls inside a container have their own tab order. To set the tab order for a group of OptionButtons inside a Frame control, select the Frame control before you choose the View ➪ Tab Order command.

Setting hot keys

You can assign an accelerator key, or *hot key*, to most dialog box controls. This enables the user to access the control by pressing Alt+the hot key. Use the Accelerator property in the Properties window for this purpose.

Tip Some controls, such as a TextBox, don't have an Accelerator property because they don't display a Caption. You still can enable direct keyboard access to these controls using a Label control. Assign an accelerator key to the Label, and put it ahead of the TextBox in the tab order.

Testing a UserForm

You can test a UserForm in three ways without actually calling it from a VBA procedure:

✦ Choose the Run ➪ Run Sub/UserForm command.

✦ Press F5.

✦ Click the Run Sub/UserForm button on the Standard toolbar.

These three techniques all trigger the UserForm's Initialize event. When a dialog box is displayed in this test mode, you can try out the tab order and the accelerator keys.

Manipulating UserForms with VBA

In this section I provide an overview of using VBA to work with custom dialog boxes.

Displaying a UserForm

To display a dialog box from VBA, you create a procedure that uses the Show method of the UserForm object. You cannot display a dialog box without using at least one line of VBA code. If your UserForm is named UserForm1, the following procedure displays the dialog box on that form:

```
Sub ShowDialog()
    UserForm1.Show
End Sub
```

This procedure must be located in a standard VBA module, not in the code module for the UserForm.

Note

VBA also has a Load statement. Loading a UserForm loads it into memory, but it is not visible until you use the Show method. To load a UserForm, use a statement like this:

```
Load UserForm1
```

If you have a complex UserForm, you might want to load it into memory before it is needed so it appears more quickly when you use the Show method. In the majority of situations, however, it's not necessary to use the Load statement.

Closing a UserForm

To close a UserForm, use the UnLoad statement. For example,

```
Unload UserForm1
```

Or, you can use the following:

```
Unload Me
```

Normally, your VBA code should include the Unload statement after the dialog box has performed its actions. For example, your dialog box may have a Command-Button that serves as an OK button. Clicking this button executes a macro. One of the statements in the macro unloads the UserForm. The UserForm remains visible on the screen until the macro that contains the Unload statement finishes.

When a UserForm is unloaded, its controls are reset to their original values. In other words, your code will not be able to access the user's choices after the

UserForm is unloaded. If the user's choice must be used later on (after the UserForm is unloaded), you need to store the value in a global variable.

A UserForm is automatically unloaded by default when the user clicks the close button (the big *X*) in the upper-right corner. No Unload statement is necessary for the UserForm to start unloading itself. With a CommandButton marked Cancel, it's generally convenient to have an event-handler procedure that contains the Unload statement, plus whatever other instructions are necessary to perform the business of the UserForm and clean up after itself. But the close button has no event of its own. So clicking the big *X* stops VBA execution of the UserForm module, and any cleanup instructions associated with the Cancel button are skipped over. The solution to this problem is to place your cleanup instructions within the UserForm_Terminate event hander. This way, both the Cancel button and the close button initiate the cleanup process. You can then keep your Unload statement within the _Click event handler for the Cancel button. You'll see more about event-handler procedures in just a few paragraphs.

 Cross-Reference The next chapter presents an example that effectively disables the close button.

UserForms also have a Hide method. When you invoke this method, the dialog box disappears, but it remains loaded in memory, so your code can still access the various properties of the controls. Here's an example of a statement that hides a UserForm:

```
UserForm1.Hide
```

Or, you can use the following:

```
Me.Hide
```

If for some reason you would like your UserForm to disappear immediately while its macro is executing, use the Hide method at the top of the procedure, and follow it with a DoEvents command. For example, in the following procedure, the UserForm disappears immediately when CommandButton1 is clicked. The last statement in the procedure unloads the UserForm.

```
Private Sub CommandButton1_Click()
    Me.Hide
    DoEvents
    For r = 1 To 10000
        Cells(r, 1) = r
    Next r
    Unload Me
End Sub
```

About event-handler procedures

In official terminology, when the user interacts with the dialog box by selecting an item from a ListBox, clicking a CommandButton, and so on, he causes an *event* to occur. For example, clicking a CommandButton raises the `Click` event for the CommandButton. Your application needs procedures that are executed when these events occur. These procedures are sometimes known as *event-handler* procedures.

Note   Event-handler procedures must be located in the code window for the UserForm. However, your event-handler procedure can call another procedure that's located in a standard VBA module.

Your VBA code can change the properties of the controls while the dialog box is displayed — that is, at run time. For example, you may assign to a ListBox control a procedure that changes the text in a Label when an item is selected. This type of manipulation becomes clearer later in this chapter.

Creating a UserForm: An Example

If you've never created a custom dialog box, you may want to walk through the example in this section. The example includes step-by-step instructions for creating a simple dialog box and developing a VBA procedure to support the dialog box.

This example uses a custom dialog box to get two pieces of information: a person's name and sex. The dialog box uses a TextBox control to get the name, and three OptionButtons to get the sex (Male, Female, or Unknown). The information collected in the dialog box is then sent to the next blank row in a worksheet.

Creating the dialog box

Figure 44-7 shows the finished custom dialog box for this example.

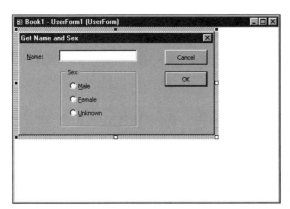

Figure 44-7: This dialog box asks the user to enter a name and a sex.

For best results, start with a new workbook with only one worksheet in it. Then follow these steps:

1. Press Alt+F11 to activate the VBE.

2. In the Project window, select the workbook's project, and choose Insert ⇨ UserForm to add an empty UserForm.

3. If the Properties window isn't visible, press F4.

4. Use the Properties window to change the UserForm's Caption property to **Get Name and Sex.**

5. Add a Label control and adjust the properties as follows:

Property	Value
Accelerator	N
Caption	Name:
TabIndex	0

6. Add a TextBox control and adjust the properties as follows:

Property	Value
Name	TextName
TabIndex	1

7. Add a Frame control and adjust the properties as follows:

Property	Value
Caption	Sex
TabIndex	2

8. Add an OptionButton control inside of the Frame and adjust the properties as follows:

Property	Value
Accelerator	M
Caption	Male
Name	OptionMale
TabIndex	0

9. Add another OptionButton control inside of the Frame and adjust the properties as follows:

Property	Value
Accelerator	F
Caption	Female
Name	OptionFemale
TabIndex	1

10. Add yet another Option Button control inside the Frame and adjust the properties as follows:

Property	Value
Accelerator	U
Caption	Unknown
Name	OptionUnknown
TabIndex	2
Value	True

11. Add a CommandButton control outside the frame and adjust the properties as follows:

Property	Value
Caption	OK
Default	True
Name	OKButton
TabIndex	3

12. Add another CommandButton control and adjust the properties as follows:

Property	Value
Caption	Cancel
Cancel	True
Name	CancelButton
TabIndex	4

Tip In some cases, you may find it easier to copy an existing control rather than create a new one. To copy a control, press Ctrl while you drag the control.

Writing code to display the dialog box

Next, you add a CommandButton to the worksheet. This button executes a procedure that displays the UserForm. Here's how:

1. Activate Excel.

2. Right-click any toolbar, and select Control Toolbox from the shortcut menu. Excel displays its Control Toolbox toolbar, which closely resembles the VBE Toolbox.

3. Use the Control Toolbox toolbar to add a CommandButton to the worksheet. Click the CommandButton tool, and then drag in the worksheet to create the button.

   If you like, you can change the caption for the worksheet CommandButton. To do so, right-click the button and select CommandButton Object ➪ Edit from the shortcut menu.

4. Double-click the button.

This activates the VBE — specifically, the code module for the worksheet is displayed, with an empty event-handler procedure for the worksheet's CommandButton.

5. Enter a single statement in the CommandButton1_Click procedure (see Figure 44-8). This short procedure uses the Show method of an object (UserForm1) to display the dialog box.

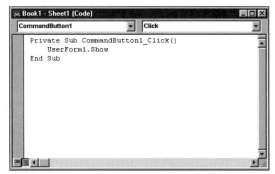

Figure 44-8: The CommandButton1_Click procedure is executed when the button is clicked.

Trying it out

The next step is to try out the procedure that displays the dialog box.

Note When you click the CommandButton on the worksheet, you'll find that nothing happens. Rather, the button is selected because Excel is still in design mode, which happens automatically when you enter a control using the Control Toolbox toolbar. To exit design mode, click the button labeled Exit Design Mode.

When you exit design mode, clicking the button displays the dialog box (see Figure 44-9).

When the dialog box is displayed, enter some text into one of the TextBoxes and click OK. You'll find that nothing happens — this is understandable because you haven't created any event-handler procedures yet.

Note Click the Close button in the dialog box's title bar to get rid of the dialog box.

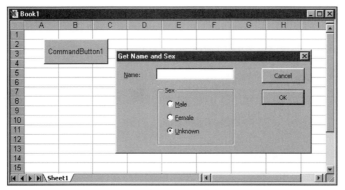

Figure 44-9: The CommandButton's Click event procedure displays the dialog box.

Adding event-handler procedures

In this section I explain how to write the procedures that handle the events that occur when the dialog box is displayed. To continue our example, do the following:

1. Press Alt+F11 to activate the VBE.

2. Make sure the UserForm is displayed, and double-click the Cancel button. The VBE activates the Code window for the UserForm, and provides an empty procedure named CancelButton_Click.

3. Modify the procedure as follows (this is the event handler for the CancelButton's Click event):

```
Private Sub CancelButton_Click()
    Unload UserForm1
End Sub
```

This procedure, which is executed when the user clicks the Cancel button, simply unloads the dialog box.

4. Press Shift+F7 to redisplay UserForm1.

5. Double-click the OK button and enter the following procedure (this is the event handler for the OKButton's Click event):

```
Private Sub OKButton_Click()
'    Make sure Sheet1 is active
     Sheets("Sheet1").Activate

'    Determine the next empty row
     NextRow = _
        Application.WorksheetFunction.CountA(Range("A:A")) + 1
'    Transfer the name
```

```
        Cells(NextRow, 1) = TextName.Text

'       Transfer the sex
        If OptionMale Then Cells(NextRow, 2) = "Male"
        If OptionFemale Then Cells(NextRow, 2) = "Female"
        If OptionUnknown Then Cells(NextRow, 2) = "Unknown"

'       Clear the controls for the next entry
        TextName.Text = ""
        OptionUnknown = True
        TextName.SetFocus
End Sub
```

6. Activate Excel and click the CommandButton again to display the UserForm.

You'll find that the dialog box controls now function correctly. Figure 44-10 shows how this looks in action.

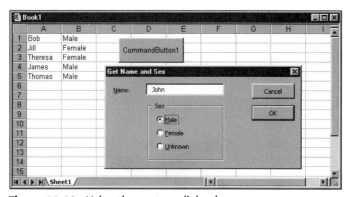

Figure 44-10: Using the custom dialog box

Here's how the OKButton_Click procedure works: First, the procedure makes sure that the proper worksheet (Sheet1) is active. It then uses Excel's COUNTA function to determine the next blank cell in column A. Here, column A is represented by the numeral 1 in the second parameter of the Cells collection; the first parameter refers to the row number. (Column B is later represented by the numeral 2 at the same position.) Next, the procedure transfers the text from the TextBox to column A. It then uses a series of If statements to determine which OptionButton was selected, and writes the appropriate text (Male, Female, or Unknown) to column B. Finally, the dialog box is reset to make it ready for the next entry. Notice that clicking OK doesn't close the dialog box. To end data entry and unload the UserForm, click the Cancel button.

Validating the data

Play around with this example some more, and you'll find that it has a small problem: It doesn't ensure that the user actually enters a name into the TextBox. The following code is inserted in the OKButton_Click procedure before the text is transferred to the worksheet. It ensures that the user enters a name (well, at least some text) in the TextBox. If the TextBox is empty, a message appears and the routine stops.

```
'   Make sure a name is entered
    If TextName.Text = "" Then
        MsgBox "You must enter a name."
        Exit Sub
    End If
```

Now it works

After making all these modifications, you'll find that the dialog box works flawlessly. In real life, you probably need to collect more information than just name and sex. However, the same basic principles apply. You just have to deal with more dialog box controls.

UserForm Events

Each UserForm control (as well as the UserForm itself) is designed to respond to certain types of events, and these events can be triggered by a user or by Excel. For example, clicking a button generates a CommandButton Click event. You can write code that is executed when a particular event occurs.

Some actions generate multiple events. For example, clicking the upward-pointing arrow of a SpinButton control generates a SpinUp event and also a Change event. When a UserForm is loaded using the Show method, Excel generates an Initialize event and an Activate event.

Cross-Reference

Excel also supports events associated with a Sheet object, a Chart object, and the ThisWorkbook object. I discuss these types of events in Chapter 46.

Learning about events

To find out which events are supported by a particular control, perform the following steps:

1. Add a control to a UserForm.

2. Double-click the control to activate the code module for the UserForm. The VBE inserts an empty event-handler procedure for the control.

3. Click the drop-down list in the upper-right corner of the module window, and you'll see a complete list of events for the control (see Figure 44-11).

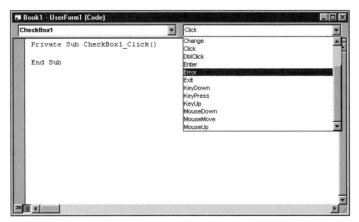

Figure 44-11: The event list for a CheckBox control

4. Select an event from the list, and the VBE creates an empty event-handler procedure for you.

Note To find out specific details about an event, consult the online help. The help system also lists the events available for each control.

Caution Event-handler procedures incorporate the name of the object in the procedure's name. Therefore, if you change the name of a control, you also need to make the appropriate changes to the control's event-handler procedure(s). The name changes are not performed automatically! To make things easy on yourself, it's a good idea to provide names for your controls before you begin creating event-handler procedures.

UserForm events

Several events are associated with showing and unloading a UserForm:

Initialize	Occurs before a UserForm is loaded or shown
Activate	Occurs when a UserForm is activated
Deactivate	Occurs when a UserForm is deactivated
QueryClose	Occurs before a UserForm is unloaded
Terminate	Occurs after the UserForm is unloaded

Note Often, it's critical that you choose the appropriate event for your event-handler procedure and that you understand the order in which the events occur. Using the Show method invokes the Initialize and Activate events (in that order). Using the Load command invokes only the Initialize event. Using the Unload command triggers the QueryClose and Terminate events (in that order). Using the Hide method doesn't trigger either of these events.

The companion CD-ROM contains a workbook that monitors all these events and displays a message box when an event occurs. If you're confused about UserForm events, studying the code in this example should clear things up.

Example: SpinButton events

To help clarify the concept of events, this section takes a close look at the events associated with a SpinButton control.

The companion CD-ROM contains a workbook that demonstrates the sequence of events that occur for a SpinButton and the UserForm that contains it. The workbook contains a series of event-handler procedures — one for each SpinButton and UserForm event. Each of these procedures simply displays a message box that tells you the event that just fired.

Table 44-1 lists all the events for the SpinButton control.

Table 44-1	
SpinButton Events	
Event	**Description**
AfterUpdate	Occurs after the control is changed through the user interface
BeforeDragOver	Occurs when a drag-and-drop operation is in progress
BeforeUpdate	Occurs before the control is changed
Change	Occurs when the Value property changes
Enter	Occurs before the control actually receives the focus from a control on the same UserForm
Error	Occurs when the control detects an error and cannot return the error information to a calling program
Exit	Occurs immediately before a control loses the focus to another control on the same form

Event	Description
KeyDown	Occurs when the user presses a key and the object has the focus
KeyPress	Occurs when the user presses any key that produces a typeable character
KeyUp	Occurs when the user releases a key and the object has the focus
SpinDown	Occurs when the user clicks the lower (or left) SpinButton arrow
SpinUp	Occurs when the user clicks the upper (or right) SpinButton arrow

A user can operate a SpinButton control by clicking it with the mouse, or (if the control has the focus) using the up-arrow or down-arrow keys.

Mouse-initiated events

When the user clicks the upper SpinButton arrow, the following events occur in this precise order:

1. Enter (triggered only if the SpinButton did not already have the focus)
2. Change
3. SpinUp

Keyboard-initiated events

The user can also press Tab to set the focus to the SpinButton, and then use the up-arrow key to increment the control. If so, the following events occur (in order):

1. Enter
2. KeyDown
3. Change
4. SpinUp

What about changes via code?

The SpinButton control can also be changed by VBA code, which also triggers the appropriate event(s). For example, the following instruction sets SpinButton1's Value property to zero, and also triggers the Change event for the SpinButton control.

```
SpinButton1.Value = 0
```

You might think that you could disable events by setting the EnableEvents property of the Application object to False. Unfortunately, this property applies only to events that involve true Excel objects: Workbooks, Worksheets, and Charts.

Pairing a SpinButton with a TextBox

A SpinButton has a Value property, but this control doesn't have a caption in which to display its value. In many cases, however, you will want the user to see the SpinButton's value. And sometimes you'll want the user to be able to change the SpinButton's value directly instead of clicking the SpinButton repeatedly.

The solution is to pair a SpinButton with a TextBox, which enables the user to specify a value by typing it into the TextBox directly, or by clicking the SpinButton to increment or decrement the value in the TextBox.

Figure 44-12 shows a simple example. The SpinButton's Min property is 1, and its Max property is 100. Therefore, clicking the SpinButton's arrows changes its Value property setting to an integer between 1 and 100.

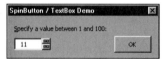

Figure 44-12: This SpinButton is paired with a TextBox.

This workbook is available on the companion CD-ROM.

The code required to "link" a SpinButton with a TextBox is relatively simple. It's basically a matter of writing event-handler procedures to ensure that the SpinButton's Value property is in sync with the TextBox's Text property.

The following procedure is executed whenever the SpinButton's Change event is triggered. That is, the procedure is executed when the user clicks the SpinButton, or changes its value by pressing the up arrow or the down arrow.

```
Private Sub SpinButton1_Change()
    TextBox1.Text = SpinButton1.Value
End Sub
```

The procedure simply assigns the SpinButton's Value to the Text property of the TextBox control. Here, the controls have their default names (SpinButton1 and TextBox1). If the user enters a value directly into the TextBox, its Change event is triggered and the following procedure is executed:

```
Private Sub TextBox1_Change()
    NewVal = Val(TextBox1.Text)
    If NewVal >= SpinButton1.Min And _
        NewVal <= SpinButton1.Max Then _
        SpinButton1.Value = NewVal
End Sub
```

This procedure starts by using VBA's Val function to convert the text in the TextBox to a value (if the TextBox contains a string, the Val function returns 0). The next statement determines if the value is within the proper range for the SpinButton. If so, the SpinButton's Value property is set to the value entered in the TextBox.

The example is set up so that clicking the OK button (which is named OKButton) transfers the SpinButton's value to the active cell. The event handler for this CommandButton's Click event is as follows:

```
Private Sub OKButton_Click()
'    Enter the value into the active cell
    If CStr(SpinButton1.Value) = TextBox1.Text Then
        ActiveCell = SpinButton1.Value
        Unload Me
    Else
        MsgBox "Invalid entry.", vbCritical
        TextBox1.SetFocus
        TextBox1.SelStart = 0
        TextBox1.SelLength = Len(TextBox1.Text)
    End If
End Sub
```

This procedure does one final check: It makes sure that the text entered in the TextBox matches the SpinButton's value. This is necessary in the case of an invalid entry. For example, should the user enter **3r** into the TextBox, the SpinButton's value would not be changed, and the result placed in the active cell would not be what the user intended. Notice that the SpinButton's Value property is converted to a string using the CStr function. This ensures that the comparison does not generate an error if a value is compared to text. If the SpinButton's value does not match the TextBox's contents, a message box is displayed. Notice that the focus is set to the TextBox object, and the contents are selected (using the SelStart and SelLength properties). This makes it very easy for the user to correct the entry.

About the Tag Property

Every UserForm and control has a Tag property. This property doesn't represent anything specific, and, by default, is empty. You can use the Tag property to store information for your own use.

For example, you may have a series of TextBox controls in a UserForm. The user may be required to enter text into some, but not all of them. You can use the Tag property to identify (for your own use) which fields are required. In this case, you can set the Tag property to a string such as **Required.** Then, when you write code to validate the user's entries, you can refer to the Tag property.

The following example is a function that examines all TextBox controls on UserForm1 and returns the number of "required" TextBox controls that are empty.

```
Function EmptyCount()
  EmptyCount= 0
  For Each ctl In UserForm1.Controls
    If TypeName(ctl) = "TextBox" Then
      If ctl.Tag = "Required" Then
        If ctl.Text = "" Then
            EmptyCount = EmptyCount + 1
        End If
      End If
    End If
  Next ctl
End Function
```

You can probably think of lots of other uses for the Tag property.

Referencing UserForm Controls

When working with controls on a UserForm, the VBA code is usually contained in the code window for the UserForm. You can also refer to dialog box controls from a general VBA module. To do so, you need to *qualify* the reference to the control by specifying the UserForm name. For example, consider the following procedure, which is located in a VBA module. It simply displays the UserForm named UserForm1.

```
Sub GetData()
    UserForm1.Show
End Sub
```

Assume that you wanted to provide a default value for the text box named TextName. You could modify the procedure as follows:

```
Sub GetData()
    UserForm1.TextName.Value = "John Doe"
    UserForm1.Show
End Sub
```

Another way to set the default value is to take advantage of the UserForm's Initialize event. You can write code in the UserForm_Initialize procedure, which is located in the code module for the UserForm. Here's an example:

```
Private Sub UserForm_Initialize()
    TextName.Value = "John Doe"
End Sub
```

Notice that when the control is referenced in the code module for the UserForm, no need exists to qualify the references with the UserForm name.

Understanding the Controls Collection

The controls on a UserForm compose a collection. For example, the following statement displays the number of controls on UserForm1:

```
MsgBox UserForm.Controls.Count
```

There is *not* a collection of each control type. For example, no collection of Command-Button controls exists. However, you can determine the type of control using the TypeName function. The following procedure uses a For Each-Next structure to loop through the Controls collection and then displays the number of CommandButton controls on UserForm1:

```
Sub CountButtons()
    cbCount = 0
    For Each ctl In UserForm1.Controls
        If TypeName(ctl) = "CommandButton" Then _
          cbCount = cbCount + 1
    Next ctl
    MsgBox cbCount
End Sub
```

Customizing the Toolbox

When a UserForm is active in the VBE, the Toolbox (see Figure 44-13) displays the controls that you can add to the UserForm. This section describes ways to customize the Toolbox.

Figure 44-13: The Toolbox contains the controls that you can add to a UserForm.

Changing icons or tip text

If you would prefer a different icon or different tip text for a particular tool, right-click the tool and select Customize *xxx* from the shortcut menu (where *xxx* is the control's name). This brings up a new dialog box that enables you to change the Tool Tip Text, edit the icon, or load a new icon image from a file.

Adding new pages

The Toolbox initially contains a single tab. Right-click this tab and select New Page to add a new tab to the Toolbox. You can also change the text displayed on the tab by selecting Rename from the shortcut menu.

Customizing or combining controls

A very handy feature enables you to customize a control and then save it for future use. You can, for instance, create a CommandButton control that's set up to serve an OK button. You can set the following properties: Width, Height, Caption, Default, and Name. Then, drag the customized CommandButton to the Toolbox. This creates a new control. Right-click the new control to rename it or change its icon.

You can also create a new Toolbox entry that consists of multiple controls. For example, you can create two CommandButtons that represent a UserForm's OK and Cancel buttons. Customize them as you want and then select them both and drag them to the Toolbox. In this case, you can use this new Toolbox control to add two customized buttons in one fell swoop.

This also works with controls that act as containers. For example, create a Frame control and add four customized OptionButtons, neatly spaced and aligned. Then drag the Frame to the Toolbox to create a customized Frame control.

Tip You might want to place your customized controls on a separate page in the Toolbox. This enables you to export the entire page so you can share it with other Excel users. To export a Toolbox page (so that it may be reloaded into a later instance of the Toolbox), right-click the tab and select Export Page.

On the CD-ROM The companion CD-ROM contains a PAG file that contains some customized controls. You can import this file as a new page in your Toolbox. Right-click a tab and select Import Page. Then locate the PAG file.

Adding new ActiveX controls

UserForms can use some other ActiveX controls developed by Microsoft or other vendors. To add an additional ActiveX control to the Toolbox, right-click the page of the Toolbox where you want the new controls to appear, and select Additional Controls. This displays the dialog box shown in Figure 44-14.

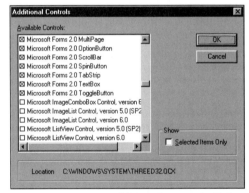

Figure 44-14: The Additional Controls dialog box enables you to add other ActiveX controls.

The Additional Controls dialog box lists all ActiveX controls that are installed on your system. Select the control(s) that you want to add, and then click OK to add an icon for each selected control.

Caution Not all ActiveX controls that are installed on your system will work in Excel UserForms. In fact, most of them probably won't work. Moreover, you need a license to use some controls in an application. If you aren't licensed to use a particular control, you'll receive an error message to that effect.

Emulating Excel's Dialog Boxes

The look and feel of Windows dialog boxes differ from program to program. When developing applications for Excel, it's best to try to mimic Excel's dialog box style whenever possible.

In fact, a good way to learn how to create effective dialog boxes is to try to copy one of Excel's dialog boxes down to the smallest detail. For example, make sure that you get all the hot keys defined and that the tab order is the same. To recreate one of Excel's dialog boxes, you need to test it under various circumstances and see how it behaves. I guarantee that your analysis of Excel's dialog boxes will improve your own dialog boxes.

Prior to Excel 97, it was impossible to duplicate some of Excel's dialog boxes. But the new capabilities introduced in Excel 97 enable you to duplicate virtually every one of them. An exception is the range selector control found (for example) in the Goal Seek dialog box. The RefEdit control, however, is a close substitute.

Creating UserForm "Templates"

You might find that when you design a new UserForm, you tend to add the same controls each time. For example, every UserForm might have two CommandButtons that serve as OK and Cancel buttons. In the previous section, I described how to create a new control that combines these two (customized) buttons into a single control. Another option is to create your UserForm "template" and then export it so it can be imported into other projects.

Start by creating a UserForm that contains all the controls and customizations that you would need to reuse in other projects. Then, make sure the UserForm is selected and choose File ➪ Export File (or press Ctrl+E). You are prompted for a filename. When you start your next project, select File ➪ Import File to load the saved UserForm.

A Dialog Box Checklist

Before you unleash a custom dialog box on end users, make sure that everything is working correctly. The following checklist should help you identify potential problems.

✦ Are similar controls the same size?

✦ Are the controls evenly spaced?

✦ Is the dialog box too overwhelming? If so, you may want to group the controls using a MultiPage control.

✦ Can every control be accessed with a hot key?

✦ Are any of the hot keys duplicated?

✦ Is the tab order set correctly?

✦ If the dialog box will be stored in an add-in, did you test it thoroughly after creating the add-in? It's important to remember that an add-in will never be the active workbook.

✦ Will your VBA code take appropriate action if the dialog box is canceled or the user presses Esc?

✦ Are there any misspellings in the text?

✦ Does the dialog box have an appropriate caption?

✦ Will the dialog box display properly at all video resolutions? Sometimes labels that display properly with a high-resolution display appear cut off in VGA display mode.

✦ Are the controls grouped logically (by function)?

✦ Do ScrollBar and SpinButton controls allow valid values only?

✦ Are ListBoxes set properly (Single, Multi, or Extended)?

Converting Dialog Sheets to UserForms

If you open an Excel 5/95 workbook that contains custom dialog boxes, they are displayed in dialog sheets in the workbook. Usually, it's not necessary to convert these dialog sheets to UserForms because Excel 97 and Excel 2000 both support dialog sheets.

Excel doesn't provide a way to convert a dialog sheet to a UserForm, but I developed a utility to do so. A copy of my DialogSheet-to-UserForm wizard is available on the companion CD-ROM. Note that this utility simply creates the UserForm. It's up to you to write the VBA code to make it function correctly.

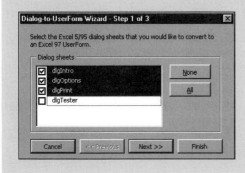

Custom Dialog Box Alternatives

In some cases, you can save yourself the trouble of creating a custom dialog box by using one of several prebuilt dialog boxes:

✦ An input box

✦ A message box

✦ A dialog box for selecting a file to open

✦ A dialog box for specifying a filename and location for a save operation

✦ A dialog box for specifying a directory (requires a Windows API call)

I describe these dialog boxes in the following sections.

Using an input box

Two InputBox functions actually exist: one from Excel and one from VBA.

VBA's InputBox function

The syntax for VBA's InputBox function is

```
InputBox(prompt[,title][,default][,xpos][,ypos][,helpfile,
context])
```

prompt	(Required) The text displayed in the input box
title	(Optional) The caption of the input box window
default	(Optional) The default value to be displayed in the dialog box
xpos, ypos	(Optional) The screen coordinates at the upper-left corner of the window
helpfile, context	(Optional) The help file and help topic

The InputBox function prompts the user for a single bit of information. The function always returns a string, so it may be necessary to convert the results to a value.

The prompt may consist of about 1,024 characters (more or less, depending on the width of the characters used). In addition, you can provide a title for the dialog box, a default value, and specify its position on the screen. You can also specify a custom help topic; if you do, the input box includes a Help button. The following example, whose output is shown in Figure 44-15, uses VBA's `InputBox` function to ask the user for his full name.

Figure 44-15: VBA's InputBox function at work

```
Sub GetName()
    Do Until UserName <> ""
        UserName = InputBox("Enter your full name: ", _
            "Identify Yourself")
    Loop
    FirstSpace = InStr(UserName, " ")
    If FirstSpace <> 0 Then
        UserName = Left(UserName, FirstSpace)
    End If
    MsgBox "Hello " & UserName
End Sub
```

Notice that this `InputBox` function is written in a `Do Until` loop to ensure that something is entered when the input box appears. If the user clicks Cancel or doesn't enter any text, UserName contains an empty string and the input box reappears. The procedure then attempts to extract the first name by searching for the first space character (using the `InStr` function), and then using the `Left` function to extract all characters before the first space. If a space character is not found, the entire name is used as entered.

As I mentioned, the `InputBox` function always returns a string. If the string returned by the `InputBox` function looks like a number, you can convert it to a value using VBA's `Val` function. Or, you can use Excel's `InputBox` method, which is described in the next section.

Excel's InputBox method

One advantage of using Excel's `InputBox` method rather than VBA's is that with Excel's you can specify the data type returned. In addition, the `InputBox` method enables the user to specify a worksheet range by dragging in the worksheet. The method's syntax is

```
object.InputBox(prompt,title,default,left,top,helpfile,context,
type)
```

prompt	(Required) The text displayed in the input box
title	(Optional) The caption in the input box window
default	(Optional) The default value to be returned by the function, if the user enters nothing
left, top	(Optional) The screen coordinates at the upper-left corner of the window
helpfile, context	(Optional) The help file and help topic
type	(Optional) A code for the data type returned, as listed in Table 44-2

Table 44-2
Codes to Determine the Data Type Returned by Excel's InputBox Method

Code	Meaning
0	A formula
1	A number
2	A string (text)
4	A logical value (True or False)
8	A cell reference, as a Range object
16	An error value, such as #N/A
64	An array of values

To specify more than one data type to be returned, use the sum of the pertinent codes. For example, to display an input box that can accept text or numbers, set type equal to 3 (that is, 1 + 2, or "number" plus "text").

Excel's InputBox method is quite versatile. For example, if you use 8 for the type argument, the user can point to a range in the worksheet. In the following code, the InputBox method returns a Range object (note the Set keyword) and then clears the values from the selected cells. The default value displayed in the input box is the current selection's address. The On Error statement ends the procedure if the input box is canceled.

```
Sub GetRange()
    Dim UserRange As Range
    Default = Selection.Address
```

```
    On Error GoTo Canceled
    Set UserRange = Application.InputBox _
        (Prompt:="Range to erase:", _
        Title:="Range Erase", _
        Default:=Default, _
        Type:=8)
    UserRange.Clear
    UserRange.Select
Canceled:
End Sub
```

Yet another advantage of using Excel's InputBox method instead of VBA's is that Excel performs input validation automatically. In the GetRange example, if you enter something other than a range address, Excel displays an informative message and enables the user to try again.

VBA's MsgBox function

I use VBA's MsgBox function in many of this book's examples as an easy way to display a variable's value. The official syntax for MsgBox is as follows:

```
MsgBox(prompt[,buttons][,title][,helpfile, context])
```

prompt	(Required) The text displayed in the message box
buttons	(Optional) A numeric expression that determines which buttons and icon is displayed in the message box (see Table 44-3)
title	(Optional) The caption in the message box window
helpfile, context	(Optional) The help file and help topic

You can easily customize your message boxes because of the flexibility of the *buttons* argument. (Table 44-3 lists the many constants that you can use for this argument.) You can specify which buttons to display, whether an icon appears, and which button is the default.

Table 44-3
Constants Used for Buttons in the MsgBox Function

Constant	Value	Description
VbOKOnly	0	Display OK button only
VbOKCancel	1	Display OK and Cancel buttons
VbAbortRetryIgnore	2	Display Abort, Retry, and Ignore buttons

Continued

Table 44-3 *(continued)*		
Constant	**Value**	**Description**
VbYesNoCancel	3	Display Yes, No, and Cancel buttons
VbYesNo	4	Display Yes and No buttons
VbRetryCancel	5	Display Retry and Cancel buttons
VbCritical	16	Display Critical Message icon
VbQuestion	32	Display Warning Query icon
VbExclamation	48	Display Warning Message icon
VbInformation	64	Display Information Message icon
VbDefaultButton1	0	First button is default
VbDefaultButton2	256	Second button is default
VbDefaultButton3	512	Third button is default
VbDefaultButton4	768	Fourth button is default
VbSystemModal	4096	All applications are suspended until the user responds to the message box (may not work under all conditions)

You can use the MsgBox function by itself (to simply display a message) or assign its result to a variable. When MsgBox does return a result, it represents the button clicked by the user. The following example displays a message and does not return a result:

```
Sub MsgBoxDemo()
    MsgBox "Click OK to continue"
End Sub
```

To get a response from a message box, you can assign the results of the MsgBox function to a variable. In the following code, I use some built-in constants (described in Table 44-3) to make it easier to work with the values returned by MsgBox:

```
Sub GetAnswer()
    Ans = MsgBox("Continue?", vbYesNo)
    Select Case Ans
        Case vbYes
'           ...[code if Ans is Yes]...
        Case vbNo
'           ...[code if Ans is No]...
    End Select
End Sub
```

Actually, it's not even necessary to use a variable to use the result of a message box. The following procedure displays a message box with Yes and No buttons. If the user doesn't click the Yes button, the procedure ends.

```
Sub GetAnswer2()
    If MsgBox("Continue?", vbYesNo) <> vbYes Then Exit Sub
'   ...[code if Yes button is not clicked]...
End Sub
```

The following function example uses a combination of constants to display a message box with a Yes button, a No button, and a question mark icon. The second button is designated as the default button (see Figure 44-16). For simplicity, I assigned these constants to the Config variable.

Figure 44-16: The buttons argument of the MsgBox function determines which buttons appear.

```
Function ContinueProcedure() as Boolean
    Config = vbYesNo + vbQuestion + vbDefaultButton2
    Ans = MsgBox("An error occurred. Continue?", Config)
    If Ans = vbYes Then ContinueProcedure = True _
        Else ContinueProcedure = False
End Function
```

If you would like to force a line break in the message, use the vbCrLf constant in the text. The following example displays the message in three lines:

```
Sub MultiLine()
    Msg = "This is the first line" & vbCrLf
    Msg = Msg & "Second line" & vbCrLf
    Msg = Msg & "Last line"
    MsgBox Msg
End Sub
```

Excel's GetOpenFilename method

If your application needs to ask the user for a filename, you can use the InputBox function. But this approach often leads to typographical errors. A better approach is to use the GetOpenFilename method of the Application object, which ensures that your application gets a valid filename as well as its complete path.

The GetOpenFilename method displays the normal Open dialog box (displayed when you select the File ➪ Open command), but does not actually open the file specified. Rather, the method returns a string that contains the path and filename selected by the user. Then you can do whatever you want with the filename. The syntax for this method is as follows (all arguments are optional):

```
object.GetOpenFilename(FileFilter, FilterIndex, Title,
ButtonText, MultiSelect)
```

The *FileFilter* argument determines what appears in the dialog box's Files of type drop-down list. The argument consists of pairs of file filter strings followed by the wildcard file filter specification, with each part and each pair separated by commas. If omitted, this argument defaults to the following:

```
"User (*.*),*.*"
```

Notice that the first part of this string (User (*.*)) is the text displayed in the Files of type drop-down list. The second part (*.*) actually determines which files are displayed.

The *FilterIndex* argument specifies which FileFilter is the default, and the title argument is text that is displayed in the title bar. If the *MultiSelect* argument is True, the user can select multiple files, all of which are returned in an array. The *ButtonText* argument is not used in Excel for Windows.

The following instruction assigns a string to a variable named Filt. This string can then be used as a FileFilter argument for the GetOpenFilename method. In this case, the dialog box enables the user to select from four different file types, plus an "all files" option.

```
Filt = "Text Files (*.txt),*.txt," & _
       "Lotus Files (*.prn),*.prn," & _
       "Comma Separated Files (*.csv),*.csv," & _
       "ASCII Files (*.asc),*.asc," & _
       "All Files (*.*),*.*"
```

The following example prompts the user for a filename. It defines five file filters. Notice that I used VBA's line continuation sequence to set up the Filter variable; doing so makes it much easier to work with this rather complicated argument.

```
Sub GetImportFileName()
'   Set up list of file filters
    Filt = "Text Files (*.txt),*.txt," & _
           "Lotus Files (*.prn),*.prn," & _
           "Comma Separated Files (*.csv),*.csv," & _
           "ASCII Files (*.asc),*.asc," & _
           "All Files (*.*),*.*"

'   Display *.* by default
    FilterIndex = 5
```

```
'    Set the dialog box caption
     Title = "Select a File to Import"

'    Get the file name
     FileName = Application.GetOpenFilename _
         (FileFilter:=Filt, _
          FilterIndex:=FilterIndex, _
          Title:=Title)

'    Exit if dialog box canceled
     If FileName = False Then
         MsgBox "No file was selected."
         Exit Sub
     End If

'    Display full path and name of the file
     MsgBox "You selected " & FileName
End Sub
```

Figure 44-17 shows the dialog box that appears when this procedure is executed.

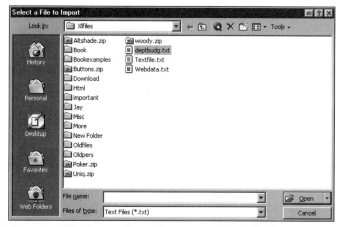

Figure 44-17: The GetOpenFilename method displays a customizable dialog box.

The following example is similar to the previous example. The difference is that the user can press Ctrl or Shift and select multiple files when the dialog box is displayed. Notice that I check for the Cancel button click by determining if `FileName` is an array. If the user doesn't click Cancel, the result is an array that consists of at least one element. In this example, a list of the selected files is displayed in a message box.

```
Sub GetImportFileName2()
'   Set up list of file filters
    Filt = "Text Files (*.txt),*.txt," & _
           "Lotus Files (*.prn),*.prn," & _
           "Comma Separated Files (*.csv),*.csv," & _
           "ASCII Files (*.asc),*.asc," & _
           "All Files (*.*),*.*"

'   Display *.* by default
    FilterIndex = 5

'   Set the dialog box caption
    Title = "Select a File to Import"

'   Get the file name
    FileName = Application.GetOpenFilename _
        (FileFilter:=Filt, _
         FilterIndex:=FilterIndex, _
         Title:=Title, _
         MultiSelect:=True)

'   Exit if dialog box canceled
    If Not IsArray(FileName) Then
        MsgBox "No file was selected."
        Exit Sub
    End If

'   Display full path and name of the files
    For i = LBound(FileName) To UBound(FileName)
        Msg = Msg & FileName(i) & vbCrLf
    Next i
    MsgBox "You selected:" & vbCrLf & Msg
End Sub
```

Excel's GetSaveAsFilename method

Like the GetOpenFilename method, Excel's GetSaveAsFilename method returns a filename and path but doesn't take any action. The syntax for this method is

```
object.GetSaveAsFilename(InitialFilename, FileFilter,
FilterIndex, Title, ButtonText)
```

All the arguments are optional.

Prompting for a directory

If you need to get a filename, use the GetOpenFileName method, as described previously. But if you need to get only a directory name, you'll find that you have no direct way to do so. However, you can use a Windows API call to display a dialog box that returns a drive and directory name.

In this section I present a function named GetDirectory that displays the dialog box shown in Figure 44-18, and returns a string that represents the selected directory. If the user clicks Cancel, the function returns an empty string.

Figure 44-18: Use an API function to display this dialog box.

The GetDirectory function takes one argument, which is optional. This argument is a string that will be displayed in the dialog box. If the argument is omitted, the dialog box displays Select a folder as the message.

On the CD-ROM The companion CD-ROM contains a workbook that demonstrates this procedure.

Following are the API declarations required at the beginning of the workbook module. This function also uses a custom data type, called BROWSEINFO.

```
'32-bit API declarations
Declare Function SHGetPathFromIDList Lib "shell32.dll" _
    Alias "SHGetPathFromIDListA" (ByVal pidl As Long, ByVal _
    pszPath As String) As Long

Declare Function SHBrowseForFolder Lib "shell32.dll" _
    Alias "SHBrowseForFolderA" (lpBrowseInfo As BROWSEINFO) _
    As Long

Public Type BROWSEINFO
    hOwner As Long
    pidlRoot As Long
    pszDisplayName As String
    lpszTitle As String
```

```
        ulFlags As Long
        lpfn As Long
        lParam As Long
        iImage As Long
    End Type
```

The `GetDirectory` function is as follows:

```
Function GetDirectory(Optional Msg) As String
    Dim bInfo As BROWSEINFO
    Dim path As String
    Dim r As Long, x As Long, pos As Integer

'   Root folder = Desktop
    bInfo.pidlRoot = 0&

'   Title in the dialog
    If IsMissing(Msg) Then
        bInfo.lpszTitle = "Select a folder."
    Else
        bInfo.lpszTitle = Msg
    End If

'   Type of directory to return
    bInfo.ulFlags = &H1

'   Display the dialog
    x = SHBrowseForFolder(bInfo)

'   Parse the result
    path = Space$(512)
    r = SHGetPathFromIDList(ByVal x, ByVal path)
    If r Then
        pos = InStr(path, Chr$(0))
        GetDirectory = Left(path, pos - 1)
    Else
        GetDirectory = ""
    End If
End Function
```

The following simple procedure demonstrates how to use the `GetDirectory` function in your code. Executing this procedure displays the dialog box. When the user clicks OK or Cancel, the `MsgBox` function displays the full path of the selected directory.

```
Sub GetAFolder()
    Dim Msg As String
    Msg = "Please select a location for the backup."
    MsgBox GetDirectory(Msg)
End Sub
```

Displaying Excel's Built-In Dialog Boxes

Code that you write in VBA can execute Excel's menu commands. And, if the command leads to a dialog box, your code can "make choices" in the dialog box — although the dialog box itself isn't displayed. For example, the following statement is equivalent to selecting the Edit ⇨ Go To command, specifying a range named InputRange, and clicking OK. However, the Go To dialog box never appears.

```
Application.Goto Reference:="InputRange"
```

In some cases, however, you may *want* to display one of Excel's built-in dialog boxes so the end user can make the choices. This is easy to do, using the Dialogs method of the Application object. Here's an example:

```
Result = Application.Dialogs(xlDialogFormulaGoto).Show
```

This statement, when executed, displays the GoTo dialog box (xlDialogFormula Goto is a predefined constant). The user can specify a named range or enter a cell address to go to. This dialog box works exactly as it does when you choose the Edit ⇨ Go To command (or press F5).

Note   Contrary to what you might think, the Result variable does not hold the range that is selected. Rather, the value assigned to Result is True if the user clicked OK, and False if the user clicked Cancel or pressed Esc.

You can get a list of all the dialog box constants using the Object Browser. Follow these steps:

1. In a VBA module, press F2 to bring up the Object Browser.

2. In the Object Browser dialog box, select Excel from the top list.

3. Type **xlDialog** in the second list.

4. Click the binoculars button.

Caution   Attempting to display a built-in dialog box in an incorrect context results in an error. For example, if you select a series in a chart and then attempt to display the xlDialogFormatFont dialog box, you'll get an error message because that dialog box is not appropriate for that selection.

On the CD-ROM   The companion CD-ROM contains a workbook with a looping macro that displays every possible built-in dialog box that can be displayed when a worksheet is active.

Most of the built-in dialog boxes also accept arguments, which correspond to the controls on the dialog box. You can specify arguments that correspond to the defaults for the dialog box. For example, the `xlDialogCellProtection` dialog box uses two arguments: locked and hidden. If you want to display that dialog box with both of these options checked, use the following statement:

```
Application.Dialogs(xlDialogCellProtection).Show True, True
```

Note   Normally, the dialog box used to protect cells is one "tab" in the Format Cells dialog box. If you use the preceding statement, however, the Protection tab appears in its own dialog box with no other tabs.

Tip   The arguments for each of the built-in dialog boxes are listed in the online help. To locate the help topic, search for *Built-In Dialog Box Argument Lists.*

Summary

In this chapter, I introduced you to custom dialog boxes and provided an overview of the controls you can use in your dialog boxes. I also presented several examples, illustrating how to create custom dialog boxes and use them with VBA.

In the next chapter, I offer many more examples of VBA procedures and dialog boxes.

✦   ✦   ✦

UserForm Techniques

This chapter presents lots of useful and informative examples that introduce you to some additional techniques that involve UserForms. You may be able to adapt these techniques to your own work. All the examples are available on the CD-ROM that accompanies this book.

Creating a Dialog Box "Menu"

Sometimes, you may want to use a dialog box as a type of menu. For example, you can present a dialog box that contains a number of buttons. Clicking a button executes a macro. Or you can use a ListBox to hold your "menu" items.

Figure 45-1 shows an example of a dialog box that uses CommandButton controls as a simple menu. Figure 45-2 shows another example that uses a ListBox as a menu.

Figure 45-1: This dialog box uses CommandButtons as a menu.

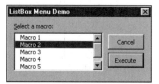

Figure 45-2: This dialog box uses a ListBox as a menu.

Setting up this sort of thing is easy, and the code behind these UserForms is very straightforward. For the CommandButton menu, each CommandButton has its own event-handler procedure. For example, the following procedure is executed when CommandButton1 is clicked:

```
Private Sub CommandButton1_Click()
    Call Macro1
    Unload Me
End Sub
```

This procedure simply calls Macro1 and closes the UserForm. The other buttons have similar event-handler procedures.

Cross-Reference

Excel, of course, also enables you to create "real" menus and toolbars. Refer to Chapters 49 and 50 for details.

Selecting Ranges

Several of Excel's built-in dialog boxes enable the user to specify a range by pointing and clicking in a sheet. For example, the Goal Seek dialog box asks the user to select two ranges.

Your custom dialog boxes can also provide this type of functionality, thanks to the RefEdit control. The RefEdit control doesn't look exactly like the range selection control used in Excel's built-in dialog boxes, but it works the same. If the user clicks the small button on the right side of the control, the dialog box disappears temporarily and a small range selector is displayed — this is exactly what happens with Excel's built-in dialog boxes.

Figure 45-3 shows a custom dialog box that contains a RefEdit control. This dialog box performs a simple mathematical operation on all nonformula (and nonempty) cells in the selected range.

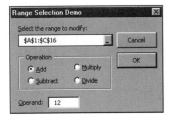

Figure 45-3: The RefEdit control here enables the user to select a range.

Following are a few things to keep in mind when using a RefEdit control:

◆ The RefEdit control returns a text string that represents a range address. You can convert this string to a `Range` object using a statement such as this:

```
Set UserRange = Range(RefEdit1.Text)
```

◆ It's a good practice to initialize the RefEdit control to display the current range selection. You can do so in the `UserForm_Initialize` procedure using a statement such as this:

```
RefEdit1.Text = ActiveWindow.RangeSelection.Address
```

◆ Don't assume that RefEdit will always return a valid range address. Pointing to a range isn't the only way get text into this control. The user can type any text, and edit or delete the displayed text. Therefore, you need to make sure the range is valid. The following code snippet is an example of a way to check for a valid range:

```
On Error Resume Next
Set UserRange = Range(RefEdit1.Text)
If Err <> 0 Then
    MsgBox "Invalid range selected"
    RefEdit1.SetFocus
    On Error GoTo 0
    Exit Sub
End If
```

◆ The user can also click the worksheet tabs while selecting a range with the RefEdit control. Therefore, you can't assume that the selection is on the active sheet. However, if a different sheet is selected, the range address is preceded by a sheet name. For example,

```
Sheet2!$A$1:$C:4
```

◆ If you need to get a single cell selection from the user, you can pick out the upper-left cell of a selected range by using a statement such as this:

```
Set OneCell = Range(RefEdit1.Text).Range("A1")
```

Cross-Reference

As I discussed in Chapter 44, you can also use VBA's `InputBox` function to enable the user to select a range.

Creating a Splash Screen

Some developers like to display some introductory information when the application is opened. This is commonly known as a *splash screen*. You are undoubtedly familiar with Excel's splash screen, which appears for a few seconds as Excel is loading. You can create a splash screen for your Excel application with a UserForm. Follow these instructions to create a splash screen for your project:

1. Create your workbook.

2. Activate the Visual Basic Editor and insert a new UserForm into the project. The code in this example assumes this form is named `UserForm1`.

3. Place any controls you like on `UserForm1`. For example, you may want to insert an Image control that has your company's logo. Figure 45-4 shows an example.

Figure 45-4: This splash screen is displayed briefly when the workbook is opened.

4. Insert the following procedure into the code module for the `ThisWorkbook` object:

```
Private Sub Workbook_Open()
    UserForm1.Show
End Sub
```

5. Insert the following procedure into the code module for `UserForm1` (this assumes a five-second delay):

```
Private Sub UserForm_Activate()
    Application.OnTime Now + _
      TimeValue("00:00:05"), "KillTheForm"
End Sub
```

6. Insert the following procedure into a general VBA module:

```
Private Sub KillTheForm()
    Unload UserForm1
End Sub
```

When the workbook is opened, the `Workbook_Open` procedure is executed. This procedure displays the UserForm. At that time, its `Activate` event occurs, which triggers the `UserForm_Activate` procedure. This procedure uses the `OnTime` method of the `Application` object to execute a procedure named `KillTheForm` at a particular time. In this case, the time is five seconds from the current time. The `KillTheForm` procedure simply unloads the UserForm.

7. As an option, you can add a small CommandButton named `CancelButton`, set its `Cancel` property to True, and insert the following event-handler procedure in the UserForm's code module:

```
Private Sub CancelButton_Click()
    KillTheForm
End Sub
```

Doing so enables the user to cancel the splash screen before the time has expired by pressing Esc. You can stash this small button behind another object so it won't be visible.

Caution

Keep in mind that the splash screen is not displayed until the workbook is entirely loaded. In other words, if you would like to display the splash screen to give the user something to look at while the workbook is loading, this technique won't fill the bill.

Disabling a UserForm's Close Button

When a UserForm is displayed, clicking the close button (the *X* in the upper-right corner) unloads the form. You might have a situation in which you don't want this to happen. For example, you may require that the UserForm be closed only by clicking a particular CommandButton.

Although you can't physically disable the close button, you can prevent the user from closing a UserForm by clicking it. You can do this by monitoring the UserForm's `QueryClose` event.

The procedure that follows, which is located in the code module for the UserForm, is executed before the form is closed (that is, when the `QueryClose` event occurs).

```
    Private Sub UserForm_QueryClose _
      (Cancel As Integer, CloseMode As Integer)
        If CloseMode = vbFormControlMenu Then
            MsgBox "Click the OK button to close the form."
            Cancel = True
        End If
    End Sub
```

The `UserForm_QueryClose` procedure uses two arguments. The `CloseMode` argument contains a value that indicates the cause of the `QueryClose` event. If `CloseMode` is equal to `vbFormControlMenu` (a built-in constant), that means the user clicked the close button. In such a case a message is displayed, the `Cancel` argument is set to True, and the form is not actually closed.

Changing a Dialog Box's Size

Many applications use dialog boxes that change their own size. For example, Excel's AutoFormat dialog box (displayed when you select Format ⟿ AutoFormat) increases its height when the user clicks the Options button.

The example in this section demonstrates how to get a custom dialog box to change its size dynamically. Changing a dialog box's size is done by altering the Width or Height property of the UserForm object.

Figure 45-5 shows the dialog box as it is first displayed, and Figure 45-6 shows it after the user clicks the Options button. Notice that the button's caption changes, depending on the size of the UserForm.

Figure 45-5: A sample dialog box in its standard mode

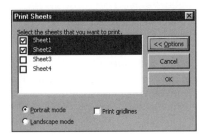

Figure 45-6: The same dialog box enlarged to show some options

On the CD-ROM   This workbook is available on the companion CD-ROM.

As you're creating the UserForm, set it to its largest size to enable you to work with the controls. Then use the UserForm_Initialize procedure to set it to its default size.

This example displays a list of worksheets in the active workbook, and enables the user to select which sheets to print. Following is the event handler that's executed when the CommandButton named `OptionsButton` is clicked:

```
Private Sub OptionsButton_Click()
    If OptionsButton.Caption = "Options >" Then
        UserForm1.Height = 164
        OptionsButton.Caption = "<< Options"
    Else
        UserForm1.Height = 128
        OptionsButton.Caption = "Options >"
    End If
End Sub
```

This procedure examines the `Caption` of the CommandButton, and sets the UserForm's `Height` property accordingly.

Note   When controls are not displayed because they are outside of the visible portion of the UserForm, the accelerator keys for such controls continue to function. In the example on the CD-ROM, the user can press the Alt+L hot key (to select the Landscape mode option) even if that option is not visible. To block access to nondisplayed controls, you can write code to disable the controls when they are not displayed.

Zooming and Scrolling a Sheet from a UserForm

When you display a dialog box, it's often helpful if the user can scroll through the worksheet to examine various ranges. Normally, this is impossible while a dialog box is displayed.

The example in this section demonstrates how to use ScrollBar controls to enable sheet scrolling and zooming while a dialog box is displayed. Figure 45-7 shows how the example dialog box is set up.

Figure 45-7: Here, ScrollBar controls enable zooming and scrolling of the worksheet.

If you look at the code for this example, you'll see that it's remarkably simple. The controls are initialized in the UserForm_Initialize procedure.

```
Private Sub UserForm_Initialize()
    LabelZoom.Caption = ActiveWindow.Zoom
'   Zoom
    With ScrollBarZoom
        .Min = 10
        .Max = 400
        .SmallChange = 1
        .LargeChange = 10
        .Value = ActiveWindow.Zoom
    End With

'   Horizontally scrolling
    With ScrollBarColumns
        .Min = 1
        .Max = 256
        .Value = ActiveWindow.ScrollColumn
        .LargeChange = 25
        .SmallChange = 1
    End With

'   Vertically scrolling
    With ScrollBarRows
        .Min = 1
        .Max = ActiveSheet.Rows.Count
        .Value = ActiveWindow.ScrollRow
        .LargeChange = 25
        .SmallChange = 1
    End With
End Sub
```

This procedure sets various properties of the ScrollBar controls using values based on the active window.

When the ScrollBarZoom control is used, the ScrollBarZoom_Change procedure is executed. This procedure sets the ScrollBar control's Value property to the ActiveWindow's Zoom property value. It also changes a label to display the current zoom factor.

```
Private Sub ScrollBarZoom_Change()
    With ActiveWindow
        .Zoom = ScrollBarZoom.Value
        LabelZoom = .Zoom & "%"
    End With
End Sub
```

Worksheet scrolling is accomplished by the following two procedures. These procedures set the ScrollRow or ScrollColumns property of the ActiveWindow object equal to the appropriate ScrollBar control value.

```
Private Sub ScrollBarColumns_Change()
    ActiveWindow.ScrollColumn = ScrollBarColumns.Value
End Sub

Private Sub ScrollBarRows_Change()
    ActiveWindow.ScrollRow = ScrollBarRows.Value
End Sub
```

ListBox Techniques

The ListBox control is extremely versatile, but it can be a bit tricky to work with. This section consists of a number of simple examples that demonstrate common techniques involving the ListBox control.

Note   In most cases, the techniques described in this section also work with a ComboBox control.

About the ListBox control

Following are a few points to keep in mind when working with ListBox controls. Examples in the sections that follow demonstrate many of these points.

✦ The items in a ListBox can be retrieved from a range of cells (specified by the RowSource property), or they can be added using VBA code (using the AddItem method).

✦ A ListBox can be set up to enable a single selection, or a multiple selection. This is determined by the MultiSelect property.

✦ It's possible to display a ListBox with no items selected (the ListIndex property is -1). However, once an item is selected, it's not possible to unselect all items.

✦ A ListBox can contain multiple columns (controlled by the ColumnCount property), and even a descriptive header (controlled by the ColumnHeads property).

✦ The vertical height of a ListBox displayed in a UserForm window isn't always the same as the vertical height when the UserForm is actually displayed.

✦ The items in a ListBox can be displayed as check boxes if multiple selection is allowed or as option buttons if a single selection is allowed. This is controlled by the ListStyle property.

Note For complete details on the properties and methods for a ListBox control, consult the online help.

Adding items to a ListBox control

Before displaying a UserForm that uses a ListBox control, you probably need to fill the ListBox with items. You can fill a ListBox at design time using items stored in a worksheet range, or at run time using VBA to add the items to the ListBox.

The two examples in this section presume that

✦ You have a dialog box on a UserForm named UserForm1.

✦ This dialog box contains a ListBox control named ListBox1.

✦ The workbook contains a sheet named Sheet1, and range A1:A12 contains the items to be displayed in the ListBox.

Adding items to a ListBox at design time

To add items to a ListBox at design time, the ListBox items must be stored in a worksheet range. Use the RowSource property to specify the range that contains the ListBox items. Figure 45-8 shows the Properties window for a ListBox control. The RowSource property is set to Sheet1!A1:A12. When the UserForm is displayed, the ListBox contains the 12 items in this range. The items appear in the ListBox at design time, as soon as you specify the range for the RowSource property.

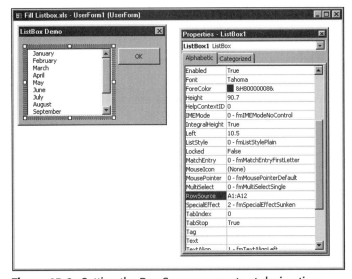

Figure 45-8: Setting the RowSource property at design time

Caution Make sure that you include the worksheet name when you specify the RowSource property. Otherwise, the ListBox uses the specified range on the active worksheet.

Adding items to a ListBox at run time

To add ListBox items at run time, you have two choices:

✦ Set the RowSource property to a range address using code.

✦ Write code that uses the AddItem method to add the ListBox items.

As you might expect, you can set the RowSource property via code rather than with the Properties window. For example, the following procedure sets the RowSource property for a ListBox before displaying the UserForm. In this case, the items consist of the cell entries in a range named Categories on the Budget worksheet.

```
UserForm1.ListBox1.RowSource = "Budget!Categories"
UserForm1.Show
```

If the ListBox items are not contained in a worksheet range, you can write VBA code to fill the ListBox before the dialog box appears. The procedure fills the ListBox with the names of the months using the AddItem method.

```
Sub ShowUserForm2()
'    Fill the list box
     With UserForm2.ListBox1
         .RowSource=""
         .AddItem "January"
         .AddItem "February"
         .AddItem "March"
         .AddItem "April"
         .AddItem "May"
         .AddItem "June"
         .AddItem "July"
         .AddItem "August"
         .AddItem "September"
         .AddItem "October"
         .AddItem "November"
         .AddItem "December"
     End With
     UserForm2.Show
End Sub
```

Caution In the preceding code, notice that I set the RowSource property to an empty string. This is to avoid a potential error that occurs if the Properties window has a nonempty RowSource setting. If you try to add items to a ListBox that has a non-null RowSource setting, you'll get a "permission denied" error.

You can also use the `AddItem` method to retrieve ListBox items from a range. Here's an example that fills a ListBox with the contents of A1:A12 on `Sheet1`.

```
For Row = 1 To 12
  UserForm1.ListBox1.AddItem Sheets("Sheet1").Cells(Row, 1)
Next Row
```

If your data is stored in a one-dimensional array, you can assign the array to the ListBox with a single instruction. For example, assume you have an array named `dData` that contains 50 elements. The following statement creates a 50-item list in `ListBox1`:

```
ListBox1.List = dData
```

Adding only unique items to a ListBox

In some cases, you may need to fill a ListBox with unique (nonduplicated) items from a list. For example, assume you have a worksheet that contains customer data. One of the columns might contain the state name of each customer (see Figure 45-9). You would like to fill a ListBox with the state name of your customers, but you don't want to include duplicate state names.

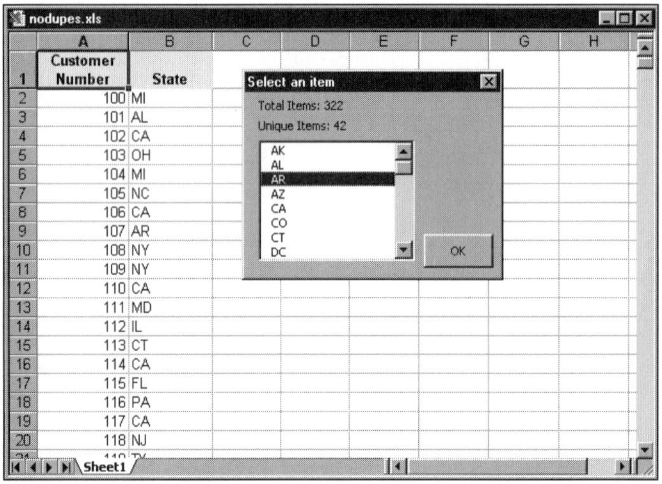

Figure 45-9: A Collection object is used to fill a ListBox with the unique items from Column B.

One technique involves using a `Collection` object. You can add items to a `Collection` object with the following syntax:

```
object.Add item, key, before, after
```

The *key* argument, if used, must be a unique text string that specifies a separate key that can be used to access a member of the collection. The important word here is *unique*. If you attempt to add a nonunique key to a collection, an error occurs and the item is not added. You can take advantage of this situation and use it to create a collection that consists only of unique items.

The following procedure demonstrates how to fill a ListBox with unique items. It starts by declaring a new `Collection` object named `NoDupes`. It assumes that range B1:B100 contains a list of items, some of which may be duplicated. The code loops through the cells in the range and attempts to add the cell's value the `NoDupes` collection. It also uses the cell's value (converted to a string) for the *key* argument. Using the `On Error Resume Next` statement causes VBA to ignore the error that occurs if the key is not unique. When an error occurs, the item is not added to the collection, which is just what you want. The procedure then transfers the items in the `NoDupes` collection to the ListBox.

```
Sub RemoveDuplicates1()
    Dim AllCells As Range, Cell As Range
    Dim NoDupes As New Collection

    On Error Resume Next
    For Each Cell In Range("B1:B100")
        NoDupes.Add Cell.Value, CStr(Cell.Value)
    Next Cell
    On Error GoTo 0

'   Add the nonduplicated items to a ListBox
    For Each Item In NoDupes
        UserForm1.ListBox1.AddItem Item
    Next Item

'   Show the UserForm
    UserForm1.Show
End Sub
```

On the CD-ROM

A slightly more sophisticated version of this example is available on the CD-ROM.

Determining the selected item

The examples in preceding sections merely display a UserForm with a ListBox filled with various items. These procedures omit a key point: how to determine which item or items were selected by the user.

Note

This discussion assumes a "single selection" ListBox object — one whose `MultiSelect` property is set to 0.

To determine which item was selected, access the ListBox's `Value` property. The following statement, for example, displays the text of the selected item in `ListBox1`:

```
MsgBox ListBox1.Value
```

If you need to know the position of the selected item in the list (rather than the content of that item) you can access the ListBox's `ListIndex` property. The next example uses a message box to display the item number of the selected ListBox item.

```
MsgBox "You selected item #" & ListBox1.ListIndex
```

Note   The numbering of items in a ListBox begins with 0, not 1. Therefore, the `ListIndex` of the first item is 0, and the `ListIndex` of the last item is equivalent to the value of the `ListCount` property minus 1.

Determining multiple selections

Normally, a ListBox's `MultiSelect` property is zero, which means that the user can select only one item in the ListBox.

If the ListBox allows multiple selections (that is, if its `MultiSelect` property is either 1 or 2), trying to access the `ListIndex`, `Value`, or `List` properties results in an error. Instead, you need to use the `Selected` property, which returns an array whose first item has an index of 0. For example, the following statement displays True if the first item in the ListBox list is selected:

```
MsgBox ListBox1.Selected(0)
```

On the CD-ROM   The companion CD-ROM contains a workbook that demonstrates how to identify the selected item(s) in a ListBox. It works for single selection and multiple selection ListBoxes.

The following code from the example workbook on the CD-ROM loops through each item in the ListBox. If the item was selected, it appends the item's text to a variable called `Msg`. Finally, the names of all the selected items are displayed in a message box.

```
Private Sub OKButton_Click()
    Msg = ""
    For i = 0 To ListBox1.ListCount - 1
        If ListBox1.Selected(i) Then _
            Msg = Msg & ListBox1.List(i) & vbCrLf
    Next i
    MsgBox "You selected: " & vbCrLf & Msg
    Unload Me
End Sub
```

Figure 45-10 shows the result when multiple ListBox items are selected.

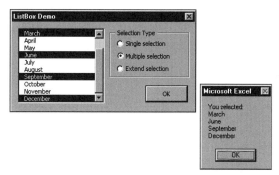

Figure 45-10: This message box displays a list of items selected in a ListBox.

Creating a ListBox with changing contents

This example demonstrates how to create a ListBox in which the contents change depending on the user's selection from a group of OptionButtons.

Figure 45-11 shows the sample dialog box. The ListBox gets its items from a worksheet range. The procedures that handle the Click event for the OptionButton controls simply set the ListBox's RowSource property to a different range. One of these procedures is as follows:

```
Private Sub obMonths_Click()
    ListBox1.RowSource = "Sheet1!Months"
End Sub
```

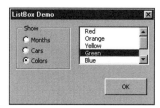

Figure 45-11: The contents of this ListBox depend on the OptionButton selected.

Clicking the OptionButton named obMonths changes the RowSource property of the ListBox to use a range named Months on Sheet1.

Building a ListBox from another list

Some applications require a user to select several items from a list. It's often useful to create a new list of the selected items. (For an example of this situation, check out the dialog box that appears when you choose the Tools ➪ Attach Toolbars command in a VBA module.)

Figure 45-12 shows a dialog box with two ListBoxes. The Add button adds the item selected in the left ListBox to the right ListBox. The Delete button removes the selected item from the list on the right. A CheckBox determines the behavior when a duplicate item is added to the list. If the *Allow duplicates* CheckBox is not checked, a message box appears if the user attempts to add an item that's already on the list.

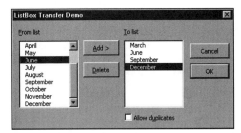

Figure 45-12: Building a list from another list

The code for this example is relatively simple. Here's the procedure that is executed when the user clicks the Add button:

```
Private Sub AddButton_Click()
    If ListBox1.ListIndex = -1 Then Exit Sub
    If Not cbDuplicates Then
'        See if item already exists
        For i = 0 To ListBox2.ListCount - 1
            If ListBox1.Value = ListBox2.List(i) Then
                Beep
                Exit Sub
            End If
        Next i
    End If
    ListBox2.AddItem ListBox1.Value
End Sub
```

The code for the Delete button is even simpler:

```
Private Sub DeleteButton_Click()
    If ListBox2.ListIndex = -1 Then Exit Sub
    ListBox2.RemoveItem ListBox2.ListIndex
End Sub
```

Notice that both routines check to make sure that an item is actually selected. If the ListBox's ListIndex property is -1, no items are selected and the procedure ends.

Moving items in a ListBox

The example in this section demonstrates how to enable the user to move the location of items up or down in a ListBox. The VBE uses this type of technique itself to enable you to control the tab order of the items in a UserForm.

Figure 45-13 shows a dialog box that contains a ListBox and two CommandButtons. Clicking the Move Up button moves the selected item up in the ListBox; clicking the Move Down button moves the selected item down.

Figure 45-13: The buttons enable the user to move items up or down in the ListBox.

The event-handler procedures for the two CommandButtons are as follows:

```
Private Sub MoveUpButton_Click()
    With ListBox1
        ItemNum = .ListIndex
        If ItemNum > 0 Then
            TempItem = .List(ItemNum - 1)
            .List(ItemNum - 1) = .List(ItemNum)
            .List(ItemNum) = TempItem
            .ListIndex = .ListIndex - 1
        End If
    End With
End Sub

Private Sub MoveDownButton_Click()
    With ListBox1
        ItemNum = .ListIndex
        If ItemNum < .ListCount - 1 And ItemNum <> -1 Then
            TempItem = .List(ItemNum + 1)
            .List(ItemNum + 1) = .List(ItemNum)
            .List(ItemNum) = TempItem
            .ListIndex = .ListIndex + 1
        End If
    End With
End Sub
```

These procedures work fairly well, but you'll find that for some reason, relatively rapid clicking doesn't always register. For example, you may click the Move Down button three times in quick succession, but the item moves only one or two positions. The solution is to add a new DblClick event handler for each CommandButton. These procedures, which simply call the Click procedures, are as follows:

```
Private Sub MoveUpButton_DblClick _
  (ByVal Cancel As MSForms.ReturnBoolean)
    Call MoveUpButton_Click
End Sub

Private Sub MoveDownButton_DblClick _
  (ByVal Cancel As MSForms.ReturnBoolean)
    Call MoveDownButton_Click
End Sub
```

Working with multicolumn ListBox controls

A normal ListBox has a single column for its contained items. You can, however, create a ListBox that displays multiple columns and, optionally, column headers. Figure 45-14 shows an example.

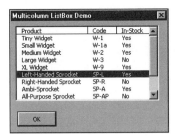

Figure 45-14: This ListBox displays a three-column list, with column headers.

To set up a multicolumn ListBox that uses data stored in a worksheet range, follow these steps:

1. Make sure the ListBox's ColumnCount property is set to the correct number of columns.

2. Specify the correct multicolumn range in the Excel worksheet as the ListBox's RowSource property.

3. To display column heads like the ListBox in Figure 45-14, set the ColumnHeads property to True. Do not include the column headings on the worksheet in the range setting for the RowSource property. VBA instead automatically uses the row directly above the first row of the RowSource range.

4. Adjust the column widths by assigning a series of values, specified in points (1/72 of one inch) separated by semicolons, to the `ColumnWidths` property. For example, for a three-column ListBox, the `ColumnWidths` property might be set to the following text string:

```
100;40;30
```

5. Specify the appropriate column as the `BoundColumn` property. The bound column specifies which column is referenced when an instruction polls the ListBox's `Value` property.

Note   To fill a ListBox with multicolumn data without using a range, you first create a two-dimensional array, and then assign the array to the ListBox's `List` property. The following statements demonstrate this technique using a 50 row by 2 column array. The result is a 50-item ListBox that has two columns.

```
Dim Data(1 To 50, 1 To 2)
' Code to fill the array goes here
ListBox1.List = Data
```

Note   There appears to be no way to specify column headers for the `ColumnHeads` property when the list source is a VBA array.

Using a ListBox to select rows

The example in this section is actually a useful utility. It displays a ListBox that consists of the entire used range of the active worksheet (see Figure 45-15). The user can select multiple items in the ListBox. Clicking the All button selects all items, and clicking the None button deselects all items. Clicking OK selects those corresponding rows in the worksheet. You can, of course, select multiple noncontiguous rows directly in the worksheet by pressing Ctrl as you click the row borders. However, you may find that selecting rows is easier using this method.

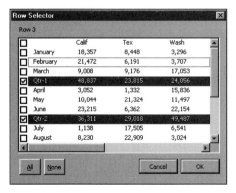

Figure 45-15: This ListBox makes it easy to select rows in a worksheet.

Selecting multiple items is possible because the ListBox's `MultiSelect` property is set to 1 - fmMultiSelectMulti. The "check boxes" on each item are displayed because the ListBox's `ListStyle` property is set to 1 - fmListStyleOption.

The UserForm's `Initialize` procedure is as follows. This procedure creates a `Range` object named `rng` that consists of the active sheet's used range — or more accurately, the narrowest rectangular range on the active worksheet containing data. Additional code sets the ListBox's `ColumnCount` and `RowSource` properties, and adjusts the `ColumnWidths` property such that the ListBox columns are proportional to the column widths in the worksheet.

```
Private Sub UserForm_Initialize()
    ColCnt = ActiveSheet.UsedRange.Columns.Count
    Set rng = ActiveSheet.UsedRange
    With ListBox1
        .ColumnCount = ColCnt
        .RowSource = rng.Address
        cw = ""
        For c = 1 To .ColumnCount
            cw = cw & rng.Columns(c).Width & ";"
        Next c
        .ColumnWidths = cw
        .ListIndex = 0
    End With
End Sub
```

The All and None buttons (named SelectAllButton and SelectNoneButton, respectively) have simple event-handler procedures and are listed here:

```
Private Sub SelectAllButton_Click()
    For r = 0 To ListBox1.ListCount - 1
        ListBox1.Selected(r) = True
    Next r
End Sub

Private Sub SelectNoneButton_Click()
    For r = 0 To ListBox1.ListCount - 1
        ListBox1.Selected(r) = False
    Next r
End Sub
```

The `OKButton_Click` procedure is listed next. This procedure creates a `Range` object named `RowRange` that consists of the rows that correspond to the selected items in the ListBox. To determine if a row was selected, the code examines the `Selected` property of the ListBox control. Notice that it uses the `Union` function to add additional ranges to the `RowRange` object.

```
Private Sub OKButton_Click()
    Dim RowRange As Range
    RowCnt = 0
    For r = 0 To ListBox1.ListCount - 1
        If ListBox1.Selected(r) Then
            RowCnt = RowCnt + 1
            If RowCnt = 1 Then
                Set RowRange = ActiveSheet.Rows(r + 1)
            Else
                Set RowRange = _
                    Union(RowRange, ActiveSheet.Rows(r + 1))
            End If
        End If
    Next r
    If Not RowRange Is Nothing Then RowRange.Select
    Unload Me
End Sub
```

Using a ListBox to activate a sheet

The example in this section is just as useful as it is instructive. This example uses a multicolumn ListBox to display a list of sheets within the active workbook. The columns represent

✦ The sheet's name

✦ The type of sheet (worksheet, chart, or Excel 5/95 dialog sheet)

✦ The number of nonempty cells in the sheet

✦ Whether the sheet is visible

Figure 45-16 shows an example of the dialog box.

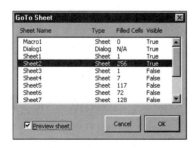

Figure 45-16: This dialog box enables the user to activate a sheet.

The code in the following `UserForm_Initialize` procedure creates a two-dimensional array, and collects the information by looping through the sheets in the active workbook. It then transfers this array to the ListBox named `ListBox1`.

```
Private Sub UserForm_Initialize()
    Dim SheetData() As String
    Set OriginalSheet = ActiveSheet
    ShtCnt = ActiveWorkbook.Sheets.Count
    ReDim SheetData(1 To ShtCnt, 1 To 4)
    ShtNum = 1
    For Each Sht In ActiveWorkbook.Sheets
        If Sht.Name = ActiveSheet.Name Then _
          ListPos = ShtNum - 1
        SheetData(ShtNum, 1) = Sht.Name
        Select Case TypeName(Sht)
            Case "Worksheet"
                SheetData(ShtNum, 2) = "Sheet"
                SheetData(ShtNum, 3) = _
                  Application.CountA(Sht.Cells)
            Case "Chart"
                SheetData(ShtNum, 2) = "Chart"
                SheetData(ShtNum, 3) = "N/A"
            Case "DialogSheet"
                SheetData(ShtNum, 2) = "Dialog"
                SheetData(ShtNum, 3) = "N/A"
        End Select
        If Sht.Visible Then
            SheetData(ShtNum, 4) = "True"
        Else
            SheetData(ShtNum, 4) = "False"
        End If
        ShtNum = ShtNum + 1
    Next Sht
    With ListBox1
        .ColumnWidths = "100 pt;30 pt;40 pt;50 pt"
        .List = SheetData
        .ListIndex = ListPos
    End With
End Sub
```

The `ListBox1_Click` procedure is as follows:

```
Private Sub ListBox1_Click()
    If cbPreview Then _
        Sheets(ListBox1.Value).Activate
End Sub
```

The value of the CheckBox control named `cbPreview` determines if the selected sheet is previewed when the user clicks an item in the ListBox.

Clicking the OK button named `OKButton` executes the `OKButton_Click` procedure, which is as follows:

```
Private Sub OKButton_Click()
    Dim UserSheet As Object
    Set UserSheet = Sheets(ListBox1.Value)
    If UserSheet.Visible Then
        UserSheet.Activate
    Else
        If MsgBox("Unhide sheet?", _
          vbQuestion + vbYesNoCancel) = vbYes Then
            UserSheet.Visible = True
            UserSheet.Activate
        Else
            OriginalSheet.Activate
        End If
    End If
    Unload Me
End Sub
```

The `OKButton_Click` procedure creates an object variable that represents the selected sheet. If the sheet is visible, it is activated. If it's not visible, the user is presented with a message box asking if it should be unhidden. If the user responds in the affirmative, the sheet is unhidden and activated. Otherwise, the original sheet (stored in an object variable named `OriginalSheet`) is activated.

Double-clicking an item in the ListBox has the same result as clicking the OK button. The following `ListBox1_DblClick` procedure simply calls the `OKButton_Click` procedure.

```
Private Sub ListBox1_DblClick(ByVal Cancel As _
  MSForms.ReturnBoolean)
    Call OKButton_Click
End Sub
```

Using the MultiPage Control

The MultiPage control is very useful for custom dialog boxes that must display many controls. The MultiPage control enables you to group the choices and place each group on a separate "tab."

Figure 45-17 shows several examples of a UserForm that contains a MultiPage control. In this case, the control has three pages, each with its own tab. As you can see, the MultiPage control is very versatile, giving you a great deal of control over its appearance and functionality. The figure shows the result of the four settings for the MultiPage's `TabOrientation` property.

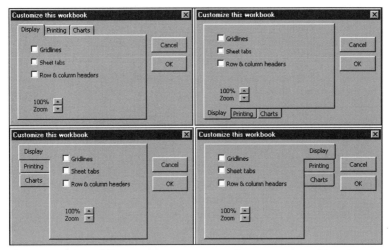

Figure 45-17: MultiPage groups your controls on pages, making them accessible from a tab.

Note The Toolbox also contains a control named TabStrip. As far as I can tell, the MultiPage control is much more versatile, and I can't think of a single reason to use the TabStrip control.

Using a MultiPage control can be a bit tricky. Following are some things to keep in mind when using this control:

✦ The tab (or page) that's displayed up front is determined by the control's Value function. A value of 0 displays the first tab, a value of 1 displays the second tab, and so on.

✦ By default, a MultiPage control has two pages. To add a new page, right-click a tab and select New Page from the shortcut menu.

✦ When you're working with a MultiPage control, just click a tab to set the properties for that particular page. The Properties window displays the properties that you can adjust.

✦ You may find it difficult to select the actual MultiPage control because clicking the control selects a page within the control. To select the control itself, you can use the Tab key to cycle among all the controls. Or you can select the MultiPage control from the drop-down list in the Properties window.

✦ If your MultiPage control has lots of tabs, you can set its MultiRow property to True to display the tabs in more than one row.

✦ If you prefer, you can display buttons instead of tabs. Just change the Style property to 1. If the Style property value is 0, the MultiPage control won't display tabs or buttons.

✦ The TabOrientation property determines the location of the tabs on the MultiPage control. Figure 45-17 shows the result of each of the four TabOrientation property settings.

✦ For each page, you can set a transition effect by changing the TransitionEffect property. For example, clicking a tab can cause the new page to "push" the former page out of the way. Use the TransitionPeriod property to set the speed of the transition effect.

Cross-Reference The next chapter contains several examples that use the MultiPage control.

Summary

In this chapter, I provided several UserForm examples that demonstrate common techniques. I also included many examples using the ListBox control.

The next chapter contains additional, more advanced examples of UserForms.

✦   ✦   ✦

Understanding Excel's Events

In several previous chapters in this book I presented examples of VBA event-handler procedures, which are specially named procedures executed when specific events occur. A simple example is the `CommandButton1_Click` procedure executed when a user clicks a CommandButton on a UserForm.

Excel is capable of monitoring a wide variety of events and executing your VBA code when a particular event occurs. The following are just a few examples of the types of events that Excel can recognize:

- ✦ A workbook is opened or closed.
- ✦ A window is activated.
- ✦ A worksheet is activated or deactivated.
- ✦ Data is entered into a cell, or the cell is edited.
- ✦ A workbook is saved.
- ✦ A worksheet is calculated.
- ✦ An object is clicked.
- ✦ The data in a chart is updated.
- ✦ A particular key or key combination is pressed.
- ✦ A cell is double-clicked.
- ✦ A particular time of day occurs.
- ✦ An error occurs.

This chapter provides comprehensive coverage of the concept of Excel events, and I include many examples that you can adapt to meet your own needs. As you'll see, understanding and implementing events can give your Excel applications a powerful edge.

Event Types That Excel Can Monitor

Excel is programmed to monitor many different events. These events can be classified in the following way:

✦ **Workbook events.** These occur for a particular workbook. Examples include Open (the workbook is opened or created), BeforeSave (the workbook is about to be saved), and NewSheet (a new sheet is added).

✦ **Worksheet events.** These occur for a particular worksheet. Examples include Change (a cell on the sheet is changed), SelectionChange (the cell pointer is moved), and Calculate (the worksheet is recalculated).

✦ **Chart events.** These occur for a particular chart. Examples include Select (a chart object is selected) and SeriesChange (a data point value in a series is changed). To monitor events for an embedded chart, use a class module.

✦ **Application events.** These occur for the application (Excel). Examples include NewWorkbook (a new workbook is created), WorkbookBeforeClose (any workbook is about to be closed), and SheetChange (a cell in any open workbook is altered).

✦ **UserForm events.** These occur for a particular UserForm or object contained on the UserForm. For example, a UserForm has an Initialize event (which occurs before the UserForm is displayed); and a CommandButton on a UserForm has a Click event (which occurs when the button is clicked).

✦ **Events not associated with objects.** The final category consists of two useful Application-level events that I call "On-" events: OnTime and OnKey. These work differently than other events.

This chapter is organized according to the preceding list. Within each section, I provide examples to demonstrate some events.

What You Should Know About Events

This section provides essential information relevant to working with events and writing event-handler procedures.

Understanding event sequences

As you'll see, some actions trigger multiple events. For example, when you insert a new worksheet into a workbook, this triggers several events at the Application level:

1. SheetDeactivate event. This occurs when the active worksheet is deactivated.

2. SheetActivate event. This occurs when the newly added worksheet is activated.

3. WorkbookNewSheet event. This occurs when a new worksheet is added.

> **Note**   Event sequencing is more complicated than you might think. The preceding events are Application-level events. When you add a new worksheet, additional events occur at the Workbook and Worksheet levels.

These three events occur in the order listed. Event sequences are not always logical. For example, you might think that the WorkbookNewSheet event occurs before the SheetActivate event, but it doesn't.

At this point, just keep in mind that events fire in a particular sequence, and knowing what the sequence is can be critical when writing event-handler procedures. Later in this chapter, I describe how to determine the order of the events that occur for a particular action (see "Monitoring Application-Level Events").

Where to put event-handler procedures

Newcomers often wonder why their event-handler procedures aren't executing when events occur. The answer almost always is that these procedures are in the wrong place.

In the Visual Basic Editor (VBE) window, each project is listed in the Project window. The project components are arranged in a collapsible list, as shown in Figure 46-1.

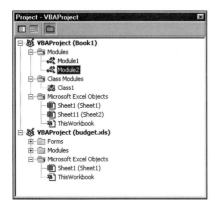

Figure 46-1: The components of each VBA project are listed in the Project window.

Each of the following components has its own code module:

✦ Sheet objects.

✦ Chart objects.

✦ ThisWorkbook object.

✦ General VBA modules. Never put event-handler procedures in a general (that is, nonobject) module.

✦ Class modules.

Even though the event-handler procedure must be located in the correct module, the procedure can call other standard procedures stored in other modules. For example, the following procedure, located in the module for the ThisWorkbook object, calls a procedure named WorkbookSetup stored in a general VBA module.

```
Private Sub Workbook_Open()
    Call WorkbookSetup
End Sub
```

Programming Events in Older Versions of Excel

Versions of Excel prior to Office 97 also supported events, but the programming protocols required to take advantage of them were different from those described in this chapter.

For example, if you have a procedure named Auto_Open stored in a general VBA module, this procedure executes when the workbook opens. In Excel 97, the Auto_Open procedure was supplemented with the Workbook_Open event-handler procedure, which was stored in the code module for the ThisWorkbook object and executed prior to Auto_Open.

With prior versions, it often was necessary to explicitly set up events. For example, if you needed to execute a procedure whenever data was entered into a cell, you had to execute a statement such as this:

```
Sheets("Sheet1").OnEntry = "ValidateEntry"
```

This statement instructed Excel to execute the procedure named ValidateEntry whenever data was entered into a cell. In Excel 97 or later versions, you simply create a procedure named Worksheet_Change and store it in the code module for the Sheet1 object.

For compatibility reasons, Excel 97 and Excel 2000 still support the older event mechanism. However, if you're developing applications for use with Excel 97 or later versions, use the techniques described in this chapter.

Disabling events

Be default, all events are enabled. To disable all events, execute the following VBA instruction:

```
Application.EnableEvents = False
```

To enable events, use this instruction:

```
Application.EnableEvents = True
```

Why do you need to disable events? The main reason is to prevent an infinite loop of cascading events from occurring.

For example, assume you've written code that executes whenever data is entered into a cell (this particular cell must contain a text string). In this case you use a procedure named Worksheet_Change to monitor the Change event for a Worksheet. Your procedure validates the user's entry, and if that entry is not a string, it displays a message and then clears the entry. The problem is that clearing the entry with your VBA code generates a new Change event, so your event-handler procedure executes again. This is not the intention, so you must disable events before you clear the cell, and then enable events again so you can monitor the user's next entry.

Another way to prevent an infinite loop of cascading events is to declare a Static Boolean variable at the beginning of your event-handler procedure, such as this:

```
Static AbortProc As Boolean
```

Whenever the procedure must make its own changes, set the AbortProc variable to True; otherwise, make sure it is set to False. Insert the following statement as the first instruction in the procedure:

```
If AbortProc Then Exit Sub
```

The event procedure is re-entered, but the True state of AbortProc trips Exit Sub, sending VBA back to the previous iteration (at the end of which AbortProc resets to False). AbortProc becomes a kind of "guard lock" mechanism.

Cross-Reference For a practical example of validating data, see "Validating Data Entry" later in this chapter.

Caution Disabling events in Excel applies to all workbooks. For example, if you disable events in your procedure and then open another workbook that has, say, a Workbook_Open procedure, that procedure will not execute.

Entering event-handler code

Every event-handler procedure has a predetermined name. You can declare the procedure by typing it, but a much better approach is to let the VBE do it for you.

Figure 46-2 shows the code module for the ThisWorkbook object. To insert a procedure declaration, select Workbook from the objects list on the left. Then select the event from the procedures list on the right. When you do this, you get a procedure "shell" that contains the procedure declaration line and an End Sub statement.

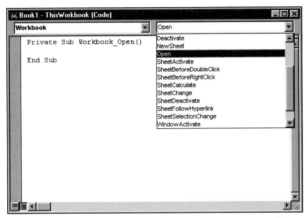

Figure 46-2: The best way to create an event procedure is to let the VBE do it for you.

For example, if you select Workbook from the objects list and Open from the procedures list, the VBE inserts the following (empty) procedure:

```
Private Sub Workbook_Open()

End Sub
```

Your code, of course, goes between these two lines.

Event-handler procedures that use arguments

Some event-handler procedures contain an argument list. For example, you may need to create an event-handler procedure to monitor the SheetActivate event for a workbook. If you use the technique described in the previous section, the VBE creates the following procedure:

```
Private Sub Workbook_SheetActivate(ByVal Sh As Object)

End Sub
```

This procedure uses one argument (Sh), which represents the activated sheet. In this case, Sh is declared as an Object data type rather than a Worksheet data type because the activated sheet also can be a Chart sheet.

Your code can, of course, make use of data passed as an argument. The following example displays the name of the activated sheet by accessing the argument's Name property. The argument becomes either a Worksheet object or a Chart object.

```
Private Sub Workbook_SheetActivate(ByVal Sh As Object)
    MsgBox Sh.Name & " was activated."
End Sub
```

Several event-handler procedures use a Boolean argument named Cancel. For example, the declaration for a Workbook's BeforePrint event is

```
Private Sub Workbook_BeforePrint(Cancel As Boolean)
```

The value of Cancel passed to the procedure is True. However, your code can set Cancel to False, which cancels the printing. The following example demonstrates this.

```
Private Sub Workbook_BeforePrint(Cancel As Boolean)
    Msg = "Have you loaded the 5164 label stock?"
    Ans = MsgBox(Msg, vbYesNo, "About to print...")
    If Ans = vbNo Then Cancel = True
End Sub
```

The Workbook_BeforePrint procedure executes before the workbook prints. This procedure displays the message box shown in Figure 46-3. If the user clicks the No button, Cancel is set to False and nothing prints.

Figure 46-3: You can cancel an operation by changing the Cancel argument.

Workbook-Level Events

Workbook-level events occur for a particular workbook. Table 46-1 lists the Workbook events, along with a brief description of each. Workbook event-handler procedures are stored in the code module for the ThisWorkbook object.

Table 46-1
Workbook Events

Event	Action That Triggers the Event
Activate	A workbook is activated.
AddinInstall	A workbook is installed as an add-in.
AddinUninstall	A workbook is uninstalled as an add-in.
BeforeClose	A workbook is about to be closed.
BeforePrint	A workbook (or anything in it) is about to be printed.
BeforeSave	A workbook is about to be saved.
Deactivate	A workbook is deactivated.
NewSheet	A new sheet is created in a workbook.
Open	A workbook is opened.
SheetActivate	Any sheet is activated.
SheetBeforeDoubleClick	Any worksheet is double-clicked. This event occurs before the default double-click action.
SheetBeforeRightClick	Any worksheet is right-clicked. This event occurs before the default right-click action.
SheetCalculate	Any worksheet is calculated (or recalculated).
SheetChange	Any worksheet is changed by the user or an external link.
SheetDeactivate	Any sheet is deactivated.
SheetSelectionChange	The selection on any worksheet is changed.
WindowActivate	Any workbook window is activated.
WindowDeactivate	Any workbook window is deactivated.
WindowResize	Any workbook window is resized.

Cross-Reference If you need to monitor events for *any* workbook, you must work with Application-level events (see "Monitoring Application-Level Events" later in this chapter).

The remainder of this section presents examples of using Workbook-level events.

Note All the example procedures that follow must be located in the code module for the ThisWorkbook object. If you put them into any other type of code module, they will not work.

Open event

One of the most common monitored events is a workbook's Open event. This event is triggered when the workbook (or add-in) opens, and executes the Workbook_Open procedure. A Workbook_Open procedure can do almost anything and often is used for the following tasks:

✦ Displaying welcome messages

✦ Opening other workbooks

✦ Setting up custom menus or toolbars

✦ Activating a particular sheet

✦ Ensuring that certain conditions are met; for example, a workbook may require that a particular add-in is installed

✦ Setting up certain automatic features; for example, you can define a key combination (see "OnKey Event" later in this chapter)

✦ Setting a worksheet's ScrollArea property (which isn't stored with the workbook)

Caution   If the user holds down the Shift key while opening a workbook, the workbook's Workbook_Open **procedure will not execute.**

The following is a simple example of a Workbook_Open procedure. It uses VBA's Weekday function to determine the day of the week. If it's Friday, a message box appears to remind the user to perform a file backup. If it's not Friday, nothing happens.

```
Private Sub Workbook_Open()
    If Weekday(Now) = 5 Then
        Msg = "Today is Friday. Make sure that you "
        Msg = Msg & "do your weekly backup!"
        MsgBox Msg, vbInformation
    End If
End Sub
```

Activate event

The following procedure executes whenever the workbook is activated. This procedure simply maximizes the active window.

```
Private Sub Workbook_Activate()
    ActiveWindow.WindowState = xlMaximized
End Sub
```

SheetActivate event

The following procedure executes whenever the user activates any sheet in the workbook. The code simply selects Cell A1. Writing On Error Resume Next causes the procedure to ignore the error that occurs if the activated sheet is a Chart sheet.

```
Private Sub Workbook_SheetActivate(ByVal Sh As Object)
    On Error Resume Next
    Range("A1").Select
End Sub
```

An alternative method to handle the case of a Chart sheet is to check the sheet type. Use the Sh argument, which is passed to the procedure.

```
Private Sub Workbook_SheetActivate(ByVal Sh As Object)
    If TypeName(Sh) = "Worksheet" Then Range("A1").Select
End Sub
```

NewSheet event

The following procedure executes whenever a new sheet is added to the workbook. The sheet is passed to the procedure as an argument. Because a new sheet can be either a worksheet or a Chart sheet, this procedure determines the sheet type. If it's a worksheet, it inserts a date and time stamp in Cell A1.

```
Private Sub Workbook_NewSheet(ByVal Sh As Object)
    If TypeName(Sh) = "Worksheet" Then _
        Range("A1") = "Sheet added " & Now()
End Sub
```

BeforeSave event

The BeforeSave event occurs before the workbook is actually saved. As you know, using the File ⇨ Save command sometimes brings up the Save As dialog box. This happens if the file has never been saved or was opened in read-only mode.

When the Workbook_BeforeSave procedure executes, it receives an argument that enables you to identify whether the Save As dialog box will appear. The following example demonstrates this.

```
Private Sub Workbook_BeforeSave _
    (ByVal SaveAsUI As Boolean, Cancel As Boolean)
    If SaveAsUI Then
        MsgBox "Click OK to display the Save As dialog box."
    End If
End Sub
```

When the user attempts to save the workbook, the `Workbook_BeforeSave` procedure executes. If the save operation brings up the Save As dialog box, the `SaveAsUI` variable is True. The preceding procedure checks this variable and displays a message only if the Save As dialog box is displayed. If the procedure sets the `Cancel` argument to True, the file is not saved.

Deactivate event

The following example demonstrates the `Deactivate` event. This procedure executes whenever the workbook is deactivated, and essentially does not enable the user to deactivate the workbook. When the `Deactivate` event occurs, the code reactivates the workbook and displays a message.

```
Private Sub Workbook_Deactivate()
    Me.Windows(1).Activate
    MsgBox "Sorry, you may not leave this workbook"
End Sub
```

Note   I do not recommend using procedures — such as this one — that attempt to "take over" Excel. It can be very frustrating and confusing for the user. Rather, I recommend training the user on how to use your application correctly.

This example illustrates the importance of understanding event sequences. When you try this procedure you'll see that it works well if the user attempts to activate another workbook. However, it's important to understand that the following actions also trigger the `Workbook_Deactivate` event:

✦ Closing the workbook

✦ Opening a new workbook

✦ Minimizing the workbook

In other words, this procedure might not perform as intended. The user may not activate a different workbook, but he or she can close the workbook, open a new workbook, or minimize the workbook. The message box still appears, but the actions occur anyway.

BeforePrint event

The `BeforePrint` event takes place when the user requests a printout or print preview, but before the printing or previewing occurs. The event uses a `Cancel` argument, so your code can cancel the printing or previewing by setting the `Cancel` variable to True.

One of Excel's deficiencies (that Microsoft seems unwilling to fix) is the incapability to print a workbook's full path name in the page header or footer. The following simple example accomplishes this feat:

```
Private Sub Workbook_BeforePrint(Cancel As Boolean)
    For Each sht In ThisWorkbook.Sheets
        sht.PageSetup.LeftFooter = _
            "&8" & ThisWorkbook.FullName
    Next sht
End Sub
```

This procedure loops through each sheet in the workbook and sets the `LeftFooter` property of the `PageSetup` object to the `FullName` property of the workbook (which is the filename and path name). It also sets the font size to 8 points.

 Note

This example exposes an inconsistency in Excel's object model. To change the font size of header or footer text, you must use a string that contains a special formatting code. In the preceding example, "&8" is the code for 8-point font. Ideally, there should be a `Font` object available for page headers and footers. To find out what other formatting codes are available, consult the online help (or record a macro while you access the Page Setup dialog box).

 Tip

When testing `BeforePrint` event handlers, save time (and paper) by previewing rather than actually printing.

BeforeClose event

The `BeforeClose` event occurs before a workbook is closed. This event often is used in conjunction with a `Workbook_Open` event handler. For example, use the `Workbook_Open` procedure to initialize items in your workbook, and use the `Workbook_BeforeClose` procedure to "clean up" or restore settings to normal before the workbook closes.

As you know, if you attempt to close a workbook that hasn't been saved, Excel displays a prompt that asks if you want to save the workbook before it closes. This is shown in Figure 46-4.

Figure 46-4: Once this message appears, Workbook_BeforeClose has done its deed.

Caution A problem can arise from this event. By the time the user sees this message, the BeforeClose event has already occurred. This means the Workbook_ BeforeClose procedure has already executed.

Consider this scenario: You need to display a custom menu when a particular workbook is open. Therefore, your workbook uses a Workbook_Open procedure to create the menu when the workbook opens, and it uses a Workbook_BeforeClose procedure to remove the menu when the workbook closes. These two event-handler procedures are as follows:

```
Private Sub Workbook_Open()
    Call CreateMenu
End Sub

Private Sub Workbook_BeforeClose(Cancel As Boolean)
    Call DeleteMenu
End Sub
```

As previously noted, Excel's "save workbook before closing" prompt occurs after the Workbook_BeforeClose event handler runs. So when the user clicks Cancel, the workbook remains open, but the custom menu item is already deleted!

One solution to this problem is to bypass Excel's prompt and write your own code in the Workbook_BeforeClose procedure, asking the user to save the workbook. The following code demonstrates this.

```
Private Sub Workbook_BeforeClose(Cancel As Boolean)
    If Not Me.Saved Then
        Msg = "Do you want to save the changes you made to "
        Msg = Msg & Me.Name & "?"
        Ans = MsgBox(Msg, vbQuestion + vbYesNoCancel)
        Select Case Ans
            Case vbYes
                Me.Save
            Case vbNo
                Me.Saved = True
            Case vbCancel
                Cancel = True
                Exit Sub
        End Select
    End If
    Call DeleteMenu
End Sub
```

This procedure determines whether the workbook has been saved. If it has, no problem: the DeleteMenu procedure executes and the workbook closes. If the workbook has not been saved, the procedure displays a message box that duplicates the one Excel normally shows. If the user clicks Yes, the menu is deleted and the workbook closes. If the user clicks No, the code sets the Saved property of the Workbook object to True (but doesn't actually save the file) and deletes the menu. If the user clicks Cancel, the BeforeClose event is canceled and the procedure ends without deleting the menu.

Worksheet Events

The events for a Worksheet object are some of the most useful. As you'll see, monitoring these events can make your applications perform feats that otherwise would be impossible.

 Note   The events in this section apply to worksheets only. No specific trappable events exist for Excel 5/95 dialog sheets or XLM macro sheets. However, you may be able to work with some relevant events by using Workbook-level events.

Table 46-2 lists the worksheet events, with a brief description of each.

Table 46-2	
Worksheet Events	
Event	*Action That Triggers the Event*
Activate	A worksheet is activated.
BeforeDoubleClick	A worksheet is double-clicked.
BeforeRightClick	A worksheet is right-clicked.
Calculate	A worksheet is calculated (or recalculated).
Change	Cells on a worksheet are changed by the user or an external link.
Deactivate	A worksheet is deactivated.
SelectionChange	The selection on a worksheet is changed.

Change event

The Change event is triggered when any cell in a worksheet is changed by the user or an external link. The Change event is not triggered when a calculation generates a different value for a formula, or when an object is added to the sheet.

When the Worksheet_Change procedure executes, it receives a Range object as its Target argument. This Range object represents the changed cell or range that triggered the event. The following example displays a message box that shows the address of the Target range.

```
Private Sub Worksheet_Change(ByVal Target As Excel.Range)
    MsgBox "Range " & Target.Address & " was changed."
End Sub
```

To get a feel for the types of actions that generate the Change event for a worksheet, enter the preceding procedure into the code module for a Worksheet object. After entering this procedure, activate Excel and, using various techniques, make changes to the worksheet. Every time the Change event occurs, a message box displays the address of the range that changed.

I discovered some interesting quirks when I ran this procedure. Actions that should trigger the event don't, and actions that should not trigger the event do!

✦ Changing the formatting of a cell does not trigger the Change event (as expected), but using the Edit ➪ Clear Formats command *does*.

✦ Filling a range using the Edit ➪ Fill command does not generate the Change event, but using AutoFill to fill the range *does*.

✦ Using the Edit ➪ Delete command does not generate the Change event, but pressing the Del key does. In fact, pressing Del generates an event even if the cell is empty at the start.

✦ Cells changed via Excel commands do not trigger the Change event. These commands include Data ➪ Form, Data ➪ Sort, Tools ➪ Spelling, and Edit ➪ Replace.

✦ If your VBA procedure changes a cell, it *does* trigger the Change event.

As you can see, it's not a good idea to rely on the Change event to detect cell changes for critical applications.

Monitoring a specific range for changes

The Change event occurs when any cell on the worksheet changes. In most cases all that matters are changes made to a specific cell or range. When the Worksheet_Change event-handler procedure is called, it receives a Range object as its argument. This Range object represents the cell or cells that changed.

Assume your worksheet has a range named InputRange, and you want to monitor changes to this range only. No Change event exists for a Range object, but you can perform a quick check within the Workhseet_Change procedure. The following procedure demonstrates this.

```
Private Sub Worksheet_Change(ByVal Target As Excel.Range)
    Dim VRange As Range
    Set VRange = Range("InputRange")
    If Union(Target, VRange).Address = VRange.Address Then
        Msgbox "The changed cell is in the input range."
    End if
End Sub
```

This example creates a range object named VRange, which represents the worksheet range that you want to monitor for changes. The procedure uses VBA's Union function to determine if VRange contains the Target range (passed to the procedure in its argument). The Union function returns an object that consists of all the cells in both of its arguments. If the range address is the same as the VRange address, then Vrange contains Target, and a message box appears. Otherwise, the procedure ends and nothing happens.

The preceding procedure has a flaw. Target may consist of a cell or a range. For example, if the user changes more than one cell at a time, Target becomes a multicell range. Therefore, the procedure requires modification to loop through all the cells in Target. The following procedure checks each changed cell and displays a message box if the cell is within the desired range.

```
Private Sub Worksheet_Change(ByVal Target As Excel.Range)
    Set VRange = Range("InputRange")
    For Each cell In Target
        If Union(cell, VRange).Address = VRange.Address Then
            Msgbox "The changed cell is in the input range."
        End if
    Next cell
End Sub
```

Tracking cell changes in a comment

The following example adds a notation to the cell's comment each time the cell changes (as determined by the Change event). The state of a CheckBox, embedded in the worksheet, determines whether the change is added to the comment.

Because the object passed to the Worksheet_Change procedure can consist of a multicell range, the procedure loops through each cell in the Target range. If the cell doesn't contain a comment, one is added. Then, new text is appended to the existing comment text (if applicable).

```
Private Sub Worksheet_Change(ByVal Target As Excel.Range)
    If CheckBox1 Then
        For Each cell In Target
            With cell
                On Error Resume Next
                OldText = .Comment.Text
                If Err <> 0 Then .AddComment
                NewText = OldText & "Changed by " & _
                  Application.UserName & " at " & Now & vbLf
                .Comment.Text NewText
                .Comment.Visible = True
                .Comment.Shape.Select
                 Selection.AutoSize = True
                .Comment.Visible = False
            End With
```

```
        Next cell
    End If
End Sub
```

Figure 46-5 shows a cell comment that has changed several times.

	A	B	C	D	E	F	G	H	
1		☑ Log changes in comments							
2		Starting Value:	1,250,000						
3		Annual Growth Rage:	5.25%						
4	Year-1	1,250,000							
5	Year-2	1,315,625							
6	Year-3	1,384,695							
7	Year-4	1,457,392							
8	Year-5	1,533,905							
9	Year-6	1,614,435							
10	Year-7	1,699,193							
11	Year-8	1,788,400							
12	Year-9	1,882,291							
13	Year-10	1,981,112							
14	Year-11	2,085,120							
15	Year-12	2,194,589							
16									
17									
18									

projections.xls

Comment box:
```
Changed by John Walkenbach at 11/14/98 8:20:14 AM
Changed by John Walkenbach at 11/14/98 8:22:20 AM
Changed by John Walkenbach at 11/14/98 8:25:26 AM
Changed by John Walkenbach at 11/14/98 8:260:34 AM
```

Figure 46-5: The Worksheet_Change procedure appends the comment with each cell change.

Note This example is primarily for instructional purposes. If you really need to track changes in a worksheet, Excel's Tools ➪ Track Changes feature does a much better job.

Validating data entry

Excel's Data Validation feature is a useful tool, but it suffers from a potentially serious problem. When you paste data to a cell that uses data validation, the pasted value not only fails to receive validation, but also deletes the validation rules associated with the cell!

In this section I demonstrate how to use a worksheet's Change event to create your own data validation procedure.

On the CD-ROM The companion CD-ROM contains two versions of this example. One uses the EnableEvents property to prevent cascading Change events, the other uses a Static variable (see "Disabling Events" earlier in this chapter).

Listing 46-1 presents a procedure that executes when a user changes a cell. The validation is restricted to the range named InputRange. Values entered into this range must be integers between 1 and 12.

Listing 46-1: Determining whether a cell entry will be validated

```
Private Sub Worksheet_Change(ByVal Target As Excel.Range)
    Dim VRange As Range, cell As Range
    Dim Msg As String
    Dim ValidateCode As Variant
    Set VRange = Range("InputRange")
    For Each cell In Target
        If Union(cell, VRange).Address = VRange.Address Then
            ValidateCode = EntryIsValid(cell)
            If ValidateCode = True Then
                Exit Sub
            Else
                Msg = "Cell " & cell.Address(False, False) _
                    & ":"
                Msg = Msg & vbCrLf & vbCrLf & ValidateCode
                MsgBox Msg, vbCritical, "Invalid Entry"
                Application.EnableEvents = False
                cell.ClearContents
                cell.Activate
                Application.EnableEvents = True
            End If
        End If
    Next cell
End Sub
```

The Worksheet_Change procedure creates a Range object (VRange) that represents the validated worksheet range. Then it loops through each cell in the Target argument, which represents the cell or cells that changed. The code determines whether each cell is contained in the range to be validated. If it is, the code passes the cell as an argument to a custom function (EntryIsValid), which returns True if the cell is a valid entry.

If the entry is not valid, the EntryIsValid function returns a string that describes the problem, and the user receives information via a message box (see Figure 46-6). When the message box is dismissed, the invalid entry is cleared from the cell and the cell is activated. Notice that events are disabled before the cell is cleared. If events were not disabled, clearing the cell would produce a Change event, which causes an endless loop.

Figure 46-6: This message box describes the problem when the user makes an invalid entry.

The EntryIsValid function procedure is presented in Listing 46-2.

Listing 46-2: Validating an entry that was just made into a restricted range

```
Private Function EntryIsValid(cell) As Variant
'    Returns True if cell is an integer between 1 and 12
'    Otherwise it returns a string that describes the problem

'    Blank
    If cell = "" Then
        EntryIsValid = True
        Exit Function
    End If

'    Numeric?
    If Not IsNumeric(cell) Then
        EntryIsValid = "Non-numeric entry."
        Exit Function
    End If

'    Integer?
    If CInt(cell) <> cell Then
        EntryIsValid = "Integer required."
        Exit Function
    End If

'    Between 1 and 12?
    If cell < 1 Or cell > 12 Then
        EntryIsValid = "Valid values are between 1 and 12."
        Exit Function
    End If

'    It passed all the tests
    EntryIsValid = True
End Function
```

SelectionChange event

The following procedure demonstrates the SelectionChange event. It executes whenever the user makes a new selection on the worksheet.

```
Private Sub Worksheet_SelectionChange(ByVal Target _
  As Excel.Range)
    Cells.Interior.ColorIndex = xlNone
```

```
With ActiveCell
    .EntireRow.Interior.ColorIndex = 36
    .EntireColumn.Interior.ColorIndex = 36
End With
End Sub
```

This procedure shades the row and column of an active cell, making it easy to identify. The first statement removes the background color of all cells. Next, the entire row and column of the active cell is shaded light yellow. Figure 46-7 shows the shading; trust me, it's yellow.

	A	B	C	D	E	F	G	H	I	J
1		Project-1	Project-2	Project-3	Project-4	Project-5	Project-6	Project-7	Project-8	Project-9
2	Jan-99	5,052	21,790	21,596	2,192	13,454	9,027	21,026	15,510	6,172
3	Feb-99	10,963	20,640	20,167	15,494	3,923	12,527	15,164	6,440	2,510
4	Mar-99	18,240	22,263	21,042	11,558	17,472	20,923	17,277	15,182	2,778
5	Apr-99	18,148	16,567	10,752	7,882	521	20,624	19,376	19,314	7,396
6	May-99	14,825	12,675	17,949	16,783	19,120	15,011	21,759	13,238	2,397
7	Jun-99	13,207	13,942	10,558	15,133	6,704	5,639	2,575	18,755	13,944
8	Jul-99	21,920	19,380	12,938	3,653	5,045	16,965	7,856	22,798	5,469
9	Aug-99	7,894	12,473	6,367	1,942	18,370	10,960	5,784	4,071	19,675
10	Sep-99	5,664	16,666	22,508	8,525	17,401	10,708	13,205	22,184	1,030
11	Oct-99	594	746	3,540	3,301	19,652	19,346	2,641	5,517	8,975
12	Nov-99	981	7,465	20,315	19,330	3,428	7,332	1,370	12,027	1,109
13	Dec-99	4,329	15,135	21,320	20,972	7,085	17,556	16,703	14,478	11,662
14	Jan-00	21,325	16,679	8,950	4,193	20,096	14,158	15,810	7,465	3,437
15	Feb-00	1,412	15,580	20,393	5,359	18,192	13,523	15,352	11,855	7,550
16	Mar-00	9,485	21,571	8,378	14,995	9,031	12,172	15,356	8,641	5,422
17	Apr-00	8,971	1,560	9,739	2,921	20,444	4,097	17,599	262	10,965
18	May-00	20,691	22,318	8,184	4,293	7,645	20,278	4,947	19,267	10,031
19	Jun-00	8,748	6,278	22,746	17,344	10,664	180	4,954	18,559	21,338
20	Jul-00	18,673	8,234	12,133	2,073	10,814	19,123	1,287	22,540	2,573
21	Aug-00	16,772	3,421	9,165	22,794	10,319	15,110	5,803	10,552	3,313
22	Sep-00	516	20,857	10,762	22,383	20,127	11,512	1,792	16,800	4,515

Figure 46-7: Moving the cell cursor causes the active cell's row and column to become shaded.

Caution   You won't want to use this procedure if your worksheet contains background shading, because it will be wiped out.

BeforeRightClick event

When the user right-clicks in a worksheet, a shortcut menu appears. If, for some reason, you want to prevent the shortcut menu from appearing, you can trap the RightClick event. The following procedure sets the Cancel argument to True, which cancels the RightClick event and, thus, the shortcut menu. Instead, a message box appears.

```
Private Sub Worksheet_BeforeRightClick _
   (ByVal Target As Excel.Range, Cancel As Boolean)
     Cancel = True
     MsgBox "The shortcut menu is not available."
End Sub
```

Cross-Reference   Chapter 50 describes other ways to disable shortcut menus.

Chart Events

By default, events are enabled only for charts that reside on a Chart sheet. To work with events for an embedded chart, you must create a class module. Table 46-3 lists the Chart events, and a brief description of each.

Table 46-3	
Events Recognized by a Chart Sheet	
Event	**Action That Triggers the Event**
Activate	A Chart sheet or embedded chart is activated.
BeforeDoubleClick	An embedded chart is double-clicked. This event occurs before the default double-click action.
BeforeRightClick	An embedded chart is right-clicked. The event occurs before the default right-click action.
Calculate	New or changed data is plotted on a chart.
Deactivate	A chart is deactivated.
DragOver	A range of cells is dragged over a chart.
DragPlot	A range of cells is dragged and dropped onto a chart.
MouseDown	A mouse button is pressed while the pointer is over a chart.
MouseMove	The position of the mouse pointer is changed over a chart.
MouseUp	A mouse button is released while the pointer is over a chart.
Resize	A chart is resized.
Select	A chart element is selected.
SeriesChange	The value of a chart data point is changed.

Using the Object Browser to Locate Events

The Object Browser is a useful tool that can help you learn about objects and their properties and methods. It also can help you find out which objects support a particular event. For example, say you want to find out which objects support the MouseMove event. Activate the VBE and press F2 to display the Object Browser window. Make sure <All Libraries> is selected and then type **MouseMove** and click the binoculars icon (see the accompanying figure).

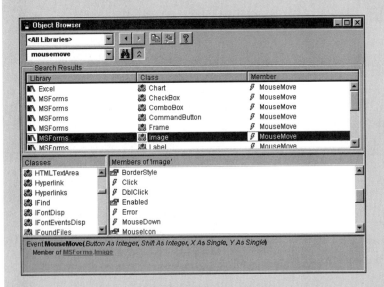

The Object Browser displays a list of matching items. Events are indicated with a small yellow lightning bolt. From this list, you can see which objects support the MouseMove event. Most of the objects are controls in the MSForms library, home of the UserForm control. But you also can see that Excel's Chart object supports the MouseMove event.

Notice how the list here is divided into three columns: Library, Class, and Member. The match for the item you're searching for may appear in any of these columns. This brings up a crucial point: The name of an event or term belonging to one library or class may be the same as that for another belonging to a different library or class, though they may not share the same meaning or functionality. In fact, you can probably bet on them being different. So be sure to click each item in the Object Browser list and check the status bar at the bottom of the list for the syntax. You might find, for instance, that one class or library treats the MouseMove event differently.

Application Events

In previous sections I discussed `Workbook` and `Worksheet` events. These events are monitored for a particular workbook. If you want to monitor events for all open workbooks or all worksheets, use Application events.

Table 46-4 lists the Application events, with a brief description of each.

Table 46-4	
Events Recognized by the Application Object	
Event	*Action That Triggers the Event*
NewWorkbook	A new workbook is created.
SheetActivate	Any sheet is activated.
SheetBeforeDoubleClick	Any worksheet is double-clicked. This event occurs before the default double-click action.
SheetBeforeRightClick	Any worksheet is right-clicked. This event occurs before the default right-click action.
SheetCalculate	Any worksheet is calculated (or recalculated).
SheetChange	Cells in any worksheet are changed by the user or an external link.
SheetDeactivate	Any sheet is deactivated.
SheetFollowHyperlink	A hyperlink is clicked.
SheetSelectionChange	The selection is changed on any worksheet except a Chart sheet.
WindowActivate	Any workbook window is activated.
WindowDeactivate	Any workbook window is deactivated.
WindowResize	Any workbook window is resized.
WorkbookActivate	Any workbook is activated.
WorkbookAddinInstall	A workbook is installed as an add-in.
WorkbookAddinUninstall	Any add-in workbook is uninstalled.
WorkbookBeforeClose	Any open workbook is closed.
WorkbookBeforePrint	Any open workbook is printed.
WorkbookBeforeSave	Any open workbook is saved.
WorkbookDeactivate	Any open workbook is deactivated.
WorkbookNewSheet	A new sheet is created in any open workbook.
WorkbookOpen	A workbook is opened.

Enabling Application-level events

To make use of Application-level events, do the following

1. Create a new class module.

2. Set a name for this class module in the Properties window under *Name*.

   By default, VBA gives each new class module a name and a number; but trying to remember which module was Class21 and which Class22 can quickly become cumbersome.

3. In the class module, declare a public Application object, using the WithEvents keyword.

4. Create a variable that you will use to refer to the declared object in the class module.

5. Write event-handler procedures in the class module.

Note   This procedure is virtually identical to the one required to use events with an embedded chart.

Determining when a workbook is opened

The example in this section stores information in a text file in order to keep track of every workbook that is opened. I start by inserting a new class module, naming it AppClass. The code in the class module is

```
Public WithEvents AppEvents As Application

Private Sub AppEvents_WorkbookOpen _
  (ByVal Wb As Excel.Workbook)
    Call UpdateLogFile(Wb)
End Sub
```

This declares AppEvents as an Application object with events. The AppEvents_WorkbookOpen procedure is called whenever a workbook is opened. This event-handler procedure calls UpdateLogFile and passes the Wb variable, which represents the Workbook that opened. I then add a VBA module and insert t he following code:

```
Dim AppObject As New AppClass

Sub Init()
'    Called by Workbook_Open
    Set AppObject.AppEvents = Application
End Sub

Sub UpdateLogFile(Wb)
```

```
        txt = Wb.FullName
        txt = txt & "," & Date & "," & Time
        txt = txt & "," & Application.UserName
        Fname = ThisWorkbook.Path & "\logfile.txt"
        Open Fname For Append As #1
        Write #1, txt
        Close #1
        MsgBox txt
End Sub
```

Notice at the top that the AppObject variable is declared as type AppClass, that is, the name of the class module. The call to Init is in the Workbook_Open procedure, which is in the code module for ThisWorkbook. Here's the procedure:

```
Private Sub Workbook_Open()
    Call Init
End Sub
```

The UpdateLogFile procedure opens a text file, or creates it if it doesn't exist. It then writes key information about the workbook that opened: filename, full path name, date, time, and username.

The Workbook_Open procedure calls the Init procedure. Therefore, when the workbook opens, the Init procedure instigates the object variable.

The text file is written to the same directory as the workbook. No error handling occurs, so the code fails when the workbook is stored on a CD-ROM drive.

Monitoring Application-level events

To get a feel for the event generation process, you might find it helpful to see a list of events that are generated as you go about your work.

The companion CD-ROM contains a workbook that displays each Application-level event as it occurs. Actually, two versions of this workbook exist. The version for Excel 2000 displays the events in a modeless UserForm, as shown in Figure 46-8. The version for Excel 97 displays each event in a message box.

The workbook contains a class module with 21 defined procedures, one for each Application-level event. Here's an example.

```
Private Sub XL_NewWorkbook(ByVal Wb As Excel.Workbook)
    LogEvent "NewWorkbook: " & Wb.Name
End Sub
```

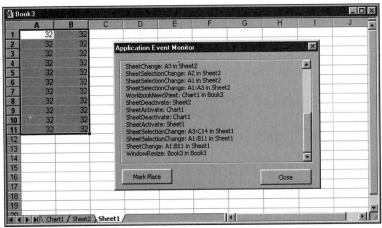

Figure 46-8: This workbook uses a class module to monitor all Application-level events.

Each of these procedures calls the LogEvent procedure and passes an argument that consists of the event name and object. Here's the LogEvent procedure:

```
Sub LogEvent(txt)
    EventNum = EventNum + 1
    With UserForm1
        With .lblEvents
            .AutoSize = False
            .Caption = .Caption & vbCrLf & txt
            .Width = UserForm1.FrameEvents.Width - 20
            .AutoSize = True
        End With
        .FrameEvents.ScrollHeight = .lblEvents.Height + 20
        .FrameEvents.ScrollTop = EventNum * 20
    End With
End Sub
```

The LogEvent procedure updates the UserForm by modifying the Caption property of the Label control named lblEvents. The procedure also adjusts the ScrollHeight and ScrollTop properties of the frame named FrameEvents, which contains Label. Adjusting these properties causes the most recently added text to show up while older text scrolls out of view.

UserForm Events

A UserForm supports many events, and each control placed on a UserForm has its own set of events. Table 46-5 lists the UserForm events that you can trap.

Table 46-5
Events Recognized by a UserForm

Event	Action That Triggers the Event
Activate	The UserForm is activated.
AddControl	A control is added at run time.
BeforeDragOver	A drag-and-drop operation is in progress while the pointer is over the form.
BeforeDropOrPaste	Data is about to be dropped or pasted; that is, the mouse button has been released.
Click	A mouse is clicked while the pointer is over the form.
DblClick	A mouse is double-clicked while the pointer is over the form.
Deactivate	The UserForm is deactivated.
Initialize	The UserForm is about to be shown.
KeyDown	A key is pressed.
KeyPress	Any ANSI key is pressed.
KeyUp	A key is released.
Layout	The size of a UserForm is changed.
MouseDown	A mouse button is pressed.
MouseMove	The mouse is moved.
QueryClose	This occurs before a UserForm is closed.
RemoveControl	A control is removed from the UserForm at run time.
Scroll	The UserForm is scrolled.
Terminate	The UserForm is terminated.
Zoom	The UserForm is zoomed.

Cross-Reference Many of the examples in Chapters 44 and 45 demonstrate event handling for UserForms and UserForm controls.

Events Not Associated with an Object

The events discussed in this chapter are associated with an object (Application, Workbook, Sheet, and so on). In this section I discuss two additional "rogue" events: OnTime and OnKey. These events are not associated with an object. Rather, they are accessed using methods of the Application object.

Note Unlike the other events discussed in this chapter, you use a general VBA module to program the "On-" events in this section.

OnTime event

The OnTime event occurs at a specified time. The following example demonstrates how to program Excel to beep and then display a message at 3:00 p.m.

```
Sub SetAlarm()
    Application.OnTime 0.625, "DisplayAlarm"
End Sub

Sub DisplayAlarm()
    Beep
    MsgBox "Wake up. It's time for your afternoon break!"
End Sub
```

In this example, the SetAlarm procedure uses the OnTime method of the Application object to set up the OnTime event. This method takes two arguments: the time (0.625, or 3:00 p.m., in the example) and the procedure to execute when the time occurs (DisplayAlarm in the example). In the example, after SetAlarm executes, the DisplayAlarm procedure is called at 3:00 p.m., bringing up the message in Figure 46-9.

Figure 46-9: This message box was programmed to appear at a particular time.

Compensating for Excel's fractional time values

Most people (myself included) find it difficult to think of time in terms of Excel's time numbering system. Therefore, you might want to use VBA's TimeValue function to represent the time. TimeValue converts a string that looks like a time into a value that Excel can handle. The following statement shows an easier way to program an event for 3:00 p.m.:

```
Application.OnTime TimeValue("3:00:00 pm"), "DisplayAlarm"
```

If you want to schedule an event that's relative to the current time—for example, 20 minutes from now—you can write an instruction like this:

```
Application.OnTime Now + TimeValue("00:20:00"), "DisplayAlarm"
```

You also can use the OnTime method to schedule a procedure on a particular day. Of course, you must keep your computer running and the workbook with the procedure open. The following statement runs the DisplayAlarm procedure at 12:01 a.m. on January 1, 2000 (assuming, of course, that no year 2000 glitches occur):

```
Application.OnTime DateValue("1/1/2000 12:01 am"), _
    "MilleniumSub"
```

Note The OnTime method has two additional arguments. If you plan to use this method, refer to the online help for complete details.

OnKey event

While you work, Excel constantly monitors what you type. Because of this, you can set up a keystroke or a key combination that, when pressed, executes a particular procedure.

The following example uses the OnKey method to set up an OnKey event. This event essentially reassigns the PgDn and PgUp keys. After the Setup_OnKey procedure executes, pressing PgDn executes the PgDn_Sub procedure, and pressing PgUp executes the PgUp_Sub procedure. The next effect is that pressing PgDn moves down one row and pressing PgUp moves up one row.

```
Sub Setup_OnKey()
    Application.OnKey "{PgDn}", "PgDn_Sub"
    Application.OnKey "{PgUp}", "PgUp_Sub"
End Sub

Sub PgDn_Sub()
    On Error Resume Next
    ActiveCell.Offset(1, 0).Activate
End Sub

Sub PgUp_Sub()
    On Error Resume Next
    ActiveCell.Offset(-1, 0).Activate
End Sub
```

Note Notice that the key codes are enclosed in brackets, not parentheses. For a complete list of the keyboard codes, consult the online help. Search for OnKey.

In the preceding examples, I used On Error Resume Next to ignore any errors generated. For example, if the active cell is in the first row, trying to move up one row causes an error. Furthermore, if the active sheet is a Chart sheet, an error occurs because no such thing as an active cell exists in a Chart sheet.

By executing the following procedure, you cancel the OnKey events and the keys return to their normal functions.

```
Sub Cancel_OnKey()
    Application.OnKey "{PgDn}"
    Application.OnKey "{PgUp}"
End Sub
```

Contrary to what you might expect, using an empty string as the second argument for the OnKey method does *not* cancel the OnKey event. Rather, it causes Excel to ignore the keystroke and do nothing at all. For example, the following instruction tells Excel to ignore Alt+F4 (the percent sign represents the Alt key):

```
    Application.OnKey "%{F4}", ""
```

Although you can use the OnKey method to assign a shortcut key for executing a macro, it's better to use the Macro Options dialog box for this task. For more details, see "Executing a Procedure Using a Ctrl+Shortcut Key Combination" in Chapter 42.

Summary

In this chapter, I described how to write code that executes when a particular event occurs.

In the next chapter, I discuss some VBA techniques that you can use to control other applications from Excel.

✦   ✦   ✦

Interacting with Other Applications

In the early days of personal computing, interapplication communication was rare. In the pre-multitasking era, users had no choice but to use one program at a time. Interapplication communication usually was limited to importing files; even copying information and pasting it into another application — something that virtually every user now takes for granted — was impossible.

Nowadays, most software is designed to support at least some type of communication with other applications. At the very least, most Windows programs support the clipboard for copy-and-paste operations between applications. Many Windows products support Dynamic Data Exchange (DDE), and leading-edge products support Automation. In this chapter, I outline the types of true multitasking operations that your Excel applications support. Of course, I also provide several examples.

Starting Another Application

It's often useful to start up another application from Excel. For example, you may want to execute a communications program or even a DOS batch file from Excel. Or, as an application developer, you may want to make it easy for a user to access the Windows Control Panel.

VBA's `Shell` function makes launching other programs relatively easy. Listing 47-1 presents a procedure that starts the Windows Character Map application, which enables the user to insert a special character.

Listing 47-1: **Launching a Windows utility application**

```
Sub RunCharMap()
    On Error Resume Next
    Program = "Charmap.exe"
    TaskID = Shell(Program, 1)
    If Err <> 0 Then
        MsgBox "Cannot start " & Program, vbCritical, "Error"
    End If
End Sub
```

You'll recognize the application this procedure launches in Figure 47-1.

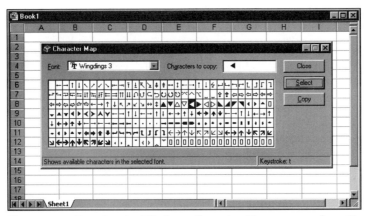

Figure 47-1: Running the Windows Character Map program from Excel

The Shell function returns a task identification number for the application. You can use this number later to activate the task. The second argument for the Shell function determines how the application is displayed (1 is the code for a normal size window, with the focus).

If the Shell function is not successful, it generates an error. So this procedure uses an On Error statement to display a message if the file cannot be found or some other error occurs.

It's important to understand that VBA does not pause while the application that was started with the Shell function is running. In other words, the Shell function runs the application *asynchronously*. If the procedure has more instructions after the Shell function is executed, they are executed concurrently with the newly loaded program. If any instruction requires user intervention (for example, displaying a message box), Excel's title bar flashes while the other application is active.

In some cases, you may want to launch an application with the Shell function, but you need your VBA code to "pause" until the application is closed. For example, the launched application may generate a file used later in your code. Although you can't pause the execution of your code, you *can* create a loop that does nothing except monitor the application's status. Listing 47-2 shows an example that displays a message box when the application launched by the Shell function has ended.

Listing 47-2: **Waiting for an application to end**

```
Declare Function OpenProcess Lib "kernel32" _
    (ByVal dwDesiredAccess As Long, _
    ByVal bInheritHandle As Long, _
    ByVal dwProcessId As Long) As Long

Declare Function GetExitCodeProcess Lib "kernel32" _
    (ByVal hProcess As Long, _
    lpExitCode As Long) As Long

Sub RunCharMap2()
    Dim TaskID As Long
    Dim hProc As Long
    Dim lExitCode As Long

    ACCESS_TYPE = &H400
    STILL_ACTIVE = &H103

    Program = "Charmap.exe"

'   Shell the task
    TaskID = Shell(Program, 1)

'   Get the process handle
    hProc = OpenProcess(ACCESS_TYPE, False, TaskID)

    If Err <> 0 Then
        MsgBox "Cannot start " & Program, vbCritical, "Error"
        Exit Sub
    End If

    Do  'Loop continuously
'       Check on the process
        GetExitCodeProcess hProc, lExitCode
'       Allow event processing
        DoEvents
    Loop While lExitCode = STILL_ACTIVE

'   Task is finished, so show message
    MsgBox Program & " is finished"
End Sub
```

While the launched program is running, this procedure continually calls the `GetExitCodeProcess` function from within a `Do-Loop` structure, testing for its returned value (`lExitCode`). When the program is finished, `lExitCode` returns a different value, the loop ends, and the VBA code resumes executing.

Both of the preceding examples are available on the companion CD-ROM.

The Windows 95 and Windows 98 operating systems provide a `Start` command, which also can be used as an argument for the `Shell` function. The `Start` command is a string literal that starts a Windows application from a DOS window. When using the `Start` command, you need to specify only the name of a *document* file — not the executable file. The program associated with that document file's extension is executed, and the file is automatically loaded. For example, the following instructions start up the installed Web browser application — that is, the application associated with the .htm extension — and load an HTML document named homepage.htm.

```
WebPage = "c:\web\homepage.htm"
Shell ("Start " & WebPage)
```

Tip If the application that you want to start is one of several Microsoft applications, you can use the `ActivateMicrosoftApp` method of the Application object. For example, the following procedure starts Word 2000:

```
Sub StartWord()
    Application.ActivateMicrosoftApp xlMicrosoftWord
End Sub
```

If Word is already running when the preceding procedure is executed, it is activated. The other constants available for this method are `xlMicrosoftPowerPoint`, `xlMicrosoftMail`, `xlMicrosoftAccess`, `xlMicrosoftFoxPro`, `xlMicrosoftProject`, and `xlMicrosoftSchedulePlus` (but no constant for Outlook).

Activating Another Application

Beware of a potential problem: You may find that if an application is already running, using the `Shell` function could start another instance of it. In most cases, you'll want to activate the instance that's running, not start another instance of it.

The `StartCalculator` procedure, as follows, uses the `AppActivate` statement to activate an application that's already running (in this case, the Windows Calculator). The argument for `AppActivate` is the caption of the application's title bar. If the `AppActivate` statement generates an error, it means the Calculator is not running. Therefore, the routine starts the application.

```
Sub StartCalculator()
    AppFile = "Calc.exe"
```

```
       On Error Resume Next
       AppActivate ("Calculator")
       If Err <> 0 Then
           Err = 0
           CalcTaskID = Shell(AppFile, 1)
           If Err <> 0 Then MsgBox ("Can't start Calculator")
       End If
End Sub
```

On the CD-ROM This example is available on the companion CD-ROM.

Note The preceding example works only if you supply the exact caption of the application's window title as the argument for AppActivate. If a window caption includes a hyphen followed by a filename (such as *Microsoft Word - testfile.doc*), you need to supply only the text prior to the hyphen.

Running Control Panel Dialog Boxes and Wizards

Windows provides quite a few system dialog boxes and wizards, most of which are accessible from the Windows Control Panel. You may need to display one or more of these from your Excel application. For example, you may want to display the Windows Date/Time Properties dialog box shown in Figure 47-2.

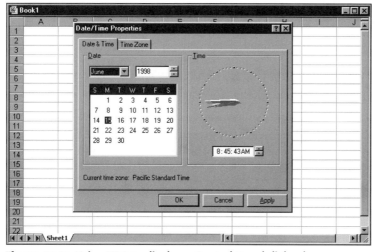

Figure 47-2: Using VBA to display a Control Panel dialog box

The key to running other system dialog boxes is knowing the argument for the Shell function. The following procedure happens to know the argument for the Date/Time dialog box.

```
Sub ShowDateTimeDlg()
    Arg = "rundll32.exe shell32.dll,Control_RunDLL timedate.cpl"
    On Error Resume Next
    TaskID = Shell(Arg)
    If Err <> 0 Then
        MsgBox ("Cannot start the application.")
    End If
End Sub
```

A workbook, depicted in Figure 47-3, that demonstrates 50 arguments is available on the companion CD-ROM.

Figure 47-3: This workbook demonstrates how to run system dialog boxes from Excel.

Automation

You can write an Excel macro to control Microsoft Word. More accurately, the Excel macro will control the most important component of Word: its so-called *automation server*. In such circumstances, Excel is called the *native* application and Word the *remote* application. Or you can write a Visual Basic application to control Excel. The process of one application's controlling another is sometimes known as OLE Automation and other times known as ActiveX Automation (Microsoft has a tendency to change its own terminology quite frequently).

The concept behind Automation is quite appealing. A developer who needs to generate a chart, for example, can just reach into another application's grab bag of objects, fetch a Chart object, and then manipulate its properties and use its methods. Automation, in a sense, blurs the boundaries between applications. An end user may be working with an Access object and not even realize it.

Note Some applications, such as Excel, can function as either a native application or a remote application. Other applications can function only as native applications or only as remote applications.

In this section, I demonstrate how to use VBA to access and manipulate the objects exposed by other applications. The examples use Microsoft Word, but the concepts apply to any application that exposes its objects for Automation — which accounts for an increasing number of applications.

Working with foreign objects

As you know, you can use Excel's Insert ➪ Object command to embed an object such as a Word document in a worksheet. In addition, you can create an object and manipulate it with VBA. (This action is the heart of Automation.) When you do so, you usually have full access to the object. For developers, this technique is generally more beneficial than embedding the object in a worksheet. When an object is embedded, the user must know how to use the Automation object's application. But when you use VBA to work with the object, you can program the object so that the user can manipulate it by an action as simple as a button click.

Early versus late binding

Before you can work with an external object, you must create an instance of the object. This can be done in either of two ways: early binding or late binding.

Early binding

At design time, you create a reference to the object library using the Tools ➪ References command in the VBE, which brings up the dialog box shown in Figure 47-4.

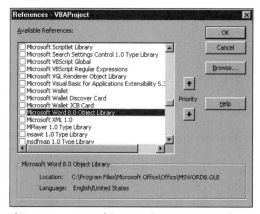

Figure 47-4: Attaching a reference to an object library file

After the reference to the object library is established, you can use the Object Browser shown in Figure 47-5 to view the object names, methods, and properties.

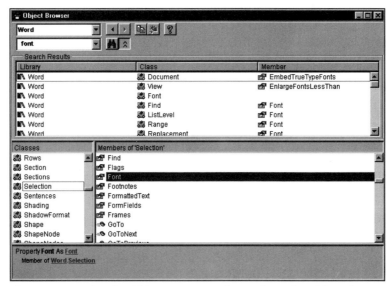

Figure 47-5: Using the Object Browser to learn about the objects in a referenced library

When you use early binding, you must establish a reference to a version-specific object library (either Microsoft Word 8.0 Object Library or Microsoft Word 9.0 Object Library) within the VBE. Then, you use a statement like the following to create the object:

```
Dim WordApp As New Word.Application
```

Late binding

At run time, you use either the `CreateObject` function to create the object or the `GetObject` function to obtain a saved instance of the object. Such an object is declared as a generic `Object` type, and its object reference is resolved at run time.

Using early binding to create the object by setting a reference to the object library usually is more efficient and yields better performance. Early binding is an option only if the object that you are controlling has a separate type library or object library file (usually with a .tlb or .olb extension). You also need to ensure that the user of the application actually has a copy of the specific library installed. Early binding also enables you to use constants that are defined in the object library. For example, Word (like Excel) contains many predefined constants that you can use in your VBA code. Another advantage in using early binding is that you can take advantage of the VBE's Object Browser and Auto List Members option to make it easier to access properties and methods; this feature doesn't work when you use late binding.

It is possible to use late binding even when you don't know which version of the application is installed on the user's system. For example, the following code, which works with both Word 97 and Word 2000, creates a Word object.

```
Dim WordApp As Object
Set WordApp = CreateObject("Word.Application")
```

If multiple versions of Word are installed, you can create an object for a specific version. The following statement, for example, uses Word 97.

```
Set WordApp = CreateObject("Word.Application.8")
```

The registry key for Word's Automation object and the reference to the Application object in VBA just happen to be the same: Word.Application. They do not, however, refer to the same thing. When you declare an object As Word.Application or As New Word.Application, the term refers to the Application object in the Word library. But when you invoke the function CreateObject("Word.Application"), the term refers to the moniker by which the latest version of Word is known in the Windows System Registry. This isn't the case for all Automation objects, although it is true for the main Office 2000 components. If the user replaces Word 97 with Word 2000, CreateObject("Word.Application") continues to work properly, referring to the new application. If Word 97 is removed, however, CreateObject("Word.Application.8"), which uses the alternate version-specific moniker for Word 97, fails to work.

The CreateObject function used on an Automation object such as Word.Application or Excel.Application always creates a new *instance* of that Automation object—that is, it starts up a new and separate copy of the automation part of the program. Even if an instance of the Automation object is already running, a new instance is started, and then an object of the specified type is created.

To use the current instance, or to start the application and have it load a file, use the GetObject function.

A simple example

The following example demonstrates how to create a Word object (using late binding). This procedure creates the object, displays the version number, closes the Word application, and then destroys the object (freeing the memory it used).

```
Sub GetWordVersion()
```

```
        Dim WordApp As Object
        Set WordApp = CreateObject("Word.Application")
        MsgBox WordApp.Version
        WordApp.Quit
        Set WordApp = Nothing
    End Sub
```

Note

The Word object that's created is invisible. If you'd like to see the object while it's being manipulated, set its Visible property to True, as follows:

```
        WordApp.Visible = True
```

Controlling Word from Excel

The example in this section demonstrates an Automation session using Word. The MakeMemos procedure creates three customized memos in Word and then saves each document to a file. The information used to create the memos is stored in a worksheet. Figure 47-6 shows these two files.

Figure 47-6: Word automatically generates three memos based on this Excel data.

The MakeMemos procedure, presented in Listing 47-3, starts by creating an object called WordApp. The routine cycles through the three rows of data in Sheet1 and uses Word's properties and methods to create each memo and save it to disk. A range named Message (also on Sheet1) contains the text used in the memo.

Listing 47-3: Generating Word 2000 data from an Excel VBA program

```
Sub MakeMemos()
'       Creates memos in word using Automation
        Dim WordApp As Object

'       Start Word and create an object
```

```
Set WordApp = CreateObject("Word.Application")

'   Information from worksheet
Set Data = Sheets("Sheet1").Range("A1")
Message = Sheets("Sheet1").Range("Message")

'   Cycle through all records in Sheet1
Records = Application.CountA(Sheets("Sheet1").Range("A:A"))
For i = 1 To Records
'       Update status bar progress message
        Application.StatusBar = "Processing Record " & i

'       Assign current data to variables
        Region = Data.Offset(i - 1, 0).Value
        SalesAmt = Format(Data.Offset(i - 1, 2).Value, _
         "#,000")
        SalesNum = Data.Offset(i - 1, 1).Value

'       Determine the file name
        SaveAsName = ThisWorkbook.Path & "\" & Region & ".doc"

'       Send commands to Word
        With WordApp
            .Documents.Add
            With .Selection
                .Font.Size = 14
                .Font.Bold = True
                .ParagraphFormat.Alignment = 1
                .TypeText Text:="M E M O R A N D U M"
                .TypeParagraph
                .TypeParagraph
                .Font.Size = 12
                .ParagraphFormat.Alignment = 0
                .Font.Bold = False
                .TypeText Text:="Date:" & vbTab & _
                    Format(Date, "mmmm d, yyyy")
                .TypeParagraph
                .TypeText Text:="To:" & vbTab & Region & _
                 " Manager"
                .TypeParagraph
                .TypeText Text:="From:" & vbTab & _
                    Application.UserName
                .TypeParagraph
                .TypeParagraph
                .TypeText Message
                .TypeParagraph
                .TypeParagraph
                .TypeText Text:="Units Sold:" & vbTab & _
                 SalesNum
                .TypeParagraph
                .TypeText Text:="Amount:" & vbTab & _
```

Continued

Listing 47-3 *(continued)*

```
                    Format(SalesAmt, "$#,##0")
            End With
                .ActiveDocument.SaveAs FileName:=SaveAsName
                .ActiveWindow.Close
        End With
    Next i

'   Kill the object
    WordApp.Quit
    Set WordApp = Nothing

'   Reset status bar
    Application.StatusBar = ""
    MsgBox Records & " memos were created and saved in " & _
        ThisWorkbook.Path
End Sub
```

Creating this macro involved several steps. I started by recording a macro in Word. I recorded my actions while creating a new document, adding and formatting some text, and saving the file. That macro provided the information I needed about the appropriate properties and methods. I then copied the macro to an Excel module. Notice that I used With-End With. I added a dot before each instruction between With and End With. For example, the original Word macro contained (among others) the following instruction:

```
Documents.Add
```

I modified the macro as follows:

```
With WordApp
    .Documents.Add
'   more instructions here
End With
```

The macro I recorded in Word used a few of Word's built-in constants. Because this example uses late binding, I had to substitute actual values for those constants. I was able to learn the values by using the Immediate window in Word's VBE.

Controlling Excel from another application

You can, of course, also control Excel from another application (such as a Visual Basic program or a Word macro). For example, you may want to perform some calculations in Excel and return the result to a Word document.

You can create any of the following Excel objects with the adjacent functions:

`Application` object	`CreateObject("Excel.Application")`
`Workbook` object	`CreateObject("Excel.Sheet")`
`Chart` object	`CreateObject("Excel.Chart")`

Figure 47-7 shows a document created by the `MakeMemos` procedure.

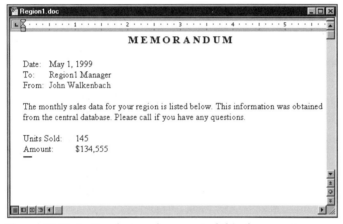

Figure 47-7: An Excel procedure created this document.

Listing 47-4 shows a procedure that is located in a VBA module in a Word 2000 document. This procedure creates an Excel `Worksheet` object — whose moniker is `"Excel.Sheet"` — from an existing workbook.

Listing 47-4: Producing an Excel worksheet on a Word 2000 document

```
Sub MakeExcelChart()
    Dim XLSheet As Object

'   Create a new document
    Documents.Add

'   Prompt for values
    StartVal = InputBox("Starting Value?")
    PctChange = InputBox("Percent Change?")
```

Continued

Listing 47-4 *(continued)*

```
'      Create Sheet object
       Wbook = ThisDocument.Path & "\projections.xls"
       Set XLSheet = GetObject(Wbook, "Excel.Sheet").ActiveSheet

'      Put values in sheet
       XLSheet.Range("StartingValue") = StartVal
       XLSheet.Range("PctChange") = PctChange
       XLSheet.Calculate

'      Insert page heading
       Selection.Font.Size = 14
       Selection.Font.Bold = True
       Selection.TypeText "Monthly Increment: " & _
         Format(PctChange, "0.0%")
       Selection.TypeParagraph
       Selection.TypeParagraph

'      Copy data from sheet & paste to document
       XLSheet.Range("data").Copy
       Selection.Paste

'      Copy chart and paste to document
       XLSheet.ChartObjects(1).Copy
       Selection.PasteSpecial _
           Link:=False, _
           DataType:=wdPasteMetafilePicture, _
           Placement:=wdInLine, DisplayAsIcon:=False

'      Kill the object
       Set XLSheet = Nothing
   End Sub
```

The initial workbook is shown in Figure 47-8. The MakeExcelChart procedure prompts the user for two values and inserts the values into the worksheet.

Recalculating the worksheet updates a chart. The data and the chart are then copied from the Excel object and pasted into a new document. The results are shown in Figure 47-9.

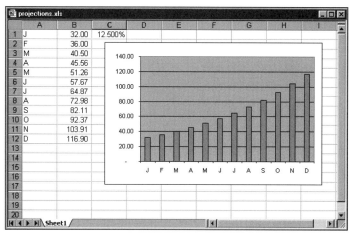

Figure 47-8: A VBA procedure in Word uses this worksheet.

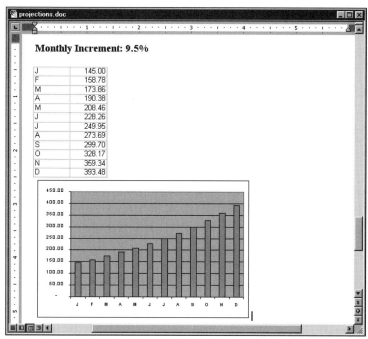

Figure 47-9: The Word VBA procedure uses Excel to create this document.

Using SendKeys

It's possible to control some applications even if they don't support Automation. You can use Excel's SendKeys method to send keystrokes to an application, simulating actions that a user might perform.

Note   SendKeys can be quite tricky to use because the keystrokes are not actually sent until VBA is finished executing. For best results, your procedures should not perform any other actions after sending keystrokes to another application. A good rule of thumb is to use SendKeys only as a last resort.

SendKeys is documented in the online help system, which describes how to send nonstandard keystrokes, such as Alt key combinations.

The CellToDialer procedure in Listing 47-5 demonstrates the use of SendKeys.

Listing 47-5: Having Excel dial the phone, one key at a time

```
Sub CellToDialer()
'   Transfers active cell contents to Dialer
'   And then dials the phone

'   Get the phone number
    CellContents = ActiveCell.Value
    If CellContents = "" Then
        MsgBox "Select a cell that contains a phone number."
        Exit Sub
    End If

'   Activate (or start) Dialer
    Appname = "Dialer"
    AppFile = "Dialer.exe"
    On Error Resume Next
    AppActivate (Appname)
    If Err <> 0 Then
        Err = 0
        TaskID = Shell(AppFile, 1)
        If Err <> 0 Then MsgBox "Can't start " & AppFile
    End If

'   Transfer cell contents to Dialer
    Application.SendKeys "%n" & CellContents, True

'   Click Dial button
    Application.SendKeys "%d"
'    Application.SendKeys "{TAB}~", True
End Sub
```

When executed from a worksheet, this procedure starts the Windows Dialer application in Figure 47-10, which dials the phone. If Dialer is not running, it starts Dialer. The macro uses `SendKeys` to transfer the contents of the active cell to the Windows Dialer application, and then "clicks" the Dial button.

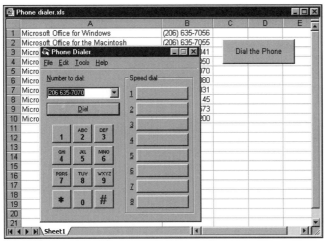

Figure 47-10: SendKeys transfers the phone number in the active cell to Windows Dialer.

Summary

In this chapter, I touched on some of the ways you can automate the process of Excel's working in tandem with other applications. These ways include using Automation to execute and/or activate other applications and using `SendKeys`.

The next chapter describes how to create custom Excel add-ins.

✦   ✦   ✦

Creating Custom Excel Add-Ins

For developers, one of the most useful features in Excel is the capability to create add-ins. This chapter discusses this concept and provides a practical example of creating an add-in.

What Is an Add-In?

Generally speaking, a spreadsheet *add-in* is something that's added to the spreadsheet to give it additional functionality. Excel 2000 includes several add-ins, including the Analysis ToolPak, AutoSave, and Solver. Some add-ins (such as the Analysis ToolPak, discussed in Chapter 38) provide new worksheet functions that can be used in formulas. Usually, the new features blend in well with the original interface, so they appear to be part of the program.

Excel's approach to add-ins is quite powerful, because any knowledgeable Excel user can create add-ins from XLS workbooks. An Excel add-in is basically a different form of an XLS workbook file. Any XLS file can be converted into an add-in, but not every workbook is a good candidate for an add-in. Add-ins are always hidden, so you can't display worksheets or chart sheets that are contained in an add-in. But, you can access its VBA subroutines and functions and display dialog boxes that are contained on dialog sheets.

The following are some typical uses for Excel add-ins:

✦ **To store one or more custom worksheet functions.** When the add-in is loaded, the functions can be used like any built-in worksheet function.

✦ **To store Excel utilities.** VBA is ideal for creating general-purpose utilities that extend the power of Excel. The Power Utility Pak that I created is an example of such a function.

✦ **To store proprietary macros.** If you don't want end users to see (or modify) your macros, store the macros in an add-in. The macros can be used, but they can't be viewed or changed.

As previously noted, Excel ships with several useful add-ins (see the sidebar "Add-Ins That Are Included with Excel"), and you can acquire other add-ins from third-party vendors or the Internet. In addition, Excel includes the tools that enable you to create your own add-ins. This process is explained later in the chapter, but first, some background is required.

Working with Add-Ins

The best way to work with add-ins is to use Excel's add-in manager, which you access by selecting Tools ➪ Add-Ins. This command displays the Add-Ins dialog box, shown in Figure 48-1. The list box contains all the add-ins that Excel knows about. Those that are checked are currently open. You can open and close add-ins from this dialog box by selecting or deselecting the check boxes.

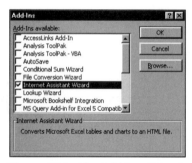

Figure 48-1: The Add-Ins dialog box

Note   Most add-in files can also be opened by selecting File ➪ Open. You'll find that after an add-in is opened, however, you can't choose File ➪ Close to close it. The only way to remove the add-in is to exit and restart Excel or to write a macro to close the add-in.

When an add-in is opened, you may or may not notice anything different. In nearly every case, however, some change is made to the menu — either a new menu or one or more new menu items on an existing menu. For example, when you open the

Analysis ToolPak add-in, a new menu item appears on the Tools menu: Data Analysis. When you open my Power Utility Pak add-in, you get a new Utilities menu, which is located between the Data and Window menus.

Add-Ins Included with Excel

The following is a list of the add-ins that are included with Excel. Some of these add-in may not have been installed. If you try to use one of these add-ins and it's not installed, you receive a prompt asking whether you want to install it.

✦ **Analysis ToolPak:** Statistical and engineering tools, plus new worksheet functions.

✦ **Analysis ToolPak — VBA:** VBA functions for the Analysis ToolPak.

✦ **AutoSave:** Automatically saves your workbook at a time interval that you specify.

✦ **Conditional Sum Wizard:** Helps you to create formulas that add values based on a condition.

✦ **File Conversion Wizard:** Converts a group of files to Excel format.

✦ **Lookup Wizard:** Helps you to create formulas that look up data in a list.

✦ **Microsoft AccessLinks Add-In:** Lets you use Microsoft Access forms and reports with Excel worksheets (Access 97 must be installed on your system).

✦ **Microsoft Bookshelf Integration:** Lets you access Microsoft Bookshelf from Excel

✦ **MS Query Add-In for Excel 5 Compatibility:** Works with Microsoft Query to bring external data into a worksheet.

✦ **ODBC Add-In:** Lets you use ODBC functions to connect to external data sources directly.

✦ **Report Manager:** Prints reports that consist of a set sequence of views and scenarios.

✦ **Solver Add-In:** A tool that helps you to use a variety of numeric methods for equation solving and optimization.

✦ **Template Utilities:** Utilities that are used by the Spreadsheet Solutions templates. This is loaded automatically when you use one of these templates.

✦ **Template Wizard with Data Tracking:** Helps you to create custom templates.

✦ **Update Add-in Links:** Updates links to MS Excel 4.0 add-ins to directly access the new built-in functionality.

✦ **Web Form Wizard:** Sets up a form on a Web server to send data to a database.

The Internet Assistant Wizard, included with Excel 97, is no longer necessary, because Excel 2000 can use HTML as a native file format.

Why Create Add-Ins?

Most Excel users have no need to create add-ins. But if you develop spreadsheets for others — or if you simply want to get the most out of Excel — you may be interested in pursuing this topic further.

The following are several reasons why you may want to convert your XLS application to an add-in:

✦ **To prevent access to your VBA code.** When you distribute an application as an add-in, the end users can't view the sheets in the workbook. If you use proprietary techniques in your VBA code, this can prevent it from being copied (or at least make it more difficult to copy).

✦ **To avoid confusion.** If an end user loads your application as an add-in, the file is not visible — and, therefore, is less likely to confuse novice users or get in the way. Unlike a hidden XLS workbook, an add-in can't be unhidden.

✦ **To simplify access to worksheet functions.** Custom worksheet functions that are stored in an add-in don't require the workbook name qualifier. For example, if you have a custom function named MOVAVG stored in a workbook named Newfuncs.xls, you would have to use a syntax such as the following to use this function in a different workbook:

```
=NEWFUNC.XLS!MOVAVG(A1:A50)
```

But if this function is stored in an add-in file that's open, the syntax is much simpler, because you don't need to include the file reference:

```
=MOVAVG(A1:A50)
```

✦ **To provide easier access.** After you identify the location of your add-in, it appears in the Add-Ins dialog box, with a friendly name and a description of what it does.

✦ **To permit better control over loading.** Add-ins can be opened automatically when Excel starts, regardless of the directory in which they are stored.

✦ **To omit prompts when unloading.** When an add-in is closed, the user never sees the Save Change In . . .? prompt.

Creating Add-Ins

Although any workbook can be converted to an add-in, not all workbooks benefit by this. In fact, workbooks that consist only of worksheets (that is, not macros or custom dialog boxes) become unusable, because add-ins are hidden.

Note   To convert a workbook to an add-in, the workbook must have at least one worksheet. Therefore, if your workbook consists only of Excel 5/95 dialog sheets or Excel 4 macro sheets, you can't convert it to an add-in.

The only types of workbooks that benefit from conversion to an add-in are those with macros. For example, you may have a workbook that consists of general-purpose macros (subroutines and functions). This type of workbook makes an ideal add-in.

Creating an add-in is quite simple. These steps describe how to create an add-in from a normal workbook file:

1. Develop your application and make sure that everything works properly. Don't forget to include a method to execute the macro or macros. You may want to add a new menu item (described later in the chapter).

2. Test the application by executing it when a *different* workbook is active. This simulates its behavior when it's an add-in, because an add-in is never the active workbook. You may find that some references no longer work. For example, the following statement works fine when the code resides in the active workbook, but fails when a different workbook is active:

```
x = Worksheets("Data").Range("A1")
```

You could qualify the reference with the name of the workbook object, like this:

```
x = Workbooks("MYBOOK.XLS").Worksheets("Data").Range("A1")
```

This method is not recommended, because the name of the workbook changes when it's converted to an add-in. The solution is to use the ThisWorkbook qualifier, as follows

```
x = ThisWorkbook.Worksheets("Data").Range("A1")
```

3. Select File ➪ Summary Info, enter a brief descriptive title in the Title field, and then enter a longer description in the Comments field. This step is not required, but it makes using the add-in easier.

4. Lock the project. This is an optional step that protects the VBA code and UserForms from being viewed. You do this in the Visual Basic Editor, using the Tools ➪ Properties command. Click the Protection tab and make the appropriate choices.

5. Save the workbook as an XLA file by selecting File ➪ Save As. Select Microsoft Excel Add-In from the Save as type drop-down list.

After you create the add-in, you need to test it. Select Tools ➪ Add-Ins and use the Browse button in the Add-Ins dialog box to locate the XLA file that you created in Step 5. This installs the add-in. The Add-Ins dialog box uses the descriptive title that you provided in Step 3.

Note   You can continue to modify the macros and UserForms in the XLA version of your file, and save your changes in the Visual Basic Editor. In versions prior to Excel 97, the changes have to be made to the XLS version and then the workbook has to be resaved as an add-in.

An Add-In Example

This section discusses the steps that are used to create a useful add-in that displays a dialog box (see Figure 48-2) in which the user can quickly change several Excel settings. Although these settings can be changed in the Options dialog box, the add-in makes these changes interactively. For example, if the Grid Lines check box is deselected, the gridlines are removed immediately.

Figure 48-2: This dialog box enables the user to change various Excel settings interactively.

This file is available on the companion CD-ROM. The file is not locked, so you have full access to the VBA code and UserForm.

Setting Up the Workbook

This workbook consists of one worksheet, which is empty. Although the worksheet is not used, it must be present, because every workbook must have at least one sheet.

Use the Visual Basic Editor to insert a VBA module (named Module1) and a UserForm (named UserForm1).

Module1

The following macro is contained in the Module1 module. This subroutine ensures that a worksheet is active. If the active sheet is not a worksheet, a message box is displayed and nothing else happens. If a worksheet is active, the subroutine displays the dialog box that is contained in UserForm1.

```
Sub ShowToggleSettingsDialog()
  If TypeName(ActiveSheet) <> "Worksheet" Then
    MsgBox "A worksheet must be active.", vbInformation
  Else
    UserForm1.Show
  End If
End Sub
```

ThisWorkbook

The ThisWorkbook object contains a macro that adds a menu item to the Tools menu when the workbook (add-in) is opened. Another macro removes the menu item when the workbook (add-in) is closed. These two subroutines, which appear in the following syntax, are explained next:

```
Private Sub Workbook_Open()
  Set NewMenuItem = Application.CommandBars _
    ("Worksheet Menu Bar").Controls("Tools").Controls.Add
  With NewMenuItem
    .Caption = "Toggle Settings..."
    .BeginGroup = True
    .OnAction = "ShowToggleSettingsDialog"
  End With
End Sub

Private Sub Workbook_BeforeClose(Cancel As Boolean)
  On Error Resume Next
  Application.CommandBars("Worksheet Menu Bar"). _
    Controls("Tools").Controls("Toggle Settings...").Delete
End Sub
```

The Workbook_Open subroutine adds a menu item (Toggle Settings) to the bottom of the Tools menu on the Worksheet Menu Bar. This subroutine is executed when the workbook (or add-in) is opened.

The Workbook_BeforeClose subroutine is executed when the add-in is closed. This subroutine removes the Toggle Settings menu item from the Tools menu.

UserForm1

Figure 48-3 shows the UserForm1 form, which has ten controls: nine check boxes and one command button. The controls have descriptive names, and the Accelerator property is set so that the controls display an accelerator key (for keyboard users).

The UserForm1 object contains the event-handler subroutines for the objects that are on the form. The following subroutine is executed before the dialog box is displayed:

```
Private Sub UserForm_Initialize()
  cbGridlines = ActiveWindow.DisplayGridlines
  cbHeaders = ActiveWindow.DisplayHeadings
  cbVerticalScrollbar = ActiveWindow.DisplayVerticalScrollBar
  cbHorizontalScrollbar =
ActiveWindow.DisplayHorizontalScrollBar
```

```
      cbFormulaView = ActiveWindow.DisplayFormulas
      cbSheetTabs = ActiveWindow.DisplayWorkbookTabs
      cbStatusBar = Application.DisplayStatusBar
      cbFormulaBar = Application.DisplayFormulaBar
      cbPageBreaks = ActiveSheet.DisplayPageBreaks
   End Sub
```

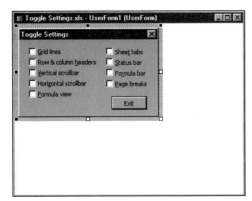

Figure 48-3: The custom dialog box

The UserForm_Initialize subroutine adjusts the settings of the CheckBox controls in the dialog box to correspond to the current settings. For example, if the worksheet is displaying gridlines, ActiveWindow.DisplayGridlines returns True. This value is assigned to the cbGridlines CheckBox—which means that the CheckBox is displayed with a check mark.

Each CheckBox also has an event-handler subroutine, listed in the following code, that is executed when the control is clicked. Each subroutine makes the appropriate changes. For example, if the Grid lines CheckBox is selected, the DisplayGridlines property is set to correspond to the CheckBox.

```
   Private Sub cbGridlines_Click on()
      ActiveWindow.DisplayGridlines = cbGridlines
   End Sub

   Private Sub cbHeaders_Click on()
      ActiveWindow.DisplayHeadings = cbHeaders
   End Sub

   Private Sub cbVerticalScrollbar_Click on()
      ActiveWindow.DisplayVerticalScrollBar = cbVerticalScrollbar
```

```
End Sub

Private Sub cbHorizontalScrollbar_Click on()
   ActiveWindow.DisplayHorizontalScrollBar =
cbHorizontalScrollbar
End Sub

Private Sub cbFormulaView_Click on()
   ActiveWindow.DisplayFormulas = cbFormulaView
End Sub

Private Sub cbSheetTabs_Click on()
   ActiveWindow.DisplayWorkbookTabs = cbSheetTabs
End Sub

Private Sub cbStatusBar_Click on()
   Application.DisplayStatusBar = cbStatusBar
End Sub

Private Sub cbFormulaBar_Click on()
   Application.DisplayFormulaBar = cbFormulaBar
End Sub

Private Sub cbPageBreaks_Click on()
   ActiveSheet.DisplayPageBreaks = cbPageBreaks
End Sub
```

The UserForm1 object has one additional event-handler subroutine for the Exit button. This subroutine, listed as follows, simply closes the dialog box:

```
Private Sub ExitButton_Click on()
   Unload UserForm1
End Sub
```

Testing the Workbook

Before you convert this workbook to an add-in, you need to test it. You should test it when a different workbook is active, to simulate what happens when the workbook is an add-in. Remember, an add-in is never the active workbook and it never displays any of its worksheets.

To test it, I saved the workbook, closed it, and then reopened it. When the workbook was opened, the `Workbook_Open` subroutine was executed. This subroutine added the new menu item to the Tools menu. Figure 48-4 shows how this looks.

Figure 48-4: The Tools menu displays a new menu item, Toggle Settings.

Selecting Tools ⇨ Toggle Setting displays the dialog box that is shown in Figure 48-5.

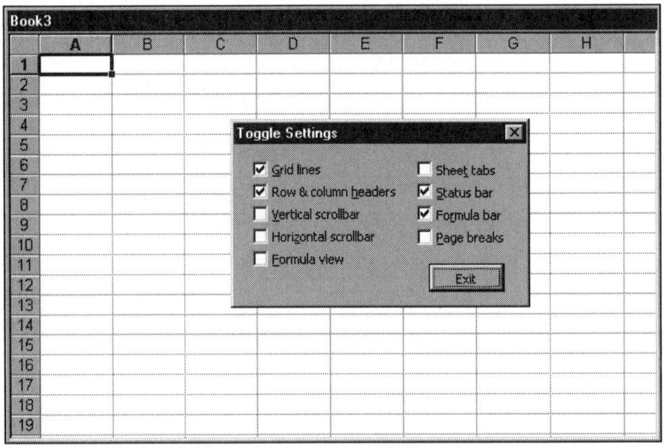

Figure 48-5: The custom dialog box in action

Adding Descriptive Information

This step is recommended but not necessary. Choose File ⇨ Properties to bring up the Properties dialog box. Then, click the Summary tab, as shown in Figure 48-6.

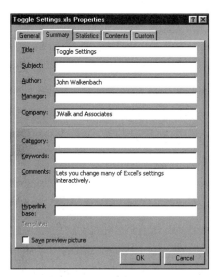

Figure 48-6: Use the Properties dialog box to enter descriptive information about your add-in.

Enter a title for the add-in in the Title field. This is the text that appears in the Add-Ins dialog box. In the Comments field, enter a description. This information appears at the bottom of the Add-Ins dialog box when the add-in is selected.

Protecting the Project

One advantage of an add-in is that it can be protected so that others can't see the source code. If you want to protect the project, follow these steps:

1. Activate the Visual Basic Editor.

2. In the Project window, click the project.

3. Select Tools ➪ [*project name*] Properties.

   VBE displays its Project Properties dialog box.

4. Click the Protection tab (see Figure 48-7).

5. Select the Lock project for viewing check box.

6. Enter a password (twice) for the project.

7. Click OK.

Figure 48-7: The Project Properties dialog box

Creating the Add-In

To save the workbook as an add-in, activate Excel, make sure the workbook is active, and then choose File ➪ Save As. Select Microsoft Excel Add-In (*.xla) from the Save as Type drop-down list. Enter a name for the add-in file and then click OK.

Opening the Add-In

To avoid confusion, close the XLS workbook before you open the add-in that was created from it. Then, select Tools ➪ Add-Ins. Excel displays its Add-Ins dialog box. Click the Browse button and locate the add-in that you just created. After you do so, the Add-Ins dialog box displays the add-in in its list. Notice that the information that you provided in the Properties dialog box appears here (see Figure 48-8). Click OK to close the dialog box and open the add-in.

When the add-in is open, the Tools menu displays a new menu item (Toggle Settings) that executes the ShowToggleSettingsDialog subroutine in the add-in.

If you activate the VBE window, you find that the add-in is listed in the Project window. However, you can't make any modifications unless you provide the password.

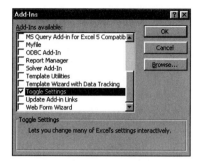

Figure 48-8: The Add-Ins dialog box, with the new add-in selected

Summary

This chapter discusses the concept of add-ins — files that add new capabilities to Excel — and explains how to work with add-ins and why you may want to create custom add-ins. The chapter closes with an example of an add-in that enables users easily to toggle on and off several Excel settings.

✦   ✦   ✦

Creating Custom Toolbars

Toolbars, of course, are a pervasive user interface element found in virtually all software these days. Excel is definitely *not* a toolbar-deficient product. It comes with more than three dozen built-in toolbars, and it's easy to construct new toolbars either manually or with VBA. In this chapter, I describe how to create and modify toolbars.

About Command Bars

Beginning with Excel 97, Microsoft introduced a completely new way of handling toolbars. Technically, a toolbar is known as a `CommandBar` object. In fact, what's commonly called a toolbar is actually one of three types of command bars:

   ✦ **Toolbar:** A floating bar with one or more clickable controls. This chapter focuses on this type of command bar.

   ✦ **Menu bar:** The two built-in menu bars are Worksheet Menu Bar and Chart Menu Bar (see Chapter 50).

   ✦ **Shortcut menu:** The menu that pops up when you right-click an object (see Chapter 50).

Cross-Reference

Because a menu bar is also a command bar, virtually all the information in this chapter also applies to menu bars. In Chapter 50, I discuss the nuances of dealing with custom menus.

Toolbar Manipulations

The following list summarizes the ways in which you can customize toolbars in Excel:

✦ **Remove controls from built-in toolbars.** You can get rid of controls that you never use and free up a few pixels of screen space.

✦ **Add controls to built-in toolbars.** You can add as many controls as you want to any toolbar. These controls can be custom buttons or buttons from other toolbars, or they can come from the stock of controls that Excel provides.

✦ **Create new toolbars.** You can create as many new toolbars as you like, with toolbar controls from any source.

✦ **Change the functionality of built-in toolbar controls.** You do this by attaching your own macro to a built-in control.

✦ **Change the image that appears on any toolbar control.** Excel includes a rudimentary but functional toolbar button editor, although several other image-changing techniques are also possible.

You can perform these customizations by using the Customize dialog box displayed when you select the View ➪ Toolbars ➪ Customize command or by writing VBA code.

Note   Don't be afraid to experiment with toolbars. If you mess up a built-in toolbar, you can easily reset it to its default state. Just choose View ➪ Toolbars ➪ Customize, select the toolbar in the list, and click the Reset button.

How Excel Handles Toolbars

Before you start working with custom toolbars, it's important to understand how Excel deals with toolbars in general. You may be surprised.

Storing toolbars

Toolbars can be attached to XLS (worksheet) or XLA (add-in) files, which makes it easy to distribute custom toolbars with your applications (see "Distributing Toolbars" later in this chapter). You can attach any number of toolbars to a workbook. When the user opens your file, all attached toolbars automatically appear.

Excel stores toolbar information in an XLB file, which resides in Windows's main directory (\WINDOWS or \WINNT). The exact name of this file varies. Why is this XLB file important? Assume that a colleague gives you an Excel workbook that has a custom toolbar stored in it. When you open the workbook, the toolbar appears. You examine the workbook but decide that you're not interested in it. Nonetheless, when you exit Excel, the custom toolbar is added to your XLB file. If you make *any* toolbar changes — from the minor adjustment of a built-in toolbar to the introduction of a custom toolbar — the XLB file is resaved when you exit Excel. Because the entire XLB file is loaded every time you start Excel, the time it takes to start and exit Excel increases significantly as the XLB file grows in size. Plus, all those toolbars eat up memory and system resources. Therefore, it's in your best interest to delete custom toolbars that you never use. Use the View ⇨ Toolbars ⇨ Customize command to do this.

When toolbars don't work correctly

Excel's approach to storing toolbars can cause problems. Suppose you've developed an application that uses a custom toolbar, and you've attached that toolbar to the application's workbook. The first time an end user opens the workbook, the toolbar is displayed. When the user closes Excel, your toolbar is saved in the user's XLB file. If the user alters the toolbar in any way — for example, if he accidentally removes a button — the next time your application is opened, the correct toolbar does *not* appear. Rather, the user sees the altered toolbar, which now lacks an important button. In other words, a toolbar attached to a workbook is not displayed if the user already has a toolbar with the same name. In many cases, this is *not* what you want to happen.

Fortunately, you can write VBA code to prevent this scenario. The trick is never to allow your custom toolbar to be added to the user's toolbar collection. The best way to do this is to create the toolbar on the fly every time the workbook is opened and then delete it when your application closes. With this process, the toolbar is never stored in the user's XLB file. You might think that creating a toolbar on the fly would be a slow process. As you'll see later in this chapter, creating toolbars with VBA is amazingly fast.

Manipulating Toolbars and Buttons Manually

Excel makes it easy for you to create new toolbars and modify existing toolbars. In fact, you may not even have to use VBA to work with toolbars, because you can do just about all your toolbar customization without it.

 Caution It's important to understand that any customizations you make to a toolbar, either built-in or custom, are "permanent." In other words, the changes remain in effect even when you restart Excel. These toolbar changes are not associated with a particular workbook. To restore a toolbar to its original state, you must reset it.

About command bar customization mode

To perform any type of manual toolbar (or menu) customization, Excel needs to be in what I call *command bar customization mode*. You can put Excel into this mode by using any of these techniques:

✦ Select View ➪ Toolbars ➪ Customize.

✦ Select Tools ➪ Customize.

✦ Right-click any toolbar or menu, and select Customize from the shortcut menu.

When Excel is in command bar customization mode, the Customize dialog box is displayed, and you can manipulate toolbars and menus any way you like. You'll find that you can right-click menus and toolbars to get a handy shortcut menu (see Figure 49-1). After you've made your customization, click the Close button in the Customize dialog box.

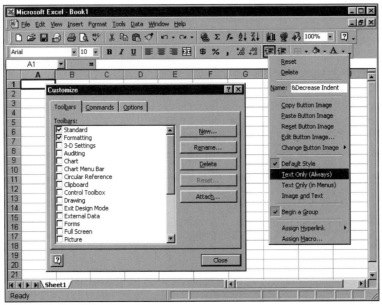

Figure 49-1: In command bar customization mode, you can alter all toolbars and menus.

The Customize dialog box includes three tabs:

✦ **Toolbars:** Lists all the available toolbars, including custom toolbars you have created. The list box also includes the two menu bars (Worksheet Menu Bar and Chart Menu Bar), plus any other custom menu bars.

✦ **Commands:** Lists by category all the available built-in commands. Use this tab to add new items to a toolbar or menu bar.

✦ **Options:** Lets you select various options that relate to toolbars and menus. These include icon size, screen tips, and menu animations.

In the sections that follow, I briefly describe how to perform some common toolbar modifications manually.

Hiding or displaying a toolbar

The Toolbars tab displays every toolbar (built-in toolbars and custom toolbars). Add a check mark to display a toolbar; remove the check mark to hide it. The changes take effect immediately.

Creating a new toolbar

Click the New button, and then enter a name in the New Toolbar dialog box. Excel creates and displays an empty toolbar. You can then add buttons (or menu commands) to the new toolbar.

Figure 49-2 shows a custom toolbar that I created manually. This toolbar, called Custom Formatting, contains the formatting tools that I use most frequently. Notice that this toolbar includes drop-down menus as well as standard toolbar buttons.

Figure 49-2: A custom toolbar that contains formatting tools

Renaming a custom toolbar

Select a custom toolbar from the list, and click the Rename button. Enter a new name in the Rename Toolbar dialog box. You cannot rename a built-in toolbar.

Deleting a custom toolbar

Select a custom toolbar from the list, and click the Delete button. You cannot delete a built-in toolbar.

Resetting a built-in toolbar

Select a built-in toolbar from the list, and click the Reset button. The toolbar is restored to its default state. If you've added any custom tools to the toolbar, they are removed. If you've removed any of the default tools, they are restored. The Reset button is disabled when a custom toolbar is selected.

Moving and copying controls

When Excel is in command bar customization mode, you can copy and move toolbar controls freely among any visible toolbars. To move a control, drag it to its new location, either within the current toolbar or on a different toolbar. To copy a control, press Ctrl while you drag that control to another toolbar. You can also copy a control within the same toolbar.

Inserting a new control

To add a new control to a toolbar, use the Commands tab of the Customize dialog box shown in Figure 49-3.

Figure 49-3: The Commands tab contains a list of every available built-in control.

Here, the controls are arranged in 17 categories. When you select a category, the controls in that category appear to the right. To find out what a control does, select it and click the Description button. To add a control to a toolbar, locate it in the Commands list, and then click and drag it to the toolbar.

Adding a toolbar button that executes a macro

To create a new toolbar button to which you will attach a macro, activate the Commands tab of the Customize dialog box, and then choose Macros from the

Categories list. Drag the command labeled Custom Button to your toolbar (by default, this button has a smiley face image). After adding the button, right-click it and select your options from the menu shown in Figure 49-4. You'll want to change the name, assign a macro, and (I hope) change the image.

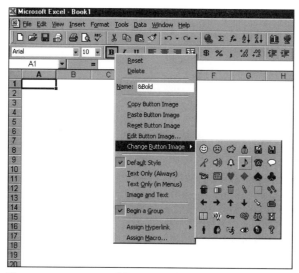

Figure 49-4: Customizing a toolbar button

Cross-Reference

Selecting Change Button Image from the shortcut menu displays a list of 42 images. This is a tiny subset of all of the available images you can use. See "Adjusting a Toolbar Button Image" later in this chapter.

Distributing toolbars

In this section, I describe how to distribute custom toolbars to others, and I outline what you need to be aware of to prevent problems.

Attaching a toolbar to a workbook

To store a toolbar in a workbook file, select View ➪ Toolbars ➪ Customize to display the Customize dialog box. Click the Attach button to bring up the Attach Toolbars dialog box, shown in Figure 49-5. This dialog box lists all the custom toolbars in the Toolbars collection in the list box on the left. Toolbars already stored in the workbook are shown in the list box on the right.

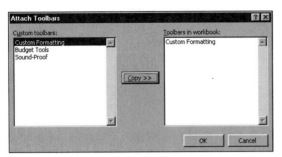

Figure 49-5: The Attach Toolbars dialog box

To attach a toolbar, select it and click the Copy button. When a toolbar in the right list box is selected, the Copy button reads "Delete"; you can click it to remove a selected toolbar from a workbook.

Note

Oddly, you have no way to attach or detach toolbars from a workbook with VBA. These operations must be performed manually.

Caution

The copy of the toolbar stored in the workbook always reflects its contents at the time you attach it. If you modify the toolbar after attaching it, the changed version is not automatically stored in the workbook. You must manually remove the old toolbar and then attach the edited toolbar.

A toolbar that's attached to a workbook automatically appears when the workbook is opened, unless the workspace already has a toolbar by the same name. See "How Excel Handles Toolbars" earlier in this chapter.

Distributing a toolbar with an add-in

Distributing an application as an add-in is often the preferred method for end users. Not surprisingly, an add-in also can include one or more custom toolbars. But you need to be aware of a potential glitch.

Here's a typical scenario: You create an application that uses a custom toolbar. The buttons on that toolbar execute VBA procedures in the application's workbook. You attach the toolbar to the workbook and save the workbook. You create an add-in from the workbook. You close the XLS version of the application. You install the add-in. You click a button on the custom toolbar *and the XLS file opens!*

Your intent, of course, is to have the toolbar buttons execute procedures in the add-in, *not* the XLS file. But when you attach the toolbar to the workbook, the toolbar is saved in its current state. In that state, the workbook includes references to the macros in the XLS file. Consequently, clicking a button opens the XLS file so that the macro can be executed. You could manually (or via VBA) change the OnAction property of each toolbar button so it refers to the add-in. A better approach, though, is to write code to create the toolbar on the fly when the add-in is opened. I discuss this topic in detail later in the chapter.

Manipulating the CommandBars Collection

The CommandBars collection — contained in the Application object — is a collection of all CommandBar objects. Each CommandBar object has a collection of Controls. All these objects have properties and methods that enable you to control toolbars with VBA procedures.

As you might expect, you can write VBA code to manipulate toolbars and other types of command bars. In this section, I provide some key background information that you should know about before you start mucking around with toolbars. As always, a thorough understanding of the object model will make your task much easier.

You manipulate Excel command bars (including toolbars) by using objects located within the CommandBars collection. This collection consists of the following items:

✦ All 40 of Excel's built-in toolbars.

✦ Any other custom toolbars that you create.

✦ A built-in menu bar named Worksheet Menu Bar. This appears when a worksheet is active.

✦ A built-in menu bar named Chart Menu Bar. This appears when a chart sheet is active.

✦ Any other custom menu bars that you create.

✦ All 50 of the built-in shortcut menus.

Command bar types

As I mentioned at the beginning of this chapter, three types of command bars actually exist, each of which is distinguished by its Type property. Possible settings for the Type property of the CommandBars collection are shown in the following table. VBA provides built-in constants for the command bar types.

Type	Description	Constant
0	Toolbar	msoBarTypeNormal
1	Menu Bar	msoBarTypeMenuBar
2	Shortcut Menu	msoBarTypePopUp

Listing all CommandBar objects

If you're curious about the objects in the CommandBars collection, the following procedure should be enlightening. Executing this procedure generates a list (shown in Figure 49-6) of all CommandBar objects in the CommandBars collection: a total of 92 built-in command bars, plus any custom menu bars or toolbars. For each command bar, the procedure lists its Index, Name, and Type property settings (displayed as *Toolbar, Menu Bar,* or *Shortcut*).

	A	B	C	D
1	1	Worksheet Menu Bar	Menu Bar	
2	2	Chart Menu Bar	Menu Bar	
3	3	Standard	Toolbar	
4	4	Formatting	Toolbar	
5	5	PivotTable	Toolbar	
6	6	Chart	Toolbar	
7	7	Reviewing	Toolbar	
8	8	Forms	Toolbar	
9	9	Stop Recording	Toolbar	
10	10	External Data	Toolbar	
11	11	Auditing	Toolbar	
12	12	Full Screen	Toolbar	
13	13	Circular Reference	Toolbar	
14	14	Visual Basic	Toolbar	
15	15	Web	Toolbar	
16	16	Control Toolbox	Toolbar	
17	17	Exit Design Mode	Toolbar	
18	18	Refresh	Toolbar	
19	19	Drawing	Toolbar	
20	20	Query and Pivot	Shortcut	
21	21	PivotChart Menu	Shortcut	
22	22	Workbook tabs	Shortcut	
23	23	Cell	Shortcut	
24	24	Column	Shortcut	
25	25	Row	Shortcut	
26	26	Cell	Shortcut	
27	27	Column	Shortcut	
28	28	Row	Shortcut	
29	29	Ply	Shortcut	

Figure 49-6: VBA code produced this list of all CommandBar objects.

```
Sub ShowCommandBarNames()
    Cells.Clear
    Row = 1
    For Each cbar In CommandBars
        Cells(Row, 1) = cbar.Index
        Cells(Row, 2) = cbar.Name
        Select Case cbar.Type
            Case msoBarTypeNormal
                Cells(Row, 3) = "Toolbar"
            Case msoBarTypeMenuBar
                Cells(Row, 3) = "Menu Bar"
            Case msoBarTypePopUp
```

```
                Cells(Row, 3) = "Shortcut"
          End Select
          Row = Row + 1
      Next cbar
  End Sub
```

Note

When you work with toolbars, you can turn on the macro recorder to see what's happening in terms of VBA code. Most (but not all) of the steps you take while customizing toolbars generate VBA code. By examining this code, you can discover how the object model for toolbars is put together. The object model actually is fairly simple and straightforward.

Creating a command bar

In VBA, you create a new toolbar using the Add method of the CommandBars collection. The following instruction creates a new toolbar with a default name, such as Custom 1. The created toolbar is initially empty (has no controls) and is not visible (its Visible property is False).

```
CommandBars.Add
```

More often, you'll want to set some properties when you create a new toolbar. The following example demonstrates one way to do this:

```
Sub CreateAToolbar()
    Dim TBar As CommandBar
    Set TBar = CommandBars.Add
    With TBar
        .Name = "MyToolbar"
        .Top = 0
        .Left = 0
        .Visible = True
    End With
End Sub
```

The CreateAToolbar procedure uses the Add method of the CommandBars collection to add a new toolbar and create an object variable, Tbar, that represents this new toolbar. Subsequent instructions provide a name for the toolbar, set its position to the extreme upper-left corner the screen, and make it visible. The Top and Left properties specify the position of the toolbar. Their settings represent screen coordinates, not Excel's window coordinates.

Referring to command bars

You can refer to a particular `CommandBar` object by its `Index` or its `Name` property. For example, the Standard toolbar has an `Index` property setting of 3, so you can refer to this toolbar in either of the following ways:

```
CommandBars(3)
CommandBars("Standard")
```

Deleting a command bar

To delete a custom toolbar, use the `Delete` method of the `CommandBar` object. You can refer to the object by its index number (if you know it) or its name. The following instruction deletes the toolbar named `MyToolbar`.

```
CommandBars("MyToolbar").Delete
```

If the toolbar doesn't exist, the instruction generates an error. To avoid the error message when you attempt to delete a toolbar that may or may not exist, the simplest solution is to ignore the error. The following code deletes `MyToolbar` if it exists. If it doesn't exist, no error message is displayed.

```
On Error Resume Next
CommandBars("MyToolbar").Delete
On Error GoTo 0
```

Another approach is to create a custom function that determines whether a particular toolbar is in the `CommandBars` collection. The following function accepts a single argument (a potential `CommandBar` object name) and returns True if the command bar exists.

```
Function CommandBarExists(n) As Boolean
    Dim cb As CommandBar
    For Each cb In CommandBars
        If UCase(cb.Name) = UCase(n) Then
            CommandBarExists = True
            Exit Function
        End If
    Next cb
    CommandBarExists = False
End Function
```

Properties of command bars

The following are some of the more useful properties of a `CommandBar` object:

BuiltIn	True if the object is one of Excel's built-in command bars.
Left	The command bar's left position in pixels.
Name	The command bar's display name.
Position	An integer that specifies the position of the command bar. Possible values are as follows:
	msoBarLeft — The command bar is docked on the left.
	msoBarTop — The command bar is docked on the top.
	msoBarRight — The command bar is docked on the right.
	msoBarBottom — The command bar is docked on the bottom.
	soBarFloating — The command bar isn't docked.
	soBarPopup — The command bar is a shortcut menu.
Protection	An integer that specifies the type of protection for the command bar. Possible values are as follows:
	msoBarNoProtection — (Default) Not protected. The command bar can be customized by the user.
	msoBarNoCustomize — Cannot be customized.
	msoBarNoResize — Cannot be resized.
	msoBarNoMove — Cannot be moved.
	msoBarNoChangeVisible — Its visibility state cannot be changed by the user.
	msoBarNoChangeDock — Cannot be docked to a different position.
	msoBarNoVerticalDock — Cannot be docked along the left or right edge of the window.
	msoBarNoHorizontalDock — Cannot be docked along the top or bottom edge of the window.
Top	The command bar's top position in pixels.
Type	Returns an integer that represents the type of command bar (a toolbar, a menu, or a shortcut menu).
Visible	True if the command bar is visible.

The VBA examples in the following sections demonstrate the use of some of the command bar properties.

Counting custom toolbars

The following function returns the number of custom toolbars. It loops through the `CommandBars` collection and increments a counter if the command bar represented by `cb` is a toolbar and if its `BuiltIn` property is False.

```
Function CustomToolbars()
    Dim cb As CommandBar
    Dim Count As Integer
    Count = 0
    For Each cb In CommandBars
        If cb.Type = msoBarTypeNormal Then
            If Not cb.BuiltIn Then
                Count = Count + 1
            End If
        End If
    Next cb
    CustomToolbars = Count
End Function
```

Preventing a toolbar from being modified

The `Protection` property of a `CommandBar` object provides you with many options for protecting a `CommandBar`. The following instruction sets the `Protection` property for a toolbar named `MyToolbar`.

```
CommandBars("MyToolbar").Protection = msoBarNoCustomize
```

After this instruction is executed, the user is unable to customize the toolbar.

The `Protection` constants are *additive*, which means that you can apply different types of protection with a single command. For example, the following instructions adjust the `MyToolbar` toolbar so that it cannot be customized or moved:

```
Set cb = CommandBars("MyToolbar")
cb.Protection = msoBarNoCustomize + msoBarNoMove
```

Animating a toolbar

The following example is quite useless, unless you're looking for a way to get the user's attention. But it does demonstrate how your VBA code can change the position of a toolbar. The following `MoveToolbar` procedure is executed when the user clicks a button on a single-button toolbar named `"Mover"`. The procedure executes a loop and randomly moves the toolbar to a different screen position each time it cycles through the loop until it ends up at its original position.

```
Sub MoveToolbar()
    With CommandBars("Mover")
        OldLeft = .Left
        OldTop = .Top
```

```
        For i = 1 To 60
            .Left = Int(vidWidth * Rnd)
            .Top = Int(vidHeight * Rnd)
            DoEvents
        Next i
        .Left = OldLeft
        .Top = OldTop
    End With
End Sub
```

In this procedure, `vidWidth` and `vidHeight` represent the width and height of the video display. These values are calculated by the `DisplayVideoInfo` procedure, which uses a Windows API function.

Creating an "autosense" toolbar

Many of Excel's built-in toolbars seem to have some intelligence; they appear when you're working in a specific context and disappear when you stop working in that context. For example, the Chart toolbar normally appears when you are working on a chart, and it disappears when you stop working on the chart. At one time, Microsoft referred to this feature as *toolbar autosensing*, but it stopped using that term in later versions. For lack of a better name, I'll continue to use *autosensing* to refer to this automatic toolbar behavior.

Note   To disable autosensing for a particular toolbar, just close the toolbar while you're working in the context in which it normally appears. To reenable it, make the toolbar visible again while you're working in its context.

You may want to program toolbar autosensing for your application. For example, you might want to make a toolbar visible only when a certain worksheet is activated or when a cell in a particular range is activated. Thanks to Excel's support for events, this sort of programming is relatively easy.

The procedure in Listing 49-1 creates a toolbar when the workbook is opened and uses one of its worksheets' `SelectionChange` events to determine whether the active cell is contained in a range named `ToolbarRange`. If so, the toolbar is visible; if not, the toolbar is hidden. In other words, the toolbar is visible only when the active cell is within a specific range of the worksheet.

Listing 49-1: This toolbar exists only when the cell pointer falls within a given range

```
Sub CreateToolbar()
'   Creates a demo toolbar named "AutoSense"
    Dim AutoSense As CommandBar
```

Continued

Listing 49-1: *(continued)*

```
    Dim Button As CommandBarButton

'   Delete the existing toolbar if it exists
    Call DeleteToolbar

'   Create the toolbar
    Set AutoSense = CommandBars.Add
    For i = 1 To 4
        Set Button = AutoSense.Controls.Add(msoControlButton)
        With Button
            .OnAction = "Button" & i
            .FaceId = i + 37
        End With
    Next i
    AutoSense.Name = "AutoSense"
End Sub
```

This procedure, which is called by the `Workbook_Open` procedure, creates a simple toolbar named `AutoSense`. The four toolbar buttons are set up to execute procedures named `Button1`, `Button2`, `Button3`, and `Button4`. The DeleteToolbar procedure (not shown) simply deletes the toolbar (if it exists) before creating a new one.

Here's the event handler procedure for the `SelectionChange` event:

```
Private Sub Worksheet_SelectionChange(ByVal Target As _
  Excel.Range)
    If Union(Target, Range("ToolbarRange")).Address = _
      Range("ToolbarRange").Address Then
        CommandBars("AutoSense").Visible = True
    Else
        CommandBars("AutoSense").Visible = False
    End If
End Sub
```

This procedure checks the active cell. If it's contained within a range named `ToolbarRange`, the `AutoSense` toolbar's `Visible` property is set to True; otherwise, it is set to False.

The workbook also contains a `Workbook_BeforeClose` procedure that calls the `DeleteToolbar` procedure (which deletes the `AutoSense` toolbar) when the workbook is closed. This technique, of course, can be adapted to provide auto-sensing capability based on other criteria.

Cross-Reference
For a comprehensive discussion of the types of events Excel recognizes, see Chapter 46.

Hiding (and later restoring) all toolbars

Some developers like to "take over" Excel when their application is loaded. For example, they like to hide all toolbars, the status bar, and the formula bar. It's only proper, however, for them to clean up when their application is closed. This includes restoring the toolbars that were originally visible.

The example in this section describes a way to hide all toolbars and then restore them when the application is closed. The HideAllToolbars procedure is called from the Workbook_Open event handler, and the RestoreToolbars procedure is called by the Workbook_BeforeClose event handler.

The code keeps track of which toolbars were visible by storing their names in a worksheet named TBSheet. When the workbook closes, the RestoreToolbars subroutine reads these cells and displays the toolbars. Using a worksheet to store the toolbar names is safer than using an array. Both procedures are shown in Listing 49-2.

Listing 49-2: Removing all toolbars and then restoring them

```
Sub HideAllToolbars()
    Dim TB As CommandBar
    Dim TBNum As Integer
    Dim TBSheet As Worksheet
    Set TBSheet = Sheets("TBSheet")
Application.ScreenUpdating = False

'   Clear the sheet
    TBSheet.Cells.Clear

'   Hide all visible toolbars and store
'   their names
    TBNum = 0
    For Each TB In CommandBars
        If TB.Type = msoBarTypeNormal Then
            If TB.Visible Then
                TBNum = TBNum + 1
                TB.Visible = False
                TBSheet.Cells(TBNum, 1) = TB.Name
            End If
        End If
    Next TB
```

Continued

Listing 49-2: *(continued)*

```
    Application.ScreenUpdating = True
End Sub

Sub RestoreToolbars()
    Dim TBSheet As Worksheet
    Set TBSheet = Sheets("TBSheet")
    Application.ScreenUpdating = False

'   Unhide the previously displayed the toolbars
    On Error Resume Next
    For Each cell In TBSheet.Range("A:A") _
      .SpecialCells(xlCellTypeConstants)
        CommandBars(cell.Value).Visible = True
    Next cell
    Application.ScreenUpdating = True
End Sub
```

Referring to controls in a command bar

A `CommandBar` object such as a toolbar contains `Control` objects. These objects are mainly toolbar buttons and menu items.

The following `Test` procedure displays the `Caption` property for the first `Control` object contained in the Standard toolbar, whose index is 3.

```
Sub Test()
    MsgBox CommandBars(3).Controls(1).Caption
End Sub
```

When you execute this procedure, you'll see the message box shown in Figure 49-7. Notice the ampersand (&). The letter following the ampersand is the underlined hot key in the displayed text.

Figure 49-7: Displaying the Caption property for a control

Rather than use an index number to refer to a control, you can use its `Caption` property setting. The following procedure produces the same result as the previous one.

```
Sub Test2()
    MsgBox CommandBars("Standard").Controls("New").Caption
End Sub
```

Note

In some cases, `Control` objects may contain other `Control` objects. For example, the first control on the Drawing toolbar contains other controls (this also demonstrates that you can include menu items on a toolbar). The concept of `Controls` within `Controls` will become clearer in Chapter 50, when I discuss menus.

Listing the controls on a command bar

The following procedure displays the `Caption` property for each `Control` object within a `CommandBar` object. This example uses the Standard toolbar.

```
Sub ShowControlCaptions()
    Dim Cbar as CommandBar
    Set CBar = CommandBars("Standard")
    Cells.Clear
    Row = 1
    For Each ctl In CBar.Controls
        Cells(Row, 1) = ctl.Caption
        Row = Row + 1
    Next ctl
End Sub
```

The output of the `ShowControlCaptions` procedure is shown in Figure 49-8.

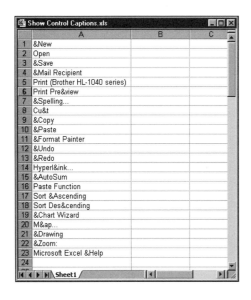

Figure 49-8: A list of the caption for each control on the Standard toolbar

Listing all controls on all toolbars

The following procedure loops through all command bars in the collection. If the command bar is a toolbar — that is, if its `Type` property is set to 1 — another loop displays the `Caption` for each toolbar button.

```
Sub ShowAllToolbarControls()
    Cells.Clear
    Row = 1
    For Each Cbar In CommandBars
        If Cbar.Type = msoBarTypeNormal Then
            Cells(Row, 1) = Cbar.Name
            For Each ctl In Cbar.Controls
                Cells(Row, 2) = ctl.Caption
                Row = Row + 1
            Next ctl
        End If
    Next Cbar
End Sub
```

Partial output of the `ShowAllToolbarControls` procedure is shown in Figure 49-9.

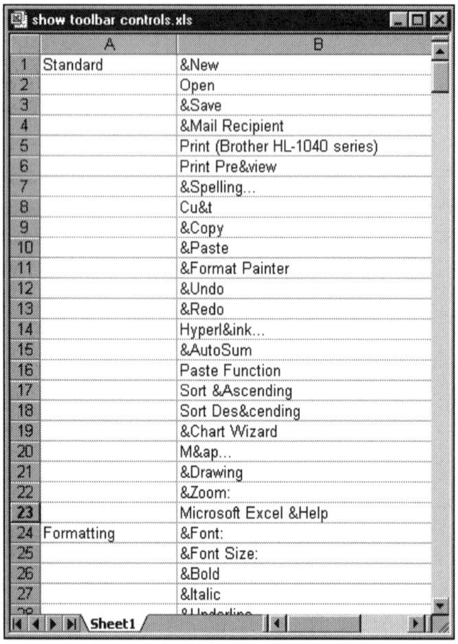
show toolbar controls.xls

	A	B
1	Standard	&New
2		Open
3		&Save
4		&Mail Recipient
5		Print (Brother HL-1040 series)
6		Print Pre&view
7		&Spelling...
8		Cu&t
9		&Copy
10		&Paste
11		&Format Painter
12		&Undo
13		&Redo
14		Hyperl&ink...
15		&AutoSum
16		Paste Function
17		Sort &Ascending
18		Sort Des&cending
19		&Chart Wizard
20		M&ap...
21		&Drawing
22		&Zoom:
23		Microsoft Excel &Help
24	Formatting	&Font:
25		&Font Size:
26		&Bold
27		&Italic

Sheet1

Figure 49-9: A list of the captions for each control on all toolbars

Adding a control to a command bar

You can add a new control to a `CommandBar` object by using the `Add` method of the `Controls` collection object. The following instruction adds a new control to a toolbar named `MyToolbar`. Its `Type` property is set to the `msoControlButton` constant, which creates a standard button.

```
CommandBars("MyToolbar").Controls.Add _
    Type:=msoControlButton
```

The toolbar button added in the preceding instruction is just a blank button; clicking it has no effect. Most of the time, you'll want to set some properties when you add a new button to a toolbar. The following code adds a new control, gives it an image through the `FaceId` property, assigns a macro by way of the `OnAction` property, and specifies a caption.

```
Sub AddButton()
    Set NewBtn = CommandBars("MyToolbar").Controls.Add _
      (Type:=msoControlButton)
    With NewBtn
      .FaceId = 300
      .OnAction = "MyMacro"
      .Caption = "Tooltip goes here"
    End With
End Sub
```

The AddButton procedure creates an object variable (NewBtn) that represents the added control. The `With-End With` construct then sets the properties for the object.

Deleting a control from a command bar

To delete a control from a `CommandBar` object, use the `Delete` method of the `Controls` collection. The following instruction deletes the first control on a toolbar named `MyToolbar`.

```
CommandBars("MyToolbar").Controls(1).Delete
```

You can also specify the control by referring to its caption. The following instruction deletes a control that has a caption of `SortButton`.

```
CommandBars("MyToolbar").Controls("SortButton").Delete
```

Properties of command bar controls

Command bar controls, of course, have a number of properties that determine how the controls look and work. Following is a list of a few of the more useful properties for command bar controls:

BeginGroup	True if a separator bar appears before the control.
BuiltIn	True if the control is one of Excel's built-in controls.
Caption	The text that is displayed for the control. If the control shows only an image, the caption appears when you move the mouse over the control.
Enabled	True if the control can be clicked.
FaceID	A number that represents a graphic image displayed next to the control's text.
OnAction	The name of a VBA procedure to be executed when the user clicks the control.
Style	Determines whether the button appears with a caption and/or image.
ToolTipText	Text that appears when the user moves the mouse pointer over the control.
Type	An integer that determines the type of the control.

Setting a control's Style property

The Style property of a command bar control determines its appearance. The Style property is usually specified using a built-in constant. For example, to display an image and text, set the Style property to msoButtonIconandCaption. Refer to the online help for other Style constants.

Figure 49-10 shows a toolbar with three controls. The first consists of only text (msoButtonCaption), the second has an icon and text (msoButtonIconand Caption), and the third has only an icon (msoButtonIcon).

Figure 49-10: The three values of the Style property for a command bar control

Note   The text displayed on a control is the control's Caption property, and its image is determined by the value of the FaceID property.

Adjusting a toolbar button image

When you're in command bar customization mode, you can right-click any toolbar button and select Change Button Image. Doing so displays a list of 42 images from which you can select. Most of the time, none of these images is exactly what you need. Therefore, you must specify the image with VBA.

The image (if any) displayed on a toolbar control is determined by its `FaceID` property. For an image to be displayed, the control's `Style` property must *not* be `msoButtonCaption`.

The following instruction sets the `FaceId` property of the first button on the `MyToolbar` toolbar image to 45, which is the code number for a mailbox icon.

```
CommandBars("MyToolbar").Controls(1).FaceId = 45
```

How does one determine the code number for a particular image? Well, there's trial and error . . . and there's also a free utility that I developed called FaceID Identifier. This add-in makes it easy to determine the `FaceID` value for a particular image. It displays all possible command bar images. When you move the mouse pointer over an image, the `FaceID` value is displayed in a text box (see Figure 49-11).

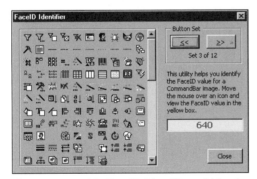

Figure 49-11: My FaceID Identifier add-in shows the FaceID values for built-in toolbar images.

On the CD-ROM The FaceID Identifier add-in is available on the companion CD-ROM.

Adjusting a control's Visible property

The following procedure—which causes lots of onscreen action—simply reverses the `Visible` property of each toolbar. Hidden toolbars are displayed, and visible toolbars are hidden. To return things to normal, execute the procedure a second time.

```
Sub ToggleAllToolbars()
    For Each cb In CommandBars
        If cb.Type = msoBarTypeNormal Then
            cb.Visible = Not cb.Visible
        End If
    Next cb
End Sub
```

Changing a control's caption dynamically

The procedure in Listing 49-3 creates a toolbar with a single button. The caption on this button displays the number format string for the active cell (see Figure 49-12). The procedure uses Worksheet events to monitor when the selection is changed. When a SelectionChange event occurs, a procedure is executed that changes the caption in the button.

Listing 49-3: **Showing the user the current cell's number format**

```
Sub MakeNumberFormatDisplay()
    Dim TBar As CommandBar
    Dim NewBtn As CommandBarButton

'   Delete existing toolbar if it exists
    On Error Resume Next
    CommandBars("Number Format").Delete
    On Error GoTo 0

'   Create a new toolbar
    Set TBar = CommandBars.Add
    With TBar
        .Name = "Number Format"
        .Visible = True
    End With

'   Add a button control
    Set NewBtn = CommandBars("Number Format").Controls.Add _
        (Type:=msoControlButton)
    With NewBtn
        .Caption = ""
        .OnAction = "ChangeNumFormat"
        .Style = msoButtonCaption
    End With
    Call UpdateToolbar
End Sub
```

	A	B	C	D	E	F	G
		Jan	Feb	Mar			
1							
2	Bob	$ 1,977.00	$ 2,324.00	$2,614.00			
3	Jill	$ 1,659.00	$ 4,816.00	$1,028.00			
4	Pam	$ 3,509.00	$ 3,992.00	$2,077.00			
5	Greg	$ 3,168.00	$ 3,166.00	$3,169.00			
6		$10,313.00	$14,298.00	$8,888.00			
7							
8	Pct. Total	30.8%	42.7%	26.5%			

dynamic caption.xls

Number Format

_($* #,##0.00_);_($* (#,##0.00);_($* "-"??_);_(@_)

Sheet1

Figure 49-12: This toolbar button displays the number format for the active cell.

Cross-Reference

For more information about events, see Chapter 46.

The following UpdateToolbar procedure simply copies the NumberFormat property of the ActiveCell to the Caption property of the button control.

```
Sub UpdateToolbar()
'    Puts the selected month in the active cell
     On Error Resume Next
     CommandBars("Number Format"). _
        Controls(1).Caption = ActiveCell.NumberFormat
     If Err <> 0 Then CommandBars("Number Format"). _
        Controls(1).Caption = ""
End Sub
```

The button's OnAction property is set to a procedure named ChangeNumFormat, as follows:

```
Sub ChangeNumFormat()
     Application.Dialogs(xlDialogFormatNumber).Show
     Call UpdateToolbar
End Sub
```

This procedure displays the Number tab of Excel's Format Cells dialog box (see Figure 49-13).

The technique described in this section works quite well, but it does have a flaw: If the user changes the number format with a button on the Formatting toolbar, the display in the Number Format is not changed, because changing the number format of a cell does not trigger a trappable event.

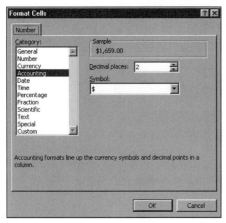

Figure 49-13: Clicking the button enables the user to select a new number format.

Using other types of command bar controls

A standard toolbar button is just one type of control that you can add to a toolbar. The control type is determined by the `Type` property of the control. Besides buttons, the online help lists many other control types. Most of these, however, cannot be added to a command bar. The built-in constants for the control types that you *can* add to a command bar are as follows:

`msoControlButton`	A standard button.
`msoControlEdit`	An edit box.
`msoControlComboBox`	A combo box.
`msoControlDropdown`	A drop-down list.
`msoControlButtonPopup`	A button that, when clicked, displays other controls. Use this control to create a menu with menu items.

Note   The `Type` property for a `Control` object is a read-only property that's set when the control is created. In other words, you can't change a control's type after it has been created.

The online help lists several other `Type` constants for a command bar control. For example, you'll find `msoControlGauge`, `msoControlGraphic Combo`, and others. These controls, however, can't be used. You are limited to controls created with any of the five constants just listed.

The `MakeMonthList` procedure in Listing 49-4 creates a new toolbar, adds a drop-down list control, and fills that control with the names of each month. It also sets the OnAction property so that clicking the control executes a procedure named PasteMonth. The resulting toolbar is shown in Figure 49-14.

Listing 49-4: Attaching a drop-down list to a command bar

```
Sub MakeMonthList()
    Dim TBar As CommandBar
    Dim NewDD As CommandBarControl

'   Delete existing toolbar if it exists
    On Error Resume Next
    CommandBars("MonthList").Delete
    On Error GoTo 0

'   Create a new toolbar
    Set TBar = CommandBars.Add
    With TBar
        .Name = "MonthList"
        .Visible = True
    End With

'   Add a DropDown control
    Set NewDD = CommandBars("MonthList").Controls.Add _
      (Type:=msoControlDropdown)
    With NewDD
        .Caption = "DateDD"
        .OnAction = "PasteMonth"
        .Style = msoButtonAutomatic

'       Fill it with month name
        For i = 1 To 12
            .AddItem Format(DateSerial(1, i, 1), "mmmm")
        Next i
        .ListIndex = 1
    End With
End Sub
```

The following is the PasteMonth procedure:

```
Sub PasteMonth()
'   Puts the selected month in the active cell
    On Error Resume Next
    With CommandBars("MonthList").Controls("DateDD")
        ActiveCell.Value = .List(.ListIndex)
    End With
End Sub
```

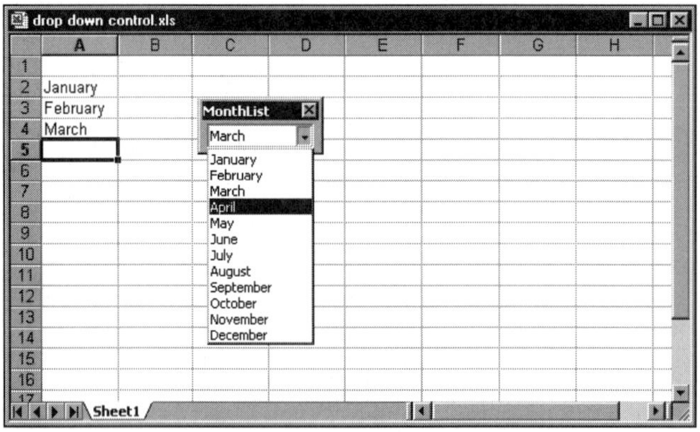

Figure 49-14: This toolbar contains a drop-down list control, with an attached macro.

The workbook has an additional twist: It uses a `Worksheet_SelectionChange` event handler. This procedure, as follows, is executed whenever the user makes a new selection on the worksheet. It determines whether the active cell contains a month name. If so, it sets the `ListIndex` property of the drop-down list control in the toolbar.

```
Private Sub Worksheet_SelectionChange(ByVal Target _
  As Excel.Range)
    For i = 1 To 12
        Set ActCell = Target.Range("A1")
        If ActCell.Value = Format(DateSerial(1, i, 1), _
        "mmmm") Then
            CommandBars("MonthList").Controls("DateDD") _
            .ListIndex = i
            Exit Sub
        End If
    Next i
End Sub
```

Summary

In this chapter, I described how to use Excel's built-in toolbars and how to customize toolbars for your applications.

The next chapter discusses two other types of command bars: menus and shortcut menus.

✦　　　✦　　　✦

Creating Custom Menus

Every Windows program has a menu system, which usually serves as the primary user interface element. The Windows standard places the menu bar directly beneath the application's title bar. In addition, many programs now implement another type of menu: shortcut menus. Typically, right-clicking a selection displays a context-sensitive shortcut menu containing commands that enable you to work with the selection.

Excel uses both types of menus, and developers have almost complete control over Excel's entire menu system, including shortcut menus. This chapter tells you everything you need to know about working with Excel's menus.

A Few Words about Excel's Menu Bar

If you've read Chapter 49, you already know that a menu bar (like a toolbar) is a `CommandBar` object. In fact, the techniques described in Chapter 49 also apply to menu bars.

So how does a menu bar differ from a toolbar? In general, a menu bar is displayed at the top of the Excel window, directly below the title bar. When clicked, the top-level controls on a menu bar display a drop-down list of menu items. A menu bar may also contain three window control buttons (Minimize, Restore, and Close) that are displayed only when a workbook window is maximized. Toolbars, on the other hand, usually consist of graphic icons and do not display any control buttons. These rules are definitely not hard and fast. You can, if desired, add traditional toolbar buttons to a menu bar or add traditional menu items to a toolbar. You can even move a menu bar from its traditional location and make it free-floating.

Beginning with Excel 97, the menus in the Microsoft Office applications are not standard Windows menus. This means that they are not affected by settings specified by the user in the Windows Display Properties dialog box shown in Figure 50-1. For example, you may select a certain text color and highlight color for your Windows menus. These colors choices will have no effect on the menus in Office applications.

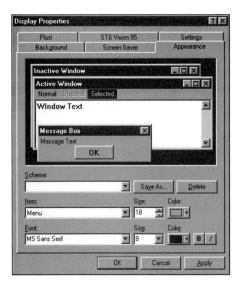

Figure 50-1: Excel's nonstandard Windows menus are not affected by global settings.

What You Can Do with Excel's Menus

Typical Excel users get by just fine with the standard menus. Because you're reading this book, however, you're probably not the typical Excel user. You may want to modify menus to make your life easier and to make life easier for the folks who use the spreadsheets that you develop.

To modify Excel's menus, you can remove elements, add elements, and change elements. In addition, you can temporarily replace Excel's standard menu bar with one of your own creation. You can change Excel's menus two ways: through the Customize dialog box or with VBA code.

When you close Excel, it saves any changes that you've made to the menu system, and these changes appear the next time you open Excel. The information about menu modifications is stored in an XLB file in your Windows directory.

See Chapter 49 for more information about the XLB file.

Note   In most cases, you won't want your menu modifications to be saved between sessions. Generally, you'll need to write VBA code to change the menus while a particular workbook is open and then change them back when the workbook closes. Therefore, you'll need VBA code to modify the menu when the workbook is opened and more VBA code to return the menus to normal when the workbook is closed.

Menu terminology

Menu terminology is often a bit confusing at first because many of the terms are similar. The following list presents the official Excel menu terminology that I refer to in this chapter:

✦ **Command bar.** An object that can function as a menu bar, a shortcut menu, or a toolbar. It is represented by the `CommandBar` object in the Office 2000 object library.

✦ **Menu bar.** The row of words that appears directly below the application's title bar. Excel has two menu bars: One is displayed when a worksheet is active, and the other is displayed when a chart sheet is active or when an embedded chart is activated.

✦ **Menu.** A single, top-level element of a menu bar. For example, both of Excel's menu bars have a File menu.

✦ **Menu item.** An element that appears in the drop-down list when you select a menu. For example, the first menu item under the File menu is New. Menu items also appear in submenus and shortcut menus.

✦ **Separator bar.** A horizontal line that appears between two menu items. The separator bar is used to group similar menu items.

✦ **Submenu.** A second-level menu that is under some menus. For example, the Edit menu has a submenu called Clear.

✦ **Submenu item.** A menu item that appears in the list when you select a submenu. For example, the Edit ➪ Clear submenu contains the following submenu items: All, Formats, Contents, and Comments.

✦ **Shortcut menu.** The floating list of menu items that appears when you right-click a selection or an object. The shortcut menu that appears depends on the current context.

✦ **Enabled.** A menu item that can be used. If a menu item isn't enabled, its text appears grayed, and it can't be used.

✦ **Checked.** The status of a menu item that represents an on/off or True/False state. A menu item can display a graphical box that is checked or unchecked. The View ➪ Status Bar menu item is an example.

✦ **Image.** A small graphic icon that appears next to some menu items. This icon is sometimes called a Face ID.

✦ **Shortcut key combination.** A keystroke combination that serves as an alternate method to execute a menu item. The shortcut key combination is displayed at the right side of the menu item. For example, Ctrl+S is the shortcut key combination for File ➪ Save.

Removing menu elements

You can remove any part of Excel's menu system: menu items, menus, and entire menu bars. For example, if you don't want the end users of your application fiddling with the display, you can remove the View menu from the Worksheet Menu Bar. You can also remove one or more menu items from a menu. If you remove the New menu item from the File menu, for example, users can't use the menu to create a new workbook. Finally, you can eliminate Excel's menu bar and replace it with one that you've created. You might do this if you want your application to be completely under the control of your macros.

Tip

It's important to remember that simply removing menu bars, menus, or menu items does not affect the alternate method of accomplishing some actions. Specifically, if corresponding shortcut keys, toolbar buttons, or shortcut menus perform the same action as a menu command, those alternate methods still work. For example, if you remove the New menu item from the File menu, the user can still use the New Workbook toolbar button, the Ctrl+N shortcut key, or the Desktop shortcut menu to create a new workbook.

Adding menu elements

You can add your own custom menus to built-in menu bars, and you can add custom menu items to a built-in menu. In fact, you can create an entirely new menu bar if you like. For example, you might develop an application that doesn't require any of Excel's built-in menus. A simple solution is to create a new menu bar that consists of custom menus and custom menu items that execute your macros. You can hide Excel's normal menu bar and replace it with your own.

Changing menu elements

If you get bored with Excel's standard menu text, you can change it to something else — for instance, you can change the Tools menu to the Stuff menu. You can also assign your own macros to built-in menu items. You have many other options for changing menu elements, including rearranging the order of the menus on a menu bar (for example, to make the Help menu appear first instead of last).

The remainder of this chapter focuses on writing VBA code to modify menus.

Cross-Reference

Chapter 49 provides background information about the Customize dialog box.

Moving Up from Excel 5/95?

If you've customized menus using Excel 5 or Excel 95, you can pretty much forget everything you ever learned. Beginning with Excel 97, menu customization has changed significantly in the following respects:

✦ A menu bar is actually a toolbar in disguise. If you don't believe me, grab the vertical bars at the very left of the menu bar and drag the bar away. You'll end up with a floating toolbar. The official (VBA) term for both menus and toolbars is command bar.

✦ The Excel 5/95 Menu Editor is gone. To edit a menu manually, you use the View ➪ Toolbars ➪ Customize command. Understand, however, that Excel 5/95 workbooks that contain menus customized using the old Menu Editor still work in Excel 97 and Excel 2000.

✦ Menu items can now have images (as you've undoubtedly noticed).

✦ You have no easy way to assign a VBA macro to a new menu item on the Tools menu. This was a piece of cake with Excel 5/95. Later in this chapter, however, I provide VBA code that you can use to add a new menu item to the Tools menu.

✦ Excel 2000 by default displays only the most recently used menu items. In my opinion, this is one of the worst ideas Microsoft has come up with. I can't imagine why anyone would want the order of her menu items to be shifting around. Fortunately, this feature can be disabled in the Options panel of the Customize dialog box.

VBA Examples

In this section, I present some practical examples of VBA code that manipulates Excel's menus.

Referencing the CommandBars Collection

The CommandBars collection is a member of the Application object. When you reference this collection in a regular VBA module, you can omit the reference to the Application object (it is assumed). For example, the following statement (contained in a standard VBA module) displays the name of the first element of the CommandBars collection:

```
MsgBox CommandBars(1).Name
```

For some reason, when you reference the CommandBars collection from a code module for a ThisWorkbook object, you must precede it with a reference to the Application object, like this:

```
MsgBox Application.CommandBars(1).Name
```

Listing menu information

The following `ListMenuInfo` procedure may be instructive. It displays the caption for each item (menu, menu item, and submenu item) on the Worksheet Menu Bar.

```
Sub ListMenuInfo()
    Row = 1
    On Error Resume Next
    For Each Menu In CommandBars(1).Controls
        For Each MenuItem In Menu.Controls
            For Each SubMenuItem In MenuItem.Controls
                Cells(Row, 1) = Menu.Caption
                Cells(Row, 2) = MenuItem.Caption
                Cells(Row, 3) = SubMenuItem.Caption
                Row = Row + 1
            Next SubMenuItem
        Next MenuItem
    Next Menu
End Sub
```

Figure 50-2 shows a portion of the `ListMenuInfo` procedure's output.

	A	B	C
112	&Insert	&Name	&Define...
113	&Insert	&Name	&Paste...
114	&Insert	&Name	&Create...
115	&Insert	&Name	&Apply...
116	&Insert	&Name	&Label...
117	&Insert	Co&mment	
118	&Insert	&Picture	&Clip Art...
119	&Insert	&Picture	&From File...
120	&Insert	&Picture	&AutoShapes
121	&Insert	&Picture	&Organization Chart
122	&Insert	&Picture	&WordArt...
123	&Insert	&Picture	From &Scanner or Camera...
124	&Insert	&Object...	
125	&Insert	Hyperl&ink...	
126	F&ormat	C&ells...	
127	F&ormat	&Row	H&eight...
128	F&ormat	&Row	&AutoFit
129	F&ormat	&Row	&Hide
130	F&ormat	&Row	&Unhide
131	F&ormat	&Column	&Width...
132	F&ormat	&Column	&AutoFit Selection
133	F&ormat	&Column	&Hide
134	F&ormat	&Column	&Unhide
135	F&ormat	&Column	&Standard Width...
136	F&ormat	S&heet	&Rename
137	F&ormat	S&heet	&Hide
138	F&ormat	S&heet	&Unhide...
139	F&ormat	S&heet	&Background...
140	F&ormat	&AutoFormat...	

Figure 50-2: A portion of the output from the ListMenuInfo procedure

A workbook that contains this procedure is available on the companion CD-ROM.

I use `On Error Resume Next` to avoid the error message that appears when the procedure attempts to access a submenu item that doesn't exist.

Menu-Making Conventions

You may have noticed that menus in Windows programs typically adhere to some established conventions. No one knows where these conventions came from, but you should follow them if you want to give the impression that you know what you're doing. When you modify menus, keep the following points in mind:

✦ Tradition dictates that the File menu is always first and the Help menu is always last.

✦ Menu text is always proper case. The first letter of each word is uppercase, except for minor words such as the, a, and and.

✦ A menu itself does not cause any action. In other words, each menu must have at least one menu item.

✦ Menu items are usually limited to three or fewer words.

✦ Every menu item should have a hot key (underlined letter) that's unique to the menu.

✦ A menu item that displays a dialog box is followed by an ellipsis (...).

✦ Menu item lists should be kept relatively short. Sometimes, submenus provide a good alternative to long lists. If you must have a lengthy list of menu items, use separator bars to group items into logical groups.

✦ If possible, disable menu items that are not appropriate in the current context. In VBA terminology, to disable a menu item, set its `Enabled` property to False.

✦ Some menu items serve as toggles. When the option is on, the menu item is preceded by a check mark.

Adding a new menu to a menu bar

In this section, I describe how to use VBA to add a new menu to the Worksheet Menu Bar. The Worksheet Menu Bar is the first item in the `CommandBars` collection, so you can reference it one of two ways:

```
CommandBars("Worksheet Menu Bar")
CommandBars(1)
```

In VBA terms, you use the `Add` method to append a new control to the `CommandBar Controls` collection. The new control is a "pop-up control" of type `msoControl Popup`. You can specify the new control's position; if you don't, the new menu is added to the end of the menu.

Adding a new menu is a two-step process:

1. Use the `Add` method to create an object variable that refers to the new control. Arguments for the `Add` method enable you to specify the control's type, its ID (useful only if you're adding a built-in menu item), its position, and whether it's a temporary control that will be deleted when Excel closes.

2. Adjust the properties of the new control. For example, you'll probably want to specify a `Caption` property and an `OnAction` property.

Adding a menu: Take 1

In this example, the objective is to add a new Budgeting menu to the Worksheet Menu Bar and to position this new menu to the left of the Help menu.

```
Sub AddNewMenu()
'   Get Index of Help menu
    HelpIndex = CommandBars(1).Controls("Help").Index

'   Create the menu
    Set NewMenu = CommandBars(1).Controls.Add _
      (Type:=msoControlPopup, _
        Before:=HelpIndex, _
        Temporary:=True)

'   Add a caption
    NewMenu.Caption = "&Budgeting"
End Sub
```

The preceding code is not a good example of how to add a menu, and it may or may not insert the menu at the proper position. It suffers from two problems:

✦ It assumes that the Help menu exists, but the user may have removed the Help menu.

✦ It assumes that the Help menu has Help as its caption, but non-English versions of Excel may have a different caption for their menus.

Adding a menu: Take 2

Listing 50-1 presents a better demonstration. It uses the `FindControl` method to attempt to locate the Help menu. If the Help menu is not found, the code adds the new menu item to the end of the Worksheet Menu Bar.

Listing 50-1: **Adding the Budgeting menu to Excel's main menu bar**

```
Sub AddNewMenu()
    Dim HelpMenu As CommandBarControl
    Dim NewMenu As CommandBarPopup

'   Find the Help Menu
    Set HelpMenu = CommandBars(1).FindControl(Id:=30010)

    If HelpMenu Is Nothing Then
'       Add the menu to the end
        Set NewMenu = CommandBars(1).Controls _
         .Add(Type:=msoControlPopup, Temporary:=True)
    Else
'       Add the menu before Help
        Set NewMenu = CommandBars(1).Controls _
         .Add(Type:=msoControlPopup, Before:=HelpMenu.Index, _
         Temporary:=True)
    End If

'   Add a caption
    NewMenu.Caption = "&Budgeting"
End Sub
```

Note

The preceding procedure creates an essentially worthless menu — it has no menu items. See "Adding a Menu Item to the Tools Menu" later in this chapter for an example of how to add a menu item to a menu.

To use the FindControl method, you must know the Id property of the control that you're looking for. Each of Excel's own built-in CommandBar controls has a unique Id property. For this example, I determined the Id property of the Help menu by executing the following statement:

```
MsgBox CommandBars(1).Controls("Help").Id
```

The message box displayed 30010, which is the value I used as the Id argument for the FindControl method. Table 50-1 shows the Id property settings for the top-level controls in Excel's menu bars.

	Table 50-1	
	Id Property Settings for Excel's Built-in Menus	
Menu	**Id Setting**	
File	30002	
Edit	30003	
View	30004	
Insert	30005	
Format	30006	
Tools	30007	
Data	30011	
Chart	30022	
Window	30009	
Help	30010	

Deleting a menu from a menu bar

To delete a menu, use the `Delete` method. The following example deletes the menu in the Worksheet Menu Bar whose caption is "Budgeting." Notice that I use `On Error Resume Next` to avoid the error message that appears if the menu does not exist.

```
Sub DeleteMenu()
    On Error Resume Next
    CommandBars(1).Controls("Budgeting").Delete
End Sub
```

Adding menu items to a menu

In the example under "Adding a new menu to a menu bar," I demonstrated how to add a menu to a menu bar. Listing 50-2 adds to the original procedure and, in so doing, demonstrates how to add menu items to the new menu.

Listing 50-2: Adding selections and submenu items to the Budgeting menu

```
Sub CreateMenu()
    Dim HelpMenu as CommandBarControl
    Dim NewMenu As CommandBarPopup

'   Delete the menu if it already exists
```

```
Call DeleteMenu

'   Find the Help Menu
    Set HelpMenu = CommandBars(1).FindControl(Id:=30010)

    If HelpMenu Is Nothing Then
'       Add the menu to the end
        Set NewMenu = CommandBars(1).Controls _
        .Add(Type:=msoControlPopup, temporary:=True)
    Else
'      Add the menu before Help
        Set NewMenu = CommandBars(1).Controls _
        .Add(Type:=msoControlPopup, Before:=HelpMenu.Index, _
        temporary:=True)
    End If

'   Add a caption for the menu
    NewMenu.Caption = "&Budgeting"

'   FIRST MENU ITEM
    Set MenuItem = NewMenu.Controls.Add _
      (Type:=msoControlButton)
    With MenuItem
        .Caption = "&Data Entry..."
        .FaceId = 162
        .OnAction = "Macro1"
    End With

'   SECOND MENU ITEM
    Set MenuItem = NewMenu.Controls.Add _
      (Type:=msoControlButton)
    With MenuItem
        .Caption = "&Generate Reports..."
        .FaceId = 590
        .OnAction = "Macro2"
End With
'   THIRD MENU ITEM
    Set MenuItem = NewMenu.Controls.Add _
      (Type:=msoControlPopup)
    With MenuItem
        .Caption = "View &Charts"
        .BeginGroup = True
    End With

'   FIRST SUBMENU ITEM
    Set SubMenuItem = MenuItem.Controls.Add _
      (Type:=msoControlButton)
    With SubMenuItem
        .Caption = "Monthly &Variance"
        .FaceId = 420
        .OnAction = "Macro3"
    End With
```

Continued

Listing 50-2 *(continued)*

```
'    SECOND SUBMENU ITEM
     Set SubMenuItem = MenuItem.Controls.Add _
       (Type:=msoControlButton)
     With SubMenuItem
         .Caption = "Year-To-Date &Summary"
         .FaceId = 422
         .OnAction = "Macro4"
     End With
End Sub
```

Specifically, the `CreateMenu` procedure builds the menu shown in Figure 50-3. This menu has three menu items, and the last menu item is a submenu with two submenu items.

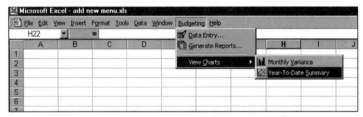

Figure 50-3: A VBA procedure created this menu and its associated menu items.

Note   You might be wondering why the code in the preceding example deletes the menu (if it already exists) and doesn't simply exit the procedure. Rebuilding the menu ensures that the latest version is added to the menu bar. This also makes it much easier on you while you're developing the code because you don't have to delete the menu manually before testing your procedure. As you may have noticed, creating menus is very fast, so the additional time required to rebuild a menu is usually negligible.

When you examine the `CreateMenu` procedure, keep the following points in mind:

✦ The control type for the first two menu items is `msoControlButton`. The type of the third menu item, however, is `msoControlPopup` because the third menu item has submenu items.

✦ No `OnAction` property exists for controls of type `msoControlPopup`.

✦ The `BeginGroup` property of the third menu item is True, which causes a separator bar to appear before the item. The separator bar is purely cosmetic and serves to "group" similar menu items together.

✦ The FaceID property determines which image (if any) appears next to the menu text. The FaceID number represents a built-in image.

✦ The text for the Caption properties uses an ampersand (&) to indicate the "hot key," or accelerator key, for the menu item. The hot key is the underlined letter that provides keyboard access to the menu item.

Adding a menu item to the Tools menu

The example in Listing 50-2 adds several menu items to a custom menu on the Worksheet Menu Bar. Often, you'll simply want to add a menu item to one of Excel's built-in menus, such as the Tools menu.

With Excel 5 and Excel 95, assigning a macro to a new menu item on the Tools menu was easy. For some reason, this feature was removed, beginning with Excel 97. With Excel 97 or later, if you want to assign a macro to a menu item on the Tools menu (or any other menu, for that matter), you must write VBA code to do so.

Listing 50-3 adds the menu item Clear All But Formulas to the Tools menu—whose Id property is set to 30007. Clicking this menu item executes a procedure named ClearAllButFormulas.

Listing 50-3: **Adding a selection to Excel's Tools menu**

```
Sub AddMenuItem()
    Dim ToolsMenu As CommandBarPopup
    Dim NewMenuItem As CommandBarButton

'   Delete the menu if it already exists
    Call DeleteMenuItem

'   Find the Tools Menu
    Set ToolsMenu = CommandBars(1).FindControl(Id:=30007)
    If ToolsMenu Is Nothing Then
        MsgBox "Cannot add menu item."
        Exit Sub
    Else
        Set NewMenuItem = ToolsMenu.Controls.Add _
          (Type:=msoControlButton)
        With NewMenuItem
            .Caption = "&Clear All But Formulas"
            .FaceId = 348
            .OnAction = "ClearAllButFormulas"
            .BeginGroup = True
        End With
    End If
End Sub
```

Figure 50-4 shows the Tools menu with the new menu item.

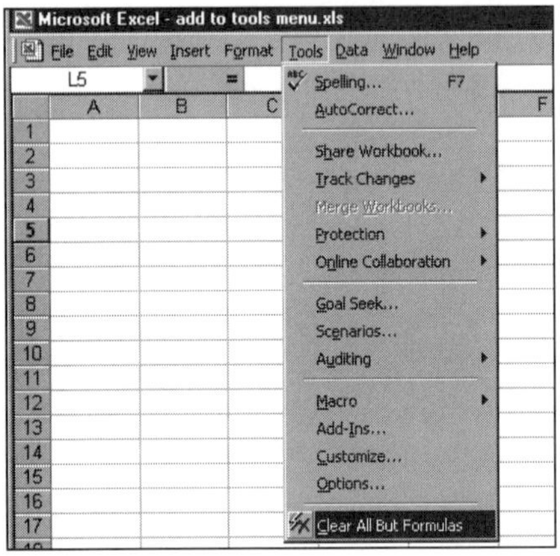

Figure 50-4: A new menu item has been added to the Tools menu.

Deleting a menu item from the Tools menu

To delete a menu item, use the `Delete` method of the `Controls` collection. The following example deletes the Clear All But Formulas menu item on the Tools menu. Note that it uses the `FindControl` method to handle the situation when the Tools menu has a different caption.

```
Sub DeleteMenuItem()
    On Error Resume Next
    CommandBars(1).FindControl(Id:=30007). _
        Controls("&Clear All But Formulas").Delete
End Sub
```

Displaying a shortcut key with a menu item

Some of Excel's built-in menu items also display a shortcut key combination that, when pressed, has the same effect as the menu command. For example, Excel's Edit menu lists several shortcut keys.

To display a shortcut key combination as part of your menu item, use the `Shortcut Text` property. Listing 50-4 creates a menu item Clear All But Formulas on the Tools menu. It sets the `ShortcutText` property to the string Ctrl+Shift+C and also uses the `MacroOptions` method to set up the shortcut key.

Listing 50-4: Adding a menu selection that features a shortcut key

```
Sub AddMenuItem()
    Dim ToolsMenu As CommandBarPopup
```

```
        Dim NewMenuItem As CommandBarButton

'       Delete the menu if it already exists
        Call DeleteMenuItem

'       Find the Tools Menu
        Set ToolsMenu = CommandBars(1).FindControl(Id:=30007)
        If ToolsMenu Is Nothing Then
            MsgBox "Cannot add a menu item - use Ctrl+Shift+C."
            Exit Sub
        Else
            Set NewMenuItem = ToolsMenu.Controls.Add _
            (Type:=msoControlButton)
            With NewMenuItem
                .Caption = "&Clear All But Formulas"
                .FaceId = 348
                .ShortcutText = "Ctrl+Shift+C"
                .OnAction = "ClearAllButFormulas"
                .BeginGroup = True
            End With
        End If

'       Create the shortcut key
        Application.MacroOptions _
          Macro:="ClearAllButFormulas", _
          HasShortcutKey:=True, _
          ShortcutKey:="C"
    End Sub
```

After this procedure is executed, the menu item is displayed as shown in Figure 50-5.

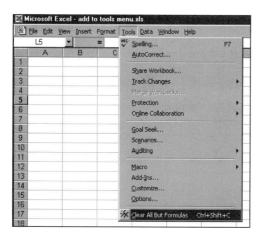

Figure 50-5: The Clear All But Formulas menu item also displays a shortcut key combination.

Fixing a menu that has been reset

Consider this scenario: You write VBA code that creates a new menu when your workbook application is opened. The user opens another workbook containing a macro that resets Excel's menu bar. Or consider this: The user plays around with the Customize dialog box, selects the Workbook Menu Bar from the list on that dialog, and clicks the Reset button. In both cases, your custom menu is zapped.

Your menu-making code is probably triggered by the Workbook_Open event, so the only way the user can get your menu back is to close and reopen the workbook. To provide another way, create a key combination that executes the procedure that builds your menu.

Apparently, applications that reset Excel's menu bar are not uncommon. Users of my Power Utility Pak add-in sometimes tell me that the Utilities menu has disappeared for no apparent reason. This is always caused by some other application that feels it must reset the Worksheet Menu Bar. Therefore, I added a key combination (Ctrl+Shift+U) that, when pressed, rebuilds the Utilities menu. The real problem, of course, is getting the user to read the documentation that describes how to recreate the menu.

Working with Events

Suppose you want to create a menu when a workbook opens. You'll also want to delete the menu when the workbook closes because menu modifications remain in effect between Excel sessions. Or suppose you want a menu to be available only when a particular workbook or worksheet is active. These sorts of things are relatively easy to program, thanks to Excel's event handlers.

The examples in this section demonstrate various menu-programming techniques used in conjunction with events.

Cross-Reference I discuss event programming in depth in Chapter 46.

Adding and deleting menus automatically

If you need a menu to be created when a workbook is opened, use the Workbook_Open event. The following code, stored in the code module for the ThisWorkbook object, executes the CreateMenu procedure.

```
Private Sub Workbook_Open()
    Call CreateMenu
End Sub
```

To delete the menu when the workbook is closed, use a procedure such as the following. This procedure is executed before the workbook closes, and it executes the DeleteMenu procedure.

```
Private Sub Workbook_BeforeClose(Cancel As Boolean)
    Call DeleteMenu
End Sub
```

A problem may arise, however, if the workbook is not saved when the user closes it. Excel's "save workbook before closing" prompt occurs after the Workbook_ BeforeClose event handler runs. So if the user clicks Cancel, the workbook remains open, but your custom menu has already been deleted!

One solution to this problem is to bypass Excel's prompt and write your own code in the Workbook_BeforeClose procedure to ask the user to save the workbook. The following code demonstrates how:

```
Private Sub Workbook_BeforeClose(Cancel As Boolean)
    If Not Me.Saved Then
        Msg = "Do you want to save the changes you made to "
        Msg = Msg & Me.Name & "?"
        Ans = MsgBox(Msg, vbQuestion + vbYesNoCancel)
        Select Case Ans
            Case vbYes
                Me.Save
            Case vbNo
                Me.Saved = True
            Case vbCancel
                Cancel = True
                Exit Sub
        End Select
    End If
    Call DeleteMenu
End Sub
```

This procedure determines whether the workbook has been saved. If it has, no problem; the DeleteMenu procedure is executed, and the workbook is closed. But if the workbook has not been saved, the procedure displays a message box that duplicates the one Excel normally shows. If the user clicks Yes, the workbook is saved, the menu is deleted, and the workbook is closed. If the user clicks No, the code sets the Saved property of the Workbook object to True (without actually saving the file) and deletes the menu. If the user clicks Cancel, the BeforeClose event is canceled, and the procedure ends without deleting the menu.

Disabling or hiding menus

When a menu or menu item is disabled, its text appears in a faint shade of gray, and clicking it has no effect. Excel disables its menu items when they are out of context. For example, the Links menu item on the Edit menu is disabled when the active workbook does not contain any links.

You can write VBA code to enable or disable both built-in and custom menus or menu items. Similarly, you can write code to hide menus or menu items. The key, of course, is tapping into the correct event.

The following procedures are stored in the code module for the ThisWorkbook object.

```
Private Sub Workbook_Open()
    Call AddMenu
End Sub

Private Sub Workbook_BeforeClose(Cancel As Boolean)
    Call DeleteMenu
End Sub

Private Sub Workbook_Activate()
    Call UnhideMenu
End Sub

Private Sub Workbook_Deactivate()
    Call HideMenu
End Sub
```

When the workbook is opened, the AddMenu procedure is called. When the workbook is closed, the DeleteMenu workbook is called. Two additional event-handler procedures are executed when the workbook is activated or deactivated. The UnhideMenu procedure is called when the workbook is activated, and the HideMenu procedure is called when the workbook is deactivated.

The HideMenu procedure sets the Visible property of the menu item to False, which effectively removes it from the menu bar. The UnhideMenu procedure does just the opposite. The net effect is that the menu is visible only when the workbook is active. These procedures, which assume that the Caption for the menu is "Budgeting", are as follows:

```
Sub UnhideMenu()
    CommandBars(1).Controls("Budgeting").Visible = True
End Sub

Sub HideMenu()
    CommandBars(1).Controls("Budgeting").Visible = False
End Sub
```

To disable the menu rather than hide it, simply access the Enabled property instead of the Visible property.

On the CD-ROM   This example is available on the companion CD-ROM.

Working with checked menu items

Several of Excel's menu items appear with or without a check mark. For example, the View ➪ Formula Bar menu item displays a check mark if the formula bar is visible and does not display a check mark if the formula bar is hidden. When you select this menu item, the formula bar's visibility is toggled, and the check mark is either displayed or not.

You can add this type of functionality to your custom menu items. Figure 50-6 shows a menu item that displays a check mark only when the active sheet is displaying grid lines. Selecting this item toggles the grid-line display and also adjusts the check mark. The check mark display is determined by the State property of the menu item control.

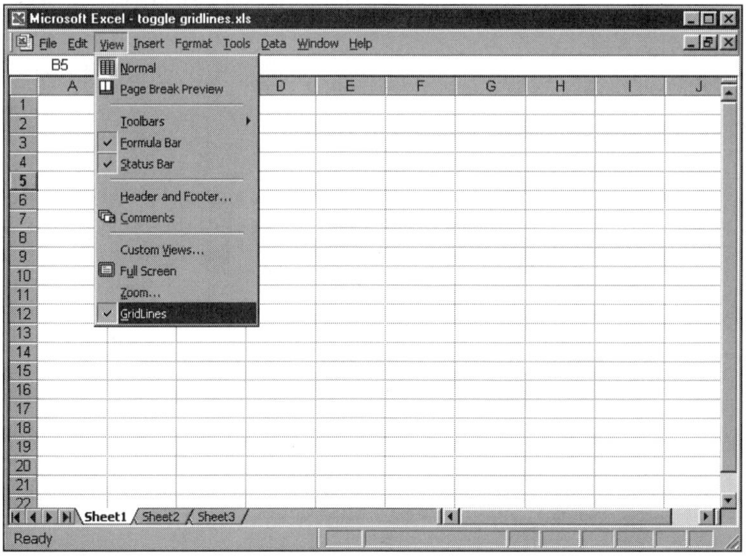

Figure 50-6: The GridLines menu item displays a check mark if the active sheet displays grid lines.

The trick here is keeping the check mark in sync with the active sheet. To do so, it's necessary to update the menu item whenever a new sheet or a new workbook is activated. This is done by setting up application-level events.

Adding the menu item

The AddMenuItem procedure shown in Listing 50-5 is executed when the workbook is opened. It creates a new GridLines menu item on the View menu.

Listing 50-5: Augmenting a built-in Excel menu

```
Dim AppObject As New XLHandler

Sub AddMenuItem()
    Dim ViewMenu As CommandBarPopup
    Dim NewMenuItem As CommandBarButton

'   Delete the menu if it already exists
    Call DeleteMenuItem

'   Find the View Menu
    Set ViewMenu = CommandBars(1).FindControl(ID:=30004)
    If ViewMenu Is Nothing Then
        MsgBox "Cannot add menu item."
        Exit Sub
    Else
        Set NewMenuItem = ViewMenu.Controls.Add _
        (Type:=msoControlButton)
        With NewMenuItem
            .Caption = "&GridLines"
            .OnAction = "ToggleGridlines"
        End With
    End If

'   Set up application event handler
    Set AppObject.AppEvents = Application
End Sub
```

The AddMenuItem procedure adds the new menu item to the Worksheet Menu Bar, not the Chart Menu Bar. Therefore, the new menu item isn't displayed when a chart sheet is active—which is just what we want!

Notice that the final statement in the AddMenuItem procedure sets up the application-level events that will be monitored. These event procedures, which are stored in a class module named XLHandler, are as follows:

```
Public WithEvents AppEvents As Excel.Application

Private Sub AppEvents_SheetActivate(ByVal Sh As Object)
    Call CheckGridlines
End Sub

Private Sub AppEvents_WorkbookActivate _
  (ByVal Wb As Excel.Workbook)
    Call CheckGridlines
End Sub
```

Toggling the grid-line display

The net effect is that when the user changes worksheets or workbooks, the following CheckGridlines procedure is executed. This procedure ensures that the check mark displayed on the GridLines menu option is in sync with the sheet.

```
Sub CheckGridlines()
    Dim TG As CommandBarButton
    On Error Resume Next
    Set TG = CommandBars(1).FindControl(Id:=30004). _
      Controls("&GridLines")
    If ActiveWindow.DisplayGridlines Then
        TG.State = msoButtonDown
    Else
        TG.State = msoButtonUp
    End If
End Sub
```

This procedure checks the active window and sets the State property of the menu item. If grid lines are displayed, it adds a check mark to the GridLines menu item. If grid lines are not displayed, it removes the check mark from the menu item.

Keeping the menu in sync with the sheet

When the menu item is selected, the OnAction property of that menu item triggers the following ToggleGridlines procedure:

```
Sub ToggleGridlines()
    On Error Resume Next
    ActiveWindow.DisplayGridlines = _
      Not ActiveWindow.DisplayGridlines
    Call CheckGridlines
End Sub
```

This procedure simply toggles the grid-line display of the active window. I use On Error Resume Next to eliminate the error message that is generated if the sheet is not a worksheet.

The Easy Way to Create Custom Menus

When Excel 97 was released, I was a bit frustrated with the code required to create a custom menu, so I developed a technique that simplifies the process considerably. My technique uses a worksheet, shown in Figure 50-7, to store information about the new menu. A VBA procedure reads the data in the workbook and creates the menu, menu items, and submenu items.

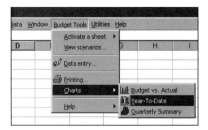

Figure 50-7: This menu was created from the data stored in a worksheet.

The worksheet consists of a table with five columns:

✦ **Level.** This is the location of the particular item relative to the hierarchy of the menu system. Valid values are 1, 2, and 3. Level 1 is for a menu; 2 is for a menu item; and 3 is for a submenu item. Normally, you'll have one level 1 item, with level 2 items below it. A level 2 item may or may not have level 3 (submenu) items.

✦ **Caption.** This is the text that appears in the menu, menu item, or submenu. To underline a character, place an ampersand (&) before it.

✦ **Position/Macro.** For level 1 items, this should be an integer that represents the position in the menu bar. For level 2 or level 3 items, this is the macro that executes when the item is selected. If a level 2 item has one or more level 3 items, the level 2 item may not have a macro associated with it.

✦ **Divider.** Enter True if a separator bar should be placed before the menu item or submenu item.

✦ **FaceID.** This optional entry is a code number that represents the built-in graphic images displayed next to an item.

Figure 50-8 shows the menu that was created from the worksheet data.

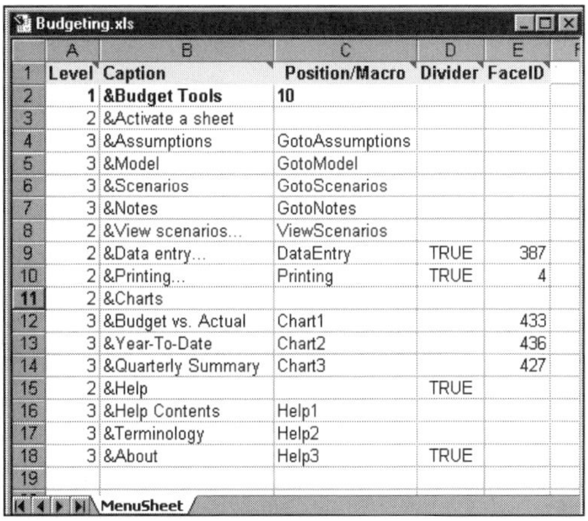

Figure 50-8: The information in this worksheet is used to create a custom menu.

	Level	Caption	Position/Macro	Divider	FaceID	
1	Level	Caption	Position/Macro	Divider	FaceID	
2	1	&Budget Tools	10			
3	2	&Activate a sheet				
4	3	&Assumptions	GotoAssumptions			
5	3	&Model	GotoModel			
6	3	&Scenarios	GotoScenarios			
7	3	&Notes	GotoNotes			
8	2	&View scenarios...	ViewScenarios			
9	2	&Data entry...	DataEntry	TRUE	387	
10	2	&Printing...	Printing	TRUE	4	
11	2	&Charts				
12	3	&Budget vs. Actual	Chart1		433	
13	3	&Year-To-Date	Chart2		436	
14	3	&Quarterly Summary	Chart3		427	
15	2	&Help		TRUE		
16	3	&Help Contents	Help1			
17	3	&Terminology	Help2			
18	3	&About	Help3	TRUE		
19						

MenuSheet

A workbook that demonstrates this technique is available on the companion CD-ROM. This workbook contains the VBA procedure that reads the worksheet data and creates the menu. To use this technique in your workbook or add-in, follow these general steps:

1. Open the example workbook from the CD-ROM.

2. Copy all the code in `Module1` to a module in your project.

3. Add procedures such as the following to the code module for the `ThisWorkbook` object:

```
Private Sub Workbook_Open()
    Call CreateMenu
End Sub

Private Sub Workbook_BeforeClose(Cancel As Boolean)
    Call DeleteMenu
End Sub
```

4. Insert a new worksheet, and name it `MenuSheet`. Better yet, copy the `MenuSheet` from the example file.

5. Customize the `MenuSheet` to correspond to your custom menu.

Note   The example workbook has no error handling, so it's up to you to make sure that everything works.

Creating a Substitute Worksheet Menu Bar

In some cases, you may want to hide Excel's standard Worksheet Menu Bar and replace it with your own. The MakeMenuBar procedure in Listing 50-6 creates a new menu bar named MyMenuBar. This menu bar consists of two menus. The first menu is the standard File menu, copied from the Worksheet Menu Bar. The second menu contains two items: Restore Normal Menu and Help.

Listing 50-6: **Replacing Excel's built-in menu with your own**

```
Sub MakeMenuBar()
    Dim NewMenuBar As CommandBar

'   Delete menu bar if it exists
    Call DeleteMenuBar

'   Add a menu bar
    Set NewMenuBar = CommandBars.Add(MenuBar:=True)
    With NewMenuBar
        .Name = "MyMenuBar"
        .Visible = True
    End With

'   Copy the File menu from Worksheet Menu Bar
    CommandBars("Worksheet Menu Bar") _
      .Controls(1).Copy Bar:=CommandBars("MyMenuBar")

'   Add a new menu
    Set NewMenu = NewMenuBar.Controls.Add _
      (Type:=msoControlPopup)
    NewMenu.Caption = "&Commands"

'   Add a new menu item
    Set NewItem = NewMenu.Controls.Add(Type:=msoControlButton)
    With NewItem
        .Caption = "&Restore Normal Menu"
        .OnAction = "DeleteMenuBar"
    End With

'   Add a new menu item
    Set NewItem = NewMenu.Controls.Add(Type:=msoControlButton)
    With NewItem
        .Caption = "&Help"
```

```
        .OnAction = "ShowHelp"
    End With
End Sub
```

Figure 50-9 shows the new menu bar.

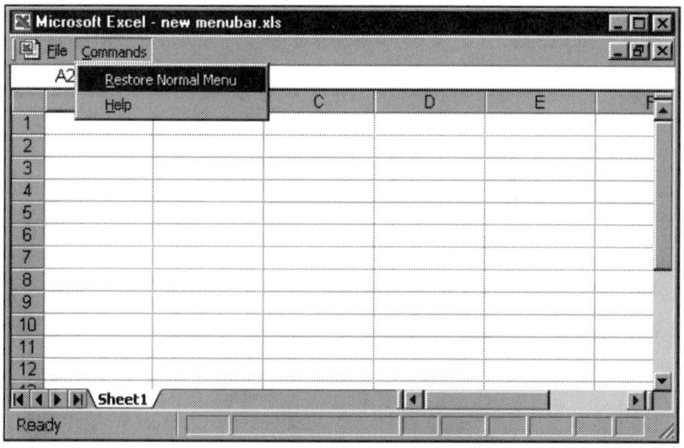

Figure 50-9: A custom menu bar replaces the standard Worksheet Menu Bar.

Notice that nothing in this procedure hides the Worksheet Menu Bar. The instruction `Set NewMenuBar = CommandBars.Add(MenuBar:=True)` adds the new command bar, and the `MenuBar` argument makes it the active menu bar. Only one menu bar can be active at a time.

Deleting the custom toolbar displays the Worksheet Menu Bar and makes it the active menu bar. The following `DeleteMenuBar` procedure returns things to normal.

```
Sub DeleteMenuBar()
    On Error Resume Next
    CommandBars("MyMenuBar").Delete
    On Error GoTo 0
End Sub
```

Working with Shortcut Menus

A shortcut menu is a pop-up menu that appears when you right-click virtually anything in Excel. You can't use Excel's Customize dialog box to remove or modify shortcut menus. The only way to customize shortcut menus is through VBA.

Menu Shenanigans

Here's a good April Fools' Day trick to play on an office mate (one with a sense of humor, that is). Create a procedure that cycles through all the menus, menu items, and submenu items and changes their captions so that they are backwards. Set things up so the routine is executed when the workbook is opened, and save the workbook in the victim's XLStart directory. The next time Excel is started, the menus look as if they're in a strange language.

For lazy pranksters, use the workbook on the CD-ROM that accompanies this book. The ReverseMenuText procedure performs its mischief by calling a custom function that reverses the text in the captions (except for the ellipses), converts the new text to proper case, and maintains the original hot keys. The net effect, as you can see in the accompanying figure, is a worksheet menu system that works exactly like the original (and is even keystroke compatible) but looks very odd.

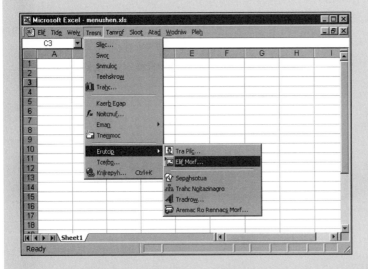

Before exiting, the routine adds an escape route: A new (legible) menu item to the Pleh menu (formerly the Help menu). This new item calls a procedure that returns the menus to normal.

Actually, this trick can be rather instructive. For example, I found out that Excel automatically resets some of the menu items when a menu is accessed; for example, the New, Save, and Save As menu items on the File menu appear as they normally do. Go figure.

Excel has lots of shortcut menus—44 in Excel 97 and 52 in Excel 2000. To work with a shortcut menu, you need to know its Caption property setting. You can use the following procedure to generate a list of all shortcut menus and the Index and Caption settings for each:

```
Sub ListShortCutMenus()
    Row = 1
    For Each cbar In CommandBars
        If cbar.Type = msoBarTypePopup Then
            Cells(Row, 1) = cbar.Index
            Cells(Row, 2) = cbar.Name
            For col = 1 To cbar.Controls.Count
                Cells(Row, col + 2) = _
                  cbar.Controls(col).Caption
            Next col
            Row = Row + 1
        End If
    Next cbar
End Sub
```

Figure 50-10 shows a portion of the output.

	A	B	C	D	E
1	20	Query and Pivot	Forma&t Report...	Pivot&Chart	&Wizard...
2	21	PivotChart Menu	Fi&eld Settings...	&Options...	&Refresh Data
3	22	Workbook tabs	Sheet1	&Sheet List	&Sheet List
4	23	Cell	Cu&t	&Copy	&Paste
5	24	Column	Cu&t	&Copy	&Paste
6	25	Row	Cu&t	&Copy	&Paste
7	26	Cell	Cu&t	&Copy	&Paste
8	27	Column	Cu&t	&Copy	&Paste
9	28	Row	Cu&t	&Copy	&Paste
10	29	Ply	&Ungroup Sheets	&Insert...	&Delete
11	30	XLM Cell	Cu&t	&Copy	&Paste
12	31	Document	&Save	Save &As...	&Print...
13	32	Desktop	&New...	&Open...	Save &Workspace...
14	33	Nondefault Drag and Drop	&Move Here	&Copy Here	Copy Here as &Values Onl
15	34	AutoFill	&Copy Cells	Fill &Series	Fill &Formats
16	35	Button	Cu&t	&Copy	&Paste
17	36	Dialog	&Paste	Ta&b Order...	&Run Dialog
18	37	Series	&Selected Object	Chart &Type...	&Source Data...
19	38	Plot Area	&Selected Object	Chart &Type...	&Source Data...
20	39	Floor and Walls	&Selected Object	3-D &View...	Cle&ar
21	40	Trendline	&Selected Object	Cle&ar	
22	41	Chart	&Selected Object	Cle&ar	
23	42	Format Data Series	&Set Print Area	&Clear Print Area	
24	43	Format Axis			
25	44	Format Legend Entry	&Mail Recipient	M&ail Recipient (as Attachment).	&Routing Recipient...
26	45	Formula Bar	Cu&t	&Copy	&Paste
27	46	PivotTable Context Menu	&Format Cells...	Forma&t Report...	Pivot&Chart
28	47	Query	Cu&t	&Copy	&Paste

Figure 50-10: A listing of all shortcut menus, plus the menu items in each

Note   Although you can refer to a shortcut menu by its `Index` property, this is not rec-ommended. For some reason, `Index` values have not remained consistent between Excel 97 and Excel 2000. For example, in Excel 97 the `CommandBar` object with an `Index` value of 21 is the Cell shortcut menu. In Excel 2000, an `Index` value of 21 refers to the PivotChart Menu shortcut menu.

Adding menu items to shortcut menus

Adding a menu item to a shortcut menu works just like adding a menu item to a regular menu. The following example demonstrates how to add a menu item to the Cell shortcut menu that appears when you right-click a cell or a row or column border. This menu item is added to the end of the shortcut menu, with a separator bar above it.

```
Sub AddItemToShortcut()
    Set NewItem = CommandBars("Cell").Controls.Add
    With NewItem
        .Caption = "Toggle Word Wrap"
        .OnAction = "ToggleWordWrap"
        .BeginGroup = True
    End With
End Sub
```

Selecting the new menu item executes a procedure named `ToggleWordWrap`. Figure 50-11 shows the new shortcut menu in action.

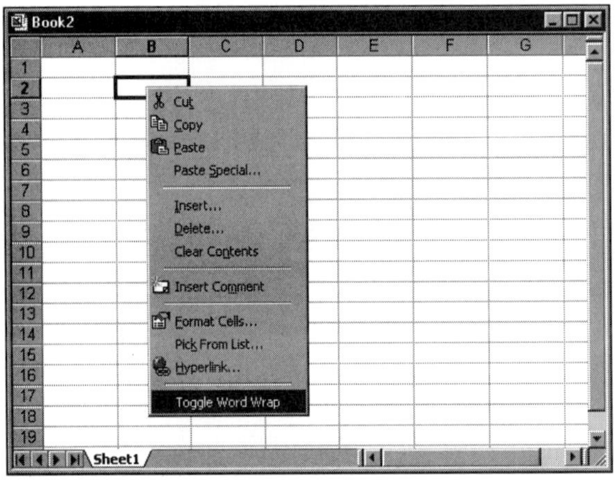

Figure 50-11: This shortcut menu has a new menu item.

Deleting menu items from shortcut menus

The following procedure uses the `Delete` method to remove the menu item added by the procedure in the previous section.

```
Sub RemoveItemFromShortcut()
    On Error Resume Next
    CommandBars("Cell").Controls("Toggle Word Wrap").Delete
End Sub
```

The On Error Resume Next statement avoids the error message that appears if the menu item is not on the shortcut menu.

The following procedure removes the Hide menu item from two shortcut menus: the one that appears when you right-click a row header and the one that appears for a column header.

```
Sub RemoveHideMenuItems()
    CommandBars("Column").Controls("Hide").Delete
    CommandBars("Row").Controls("Hide").Delete
End Sub
```

Disabling shortcut menu items

As an alternative to removing menu items, you may want to disable one or more items on certain shortcut menus while your application is running. When an item is disabled, it appears in a light gray color, and clicking it has no effect. The following procedure disables the Hide menu item from the Row and Column shortcut menus.

```
Sub DisableHideMenuItems()
    CommandBars("Column").Controls("Hide").Enabled = False
    CommandBars("Row").Controls("Hide").Enabled = False
End Sub
```

Disabling shortcut menus

You can also disable entire shortcut menus. For example, you may not want the user to access the commands generally made available by right-clicking a cell. The following DisableCell procedure disables the Cell shortcut menu. After the procedure is executed, right-clicking a cell has no effect.

```
Sub DisableCell()
    CommandBars("Cell").Enabled = False
End Sub
```

If you want to disable all shortcut menus, use the following procedure:

```
Sub DisableAllShortcutMenus()
    Dim cb As CommandBar
    For Each cb In CommandBars
        If cb.Type = msoBarTypePopup Then _
          cb.Enabled = False
    Next cb
End Sub
```

Tip   Disabling the shortcut menus "sticks" between sessions. Therefore, you'll probably want to restore the shortcut menus before closing Excel. To restore the shortcut menus, modify the preceding procedure to set the `Enabled` property to True.

Note   In the initial release of Excel 97, the Toolbar List shortcut menu cannot be disabled. This is the shortcut menu that appears when you right-click any command bar. In other words, you have no way to prevent the user from displaying this shortcut menu. This problem was corrected in SR-1 and SR-2.

Resetting shortcut menus

The `Reset` method restores a shortcut menu to its original condition. The following procedure resets the Cell shortcut menu to its normal state.

```
Sub ResetCellMenu()
    CommandBars("Cell").Reset
End Sub
```

Creating new shortcut menus

It's possible to create an entirely new shortcut menu. Listing 50-7 creates a shortcut menu named `MyShortcut` and adds six menu items to it. These menu items display one of the tabs in the Format Cells dialog box.

Listing 50-7: Creating an entirely new and separate shortcut menu

```
Sub CreateShortcut()
    Set myBar = CommandBars.Add _
      (Name:="MyShortcut", Position:=msoBarPopup, _
      Temporary:=True)

'    Add a menu item
    Set myItem = myBar.Controls.Add(Type:=msoControlButton)
    With myItem
        .Caption = "&Number Format..."
        .OnAction = "ShowFormatNumber"
        .FaceId = 1554
    End With

'    Add a menu item
    Set myItem = myBar.Controls.Add(Type:=msoControlButton)
    With myItem
        .Caption = "&Alignment..."
        .OnAction = "ShowFormatAlignment"
        .FaceId = 217
    End With

'    Add a menu item
```

```
        Set myItem = myBar.Controls.Add(Type:=msoControlButton)
        With myItem
            .Caption = "&Font..."
            .OnAction = "ShowFormatFont"
            .FaceId = 291
        End With

'       Add a menu item
        Set myItem = myBar.Controls.Add(Type:=msoControlButton)
        With myItem
            .Caption = "&Borders..."
            .OnAction = "ShowFormatBorder"
            .FaceId = 149
            .BeginGroup = True
        End With

'       Add a menu item
        Set myItem = myBar.Controls.Add(Type:=msoControlButton)
        With myItem
            .Caption = "&Patterns..."
            .OnAction = "ShowFormatPatterns"
            .FaceId = 1550
        End With

'       Add a menu item
        Set myItem = myBar.Controls.Add(Type:=msoControlButton)
        With myItem
            .Caption = "Pr&otection..."
            .OnAction = "ShowFormatProtection"
            .FaceId = 2654
        End With
    End Sub
```

Figure 50-12 shows how this new shortcut menu looks.

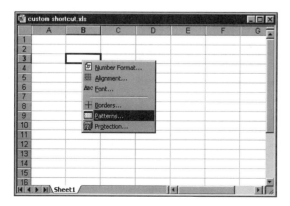

Figure 50-12: This new shortcut menu was created with VBA.

After the shortcut menu is created, you can display it with the ShowPopup method. The following procedure, located in the code module for a Worksheet object, is executed when the user right-clicks a cell.

```
Private Sub Worksheet_BeforeRightClick _
   (ByVal Target As Excel.Range, Cancel As Boolean)
      If Union(Target.Range("A1"), Range("data")).Address = _
         Range("data").Address Then
            CommandBars("MyShortcut").ShowPopup
            Cancel = True
      End If
End Sub
```

If the cell the user right-clicks is within a range named data, the MyShortcut menu appears. Setting the Cancel argument to True ensures that the normal shortcut menu is not displayed.

The companion CD-ROM contains an example that creates a new shortcut menu and displays it in place of the normal Cell shortcut menu.

Summary

In this chapter, I covered the topic of custom menus and presented many examples that demonstrate how to modify and create standard menus and shortcut menus.

The next chapter continues the discussion of application development, covering the topic of user help.

✦   ✦   ✦

Providing Help for Your Applications

Computer users have become rather spoiled over the years. Not too many years ago, software rarely provided online help. And the "help" provided often proved less than helpful. Now, just about all commercial software provides online help; and more often than not, online help serves as the primary documentation. Thick software manuals are an endangered species (good riddance!).

In this chapter, I discuss the concept of providing help for your Excel applications. As you'll see, you have lots of options.

Help for Your Excel Applications?

If you develop a nontrivial application in Excel, you may want to consider building in some sort of help for end users. Doing so makes the users feel more comfortable with the application and may eliminate those time-wasting phone calls from users with basic questions. Another advantage is that online help is always available (the instructions can't be misplaced or buried under a pile of books).

You can add user help to your applications in a number of ways, ranging from simple to complex. The method you choose depends on your application's scope and complexity and how much effort you're willing to put into this phase of development. Some applications may require only a brief set of instructions on how to start them. Others may benefit from a full-blown, searchable help system. Most often, applications need something in between.

This chapter classifies online help into two categories:

✦ **Unofficial Help System.** This method of displaying help uses standard Excel components (such as a UserForm).

✦ **Official Help System.** This help system uses either a compiled HLP file produced by the Windows Help System or a compiled CHM file produced by the HTML Help System.

Creating a compiled Help file is not a trivial task, but it may be worth the effort if your application is complex or if it will be used by a large number of people.

About the Examples in This Chapter

In this chapter, I use a simple workbook application to demonstrate various ways of providing help. The application uses data stored in a worksheet to generate and print form letters.

As you can see in the following figure, cells display the total number of records in the database (C2, calculated by a formula), the current record number (C3), the first record to print (C4), and the last record to print (C5). To display a particular record, the user enters a value into cell C3. To print a series of form letters, the user specifies the first and last record numbers in cells C4 and C5.

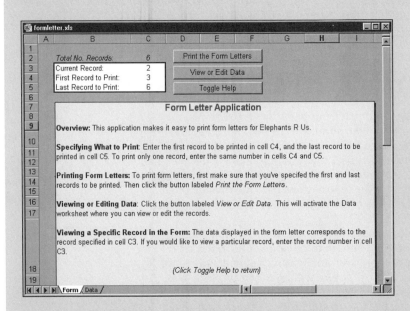

The application is simple, but it does consist of several discrete components in order to demonstrate various ways of displaying context-sensitive help.

The form letter workbook consists of the following components:

Form	A worksheet that contains the text of the form letter.
Data	A worksheet that contains a seven-field database.
HelpSheet	Present only in the examples that store help text on a worksheet.
PrintMod	A VBA module that contains macros to print the form letters.
HelpMod	A VBA module that contains macros that control the help display. The content of this module varies, depending on the type of help being demonstrated.
UserForm1	Present only if the help technique involves a UserForm.

On the CD-ROM The workbook is available on the companion CD-ROM. You might want to take a few minutes to familiarize yourself with the application.

Help Systems That Use Excel Components

Perhaps the most straightforward method of providing help to your users is to use the features contained in Excel itself. The primary advantage is that you don't need to learn how to create WinHelp or HTML Help files — which can be a major undertaking and may take longer to develop than your application!

In this section, I provide an overview of some help techniques that use the following built-in Excel components:

✦ **Cell comments.** This is about as simple as it comes.

✦ **A Text Box control.** A simple macro is all it takes to toggle the display of a Text Box that shows help information.

✦ **A worksheet.** A simple way to add help is to insert a worksheet, enter your help information, and name its tab "Help." When the user clicks the tab, the worksheet is activated.

✦ **A custom UserForm.** A number of techniques involve displaying help text in a UserForm.

Using cell comments for help

Perhaps the simplest way to provide user help is to use cell comments. This technique is most appropriate for describing the type of input that's expected in a cell. When the user moves the mouse pointer over a cell that contains a comment, that comment appears in a small window. Another advantage is that this technique does not require any macros.

Automatic display of cell notes is an option. The following VBA instruction ensures that cell comment indicators are displayed for cells that contain comments:

```
Application.DisplayCommentIndicator = xlCommentIndicatorOnly
```

On the CD-ROM

A workbook that demonstrates the use of cell comments for help is available on the companion CD-ROM.

Using a Text Box for help

Using a Text Box to display help information is also easy to implement. Simply create a Text Box using the Text Box button on the Drawing toolbar, enter the help text, and format it to your liking. Figure 51-1 shows an example of a text box set up to display help information.

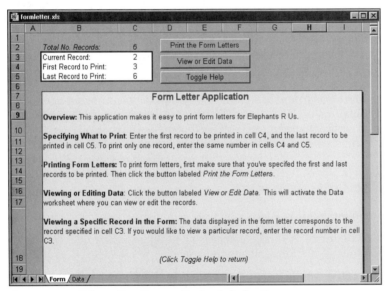

Figure 51-1: Using a Text Box to display help for the user

Tip

Using the Text Box from the Drawing toolbar is preferable to using an ActiveX Text Box from the Control Toolbox toolbar because it allows rich text formatting. In other words, the Text Box from the Drawing toolbar enables you to apply formatting to individual characters within the Text Box.

Most of the time, you won't want the Text Box to be visible. Therefore, you might want to add a button to your application to execute a macro that toggles the Visible property of the Text Box. An example of such a macro follows. In this case, the Text Box is named HelpText.

```
Sub ToggleHelp()
    ActiveSheet.TextBoxes("HelpText").Visible = _
        Not ActiveSheet.TextBoxes("HelpText").Visible
End Sub
```

Using a worksheet to display help text

Another easy way to add help to your application is to create a macro that activates a separate worksheet that holds the help information. Just attach the macro to a button control, toolbar button, or menu item, and voilà! . . . quick-and-dirty help.

Figure 51-2 shows a sample help worksheet. I designed the range that contains the help text to simulate a page from a yellow notebook pad — a fancy touch that you may or may not like.

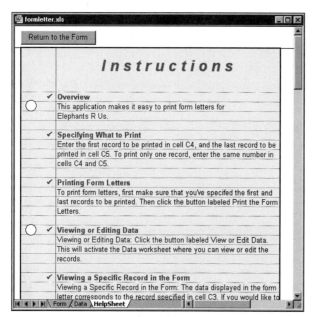

Figure 51-2: Putting user help in a separate worksheet is an easy way to go.

To keep the user from scrolling around the HelpSheet worksheet, the macro sets the ScrollArea property of the worksheet. Because this property is not stored with the workbook, it's necessary to set it when the worksheet is activated. I also protected the worksheet to prevent the user from changing the text, and I "froze" the first row so that the Return button is always visible, regardless of how far down the sheet the user scrolls.

The main disadvantage of using this technique is that the help text isn't visible along with the main work area. One possible solution is to write a macro that opens a new window to display the sheet.

Displaying help in a UserForm

Another way to provide help to the user is to display the text in a UserForm. In this section, I describe several techniques that involve UserForms.

Using Label controls to display help text

Figure 51-3 shows a UserForm that contains two Label controls: one for the title, one for the actual text. A SpinButton control enables the user to navigate among the topics. The text itself is stored in a worksheet, with topics in column A and text in column B.

Figure 51-3: Clicking the SpinButton determines the text displayed in the Labels.

Clicking the SpinButton executes the following procedure. This procedure simply sets the Caption property of the two Label controls to the text in the appropriate row of the worksheet (named HelpSheet).

```
Private Sub SpinButton1_Change()
    HelpTopic = SpinButton1.Value
    LabelTopic.Caption = Sheets("HelpSheet")._
      Cells(HelpTopic, 1)
    LabelText.Caption = Sheets("HelpSheet").Cells(HelpTopic, 2)
    Me.Caption = APPNAME & ": Topic " & HelpTopic & "/" _
      & SpinButton1.Max
End Sub
```

Here, APPNAME is a global constant that contains the application's name.

Using a "scrolling" Label to display help text

This technique displays help text in a single Label control. Because a Label control cannot contain a vertical scrollbar, the Label is placed inside a Frame control, which can contain a scrollbar. Figure 51-4 shows an example of a UserForm set up in this manner. The user can scroll through the text by using the Frame's scrollbar.

Figure 51-4: Inserting a Label control inside a Frame control adds scrolling to the Label.

The text displayed in the Label is read from a worksheet named HelpSheet when the UserForm is initialized. Listing 51-1 presents the UserForm_Initialize procedure for this worksheet. Notice that the code adjusts the Frame's ScrollHeight property to ensure that the scrolling covers the complete height of the Label. Again, APPNAME is a global constant that contains the application's name.

Listing 51-1: Making the label control display scrollable text from the worksheet

```
Private Sub UserForm_Initialize()
    Me.Caption = APPNAME & " Help"
    LastRow = Sheets("HelpSheet").Range("A65536") _
    .End(xlUp).Row
    txt = ""
    For r = 1 To LastRow
      txt = txt & Sheets("HelpSheet").Cells(r, 1) _
        .Text & vbCrLf
    Next r
    With Label1
        .Top = 0
        .Caption = txt
        .Width = 160
        .AutoSize = True
    End With
    With Frame1
        .ScrollHeight = Label1.Height
        .ScrollTop = 0
    End With
End Sub
```

Because a Label cannot display formatted text, I used horizontal lines in the `HelpSheet` worksheet to delineate the help topics.

Using a DropDown control to select a help topic

The example in this section improves upon the previous example. Figure 51-5 shows a UserForm that contains a DropDown control and a Label control. The user can select a topic from the DropDown or view the topics sequentially by clicking the Previous or Next button.

Figure 51-5: Designating the topic of the label's text with a drop-down list control

This example is a bit more complex than the example in the previous section, but it's also a lot more flexible. It uses the Label-within-a-scrolling-Frame technique (described previously) to support help text of any length.

The help text is stored in a worksheet named `HelpSheet` in two columns (A and B). The first column contains the topic headings and the second column contains the text. The ComboBox items are added in the `UserForm_Initialize` procedure, as follows. The `CurrentTopic` variable is a module-level variable that stores an integer that represents the help topic.

```
Private Sub UserForm_Initialize()
    Set HelpSheet = ThisWorkbook.Sheets(HelpSheetName)
    TopicCount = Application.WorksheetFunction. _
      CountA(HelpSheet.Range("A:A"))
    For Row = 1 To TopicCount
        ComboBoxTopics.AddItem HelpSheet.Cells(Row, 1)
    Next Row
    ComboBoxTopics.ListIndex = 0
    CurrentTopic = 1
    UpdateForm
End Sub
```

The `UpdateForm` procedure is shown in Listing 51-2. This procedure handles the details of setting the Label's caption, adjusting the Frame's scrollbar, and enabling or disabling the Previous and Next buttons.

Listing 51-2: **Making the Label mind the Frame's directive**

```
Private Sub UpdateForm()
    ComboBoxTopics.ListIndex = CurrentTopic - 1
    Me.Caption = HelpFormCaption & _
      " (" & CurrentTopic & " of " & TopicCount & ")"

    With LabelText
        .Caption = HelpSheet.Cells(CurrentTopic, 2)
        .AutoSize = False
        .Width = 212
        .AutoSize = True
    End With
    With Frame1
        .ScrollHeight = LabelText.Height + 5
        .ScrollTop = 1
    End With

    On Error Resume Next
    If CurrentTopic = 1 Then PreviousButton.Enabled = False _
      Else PreviousButton.Enabled = True
    If CurrentTopic = TopicCount Then _
      NextButton.Enabled = False _
      Else NextButton.Enabled = True
    If NextButton.Enabled Then NextButton.SetFocus _
      Else PreviousButton.SetFocus
End Sub
```

Using the WinHelp and HTML Help Systems

Currently, the most common help system used in Windows applications is the Windows Help System (WinHelp). This system displays HLP files and supports hypertext jumps that let the user display another related topic. However, it seems that Microsoft is attempting to phase out WinHelp in favor of HTML Help. Most of the new applications from Microsoft, including Office 2000, use HTML Help.

Both these help systems enable the developer to associate a context ID with a particular Help topic. This makes it possible to display a particular help topic in a context-sensitive manner.

In this section, I briefly describe these two help-authoring systems. Details on creating such help systems are well beyond the scope of this book.

Note   If you plan to develop a large-scale help system, I strongly recommend that you purchase a help-authoring software product to make your job easier. Help-authoring software makes it much easier to develop Help files because the software takes care of lots of the tedious details for you. Many products are available, including shareware and commercial offerings. Perhaps the most popular help-authoring product is RoboHELP, from Blue Sky Software. RoboHELP creates both WinHelp and HTML help systems. For more information, visit the company's Web site at www.blue-sky.com.

About WinHelp

Figure 51-6 shows a typical help topic displayed in WinHelp. Some words, called jump words, are underlined and displayed in a different color. Clicking a jump word that has a dotted underline makes WinHelp display another window with more explanation — often a definition. Clicking a jump word that has a solid underline makes WinHelp either jump to a new topic or display a secondary help window.

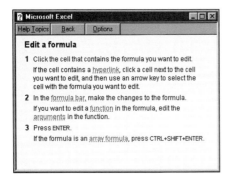

Figure 51-6: An example of WinHelp

WinHelp's main disadvantage is that creating the HLP files takes a great deal of knowledge and effort. An entire Usenet newsgroup is devoted to this topic (comp.os.ms-windows.programmer.winhelp), and I'm constantly amazed at the level of discussions in this group. It's clear that creating a good WinHelp file requires lots of experience and some good programming skills to boot.

To create an HLP file, you need a word processing program that can read and write RTF (Rich Text Format) files. Most major word processors can do this, including Microsoft Word. You also need a copy of the Microsoft Help Workshop, which includes the Help compiler. You can download the Help Workshop from Microsoft's FTP site at `ftp://ftp.microsoft.com/softlib/mslfiles/hcwsetup.exe`.

On the CD-ROM The companion CD-ROM contains a simple compiled HLP file, along with the RTF file and the project file (an HPJ file) that were used to create it.

About HTML Help

As I mentioned, Microsoft is positioning HTML Help as the new Windows standard for online help. This system essentially compiles a series of HTML files into a compact help system. Unlike WinHelp, which uses RTF-formatted documents, HTML Help accepts documents in HTML format. Figure 51-7 shows an example of an HTML Help system.

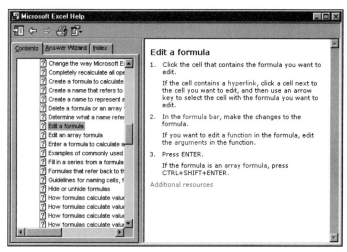

Figure 51-7: An example of HTML Help

HTML Help is displayed in a browser window, and the table of contents, index, and search tools are displayed in a separate pane. In addition, the help text can contain standard hyperlinks that display another topic or even a document on the Internet.

Like WinHelp, you need a special compiler to create an HTML Help system. The HTML Help Workshop is available free from Microsoft's Web site at `www.microsoft.com/workshop/author/htmlhelp`.

On the CD-ROM The companion CD-ROM contains an example of a simple HTML Help system, along with the files used to create it.

Associating a Help File with Your Application

If you use one of the "official" Help file systems (that is, WinHelp or HTML Help), you can associate a particular Help file with your application in one of two ways: by using the Project Properties dialog box or by writing VBA code.

In the VB Editor, select Tools ➪ *xxx* Properties (where *xxx* corresponds to your project's name). In the Project Properties dialog box, click the General tab, and specify a Help file for the project — either an HLP file or a CHM file.

It's a good practice to keep your application's Help file in the same directory as the application. The following instruction sets up an association to Myfuncs.hlp, which is assumed to be in the same directory as the workbook.

```
ThisWorkbook.VBProject.HelpFile = _
    ThisWorkbook.Path & "\Myfuncs.hlp"
```

After a Help file is associated with your application, you can call up a particular Help topic in the following situations:

✦ When the user presses F1 while a custom worksheet function is selected in the Paste Function dialog box.

✦ When the user presses F1 while a UserForm is displayed. The Help topic associated with the control that has the focus is displayed.

Associating a help topic with a VBA function

If you create custom worksheet functions using VBA, you may want to associate a Help file and context ID with each function. Once these items are assigned to a function, the Help topic can be displayed from the Paste Function dialog box by pressing F1.

To specify a context ID for a custom worksheet function, follow these steps:

1. Create the function as usual.

2. Make sure that your project has an associated Help file (refer to the preceding section).

3. In the VB Editor, press F2 to activate the Object Browser.

4. Select your project from the Project/Library drop-down list.

5. In the Classes window, select the module that contains your function.

6. In the Members of window, select the function.

7. Right-click the function, and select Properties from the shortcut menu. This displays the Member Options dialog box, as shown in Figure 51-8.

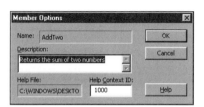

Figure 51-8: Specify a context ID for a custom function in the Member Options dialog box.

8. Enter the context ID of the Help topic for the function. You can also enter a description of the function.

Note   The Member Options dialog box does not let you specify the Help file. It always uses the Help file associated with the project.

You may prefer to write VBA code that sets up the context ID and Help file for your custom functions. You can do this using the MacroOptions method. The following procedure uses the MacroOptions method to specify a description, Help file, and context ID for two custom functions (AddTwo and Squared).

```
Sub SetOptions()
'    Set options for the AddTwo function
     Application.MacroOptions Macro:="AddTwo", _
         Description:="Returns the sum of two numbers", _
         HelpFile:=ThisWorkbook.Path & "\Myfuncs.hlp", _
         HelpContextID:=1000

'    Set options for the Squared function
     Application.MacroOptions Macro:="Squared", _
         Description:="Returns the square of an argument", _
         HelpFile:=ThisWorkbook.Path & "\Myfuncs.hlp", _
         HelpContextID:=2000
End Sub
```

On the CD-ROM   A workbook on the companion CD-ROM demonstrates this technique.

Displaying Help from a custom dialog box

Each control on a UserForm — as well as the UserForm itself — can have a Help topic associated with it. The Help file for the topic is the file associated with the project. The type of help provided is determined by the value of the following two UserForm properties:

✦ **WhatsThisButton.** If True, the UserForm displays a small question mark button in its title bar, like the one in Figure 51-9. The user can click this button and then click a UserForm control to get help regarding the control.

✦ **WhatsThisHelp.** If True, the help provided for each control is in the form of a small pop-up window that displays the Help topic's title only.

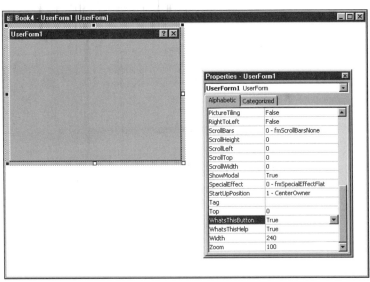

Figure 51-9: A WhatsThisButton setting of True brings up a small question mark button.

The WhatsThisHelp property must be True for the WhatsThisButton property to be True. In other words, only three combinations of values for WhatsThisHelp and WhatsThisButton are possible. Table 51-1 summarizes the effects of various settings.

Table 51-1
Settings for WhatsThisHelp and WhatsThisButton Properties

WhatsThisHelp	WhatsThisButton	Result
True	True	Question mark button is displayed; F1 gives pop-up help.
True	False	No question mark button is displayed; F1 gives pop-up help.
False	False	No question mark button is displayed; F1 gives full help.

A workbook that demonstrates these settings is available on the companion CD-ROM.

Using the Office Assistant to Display Help

You're probably familiar with the Office Assistant — the cutesy screen character that's always ready to help out. In my experience, people either love or hate this feature (you can count me among the latter group). The Office Assistant is quite programmable, and you can even use it to display help for the user.

Figure 51-10 shows the Office Assistant displaying some help text.

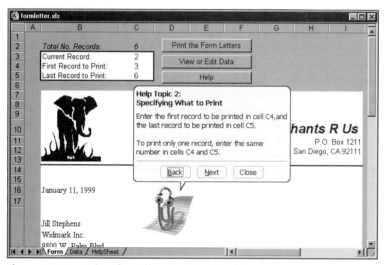

Figure 51-10: Using the Office Assistant to deliver custom help

The main procedure for using the Office Assistant to display help is shown in Listing 51-3. The help text is stored in two columns on a worksheet named `HelpSheet`. Column A contains the topics, and column B contains the help text.

Listing 51-3: **Calling up the Office Assistant to display custom help**

```
Public Const APPNAME As String = "Elephants R Us"
Dim Topic As Integer
Dim HelpSheet As Worksheet
```

Continued

Listing 51-3: *(continued)*

```
Sub ShowHelp()
    Set HelpSheet = ThisWorkbook.Worksheets("HelpSheet")
    Application.Assistant.On = True
    Topic = 1
    With Assistant.NewBalloon
        .Heading = "Help Topic " & Topic & ": " & _
            vbCrLf & HelpSheet.Cells(Topic, 1)
        .Text = HelpSheet.Cells(Topic, 2)
        .Button = msoButtonSetNextClose
        .BalloonType = msoBalloonTypeButtons
        .Mode = msoModeModeless
        .Callback = "ProcessRequest"
        .Show
    End With
End Sub
```

The procedure begins by making sure the Office Assistant is turned on. Then, it creates a new Balloon object (you'll recall that the Office Assistant's help text is displayed in a balloon) and uses the first help topic in the HelpSheet worksheet to set the Heading and Text properties. It sets the Button property so it displays Next and Close buttons like a wizard. The procedure then sets the Mode property to msoModeModeless so the user can continue working while the help is displayed. The Callback property contains the procedure name that is executed when a button is clicked. Finally, the Assistant balloon is displayed using the Show method.

The ProcessRequest procedure, shown in Listing 51-4, is called when any of the buttons is clicked.

Listing 51-4: Engaging the customized help through the Office Assistant

```
Sub ProcessRequest(bln As Balloon, lbtn As Long, lPriv _
    As Long)
    NumTopics = _
        WorksheetFunction.CountA(HelpSheet.Range("A:A"))
    Assistant.Animation = msoAnimationCharacterSuccessMajor
    Select Case lbtn
        Case msoBalloonButtonBack
            If Topic <> 1 Then Topic = Topic - 1
        Case msoBalloonButtonNext
            If Topic <> NumTopics Then Topic = Topic + 1
```

```
            Case msoBalloonButtonClose
                bln.Close
                Exit Sub
        End Select
        With bln
            .Close
            Select Case Topic
                Case 1
                    .Button = msoButtonSetNextClose
                Case NumTopics
                    .Button = msoButtonSetBackClose
                Case Else
                    .Button = msoButtonSetBackNextClose
            End Select
            .Heading = "Help Topic " & Topic & ": " & _
                vbCrLf & HelpSheet.Cells(Topic, 1)
            .Text = HelpSheet.Cells(Topic, 2)
            .Show
        End With
    End Sub
```

The `ProcessRequest` procedure displays one of several animations and then uses a `Select Case` construct to take action depending on which button was clicked. The button clicked is passed to this procedure through the `lbtn` variable. The procedure also specifies which buttons to display based on the current topic.

If you have an interest in programming the Assistant, I refer you to the online help for the details.

This example is available on the companion CD-ROM.

Other Ways of Displaying WinHelp or HTML Help

VBA provides several different ways to display specific help topics. I describe these in the following sections.

Using the Help method

Use the `Help` method of the `Application` object to display a Help file—either a WinHelp HLP file or an HTML Help CHM file. This method works even if the Help file doesn't have any context IDs defined.

The syntax for the Help method is as follows:

```
Application.Help(helpFile, helpContextID)
```

Both arguments are optional. If the name of the Help file is omitted, Excel's Help file is displayed. If the context ID argument is omitted, the specified Help file is displayed with the default topic.

The following example displays the default topic of Myapp.hlp, which is assumed to be in the same directory as the workbook that it's called from. Note that the second argument is omitted.

```
Sub ShowHelpContents()
    Application.Help ThisWorkbook.Path & "\Myapp.hlp"
End Sub
```

The following instruction displays the help topic with a context ID of 1002 from an HTML Help file named Myapp.chm.

```
Application.Help ThisWorkbook.Path & "\Myapp.chm", 1002
```

Displaying Help from a message box

When you use VBA's MsgBox function to display a message box, you include a Help button by providing the vbMsgBoxHelpButton constant as the function's second argument. You'll also need to include the Help file name as its fourth argument. The context ID (optional) is its fifth argument. The following code, for example, generates the message box shown in Figure 51-11.

Figure 51-11: A message box with a Help button

```
Sub MsgBoxHelp()
    Msg = "Do you want to exit now?"
    Buttons = vbQuestion + vbYesNo + vbMsgBoxHelpButton
    He
lpFile = ThisWorkbook.Path & "\AppHelp.hlp"
    ContextID = 1002
    Ans = MsgBox(Msg, Buttons, , HelpFile, ContextID)
    If Ans = vbYes Then Call CloseDown
End Sub
```

Displaying Help from an input box

VBA's `InputBox` function can also display a Help button if its sixth argument contains the Help file name. The following example produces the `InputBox` shown in Figure 51-12.

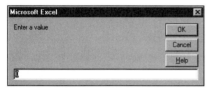

Figure 51-12: An InputBox with a Help button

```
Sub ShowInputBox()
    Msg = "Enter a value"
    DefaultVal = 0
    HelpFile = ThisWorkbook.Path & "\AppHelp.hlp"
    ContextID = 1002
    x = InputBox(Msg, , DefaultVal, , , HelpFile, ContextID)
End Sub
```

Summary

In this chapter, I presented several alternative methods of providing online help for end users, including "official" help systems (WinHelp or HTML Help) and "unofficial" help systems that use Excel-specific techniques to display help.

✦   ✦   ✦

Using Online Help: A Primer

Excel's online Help system has always been good. But the Help available with Excel 2000 is better than ever. However, the online Help system can be a bit intimidating for beginners, because you can get help in many ways. This appendix assists you in getting the most out of this valuable resource.

Why Online Help?

In the early days of personal computing, software programs usually came bundled with bulky manuals that described how to use the product. Some products included rudimentary help that could be accessed online. Over the years, that situation gradually changed. Now, online help is usually the *primary* source of documentation, which may be augmented by a written manual.

After you become accustomed to it, you'll find that online help (if it's done well) offers many advantages over written manuals:

+ You don't have to lug around a manual — especially important for laptop users who do their work on the road.

+ You don't have to thumb through a separate manual, which often has a confusing index.

+ You can search for specific words and then select a topic that's appropriate to your question.

+ In some cases (for example, writing VBA code), you can copy examples from the Help window and paste them into your application.

+ Help sometimes includes embedded buttons that you can click to go directly to the command that you need.

Types of Help

Excel offers several types of online Help:

✦ **Tooltips:** Move the mouse pointer over a toolbar button and the button's name appears.

✦ **Office Assistant:** The animated Office Assistant monitors your actions while you work. If a more efficient way to perform an operation exists, the Assistant can tell you about it.

✦ **Dialog box help:** When a dialog box is displayed, click the Help button in the title bar (it has a question mark on it) and then click any part of the dialog box. Excel pops up a description of the selected control. Figure A-1 shows an example.

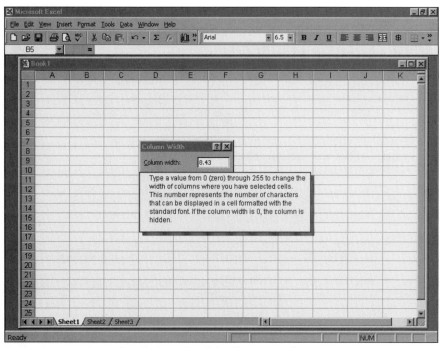

Figure A-1: Getting a description of a dialog box control.

✦ **"What's This" help:** Press Shift+F1, and the mouse pointer turns into a question mark. You can then click virtually any part of the screen to get a description of the object.

✦ **1-2-3 help:** The Help ➪ Lotus 1-2-3 Help command provides help designed for those who are familiar with 1-2-3's commands.

✦ **Internet-based help:** You can access a variety of Internet resources directly from Excel.

✦ **Detailed help:** This is what's usually considered online help. As you'll see, you have several ways to locate a particular Help topic.

Accessing Help

When you work with Excel 2000, you can access the online Help system by using the Help menu, shown in Figure A-2. The various options are described in the sections that follow.

Figure A-2: The Help menu.

The Office Assistant

Selecting Microsoft Excel Help displays the Office Assistant, shown in Figure A-3. Type a brief description of the subject about which you want help, and the Assistant displays a list of Help topics. Chances are good that one of these topics will lead to the help that you need; click a list item to view a Help topic.

The information that you type doesn't have to be in the form of a question. Rather, you can simply enter one or more keywords that describe the topic. For example, if you want to find out how to turn off gridlines, you can type **gridlines off**.

Tip

You have a great deal of control over the Office Assistant. Right-click the Assistant and select Options from the shortcut menu. Excel displays the dialog box shown in Figure A-4. The Gallery tab lets you select a new character for the Assistant. The Options tab lets you determine whether to use the Assistant and, if you do, how the Assistant behaves. If you find that the Office Assistant is distracting, remove the check from the Use the Office Assistant check box. You can turn on the Office Assistant again by choosing the Show the Office Assistant command on the Help menu.

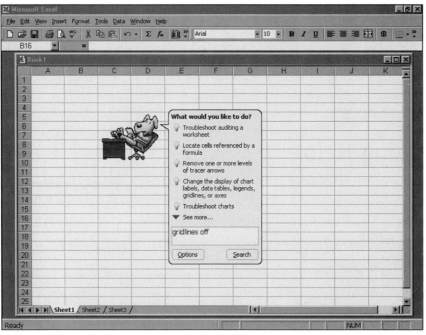

Figure A-3: The Office Assistant.

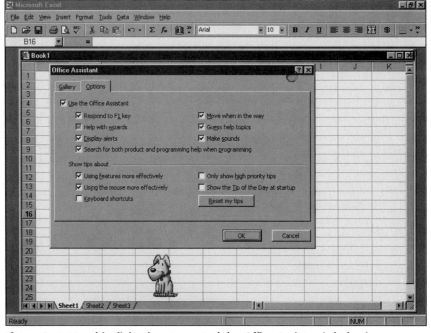

Figure A-4: Use this dialog box to control the Office Assistant's behavior.

The Help window

Whether you use the Office Assistant or turn it off, the Help window appears tiled to the right of the Excel window (see Figure A-5); all Office 2000 products let the Help window share your monitor space with an Office product.

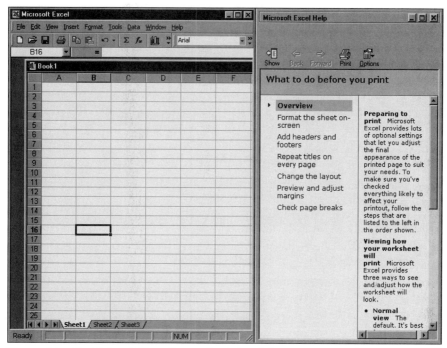

Figure A-5: The Help window tiles to the right of the program window so you can view Help while working.

Tip

On most Help topics, you'll find links to related Help topics that look like Web links (they appear underlined). You'll also see links to the Web. Help text for all Office products is written in HTML. As you'll read in a moment, navigating through Help topics is like using a browser.

If you click the Show button in the Help window, the Help window expands to include two panes; in the right pane, Help topics continue to appear, but in the left pane, you'll see three tabs. Each of the following tabs provides a different way to find the information that you need.

Contents tab

Figure A-6 shows the Contents tab. This tab is arranged alphabetically by subject; you can compare the Contents tab to the table of contents in a book, because they both organize information by similar topic. When you double-click a book icon (or single-click the plus sign to the left of the book icon), the book expands to show Help topics (each with a question-mark icon). To close a book, double-click it again or single-click the minus sign to the left of the book. To display a Help topic, single-click the topic title.

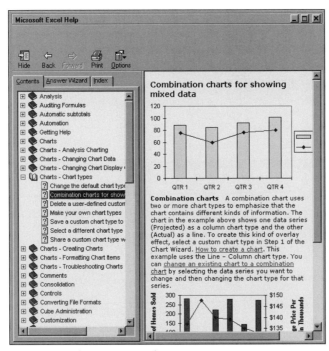

Figure A-6: The Contents tab.

The Help topic remains onscreen until you either close Help or select another Help topic.

Answer Wizard tab

The Answer Wizard tab works in much the same way as the Office Assistant works. Type a question or some words related to the subject about which you want help, and then click the Search button (see Figure A-7). Topics appear at the bottom of the window. Double-click a topic in the bottom of the window and the Help topic appears in the right pane of the Help window.

Index tab

Figure A-8 shows the Index tab of the Help Topics dialog box. The keywords are arranged alphabetically, much like an index for a book. You can enter in the box at the top the first few letters of a keyword for which you'd like to search. Click the Search button to display related topics at the bottom of the box. Double-click a topic at the bottom of the box to display it in the right pane of the Help window.

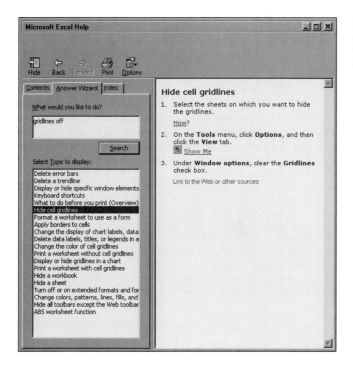

Figure A-7: The Answer Wizard tab of the Help window.

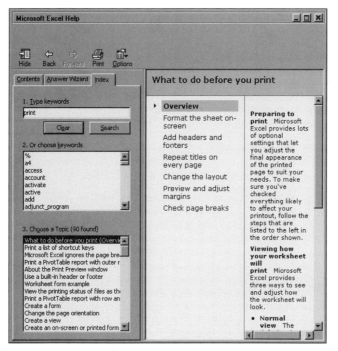

Figure A-8: The Index tab of the Help topics dialog box.

Mastering Help

After you select a Help topic, you can navigate through Help in the same way that you use a browser to navigate on the Web. The Back and Forward buttons let you view Help topics that you previously viewed, in the order that you viewed them. Use the Print button to print a Help topic. Click the Options button to display a drop-down menu that contains commands that perform the same functions as the Show, Hide, Back, Forward, and Print buttons. You'll also find a Stop command and a Refresh command; you can use these if you connect to the Web for Help and want to stop loading a page or refresh the Web page you're viewing.

The information provided in this appendix gets you started using Excel's online Help. Everyone develops his or her own style for using this help, and I urge you to explore this resource. Even if you think you understand a topic in Excel fairly well, you can often discover one or two subtle features that you didn't know about. A thorough understanding of how to use the online Help system will definitely make you a more productive Excel user.

✦　　✦　　✦

Online Excel Resources

If I've done my job, the information provided in this book will be useful to you. It is, however, by no means comprehensive. In addition, new issues tend to crop up, so you'll want to make sure that you're up-to-date. Therefore, I've compiled a list of additional resources that may help you become more proficient in Excel application development. I've classified these resources into three categories:

◆ Microsoft technical support

◆ Internet newsgroups

◆ Internet Web sites

Microsoft Technical Support

Technical support is the common term for assistance provided by a software vendor. In this case, I'm talking about assistance that comes directly from Microsoft. Microsoft's technical support is available in several different forms.

Support options

To find out your support options, choose the Help ⇨ About Microsoft Excel command. Then click the Tech Support button. This opens a help file that lists all the support options offered by Microsoft, including both free and fee-based support.

My experience is that you should use vendor standard telephone support only as a last resort. Chances are, you'll run up a big phone bill (assuming you can even get through) and spend lots of time on hold, but you may or may not find an answer to your question.

The truth is, the people who answer the phone are equipped to answer only the most basic questions. And the answers to these basic questions are usually readily available elsewhere.

Microsoft Knowledge Base

Your best bet for solving a problem may be the Microsoft Knowledge Base. This is the primary Microsoft product information source—an extensive, searchable database that consists of tens of thousands of detailed articles containing technical information, bug lists, fix lists, and more.

You have free and unlimited access to the Knowledge Base via the Internet. The URL is: http://support.microsoft.com.

Microsoft Excel Home Page

The official home page of Excel is at:

www.microsoft.com/excel

Microsoft Office update

For information about Office 2000 (including Excel), try this site:

http://officeupdate.microsoft.com

Internet Newsgroups

Usenet is an Internet service that provides access to several thousand special interest groups that enable you to communicate with people who share common interests. Thousands of newsgroups exist covering virtually every topic you can think of (and many that you haven't). Typically, questions posed on a newsgroup are answered within 24 hours—assuming, of course, that the questions are asked in a manner that makes others want to reply.

Note

Besides an Internet connection, you need special newsreader software to access newsgroups. Microsoft Outlook Express (free) is a good choice. This product is available on your Office 2000 CD-ROM.

About the URLs Listed Here

As you know, the Internet is a dynamic entity that tends to change rapidly. Web sites are often reorganized, so a particular URL listed in this appendix may not be available when you try to access it. Each URL was accurate at the time of this writing, but it's possible that a URL may have changed by the time you read this.

Spreadsheet newsgroups

The primary Usenet newsgroup for general spreadsheet users is

```
comp.apps.spreadsheets
```

This newsgroup is intended for users of any brand of spreadsheet, but about 90 percent of the postings deal with Excel.

Microsoft newsgroups

Microsoft has an extensive list of newsgroups, including quite a few devoted to Excel. If your Internet service provider doesn't carry the Microsoft newsgroups, you can access them directly from Microsoft's news server. You'll need to configure your newsreader software or Web browser to access Microsoft's news server, which is at this address:

```
msnews.microsoft.com
```

Table B-1 lists the key newsgroups you'll find on Microsoft's news server.

Table B-1	
Microsoft.com's Excel-Related Newsgroups	
Newsgroup	**Topic**
`microsoft.public.excel`	Programming Excel with VBA or XLM macros.programming
`microsoft.public.excel.123quattro`	Converting 1-2-3 or Quattro Pro sheets into Excel sheets
`microsoft.public.excel.worksheet.functions`	Worksheet functions
`microsoft.public.excel.charting`	Building charts with Excel
`microsoft.public.excel.printing`	Printing with Excel

Continued

Table B-1 *(continued)*	
Microsoft.com's Excel-Related Newsgroups	
Newsgroup	**Topic**
`microsoft.public.excel.queryDAO`	Using Microsoft Query and Data Access Objects (DAO) in Excel
`microsoft.public.excel.datamap`	Using the Data Map feature in Excel
`microsoft.public.excel.crashesGPFs`	Help with General Protection Faults or system failures
`microsoft.public.excel.misc`	General topics that do not fit one of the other categories
`microsoft.public.excel.links`	Using links in Excel
`microsoft.public.excel.macintosh`	Excel issues on the Macintosh operating system
`microsoft.public.excel.interopoledde`	OLE, DDE, and other cross-application issues
`microsoft.public.excel.setup`	Setting up and installing Excel
`microsoft.public.excel.templates`	Spreadsheet Solutions templates and other XLT files
`microsoft.public.excel.sdk`	Excel Software Development issues

Searching newsgroups

Many people don't realize that you can perform a keyword search on past newsgroup postings. Often, this is an excellent alternative to posting a question to the newsgroup because you can get the answer immediately. The best source for searching newsgroup postings is DejaNews, at the following Web address:

`www.dejanews.com`

For example, assume you're having a problem with the ListBox control on a UserForm. You can perform a search using the following keywords: **Excel**, **ListBox**, and **UserForm**. The DejaNews search engine will probably find dozens of newsgroup postings that deal with these topics. It may take a while to sift through the messages, but there's an excellent chance that you'll find an answer to your question.

Tips for Posting to a Newsgroup

1. Make sure that your question has not already been answered. Check the FAQ (if one exists) and also perform a DejaNews search (see "Searching newsgroups" in this appendix).

2. Make the subject line descriptive. Postings with a subject line such as "Help me!" and "Excel Question" are less likely to be answered than postings with a subject such as "VBA Code to Resize a Chart in Excel 2000."

3. Specify the spreadsheet product and version that you are using. In many cases, the answer to your question depends on your version of Excel.

4. Make your question as specific as possible.

5. Keep your question brief and to the point, but provide enough information so it can be adequately answered.

6. Indicate what you've done to try to answer your own question.

7. Post in the appropriate newsgroup, and don't cross-post to other groups unless the question applies to multiple groups.

8. Don't type in all uppercase or all lowercase, and check your grammar and spelling.

9. Don't include a file attachment.

10. Avoid posting in HTML format.

11. If you would like an e-mail reply, don't use an "anti-spam" e-mail address that requires the responder to modify your address. Why cause extra work for someone who's doing *you* a favor?

Internet Web Sites

If you have access to the World Wide Web, you'll find some very useful Web sites. I list a few of my favorites here.

The Spreadsheet Page

This is my own Web site. All humility aside, this is the best site on the Web for developer information. It contains files to download, developer tips, instructions for accessing Excel Easter Eggs, spreadsheet jokes, and links to other spreadsheet sites. The URL is

```
www.j-walk.com/ss
```

Note This site also contains updates on the topics covered in my books, including the book you're reading now.

Chip Pearson's Excel Pages

This site contains dozens of useful examples of VBA and clever formula techniques. The URL is

```
http://www.cpearson.com/excel.htm
```

Stephen Bullen's Excel Page

Stephen is an Excel developer based in the United Kingdom. His Web site contains some fascinating examples of Excel code, including a section titled "They Said it Couldn't be Done." The URL is

```
www.bmsltd.co.uk/excel
```

Spreadsheet FAQ

Many newsgroups have FAQ—a list of frequently asked questions. The purpose of FAQs is to prevent the same questions from being asked over and over. The FAQ for the comp.apps.spreadsheets newsgroup is available at

```
www.faqs.org/faqs/spreadsheets/faq
```

✦   ✦   ✦

Worksheet Function Reference

This appendix contains a complete listing of Excel's worksheet functions. The functions are arranged alphabetically by categories used by the Paste Function dialog box. Some of these functions (indicated in the lists that follow) are available only when a particular add-in is attached.

For more information about a particular function, including its arguments, select the function in the Function Wizard and click the Help button.

Table C-1	
Database Category Functions	
Function	**What It Does**
DAVERAGE	Returns the average of selected database entries
DCOUNT	Counts the cells containing numbers from a specified database and criteria
DCOUNTA	Counts nonblank cells from a specified database and criteria
DGET	Extracts from a database a single record that matches the specified criteria
DMAX	Returns the maximum value from selected database entries
DMIN	Returns the minimum value from selected database entries
DPRODUCT	Multiplies the values in a particular field of records that match the criteria in a database

Continued

Table C-1 *(continued)*

Function	What It Does
DSTDEV	Estimates the standard deviation based on a sample of selected database entries
DSTDEVP	Calculates the standard deviation based on the entire population of selected database entries
DSUM	Adds the numbers in the field column of records in the database that match the criteria
DVAR	Estimates variance based on a sample from selected database entries
DVARP	Calculates variance based on the entire population of selected database entries
SQL.CLOSE**	Terminates a SQL.OPEN connection
SQL.BIND**	Specifies where to place SQL.EXEC.QUERY results
SQL.ERROR**	Returns error information on SQL* functions
SQL.EXEC.QUERY**	Executes a SQL statement on a SQL.OPEN connection
QUERYGETDATA***	Gets external data using Microsoft Query
QUERYGETDATADIALOG***	Displays a dialog box to get data using Microsoft Query
SQL.GET.SCHEMA**	Returns information on a SQL.OPEN connection
SQL.OPEN**	Makes a connection to a data source via ODBC
QUERYREFRESH***	Updates a data range using Microsoft Query
SQL.REQUEST**	Requests a connection and executes a SQL query
SQL.RETRIEVE**	Retrieves SQL.EXEC.QUERY results
SQL.RETRIEVE.TO.FILE**	Retrieves SQL.EXEC.QUERY results to a file

* Available only when the Analysis ToolPak add-in is attached
** Available only when the ODBC add-in is attached
*** Available only when the MS Query add-in is attached

Table C-2
Date and Time Category Functions

Function	What It Does
DATE	Returns the serial number of a particular date
DATEVALUE	Converts a date in the form of text to a serial number
DAY	Converts a serial number to a day of the month

Function	What It Does
DAYS360	Calculates the number of days between two dates, based on a 360-day year
EDATE*	Returns the serial number of the date that is the indicated number of months before or after the start date
EOMONTH*	Returns the serial number of the last day of the month before or after a specified number of months
HOUR	Converts a serial number to an hour
MINUTE	Converts a serial number to a minute
MONTH	Converts a serial number to a month
NETWORKDAYS*	Returns the number of whole workdays between two dates
NOW	Returns the serial number of the current date and time
SECOND	Converts a serial number to a second
TIME	Returns the serial number of a particular time
TIMEVALUE	Converts a time in the form of text to a serial number
TODAY	Returns the serial number of today's date
WEEKDAY	Converts a serial number to a day of the week
WEEKNUM*	Returns the week number in the year
WORKDAY*	Returns the serial number of the date before or after a specified number of workdays
YEAR	Converts a serial number to a year
YEARFRAC*	Returns the year fraction representing the number of whole days between start_date and end_date

* Available only when the Analysis ToolPak add-in is attached

Table C-3
Engineering Category Functions

Function	What It Does
BESSELI*	Returns the modified Bessel function In(x)
BESSELJ*	Returns the Bessel function Jn(x)
BESSELK*	Returns the modified Bessel function Kn(x)
BESSELY*	Returns the Bessel function Yn(x)
BIN2DEC*	Converts a binary number to decimal

Continued

Table C-3 *(continued)*

Function	What It Does
BIN2HEX*	Converts a binary number to hexadecimal
BIN2OCT*	Converts a binary number to octal
COMPLEX*	Converts real and imaginary coefficients into a complex number
CONVERT*	Converts a number from one measurement system to another
DEC2BIN*	Converts a decimal number to binary
DEC2HEX*	Converts a decimal number to hexadecimal
DEC2OCT*	Converts a decimal number to octal
DELTA*	Tests whether two values are equal
ERF*	Returns the error function
ERFC*	Returns the complementary error function
GESTEP*	Tests whether a number is greater than a threshold value
HEX2BIN*	Converts a hexadecimal number to binary
HEX2DEC*	Converts a hexadecimal number to decimal
HEX2OCT*	Converts a hexadecimal number to octal
IMABS*	Returns the absolute value (modulus) of a complex number
IMAGINARY*	Returns the imaginary coefficient of a complex number
IMARGUMENT*	Returns the argument theta, an angle expressed in radians
IMCONJUGATE*	Returns the complex conjugate of a complex number
IMCOS*	Returns the cosine of a complex number
IMDIV*	Returns the quotient of two complex numbers
IMEXP*	Returns the exponential of a complex number
IMLN*	Returns the natural logarithm of a complex number
IMLOG2*	Returns the base-2 logarithm of a complex number
IMLOG10*	Returns the base-10 logarithm of a complex number
IMPOWER*	Returns a complex number raised to an integer power
IMPRODUCT*	Returns the product of two complex numbers
IMREAL*	Returns the real coefficient of a complex number
IMSIN*	Returns the sine of a complex number
IMSQRT*	Returns the square root of a complex number

Function	What It Does
IMSUB*	Returns the difference of two complex numbers
IMSUM*	Returns the sum of complex numbers
OCT2BIN*	Converts an octal number to binary
OCT2DEC*	Converts an octal number to decimal
OCT2HEX*	Converts an octal number to hexadecimal

* Available only when the Analysis ToolPak add-in is attached

Table C-4
Financial Category Functions

Function	What It Does
ACCRINT*	Returns the accrued interest for a security that pays periodic interest
ACCRINTM*	Returns the accrued interest for a security that pays interest at maturity
AMORDEGRC*	Returns the depreciation for each accounting period
AMORLINC*	Returns the depreciation for each accounting period
COUPDAYBS*	Returns the number of days from the beginning of the coupon period to the settlement date
COUPDAYS*	Returns the number of days in the coupon period that contains the settlement date
COUPDAYSNC*	Returns the number of days from the settlement date to the next coupon date
COUPNCD*	Returns the next coupon date after the settlement date
COUPNUM*	Returns the number of coupons payable between the settlement date and maturity date
COUPPCD*	Returns the previous coupon date before the settlement date
CUMIPMT*	Returns the cumulative interest paid between two periods
CUMPRINC*	Returns the cumulative principal paid on a loan between two periods
DB	Returns the depreciation of an asset for a specified period, using the fixed-declining balance method
DDB	Returns the depreciation of an asset for a specified period, using the double-declining balance method or some other method that you specify
DISC*	Returns the discount rate for a security

Continued

Table C-4 (continued)

Function	What It Does
DOLLARDE*	Converts a dollar price, expressed as a fraction, into a dollar price, expressed as a decimal number
DOLLARFR*	Converts a dollar price, expressed as a decimal number, into a dollar price, expressed as a fraction
DURATION*	Returns the annual duration of a security with periodic interest payments
EFFECT*	Returns the effective annual interest rate
FV	Returns the future value of an investment
FVSCHEDULE*	Returns the future value of an initial principal after applying a series of compound interest rates
INTRATE*	Returns the interest rate for a fully invested security
IPMT	Returns the interest payment for an investment for a given period
IRR	Returns the internal rate of return for a series of cash flows
ISPMT	Returns the interest associated with a specific loan payment.
MDURATION*	Returns the Macauley modified duration for a security with an assumed par value of $100
MIRR	Returns the internal rate of return where positive and negative cash flows are financed at different rates
NOMINAL*	Returns the annual nominal interest rate
NPER	Returns the number of periods for an investment
NPV	Returns the net present value of an investment based on a series of periodic cash flows and a discount rate
ODDFPRICE*	Returns the price per $100 face value of a security with an odd first period
ODDFYIELD*	Returns the yield of a security with an odd first period
ODDLPRICE*	Returns the price per $100 face value of a security with an odd last period
ODDLYIELD*	Returns the yield of a security with an odd last period
PMT	Returns the periodic payment for an annuity
PPMT	Returns the payment on the principal for an investment for a given period
PRICE*	Returns the price per $100 face value of a security that pays periodic interest
PRICEDISC*	Returns the price per $100 face value of a discounted security

Function	What It Does
PRICEMAT*	Returns the price per $100 face value of a security that pays interest at maturity
PV	Returns the present value of an investment
RATE	Returns the interest rate per period of an annuity
RECEIVED*	Returns the amount received at maturity for a fully invested security
SLN	Returns the straight-line depreciation of an asset for one period
SYD	Returns the sum-of-years' digits depreciation of an asset for a specified period
TBILLEQ*	Returns the bond-equivalent yield for a Treasury bill
TBILLPRICE*	Returns the price per $100 face value for a Treasury bill
TBILLYIELD*	Returns the yield for a Treasury bill
VDB	Returns the depreciation of an asset for a specified or partial period using a declining balance method
XIRR*	Returns the internal rate of return for a schedule of cash flows that is not necessarily periodic
XNPV*	Returns the net present value for a schedule of cash flows that is not necessarily periodic
YIELD*	Returns the yield on a security that pays periodic interest
YIELDDISC*	Returns the annual yield for a discounted security; for example, a Treasury bill
YIELDMAT*	Returns the annual yield of a security that pays interest at maturity

* Available only when the Analysis ToolPak add-in is attached

Table C-5
Information Category Functions

Function	What It Does
CELL	Returns information about the formatting, location, or contents of a cell
COUNTBLANK	Counts the number of blank cells within a range
ERROR.TYPE	Returns a number corresponding to an error type
INFO	Returns information about the current operating environment
ISBLANK	Returns TRUE if the value is blank
ISERR	Returns TRUE if the value is any error value except #N/A
ISERROR	Returns TRUE if the value is any error value

Continued

Table C-5 (continued)

Function	What It Does
ISEVEN*	Returns TRUE if the number is even
ISLOGICAL	Returns TRUE if the value is a logical value
ISNA	Returns TRUE if the value is the #N/A error value
ISNONTEXT	Returns TRUE if the value is not text
ISNUMBER	Returns TRUE if the value is a number
ISODD*	Returns TRUE if the number is odd
ISREF	Returns TRUE if the value is a reference
ISTEXT	Returns TRUE if the value is text
N	Returns a value converted to a number
NA	Returns the error value #N/A
TYPE	Returns a number indicating the data type of a value

* Available only when the Analysis ToolPak add-in is attached

Table C-6
Logical Category Functions

Function	What It Does
AND	Returns TRUE if all of its arguments are TRUE
FALSE	Returns the logical value FALSE
IF	Specifies a logical test to perform
NOT	Reverses the logic of its argument
OR	Returns TRUE if any argument is TRUE
TRUE	Returns the logical value TRUE

Table C-7
Lookup and Reference Category Functions

Function	What It Does
ADDRESS	Returns a reference as text to a single cell in a worksheet
AREAS	Returns the number of areas in a reference
CHOOSE	Chooses a value from a list of values

Function	*What It Does*
COLUMN	Returns the column number of a reference
COLUMNS	Returns the number of columns in a reference
GETPIVOTDATA	Returns data stored in a PivotTable
HLOOKUP	Looks in the top row of an array and returns the value of the indicated cell
HYPERLINK	Creates a shortcut that opens a document on your hard drive, a server, or the Internet
INDEX	Uses an index to choose a value from a reference or array
INDIRECT	Returns a reference indicated by a text value
LOOKUP	Looks up values in a vector or array
MATCH	Looks up values in a reference or array
OFFSET	Returns a reference offset from a given reference
ROW	Returns the row number of a reference
ROWS	Returns the number of rows in a reference
TRANSPOSE	Returns the transpose of an array
VLOOKUP	Looks in the first column of an array and moves across the row to return the value of a cell

Table C-8
Math and Trig Category Functions

Function	*What It Does*
ABS	Returns the absolute value of a number
ACOS	Returns the arccosine of a number
ACOSH	Returns the inverse hyperbolic cosine of a number
ASIN	Returns the arcsine of a number
ASINH	Returns the inverse hyperbolic sine of a number
ATAN	Returns the arctangent of a number
ATAN2	Returns the arctangent from x and y coordinates
ATANH	Returns the inverse hyperbolic tangent of a number
CEILING	Rounds a number to the nearest integer or to the nearest multiple of significance

Continued

Table C-8 (continued)

Function	What It Does
COMBIN	Returns the number of combinations for a given number of objects
COS	Returns the cosine of a number
COSH	Returns the hyperbolic cosine of a number
COUNTIF	Counts the number of nonblank cells within a range that meets the given criteria
DEGREES	Converts radians to degrees
EVEN	Rounds a number up to the nearest even integer
EXP	Returns e raised to the power of a given number
FACT	Returns the factorial of a number
FACTDOUBLE	Returns the double factorial of a number
FLOOR	Rounds a number down, toward 0
GCD*	Returns the greatest common divisor
INT	Rounds a number down to the nearest integer
LCM*	Returns the least common multiple
LN	Returns the natural logarithm of a number
LOG	Returns the logarithm of a number to a specified base
LOG10	Returns the base-10 logarithm of a number
MDETERM	Returns the matrix determinant of an array
MINVERSE	Returns the matrix inverse of an array
MMULT	Returns the matrix product of two arrays
MOD	Returns the remainder from division
MROUND*	Returns a number rounded to the desired multiple
MULTINOMIAL*	Returns the multinomial of a set of numbers
ODD	Rounds a number up to the nearest odd integer
PI	Returns the value of pi
POWER	Returns the result of a number raised to a power
PRODUCT	Multiplies its arguments
QUOTIENT*	Returns the integer portion of a division

Function	*What It Does*
RADIANS	Converts degrees to radians
RAND	Returns a random number between 0 and 1
RANDBETWEEN*	Returns a random number between the numbers that you specify
ROMAN	Converts an Arabic numeral to Roman, as text
ROUND	Rounds a number to a specified number of digits
ROUNDDOWN	Rounds a number down, toward 0
ROUNDUP	Rounds a number up, away from 0
SERIESSUM*	Returns the sum of a power series based on the formula
SIGN	Returns the sign of a number
SIN	Returns the sine of the given angle
SINH	Returns the hyperbolic sine of a number
SQRT	Returns a positive square root
SQRTPI*	Returns the square root of ($number \times$ pi)
SUBTOTAL	Returns a subtotal in a list or database
SUM	Adds its arguments
SUMIF	Adds the cells specified by a given criteria
SUMPRODUCT	Returns the sum of the products of corresponding array components
SUMSQ	Returns the sum of the squares of the arguments
SUMX2MY2	Returns the sum of the difference of squares of corresponding values in two arrays
SUMX2PY2	Returns the sum of the sum of squares of corresponding values in two arrays
SUMXMY2	Returns the sum of squares of differences of corresponding values in two arrays
TAN	Returns the tangent of a number
TANH	Returns the hyperbolic tangent of a number
TRUNC	Truncates a number to an integer

* Available only when the Analysis ToolPak add-in is attached

Table C-9
Statistical Category Functions

Function	What It Does
AVEDEV	Returns the average of the absolute deviations of data points from their mean
AVERAGE	Returns the average of its arguments
AVERAGEA	Returns the average of its arguments and includes evaluation of text and logical values
BETADIST	Returns the cumulative beta probability density function
BETAINV	Returns the inverse of the cumulative beta probability density function
BINOMDIST	Returns the individual term binomial distribution probability
CHIDIST	Returns the one-tailed probability of the chi-squared distribution
CHIINV	Returns the inverse of the one-tailed probability of the chi-squared distribution
CHITEST	Returns the test for independence
CONFIDENCE	Returns the confidence interval for a population mean
CORREL	Returns the correlation coefficient between two data sets
COUNT	Counts how many numbers are in the list of arguments
COUNTA	Counts how many values are in the list of arguments
COUNTBLANK	Counts the number of blank cells in the argument range
COUNTIF	Counts the number of cells that meet the criteria you specify in the argument
COVAR	Returns covariance, the average of the products of paired deviations
CRITBINOM	Returns the smallest value for which the cumulative binomial distribution is less than or equal to a criterion value
DEVSQ	Returns the sum of squares of deviations
EXPONDIST	Returns the exponential distribution
FDIST	Returns the F probability distribution
FINV	Returns the inverse of the F probability distribution
FISHER	Returns the Fisher transformation
FISHERINV	Returns the inverse of the Fisher transformation
FORECAST	Returns a value along a linear trend
FREQUENCY	Returns a frequency distribution as a vertical array

Function	What It Does
FTEST	Returns the result of an F-test
GAMMADIST	Returns the gamma distribution
GAMMAINV	Returns the inverse of the gamma cumulative distribution
GAMMALN	Returns the natural logarithm of the gamma function, $G(x)$
GEOMEAN	Returns the geometric mean
GROWTH	Returns values along an exponential trend
HARMEAN	Returns the harmonic mean
HYPGEOMDIST	Returns the hypergeometric distribution
INTERCEPT	Returns the intercept of the linear regression line
KURT	Returns the kurtosis of a data set
LARGE	Returns the *k*th largest value in a data set
LINEST	Returns the parameters of a linear trend
LOGEST	Returns the parameters of an exponential trend
LOGINV	Returns the inverse of the lognormal distribution
LOGNORMDIST	Returns the cumulative lognormal distribution
MAX	Returns the maximum value in a list of arguments, ignoring logical values and text
MAXA	Returns the maximum value in a list of arguments, including logical values and text
MEDIAN	Returns the median of the given numbers
MIN	Returns the minimum value in a list of arguments, ignoring logical values and text
MINA	Returns the minimum value in a list of arguments, including logical values and text
MODE	Returns the most common value in a data set
NEGBINOMDIST	Returns the negative binomial distribution
NORMDIST	Returns the normal cumulative distribution
NORMINV	Returns the inverse of the normal cumulative distribution
NORMSDIST	Returns the standard normal cumulative distribution
NORMSINV	Returns the inverse of the standard normal cumulative distribution
PEARSON	Returns the Pearson product moment correlation coefficient
PERCENTILE	Returns the *k*th percentile of values in a range
PERCENTRANK	Returns the percentage rank of a value in a data set

Continued

	Table C-9 (continued)	
Function	**What It Does**	
PERMUT	Returns the number of permutations for a given number of objects	
POISSON	Returns the Poisson distribution	
PROB	Returns the probability that values in a range are between two limits	
QUARTILE	Returns the quartile of a data set	
RANK	Returns the rank of a number in a list of numbers	
RSQ	Returns the square of the Pearson product moment correlation coefficient	
SKEW	Returns the skewness of a distribution	
SLOPE	Returns the slope of the linear regression line	
SMALL	Returns the kth smallest value in a data set	
STANDARDIZE	Returns a normalized value	
STDEV	Estimates standard deviation based on a sample, ignoring text and logical values.	
STDEVA	Estimates standard deviation based on a sample, including text and logical values	
STDEVP	Calculates standard deviation based on the entire population, ignoring text and logical values.	
STDEVPA	Calculates standard deviation based on the entire population, including text and logical values.	
STEYX	Returns the standard error of the predicted y-value for each x in the regression	
TDIST	Returns the student's t-distribution	
TINV	Returns the inverse of the student's t-distribution	
TREND	Returns values along a linear trend	
TRIMMEAN	Returns the mean of the interior of a data set	
TTEST	Returns the probability associated with a *student's t-Test*	
VAR	Estimates variance based on a sample, ignoring logical values and text	
VARA	Estimates variance based on a sample, including logical values and text	
VARP	Calculates variance based on the entire population, ignoring logical values and text	
VARPA	Calculates variance based on the entire population, including logical values and text	
WEIBULL	Returns the Weibull distribution	
ZTEST	Returns the two-tailed P-value of a z-test	

Table C-10
Text Category Functions

Function	What It Does
CHAR	Returns the character specified by the code number
CLEAN	Removes all nonprintable characters from text
CODE	Returns a numeric code for the first character in a text string
CONCATENATE	Joins several text items into one text item
DOLLAR	Converts a number to text, using currency format
EXACT	Checks to see whether two text values are identical
FIND	Finds one text value within another (case-sensitive)
FIXED	Formats a number as text with a fixed number of decimals
LEFT	Returns the leftmost characters from a text value
LEN	Returns the number of characters in a text string
LOWER	Converts text to lowercase
MID	Returns a specific number of characters from a text string, starting at the position that you specify
PROPER	Capitalizes the first letter in each word of a text value
REPLACE	Replaces characters within text
REPT	Repeats text a given number of times
RIGHT	Returns the rightmost characters from a text value
SEARCH	Finds one text value within another (not case-sensitive)
SUBSTITUTE	Substitutes new text for old text in a text string
T	Converts its arguments to text
TEXT	Formats a number and converts it to text
TRIM	Removes spaces from text
UPPER	Converts text to uppercase
VALUE	Converts a text argument to a number

✦　　✦　　✦

Importing 1-2-3 Formulas

Lotus 1-2-3 used to be the leading spreadsheet. That distinction, of course, now belongs to Excel. Many users, however, continue to use 1-2-3. You may be in a position in which you need to import a file generated by 1-2-3. If so, the information in this appendix may be helpful to you.

About 1-2-3 Files

Many versions of 1-2-3 have surfaced over the years, and 1-2-3 files exist in several formats. Table D-1 describes the 1-2-3 files you may encounter.

Table D-1	
Lotus 1-2-3 File Types	
File Extension	**Description**
WKS	Generated by 1-2-3 for DOS Release 1.0 and 1.0a. These files consist of a single sheet. Excel can read and write these files.
WK1	Generated by 1-2-3 for DOS Release 2.x. These files consist of a single sheet, and may have a companion *.FMT or *.ALL file that contains formatting information. Excel can read these files, but saves only the active sheet.
WK3	Generated by 1-2-3 for DOS Release 3.x and 1-2-3 for Windows Release 1.0. These files may contain multiple sheets, and may have a companion *.FM3 file that contains formatting information. Excel can read and write these files.

Continued

Table D-1 *(continued)*	
File Extension	**Description**
WK4	Generated by 1-2-3 for Windows Release 4.0. These files may contain multiple sheets. Excel can read and write these files.
123	Generated by 1-2-3 for Windows Release 5 and Millennium Edition. Excel can neither read nor write these files.

Note   When importing or exporting 1-2-3 files, do not expect a perfect translation. Excel's online help describes the limitations.

Lotus 1-2-3 Formulas

In some cases, you may find that the formulas in an imported 1-2-3 file work perfectly in Excel. In other cases, some formulas may not convert correctly and you may need to do some tweaking or rewriting.

Excel evaluates some formulas differently than 1-2-3. These formulas fall into three categories:

✦ Those that use text in calculation

✦ Those that use logical operators (TRUE and FALSE)

✦ Those that use database criteria

To force Excel to use 1-2-3's method of evaluating formulas, select Tools ➪ Options. In the Options dialog box, click the Transition tab and place a checkmark next to the Transition formula evaluation option.

Got a Case of File Bloat?

When you import a 1-2-3 file and save it as an Excel file, you may find that the file becomes very large, making it very slow to open and save. The most likely cause is that the imported 1-2-3 file contains entire columns that are preformatted. When Excel imports such a file, it converts all formatted cells — even if they're empty. The solution is to select all blank rows below the last-used cell in your worksheet, and then delete those rows. Resave the workbook, and it should be a more manageable size.

Note When you open a 1-2-3 file, the Transition formula evaluation checkbox is selected automatically for that sheet to ensure that Excel calculates the formulas according to Lotus 1-2-3 rules.

If you plan to make extensive use of an imported 1-2-3 file, you might want to consider translating any formulas that aren't evaluated correctly, and turning off the Transition formula evaluation option. Doing so helps to avoid confusion among users unfamiliar with 1-2-3.

The following sections provide some tips on how to convert your 1-2-3 formulas so they work properly in Excel (without the Transition formula evaluation setting).

Text in calculations

In 1-2-3, cells that contain text are considered to have a value of 0 when the cell is used in a formula that uses mathematical operators. Excel, on the other hand, returns an error.

Note If the Transition formula evaluation option is set, Excel considers text to have a value of 0.

The following formula is perfectly valid in 1-2-3 (and it returns 12). In Excel, the formula returns a #VALUE! error.

```
="Dog"+12
```

Similarly, if cell A1 contains the text *Dog*, and cell A2 contains the value 12, the following formula is valid in 1-2-3, but returns an error in Excel:

```
=A1+A2
```

Excel, however, does permit references to text cells in function arguments, and it treats such values as 0. For example, the following formula works fine in both 1-2-3 and Excel, even if the range A1:A10 contains text:

```
=SUM(A1:A10)
```

You can take advantage of this fact to convert a 1-2-3 formula such as =A1+A2 to the following:

```
=SUM(A1,A2)
```

Let Excel Teach You

If you're moving up from an older DOS version of 1-2-3, you may be surprised to know that Excel can help you with the transition. The secret lies in the Help ➪ Lotus 1-2-3 Help command. Selecting this command displays a dialog box with the 1-2-3 commands listed along the left side (see the accompanying figure).

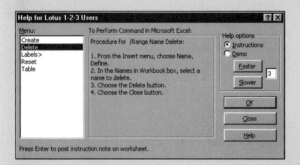

Select the 1-2-3 command sequence, and Excel displays instructions, or even demonstrates the corresponding menu command. For example, if you're a veteran 1-2-3 for DOS user, you know that you use /rnd (for Range Name Delete) to delete a name. If you enter this command sequence in Excel's Help for Lotus 1-2-3 Users dialog box, you see instructions that describe how to perform that operation in Excel.

Logical operators

Boolean expressions in 1-2-3 are evaluated to 1 or 0. Excel displays these values as TRUE or FALSE. TRUE is equivalent to 1-2-3's 1, and FALSE is equivalent to 1-2-3's 0.

Note　If the Transition formula evaluation option is set, Excel displays 0 for FALSE and 1 for TRUE.

In 1-2-3, for example, the following formula displays either 1 or 0, depending on the contents of cells A1 and A2. In Excel, the formula returns either TRUE or FALSE.

```
=A1<A2
```

This distinction may be important if your worksheet uses IF functions that check for 0 or 1. For example, the following formula has different results in 1-2-3 and Excel:

```
=IF(A1<A2=1,B1,B2)
```

To fix this formula so it works properly in Excel, change it to:

```
=IF(A1<A2,B1,B2)
```

Lotus 1-2-3 uses the following logical operators: #AND#, #NOT#, and #OR#. Excel uses logical functions (AND, NOT, and OR) in place of these. For example, the following 1-2-3 formula returns the string *yes* if cell A1=12 and cell A2=12, and the string *no* if both cells are not equal to 12:

```
@IF(A1=12#AND#A2=12,"yes","no")
```

The equivalent 1-2-3 formula is:

```
=IF(AND(A1=12,A2=12),"yes","no")
```

What About 1-2-3 Macros?

Excel can execute some 1-2-3 macros — the keystroke macros developed using early versions of 1-2-3. These macros are stored directly in a worksheet and represent keystrokes sent to the interface. Don't expect perfect compatibility, however.

Typically, these keystroke macros are given a range name such as \t. This macro is executed by typing Ctrl+T. These special names are valid if they are contained in an imported file. But, you'll find that you cannot create such a name in Excel.

If you convert 1-2-3 files to Excel, the best approach is to recreate the macros using VBA. You'll get much better performance and the macros will be easier to maintain.

Database criteria

If your imported worksheet uses database criteria ranges (i.e., advanced filtering), be especially careful. Database criteria ranges are evaluated differently when you extract data, find data, and use database functions. For example, the criteria "Ben" finds only rows where the value *Ben* is contained in the cell. In Excel, the criteria "Ben" finds rows in which the contents of the cell begins with *Ben* — including *Benjamin*, *Benny*, and *Benito*.

Note   If the Transition formula evaluation option is set, Excel works exactly like 1-2-3 in using database criteria.

Lotus 1-2-3 Function Compatibility

Most of the worksheet functions in 1-2-3 have equivalents in Excel. In some cases, however, the correspondence is not perfect. Fortunately, Excel's online help provides a thorough description of the differences between the worksheet functions available in 1-2-3 and in Excel.

Function equivalents

Table D-2 lists 1-2-3 functions that have equivalent Excel functions. It's important to understand that in some cases the correspondence is not exact. Also, for some Excel functions, you must enter the arguments in a different order.

Table D-2	
Excel Equivalents for 1-2-3 Functions	
Lotus 1-2-3 Function	*Equivalent Excel Function*
@	INDIRECT
@@	INDIRECT
@ABS	ABS
@ACCRUED	ACCRINT
@ACOS	ACOS
@ACOSH	ACOSH
@ASIN	ASIN
@ASINH	ASINH
@ATAN	ATAN
@ATAN2	ATAN2
@ATANH	ATANH
@AVEDEV	AVEDEV
@AVG	AVERAGEA
@BESSELI	BESSELI
@BESSELJ	BESSELJ
@BESSELK	BESSELK
@BESSELY	BESSELY
@BIN2DEC	BIN2DEC
@BIN2HEX	BIN2HEX
@BIN2OCT	BIN2OCT
@BINOMIAL	BINOMDIST
@CELL	CELL
@CELLPOINTER	CELL
@CHAR	CHAR
@CHAR	CHAR

Lotus 1-2-3 Function	Equivalent Excel Function
@CHIDIST	CHIINV
@CHIDIST	CHIDIST
@CHOOSE	CHOOSE
@CLEAN	CLEAN
@CODE	CODE
@COLS	COLUMNS
@COLUMN	COLUMN
@COMBIN	COMBIN
@CONFIDENCE	CONFIDENCE
@CONVERT	CONVERT
@CORREL	CORREL, PEARSON
@COS	COS
@COSH	COSH
@COUNT	COUNTA
@COUNTBLANK	COUNTBLANK
@COUNTIF	COUNTIF
@COUPDAYBS	COUPDAYBS
@COUPDAYS	COUPDAYS
@COUPDAYSNC	COUPDAYSNC
@COUPNCD	COUPNCD
@COUPNUM	COUPNUM
@COUPPCD	COUPPCD
@COV	COVAR
@CRITBINOMIAL	CRITBINOM
@CTERM	NPER
@D360	DAYS360
@DATE	DATE
@DATEVALUE	DATEVALUE
@DAVG	DAVERAGE
@DAVG	DAVERAGE
@DAY	DAY

Continued

Table D-2 (*continued*)

Lotus 1-2-3 Function	Equivalent Excel Function
@DAYS	DAYS360
@DAYS360	DAYS360
@DB	DB
@DCOUNT	DCOUNTA
@DDB	DDB
@DEC2BIN	DEC2BIN
@DEC2FRAC	DOLLARFR
@DEC2HEX	DEC2HEX
@DEC2OCT	DEC2OCT
@DEGTORAD	RADIANS
@DEVSQ	DEVSQ
@DGET	DGET
@DISC	DISC
@DMAX	DMAX
@DMAX	DMAX
@DMIN	DMIN
@DPURECOUNT	DCOUNT, DCOUNTA
@DSTD	DSTDEVP
@DSTDS	DSTDEV
@DSUM	DSUM
@DURATION	DURATION
@DVAR	DVARP
@DVARS	DVAR
@ERF	ERF
@ERFC	ERFC
@EVEN	EVEN
@EXACT	EXACT
@EXP	EXP
@EXPONDIST	EXPONDIST
@FACT	FACT

Lotus 1-2-3 Function	Equivalent Excel Function
@FALSE	FALSE
@FDIST	FINV, FDIST
@FIND	FIND
@FISHER	FISHER
@FISHERINV	FISHERINV
@FORECAST	FORECAST
@FRAC2DEC	DOLLARDE
@FTEST	FTEST
@FV	FV
@FVAL	FV
@GAMMALN	GAMMALN
@GEOMEAN	GEOMEAN
@HARMEAN	HARMEAN
@HEX2BIN	HEX2BIN
@HEX2DEC	HEX2DEC
@HEX2OCT	HEX2OCT
@HLOOKUP	HLOOKUP
@HOUR	HOUR
@HYPGEOMDIST	HYPGEOMDIST
@IF	IF
@INDEX	INDEX
@INFO	INFO
@INT	TRUNC
@INTRATE	INTRATE
@IPAYMT	CUMIPMT, IMPT
@IRATE	RATE
@IRR	IRR
@ISEMPTY	ISBLANK
@ISERR	ISERR, ISERROR
@ISNUMBER	ISNONTEXT, ISNUMBER
@ISRANGE	ISREF

Continued

Table D-2 (continued)	
Lotus 1-2-3 Function	**Equivalent Excel Function**
@ISSTRING	ISTEXT
@KURTOSIS	KURT
@LARGE	LARGE
@LEFT	LEFT
@LENGTH	LEN
@LN	LN
@LOG	LOG, LOG10
@LOGINV	LOGINV
@LOGNORMDIST	LOGNORMDIST
@LOWER	LOWER
@MATCH	MATCH
@MAX	MAXA
@MDURATION	MDURATION
@MEDIAN	MEDIAN
@MID	MID
@MIN	MINA
@MINUTE	MINUTE
@MIRR	MIRR
@MOD	MOD
@MODE	MODE
@MONTH	MONTH
@N	N
@NA	NA
@NEGBINOMDIST	NEGBINOMDIST
@NETWORKDAYS	NETWORKDAYS
@NEXTMONTH	EOMONTH, EDATE
@NORMAL	NORMINV, NORMDIST, NORMSDIST
@NORMSINV	NORMSINV
@NOW	NOW

Lotus 1-2-3 Function	Equivalent Excel Function
@NPER	NPER
@NPV	NPV
@OCT2BIN	OCT2BIN
@OCT2DEC	OCT2DEC
@OCT2HEX	OCT2HEX
@ODD	ODD
@PAYMT	PMT
@PERCENTILE	PERCENTILE
@PERMUT	PERMUT
@PI	PI
@PMT	PMT
@POISSON	POISSON
@PPAYMT	CUMPRINC, PPMT
@PRANK	PERCENTRANK
@PRICE	PRICE
@PRICEDISC	PRICEDISC
@PRICEMAT	PRICEMAT
@PROB	PROB
@PRODUCT	PRODUCT
@PROPER	PROPER
@PUREAVG	AVERAGE, AVERAGEA
@PURECOUNT	COUNT, COUNTA
@PUREMAX	MAX, MAXA
@PUREMIN	MIN, MINA
@PURESTD	STDEVP, STDEVPA
@PURESTDS	STDEV, STDEVA
@PUREVAR	VARP, VARPA
@PUREVARS	VAR, VARA
@PV	PV
@PVAL	PV
@QUARTILE	QUARTILE

Continued

Table D-2 *(continued)*	
Lotus 1-2-3 Function	**Equivalent Excel Function**
@QUOTIENT	QUOTIENT
@RADTODEG	DEGREES
@RAND	RAND
@RANDBETWEEN	RANDBETWEEN
@RANK	RANK
@RATE	RATE
@RECEIVED	RECEIVED
@REGRESSION	INTERCEPT
@REPEAT	REPT
@REPLACE	REPLACE
@RIGHT	RIGHT
@RIGHT	RIGHT
@ROUND	ROUND
@ROUNDDOWN	INT, ROUNDDOWN
@ROUNDM	CEILING, FLOOR
@ROUNDUP	ROUNDUP
@ROW	ROW
@ROWS	ROWS
@RSQ	RSQ
@S	T
@SECOND	SECOND
@SERIESSUM	SERIESSUM
@SIGN	SIGN
@SIN	SIN
@SINH	SINH
@SKEWNESS	SKEW
@SLN	SLN
@SMALL	SMALL
@SQRT	SQRT
@SQRTPI	SQRTPI
@STANDARDIZE	STANDARDIZE

Lotus 1-2-3 Function	Equivalent Excel Function
@STD	STDEVPA
@STDS	STDEVA
@STEYX	STEYX
@STRING	FIXED, TEXT
@SUM	SUM
@SUMIF	SUMIF
@SUMPRODUCT	SUMPRODUCT
@SUMSQ	SUMSQ
@SUMX2MY2	SUMX2MY2
@SUMX2PY2	SUMX2PY2
@SUMXMY2	SUMXMY2
@SYD	SYD
@TAN	TAN
@TANH	TANH
@TBILLEQ	TBILLEQ
@TBILLPRICE	TBILLPRICE
@TBILLYIELD	TBILLYIELD
@TDIST	TDIST, TINV
@TERM	NPER
@TIME	TIME
@TIMEVALUE	TIMEVALUE
@TODAY	TODAY
@TRIM	TRIM
@TRIMMEAN	TRIMMEAN
@TRUE	TRUE
@TRUNC	TRUNC
@TTEST	TTEST
@UPPER	UPPER
@VALUE	VALUE
@VAR	VARPA
@VARS	VARA

Continued

Table D-2 (continued)	
Lotus 1-2-3 Function	**Equivalent Excel Function**
@VDB	VDB
@VLOOKUP	VLOOKUP
@WEEKDAY	WEEKDAY
@WEIBULL	WEIBULL
@WORKDAY	WORKDAY
@YEAR	YEAR
@YEARFRAC	YEARFRAC
@YIELD	YIELD
@YIELDDISC	YIELDDISC
@YIELDMAT	YIELDMAT
@ZTEST	ZTEST

Converting database functions

There's a common problem with 1-2-3's database functions (for example, @DSUM and @DCOUNT). Lotus 1-2-3 enables you to specify your criteria as an argument. Refer to Figure D-1, which shows a 1-2-3 file imported into Excel. The following formula (in cell E4) was not translated correctly and displays a #NAME? error.

```
=DCOUNTA(A1:C18,"Product",AND(PRODUCT="Widget",MONTH="January"))
```

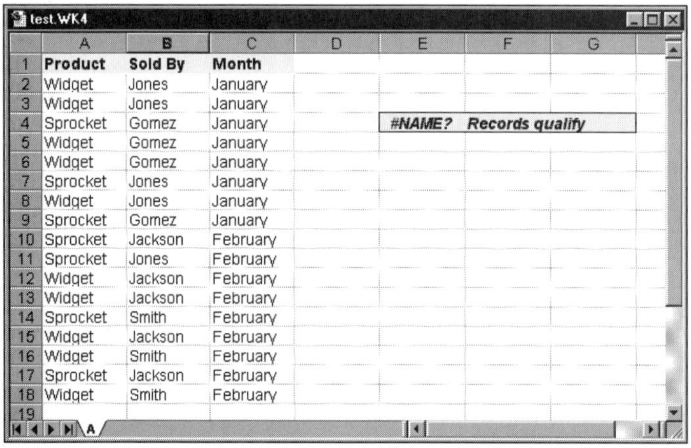

Figure D-1: This imported 1-2-3 file uses a @DCOUNT function with a criterion argument not supported by Excel.

The original 1-2-3 formula was written to return the count of records in which the Product is *Widget* and the Month is *January*. The original 1-2-3 formula (before conversion by Excel) was:

```
@DCOUNT(A1:C18,"Product",PRODUCT="Widget" #AND#MONTH="January")
```

Unfortunately, Excel's database functions do not let you specify the criteria as an argument. Rather, you need to:

✦ Set up a special criteria range for the DCOUNTA function

✦ Use a different function — in this case, the COUNTIF function.

Figure D-2 shows a criteria range in E1:F2. The following formula returns the count of records in which the Product is *Widget* and the Month is *January*.

```
=DCOUNT(A1:C18,"Product",E1:F2)
```

Figure D-2: Using a criteria range for the DCOUNT formula

Alternatively, you can use an array formula, which doesn't require a criteria range. The following formula is the Excel equivalent of the incorrectly translated @DCOUNT formula:

```
{=SUM((A2:A18="Widget")*(C2:C18="January"))}
```

✦   ✦   ✦

Excel's Shortcut Keys

This appendix lists the most useful shortcut keys that are available in Excel. The shortcuts are arranged by context.

The keys listed assume that you are not using the Transition Navigation Keys, which are designed to emulate Lotus 1-2-3. You can select this option in the Transition tab of the Options dialog box.

Table E-1 Moving Through a Worksheet	
Key(s)	**What It Does**
Arrow keys	Move left, right, up, or down one cell
Home	Moves to the beginning of the row
Home*	Moves to the upper-left cell displayed in the window
End*	Moves to the lower-left cell displayed in the window
Arrow keys*	Scrolls left, right, up, or down one cell
PgUp	Moves up one screen
Ctrl+PgUp	Moves to the previous sheet
PgDn	Moves down one screen
Ctrl+PgDn	Moves to the next sheet
Alt+PgUp	Moves one screen to the left
Alt+PgDn	Moves one screen to the right
Ctrl+Home	Moves to the first cell in the worksheet (A1)
Ctrl+End	Moves to the last active cell of the worksheet

Continued

Table E-1 *(continued)*

Key(s)	What It Does
Ctrl+arrow key	Moves to the edge of a data block; if the cell is blank, moves to the first nonblank cell
Ctrl+Backspace	Scrolls to display the active cell
End+Home	Moves to the last nonempty cell on the worksheet
F5	Prompts for a cell address to go to
F6	Moves to the next pane of a workbook that has been split
Shift+F6	Moves to the previous pane of a workbook that has been split
Ctrl+Tab	Moves to the next window
Ctrl+Shift+Tab	Moves to the previous window

* With Scroll Lock on

Table E-2
Selecting Cells in the Worksheet

Key(s)	What It Does
Shift+arrow key	Expands the selection in the direction indicated
Shift+spacebar	Selects the entire row
Ctrl+spacebar	Selects the entire column
Ctrl+Shift+	Selects the entire worksheet spacebar
Shift+Home	Expands the selection to the beginning of the current row
Ctrl+*	Selects the block of data surrounding the active cell
F8	Extends the selection as you use navigation keys
Shift+F8	Adds other nonadjacent cells or ranges to the selection; pressing Shift+F8 again ends Add mode
F5	Prompts for a range or range name to select
Ctrl+G	Prompts for a range or range name to select
Ctrl+A	Selects the entire worksheet
Shift+Backspace	Selects the active cell in a range selection

Table E-3
Moving Within a Range Selection

Key(s)	What It Does
Enter	Moves the cell pointer down to the next cell in the selection
Shift+Enter	Moves the cell pointer up to the preceding cell in the selection
Tab	Moves the cell pointer right to the next cell in the selection
Shift+Tab	Moves the cell pointer left to the preceding cell in the selection
Ctrl+period (.)	Moves the cell pointer to the next corner of the current cell range
Ctrl+Tab	Moves the cell pointer to the next cell range in a nonadjacent selection
Ctrl+Shift+Tab	Moves the cell pointer to the previous cell range in a nonadjacent selection
Shift+Backspace	Collapses the cell selection to just the active cell

Table E-4
Editing Keys in the Formula Bar

Key(s)	What It Does
F2	Begins editing the active cell
F3	Pastes a name into a formula
Arrow keys	Moves the cursor one character in the direction of the arrow
Home	Moves the cursor to the beginning of the line
Esc	Cancels the editing
End	Moves the cursor to the end of the line
Ctrl+right arrow	Moves the cursor one word to the right
Ctrl+left arrow	Moves the cursor one word to the left
Del	Deletes the character to the right of the cursor
Ctrl+Del	Deletes all characters from the cursor to the end of the line
Backspace	Deletes the character to the left of the cursor

Table E-5
Formatting Keys

Key(s)	What It Does
Ctrl+1	Format ⇨ [Selected Object]
Ctrl+B	Sets or removes boldface
Ctrl+I	Sets or removes italic
Ctrl+U	Sets or removes underlining
Ctrl+5	Sets or removes strikethrough
Ctrl+Shift+~	Applies the general number format
Ctrl+Shift+!	Applies the comma format with two decimal places
Ctrl+Shift+#	Applies the date format (day, month, year)
Ctrl+Shift+@	Applies the time format (hour, minute, a.m./p.m.)
Ctrl+Shift+$	Applies the currency format with two decimal places
Ctrl+Shift+%	Applies the percent format with no decimal places
Ctrl+Shift+&	Applies border to outline
Ctrl+Shift+_	Removes all borders
Alt+'	Selects Format ⇨ Style

Table E-6
Other Shortcut Keys

Key(s)	What It Does
Alt+=	Inserts the AutoSum formula
Alt+Backspace	Selects Edit ⇨ Undo
Alt+Enter	Starts a new line in the current cell
Ctrl+;	Enters the current date
Ctrl+0 (zero)	Hides columns
Ctrl+1	Displays the Format dialog box for the selected object
Ctrl+6	Cycles among various ways of displaying objects
Ctrl+7	Toggles the display of the standard toolbar
Ctrl+8	Toggles the display of outline symbols
Ctrl+9	Hides rows
Ctrl+A	After typing a function name in a formula, displays the Formula Palette

Key(s)	What It Does
Ctrl+C	Selects Edit ⇨ Copy
Ctrl+D	Selects Edit ⇨ Fill Left
Ctrl+Delete	Selects Edit ⇨ Cut
Ctrl+F	Selects Edit ⇨ Find
Ctrl+H	Selects Edit ⇨ Replace
Ctrl+Insert	Selects Edit ⇨ Copy
Ctrl+K	Selects Insert ⇨ Hyperlink
Ctrl+N	Selects File ⇨ New
Ctrl+O	Selects File ⇨ Open
Ctrl+P	Selects File ⇨ Print
Ctrl+R	Selects Edit ⇨ Fill Right
Ctrl+S	Selects File ⇨ Save
Ctrl+Shift+(	Unhides rows
Ctrl+Shift+)	Unhides columns
Ctrl+Shift+:	Enters the current time
Ctrl+Shift+A	After typing a valid function name in a formula, inserts the argument names and parentheses for the function
Ctrl+V	Selects Edit ⇨ Paste
Ctrl+X	Selects Edit ⇨ Cut
Ctrl+Z	Selects Edit ⇨ Undo
Delete	Selects Edit ⇨ Clear
Shift+Insert	Selects Edit ⇨ Paste

Table E-7
Function Keys

Key(s)	What It Does
F1	Displays Help or the Office Assistant
Shift+F1	Displays the What's This cursor
Alt+F1	Inserts a chart sheet
Alt+Shift+F1	Inserts a new worksheet
F2	Edits the active cell

Continued

Table E-7 *(continued)*

Key(s)	What It Does
Shift+F2	Edits a cell comment
Alt+F2	Issues Save As command
Alt+Shift+F2	Issues Save command
F3	Pastes a name into a formula
Shift+F3	Pastes a function into a formula
Ctrl+F3	Defines a name
Ctrl+Shift+F3	Displays the Creates Names dialog box, to create names using row and column labels
F4	Repeats the last action
Shift+F4	Repeats the last Find (Find Next)
Ctrl+F4	Closes the window
Alt+F4	Exits the program
F5	Displays the Go To dialog box
Shift+F5	Displays the Find dialog box
Ctrl+F5	Restores the window size
F6	Moves to the next pane
Shift+F6	Moves to the previous pane
Ctrl+F6	Moves to the next workbook window
Ctrl+Shift+F6	Moves to the previous workbook window
F7	Issues Spelling command
Ctrl+F7	Moves the window
F8	Extends a selection
Shift+F8	Adds to the selection
Ctrl+F8	Resizes the window
Alt+F8	Displays the Macro dialog box
F9	Calculates all sheets in all open workbooks
Shift+F9	Calculates the active worksheet
Ctrl+F9	Minimizes the workbook
F10	Makes the menu bar active
Shift+F10	Displays a shortcut menu

Key(s)	What It Does
Ctrl+F10	Maximizes or restores the workbook window
F11	Creates a chart
Shift+F11	Inserts a new worksheet
Ctrl+F11	Inserts an Excel 4.0 macro sheet
Alt+F11	Displays Visual Basic Editor
F12	Issues Save As command
Shift+F12	Issues Save command
Ctrl+F12	Issues Open command
Ctrl+Shift+F12	Issues Print command

✦   ✦   ✦

VBA Statements and Function Reference

This appendix contains a complete listing of all VBA statements and built-in functions. For details, consult Excel's online help.

Table F-1 Summary of VBA Statements	
Statement	**Action**
AppActivate	Activates an application window
Beep	Sounds a tone using the computer's speaker
Call	Transfers control to another procedure
ChDir	Changes the current directory
ChDrive	Changes the current drive
Close	Closes a text file
Const	Declares a constant value
Date	Sets the current system date
Declare	Declares a reference to an external procedure in a DLL
DefBool	Sets the default data type to Boolean for variables that begin with a specified letter
DefByte	Sets the default data type to byte for variables that begin with a specified letter

Continued

Table F-1
Summary of VBA Statements

Statement	Action
DefDate	Sets the default data type to date for variables that begin with a specified letter
DefDec	Sets the default data type to decimal for variables that begin with a specified letter
DefDouble	Sets the default data type to double for variables that begin with a specified letter
DefInt	Sets the default data type to integer for variables that begin with a specified letter
DefLng	Sets the default data type to long for variables that begin with a specified letter
DefObj	Sets the default data type to object for variables that begin with a specified letter
DefSng	Sets the default data type to single for variables that begin with a specified letter
DefStr	Sets the default data type to string for variables that begin with a specified letter
DeleteSetting	Deletes a section or key setting from an application's entry in the Windows Registry
Dim	Declares an array locally
Do-Loop	Loops
End	Exits the program
Enum*	Declares a type for enumeration
Erase	Reinitializes an array
Error	Simulates a specific error condition
Event*	Declares a user-defined event
Exit Do	Exits a block of Do-Loop code
Exit For	Exits a block of Do-For code
Exit Function	Exits a Function procedure
Exit Property	Exits a Property procedure
Exit Sub	Exits a subroutine procedure

Statement	Action
FileCopy	Copies a file
For Each-Next	Loops
For-Next	Loops
Statement	Action
Function	Declares the name and arguments for a Function procedure
Get	Reads data from a text file
GoSub-Return	Branches
GoTo	Branches
If-Then-Else	Processes statements conditionally
Implements*	Specifies an interface or class that will be implemented in a class module
Input #	Reads data from a sequential text file
Kill	Deletes a file from a disk
Let	Assigns the value of an expression to a variable or property
Line Input #	Reads a line of data from a sequential text file
Load	Loads an object but doesn't show it
Lock-Unlock	Controls access to a text file
LSet	Left-aligns a string within a string variable
Mid	Replaces characters in a string with other characters
MkDir	Creates a new directory
Name	Renames a file or directory
On Error	Branches on an error
On-GoSub	Branches on a condition
On-GoTo	Branches on a condition
Open	Opens a text file
Option Base	Changes default lower limit
Option Compare	Declares the default comparison mode when comparing strings
Option Explicit	Forces declaration of all variables in a module
Option Private	Indicates that an entire module is Private
Print #	Writes data to a sequential file

Continued

Table F-1 *(continued)*

Statement	Action
Private	Declares a local array
Property Get	Declares the name and arguments of a Property Get procedure
Property Let	Declares the name and arguments of a Property Let procedure
Property Set	Declares the name and arguments of a Property Set procedure
Public	Declares a public array
Put	Writes a variable to a text file
RaiseEvent	Fires a user-defined event
Randomize	Initializes the random number generator
ReDim	Changes the dimensions of an array
Rem	Specifies a line of comments (same as an apostrophe ['])
Reset	Closes all open text files
Resume	Resumes execution when an error-handling routine finishes
RmDir	Removes an empty directory
RSet	Right-aligns a string within a string variable
SaveSetting	Saves or creates an application entry in the Windows registry
Seek	Sets the position for the next access in a text file
Select Case	Processes statements conditionally
SendKeys	Sends keystrokes to the active window
Set	Assigns an object reference to a variable or property
SetAttr	Changes attribute information for a file
Static	Changes the dimensions of an array, keeping the data intact
Stop	Pauses the program
Sub	Declares the name and arguments of a Sub procedure
Time	Sets the system time
Type	Defines a custom data type
Unload	Removes an object from memory
While-Wend	Loops
Width #	Sets the output line width of a text file
With	Sets a series of properties for an object
Write #	Writes data to a sequential text file

* Not available in Excel 97 and earlier editions

Invoking Excel Functions in VBA Instructions

If a VBA function that's equivalent to one you use in Excel is not available, you can use Excel's worksheet functions directly in your VBA code. Just precede the function with a reference to the `WorksheetFunction` object. For example, VBA does not have a function to convert radians to degrees. Because Excel has a worksheet function for this procedure, you can use a VBA instruction such as the following:

```
Deg = Application.WorksheetFunction.Degrees(3.14)
```

The `WorksheetFunction` object was introduced in Excel 97. For compatibility with earlier versions of Excel, you can omit the reference to the `WorksheetFunction` object and write an instruction such as the following:

```
Deg = Application.Degrees(3.14)
```

Table F-2 Summary of VBA Functions	
Function	**Action**
Abs	Returns the absolute value of a number
Array	Returns a variant containing an array
Asc	Converts the first character of string to its ASCII value
Atn	Returns the arctangent of a number
CallByName*	Executes a method, or sets or returns a property of an object
CBool	Converts an expression to a Boolean data type
CByte	Converts an express to a byte data type
CCur	Converts an expression to a currency data type
CDate	Converts an expression to a date data type
CDbl	Converts an expression to a double data type
CDec	Converts an expression to a decimal data type
Choose	Selects and returns a value from a list of arguments
Chr	Converts a character code to a string
CInt	Converts an expression to an integer data type
CLng	Converts an expression to a long data type

Continued

Table F-2 *(continued)*

Function	Action
Cos	Returns the cosine of a number
CreateObject	Creates an OLE Automation object
CSng	Converts an expression to a single data type
CStr	Converts an expression to a string data type
CurDir	Returns the current path
CVar	Converts an expression to a variant data type
CVDate	Converts an expression to a date data type
CVErr	Returns a user-defined error number
Date	Returns the current system date
DateAdd	Adds a time interval to a date
DateDiff	Returns the time interval between two dates
DatePart	Returns a specified part of a date
DateSerial	Converts a date to a serial number
DateValue	Converts a string to a date
Day	Returns the day of the month of a date
DDB	Returns the depreciation of an asset
Dir	Returns the name of a file or directory that matches a pattern
DoEvents	Yields execution so the operating system can process other events
Environ	Returns an operating environment string
EOF	Returns True if the end of a text file has been reached
Error	Returns the error message that corresponds to an error number
Exp	Returns the base of the natural logarithms (e) raised to a power
FileAttr	Returns the file mode for a text file
FileDateTime	Returns the date and time when a file was last modified
FileLen	Returns the number of bytes in a file
Fix	Returns the integer portion of a number
Format	Displays an expression in a particular format

Function	Action
FormatCurrency*	Returns an expression formatted with the system currency symbol
FormatDateTime*	Returns an expression formatted as a date or time
FormatNumber*	Returns an expression formatted as a number
FormatPercent*	Returns an expression formatted as a percentage
FreeFile	Returns the next available file number when working with text files
FV	Returns the future value of an annuity
GetAllSettings	Returns a list of settings and values from the Windows Registry
GetAttr	Returns a code representing a file attribute
GetObject	Retrieves an OLE Automation object from a file
GetSetting	Returns a specific setting from the application's entry in the Windows Registry
Hex	Converts from decimal to hexadecimal
Hour	Returns the hour of a time
Iif	Evaluates an expression and returns one of two parts
Input	Returns characters from a sequential text file
InputBox	Displays a box to prompt a user for input
InStr	Returns the position of a string within another string
InStrRev*	Returns the position of a string within another string, from the end of the string
Int	Returns the integer portion of a number
IPmt	Returns the interest payment for a given period of an annuity
IRR	Returns the internal rate of return for a series of cash flows
IsArray	Returns True if a variable is an array
IsDate	Returns True if a variable is a date
IsEmpty	Returns True if a variable has been initialized
IsError	Returns True if an expression is an error value
IsMissing	Returns True if an optional argument was not passed to a procedure

Continued

Table F-2 *(continued)*

Function	Action
IsNull	Returns True if an expression contains no valid data
IsNumeric	Returns True if an expression can be evaluated as a number
IsObject	Returns True if an expression references an OLE Automation object
Join*	Combines strings contained in an array
LBound	Returns the smallest subscript for a dimension of an array
LCase	Returns a string converted to lowercase
Left	Returns a specified number of characters from the left of a string
Len	Returns the number of characters in a string
Loc	Returns the current read or write position of a text file
LOF	Returns the number of bytes in an open text file
Log	Returns the natural logarithm of a number
LTrim	Returns a copy of a string with no leading spaces
Mid	Returns a specified number of characters from a string
Minute	Returns the minute of a time
MIRR	Returns the modified internal rate of return for a series of periodic cash flows
Month	Returns the month of a date
MsgBox	Displays a modal message box
Now	Returns the current system date and time
NPer	Returns the number of periods for an annuity
NPV	Returns the net present value of an investment
Oct	Converts from decimal to octal
Partition	Returns a string representing a range in which a value falls
Pmt	Returns a payment amount for an annuity
Ppmt	Returns the principal payment amount for an annuity
PV	Returns the present value of an annuity
QBColor	Returns an RGB color code
Rate	Returns the interest rate per period for an annuity

Function	Action
Replace*	Returns a string in which a substring is replaced with another string
RGB	Returns a number representing an RGB color value
Right	Returns a specified number of characters from the right of a string
Rnd	Returns a random number between 0 and 1
Round	Returns a rounded number
RTrim	Returns a copy of a string with no trailing spaces
Second	Returns the seconds portion of a specified time
Seek	Returns the current position in a text file
Sgn	Returns an integer that indicates the sign of a number
Shell	Runs an executable program
Sin	Returns the sine of a number
SLN	Returns the straight-line depreciation for an asset for a period
Space	Returns a string with a specified number of spaces
Spc	Positions output when printing to a file
Split*	Returns a one-dimensional array containing a number of substrings
Sqr	Returns the square root of a number
Str	Returns a string representation of a number
StrComp	Returns a value indicating the result of a string comparison
StrConv	Returns a converted string
String	Returns a repeating character or string
StrReverse*	Returns a string, reversed
Switch	Evaluates a list of Boolean expressions and returns a value associated with the first True expression
SYD	Returns the sum-of-years' digits depreciation of an asset for a period
Tab	Positions output when printing to a file
Tan	Returns the tangent of a number

Continued

Table F-2 *(continued)*

Function	Action
Time	Returns the current system time
Timer	Returns the number of seconds since midnight
TimeSerial	Returns the time for a specified hour, minute, and second
TimeValue	Converts a string to a time serial number
Trim	Returns a string without leading spaces and/or trailing spaces
TypeName	Returns a string that describes the data type of a variable
UBound	Returns the largest available subscript for a dimension of an array
UCase	Converts a string to uppercase
Val	Returns the numbers contained in a string
VarType	Returns a value indicating the subtype of a variable
WeekdateName*	Returns a string indicating a day of the week
Weekday	Returns a number representing a day of the week
Year	Returns the year of a date

* Not available in Excel 97 and earlier editions

✦   ✦   ✦

VBA Error Codes

This appendix contains a complete listing of the error codes for all trappable errors. This information is useful for error trapping. For complete details, consult the online help.

Note Codes marked with an asterisk are not supported by Excel 97 or earlier editions.

Error Code	Message
3	Return without GoSub
5	Invalid procedure call
6	Overflow
7	Out of memory
9	Subscript out of range
10	This array is fixed or temporarily locked
11	Division by zero
13	Type mismatch
14	Out of string space
16	Expression too complex
17	Can't perform requested operation
18	User interrupt occurred
20	Resume without error
28	Out of stack space
35	Sub, Function, or Property not defined
47	Too many code resources or DLL application clients
48	Error in loading code resource or DLL
49	Bad code resource or DLL calling convention
51	Internal error
52	Bad filename or number
53	File not found

Continued

Error Code	Message
54	Bad file mode
55	File already open
57	Device I/O error
58	File already exists
59	Bad record length
61	Disk full
62	Input past end of file
63	Bad record number
67	Too many files
68	Device unavailable
70	Permission denied
71	Disk not ready
74	Can't rename with different drive
75	Path/File access error
76	Path not found
91	Object variable or With block variable not set
92	For loop not initialized
93	Invalid pattern string
94	Invalid use of Null
97	Can't call Friend procedure on an object that is not an instance of the defining class
98*	A property or method call cannot include a reference to a private object, either as an argument or as a return value
298	System DLL could not be loaded
320	Can't use character device names in specified filenames
321	Invalid file format
322	Can't create necessary temporary file
325	Invalid format in resource file
327	Data value named not found
328	Illegal parameter; can't write arrays
335	Could not access system registry
336	Component not correctly registered
337	Component not found

Error Code	Message
338	Component did not run correctly
360	Object already loaded
361	Can't load or unload this object
363	Control specified not found
364	Object was unloaded
365	Unable to unload within this context
368	The specified file is out of date. This program requires a later version
371	The specified object can't be used as an owner form for Show
380	Invalid property value
381	Invalid property-array index
382	Property Set can't be executed at run time
383	Property Set can't be used with a read-only property
385	Need property array index
387	Property Set not permitted
393	Property Get can't be executed at run time
394	Property Get can't be executed on write-only property
400	Form already displayed; can't show modally
402	Code must close topmost modal form first
419	Permission to use object denied
422	Property not found
423	Property or method not found
424	Object required
425	Invalid object use
429	Component can't create object or return reference to this object
430	Class doesn't support Automation
432	Filename or class name not found during Automation operation
438	Object doesn't support this property or method
440	Automation error
442	Connection to type library or object library for remote process has been lost
443	Automation object doesn't have a default value
445	Object doesn't support this action

Continued

Error Code	Message
446	Object doesn't support named arguments
447	Object doesn't support current locale setting
448	Named argument not found
449	Argument not optional or invalid property assignment
450	Wrong number of arguments or invalid property assignment
451	Object not a collection
452	Invalid ordinal
453	Specified code resource not found
454	Code resource not found
455	Code resource lock error
457	This key is already associated with an element of this collection
458	Variable uses a type not supported in VBA
459	This component doesn't support the set of events
460	Invalid Clipboard format
461	Method or data member not found
462*	The remote server machine does not exist or is unavailable
463*	Class not registered on local machine
480	Can't create AutoRedraw image
481	Invalid picture
482	Printer error
483	Printer driver does not support specified property
484	Problem getting printer information from the system. Make sure the printer is set up correctly
485	Invalid picture type
486	Can't print form image to this type of printer
520	Can't empty Clipboard
521	Can't open Clipboard
735	Can't save file to TEMP directory
744	Search text not found
746	Replacements too long
31001	Out of memory
31004	No object

Error Code	Message
31018	Class is not set
31027	Unable to activate object
31032	Unable to create embedded object
31036	Error saving to file
31037	Error loading from file

* Not supported by Excel 97 or earlier editions

✦　　✦　　✦

ANSI Code Reference

This appendix contains the ANSI codes, the character (if any) they produce, their hex value, binary value, and the keystroke (if any) that generates the code.

Note   For keystrokes that use the Alt key, you must use the numeric keypad with Num Lock on.

ANSI Code	Character	Hex Code	Binary Code	Keystroke
1	\<None\>	&H01	0000 0001	\<None\>
2	\<None\>	&H02	0000 0010	\<None\>
3	\<None\>	&H03	0000 0011	\<None\>
4	\<None\>	&H04	0000 0100	\<None\>
5	\<None\>	&H05	0000 0101	\<None\>
6	\<None\>	&H06	0000 0110	\<None\>
7	\<None\>	&H07	0000 0111	\<None\>
8	\<Backspace\>	&H08	0000 1000	Backspace
9	\<Tab\>	&H09	0000 1001	Tab
10	\<Line feed\>	&H0A	0000 1010	\<None\>
11	\<None\>	&H0B	0000 1011	\<None\>
12	\<None\>	&H0C	0000 1100	\<None\>
13	\<Carriage return\>	&H0D	0000 1101	Return
14	\<None\>	&H0E	0000 1110	\<None\>
15	\<None\>	&H0F	0000 1111	\<None\>
16	\<None\>	&H10	0001 0000	\<None\>
17	\<None\>	&H11	0001 0001	\<None\>
18	\<None\>	&H12	0001 0010	\<None\>
19	\<None\>	&H13	0001 0011	\<None\>
20	\<None\>	&H14	0001 0100	\<None\>
21	\<None\>	&H15	0001 0101	\<None\>
22	\<None\>	&H16	0001 0110	\<None\>
23	\<None\>	&H17	0001 0111	\<None\>
24	\<None\>	&H18	0001 1000	\<None\>
25	\<None\>	&H19	0001 1001	\<None\>
26	\<None\>	&H1A	0001 1010	\<None\>
27	\<None\>	&H1B	0001 1011	\<None\>
28	\<None\>	&H1C	0001 1100	\<None\>
29	\<None\>	&H1D	0001 1101	\<None\>
30	\<None\>	&H1E	0001 1110	\<None\>
31	\<None\>	&H1F	0001 1111	\<None\>

ANSI Code	Character	Hex Code	Binary Code	Keystroke
32	<Space>	&H20	0010 0000	Space
33	!	&H21	0010 0001	!
34	"	&H22	0010 0010	"
35	#	&H23	0010 0011	#
36	$	&H24	0010 0100	$
37	%	&H25	0010 0101	%
38	&	&H26	0010 0110	&
39	'	&H27	0010 0111	'
40	(	&H28	0010 1000	(
41	)	&H29	0010 1001	)
42	*	&H2A	0010 1010	*
43	+	&H2B	0010 1011	+
44	,	&H2C	0010 1100	,
45	-	&H2D	0010 1101	-
46	.	&H2E	0010 1110	.
47	/	&H2F	0010 1111	/
48	0	&H30	0011 0000	0
49	1	&H31	0011 0001	1
50	2	&H32	0011 0010	2
51	3	&H33	0011 0011	3
52	4	&H34	0011 0100	4
53	5	&H35	0011 0101	5
54	6	&H36	0011 0110	6
55	7	&H37	0011 0111	7
56	8	&H38	0011 1000	8
57	9	&H39	0011 1001	9
58	:	&H3A	0011 1010	:
59	;	&H3B	0011 1011	;
60	<	&H3C	0011 1100	<
61	=	&H3D	0011 1101	=
62	>	&H3E	0011 1110	>

Continued

ANSI Code	Character	Hex Code	Binary Code	Keystroke
63	?	&H3F	0011 1111	?
64	@	&H40	0100 0000	@
65	A	&H41	0100 0001	A
66	B	&H42	0100 0010	B
67	C	&H43	0100 0011	C
68	D	&H44	0100 0100	D
69	E	&H45	0100 0101	E
70	F	&H46	0100 0110	F
71	G	&H47	0100 0111	G
72	H	&H48	0100 1000	H
73	I	&H49	0100 1001	I
74	J	&H4A	0100 1010	J
75	K	&H4B	0100 1011	K
76	L	&H4C	0100 1100	L
77	M	&H4D	0100 1101	M
78	N	&H4E	0100 1110	N
79	O	&H4F	0100 1111	O
80	P	&H50	0101 0000	P
81	Q	&H51	0101 0001	Q
82	R	&H52	0101 0010	R
83	S	&H53	0101 0011	S
84	T	&H54	0101 0100	T
85	U	&H55	0101 0101	U
86	V	&H56	0101 0110	V
87	W	&H57	0101 0111	W
88	X	&H58	0101 1000	X
89	Y	&H59	0101 1001	Y
90	Z	&H5A	0101 1010	Z
91	[	&H5B	0101 1011	[
92	\	&H5C	0101 1100	\
93	]	&H5D	0101 1101	]

ANSI Code	Character	Hex Code	Binary Code	Keystroke
94	^	&H5E	0101 1110	^
95	_	&H5F	0101 1111	_
96	`	&H60	0110 0000	`
97	a	&H61	0110 0001	a
98	b	&H62	0110 0010	b
99	c	&H63	0110 0011	c
100	d	&H64	0110 0100	d
101	e	&H65	0110 0101	e
102	f	&H66	0110 0110	f
103	g	&H67	0110 0111	g
104	h	&H68	0110 1000	h
105	i	&H69	0110 1001	i
106	j	&H6A	0110 1010	j
107	k	&H6B	0110 1011	k
108	l	&H6C	0110 1100	l
109	m	&H6D	0110 1101	m
110	n	&H6E	0110 1110	n
111	o	&H6F	0110 1111	o
112	p	&H70	0111 0000	p
113	q	&H71	0111 0001	q
114	r	&H72	0111 0010	r
115	s	&H73	0111 0011	s
116	t	&H74	0111 0100	t
117	u	&H75	0111 0101	u
118	v	&H76	0111 0110	v
119	w	&H77	0111 0111	w
120	x	&H78	0111 1000	x
121	y	&H79	0111 1001	y
122	z	&H7A	0111 1010	z
123	{	&H7B	0111 1011	{
124			&H7C	0111 1100		

Continued

ANSI Code	Character	Hex Code	Binary Code	Keystroke
125	}	&H7D	0111 1101	}
126	~	&H7E	0111 1110	~
127	□	&H7F	0111 1111	Del
128	□	&H80	1000 0000	Alt+0128
129	□	&H81	1000 0001	Alt+0129
130	,	&H82	1000 0010	Alt+0130
131	ƒ	&H83	1000 0011	Alt+0131
132	„	&H84	1000 0100	Alt+0132
133	…	&H85	1000 0101	Alt+0133
134	†	&H86	1000 0110	Alt+0134
135	‡	&H87	1000 0111	Alt+0135
136	ˆ	&H88	1000 1000	Alt+0136
137	‰	&H89	1000 1001	Alt+0137
138	Š	&H8A	1000 1010	Alt+0138
139	‹	&H8B	1000 1011	Alt+0139
140	Œ	&H8C	1000 1100	Alt+0140
141	□	&H8D	1000 1101	Alt+0141
142	□	&H8E	1000 1110	Alt+0142
143	□	&H8F	1000 1111	Alt+0143
144	□	&H90	1001 0000	Alt+0144
145	'	&H91	1001 0001	Alt+0145
146	'	&H92	1001 0010	Alt+0146
147	"	&H93	1001 0011	Alt+0147
148	"	&H94	1001 0100	Alt+0148
149	•	&H95	1001 0101	Alt+0149
150	–	&H96	1001 0110	Alt+0150
151	—	&H97	1001 0111	Alt+0151
152	~	&H98	1001 1000	Alt+0152
153	™	&H99	1001 1001	Alt+0153
154	š	&H9A	1001 1010	Alt+0154
155	›	&H9B	1001 1011	Alt+0155

ANSI Code	Character	Hex Code	Binary Code	Keystroke
156	œ	&H9C	1001 1100	Alt+0156
157	□	&H9D	1001 1101	Alt+0157
158	□	&H9E	1001 1110	Alt+0158
159	Ÿ	&H9F	1001 1111	Alt+0159
160	<None>	&HA0	1010 0000	Alt+0160
161	¡	&HA1	1010 0001	Alt+0161
162	¢	&HA2	1010 0010	Alt+0162
163	£	&HA3	1010 0011	Alt+0163
164		&HA4	1010 0100	Alt+0164
165	¥	&HA5	1010 0101	Alt+0165
166	¦	&HA6	1010 0110	Alt+0166
167	§	&HA7	1010 0111	Alt+0167
168	¨	&HA8	1010 1000	Alt+0168
169	©	&HA9	1010 1001	Alt+0169
170	ª	&HAA	1010 1010	Alt+0170
171	«	&HAB	1010 1011	Alt+0171
172	¬	&HAC	1010 1100	Alt+0172
173	-	&HAD	1010 1101	Alt+0173
174	®	&HAE	1010 1110	Alt+0174
175	¯	&HAF	1010 1111	Alt+0175
176	°	&HB0	1011 0000	Alt+0176
177	±	&HB1	1011 0001	Alt+0177
178	²	&HB2	1011 0010	Alt+0178
179	³	&HB3	1011 0011	Alt+0179
180	´	&HB4	1011 0100	Alt+0180
181	µ	&HB5	1011 0101	Alt+0181
182	¶	&HB6	1011 0110	Alt+0182
183	·	&HB7	1011 0111	Alt+0183
184	¸	&HB8	1011 1000	Alt+0184
185	¹	&HB9	1011 1001	Alt+0185
186	º	&HBA	1011 1010	Alt+0186

Continued

ANSI Code	Character	Hex Code	Binary Code	Keystroke
187	»	&HBB	1011 1011	Alt+0187
188	¼	&HBC	1011 1100	Alt+0188
189	½	&HBD	1011 1101	Alt+0189
190	¾	&HBE	1011 1110	Alt+0190
191	¿	&HBF	1011 1111	Alt+0191
192	À	&HC0	1100 0000	Alt+0192
193	Á	&HC1	1100 0001	Alt+0193
194	Â	&HC2	1100 0010	Alt+0194
195	Ã	&HC3	1100 0011	Alt+0195
196	Ä	&HC4	1100 0100	Alt+0196
197	Å	&HC5	1100 0101	Alt+0197
198	Æ	&HC6	1100 0110	Alt+0198
199	Ç	&HC7	1100 0111	Alt+0199
200	È	&HC8	1100 1000	Alt+0200
201	É	&HC9	1100 1001	Alt+0201
202	Ê	&HCA	1100 1010	Alt+0202
203	Ë	&HCB	1100 1011	Alt+0203
204	Ì	&HCC	1100 1100	Alt+0204
205	Í	&HCD	1100 1101	Alt+0205
206	Î	&HCE	1100 1110	Alt+0206
207	Ï	&HCF	1100 1111	Alt+0207
208		&HD0	1101 0000	Alt+0208
209	Ñ	&HD1	1101 0001	Alt+0209
210	Ò	&HD2	1101 0010	Alt+0210
211	Ó	&HD3	1101 0011	Alt+0211
212	Ô	&HD4	1101 0100	Alt+0212
213	Õ	&HD5	1101 0101	Alt+0213
214	Ö	&HD6	1101 0110	Alt+0214
215	×	&HD7	1101 0111	Alt+0215
216	Ø	&HD8	1101 1000	Alt+0216
217	Ù	&HD9	1101 1001	Alt+0217

ANSI Code	Character	Hex Code	Binary Code	Keystroke
218	Ú	&HDA	1101 1010	Alt+0218
219	Û	&HDB	1101 1011	Alt+0219
220	Ü	&HDC	1101 1100	Alt+0220
221	Ý	&HDD	1101 1101	Alt+0221
222	þ	&HDE	1101 1110	Alt+0222
223	ß	&HDF	1101 1111	Alt+0223
224	à	&HE0	1110 0000	Alt+0224
225	á	&HE1	1110 0001	Alt+0225
226	â	&HE2	1110 0010	Alt+0226
227	ã	&HE3	1110 0011	Alt+0227
228	ä	&HE4	1110 0100	Alt+0228
229	å	&HE5	1110 0101	Alt+0229
230	æ	&HE6	1110 0110	Alt+0230
231	ç	&HE7	1110 0111	Alt+0231
232	è	&HE8	1110 1000	Alt+0232
233	é	&HE9	1110 1001	Alt+0233
234	ê	&HEA	1110 1010	Alt+0234
235	ë	&HEB	1110 1011	Alt+0235
236	ì	&HEC	1110 1100	Alt+0236
237	í	&HED	1110 1101	Alt+0237
238	î	&HEE	1110 1110	Alt+0238
239	ï	&HEF	1110 1111	Alt+0239
240		&HF0	1111 0000	Alt+0240
241	ñ	&HF1	1111 0001	Alt+0241
242	ò	&HF2	1111 0010	Alt+0242
243	ó	&HF3	1111 0011	Alt+0243
244	ô	&HF4	1111 0100	Alt+0244
245	õ	&HF5	1111 0101	Alt+0245
246	ö	&HF6	1111 0110	Alt+0246
247	÷	&HF7	1111 0111	Alt+0247
248	ø	&HF8	1111 1000	Alt+0248

Continued

ANSI Code	Character	Hex Code	Binary Code	Keystroke
249	ù	&HF9	1111 1001	Alt+0249
250	ú	&HFA	1111 1010	Alt+0250
251	û	&HFB	1111 1011	Alt+0251
252	ü	&HFC	1111 1100	Alt+0252
253	ý	&HFD	1111 1101	Alt+0253
254		&HFE	1111 1110	Alt+0254
255	ÿ	&HFF	1111 1111	Alt+0255

✦   ✦   ✦

What's on the CD-ROM?

This appendix describes the contents of the companion CD-ROM.

CD-ROM Overview

The CD-ROM consists of four components:

✦ **Chapter Example:**. Excel workbooks discussed in the text.

✦ **Power Utility Pak 2000:** A 30-day trial version of the author's popular Excel add-in (works with Excel 97 or Excel 2000). Use the coupon in this book to order the full version at a significant discount. The complete VBA source code also is available for a small fee.

✦ **Sound-Proof:** The demo version of the author's audio proofreader add-in.

Note

All CD-ROM files are read-only. Therefore, if you open a file from the CD-ROM and make any changes to it, you need to save it to your hard drive. Also, if you copy a file from the CD-ROM to your hard drive, the file retains its read-only attribute. To change this attribute after copying a file, right-click the file name or icon and select Properties from the shortcut menu. In the Properties dialog box, click the General tab and remove the checkmark from the Read-only checkbox.

Chapter Examples

Each chapter of this book that contains example workbooks has its own subdirectory on the CD-ROM. For example, the example files for Chapter 2 are found in the following directory:

```
chapters\chap02\
```

Following is a list of the chapter examples, with a brief description of each.

Chapter 2

handson.xls   The end-result of the hands-on exercise.

Chapter 5

formats.xls   A workbook that contains a variety of custom number formats.

Chapter 9

amortize.xls   A workbook that demonstrates the use of PMT, PPMT, and IPMP function to calculate a fixed-rate amortization schedule.

mileage.xls   A workbook that demonstrates the use of the INDEX and MATCH functions to display the mileage between various cities.

indirect.xls   A workbook that demonstrates the use of the INDIRECT function.

megaform.xls   A workbook that demonstrates the use of a lengthy "megaformula" to remove the middle names and middle initials from a list of names.

Chapter 10

identifying text in cells.xls   Examples of three functions (ISTEXT, CELL, and TYPE) that are supposed to identify the type of data in a cell.

character set.xls   Displays all characters for a selected font. Requires Excel 97 or later.

`text histogram.xls`	Displays a histogram using text characters rather than a chat.
`text formula examples.xls`	Contains the example formulas described in the chapter.

Chapter 11

`day of the week count.xls`	Counts the number of each day of the week for a particular year.
`ordinal dates.xls`	Formulas that express a date as an ordinal number (for example, June 13th, 1999).
`holidays.xls`	Formulas that calculate the dates of various holidays.
`calendar array.xls`	A single array formula that displays a monthly calendar.
`jogging log.xls`	Formulas to keep track of jogging data.
`time sheet.xls`	A workbook (with VBA macros) to keep track of hours worked in a week. This example is not discussed in Chapter 10.

Chapter 11

`day of the week count.xls`	Counts the number of each day of the week for a particular year.
`ordinal dates.xls`	Formulas that express a date as an ordinal number (for example, June 13th, 1999).
`holidays.xls`	Formulas that calculate the dates of various holidays.
`calendar array.xls`	A single array formula that displays a monthly calendar.
`jogging log.xls`	Formulas to keep track of jogging data.
`time sheet.xls`	A workbook (with VBA macros) to keep track of hours worked in a week. This example is not discussed in Chapter 10.

Chapter 12

`basic counting.xls`	Formulas that demonstrate basic counting techniques

Chapter 13

Chapter 15

toolbar.xls A workbook that contains a custom toolbar to assist with formatting.

Chapter 19

gantt.xls A workbook that demonstrates how to create a Gantt chart.

comphist.xls A workbook that demonstrates how to create a comparative histogram.

autochart.xls A workbook that contains a chart that updates automatically when you add new data to the data range.

Chapter 23

outline.xls A budgeting workbook that demonstrates the use of row and column outlining.

textout.xls A workbook that demonstrates the use of an outline to display various levels of text.

Chapter 26

single-cell array formulas.xls Examples of array formulas that occupy a single cell

logical functions.xls Demonstrates how to use logical functions in an array formula

sum every nth.xls Two techniques to sum every nth value

multi-cell array formulas.xls Examples of array formulas that occupy multiple cells

calendar array.xls An array formula that displays a calendar

SORTED function.xls A custom VBA function that returns a sorted range

Chapter 31

tictac.xls	An Excel version of tick-tack-toe.
movetile.xls	An Excel version of the common moving tile puzzle.
keno.xls	An Excel version of Keno.
kenoodds.xls	A workbook that calculates the odds of winning in Keno.
animshap.xls	A workbook that that contains some animated Shape objects.
pattern.xls	Create colorful symmetrical patterns in Excel.
guitar.xls	A workbook that displays a guitar fretboard and the notes in various scales and keys.
menushen.xls	A workbook that contains a macro which reverses the text in Excel's menus.
wordsrch.xls	A workbook that creates word search puzzles.
asciiart.xls	A workbook that contains examples of ASCII art.
sounder.xls	A workbook that lets you play sound files (WAV or MID format).
trigfun.xls	A workbook that displays interesting charts that use trigonometric functions.
xysketch.xls	A workbook that lets you draw simple figure that are actually X-Y charts.

Chapter 34

budget.dbf	A dBASE file used for the examples in this chapter.

Chapter 35

banking.xls	A workbook used for several pivot table examples.
consolid.xls, file1.xls, file2.xls, file3.xls	These four files are used in the pivot table consolidation example.
pivchart.xls	A workbook that demonstrates pivot charts.

survey.xls
A workbook that demonstrates survey data analysis using pivot tables.

geog.xls
A workbook that demonstrates geographic analysis using a pivot table.

pivdates.xls
A workbook that demonstrates how to group pivot table data by dates.

Chapter 37

shipping.xls
A workbook set up to demonstrate the shipping costs example using Solver.

schedule.xls
A workbook set up to demonstrate the staff scheduling example using Solver.

allocate.xls
A workbook set up to demonstrate the resource allocation example using Solver.

invest.xls
A workbook set up to demonstrate the investment portfolio example using Solver.

Chapter 40

commentobject.xls
Examples of VBA code that manipulates Comment.xls objects.

Chapter 42

sheet sorter.xls
The sheet-sorting application.

better sheet sorter.xls
The sheet-sorting application, improved so that it better handles sheet names that end in numbers.

Chapter 43

funcs.xls
A workbook that contains several examples of custom worksheet functions written in VBA.

Chapter 44

get a filename.xls
Demonstrates how to use the GetOpenFilename method.

get directory.xls	Demonstrates API functions that display a dialog box that enables the user to select a directory.
excel dialogs.xls	Contains a procedure that displays all of Excel's built-in dialog boxes.
excel dialogs.xls	Contains a procedure that displays all of Excel's built-in dialog boxes.
dlgwiz.xls	Converts Excel 5/95 dialog sheets to UserForms. See dlgwiz.doc for additional information about this add-in.
worksheet controls.xls	Demonstrates the use of dialog box controls placed on a worksheet.
all controls.xls	Demonstrates all UserForm controls.
get name and sex.xls	Is the end result of the hands-on example described in Chapter 14.
userform events.xls	Demonstrates the sequence of events pertaining to UserForms.
spinbutton events.xls	Demonstrates the sequence of events pertaining to SpinButton controls.
spinbutton textbox.xls	Demonstrates how to pair a SpinButton control with a TextBox control.
newcontrols.pag	Contains customized controls for your Toolbox. To import this file as a new page, right-click a Toolbox tab, and select Import Page.

Chapter 45

dialog box menus.xls	Demonstrates two simple menu systems using CommandButton controls and a ListBox control.
refedit.xls	Demonstrates the RefEdit control.
splash.xls	Demonstrates a splash screen that is displayed when the workbook is opened.
queryclose.xls	Demonstrates a technique that ensures that the user can't close a UserForm by clicking its Close button.
change size.xls	Demonstrates a dialog box that changes sizes.

zoom.xls	Demonstrates the use of the Zoom property to zoom a dialog box.
zoom and scroll sheets	Demonstrates how to use dialog box controls to zoom and scroll a worksheet.
fill listbox.xls	Demonstrates two ways to add items to a ListBox control.
unique.xls	Demonstrates how to fill a ListBox control with unique items.
selected items.xls	Demonstrates how to identify selected items in a ListBox control.
multiple lists.xls	Demonstrates how to display multiple lists in a single ListBox control.
item transfer.xls	Demonstrates how to let the user transfer items between two ListBox controls.
move items.xls	Demonstrates how to enable the user to move items within a ListBox control.
select rows.xls	Demonstrates how to use a multicolumn ListBox control to enable the user to select rows in a worksheet.
activate sheet.xls	Demonstrates how to display a list of sheet names in a ListBox control.

Chapter 46

track changes.xls	Demonstrates a procedure that uses comments to track changes made to cells.
validate entry1.xls	Demonstrates how to validate data entered into a cell; uses the EnableEvents property.
validate entry2.xls	Demonstrates how to validate data entered into a cell; does not use the EnableEvents property.
log file.xls	Demonstrates how to keep track of every workbook that is opened by storing information in a text file.
application events 2k.xls	Demonstrates how to monitor Application-level events (Excel 2000 version, which uses a modeless UserForm).

hide **and** restore.xls	Contains procedures that hide and then later restore toolbars.
list all controls.xls	Contains a procedure that displays the Caption property for each control on every toolbar.
faceids.xla	Is an add-in that makes it very easy to determine the FACEId property setting for a particular image. This add-in uses additional files and is contained in a separate \faceids subdirectory.
toggle toolbars.xls	Contains a procedure that toggles the Visible property of each CommandBar.
dynamic caption.xls	Creates a toolbar button that displays the number format string for the active cell.
month list.xls	Demonstrates the use of a drop-down list control on a CommandBar.

Chapter 50

list menu info.xls	Contains a procedure that displays the caption for each item (menu, menu item, and submenu item) on the Worksheet Menu Bar.
add new menu.xls	Contains a procedure that adds a new menu with menu items.
add tools item.xls	Contains a procedure that adds a new menu item to the Tools menu on the Worksheet Menu Bar.
shortcut key.xls	Contains a procedure that adds new menu items with a shortcut key.
hide menu.xls	Demonstrates how to display a menu only when a particular workbook is active.
toggle gridlines.xls	Demonstrates how to display a "toggle" menu with a check mark.
menu maker.xls	Demonstrates an easy way to create a menu with information contained in a worksheet.
new menubar.xls	Demonstrates how to replace Excel's menu bar with one of your own.
menu shenanigans.xls	Contains a procedure that reverses the text in all menus and menu items.

list shortcut menus.xls   Contains a procedure that lists all shortcut
                          menus.

new shortcut menu.xls   Contains a procedure that creates a new
                          shortcut menu.

Note   Some of the examples in Chapter 51 use multiple files, and many use the same
file name. Therefore, each example is contained in a separate subdirectory.

Chapter 51

\comments\formletter   Demonstrates how to display help by using
                           cell comments.

\textbox\formletter.xls   Demonstrates how to display help by using a
                           TextBox control on a worksheet.

\worksheet\formletter   Demonstrates how to display help by
                           activating a worksheet.

\userform1\formletter   Demonstrates how to display help by using
                           Label controls in a UserForm.

\userform2\formletter   Demonstrates how to display help by using a
                           "scrolling" Label control in a UserForm.

\userform3\formletter   Demonstrates how to display help by using a
                           DropDown control and a Label control in a
                           UserForm.

\winhelp\formletter.xls   Demonstrates a simple WinHelp Help system
                           (includes the source files).

\htmlhelp\formletter   Demonstrates a simple HTML Help system
                           (includes the source files).

\function\myfuncs.xls   Demonstrates how to display help for custom
                           functions.

\assistant\formletter   Demonstrates how to display help by using
                           the Office Assistant.

\other\myapp.xls   Demonstrates other ways to display help:
                           with the Help method, from a message box,
                           and from an input box.

Power Utility Pak 2000

Power Utility Pak 2000 (PUP 2000) is a comprehensive collection of Excel add-ins that I developed. It includes 50 general-purpose utilities, 40 custom worksheet functions, and enhanced shortcut menus. When the PUP 2000 add-in is installed, Excel displays a new menu. The companion CD-ROM contains a 30-day trial version of this product.

Registering Power Utility Pak

The normal registration fee for Power Utility Pak is $39.95. However, you can use the coupon in this book to get a copy of PUP 2000 for only $9.95, plus shipping and handling. Also, you can purchase the complete VBA source code for an additional $20.00.

Installing the trial version

To install the trial version of Power Utility Pak

1. Make sure Excel is not running.
2. Locate the PUP2000.EXE file on the CD-ROM. This file is located in the \Power Utility Pak directory.
3. Double-click PUP2000.EXE. This expands the files to a directory you specify on your hard drive. For best results, use the proposed directory.
4. Start Excel.
5. Select Tools ➪ Add-Ins, and click the Browse button. Locate the PUP2000.XLA file in the directory you specified in Step 3.
6. In the Add-Ins dialog box, make sure Power Utility Pak 2000 is checked in the add-ins list.
7. Click OK to close the Add-Ins dialog box.

This procedure installs Power Utility Pak, and it will be available whenever you start Excel. When the product is installed, you'll have a new menu: PUP 2000. Access the Power Utility Pak features from the PUP 2000 menu.

Note Power Utility Pak includes extensive online help. Select Utilities ➪ Help to view the Help file.

Uninstalling Power Utility Pak

If you decide that you don't want Power Utility Pak, follow these instructions to remove it from Excel's list of add-ins:

1. In Excel, select Tools ⇨ Add-Ins.

2. In the Add-Ins dialog box, remove the checkmark from Power Utility Pak 2000.

3. Click OK to close the Add-Ins dialog box.

After performing these steps, you can reinstall Power Utility Pak at any time during the 30-day trial period by placing a checkmark next to the Power Utility Pak 2000 item in the Add-Ins dialog box.

Note   To permanently remove Power Utility Pak from your system, after you've uninstalled it from Excel using the previous steps, delete the directory into which you originally installed it.

Sound-Proof

Sound-Proof is an Excel add-in I developed. It uses a synthesized voice to read the contents of selected cells. It's the perfect proofreading tool for anyone who does data entry in Excel.

Cells are read back using natural language format. For example, 154.78 is read as "One hundred fifty-four point seven eight." Date values are read as actual dates (for example, "June fourteen, nineteen ninety-eight") and time values are read as actual times (for example, "Six forty-five AM").

The companion CD-ROM contains a demo version of Sound-Proof. The full version is available for $19.95. Ordering instructions are provided in the online Help file.

Note   The only limitation in the demo version is that it reads no more than 12 cells at a time.

Installing the demo version

To install the demo version of Sound-Proof

1. Make sure Excel is not running.

2. Locate the SPDEMO.EXE file on the CD-ROM. This file is located in the Sound Proof\ directory.

3. Double-click SPDEMO.EXE. This expands the files to a directory you specify on your hard drive.

4. Start Excel.

5. Select Tools ⇨ Add-Ins, and click the Browse button. Locate the SOUNDPRF.XLA file in the directory you specified in Step 3.

6. In the Add-Ins dialog box, make sure Sound-Proof is checked in the add-ins list.

7. Click OK to close the Add-Ins dialog box.

This process enables you to install Sound-Proof so that it will be available whenever you start Excel. Once the product is installed, you'll have a new menu command: Tools ⇨ Sound-Proof. This command displays the Sound-Proof toolbar.

Uninstalling Sound-Proof

If you decide that you don't want Sound-Proof, follow these instructions to remove it from Excel's list of add-ins:

1. In Excel, select Tools ⇨ Add-Ins.

2. In the Add-Ins dialog box, remove the checkmark from Sound-Proof.

3. Click OK to close the Add-Ins dialog box.

After performing these steps, you can reinstall Sound-Proof at any time by placing a checkmark next to the Sound-Proof item in the Add-Ins dialog box.

Note

To permanently remove Sound-Proof from your system, after you have performed the previous steps to uninstall the add-in, delete the directory into which you originally installed it.

✦   ✦   ✦

Index

Continued

Continued

Continued

Continued

IDG Books Worldwide, Inc.
End-User License Agreement

READ THIS. You should carefully read these terms and conditions before opening the software packet(s) included with this book ("Book"). This is a license agreement ("Agreement") between you and IDG Books Worldwide, Inc. ("IDGB"). By opening the accompanying software packet(s), you acknowledge that you have read and accept the following terms and conditions. If you do not agree and do not want to be bound by such terms and conditions, promptly return the Book and the unopened software packet(s) to the place you obtained them for a full refund.

1. **License Grant.** IDGB grants to you (either an individual or entity) a nonexclusive license to use one copy of the enclosed software program(s) (collectively, the "Software") solely for your own personal or business purposes on a single computer (whether a standard computer or a workstation component of a multiuser network). The Software is in use on a computer when it is loaded into temporary memory (RAM) or installed into permanent memory (hard disk, CD-ROM, or other storage device). IDGB reserves all rights not expressly granted herein.

2. **Ownership.** IDGB is the owner of all right, title, and interest, including copyright, in and to the compilation of the Software recorded on the disk(s) or CD-ROM ("Software Media"). Copyright to the individual programs recorded on the Software Media is owned by the author or other authorized copyright owner of each program. Ownership of the Software and all proprietary rights relating thereto remain with IDGB and its licensers.

3. **Restrictions On Use and Transfer.**

   (a) You may only (i) make one copy of the Software for backup or archival purposes, or (ii) transfer the Software to a single hard disk, provided that you keep the original for backup or archival purposes. You may not (i) rent or lease the Software, (ii) copy or reproduce the Software through a LAN or other network system or through any computer subscriber system or bulletin-board system, or (iii) modify, adapt, or create derivative works based on the Software.

   (b) You may not reverse engineer, decompile, or disassemble the Software. You may transfer the Software and user documentation on a permanent basis, provided that the transferee agrees to accept the terms and conditions of this Agreement and you retain no copies. If the Software is an update or has been updated, any transfer must include the most recent update and all prior versions.

4. Restrictions On Use of Individual Programs. You must follow the individual requirements and restrictions detailed for each individual program in the "What's on the CD-ROM" appendix of this Book. These limitations are also contained in the individual license agreements recorded on the Software Media. These limitations may include a requirement that after using the program for a specified period of time, the user must pay a registration fee or discontinue use. By opening the Software packet(s), you will be agreeing to abide by the licenses and restrictions for these individual programs that are detailed in the "What's on the CD-ROM" appendix and on the Software Media. None of the material on this Software Media or listed in this Book may ever be redistributed, in original or modified form, for commercial purposes.

5. Limited Warranty.

(a) IDGB warrants that the Software and Software Media are free from defects in materials and workmanship under normal use for a period of sixty (60) days from the date of purchase of this Book. If IDGB receives notification within the warranty period of defects in materials or workmanship, IDGB will replace the defective Software Media.

(b) IDGB AND THE AUTHORS OF THE BOOK DISCLAIM ALL OTHER WARRANTIES, EXPRESS OR IMPLIED, INCLUDING WITHOUT LIMITATION IMPLIED WARRANTIES OF MERCHANTABILITY AND FITNESS FOR A PARTICULAR PURPOSE, WITH RESPECT TO THE SOFTWARE, THE PROGRAMS, THE SOURCE CODE CONTAINED THEREIN, AND/OR THE TECHNIQUES DESCRIBED IN THIS BOOK. IDGB DOES NOT WARRANT THAT THE FUNCTIONS CONTAINED IN THE SOFTWARE WILL MEET YOUR REQUIREMENTS OR THAT THE OPERATION OF THE SOFTWARE WILL BE ERROR FREE.

(c) This limited warranty gives you specific legal rights, and you may have other rights that vary from jurisdiction to jurisdiction.

6. Remedies.

(a) IDGB's entire liability and your exclusive remedy for defects in materials and workmanship shall be limited to replacement of the Software Media, which may be returned to IDGB with a copy of your receipt at the following address: Software Media Fulfillment Department, Attn.: *Microsoft Excel 2000 Bible, Gold Edition*, IDG Books Worldwide, Inc., 7260 Shadeland Station, Ste. 100, Indianapolis, IN 46256, or call 1-800-762-2974. Please allow three to four weeks for delivery. This Limited Warranty is void if failure of the Software Media has resulted from accident, abuse, or misapplication. Any replacement Software Media will be warranted for the remainder of the original warranty period or thirty (30) days, whichever is longer.

(b) In no event shall IDGB or the authors be liable for any damages whatsoever (including without limitation damages for loss of business profits, business interruption, loss of business information, or any other pecuniary loss) arising from the use of or inability to use the Book or the Software, even if IDGB has been advised of the possibility of such damages.

(c) Because some jurisdictions do not allow the exclusion or limitation of liability for consequential or incidental damages, the above limitation or exclusion may not apply to you.

7. U.S. Government Restricted Rights. Use, duplication, or disclosure of the Software by the U.S. Government is subject to restrictions stated in paragraph (c)(1)(ii) of the Rights in Technical Data and Computer Software clause of DFARS 252.227-7013, and in subparagraphs (a) through (d) of the Commercial Computer — Restricted Rights clause at FAR 52.227-19, and in similar clauses in the NASA FAR supplement, when applicable.

8. General. This Agreement constitutes the entire understanding of the parties and revokes and supersedes all prior agreements, oral or written, between them and may not be modified or amended except in a writing signed by both parties hereto that specifically refers to this Agreement. This Agreement shall take precedence over any other documents that may be in conflict herewith. If any one or more provisions contained in this Agreement are held by any court or tribunal to be invalid, illegal, or otherwise unenforceable, each and every other provision shall remain in full force and effect.

my2cents.idgbooks.com

Register This Book — And Win!

Visit **http://my2cents.idgbooks.com** to register this book and we'll automatically enter you in our fantastic monthly prize giveaway. It's also your opportunity to give us feedback: let us know what you thought of this book and how you would like to see other topics covered.

Discover IDG Books Online!

The IDG Books Online Web site is your online resource for tackling technology — at home and at the office. Frequently updated, the IDG Books Online Web site features exclusive software, insider information, online books, and live events!

10 Productive & Career-Enhancing Things You Can Do at www.idgbooks.com

- Nab source code for your own programming projects.

- Download software.

- Read Web exclusives: special articles and book excerpts by IDG Books Worldwide authors.

- Take advantage of resources to help you advance your career as a Novell or Microsoft professional.

- Buy IDG Books Worldwide titles or find a convenient bookstore that carries them.

- Register your book and win a prize.

- Chat live online with authors.

- Sign up for regular e-mail updates about our latest books.

- Suggest a book you'd like to read or write.

- Give us your 2¢ about our books and about our Web site.

You say you're not on the Web yet? It's easy to get started with IDG Books' *Discover the Internet,* available at local retailers everywhere.

CD-ROM Installation Instructions

The Microsoft Excel 2000 Bible, Gold Edition CD-ROM contains author John Walkenbach's Power Utility Pak 2000, his Sound-Proof add-in, and a complete set of workbook files for the macros discussed in the book.

Appendix I contains detailed descriptions of these items, along with installation guidelines. When you copy the workbook files from the CD-ROM to your own disk, you should remove the read-only attribute by right-clicking the file and selecting Properties; then uncheck the read-only check box.